Guide to Pronunciation

After each black-type word in this dictionary there is a special spelling of the word which shows you how to say it. The special spelling has parentheses ( ) around it. Here is an example of a black-type word with its special spelling: **cat** (KAT).

On the next page is a guide to the special spellings.

This is how to use the guide. Each line tells about one sound. In the first column you will see the letters that stand for that sound. In the second column are some words in which the sound occurs. If you say those words and listen to the parts in black type, you will hear the sound. In the third column are the special spellings for those words. You can use them to practice sounding out the letters.

Some of the special spellings have both capital letters and small ones.The capital letters are the accented ones. We say them a little louder than we do the others.

In many of the special spellings there is a ə. This is a quiet little sound that is often found in the unaccented, or softly-said, parts of words. ə is just a very weak vowel. The guide will tell you more about ə.

Some of the special spellings give you a choice. They tell you that people very often say a word more than one way. These spellings look like this: (bee- *or* bə-GIN). This means that the first part of the word can be said (bee) or (bə), giving you either (bee-GIN) or (bə-GIN). Sometimes the whole word is spelled out twice, as in (kahn-KREET *or* KAHN-kreet). Then you know that it is either (kahn-KREET) or (KAHN-kreet), as you choose.

Vowel Sounds

a	had, sat	(HAD) (SAT)
ah	far, calm	(FAHR) (KAHM)
air	pear, scare	(PAIR) (SKAIR)
aw	law, cause	(LAW) (KAWZ)
ay	bay, rate	(BAY) (RAYT)
e	met, bet	(MET) (BET)
ee	me, fairy	(MEE) (FAIR-ee)
er	fur, after	(FER) (AF-ter)
i	sit, bid	(SIT) (BID)
oh	go, rowboat	(GOH) (ROH-boht)
oi	oil, boy	(OIL) (BOI)
oo	root, soup	(ROOT) (SOOP)
or	for, border	(FOR) (BOR-der)
ow	how, sound	(HOW) (SOWND)
u	fun, cup	(FUN) (KUP)
uh	could, pull	(KUHD) (PUHL)
y	fly, sight	(FLY) (SYT)
yoo	fuse, view	(FYOOZ) (VYOO)
ə	soda	(SOH-də)
ə	silent	(SY-lənt)
ə	pencil	(PEN-səl)
ə	bacon	(BAY-kən)
ə	circus	(SER-kəss)

Consonant Sounds

ch	church, nature	(CHERCH) (NAY-cher)
g	get, great	(GET) (GRAYT)
j	just, age	(JUST) (AYJ)
ks	mix, six	(MIKS) (SIKS)
ng	king, finger	(KING) (FING-ger)
th	three, thin	(THREE) (THIN)
th	then, further	(THEN) (FER-ther)
zh	vision	(VIZH-ən)

Say the other consonants just as you always do when you find them in a word.

Every time you see a "y" with a vowel following it, sound it like the "y" in "yoo," just as you do in "yet."

The Courtis-Watters

ILLUSTRATED GOLDEN DICTIONARY

for Young Readers

REVISED AND EXPANDED

BY STUART A. COURTIS

Professor of Education, Emeritus, University of Michigan

AND GARNETTE WATTERS

Formerly Director of the Language Department, Public Schools, Hamtramck, Michigan

ALLEN WALKER READ

Consultant on Pronunciation, Professor of English, Columbia University

GOLDEN PRESS NEW YORK

REVISED EDITION, 1965
Library of Congress Catalog Card Number: 65-18917
 Designed and produced by Artists and Writers Press, Inc. Printed in the U.S.A. by Western Printing and Lithographing Company. Published by Golden Press, Inc., New York.

ACKNOWLEDGMENTS

To ALL teachers and other persons in the public schools of Hamtramck, Michigan, who participated in the research which preceded the compilation of this book, we extend our gratitude and appreciation. Especially do we acknowledge the valuable assistance and advice given so willingly by Miss Clara Horine, formerly Director of Language Education in the Hamtramck Public Schools.

We are greatly indebted to Irving A. Leitner, noted author and teacher, who has written the definitions for the 1,500 new entries in this specially revised edition.

We are very proud to have had the help of Professor Allen Walker Read, who supervised the preparation of the pronunciations for each entry. Professor Read is a member of the faculty of Columbia University and a widely known authority on phonetics and word usage.

And we further extend our deep appreciation and gratitude to all other teachers everywhere who have given of their time and effort to read and evaluate the manuscript.

ABOUT THE AUTHORS OF THIS BOOK

THE AUTHORS of this new dictionary are recognized experts. Their qualifications for preparing such a book are outstanding, since both are authorities with long experience in the field of language education.

Stuart A. Courtis is Professor of Education, Emeritus, at the University of Michigan. Dr. Courtis has long been an authority on the preparation of educational materials for children. He is well known for the *Courtis Arithmetic Standardized Tests*, many standard reading tests and texts, and professional books for educators.

Garnette Watters formerly taught literature, art, and music in the Hamtramck, Michigan, public schools. For twenty-five years she was a director of the system's Language Department. Mrs. Watters is co-author of a number of textbooks on language studies.

TO PARENTS AND TEACHERS

A NEW age, a new need, and a new idea have resulted in the development of this new dictionary, designed for young readers of grade-school age.

Your boys and girls are rapidly growing up, physically and mentally. A dictionary adequate to their needs must grow up with them. Many new words are coming into the language of our new machine and space age. This has created the need for a more advanced dictionary, written on a level that young boys and girls can understand. This dictionary, the first of its kind, was created to meet this need. To the basic word list comprising our previous, more elementary *Illustrated Golden Dictionary*, many hundreds of space-age words have been added.

Every detail—size of print, page arrangement, understandable definitions with illustrating sentences, new and better pictures, classification of words according to parts of speech, and a new comprehensive pronunciation system—has been planned for the single purpose of helping "growing up" boys and girls to learn by themselves and enjoy doing it.

In addition to the basic words, their variants, such as plurals, comparative forms, and verb parts, are listed. Parts of speech are indicated and the words defined accordingly, thereby promoting growth in language skills. The words are defined in the language of the growing child to make the use of the dictionary a pleasure, rather than a difficult chore. Only the meanings that a child is likely to encounter are included.

The newest self-help device introduced is a pronunciation system consisting wholly of respelling the words according to sound. This is explained on the endpapers of the dictionary.

In our previous dictionaries for young children, we used a vocabulary drawn from the writings and conversations of children in the first, second, third, and fourth grades, and from the vocabularies used in eighty-six carefully selected primers, readers, and other texts used in the early and middle grades. These were checked against and supplemented with words from standard word lists, such as Gates, Horn, Thorndike, and Buckingham-Dolch. The words finally selected were those most frequently encountered and used by young readers.

This list has now been expanded by more than 1,500 entries and thousands of variants, selected in a similar manner from more advanced books.

Parents and teachers who introduce children to this book can do so with confidence that every effort has been made to make it as clear, understandable, and useful as possible. It is most important that the child be encouraged to use the book by himself: to make it his ever-handy companion in learning.

More and more parents and teachers are coming to see that true education is really a maturation process, like cutting teeth or learning to walk; that the methods and results of education must be measured not only in terms of knowledge and skill, but also in terms of personality values. Learning to help oneself to master a difficulty is a personality development which far outweighs in value the knowledge of words and their meanings. The knowledge gained through purposeful activity is likely to be useful and long remembered.

The teacher using this dictionary as supplementary material can help the child in developing self-direction and self-control, and, at the same time, set him free for functional reading on a wider and higher scale than he could possibly attain so long as he is dependent on her help alone. Similarly, parents, by their interest and participation in the child's self-help activities, can encourage their children to use the dictionary. Older children will be interested, too, in helping younger children.

All ages enjoy just thumbing through the dictionary, looking at pictures, reading definitions, and noticing various special features. Younger children enjoy recognizing the contents of the pictures and naming them. They tend to imitate the behavior of their older brothers and sisters and soon learn many words incidentally. The whole family, in fact, can have a good time with the book. Out of such enjoyable experiences comes the development of understanding, a skill of lasting value.

This dictionary will be found suitable for use by readers at different stages of development. Slow learners in more advanced grades will find that it gives them just the help they need. Many adults in special English classes for foreigners or advanced citizenship classes can use it to great advantage.

It would be unreasonable to expect of this book either the simplicity essential for beginning readers or the complexity of an adult dictionary. Books for children must mature with the children. Other books provide fundamental dictionary experiences for beginners; the present volume is several steps higher in complexity.

We confidently and joyously entrust to you the introduction of this book to the children, because we know you want to help them as much as we do ourselves.

—The Authors

TO THE BOYS AND GIRLS WHO USE THIS BOOK

THE people who made this dictionary did their best to make it *easy to use*, *easy to read*, and *easy to understand*.

The entry words, or words that are explained, are in alphabetical order. These words are printed in **black type** to help you find them quickly. Here is a sample entry. Read all the parts of it so that you can see how to understand all the other entries in the book:

> **ac•count** (ə-KOWNT) *n. accounts.* 1. A record of money paid out and received.—Father has a bank *account*. The bank takes care of his money and keeps a record of the money he puts in and takes out.—Mother keeps an *account* of the money she spends for food. She writes down all the figures carefully. 2. An explanation; a telling.—When Mary returned from the zoo, she gave an *account* of what she had seen. She told all about it.
>
> —*v. accounts, accounted, accounting.* Give an explanation or reason.—One of the pencils is missing. Susan could not *account* for it.
>
> —*On account of* means because of.—Bob was absent from school *on account of* illness.

The dot in the entry word **ac•count** shows how the word is divided into syllables. It shows you where the word can be divided at the end of a line when you are writing it.

(ə-KOWNT) is a special spelling of the word that shows you how to say the word. There is a guide in the front of this volume that will help you to understand this special spelling.

The *n.* shows you that the entry word is a noun, and the *v.* below shows you that it is also a verb. The abbreviations used for other parts of speech are: *adj.* for adjective; *adv.* for adverb; *conj.* for conjunction; *prep.* for preposition; *art.* for article; *pron.* for pronoun; *interj.* for interjection. You will also find definitions for many terms that do not belong in any special part-of-speech group. There are two other abbreviations used throughout this dictionary. They are *sing.* for singular and *pl.* for plural.

Accounts is a word that is related to the noun **account**. It is the plural. Sometimes you will find other related words at the beginning of an entry.

Next comes the meaning of the word and a sentence that uses the word. Sometimes a word has more than one meaning. That is why the numbers 1 and 2 are used here. Sometimes it is very hard to explain what an entry word means. When this is so, you will not find any definition or explanation after the entry word. Instead, you will find one or more sentences. From these sentences you will be able to get the meaning of the entry word.

The dash in the margin in front of the *v.* tells you that **account** can also be a verb, and that the verb form of the word is spelled the same way that the noun form is. Since it is also pronounced the same way, there is no special spelling to tell you how to say it.

Accounts, accounted, and *accounting* are words that are related to the verb **account.** They are some other forms of the verb: the third person present, the third person past, and the present participle.

The next dash in the margin points out a special use of **account**. In some entries this dash points out a word that is closely related to the entry word.

Pictures have been used whenever possible to tell you more about the meaning of a word. There are more than 3,000 of them.

In the back of this book you will find many lists of things that you will want to know, such as weights and measures, abbreviations, large cities, presidents of the United States, and rules for using capital letters.

The more words you know about and understand, the more you will enjoy using them. Whenever, in reading or spelling, you meet a word you want to know more about, use your dictionary to learn its meaning. You will soon find this dictionary is one of the most important books in your library.

A a

A, a (AY) *n. A's, a's.* 1. The first letter of the alphabet.
2. The sixth note of the c scale in music: c, d, e, f, g, *a*, b, c.
–(AY, U, or ə) *adj.* or *art.* One or any.–We made *a* kite.–Can you lend me *a* pencil?

ab•a•cus (AB-ə-kəss) *n. abacuses.* An old-fashioned calculator for working out problems in addition, subtraction, etc. The *abacus* works by sliding beads along rods or grooves set in a frame.

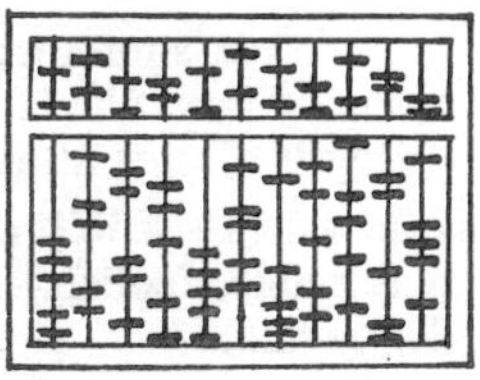

–Many Chinese businessmen still use *abacuses* for totaling their bills.

a•ban•don (ə-BAN-dən) *v. abandons, abandoned, abandoning.* Leave forever.–The birds *abandoned* their nest. They left it and never went back to it.

a•bashed (ə-BASHT) *adj.* So embarrassed or ashamed that self-confidence is lost.–I was *abashed* when I forgot my multiplication tables. I sat there and blushed.

ab•bre•vi•ate (ə-BREE-vee-ayt) *v. abbreviates, abbreviated, abbreviating.* Shorten.–We *abbreviate* the words United States of America by writing them U.S.A. Other words may be *abbreviated* by leaving out certain letters. –"Dr." is the word "doctor" *abbreviated.*

ab•bre•vi•a•tion (ə-bree-vee-AY-shun) *n. abbreviations.* A shortened form.–The *abbreviation* for the word "foot" is "ft." "Pt." is the *abbreviation* for "pint."

ab•di•cate (AB-də-kayt) *v. abdicates, abdicated, abdicating.* Give up supreme power, position, etc., which one has by right, such as the power of a king.–King Edward VIII, of Great Britain, decided to *abdicate* his throne rather than give up the woman he loved. After King Edward VIII *abdicated,* he became the Duke of Windsor.

ab•do•men (AB-də-mən *or* ab-DOH-mən) *n.* 1. The belly; the hollow part of the body between the diaphragm and the pelvis; or, the section holding the stomach, spleen, intestines, etc.–Tom told the doctor about the pains in his *abdomen.*
2. The rear part of the body of insects.

ab•dom•i•nal (ab-DAHM-ən-əl) *adj.* In or of the abdomen.–Tom had felt *abdominal* pains all day. He was sure it was because he had eaten too much candy.

a•bide (ə-BYD) *v. abides, abode, abiding.* 1. Live up to; keep.–Bob always *abides* by the rules of the school. He obeys them.
2. Stand; endure.–Jack says he cannot *abide* being treated like a child.
3. Stay.–The traveler asked if he might *abide* with us overnight.

a•bil•i•ty (ə-BIL-ə-tee) *n. abilities.* Skill or knowledge; power to do something.–Bob is a student of unusual *ability.*–I don't doubt your *ability* to solve the problem.

a•ble (AY-bəl) *adj. abler, ablest.* 1. Having knowledge or power.–Jack is *able* to spell many words. He can spell them.–Bob is *able* to do his arithmetic without help.
2. Strong enough.–The baby is *able* to push the door open.–Grandmother was *able* to sit up today for the first time since her sickness.
3. Capable; fine.–Bob is an *able* student. His work is better than most students' work.

a•board (ə-BORD) *adv.* On a boat, a bus, a train or a plane.–When the conductor calls, "All *aboard,*" he wants all passengers to get onto the train.

a•bol•ish (ə-BAHL-ish) *v. abolishes, abolished, abolishing.* 1. Put an end to, or do away with something.–After the Civil War, slavery in the United States was *abolished.*
2. Make null and void, as a law.–If Congress were to *abolish* taxes, the Government would lose its most important source of income.

ab•o•li•tion (ab-ə-LISH-ən) *n.* The complete doing away with something; specifically, in the United States, of slavery.–Many sympathetic men worked for the *abolition* of slavery for many years.

ab•o•rig•i•nes (ab-ə-RIJ-ə-neez) *n. pl.* The very first people known to have lived in a place.–The *aborigines* in South Africa were known as the Bushmen and the Hottentots.

a·bound (ə-BOWND) *v. abounds, abounded, abounding.* 1. Be plentiful, or overflowing in number.–The forest *abounds* with birds and animals.
2. Be fully supplied with.–Baby is *abounding* in energy. He plays for hours without tiring.

a·bout (ə-BOWT) *adj., adv.,* and *prep.* 1. Around; in all directions.–The dog looked *about* him.
2. Nearly; almost.–John's kite is *about* finished.
3. More or less; around.–Mary is *about* ten years old.
4. Of.–Tell us the story *about* King Midas.
5. Around.–Flowers grow all *about* the house.
6. The other way.–The captain said, "*About*, face!" He meant, "Face the opposite direction."
7. Moving from place to place; up.–After her long illness, Jane was finally *about* again.

a·bove (ə-BUV) *adj., adv.,* and *prep.* 1. Overhead.–He saw many clouds floating *above*.
2. Higher than; over.–The picture on the wall is *above* the table.
3. Better than. – Bill thinks himself *above* the other boys.
4. More than.–That price is *above* what I wanted to pay.
5. Foregoing.–Refer to the *above* paragraph for that information.

a·breast (ə-BREST) *adv.* Side by side.–The children in the parade marched eight *abreast*. Eight children marched side by side.

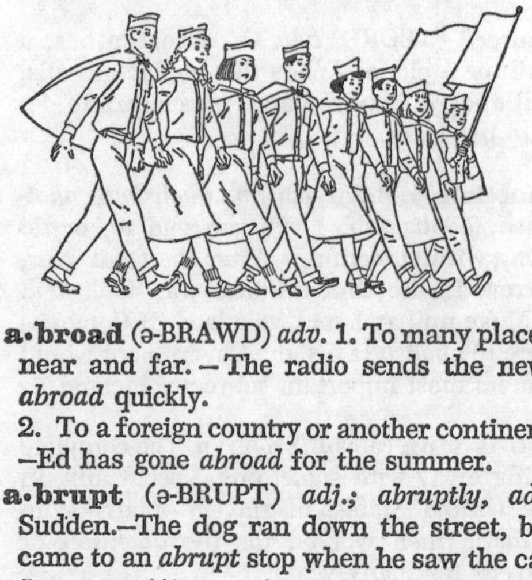

a·broad (ə-BRAWD) *adv.* 1. To many places, near and far. – The radio sends the news *abroad* quickly.
2. To a foreign country or another continent. –Ed has gone *abroad* for the summer.

a·brupt (ə-BRUPT) *adj.; abruptly, adv.* Sudden.–The dog ran down the street, but came to an *abrupt* stop when he saw the cat.

ab·sence (AB-sənss) *n.* 1. Time spent away. –John returned to school after an *absence* of three days.
2. A lack.–These potatoes taste flat because of the *absence* of salt. They have no salt.

ab·sent (AB-sənt) *adj.* Away; not present; not at a certain place.–John has never been *absent* from school.

ab·so·lute (AB-sə-loot) *adj.; absolutely, adv.* 1. Perfect; whole; complete.–John answered the question with *absolute* truth.
2. Free from limit or restriction. – In the United States, the President does not have *absolute* power.
3. Positive; certain. – Jim found *absolute* proof that his answer had been correct.

ab·sorb (ab-SORB *or* -ZORB) *v. absorbs, absorbed, absorbing.* 1. Soak up.–A blotter *absorbs* ink.
2. Hold one's interest completely.–This story *absorbs* Mary. She is so interested that she is giving it all her attention.

ab·surd (ab-SERD) *adj.; absurdly, adv.* Not reasonable; foolish.–It is *absurd* to expect a dog to talk.

a·bun·dance (ə-BUN-dənss) *n.* A great amount; plenty.–There is an *abundance* of wheat in this country. We have more than is needed.

a·bun·dant (ə-BUN-dənt) *adj.; abundantly, adv.* Plentiful.–Rubber trees are *abundant* in South America.

a·buse (ə-BYOOSS) *n. abuses.* Bad or wrong treatment.–*Abuse* of people does not make friends for you.
–(ə-BYOOZ) *v. abuses, abused, abusing.* 1. Take wrong advantage of; make the wrong use of.–The children do not *abuse* the privilege of a morning recess.
2. Treat unkindly.–Do not *abuse* your dog, and he will be your friend.
3. Scold rudely. – I heard the angry man *abuse* the boy.

a·byss (ə-BISS) *n.* 1. A "bottomless" space; a very deep pit.–Many people fell into the *abyss* when the earth split open during the earthquake.
2. Endless time or emptiness.–The rocket was fired into the *abyss* of space.

a·cad·e·my (ə-KAD-ə-mee) *n. academies.* 1. A school of higher learning, such as a college; now also a private high school.–The United States Military *Academy* is located at West Point, N. Y.
2. A place of training, usually in a special subject.–Before giving his first concert, the pianist studied at a music *academy* for years.
3. An organization of scholars.–The French *Academy* was founded in the seventeenth century.

ac•cel•er•ate (ak-SEL-er-ayt) *v. accelerates, accelerated, accelerating.* 1. Speed up; quicken; move faster.–The men in the factory worked overtime to *accelerate* production.
2. Move up in time.–Father *accelerated* his departure by one day. He left earlier than he had planned.

ac•cel•er•a•tor (ak-SEL-er-ay-ter) *n. accelerators.* Anything used to make something go faster.–If you step on the *accelerator* of an automobile, it feeds more gas to the motor, and makes the car go faster.

ac•cent (AK-sent) *n.* Increased force given to a word or part of a word in speaking.–Put the *accent* on the first syllable in the word "accent."
–(ak-SENT) *v. accents, accented, accenting.* 1. Speak a word or part of a word with increased force.–In this dictionary, the syllable you should *accent* in a word is printed in capital letters.
2. Emphasize; call to the attention.–Ellen *accented* her blond hair by wearing a bright red ribbon.

ac•cept (ak-SEPT) *v. accepts, accepted, accepting.* 1. Take.–Bob will *accept* the gift offered him.
2. Say yes to.–Mary will *accept* the invitation to Bob's party.
3. Agree to the truth of.–Bob was absent from school. The teacher *accepted* the excuse from his father. She was satisfied with the excuse.

ac•cess (AK-sess) *n.* 1. Permission to enter or approach; admittance.–The children had *access* to the school playground after school was closed.
2. A place of entry or passage.–The point of *access* to the harbor was through the channel.

ac•ces•si•ble (ak-SESS-ə-bəl) *adj.* 1. Open to passage; free of obstruction.–The road was *accessible* in spite of the construction work in progress. You could drive on it.
2. Able to be had or obtained.–The records of the firm are *accessible* for examination.

ac•ces•so•ry (ak-SESS-ə-ree) *n. accessories.* 1. Something that adds comfort or usefulness to a more important thing; something extra but not really necessary.–Many *accessories*, such as radios, clocks, and mirrors, are available for automobiles at extra cost.
2. A person involved in a crime even though he does not commit the actual crime.–The man became an *accessory* to the theft because he hid the thief.

ac•ci•dent (AK-si-dənt) *n. accidents.* 1. A happening that is not wanted or expected.–These are *accidents:* A man slipped and fell on the ice; a boy fell into the water; two automobiles struck each other.
2. Chance.–It was just by *accident* that I found you at home.

ac•ci•den•tal (ak-si-DEN-təl) *adj.; accidentally, adv.* Just by chance; not intended.–When I bumped into Mother, it was *accidental.*

ac•claim (ə-KLAYM) *n.* Loud applause or approval.–The pianist received great *acclaim* for his fine concert.
–*v. acclaims, acclaimed, acclaiming.* Cheer loudly; shout approval; applaud.–The people *acclaimed* the President as his car drove by in the parade.

ac•com•mo•date (ə-KAHM-ə-dayt) *v. accommodates, accommodated, accommodating.* 1. Make room for.–The teacher could *accommodate* only twenty children in her room.
2. Help; aid. – You will *accommodate* me very much by sewing for me.

ac•com•pa•ny (ə-KUM-pə-nee) *v. accompanies, accompanied, accompanying.* 1. Go with.–Our teacher will *accompany* us to the zoo.
2. Play music along with (a soloist).–Mary will sing and Mother will *accompany* her on the piano.

ac•com•plish (ə-KAHM-plish) *v. accomplishes, accomplished, accomplishing.* Do successfully; finish.–It is hard to *accomplish* your work when you are tired.

ac•cord (ə-KORD) *n.* Agreement.–The boys were in *accord* as to who broke the window. All agreed that Jack did it.
–*v. accords, accorded, according.* Agree; be in harmony.–John's story *accorded* with Dick's, so they did not argue.
–*According to* means by or on the authority of.–*According to* the teacher's record, you were absent only one day.
–*Of one's own accord* means by one's own decision, without being told or advised.–Jack usually has to be asked to mow the lawn, but today he did it *of his own accord.*

ac•cor•di•on (ə-KOR-dee-ən) *n. accordions.* A musical instrument consisting of bellows, metal reeds, and keys that look like piano keys. The *accordion* is played by pressing the keys down with the right hand, and moving the bellows back and forth with the left hand. The left hand also presses down buttons called stops.

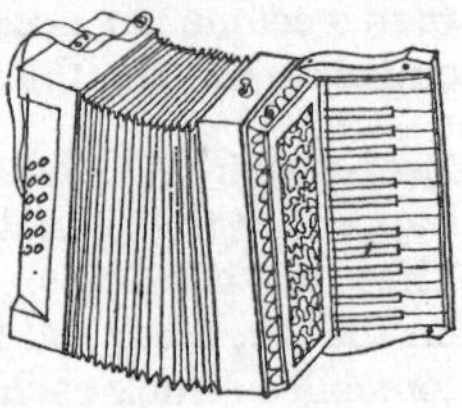

ac•count (ə-KOWNT) *n. accounts.* 1. A record of money paid out and received.–Father has a bank *account.* The bank takes care of his money and keeps a record of the money he puts in and takes out.–Mother keeps an *account* of the money she spends for food. She writes down all the figures carefully.
2. An explanation; a telling.–When Mary returned from the zoo, she gave an *account* of what she had seen. She told all about it.
–*v. accounts, accounted, accounting.* Give an explanation or reason.–One of the pencils was missing. Susan could not *account* for it.
–*On account of* means because of.–Bob was absent from school *on account of* illness.

ac•cu•mu•late (ə-KYOO-myə-layt) *v. accumulates, accumulated, accumulating.* Gather together; collect in one place; pile up.–Slowly but surely a crowd *accumulated* to hear the speaker.–A good gardener does not let weeds *accumulate.*

ac•cu•ra•cy (AK-yə-rə-see) *n.* Correctness; being without mistakes.–Bob was praised for his *accuracy* in arithmetic.

ac•cu•rate (AK-yə-rət) *adj.; accurately, adv.* Correct; exact; right.–A banker must be *accurate* in counting money. He must not make mistakes.

ac•cuse (ə-KYOOZ) *v. accuses, accused, accusing.* Charge with doing wrong; blame.–The man will *accuse* you of being lazy if you do not work harder.–The boy was *accused* of stealing, but he was not guilty.

ac•cus•tom (ə-KUS-təm) *v. accustoms, accustomed, accustoming.* Become used to.–It is hard for some people to *accustom* themselves to cold.
–*Accustomed to* means used to; fitted for by practice or custom.–Mary is *accustomed to* sleeping in a cold room.

ace (AYSS) *n. aces.* 1. A playing card with only one spot on it.–To our surprise, Father had three *aces.*
2. A person of the highest skill.–The opposing team had an *ace* in left field. He made four wonderful catches during the game.

ache (AYK) *n. aches.* A dull pain that lasts for some time.–John has a stomach *ache.*
–*v. aches, ached, aching.* Have a dull pain that lasts for some time.–John's stomach *ached.*

a•chieve (ə-CHEEV) *v. achieves, achieved, achieving.* 1. Get with effort; accomplish.–I *achieved* my goal. I earned enough money for a bicycle.
2. Get; win.–The man *achieved* fame by his invention.

a•chieve•ment (ə-CHEEV-mənt) *n. achievements.* An accomplishment, especially in the face of hardship or difficulty; a noteworthy attainment; a successful act.–The climbing of Mt. Everest, the highest mountain in the world, was a great *achievement.*

ac•id (ASS-id) *n. acids.* A sour-tasting substance which causes a change in some metals. Lemons and green apples are sour because they have *acids* in them. When you cut a lemon or peel a sour apple with a steel knife, the *acid* in the fruit makes the knife become dark. *Acids* can be made so strong that they will eat holes in things.–Father spilled *acid* from the automobile battery on his shoe and it burned a hole in the shoe.
–*adj.* Sour.–Vinegar has an *acid* taste.

ac•knowl•edge (ak-NAHL-ij) *v. acknowledges, acknowledged, acknowledging.* 1. Show that something has been received; answer to or express thanks for.–As soon as Mary received the invitation, she *acknowledged* it.
2. Admit; confess.–Jack would not *acknowledge* his mistake.

a•corn (AY-korn) *n. acorns.* The seed of an oak tree.

a•cous•tics (ə-KOOSS-tiks) *n. sing.* and *pl.* The science of making and transmitting sounds and their effects, such as echoes and vibrations, or all of the qualities of sound put together.–*Acoustics* have to do with hearing. – The architects studied *acoustics* before drawing up plans for the new auditorium.–The *acoustics* of the theater allowed even a whisper to be heard from the stage.

ac•quaint (ə-KWAYNT) *v. acquaints, acquainted, acquainting.* Make familiar; make known to.–I will *acquaint* you with the work that is to be done.
–*Acquainted* means knowing or knowing about.–Bob and Jack are *acquainted.* They know each other.–The men are *acquainted* with airplane building.

ac•quaint•ance (ə-KWAYN-tənss) *n. acquaintances.* A person one knows personally, but not well.–Dr. Brown is an *acquaintance* of mine. He is not a close friend, but I know him.

ac•quire (ə-KWYR) *v. acquires, acquired, acquiring.* Get for one's own.–Father would like to *acquire* the house on the corner.

ac•quit (ə-KWIT) *v. acquits, acquitted, acquitting.* 1. Declare not guilty; clear from accusation.–The jury *acquitted* the prisoner of the charges against him.
2. Behave (oneself).–The British soldiers *acquitted* themselves well at Waterloo.

a•cre (AY-ker) *n. acres.* A unit of land measurement that equals 160 square rods, or 43,560 square feet.–The farmer sold three *acres* of land.

ac•ro•bat (AK-rə-bat) *n. acrobats; acrobatic, adj.* A person who does stunts.–The *acrobat* we saw at the circus could walk a tightrope and do stunts on a trapeze.

a•cross (ə-KRAWSS) *adv.* and *prep.* From one side to the other.–The dog ran *across* the street.–There is a bridge *across* the river. –Mother sewed a hem *across* one end of the towel.

act (AKT) *n. acts.* 1. A thing done.–Skating, eating, sleeping, and playing are *acts.*
2. A deed. – A Boy Scout does a kind *act* every day.
3. A main division of a play or other stage entertainment.–The children are giving a play during Christmas Week. It has two *acts.*
–*v. acts, acted, acting.* 1. Take a part in a play or other entertainment.–Mary *acted* in the school play.
2. Do; behave.–Mother told the children to *act* properly in school.

ac•tion (AK-shən) *n. actions.* 1. Doing or acting.–Through quick *action* on the part of the lifeguard, the boy was saved from drowning.
2. A thing done.–Mother told Bob that his *actions* were not those of a gentleman.

ac•tive (AK-tiv) *adj.; actively, adv.* Busy; lively; moving a great deal.–Mr. Smith is very *active.* He is always doing something.

ac•tiv•i•ty (ak-TIV-ə-tee) *n. activities.* 1. Motion; being busy or moving about.–There is a lot of *activity* on our playground after school.
2. Something being done.–Drawing pictures is an *activity.*

ac•tor (AK-ter) *n. actors.* A man who acts or takes part in a play or moving picture.

ac•tress (AK-trəss) *n. actresses.* A woman who acts or takes a part in a play or moving picture.

ac•tu•al (AK-tyoo-əl *or* AK-chəl) *adj.; actually, adv.* Real; true.–I have no *actual* proof that Bob took the cookies, but I think he did.

ad•age (AD-ij) *n. adages.* A proverb; a saying accepted as true after long usage.–Many criminals get caught trying to disprove the old *adage* that there is no perfect crime.

a•dapt (ə-DAPT) *v. adapts, adapted, adapting.* Adjust; make to do or to fit something other than what the item was originally meant for.–Boy Scouts learn to *adapt* to various outdoor conditions, such as storms, lack of shelter, etc.–The electrician *adapted* the direct current motor to work on alternating current.
–*adaptation, n. adaptations.*

add (AD) *v. adds, added, adding.* 1. Put together; put with; join.–We *add* ten apples and two apples and get twelve apples.–*Add* yellow paint to blue, and you will have green.
2. Cause an increase of. – Your good luck *adds* to my happiness.
3. To say further.–Bill said it was time to meet the train. Dick *added* that they had to hurry.

ad·di·tion (ə-DISH-ən) *n. additions.* 1. Adding or putting numbers together to find the sum or answer. 2 + 4 = 6 is *addition.*
2. Putting with.–The *addition* of salt to vegetables makes them taste better.
3. A part or thing added.–We have a new *addition* on our school, with six rooms in it.

ad·di·tion·al (ə-DISH-ən-əl) *adj.; additionally, adv.* Extra; some more.–So many children came to the party that *additional* tables and chairs had to be used.

ad·dress (ə-DRESS *or* AD-rəss) *n. addresses.*
1. A speech; a talk.–Bob will give an *address* on safety at the meeting today.
2. Number, street, and place where one lives or where mail may be sent.–My *address* is 29 Smith Street, Lima, Ohio.

–*v. addresses, addressed, addressing.* 1. Speak to; give a talk to.–Father stood up to *address* the men.
2. Write an address on.–Mary *addressed* the letter to her friend.

ad·e·noid (AD-noid *or* AD-ən-oid) *n. adenoids.* A growth at the back of the nose and in the throat.–Bob had his tonsils and *adenoids* removed.

ad·e·quate (AD-ə-kwət) *adj.; adequately, adv.* Enough to meet the need; sufficient.–There was *adequate* food for all the guests. Everyone had enough to eat.

ad·he·sive·tape (ad-HEE-siv *or* -ziv tayp). A strip of cloth with a sticky substance on one side, used especially for fastening bandages. – Mother fastened the bandage to Mary's knee with *adhesive tape.*

ad·ja·cent (ə-JAY-sənt) *adj.; adjacently, adv.* Next to but not necessarily touching; neighboring.–John and Henry live in *adjacent* houses separated by a driveway.

ad·jec·tive (AJ-ik-tiv) *n. adjectives.* A word that tells you something about the noun or pronoun with which it is used, such as its description, quality, quantity, etc. – *Adjectives* include such words as: blue, English, good, bad, many, all, these, those, etc.

ad·join (ə-JOIN) *v. adjoins, adjoined, adjoining.* Be next to and actually touching; be joined with or to.–The kitchen *adjoins* the dining room in Susan's apartment.

ad·journ (ə-JERN) *v. adjourns, adjourned, adjourning.* Be dismissed; end (a meeting or gathering).–The club meeting *adjourned* because the chairman had to leave.

ad·just (ə-JUST) *v. adjusts, adjusted, adjusting.* 1. Change to make right.–John will *adjust* the window shade so that the sun will not shine in your eyes.
2. Correct; make right.–The grocer will *adjust* your grocery bill if there is a mistake.
3. Become suited to; adapt to.–The kitten *adjusted* to her new home quickly.
–*adjustment, n. adjustments.*

ad·min·is·ter (əd-MIN-əss-ter) *v. administers, administered, administering.* 1. Manage or direct. – The coach *administers* all the sports activities for the school.
2. Give. – The nurse *administered* first aid to the patient.

ad·min·is·tra·tion (əd-min-əss-TRAY-shən) *n. administrations.* 1. The managing, regulating and conducting of a business, school, institution, etc. – The company increased its sales through better *administration.*
2. The people or executives who are in charge of conducting and managing a business, school, institution, etc. – When the Board of Directors resigned, a new *administration* took over the direction of the hospital.
3. The time during which an official or his political party holds public office.–The Civil War was fought during Abraham Lincoln's *administration.*
4. The people in public office and their activities.–The new *administration* was determined to get rid of graft.
5. The giving of something, such as medicine, oaths, etc.–The *administration* of drugs should be done only on the advice of a doctor. –The spectators were silent during the *administration* of the oath of office.

ad·mi·ra·ble (AD-mə-rə-bəl) *adj.; admirably, adv.* Deserving the highest praise; wonderful.–John's efforts to save the drowning boy were *admirable.* He pulled him from the water and gave him artificial respiration.

ad·mi·ral (AD-mer-əl) *n. admirals.* An officer in the navy ranking above commodore.–The *admiral* ordered the ships into battle.

ad·mi·ra·tion (ad-mer-AY-shən) *n.* High regard and approval; esteem.–Actors and actresses often receive the *admiration* of the public.–To be held in *admiration* by one's fellow man is a great honor.–Mary is so pretty that she is often embarrassed by the *admiration* of strangers.

ad·mire (əd-MYR) *v. admires, admired, admiring.* 1. Look up to with respect, wonder, and approval.–Most boys *admire* baseball heroes.
2. Like and enjoy–The children *admired* the beautiful view from the mountain top.

ad·mis·sion (əd-MISH-ən) *n. admissions.* 1. The act of entering or getting in; admittance.–The boys voted for the *admission* of four more members into the club.
2. A price to be paid for getting in to see a movie, game, etc.–The *admission* to the ball game is $1.
3. A confession; telling the truth.–The boy's *admission* of having done wrong solved the mystery of the missing pencils.

ad·mit (əd-MIT) *v. admits, admitted, admitting.* 1. Let in.–Children were not *admitted* to the theater unless they were with a grownup.
2. Confess; acknowledge.–Jack does not like to *admit* that he has made a mistake.

a·do·be (ə-DOH-bi *or* -bee) *n.* and *adj.* A kind of brick that is dried in the sun.–Some American Indians live in houses made of *adobe.*

a·dopt (ə-DAHPT) *v. adopts, adopted, adopting.* 1. Take and treat as one's own.–The family will *adopt* the baby whose parents were lost in the storm. They will take the baby into their home and treat it as their own child.
2. Accept as one's own.–Usually people who come to America from abroad *adopt* American customs. They follow American ways.
3. To approve.–The committee *adopted* the plan proposed by Mr. Peters.
–adoption, n. adoptions.

a·dor·a·ble (ə-DOR-ə-bəl *or* ə-DOHR-ə-bəl) *adj.* Very sweet and lovable.–We think the baby is *adorable.*

a·dore (ə-DOR) *v. adores, adored, adoring.* Love and admire greatly.–Mary *adores* her piano teacher. She thinks her piano teacher is wonderful.

a·dorn (ə-DORN) *v. adorns, adorned, adorning.* Beautify; dress with decorations; make pleasing to the eye.–The queen was *adorned* with silks and jewels. – The bridesmaids helped to *adorn* the bride.

a·dult (ə-DULT *or* AD-əlt) *n. adults* and *adj.* A grownup; a person who has grown to be a man or a woman.–Your parents are *adults.*

ad·vance (əd-VANSS) *n. advances.* Forward movement; progress.–The army's *advance* was ten miles.–Recent *advances* in medicine have led to the cure of many diseases.
–v. advances, advanced, advancing. 1. Go forward; go ahead.–The officer told the men to *advance.*
2. Offer; bring forward.–The senior class *advanced* an amazing new program for the prom.
3. Give ahead of time.–Father will *advance* us part of next week's spending money if we all do our chores.
4. Raise.–They *advance* the theater prices in the evening.
5. Promote or be promoted.–Captain Winters was pleased to be *advanced* to the rank of major.

ad·van·tage (əd-VAN-tij) *n. advantages.* 1. A benefit; something good that makes a thing more wanted.–This book has an *advantage* over the other in that it is simpler. It is better than the other because it is simpler.–It would be of *advantage* to Bob to go on the trip with the basketball team. It would be good for him.
2. An opportunity.–Mary has had more *advantages* than most children. She has had music and dancing lessons, and chances to make friends.

ad·ven·ture (əd-VEN-tyoor *or* -cher) *n. adventures.* 1. An exciting and daring thing to do.–Admiral Byrd's trip to the South Pole was a great *adventure.*
2. An exciting experience.–Riding in an airplane proved to be a wonderful *adventure* for Bob and his sister, Sue.

ad•verb (AD-verb) *n. adverbs; adverbial, adj.* A word which tells something about a verb, an adjective, or another adverb. *Adverbs* usually answer one of the following questions: how?, when?, where?, etc. Most *adverbs* are formed by adding the suffix "-ly" to adjectives or participles (slow-*ly*; halting-*ly*).

ad•ver•tise (AD-ver-tyz) *v. advertises, advertised, advertising.* Make something known to the public through the newspapers, billboard signs, radio, etc. – Stores *advertise* things they have to sell.

ad•ver•tise•ment (əd-VER-tiss-mənt *or* ad-ver-TYZ-mənt) *n. advertisements.* A public notice.–If you do not find your dog, put an *advertisement* in the paper asking the person who finds him to bring him back.–Mother reads the department-store *advertisements* to see what is on sale.

ad•vice (əd-VYSS) *n.* Suggestions; ideas about what to do.–Mary had trouble with her arithmetic. Her teacher gave her some *advice*. She told Mary that she should learn her tables better.

ad•vise (əd-VYZ) *v. advises, advised, advising.* 1. Give advice or suggestions.–I *advise* you to see a doctor if you are not feeling well.

2. Tell.–A telegram *advised* us that our aunt would come to stay with us.

ad•vis•er or **ad•vi•sor** (əd-VYZ-er) *n. advisers* or *advisors.* One who gives guidance, counsel, or advice.–John asked the student *adviser* to help him with a problem.–The President and his *advisers* held a meeting.

ad•vo•cate (AD-və-kət) *n. advocates.* A pleader; one who supports or argues for something.–Many workers are *advocates* of higher wages.

–(AD-voh-kayt *or* AD-və-kayt) *v. advocates, advocated, advocating.* Recommend; urge support of.–The governor *advocated* passage of laws to aid school construction.

a•er•ate (AY-er-ayt *or* AIR-ayt) *v. aerates, aerated, aerating.* 1. Pass air or oxygen through.–Mother *aerated* the room to clear it of stale odors.

2. To mix with a gas, usually with carbon dioxide. – Soda water is usually made by *aerating* water with carbon dioxide.

a•e•ri•al (AIR-ee-əl *or* AY-ree-əl) *n. aerials.* A radio or television antenna.–The receiver was able to pick up more broadcasts once the *aerial* was attached.

–*adj.; aerially, adv.* Of, in, or like air.–A helicopter is an *aerial* means of transportation.

a•er•o•nau•tics (ay-roh-NAW-tiks *or* air-ə-NAW-tiks) *n.* The science or study of the operation of aircraft.–Advances in *aeronautics* have enabled engineers to design planes that fly faster than the speed of sound.

af•fair (ə-FAIR) *n. affairs.* 1. A matter of interest or business.–Father had many *affairs* to look after in the city.

2. A happening.–In small towns circus parades are big *affairs*.

af•fect (ə-FEKT) *v. affects, affected, affecting.* Change; make a difference in.–Because Bob studied at home, his absence from school did not *affect* his school marks.

af•fec•tion (ə-FEK-shən) *n.* Love; tender feeling.–Mother has much *affection* for all her children.

af•fec•tion•ate (ə-FEK-shən-ət) *adj.; affectionately, adv.* Fond; loving.–Jack is very *affectionate*. He shows his fondness for his family and friends.–The children are *affectionate* toward Mother. They kiss her.

af•firm (ə-FERM) *v. affirms, affirmed, affirming.* 1. State positively. – When questioned by the reporter, the mayor *affirmed* that he was planning to run for re-election.

2. Make officially valid; ratify.–The Senate will *affirm* the agreements reached at the international conference.

af•firm•a•tive (ə-FERM-ə-tiv) *adj.; affirmatively, adv.* Consenting or saying yes.–When Bob asked Mother if he might go camping, her answer was *affirmative*. She said yes.

af•ford (ə-FORD) *v. affords, afforded, affording.* 1. Spare the money.–Jack spent so much money for candy that he could not *afford* to buy the magazine.

2. Spare; give up. – Mother had so much housework to do that she could not *afford* the time to go to the movies.

3. Give.–Going to school *affords* you the opportunity to work and play with other boys and girls.

a•fraid (ə-FRAYD) *adj.* Scared; frightened. –Who's *afraid* of the big, bad wolf?

Af•ri•ca (AF-ri-kə) *n.; African, adj.* One of the seven continents of the earth. *Africa* is south of Europe. Much of *Africa* is very hot.

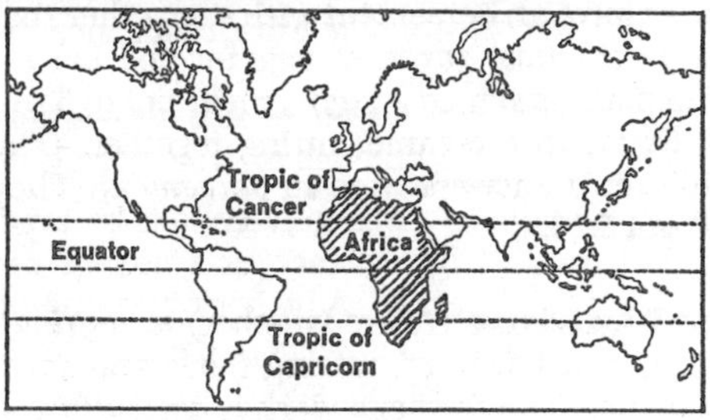

aft•er (AF-ter) *adj., adv., conj.,* and *prep.* 1. Behind. – Bob walked in the line *after* Jack.
2. Later; later than. – Father gets home shortly *after* six o'clock.
3. In search of; following.–The police have gone *after* the burglars.
4. In view of; because of. – *After* all my warnings, how could you have done it?

aft•er•noon (af-ter-NOON) *n. afternoons.* The time from noon until the sun goes down; the time between noon and evening.–Sally takes a nap in the *afternoon.*

aft•er•ward or **aft•er•wards** (AF-ter-werd *or* AF-ter-werdz) *adv.* Later; following that time.–Mother came home at six o'clock and Father came soon *afterward.*–We work first. We play *afterwards.*

a•gain (ə-GEN *or* -GAYN) *adv.* One more time; another time.–The bell rang once, then *again.* It rang a second time.–May I see the book *again?*

a•gainst (ə-GENST) *prep.* 1. On.–The ladder leaned *against* the house. The top end touched the house.–The branches hitting *against* the window panes frightened me.
2. Opposite.–John is running for class president *against* Bob. He is trying to win more votes than Bob.
3. Opposed to; contrary to; not in favor of.–Father is *against* Sally's eating much candy.
4. Next to.–In winter the tree branches look like fingers *against* the sky.–Gray looks nice *against* red.

a•gate (AG-ət) *n. agates.* A type of quartz with colored stripes or clouds inside that can be seen from the outside.–Children's marbles are often made of *agate.*

age (AYJ) *n. ages.* 1. Number of years old.–What is your *age?* I am eight years old. I am eight years of *age.*
2. A time or period.–We are living in a machine *age.* Machines are used for a great many things these days.
3. A time in one's life.–We learn to walk at an early *age.*
–*v. ages, aged, aging.* Grow old.–Grandfather is *aging.*

a•gen•da (ə-JEN-də) *n. agendas.* A list of subjects to be discussed at a meeting; a program of things to be done.–The mayor placed the problem of smoke control on his *agenda* for the next meeting.–We did many things during vacation that were not on our *agenda.* We did things we had not planned to do.

a•gent (AY-jənt) *n. agents.* A person or organization working for or selling things for someone else.–An *agent* came to the door selling brooms.–The ticket *agent* sells tickets for the railroad company.

ag•gra•vate (AG-rə-vayt) *v. aggravates, aggravated, aggravating.* 1. Make worse; increase in seriousness.–The patient's condition was *aggravated* by a high temperature.
2. Make angry; vex; irritate.–Tom *aggravates* his mother when he is late for dinner.

ag•gres•sion (ə-GRESH-ən) *n.* Attack, especially the first, by one nation or person upon another without just reason or excuse.–The United Nations seeks to prevent *aggression* in the interest of world peace.

ag•i•tate (AJ-ə-tayt) *v. agitates, agitated, agitating.* 1. Stir up or excite; disturb.–Father was *agitated* by the news that his favorite candidate had lost.
2. Shake rapidly and violently; set in irregular motion.–The instructions read: *Agitate* contents before opening can.
3. Arouse or excite public interest.–When Mr. Jones *agitated* for better schools, many people in the community became aware of the need.

a•go (ə-GOH) *adj.* and *adv.* Past; before now.–Father went to work at least an hour *ago.*–Mary likes to read stories of long *ago,* when there were knights and people believed in magic.

ag•o•ny (AG-ə-nee) *n.* Great pain or suffering.–The child screamed as though he were in *agony.*

a•gree (ə-GREE) *v. agrees, agreed, agreeing.* 1. Think the same; think alike.–The boys do not *agree* about whose turn it is to ride the bicycle. Jack says it is his turn, and Bill says it is his turn.
2. Consent.–Bob would not *agree* to the plan. He said no.
3. Match; equal the same.–The boys both added the numbers, but their answers did not *agree*. They got different answers.
4. Be suited; go together well.–Chocolate does not *agree* with some people.–Strawberries do not *agree* with some people.

a•gree•a•ble (ə-GREE-ə-bəl) *adj.; agreeably, adv.* 1. Pleasant.–The actress is a very *agreeable* person to meet and talk to.–Snow White found that the apple had an *agreeable* taste.
2. Suitable; convenient; to one's liking.–If the hour is *agreeable* to you, we will start early in the morning.
3. Willing to accept or consent to.–If you are *agreeable* to our plan, meet us early.

a•gree•ment (ə-GREE-mənt) *n. agreements.* 1. An understanding; arrangement.–Bob and Mary have an *agreement* with each other that they will take turns caring for the baby.–The nations signed an *agreement* not to fight.
2. Equal to the same; fitting together.–The children's answers were in *agreement*. They all got 225.

ag•ri•cul•ture (AG-rə-kul-cher) *n.; agricultural, adj.* Farming; raising foods and farm animals.–The farmer's work is *agriculture*.–Much of the central part of our country is given to *agriculture*.

ah (AH) *interj. Ah* shows a feeling of happiness, sorrow, victory, or the like.–*Ah*, now at last I can go to the circus!

AGRICULTURE

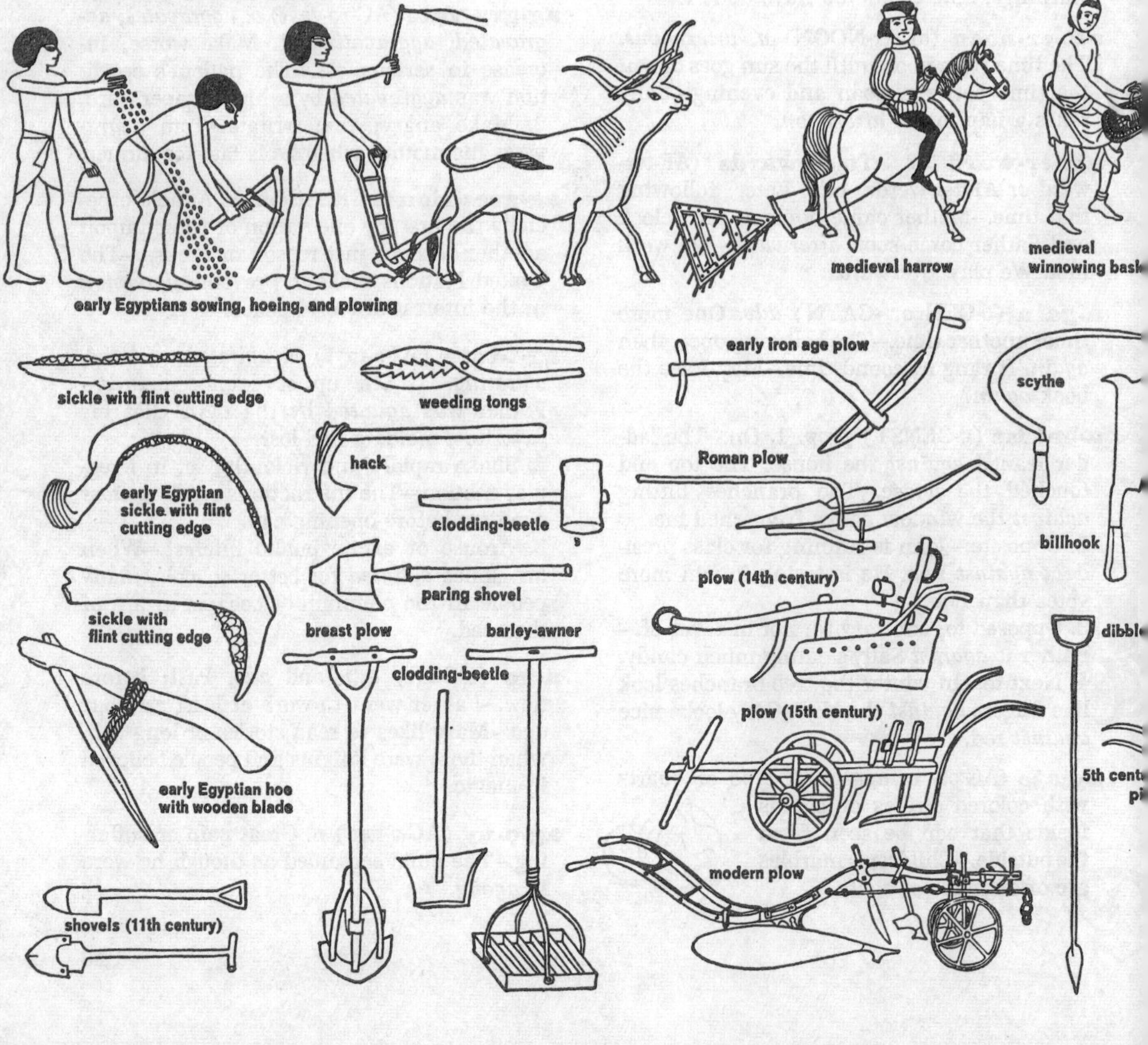

a·head (ə-HED) *adj.* and *adv.* 1. In front.–Bill could not get *ahead* of Jack in the line because the children behind wouldn't let him.–When the boy *ahead* stopped, I bumped into him.
2. On; forward.–The rain kept the carpenters from going *ahead* with their building. They could not continue.–The policeman told us that if we drove straight *ahead* we would come to the street we wanted.
3. Before.–The train arrived *ahead* of time.
4. Leading.–Bob's baseball team is *ahead* by three runs.

aid (AYD) *n.* 1. Help.–Without your *aid,* I could not have done the work.
2. (Also spelled *aide.*) A helper or assistant.–The children take turns being their teacher's *aid.*
–*v. aids, aided, aiding.* Give help to.–Thank you for *aiding* me with the work.
–*First aid* means help for the sick or injured; quick treatment.–A good Boy Scout learns *first aid.*

ail (AYL) *v. ails, ailed, ailing.* 1. Be wrong with.–I don't understand what *ails* Jack. I don't understand what's the matter with him.
2. Be sick.–Grandmother is *ailing* today.

ai·ler·on (AY-ler-ahn) *n. ailerons.* A hinged flap on the back edge of each wing of an airplane. The pilot uses the *ailerons* to tip the plane sideways when turning.

aim (AYM) *n. aims.* 1. Pointing.–He missed the target because his *aim* was bad.
2. A purpose or thing one tries for.–Bob's *aim* is to be an engineer.
–*v. aims, aimed, aiming.* 1. Point.–The Boy Scout *aimed* the arrow at the target.
2 Try.–We *aim* to do our best work.

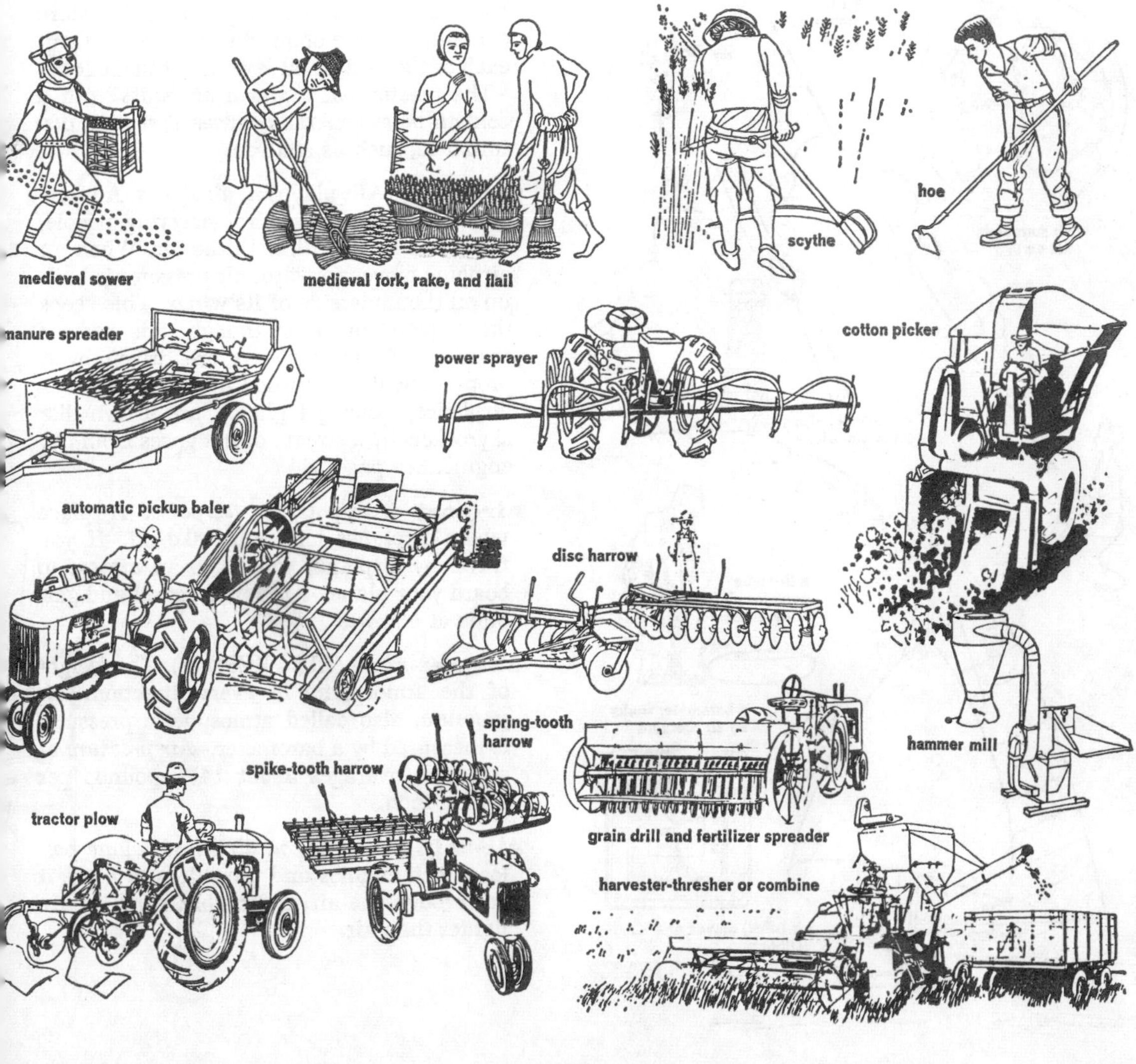

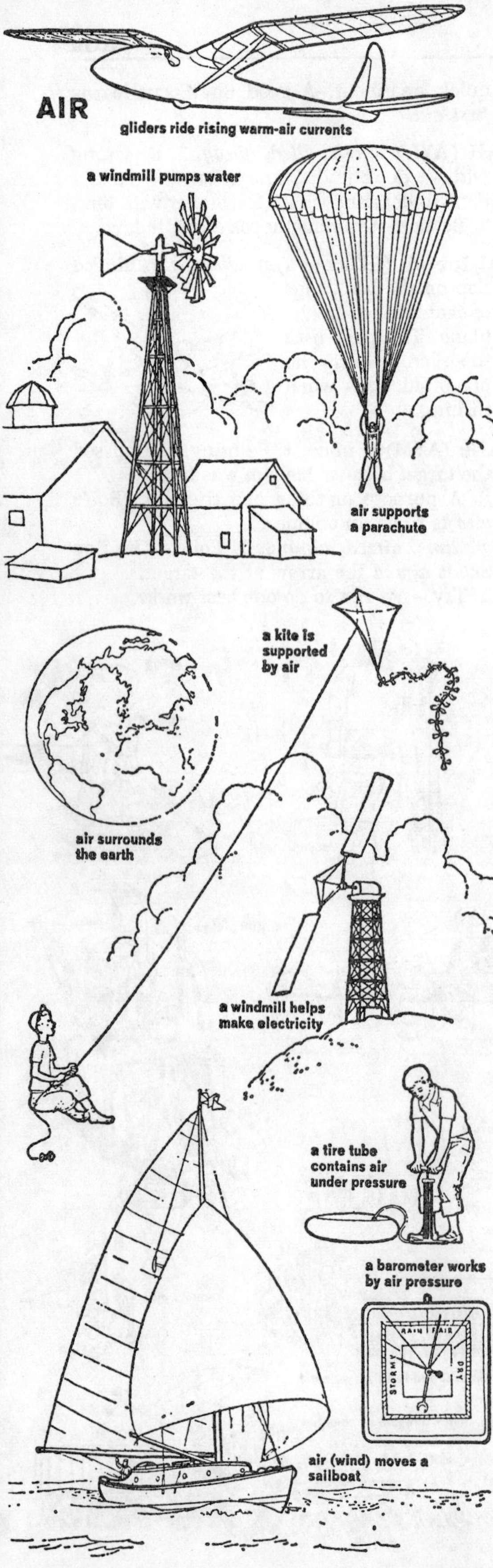
AIR
gliders ride rising warm-air currents
a windmill pumps water
air supports a parachute
a kite is supported by air
air surrounds the earth
a windmill helps make electricity
a tire tube contains air under pressure
a barometer works by air pressure
RAIN
FAIR
STORMY
DRY
air (wind) moves a sailboat

air (AIR) *n.* 1. A mixture of gases which is all about us, but which we cannot see. We breathe *air*. We put *air* into balloons, automobile tires, etc. Birds fly through the *air*.—Mother opened the windows to let in some *air*. 2. Appearance; manner.—There was an *air* of mystery about the old, deserted house.
—*v. airs, aired, airing.* Expose to fresh air.—Mother *airs* the beds before she makes them. She turns back the covers and lets the air in on them.

air-con·di·tion (AIR kən-DISH-ən) *v. air-conditions, air-conditioned, air-conditioning.* Control the air in a room, theater, etc., by cooling, heating, purifying, etc.—The owners *air-conditioned* the store for comfort.

air cur·rent (AIR kur-ənt) *air currents.* Wind, movement or stream of air, or a body of air.—Pilots and airplane navigators are interested in *air currents* at various altitudes.

air mass (AIR MASS) *air masses.* A large body of air in which temperature, moisture content, etc., are about the same throughout each of the horizontal layers that make it up. —The meeting of a warm *air mass* with a cold *air mass* generally causes a weather disturbance, such as a storm.

air·plane (AIR-playn) *n. airplanes.* A transportation vehicle used for carrying people, mail, and freight through the air. When an *airplane* moves forward, air pressure is built up on the underside of its wings. This keeps the *airplane* up, even though it is heavier than air. Some *airplanes* are driven by a propeller which is turned by a motor. Other *airplanes*, called jet planes, are driven like skyrockets by a stream of hot gases from the engine. See page 324.

air·port (AIR-port) *n. airports.* A place where airplanes land and take off.—If you travel by airplane, you go to an *airport* to board your plane.—Airplanes get oil and gasoline at *airports*.

air pres·sure (AIR PRESH-er). The weight of the atmosphere in every direction. *Air pressure*, also called atmospheric pressure, is measured by a barometer.—*Air pressure* at sea level averages about 14½ pounds per square inch.

air·ship (AIR-ship) *n. airships.* A long balloon with engines and propellers to make it go through the air; a dirigible. *Airships* are lighter than air.

air•way (AIR-way) *n. airways.* A route or path in the air which is followed by airplanes carrying passengers or freight. Some *airways* are marked at night by beacons, or guide lights, on the ground below.

aisle (YL) *n. aisles.* A path between rows of seats.–The children pick up the papers in the *aisle* to the right of their desks.–The usher at the theater led us down the *aisle.*

a•jar (ə-JAHR) *adj.* Open a little way.–Mother left the door *ajar* so that the dog could get back into the house.

Al•a•bam•a (al-ə-BAM-ə) *n.* A state in southeastern United States, noted for large cotton crops, manufacturing of iron and steel products, and lumbering. Much livestock feeds in the rich pastures of the foothills.

a•larm (ə-LAHRM) *n. alarms.* 1. A warning signal.–The red light at the railroad crossing gives the *alarm* when a train is coming. – We heard the burglar *alarm* ringing in the jewelry store.
2. A sudden fright.–Jack turned pale with *alarm* when he slipped and almost fell off the ladder.

–*v. alarms, alarmed, alarming.* Frighten; fill with dread.–Mother was *alarmed* because of the baby's cough, so she called the doctor.

a•las (ə-LASS) *interj. Alas* is used to express feelings of sadness or pity.–"*Alas,* I cannot go to the ball," said Cinderella.

A•las•ka (ə-LASS-kə) *n.* The 49th state to be admitted to the union of the United States. The territory of *Alaska* was originally purchased from Russia in 1867. *Alaska* is in the northwestern part of North America.

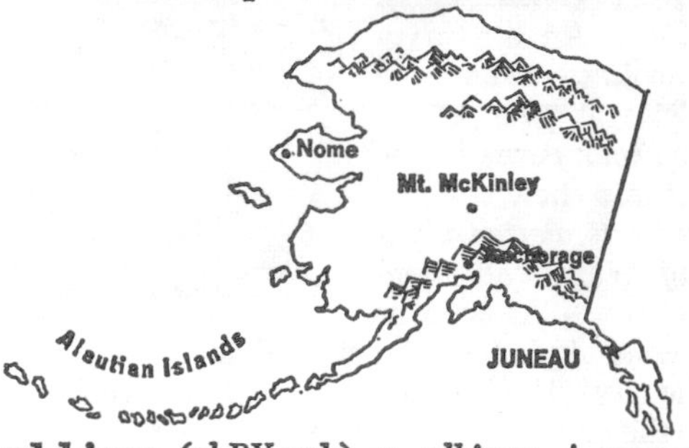

al•bi•no (al-BY-noh) *n. albinos.* A person born with a shortage of coloring matter in the skin, eyes, and hair. *Albinos* often have very light hair and milky-colored skin.

al•bum (AL-bəm) *n. albums.* A book with empty pages to be written in or have pictures, stamps, etc., pasted in.–The children pasted the pictures they took at the beach in the *album.*–The actress signed her name in Mary's *album.*

al•co•hol (AL-kə-hawl) *n.* A colorless liquid that looks like water. It is made chiefly by fermenting grains, such as corn, or from molasses or wood. Some drinks, such as whisky and beer, have *alcohol* in them. *Alcohol* is often used in medicines, and in making perfumes. Some kinds of *alcohol* are poisonous. One kind, if mixed with the water in the radiator of an automobile, will keep the water from freezing.

al•cove (AL-kohv) *n. alcoves.* A small room or area set off from a larger room.–The extra guest slept on a cot in the bedroom *alcove.*

al•der (AWL-der) *n. alders.* A kind of shrub or tree.—The bark of the *alder* is used to dye and tan leather.

a•lert (ə-LERT) *n. alerts.* An alarm; a warning.—When the *alert* was given, everyone took cover in the air raid shelter.
—*v. alerts, alerted, alerting.* Warn; call attention to.—As soon as enemy airplanes were sighted, sirens *alerted* the city.—The Boy Scout *alerted* the campers to the danger of forest fire.
—*adj.; alertly, adv.* Quick to notice or understand things.—Jack is very *alert* in class. He is wide awake and always pays attention.

al•fal•fa (al-FAL-fə) *n.* A plant with leaves like clover and with purple blossoms. Cattle and horses eat *alfalfa.* The roots of *alfalfa* are very long, and can get moisture from deep in the ground when the topsoil is dry.

al•gae (AL-jee) *n. pl.* Plants without true roots, stems, or leaves. *Algae* are usually one-celled and contain chlorophyll. Most seaweeds and fresh-water mosses are forms of *algae.*

al•ge•bra (AL-jə-brə) *n.* 1. Branch of mathematics that deals with numbers and their properties by using symbols, such as +, −, =, *x, a, b, c.* In *algebra,* the sum of 5 and 3 may be written: $a + b = x$, where *a* stands for 5, *b* stands for 3, and *x* stands for the sum.
2. A textbook on the subject.—John left his *algebra* in school.

al•i•bi (AL-ə-by) *n. alibis.* A defense or statement by an accused person in which he declares that at the time a deed was done he was elsewhere.—The prisoner's *alibi* was that he was out of town at the time of the theft.

al•ien (AYL-yən *or* AY-lee-ən) *n. aliens.* A foreign person; one who lives in a country but is not a citizen of that country.—An American in France would be an *alien.*

a•light (ə-LYT) *v. alights, alighted, alighting.* 1. Get off.—When the train stops, we will *alight.*
2. Land; come down from the air and settle.—The airplane is about to *alight.*—The bee *alights* on the flower to get the sweet nectar.

a•like (ə-LYK) *adj.* and *adv.* Very much the same; similar.—These dresses are so much *alike* that you can hardly tell them apart.—Bob and Mary look much *alike.* They both have blue eyes, light hair, and freckles.

al•i•men•ta•ry ca•nal (al-ə-MEN-tə-ree kə-NAL). The tube through which food travels in the body from the time it is eaten until the time it is digested, absorbed, and the waste products eliminated. The *alimentary canal* includes the mouth, stomach, small and large intestines, etc.

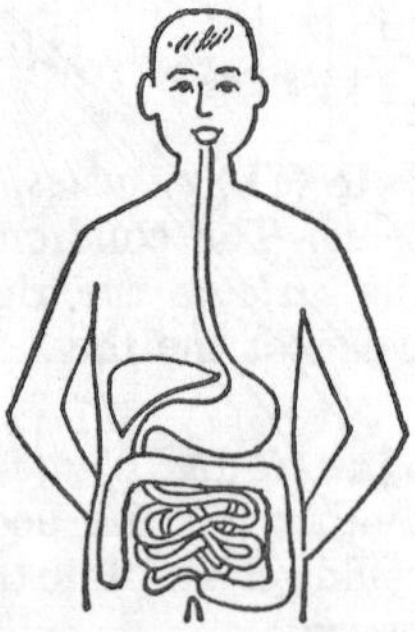

a•live (ə-LYV) *adj.* 1. Living; not dead.—The cat that had fallen into the water was still *alive.* He was saved in time.
2. Keeping active.—The players tried to keep the volleyball game *alive* by not letting the ball come to a stop.
3. Full of motion.—There were so many birds flying that the sky looked *alive.*

all (AWL) *n., adj., adv.,* and *pron.* 1. Everything.—Although Bill gave his *all,* his team lost the game.—*All* is well.
2. Every bit of; the whole of.—We went fishing *all* the time last summer.—Grandfather has lived in this city *all* his life. He has never lived anywhere else.
3. Everybody.—In this country, there is enough food for *all.*
4. Each one of.—*All* of us went to the movies.
5. Apiece.—At the end of the game, the score was tied at four *all.* Neither team had won.
6. Completely.—You don't have to live on a desert island to be *all* alone.

al•le•giance (ə-LEE-jənss) *n.* Loyalty, devotion, and faithfulness.—Citizens show their *allegiance* to their country in different ways. They display flags on national holidays, take part in parades, serve in the armed forces.

al•ler•gic (ə-LER-jik) *adj.* Having extreme sensitivity that causes various body reactions, such as rashes and swelling.—Henry is *allergic* to feathers. They make him sneeze.

al·ler·gy (AL-er-jee) *n. allergies.* A special sensitivity in the body that causes certain illnesses, such as hay fever and hives.–John has an *allergy* which causes him to break out in a rash whenever he eats chocolate.

al·ley (AL-ee) *n. alleys.* 1. A narrow roadway. *Alleys* are built between or behind buildings for service trucks, delivery trucks, etc.–We put the rubbish in the *alley* so that it can be collected easily.

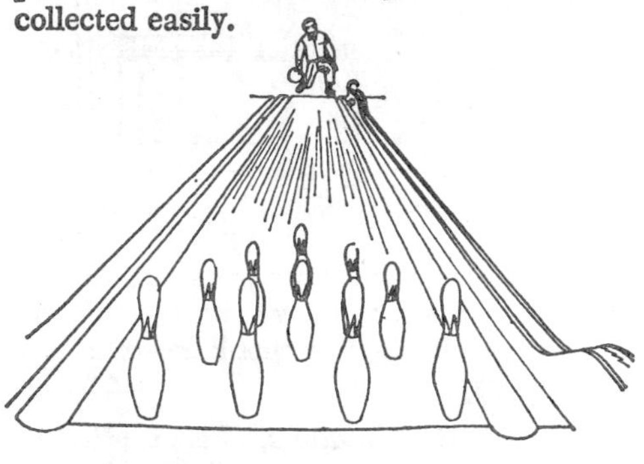

2. A smooth pathway made of boards.–Father bowls in a bowling *alley.*

al·li·ance (ə-LY-ənss) *n. alliances.* 1. A joining together of people, nations, clubs, etc., often in their own interests.–When Mary Greene and John Smith were married, a family *alliance* was formed by the Greenes and the Smiths.–Five nations formed an *alliance* to help one another in emergencies.
2. The agreement itself.–The *alliance* proved that the nations were friendly.
3. The members who join in such an agreement.

al·li·ga·tor (AL-ə-gay-ter) *n. alligators.* A large crawling animal with four short legs, large and strong jaws, and a long pointed tail. *Alligators* live in the warmer parts of North America, both in water and on land. The *alligator's* tough hide is sometimes made into leather for shoes, purses, etc.

al·lit·er·a·tion (ə-lit-er-AY-shən) *n.* Repetition of the same sound or letter at the beginning of each word in a series of words. The words do not necessarily have to be next to one another, as: The strong, silent man sat in the sixth row. – *Alliteration* is often found in poetry.

al·low (ə-LOW) *v. allows, allowed, allowing.* 1. Permit; let.–Mary's mother *allows* her to play the piano any time. She lets Mary play without asking her permission.
2. Give; let have.–Our teacher *allows* us five pages to write our test on.

al·low·ance (ə-LOW-ənss) *n. allowances.* A set amount given.–Some fathers give their children an *allowance* of money each week. They give them a certain amount to spend.
–*Make allowance for* means take into consideration. – You should *make allowance for* Bill's mistake. He did not have all the facts.

al·loy (AL-oi *or* ə-LOI) *n. alloys.* 1. A mixture of two or more metals, or of a metal and another substance, such as carbon. The mixture generally produces some special quality, such as hardness, springiness.–Brass is an *alloy* of copper and zinc.
2. An impure or cheap mixture of metals.–The candlesticks were made of an *alloy* of copper and silver.

all right (AWL RYT). 1. Correct.–John's answer was *all right.*
2. Satisfactory or agreeable.–If it is *all right* with you, we will meet at the school.
3. Yes; very well.–When Mary asked if she might go, Mother said, *"All right."*

al·ly (AL-y) *n. allies.* 1. A nation tied to another nation by treaty.–The United States and Great Britain are *allies.*
2. An associate; a helper. – John gave his friend a fly swatter and asked him to become his *ally* in his battle against the flies.
–(ə-LY) *v. ally, allied, allying.* To unite or to join.–The two cowboys *allied* themselves to catch the wild horse.

al·ma·nac (AWL-mə-nak) *n. almanacs.* A yearly booklet that tells about the days, weeks, and months of the year, and about the moon, stars, weather, etc.

al·most (AWL-mohst) *adv.* Nearly. – Jack had *almost* enough money to go to the circus.

a·loft (ə-LAWFT) *adv.* High in the air.–The balloon was sent *aloft* during the night.–The captain sent the sailor *aloft.* So he climbed to the top of the mast, or rigging, of the ship.

a·lone (ə-LOHN) *adj.* and *adv.* 1. By oneself; without others.–My grandmother lives *alone.*
2. Only; by itself; without other things.–Sunshine *alone* will not make the plants grow. They also need water.

a•long (ə-LAWNG) *adv.* 1. Onward.—The policeman told the driver of the car to go *along.*
2. With (one).—We are going to town, and Bob will go *along.*
—*prep.* Throughout the length of; beside.—The man walked *along* the street. — Bob walked *along* the wall. He walked beside the wall.

a•loud (ə-LOWD) *adv.* With sound; out loud. —Speak *aloud,* do not whisper, if you want people to hear you.—Mother reads *aloud* to us on rainy days.

al•pha•bet (AL-fə-bət) *n. alphabets.* A set of all the letters used in any language, arranged or put in a certain order. — In the English language, the *alphabet* is sometimes called the ABC's, and has 26 letters.

al•pha•bet•i•cal (al-fə-BET-ik-əl) *adj.; alphabetically, adv.* According to or in the order of the alphabet.—The children arranged their spelling words in *alphabetical* order.—In an English dictionary, all the words starting with "a" come first, those starting with "b" come next, and so on, all in *alphabetical* order.

al•read•y (awl-RE-dee) *adv.* By or before this time.—We thought Father would be here *already.*

al•so (AWL-soh) *adv.* Too; in addition.—Bob is in the fifth grade. Mary is in the fifth grade *also.*

al•tar (AWL-ter) *n. altars.* A raised place at the front of a church where sacred ceremonies are held.—The monk knelt at the *altar* to pray.

al•ter (AWL-ter) *v. alters, altered, altering.* Change; make different; adjust.—Mother's dress did not fit well, so she *altered* it.

al•ter•nate (AWL-ter-nət) *n. alternates.* Substitute; one that takes the place of another.—The lead actor was sick, so his *alternate* took his part in the play.
—(AWL-tər-nayt) *v. alternates, alternated, alternating.* Change regularly; do or take place in turn, first one, then the other.—The two workers *alternate* their hours. First one works at night for a week, then the other works at night for a week, and so on.
—(AWL-tər-nət) *adj.; alternately, adv.* Taking turns.—People walk by using their left and right legs in *alternate* order.

al•ter•nat•ing cur•rent (AWL-ter-nayt-ing KER-ənt). Electric current that changes its direction of flow at regular intervals.—Most houses in New York City are wired for *alternating current.*

al•though (awl-THOH) *conj.* Even if; though.—*Although* I haven't a new hat, I shall go to church on Easter.

al•tim•e•ter (al-TIM-ə-ter) *n. altimeters.* An instrument for measuring heights or altitudes.—The pilot checked his *altimeter* to see how high he was flying.

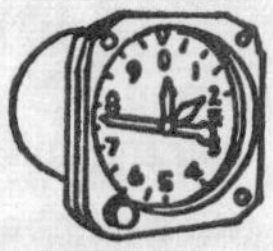

al•ti•tude (AL-tə-tood *or* -tyood) *n. altitudes.* Height; distance from the earth or from the level of the oceans, called sea-level.—What is the *altitude* of this hill? How high is it?—Birds fly at different *altitudes.*

al·to (AL-toh) *n. altos* and *adj.* 1. A part in music sung by women who have low voices. 2. A woman with a singing voice suitable to sing this part.

al·to·geth·er (awl-tə-GETH-er) *adv.* Wholly; entirely.—The farmer's work was not *altogether* satisfactory. He was not entirely pleased with it.

a·lu·mi·num (ə-LOOM-ə-nəm *or* əl-LYOOM-ə-nəm) *n.* A dull, silver-colored metal that is very light. It is used for cooking utensils, airplanes, and many other things that must be strong but light.

al·ways (AWL-wayz) *adv.* At all times.—*Always* think before you speak.

am (AM) *v.* One form of the verb *be*, used only with I.—I *am* going to play ball.—I *am* in the fifth grade.

am·a·teur (AM-ə-tyoor *or* -cher *or* AM-ə-ter) *n. amateurs* and *adj.* One who works or plays at some activity just for pleasure and not for pay.—The Eagles Club is a hockey club. All its members are *amateurs.*

a·maze (ə-MAYZ) *v. amazes, amazed, amazing.* Surprise.—Mary's ability to play the piano will *amaze* you.
—*amazement, n. amazements.*

am·bas·sa·dor (am-BASS-ə-der *or* -dohr) *n. ambassadors.* 1. A minister of state sent by one government as its highest official representative to another government.—The new *ambassador* presented his official papers and was cordially received.
2. Any official messenger.—The union's *ambassador* spoke at the labor convention.

am·ber (AM-ber) *n.* A hard, yellowish gum used in making beads and other articles of jewelry. Amber is the fossil resin of pines that grew long ago.
—*adj.* Yellowish.—The *amber* traffic light tells the driver to get ready to stop.

am·bi·dex·trous (am-bi-DEKS-trəss) *adj.* Having the ability to use either hand with equal skill; being both right- and left-handed.—Tom is *ambidextrous.* He can play tennis holding his racket in either hand.

am·bi·tion (am-BISH-ən) *n. ambitions.* 1. An aim; a goal.—Mary's *ambition* is to become a great musician.
2. A great desire for success.—The reason Bob makes better grades than Bill is that he has more *ambition.*

am·bi·tious (am-BISH-əss) *adj.; ambitiously, adv.* Full of ambition; wanting success.—People who are *ambitious* are apt to be successful.

am·bu·lance (AM-byə-lənss *or* AM-byoo-lənss) *n. ambulances.* A specially designed car for carrying sick and injured people.—Mary was taken to the hospital in an *ambulance.*

a·men (AH-MEN *or* AY-MEN). A word said at the end of a prayer, meaning "So be it!"

a·mend (ə-MEND) *v. amends, amended, amending.* Change, especially for the better.—The boy *amended* his answer. He gave more information.

a·mend·ment (ə-MEND-mənt) *n. amendments.* 1. A change or correction, usually for the better; an improvement.—The author made several *amendments* to eliminate repetition in his book.
2. A legislative correction, change, addition, or substitution, in a bill, law, etc.—The senator proposed an *amendment* to the bill under discussion.

A·mer·i·ca (ə-MAIR-ə-kə) *n.; American, adj.* 1. The continents of North *America* and South *America.*—The United States is in North *America.*
2. The name *America* can mean either North *America* or South *America.*
3. The United States is often called *America*; its citizens are known as *Americans.*

am·mo·ni·a (ə-MOHN-yə) *n.* A colorless gas with a sharp, strong odor. *Ammonia* is mixed with water and used for cleaning. *Ammonia* gas is often used in making ice.

am·mu·ni·tion (am-yə-NISH-ən *or* am-yoo-NISH-ən) *n.* Gunpowder, shells, bullets, etc., used in shooting guns and cannon.

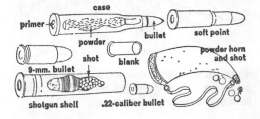

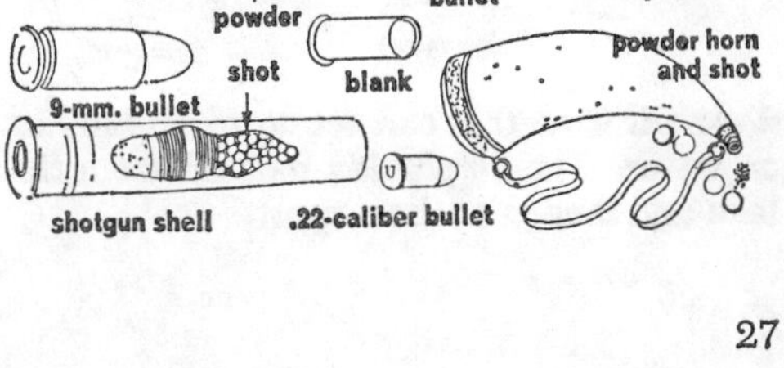

am•ne•si•a (am-NEE-zhə) *n.* Loss of memory. *Amnesia* may be caused by injury to the brain, severe shock, high fever, etc.

a•moe•ba or **a•me•ba** (ə-MEE-bə) *n. amoebas* or *amebas.* A one-celled animal that can be seen only with the aid of a microscope. The *amoeba* moves by constantly changing its shape. It flows in different directions and pulls its body after it. The *amoeba* can be found in fresh-water ponds or in stale water.

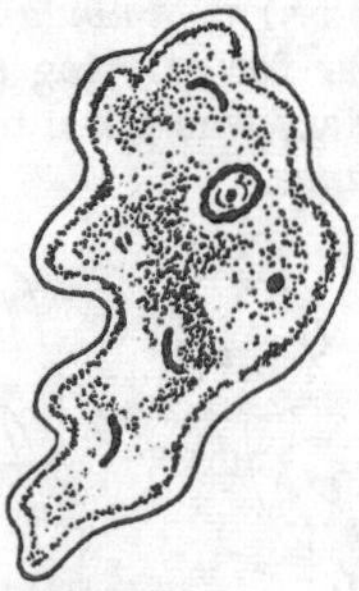

a•mong (ə-MUNG) *prep.* 1. In the midst of. –There was a spy *among* the soldiers in the camp.
2. To each of.–Mother divided the cake *among* the children. She gave each child some.
3. Together with.–We are *among* friends.

a•mount (ə-MOWNT) *n. amounts.* 1. Total; entire quantity.–Mother spent $4 for a hat and $2 for gloves. The *amount* of money she spent was $6.
2. A quantity.–Each year a large *amount* of sugar is made from sugar beets.
–*v. amounts, amounted, amounting.* Attain; reach.–Bill will never *amount* to anything. He is too lazy to succeed.
–*Amount to* can mean come to, total, or become.–The money he spent *amounted* to $6. –A day without any housework *amounts to* a vacation for Mother.

am•pere (AM-pir) *n. amperes.* A unit for measuring the strength of an electric current.

am•phib•i•an (am-FIB-ee-ən) *n. amphibians* and *adj.* 1. A plant or animal that can live both on land and in the water, such as a frog, a salamander, etc. *Amphibians* belong to the class of vertebrate animals, or those with backbones.

eastern newt (salamander)

2. An airplane that can set down on land or on water.–The *amphibian* took off from the lake and landed at the airport.

am•ple (AM-pəl) *adj.* Enough.–There was *ample* cake for all the guests at the birthday party.

am•pli•fy (AM-plə-fy) *v. amplifies, amplified, amplifying.* 1. Enlarge upon a subject by adding details, illustrations, examples, etc.–The teacher asked Robert to *amplify* his discussion by including more dates and facts.
2. Exaggerate; make more important.–The writer *amplified* his tale beyond belief.
3. Increase, as power or current.–Tom's new hi-fi set *amplifies* the sound twice as much as the old model did. It is much louder.

am•pu•tate (AM-pyə-tayt) *v. amputates, amputated, amputating.* Cut off.–The doctor did not have to *amputate* the man's injured finger. It finally healed.
–*amputation, n. amputations.*

a•muse (ə-MYOOZ) *v. amuses, amused, amusing.* Entertain; make laugh; please with humor.–Clowns *amuse* the children by doing tricks and funny stunts.

a•muse•ment (ə-MYOOZ-mənt) *n. amusements.* 1. An entertaining thing; a sport or pastime.–Fishing, racing, and puppet shows are Jack's favorite *amusements.*
2. Entertainment; pleasure.–The clown does tricks for the *amusement* of the children.

an (AN) *adj.* or *art.* (Used instead of "a" when the following word begins with a vowel.)
1. One or any.–Grandfather is *an* old man. –Baby has *an* orange.
2. For each.–There are four lines *an* inch on the paper. There are four lines in, or for, every inch.

a•nal•y•sis (ə-NAL-ə-səss) *n. analyses.* An examination made by separating into parts. –The farmer made an *analysis* of the soil to see if it contained the proper materials to make corn grow.

an•a•lyze (AN-əl-yz) *v. analyzes, analyzed, analyzing.* 1. Separate a thing into parts to find out what it is made of.–In science class we *analyzed* a bar of soap.
2. Examine each part of a thing or situation in detail.–The teacher *analyzed* the arithmetic problem by going over each part.

a•nat•o•my (ə-NAT-ə-mee) *n.* 1. The science or study of the structure of plants or animals, or of any of their parts.–The understanding of *anatomy* is an important part of medical training.
2. The dividing and separating of the various parts of a plant or animal for examination. – *Anatomy* adds to man's knowledge of himself and his environment.
3. The structure of the body or its parts.–Artists study *anatomy* in order to be able to draw the human form accurately.
4. A skeleton.–The laboratory acquired an *anatomy* for study.

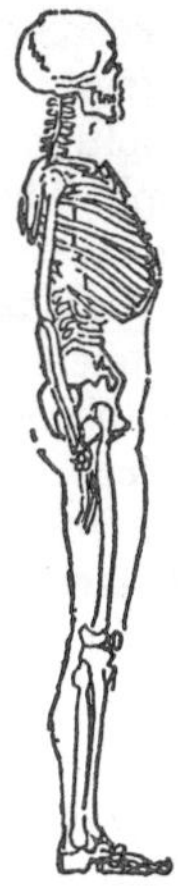

an•ces•tor (AN-sess-ter) *n. ancestors.* A person who came before in a family line.–Your father, your mother, and your grandparents are your *ancestors.* Your grandparents' *ancestors* are also yours. They are your family from away back.

an•chor (ANG-ker) *n. anchors.* A heavy metal object, usually with two points, used to hold boats in place in the water. One end of a rope or chain is fastened to the *anchor* and the other to the boat. When the *anchor* is dropped into the water, it digs into the bottom and keeps the boat from moving about.

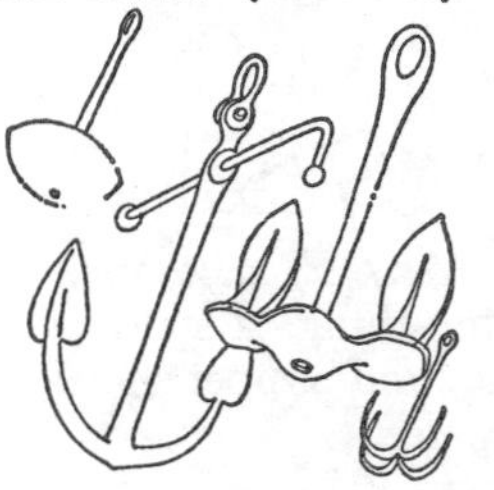

–*v. anchors, anchored, anchoring.* 1. Fasten in place with an anchor.–Fishermen sometimes *anchor* their boats while they fish.
2. Fix or fasten.–The flagpole was *anchored* to the roof with bolts.

an•cient (AYN-shənt *or* -chənt) *adj.* 1. Of times long ago.–Mummies are relics of *ancient* Egypt.
2. Very old.–The custom of celebrating Christmas is *ancient.*–That chair is so *ancient* it looks as though it will fall apart. Let's buy a new one.

and (AND) *conj.* 1. The word *and* is used to join words *and* groups of words.
2. Added to.–Four *and* four is eight.
–*And* is used for the word "to" when used after "come," "go," and some other words.–Come *and* see my new hat.–Go *and* buy the toys.

an•e•mom•e•ter (an-ə-MAHM-ə-ter) *n. anemometers.* An instrument for measuring the wind.–The meteorologist checked the *anemometer* in the weather observatory before preparing his forecast.

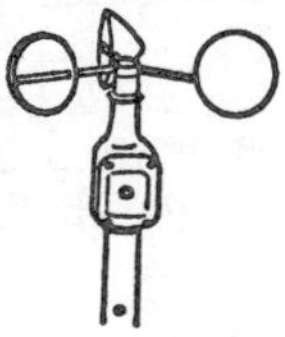

an•es•thet•ic (an-əss-THET-ik) *n. anesthetics.* A substance used by doctors and dentists to lessen or eliminate pain by producing a lack of feeling or sensitivity.–The doctor gave his patient an *anesthetic* before the operation.

an•gel (AYN-jəl) *n. angels.* 1. A winged messenger of God.
2. Sometimes people are called *angels* because of their goodness and loveliness.

an•ger (ANG-ger) *n.* A fighting feeling; a feeling caused by receiving unfair treatment or by being kept from doing what one wishes.
–Even though the bully continued to tease him, John did not show his *anger.* John did not let the bully see how annoyed and furious he felt.
–*v. angers, angered, angering.* Make angry.–His father's refusal to let him go to the game *angered* Jack.

an•gle (ANG-gəl) *n. angles.* A point where two lines meet, or the space between two lines meeting at a point.

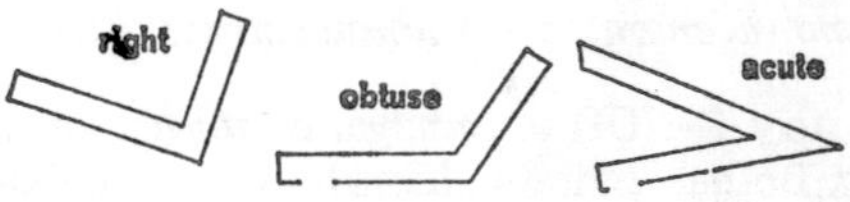

an•gle•worm (ANG-gəl-werm) *n. angleworms.* Earthworms are called *angleworms* because they are used for bait in angling or fishing.

an•gri•ly (ANG-grə-lee) *adv.* In an angry or displeased manner.–Jack spoke *angrily* to his dog when it would not go home.

an•gry (ANG-gree) *adj. angrier, angriest.*
1. Feeling like fighting or doing injury; feeling anger.–When the boys tied Bob's hands behind him, he became *angry.*
2. Severe; dangerous. – The *angry* waves nearly wrecked the boat.
3. Red and sore. – The cut on Bob's arm looked *angry.*

an•i•mal (AN-ə-məl) *n. animals.* Any living thing other than a plant. Most *animals* are able to move, and eat plants or other *animals.* A tiny spider is an *animal* and a great elephant is an *animal*, too. See page 327.

an•kle (ANG-kəl) *n. ankles.* The joint between the foot and the leg. – Mary sprained her *ankle* badly when she jumped off the fence behind the house.

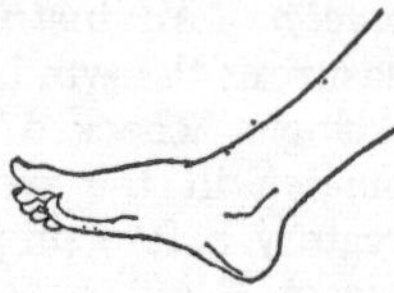

an•nex (AN-eks) *n.* An addition to something, as an extra building, room, etc.; an additional section in a book, statement, contract, etc.–The basketball game took place in the gym *annex.*

an•ni•ver•sa•ry (an-ə-VERSS-ə-ree) *n. anniversaries.* A date of the year on which something happened in an earlier year.–September 12 is Mother's and Father's wedding *anniversary.* They were married many years ago on that date.–The *anniversary* of your birth is your birthday.

an•nounce (ə-NOWNSS) *v. announces, announced, announcing.* 1. Tell to everyone or to a large group of people; make a public notice of.–John will *announce* who the characters in the play will be.–When visitors call at the school, the teacher will *announce* their arrival to the class.

2. Make known to everyone by printing in a newspaper, telling by means of radio, etc. –The newspapers will *announce* the date of the first ball game.

–*announcement, n. announcements.*

an•noy (ə-NOI) *v. annoys, annoyed, annoying.* Bother; irritate; disturb.–Our neighbor's radio *annoys* Father.

–*annoyance, n. annoyances.*

an•nu•al (AN-yoo-əl) *adj.; annually, adv.* 1. Once a year.–Thanksgiving is an *annual* holiday.

2. Yearly.–The *annual* rent for our house is $800.

a•non•y•mous (ə-NAHN-ə-məss) *adj.* By an unknown or unidentified gift-giver or writer. –The school received a collection of *anonymous* poetry last month from an *anonymous* donor.

an•oth•er (ə-NUTH-er) *adj.* 1. One more.–Mary sang *another* song when the children asked her to.

2. A different.–Father put on *another* suit to go out.

–*pron.* A different person or thing.–This apple is spoiled. May I have *another*?

an•swer (AN-ser) *n. answers.* 1. A reply.–The teacher asked a question and Jack gave the correct *answer.*–We wrote the *answers* to the test.

2. Solution.–The *answer* to the mystery is simple. The butler did it.

–*v. answers, answered, answering.* 1. Go to see what is wanted or who is calling.–When the telephone rings, Mary *answers* it.–Will you *answer* the doorbell?

2. Reply to.–Did you *answer* the question?

3. Be responsible.–I cannot *answer* for Bill's mistakes. I was not there.

ant (ANT) *n. ants.* A small insect, with a body divided into sections like little beads. Some *ants* are black, some red. They live together in big "colonies," and dig their homes, called *ant* hills, in the ground. Some *ants* do a great deal of damage.

an•tag•o•nize (an-TAG-ə-nyz) *v. antagonizes, antagonized, antagonizing.* Make angry and hostile. – Johnny *antagonized* his brother by riding his bicycle.–The lion tamer is careful not to *antagonize* the animals when he enters the cage.

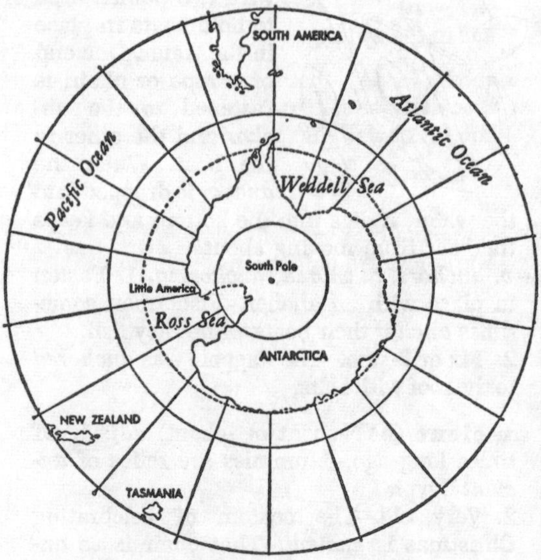

SOUTH POLAR AREA

Ant•arc•ti•ca (ant-AHRK-tə-kə) *n.; Antarctic, adj.* The name of a large continent on which the South Pole is located. No one lives in *Antarctica,* which is almost completely covered by ice. It is surrounded by the *Antarctic* Ocean.

an·te·lope (AN-tə-lohp) *n. antelopes.* An animal similar to a deer.

an·ten·na (an-TEN-ə) *n. antennas.* 1. An aerial; a wire or arrangement of wires attached to a radio receiver or transmitter for receiving or sending out radio waves.—The station went off the air when its *antenna* was damaged.
2. *pl. antennae.* The "feelers" or sensitive, movable, wandlike organs on the heads of insects, centipedes, crabs, etc.—The lobster waved its *antennae* in the water.

an·them (AN-thəm) *n. anthems.* A song. especially a solemn or a sacred one.—The church choir sang an *anthem* on Easter.

an·thol·o·gy (an-THAL-ə-jee) *n. anthologies.* A collection of stories, poems, writings, etc., usually of outstanding quality.—Many of Mark Twain's stories are printed in *anthologies.*

an·thro·poid (AN-thrə-poid) *n. anthropoids.* An ape, resembling man, such as the gorilla or gibbon.—*Anthropoids* are found in certain parts of Africa and southeastern Asia.

an·ti·bi·ot·ic (an-tee- *or* an-tə-by-AHT-ik) *n. antibiotics.* A substance manufactured by certain bacteria or fungi which is used by doctors to prevent infection by other bacteria.—Penicillin and streptomycin are *antibiotics* which are widely used to fight disease.

an·tic·i·pate (an-TISS-ə-payt) *v. anticipates, anticipated, anticipating.* 1. Expect; look forward to.—The family was *anticipating* the arrival of the new car Father had bought.
2. Deal with something before someone else does.—Peter *anticipated* the question in the debate. He answered it before his opponent spoke.
3. Experience something before it actually happens.—The children are *anticipating* the fun of going to the circus.

an·tic·i·pa·tion (an-tiss-ə-PAY-shən) *n.* Expectation.—John's *anticipation* of a reward was justified. He received ten dollars for finding and returning the lost purse.

an·ti·dote (AN-tə-doht) *n. antidotes.* 1. Something given to counteract or cure poisoning.—Table salt dissolved in warm water, starch paste, or milk are *antidotes* for many poisons.
2. Anything that corrects the bad effects of something else.—Keeping busy is an *antidote* for mischief.

an·tique (an-TEEK) *n. antiques* and *adj.* Something made long ago, and valuable because of its age.—Aunt Ella gives Mother *antiques.* Last year she gave us an *antique* desk made two hundred years ago.

an·ti·sep·tic (an-tə-SEP-tik) *n.* and *adj.* Something that prevents or stops infection, growth of bacteria, etc., or has the ability to do so.—Iodine is an *antiseptic.*

an·ti·tox·in (an-ti-TAHK-sən) *n. antitoxins.* A substance, or antibody, formed in the blood that fights disease.—Many serums are made with *antitoxins* to fight tetanus, scarlet fever, diphtheria, etc.

ant·ler (ANT-ler) *n. antlers.* The solid horn, usually branched, of an animal in the deer family, such as the moose, reindeer, or caribou. — Deer shed their *antlers* and grow new ones each year.

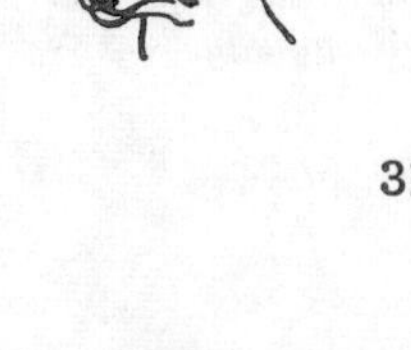

an•to•nym (AN-tə-nim) *n. antonyms.* A word that means the opposite of another word.–"Light" is the *antonym* of "dark."–"Up" is the *antonym* of "down."

an•vil (AN-vil *or* -vəl) *n. anvils.* An iron block on which metal or iron is pounded into shape. –A blacksmith shapes metal horseshoes on an *anvil.*

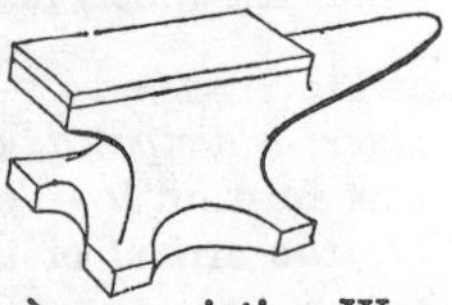

anx•i•e•ty (ang-ZY-ə-tee) *n. anxieties.* Worry, mental uneasiness, or the state of being very much concerned about something.–The coach's *anxiety* was due to the fact that his star player had been injured.

anx•ious (ANGK-shəss) *adj.; anxiously, adv.* 1. Worried; nervous; concerned.–Mother is *anxious* about the baby's cough.
2. Eager; impatient.–Mary was *anxious* for Father to come home so she could show him her new hair-do.

an•y (EN-ee) *adj.* 1. No particular one.–Grandmother told me to take *any* flower I wanted from the garden.–I'd like to go to town with you *any* day you say.
2. Even one; a little.–I do not want *any* candy.
3. Some.–Father asked us if we wanted *any* money to go shopping.
4. An unlimited or large amount.–Jim can walk *any* distance.
5. Every.–*Any* riddle can be answered.
–*adv.* To any degree; in any measure.–Is a man with five million dollars *any* happier than a man with four million dollars?

an•y•bod•y (EN-ee-bah-dee) *pron.* Anyone; any person.–We did not hear *anybody* knock at the door.

an•y•how (EN-ee-how) *adv.* 1. Anyway; in spite of something; nevertheless.–It looks like rain, but Father says we may go *anyhow.*
2. Besides; also.–Mary stayed home because of her cold, but she wanted to stay home and play *anyhow.*

an•y•one (EN-ee-wun) *pron.* Any person; no one in particular.–*Anyone* who wants to read may get a book from the table.

an•y•thing (EN-ee-thing) *adv.* At all; in any way.–Are your friends *anything* like mine?
–*pron.* Something; one thing.–Have you had *anything* to eat?

an•y•way (EN-ee-way) *adv.* Anyhow; no matter what happens.–It is cold out, but we will go *anyway.*

an•y•where (EN-ee-hwair) *adv.* Any place.–Sally lost her scarf and could not find it *anywhere.*

a•part (ə-PAHRT) *adv.* 1. Away; off; to one side.–The children who whispered sat *apart* from the others.
2. One from the other.–The twins look so much alike that only their mother can tell them *apart.*
3. To pieces.–The officer took his gun *apart* to clean it.

a•part•ment (ə-PAHRT-mənt) *n. apartments.* 1. A room or group of rooms forming a home, rented or sometimes owned, within a larger building.–Aunt Ella lives in a four-room *apartment* in a building which has thirty-six *apartments.*

2. One's own room or chamber.–The window in my *apartment* faces the park.

ape (AYP) *n. apes.* An animal that belongs to the monkey family. Unlike most monkeys, the *ape* does not have a tail. *Apes* are in many ways manlike.
–*v. apes, aped, aping.* Imitate; act like. –Mary likes to *ape* her mother.

a•phid (AY-fid *or* AF-id) *n. aphids.* An insect with sucking mouth parts, such as the plant louse or locust, which lives by sucking the juices of plants.–*Aphids* often cause great damage to farmers' crops.

a•piece (ə-PEESS) *adv.* For each one.–Two dollars *apiece* is too much to pay for kites.–If apples are five cents *apiece,* two apples will cost a dime.

a•pol•o•get•ic (ə-pahl-ə-JET-ik) *adj.; apologetically, adv.* Making excuses for, or defending something; feeling that it is necessary to do so.–Tom was *apologetic* for having stayed out late without letting his parents know where he was.

a·pol·o·gize (ə-PAHL-ə-jyz) *v. apologizes, apologized, apologizing.* Admit making a mistake or doing wrong, and say that one is sorry.–Jack knew that he had been rude, and *apologized.*

a·pol·o·gy (ə-PAHL-ə-jee) *n. apologies.* Words saying that one has done wrong and is sorry.–The teacher accepted Jack's *apology* for interrupting her.

a·pos·tro·phe (ə-PAHSS-trə-fee) *n. apostrophes.* A mark or sign [’] that looks like a comma, but is used above a word. 1. The *apostrophe* takes the place of a letter or letters that are left out.–It's time to go.–We've got only an hour.
2. The *apostrophe* shows that someone owns something.–Bob's kite got away.–It was Bob's.
3. Sometimes an *apostrophe* is used in front of the "s" to make a word mean more than one.–There are two "e's" in the word fee.–Three 6's are 18.

a·poth·e·car·y (ə-PAHTH-ə-kair-ee) *n. apothecaries.* A druggist or pharmacist.–*Apothecaries* once were permitted to prescribe as well as to sell drugs in England.

ap·pa·ra·tus (ap-ə-RAY-təss *or* ap-ə-RAT-əss) *n. apparatuses.* The tools or things used in doing a piece of work.–A towing truck has *apparatus* for hauling away cars.–A washing machine is an *apparatus* for doing the wash.

ap·par·el (ə-PAR-əl *or* ə-PAIR-əl) *n.* One's clothes; dresses, suits, and other clothing.–Cinderella's rags turned to beautiful evening *apparel.*

ap·par·ent (ə-PAR-ənt *or* ə-PAIR-ənt) *adj.; apparently, adv.* 1. Evident; clear or plain.–It is *apparent* that sleep is necessary for health.
2. Visible.–Although the fog was heavy, the ship's outline was still *apparent.* You could see it.
3. Appearing or seeming.–John is the *apparent* choice for class president. It appears that he will be elected.

ap·peal (ə-PEEL) *n. appeals.* 1. A request.–The children made an *appeal* to the teacher for more time to finish the test.
2. Power of attraction.–The West had a great *appeal* to the pioneers of the American frontier.
–*v. appeals, appealed, appealing.* 1. Attract; seem pleasant and inviting.–Traveling in the jungle does not *appeal* to Mother.–This picture *appeals* to me. I like the colors in it.
2. Plead; ask; call upon.–After Father said no, Jack *appealed* to Mother.–The President *appealed* to his countrymen to end all wars.

ap·pear (ə-PEER) *v. appears, appeared, appearing.* 1. Come to be seen; show oneself.–The baseball team did not *appear* until it was time for the game to begin.
2. Seem or look; give the impression.–The old man *appeared* to be a tramp, because he was poorly dressed.

ap·pear·ance (ə-PEER-ənss) *n. appearances.* 1. Showing of oneself.–Mother did not make an *appearance* until after the dishes were washed. She did not come in till then.
2. A public showing.–Shirley Temple made her first *appearance* in the movies when she was a very little girl.
3. The way someone or thing looks.–Indians used to use bright paint on their faces to improve their *appearance.*–Mary's tired *appearance* worried Mother.–The new drapes improved the *appearance* of the room.

ap·pen·di·ci·tis (ə-pen-də-SY-təss) *n.* Swelling and inflammation of the appendix.–A common treatment for *appendicitis* is the removal of the appendix from the body.

ap·pen·dix (ə-PEN-diks) *n. appendixes* or *appendices.* 1. A thin tube, about three inches long, growing from a part of the large intestine, and having no known body function.–The doctor said that Tom's pains were due to an inflamed *appendix.*
2. A section added to a book, document, etc., to give more information, such as notes, maps, and tables.–The author added a bibliography to his book as an *appendix.*

ap·pe·tite (AP-ə-tyt) *n. appetites.* 1. A desire for food and drink.–Sometimes when people are ill they have no *appetite.*
2. A desire.–Bob's *appetite* for learning is never satisfied. He always wants to know more.

ap·pe·tiz·ing (AP-ə-tyz-ing) *adj.* Delicious; good to eat, or appearing to be.–Mother put cream cheese on the salad to make it *appetizing.*

ap·plaud (ə-PLAWD) *v. applauds, applauded, applauding.* Clap the hands to show that one approves, agrees, is enjoying a performance, etc.–The children *applauded* Mary's performance in the show.
–applause, n.

ap·ple (AP-əl) *n. apples.* A round fruit that grows on a tree and is red, yellow, or green. *Apples* are good to eat.–Green *apples* are used in making *apple* pie.

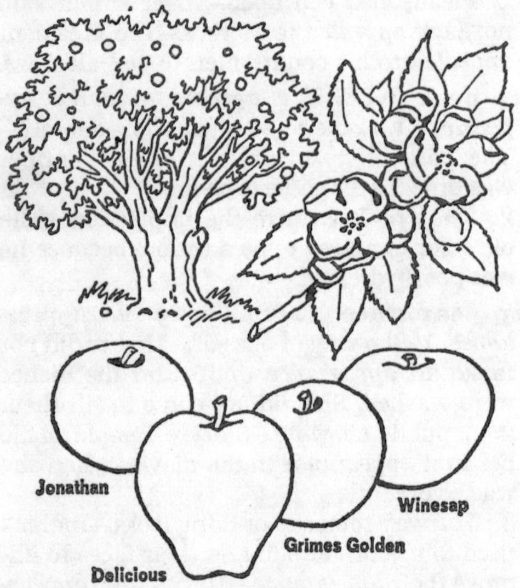

ap·pli·ance (ə-PLY-ənss) *n. appliances.* A useful item, device, piece of equipment, etc. Mother's washing machine, toaster, and electric iron are *appliances.*

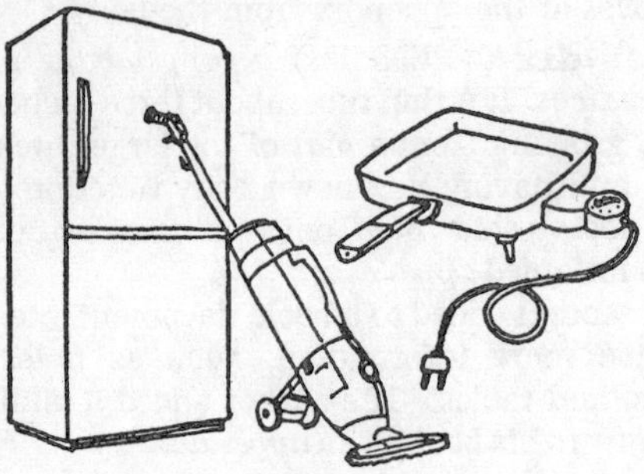

ap·ply (ə-PLY) *v. applies, applied, applying.* 1. Put on.–Doctors *apply* iodine to cuts and sores.
2. Give close attention.–Good readers *apply* themselves to their reading.
3. Fit; suit; refer to.–Spelling rules do not *apply* to all words. They cannot be used to spell all words.–The teacher said her warning did not *apply* to the children who did their work on time.
4. Ask (for something).–Uncle Jim will *apply* for the job.
5. Put to use.–Spelling rules are of no help unless you can *apply* them correctly.
–application, n. applications.

ap·point (ə-POINT) *v. appoints, appointed, appointing.* Select; choose.–The teacher *appointed* Mary to collect the books.

ap·point·ment (ə-POINT-mənt) *n. appointments.* 1. An agreement to be somewhere.–Bob has an *appointment* with the dentist this afternoon at three.
2. A naming or choosing of a person for an office or a job.–Bob is trying to get an *appointment* to the Safety Patrol.

ap·pos·i·tive (ə-PAHZ-ə-tiv) *n. appositives.* A word or phrase placed near a noun to further explain it, such as "our scout leader" in: Mr. Black, our scout leader, took us on a camping trip. An *appositive* is usually set off by commas.

ap·pre·ci·ate (ə-PREE-shee-ayt) *v. appreciates, appreciated, appreciating.* 1. See the value or good of.–Bob *appreciates* the friendship of his schoolmates.–I *appreciate* my good health.
2. Enjoy; get pleasure from.–Mary *appreciates* good music.
3. Be grateful for.–Bill *appreciated* the gift his sister bought him.
4. Sympathize; understand.–I can *appreciate* your problems. I had them once, too.

ap·pre·ci·a·tion (ə-pree-shee-AY-shən) *n.* 1. Thankfulness; gratitude.–The man expressed his *appreciation* for the help his neighbors had given him.
2. Enjoyment.–*Appreciation* of good music makes people's lives more fun.

ap·pren·tice (ə-PREN-təss) *n. apprentices.* A beginner; somebody who is learning a trade or art under a skilled worker.–Robert would like to become a printer's *apprentice* although most of his friends are electricians' *apprentices.*

ap•proach (ə-PROHCH) *n. approaches.* A passageway; a means of reaching or getting to.–The *approach* to the house led through a rose garden.–The *approach* to the city is a bridge across the river.
–*v. approaches, approached, approaching.* Come or go near to.–*Approach* Baby's crib quietly, in case she is asleep.–Christmas is fast *approaching.*

ap•pro•pri•ate (ə-PROH-pree-ayt) *v. appropriates, appropriated, appropriating.* 1. Take for one's own.–Jim *appropriated* my bat and ball before I could give them to him.
2. Set aside for a certain purpose.–Our club *appropriated* one month's dues to pay for the Christmas party.
–(ə-PROH-pree-ət) *adj.; appropriately, adv.* Suitable; fit.–Susan wore a blue dress because her new bright red one did not seem *appropriate.*

ap•prove (ə-PROOV) *v. approves, approved, approving.* Like; be in favor of; think well of.–Father does not *approve* of our staying up late at night.–Father tasted the cake and *approved* it. He said it was good.
–*approval, n. approvals.*

ap•prox•i•mate (ə-PRAHK-sə-mayt) *v. approximates, approximated, approximating.* 1. Come near or close to; approach.–Although this car is cheaper, it *approximates* the more expensive models. Except for price, there is not much difference.
2. Have a similarity or likeness.–Some people think the sound of a violin *approximates* the sound of the singing of a human voice.
–(ə-PRAHK-sə-mət) *adj.; approximately, adv.* 1. Having a likeness to; close to.–John made an *approximate* copy of his first picture. The two pictures are similar, but not identical.
2. Almost right, not exact but close to it; nearly.–The *approximate* time is two o'clock. The exact time is 1:56.

a•pri•cot (AYP- *or* AP-rə-kaht) *n. apricots.* An orange-colored fruit of the peach family. *Apricots* are good to eat raw, stewed, dried, and in pies, jams, etc.

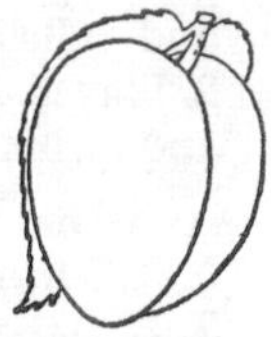

A•pril (AY-prəl) *n. Aprils.* The fourth month of the year. *April* has thirty days.

a•pron (AY-prən) *n. aprons.* A garment worn over the front of one's clothing to keep it clean.–Mother wears an *apron* when she washes the dishes.

apt (APT) *adj.; aptly, adv.* 1. Likely.–Mother is not *apt* to forget my birthday.–It is *apt* to rain today.
2. Promising; gifted. – Mary is an *apt* pupil in music. She learns quickly.
3. Suitable.–That is an *apt* statement. It fits the occasion perfectly.

ap•ti•tude (AP-ti-tyood *or* -tood) *n.* 1. Natural ability or talent.–Mary has great *aptitude* for music.
2. Speed in learning.–The teacher realized that she was going too fast for the *aptitude* of the pupils. Therefore, she carefully explained the instructions again.

aq•ua•plane (AK-wə-playn) *n. aquaplanes.* A board or platform used to carry a standing person while being towed by a motorboat.–Tom fell off the *aquaplane* and swam ashore.

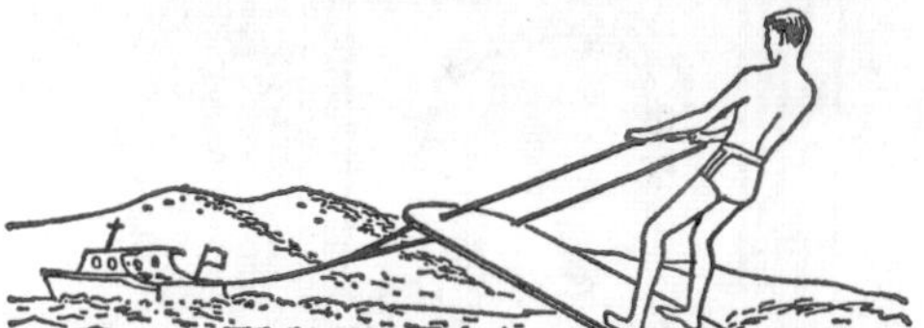

a•quar•i•um (ə-KWAIR-ee-əm) *n. aquariums.* 1. A tank or bowl of water for raising water animals and plants.–The teacher put the goldfish and seaweed in the *aquarium.*

2. A building in which water plants and animals are kept.–Our class visited the *aquarium* in the neighboring city.

a·quat·ic (ə-KWAT-ik) *adj.* 1. Living or growing in, or often visiting, water.–Ducks and gulls are *aquatic* birds.
2. Played or done in or on water.–Water polo and swimming are *aquatic* sports.

Ar·a·bic nu·mer·als (AR-ə-bik NOO- *or* NYOO-mər-əlz).The figures 0, 1, 2, 3, 4, 5, 6, 7, 8, 9. *Arabic numerals* were first used in India. They were brought into use in Europe by the Arabs between the ninth and twelfth centuries.

ar·bi·trate (AHR-bə-trayt) *v. arbitrates, arbitrated, arbitrating.* Settle a dispute between two parties by having a third party make the decision.–The union and the company *arbitrated* their disagreement about working conditions.

ar·bi·tra·tion (ahr-bə-TRAY-shən) *n.* A way of bringing a dispute to an end by having a third party make a decision about the issues involved, with both sides agreeing in advance to accept the decision.–*Arbitration* has often been used to settle disagreements between people, nations, clubs, etc.

ar·bor (AHR-ber) *n. arbors.* 1. A shaded place.–The branches of the trees formed an *arbor.*

2. A trellis or wooden frame covered with vines or branches to make shade.
–*Arbor Day* is the special day set aside each year for planting trees.

ar·bu·tus (ahr-BYOO-təss) *n.* An early spring flower, also called trailing *arbutus,* which crawls or trails along the ground. It is pink or white, and very fragrant.

arc (AHRK) *n. arcs.* A curved line, or a line that is a part of a circle.

arch (AHRCH) *n. arches.* A structure curved like part of a circle. *Arches* are built of wood, stone, brick, or any other building material. Sometimes gates, doors, and bridges have *arches* over them.
–*v. arches, arched, arching.* Shape like an arch; curve upward.–The kitten *arches* her back when she is angry.

ar·chae·ol·o·gist or **ar·che·ol·o·gist** (ahr-kee-AHL-ə-jist) *n. archaeologists* or *archeologists.* A person who studies or specializes in the field of archaeology.–Harry wants to become an *archaeologist* because he likes to dig and discover things.

ar·chae·ol·o·gy or **ar·che·ol·o·gy** (ahr-kee-AHL-ə-jee) *n.* 1. The science or study of past life and history by means of digging up or uncovering buried cities, temples, tools, etc. – *Archaeology* has provided man with much knowledge about ancient peoples.
2. The things or remains dug up or uncovered for scientific and historical study. – The Sphinx and the pyramids are part of the *archaeology* of Egypt.

ar•chi•tect (AHR-kə-tekt) *n. architects.* A person who designs buildings and sees that they are built according to his plans.

arc•tic (AHRK-tik) *adj.* The most northern part of the world; the region near the North Pole.

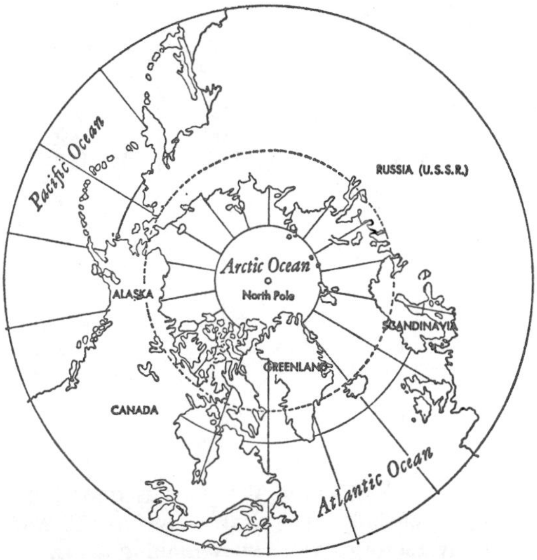

are (AHR) *v.* One form of the verb *be,* used with we, you, or they.–We *are* going.–They *are* coming.–You *are* here.

a•re•a (AIR-ee-ə) *n. areas.* 1. An amount of space enclosed by boundaries.–We have an acre of land; the *area* of our land is an acre.
2. A section or piece of land.–The *area* in front of the house was covered with grass.
3. The extent or scope, as of a subject.–There is much experimenting still to be done in the *area* of rocket research.

a•re•na (ə-REE-nə) *n. arenas.* 1. A place where public contests, battles, shows, etc., take place.–Tom's father took him to see the fights in the boxing *arena.*
2. The place in ancient Rome where gladiators, or warriors, fought before large public audiences. – Men often fought lions in the *arenas* of ancient Rome.

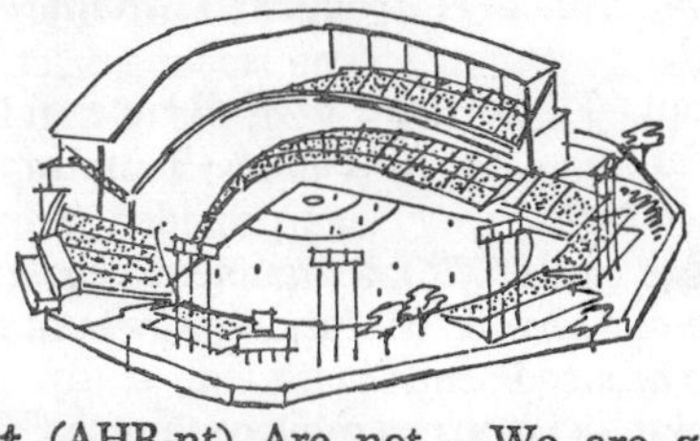

aren't (AHR-nt). Are not. – We are going. They *aren't.*

ar•gue (AHR-gyoo) *v. argues, argued, arguing.* Discuss things disagreed upon; talk for and against something.–John and Mary often *argue* with each other about whether girls or boys are smarter.

ar•gu•ment (AHR-gyoo-mənt) *n. arguments.* 1. A dispute; a discussion of a thing disagreed upon.–The children had an *argument* about whose turn it was to wash the dishes. Mary said it was Ruth's turn. Ruth said it was Mary's turn.
2. A reason given for or against a question. –Bob offered a good *argument* in favor of holding the party Saturday afternoon.

a•rise (ə-RYZ) *v. arises, arose, arising.* 1. Get up; get out of bed. – Mother *arises* at six o'clock every morning.
2. Come up.–If an argument *arises* over the work to be done, Mother will settle it.

a•ris•to•crat (ə-RISS-tə-krat) *n. aristocrats; aristocratic, adj.* 1. A member of a high or ruling class in a society or government called an aristocracy, such as a duke, prince, etc.–The king invited all the *aristocrats* of his court to a banquet.
2. A person who acts, thinks, or has the manners and tastes of a superior person.–Mary walked like an *aristocrat* in her new gown. She held her head high. She looked proud and poised.

a•rith•me•tic (ə-RITH-mə-tik) *n.* The study of using numbers.–In *arithmetic* class children learn how to work with numbers. They learn how to add, subtract, multiply, and divide.

Ar•i•zo•na (ar-ə-ZOH-nə) *n.* A state in southwestern United States, known for its healthful climate, its beautiful Grand Canyon National Park, and the Painted Desert. Cotton, lettuce, and fruits are raised on the rich farmlands.

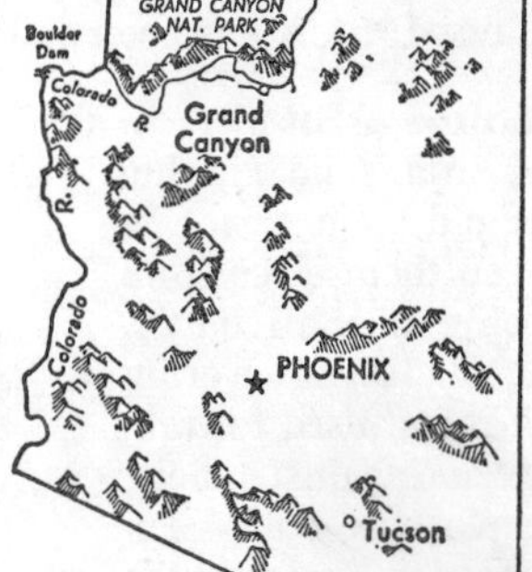

ark (AHRK) *n.* The Bible tells us that Noah was saved from the great Flood in a large boat called the *ark.* He took his family and a pair of each kind of animal on the *ark* with him.

Ar•kan•sas (AHR-kən-saw) *n.* A state in south central United States, known for its rich crops of cotton, manufactured lumber products, petroleum, and minerals. Nearly every known mineral is found in *Arkansas.*

arm (AHRM) *n. arms.* 1. One of the two upper limbs of a person. Human beings have four limbs, or branches of the body. The two upper limbs are called *arms.* The two lower limbs are the legs.

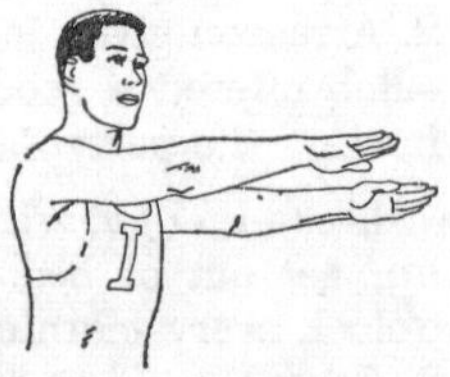

2. A part at the side or end of a seat to support a person's arms.–Jack rests his arms on the *arms* of his chair.
–*v. arms, armed, arming.* Prepare for war; take up weapons.–A country *arms* to protect itself from its enemies.

arm•chair (AHRM-chair) *n. armchairs.* A chair with side pieces to support a person's arms.

ar•mi•stice (AHR-məss-təss) *n.* A temporary peace agreement; a truce.–The two countries which were at war made an *armistice* until they could make a final treaty. They stopped fighting for a time.

Ar•mi•stice Day (AHR-məss-təss day) November 11. In 1918, during the first World War, an armistice was signed on this date. November 11 has since been known as *Armistice Day,* in memory of the end of fighting. Since 1954, it has been called Veterans Day.

ar•mor (AHR-mer) *n.; armored, adj.* 1. A suit of iron.–The knights of old wore *armor* to keep themselves from being hurt in battle.
2. A sheet or covering of metal used for protection against bullets, explosives, etc. – Policemen sometimes wear steel jackets as an *armor.*–A covering of strong metal *armor* protects the bank's money when it travels in an *armored* car.

ARMS

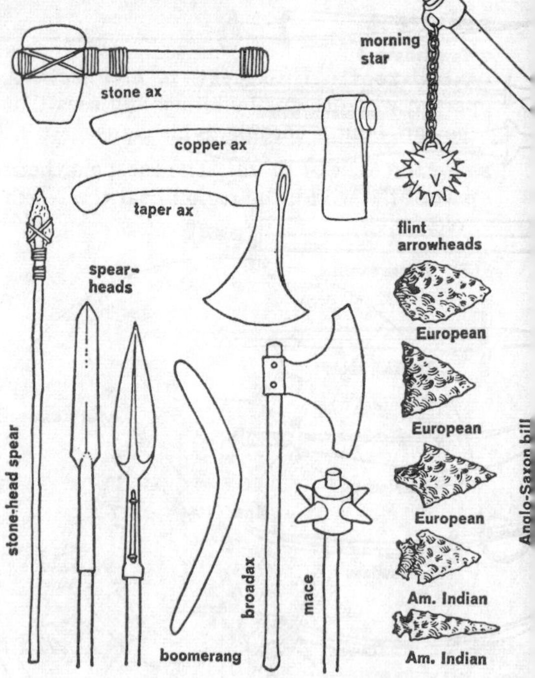

arms (AHRMZ) *n. pl.* Weapons used for fighting, especially in warfare.–During the war many factories were busy making *arms.*

ar•my (AHR-mee) *n. armies.* 1. An organized group of men trained in the use of arms and the methods of war.
2. A great number.–An *army* of boys and girls took part in the sports events.

a•ro•ma (ə-ROH-mə) *n. aromas.* A special and pleasant smell; fragrance.–The *aroma* of Mother's cooking made everybody's mouth water.

a•rose (ə-ROHZ) *v.* One form of the verb *arise.*–The speaker *arose* from his chair. He got up.

a•round (ə-ROWND) *adv.* and *prep.* 1. Along all sides.–The children ran quickly *around* the schoolhouse.
2. To another side of.–Jack walked *around* the corner.
3. About or near.–Mother told us not to play *around* the fire.
4. In a circle.–The dog ran *around* and *around.*
5. About.–I'll be there *around* nine o'clock.
6. In an opposite direction.–Turn *around* and face me!

a•rouse (ə-ROWZ) *v. arouses, aroused, arousing.* 1. Awaken.–At six o'clock, Mother tried to *arouse* Father.
2. Excite.–The circus *aroused* Sally so much that she could not sleep.

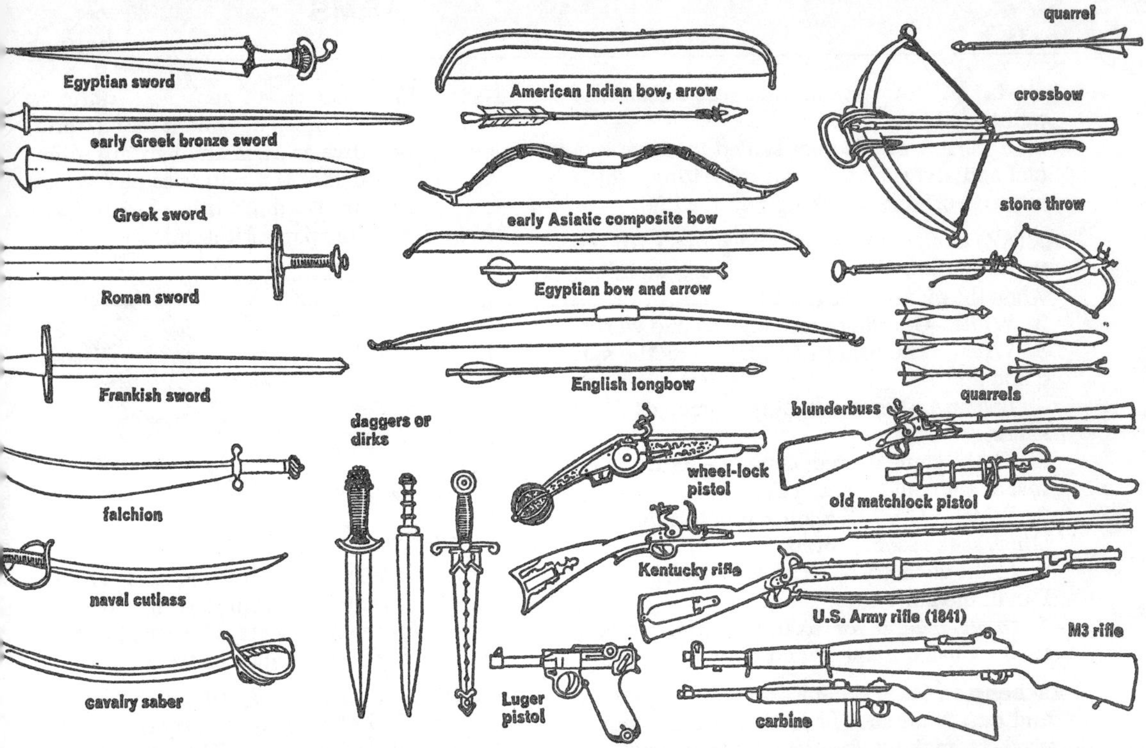

ar·range (ə-RAYNJ) *v. arranges, arranged, arranging.* 1. Put in some order; place according to a plan.—Jack *arranged* the books on the shelves.—Mary *arranged* the silver on the table.

2. Make plans.—The chairman will *arrange* for the picnic.

ar·range·ment (ə-RAYNJ-mənt) *n. arrangements.* 1. A way or plan of putting things in a place.—The *arrangement* of the flowers in the bowl was pretty.

2. A plan.—Jack's *arrangements* for the party were pleasing to the rest of the class.

ar·ray (ə-RAY) *v. arrays, arrayed, arraying.* 1. Dress in beautiful costumes, uniforms, clothes, etc.—The actors were *arrayed* in Oriental costumes.

2. Line up, place, or arrange soldiers for battle, parade, formal review, etc.—The sergeant grew angry waiting for the troops to *array* themselves properly.

ar·rest (ə-REST) *v. arrests, arrested, arresting.* 1. Seize and take to jail under the law.—Policemen have the power to *arrest* people who do not obey the laws.

2. Stop.—The flood was *arrested* when the rain stopped.

ar·riv·al (ə-RYV-əl) *n.* Coming.—Our *arrival* did not surprise Grandmother.—The *arrival* of spring was welcomed by all of us.

ar·rive (ə-RYV) *v. arrives, arrived, arriving.* Come; get to a place.—The train will *arrive* at six o'clock.—If our friends *arrive* at the park first, they will wait for us.

ar·ro·gance (AR-ə-gənss) *n.; arrogant, adj.; arrogantly, adv.* Annoying pride and vanity; unjustified display of self-importance.—Even though Frank was a star basketball player, his *arrogance* caused him to lose friends.

ar·row (AR-oh) *n. arrows.* 1. A pointed stick that is shot from a bow.—Indians used bows and *arrows* to shoot wild animals.

2. A sign which points in a certain direction.—You will find the park if you follow the *arrows.*

art (AHRT) *n. arts.* 1. Drawing, painting, or sculpture.—In our school children go to the *art* class twice a week.

2. Pictures, sculpture, etc.—Mr. Jones, the *art* teacher, produced some very nice *art.*

3. A thing that requires much practice or skill.—Playing the piano well is an *art.*

ar·ter·y (AHR-ter-ee) *n. arteries.* One of the tubes in the body that carry blood from the heart to other parts of the body.

ar·ti·cle (AHR-tik-əl) *n. articles.* 1. An object; a separate part or piece.—Overcoats, hats, and shoes are *articles* of clothing.

2. A written composition giving information.—The newspaper reporter wrote an *article* about safety.

ar·ti·fi·cial (ahr-tə-FISH-əl) *adj.; artificially, adv.* Not real; not found in nature; made as an imitation.—Some *artificial* flowers are made of paper.

art•ist (AHR-təst) *n. artists.* 1. A person who paints or draws pictures.
2. A person who is very skilled in some special activity, such as music or writing, which requires original thinking and feeling.

as (AZ) *adv., conj., prep.,* and *pron.* 1. In the manner that.–Stand *as* you were standing when the picture was taken.
2. While.–Grandmother sings *as* she works.
3. When.–The fisherman arrived *as* the sun came up.
4. Because.–We must stay home, *as* it is raining.
5. To the same degree; equally.–Joan ran *as* fast as she could to catch Tom.
6. Which.–Our ball team was better than the other, *as* the score proved.
7. In the capacity of.–Tim appeared *as* Peter Pan in the play.
–*Such as* means for example.–Many trees, *such as* oaks, maples, and elms, grow here.

as•bes•tos (ass-PESS-təss *or* az-BESS-təss) *n.* and *adj.* A mineral fiber that will not burn, used in making fireproof articles such as screens, ironing pads, etc.–Theater curtains usually are made of *asbestos.*

as•cend (ə-SEND) *v. ascends, ascended, ascending.* Go up; rise. – The climbers prepared to *ascend* the mountain.–The balloon *ascended* to a height of five hundred feet.–After twenty years with the firm, Harry had *ascended* from office boy to vice-president.

ash (ASH) *n. ashes.* A tree which belongs to the olive family. The wood of the *ash* is used in making furniture, and for many other things.

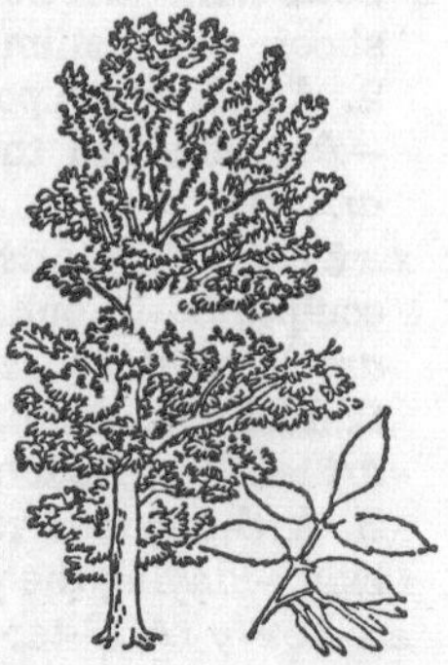

a•shamed (ə-SHAYMD) *adj.* Feeling guilt; unhappy because of failure or wrongdoing.–The boy was *ashamed* because he had pulled the little girl's hair.

ash•es (ASH-əz) *n. pl.* The dusty material that remains after anything has been burned.–Grandfather emptied the *ashes* from his pipe.

a•shore (ə-SHOR) *adj.* and *adv.* 1. To the shore; onto the land.–Sailors on the ship will go *ashore* when the ship arrives in port.
2. On land.–The sailors will stay *ashore* for several days.

A•sia (AY-zhee-ə *or* AY-zhə) *n.; Asiatic* or *Asian, adj.* The largest continent in the world. More people live in *Asia* than in any other continent. Some of the countries of *Asia* are India, Pakistan, Burma, China, Japan, Indonesia, Korea, and part of Russia.

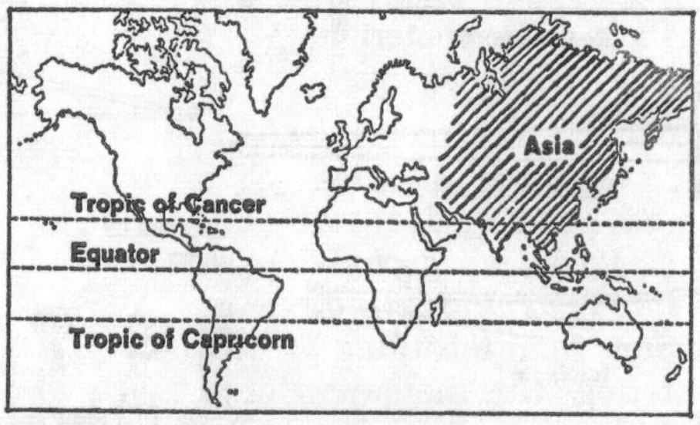

a•side (ə-SYD) *adv.* 1. To one side; apart.–The officers sat *aside* from the other men.
2. In safekeeping; away.–Mother puts *aside* some money for the rent each week.

ask (ASK) *v. asks, asked, asking.* 1. Request.–Mary *asked* Mother for an apple.
2. Request an answer to.–The teacher *asked* many questions in class today.
3. Inquire.–Did you *ask* about the time of the party?–*Ask* if we may go.
4. Invite.–Ann *asked* Jack to come to her party.

a•sleep (ə-SLEEP) *adj.* and *adv.* 1. Sleeping; not awake.–The baby is *asleep.*
2. Numb.–Father's arm is *asleep* because he was lying on it and stopped the circulation of blood. He has no feeling in it.

as•par•a•gus (əss-PAR-ə-gəss) *n.* A vegetable whose shoots or young stems are good to eat. If the shoots are not picked for eating, they grow to be large, fern-like plants with branches. Sometimes the branches are used in bouquets.

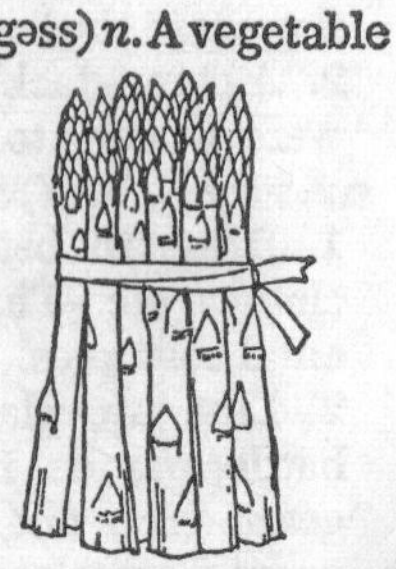

as•pect (ASS-pekt) *n. aspects.* 1. Appearance or look, especially at a particular time.–When night fell, the forest took on a frightening *aspect.* – The menacing *aspect* of the wrestler was just an act.
2. A particular point of view or side.–The judge told the jury to examine the case in all its *aspects.*
3. Direction something is facing.–The southern *aspect* of the house makes it warm and sunny.

as•pen (ASS-pən) *n. aspens.* A kind of poplar tree. The leaves of the *aspen* shake or quiver if there is a breeze.

as•phalt (ASS-fawlt) *n.* A dark, tarlike substance that is mixed with other materials and used to pave roads.

as•phyx•i•ate (əss-FIKS-ee-ayt) *v. asphyxiates, asphyxiated, asphyxiating.* Stop from breathing by cutting off or interfering with the supply of air; suffocate, as with gas fumes.—The man was almost *asphyxiated* by leaking gas.

as•pir•in (ASS-per-ən *or* ASSP-rən) *n.* A medicine that helps to relieve pain.—When Father had a headache, he took an *aspirin* tablet.

as•sas•si•nate (ə-SASS-ən-ayt) *v. assassinates, assassinated, assassinating.* Kill suddenly and by surprise.—An enemy agent tried to *assassinate* the king, but failed.

as•sem•ble (ə-SEM-bəl) *v. assembles, assembled, assembling.* 1. Come together.—The children *assemble* each morning to salute the flag.
2. Put together.—The girls *assembled* the parts of the jigsaw puzzle.

as•sem•bly (ə-SEM-blee) *n. assemblies.* 1. A meeting.—All the classes went to the *assembly.*
2. Putting together.—The *assembly* of an automobile is done by many men working on an *assembly* line.

as•sign (ə-SYN) *v. assigns, assigned, assigning.* 1. Give out (work to be done).—Our teacher will *assign* our spelling lesson later.
2. Appoint.—The safety-patrol boys have been *assigned* to their places of duty. They have been told where to work.
—*assignment, n. assignments.*

as•sist (ə-SIST) *v. assists, assisted, assisting.* Help.—Mary will *assist* Mother in caring for the baby.

as•sist•ance (ə-SISS-tənss) *n.* Help or aid.—The needy family was grateful for the *assistance* of the school.

as•sist•ant (ə-SISS-tənt) *n. assistants.* A helper; a person who helps.—The principal's *assistant* helps him manage the school.

as•so•ci•ate (ə-SOH-shee-ət *or* ə-SOH-see-ət) *n. associates.* Companion; ally; partner.—Jack and his *associates* like to play baseball.
—Father and his *associate* are opening a new store.
—(ə-SOH-shee-ayt *or* ə-SOH-see-ayt) *v. associates, associated, associating.* 1. Be in company (with someone); be together.—Jack does not like to *associate* with Bill.
2. Think of in connection.—I *associate* strawberries with shortcake.

as•sort•ed (ə-SOR-tid) *adj.* Made up of different kinds, or of various types or classifications.—Mary received *assorted* gifts on her birthday.
—*assortment, n. assortments.*

as•sume (ə-SYOOM *or* -SOOM) *v. assumes, assumed, assuming.* 1. Take for granted, usually without reason for doing so; suppose.—John *assumed* that the car would make the trip easily, but he was wrong. It broke down on the way.
2. Undertake; take on oneself.—Tom will *assume* his duties at the office on Monday.
3. Pretend to be or to have; put on an appearance.—The poor man *assumed* an air of wealth. He spent more money than he could afford.

as•ter (ASS-ter) *n. asters.* A flower that has a yellow center. *Asters* bloom in late summer. They are of various colors.

as•ter•isk (ASS-ter-isk) *n. asterisks.* A starlike symbol [*] used next to a word, phrase, or sentence in printing and writing to mark a point of reference given elsewhere, often at the foot of the page. A series of *asterisks* frequently indicates an omission in text.

ASTRONOMY

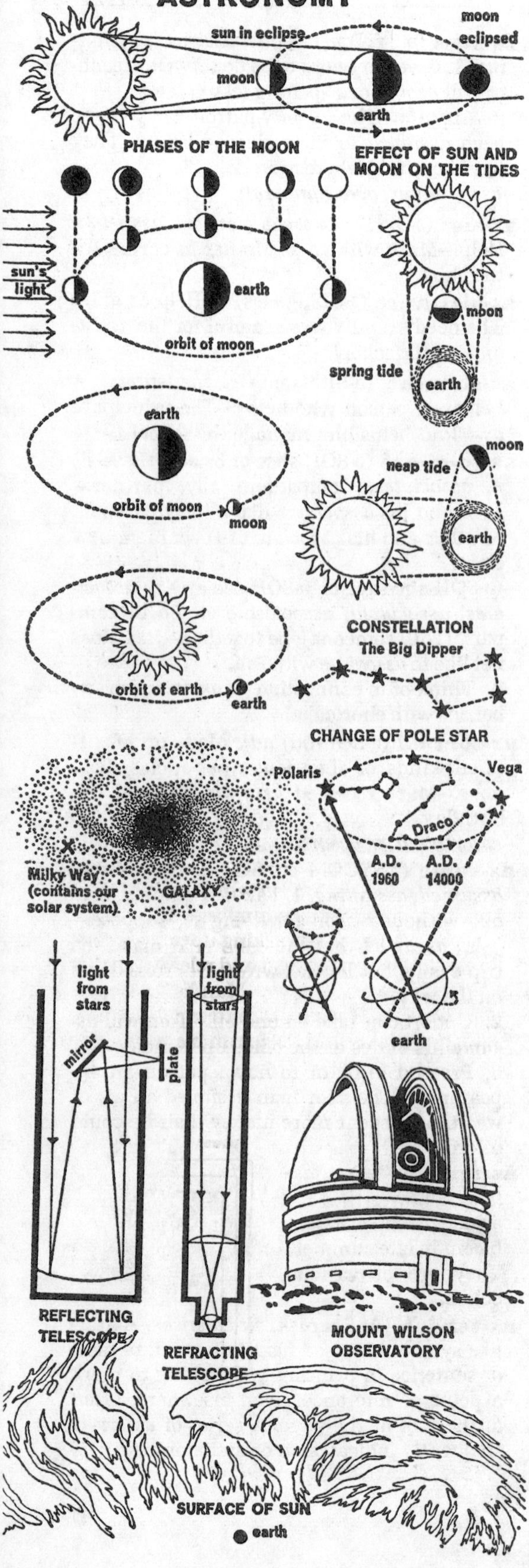

as·ter·oid (ASS-ter-oid) *n. asteroids.* 1. A small starlike body, or minor planet, that revolves in a path between the planets Mars and Jupiter.–There are hundreds of *asteroids* known to be revolving around the sun.
2. A starfish.–The sea *asteroid* lives on mussels and oysters and is commonly found off the North Atlantic and North Pacific coasts.

asth·ma (AZ-mə) *n.* A disease which makes breathing very difficult and causes one to cough.–Grandmother's *asthma* is much better this winter.

as·ton·ish (ə-STAHN-ish) *v. astonishes, astonished, astonishing.* Amaze; fill with surprise.–When Jack looked up and saw his dog standing in the schoolroom doorway, he was *astonished.*
–astonishment, n.

as·ton·ish·ing (ə-STAHN-ish-ing) *adj.* Amazing; surprising.–An *astonishing* thing happened today. Three little kittens were following a big hen.

a·stray (ə-STRAY) *adv.* Away from home; wandering.–Our cat has gone *astray.*

as·trol·o·ger (ə-STRAHL-ə-jer) *n. astrologers.* A fortune-teller who makes his predictions by the stars.–*Astrologers* had great influence in the courts of ancient kings.

as·trol·o·gy (ə-STRAHL-ə-jee) *n.* The telling of fortunes by studying the positions of the stars and planets.

as·tro·naut (AS-troh-naht) *n. astronauts.* A pilot or passenger on a space ship.

as·tron·o·mer (ə-STRAHN-ə-mer) *n. astronomers.* A person who studies the sun, moon, stars, and other heavenly bodies.

as·tron·o·my (ə-STRAHN-ə-mee) *n.* The study of the sun, moon, stars, and other heavenly bodies.–The invention of the telescope made *astronomy* far easier.

a·sy·lum (ə-SY-ləm) *n. asylums.* A place where people who are unable to take care of themselves, as from blindness or sickness of the mind, are cared for.

at (AT) *prep.* 1. *At* may indicate a place (where) or a time (when).–We met *at* the corner.–The sun came up *at* six o'clock.
2. In the direction of.–Bob threw a stone *at* the tree.

ate (AYT) *v.* One form of the verb *eat.*–The horse *ate* his oats.

ATHLETICS

ath•lete (ATH-leet) *n. athletes.* A person who is skillful in some sport.–A football player is an *athlete.*

ath•let•ic (ath-LET-ik) *adj.* 1. Like an athlete; good at sports.–Some boys and girls are more *athletic* than others; they are better at sports. 2. Having to do with sports.–The school has a new *athletic* field.–Bob is organizing an *athletic* club.

ath•let•ics (ath-LET-iks) *n. pl.* Games and other sports that require action and strength.–Baseball and swimming are kinds of *athletics.*

at•las (AT-ləss) *n. atlases.* A book of maps or tables, often giving additional information, such as population figures, historical facts, etc.–Harry looked up the size and location of Greece in his *atlas.*

at•mos•phere (AT-məss-feer) *n.; atmospheric, adj.* 1. The air enveloping the earth; the air.–The earth's *atmosphere* is invisible, tasteless, and odorless.
2. The mood of influences surrounding something.–When Father stays home from the office, there is a holiday *atmosphere* in the house.

at•om (AT-əm) *n. atoms; atomic, adj.* The smallest bit or particle of which anything is made up.

at•om bomb (AT-əm BAHM) *atom bombs.* The most powerful bomb ever used in warfare. A single *atom bomb* can blow up an entire city. When the *atom bomb* explodes, the atoms, or tiniest particles of the material it is made of, are broken up and changed. In this process, a tremendous amount of energy or force is released.

a•tom•ic en•er•gy (ə-TAHM-ik EN-er-jee). The strength, power, or force stored inside atoms. This power is released by a process called "nuclear fission" in which certain tiny parts of atoms are broken up into still smaller parts. During this breaking up process tremendous heat is produced and released in the form of power, or energy.–Man hopes to use *atomic energy* in the future to supply all his needs for power, such as to run machines, fly planes, move ships, etc.

ATOMIC POWER

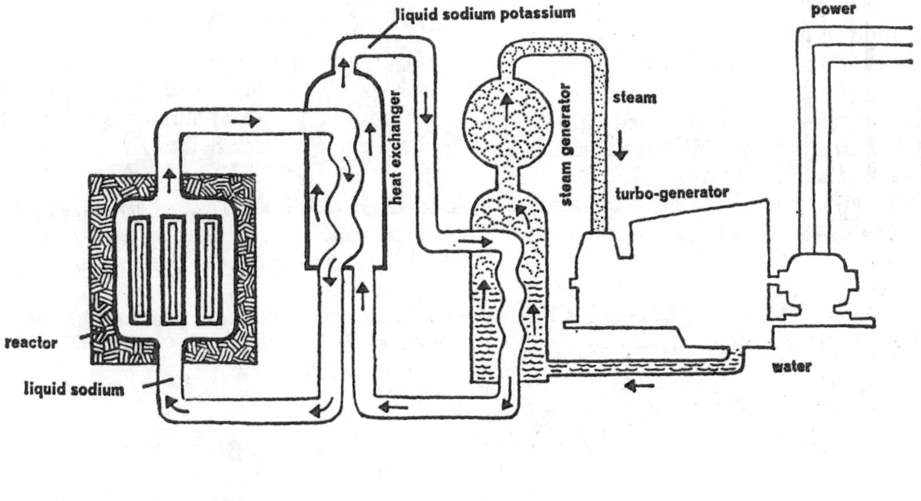

at·tach (ə-TACH) *v. attaches, attached, attaching.* 1. Fasten; join.–When Tom *attaches* the string to his kite, it will be finished.
–*Attached to* can mean fond of.–Mother is very *attached to* Baby.

at·tach·ment (ə-TACH-mənt) *n. attachments.* 1. Something to be attached to another object.–The vacuum cleaner has *attachments* to do different kinds of work.
2. Fondness; love.–Parents have a great *attachment* for their children.

at·tack (ə-TAK) *n. attacks.* 1. A use of force against a person or place.–The army started an *attack* on the city.
2. An occurrence or happening of a disease. –Mary had an *attack* of the measles.
–*v. attacks, attacked, attacking.* 1. Start a fight with.–The boxer *attacked* his opponent swiftly.
2. Start to work on; tackle.–Bob *attacked* the puzzle eagerly.

at·tain (ə-TAYN) *v. attains, attained, attaining.* 1. Achieve; accomplish; reach one's goal. –Father *attained* his ambition. He finished building a summerhouse for the family.
2. Arrive at; come to.–The plane should *attain* its destination by morning.

at·tempt (ə-TEMPT) *n. attempts.* A try.–Larry made several *attempts* at jumping the fence before he succeeded.
–*v. attempts, attempted, attempting.* Try; make an effort.–Aviators do not *attempt* to fly during a hurricane.

at·tend (ə-TEND) *v. attends, attended, attending.* 1. Be present at.–Father and Mother will *attend* the May Day entertainment.
2. Look after.–The chairman of the class will *attend* to the plans for the ball game.
3. Go with; accompany. – Seeing-eye dogs *attend* blind people. The dogs lead the blind people and help them find their way about.

at·tend·ance (ə-TEN-dənss) *n.* 1. Being present.–Bob has a good record of *attendance* at school.
2. The number present.–The average class *attendance* is thirty pupils.

at·ten·tion (ə-TEN-shən) *n. attentions.* 1. Thought; notice.–When Jack called Father's *attention* to the smoke coming from the store, Father called the Fire Department.
2. A courtesy; a little thing done for someone.–Grandmother appreciates little *attentions.*
–*Pay attention* means notice and think carefully about what is being said or done.–Children who *pay attention* learn quickly.

at·tic (AT-ik) *n. attics.* The space or room just under the roof of a house.–We have several old trunks in the *attic.*

at·ti·tude (AT-ə-tyood *or* -tood) *n. attitudes.* One's thoughts and feelings about something; a way of looking at or dealing with.–What is your teacher's *attitude* toward the boy's laziness?

at·tor·ney (ə-TER-nee) *n. attorneys.* A lawyer; a person given legal or lawful right to act for another person.–Grandfather had an *attorney* collect the money which was due him.

at·tract (ə-TRAKT) *v. attracts, attracted, attracting.* Draw; pull; get.–A horseshoe magnet *attracts* steel to itself.–Mary tried to *attract* attention by looking very sad.
–*attraction, n. attractions.*

at·trib·ute (AT-rə-byoot) *n. attributes.* An identifying quality; a characteristic of a person or thing.–Accuracy is an *attribute* of a scholar.–You can easily recognize Bill by the sound of his voice. One of his *attributes* is speaking clearly, in a soft tone.
–(ə-TRIB-yoot) *v. attributes, attributed, attributing.* 1. Give credit to someone or thing as having been the cause of something else. –The champion *attributed* his victory to hard training and clean living.–Father *attributes* his happiness to Mother and the children.
2. Regard as belonging to or going with.–Wisdom and knowledge of the law are *attributed* to the old judge.

auc·tion (AWK-shən) *n. auctions.* A public sale at which people offer money for things, which are finally sold to the person who will pay the most.
–*v. auctions, auctioned, auctioning.* Sell at auction.

au•di•ble (AW-də-bəl) *adj.; audibly, adv.* Loud enough to be heard.—The child's voice is soft, yet *audible.*

au•di•ence (AW-dee-ənss *or* AWD-yənss) *n. audiences.* 1. A group of people watching or listening to a performance, as a game, a moving picture, a play, etc.—Because of the rain, the *audience* at the concert was small.

2. A hearing; a chance to say what one has to say.—The mayor gave the man an *audience.*

au•di•tion (aw-DISH-ən) *v. auditions, auditioned, auditioning.* Give a hearing to, as to a singer or performer, to test for ability or talent.—The producer of the play will *audition* John and Mary for the parts of Hansel and Gretel.

au•di•to•ri•um (aw-də-TOR-ee-əm) *n. auditoriums.* A room or a hall for an audience, or a large group of people, to sit.—We hold our school entertainments in the *auditorium.*

au•ger (AW-ger) *n. augers.* A tool for making holes.—When Father built a swing for Sally, he used an *auger* to make two holes in the board for the ropes to go through.

Au•gust (AW-gəsst) *n. Augusts.* The eighth month of the year. *August* has thirty-one days.

aunt (ANT *or* AHNT) *n. aunts.* The sister of one's father or mother. The wives of your father's and your mother's brothers are your *aunts* by marriage.—Our *Aunt* Ann is Father's sister.

au•ri•cle (AW-ri-kəl) *n. auricles.* One of the chambers of the heart through which blood flows on its way from the veins back to the arteries.

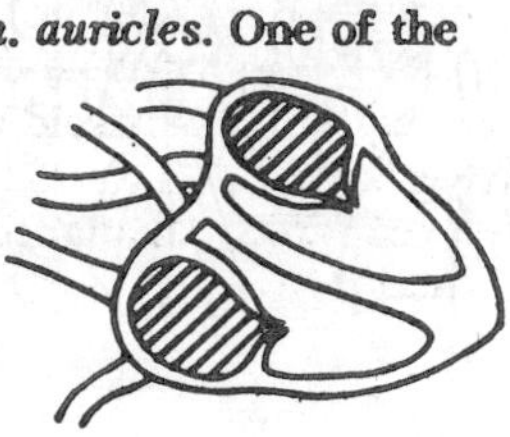

au•ro•ra bo•re•al•is (ə-RAW-rə baw-ree-AL-əss). A spectacle of lights appearing at night in the northern skies, especially in the arctic regions; the northern lights.—In the Middle Ages the *aurora borealis* was looked upon as an evil omen. Today the *aurora borealis* is believed to come from electrical disturbances in the atmosphere.

Aus•tral•ia (awss-TRAYL-yə) *n.; Australian, adj.* The smallest continent in the world. *Australia* is an island continent located in the South Pacific. It consists of only one country, and is part of the British Commonwealth of Nations.

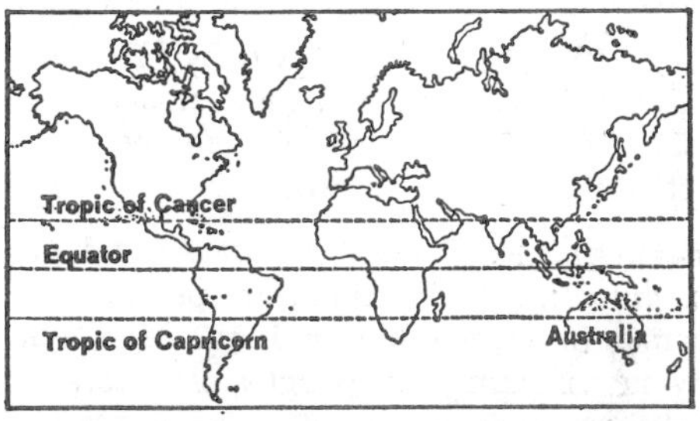

au•then•tic (aw-THEN-tik) *adj.* 1. Genuine; real.—John's father has an *authentic* letter signed by President Truman.
2. True; reliable.—Mary's story about the fire was *authentic.* She was there and saw it.

au•thor (AW-ther) *n. authors.* 1. A writer; one who makes up and writes articles, stories, poems, or books.—Robert Louis Stevenson was a famous *author.*—Who is your favorite *author?*
2. One who begins something.—Are you the *author* of this plan? Did you start it?

au•thor•i•ty (aw-THAWR-ə-tee) *n. authorities.* 1. The right to give orders, or to say that something shall be done.—The superintendent has the *authority* to close all the schools in case of bad weather.
2. A place, person, or book from which information is taken.—A dictionary is a good *authority* on how to spell words.
3. The people in charge.—Jack reported to the *authorities* that he had found the lost dog.

au·thor·ize (AW-ther-yz) *v. authorizes, authorized, authorizing.* 1. Give permission or power to someone to do something.–The manager of the store *authorized* the salesman to accept payment by check.
2. Make legal or official.–The mayor *authorized* the purchase of the land for a park.
3. Justify; permit.–The fact that a lion is loose in the zoo *authorizes* the guards to carry guns to protect the public.

au·to (AW-toh) *n. autos.* An automobile; a car.–Children should not try to drive an *auto* until they are old enough to have a license.

au·to·bi·og·ra·phy (aw-tə-by-AHG-rə-fee) *n. autobiographies.* A history or account of one's life written by oneself.–Famous people often write *autobiographies.*

au·to·graph (AW-tə-graf *or* AW-toh-graf) *n. autographs.* The signature or name of a person in his own handwriting.–Mary's hobby is collecting *autographs* of actors and actresses.

au·to·mat·ic (awt-ə-MAT-ik *or* aw-toh-MAT-ik) *adj.; automatically, adv.* 1. Working by itself.–Father bought an *automatic* pump to pump the water from the basement.
2. Done without thought and effort.–Breathing is *automatic.*

au·to·ma·tion (aw-toh-MAY-shən) *n.* The use of self-regulating or automatic machines. –Some factories run by *automation.*

au·to·mo·bile (AWT-ə-moh-beel *or* awt-ə-moh-BEEL *or* aw-to-MOH-beel) *n. automobiles.* A vehicle that moves under its own power; a motor car.

au·tumn (AWT-əm) *n. autumns* and *adj.* 1. The time of year between the hot weather of summer and the cold weather of winter.–Leaves fall from the trees in *autumn.*
2. One of the four seasons of the year, from September 21 to December 21.

a·vail·a·ble (ə-VAYL-ə-bəl) *adj.* 1. Ready to be used; usable; handy.–All *available* fire-fighting equipment was used to fight the blaze.–Mother had money *available* to pay the milkman.
2. Able to be had or obtained.–There were ten men *available* for the job.

av·a·lanche (AV-ə-lanch) *n. avalanches.* 1. A great quantity of snow, earth, etc., sliding down a mountainside.–The *avalanche* buried the trees in the narrow valley.

2. A huge amount.–The ball player received an *avalanche* of fan mail.

av·e·nue (AV-ə-nyoo *or* AV-ən-oo) *n. avenues.* A wide street.–A new *avenue* is being built at the edge of the city because traffic is so heavy there.

av·er·age (AV-rij *or* AV-ə-rij) *n. averages.* 1. On Monday Bob had a mark of 80 in spelling; on Tuesday he had 90. To find his *average* spelling grade for the 2 days, he added both marks together and divided by 2 (the number of days). $80 + 90 = 170$. $170 \div 2 = 85$, his *average* mark.
2. Usual; normal.–The attendance at school today is better than *average.*

a·vi·ar·y (AY-vee-air-ee) *n. aviaries.* A large bird house or cage; a living place for birds in captivity.–Father took the children to the *aviary* in the zoo.

NTIQUE AUTOMOBILES

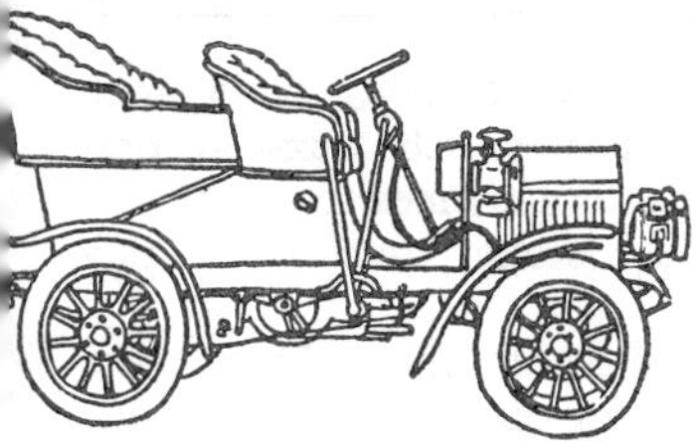
Studebaker (1904)

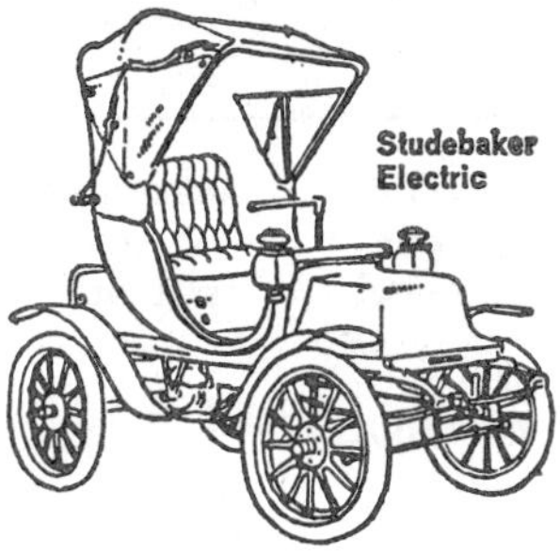
Studebaker Electric

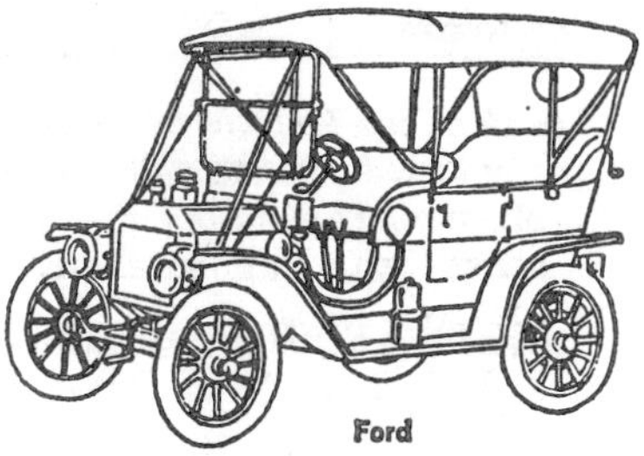
Ford

AUTOMOBILES

ORTS CARS

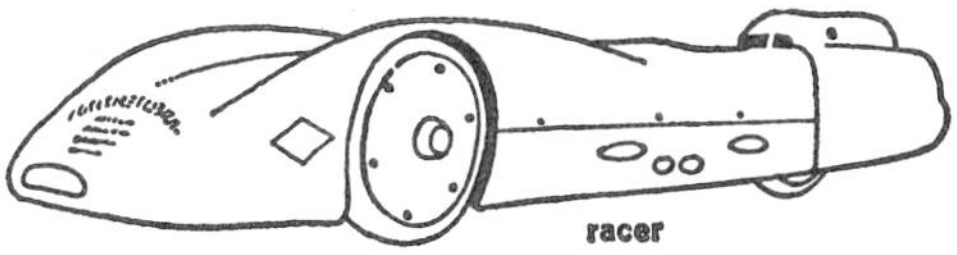
racer

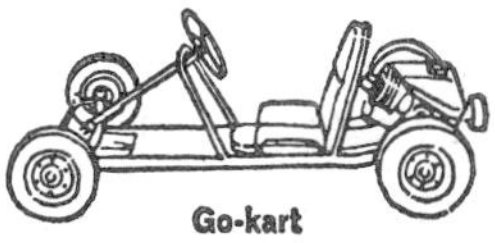
Go-kart

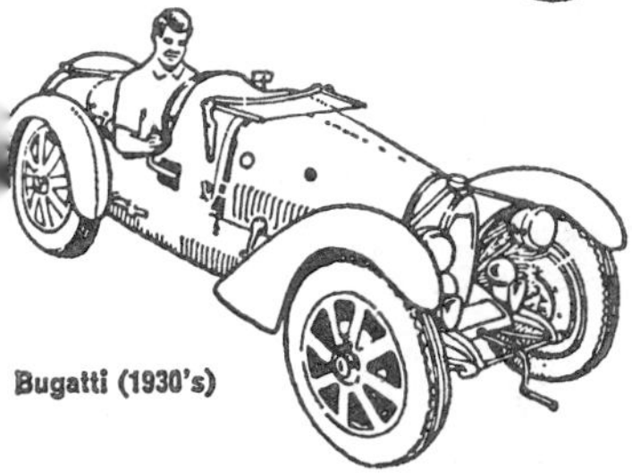
Bugatti (1930's)

Cord Convertible (1937)

dragster

EDANS

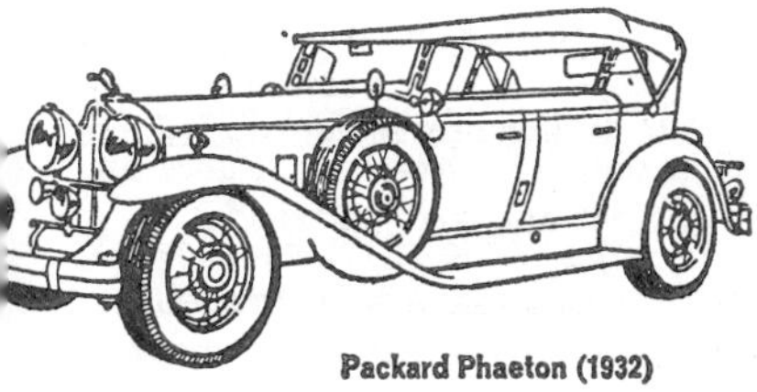
Packard Phaeton (1932)

Rolls Royce Limousine

Volkswagon Sedan

USES AND TRUCKS

truck

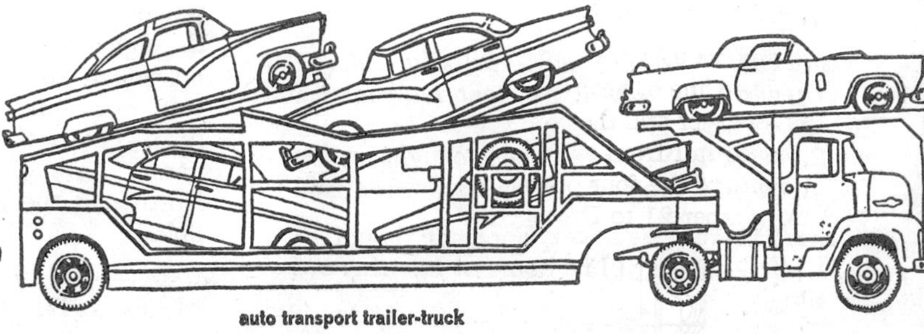
auto transport trailer-truck

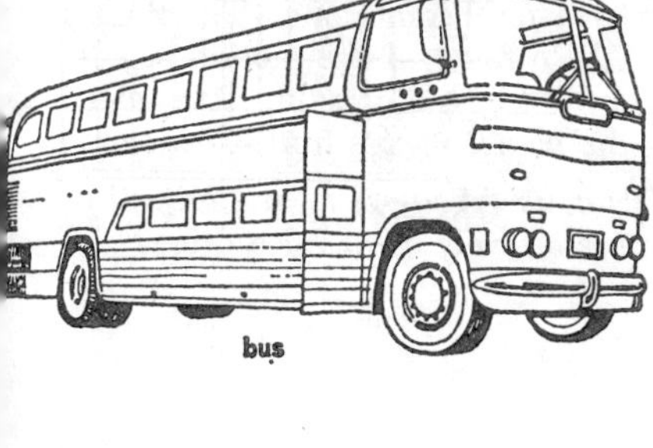
bus

fire truck

Army truck (jeep)

a•vi•a•tor (AY-vee-ay-ter *or* AV-ee-ay-ter) *n. aviators.* A man who flies an airplane; an airplane pilot.–*Aviators* must know a great deal about weather and mechanics.

a•void (ə-VOID) *v. avoids, avoided, avoiding.* 1. Keep away from.–Try to *avoid* bad company.
2. Keep from.–*Avoid* talking when others are talking.

a•wait (ə-WAYT) *v. awaits, awaited, awaiting.* Wait for.–Mother will *await* me at the corner store.

a•wake (ə-WAYK) *v. awakes, awoke* or *awaked, awaking.* Wake up.–It is hard for Bob to *awake* in the morning.
–*adj.* Not asleep.–Baby is *awake*. She woke up.

a•wak•en (ə-WAYK-ən) *v. awakens, awakened, awakening.* 1. Wake up.–It is hard for Bob to *awaken* in the morning.
2. Arouse.–It is easy for the scout leader to *awaken* the interest of the boys.

a•ware (ə-WAIR) *adj.* Conscious; knowing; noticing.–John was so interested in his reading that he was not *aware* of the time. He did not realize what time it was.

a•way (ə-WAY) *adj.* and *adv.* 1. To another place.–The family went *away* for the summer.–The dog ran *away*.
2. In or at another place.–The family is *away* now.
–*Right away* means at once.–When Mary cut herself, Mother put a bandage on the cut *right away*.

awe (AW) *n.* Fear and respect; wonder.–The girls watched the lightning with a feeling of *awe*.

aw•ful (AW-fuhl) *adj.; awfully, adv.* 1. Dreadful.–An *awful* accident happened at the corner.
2. Fearful.–When the house caught on fire, an *awful* feeling came over me. I was afraid.

a•while (ə-HWYL) *adv.* For some time; for a while.–Father will be home *awhile* this evening.

awk•ward (AWK-werd) *adj.; awkwardly, adv.* Clumsy.–The boy's large shoes made him *awkward*. He could not move gracefully.

awl (AWL) *n. awls.* A pointed tool for punching holes.–Father used an *awl* to make the holes in the horse's harness.

awn•ing (AWN-ing) *n. awnings.* A canvas or metal cover to keep out the sun.–Father put up *awnings* at the windows.

a•woke (ə-WOHK) *v.* One form of the verb *awake*.–When the baby *awoke*, she started to cry.

ax or **axe** (AKS) *n. axes.* A sharp-edged tool with a long handle.–The woodsman uses an *ax* to cut down trees and to chop wood.

ax•is (AKS-iss) *n. axes.* A line, either real or imaginary, that passes through an object and on which the object turns or appears to turn.–The earth's *axis* passes through the North and the South Poles.

ax•le (AKS-əl) *n. axles.* A bar or rod to which wheels are fastened and on which they turn.

aye or **ay** (Y) *adv.* Yes.–If you vote *aye*, you vote yes, or in favor of something.–The chairman said, "All in favor of the motion to adjourn say *aye*."–The sailor said, "*Aye, aye,* sir," when the captain gave him his orders.

az•ure (AZH-er *or* AY-zher) *n.* and *adj.* Sky blue.–*Azure* is a lovely color for a dress.

B b

B, b (BEE) *n. B's, b's.* The second letter of the alphabet.

baa (BAH) *n.* The cry of a sheep.–The farmer heard the *baa* of the lost sheep.

babe (BAYB) *n. babes.* A baby; an infant.–The *babe* was fast asleep in his mother's arms.

ba•boon (ba-BOON) *n. baboons.* A large kind of monkey with a face like a dog.

ba•by (BAY-bee) *n. babies.* A very young child who cannot walk or talk; an infant.–Our new *baby* must be fed every four hours.
–*v. babies, babied, babying.* Treat like a small baby.–When Jack was sick, his mother *babied* him.

bach•e•lor (BACH-ə-ler) *n. bachelors.* A man who has not been married.–Father's brother is still a *bachelor.* He has no wife.

back (BAK) *n. backs.* 1. The part of anything that is opposite the front, as the *back* of the room, the *back* of a chair.
2. The side of the body opposite the chest.–Bob usually sleeps on his *back.*
–*v. backs, backed, backing.* 1. Go or make go rear end first.–Father *backed* the car out of the garage.
2. Encourage; supply money for.–Father *backed* my uncle in his shoe business.
–*adv.* In return.–My uncle will pay *back* the money Father let him have for his business.

back•bone (BAK-bohn) *n. backbones.* 1. The spine or main set of bones in the back of people and animals. The *backbone* is made up of many small bones.
2. Courage.–Jack has enough *backbone* to stand up for his rights. He will make sure he receives fair treatment.

back•ground (BAK-grownd) *n. backgrounds.* 1. The part of a picture that seems to be behind all the main objects in the picture.–Mary painted a picture with a blue *background* to look like the sky.
2. A person's past experiences.–John told us about the candidate's *background.*
–*In the background* means in a place where one is not noticed much.–The little girl kept herself *in the background* at the party.

back•ward (BAK-werd) *adj.* and *adv.* 1. Opposite the front; toward the starting point.–The children looked *backward* as they walked.
2. Slow in learning.–Ned is a *backward* pupil.
3. Shy.–Some girls are *backward* about playing with boys.
4. (Also spelled *backwards.*) With the back first.–It is not safe to walk *backwards.*

ba•con (BAY-kən) *n.* Meat from the sides of a pig, salted and smoked. *Bacon* has stripes of lean and fat.–On Sunday morning, Mother cooks eggs and *bacon.*

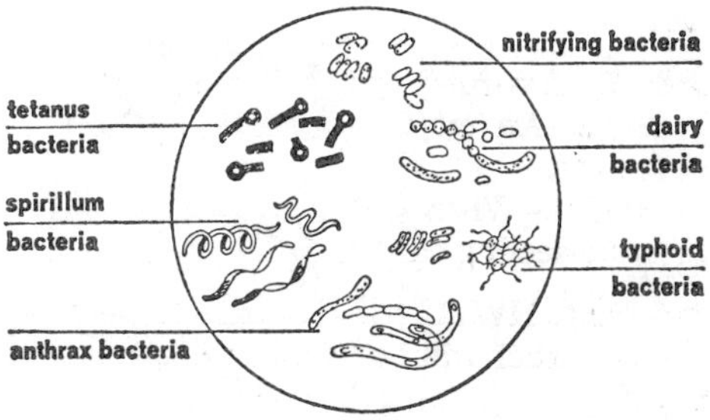

bac•te•ri•a (bak-TIR-ee-ə) *n. pl.* Plants that are so small they cannot be seen except through a microscope.–The doctor is trying to find the *bacteria* that cause the unusual disease.–Some kinds of *bacteria* are useful, like the *bacteria* that help make milk into cheese.

bad (BAD) *adj. worse, worst; badly, adv.* 1. Evil; wicked.–Stealing is *bad.*–Some people are *bad;* they do evil things.
2. Unfortunate; not what is wanted.–It was too *bad* that the storm ruined the farmer's corn.
3. Severe.–Bob had a *bad* cold, but he is well now.
4. Rotten; spoiled.–This is a *bad* apple.
5. Harmful.–It is *bad* for your health not to get enough sleep.

bade (BAD *or* BAYD) *v.* One form of the verb *bid.*–Our guests *bade* us good-by. They said good-by.

badge (BAJ) *n. badges.* A sign or button that shows the wearer belongs to a certain group. – The traffic policeman wore a *badge.* – Children in our class made paper *badges* which they wore to show that they were in the seventh grade.

badg•er (BAJ-er) *n. badgers.* A gray animal that has long front claws, with which it digs holes in the ground to live in.

baf•fle (BAF-əl) *v. baffles, baffled, baffling.* Confuse; defeat; puzzle. – The detectives were *baffled* by the crime because there were no clues.

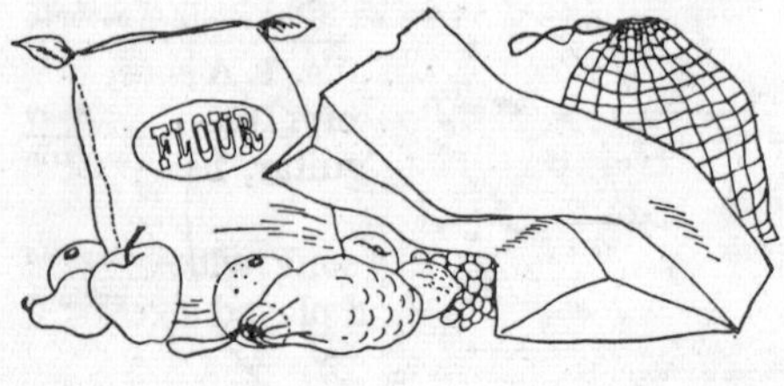

bag (BAG) *n. bags.* 1. A sack; a deep container made of paper, cloth, or other soft material.–The grocer put the fruit in a paper *bag.*
2. A purse or hand*bag.* – Mother's *bag* is made of leather.
3. A suitcase or traveling *bag.*–The porter helped us with our *bags* at the train.

bag•gage (BAG-ij) *n.* Trunks, suitcases, hatboxes, etc.–On a long trip, you need several pieces of *baggage* to carry your clothes in.

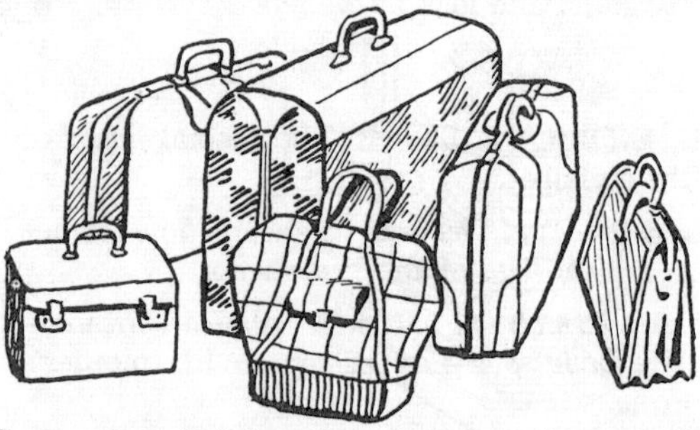

bag•pipe (BAG-pyp) *n. bagpipes.* A musical wind instrument usually played in Scotland. It has a leather windbag and pipes from which the music comes. One pipe plays the tune and the others make a soft sound which goes on at the same time.

bail (BAYL) *n.* The money put up to get a prisoner released until it is time for his trial. –The prisoner got out of jail on $2,500 *bail.*
–v. bails, bailed, bailing. 1. Get someone out of jail by promising to pay a certain amount of money if the person under arrest fails to report to the court when he is sent for.
2. Scoop water out of.–Sally watched Father *bail* the boat.

bait (BAYT) *n. baits.* 1. Food used to tempt fish when you want to catch them.–Angleworms and crickets are sometimes used for *bait* on the fishhook.
2. Anything used to lure an animal or person into being caught.
–v. baits, baited, baiting. 1. Put bait on.–Mother *baited* the mousetrap with a piece of bacon.
2. Tease.–John *baited* his opponent. He said his opponent was a dull fellow.

bake (BAYK) *v. bakes, baked, baking.* 1. Cook in an oven.–Mary will *bake* cookies today.–Grandmother *baked* a ham.
2. Dry and harden by heat.–Vases, bricks, and tiles are *baked* in a kind of large oven called a kiln.

bak•er (BAYK-er) *n. bakers.* A person who makes cookies, bread, pies, etc., to sell.–Jack went to the *baker's* to buy a coffee cake for breakfast.

bak•er•y (BAYK-er-ee *or* BAYK-ree) *n. bakeries.* A store where cookies, bread, and other baked goods are made and sold.—Jack likes to stand and look at the *bakery* counter.

bak•ing (BAYK-ing) *n.* Things baked.—Jack asked Father whether he liked Mother's *baking* or Grandmother's *baking* best.
—*v.* One form of the verb *bake.* — Mother is *baking* a yellow birthday cake for Sally.

bak•ing pow•der (BAYK-ing POW-der). A specially prepared powder containing flour or starch and certain chemicals, used in baking to make dough rise and become light.

bak•ing so•da (BAYK-ing SOH-də). Sodium bicarbonate, used as a baking powder or a medicine for indigestion.

bal•ance (BAL-ənss) *n. balances.* 1. Steadiness.—It is hard to keep your *balance* on a bicycle when you ride very slowly.—Mary loses her *balance* when she walks in Mother's high-heeled shoes. She falls over.
2. The rest, or remainder; what is left. — Mother paid the grocer $4 on her bill today and will pay the *balance* tomorrow.
—*v. balances, balanced, balancing.* Keep weight, amount, force, etc., equal or the same on both sides of anything.—When the clown walked the tightrope, he carried an umbrella to *balance* himself.—Mother made some pale yellow curtains to *balance* the dark colors in the living room.

bal•co•ny (BAL-kə-nee) *n. balconies.* A platform with a railing around it, which sticks out from a building or into a room or theater. —The children sat in the *balcony* of the theater.—There was a *balcony* outside our window in the hotel.

bald (BAWLD) *adj. balder, baldest.* 1. Without hair.—Father's head is growing *bald.* He is getting *bald*-headed.

2. Bare, or without trees or plants.—The mountain tops are *bald.* The rocks show above the point where the trees stop growing.

bale (BAYL) *n. bales.* A bundle of material pressed closely together and bound.—Cotton and wool are made into *bales* to be shipped.

balk (BAWK) *v. balks, balked, balking.* 1. Stop short and refuse to go on.—Mules are stubborn and often *balk.* — Jack *balked* at taking violin lessons.
2. Hinder.—Bad weather *balked* our plans.

ball (BAWL) *n. balls.* 1. Any round thing.— The kitten is a little *ball* of fur.—Jack bought a bag of lemon *balls.*—Grandmother winds her wool into a *ball.*—The earth is a *ball.*
2. A round object used in playing tennis, football, baseball, basketball, golf, etc. — Foot*balls* are oval in shape.

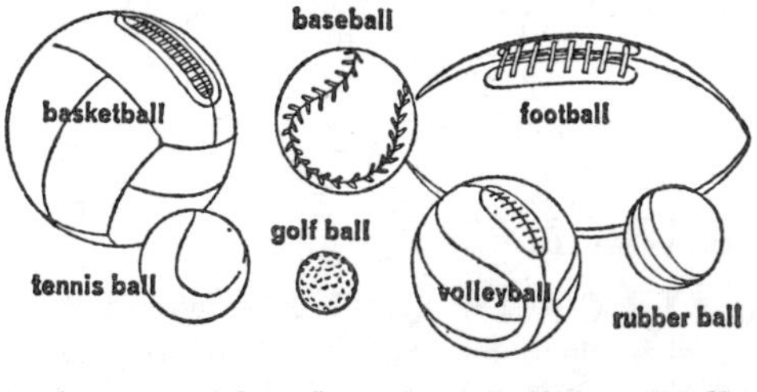

3. A game played with a ball, especially baseball.—Bob and Jack play *ball* every Saturday.
4. A dancing party.—Cinderella went to the *ball* in a handsome carriage.

bal•lad (BAL-id) *n. ballads.* 1. A short poem which tells a romantic story. It is often sung. —When Tom plays his guitar, he also likes to sing *ballads.*
2. A popular romantic song with a simple melody.—The dance band played a *ballad* for its last number.

bal•last (BAL-əst) *n.* Something heavy, such as sand or rocks, to give balance. When a ship is not fully loaded with freight, *ballast* is put in it to keep it steady, or in position. *Ballast* is used in balloons, also.

ball bear·ing (bawl BAIR-ing) *ball bearings.* A machine part in which a section moves, turns, or slides on steel balls; a steel ball in such a machine part.–The wheels on Harry's roller skates turn on *ball bearings.*

bal·let (BAL-ay *or* bal-AY) *n.* and *adj.* 1. A special kind of detailed dance in which all the movements are graceful, expressive, and pleasing to the eye.–Robert took his friend Mary to see the *ballet.*

2. A dance company made up of ballet dancers.–The Bolshoi *Ballet* is one of the world's most famous *ballet* companies.

bal·loon (bə-LOON) *n. balloons.* A bag filled with heated air, or a gas lighter than air, so that it will rise into the air when set free. Some toy *balloons* have cold air in them and do not rise.

bal·lot (BAL-ət) *n. ballots.* A voting ticket used in elections. On it you mark the names of the people you want to elect.

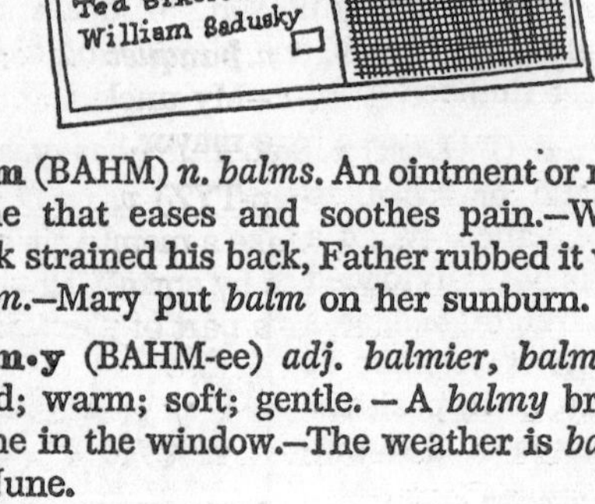

balm (BAHM) *n. balms.* An ointment or medicine that eases and soothes pain.–When Jack strained his back, Father rubbed it with *balm.*–Mary put *balm* on her sunburn.

balm·y (BAHM-ee) *adj. balmier, balmiest.* Mild; warm; soft; gentle. – A *balmy* breeze came in the window.–The weather is *balmy* in June.

bal·sam (BAWL-səm) *n.* 1. A sticky substance that comes from trees and is used in making balms, or soothing medicines.

2. A kind of evergreen tree somewhat like the pine. – Grandmother has a little pillow stuffed with sweet-smelling *balsam* needles.

bam·boo (bam-BOO) *n.* A stout, hollow grass that grows very thick and high. *Bamboo* grows in very hot places. The shoots of the *bamboo* are eaten as a vegetable in some countries.

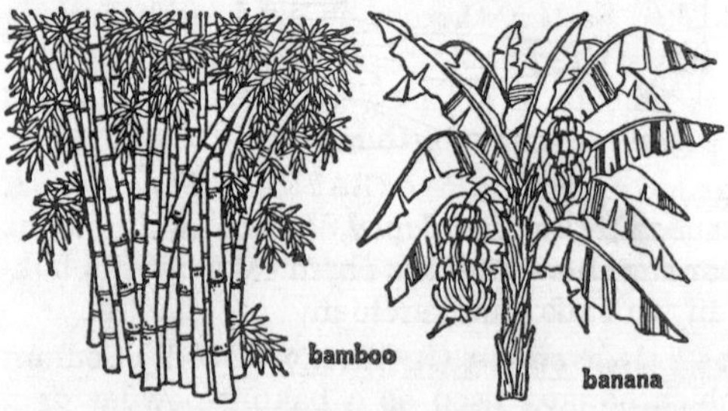

ba·na·na (bə-NAN-ə) *n. bananas.* A long fruit with a heavy yellow or red skin. *Bananas* grow in large bunches on trees in warm climates. The part of the *banana* which you eat is soft and has a rich, creamy color.

band (BAND) *n. bands.* 1. A flat strip; a long, narrow piece.–Mother trimmed Mary's new dress with a *band* of black velvet.

2. A stripe; a long, narrow marking. – A zebra is light-colored with black *bands.*

3. A group.–While on our vacation, we saw a *band* of gypsies.

4. A group of musicians who play music together.–Instruments that you blow, or wind instruments, and drums, are generally played in *bands.*

–*v. bands, banded, banding.* Gather together in a group.–Gypsies *band* together to travel.

band•age (BAN-dij) *n. bandages.* A band or strip of cloth used in binding up wounds or injuries.—When Bob cut his finger, the school nurse put a *bandage* around it to keep it clean.

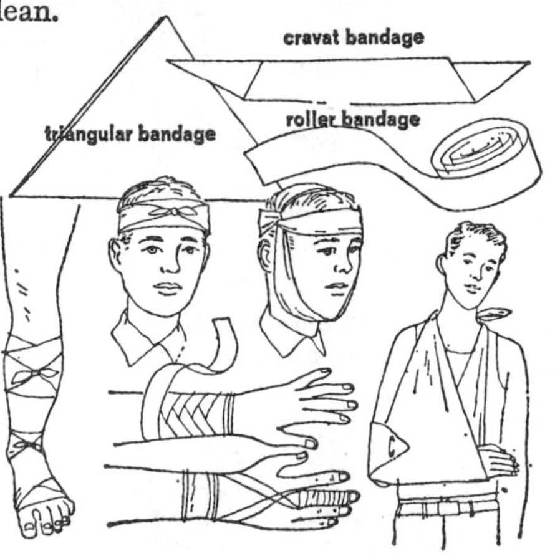

—*v. bandages, bandaged, bandaging.* Put a bandage on.—Jack *bandaged* the puppy's hurt tail with his handkerchief.

ban•dan•na or **ban•dan•a** (ban-DAN-ə) *n. bandannas* or *bandanas.* A very large colored handkerchief, often with red, white, or blue designs.—Mary wore a blue *bandanna* around her neck.

ban•dit (BAN-dət) *n. bandits.* A robber, especially one in the woods or desert.—Long ago in the West, many stagecoaches were held up by *bandits.*

bang (BANG) *n. bangs.* A loud, sharp, sudden noise.—The car door blew shut with a *bang.*—When we heard the *bang* of a rifle, we knew someone was hunting nearby.
—*v. bangs, banged, banging.* 1. Slam.—In the middle of the night someone *banged* the barn door.
2. Hit.—It is not polite to *bang* your plate with your silverware.

ban•ish (BAN-ish) *v. banishes, banished, banishing.* Force to leave one's home country or regular place.—The king *banished* the duke who had tried to betray him.—The teacher *banished* Bill from the classroom for squirting ink at Mary.

ban•is•ter (BAN-əss-ter) *n. banisters.* A handrailing along a flight of stairs.—Prevent accidents by taking hold of the *banister* when you go up or down stairs.

ban•jo (BAN-joh) *n. banjos.* A simple musical instrument with five to nine strings, which is played with the fingers or a pick.

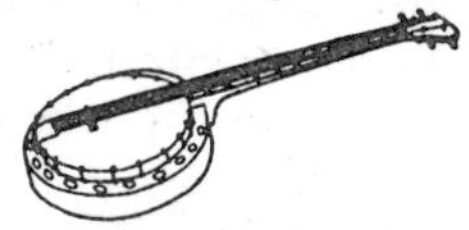

bank (BANGK) *n. banks.* 1. A long pile.—The children made a *bank* of sand along the beach.
2. The ground on the sides of a river, lake, stream, etc.—While fishing, Father slipped and fell off the *bank* into the water.
3. A business company which keeps people's money for them, lends money for a charge, etc. The *bank* makes money with the money which the people put in, or deposit.

4. A locked container for putting money in to save.—Mary has a small iron *bank* in the shape of a pig. She puts pennies in it.

bank•er (BANGK-er) *n. bankers.* A man whose business or work is running a bank.

ban•ner (BAN-er) *n. banners.* A flag, pennant, or streamer, with pictures, writing, etc., on it.—The Boy Scouts carried many *banners* in the parade.—"The Star-Spangled *Banner*" means "The Star-Spangled Flag."

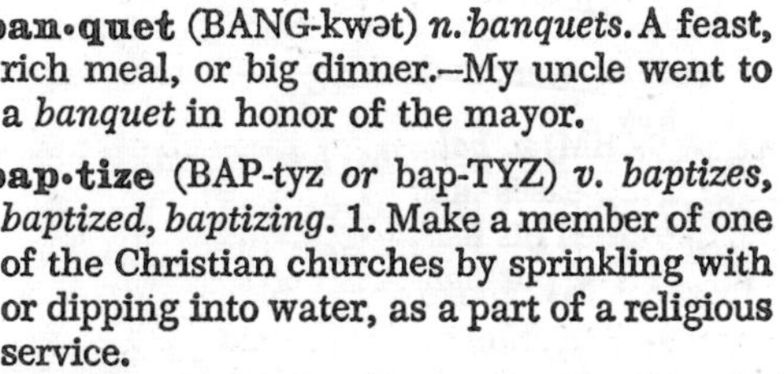

ban•quet (BANG-kwət) *n. banquets.* A feast, rich meal, or big dinner.—My uncle went to a *banquet* in honor of the mayor.

bap•tize (BAP-tyz *or* bap-TYZ) *v. baptizes, baptized, baptizing.* 1. Make a member of one of the Christian churches by sprinkling with or dipping into water, as a part of a religious service.
2. Give a name to a person at the time he is *baptized,* or taken into a church.
—*baptism, n. baptisms.*

bar (BAHR) *n. bars.* 1. A long, solid piece of steel or wood.–Grandfather put a *bar* under the box to lift it.

2. A cake or piece (of something).–Mother bought three *bars* of soap.–Jack bought a candy *bar.*

3. A band or stripe.–There was a long *bar* of light across the sky at sunset.–The army officer has *bars* on his sleeve to tell how long he has been in the army.

4. A bank of sand at the mouth of a river.–A ship ran aground on the *bar.*

5. Anything that hinders or keeps back.–A tree across the road keeping back the cars that wanted to pass would be a *bar.*

6. An up-and-down line on a music staff to mark the measures. The double *bars* at the end of the music tell that the music has ended.

7. A place in a courtroom, enclosed by a railing, where prisoners stand.–The prisoner stood at the *bar.*

8. A long, high counter where drinks are served.–The boys gathered at the milk *bar.*

–*v. bars, barred, barring.* Forbid; keep out or away.–John was *barred* from the team because he was underweight.–A tree *barred* the way.

barb (BAHRB) *n. barbs; barbed, adj.* A short, sharp point. – The fence had *barbs* on the wire to keep the livestock in.–The arrows which the Indian hunter used had sharp *barbs* on them.–Grandmother's crochet hook has a *barb* on it.

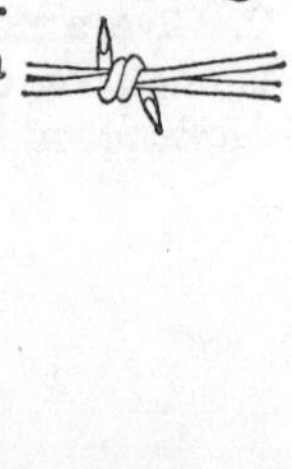

bar•ba•ri•an (bahr-BAIR-ee-ən) *n. barbarians* and *adj.* A savage; a member of a tribe of people who are not civilized. *Barbarians* live mostly by hunting.

bar•be•cue (BAHR-bə-kyoo) *n. barbecues.* 1. A feast at which a cow, hog, or other animal is roasted whole.–The man held a great *barbecue* on his ranch.

2. An outdoor party at which food is cooked over a fire.

–*v. barbecues, barbecued, barbecuing.* Roast over an open fire.–Many restaurants *barbecue* meat for sandwiches.

bar•ber (BAHR-ber) *n. barbers.* A person who cuts and shampoos hair, shaves men, and trims their beards or mustaches.

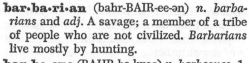

bar•ber•ry (BAHR-bair-ee) *n. barberries.* A low, bushy plant that has red berries and thorns.

bare (BAIR) *v. bares, bared, baring.* Uncover. –When the flag went by, the men *bared* their heads.

–*adj.* 1. Uncovered.–When the flag went by, the men stood with *bare* heads.

2. Without leaves.–In winter, the maple trees are *bare.*

3. Empty.–The cupboard was *bare.*

bare•foot (BAIR-fuht) *adj.* and *adv.* Without shoes or stockings on.–Bob is often *barefoot* in hot weather.

bare•head•ed (BAIR-hed-əd) *adj.* and *adv.* With the head bare; without a hat.

bare•ly (BAIR-lee) *adv.* Scarcely.–We had *barely* enough sugar to bake the cake.

bar•gain (BAHR-gən) *n. bargains.* 1. An agreement. – John and his father made a *bargain.* John said he would mow the lawn once a week, and his father said he would pay John fifty cents.

2. Something good bought for a low price.–Mother's dress was a *bargain.* She paid less for it than it was actually worth.

–*v. bargains, bargained, bargaining.* Argue about price.–The gypsy tried to *bargain* with the peddler. She tried to make him lower his price.

barge (BAHRJ) *n. barges.* A large, flat-bottomed boat towed or pushed by another boat. —Iron, coal, steel, and other products are often shipped down rivers and canals on *barges.*

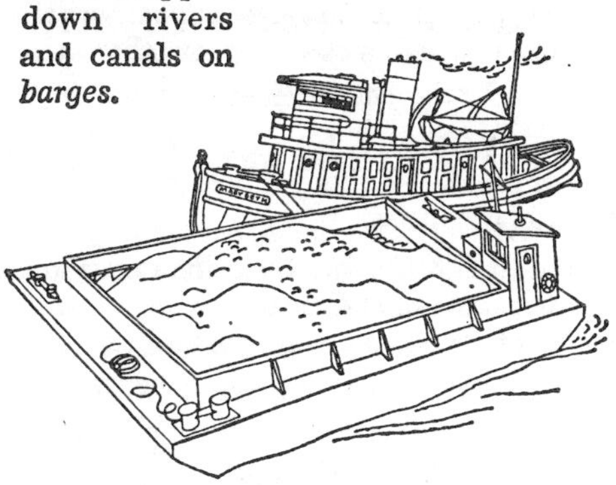

bar•i•tone (BAR-ə-tohn) *n. baritones.* A singer whose voice is not as low as a bass and not as high as a tenor.—Harry is a *baritone.* —*adj.* A part in music suitable for a man with such a voice.—Harry will sing the *baritone* role in the show.

bark (BAHRK) *n. barks.* 1. The hard outside covering of a tree.

2. A sharp, loud sound made by a dog.
—*v. barks, barked, barking* Make a short, sharp cry, as a dog.—Some dogs *bark* at all strangers.

bar•ley (BAHR-lee) *n.* The seed or grain of a grasslike plant. *Barley* is good to eat.—Mother puts *barley* in soup.

barn (BAHRN) *n. barns.* A large building on a farm in which farm animals and their feed are kept.

bar•na•cle (BAHR-nə-kəl) *n. barnacles.* A shellfish that attaches itself to the hulls of ships, rocks, docks, etc., and clings very hard. — The captain had the *barnacles* scraped from the bottom of his ship.

barn•yard (BAHRN-yahrd) *n. barnyards.* A yard or space around a barn.—Sometimes the cows and horses come out of the barn into the *barnyard.*

ba•rom•e•ter (bə-RAHM-ə-ter) *n. barometers.* 1. An instrument for gauging atmospheric pressure. It helps us predict weather changes, measure altitude, etc.

—The *barometer* is falling; we shall have rain for the weekend.
2. Any measure of changes.—The *barometer* of public opinion showed strong support for the new traffic laws.

bar•racks (BAR-əks) *n. pl.* A place where soldiers live, usually a building or group of buildings on an army base.—The soldiers keep their *barracks* neat and clean.

bar•rel (BAR-əl) *n. barrels.* 1. A large container made of curved slats or staves that are held together with wooden or steel bands. *A barrel* is flat on the ends and a little larger in the middle than at the ends.—The farmer keeps oil in a large *barrel.*

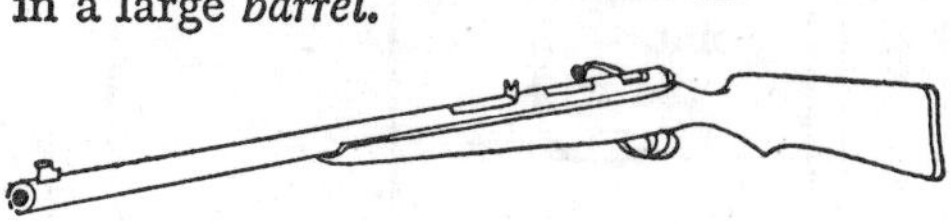

2. The long metal tube of a gun, through which the bullet passes.—Father's shotgun has a long, shiny *barrel.*

bar•ren (BAR-ən) *adj.* 1. Bare; not growing anything.—The soil was dry and *barren.* Not even weeds were growing in it.
2. Uninteresting; without charm.—The land was without trees; it was flat, sandy, and *barren.*

bar•ri•er (BAR-ee-er) *n. barriers.* An obstruction to movement or progress.—The deep hole in the road was a *barrier* to traffic. —The soldiers put up wire *barriers* to slow down the enemy.—High tariffs are *barriers* to trade among nations.

bar•ter (BAHR-ter) *n.* Trading things without the use of money. — Before the use of money, people exchanged what they had for what they needed by *barter.*
—*v. barters, bartered, bartering.* Trade.—The farmer *bartered* his cow for a plow.

base (BAYSS) *n. bases.* 1. The bottom part of anything, which holds up the rest of the structure.—The house stands on its *base* of stone.—The *base* of the lamp is made of brass.
2. One of the four goals or stopping places for a runner in baseball.—The player reached third *base* safely.
3. A place to which a ship, airplane, etc., returns for supplies, repairs, orders, shelter.—The bomber returned to its *base* safely.
—*v. bases, based, basing.* Build; set up (on something).—The man who *bases* his business on honesty and fairness is likely to succeed.

base•ball (BAYSS-bawl) *n. baseballs.* 1. A game played by two teams of nine persons each, on a diamond-shaped field with four bases. *Baseball* is played with a ball and bat.
2. The ball used in playing baseball.

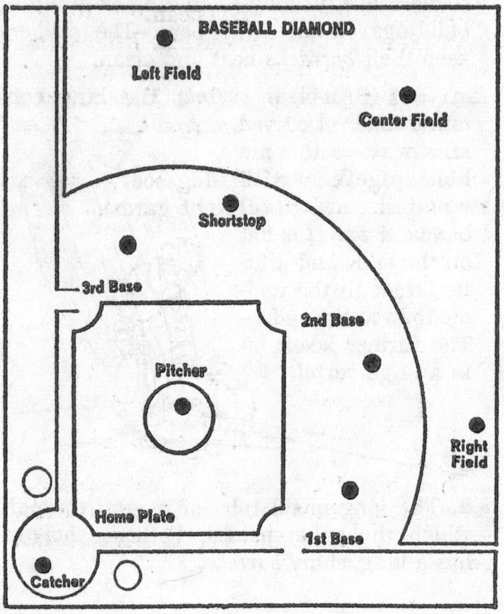

base•ment (BAYSS-mənt) *n. basements.* The lowest part of a building; the part below the level of the ground.—Our washing machine is in the *basement* of our new house.

bash•ful (BASH-fuhl) *adj.; bashfully, adv.* Shy or timid.—The baby is *bashful.* He doesn't like to be noticed.

bas•ic (BAY-sik) *adj.; basically, adv.* Fundamental; essential.—One of the *basic* requirements of a good education is reading.

ba•sin (BAY-sən) *n. basins.* 1. A bowl not very deep but wide at the top. — Mother washes the vegetables in a *basin.* — A bowl fixed to the wall or floor and equipped with water faucets and a drain is called a wash*basin.*

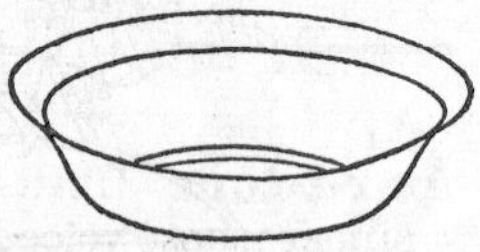

2. All the land drained by a single river.—The Mississippi River has a large river *basin.*

ba•sis (BAY-siss) *n. bases.* 1. Foundation; support upon which something rests, in a nonmaterial sense, as for an idea, theory, etc. —The prisoner claimed that the charges against him had no *basis* in fact.
2. The most important part, or the principal ingredient.—Father says the *basis* of good character is honesty.

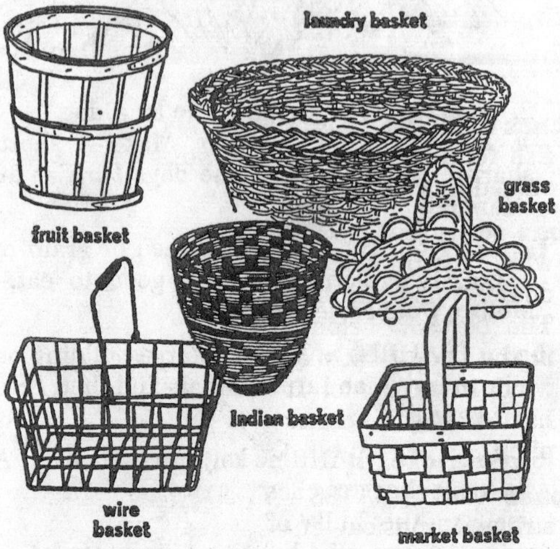

bas•ket (BASS-kət) *n. baskets.* A container made of woven grasses, reeds, ropes, etc.—Grandmother keeps her thread in a sewing *basket.*

bas•ket•ball (BASS-kət-bawl) *n. basketballs.* 1. A game played with a large, round, leather-covered ball filled with air. At each end of the playing space is a bottomless basket placed high over the heads of the players. They try to throw the ball into the basket. The game is played indoors by two teams of five persons.
2. The ball used in playing basketball.

bas•ket•ful (BASS-kət-fuhl) *n. basketfuls.* As much or as many as a basket will hold.—Grandfather brought us a *basketful* of apples.

bass (BAYSS) *n.* The lowest part in music.—Some men sing *bass.*
—*adj.* Very low in pitch; deep in sound.—My father has a *bass* voice.

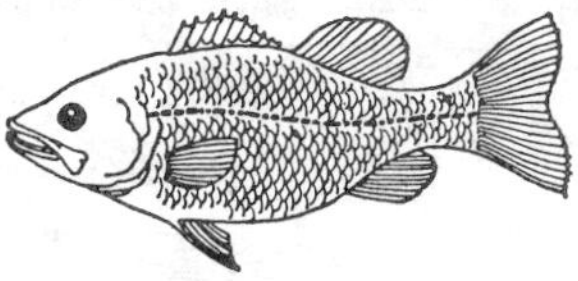

bass (BASS) *n. bass* or *basses.* A kind of food fish found in fresh or salt water and much valued by sportsmen.

bas•soon (bə-SOON) *n. bassoons.* A musical wind instrument of double wooden tubes. The *bassoon* belongs in the oboe family of wind instruments. It has a low baritone pitch.

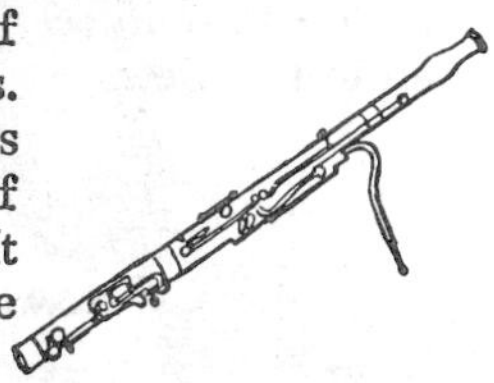

bass viol (BAYSS VY-əl) *bass viols.* A stringed musical instrument belonging to the family of viols. The *bass viol* has a low pitch and is played standing up because of its large size.

baste (BAYST) *v. bastes, basted, basting.* 1. Sew together by hand with long, loose stitches.—Before Mother stitched her dress on the sewing machine, she *basted* it.
2. Drop melted fat over roasting meat. *Basting* a roast or a fowl keeps it from becoming dry and hard on the outside.

bat (BAT) *n. bats.* 1. A strong wooden stick for hitting balls or other objects.—John hit the ball with the *bat.*—Baseball *bats* are often made of maple or hickory because these woods are strong.

2. A short-furred animal that flies at night. *Bats* look like mice with wings. Some *bats* eat fruit; others live on insects.
—*v. bats, batted, batting.* Try to hit the ball in the game of baseball.—It is Bob's turn to *bat.*

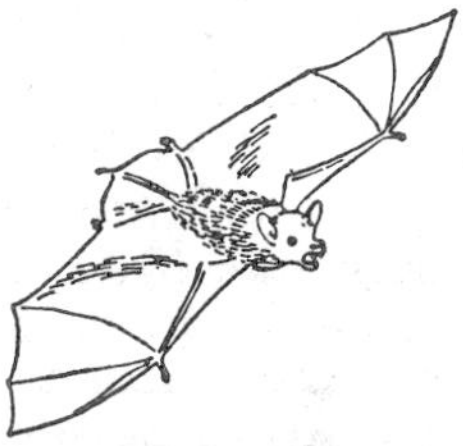

bath (BATH) *n. baths.* 1. A cleaning or washing of the body with water.—Every day Mother gives the baby a *bath.*
2. Water for a bath.—Mary helps Mother get the *bath* ready for the baby.

bathe (BAYTH) *v. bathes, bathed, bathing.* 1. Take a bath; wash the body.—Bob *bathes* every day.
2. Give a bath to; wash.—Mother will *bathe* the baby this afternoon.
3. Go into water for pleasure.—It is fun to *bathe* in a lake or in the ocean.

bath•house (BATH-howss) *n. bathhouses.* A building with dressing rooms for changing clothes for bathing.—When the children went swimming, they changed their clothes in the *bathhouse.*

bath•ing suit (BAYTH-ing soot *or* syoot) *bathing suits.* A short, light garment worn for swimming.

bath•robe (BATH-rohb) *n. bathrobes.* A loose-fitting robe, worn to and from the bathroom, and often for warmth over night clothes.

bath·room (BATH-room) *n. bathrooms.* A room with a bathtub; often, a room with bathtub or shower, washbasin, and toilet.

ba·ton (bə-TAHN) *n. batons.* 1. A wand or stick used by an orchestra leader to conduct the orchestra.

2. A staff of authority. –Officers in the British army often carry *batons.*

bat·tal·ion (bə-TAL-yən) *n. battalions.* 1. A military force made up of a large number of men under the command of a high-ranking officer; or, a body of soldiers prepared for battle.–The colonel ordered his *battalion* to advance.–The *battalion* was ready to attack. 2. Any large group of people organized for a common purpose.–A *battalion* of Girl Scouts set out to sell cookies.

bat·ter (BAT-er) *n. batters.* 1. A mixture of flour, eggs, milk, sugar, butter, etc.–Mother is beating the *batter.* When the *batter* is baked, it will be a cake.–Some *batters* make pancakes, waffles, etc.
2. A baseball player while taking his turn to try to bat or hit the ball.–John is the best *batter* in the ball game.

–*v. batters, battered, battering.* Hit or pound on hard and often.–The waves *battered* the old dock to pieces.

bat·ter·y (BAT-er-ee *or* BAT-ree) *n. batteries.* 1. A device that makes or stores electricity by chemical changes of the materials inside it.–An automobile has a *battery* which makes the lights burn and helps start the motor.

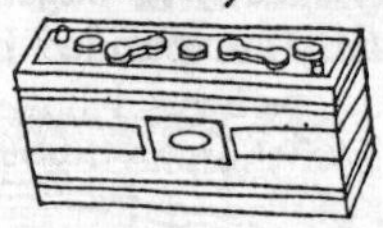

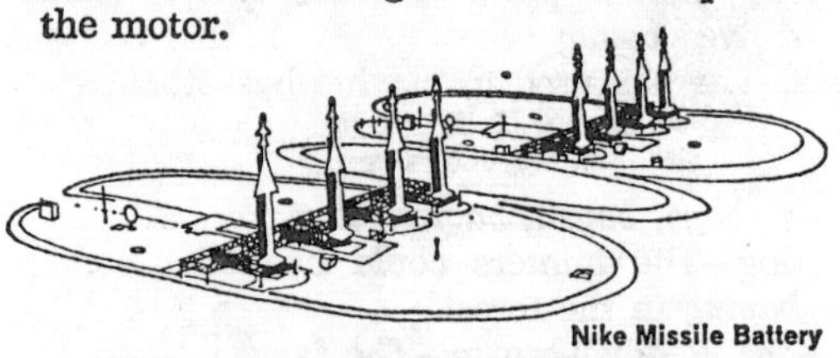

Nike Missile Battery

2. A group of guns.–The United States has *batteries* of big guns to defend its coasts.

bat·tle (BAT-l) *n. battles.* 1. A fight between two armed forces.–Our army won a big *battle.*
2. A contest.–The spelling bee was quite a *battle.*
–*v. battles, battled, battling.* Fight.–Doctors *battle* disease.

bat·tle·field (BAT-l-feeld) *n. battlefields.* A place where a battle or fight between armies takes place.

bat·tle·ship (BAT-l-ship) *n. battleships.* A warship of the largest class, with powerful guns on it.–*Battleships* carry thousands of men in the crew.

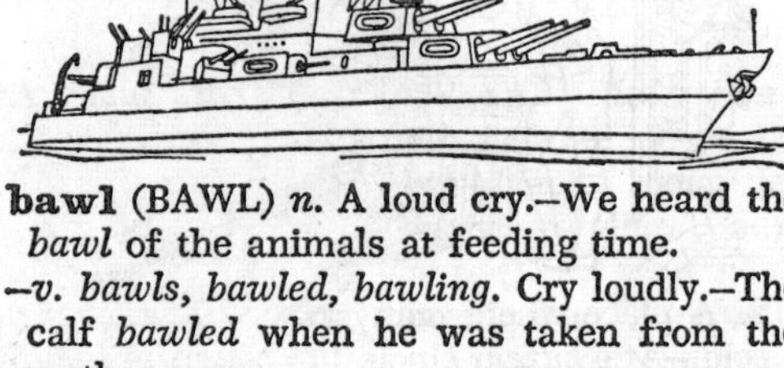

bawl (BAWL) *n.* A loud cry.–We heard the *bawl* of the animals at feeding time.
–*v. bawls, bawled, bawling.* Cry loudly.–The calf *bawled* when he was taken from the mother cow.

bay (BAY) *n. bays.* A broad body of water partly surrounded by land.

–v. bays, bayed, baying. Bark or howl, as a dog.–The hunters could hear the hounds *baying* in the forest.
–adj. Reddish-brown.–The farmer has a *bay* horse.

bay•ber•ry (BAY-bair-ee) *n. bayberries.* A bush that grows near water and has grayish-white berries sometimes used for winter bouquets and in making candles.

bay•o•net (BAY-oh-nət *or* bay-ə-NET) *n. bayonets.* A kind of short sword fastened to the barrel of a rifle.

bay•ou (BY-oo) *n. bayous.* A marshy stream of water leading into or out of a larger body of water, such as a river, lake, gulf, etc.–There are swamps along the *bayous* of southern Louisiana.

bay win•dow (BAY WIN-doh) *bay windows.* A window made of smaller windows which stand out from the wall of a building. A *bay window* lets in much light.

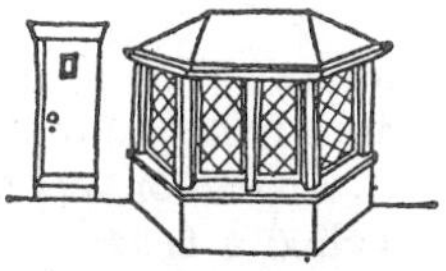

ba•zaar (bə-ZAHR) *n. bazaars.* 1. A sale of things donated to raise funds for a church, a charity, etc.–The church is having a Christmas *bazaar.*

2. A place where many kinds of things are sold.–At a *bazaar* Uncle Jim bought a beautiful oriental rug from the man who made it.

be (BEE) *v. is, was, being.* You will *be* late unless you hurry.–John can *be* a good boy if he tries.–The word *be* has many forms.

beach (BEECH) *n. beaches.* A flat, sandy shore along an ocean, lake, or river.
–v. beaches, beached, beaching. Pull completely out of the water; rest on the beach.–John *beached* his canoe and headed for camp.

bea•con (BEE-kən) *n. beacons.* 1. A signal fire or light.–The Boy Scouts made a *beacon* in the woods to attract the attention of the scoutmaster.
2. A light along the shore to guide ships.–Ships at sea depend upon *beacons* to keep them from running onto the rocks at night.

bead (BEED) *n. beads.* 1. A round ball of wood, pressed paper, glass, metal, etc., with a hole through it for a string. *Beads* are usually brightly colored.–Children like to string *beads* into necklaces.

2. A drop.–Small *beads* of dew settled on the flowers during the night.
–v. beads, beaded, beading. Trim or decorate with beads.–The dressmaker will *bead* the front of the dress.

bea•gle (BEE-gəl) *n. beagles.* A kind of dog used for hunting small game.–The *beagle* chased the rabbit.

beak (BEEK) *n. beaks.* The long, pointed parts extending out from a bird's mouth. Birds eat with their *beaks.*

beak•er (BEEK-er) *n. beakers.* 1. A large drinking cup with a wide mouth.—The king made a toast, then drank a *beaker* of wine.
2. A vessel with a pouring lip, often used by chemists.—The chemist poured the contents of the *beaker* into a test tube.

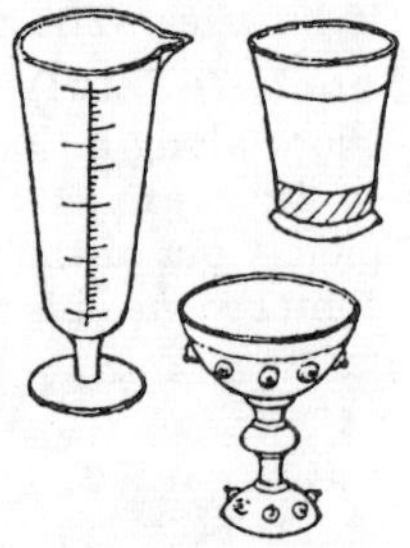

beam (BEEM) *n. beams.* 1. A ray or line (of light).—We saw the airplane in the search-light's *beam.*

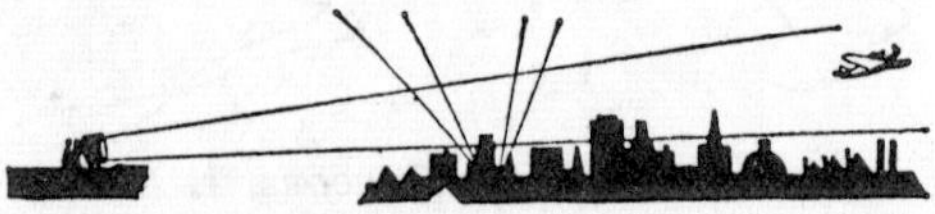

2. A strong bar that supports a floor.—The carpenter fastened the floor of the house to long wooden *beams.*

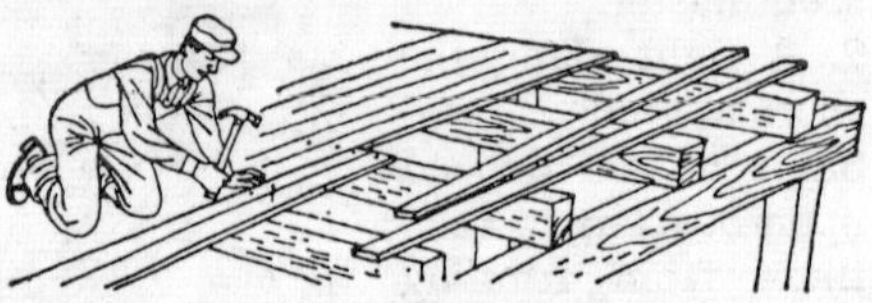

—*v. beams, beamed, beaming.* 1. Shine.—The moon *beams* over the hilltop.
2. Smile.—Bob *beamed* as he read the good news.

bean (BEEN) *n. beans.* A vegetable plant that grows seeds in pods. The seeds are good to eat, and so are the pods of some *beans,* when young and tender.

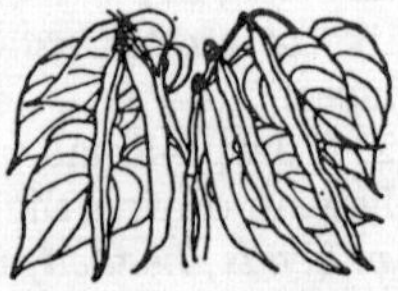

bear (BAIR) *n. bears.* A large, hairy animal that has a very short tail and large, flat paws.

There are several kinds: the polar *bear,* which is white; the black *bear;* and the grizzly *bear,* which is grayish or brownish, and sometimes very fierce.

—*v. bears, bore, bearing.* 1. Produce.—Apple trees *bear* apples.—Cherry trees *bear* cherries.
2. Carry.—Father *bears* the responsibility for supporting his family.
3. Press.—*Bear* down on the doorknob and the door will open easily.
—*Bear on* may mean to have to do with.—The facts which the witness gave did not *bear on* the case. They had nothing to do with it.

beard (BEERD) *n. beards.* 1. The hair that grows on a man's chin and face. — Great-grandfather has a long, gray *beard.*
2. The long, hairlike straws on the heads of grain.—Wheat, oats, and other grains have *beards.*

bear•er (BAIR-er) *n. bearers.* A carrier; one who holds or carries something.—Bob was the *bearer* of the torch in the graduation ceremony.—The bank paid the money to the *bearer* of the check.

bear•ing (BAIR-ing) *n. bearings.* 1. A relation; something to do with (something else). —The statements which the witness made had no *bearing* on the case. They had nothing to do with it.
2. Way or direction.—The fireman lost his *bearings* in the thick smoke. He did not know where he was.

beast (BEEST) *n. beasts; beastly, adj.* 1. A four-footed animal.
2. An evil or very coarse person is sometimes called a *beast.*

beat (BEET) *n. beats.* 1. A throbbing sound. —The doctor listened to the *beat* of the baby's heart.—We heard the *beat* of the Indians' drums in the distance.
2. An accent or count in music.—In this piece of music there are four *beats* to a measure.
3. A route, or round of duties.—John met a policeman walking his *beat.*
—*v. beats, beat, beating.* 1. Whip; hit; strike; thrash.—The bad boy *beat* his dog. He hit the dog again and again.
2. Whip.—Mother *beat* the cake batter until it was smooth. She stirred it with a whipping motion.
3. Defeat.—Our baseball team can *beat* all the other teams in our school.

beat•en (BEET-n) *v.* One form of the verb *beat.*–The marks on the horse's back showed that it had been *beaten.*
–*adj.* 1. Well worn; used often.–Robin followed the *beaten* path through the forest.
2. Defeated.–After the battle, the *beaten* army retreated.

beat•er (BEET-er) *n. beaters.* A person or tool that beats, especially a kitchen utensil for beating eggs, whipping cream, and mixing things.

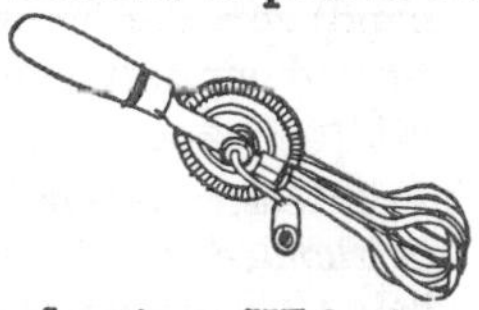

beat•ing (BEET-ing) *n. beatings.* Whipping; thrashing.–Mr. Jones gave his dog a *beating.*

beau (BOH) *n. beaux.* A sweetheart; a man who is courting a girl.–My sister has a *beau.*

beau•ti•ful (BYOO-tə-fuhl) *adj.; beautifully, adv.* 1. Lovely to look at; very pretty.–Mary has a *beautiful* hat.
2. Producing pleasant feelings.–Our teacher read a *beautiful* poem.–Birds have *beautiful* songs.–Music has *beautiful* sounds.

beau•ti•fy (BYOO-tə-fy) *v. beautifies, beautified, beautifying.* Make beautiful.–You can *beautify* yourself by keeping your hair combed nicely.–New curtains *beautify* the living room.

beau•ty (BYOO-tee) *n. beauties.* 1. Loveliness; prettiness; a quality that produces pleasant feelings.–Grandmother's garden is a place of *beauty.*
2. A lovely or beautiful person or thing.–That child is a *beauty.*–Bob's new bicycle was a *beauty.*

bea•ver (BEE-ver) *n. beavers.* A brown-furred animal that lives in ponds and streams, and is about two feet long. It has a broad, flat tail. Its fur is used for coats and hats. *Beavers* cut down trees to build their homes and make dams.

be•came (bee- *or* bə-KAYM) *v.* One form of the verb *become.*–The weather *became* cold.

be•cause (bee- *or* bə-KAWZ) *conj.* For the reason that.–Mary could not go to the party, *because* she had to take care of the baby.

beck•on (BEK-ən) *v. beckons, beckoned, beckoning.* Signal.–The teacher *beckoned* to John by nodding her head.

be•come (bee- *or* bə-KUM) *v. becomes, became, becoming.* 1. Come to be.–If it *becomes* warmer tomorrow, we will have a picnic.
2. Look well on; suit.–Red hats do not *become* red-headed people.
–*Become of* means happen to.–What has *become of* John's pet?

be•com•ing (bee- *or* bə-KUM-ing) *adj.; becomingly, adv.* Suitable; attractive.–Mary wears a very *becoming* hat. It is suitable to her.
–*v.* One form of the verb *become.*–As it is *becoming* late, I must go.

bed (BED) *n. beds.* 1. A padded piece of furniture to lie or sleep on.
2. A small piece of ground planted with plants.–Grandmother has a pansy *bed.*

3. The bottom of a body of water.–The river's *bed* is sandy.
4. A sleeping place.–The farmer made a *bed* of straw for his cattle.

bed•ding (BED-ing) *n.* Blankets, bedspreads, quilts, sheets, and other things used on beds.

bed•room (BED-room) *n. bedrooms.* A room with beds for sleeping.

bed•time (BED-tym) *n.* Time to retire or go to bed.–Mary's *bedtime* is nine o'clock.

bee (BEE) *n. bees.* A small insect which has four gauzy wings. The front wings are larger than the back wings. *Bees* sting people only to protect themselves. *Bees,* like ants, live in colonies. Some *bees* make honey.

beech (BEECH) *n. beeches.* A tree with a light gray bark. The wood of the *beech* tree is very hard. The tree bears three-cornered nuts that are good to eat. They are called *beech*nuts.

beef (BEEF) *n.* The meat of a cow, steer, or bull.—For dinner Mother cooked a roast of *beef.*

bee•hive (BEE-hyv) *n. beehives.* A box or small house built for bees to live in.—Some bees live and make honey in a *beehive.*

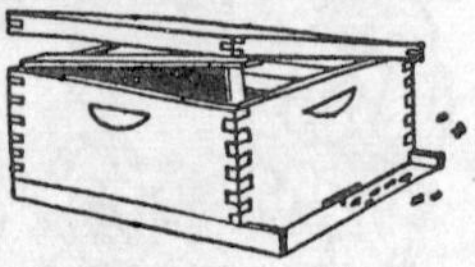

been (BIN) *v.* One form of the verb *be.*—It has *been* a long time since I saw you.—We have *been* waiting fifteen minutes for you.

beer (BIR) *n. beers.* A fermented, bubbling drink which has malt and hops in it.

beet (BEET) *n. beets.* A vegetable with a large red or white root. The red root of the common *beet* is usually cooked with the skin on to keep the color in. The leaves are sometimes cooked and eaten, too. Some sugar is made from sugar *beets,* which have white roots.

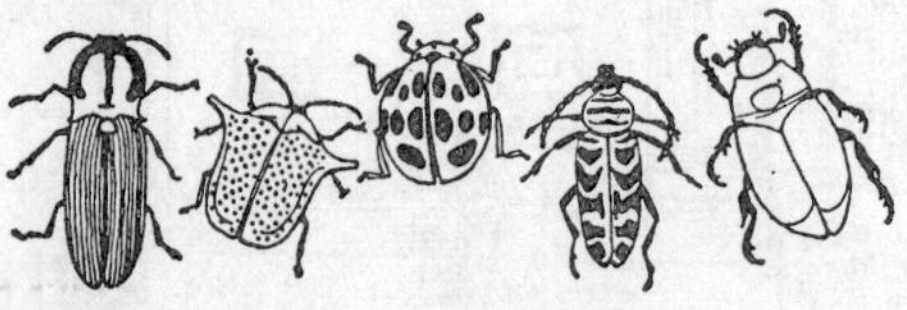

bee•tle (BEE-tl) *n. beetles.* An insect with four wings. One pair of wings forms a hard covering over the other pair to protect them when the *beetle* is not flying. Some *beetles* cannot fly. Ladybugs are *beetles.*

be•fore (bə-FOR *or* bee-FOHR) *adv., conj.,* and *prep.* 1. Earlier than.—John arrived *before* Bob did.

2. At any time in the past.—We never played ball *before.*

3. In front of.—The seeing-eye dog walked *before* the blind man.

be•fore•hand (bə-FOR-hand *or* bee-FOHR-hand) *adv.* Earlier or before the time.—When we had our party, Mother prepared the lunch *beforehand.*

be•friend (bee- *or* bə-FREND) *v. befriends, befriended, befriending.* Act as a friend to; help.—The policeman *befriended* the lost boy. He took him to the police station and played with him until his parents arrived.—Mary *befriends* stray cats. She gives them milk.

beg (BEG) *v. begs, begged, begging.* Ask; ask again and again.—The dog *begs* for food by barking.—Bob *begged* Mother for money to go to a movie.

be•gan (bee- *or* bə-GAN) *v.* One form of the verb *begin.*—When the baby fell down she *began* to cry.

beg•gar (BEG-er) *n. beggars.* A person who begs or asks for money and other things; a very poor person who does not work for his own living.—In a large city you can see many *beggars.*

be•gin (bee- *or* bə-GIN) *v. begins, began, beginning.* Start.—If you *begin* your work now, you will be through in time for supper.

be•gin•ner (bee- *or* bə-GIN-er) *n. beginners.* A person trying to do something for the first time.—Mary has taken lessons on the piano for a long time, but Bob is just a *beginner.* —You were a *beginner* in school when you went for the first time.

be•gin•ning (bee- *or* bə-GIN-ing) *n. beginnings.* The start or first part.—We arrived at the movie just in time for the *beginning.*—John started the book at the *beginning.*

be•go•ni•a (bə-GOHN-yə) *n. begonias.* A plant with shiny leaves that are usually red or green. *Begonias* can have red, white, pink, or yellow blossoms.

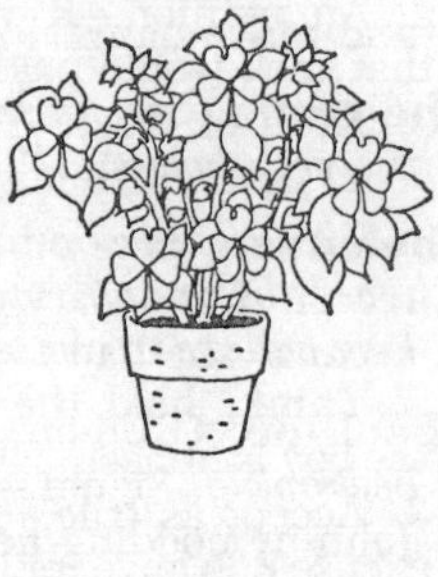

be•gun (bee- *or* bə-GUN) *v.* One form of the verb *begin.* — The flowers have *begun* to bloom.

be•have (bee- *or* bə-HAYV) *v. behaves, behaved, behaving.* 1. Act; do.–Some children *behave* well, and some *behave* badly.
2. Act properly.–Mother said to Bob, "Why don't you *behave?*"

be•hav•ior (bee- *or* bə-HAYV-yer) *n.* Actions; the way one acts.–Mary's *behavior* is excellent; she is polite.

be•hind (bee- *or* bə-HYND) *adj., adv.,* and *prep.* 1. Late.–The milkman is *behind* with his milk delivery.
2. In back of.–Mary walked first, and John walked *behind.*–They went to see the sheriff put the criminal *behind* bars.

be•hold (bee- *or* bə-HOLD) *v. beholds, beheld, beholding.* Look at; see.–*Behold* the sun peeping through the clouds.

beige (BAYZH) *adj.* Having the color of natural or undyed wool; of a light tan or light brown shade.–Mother hung *beige* curtains on her bedroom windows.

be•ing (BEE-ing) *n. beings.* 1. Existence.–When oil was found here, a town came into *being.* It began.
2. A human *being* is a man, woman, or child. –The President is a very important *being.*

bel•fry (BEL-free) *n. belfries.* A tower or small room built for a bell, high up on a church roof or other building.

be•lief (bee- or bə-LEEF) *n. beliefs.* 1. Anything we believe as true.–Small children often have a *belief* in magic.
2. An opinion.–It was the teacher's *belief* that Jack would pass if he worked hard.
3. Faith or trust.–The men expressed their *belief* in their leader.

be•lieve (bee- *or* bə-LEEV) *v. believes, believed, believing.* 1. Have faith or trust (in). –We *believe* in our leader.
2. Think; hold the opinion.–I *believe* that the boy is honest.
3. Accept as true.–The teacher *believes* the excuse Bob gave for being tardy.

bell (BEL) *n. bells.* 1. A cuplike instrument, usually made of a mixture of tin and other metals, with a "tongue" hanging inside. When the *bell* is shaken, the tongue strikes against the inside, making a musical tone. Some *bells* can be played upon to make tunes.

2. Any device for making a ringing sound.–The door*bell* works by electricity.

bel•low (BEL-oh) *n. bellows.* A loud roar or cry.–We heard the *bellow* of the bull.
–*v. bellows, bellowed, bellowing.* Make a loud roar.–Oxen *bellow.*

bel•lows (BEL-ohz) *n. sing.* and *pl.* A device for making a strong gust of air. The bagpipe and the accordion have *bellows* to help make musical sounds. A *bellows* takes in air, then blows it out when squeezed. In olden times *bellows* were used to blow air into a fire to make it burn more quickly.

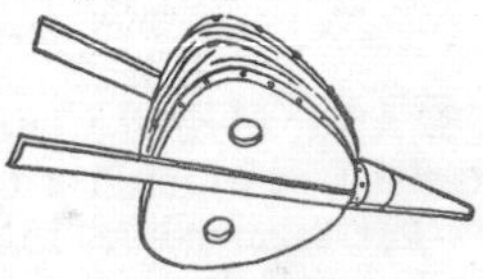

bel•ly (BEL-ee) *n. bellies.* The lower front part of a person's body; the abdomen. The underside of an animal's body is its *belly.*–Our kitten is black, with white chin and *belly* and white paws.

be•long (bee- *or* bə-LAWNG) *v. belongs, belonged, belonging.* 1. Be owned by.–This pencil *belongs* to me. It is mine.
2. Be a member of.–Father *belongs* to the Men's Club.
3. Have as its right or proper place.–Jack's hat *belongs* in the clothes closet.

be•long•ings (bee- *or* bə-LAWNG-ingz) *n.pl.* Things one owns; property.–We took all our *belongings* out of our desks when the term ended.–Mother sewed Jack's name on all his *belongings* when he went to camp.

be•lov•ed (bee-LUVD *or* bə-LUV-əd) *n.* and *adj.* One who is loved.–Grandmother said to me, "Good night, *beloved.*"

be•low (bee- *or* bə-LOH) *adv.* and *prep.* 1. Under; farther down than; lower than.–Hang this picture *below* the other one. Let the other one hang above it.
2. To a lower deck on a ship.–When the third mate's watch was over, he went *below.*

belt (BELT) *n. belts.* 1. A band or narrow strip of leather, cloth, metal, etc., worn about the waist.

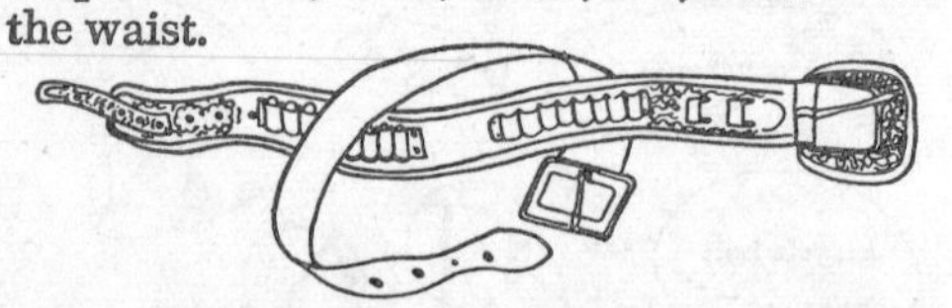

2. In machinery, a broad leather loop placed around two wheels that are some distance apart, to make the wheels turn together.

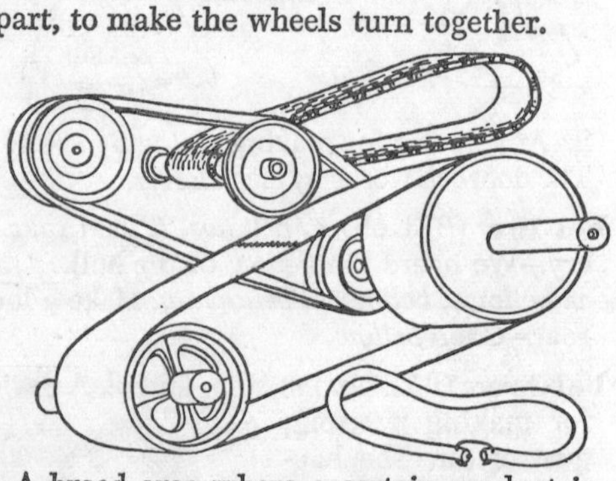

3. A broad area where a certain product is raised, or which has a particular climate, etc. –The farmer lives in the corn *belt,* a region where much corn is grown.

bench (BENCH) *n. benches.* 1. A long seat. –We sat on the *bench* in the park.

2. A long table to work on, sometimes with drawers for keeping tools in.–Father has a work*bench* in the garage.
3. The place where the judge sits in court.–The judge walked to the *bench.*

bend (BEND) *n. bends.* A curve or turn.–The train goes slowly around the *bend* in the railroad tracks.
–*v. bends, bent, bending.* 1. Curve or become crooked.–The nail may *bend* unless you hit it squarely on the head.
2. Stoop.–It's hard for the fat baby to *bend* over.

be•neath (bee- *or* bə-NEETH) *adj., adv.* and *prep.* Below; under; lower than.–The flowers were planted *beneath* the dining room window.–As fall came, their petals died and fell on the ground *beneath.*

ben•e•fac•tor (BEN-ə-fak-ter *or* ben-ə-FAK-ter) *n. benefactors.* One who gives a gift of money, or who, in some way, helps.–Father became a *benefactor* of the hospital when he bought a bed for the clinic.–When Uncle John died, he left his money to his nephew. Uncle John was his nephew's *benefactor.*

ben•e•fi•cial (ben-ə-FISH-əl) *adj.* Helpful; good for.–Regular daily exercise is *beneficial* to the body.

ben•e•fit (BEN-ə-fit) *n. benefits.* 1. A show to raise money to help a particular group of people, etc.–The children gave a *benefit* for the orphanage.
2. Use; advantage.–The camp has the *benefit* of a lake near by.–The school children have the *benefit* of a new library.
–*v. benefits, benefited, benefiting.* 1. Help; be good for.–The doctor said a long rest would *benefit* Mother.–The sunshine will *benefit* the children.
2. Be helped.–The farmers will *benefit* by the new road.–The children will *benefit* by the sunshine.

bent (BENT) *v.* One form of the verb *bend.* –The children *bent* the wire in the fence so that it touched the ground.
–*adj.* Not straight.–The wrecked car had two *bent* fenders.

be•ret (be-RAY *or* BAIR-ay) *n. berets.* A soft, round cap.–Pictures of artists sometimes show them wearing *berets* and floppy bow ties.

ber•ry (BAIR-ee) *n. berries.* A small fruit with many seeds. There are many kinds of

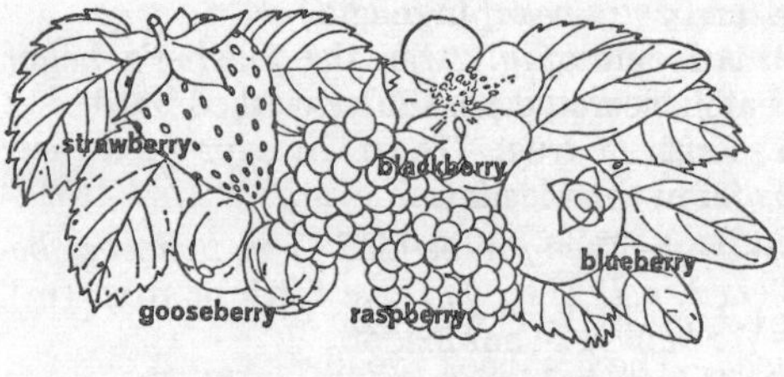

berries, such as rasp*berries,* straw*berries,* huckle*berries,* and goose*berries.* Sometimes the hard seeds of grains are called *berries.*

berth (BERTH) *n. berths.* A bunk or bed hung against a wall.
—A person who travels at night on a ship or train may sleep in a *berth.* The upper *berth* is above the lower one. One needs a ladder to get into the upper *berth.*

be•side (bee- *or* bə-SYD) *prep.* At the side of; close to.—A spider sat down *beside* Little Miss Muffet.

be•sides (bee- *or* bə-SYDZ) *adv.* and *prep.* In addition to; other than; too.—*Besides* these problems, we must work those on page 10.—We read pages 10 and 11 *besides* page 9.—We have many rabbits *besides* the ones in this pen.

best (BEST) *adj.* One form of the word *good.* Better than any other.—Mary is the *best* writer in the class.—The first apple Bob ate was good, the second was better, and the third was *best* of all.
—*adv.* One form of the word *well.*—Of all the boys, Ed plays *best.*

be•stow (bee- *or* bə-STOH) *v. bestows, bestowed, bestowing.* Give; grant. — After the contest the judges will *bestow* medals on the winners.

bet (BET) *n. bets.* An agreement to pay or give something to someone else if he turns out to be right about a thing and you are wrong.—The children made a *bet* about the game.
—*v. bets, bet, betting.* Make or offer to make such an agreement.—Mary *bet* five cents that John's team would win; Bob *bet* five cents that it would lose. John's team won, so Bob paid Mary.

be•tray (bee- *or* bə-TRAY) *v. betrays, betrayed, betraying.* 1. Be false to; give away (a person, secret, etc.).—Bob would never *betray* a secret.
2. Show what was being hidden; indicate.—Father's smile *betrayed* that he was joking.

bet•ter (BET-er) *adj.* One form of the word *good.*—The first book I read was good, but the second was *better.* It was more interesting.
—*adv.* One form of the word *well.*—My brother plays baseball *better* than I do.

be•tween (bee- *or* bə-TWEEN) *adv.* and *prep.* 1. Separating.—The fence *between* the yards was made of wire.—There are six hours *between* noon and six o'clock.
2. Father divided the money *between* the two boys. He gave each of them a share.
3. Joining or involving.—There is good friendship *between* us.—It was an argument *between* Jane and Bill.

bev•er•age (BEV-er-ij *or* BEV-rij) *n. beverages.* Something to drink.—We always have a *beverage* with our lunch. Usually it is milk.

be•ware (bee- *or* bə-WAIR) *v.* Be careful.—*Beware* of fire or you may be burned. Keep away from fire.—*Beware* of crossing the street when the light is red.

be•wil•der (bee- *or* bə-WIL-der) *v. bewilders, bewildered, bewildering.* Perplex; utterly confuse.—The boys were *bewildered* in the forest.—The variety of dresses in the store was *bewildering.* Mother didn't know which one to buy.

be•yond (bee-YAHND) *adv.* and *prep.* 1. On the other side of; farther than.—We stopped at a farmhouse a mile *beyond* the city.—The baby tried to get the cup, but it was *beyond* her reach.—*Beyond* the mountains the sun is still shining.
2. Later than.—Do not stay *beyond* four o'clock.

bib (BIB) *n. bibs.* A napkin fastened about one's neck. — Mother put a *bib* on the baby so that she would not soil her pretty dress at supper.

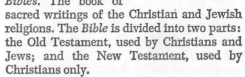

Bi•ble (BY-bəl) *n. Bibles.* The book of sacred writings of the Christian and Jewish religions. The *Bible* is divided into two parts: the Old Testament, used by Christians and Jews; and the New Testament, used by Christians only.

bib•li•og•ra•phy (bib-lee-AHG-rə-fee) *n. bibliographies.* 1. A list of books, authors, articles, etc., which deals with a particular subject.—The author prepared a *bibliography* to be printed at the end of his book.
2. The study or history of books, including dates of publication, styles, etc.—Booksellers and collectors are usually well-informed on *bibliography.*

bi•cy•cle (BY-si-kəl) *n. bicycles.* A vehicle with two wheels, handlebars to guide it with, a seat, and two pedals to make it go.

bid (BID) *n. bids.* The amount of money offered.–My *bid* for the ball was five cents.
–*v. bids, bade, bidding.* 1. Tell.–Always *bid* your mother good-by before you start for school.
2. Order or command.–I *bid* you to obey the law.
3. Offer to pay.–John *bid* fifty cents for the baseball bat.
4. Invite.–John *bade* us come to the party.

big (BIG) *adj. bigger, biggest.* Large; great in size.–Our dog caught a *big* rat.–Once Baby was small; now she is *big*.

bill (BIL) *n. bills.* 1. The beak or hard pointed mouth of a bird. –Birds use their *bills* to pick up food.

2. A printed advertisement.–A boy left a *bill* on our porch telling about the sale of ponies.

3. A written notice or statement telling how much is owed.–The milkman left Mother a *bill* for $4.15.
4. A piece of paper money.–Grandmother gave Bob a dollar *bill*.
5. A suggestion for a law.–The new *bill* was presented to Congress, and it became law.

bil•lion (BIL-yən) *n. billions.* The number represented by 1 followed by nine zeros. There are a thousand millions in a *billion*.
1,000 is one thousand.
1,000,000 is one million.
1,000,000,000 is one *billion*.

bil•low (BIL-oh) *n. billows.* 1. A large, smooth wave of water.–We sat by the ocean and watched the *billows* rise and fall.

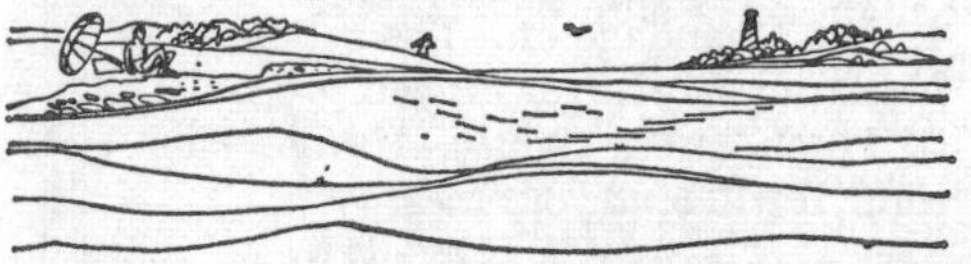

2. A wave.–*Billows* of smoke rose from the big fire.
–*v. billows, billowed, billowing.* Swell; bulge; wave.–The sails were *billowing* in the wind.

bin (BIN) *n. bins.* A large box or crib.–The farmer keeps his grain in a *bin*.–We keep coal in a coal*bin*.

bind (BYND) *v. binds, bound, binding.* 1. Tie. –Father will *bind* the papers into a bundle before giving them to the Red Cross.
2. Sew a narrow piece of cloth over the edge of.–Mother will *bind* the sleeves of Mary's dress.

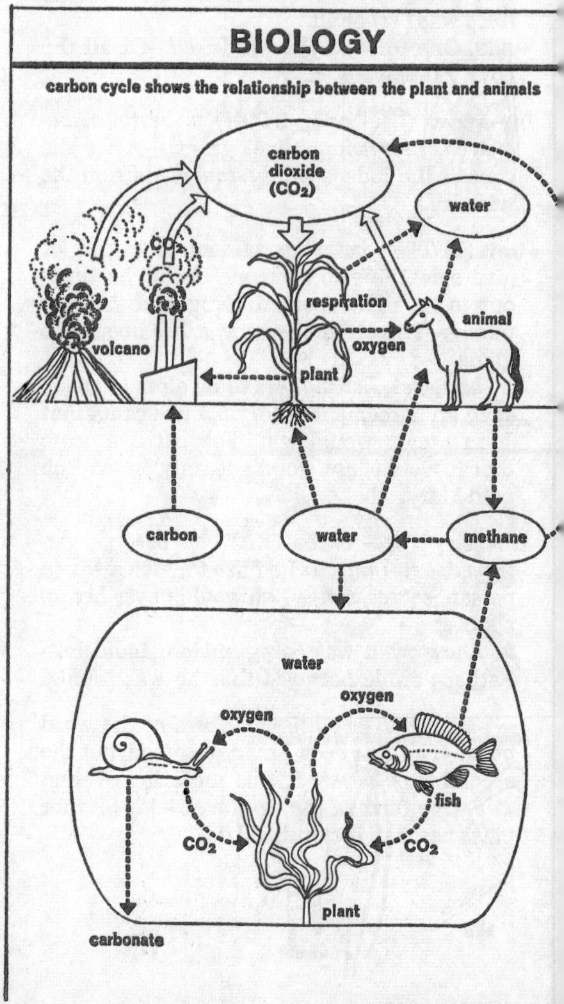

3. Put the pages of a book together and into a cover.–The leaves of Bob's book have come apart, so Father will have to *bind* it.
4. Put a bandage on.–The school nurse will *bind* your sore finger for you.
5. Pinch; press tightly.–If your shoe is too tight, it will *bind* your toes.

bind·ing (BYND-ing) *n. bindings.* 1. A book cover.–The *binding* of Bob's book is blue.
2. A strip of cloth to cover the raw edge of material. – The *binding* on Mary's sleeve is red.

bin·oc·u·lars (bə-NAHK-yə-lerz *or* by-NAHK-yoo-lerz) *n. pl.* A field glass or double telescope, held to both eyes at once to bring distant objects into closer view.–The captain looked through his *binoculars* to see the distant ship.

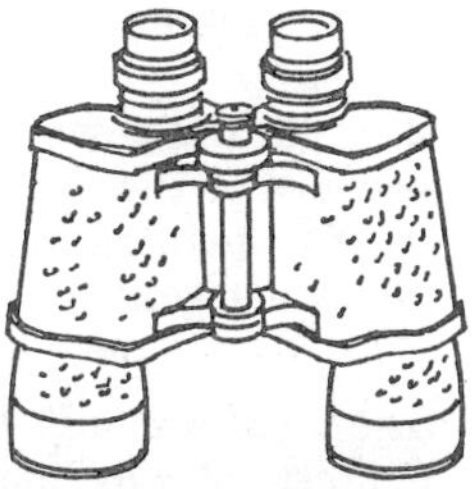

bi·og·ra·phy (by-AHG-rə-fee) *n. biographies.* A story of one person's life written by another person.–John is reading Abraham Lincoln's *biography.*

bi·o·log·i·cal (by-oh-LAHJ-ə-kəl) *adj.* Related to life, to the science or study of life, or to biology.–Breathing and sleeping are *biological* processes.

bi·ol·o·gy (by-AHL-ə-jee) *n.* The science or study of plants and animals, covering growth, history, etc.–Students learn to use the microscope in certain courses in *biology.*

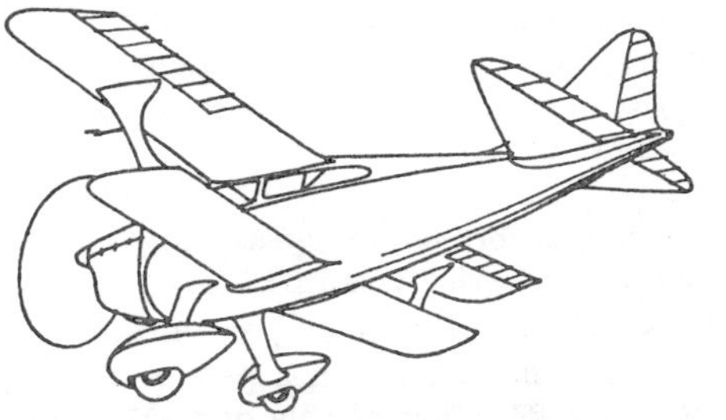

bi·plane (BY-playn) *n. biplanes.* An airplane with a lower and an upper wing on each side.

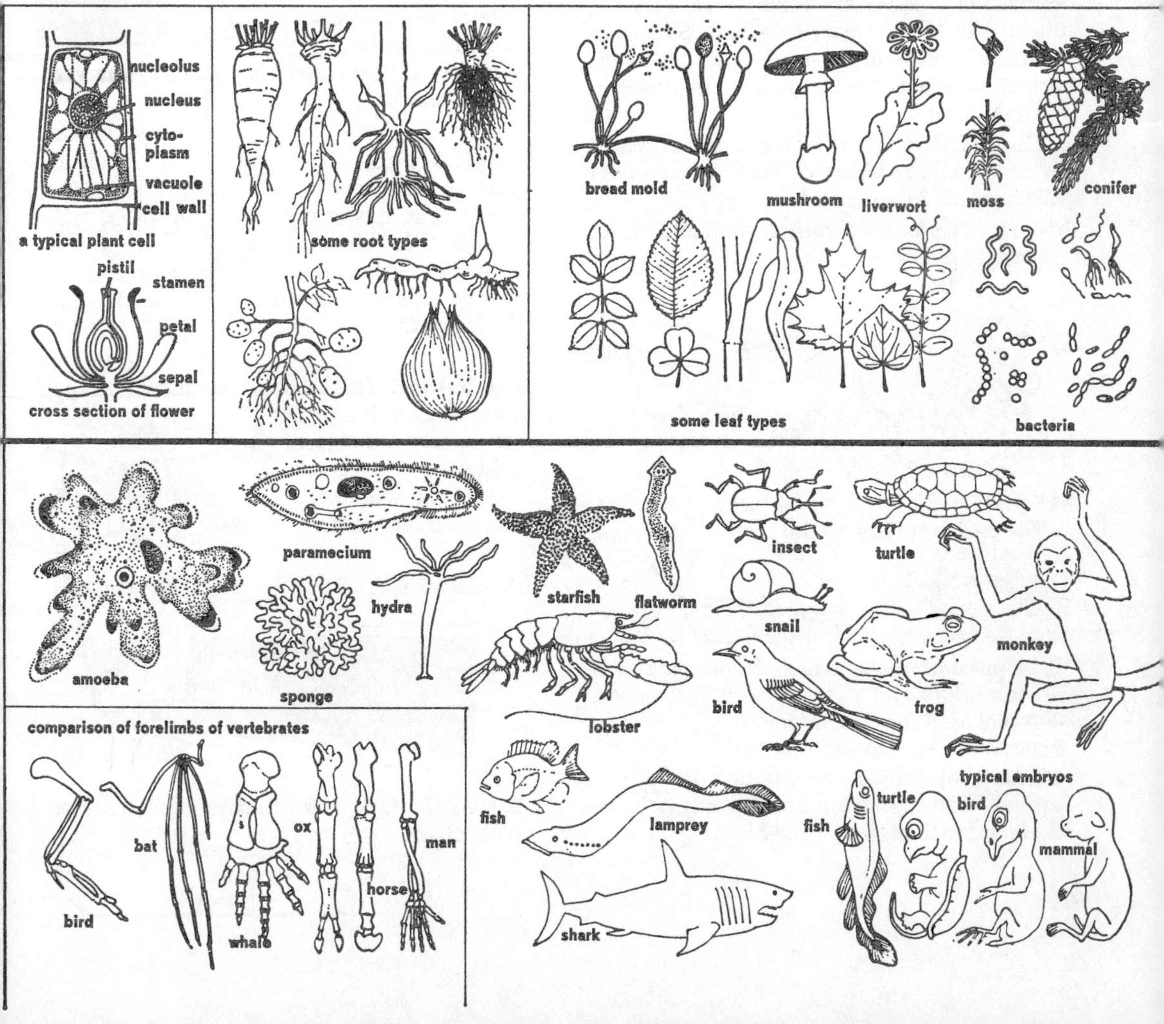

birch (BERCH) *n. birches.* A kind of tree with smooth, peeling bark. *Birch* wood is used in making furniture, and for woodwork in houses. Indians used *birch*bark for canoes.

bird (BERD) *n. birds.* A feathered animal with wings. Most *birds* can fly. Sparrows and robins are *birds*; so are chickens and ducks. See page 326.

birth (BERTH) *n. births.* 1. Being born; beginning to live.–My parents came to America before my *birth.*
2. Beginning of anything.–When a new country is formed, we speak of its *birth.* The *birth* of America was in 1776.

birth•day (BERTH-day) *n. birthdays* and *adj.* The day on which a person is born, or yearly celebration of this day.–March 31 is Father's *birthday.*

bis•cuit (BISS-kət) *n. biscuits.* A small patty or cake of bread. Sometimes we eat *biscuits,* instead of bread baked in a loaf. Some *biscuits* are made of bread dough, and some are made of a dough that has baking powder, or soda, in it.

bish•op (BISH-əp) *n. bishops.* A clergyman of high rank. A *bishop* is head of a number of churches in a district.

bi•son (BY-sən *or* BY-zən) *n. sing.* and *pl.* An American buffalo.

bit (BIT) *n. bits.* 1. A small piece or amount. –The mouse ate a *bit* of the cheese in the trap.

2. A piece of metal which forms part of a horse's bridle and goes through his mouth.
3. A tool used for making round holes. A *bit* fits into a tool called a brace, by which the *bit* is turned.–Father made a hole in the board with his brace and *bit.*

bite (BYT) *n. bites.* 1. An amount of something taken into the mouth at one time.–Bob asked Grandmother for a *bite* of apple.
2. A sore spot made by the sting of an insect. –Mother had a mosquito *bite* on her arm.
–*v. bites, bit, biting.* 1. Chop with the teeth; take into the mouth by cutting off with the teeth.–Animals have sharp teeth with which to *bite* their food.
2. Sting.–Mosquitoes *bite.*

bit•ten (BIT-n) *v.* One form of the verb *bite.*–Do not put your hands into the animals' cages at the zoo, or you may be *bitten.*

bit•ter (BIT-er) *adj.; bitterly, adv.* 1. Sharp and unpleasant to the taste.–Some medicines are *bitter.*
2. Cold and raw.–We could not go skating because of the *bitter* wind.
3. Disappointed and angry.–Bob was *bitter* about not getting on the team.

black (BLAK) *adj. blacker, blackest.* 1. The darkest color or hue; the opposite of white.–Coal is *black.*
2. Dark; without light.–When the door of the closet blew shut, it was very *black* inside.

black•ber•ry (BLAK-bair-ee) *n. blackberries.* A purplish-black berry that has many seeds. *Blackberries* grow on *blackberry* bushes.–Father's favorite pie is made from *blackberries.*

black•bird (BLAK-berd) *n. blackbirds.* A kind of bird that is all or nearly all black. Red-winged *blackbirds* are black with some red on their wings.

black•board (BLAK-bord) *n. blackboards.*

A smooth, dark board that you can write on with chalk.

black•smith (BLAK-smith) *n. blacksmiths.* A person who shapes iron or other metal into different things. A *blacksmith* makes horseshoes and fits them to horses' feet.

blad•der (BLAD-er) *n. bladders.* 1. A sac in people and animals in which urine from the kidneys is stored before it leaves the body.
2. Any balloonlike bag that can be filled with air, gas, or fluid.–Tom pumped air into the *bladder* of his football.

blade (BLAYD) *n. blades.* 1. A flat, thin part used for cutting; any flat part.–The *blade* of the knife was so dull that we could not cut the meat.–The *blade* of the oar is pushed through the water to make the rowboat go.–The propeller *blade* cut the air as it whirled.

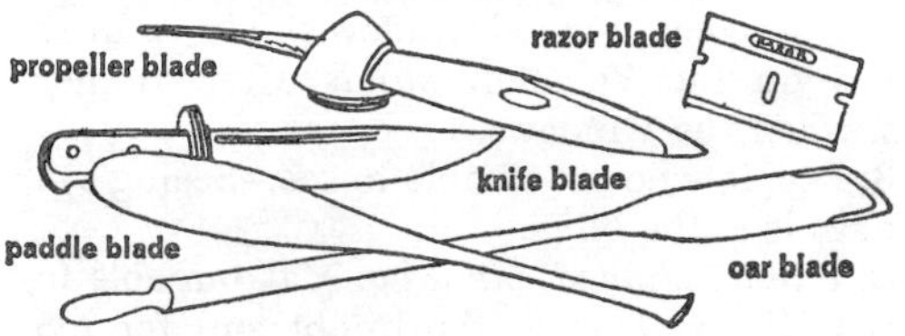

2. A long, flat leaf.–The horse ate every *blade* of grass that Sally gave him.

blame (BLAYM) *n.* Guilt; responsibility.–Bill broke the window, and then tried to put the *blame* on Jack. He tried to make people think Jack had broken it.
–*v. blames, blamed, blaming.* Believe that (someone) is at fault; accuse.–The man did not *blame* us for the accident.
–*To blame* means at fault, responsible for.–Mary was not *to blame* for the baby's fall. She didn't make him fall. She tried to stop him, but couldn't.

blank (BLANGK) *n. blanks.* 1. An empty space.–The children filled in the *blanks* on the cards with their names and addresses.
2. A card or paper to be filled out with special information.–Bob had to fill out a *blank* to apply for the job. He had to fill in spaces with his name, age, what training he had had, etc.
–*adj. blanker, blankest; blankly, adv.* Empty; containing nothing.–The stamp album we gave Father had *blank* pages for pasting the stamps on.

blan•ket (BLANG-kət) *n. blankets.* 1. A woven cover.–In summer Mother puts a cotton *blanket* on our bed, but in the winter she puts on a woolen *blanket.*

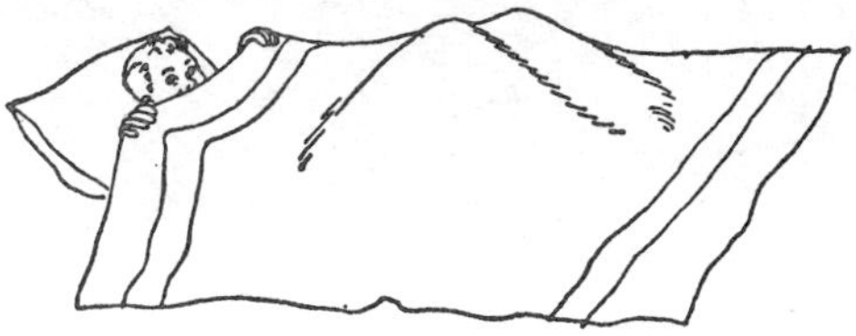

2. A covering.–During the sandstorm, a *blanket* of dust settled on the floors.

blare (BLAIR) *v. blares, blared, blaring.* Make a loud, harsh sound, such as a horn.–The trumpets *blared* forth a greeting to the king.

blast (BLAST) *n. blasts.* 1. A great rush (of wind).–The door was thrown open by a *blast* of wind.
2. A sound made by blowing.–We could hear the *blast* of horns across the lake.
3. An explosion.–While we watched the burning building, we heard a loud *blast.*
–*v. blasts, blasted, blasting.* Blow up.–The men building the new road had to *blast* the rocks with dynamite.

blaze (BLAYZ) *n. blazes.* 1. Bright flames.–The Boy Scouts sat around the *blaze* of the campfire.

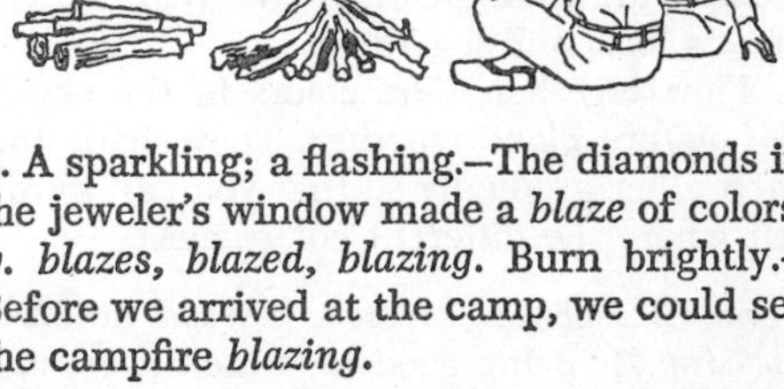

2. A sparkling; a flashing.–The diamonds in the jeweler's window made a *blaze* of colors.
–*v. blazes, blazed, blazing.* Burn brightly.–Before we arrived at the camp, we could see the campfire *blazing.*

bleach (BLEECH) *n. bleaches.* A product which makes things white.–Mary spilled the *bleach* on her dress. Soon she had a big colorless spot on her dress.
–*v. bleaches, bleached, bleaching.* Make white or stainless.–Mother hangs the clothes in the sun to *bleach* them.

bleach•ers (BLEECH-erz) *n. pl.* A set of seats in a stadium or ball park that has no roof over it.–Jack sat in the *bleachers* at the ball game.

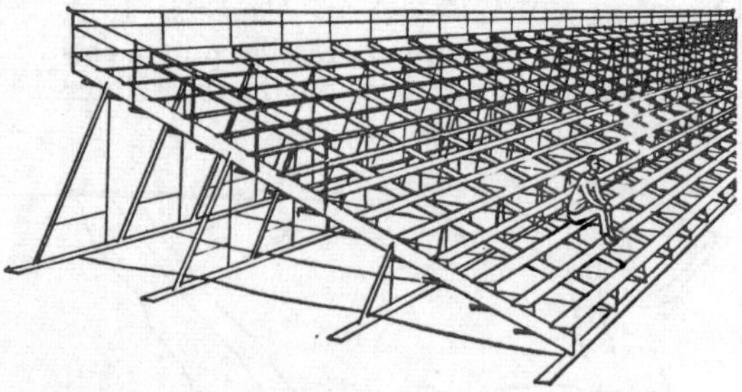

bleak (BLEEK) *adj. bleaker, bleakest.* 1. Cold and bare; swept by winds.–The arctic regions of the earth are *bleak* and icy.
2. Without cheer; dreary.–Yesterday was a *bleak* day. It rained without a stop. It was the *bleakest* day we've had in a long time.

bleat (BLEET) *n. bleats.* A high, thin cry.–We could hear the *bleat* of the lost sheep.
–*v. bleats, bleated, bleating.* Make such a cry.–Sheep and lambs *bleat* when they are hungry.

bled (BLED) *v.* One form of the verb *bleed.* –When Mary cut her finger, it *bled.*

bleed (BLEED) *v. bleeds, bled, bleeding.* Give out or flow blood.–Mother let her cut finger *bleed* for a few minutes before she bandaged it, so that the dirt would be washed out of the cut.

blend (BLEND) *v. blends, blended, blending.* 1. Mix pleasantly; harmonize.–The children's voices *blend* well. They mix so that you hear all the voices as one.–Will this green hat *blend* with your green dress? Will the two greens look well together?
2. Flow together.–The colors in the sky in the picture *blend* together. They shade into each other gradually so that you can hardly tell where the different colors meet.

bless (BLESS) *v. blesses, blessed* or *blest, blessing.* 1. Bring good to; watch over; look upon with favor.–God *bless* America. God guard and preserve America.–Mary has been *blessed* with great talent for music.
2. Make holy; make fit for a holy purpose.–The priest *blessed* the palms which the people received on Palm Sunday.
3. Praise.–*Bless* the Lord.

bless•ing (BLESS-ing) *n. blessings.* 1. A prayer before a meal.–Grandfather says a *blessing* before every meal.
2. A prayer or wish that good may come to someone or something.–"*Blessings* on thee, little man."
3. A good or desirable thing.–What a *blessing* that you were not hurt in the accident!

blew (BLOO) *v.* One form of the verb *blow.*–The wind *blew* so hard that it uprooted an old tree.–Sally *blew* her whistle twice.

blimp (BLIMP) *n. blimps.* An inflatable, balloonlike airship with a small cabin underneath it where the crew works. A *blimp's* shape depends on the pressure of gas or air with which it is filled.–*Blimps* today are used mainly for scouting and observation purposes.

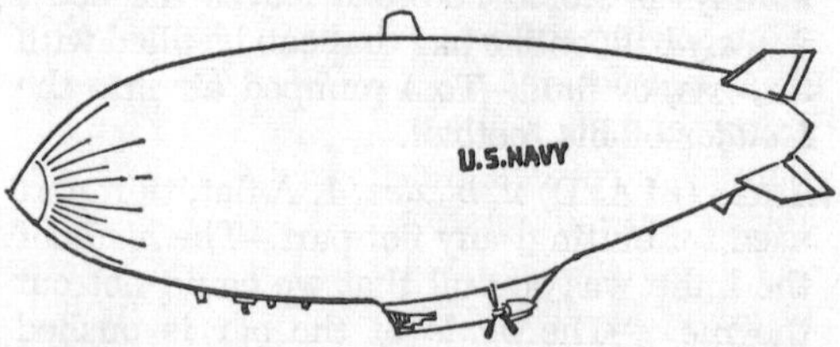

blind (BLYND) *n. blinds.* 1. A shutter.–The white house has green *blinds.*
2. A wooden or metal window shade.–Father put up the Venetian *blinds* after Mother washed the windows.
3. People who are unable to see.–Seeing-eye dogs lead the *blind.*
–*v. blinds, blinded, blinding.* Make unable to see.–If you look at the bright sun for too long, it will *blind* you. You will be unable to see for a while.
–*adj.* 1. Without eyesight; unable to see.–The *blind* man could not see the elephant at all.
2. Having no way out.–A dead-end street, or a street that does not go through, is a *blind* street.
–*Blind to* means refusing to take notice of.–Grandmother is *blind to* Jack's faults.

blind•fold (BLYN-fohld) *n. blindfolds.* A cover for the eyes.–The children use a cloth for a *blindfold.*
–*v. blindfolds, blindfolded, blindfolding.* Cover the eyes of.–In the game of "pin the tail on the donkey," the children are *blindfolded* when it is their turn to try.

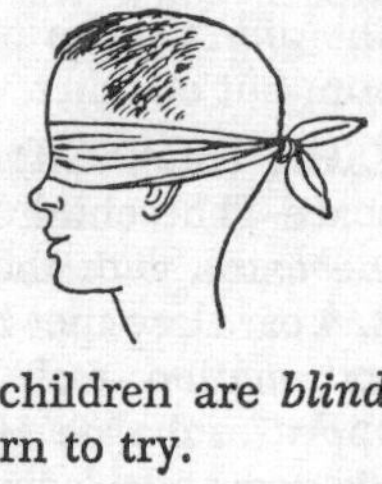

blind•ness (BLYND-nəss) *n.* Absence of sight; inability to see.–The operation cured the woman's *blindness*. It made her able to see again.

blink (BLINGK) *v. blinks, blinked, blinking.* 1. Wink quickly; open and shut the eyes quickly and without always realizing it.–The sun shining through the windshield made the driver *blink*.
2. Shine shakily; shine on and off.–We saw the many lights of the city *blinking* through the dark.

bliss (BLISS) *n.; blissful, adj.; blissfully, adv.* Perfect happiness.–When school is out, the children are in *bliss*.

blis•ter (BLISS-ter) *n. blisters.* 1. A place where the skin is raised, with water underneath.–Where Mary burned her arm there is a large *blister*.–Jack has *blisters* on his hands from rowing the boat so long.
2. A spot covered with a thin skin of something, and filled with air inside.–After the painter varnished the floor, a large *blister* formed on the wood.
–*v. blisters, bistered, blistering.* Make a blister on.–Father *blistered* his hand while hoeing in the garden.

bliz•zard (BLIZ-erd) *n. blizzards.* A cold, windy snowstorm.–The hunter was caught in a *blizzard*.

block (BLAHK) *n. blocks.* 1. A piece of stone, wood, ice, etc., in the form of a cube or with squared edges.–The courthouse is built of big *blocks* of granite.
2. A toy made of small pieces of wood or plastic.–Let us build a house of *blocks*.

3. A square of land and buildings built close together and facing four different streets.–Jack walked his dog around the *block*.

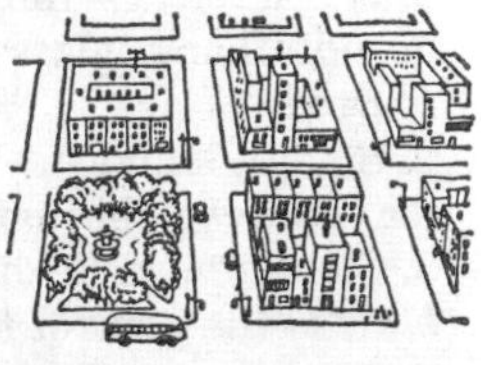

4. The distance from one street corner to the next.–The school is three *blocks* away.
–*v. blocks, blocked, blocking.* 1. Be in the way of; close up.–A tree fell across the road and *blocked* traffic.
2. Put into shape.–Mother had her felt hat cleaned and *blocked*.

block•ade (blah-KAYD) *n. blockades.* 1. The shutting off of a port, city, country, etc., usually by sea forces, to stop anyone from getting in or out.–The naval *blockade* was unsuccessful because the city was supplied by air.
2. Any obstruction to passage.–The police set up road *blockades* to prevent the escape of the fugitive.
–*v. blockades, blockaded, blockading.* Prevent passage in or out of a city, port, country, etc., by armed forces or ships.–The navy *blockaded* the harbor.

blond or **blonde** (BLAHND) *n. blonds* or *blondes.* A person whose hair, eyes, and skin are very light-colored.
–*adj. blonder, blondest.* Fair in coloring.–Sally is *blond*; Jack is dark.

blood (BLUD) *n. blood* or *bloods.* A liquid in the veins and arteries that carries nourishment through the body and carries away waste. *Blood* is pumped to all parts of the body by the heart. *Blood* is red when it is in the air.–When Mother cut her finger, *blood* came from the cut.

blood•y (BLUD-ee) *adj. bloodier, bloodiest.* Covered with blood.–The clothes of the man who was in the fight were *bloody*.

bloom (BLOOM) *n. blooms.* A blossom or flower.–The lily has a white *bloom*.
–*v. blooms, bloomed, blooming.* Have flowers; blossom.–Violets *bloom* early in the spring.

blos•som (BLAHSS-əm) *n. blossoms.* A flower.–The bride carried orange *blossoms*.
–*v. blossoms, blossomed, blossoming.* Bloom; produce flowers.–Lilacs *blossom* in the spring.

blot (BLAHT) *n. blots.* A spot.–Mary got a *blot* of ink on her homework when her pen leaked.
–*v. blots, blotted, blotting.* Soak; absorb.–When she spilled the ink, she used a blotter to *blot* it up.

blot•ter (BLAHT-er) *n. blotters.* A soft, fuzzy paper for soaking up ink, water, etc.–We used a *blotter* to take up the spilled ink.

blouse (BLOWSS) *n. blouses.* 1. A loose waist, or upper garment.—Some girls and women wear skirts and *blouses.*
2. The coat of a soldier's uniform.—United States soldiers wear *blouses* over their shirts.

blow (BLOH) *n. blows.* 1. A hit.—The boxer struck hard *blows.*
2. A shock, misfortune, or terrible happening.—It was a great *blow* to the rich man when he lost his money.

—*v. blows, blew, blowing.* 1. Drive or force air, breath, or wind.—I heard the wind *blow* through the trees last night.—The policeman *blows* his whistle for the cars to stop.—Father *blows* up Sally's balloons for her.
2. Carry by blowing.—The wind *blows* the seeds of many plants far and wide, so that they grow in different places.
—*Blow up* means cause to explode.—The soldiers will *blow up* the bridge with dynamite so that the enemy cannot cross it.

blub·ber (BLUB-er) *n.* The fat of whales, walruses, and other sea animals. Some oil is made from *blubber.*
—*v. blubbers, blubbered, blubbering.* Weep and sob noisily.—Grandfather told Jack to stop *blubbering.*

blue (BLOO) *adj. bluer, bluest.* 1. The color of the sky.—The colors of the American flag are red, white, and *blue.*
2. Sad.—Mother felt *blue* the day she heard the bad news.

blue·ber·ry (BLOO-bair-ee) *n. blueberries.* A kind of berry that is blue in color and good to eat.

blue·bird (BLOO-berd) *n. bluebirds.* A bird with blue back and wings, and orange breast. The *bluebird* is related to the robin, but is much smaller.

blue jay (BLOO-jay) *n. blue jays.* A bird somewhat larger than the robin, with a topknot or crest on its head. Its back is blue with black markings, and its breast is a mixture of white and blue. The *blue jay* chatters noisily.

bluff (BLUF) *n. bluffs.* A high, steep bank or cliff.—From the boat we saw the *bluff* along the shore.
—*v. bluffs, bluffed, bluffing.* Frighten off by pretending to have the advantage.—Bob *bluffed* the new boy who wanted to play marbles by pretending that he was a champion player.

blun·der (BLUN-der) *n. blunders.* A bad mistake.—Bob made a *blunder* in English class. He said "Ain't it the truth?" for "Isn't it the truth?"
—*v. blunders, blundered, blundering.* Make a bad mistake.

blunt (BLUNT) *v. blunts, blunted, blunting.* Make dull.—Bob *blunted* his knife by trying to cut a stone with it.
—*adj.* 1. Dull.—Grandfather's knife is *blunt.*
2. Likely to speak frankly; to say what one thinks.—The officer was very *blunt.* He called the man a thief.

blur (BLER) *v. blurs, blurred, blurring.* 1. Make unclear.—Jim cannot see with his grandfather's glasses. His sight becomes *blurred.*
2. Smear; smudge.—Water spilled on the letter, *blurring* the handwriting.
3. Cloud up; make dim.—Smoke from the fire *blurred* the view of the mountain.

blush (BLUSH) *n. blushes.* A turning red from shame or embarrassment.—The *blush* on Mary's cheeks made her more beautiful.
—*v. blushes, blushed, blushing.* Turn red from shame or embarrassment.—Every time Mother spoke of Bob's mistake, he *blushed.*—Children who are bashful or shy *blush* easily.

blus•ter (BLUSS-ter) *v. blusters, blustered, blustering.* 1. Blow noisily.—We heard the wind *blustering* in the trees.
2. Talk noisily, with bluffing.—When Jack is angry, he *blusters* about "getting even."

bo•a con•stric•tor (BOH-ə kən-strik-ter) *boa constrictors.* A very large snake found in South and Central America. The *boa constrictor* is not poisonous. It kills its victims by crushing them in its coils. The *boa constrictor* often grows ten feet long.

boar (BOR) *n. boars.* A wild male pig, or hog.

board (BORD) *n. boards.* 1. A long piece of wood.—Father ordered *boards* from the lumber yard to repair the porch with.

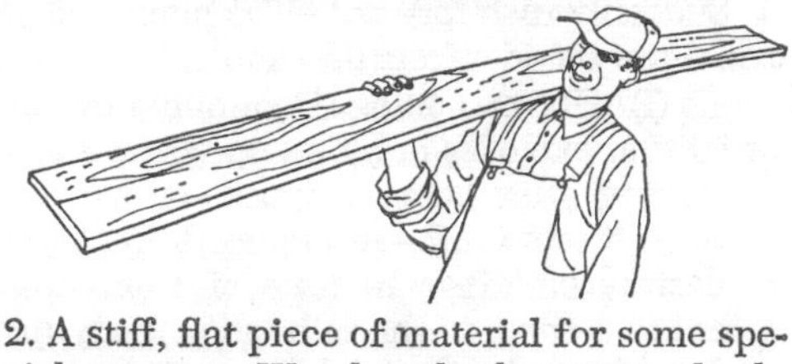

2. A stiff, flat piece of material for some special purpose.—We play checkers on a checker*board.*—The man puts his paper on a drawing *board* when he draws.

checkerboard

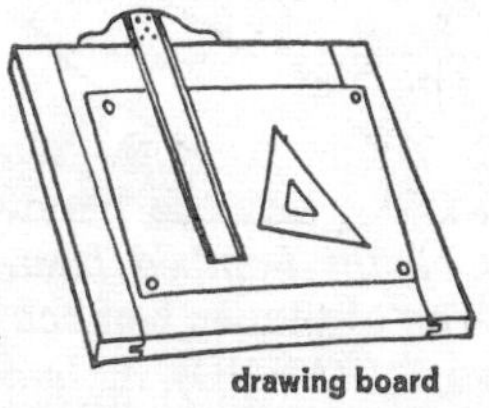

drawing board

3. Meals for which one pays.—Mrs. Jones will give the workers *board.*
4. A group of persons chosen to manage something.—The school *board* is a group of men chosen by the voters to take care of operating the schools.
—*v. boards, boarded, boarding.* 1. Live at another's house, paying for one's meals and room.—Mr. Smith *boards* at Mrs. Jones's house.
2. Go onto or into a ship, train, etc.—The sailors *boarded* their ship.
—*On board* means on or in a ship, train, etc.—The sailors went *on board* the ship.

boast (BOHST) *v. boasts, boasted, boasting.* Brag or talk too much about oneself and what one can do.—The boy who *boasted* all the time couldn't find anyone to play with him.

boast•ful (BOHST-fuhl) *adj.; boastfully, adv.* Bragging or boasting often.

boat BOHT) *n. boats.* A vessel for traveling on water. *Boats* moved by oars are called row*boats*. *Boats* moved by the wind blowing on sails are called sail*boats*. Some *boats* are moved by steam power and carry many people. They are steam*boats*. Small *boats* are often carried on big ships. See page 325.

bob (BAHB) *n. bobs.* 1. A float on a fishing line which moves up and down when a fish bites on the bait.
2. A quick nod.—Uncle Dick offered me a horse. I was so surprised, I could only answer by a *bob* of my head.
—*v. bobs, bobbed, bobbing.* 1. Cut hair quite short.—The barber will *bob* Mary's hair so her head will be cool in the summer.
2. Move up and down.—The floating bottle *bobbed* on the waves.

bob•bin (BAHB-ən) *n. bobbins.* A spool or reel.—Grandmother had to wind the *bobbin* with thread before she could sew on the sewing machine.—Wire, thread, yarn, and string are often wound on *bobbins.*

bob•cat (BAHB-kat) *n. bobcats.* A lynx; a wildcat, found in North America. *Bobcats* hunt and live on small animals and birds. Large *bobcats* often attack deer.

bob•o•link (BAHB-ə-lingk) *n. bobolinks.* A kind of songbird. Its breast is black, and its dark back is marked with yellow and white.

bob•sled (BAHB-sled) *n. bobsleds.* A sled with two pairs of runners.–The children like to slide downhill together on Jack's *bobsled.*

bob•white (BAHB-HWYT) *n. bobwhites.* A bird also called the quail. It has a ruddy back, and white on the throat. Its call is a whistle that sounds like its name.

bod•y (BAHD-ee) *n. bodies.* 1. All of a person or animal other than the mind.–Keep your *body* healthy and your mind will work better.
2. All of a person except his head, arms, and legs; the trunk or torso.
3. A dead person or animal.
4. A large mass or quantity, all together.–An ocean is a vast *body* of water.

bod•y•guard (BAHD-ee-gahrd) *n. bodyguards.* A man who goes around with a person to protect him from harm.–The President has *bodyguards* to keep him safe.

bog (BAHG) *n. bogs.* A marsh; a swampy place.–Cranberries grow in *bogs.*

bog•gy (BAHG-ee) *adj.* Swampy.–Low land near a river is often *boggy.*

boil (BOIL) *n. boils.* A hard, swollen, sore place with pus in it.–The *boil* on my arm has nearly gone.
–*v. boils, boiled, boiling.* Bubble and give off steam or vapor.–Water will *boil* if heated enough. If water *boils* long enough, it will all become steam and disappear into the air.
–*adj.* Cooked in boiling liquid.–Bob likes eggs fried; Mary likes *boiled* eggs best.

boil•er (BOIL-er) *n. boilers.* 1. A large metal pan or container for boiling things in.–Mother boils the clothes in a wash *boiler.*

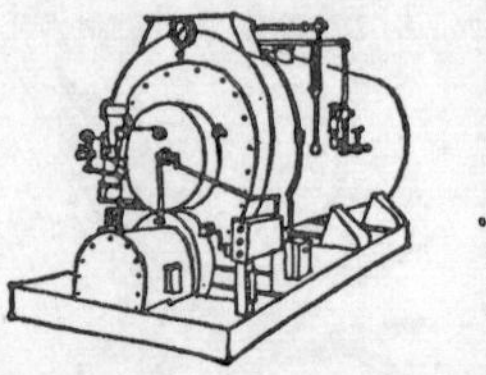

2. A tank in which water is heated to make steam.–In factories water is heated in *boilers* to make steam to run the machines.

bois•ter•ous (BOISS-ter-əss) *adj.* Loud, noisy, and rough.–The children were so *boisterous* in their play that they woke the baby.

bold (BOHLD) *adj. bolder, boldest; boldly, adv.* 1. Willing to face danger; not afraid.–The knights of old were very *bold.* They were brave and daring.
2. Rough or rude.–Children are not well liked if they are *bold.*
3. Bright; clearly seen.–The tree in the picture is very *bold.* It stands out strongly.

boll (BOHL) *n. bolls.* The part of the cotton or flax plant which contains the seeds.–The boll weevil, a grayish beetle, often attacks cotton plants by laying its eggs in the cotton *bolls.*

bolt (BOHLT) *n. bolts.* 1. A sliding bar, as on a door.–Mr. Smith fastened the door with a *bolt.*

2. A metal rod with a head at one end and screw threads along its length so that a nut can be screwed onto it.–Some parts of an automobile are held together with *bolts.*

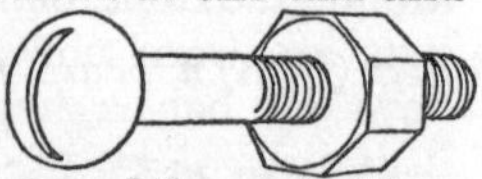

3. A roll (of cloth).–The dressmaker used a whole *bolt* of cloth to make the costumes.
4. A stroke of lightning.–We saw a *bolt* of lightning. It was followed by thunder.
–*v. bolts, bolted, bolting.* 1. Fasten, or hold, with a bolt.–Father *bolted* the door before going to bed.–The top of the desk was *bolted* to the frame. It was fastened with bolts and nuts.
2. Suddenly rush forward.–The horse *bolted* and threw its rider from the saddle.

bomb (BAHM) *n. bombs.* A container of material that explodes or blows up when it hits something after being dropped, or when a clock in it sets it off.–Airplanes drop *bombs* to destroy buildings in time of war.–The spies hid a *bomb* in the railroad station, and an hour later the station blew up.

–*v. bombs, bombed, bombing.* Drop bombs on.–The airplanes *bombed* the city.

bond (BAHND) *n. bonds.* 1. A written or printed statement given by the government or a business firm in return for a loan of money. The *bond* promises to pay back the money at a certain time with interest.
2. A tie.–The secret was a *bond* between them.

bond•ed (BAHND-əd) *adj.* In slavery; sold to serve for a certain amount of time.—John wanted to come to America. Mr. Smith promised to take him there if John would be his *bonded* servant for seven years.

bone (BOHN) *n. bones; bony, adj.* One of the hard, stiff pieces that make up the skeleton, or framework, of the body. — Dogs like to gnaw the meat from *bones.*

bon•fire (BAHN-fyr) *n. bonfires.* A big fire outdoors.—Father made a *bonfire* in the alley and burned up the rubbish.

bon•net (BAHN-ət) *n. bonnets.* A close-fitting hat with a brim around the front. *Bonnets* are worn nowadays by babies and little girls.

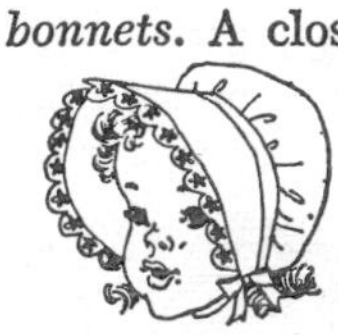

bon•ny or **bon•nie** (BAHN-ee) *n.* Pretty one; loved one.—"My *bonny* lies over the ocean."
—*adj. bonnier, bonniest.* 1. Pretty; fair.—Susan wore a *bonny* hat in the Easter parade.
2. Healthy; well filled out.—Ruth was the *bonniest* baby in the nursery.

bo•nus (BOH-nəss) *n. bonuses.* A gift of money in addition to the amount earned.—Each Christmas Father gets a *bonus* from his employer.

boo (BOO) *n. boos.* An exclamation used to frighten.—Sally shouted *"Boo!"* at Father to frighten him.
—*v. boos, booed, booing.* Show that one is not pleased with something by yelling *boo!*—When the first baseman struck out, the people *booed* him.

book (BUHK) *n. books.* Sheets of paper or pages, printed or blank, fastened together within a cover. —The children made *books* to draw pictures in by sewing sheets of paper together and putting a cover around them.—Each volume in this dictionary is a *book.*

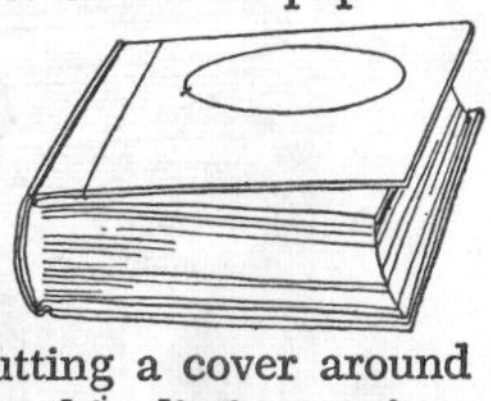

book•case (BUHK-kayss) *n. bookcases.* A cupboard or case of shelves for putting books in. Some *bookcases* are open in the front and some have glass doors.

book•let (BUHK-lət) *n. booklets.* A thin paper-covered book. — The children made *booklets* of poems for their mothers.

boom (BOOM) *n. booms.* 1. A deep, loud, hollow sound.—The children heard the *boom* of the cannon.
2. A time when much money is made.—There is a *boom* in the oil fields.
—*v. booms, boomed, booming.* Do much business; become rich.—Towns near the new oil fields are *booming.* They are very prosperous.

boost (BOOST) *n. boosts.* 1. A lift up.—Father gave Mary a *boost* to help her onto the horse.
2. A rise; an increase.—There was a *boost* in the price of oil. The price went up.
—*v. boosts, boosted, boosting.* 1. Give a lift or shove.—Bob *boosted* Jack over the fence. He gave him a little push.
2. Raise.—A war *boosts* prices because things are hard to get.

boot (BOOT) *n. boots.* A covering for the foot and leg. *Boots* are made of rubber or leather. Rubber *boots* are often worn over shoes. That way the shoes do not get wet. Some *boots* cover the legs to the knees. Rubber *boots* sometimes reach to the hips.

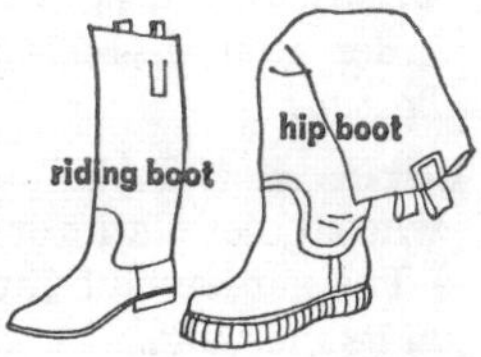

booth (BOOTH) *n. booths.* 1. A closet or tiny room for telephoning. voting, etc. — Father went into a *booth* to phone Mother.
2. A covered stand or stall. — My sister sold candy in a *booth* at the fair.

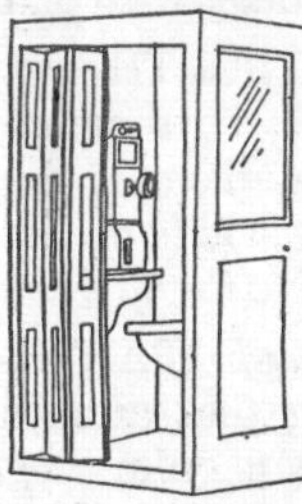

bor•der (BOR-der) *n. borders.* 1. An outer edge; a margin.—The teacher told us to draw a 1-inch *border* all around our picture to make a frame.—Wild flowers grow at the *border* of the woods.— —Our big rug in the hall has a dark blue *border.*
2. A legal boundary.—The travelers crossed the *border* into the neighboring country.
—*v. borders, bordered, bordering.* Be next (to); touch. — Our farm *borders* on Mr. Smith's farm on the south. Mr. Smith's farm starts where ours ends on the south.

bore (BOR) *n. bores.* A person or thing that is not interesting.–Mary finds arithmetic a *bore.* On the other hand, she thinks history is very interesting.
–*v. bores, bored, boring.* 1. Pierce; drill.–The carpenter can *bore* holes in a board with his brace and bit.
2. Weary; tire; make one lose interest.–People who talk too much about themselves *bore* others. – The long, dull story *bored* the children.

borne (BORN) *v.* One form of the verb *bear.* –Jack has *borne* abuse from Bill as long as he can; he can stand it no longer.

bor•row (BAHR-oh) *v. borrows, borrowed, borrowing.* Take or use for a time, and then give back to the owner.–May I *borrow* your red pencil? Will you lend it to me?–I *borrowed* Father's hammer to build a kite.

boss (BAWSS) *n. bosses.* A person who directs others in their work.–My *boss* at the office is strict but fair.
–*v. bosses, bossed, bossing.* Tell what to do; order around.–Most people do not like to be *bossed.*

bot•a•nist (BAHT-ə-nəst) *n. botanists.* One who studies plants or is a specialist in botany. –The garden club invited a *botanist* to speak at its meeting.

bot•a•ny (BAHT-ə-nee) *n.* The science or study of plants; the special branch of biology that deals with plant life.

both (BOHTH) *adj., conj.,* and *pron.* The two. –*Both* boys came into the kitchen. Mother asked them if they wanted pie or cookies. They said *both. Both* pie and cookies sounded good to them.

both•er (BAHTH-er) *n. bothers.* Trouble; thing that annoys.–Mother thinks darning socks is quite a *bother.*
–*v. bothers, bothered, bothering.* 1. Take the trouble.–I didn't *bother* to look for the paper.
2. Trouble; annoy.–The noise *bothers* Mother.

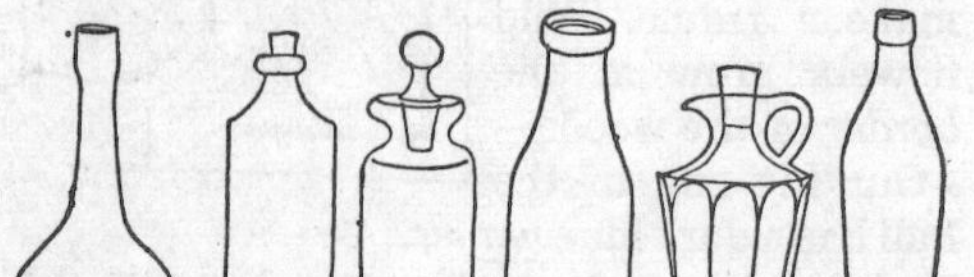

bot•tle (BAHT-l) *n. bottles.* 1. A glass container with a narrow neck.–Many medicines are kept in *bottles.*
2. As much as a bottle will hold.–The baby drank a whole *bottle* of milk.
–*v. bottles, bottled, bottling.* Put into bottles.– The farmer sends his milk in large cans to the city to be *bottled.*

bot•tom (BAHT-əm) *n. bottoms.* 1. The lowest part.–The olives at the *bottom* of the bottle are hard to reach.
2. Under part.–The *bottoms,* or soles, of my feet are sore from walking barefoot.
3. The ground beneath a body of water.– The lake was so clear that we saw pebbles on the *bottom.*
–*adj.* Lowest.–The book you are looking for is on the *bottom* shelf.

bough (BOW) *n. boughs.* A branch. – The *boughs* of the trees swing back and forth in the wind.

bought (BAWT) *v.* One form of the verb *buy.*–Father has *bought* this house; he owns it now.

boul•der (BOHL-der) *n. boulders.* A large rock which is smooth and rounded. *Boulders* are generally separate and individual rocks.–The *boulder* fell off the cliff.

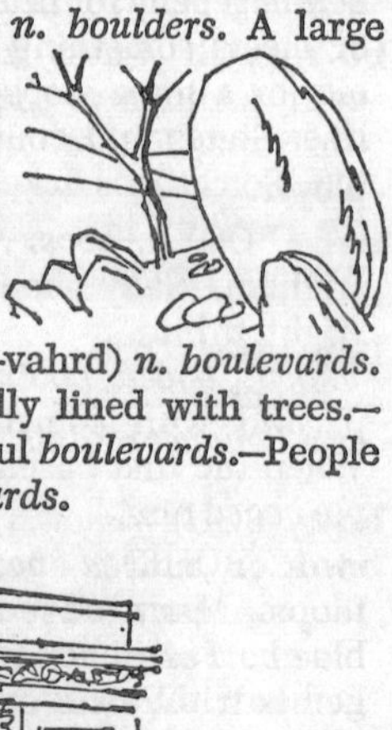

bou•le•vard (BUHL-ə-vahrd) *n. boulevards.* A broad avenue, usually lined with trees.– Paris has many beautiful *boulevards.*–People like to stroll on *boulevards.*

bounce (BOWNSS) *n. bounces.* Spring; jump.–This old tennis ball is still good. It still has a lot of *bounce* left.
–*v. bounces, bounced, bouncing.* 1. Hit something and spring back.–The rubber ball *bounced* up and down on the floor when it was dropped.–The car *bounced* into the air when it went over the rut.
2. Make *bounce.*–Sally *bounces* her ball.
3. Jump; spring; bound.–Jack *bounces* out of bed on Saturdays.

bound (BOWND) *v. bounds, bounded, bounding.* 1. Headed; going in the direction of.–Uncle Jim is *bound* for Washington.
2. Be next to; surround; mark the end of.–The Atlantic Ocean *bounds* North America on the east. It is on the eastern edge of North America.–A picket fence *bounds* our yard. It goes all around it.
3. Leap.–We saw a rabbit go *bounding* across the road.–When the bell rang, the children *bounded* from their seats and rushed from the room.
4. One form of the verb *bind.*–Grandmother's Bible is *bound* in real leather.

bound•a•ry (BOWN-də-ree) *n. boundaries.* The edge, end, or line where something stops or meets something else. The line where a city or a town stops is called the *boundary* line. States and countries have *boundaries,* too. Sometimes lakes and mountains form the dividing line. Lake Michigan forms the western *boundary* of the state of Michigan.

bou•quet (boh- *or* boo-KAY) *n. bouquets.* A bunch of flowers.–Mary brought her mother a *bouquet* of daisies.

bow (BOH) *n. bows.* 1. A kind of knot with two or more open loops.–Mary wore a blue *bow* of ribbon on her hair.–We tie our shoelaces in a *bow.*

2. A weapon used for shooting arrows. It is a curved, easily bent stick with a string fastened to each end.–Indians used *bows* and arrows to hunt animals with.

3. A slender stick with coarse hairs fastened onto it, used to draw across the strings of a violin or other stringed instrument to make music.

bow (BOW) *n. bows.* The front part of a boat. –The girls sat in the *bow* of the boat. The boys sat in the stern.
–*v. bows, bowed, bowing.* 1. Bend down; incline; stoop.–The children *bow* their heads when they say their prayers.
2. Bend the body or head forward as a greeting, to express thanks, etc.–The people clapped their hands when Mary sang. She came back to the stage and *bowed.*–Father lifts his hat and *bows* a little when he meets the teacher on the street.

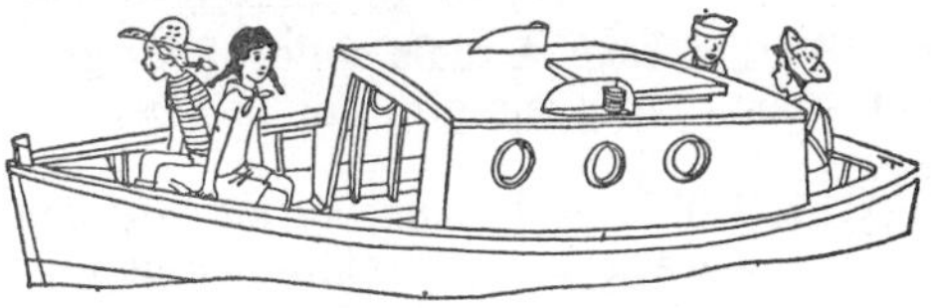

bow•els (BOW-əlz) *n. pl.* 1. A long, coiled tube in the body, also called the intestines. Food passes from the stomach into the *bowels.* The *bowels* send food into the blood stream to nourish other parts of the body. The waste parts of food pass out of the body through the end of the *bowels.*
2. Deep, inside part.–Precious metals lie buried in the *bowels* of the earth.

bowl (BOHL) *n. bowls.* A deep, round dish.–We eat soup from a *bowl.*–Mother mixes cakes in a mixing *bowl.*

2. As much as a bowl will hold.–Goldilocks ate the Baby Bear's *bowl* of porridge all up.
–*v. bowls, bowled, bowling.* Play the game of *bowling* by rolling a large ball down a smooth wooden alley to knock down large wooden pins. This game is played also on grass.

box (BAHKS) *n. boxes.* 1. A cardboard, wood, or metal container made to hold things.–We put the Christmas gifts in *boxes.*–We bought a *box* of soap powder.

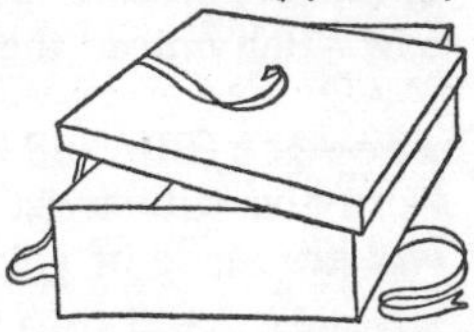

2. As much as a box holds.–We used a *box* of soap powder.
3. A private section in a theater balcony.–Mary went to the show and sat in a *box.*
–*v. boxes, boxed, boxing.* 1. Fight with the fists according to certain rules.–George can *box* better than Jim. He has knocked Jim out twice.
2. Put in a box.–Mary *boxes* pretzels at the factory. She puts pretzels into boxes.

box·er (BAHK-ser) *n. boxers.* One who boxes; a prize fighter.—Joe Louis was a great *boxer.*

boy (BOI) *n. boys.* A male child.—*Boys* grow to be men.—Mary is a girl. Bob is a *boy.*

boy·ish (BOI-ish) *adj; boyishly, adv.; boyishness, n.* Like a boy, or male child.—Sometimes grown men say and do *boyish* things. They act like boys.

brace (BRAYSS) *n. braces.* **1.** Something used to hold up a thing or give it support.—The table leg was loose, so Grandfather put a *brace* on it.—Crippled people often wear *braces* on their backs, arms, or legs.—Mary wears *braces* on her teeth to straighten them.

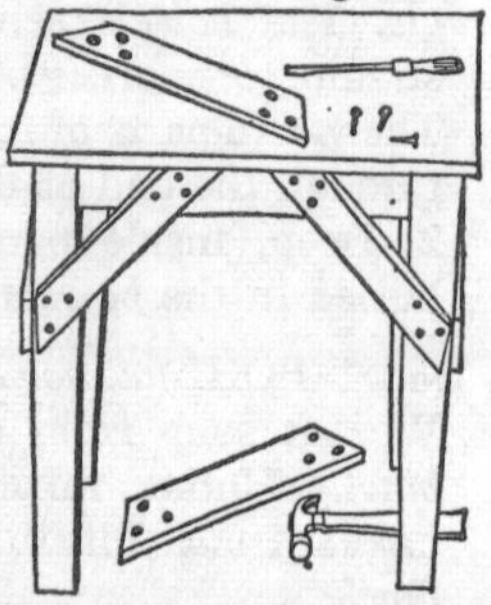

2. A tool used with a bit to make a hole. The *brace* is the holder for the bit.

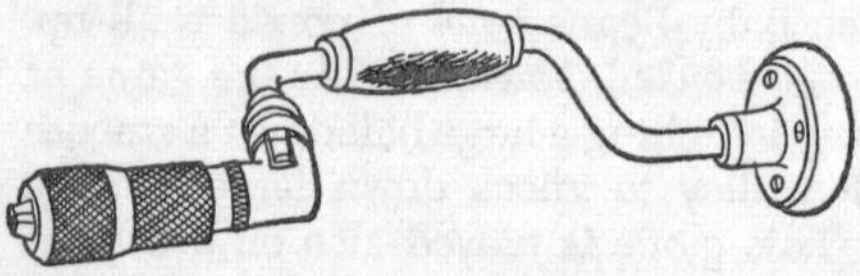

—*v. braces, braced, bracing.* Strengthen; support.—Bob *braced* the table.

brace·let (BRAYSS-lət) *n. bracelets.* A band worn about the wrist as an ornament. *Bracelets* are made of gold, silver, beads, etc.

brack·et (BRAK-ət) *n. brackets.* **1.** An L-shaped piece of metal or wood used to hold up or support one end of something, such as a shelf.—Father fastened the *brackets* on the wall and then screwed the shelf to them.

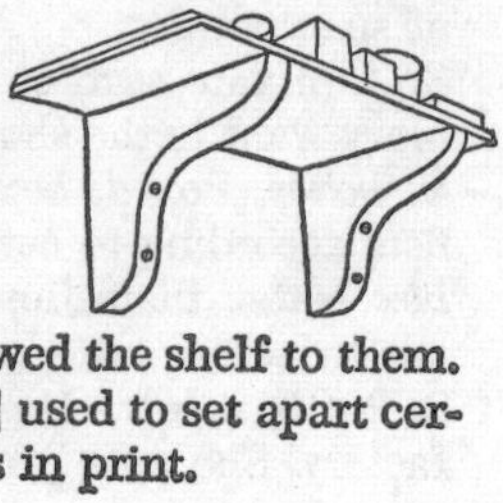

2. One of two marks [ ] used to set apart certain words or numbers in print.

brag (BRAG) *v. brags, bragged, bragging.* Boast; talk much about one's ability, possessions, or doings.—Boys and girls who *brag* are not usually liked.—Ed *brags* about his new boat.

braid (BRAYD) *n. braids.* **1.** A lock of hair that has been divided into three or more parts and woven into one large strand.—Sometimes Mary wears her hair in two *braids.*
2. Strips of material that have been twisted or woven into one strand. They are used as trimming.—The captain's suit was trimmed with gold *braid.*
—*v. braids, braided, braiding.* Make into a braid.—Mary's hair is long enough to *braid.*

Braille (BRAYL) *n.* (Also spelled without a capital "b.") A system of raised dots which represent all the letters of the alphabet. By touching these dots a blind person can spell out the letters of a word. So he can "read" the word.—Many books are printed in *braille* for the blind.

brain (BRAYN) *n. brains.* The large, grayish mass of nerves inside the skull, or head, of persons and animals. The *brain* contains nerve cells that control our thinking and the movements of our bodies.

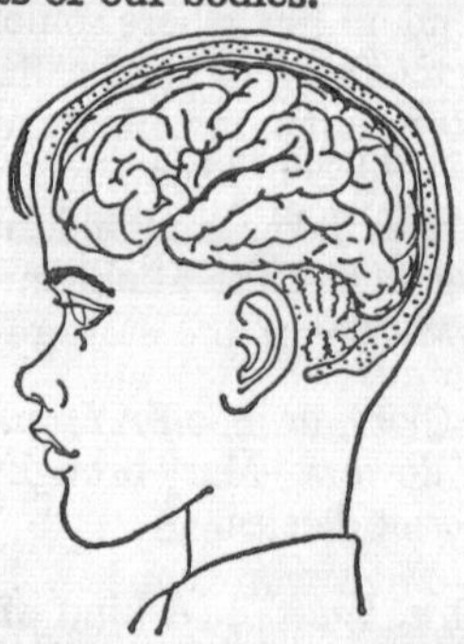

brake (BRAYK) *n. brakes.* A device used to slow down or stop bicycles, cars, etc.—Mother stepped on the *brake* when she saw the traffic light turn red.

bram·ble (BRAM-bəl) *n. brambles.* A shrub with thorns on it.—Grandfather planted *brambles* along the back fence.

bran (BRAN) *n.* The outer covering of grains. When wheat is made into flour, it is cracked open and sifted. The fine powdered part is the flour, and the remaining hull, or husk, is the *bran.*

branch (BRANCH) *n. branches.* **1.** A limb or stem of a tree. The trunk of the tree is the main part that grows up from the ground. The roots are joined to the bottom of the trunk, and the *branches* are joined to the upper part. Leaves grow on the *branches*.

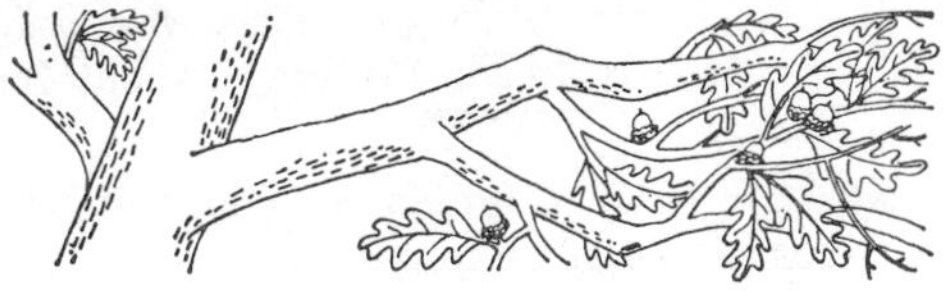

2. A division of a larger thing, such as one of the small rivers that flow into a large river.
3. One office or agency of a large organization.–The library at the corner is a *branch* of the downtown library.
–*v. branches, branched, branching.* Go more than one way; reach out in different directions.–At the bottom of the hill the road *branched* off in several directions. John did not know which way to go.

brand (BRAND) *n. brands.* 1. A mark or symbol which is burned on with a hot iron.–Cattle are often marked with a *brand* so that their owners will be able to tell them apart from other cattle.

2. A particular kind or make.–Uncle Jim always uses this *brand* of mustard.
–*v. brands, branded, branding.* Mark with a hot iron.

brass (BRASS) *n.* A yellowish metal made by putting copper, zinc, and other metals together. *Brass* is used to make dishes, candlesticks, bells, musical instruments, etc.

brave (BRAYV) *n. braves.* An Indian warrior of North America.
–*v. braves, braved, braving.* Face with courage; defy.–The hunters *braved* the storm. They went out into it.
–*adj. braver, bravest.* Ready to face danger; not afraid.–Mike won a medal because he was a very *brave* soldier.

brave•ly (BRAYV-lee) *adv.* Without fear; with courage.–The animal trainer walked *bravely* into the lions' cage.

brav•er•y (BRAY-ver-ee) *n.* Courage; being unafraid.–The officer was given a medal for his *bravery.*

bray (BRAY) *n. brays.* A loud, harsh cry.–One night at the farm we heard the *bray* of a donkey.
–*v. brays, brayed, braying.* Make a loud, harsh cry.–Donkeys *bray.*

bread (BRED) *n. breads.* 1. A food made of wheat flour, bran, rye flour, cornmeal, etc., and baked in loaves in an oven.
2. Food.–"Give us this day our daily *bread*" means give us this day our daily food.
–*v. breads, breaded, breading.* Put a coating of crumbs on.–Mother *breaded* veal chops for dinner. She dipped them in egg and bread crumbs and fried them in deep fat.

breadth (BREDTH) *n.* Width or distance across.–The length of the board is four feet and the *breadth* is eight inches.

break (BRAYK) *n.* 1. A crack.–There is a bad *break* in the fence. It will have to be repaired.
2. Interruption; rest.–The actors took a five-minute *break.* They rested for five minutes before going on with the rehearsal.
–*v. breaks, broke, breaking.* 1. Crack.–Jack did not *break* any bones in his arm when he fell on it.
2. Smash; separate into pieces.–Dishes *break* easily if they are dropped.–Jerry dropped the dish and *broke* it.
3. Disobey; not keep (rules).–The children did not mean to *break* the rules of the school.
4. Force one's way.–The rabbit *breaks* out of its pen nearly every day.
5. Tell gently.–The teacher *broke* the bad news to the children.
6. Change; give up.–Bad habits are hard to *break.*
7. Appear; come out.–A rash has *broken* out all over Mary's face.
8. Plow.–Farmers *break* the ground before planting the seeds.
9. Quickly come forth, appear, or develop.–The storm *broke* suddenly.–Uncle Jim enlisted when the war *broke* out.

break•er (BRAYK-er) *n. breakers.* A wave that crashes down into foam as it comes toward and hits the shore.–The *breakers* rolled into shore with great force as the storm rose.

break•fast (BREK-fəst) *n. breakfasts.* The first meal of the day. It breaks the long fast, or time without food, of the night.–Fruit, cereal, an egg, toast, and milk make a good *breakfast.*

breast (BREST) *n. breasts.* Chest, or upper part of the front of the body.–He lay with his hands upon his *breast.*–Some people like the *breast* of a chicken best.

breath (BRETH) *n. breaths.* 1. Air taken into and let out of the lungs.–Mary blew her *breath* against the window glass to make a smear.
2. A stir; a movement (of air).–It was so warm that there was not a *breath* of air.

BRIDGES

rope bridge

viaduct

suspension bridge

continuous span bridge

breathe (BREETH) *v. breathes, breathed, breathing.* Take air into the lungs and let it out again.–Jack ran so fast that it was hard for him to *breathe.*

breath•less (BRETH-ləss) *adj.; breathlessly, adv.; breathlessness, n.* Unable to breathe; panting; out of breath.–The race left the boys *breathless.*–Mary was *breathless* with excitement at the concert.

breech•es (BRICH-əz) *n. pl.* Short trousers that fit tight over the knees. – In George Washington's day, men wore *breeches.*
–A *breeches buoy* is a canvas seat on a rope and pulley, used to save people from sinking ships.

breed (BREED) *n. breeds.* A certain kind or family.–On this ranch they raise a fine *breed* of horses.–Jersey cows are a *breed* of cows.
–*v. breeds, bred, breeding.* 1. Raise.– The farmer *breeds* horses.
2. Produce young.–Sheep *breed* often.

breeze (BREEZ) *n. breezes; breezy, adj.* A gentle wind.–The *breeze* stirred the leaves.

brew (BROO) *n. brews.* A drink that has been specially mixed.–The coffee tasted like witches' *brew.* It tasted terrible.
–*v. brews, brewed, brewing.* 1. Make (beer, etc.).–Beer is *brewed* from hops and malt.
2. Form, start, or be about to break out.– Mother can always tell when the children are *brewing* mischief. – The black clouds showed that a storm was *brewing.*

bri•ar or **bri•er** (BRY-er) *n. briars* or *briers.* A plant that has thorns or sharp points along its stem.–Blackberries and wild roses are called *briars.*

bribe (BRYB) *n. bribes.* Money or gifts given to a person to get him to do something dishonest or something he does not want to do.– Jack gave Bob an apple as a *bribe,* so Bob would help him solve the problem.
–*v. bribes, bribed, bribing.* Give a bribe to.– The criminals tried to *bribe* the judge.

brick (BRIK) *n. bricks.* 1. A block of clay or mud that has been baked to make it hard. –Some houses are made of *bricks.*
2. Something shaped

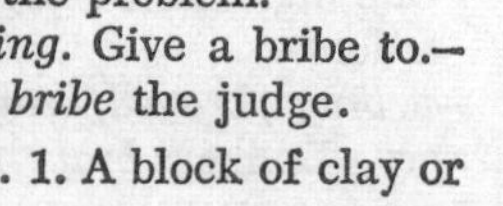

arcade bridge, Venice

wooden covered bridge

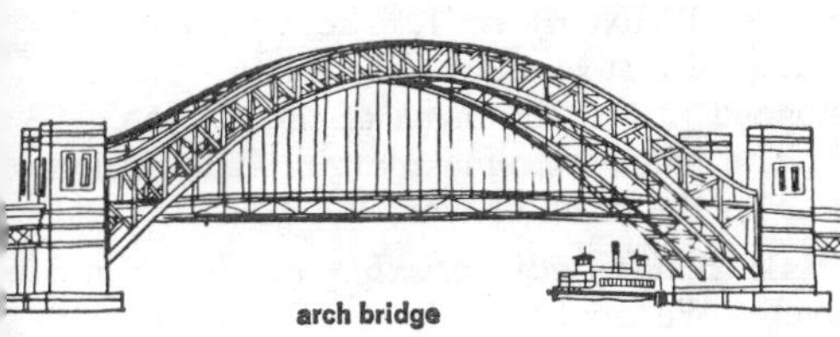
arch bridge

cantilever bridge

bascule bridge

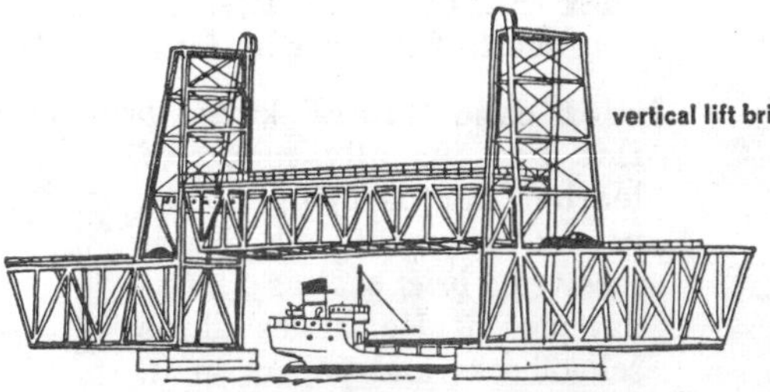
vertical lift bridge

like the *bricks* used for houses is often called a *brick*, as a *brick* of ice cream, a *brick* of cheese, etc.

brid•al (BRYD-l) *adj.* Of or for a bride.–My sister received many *bridal* gifts when she got married.–She threw her *bridal* bouquet to the guests.

bride (BRYD) *n. brides.* A woman who is about to be married, is being married, or has just been married.–My sister received many gifts when she was a *bride.*

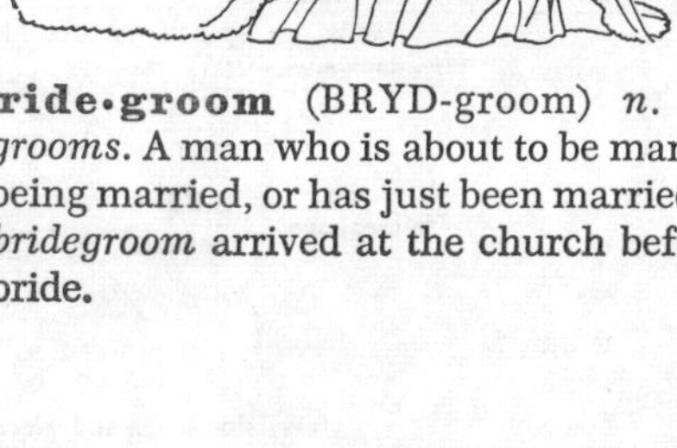

bride•groom (BRYD-groom) *n. bridegrooms.* A man who is about to be married, is being married, or has just been married.–The *bridegroom* arrived at the church before the bride.

brides•maid (BRYDZ-mayd) *n. bridesmaids.* A young woman who attends a bride and walks down the aisle with her at the wedding.

bridge (BRIJ) *n. bridges.* 1. Something built over a river or a low place for people or vehicles to cross on.–The cars crossed the river on the *bridge.*

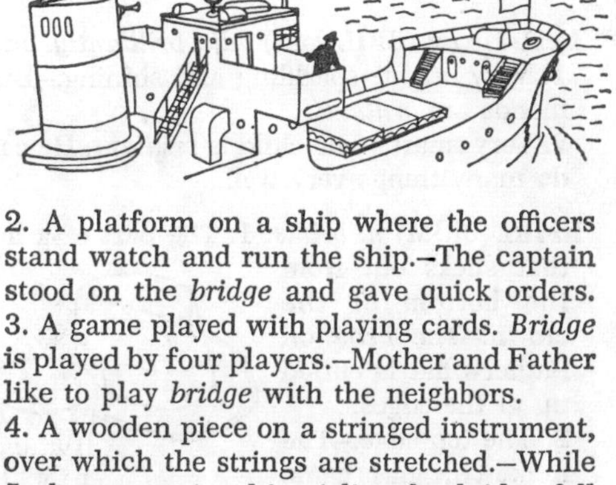

2. A platform on a ship where the officers stand watch and run the ship.–The captain stood on the *bridge* and gave quick orders.
3. A game played with playing cards. *Bridge* is played by four players.–Mother and Father like to play *bridge* with the neighbors.
4. A wooden piece on a stringed instrument, over which the strings are stretched.–While Jack was tuning his violin, the *bridge* fell over.
–*v. bridges, bridged, bridging.* Close up; make travel across easier.–Don hit a home run. That *bridged* the gap between his batting average and Tom's.

bri•dle (BRYD-l) *n. bridles.* The part of a horse's harness that fits on the horse's head. When you pull the reins which are fastened to the *bridle,* the horse slows down or turns.

–v. bridles, bridled, bridling. 1. Put a bridle on.–Jim *bridled* the horse.
2. Control.–Lou tried to *bridle* his bad temper. He tried not to yell so often.
3. Seem offended or angered.–Jack *bridled* when I told him I thought he could not do the work.

brief (BREEF) *adj. briefer, briefest; briefly, adv.* Short.–Bob wrote his father a *brief* note.

brief case (BREEF kayss) *brief cases.* A flat bag, usually made of leather, for carrying books, papers, documents, etc.–Harry received a *brief case* as a birthday present. He carries all his schoolbooks and papers in it.

bri•er (BRY-er) *n. briers.* Another way of spelling the word *briar,* meaning a plant with thorns.

bright (BRYT) *adj. brighter, brightest; brightly, adv.* 1. Shining. – A *bright* light shone through the window.
2. Giving much light.–Sometimes the moon is very *bright.* It gives much light.
3. (Of a color) Clear; not mixed with duller shades.–Mary has a *bright* blue dress.
4. Smart.–Ned is the *brightest* boy in school.

bril•liant (BRIL-yənt) *adj.; brilliantly, adv.* 1. Very bright; sparkling and shining.–Diamonds are *brilliant.*
2. Very smart.–The child is *brilliant.* He can do many things very well.

brim (BRIM) *n. brims.* 1. The part of a hat that sticks out from the bottom of the crown.–The *brim* on Father's hat is curled up at the edges.
2. The top edge.–The milk in the glass came up to the *brim.*

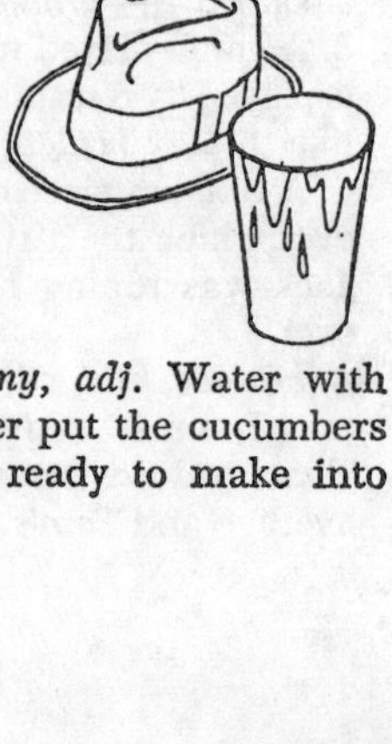

brine (BRYN) *n.; briny, adj.* Water with much salt in it.–Mother put the cucumbers in *brine* to get them ready to make into pickles.

bring (BRING) *v. brings, brought, bringing.* 1. Cause to come with oneself; carry, lead, or accompany.–I will *bring* Jack to the party. I will see that he comes with me.–*Bring* your coat along. It may rain.
2. Cause.–The heavy rain *brought* floods in the valley.

brink (BRINGK) *n.* 1. The very edge or border of a steep place, like a cliff.–The car stopped just at the *brink* of the canyon.
2. The edge; extreme margin.–The nation was on the *brink* of war.

brisk (BRISK) *adj.; briskly, adv.* Quick and lively.–We went for a *brisk* walk in the cold morning air.

bris•tle (BRISS-əl) *n. bristles.* One of the stiff hairs in brushes or in the coats of certain animals. Some brushes are made from the *bristles* of a hog.

brit•tle (BRIT-l) *adj.* Hard, but very easily snapped, cracked, or broken.–Egg shells and glass are *brittle.* They crack easily.

broad (BRAWD) *adj. broader, broadest.* 1. Wide; of large surface from side to side.–The desert is long and *broad.*–The *broad* river flows slowly.
2. Full; clear.–It was *broad* daylight when I awoke.

broad•cast (BRAWD-kast) *v. broadcasts, broadcast* or *broadcasted, broadcasting.* Send out in all directions; send out over the radio. –The news was *broadcast* over the radio.

television master control console

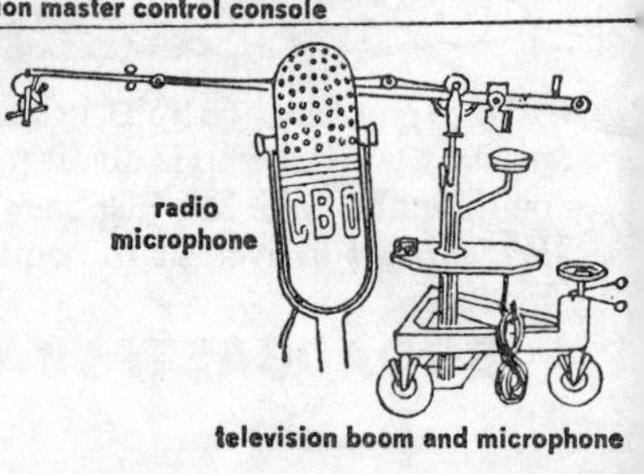

radio microphone

television boom and microphone

broad-mind•ed (BRAWD-myn-dəd) *adj.* Fair; having no prejudice.—Jane's parents are very *broad-minded.* They let her stay out late when she has a good reason.

broil (BROIL) *v. broils, broiled, broiling.* Cook on an open fire or in an oven broiler.—We went on a picnic and *broiled* steak.

broke (BROHK) *v.* One form of the verb *break.*—The glass *broke* when it fell from the shelf.

bro•ken (BROHK-ən) *v.* One form of the verb *break.*—The windshield of the car was *broken* into pieces by a flying stone.
—*adj.* 1. Shattered.—Mother threw away the *broken* dish.
2. Not kept.—Jack explained the reasons for his *broken* promise. He told why he hadn't done what he had said he would do.

bron•chi•al tubes (BRAHNG-kee-əl tyoobz *or* toobz). The two main branches of the windpipe, leading into the lungs. There are a number of smaller tubes which branch off from the main tubes. *Bronchial tubes* are also called bronchi.

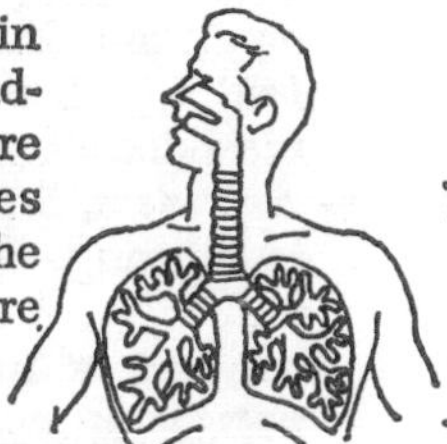

bron•chi•tis (brahn-KȲ-təss) *n.* An inflammation of the bronchial tubes.

bron•co (BRAHNG-koh) *n. broncos.* A small, somewhat wild horse used in western North America.—Bob liked the moving picture that showed cowboys riding *broncos.*

bronze (BRAHNZ) *n.* and *adj.* A yellowish metal made by melting copper and tin together. *Bronze* is made into dishes, jewelry, statues, etc.

brood (BROOD) *n. broods.* 1. A group of birds hatched out at one time.—There were seven chickens in the *brood.*
2. A mother's children are her *brood.*
—*v. broods, brooded, brooding.* Think sadly and silently; mope.—Jack *broods* over the loss of his dog.

BROADCASTING

brook (BRUHK) *n. brooks.* A small stream of water.–We fish in the *brook.*

broom (BROOM *or* BRUHM) *n. brooms.* A stiff brush with a long handle. The brush part of a *broom* is sometimes made of straws. *Brooms* are used to sweep rugs, floors, etc.

broom•stick (BROOM- *or* BRUHM-stik) *n. broomsticks.* The handle of a broom.–Grandfather cut off a *broomstick* and the boys used it for a bat.

broth (BRAWTH) *n.* The water in which meat or fish has been boiled.–We ate crackers and chicken *broth* for lunch.

broth•er (BRUTH-er) *n. brothers.* A boy or man born of the same parents as another child or person. If two boys or men have the same mother and father, they are *brothers.* –Bob is Mary's *brother.* Bob and Mary have the same father and mother.

broth•er•hood (BRUTH-er-huhd) *n.* 1. The close feeling between brothers; being like brothers.–Because John and Henry are such close friends, people often think they are brothers. They have a strong feeling of *brotherhood.*

2. A fraternal, labor, religious, or professional organization.–Frank is a railroad engineer. He belongs to the *Brotherhood* of Railroad Trainmen.

3. The people in a particular business or profession.–The entire *brotherhood* of plumbers went to the annual picnic.

broth•er-in-law (BRUTH-er-ən-law) *n. brothers-in-law.* The husband of one's sister, or the brother of one's husband or wife.

brought (BRAWT) *v.* One form of the verb *bring.*–Today I *brought* my lunch to school.

brow (BROW) *n. brows.* 1. Eyebrow; the short hairs above the eyes.–The girl had very heavy *brows.*

2. Forehead.–The fireman was so hot that his *brow* was covered with drops of sweat.

brown (BROWN) *n.* and *adj.* A darkish color; the color of moist earth or of chocolate.–Some people have blue eyes; others have *brown* eyes.

brown•ie (BROW-nee) *n. brownies.* 1. An elf or fairy that does helpful things for people. –The children enjoyed the story about the *brownies.*

2. A flat chocolate cake with nuts in it.–Bob and Jack like to eat *brownies.*

browse (BROWZ) *v. browses, browsed, browsing.* 1. Spend time looking here and there in a shop, book, etc.–Father likes to *browse* through the library before borrowing a book to read.

2. Graze or nibble.–The sheep were *browsing* in the meadow.

bruise (BROOZ) *n. bruises.* An injury to flesh caused by a blow, bump, etc., that does not break the skin.–Mary has a black-and-blue *bruise* on her arm. She got it by falling on the sidewalk.

–*v. bruises, bruised, bruising.* Cause a bruise by injuring.–Mary *bruised* her arm when she fell.

bru•net or **bru•nette** (broo-NET) *n. brunets* or *brunettes* and *adj.* A person whose hair and eyes are dark-colored.

brush (BRUSH) *n. brushes.* A tool with stiff hairs or bristles for scrubbing, etc. *Brushes* are made of stiff hairs, straw, wire, etc., set in some material such as wood, metal, or hard rubber.

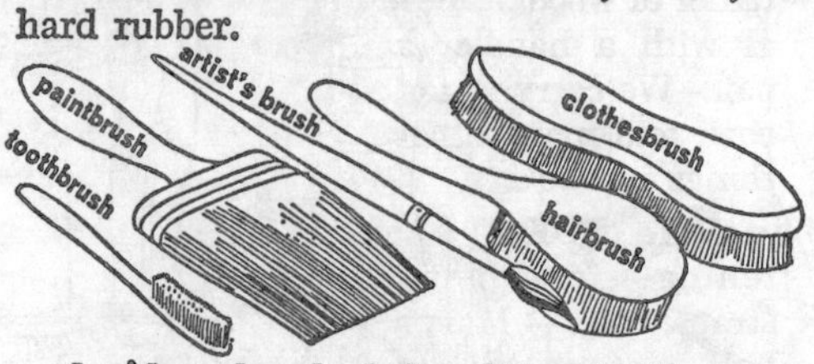

–*v. brushes, brushed, brushing.* 1. Clean or rub with a brush.–We *brush* our teeth with a tooth*brush.*–We *brush* our hair.

2. Rub against; touch.–A dog *brushed* my hand as he passed by.

brute (BROOT) *n. brutes* and *adj.* 1. A beast. –Animals are *brutes.* They cannot think or feel in the way people do.
2. A cruel, unkind person.–Mary called Bill a *brute* when he twisted her arm.

bub•ble (BUB-əl) *n. bubbles.* A little ball of air or other gas formed in a liquid, or with a thin film of liquid around it.–Ginger ale is full of little *bubbles.*–Children like to blow soap *bubbles* and let them float through the air.

–*v. bubbles, bubbled, bubbling.* To form, or rise, in bubbles.–When you make candy, the heat makes the candy *bubble* while it is cooking.–Boiling water *bubbles.*

buc•ca•neer (buk-ə-NEER) *n. buccaneers.* A pirate.–*Buccaneers* sailed the seas in the seventeenth and eighteenth centuries. They often attacked Spanish ships on their way to America.

buck (BUK) *n. bucks.* 1. A father or male deer. A *buck* has horns.

2. The male of goats, rabbits, and many other animals are called *bucks,* too.
–*v. bucks, bucked, bucking.* Jump up and down violently (said of a horse, steer, etc.)–The wild horse *bucked* to throw the cowboy off.

buck•et (BUK-ət) *n. buckets.* An open container of wood or metal with a handle; a pail.–We carry water, coal, and many other things in *buckets.*

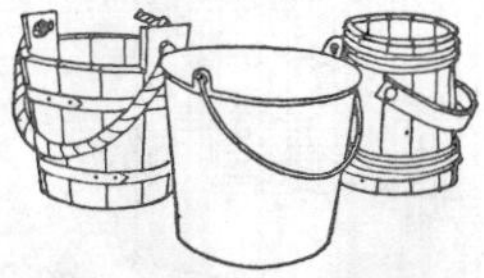

buck•le (BUK-əl) *n. buckles.* A kind of fastening for belts, straps, etc. – Mary's belt fastens with a brass *buckle.*

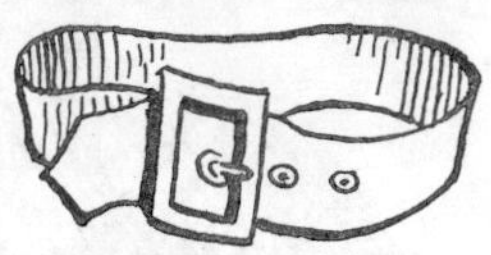

–*v. buckles, buckled, buckling.* 1. Fasten with a buckle.–The milkman *buckled* the horse's harness.
2. Bend.–The shelf *buckled* when too many books were put on it.

buck•skin (BUK-skin) *n.* and *adj.* The soft, yellowish or grayish leather made from the skin of a deer or a sheep.–John has a jacket made of *buckskin.* He wears his *buckskin* jacket almost everywhere he goes.

buck•wheat (BUK-hweet) *n.* A kind of plant with seeds that can be ground into a flour. *Buckwheat* flour is used to make pancakes.

bud (BUD) *n. buds.* A blossom or leaf of a plant before it unfolds.
–*v. buds, budded, budding.* Form buds.–The trees are beginning to *bud.*

budg•et (BUJ-ət) *n. budgets.* 1. A plan showing how much will be spent for what.–Mother makes out a *budget* each week. Then she knows how much money she can spend for groceries.
2. A plan showing how much money the government will get and how much it will spend during a certain amount of time.–The President sends his annual *budget* to Congress for approval.
–*v. budgets, budgeted, budgeting.* Make a plan for spending a certain amount of money, time, etc., for particular things.–Tom *budgets* his allowance so that he won't run short. –Father *budgets* his time so that he won't waste a minute.

buf•fa•lo (BUF-ə-loh) *n. buffaloes.* A kind of wild ox. *Buffaloes* look something like the bulls you see on farms. American *buffaloes* are also called bison.

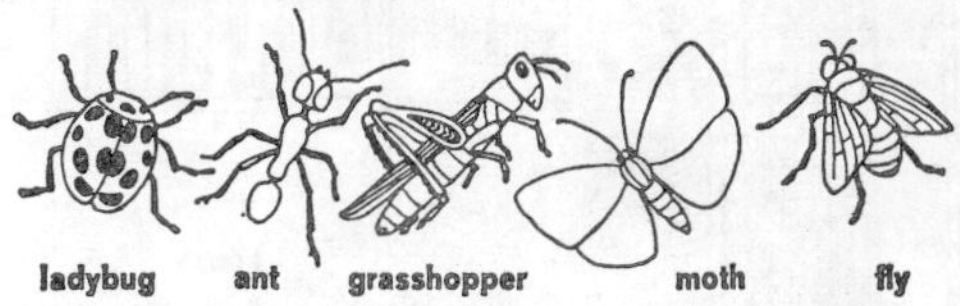

ladybug ant grasshopper moth fly

bug (BUG) *n. bugs.* An insect.–Jack has ladybugs, ants, flies, potato *bugs,* and many others in his collection.

BUILDINGS

factory
school
modern office building
auditorium
train station (depo
theater
observatory
hangars
skyscraper
log cabin
church
house
wooden house constructio
Price Tower, Bartlesville, Oklahoma

bug·gy (BUG-ee) *n. buggies.* A small, light carriage drawn by a horse.–Almost everyone rides in an automobile today. But some people still ride in *buggies.*

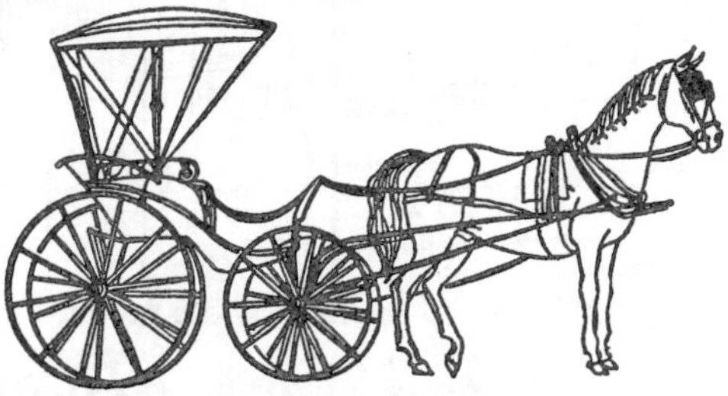

bu·gle (BYOO-gəl) *n. bugles.* A kind of small brass horn with a coiled tube. – The bugler in the army blows the *bugle* to tell the soldiers it is time to come to meals, go to bed, get up, etc.

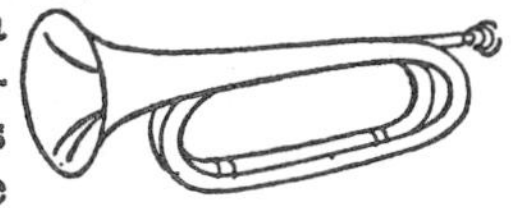

bu·gler (BYOO-gler) *n. buglers.* A person who blows a bugle.

build (BILD) *v. builds, built, building.* Construct; make; put together.–Beavers *build* dams.–Bricklayers *build* walls.

build·er (BILD-er) *n. builders.* A person who makes or designs buildings, bridges, etc.–The *builder* of our house said it would last a hundred years.

build·ing (BILD-ing) *n. buildings.* A structure that provides shelter and protection. Houses, stores, garages, etc., are *buildings.*

bulb (BULB) *n. bulbs.* 1. A thick root, often round, of certain plants. Some plants grow from seeds, and some grow from *bulbs.* Onions are *bulbs.* Lilies and irises grow from *bulbs.*

2. A thin glass globe or container containing thin wires which light up when electricity passes through; a light *bulb.*–Father put a new *bulb* in the lamp.

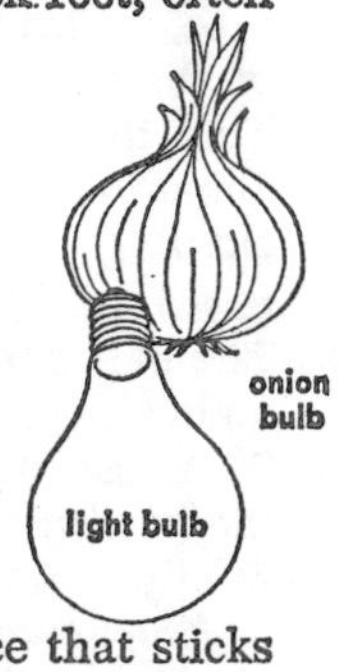

bulge (BULJ) *n. bulges.* A place that sticks out; a swelling.–Mother told Bob that his pocket would have a *bulge* if he put his baseball in it.

–*v. bulges, bulged, bulging.* Swell out.–Mother's pocketbook was so full that it *bulged.*

bulk (BULK) *n.* 1. The largest part.–The old man left the *bulk* of his fortune to charity when he died.

2. Greatness in size; magnitude.–The *bulk* of the iceberg surprised us. It extended under the water for a great distance.

bulk·y (BULK-ee) *adj. bulkier, bulkiest.* Large and clumsy; not easily managed because of its size.–The packages were too *bulky* to carry, so Mother had them delivered.

bull (BUHL) *n. bulls.* A male or he animal, especially one of the ox or cow kind. A milk cow is a female, or she animal; a *bull* is a male, or he animal, of the same kind. The male elephant and some other large animals are called *bulls,* too.

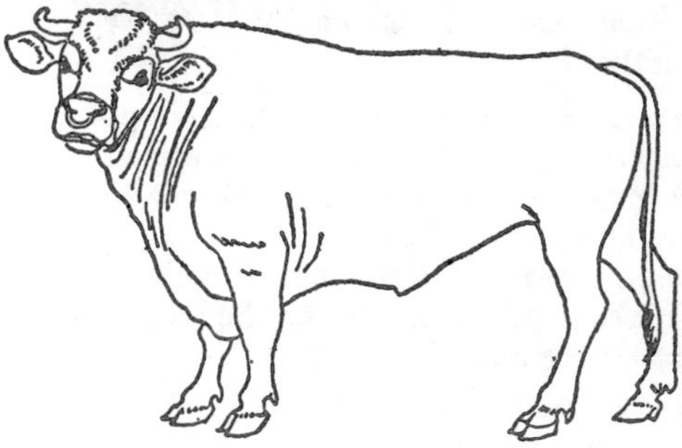

bull·dog (BUHL-dawg) *n. bulldogs.* A strong, short-haired dog with a short face.

bull·doz·er (BUHL-dohz-er) *n. bulldozers.* A caterpillar tractor with a wall-like shield in front. It is used to clear land by moving earth, rocks, rubble, etc. – Two powerful *bulldozers* rapidly cleared the tree stumps from the area.

bul·let (BUHL-ət) *n. bullets.* A piece of lead with a rounded point that is shot from a gun.–The *bullet* from Ed's gun hit the target.

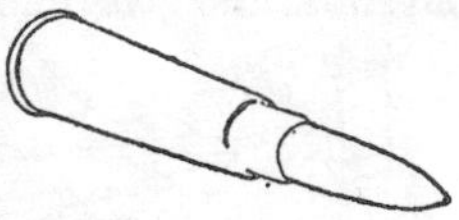

bul·le·tin (BUHL-ə-tən) *n. bulletins.* A notice, announcement, or printed booklet of information.–Newspapers print news *bulletins,* or short articles telling the latest news. –The radio stations sent out news *bulletins* about the hurricane.–Father received a *bulletin* on farming from the Department of Agriculture. It told how to plant seeds.

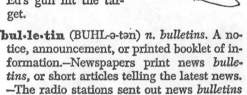

bull•frog (BUHL-frawg) *n. bullfrogs.* The largest of our frogs. The bullfrog is usually a dull green in color and makes a deep croaking noise.

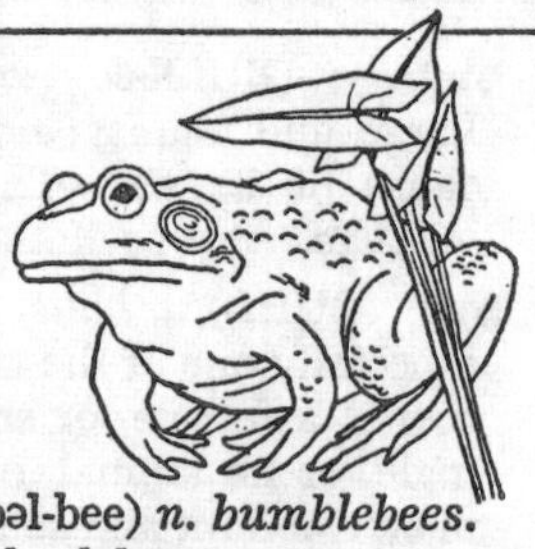

bum•ble•bee (BUM-bəl-bee) *n. bumblebees.* A large kind of bee. Its back has yellow and black stripes across it. *Bumblebees* buzz loudly when they fly.

bump (BUMP) *n. bumps.* **1.** A swollen place. –Baby fell and made a *bump* on her head.
2. A raised place; a hump.–The road was full of *bumps* after the rain.
–*v. bumps, bumped, bumping.* Hit or strike.– Father stopped the car so that he would not *bump* the car ahead.

bump•er (BUMP-er) *n. bumpers.* A heavy bar to protect a vehicle if it bumps into something. – The *bumper* on the front of a car protects it when it bumps against another car.

bun (BUN) *n. buns.* A kind of sweetened roll or biscuit.–When Mother makes bread, she usually makes a pan of *buns* for us.

bunch (BUNCH) *n. bunches.* A number of things held together; a cluster or group.–We took a *bunch* of flowers to our teacher.– Grapes grow in *bunches.*

bun•dle (BUN-dəl) *n. bundles.* A package or bunch bound up together.–Mother gave a *bundle* of newspapers to the Red Cross. They were tied together.
–*v. bundles, bundled, bundling.* Wrap; bind together.–We are going to *bundle* up these old shoes and give them away.

bun•ga•low (BUNG-gə-loh) *n. bungalows.* A small, one-story house.

bunk (BUNGK) *n. bunks.* A plain, narrow bed, usually fixed to a wall or floor.–The twins sleep in *bunks,* one above the other.

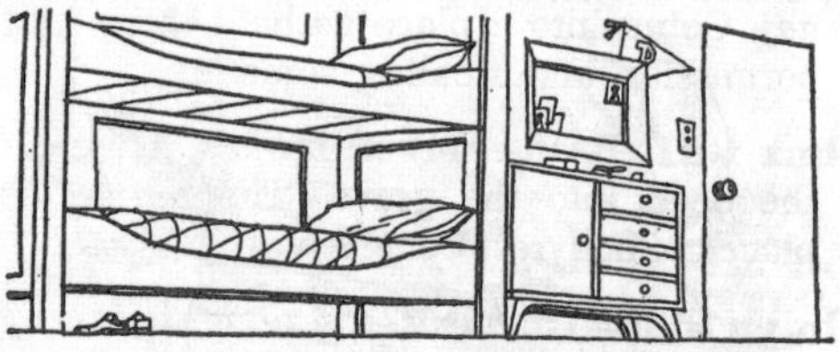

bun•ny (BUN-ee) *n. bunnies.* A pet rabbit.– Jack is fond of his *bunny.*

bun•ting (BUNT-ing) *n. buntings.* **1.** A bird that is much like a sparrow.
2. A cloth used to make flags and banners.

buoy (BOO-ee *or* BOI) *n. buoys.* **1.** A floating marker. – *Buoys* are anchored in the river to guide the ships.
2. A floating object used to keep a person up in the water.–The sailors clung to life *buoys* to keep from sinking.

bur or **burr** (BER) *n. burs* or *burrs.* A thorny part of a plant. Seeds of some plants and trees are held in a case, or cover, that has prickers or thorns all over the outside. This thorny cover is a *bur.*– Some thorny *burs* cling to your clothing if you touch them.

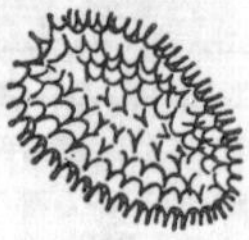

bur•den (BER-dn) *n. burdens.* **1.** A load.– The old man was carrying a heavy *burden* on his back.
2. A task that must be done.–Father bears the *burden* of earning money to support the family.
3. The amount a ship can carry.–The ship's *burden* is 2,500 tons.

bu•reau (BYOOR-oh) *n. bureaus.* **1.** A chest of drawers. – Father keeps his shirts in a *bureau* in the bedroom.
2. A branch or department, as of a government, for managing or studying a particular thing.–Farmers were warned by the Weather *Bureau* that there would be a frost.

bur•glar (BER-gler) *n. burglars.* A person who breaks into a house, store, etc., to steal.

bur•gla•ry (BER-glə-ree) *n. burglaries* and *adj.* Going into a place without the owner's permission and stealing something.

bur•i•al (BAIR-ee-əl) *n. burials.* Laying of the dead into the grave.–The *burial* took place in Shadyrest Cemetery.

burn (BERN) *n. burns.* A sore made by something very hot.–Mother had a small *burn* on her arm from the iron.
–*v. burns, burned* or *burnt, burning.* 1. Be on fire; make flames.–The coal in the furnace is *burning.*
2. Hurt by fire.–Children who play with fire may be *burned.*
3. Be destroyed by fire.–The house *burned* to the ground.
4. Cause to burn; set on fire.–The children *burned* the leaves in the alley.
5. To sting, as if from something hot.–Iodine *burns* when you put it into a cut.

bur•ro (BER-oh) *n. burros.* A small donkey used to carry loads.–The old man piled his belongings on the back of his *burro* and set out for the hills.

bur•row (BER-oh) *n. burrows.* A nest or hole made in the ground by an animal.
–*v. burrows, burrowed, burrowing.* Dig into the ground; dig a hole to live in.–Rabbits, gophers, and moles *burrow.*

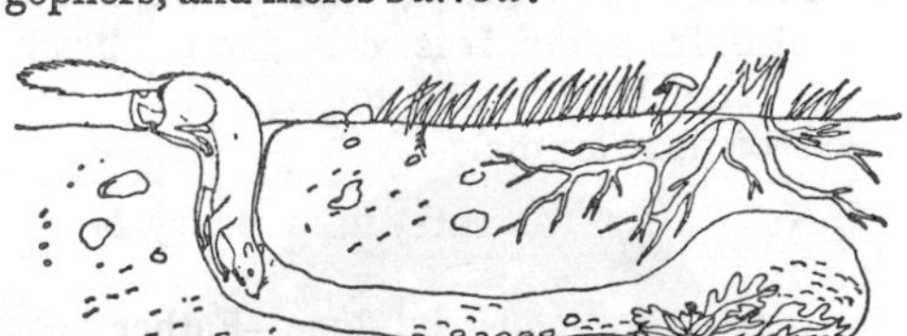

burst (BERST) *v. bursts, burst, bursting.* 1. Break open.–Mary blew so much air into the balloon that it *burst.*
2. Break into many pieces.–The firecrackers *burst* while they were in the air.
3. Rush suddenly.–John *burst* into the room, and told of the fire.

bur•y (BAIR-ee) *v. buries, buried, burying.* 1. Put into the ground and cover up.–Dogs *bury* bones.–When people or animals die, their bodies are usually *buried.*
2. Cover completely. – Jack's baseball mitt was *buried* under his clothes in the trunk.

bus (BUSS) *n. busses* or *buses.* A large vehicle with many seats. Many people traveling from town to town ride on a *bus.* Some *buses* have two decks or floors with seats on each deck.

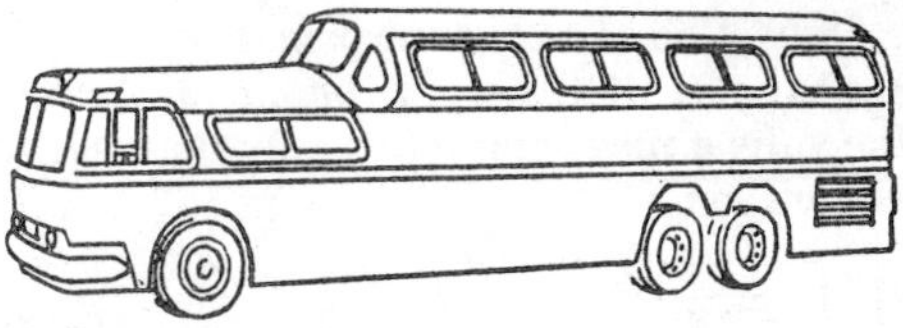

bush (BUHSH) *n. bushes.* A low plant that has many branches or stems near, or coming from, the ground. Shrubs are *bushes.* Roses and berries grow on *bushes.*

bush•el (BUHSH-əl) *n. bushels.* A measure of certain dry things such as grain. We may buy tomatoes and potatoes either by the pound or by the *bushel.* A *bushel* is equal to 32 dry quarts, or 4 pecks.

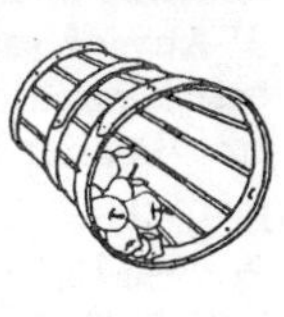

bush•y (BUHSH-ee) *adj.* 1. Thick with fur or hair.–The squirrel has a *bushy* tail.
2. Overgrown with bushes. – The path is *bushy.*

bus•i•ly (BIZ-ə-lee) *adv.* In a busy manner. –Father worked *busily* all day long.

busi•ness (BIZ-nəss) *n. businesses.* 1. The work a man does to earn a living.–Painting houses is a painter's *business.*
2. A group of people organized to earn a living.–Father is in the shoe *business.* The company he works for sells shoes.
3. An amount of buying and selling.–The second-hand automobile dealers do a big *business.* They buy and sell many used automobiles.

bus•tle (BUSS-əl) *v. bustles, bustled, bustling.* Move hurriedly, excitedly, and noisily. –The children *bustle* about doing their work.

bus•y (BIZ-ee) *adj. busier, busiest.* 1. Active; at work.–Mother will be *busy* until her work is done.
2. Alive with activity or work.–The art room is a *busy* place.–Yesterday was a *busy* day.

but (BUT) *adv.*, *conj.*, and *prep.* 1. Except.–All the boys *but* one are here.
2. However; yet.–The boys may play ball now, *but* they must work later.–They are tired *but* happy.
3. Only.–John has *but* one pencil.

butch•er (BUHCH-er) *n. butchers.* A man who runs a meat market or cuts up meat to sell for food.

butte (BYOOT) *n. buttes.* A steep hill standing by itself, apart from other hills or mountains.–The treasure was buried at the foot of the *butte.*

but•ter (BUT-er) *n. butters.* 1. The solid yellow fat that comes from cream when it is churned or beaten.–We eat *butter* on bread.
2. Any of several spreads for bread. *Butter* can be made from apples, peaches, plums, etc.–Peanut *butter* is made from ground-up peanuts.
–*v. butters, buttered, buttering.* Put or spread butter on.–Mother *buttered* Baby's bread.

but•ter•cup (BUT-er-cup) *n. buttercups.* A small, bright yellow flower with large leaves.

but•ter•fly (BUT-er-fly) *n. butterflies.* An insect that has four beautifully colored wings. *Butterflies* fly in the daytime.

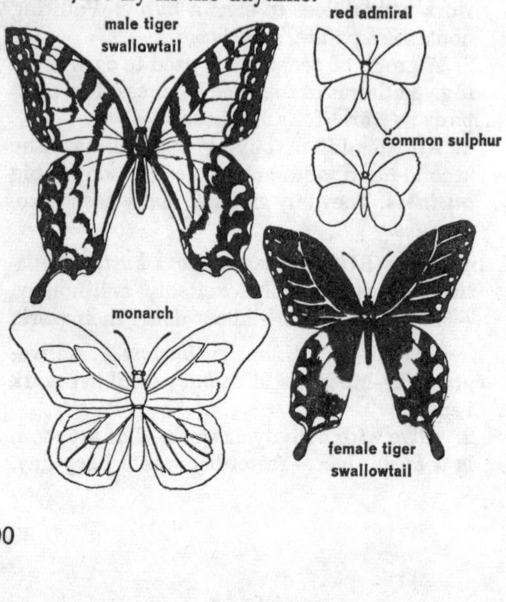

but•ter•milk (BUT-er-milk) *n.* The milk (sometimes sour) that is left when the butterfat is taken out of cream.

but•ton (BUT-n) *n. buttons.* 1. A piece of glass, pearl, brass, etc., used as a fastener or decoration on clothing, cloth covers, etc.–Mother sewed the green *buttons* onto Sally's dress with green thread.

2. A small, round device which is pressed to make something work.–John pressed the *button* and the bell rang.
–*v. buttons, buttoned, buttoning.* Fasten with buttons.–Baby cannot *button* her dress.

but•ton•hole (BUT-n-hohl) *n. buttonholes.* A hole in clothing, etc., through which a button goes.–The *buttonholes* on Father's coat are too small for the buttons to go through.

buy (BY) *v. buys, bought, buying.* Get (anything) by paying money for it.–Father went to the store to *buy* some oranges.

buy•er (BY-er) *n. buyers.* 1. A person who buys things.
2. A person who chooses and buys goods to be sold in a store.–Mrs. Jones is the dress *buyer* for the big store in town.

buzz (BUZ) *n. buzzes.* A humming or murmuring noise.–Before the show started, we could hear the *buzz* of people talking softly.
–*v. buzzes, buzzed, buzzing.* Make a buzz.–Bees and other insects *buzz.*

buz•zard (BUZ-erd) *n. buzzards.* 1. A large bird that lives by eating small animals such as mice, frogs, etc. It is related to the hawk.
2. A large bird related to the vulture that feeds on dead animals.

by (BY) *adv.* and *prep.* 1. Close to; near.–John sits *by* Jack.
2. Through the use of; with; through the effort or activity of.–Four divided *by* two is two.–The window was broken *by* the ball.–We are going to Chicago *by* train.
3. Along.–They traveled *by* this route.
4. Not later than.–We will be there *by* seven o'clock.
5. Past.–In times gone *by*, farmers cut hay with scythes.–We went right *by* the house.

C c

C, c (SEE) *n. C's, c's.* 1. The third letter of the alphabet.
2. Roman numeral meaning 100.

cab (KAB) *n. cabs.* 1. An automobile which is rented or hired with its driver; a taxi*cab*.—Father took a *cab* to work while his car was being repaired.
2. A closed carriage drawn by a horse.—When Grandfather was young, he rode in a *cab*. Now he rides in an automobile.
3. The space in a locomotive or truck where the driver or engineer sits.—The truck driver looked out of his *cab* through the window.

cab•bage (KAB-ij) *n. cabbages.* A vegetable which grows in a head like head lettuce, but has leaves more tightly pressed together. *Cabbage* is white, green, or red. Sauerkraut is made of *cabbage*.

cab•in (KAB-in) *n. cabins.* 1. A small house, especially one built of rough timbers or logs.—Abraham Lincoln was born in a *cabin*.

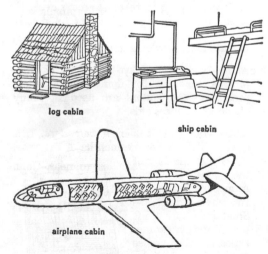

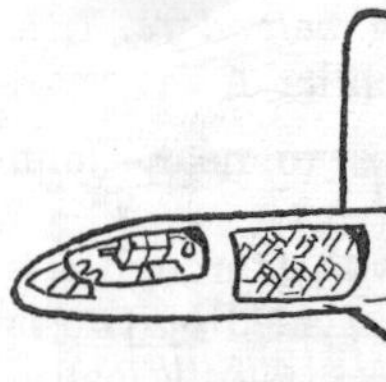

log cabin

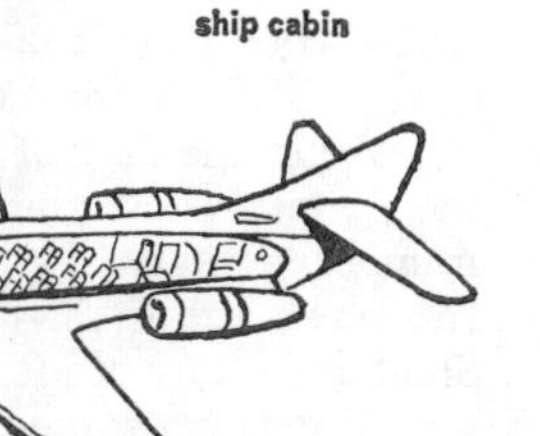

ship cabin

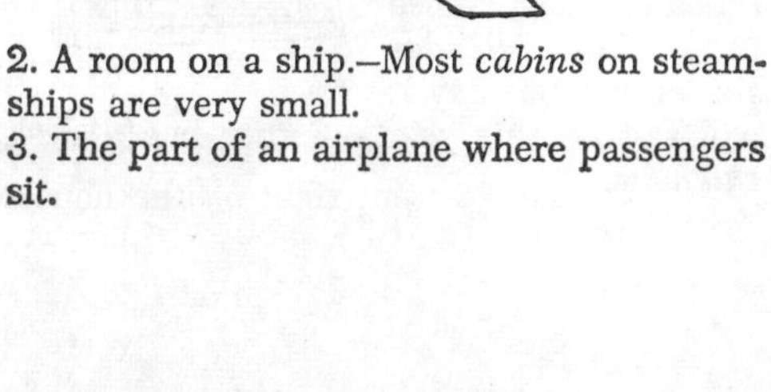

airplane cabin

2. A room on a ship.—Most *cabins* on steamships are very small.
3. The part of an airplane where passengers sit.

cab•i•net (KAB-in-ət) *n. cabinets.* 1. A set of shelves, a chest of drawers, or a case.—We keep medicines in the bathroom *cabinet*.—Father keeps papers in a filing *cabinet*.

2. A group of men chosen to help run the government. – The President appoints the members of his *cabinet* with the consent of the Senate.

ca•ble (KAY-bəl) *n. cables.* 1. A heavy, metal rope or chain. Many wires wound together make a wire rope or *cable*.—The ship was held to the dock with large *cables*.
2. A large, protected bundle of wires laid under the ocean and used to send telegraph messages to foreign countries.

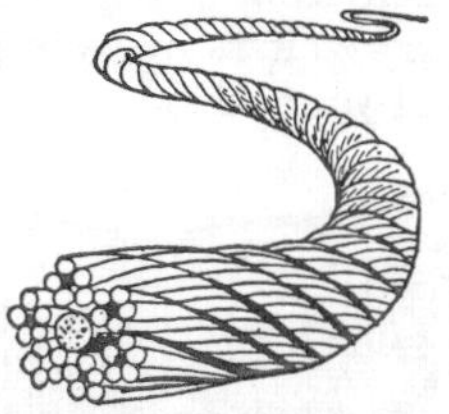

3. A message sent under the ocean by cable; a *cable*gram.
—*v. cables, cabled, cabling.* Send a message by cable.—While in France, Ed *cabled* his father for more money.

ca•ble•gram (KAY-bəl-gram) *n. cablegrams.* A message sent by a cable.—Uncle Frank sent Father a *cablegram* from England.

ca•boose (kə-BOOSS) *n. cabooses.* A small box-shaped car at the end of a freight train. The trainmen sleep and cook in the *caboose*.

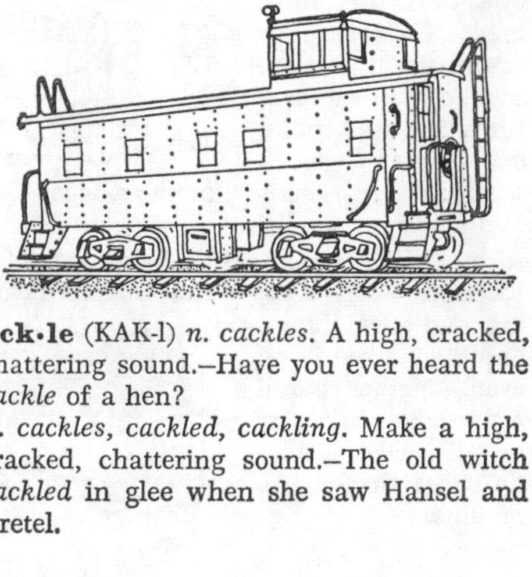

cack•le (KAK-l) *n. cackles.* A high, cracked, chattering sound.—Have you ever heard the *cackle* of a hen?
—*v. cackles, cackled, cackling.* Make a high, cracked, chattering sound.—The old witch *cackled* in glee when she saw Hansel and Gretel.

cac•tus (KAK-təss) *n. cactuses* or *cacti.* A plant that has prickles, or thorns, instead of leaves. The *cactus* needs very little water, and can live in very hot places. Some *cactuses* grow into funny shapes. Many grow in deserts. Some are small enough to grow indoors in flowerpots.

ca•det (kə-DET) *n. cadets.* A student at a military school.

ca•fé (kə-FAY *or* kaf-AY) *n. cafés.* A restaurant.–After the show we stopped at a *café* to get a bite to eat.

caf•e•te•ri•a (kaf-ə-TIR-ee-ə) *n. cafeterias.* A kind of restaurant in which you serve yourself from a long counter of food. There are no waiters or waitresses to take your order at your table.

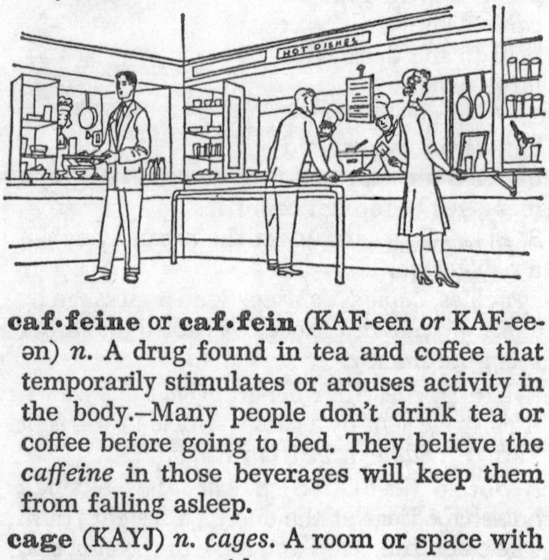

caf•feine or **caf•fein** (KAF-een *or* KAF-ee-ən) *n.* A drug found in tea and coffee that temporarily stimulates or arouses activity in the body.–Many people don't drink tea or coffee before going to bed. They believe the *caffeine* in those beverages will keep them from falling asleep.

cage (KAYJ) *n. cages.* A room or space with one or more sides made of wire or bars. –Animals at the zoo are kept in *cages.*– Birds that are kept indoors live in *cages.*

–*v. cages, caged, caging.* Put into a cage.–The hunters *caged* the lion.

cake (KAYK) *n. cakes.* 1. A food made of a batter of flour, eggs, butter, sugar, flavoring, and other things, and then baked in an oven.–Mother baked a birthday *cake* for me.–Cup*cakes* are little *cakes* shaped like muffins.

2. Anything molded or cut into a small rounded or squared shape.–Meat, salmon, mashed potatoes, and many other foods can be patted or formed into *cakes* and fried like pan*cakes.*–Mother bought three *cakes* of soap.–We saw a big *cake* of ice in the river.
–*v. cakes, caked, caking.* Become hard or solid. –The paint will *cake* on your brushes if they are not cleaned after painting with them.

ca•lam•i•ty (kə-LAM-ə-tee) *n. calamities.* A great misfortune, either personal or public, such as a flood, fire, or the loss of one's savings; a disaster.–The earthquake was a great *calamity.*

cal•ci•um (KAL-see-əm) *n.* A soft metallic substance found in combination with other substances, such as in mineral chalk, limestone, etc. *Calcium* is necessary to the body for sound teeth and bones. *Calcium* is found in many foods, such as in milk, cereals, fish.

cal•cu•late (KAL-kyə-layt) *v. calculates, calculated, calculating.* 1. Figure out by mathematics, such as by adding, subtracting, dividing, or multiplying.–Father *calculates* his monthly expenses by adding up all his bills.

2. Estimate; guess.–The bricklayer *calculated* that he would need 1000 bricks for the wall.
3. Carefully plan or weigh.–Father's decision to sell the house was *calculated* for a long time.
–*calculation, n. calculations.*

cal•cu•la•tor (KAL-kyə-layt-er) *n. calculators.* A machine for doing mathematical problems.–*Calculators* are used in many offices as business aids.

cal•en•dar (KAL-ən-der) *n. calendars.* 1. A chart which shows the months of the year, the weeks, the days of the month, and the number of each day in each month.–Sometimes July 4th is on Monday, sometimes Tuesday, and so forth. The *calendar* shows us what day it will fall on this year.–Father has a desk *calendar.*

2. A list of events, persons, or things, arranged in an orderly way.–Our club's *calendar* showed that no meetings were scheduled for May.

calf (KAF) *n. calves.* 1. The young of a cow. The babies of some other animals, such as the elephant and the moose, are also called *calves.*

2. The thick, muscular part of the back of the leg that is just below the knee.

Cal•i•for•nia (cal-ə-FOR-nyə) *n.* A state on the west coast of the United States, noted for its fine climate and its beauty. Fine fruit groves and truck farms produce several crops each year. Many motion pictures are made in *California.*

call (KAWL) *n. calls.* 1. A cry; a voice.–We heard the robin's *call.*
2. A shout.–We heard a loud *call* for help from the middle of the lake.
3. A visit.–Mary paid us a short *call.*
–*v. calls, called, calling.* 1. Shout; cry out.–Bill *called* me from the window as I passed.
2. Speak someone's name.–My real name is Robert, but my friends *call* me Bob.
3. Send for; ask to come.–We *called* Father to dinner. We asked him to come.
4. Telephone.–I *called* Bill but there was no answer. I'll make another telephone call to him in the morning.
5. Invite; summon; bring together.–The President *called* an emergency session of Congress.
–*Call on* means ask the help of; turn to.–We can always *call on* Father when we are in difficulty.
–*Call on* also means make a visit to.–The minister *calls on* Grandmother.

call•er (KAWL-er) *n. callers.* A visitor.–Mother is cleaning the house because we are expecting a *caller.*

cal•lous (KAL-əss) *adj.; callously, adv.* 1. Having a callus.–Jack had a *callous* area on his thumb.
2. Heartless; without pity.–The *callous* general ordered the mules killed.

cal•lus (KAL-əss) *n. calluses.* A spot on which the skin has become hard and thick.–The farmer had a *callus* on the palm of his right hand where the handle of his hoe had kept rubbing.

calm (KAHM) *n.* Quiet; peacefulness; lack of motion.–A great *calm* settled over the audience as the pianist began his performance.–Grandmother enjoys the *calm* of the country. She dislikes the busyness of the city.
–*v. calms, calmed, calming.* Soothe or pacify; make still.–Father tried to *calm* Baby by giving her his watch to play with.
–*adj. calmer, calmest; calmly, adv.* Undisturbed; unexcited; serene.–Bob is always *calm,* no matter what happens, but Jack gets upset easily.

cal•o•rie or **cal•o•ry** (KAL-oh-ree *or* KAL-ə-ree) *n. calories.* A unit measure of heat, used to measure the amount of heat or energy produced in the body by eating various foods.–On the average, a dish of ice cream contains about 200 *calories;* a dish of oatmeal, about 65.

calves (KAVZ) *n. pl.* Two or more baby cows.–Grandmother's cow had one calf last spring, but twin *calves* this year.

came (KAYM) *v.* One form of the verb *come.*–The children *came* to school at nine o'clock.

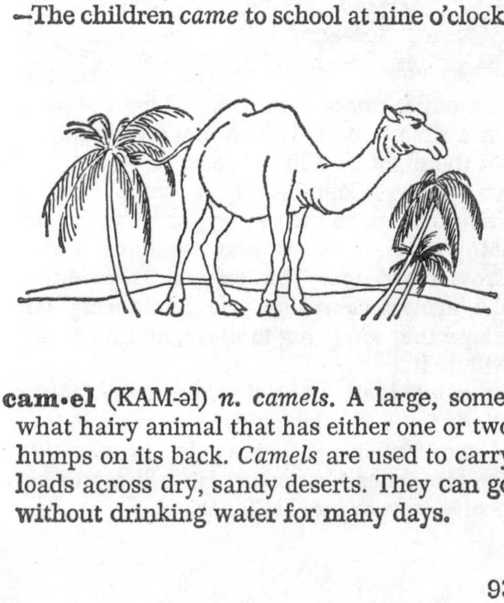

cam•el (KAM-əl) *n. camels.* A large, somewhat hairy animal that has either one or two humps on its back. *Camels* are used to carry loads across dry, sandy deserts. They can go without drinking water for many days.

cam•er•a (KAM-er-ə *or* KAM-rə) *n. cameras.* A machine for taking photographs of things by exposing to light a special film or plate.—When we go on our vacation, we take our *camera* so that we can take pictures.

cam•ou•flage (KAM-ə-flahzh) *n.* Something used to make a thing hard to see or recognize. — The soldier's covering of leaves was a good *camouflage.* It made him look like a part of the woods.

—*v. camouflages, camouflaged, camouflaging.* Change the appearance of a thing so that it will not be seen or recognized easily.—The soldiers *camouflaged* the tops of the buildings by painting them to look like trees.

camp (KAMP) *n. camps.* A place where people live in tents or simple buildings placed close together, in the country.—The boys are going to the Boy Scout *camp.*

—*v. camps, camped, camping.* Live outdoors for a time, especially in a tent.—We *camped* for the night by a little brook.

cam•paign (kam-PAYN) *n. campaigns.* A drive or plan to get money, or to get something done.—Once a year we have a Red Cross *campaign.*—The general is planning the army's *campaign.* He is figuring out where they are going to move, and how they will do it.

—*v. campaigns, campaigned, campaigning.* Work for a special purpose according to a plan or system.—Father is going to *campaign* for Mr. Jones for mayor. He will try to get people to vote for Mr. Jones.

camp•er (KAM-per) *n. campers.* A person who lives for a time outdoors in a tent, rough building, sleeping bag, etc., and lives very simply. One who goes to a camp is also a *camper.*

cam•phor (KAM-fer) *n.* A gum that comes from the *camphor* tree. *Camphor* is used in medicines. It has a strong, sharp odor.—Mother uses balls of *camphor* in closets and drawers to keep moths away.

can (KAN) *v. can, could.* 1. Know how to; have the ability to.—Jack *can* skate.—Sally *can* draw very well for her age.

2. Be able to; have the strength to.—Father *can* push the auto.—*Can* you lift this?

3. Be allowed to; may.—Bill asked Mother if he *could* go to the movies. She told him, "Yes, Bill, you *can.*"

can (KAN) *n. cans; canned, adj.* A container, usually made of tin or other metal.—Vegetables, soups, fruits, and many other foods may be bought in *cans.*—We put garbage in a metal *can.*

—*v. cans, canned, canning.* Put in cans or jars, and seal tightly.—Last year Grandmother *canned* a bushel of tomatoes.

ca•nal (kə-NAL) *n. canals.* A waterway that looks like a river, but has been dug by man. *Canals* are deep enough for boats to sail on them. A *canal* makes it possible for boats to travel from one body of water to another.

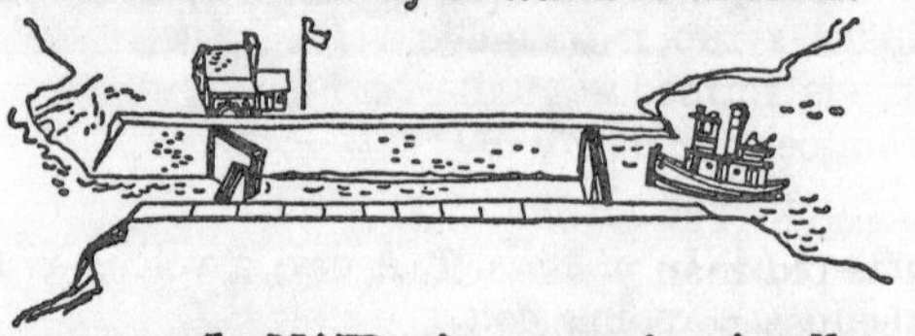

ca•nar•y (kə-NAIR-ee) *n. canaries.* A yellowish songbird. Many people have *canary* birds in wire cages in their homes.

can•cel (KAN-səl) *v. cancels, canceled, canceling.* 1. Withdraw; call off; decide that something that was to happen shall not take place.—Mother ordered a new coat, and then *canceled* the order when she decided to use her old coat instead. She told the store not to send her the coat.—Because of rain, the ball game was *canceled.*

2. Mark out; draw lines through. — When Mary wrote the word wrong, she *canceled* it. She crossed it out.—The post office *cancels* postage stamps on letters. It makes marks through them with a rubber stamp to show that they have been used.

3. Balance; make up for.—Although Bill used to be a bad boy, he is so good now that it *cancels* his earlier behavior.

can·cer (KAN-ser) *n. cancers.* A kind of growing sore on or inside the body. *Cancer* causes many deaths.

can·di·date (KAN-də-dayt) *n. candidates.* A person who is being considered for a certain position; a person who is running for office. —Mr. Jones is a *candidate* for mayor. He is running for mayor.

can·dle (KAN-dl) *n. candles.* A stick of wax with a wick, or string, running through it. When the wick is lighted, it slowly burns up the wax to give light.—We burn *candles* at Christmas time, on birthday cakes, and in church.

can·dle·stick (KAN-dl-stik) *n. candlesticks.* A holder for a candle. We put candles in *candlesticks. Candlesticks* are made of glass, brass, wood, silver, and many other things.

can·dy (KAN-dee) *n. candies; candied, adj.* A sweet food made by boiling down sugar or syrup until it is thick enough to be shaped into pieces. *Candy* is flavored and often covered with chocolate or other coating. Some *candy* is hard and some is soft and chewy. *—v. candies, candied, candying.* To cook in sugar, syrup, marshmallow, etc., until a coating is formed. – Mother *candied* the sweet potatoes for dinner.

cane (KAYN) *n. canes.* 1. A walking stick.—The old man walks with a *cane* to lean on, because he is lame.

2. Rattan, or parts of a palm tree that have been cut into narrow strips. – The chair seat is woven with *cane.*

3. A large, grasslike plant.—Sugar is made from sugar beets and from sugar *cane.*

4. A name often given to the hollow stem of the bamboo, a giant grass plant.

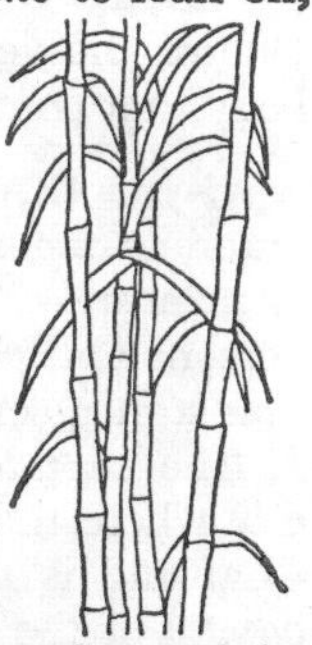

canned (KAND) *v.* and *adj.* One form of the verb *can.*—Mother *canned* many quarts of peaches.

can·ni·bal (KAN-ə-bəl) *n. cannibals.* A person who eats human flesh.—*Cannibals* still may be found in certain parts of the world, such as in the jungles of South America or Africa.

can·non (KAN-ən) *n. cannon* or *cannons.* A big gun. Some *cannons* are mounted on wheels so they can be moved easily.—The soldiers fired the *cannon* at the fort.

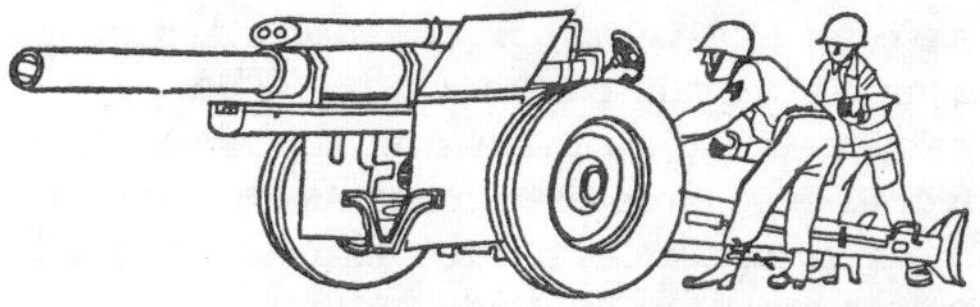

can·not (KAN-naht). Is not able to.—Because of her cold, Mary *cannot* go to school today.

ca·noe (kə-NOO) *n. canoes.* A light, narrow boat that is pointed at both ends. A *canoe* is pushed swiftly through the water by paddles worked by hand.

can·o·py (KAN-ə-pee) *n. canopies; canopied, adj.* 1. A covering either fixed or carried over a throne, holy object, bed, people, etc.—The *canopy* over the king's throne was made of gold.

2. Any overhanging covering or shade, such as over an entrance to a store or building, etc.—Mother bought a carriage with a *canopy* for the baby.

can·ta·loupe or **can·ta·loup** (KAN-tə-lohp) *n. cantaloupes.* A kind of large fruit that grows on a vine which crawls along the ground; the muskmelon. The outer skin of the *cantaloupe* is rough, and the inner part, which we eat, is orange and juicy.

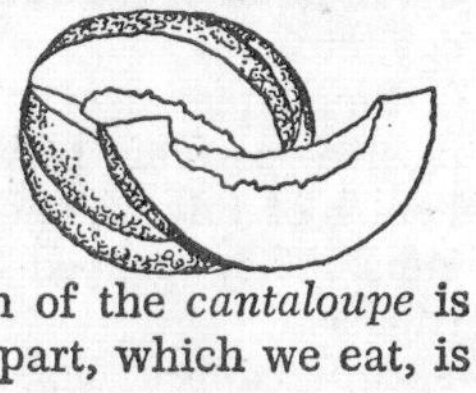

can·teen (kan-TEEN) *n. canteens.* 1. A store at an army camp. – The soldiers buy candy, cigarettes, foods, soft drinks, and other things at the *canteen.*

2. A bottle-shaped metal container.—Soldiers carry *canteens* filled with water.

can•ter (KAN-ter) *v. canters, cantered, cantering.* Move or ride with an easy gallop.—After winning the race, the jockey slowed his horse and *cantered* to the judges' stand.

can•vas (KAN-vəss) *n. canvases.* A strong, coarsely woven cotton cloth.—The paper-hanger spread a *canvas* over the rug to protect it.—The cloth used for tents and sails on boats is *canvas.*—Pictures painted with oil paints are often painted on *canvas.*

can•vass (KAN-vəss) *v. canvasses, canvassed, canvassing.* Go from door to door; inquire, search, or ask everywhere.—Jack's dog is lost. Jack is going to *canvass* the neighborhood for him.—The Girl Scouts *canvassed* the town taking orders for cookies.

can•yon (KAN-yən) *n. canyons.* A deep, narrow valley with very steep sides. Sometimes there is a stream at the bottom of a *canyon.*

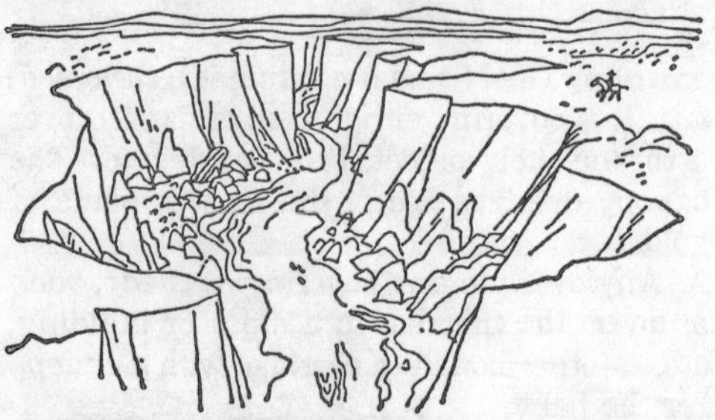

cap (KAP) *n. caps.* 1. A small hat that fits the head closely. Some *caps* have bills, or small brims, in front to shade the eyes.—Soldiers, sailors, nurses, cooks, etc. wear special *caps* made for them.

2. The covering for the top of almost anything, as a bottle *cap,* a *cap* on the radiator of a car, a fruit-jar *cap,* etc.

3. Small pieces of paper with a little explosive powder between them.—On the Fourth of July we had some *caps* for our toy guns. They popped when we pulled the trigger.

—*v. caps, capped, capping.* Put a cap or cover on.—Mother *capped* the fruit jars.

ca•pa•ble (KAY-pə-bəl) *adj.; capably, adv.* Able; knowing enough and having strength enough to do a thing well; qualified; good at doing something.—Jack is *capable* of doing better work than he has done lately.—Mother does not worry about leaving the baby with Mary, because Mary is so *capable.*

ca•pac•i•ty (kə-PASS-ə-tee) *n. capacities.* 1. Amount or number that can be contained or held.—The bottle has a *capacity* of one quart.—The church has a seating *capacity* of eight hundred.

2. Position.—He will go camping with us in the *capacity* of guide.

cape (KAYP) *n. capes.* 1. An outer garment, or cloak, without sleeves. It hangs from the shoulders over the arms and body. Some *capes* are long and some short.

2. A narrow piece of land that extends or stretches out into the sea. A *cape* is surrounded on three sides by the ocean.—We spent the summer on *Cape* Cod.

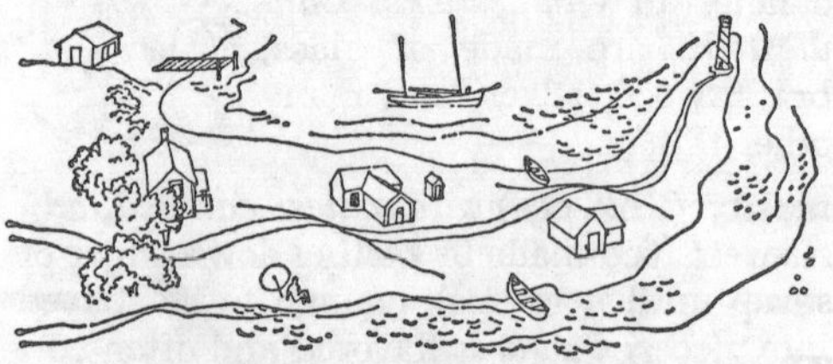

ca•per (KAY-per) *n. capers.* Playful leaping and jumping.—We watched the *capers* of the lambs.

—*v. capers, capered, capering.* Jump and spring about in a lively way.—The horse was *capering* about in the field.

cap•il•lar•y (KAP-ə-lair-ee) *n. capillaries.* One of the very small blood vessels in the body that connect veins and arteries.

cap•i•tal (KAP-ə-tl) *n. capitals.* 1. A large letter, as opposed to a small letter, in writing or printing.—The first letter of the names of persons and places are written in *capitals.*—You start a sentence with a *capital.*

2. The *capital* of a state or country is the city where the government meets regularly.—Lansing is the *capital* of Michigan.—The *capital* of the whole United States is Washington, D.C.

3. Money or property.—Mr. Jones did not have enough *capital* to start the new business, so he borrowed some from a bank.

—*Capital punishment* means a death penalty for certain crimes.—In some states, *capital punishment* is used for people who have killed someone.

cap·i·tal·ism (KAP-ə-tl-iz-əm) *n.* An economic system in which goods and property are for the most part privately owned and controlled. Under *capitalism,* people work for their own profit in competition with others.

cap·i·tol (KAP-ə-tl) *n. capitols.* 1. In the United States, a building where the lawmakers of a state meet. Each state has a *capitol.*
2. (Spelled with a capital "C.") The building in Washington, D.C., where Congress meets, is the *Capitol.*

cap·size (kap-SYZ) *v. capsizes, capsized, capsizing.* Upset; turn over.—The canoe *capsized* in the water when one of the boys stood up.

cap·sule (KAP-syool *or* -səl) *n. capsules.* 1. A small container, usually made of gelatin, for holding medicine so that the medicine may be swallowed without actually being tasted.—The nurse gave her patient two *capsules* with a glass of water.

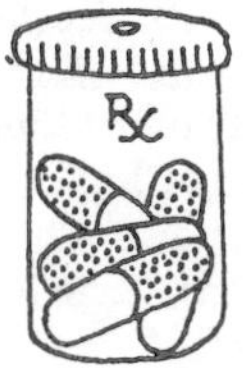

2. Any small case or container.—The chemist filled a glass *capsule* with acid.
3. The seed case of certain plants, such as the poppy or violet.

cap·tain (KAP-tən) *n. captains.* 1. A leader.—The football *captain* was hurt.
2. An army officer ranking next above first lieutenant.
3. A naval officer ranking next above commander.
4. Anyone who commands a ship.—The *captain* of the ship gave the sailors their orders.

cap·ti·vate (KAP-tə-vayt) *v. captivates, captivated, captivating.* Charm; attract and delight; fascinate.—The beautiful music *captivated* the audience.—The speaker has the ability to *captivate* those who hear him.

cap·tive (KAP-tiv) *n. captives.* A prisoner.—The *captives* in the prison camp had to wear chains.

cap·tiv·i·ty (kap-TIV-ə-tee) *n.* Condition of being held prisoner.—Lions in the zoo are in *captivity.*—People in prisons are in *captivity.* They are kept in prison against their wishes.

cap·ture (KAP-cher) *n.* 1. Catching, or being caught.—The *capture* of the wild animals was brought about by the skill and daring of the hunters.—After their *capture,* the animals were sent to a zoo in a far-away city.
2. The thing taken; the prey.—After the hunt, Bill wanted to see Jim's *capture.* He wanted to see what Jim had caught.
—*v. captures, captured, capturing.* Take alive, or seize.—The enemy *captured* fifty of our men. They took fifty prisoners.

car (KAHR) *n. cars.* 1. An automobile.—Mother drove the *car* downtown to meet Father.

2. A carriage, cart, or anything built on wheels for carrying people or goods.—We walked through the *cars* of the train to find a seat.—Baby likes to ride her kiddy *car.*—We stand on the corner to wait for the street*car.*

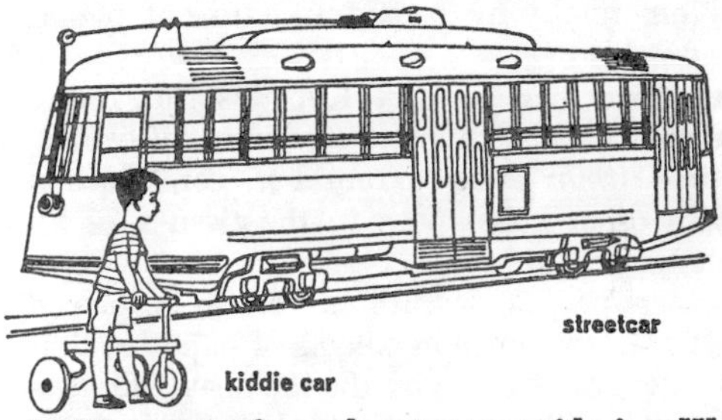

3. The part of an elevator you ride in.—We rode to the fifth floor in the elevator *car.*

car·a·mel (KAR-ə-məl *or* KAHR-məl) *n. caramels.* A gummy or chewy candy made with brown sugar, butter, milk, etc.—Most children like *caramels.*
—*adj.* Flavored with sugar browned by burning it a little.—We made *caramel* pudding.

car·at (KAR-ət) *n. carats.* 1. A unit of weight for determining the value of precious gems, such as diamonds, pearls, rubies, etc.—John gave Mary a large diamond engagement ring. The diamond weighed 2 *carats.*
2. One twenty-fourth part, used in stating the fineness of gold.—Pure gold is 24 *carats.* A 10-carat gold chain has 10 *carats* of pure gold and 14 *carats* of gold alloy.

car•a•van (KAR-ə-van) *n. caravans.* 1. A group of people traveling together through wilderness or desert country.–There were many camels in the *caravan* that set out across the desert.

2. A wagon in which people travel and live. –Gypsies often live in *caravans.*

car•bo•hy•drate (kahr-boh-HY-drayt) *n. carbohydrates.* A chemical substance or compound made up of carbon, hydrogen, and oxygen. *Carbohydrates* are found in sugars, starches, and in all green plants. They are necessary in the diet for the maintenance of good health. *Carbohydrates* are also used commercially in the manufacture of paper, cotton, etc.

car•bon (KAHR-bən) *n.* 1. A substance found in coal, coke, charcoal, petroleum, diamonds, etc. *Carbon* may be found in combination with other substances in the tissues of all plants and animals.
2. A paper, made with carbon, to be placed between two or more sheets of paper so that whatever is written on the top sheet is reproduced on the next sheet; the carbon copy itself.

car•bon di•ox•ide (KAHR-bən dy-AHK-syd). A colorless gas that does not burn. *Carbon dioxide* is used in fire extinguishers and in making carbonated drinks, or soda water. *Carbon dioxide* is formed naturally in the process of breathing. Oxygen and other parts of the air are taken into the lungs. *Carbon dioxide* is given off.

car•bon mon•ox•ide (KAHR-bən mə-NAHK-syd). A poisonous gas without odor or color. It is formed when carbon burns in air that does not contain enough oxygen.–*Carbon monoxide* is present in automobile exhaust fumes. Car engines, therefore, should not be run in closed garages because of the danger of *carbon monoxide* poisoning.

car•bu•ret•or (KAHR-bə-ray-ter *or* KAHR-byə-ray-ter) *n. carburetors.* A piece of equipment, usually part of an automobile engine, which mixes air and gasoline to make the fuel combination more explosive. – Father said he wasn't getting enough power out of his car engine because the *carburetor* was out of order.

card (KAHRD) *n. cards.* A piece of heavy paper or cardboard, blank or printed.–The teacher gave us our report *cards* today.–Uncle Jim sent us a post*card* from New York.–The tickets used for the ball game were little green *cards.* – We play bridge and other card games with a deck or pack of playing *cards.*

card•board (KAHRD-bord) *n. cardboards.* Heavy, stiff paper. – Posters, boxes, book-covers, and many other things may be made of *cardboard.*

car•di•nal (KAHRD-nl) *n. cardinals.* 1. One of the high officials of the Roman Catholic Church.
2. A songbird with red feathers, and with black feathers on the front of the head. – The *cardinal* has several beautiful songs and a whistling call.

–*adj.* 1. Bright red.–Mary has a *cardinal* silk scarf.
2. Of great or prime importance.–One of life's *cardinal* lessons is learning how to get along with others.

care (KAIR) *n. cares.* 1. Anxiety or concern. –After the accident, I had many *cares.* But as soon as I spoke to the doctor, I was no longer worried.
2. Caution; serious attention. – Take *care* that you don't fall. That mountain road is dangerous.–The children did their work with *care.*
3. Protection or custody.–Jim is under a doctor's *care.* He will be looked after until his illness is over.–We didn't know Bill's address, so we sent a letter to him in *care* of his Mother. She knew where he was living, and would forward his mail to him.
–*v. cares, cared, caring.* 1. Be concerned or interested; anxious.–Tom didn't *care* how strong Bill was. He wasn't going to let himself be pushed around.

2. Have love or affection for someone or thing.–Parents *care* deeply for their children.
3. Have an inclination or desire. – I don't *care* to see that movie. I've already seen it once.
–*Care for* means to watch over or look after; deal with.–Grandmother will *care for* the children while Mother is away.–That flower garden is beautiful. It has been well *cared for*.

ca•reer (kə-REER) *n. careers.* A life's work, occupation, or profession. – Peter hopes to make the field of medicine his *career*.

care•ful (KAIR-fuhl) *adj.; carefully, adv.; carefulness, n.* Using thought and effort; paying attention; watchful. – Bob is a *careful* worker.–Mary is *careful* to see that the baby doesn't fall.

care•less (KAIR-ləss) *adj.; carelessly, adv.; carelessness, n.* Not interested; thoughtless; not trying or paying attention.–Bill's poor writing shows that he is *careless*.–Do not be *careless* when crossing the street or you may be hurt.

care•tak•er (KAIR-tayk-er) *n. caretakers.* A person who is hired to look after a building or other property.–The man who cares for the animals at the zoo is a *caretaker*.

car•go (KAHR-goh) *n. cargoes* or *cargos.* A load of anything carried by a ship or plane. –The ship was loaded with a heavy *cargo*.

car•na•tion (kahr-NAY-shən) *n. carnations.* A kind of large, red, white, or pink flower which has a very spicy, pleasing odor.

car•ni•val (KAHR-nə-vəl) *n. carnivals.* 1. A time for merrymaking and being gay.–The school is having a *carnival* next Monday evening.
2. An amusement show, with booths, merry-go-round, ferris wheels, etc.

car•niv•o•rous (kahr-NIV-ə-rəss) *adj.* Flesh-eating, as in the case of animals that live by feeding on other animals.–Lions and tigers are *carnivorous* beasts.

car•ol (KAR-əl) *n. carols.* A song of joy, especially a Christmas hymn.–The choir sings *carols* at Christmas time.
–*v. carols, caroled, caroling.* Sing happily.–Children were *caroling* on the porch.–Birds *carol* in the spring.

car•pen•ter (KAHR-pən-ter) *n. carpenters.* A person who builds things from wood. – Father hired a *carpenter* to lay a new floor.

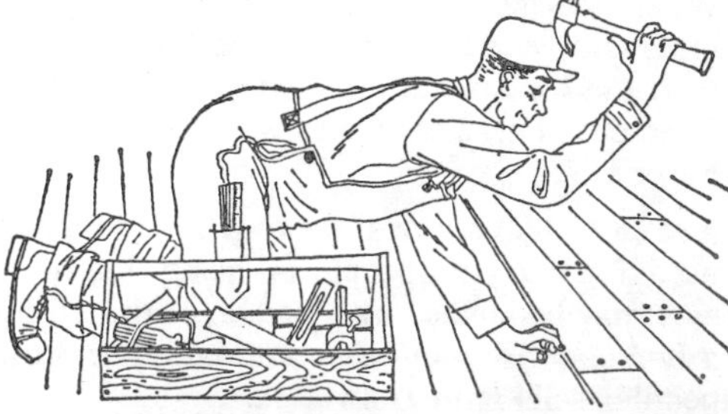

car•pet (KAHR-pət) *n. carpets.* A rug fastened to a floor; any rug.–We put a *carpet* on the living-room floor.
–*v. carpets, carpeted, carpeting.* Cover smoothly, as with a carpet.–The field is *carpeted* with grass and fallen leaves.

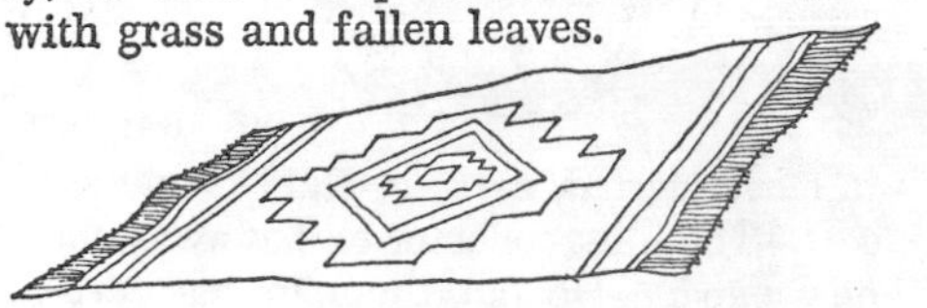

car•riage (KAR-ij) *n. carriages.* 1. A wheeled vehicle drawn by horses and usually used to carry people.–Automobiles have taken the place of *carriages*.

2. Posture; way of holding the body. – The man's *carriage* showed that he was a soldier.

car•rot (KAR-ət) *n. carrots.* A vegetable with an orange root that is good to eat. *Carrots* grow in the ground the way beets do.– Some farmers raise *carrots* to feed to their cattle.

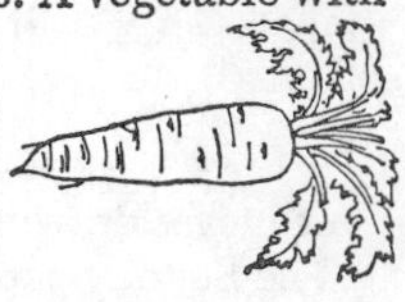

car•ry (KAR-ee) *v. carries, carried, carrying.* 1. Transport; take from place to place.—Streetcars *carry* many passengers each day. They take the passengers from one place to another.—The wind *carries* leaves through the air.
2. Sustain; bear the burden.—Can you *carry* that bag?
3. Pass by vote; uphold successfully.—The suggestion to have a picnic was *carried.*
4. Have for sale; keep on hand.—Department stores *carry* many kinds of goods.
5. Hold or bear. – Jim is very proud. He stands erect, *carrying* his head high.
—*Carry on* means to advance or continue.—When the general was wounded, he asked his men to *carry on* the fight without him.
—*Carry out* means to do what you are told or directed to do.—The general's men *carried out* his orders.

cart (KAHRT) *n. carts.* A two-wheeled wagon used for carrying people or heavy loads. A *cart* may be pushed by a person or drawn by a horse, donkey, or other animal.—The fruit peddler sells fruit from a *cart.*

—*v. carts, carted, carting.* Haul or carry in a cart.—The junk collector *carted* away the old newspapers. He put them in his *cart* and carried them away.

car•ti•lage (KAHR-tə-lij) *n.* The tough, elastic, and flexible tissue which makes up most of the skeleton of young animals; gristle. *Cartilage* is generally white or yellowish in color.

car•ton (KAHR-tn) *n. cartons.* A stiff paper or pasteboard box.—The farmer sells eggs in *cartons.*

car•toon (kahr-TOON) *n. cartoons.* A funny

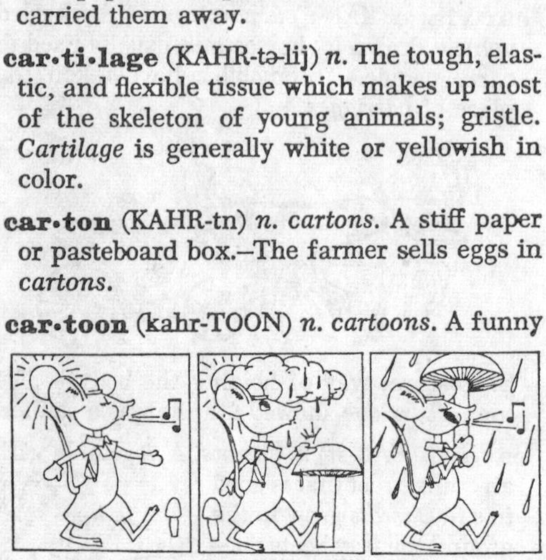

or clever drawing of people or happenings.—The Sunday paper has colored *cartoons* in it.

car•tridge (KAHR-trij) *n. cartridges.* A case or shell that holds an explosive.—*Cartridges* are used in guns.

carve (KAHRV) *v. carves, carved, carving.* 1. Cut into shape.—The statue was *carved* from stone. – Children like to *carve* figures from soap.
2. Cut into pieces.—Mother *carved* the meat in the kitchen.
3. Cut a design on.—John is *carving* his initials on the tree.

carv•er (KAHR-ver) *n. carvers.* A person who cuts or carves things.—The wood *carver* made little figures of people from wood.

case (KAYSS) *n. cases.* 1. A box or carton.—Father bought a *case* of canned tomatoes.
2. A covering or holder.—Jack's new knife came in a leather *case.*
3. A condition or instance.—In *case* of accident, call the police department.—Baby had a slight *case* of the measles.
4. A matter to be settled by law.—The farmer who was cheated took the *case* to court.

cash (KASH) *n.* Money; money on hand.—Bob didn't have enough *cash* to pay for the bicycle. He had enough money in his bank account but not enough with him.
—*v. cashes, cashed, cashing.* Exchange for money.—The workman took his check to the bank to have it *cashed.*

cash•ier (kash-IR) *n. cashiers.* A person who handles or is responsible for handling money, or cash.—A *cashier* at the bank takes care of the money.—A *cashier* in a store handles the money, makes change, etc., when something is bought.

cas•ing (KAYSS-ing) *n. casings.* A frame.—The window *casing* needs to be painted.

cask (KASK) *n. casks.* A barrel.—The grocer bought a *cask* of vinegar.

cas•ket (KASS-kət) *n. caskets.* 1. A coffin or large box in which a person is buried.
2. A small box for jewelry.—The children gave their teacher a silver *casket.*

cas•se•role (KASS-ə-rohl) *n. casseroles.* A covered dish in which food can be baked and from which food can be served at the table.—In restaurants chicken pie is often served to each person in a small *casserole.*

cast (KAST) *n.* 1. Actors in a play or motion picture. – The *cast* for the school play has been chosen.
2. A hard plaster dressing that is set around a part of the body to help broken bones heal. –When Bill broke his leg, the doctor put a plaster *cast* on it.
3. A throw.–The fisherman's *cast* was perfect. He had thrown the line just where he had aimed.
4. Anything that has been formed in a mold.
–*v. casts, cast, casting.* 1. Throw.–The fisherman *cast* the fish hook and bait into the water.
2. Form into a shape.–Many parts of an automobile are *cast* from metal. The metal is melted, poured into molds of different shapes, and allowed to harden.
3. Assign actors to play the parts in a play. –Bob's sister, Mary, was *cast* as the heroine in the school play.
4. To *cast* a vote or ballot means to vote.– Father *cast* his vote for Mr. Jones for mayor.

cas•ta•nets (kass-tə-NETSS) *n. pl.* Wooden or ivory clappers held in the hands and clapped together to the rhythm of music. – The dancer kept time with *castanets.*

cast•er (KASS-ter) *n. casters.* 1. A small roller or wheel on the leg of a table, bed, etc. – The *casters* on the table legs allow the table to be moved easily.

2. A holder for salt and pepper shakers, vinegar bottles, etc.– Grandmother has a silver *caster* on her dining-room table.

cas•tle(KASS-əl) *n. castles.* 1. A large building of olden times, used as a fort and dwelling place. *Castles* had towers, high walls, and moats or waterways about them to hold off enemies.

2. A very large and grand house. – Princes and noblemen live in *castles.*

cas•tor oil (KASS-ter oil). An oil made from the seeds of the castor-oil plant. *Castor oil* is taken as medicine to bring about a movement of the bowels.

cas•u•al (KAZH-yoo-əl) *adj.; casually, adv.* 1. Without plan; happening by accident or chance.–John's visit was *casual.* He dropped in while passing through town.
2. Unconcerned; easy in appearance.–The man had an unworried, *casual* air about him.

cas•u•al•ty (KAZH-yoo-əl-tee *or* KAZH-əl tee) *n. casualties.* 1. An accident.–The explosion was a serious *casualty.*
2. In war, a soldier killed, wounded, or taken ill. – There are often more *casualties* from disease than from battle.

cat (KAT) *n. cats.* 1. A small, furred animal kept as a pet. – *Cats* are tame. They catch mice and rats.

2. Any of the family of animals including pet *cats* and wild *cats,* such as the lion, tiger, and leopard.

cat•a•log or **cat•a•logue** (KAT-ə-lawg) *n. catalogs* or *catalogues.* 1. A book that describes and pictures things and tells how much they cost.
2. An orderly list.–The teacher made a *catalog* of the names of all the boys and girls in the school.
–*v. catalogs, cataloged, cataloging.* Make an orderly list of. – The librarian *catalogs* the books in the library.

ca•tal•pa (kə-TAL-pə) *n. catalpas.* A kind of short tree with large heart-shaped leaves, white, bell-shaped flowers, and long seed pods that turn brown when ripe.

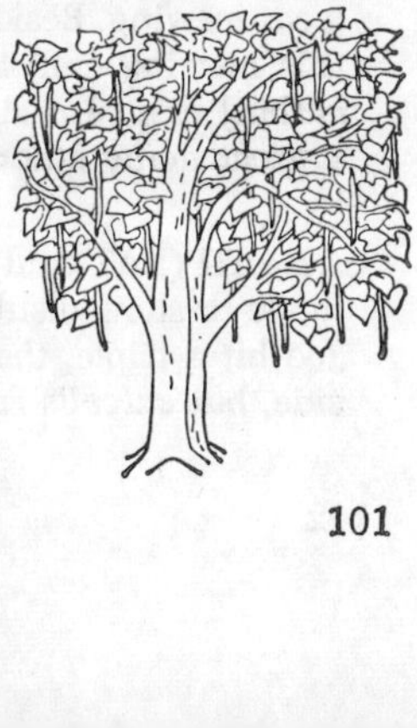

CATAPULTS

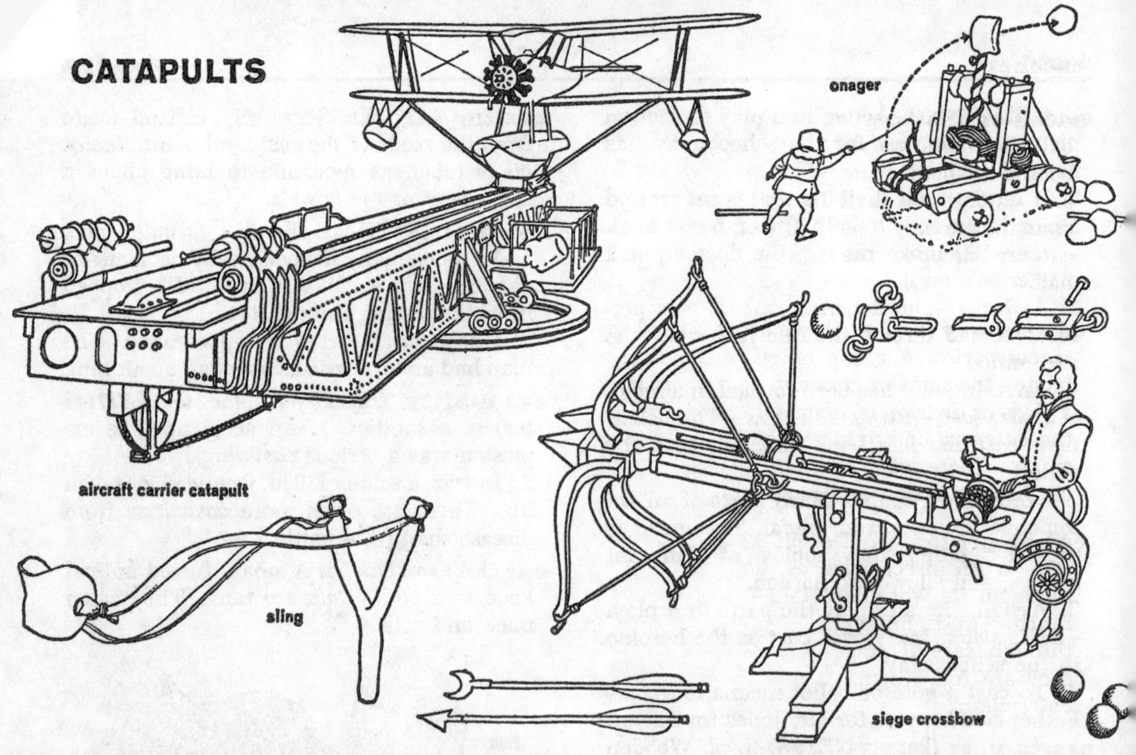

cat·a·pult (KAT-ə-puhlt) *n. catapults.* 1. A weapon used in ancient times for hurling rocks, spears, arrows, etc., against an enemy. 2. A modern machine for hurling aircraft into the air from the deck of a ship. – The *catapults* launched the planes one after another from the deck of the aircraft carrier. 3. A slingshot.–Sam made a *catapult* with a rubber band and a forked stick.
–*v. catapults, catapulted, catapulting.* Throw from a catapult, or as if from a catapult; hurl.–John was *catapulted* from his bicycle when the front tire hit a rock.

ca·tas·tro·phe (kə-TASS-trə-fee) *n. catastrophes.* A great disaster, misfortune, or calamity. – The Chicago Fire of 1871 was a giant *catastrophe.* Over 17,000 buildings were destroyed in the blaze.

cat·bird (KAT-berd) *n. catbirds.* A gray bird whose call sounds like a cat mewing. Besides this mewing call, the *catbird* can also sing a great many other beautiful songs.

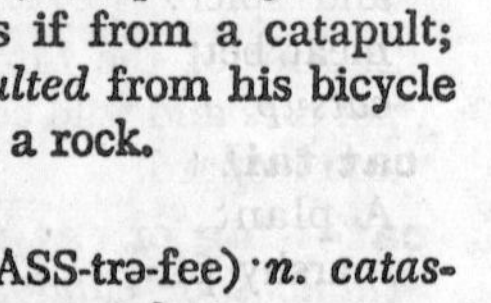

cat·call (KAT-cahl) *n. catcalls.* A loud noise made to show dislike or disapproval.–When Joe hit a triple, there were cheers from our side, but *catcalls* from our opponents.

catch (KACH) *n. catches.* 1. The act of taking hold, seizing, or grabbing.–Mother threw the ball into the baby's hands. "Good *catch*," she said.
2. A game in which a ball is thrown from person to person.–"Does anyone want to play *catch*?" asked Bill.
3. Something captured or taken.–The fisherman came home with a good *catch.*
4. A fastener.–The *catch* on the screen holds it in place.
–*v. catches, caught, catching.* 1. Get or take and hold on to; seize and hold.–I saw the ball player *catch* the ball. He got it while it was still in the air.–Fishermen *catch* fish.–Traps are used to *catch* some animals.
2. Come up to.–John started to run, and Bob could not *catch* him.
3. Discover; find out; surprise.–Just as Mary was getting a cooky from the jar, Mother *caught* her.
4. Get; receive.–Bob was careful not to *catch* a cold.
5. Become tangled with. – The dog's leash *caught* on a bush.
–*Catch fire* means to start burning.–Do not play with fire. Your clothes may *catch fire.*
–*Catch up with* means to get to the same place as.–Mary worked so many problems at home that it was hard for the class to *catch up with* her.–We started to the park first, and the others could not *catch up with* us.

catch·er (KACH-er) *n. catchers.* The baseball player who stands behind the home plate and catches the ball from the pitcher.—The *catcher* dropped the ball.

cat·e·go·ry (KAT-ə-goh-ree *or* KAT-ə-gor-ee) *n. categories.* A group of people or things having the same or common characteristics; a class or division of items.—John belongs in the *category* of bright students. He is very smart.—There were two *categories* of books on display, fiction and biography.

cat·er·pil·lar (KAT-er-pil-er) *n. caterpillars.* 1. An insect, such as the moth, in its wormlike stage.—Moths and butterflies go through several stages before they are full grown. At one stage they are *caterpillars.*

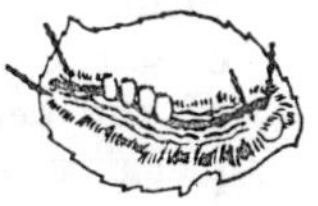

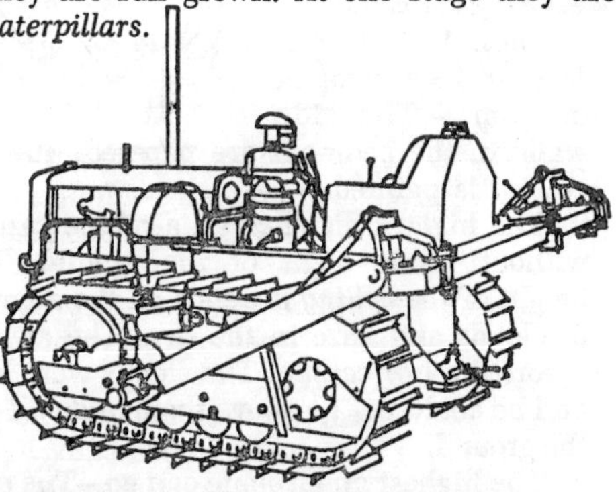

2. (Spelled with a capital "C.") The trade name of a tractor that runs on two flat metal belts.—Heavy loads can be pulled over rough ground by *Caterpillars.*

cat·fish (KAT-fish) *n.* A fish that has a flat head with long feelers that look like a cat's whiskers.

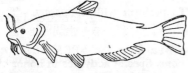

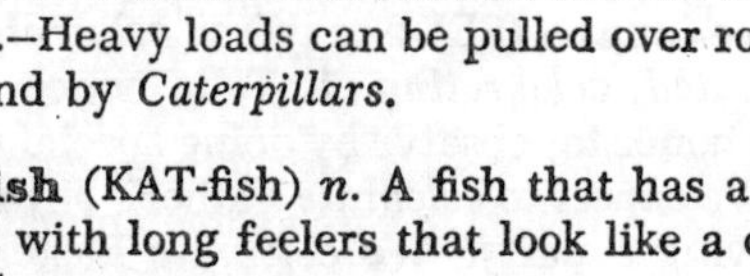

cat·gut (KAT-gut) *n.* and *adj.* A strong string made from the dried intestines of certain animals. The strings of violins and other stringed instruments are made of *catgut.*

ca·thar·tic (kə-THAHR-tik) *n. cathartics* and *adj.* Something which cleans out the intestinal tract; a strong medicine that makes the bowels move.

ca·the·dral (kə-THEE-drəl) *n. cathedrals.* The main church in a certain district.—A bishop has charge of a *cathedral.*

Cath·o·lic (KATH-ə-lik) *n. Catholics* and *adj.* 1. A person who belongs to the *Catholic* Church.

2. The *Catholic* Church, sometimes called the Roman *Catholic* Church, is a religious group led by the Pope in Rome.

cat·kin (KAT-kin) *n. catkins.* The fluffy flower of the willow and birch trees.

catkin

cat·nip (KAT-nip) *n.* A plant something like mint. Cats are fond of *catnip.* It has a pleasing odor.

cat·sup or **catch·up** or **ketch·up** (KAT-səp *or* KACH- *or* KECH-əp). A sauce made from tomatoes, vinegar, onions, and spices.—Some people like meat better if it is eaten with *catsup.*

cat·tail (KAT-tayl) *n. cattails.* A plant that grows in wet, marshy places. The leaves are long and narrow. The flower is a long, furry, brown spike that stands on a long, stiff stem.

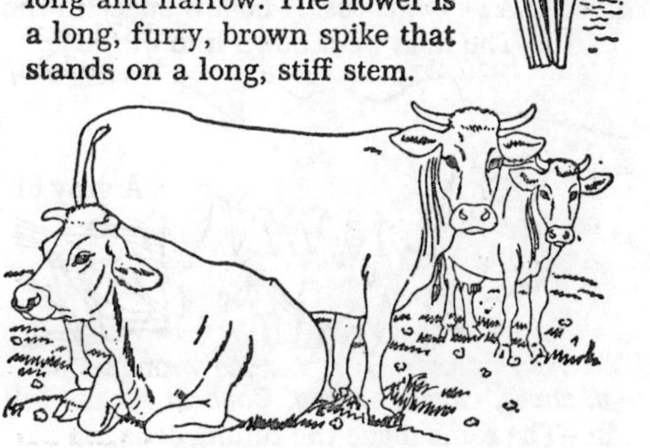

cat·tle (KAT-l) *n.* Cows, bulls, and steers.—Some farmers raise grain, and others raise *cattle.*

caught (KAWT) *v.* One form of the verb *catch.*–Bob caught the apple as it fell from the tree.

cau•li•flow•er (KAW-lə-flow-er) *n. cauliflowers.* A cabbagelike vegetable that is good to eat. It grows in a head made up of solid white flowers with leaves around them.

cause (KAWZ) *n. causes.* 1.That which makes something happen.–Sickness was the *cause* of Mary's absence from school.

2. A thing which people believe in.–Soldiers fight for the *cause* of freedom.

–*v. causes, caused, causing.* Bring about; make happen.–A lighted match thrown into the grass *caused* the fire.–Wind *causes* the iceboat to go.

cau•tion (KAW-shən) *n. cautions.* Care; watchfulness.–Cross the street with *caution.* Take no chances.

–*v. cautions, cautioned, cautioning.* Warn.–The policeman *cautioned* the driver to stay in line.

cau•tious (KAW-shəss) *adj.; cautiously, adv.* Careful.–Children are very *cautious* in crossing the streets.

cav•al•ry (KAV-əl-ree) *n. cavalries.* Soldiers who ride horses.–The *cavalry* led the parade.

cave (KAYV) *n. caves.* A hollow space in the earth.–The men went down into the *cave.*

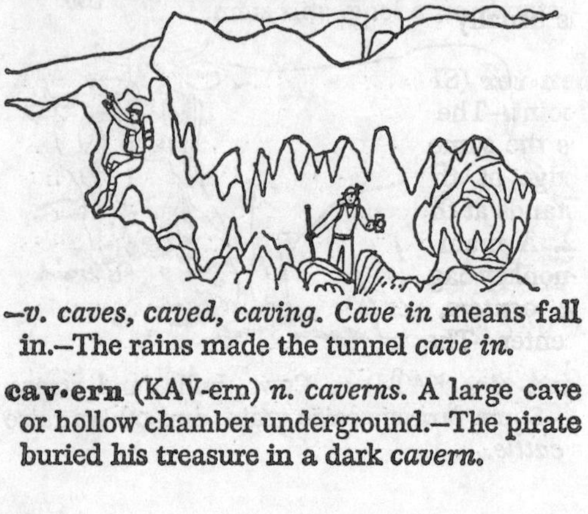

–*v. caves, caved, caving. Cave in* means fall in.–The rains made the tunnel *cave in.*

cav•ern (KAV-ern) *n. caverns.* A large cave or hollow chamber underground.–The pirate buried his treasure in a dark *cavern.*

cav•i•ty (KAV-ə-tee) *n. cavities.* A hole or hollow space.–The dentist filled a *cavity* in Mother's tooth.

caw (KAW) *n. caws.* The cry of a crow.

–*v. caws, cawed, cawing.* Make the cry of a crow.–Crows *caw.*

cease (SEESS) *v. ceases, ceased, ceasing.* Stop; quit.–Father told John to *cease* shouting.–We shall go when the rain *ceases.*

ce•dar (SEE-der) *n. cedars.* A tree with flat, weblike leaves that stay green all winter. The red wood of the *cedar* is used to make furniture, for lining closets, etc. The wood of the *cedar* has a pleasing odor.

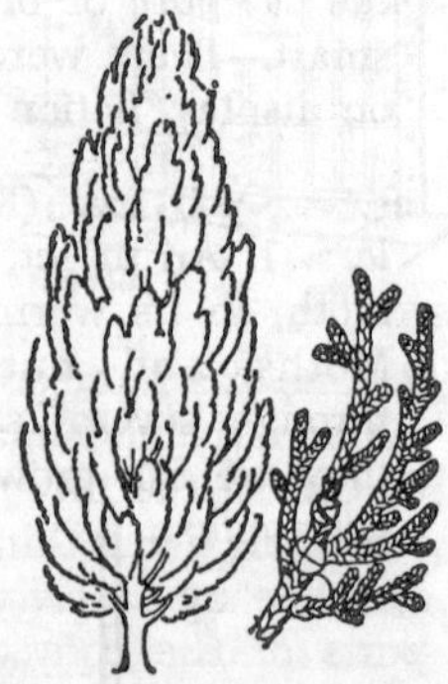

ceil•ing (SEE-ling) *n. ceilings.* 1. The overhead surface or top of a room. – The side walls in the bedroom are papered, but the *ceiling* is painted.

2. The highest distance an airplane can go without losing sight of the ground. The height of the *ceiling* depends on the amount of clouds and haze in the sky.–The aviator reported a low *ceiling.* The clouds were low, and he could not go above them and still see the ground.

3. The highest an airplane can go.–The *ceiling* of this plane is 30,000 feet.

cel•e•brate (SEL-ə-brayt) *v. celebrates, celebrated, celebrating.* 1. Take notice of and do honor to; observe by doing special things. –We expect to *celebrate* Father's birthday by having a party.–We *celebrate* Easter every year.

2. To perform with ceremony. – The marriage was *celebrated* in church.

cel•e•bra•tion (sel-ə-BRAY-shən) *n. celebrations.* Special activities in honor of some event or holiday.–We went to the *celebration* honoring the men who built the new bridge.

ce•leb•ri•ty (sə-LEB-rə-tee) *n. celebrities.* 1. A well-known, famous, or recognized person. –Tom is a school *celebrity.* He is well-known by all the students.

2. Fame; being well-known and recognized. –Tom's *celebrity* is due to the fact that he is the best athlete in school.

cel•er•y (SEL-ə-ree) *n.* A vegetable that grows in stalks which are cut apart and eaten raw, often in salads. It can be cooked or used in soups, also.

cell (SELL) *n. cells.* 1. A small room in a jail.—The robber was put into a *cell.*

jail cell

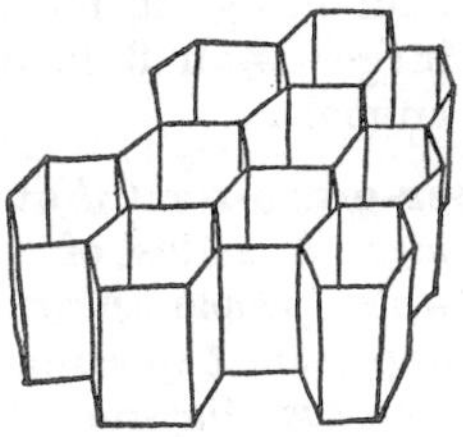

honeycomb cell

2. One of a number of small spaces or parts. —A honeycomb is made up of small *cells.*
3. One of the tiny parts of living matter of which all living things are made. Your body is made up of *cells.* The *cells* in different parts of the body are somewhat different from one another.

cel•lar (SEL-er) *n. cellars.* The space under a building, below the ground.—The furnace of our house is in the *cellar.*

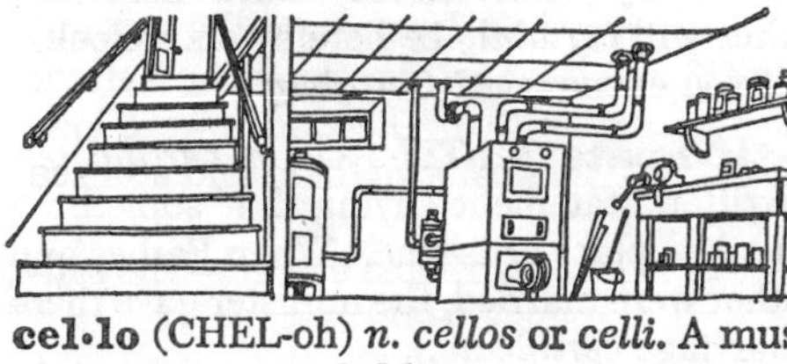

cel•lo (CHEL-oh) *n. cellos* or *celli.* A musical instrument much like the violin, but larger and deeper in tone. It is stood on the floor between the knees to be played. It has four strings.—Bill is learning to play the *cello.*

Cel•lo•phane (SEL-ə-fayn) *n.* A material made from the woody parts of plants and trees. It is waterproof, and one can see through it. It is used for wrapping foods and for many other things. *Cellophane* is usually spelled with a capital C because the word is a trade mark.

cel•lu•lose (SEL-yə-lohss) *n.* The main ingredient in the cell walls of plants and in the wood of trees.—*Cellulose* is widely used to make cotton, rayon, paper, medicine, and many other things.

ce•ment (sə-MENT) *n. cements.* 1. A powder made by burning clay with a kind of rock known as limestone. *Cement,* when mixed with water and sand, dries hard. It is used in making sidewalks, roads, floors, etc., and for holding bricks and stones together in walls and buildings.
2. Any material, such as glue, that holds things together.—Mother used a china *cement* to mend the broken vase.
—*v. cements, cemented, cementing.* Stick.—She *cemented* the pieces together.

cem•e•ter•y (SEM-ə-tair-ee) *n. cemeteries.* A graveyard, or place where the dead are buried.—The soldier was buried in Mount Hope *Cemetery.*

cen•sor (SEN-ser) *n. censors.* A person who examines movies, books, etc. to make sure that they don't say anything they shouldn't. He is usually an official of the government or of some organization.—In wartime *censors* read the soldiers' letters to make sure they haven't given away any secrets.
—*v. censors, censored, censoring.* Examine to make sure that nothing thought objectionable is said; cut out bad parts or stop distribution of.—Some people want to *censor* comic books. They want to take out the stories about crime.

cen•sus (SEN-səss) *n. censuses.* A count of the people living in a certain place. The *census* tells how many people there are, how old they are, etc.

cent (SENT) *n. cents.* A small piece of money used in Canada and the United States; a penny. A *cent* is made of copper, tin, and zinc. Five *cents* make a nickel. Ten *cents* make a dime. One hundred *cents* make a dollar. One *cent* is usually written 1¢.

cen•ter (SEN-ter) *n. centers.* 1. The middle point.—The *center* of a circle is the point that is the same distance from all points on the edge of the circle. — The baseball pitcher stands at the *center* of the baseball diamond.
2. A main point or place.—At the zoo, the monkey cage is usually the *center* of interest.
—*v. centers, centered, centering.* Put in the center.—The teacher told us to *center* our drawings on the page. She wanted us to leave an equal amount of space on all sides of our drawings.

cen•ti•grade (SEN-tə-grayd) *adj.* Having 100 degrees, or parts.—The *centigrade* thermometer measures temperature on a scale based on 100°. The freezing point of water is at 0° C., and the boiling point is at 100°.

cen•ti•pede (SEN-tə-peed) *n. centipedes.* A bug with a body made up of many sections or joints. At each joint is a pair of legs. *Centipedes* can run very fast. The name *centipede* means "hundred feet," but it does not really have that many.

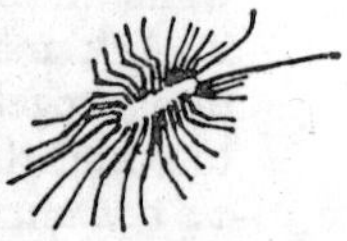

cen•tral (SEN-trəl) *adj.; centrally, adv.* 1. Middle.—The city hall is in the *central* part of town. It is not on the edge.
2. Leading; chief.—The cowboys were the *central* interest at the circus.

cen•tu•ry (SEN-chə-ree) *n. centuries.* One hundred years.—Few people live a *century.*—From 1850 to 1950 is one *century.*

ce•ram•ics (sə-RAM-iks) *n. pl.; ceramic, adj.* 1. The art of making things such as bowls, pottery, etc., out of baked clay or earth.—Susan is studying *ceramics* as a hobby.
2. The objects so made.—The museum plans an exhibition of ancient *ceramics.*

ce•re•al (SEER-ee-əl) *n. cereals.* 1. Food such as rice, oatmeal, ground wheat, corn, and other things made from grain.—For breakfast many people eat some kind of *cereal.*
2. Any of the grasses that produce the grain from which cereals are made.

cer•e•bel•lum (sair-ə- *or* sair-ee-BEL-əm) *n.* The part of the brain that controls both the functioning of the body's muscles and the body's equilibrium, or balance. The *cerebellum* in human beings is located at the rear of the brain.

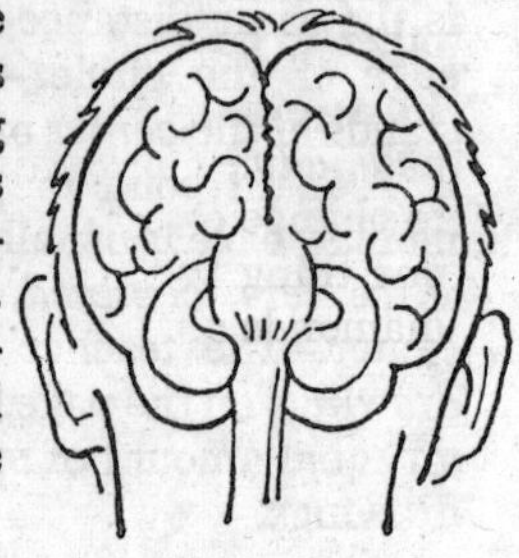

cer•e•brum (SAIR-ə-brəm *or* sə-REE brəm) *n.* The upper front part of the brain; the part in which thinking takes place. The *cerebrum* is divided into two sections called "hemispheres." The *cerebrum* in human beings is much larger than it is in animals.

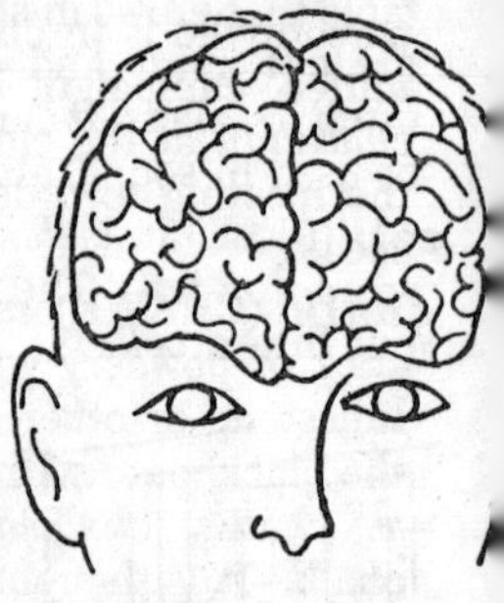

cer•e•mo•ny (SAIR-ə-moh-nee) *n. ceremonies.* A series of solemn, formal actions which people perform in a regular way at an important happening. There are church *ceremonies,* flag-raising *ceremonies,* wedding *ceremonies,* patriotic *ceremonies,* etc.

cer•tain (SER-tən) *adj.* 1. Positive; sure; knowing without any doubt.—Bob was not *certain* he could go until he asked Father.—I am *certain* the sky is blue.—The weather report said that rain was *certain.*
2. Some; special; particular. – *Certain* fish live in salt water and *certain* others live in fresh water.—There is a *certain* book I want, but I can't find it.

cer•tain•ly (SER-tən-lee) *adv.* Surely. – Father will *certainly* be here by six o'clock.—Will you excuse me? *Certainly.*

cer•tif•i•cate (ser-TIF-ə-kət) *n. certificates.* A written statement saying that something has taken place or is true.—When Father and Mother were married, the minister gave them a marriage *certificate.*

chain (CHAYN) *n. chains.* 1. A number of links or rings fastened together. – Father's watch *chain* is made of gold.—Children like to make *chains* of daisies and dandelions.
2. An unbroken line of things. – Several mountains joined together are called a mountain *chain.*
—*v. chains, chained, chaining.* Fasten with a chain.—Jack *chained* his dog to a stake so he could not run away.

chair (CHAIR) *n. chairs.* A seat with legs and a back. We sit in a *chair.* Some *chairs* have rockers and are called rocking *chairs.* A *chair* with arms is an arm*chair.*

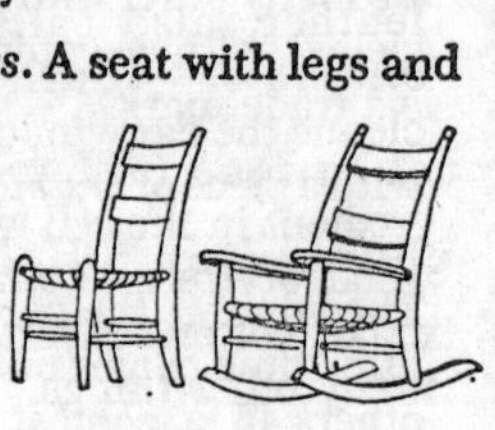

chair•man (CHAIR-mən) *n. chairmen.* A person who is in charge of a meeting, committee, campaign, etc. – Jack will be the *chairman* at the class meeting. He will call the meeting to order and call on people to speak.

chalk (CHAWK) *n. chalks; chalky, adj.* A stick of powdery white material made from limestone or other soft stone.–We write on the blackboard with *chalk.*

–*v. chalks, chalked, chalking.* Mark with chalk.–It is thoughtless to *chalk* up people's sidewalks.

chal•lenge (CHAL-ənj) *n. challenges.* A dare.–Tom accepted the *challenge.*

–*v. challenges, challenged, challenging.* Dare; invite to enter a contest, etc.–The small boy *challenged* the big boy to a fight.

cham•ber (CHAYM-ber) *n. chambers.* 1. A bedroom; a private room.–Sleeping Beauty was found in a *chamber* at the top of the palace.

2. *Chambers* means an apartment or group of rooms in which people live or work.

3. A room or auditorium where a body of lawmakers meets; or the body of lawmakers itself.–The Senate is the upper *chamber* of Congress.

4. A committee or department, as a *chamber* of commerce.

5. The part of a gun that holds the bullets or powder.

cha•me•le•on (kə-MEE-lee-ən *or* kə-MEEL-yən) *n. chameleons.* 1. A lizard that can change its color. When a *chameleon* is on the grass, he is green. When a *chameleon* is on the ground, he is brown.

2. A person who is always changing his mind.–Jack is a *chameleon* about desserts. He never chooses the same one twice.

cham•ois (SHAM-ee) *n. sing.* and *pl.* A kind of antelope that is something like a goat. The skin of a *chamois* is made into a soft leather, also called *chamois.* – Father cleans the car window with a piece of *chamois.*

cham•pi•on (CHAMP-ee-ən) *n. champions.* The winner; the person or group which time after time comes out first, or ahead of all the others in a contest of any kind.–The New York Yankees have been world *champions* in baseball many times.

chance (CHANSS) *n. chances.* 1. Luck; an accident, or an unexpected happening.–Our team won by *chance.* It wasn't really better than the other team.–Mary met her teacher by *chance.* The meeting was not planned.

2. An opportunity.–Jack has a *chance* to pass the test if he studies at home.–Grandfather did not have the *chance* to get an education when he was young.

3. Possibility.–There is a *chance* that it may rain.

4. Risk.–You are taking *chances* if you cross a street without looking both ways first.

–*v. chances, chanced, chancing.* Happen without plan.–We *chanced* to hear the radio program. We happened to turn on the radio just when the program was on.

chan•de•lier (shan-də-LEER) *n. chandeliers.* A hanging light fixture with several sockets for bulbs or candles.–The *chandelier* hangs from the ceiling over the table. It has several bulbs fastened to it.

change (CHAYNJ) *n.* 1. Money due in return because more has been given than the price of what was bought.–Mary bought 75¢ worth of groceries, and gave the grocer a dollar. The grocer gave her 25¢ *change.*

2. Small pieces of money.–We did not have the *change* to pay the newsboy.

–*v. changes, changed, changing.* 1. Make or become different.–Mother *changed* her old dress by shortening the skirt and putting on a new collar. She made it look like a new dress.–The weather *changed.* The rain stopped and the sun shone brightly.

2. Substitute or put in place of; exchange or trade. – When Baby fell into the puddle, Mother had to *change* her clothes. She put dry clothes on Baby in place of the wet ones. –The twins like to *change* seats with each other to confuse the teacher.

change•a•ble (CHAYNJ-ə-bəl) *adj.; changeably, adv.; changeableness, n.* Able or likely to change or become different; turning from one thing to something else.–The colors in diamonds are *changeable.* The colors change from one color to another when you turn them in the light.–Mary is very *changeable.* She likes a thing one day and does not like it at all the next day.

chan•nel (CHAN-əl) *n. channels.* 1. A narrow body of water that joins two larger bodies of water.

2. The deeper part of a river or harbor.—A ship passed through the *channel.*

chap (CHAP) *n. chaps.* A man or boy; a fellow.—Jack is a good *chap.*

—*v. chaps, chapped, chapping.* Make rough and broken (of skin).—When my hands are *chapped* from the cold, I put cold cream on them.

chap•el (CHAP-əl) *n. chapels.* 1. A small room or place for prayer inside a large church. — Grandmother prays in the *chapel* of the old church.

2. A place for prayer separate from a church and usually much smaller.—There are many small *chapels* along the country roads of Quebec, Canada.

chap•er•on (SHAP-er-ohn) *n. chaperons.* An older person who watches over the activities of a young girl or a group of young people.—Mrs. Jones, one of our teachers, acted as *chaperon* at the school dance.

chap•lain (CHAP-lən) *n. chaplains.* 1. A priest, minister, or rabbi in the Armed Forces.

2. A priest, minister, or rabbi who is part of the staff of an institution like a school or a prison.—Our *chaplain* conducts services every Sunday morning in the school chapel.

chaps (CHAPSS) *n. pl.* Thick leather leggings, usually open at the back. Cowboys wear *chaps* over their trousers for protection.

chap•ter (CHAP-ter) *n. chapters.* 1. A part or section of a book. *Chapters* usually have numbers and titles to tell what each *chapter* is about.

2. A smaller division of a group.—The Red Cross has a *chapter* in each city.

char•ac•ter (KAR-ik-ter) *n. characters.* 1. A person in a play, book, etc.—Tom Sawyer is a *character* in a book.

2. One's nature, or the way a person really is, inside his mind. The ways you think, feel, and act make up your *character.* If you do good things and have good thoughts and feelings toward others, you are a person of good *character.*

3. Strength of mind; honesty, sincerity, courage, and other good qualities taken together. —Father is a man of *character.*—Bob has too much *character* to blame someone else for something he himself did.

4. A person who is noticeable because of odd behavior.—The old woman who goes around feeding the cats at night is quite a *character* in town.

5. A letter or sign.—The *characters* used in writing Chinese are different from those used in English.

char•ac•ter•is•tic (kar-ik-ter-ISS-tik) *n. characteristics.* A trait; a special feature; something that makes one different from another.—John's special *characteristic* is a small scar on his arm.—The giraffe's long neck and huge size are its most obvious *characteristics.*

—*adj.* Typical.—Ellen answered the question with *characteristic* honesty. She always tells the truth.

char•coal (CHAHR-kohl) *n.* A black, coal-like material made by partly burning wood in ovens with little air. It is often used as a fuel.—We went for a picnic, and made a fire in an outdoor stove with *charcoal.*

charge (CHAHRJ) *n. charges.* 1. Something one is accused of.—The witness said that the *charge* against the man was not true. He had not done the thing he was accused of doing.

2. Care.—The teacher told Mary to take *charge* of the class while she was out of the room.

—*v. charges, charged, charging.* 1. Ask a price of.—Bob *charges* 50¢ an hour for mowing lawns.

2. Accuse.—The officer *charged* the man with driving sixty miles an hour.

3. Put on a bill to be paid later.—When Mary bought the groceries, she had them *charged,* since she did not have any money with her.—When Mother buys clothes, she *charges* them to Father's account.

4. Rush at; attack.—The angry bull *charged* the farmer.

5. Load; fill.—The soldiers *charged* the gun with shot.

char•i•ot (CHAR-ee-ət) *n. chariots.* A two-wheeled vehicle in which the rider or riders stand. It is drawn by horses.–The ancient Greeks and Romans used *chariots* in battle, in parades, and in races.

char•i•ty (CHAR-ə-tee) *n. charities.* 1. Help given to poor, sick, and helpless people.–Each year Father gives something to *charity.* –Hospitals and homes for the needy and the helpless, who can afford to pay little or nothing, are *charities.*
2. Kindness; willingness to overlook faults.–The teacher treats small children with *charity.*

charm (CHAHRM) *n. charms.* 1. Attraction. –The story of Huckleberry Finn holds much *charm* for boys. They like it.
2. A quality which gives pleasure.–Mary's sweetness is her greatest *charm.*
3. A small object like a locket.–Father wears a gold watch *charm.*–Long ago people wore *charms* because they thought *charms* would keep them from harm.

–*v. charms, charmed, charming.* 1. Delight; please.–I was *charmed* with the book when I read it.
2. Hypnotize; make obedient and helpless.–The man says that he *charms* snakes. He says he can make them do as he wishes.

charm•ing (CHAHRM-ing) *adj.; charmingly, adv.* Pleasant; delightful; attractive.–Grandmother is a *charming* person. – The story of Cinderella is *charming.*

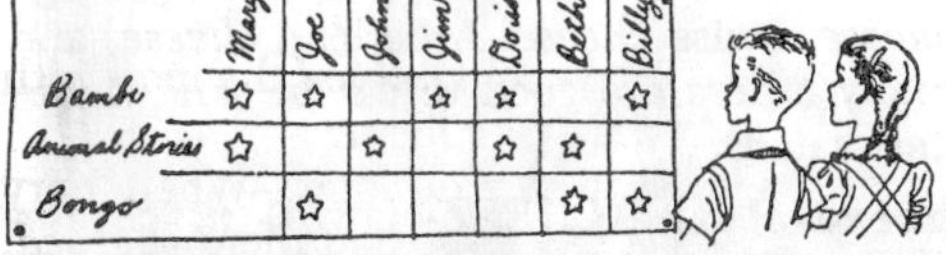

chart (CHAHRT) *n. charts.* 1. A list or diagram made to show certain information at a glance.–The children made a *chart* on a large sheet of paper to show what books each of them had read. – The mayor drew a *chart* which showed how the parts of the city government worked together.
2. A map which shows where different important points are. – Sailors are guided in their sailing by *charts.*
–*v. charts, charted, charting.* 1. Record on a chart. – Jack *charted* his marks in all his subjects.
2. Make a map of.–Admiral Byrd *charted* the country which he visited.

chase (CHAYSS) *v. chases, chased, chasing.* 1. Run after and try to catch.–Dogs like to *chase* cats.
2. Drive away.–The old man *chased* the boys from the orchard.

chasm (KAZ-əm) *n. chasms.* A long, steep, deep opening in the ground. *Chasms* are made by earthquakes and by the eating force of rivers.

chat (CHAT) *n. chats.* A friendly talk about little things.–Mother had a *chat* with her neighbor.
–*v. chats, chatted, chatting.* Talk in a friendly way about this and that.–Mary likes to *chat* with her friends before school begins.

chat•ter (CHAT-er) *n.* Light, quick noises or voices.–We heard the *chatter* of the birds in the trees. They sounded as if they were talking to one another.
–*v. chatters, chattered, chattering.* Talk fast or make quick little noises.–Mother asked the children to stop *chattering* while she was at the telephone.–The room is so cold that my teeth *chatter.* They hit together, making a *chattering* sound.

chauf•feur (SHOH-fer *or* shoh-FER) *n. chauffeurs.* A person who drives an automobile for pay.–If you are a *chauffeur,* you must have a *chauffeur's* license, or special driver's license.

cheap (CHEEP) *adj. cheaper, cheapest; cheaply, adv.* 1. Costing only a little money.–Bob bought a *cheap* knife.
2. Poor in quality.–This material is *cheap.* It is not good material.

cheat (CHEET) *n. cheats.* A person who is unfair and dishonest. – The man is not a *cheat.* He will not sell his goods for more than they are worth.
–*v. cheats, cheated, cheating.* Be unfair or dishonest; get something for oneself by a trick or dishonest act.–During the test the teacher left the room, since she knew she could trust the children not to *cheat.* She knew they would not look at each other's papers or look in their books.

check (CHEK) *n. checks.* 1. The mark [√] meaning something is correct, or calling special attention to something.—Jack put a *check* after each word spelled right.
2. A written order which can be exchanged for money at the bank.—The workmen were paid by *check.*

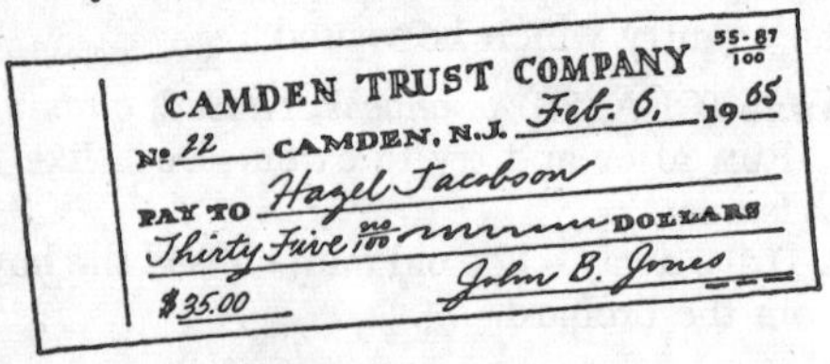

3. Any kind of receipt given to prove that one owns something, has bought something at a certain store, etc.—The girl at the counter took our packages and gave us a *check.* We gave the *check* back to her when we claimed the packages.—The man in the store gave us a sales*check.*

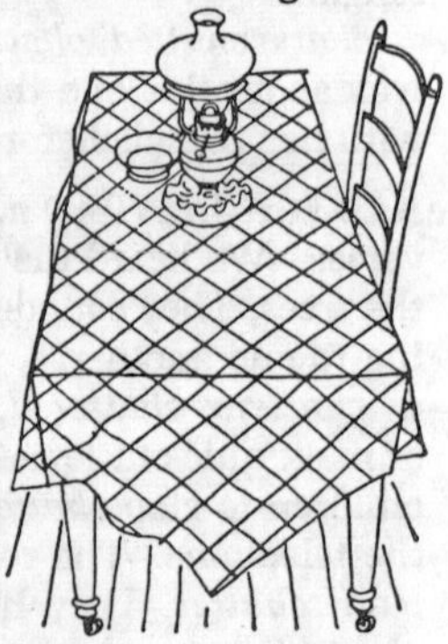

4. One of the small squares in a pattern of squares. — Grandmother's tablecloth is made of green and white *checks.*
—*v. checks, checked, checking.* 1. Turn in for a time, to be called for later. — Father *checked* his hat and coat in the restaurant.
2. Compare.—The teacher told us to *check* our words with those in the spelling book.
3. Be the same as. — Jack's spelling words *check* with mine.
4. Stop.—Grandfather *checked* the runaway horses by pulling on the reins.

check•er•board (CHEK-er-bord) *n. checkerboards.* A board marked with red and black squares, on which the game of checkers is played.

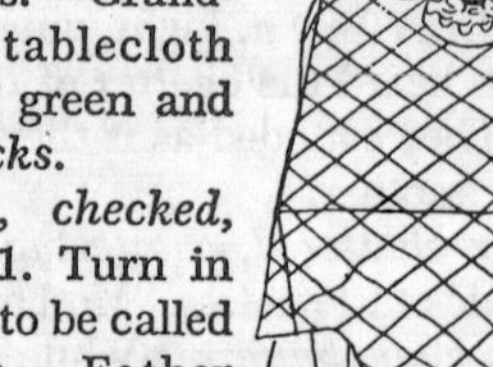

check•ered (CHEK-erd) *adj.* Marked with a pattern of small squares. — Grandmother's tablecloth is of green and white *checkered* linen.

check•ers (CHEK-erz) *n.* A game played on a checkerboard, which is a board marked off into squares. The game is played with two sets of round, flat pieces called *checkers.* Usually one set of *checkers* is red and the other is black.

cheek (CHEEK) *n. cheeks.* The side of the face below the eyes and at the side of the mouth.—Baby has round, rosy *cheeks.*

cheep (CHEEP) *n. cheeps.* A small chirping cry.—The bird's *cheep* meant that it was hungry.
—*v. cheeps, cheeped, cheeping.* Make peeping or chirping noise.—We could hear the little chicks *cheeping* in the barn.

cheer (CHEER) *n. cheers.* A shout of joy or approval.—When Jack made a home run, a *cheer* rose from the crowd.
—*v. cheers, cheered, cheering.* 1. Raise the spirits of.—The letters and flowers *cheered* the sick boy.
2. Shout encouragement and approval.—The crowd *cheered* the team when it came onto the field.

cheer•ful (CHEER-fuhl) *adj.; cheerfully, adv.; cheerfulness, n.* 1. Happy; in good spirits.—A sunny day makes us *cheerful.*
2. Bright; pleasant. — Mary has a *cheerful* smile.—This is a *cheerful* morning.

cheer•y (CHEER-ee) *adj. cheerier, cheeriest; cheerily, adv.* Bright and cheerful.—The Boy Scouts sat by the *cheery* fire and sang songs.

cheese (CHEEZ) *n. cheeses.* A food made by separating the solid or thick part of milk from the watery part and pressing it into a

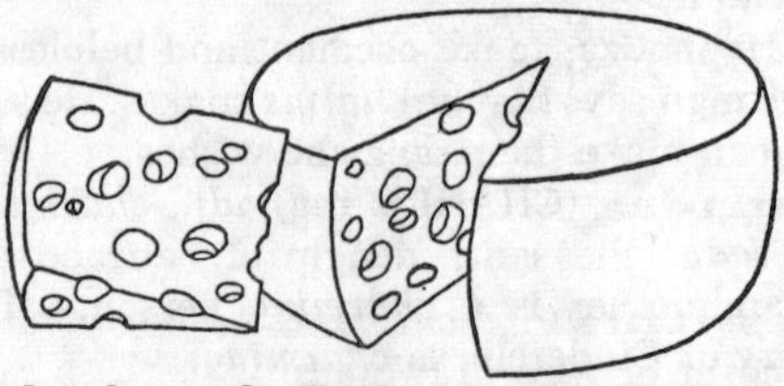

solid cake or loaf.—Cream *cheese,* cottage *cheese,* Swiss *cheese,* American *cheese,* and many others are good to eat in sandwiches and salads.

cheese•cloth (CHEEZ-clawth) *n. cheesecloths.* Thin cotton cloth that is loosely woven. — Grandmother strained the juice through a piece of *cheesecloth.*

chem•i•cal (KEM-i-kəl) *n. chemicals.* A substance used in, or made by, the science of chemistry. — Acids, gases, alcohols, resins, etc., are *chemicals.*

chem•ist (KEM-ist) *n. chemists.* A person who works in the field of chemistry or who is learned in the science.–Tom wants to be a *chemist* when he grows up.

chem•is•try (KEM-iss-tree) *n.* A science; the study of what substances are made of, the changes that take place inside them, and how they affect other substances. You are learning something about *chemistry* when you learn that water is made of oxygen and hydrogen. *Chemistry* has enabled men to make many new substances, such as plastics and drugs.

cher•ish (CHAIR-ish) *v. cherishes, cherished, cherishing.* 1. Treat or care for tenderly; hold dear.–Sally *cherishes* her pet kitten.
2. Keep in the mind.–Mary *cherishes* the hope that she will be an actress some day.

cher•ry (CHAIR-ee) *n. cherries.* A small, round, smooth red or white fruit that grows on *cherry* trees. Some *cherries* are sweet and some are sour. They have long stems and a very hard stone.

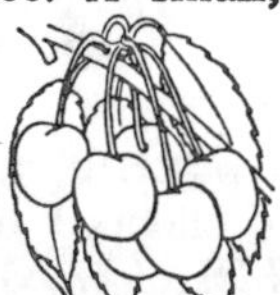

chess (CHESS) *n.* A game of skill played with 32 pieces, or chessmen, by two players, each having 16 pieces with which to play. The game is played on a board like that used in the game of checkers. *Chess* is believed by many authorities to have been played first in India about 1000 years ago.

chest (CHEST) *n. chests.* 1. A large box with a cover or with drawers in it.–Father keeps his tools in a tool *chest.*–A bureau is a *chest* of drawers.

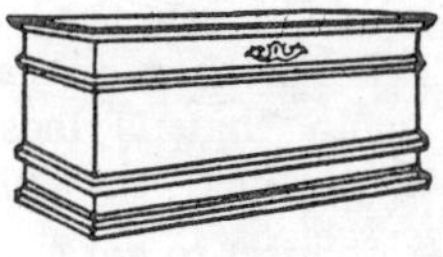

2. The upper front part of the body.–Jack won a medal in the race. He wore it on his *chest.*

chest•nut (CHESS-nut) *n. chestnuts.* A nut that is good to eat. The *chestnut* is covered with a brown shell. It grows in a prickly green covering. The tree on which *chestnuts* grow is the *chestnut* tree. The wood of the tree is used for furniture and in building houses.
–*adj.* Reddish brown.–The farmer has a *chestnut* horse.

chew (CHOO) *v. chews, chewed, chewing.* Cut or grind into tiny bits with the teeth.–*Chew* your food well before you swallow it.

chick (CHIK) *n. chicks.* A little chicken.–The farmer has twenty *chicks.*–Little birds are *chicks,* too.

chick•a•dee (CHIK-ə-dee) *n. chickadees.* A small gray bird with black on the top of its head. The *chickadee* is named after its call.

chick•en (CHIK-ən) *n. chickens.* A kind of large fowl or bird raised for its meat and eggs. The meat of a *chicken* is good to eat. Hens and roosters are *chickens.* Hens lay eggs.

chick•en pox (CHIK-ən pahks). A sickness which causes a person to break out with red itchy spots.–When children have *chicken pox,* they should stay at home, so they will not give the disease to others.

chief (CHEEF) *n. chiefs.* 1. A leader.–Pontiac was an Indian *chief.*
2. Head; person in charge.–The *chief* of the police department has charge of all the policemen in the city.
–*adj.; chiefly, adv.* Most important; main. –The *chief* thing in Mother's life is her family.

chif•fo•nier (shif-ə-NEER) *n. chiffoniers.* A tall chest of drawers.—Mother keeps the towels in the *chiffonier.*

child (CHYLD) *n. children.* A person who has not yet grown up.—A baby is a *child.*—A young boy or a young girl is a *child.*

chil•dren (CHIL-drən) *n. pl.* More than one child. — Many *children* play in the park.

chill (CHIL) *n. chills.* 1. A shivering feeling of cold.—People who have fever often have *chills.*

2. Coldness.—The north wind has a *chill* in it that makes one shiver.

—*v. chills, chilled, chilling.* Make cool or colder.—We put melon on ice to *chill* it.

chill•y (CHIL-ee) *adj. chillier, chilliest.* Cool or slightly cold.—Mary was *chilly,* so she put on her sweater.

chime (CHYM) *n. chimes.* 1. One of a number of bells or metal tubes that are in tune with each other so music can be played on them.—We heard the *chimes* in the church tower.

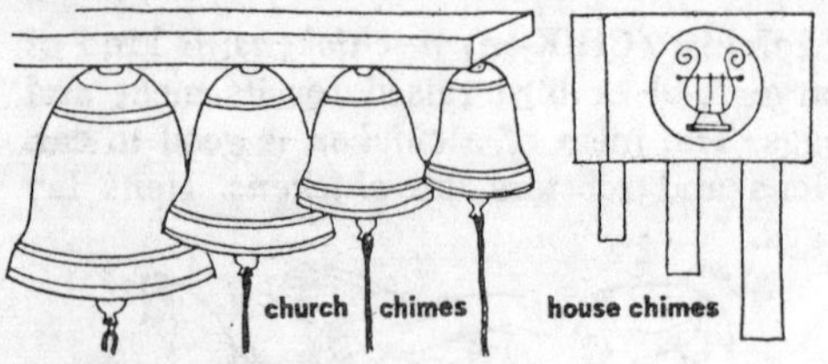

2. Music of chimes.—The *chimes* came to us across the fields.

—*v. chimes, chimed, chiming.* Make ringing musical sounds. — Our clock *chimes* every fifteen minutes.

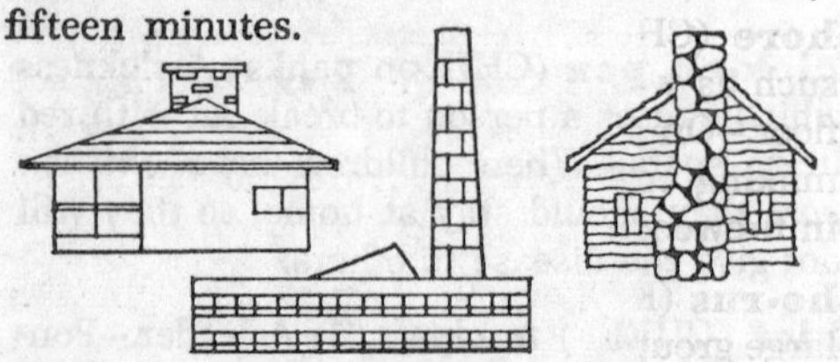

chim•ney (CHIM-nee) *n. chimneys.* 1. A long tube to draw smoke from a fire and to make a draft on the fire so that it will burn better. A *chimney* is often made of bricks or stone, and runs up through the roof of a building. It is hollow in the middle to let air, gas, and smoke pass through from the furnace, stove, or fireplace.

2. A glass tube on a kerosene lamp to protect the flame from wind and make it look larger.

chim•pan•zee (chim-pən-ZEE *or* chim-PAN-zee) *n. chimpanzees.* A brown African ape with large ears and teeth, and paws something like a man's hands. A *chimpanzee* has no tail.

chin (CHIN) *n. chins.* The lowest part of the face. — When you chew or talk, your *chin* moves up and down.

chi•na (CHY-nə) *n.* 1. A white material made of baked clay and used for making dishes.

2. Dishes made of china.—Mary put the *china* on the table.

chip (CHIP) *n. chips.* 1. A small piece broken or chopped off something. — We gathered *chips* of wood to start the fire.

2. A small, round, flat piece like a coin.—We used *chips* to keep our score in the game.

3. A thin, crisp piece of food.—Mary took potato *chips* to the picnic.

—*v. chips, chipped, chipping.* Break off small parts of.—Be careful not to *chip* the dishes.

—*Chip in* means to give or put in one's share; to contribute one's time, effort, or money.—We all *chipped in* at the bazaar. Each of us did his share to make it a success.

chip•munk (CHIP-məngk) *n. chipmunks.* A small, squirrel-like animal with black and white stripes on its back.

chirp (CHERP) *n. chirps.* Light, quick singing sound made by birds and insects.

—*v. chirps, chirped, chirping.* Make light, quick, singing sounds.

chis•el (CHIZ-əl) *n. chisels.* A cutting tool with a long, flat blade that has a sharp edge at the end.—The carpenter uses a *chisel* to cut off small pieces of wood.—The mason uses a *chisel* to carve or cut stone.

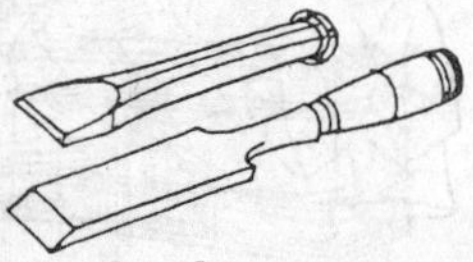

—*v. chisels, chiseled, chiseling.* Cut with a chisel.—Father *chiseled* off the edge of the shelf so that it would fit into place.

chlo•rine (KLOR-een) *n.; chlorinated, adj.* A greenish-yellow gas that has a strong, unpleasant odor and is very irritating when breathed. *Chlorine* is often used to sterilize drinking water.

chlo•ro•form (KLOR-ə-form) *n.* A pleasant-tasting, colorless liquid often used by doctors as an anesthetic to put patients to sleep for an operation.

chlo•ro•phyll (KLOR-ə-fil) *n.* The substance in plants which makes them green. *Chlorophyll* is necessary for the production of carbohydrates in plants.

choc•o•late (CHAWK-lət) *n. chocolates* and *adj.* 1. A food made by grinding the seeds or beans of the cacao tree.

cacao bean

2. A drink made by mixing chocolate, milk, and sugar.—We drink hot *chocolate* in winter.
3. Chocolate candy or a piece of chocolate candy.—*Chocolates* are often filled with a sweet cream.

4. Dark brown.—The pocketbook was *chocolate.* It had a dark-brown color.

choice (CHOISS) *n. choices.* 1. A selection; something chosen.—The black hat with the white feather was my first *choice.*
2. A chance to choose.—We were so late that we did not have a *choice* of food. We ate just what was left.
—*adj.* Finest or best.—The butcher offered Mother his *choice* steaks.

choir (KWYR) *n. choirs.* 1. A number of singers who sing together, especially in a church.—The *choir* will sing hymns tonight.
2. Part of the church where the church singers sit.—The *choir* in our church was painted.

choke (CHOHK) *n. chokes.* A device that regulates the amount of air in the mixture of gasoline and air that runs a gasoline engine.
—*v. chokes, choked, choking.* 1. Have a blocking or checking of the breathing.—Food got caught in the boy's throat and he *choked.*—Father's collar was so tight it almost *choked* him.
2. Clog; fill up.—Weeds *choked* the garden.—The river was *choked* with logs, and boats could not get through.

choose (CHOOZ) *v. chooses, chose, choosing.* 1. Select; pick out.—It is hard to *choose* a purse when there are so many to *choose* from.
2. See fit; decide.—The teacher *chose* to go to the hospital. She decided to go.

chop (CHAHP) *n. chops.* A cut of meat with a rib in it.—We ate pork *chops* for dinner.—Lamb *chops* and veal *chops* also are good to eat.
—*v. chops, chopped, chopping.* 1. Cut by striking with a sharp tool. — The woodman will *chop* down the tree with an ax.

2. Cut into small pieces.—Mother *chopped* cabbage for a salad.

chop•stick (CHAHP-stik) *n. chopsticks.* One of a pair of long sticks used by the Chinese to eat with. We lift food to our mouths with spoons or forks. The Chinese use *chopsticks.*

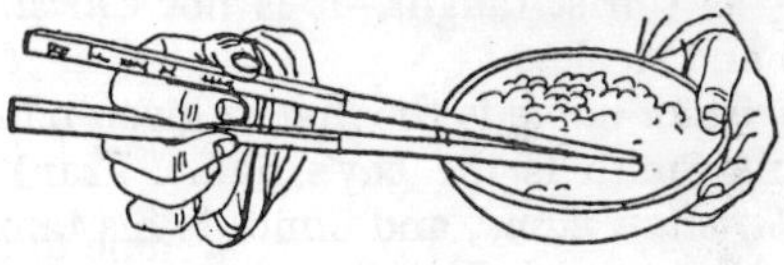

chord (KORD) *n. chords.* In music, three or more musical tones sounded together to make a pleasing tone.

chore (CHOR) *n. chores.* A small odd job such as washing the dishes or sweeping the floor.—On a farm the boy's *chores* include milking cows, feeding horses, and bringing in firewood.

cho•rus (KOR-əss) *n. choruses.* 1. A choir; a large group of singers.
2. A part of a song repeated after each verse.—The girls sang the verses, or stanzas, of the songs and the boys sang the *chorus.*
3. A song sung by a chorus.

chose (CHOHZ) *v.* One form of the verb *choose.*—The hat Mother *chose* was black.

cho•sen (CHOH-zən) *v.* One form of the verb *choose.*—Bob was *chosen* to give the gift to the teacher.

chow (CHOW) *n. chows.* A kind of dog first raised in China. *Chows* have thick brown or black hair, black tongues, and short, bushy tails which rest on the tops of their backs.

chow·der (CHOW-der) *n. chowders.* A soup or stew made from clams or fish, with vegetables and seasoning.

Christ (KRYST) *n.* Jesus; the founder of the Christian religion, worshiped by Christians as The Saviour and Son of God.

chris·ten (KRISS-ən) *v. christens, christened, christening.* 1. Baptize; give a name to a person when he is baptized into the Christian church.
2. Name.–The ship was *christened* "The Ocean Queen."
–*christening, n. christenings.*

Chris·tian (KRISS-chən) *n. Christians.* A person who believes in and follows the teachings of Christ.
–*adj.* Having to do with Christ's teachings; doing as Christ taught.–It is not *Christian* to lie and steal.
–A *Christian name* is the first or given name. –Frank Smith is the boy's name. Frank is his *Christian name,* and Smith is his family name.

Chris·ti·an·i·ty (kriss-chee-AN-ə-tee) *n.* The religion and teachings of Christ.

Christ·mas (KRISS-məss) *n. Christmases.* The 25th day of December; the celebration of the birth of Christ.

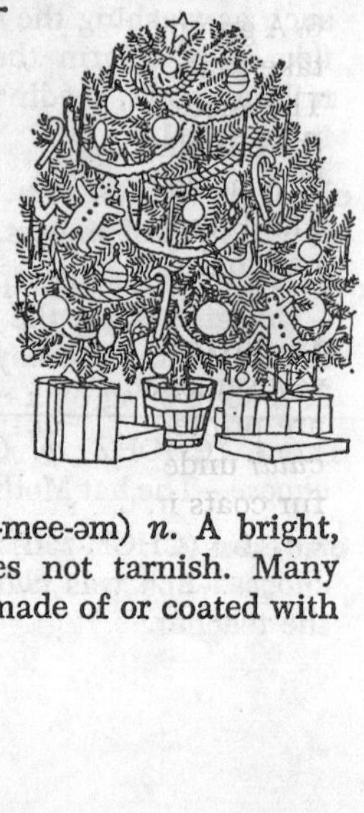

Christ·mas tree (KRISS-məss tree) *Christmas trees.* An evergreen or pine tree decorated with ornaments to celebrate Christmas.–On Christmas eve we lit the light bulbs that were on our *Christmas tree.*

chro·mi·um (KROH-mee-əm) *n.* A bright, shiny metal that does not tarnish. Many automobile parts are made of or coated with *chromium.*

chron·o·log·i·cal or·der (krahn-ə-LAHJ-i-kəl or-der). A listing of events or telling of things according to time, or in the order they happened, as first this took place, then that, and so on.–John arranged the correspondence in his file in *chronological order,* or according to the date he received each letter: January, March, May, June, etc.

chrys·a·lis (KRISS-ə-ləss) *n. chrysalises.* 1. A stage of development in the life of an insect, such as the moth or butterfly, when it is enclosed in a cocoon.–The butterfly was not fully grown. It was a *chrysalis.*

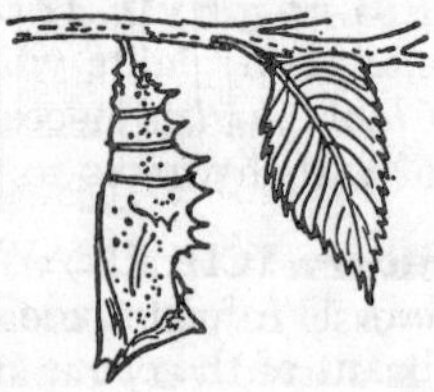

2. The cocoon or case itself.–The butterfly came out of its *chrysalis.*

chrys·an·the·mum (kri-SAN-thə-məm) *n. chrysanthemums.* A late fall flower of many colors. The very smallest blossoms are about the size of a quarter, the largest about the size of a tea plate.

chub·by (CHUB-ee) *adj. chubbier, chubbiest.* Round and fat. –Sally's Teddy bear is *chubby.*

chuck·le (CHUK-əl) *n. chuckles.* A low laugh.–We heard Father's *chuckle* as he watched the puppies play.
–*v. chuckles, chuckled, chuckling.* Laugh quietly.–Father *chuckled* at the funny way the puppies played together.

chug (CHUG) *n. chugs.* The sound of an engine.–We heard the *chug* of the boat going up the river.
–*v. chugs, chugged, chugging.* Make a sound like that of an engine.–The boat *chugged* up the river.

chum (CHUM) *n. chums.* A close friend.–Mary and Ruth have been *chums* for a long time.

chum·my (CHUM-ee) *adj. chummier, chummiest.* Friendly.–The boys were very *chummy.* They were together a great deal.

chunk (CHUNGK) *n. chunks.* A large lump.–Jack threw a *chunk* of coal into the furnace.

church (CHERCH) *n. churches.* 1. A building where Christians gather to worship.–On Sundays we go to our *church.*
2. An organization of Christians for worship

and Christian activities. – The Methodist *Church* built a playground in the neighborhood.

churn (CHERN) *n. churns.* A machine or a vessel in which cream is stirred very rapidly to separate the butter from the milk.–The farmer makes butter in a *churn.*

–*v. churns, churned, churning.* Whip or shake cream rapidly in a churn to make butter.–Mary helped Grandmother to *churn* the butter.

ci•ca•da (si-KAY-də) *n. cicadas.* A large winged insect, often identified by the shrill sound made by the male; a locust.–The harsh song of *cicadas* can sometimes be heard over distances of a quarter of a mile.

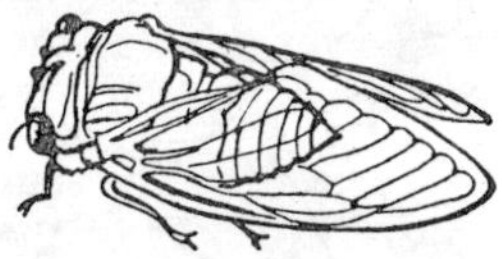

ci•der (SY-der) *n.* A drink made by pressing the juice out of apples. After *cider* stands for a long time it gets sour and turns into vinegar.–At the Halloween party, we drank *cider.*

ci•gar (si-GAHR) *n. cigars.* Tobacco leaves rolled tightly into a large solid roll.–Father smoked a *cigar* after dinner.

cig•a•rette (SIG-ə-ret *or* sig-ə-RET) *n. cigarettes.* A small roll of finely cut tobacco rolled up in a thin piece of paper.–Some people smoke cigars or pipes; some smoke *cigarettes.*

cin•der (SIN-der) *n. cinders.* A hard piece of partly burned coal, wood, etc. If coal or wood is completely burned, it leaves a powder called ashes. Some *cinders* have many little holes in them. They look like hard sponges.

cin•na•mon (SIN-ə-mən) *n.* A kind of tree that has an inner bark used as a spice for flavoring. This spice also is called *cinnamon.*
–*adj.* 1. Flavored with cinnamon spice.–Mother bakes *cinnamon* rolls for breakfast on Sundays.
2. Reddish brown.–Some bears have a *cinnamon* color.–Mother has a *cinnamon* suit.

ci•pher (SYF-er) *n. ciphers.* The figure "0." The *cipher* is also called a zero.

cir•cle (SER-kəl) *n. circles.* 1. A ring that is perfectly round. Every point on a *circle* is the same distance away from the center as any other point.

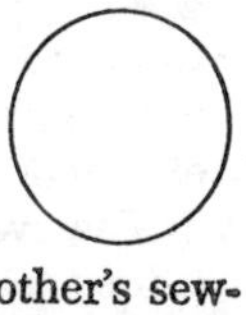

2. A group of people who meet to do things together; a club.–Mother's sewing *circle* meets on Thursday afternoons.
–*v. circles, circled, circling.* Move in a ring or circle.–The airplane *circled* around the field before it landed.–The children all held hands and *circled* around to play Farmer in the Dell.

cir•cuit (SER-kət) *n. circuits.* 1. A movement in a circle.–The second hand of a clock makes a complete *circuit* once every sixty seconds.
2. The path around which such a movement takes place.–The *circuit* is brief.
3. A trip made regularly to do certain things; the route itself.–The salesman's *circuit* took him around the city.
4. The area within a circumference or boundary; the circumference itself. – The boys wrestled within the *circuit* of the ring. The *circuit* was marked off with chalk.
5. The path, complete or otherwise, of an electric current.–The lights went out when the *circuit* was broken.
6. A group of theaters at which performances take place periodically, one after another.–The motion picture was shown throughout the *circuit.*
7. A hookup of radio or television stations.–The President's broadcast was heard over a national radio *circuit.*

cir•cu•lar (SER-kyə-ler) *n. circulars.* An advertisement or handbill of which many copies are printed and given out.–We found a *circular* under our door telling us where to store fur coats in the summer.
–*adj.* Round; shaped like a circle.–In playing Farmer in the Dell, the children move in a *circular* formation.

cir·cu·late (SER-kyə-layt) *v. circulates, circulated, circulating.* 1. Spread around.—Nowadays, with the radio, etc., it doesn't take long for news to *circulate.*—We opened the door to let the air *circulate* freely in the room.
2. Send around; put out; give out publicly.—The neighbors *circulated* a paper asking people to vote for Mr. Jones.

cir·cu·la·tion (ser-kyə-LAY-shən) *n.* 1. The act of going around, either in a circle or otherwise.—The *circulation* of the wheel was stopped by the brake.
2. The passage of things from person to person or place to place.—The news was in *circulation.* Everybody was telling everybody else about it.
3. The average number of newspapers, magazines, etc., sold or distributed in a given time.—The newspaper increased its *circulation* last month. Two hundred more copies were sold.
4. The movement of the blood through the body.—The doctor said John's *circulation* was slow.

cir·cu·la·to·ry (SER-kyə-lə-tor-ee) *adj.* Having to do with circulation, especially of the blood.—The *circulatory* system of the body contains thousands of blood vessels.

cir·cum·fer·ence (ser-KUM-fer-ənss) *n. circumferences.* The distance around a thing, especially a circle.—Mother measured the *circumference* of Mary's waist by putting a tape measure around it.

cir·cum·stance (SER-kəm-stanss) *n. circumstances.* A state, fact, or condition.—We are sometimes excused for lateness, depending on the *circumstances.* It depends on why we are late.—The policeman asked the witness to describe the *circumstances* of the accident. He asked the witness to tell how it happened.—The poor family is in reduced *circumstances.* They have much less money than they once had.

cir·cus (SER-kəss) *n. circuses.* A show in which clowns, horses, other animals, and acrobats perform. *Circuses* travel from town to town, and often hold their shows in tents. Some *circuses* are shown in buildings.

CIRCUS

cis•tern (SISS-tern) *n. cisterns.* A large tank or cement-lined hole in the ground for holding rain water.—Grandfather has a *cistern* on his farm.

cit•i•zen (SIT-ə-zən) *n. citizens.* A person who belongs to a particular country, city, etc. You are a *citizen* of the country in which you were born. If you were born in one country and want to become a *citizen* of another country, you must take out citizenship papers, pass certain tests, and pledge that you want to be a *citizen* of that country more than of any other. The government of a country gives its *citizens* protection and certain rights, and expects them to be good *citizens* in return.

cit•i•zen•ship (SIT-ə-zən-ship) *n.* The condition of belonging to a country, city, or other place, and having the rights and duties of a citizen. To become a citizen of a new country, one must give up his *citizenship* in any other country.

cit•rus fruits (SIT-rəss froots). Fruits such as lemons, limes, oranges, and grapefruits. *Citrus fruits* are generally grown in warm climates, such as in the states of Florida and California.

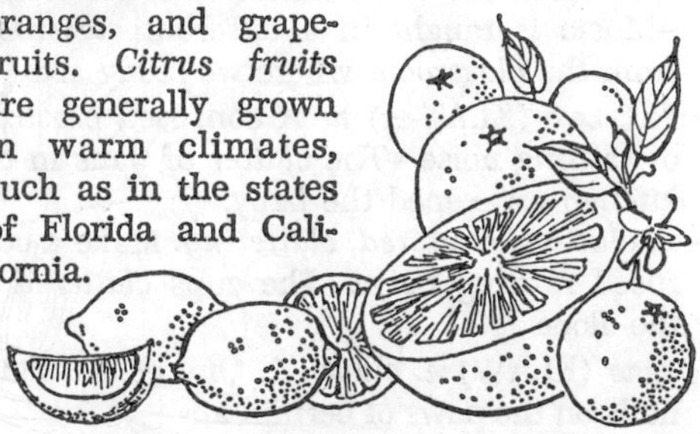

cit•y (SIT-ee) *n. cities.* A large town; a place where many people live close together. The people of a *city* elect a mayor and other officers to take care of the *city's* affairs. New York, Chicago, and London are large *cities.*

civ•ic (SIV-ik) *adj.* Having to do with the duties or affairs of a city, of citizens, or of citizenship.—It is a *civic* duty to keep the city clean. It is a matter of *civic* pride.

ci•vil•ian (sə-VIL-yən) *n. civilians.* A person who is not in the army, the navy, the air force, or any other military service.

civ•i•li•za•tion (siv-əl-ə-ZAY-shən) *n. civilizations.* 1. The standard of government, education, science, art, etc., that a nation or people has.—American *civilization* is famous for its science and inventions.

2. The way of life of a nation or people at a certain period.—Mummies are relics of an earlier *civilization.* — In school we talked about the early Indian *civilization.*

civ•i•lize (SIV-ə-lyz) *v. civilizes, civilized, civilizing.* Educate and train a person so that he can live peacefully with other people and enjoy the many good things of civilization.

clad (KLAD) *v.* One form of the verb *clothe.* —The beggar was *clad* in ragged clothes.

claim (KLAYM) *n. claims.* A right.—The miner had no *claim* to the land; he just took it.

—*v. claims, claimed, claiming.* 1. Say or make known that one owns something. — Jack *claimed* the ball which Joe found. He said it was his.

2. Say; declare as true.—Jack *claims* that he is a faster runner than Bob.

3. Take up (time, attention, etc.).—Arithmetic is hard for Mary; it *claims* most of her time.

clam (KLAM) *n. clams.* A shellfish something like an oyster. *Clams* grow in shells. They live in sand or mud. Some *clams* are good to eat, either raw or cooked. *Clams* are also good in a soup called *clam* chowder.

clamp (KLAMP) *n. clamps.* A device for holding things tightly together.—We put a *clamp* on the boards after we glued them together.

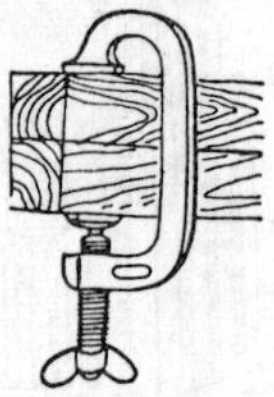

—*v. clamps, clamped, clamping.* Fasten together with clamps.—We *clamped* the boards together after we glued them.

clang (KLANG) *n. clangs.* A loud ringing noise, like that of a bell or pieces of metal hitting together.—As we passed the machine shop, we heard the *clang* of the workman's hammer.

—*v. clangs, clanged, clanging.* Ring harshly.—The mechanic's hammer *clanged* as he hit the axle.

clank (KLANGK) *n. clanks.* A dull, short ringing sound.—We heard the *clank* as the bumper of the car struck the stone wall.

—*v. clanks, clanked, clanking.* Make a clank.—The runaway dog had a heavy, broken chain *clanking* behind him.

clap (KLAP) *n. claps.* A loud noise or crash.—The loud *clap* of thunder frightened us.

—*v. claps, clapped, clapping.* 1. Hit the palms of the hands together; applaud.—The children *clapped* when the concert was over.

2. Slap or strike in a friendly way.—Grandfather *clapped* Bob on the shoulder.

clar•i•fy (KLAR-ə-fy) *v. clarifies, clarified, clarifying.* Make clear; make easier to understand.—The teacher's explanation *clarified* the difficult problem.

clar•i•net (klar-ə-NET) *n. clarinets.* A musical instrument made of wood. It is played by blowing into one end through a mouthpiece while the keys are worked by the fingers. The mouthpiece has a thin strip of cane, called a reed, fastened to it.

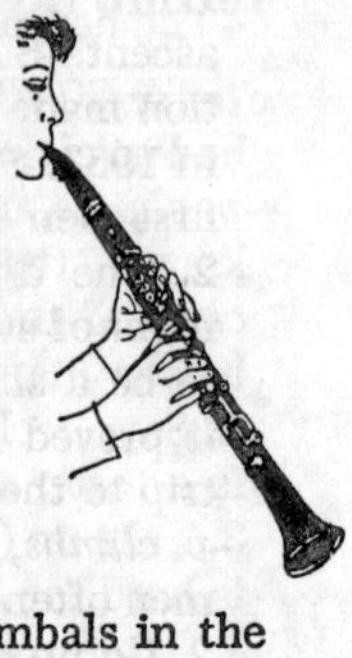

clash (KLASH) *n. clashes.* 1. A harsh, flat, ringing sound.—When the cars came together, we heard a loud *clash.*—The cymbals in the band make a *clash.*

2. An argument or disagreement.—Every time those boys see each other they have a *clash.*

—*v. clashes, clashed, clashing.* 1. Make a clash.—The dishpan *clashed* when it hit the floor.

2. Fail to harmonize or go well together.—The colors of the girl's skirt and coat *clashed.*

clasp (KLASP) *n. clasps.* 1. A fastener.—The *clasp* on the belt broke.

2. A clip used as an ornament.—I have two blue *clasps* to wear on my new dress.

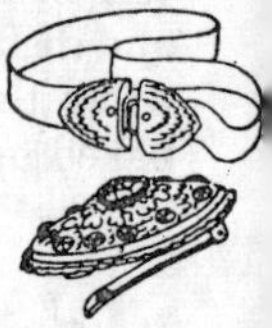

—*v. clasps, clasped, clasping.* 1. Fasten.—Mary *clasped* the belt with a new buckle.

2. Hold tightly.—Father *clasped* the baby in his arms.—The children formed a circle and *clasped* hands.

class (KLASS) *n. classes.* 1. A group.—The teacher divided the children into *classes,* which she will teach separately.

2. A group of things somewhat alike.—The farmer sorted the potatoes into *classes,* or grades. He put each potato with others like it in size and quality.

3. A large number of people who live somewhat alike or who make their living in much the same way.—Farmers are sometimes called the farming *class.*

4. A gathering of students for studying a certain thing.—The children study art in art *class.*

—*v. classes, classed, classing.* Put into a class or group.—These books are *classed* with the better ones.

clas•si•fy (KLASS-ə-fy) *v. classifies, classified, classifying.* Arrange in groups or classes; place all persons or things that are the same or similar in the same group.—The children were *classified* by height. Short children were seated in front, tall children in back.

class•mate (KLASS-mayt) *n. classmates.* A person in the same class at school with one.—Three of Bob's *classmates* were absent yesterday.

class•room (KLASS-room) *n. classrooms.* A schoolroom; room where students are taught.—Music is taught in a different *classroom* from the *classroom* where we study art.

clat•ter (KLAT-er) *n.* A confused crashing or rattling noise.—The *clatter* of pans in the kitchen awakened the baby.

—*v. clatters, clattered, clattering.* Make a confused rattling noise.—The cups *clattered* to the floor.

claw (KLAW) *n. claws.* 1. One of the sharp nails on the paws of certain animals.—Cats have sharp *claws.*

2. One of the pincers of a crab or lobster.

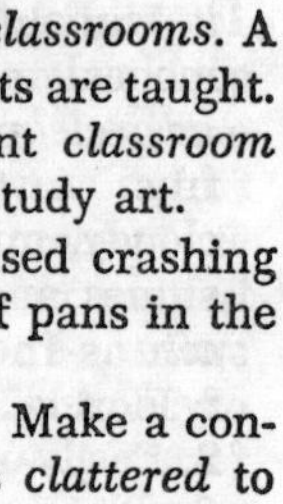

—*v. claws, clawed, clawing.* Scratch and tear with claws.—The cat *clawed* Mary's stocking.

clay (KLAY) *n. clays.* A kind of earth that can be molded easily. Tile, bricks, pottery, and dishes are made of certain kinds of *clay.* After they are shaped and dried, they are baked hard.–Indians made dishes of *clay.*

clean (KLEEN) *adj. cleaner, cleanest.* 1. Free from dirt; not soiled.–Mother told Bob to be sure his hands were *clean* before dinner.
2. Exactly right; accurate; well done.–The ball player made a *clean* hit.
–*v. cleans, cleaned, cleaning.* Remove dirt from; make clean.–Mary *cleaned* the kitchen.

clean•er (KLEEN-er) *n. cleaners.* 1. A person hired to clean anything.–Grandmother has a *cleaner* to help her each week.–Father sent his suit to the *cleaner.*
2. Something used to remove dirt.–Soap is a *cleaner.*–Mary cleans her white shoes with a white shoe *cleaner.*

clear (KLIR) *v. clears, cleared, clearing.* 1. Remove things from.–Mary *cleared* the dining-room table for Mother.–The woodsmen *cleared* the land. They removed the trees and brush.
2. Pass over without touching.–The jumper *cleared* the bar by four inches. He went over it without coming nearer to it than four inches.
–*adj. clearer, clearest; clearly, adv.* 1. Free from anything that holds back light; not cloudy, misty, or muddy.–When the sun shines and there are no clouds, the sky is *clear.*–The river was muddy, but the lake was *clear.*
2. Easily understood.–The problem was *clear.*
3. Plain; easily seen or heard.–The boy's voice was *clear.* Everyone in the audience could hear and understand him.
–*adv.* Completely.–John swam *clear* out of sight. We could not see him at all.

cleav•er (KLEEV-er) *n. cleavers.* A heavy, sharp hand tool used by butchers for chopping meat.

cler•gy•man (KLER-ji-mən) *n. clergymen.* A person officially named or chosen to hold religious services.–Priests and ministers are *clergymen.*

clerk (KLERK) *n. clerks.* 1. A person who types letters, puts away papers, and takes care of other work in an office.–My sister is a *clerk* for the City Gas Company.–A city or county *clerk* is an officer in the city government who takes care of records for the city or county.
2. A person who sells customers in a store what they want to buy.–Bob worked as a *clerk* in the grocery store on Saturdays.

clev•er (KLEV-er) *adj. cleverer, cleverest; cleverly, adv.* 1. Skillful and quick.–That man is a *clever* artist. He can draw quickly and well.
2. Smart.–Bob's dog does many *clever* tricks.

click (KLIK) *n. clicks.* A sharp, short, hard noise.–We heard the *click* of the horse's hoofs on the pavement.
–*v. clicks, clicked, clicking.* Make a sharp, short, hard noise.–The horses' hoofs *clicked* on the pavement.–The lock *clicked* as the key turned.

cli•mate (KLY-mət) *n. climates.* The average weather conditions in an area.–Mary described the *climate* of her state. She said it was very warm in summer, and not too cold in winter, and that there was plenty of rain.

cli•max (KLY-maks) *n.* The most exciting or interesting point in a play, story, motion picture, etc.–The *climax* of the novel was reached when the hero was finally rescued.

climb (KLYM) *n. climbs.* 1. A going up; an ascent.–Sir Edmund Hillary and his expedition made their famous Mount Everest *climb* in 1953. Sir Edmund and his guide were the first men to reach the top of Mount Everest.
2. The distance up a hill, a mountain, a flight of stairs, etc.–We thought it was going to be a short trip to the top of the hill, but it proved to be a long *climb.* It was a long trip to the top of the hill.
–*v. climbs, climbed, climbing.* 1. Go up.–Firemen often *climb* high ladders to put out fires.
2. Go up and down.–Monkeys *climb* trees.–Baby *climbs* the stairs when no one is looking.
3. Grow along.–The grapevine *climbed* up the tree. It grew up along the tree trunk.

cling (KLING) *v. clings, clung, clinging.* Hold fast to something firm.–Some snow *clings* to your shoes.

clin·ic (KLIN-ik) *n. clinics.* A place where diseases are studied and medical help is given.—Doctors learn how to treat diseases at a *clinic*, and patients are cared for there.

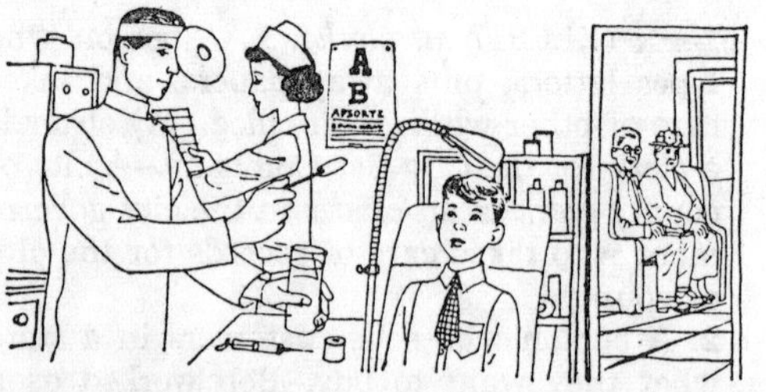

clink (KLINGK) *n.* A short, sharp, ringing noise.—We knew that Bob had money, because we heard the *clink* it made in his pocket.
—*v. clinks, clinked, clinking.* Make a short, sharp, ringing noise.—The coin *clinked* when it dropped to the sidewalk.

clip (KLIP) *n. clips.* 1. Rate of speed.—The auto was going at a fast *clip.*
2. A wire fastener.—The teacher put a *clip* on the papers to hold them together.

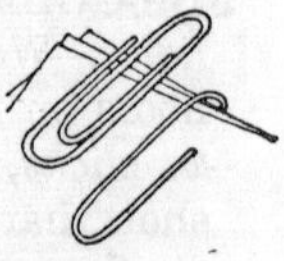

3. An ornament that clasps on.
—The only ornament the dress had was a large, gold *clip.*
—*v. clips, clipped, clipping.* Cut; cut off.—Do not *clip* the grass too short.—In warm weather Father *clips* the dog's hair.

clip·pers (KLIP-erz) *n. pl.* A pair or set of scissors-like blades used for cutting hair, grass, etc., very short.—The gardener cut the bushes with *clippers.*—The barber trims Bob's hair with *clippers.*

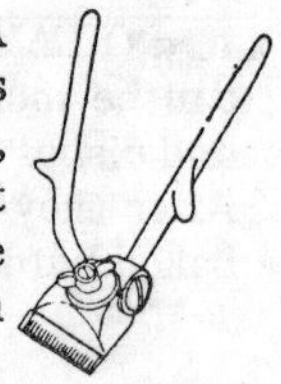

cloak (KLOHK) *n. cloaks.* A loose outer garment. Some *cloaks* have sleeves, like coats, and some are without sleeves, like capes.

clock (KLAHK) *n. clocks.* An instrument that shows the passage of time. *Clocks* tell the time of day. Some *clocks* run by electricity and some have to be wound. A watch can be worn or carried, but a *clock* must be level to keep good time.

clock·wise (KLAHK-wyz) *adj.* and *adv.* In the same direction that a clock's hands turn. —John ran around the track *clockwise.* His friend ran the other way, or counter*clockwise.*

CLOCKS

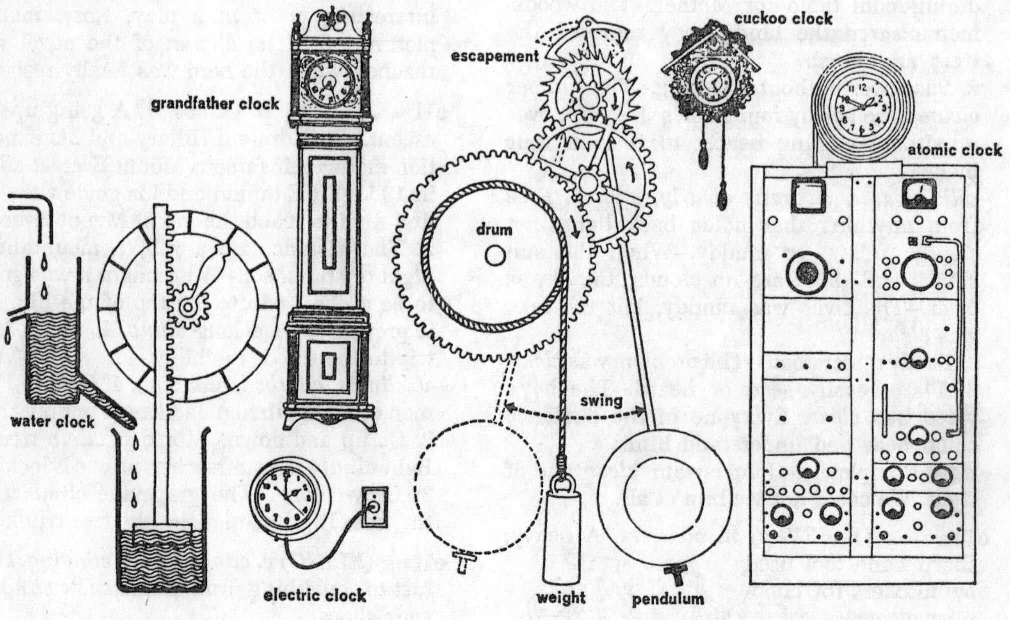

clog (KLAHG) *n. clogs.* A shoe with a wooden sole.–The children wore *clogs* to the beach.
–*v. clogs, clogged, clogging.* Block; stop up.–People are not allowed to *clog* the aisles in a theater.

close (KLOHZ) *n.* End.–The *close* of school is not far off.
–*v. closes, closed, closing.* 1. Come to an end. –School will *close* in June.
2. Shut.–If it is cold, *close* the window.

close (KLOHSS) *adj. closer, closest.* 1. Near (a place).–Bob sits *close* to Mary.
2. Near (in time).–It is getting *close* to school time.
3. Very dear.–Bob and Joe are *close* friends.
4. Almost even.–The score of the ball game was *close.* It was three to two.
5. Stuffy; stifling.–The room was so *close* that we opened all the windows to let in plenty of fresh air.

close·ly (KLOHSS-lee) *adv.* 1. Tightly.–Bob's shoes fit *closely.*
2. Very near.–The dog followed *closely* behind.

clos·et (KLAHZ-it) *n. closets.* A small room for storage.–We keep clothes, linens, and blankets in *closets.*

clot (KLAHT) *v. clots, clotted, clotting.* Thicken; make into a soft lump.–When Mary's finger stopped bleeding, the blood *clotted* over the cut. Bleeding stops when the blood *clots.*

cloth (KLAWTH) *n. cloths.* 1. Material made of threads of cotton, wool, silk, etc., woven together. Clothes, tablecloths, and sheets are made of *cloth.*
2. A piece of cloth.–We dust with a dust*cloth.* –We use a table*cloth* on the dining table.

clothe (KLOHTH) *v. clothes, clothed* or *clad, clothing.* 1. Dress.–The tramp was *clothed* in torn garments.
2. Cover.–The fields were *clothed* with ice and snow.

clothes (KLOHTHZ) *n. pl.* 1. Articles of dress; garments; things worn to cover the body.–We buy our *clothes* at a large clothing store.
2. Bed*clothes* are coverings used on a bed.–In winter we use more bed*clothes* than in summer.

cloth·ing (KLOHTH-ing) *n.* Clothes; things worn to cover the body.–We wear heavier *clothing* in winter than in summer.

CLOTHES

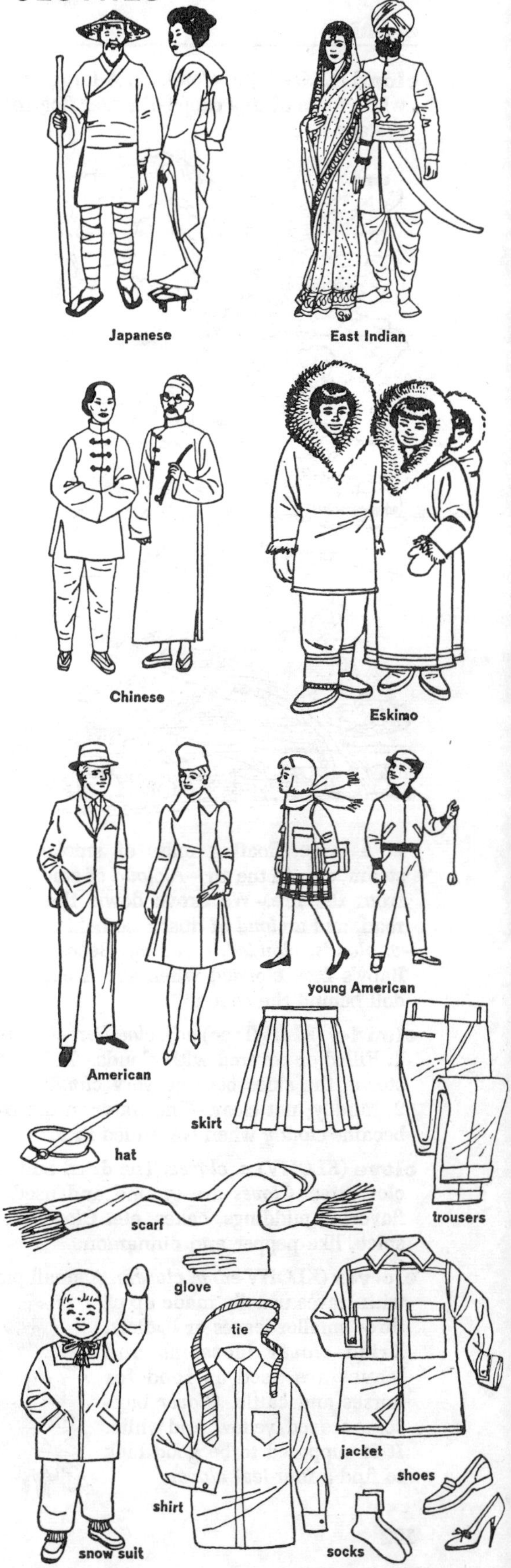

cloud (KLOWD) *n. clouds.* 1. A large gray or white mass of tiny drops of water floating in the sky.

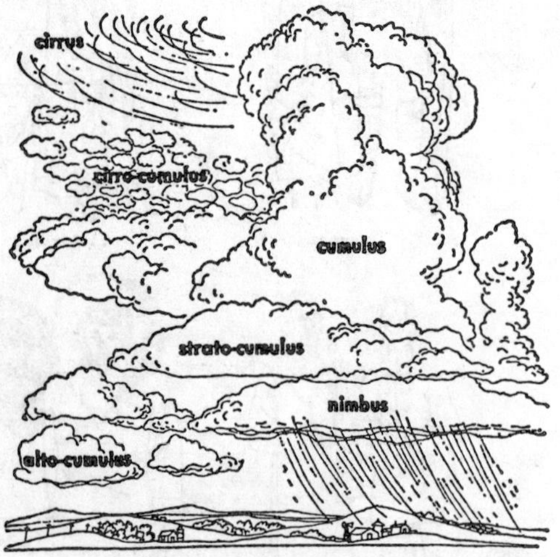

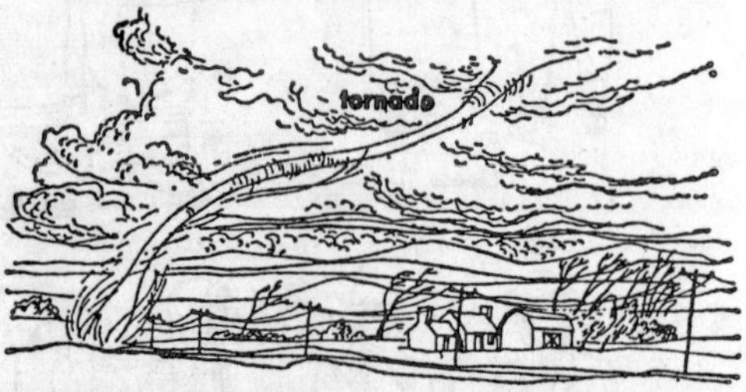

2. A large, floating mass of smoke, dust, steam, etc., in the air.—A *cloud* of smoke rose from the fire.—We drove down the gravel road, and a *cloud* of dust rose behind us.

—*v. clouds, clouded, clouding.* Become sad.—Baby's face *clouded* when she dropped her doll behind the couch.

cloud•y (KLOWD-ee) *adj. cloudier, cloudiest.* 1. Filled or covered with clouds.—Before the storm, the skies became very *cloudy.*

2. Muddy; not clear.—The water in the river became *cloudy* when we waded in it.

clove (KLOHV) *n. cloves.* The dried bud of a *clove* tree. *Cloves* are ground and used for flavoring puddings, cakes, etc. *Cloves* are a spice, like pepper and cinnamon.

clo•ver (KLOHV-er) *n. clovers.* A small plant with leaves usually made up of three smaller leaves or leaflets. Dried *clover* blossoms and leaves are used as food for horses and cattle. *Clover* blossoms are red, yellow, and white. It is supposed to be good luck to find a four-leaf *clover.*

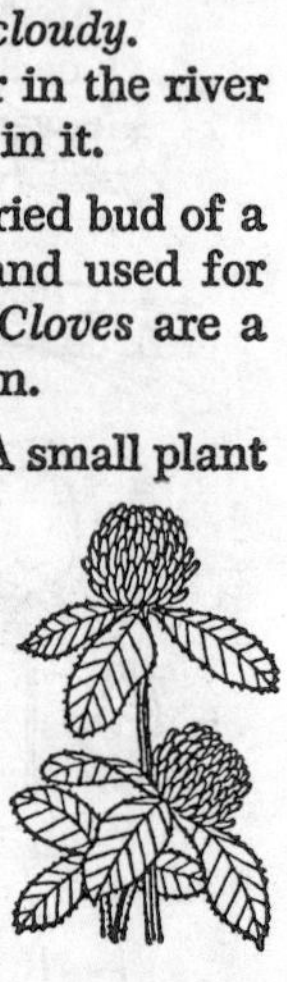

clown (KLOWN) *n. clowns.* A man with a painted face who wears a costume of many bright colors and does funny tricks at the circus. — Children laugh at the *clowns.*

club (KLUB) *n. clubs.* 1. A heavy wooden stick for use as a weapon.—The policeman carries a *club.*

2. Any stick used for beating or striking things. — Jack carried the golf *clubs* for the players.

3. A group of people who have joined together for a special purpose, often for pleasure and recreation. — We belong to a writing *club.* We have meetings at which we plan writing stories.

—*v. clubs, clubbed, clubbing.* Hit with a heavy club. — The policeman *clubbed* the mad dog that was biting people.

cluck (KLUK) *n.* The sound a hen makes.—The old hen calls her little chicks by saying, *"Cluck, cluck."*

—*v. clucks, clucked, clucking.* Make the sound of a hen.—The hen *clucked* to her cheeping baby chicks.

clue (KLOO) *n. clues.* Anything that helps to solve a difficult problem or mystery; a hint. —A pair of glasses lost by the robber was the *clue* that helped to solve the mystery of the robbery.

clump (KLUMP) *n. clumps.* Close group or grove.—A thick *clump* of trees stands on the hill.

—*v. clumps, clumped, clumping.* Walk heavily and noisily.—The tired soldier *clumped* along the road.

clum•sy (KLUM-zee) *adj. clumsier, clumsiest; clumsily, adv.* 1. Awkward; not graceful. —Jack is a *clumsy* boy. His feet seem to get in his way, and he doesn't seem to know what to do with his hands. He is always falling over something, or knocking something down by accident.

2. Poorly done or made. — Older boys often think that the airplane models their younger brothers make are *clumsy.*

clung (KLUNG) *v.* One form of the verb *cling.*—The man in the water *clung* to the overturned boat.

clus·ter (KLUSS-ter) *n. clusters.* A bunch or group.—Grapes grow in *clusters.*—Mother arranged a *cluster* of leaves on the mantel.
—*v. clusters, clustered, clustering.* Gather; form into a group. – The children *cluster* around Father when he comes home.

clutch (KLUCH) *n. clutches.* 1. A tight grasp or hold. – The witch got Hansel and Gretel into her *clutches,* but they escaped. – Father kept a tight *clutch* on Sally's hand.
2. A device that joins two parts of a machine so that it will run, or which throws the parts out of gear, or apart, when you do not want the machine to run.—To stop the auto, push with your right foot on the brake, and with your left foot on the *clutch.*
—*v. clutches, clutched, clutching.* Grasp or hold tightly. – The old woman *clutched* the Boy Scout's arm as they crossed the icy street.

coach (KOHCH) *n. coaches.* 1. A closed carriage drawn by horses.—The fairy godmother changed the pumpkin into a golden *coach.*

2. A passenger car on a train.—We rode in a *coach* when we went to see Grandmother.

3. A teacher or instructor.—The football *coach* trains the boys to play football.
—*v. coaches, coached, coaching.* Teach or help to learn.—Jack *coaches* Mary in arithmetic, and she helps him with his music.

coal (KOHL) *n. coals.* 1. A fuel that is sold in small, black chunks. It is burned to give heat and power. *Coal* is a mineral that comes from mines in the earth.

2. A piece of wood or coal that is red-hot.—We cooked our steak over the hot *coals* of the campfire.

coarse (KORSS) *adj. coarser, coarsest; coarsely, adv.* 1. Not fine; not in small pieces.—The cook chopped the cabbage into *coarse* pieces for the salad.—Drip coffee is ground fine; it is not *coarse.*
2. Poor; rough.—The poor family ate *coarse* food. They could not afford better foods.
3. Having rough manners and rude ways.—Mary says that Jack is *coarse* when he teases her or takes big mouthfuls at the table.

coast (KOHST) *n. coasts.* Seashore; the land along the water.—A boat was anchored just off the *coast.*—We went to the *coast* for our summer vacation.
—*v. coasts, coasted, coasting.* Slide; move along with no effort.—Children *coast* downhill on their sleds.—Boys *coast* downhill on their bicycles.

coat (KOHT) *n. coats.* 1. A garment with sleeves that is worn over other clothing.—In winter I wear my heavy *coat.*

2. A covering. – The painter gave the house two *coats* of paint. – The swimmers have a dark *coat* of tan.
—*v. coats, coated, coating.* Cover.—A heavy snow *coated* all the roads.

coax (KOHKS) *v. coaxes, coaxed, coaxing.* Persuade; get to say yes.—Bob tried to *coax* Mother to let him go swimming. He said it was a warm day, he would be very careful, and he hadn't been swimming for a long time.

cob (KAHB) *n. cobs.* A corncob; the long, hard, woodlike center. Corn grows on a *cob.* – Some pipes are carved out of *cobs.*

co•bra (KOH-brə) *n. cobras.* A very poisonous snake that can spread the skin about its neck into a hood when angry or excited. *Cobras* are found mostly in Asia and Africa.

cob•web (KAHB-web) *n. cobwebs.* A network of very fine threads spun by a spider. Flies and insects get caught and tangled up in *cobwebs,* and the spider eats them. *Cobwebs* are often spun in high corners of rooms.

cock (KAHK) *n. cocks.* A rooster. The hen is the female bird, and the *cock* is the male bird. The males of many kinds of birds are called *cocks.*
–*v. cocks, cocked, cocking.* Turn up.–The man *cocked* his hat on one side.–Jack's dog Spot *cocks* his head when he hears Jack coming.

cock•er span•iel (kahk-er SPAN-yəl) *cocker spaniels.* A small hunting dog. *Cocker spaniels* have long curly hair, short tails, long floppy ears, and shaggy paws.

cock•pit (KAHK-pit) *n. cockpits.* 1. The space for the pilots in airplanes.–The pilot waved from the *cockpit* before he took off.
2. A small space below deck on small boats and yachts.–During the rainstorm the crew sat in the *cockpit* of the boat and told stories.

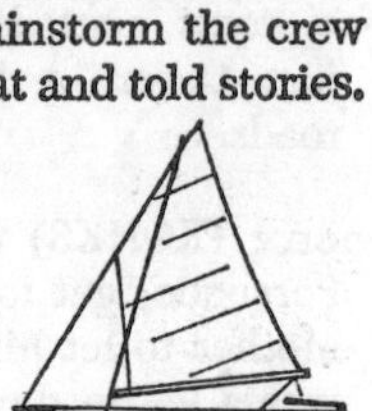

cock•roach (KAHK-rohch) *n. cockroaches.* A long, brown insect that gets into stores, kitchens, ships, and other places where there is food. *Cockroaches* run very fast and travel at night.–Mother gets rid of *cockroaches* by spreading a poison powder around.

co•coa (KOH-koh) *n.* Ground or powdered chocolate. Children drink hot *cocoa.* It is made from powdered chocolate, sugar, and hot milk.

co•co•nut or **co•coa•nut** (KOH-kə-nut) *n. coconuts* or *cocoanuts.* The large, hard-shelled, brown fruit of the coco palm tree. The *coconut* has two shells; the outside shell is very hard to break. Inside is a layer of white nutmeat that is good to eat. The center of the *coconut* is filled with a clear liquid, called milk, that is good to drink. The white meat of the *coconut* is often shredded and used on cakes, in puddings, pies, and candies.

co•coon (kə-KOON) *n. cocoons.* The silky case or covering made by a caterpillar to live in while it is changing into a butterfly or moth.

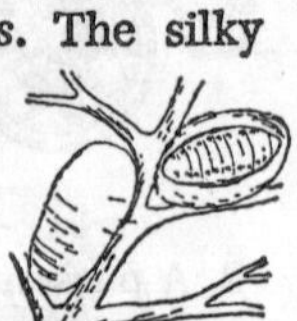

cod or **cod•fish** (KAHD-fish) *n. sing.* and *pl.* A kind of fish that lives in cold, deep salt water. Many people eat *cod.* The oil from the liver of the *codfish* is used as a medicine.

code (KOHD) *n. codes.* 1. Any set of signals; a group of words or letters, etc., used for sending messages.–The Boy Scouts' *code* for sending messages is a set of flag-waving signals.–Jack and Bob write notes to each other in *code.*
2. A rule, law, or standard by which people live.–A Boy Scout must have a high *code* of honor.

cof·fee (KAWF-ee) *n. coffees.* A drink made from the dried, roasted seeds of the *coffee* plant. Many people drink *coffee*. The seeds of the *coffee* plant are also called *coffee*.

cof·fin (KAWF-ən) *n. coffins.* A long box in which the body of a dead person is placed for burial.–The body of the old man who was drowned was buried in a gray *coffin*.

cog (KAHG) *n. cogs.* One of a row of little points or teeth which stick out from a part on a machine. A *cog*wheel is not smooth on the edge; it has *cogs* that fit into the *cogs* of other wheels to make them turn.

coil (KOIL) *n. coils.* A ring or spiral made by winding something around and around.–After the gardener finished sprinkling the garden, he wound the hose into a *coil*.–*Coils* of wire are used in many electrical devices.

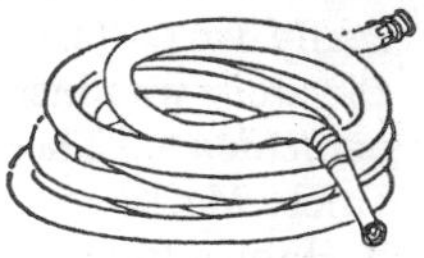

–*v. coils, coiled, coiling.* Wind round and round.–The monkey *coiled* his tail around the branch and swung on it.

coin (KOIN) *n. coins.* A piece of metal money; a penny, nickel, dime, etc.–Jack put some *coins* into his savings bank.–*Coins* are stamped to tell how much money they are worth and in what year they were made.

–*v. coins, coined, coining.* 1. Shape and stamp a piece of metal to make money.–The government *coins* money.

2. Make up.–The children *coined* a new class motto.

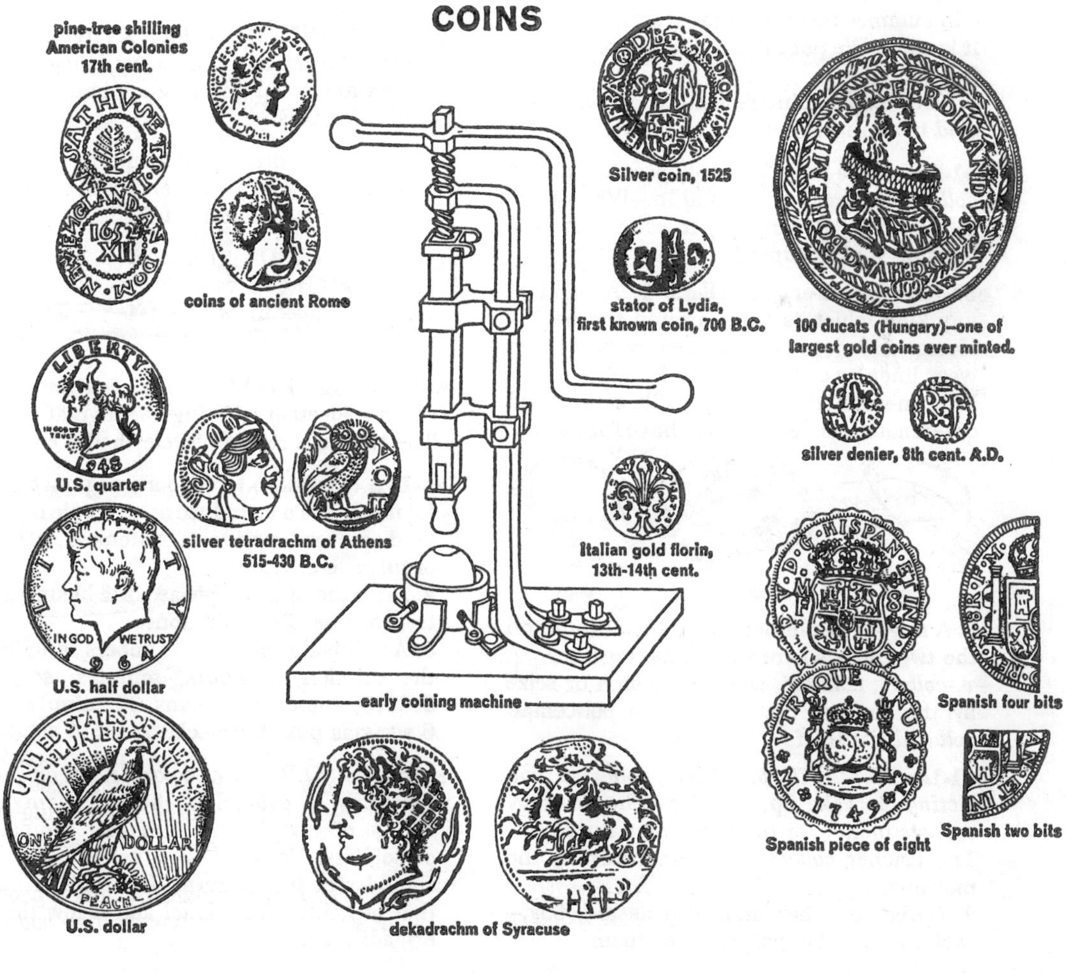

co•in•ci•dence (koh-IN-sə-dənss) *n. coincidences.* 1. Something that looks planned but really isn't.—The fact that the old judge in the story was just like Uncle Mark was pure *coincidence.* The author didn't even know Uncle Mark.
2. Happening at the same time or same place. —The *coincidence* of the three bomb scares made the police think that the same group was responsible for them all. Bombs were found at the same time in three of the city's theaters.

coke (KOHK) *n.* A fuel used in refining metals. *Coke* is made by heating soft coal until some of the gases in the coal have passed off. *Coke* has a grayish color.

cold (KOHLD) *n. colds.* A very common sickness that causes coughing and sneezing, a running nose, and, sometimes, a sore throat and fever.—If you have a *cold,* stay at home so that you will not spread it to other people.
—adj. colder, coldest; coldly, adv. 1. Not warm. —In summer the weather is warm. In winter it is *cold.*—We put milk in the icebox to keep it *cold.*
2. Not friendly or interested.—The man seems *cold* to strangers because he is shy.

col•lapse (kə-LAPSS) *v. collapses, collapsed, collapsing.* Break down; fall in.—When Baby sat in the doll carriage, it *collapsed.*—The burning roof *collapsed.*

col•lar (KAHL-er) *n. collars.* 1. A band of any kind which is worn around the neck.—Horses and dogs wear leather *collars.*—Men wear linen or cotton *collars* on their shirts.—Women wear *collars* of lace, silk, cotton, and other materials.—Some coats have fur *collars.*

2. A ring.—The plumber put a metal *collar* on the two pipes where they came together.
—v. collars, collared, collaring. Catch or seize by the back of the collar.—The policeman *collared* the thief.

col•lect (kə-LEKT) *v. collects, collected, collecting.* 1. Take up; call for.—The newsboy *collects* money for the paper on Saturdays.—The teacher *collects* our homework in the morning.
2. Gather together and keep as a hobby.—Jack *collects* stamps. He saves them.
3. Gather together in a group; pile up.—A large crowd *collected* to see the circus parade. —Leaves *collect* on the sidewalks in the fall.

col•lec•tion (kə-LEK-shən) *n. collections.* 1. A group of things selected and kept, as a hobby or to be shown.—Father has a *collection* of old pieces of money.
2. A sum of money made up by many contributions, or by many people each giving something.—The children took up a *collection* to buy flowers for their sick classmate. They each gave something to get enough money together.

col•lege (KAHL-ij) *n. colleges.* A school higher up or more advanced than a high school. Many boys and girls go to *college.* A *college* gives degrees to show that one has completed his studies satisfactorily.

col•lide (kə-LYD) *v. collides, collided, colliding.* Come together with force; crash against each other.—The two cars *collided* on the road.

col•lie (KAHL-ee) *n. collies.* A large dog with a long, bushy tail and heavy, shaggy hair. *Collies* are sheep dogs.—Many children have *collies* for pets.

col•li•sion (kə-LIZH-ən) *n. collisions.* The coming together of things with great force.—The two boys riding bicycles had a *collision.*

co•lon (KOH-lən) *n.* A mark of punctuation [:] used: 1. To introduce an example of some kind, an explanation, a statement, a series of items, etc.
2. After the opening phrase of a business letter, such as "Dear Mr. Jones:".
3. As a divider between numbers to indicate the division of hours, minutes, seconds. 5:32:6, therefore, means 32 minutes and 6 seconds past 5 o'clock.

colo•nel (KER-nəl) *n. colonels.* An officer in the army. A *colonel* in the U.S. Army has charge of a regiment or several companies of soldiers. He wears a silver eagle on the shoulder of his uniform. His rank is above that of lieutenant *colonel* and below that of brigadier general.

COLONIAL PERIOD

early colonial dwellings

typical colonial interior

co•lo•ni•al (kə-LOH-nee-əl) *adj.* Having to do with colonies.–When the first British people came to America, they formed thirteen colonies. They built certain styles of houses and furniture, wore certain styles of clothing, and had certain customs. We call this time the *colonial* period.

col•o•nist (KAHL-ə-nist) *n. colonists.* One of a group of people founding a colony or settlement; a settler; a person who lives in a colony.–The first *colonists* in America were brave and hardy people. They settled in an unknown land.

col•o•nize (KAHL-ə-nyz) *v. colonizes, colonized, colonizing.* Make settlements in; also, settle in a colony. – The French *colonized* parts of North Africa.

col•o•ny (KAHL-ə-nee) *n. colonies.* 1. A group of people who go from their own country to a new one, and live together in a settlement or town.–A *colony* of French people live in the southern part of our city.

2. A group of certain insects, animals, or plants that live together, as a *colony* of bees or a *colony* of ants.

col•or (KUL-er) *n. colors.* Blue is the *color* of the sky.–Green is the *color* of the grass.–Yellow is the *color* of the sun.–Red and green are the *colors* used at Christmas time.

–*v. colors, colored, coloring.* Put color on.–The children *color* eggs for Easter. They paint or dye them.

–*The colors* means the flag.–The soldiers marched up the street with *the colors* flying.

Col•o•rad•o (kahl-ə-RAD-oh *or* kahl-ə-RAHD-oh) *n.* A mountainous state in western United States, rich in minerals, especially coal. *Colorado* raises watermelons, cantaloupes, and more sugar beets than any other state.

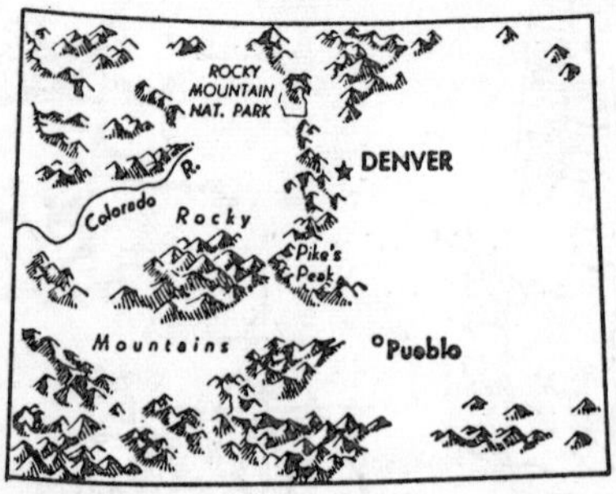

col•or•less (KUL-er-ləss) *adj.* 1. Without any color.–The boy was so frightened that his face was *colorless*.–The water that we drink is *colorless*.
2. Dull; the same all the time.–Cinderella's life was *colorless* until she went to the ball.–The bashful boy told the story in a *colorless* voice, without emphasizing anything.

colt (KOHLT) *n. colts.* A baby horse. *Colts* have very long, wobbly legs. – Grandfather's mare has a *colt.*

col•um•bine (KAHL-əm-byn) *n. columbines.* A flower that grows both wild and in gardens. *Columbines* are of many different colors.

col•umn (KAHL-əm) *n. columns.* 1. A tall, up-and-down support, usually thin, used in buildings.–The porch roof is held up by white *columns.*
2. A long, straight up-and-down line or row.–In arithmetic class we added several *columns* of figures.–The pages in this dictionary are divided into *columns*. – A *column* of smoke came from the chimney.
3. A long single row or line.–The boys marched in a *column* across the ball field.

4. A special part of a newspaper written regularly by one person.–The household *column* in the newspaper tells how to cook and keep house.

comb (KOHM) *n. combs.* 1. A long piece of metal, rubber, or other material with close-set teeth used to straighten out hair or wool.–Coarse *combs* are used to untangle sheep wool before it is spun into threads.

2. A crest; a ridge that sticks up.–Roosters have red *combs* on their heads.

3. A wax framework which bees make to store honey in.–Pieces of honey*comb* are often packed with the honey that comes in jars.

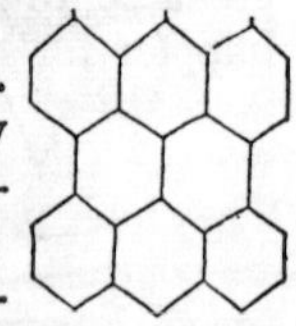

–*v. combs, combed, combing.* 1. Straighten and untangle by running a comb through.–Mother *combed* Baby's hair.
2. Look all over; search thoroughly.–Mother *combed* the house in search of her thimble.

com•bi•na•tion (kahm-bə-NAY-shən) *n. combinations.* Several things put together or combined.–The *combination* of celery, cabbage, pineapple, and salad dressing makes a tasty salad.

com•bine (kəm-BYN) *v. combines, combined, combining.* Mix or put together.–If you *combine* blue paint and yellow paint, you will have green paint.

com•bus•ti•ble (kəm-BUSS-tə-bəl) *adj.* Capable of burning.–Coal is *combustible.*

com•bus•tion (kəm-BUSS-chən) *n. combustions.* Burning; the process of burning.–We do not keep piles of paper in the basement because of the danger of *combustion.*

come (KUM) *v. comes, came, coming.* 1. Move toward.–The horse will *come* to the fence if you hold out your hand.
2. Attend; arrive and stay.–My teacher is *coming* to my party. She *came* last year, too.
3. Happen; take place.–Christmas *comes* once a year.
4. Reach.–Mother's short jacket *comes* down to her waist.
–*Come about* means happen.–How did the accident *come about*?

co•me•di•an (kə-MEED-ee-ən) *n. comedians.* A funny person who entertains other people. –The *comedian* in the show told funny jokes and stories.

com•e•dy (KAHM-ə-dee) *n. comedies.* A funny play or motion picture.–There was a *comedy* before the feature picture.

com•et (KAHM-it) *n. comets.* A bright heavenly body that has a tail of light. *Comets* move about the sun.

com•fort (KUM-fert) *n. comforts.* 1. Something which cheers.–The hunter's dog was a great *comfort* to him. The dog made life happier for him.
2. State of ease; freedom from trouble or worry.–The family lives in great *comfort.* They have plenty of money, food, and clothes.
–*v. comforts, comforted, comforting.* Cheer up; make peaceful or happy.–The policeman tried to *comfort* the lost child and make him forget his fears.

com•fort•a•ble (KUM-fer-tə-bəl *or* KUMF-ter-bəl) *adj.; comfortably, adv.* 1. Giving rest and peace for the body.–The new bed is *comfortable* to sleep in.
2. Free from trouble, pain, etc.; contented.–The family is *comfortable* in the new house.

com•fort•er (KUM-fer-ter) *n. comforters.* 1. One that cheers and makes comfortable.–The old woman is a great *comforter* to the sick and poor. She brings them cheer and makes them happier.

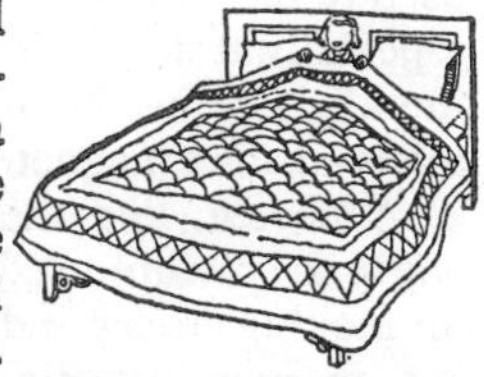

2. A quilt; a thick, padded covering.–The new *comforter* on my bed keeps me warm.

com•ic (KAHM-ik) *adj.* Funny.–The clown was a *comic* sight, balancing the little dog on his head.
–*Comics* are funny pictures or cartoons.–The Sunday newspaper has colored *comics* in it.

com•i•cal (KAHM-i-kəl) *adj.; comically, adv.* Funny.–The clown told many *comical* stories. They made us laugh.

com•ma (KAHM-ə) *n. commas.* A punctuation mark [,] used in sentences to help you read and understand them properly.

com•mand (kə-MAND) *n. commands.* 1. An order; a direction.–The soldiers obeyed the captain's *commands.*
2. Charge; control.–The captain is in *command* of the ship. Everyone there must obey him.
–*v. commands, commanded, commanding.* Order; tell to do.–The captain *commanded* the soldiers to halt.

com•mand•er (kə-MAND-er) *n. commanders.* 1. A person who has charge of or control over people.–The captain was the *commander* of the company of soldiers.
2. An officer in the navy ranking just below captain.

com•mence (kə-MENSS) *v. commences, commenced, commencing.* Begin.–The teacher said to *commence* writing.

com•mence•ment (kə-MENSS-mənt) *n. commencements.* 1. Beginning.–The audience waited for the *commencement* of the performance.
2. The day of graduation; the occasion on which students receive diplomas, degrees, etc., for having successfully completed a course of study.–Tom's family was proud of him on the day of his *commencement.*

com•ment (KAHM-ent) *n. comments.* 1. A remark.–After his speech, the speaker made a few additional *comments.*
2. A critical opinion. It can be good or bad.–The teacher wrote a *comment* on everyone's paper. She said mine was well written. She told John he had misspelled several words.

com•men•ta•tor (KAHM-ən-tayt-er) *n. commentators.* 1. A person who analyzes or speaks about the news.–Father turned on the radio to hear his favorite *commentator.*
2. A person who makes comments (on something).–That comedian is a great *commentator* on our manners. He makes us laugh at the silly things we do.

com•merce (KAHM-erss) *n.* Buying and selling of goods.–There is much *commerce* between England and the United States.

com•mer•cial (kə-MER-shəl) *adj.; commercially, adv.* Having to do with business or commerce.–Banks, department stores, grocery stores, and candy shops are all *commercial* enterprises.

com•mit•tee (kə-MIT-ee) *n. committees.* A group of people named to do certain things for a larger group.–The *committee* on decorations chose the decorations for the club party.

com•mon (KAHM-ən) *adj.; commonly, adv.* 1. Frequent; usual.–Storms are *common* near the seashore.
2. Ordinary; seen often. – Dandelions are *common* weeds.
3. Shared.–Grandfather gave Joe, Jack, and John a pony. The pony is the *common* property of all the boys.
–*In common* means shared.–Jack and Bob have many things *in common.* There are many things in which they share an interest.

com•mon•place (KAHM-ən-playss) *adj.* 1. Ordinary; common; customary. – Automobiles on the streets of New York City are *commonplace.*
2. Uninteresting; dull.–The speaker made a *commonplace* speech. It was long and boring.

com•mo•tion (kə-MOH-shən) *n. commotions.* A disturbance; noisy disorder and confusion.–A *commotion* arose when everybody tried to leave the hall at the same time.

com•mu•ni•cate (kə-MYOO-nə-kayt) *v. communicates, communicated, communicating.* 1. Send a message or exchange messages or information with.–When Father gets to Washington, he will *communicate* with us. He will telephone or write us, or send us a telegram.
2. Pass on.–If you have a case of measles, stay at home so that you will not *communicate* it to others.

com•mu•ni•ca•tion (kə-myoo-nə-KAY-shən) *n. communications.* 1. News, information, or message sent. – We do not know whether the *communication* came by letter, telephone, or telegram.
2. A way or means of sending messages.–During the storm there was no *communication* between the cities.

com•mu•nism (KAHM-yə-niz-əm) *n.* A form of socialism; a system of social organization based on the theory that goods and property should be owned and controlled by the community as a whole, not by private individuals. As practiced in Russia at present, *communism* is characterized by the use of authoritarian government control as a means of reaching its final goals: equal distribution of wealth and abolishment of the state.

com•mu•nist (KAHM-yə-nist) *n. communists.* A person who believes in the ideas of communism, or who is part of a state that practices communism.

com•mu•ni•ty (kə-MYOO-nə-tee) *n. communities.* A group of people who live together in a town or settlement.–Money was given by the *community* to build a playground.

com•pan•ion (kəm-PAN-yən) *n. companions.* 1. One who goes about with another.–The crippled woman has a traveling *companion.*–The old man and his dog are faithful *companions.* They go around together all the time.
2. A friend; a comrade.–The men were *companions* at school. They enjoyed each other's company.

com•pa•ny (KUM-pə-nee) *n. companies.* 1. Guests; people who are visiting.–Our *company* could not stay for dinner.
2. In the army, a unit of soldiers commanded by a captain.
3. A business firm or organization into which people put money in order to make profit.–A new *company* has just been formed in our town to sell building materials.
4. Companionship; being with or together.–Bob enjoys Jack's *company.*

com•pare (kəm-PAIR) *v. compares, compared, comparing.* Examine to see how things are different or alike.–The boys *compared* their knives. They looked at the knives to see how they were alike and how they were different.

com•pass (KUM-pəss) *n. compasses.* 1. An instrument with a needle or pointer which points to the north. *Compasses* are used to tell directions, especially at sea and in the air. The needle of a *compass* is a magnet.
2. A device, like the one in the picture, used for making circles and for measuring distances. It is sometimes called a pair of *compasses,* because it has two points.

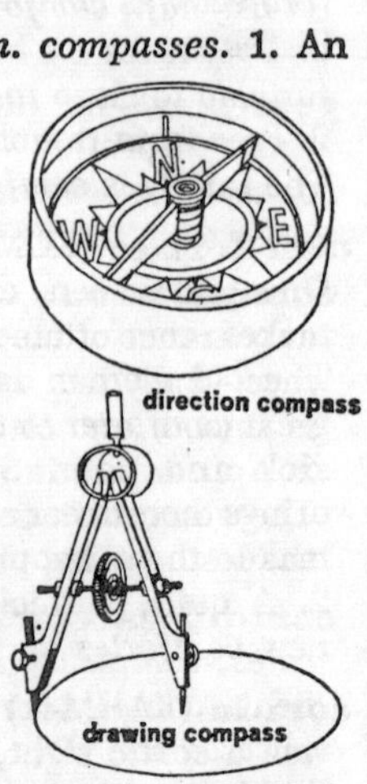

com•pel (kəm-PEL) *v. compels, compelled, compelling.* Force.–The deep snow *compels* us to stay home today.–The law *compelled* the man to send his children to school.

com•pete (kəm-PEET) *v. competes, competed, competing.* Try to outdo or win over another; engage or take part in a contest.–Mary and Bob will *compete* in the spelling bee.–The brothers *competed* in the race.

com·pe·ti·tion (kahm-pə-TISH-ən) *n. competitions.* A contest.–One boy from our school is in the swimming *competition* for the city championship.

com·plain (kəm-PLAYN) *v. complains, complained, complaining.* 1. Find fault.–Father never *complains* about the food we eat. He thinks it is all right.
2. Talk about one's troubles.–The poor old man never *complains.*

com·plaint (kəm-PLAYNT) *n. complaints.* 1. A statement accusing one of wrongdoing; a statement that something is not right.–The *complaint* said that the man was driving on the wrong side of the street.–The woman made a *complaint* to the store that the dress she bought had a hole in it.
2. A trouble; a thing to complain about.–The boy's *complaint* was that his stomach hurt.

com·plete (kəm-PLEET) *v. completes, completed, completing.* Finish.–It will take a long time to *complete* the building of the house. –Have you *completed* your work?
–*adj.* 1. Whole; full; entire.–John has a *complete* set of tools for building model airplanes.
2. Perfect; thorough.–Our play was a *complete* success. Everyone liked it.
3. Finished.–After five months of work, the project was *complete.* It took five months to finish it.

com·plete·ly (kəm-PLEET-lee) *adv.* Entirely; altogether.–Mary's work is *completely* done.–The boy was *completely* happy. Nothing was troubling him.

com·plex·ion (kəm-PLEK-shən) *n.* 1. The appearance of the skin, especially that of the face.–Baby has a fair *complexion.* Her skin is smooth and clear.
2. Appearance in general; how things look.–The game took on a new *complexion* when the losing team tied the score.

com·pli·cate (KAHM-plə-kayt) *v. complicates, complicated, complicating.* Make difficult, complex, involved.–Heavy rains *complicated* the work of the farmer.–Too many big words *complicate* the reading of the story.

com·pli·ment (KAHM-plə-mənt) *n. compliments.* A statement of praise.–The teacher gave Mary a *compliment* about her neatly written paper. She said nice things about it.
–(KAHM-plə-ment) *v. compliments, complimented, complimenting.* Praise.–The coach *complimented* Bob for his good plays in the game.

com·pose (kəm-POHZ) *v. composes, composed, composing.* 1. Make up; put together; create.–Some people *compose* music; others *compose* poems.
2. Make by putting different things together. –Hot chocolate is *composed* of hot milk, chocolate, and sugar.
3. Make calm; control.–The actress *composed* herself very well. She no longer looked excited.

com·pos·er (kəm-POHZ-er) *n. composers.* A person who composes, especially one who writes music.

com·po·si·tion (kahm-pə-ZISH-ən) *n. compositions.* 1. Something made up and written down.–Poems, stories, music, and books are
2. A mixture.–Concrete is a *composition* of sand, cement, and water.

com·pound (KAHM-pownd) *n. compounds* and *adj.* 1. Something made by the combination or mixture of two or more things, elements, or parts.–Many cosmetics are *compounds* of oils, perfumes, powders, and coloring materials.
2. A word made up by the combination of two or more words.–"Grapevine" and "do-it-yourself" are *compounds.*

com·pre·hend (kahm-pree-HEND) *v. comprehends, comprehended, comprehending.* Understand; know the meaning of.–Pierre *comprehends* the French language. He was born in France.

com·pul·so·ry (kəm-PUL-sə-ree) *adj.* Required; enforced, often with the understanding that some punishment will follow if the particular thing is not done or observed.–Fire drills are *compulsory* in many schools.

com·pu·ter (kahm-PYOO-ter) *n. computers.* An instrument which carries out mathematical operations.–A *computer* can solve in seconds a problem that might take days for mathematicians.

com·rade (KAHM-rad) *n. comrades.* A friend; a companion.–The young men were *comrades* in the army. They spent much time together.

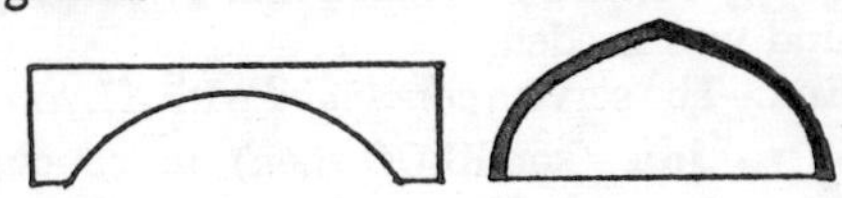

con·cave (KAHN-kayv *or* kahn-KAYV) *adj.* Curved inwardly, or hollowed out in a curve, as the inside of a canoe. A ball or sphere viewed from the inside is *concave.*

con•ceal (kən-SEEL) *v. conceals, concealed, concealing.* Hide.–The robber *concealed* his gun under his coat.

con•ceit (kən-SEET) *n.* Too high an opinion or judgment of oneself.–The boy's *conceit* caused people to dislike him.

con•ceit•ed (kən-SEET-əd) *adj.* Vain; too proud.–The woman is very *conceited.* She thinks that she is better than anyone else.

con•cen•trate (KAHN-sən-trayt) *v. concentrates, concentrated, concentrating.* 1. Mass, gather, or bring together at one point.–The general *concentrated* his troops in front of the palace.
2. Pay attention.–The teacher told the pupils to *concentrate* on their homework.

con•cern (kən-SERN) *n. concerns.* 1. Worry; serious consideration.–Bob showed much *concern* when he saw how big the football players were on the opposing team.
2. A business company.–A new *concern* has opened a shop around the corner.
–*v. concerns, concerned, concerning.* 1. Relate to; have an effect on.–The war *concerned* everyone, soldiers and civilians alike. –The railroad strike *concerned* all of us. It mattered to all of us.
2. Be worried or anxious.–When Bill was late, Mother was *concerned* about him.
3. Have to do with; be about.–The telephone message *concerned* Father only.

con•cert (KAHN-sert) *n. concerts.* 1. A musical program in which several pieces are performed.–Three symphonies were played at last night's *concert.*–The *concert* was given good reviews by the critics.
2. Harmony or agreement.–The children sang and said poems in *concert.*

conch (KAHNCH *or* KAHNK) *n. conches* or *conchs.* A spiral-shaped shell. – We found a large *conch* on the seashore.

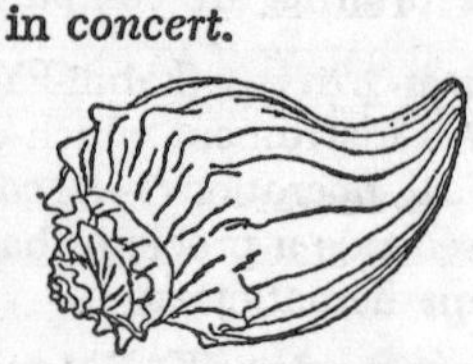

con•clude (kən-KLOOD) *v. concludes, concluded, concluding.* 1. Decide after thinking. –The city officials *concluded* that a new playground was needed.
2. End.–The service *concluded* with a hymn.

con•clu•sion (kən-KLOO-zhən) *n. conclusions.* 1. An end.–The story running in the paper came to a *conclusion* in today's paper.
2. What one decides after thinking.–What *conclusion* did you reach? What did you decide?

con•crete (KAHN-kreet *or* kahn-KREET) *n.* Stone made by mixing sand, gravel, cement, and water, and allowing it to harden. *Concrete* is used in building roads, houses, sidewalks, bridges, and other structures.

–*adj.* 1. Specific; not general.–The teacher asked for a *concrete* answer.
2. Real; actual.–The figure I glimpsed in the dark hall was *concrete.* It was not a ghost at all, but only my father.

con•demn (kən-DEM) *v. condemns, condemned, condemning.* 1. Strongly disapprove; state to be wrong.–The use of fighting to settle an argument should be *condemned.*
2. Declare or pronounce guilty.–The jury did not *condemn* the prisoner. They said he was innocent.
3. Doom.–The judge *condemned* the killer to death.
4. Pronounce unsafe or not fit for use.–The broken-down building was *condemned* as a firetrap.

con•den•sa•tion (kahn-dən-SAY-shən) *n. condensations.* 1. The act of making more compact or brief.–The book was improved by *condensation.* Unnecessary information was cut out.
2. The condensed item itself.–The *condensation* was easier to read.
3. The act of changing one form of something into a denser form, such as changing steam into water.

con•dense (kən-DENSS) *v. condenses, condensed, condensing.* 1. Make shorter and more compact; concentrate.–Father told John to *condense* his story and come to the point.
2. Change from gas or vapor to liquid.– When water vapor in the air *condenses,* it becomes rain.

con·di·tion (kən-DISH-ən) *n. conditions.* 1. State of health.—After taking his medicine, the boy's *condition* got better.
2. State of repair.—The old house is in poor *condition.* It needs painting and repairing.
3. Something needed to make something else possible.—Hard work is one of the *conditions* of success. Without it, there is little chance of succeeding.
4. Limitation; special circumstance.—Only under certain *conditions* will I sign that contract. I will not sign until parts of it have been changed.
—*v. conditions, conditioned, conditioning.* 1. Make ready; put in good repair.—I had my car *conditioned* for the trip.
2. Limit; qualify.—I must *condition* what I'm about to say because I don't want you to get the wrong idea.
3. Get used to; prepare.—Bob *conditioned* himself to the task. Now the hard work no longer bothers him.—The dog was *conditioned* to raise his right paw every time Bill snapped his fingers.
—*On condition that* means if or provided.—The farmer will give Bob a dog *on condition that* Bob gets all A's on his report card.

con·duct (KAHN-dukt) *n.* Behavior; way of acting.—The boy's *conduct* is very good.
—(kən-DUKT) *v. conducts, conducted, conducting.* 1. Guide; go along with.—The man will *conduct* us through the cave.
2. Direct; take charge of.—The chairman *conducts* our class meetings.
3. Direct or lead musicians in playing or singing.—Our music teacher will *conduct* at the concert.
—*Conduct oneself* means behave.—The boys *conduct themselves* well.

con·duc·tor (kən-DUK-ter) *n. conductors.* 1. A leader of a band, orchestra, or chorus. —Mr. Miller is the *conductor* of the school band.
2. A person who takes fares and looks after passengers on a public vehicle.—We gave our tickets to the *conductor* on the streetcar.—Trains and buses have *conductors,* too.
3. Something through which electricity or heat will pass.—Copper wire is a *conductor* of electricity.—An aluminum pan is a good *conductor* of heat. It allows the heat to pass from the stove to the contents of the pan.

cone (KOHN) *n. cones.* 1. A long or tall figure that is round at one end and pointed at the other.
2. A crisp, cone-shaped, hollow cake to be filled with ice cream.—Children like ice-cream *cones.*

3. The seed pod of an evergreen tree.—The pine tree has *cones.*

con·fer·ence (KAHN-fer-ənss) *n. conferences.* A meeting, usually for the purpose of discussing specific subjects or problems.—A *conference* was called to discuss a way of improving attendance at club meetings.

con·fess (kən-FESS) *v. confesses, confessed, confessing.* 1. Admit or own up that one has done wrong.—Jack *confessed* that he broke the window.
2. Tell, say, or make known something one did not want to tell.—I must *confess* I do not like arithmetic.

con·fes·sion (kən-FESH-ən) *n. confessions.* 1. A statement saying that one has done wrong.—The guilty man signed a *confession.* —Priests hear the *confessions* of people who want to tell of something wrong they have done.
2. An acknowledgment or admission of something one did not want to tell.—At the boy's *confession* that he had not had breakfast, Mother gave him some cereal and toast.

con·fide (kən-FYD) *v. confides, confided, confiding.* Tell private things to someone, with faith that they will be kept secret.—Mary *confides* in Mother.—Jack *confided* his plan to Bob.

con•fi•dence (KAHN-fə-dənss) *n. confidences.* 1. A feeling of faith in oneself.–Mary spoke with *confidence.* She was sure she was right.
2. Trust.–Mother has *confidence* in Bob's honesty.
3. Secrecy; an agreement not to tell.–Mary told Ruth her secret in *confidence.*
4. A secret.–Mary told Ruth a *confidence.*

con•fi•dent (KAHN-fə-dənt) *adj.* Sure; having no doubts.–I am *confident* that my new dress will come today.–Bob is a *confident* person. He is sure he can do what he sets out to do.

con•fi•den•tial (kahn-fə-DEN-shəl) *adj.; confidentially, adv.* Secret; private; not to be made public.–What Mary told Ruth is *confidential.* It is a secret between them.

con•fuse (kən-FYOOZ) *v. confuses, confused, confusing.* 1. Mix up one's thinking.–So many things happened at once this morning that it *confused* Mother. She didn't know what she was doing.
2. Mistake one for another.–The doctor told us not to *confuse* the two medicines, because they looked alike.

con•fu•sion (kən-FYOOZH-ən) *n.* A mixed-up condition; disorder.–If your mind is in *confusion,* you may say and do things you do not mean.–Bob's desk was in *confusion.* There were papers, pencils, inky handkerchiefs, marbles, and many other things all mixed up together in it.

con•grat•u•late (kən-GRACH-ə-layt) *v. congratulates, congratulated, congratulating.* Give someone one's good wishes or praise for something he has done well or something nice that has happened to him.–The teacher *congratulated* Jack on winning the sailing race.

con•grat•u•la•tions (kən-grach-ə-LAY-shənz) *n. pl.* Good wishes or praise given to a person for something he has done well or because something nice has happened.–The children gave the teacher their *congratulations* on his birthday.

con•gre•ga•tion (kahng-grə-GAY-shən) *n. congregations.* 1. The people attending a church service.–The minister spoke to a large *congregation.*
2. A crowd or gathering of people.–There was a great *congregation* at the all-star game.

con•gress (KAHNG-grəss) *n. congresses.* 1. (Always spelled with a capital "C.") A group of persons elected by the people of every state to make the laws for the United States.–*Congress* meets in the Capitol building in Washington, D. C. *Congress* is divided into two parts, or bodies. One is the Senate, and the other is the House of Representatives.
2. A large meeting or gathering of people to make plans, laws, etc.

con•junc•tion (kən-JUNGK-shən) *n. conjunctions.* 1. A combination, union, or joining together.–The *conjunction* of good weather, good food, and good company made things just right for a happy picnic.
2. A word used to connect words or groups of words. "And," "but," "or," and "if" are *conjunctions.*

con•nect (kə-NEKT) *v. connects, connected, connecting.* 1. Join; unite; put together.–We watched the men *connect* the trailer to the car.–The girls *connected* the pieces of rope to make a jumping rope.
2. Associate (in thought).–I *connect* the word "bed" with sleep and the word "bread" with eat. I think of them as being used with, or related to, each other.
3. Be engaged in business.–Father is *connected* with a radio repair company.

Con•nec•ti•cut (kə-NET-i-kət) *n.* A small state on the east coast of the United States, known for farming, tobacco-raising, and the manufacturing of watches, clocks, silverware, machinery, and many other articles.

con•nec•tion (kə-NEK-shən) *n. connections.* 1. The act of uniting or connecting.–Father connected the hose to the outside faucet. After making the *connection,* he watered the grass.
2. A place where things are joined together. –The hose leaks right at the *connection* with the faucet.
3. A relation; a going with or belonging together.–I am thinking of something in *connection* with a finger. It would be ring, thimble, glove, or hand.–Although both our names are Smith, there is no *connection* between our families. We are not related.
4. Business doings or relation.–Father has no *connection* with the flower shop. He does not have anything to do with it.

con·quer (KAHNG-ker) *v. conquers, conquered, conquering.* 1. Overcome or get rid of.—At last Jack has *conquered* his bad habit of being late.
2. Defeat; overcome; win over.—The smaller army can *conquer* the larger one if it gets more airplanes.

con·science (KAHN-shənss) *n.* Inner knowledge of what is right and what is wrong; the feeling inside a person that causes him to do the right thing when he has the choice of doing the wrong thing.—Tom's *conscience* troubled him because he had told a lie. He admitted the truth and felt better.

con·sci·en·tious (kahn-shee-EN-shəss) *adj.; conscientiously, adv.* Done with honesty, care, and painstaking effort, as one would do in keeping with one's conscience.—John did a *conscientious* job on his homework.

con·scious (KAHN-shəss) *adj.* 1. Aware (of something).—Mary was *conscious* of the heat, but it did not bother her.
2. Mentally awake.—The fall knocked Jim out. But he became *conscious* again in less than a minute.
3. Deliberate; on purpose.—Walter broke the stick. It was a *conscious* act. He wanted to break it.

con·sec·u·tive (kən-SEK-yə-tiv) *adj.; consecutively, adv.* Following one after another without interruption.—June, July, and August are *consecutive* months. But June, September, and December are not *consecutive* months.

con·sent (kən-SENT) *n. consents.* Permission.—Mother has given me her *consent* to go out. She has said that I may go.
—*v. consents, consented, consenting.* Agree; give permission; allow.—Grandfather would not *consent* to my riding the frisky pony.—Mother *consented* to my going out tonight.

con·se·quence (KAHN-sə-kwenss) *n. consequences.* 1. Result; something that happens because of something else that has taken place before.—John's car broke down, and as a *consequence,* he had to buy another one.
2. Importance, as in society, business, government, etc.—The mayor is a man of *consequence.*

con·ser·va·tion (kahn-ser-VAY-shən) *n.* The act of preserving, keeping safe, or protecting.—The *conservation* of fresh water is a problem in dry areas.

con·serv·a·tive (kən-SERV-ə-tiv) *n. conservatives.* A person opposed to change or new ideas.
—*adj.* Opposed to change; cautious.—A *conservative* company hesitates to try new business methods.

con·serve (kən-SERV) *v. conserves, conserved, conserving.* Preserve; guard; protect; keep from being wasted.—The boxer *conserved* his energy for the final rounds of the fight.

con·sid·er (kən-SID-er) *v. considers, considered, considering.* 1. Think about.—We will *consider* going to Washington for our vacation.
2. Remember; keep in mind; take account of.—The child looks fine, when you *consider* her long sickness.—Jack says Mary plays ball well *considering* she is only a girl.
3. Regard; think of as.—The coach *considers* Bob a good ball player.
—*consideration, n. considerations.*

con·sid·er·a·ble (kən-SID-er-ə-bəl) *adj.; considerably, adv.* 1. Quite a bit; much.—We have had *considerable* snow this winter.
2. Something of importance; worthy of consideration.—This problem is *considerable.*

con·sid·er·ate (kən-SID-er-ət) *adj.; considerately, adv.* Respectful; showing regard; courteous.—Jane gave her seat in the bus to the old man. She is a thoughtful person. It was a *considerate* thing to do.

con·sid·er·a·tion (kən-sid-er-AY-shən) *n. considerations.* 1. Thoughtful attention.—Mother asked Bob to give careful *consideration* to her question. She wanted him to think about it carefully before he answered.
2. Thoughtfulness or respect.—We should show *consideration* for the wishes of others.
3. A reason; something that must be taken into account.—What *considerations* made you give that answer?

con·sist (kən-SIST) *v. consists, consisted, consisting.* Be made up.—An hour *consists* of sixty minutes.

con·sist·ent (kən-SISS-tənt) *adj.; consistently, adv.* Being in harmony or in agreement with.—Tom's behavior is *consistent* with his appearance. He looks like a gentleman and acts like one.

con·so·nant (KAHN-sə-nənt) *n. consonants.* Any letter of the alphabet except a, e, i, o, u, and sometimes y.

con·spic·u·ous (kən-SPIK-yoo-əss) *adj.; conspicuously, adv.* 1. Prominent; easily noticed.–The newspaper headline was *conspicuous.* It was very big.
2. Noteworthy; striking.–The soldier won a medal for *conspicuous* bravery.

con·sta·ble (KAHN-stə-bəl) *n. constables.* A policeman.–The *constable* took the lost child to its home.

con·stant (KAHN-stənt) *adj.; constantly, adv.* 1. Without stopping; uninterrupted.–There is a *constant* flow of water from the Mississippi River into the Gulf of Mexico.
2. Loyal; faithful.–A dog is known to be a *constant* companion.
3. Firm; steadfast; unchanging.–The mayor is *constant* in his determination to maintain a clean city.
4. Happening again and again.–Susan's cat has disappeared again. His disappearance is a *constant* occurrence.

con·stel·la·tion (kahn-stə-LAY-shən) *n. constellations.* A group of stars that, as seen from the earth, seemed to ancient people to form pictures in the sky. The Big Dipper, also called Ursa Major, or the Big Bear, is easy to recognize. The *constellations* appear in different parts of the sky at different times of the year.

con·sti·tu·tion (kahn-stə-TOO-shən *or* kahn-sta-TYOO-shən) *n. constitutions.* 1. The physical make-up of a person or animal.–The sick boy has a poor *constitution.* His body is weak.
2. The most important rules of a group.–The *Constitution* of the United States is a group of rules which guides us in our lawmaking and public affairs and grants us our rights.–Clubs often have *constitutions.*

con·struct (kən-STRUKT) *v. constructs, constructed, constructing.* Build; make.–The children *constructed* a house of blocks.–The men *constructed* a bridge.

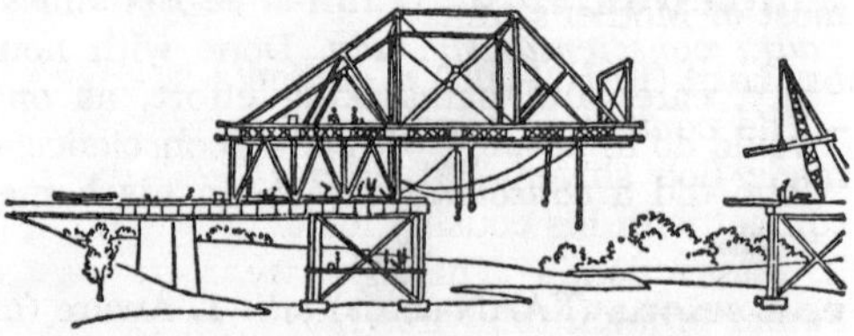

con·struc·tion (kən-STRUK-shən) *n. constructions.* 1. The act of building.–The *construction* of the bridge took a year.
2. The way of building.–The *construction* of that building is unusual; it is built of glass and concrete.
3. Something built.–The Empire State Building is a well-known *construction.*

CONSTELLATIONS OF SPRING AND WINTER

con•sult (kən-SULT) *v. consults, consulted, consulting.* 1. Get advice or information from.–Bob *consulted* the coach about improving his batting average.–Mary *consults* a dictionary whenever she has trouble spelling a word.
2. Consider together.–The boys *consulted* over the weather map before leaving for the picnic.

con•sume (kən-SOOM *or* -SYOOM) *v. consumes, consumed, consuming.* 1. Eat or drink up.–Pigs *consume* much food and water.
2. Destroy.–Fire *consumed* the building.
3. Use up.–Taking care of the baby *consumes* most of Mother's time.

con•tact (KAHN-takt) *n. contacts.* 1. Touch. – The *contact* of the sick boy's cold hand made Bob shiver.–Father has been out of *contact* with his cousins for many years.
2. Connection. – The light went on when Father brought the wires into *contact.*
–*v. contacts, contacted, contacting.* Get in touch with (used informally).– We tried to *contact* you by telephone, but no one answered.

con•ta•gious (kən-TAY-jəss) *adj.* Catching. –Measles, chickenpox, and some other diseases are *contagious.* They can be spread to other people by touch.

con•tain (kən-TAYN) *v. contains, contained, containing.* 1. Hold; have in it.–This bottle *contains* one pint.–The old trunk *contained* many wonderful things.
2. Consist of; be made up of.–One dollar *contains* twenty nickels.–6 *contains* three 2's.
3. Hold back; control one's feelings.–Mary was so excited that she could scarcely *contain* herself.

con•tain•er (kən-TAYN-er) *n. containers.* A box, barrel, carton, can, jug, or anything else for holding something.–Milk is often sold in cardboard *containers.*–A garbage can is a garbage *container.*

con•tent (kən-TENT) *adj.* Satisfied; pleased; at peace.–Jack was *content* with the mark he got on his spelling paper.
–*v. contents, contented, contenting.* Satisfy.– Cookies and milk *contented* the hungry child.

con•tents (KAHN-tentss) *n. pl.* What something written says; what a thing holds or has in it.–Mother did not tell us the *contents* of Grandfather's letter, so we were very curious to know what he said.–Sally stuck her finger into the jar to find out its *contents.*

Leo

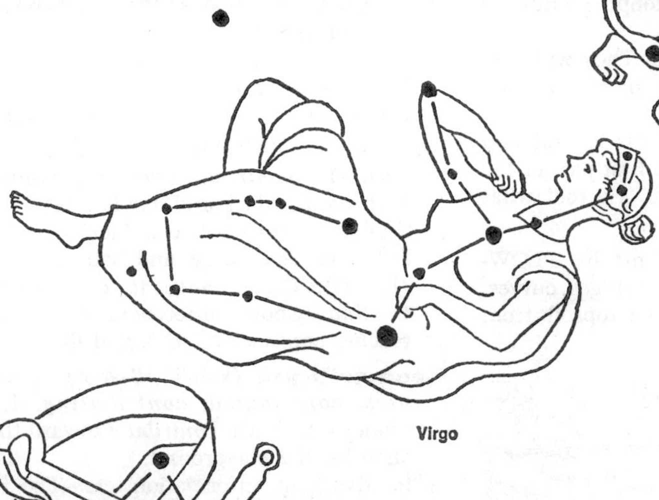

Virgo

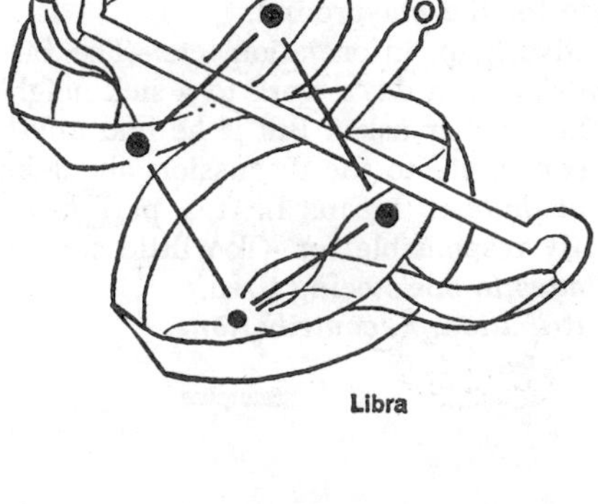

Libra

con•test (KAHN-test) *n. contests.* 1. A game in which people try to win.–We have running *contests*, broad-jumping *contests*, music *contests*, drawing *contests*, etc.–Today our class had a spelling bee, or *contest*, and our team won.
2. A fight or dispute.–There was such a *contest* over which movie the boys should see that they decided to draw straws.

con•ti•nent (KAHN-tə-nənt) *n. continents.* One of the seven largest pieces of land on the earth. The world is divided into *continents*, and then into countries. Each *continent* may contain many countries. North America, South America, Europe, Asia, Africa, Antarctica, and Australia are the names of the *continents*.

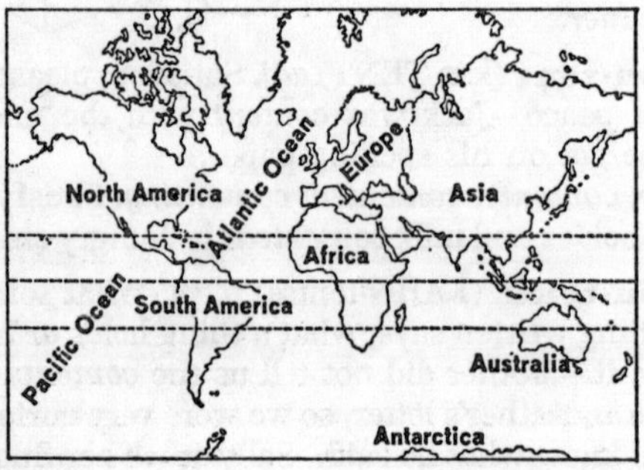

con•tin•ue (kən-TIN-yoo) *v. continues, continued, continuing.* 1. Keep on with.–We *continued* our work without stopping until we were finished.
2. Not stop; proceed; go on.–They will *continue* traveling until they have gone all around the world.
3. Take up where something is left off and go on with it.–Mary told the first part of the story, and Jack *continued* it. He told what happened next.

con•tour plow•ing (kahn-tuhr PLOW-ing). Plowing along the earth's ridges, curves, slopes, etc., to help keep the topsoil from being washed away by rain.

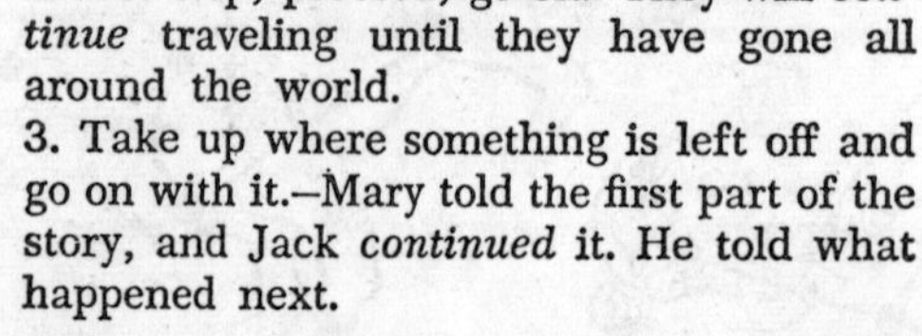

con•tract (KAHN-trakt) *n. contracts.* An agreement, usually written, between two or more people.–The *contract* said that the builder would build our house for $12,000.

con•tract (kən-TRAKT) *v. contracts, contracted, contracting.* 1. Agree by contract.–Father *contracted* to pay $60 a month on the mortgage.
2. Get smaller.–Most metals *contract* when they get cooler.
3. Make smaller.–In speaking, we often *contract* "is not" to "isn't."

con•trac•tion (kən-TRAK-shən) *n. contractions.* 1. Shrinking; drawing together; contracting.–When using metal, builders have to make allowance for its *contraction* in cold weather and its expansion in hot weather.
2. A shortened form, as a word made shorter by leaving out letters.–"Isn't" is a *contraction* of "is not."

con•tra•dict (kahn-trə-DIKT) *v. contradicts, contradicted, contradicting.* 1. Say the opposite of what another person has said.–Tom *contradicted* his friend Harry. Harry said the party was dull. Tom said it was gay.
2. Say that something is not true–The prisoner offered proof to *contradict* the charges against him.
3. Be in opposition to, or in disagreement with.–The two statements *contradicted* each other. Since each was different, we didn't know which one to believe.

con•tra•ry (KAHN-trair-ee) *adj.* 1. Opposite; against; not agreeing with.–Driving on the left side of the street is *contrary* to law in the United States. We are supposed to drive on the right side.
2. Stubborn; not agreeable.–Dickie is *contrary*. He never does what someone else wants him to do. He does only what he wants to do.

con•trast (KAHN-trast) *n. contrasts.* Difference.–The *contrast* between night and day is that night is dark and day is light.–There is a great *contrast* between Jack's writing and Bob's. Jack's is large, and Bob's is small.
–(kən-TRAST) *v. contrasts, contrasted, contrasting.* Show differences between.–The teacher *contrasted* Jack's and Bob's writing.

con•trib•ute (kən-TRIB-yoot) *v. contributes, contributed, contributing.* 1. Give money.–Jack will *contribute* toward the new slide for the playground.
2. Give help, information, etc.–The farmer *contributed* a day's work to a sick neighbor.
–The teacher asked Bill if he had anything to *contribute* to the discussion about birds.
–*Contribute to* means have a part in or be partly responsible for.–Too little sleep *contributes to* one's being tired.
–*contribution, n. contributions.*

con•trol (kən-TROHL) *n. controls.* 1. The power to manage.–The driver lost *control* over his automobile, and it went into the ditch.
2. Direction; management; care.–The fire chief has many men under his *control.* He tells them what to do.–The children are not under the teacher's *control* during the summer vacation.
3. A device that guides or makes a machine do certain things.–The pilot knows how to handle the airplane's *controls.*
–*v. controls, controlled, controlling.* Keep back; check.–Jack *controlled* his tears when the ball hit him.

con•ven•ient (kən-VEEN-yənt) *adj.; conveniently, adv.* 1. Handy; arranged so that it is easy to get around or do things.–Our kitchen is very *convenient.*–The hammer is in a *convenient* place.–It is *convenient* to have a telephone.
2. Suitable; to one's liking and comfort.–If it is *convenient* for you, I will come at seven.

con•vent (KAHN-vent) *n. convents.* A building or a number of buildings where nuns live. A nun devotes or gives all her life to her religion.

con•ven•tion (kən-VEN-shən) *n. conventions.* A meeting of many people of an organization for a special purpose.–The doctors are holding a *convention* in the city next week.–At a *convention* people talk about problems that they are all interested in.

con•ver•sa•tion (kahn-ver-SAY-shən) *n. conversations.* A talk between two or more people.–Jack and Mary had a long *conversation* about the play.

con•vex (KAHN-vekss *or* kahn-VEKSS) *adj.* Curved or bulging outwardly, like the outside of a circle.–A ball or sphere viewed from the outside is *convex.*

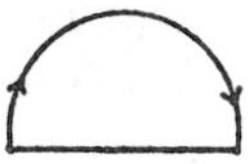

con•vict (KAHN-vikt) *n. convicts.* Person who has been proven guilty in court of a crime and sent to prison.–The *convict* was freed for good behavior.
–(kən-VIKT) *v. convicts, convicted, convicting.* Find or prove guilty in court.–The driver was *convicted* of driving too fast.

coo (KOO) *n. coos.* A soft, low sound.–We heard the *coo* of the pigeon.
–*v. coos, cooed, cooing.* Make a soft, low sound.–Pigeons *coo.*

cook (KUHK) *n. cooks.* A person who prepares food.–The *cook* at the restaurant wears a tall, white cap.
–*v. cooks, cooked, cooking.* Prepare food to eat by using heat.–We *cook* food. We broil, boil, fry, bake, or roast food over a fire or in an oven.

cook•ie or **cook•y** (KUHK-ee) *n. cookies.* A small, thin, sweet cake.–*Cookies* are baked in the oven.

cool (KOOL) *v. cools, cooled, cooling.* Remove heat from; make slightly cold.–The room was *cooled* by air conditioning.–We *cooled* the melon in the refrigerator.
–*adj. cooler, coolest.* 1. Without much heat; slightly cold.–Food that stands too long after being taken from the stove becomes *cool.*–We wear light clothes in the summer to keep us *cool.*
2. Calm; not excited.–When the fire alarm sounded, the children were very *cool.*
3. Unfriendly.–The new boy is *cool* toward us. We think it is just because he is shy.

coop (KOOP) *n. coops.* A small, cagelike pen. –Grandmother keeps her chickens in *coops.*

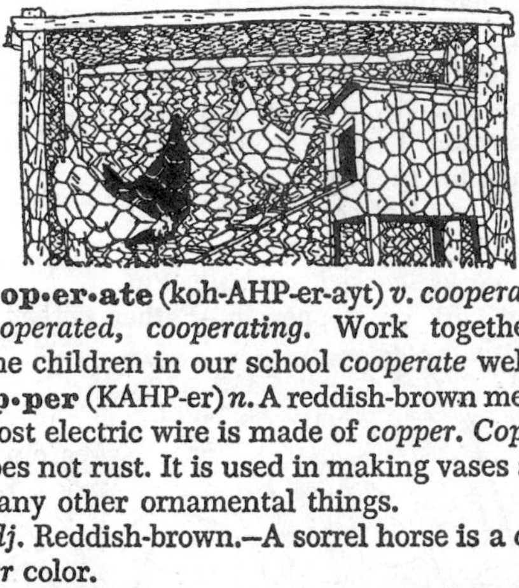

co•op•er•ate (koh-AHP-er-ayt) *v. cooperates, cooperated, cooperating.* Work together.–The children in our school *cooperate* well.

cop•per (KAHP-er) *n.* A reddish-brown metal. Most electric wire is made of *copper. Copper* does not rust. It is used in making vases and many other ornamental things.
–*adj.* Reddish-brown.–A sorrel horse is a *copper* color.

cop•y (KAHP-ee) *n. copies.* 1. Anything that is made exactly like something else.–My dress is a *copy* of one I saw in the store window.–That picture is a *copy* of one painted by a great artist.
2. One of a number of books, magazines, etc., just alike.–Mary got a *copy* of "Little Women" from the library.
–*v. copies, copied, copying.* Set down or make just exactly like something else.–The teacher wrote a poem on the blackboard for us to *copy.*

cop·y·right (KAHP-ee-ryt) *n. copyrights.* The sole right to print, sell, reproduce, or otherwise control a literary or artistic work for a certain number of years. *Copyrights* are protected by law.

cor·al (KOR- *or* KAHR-əl) *n. corals.* A hard, shell-like substance formed in the sea from the skeletons of very small sea animals. It is red, white, or pink, and is used in jewelry, beads, etc.
—*adj.* Reddish-pink.—The clerk showed us a *coral* dress.

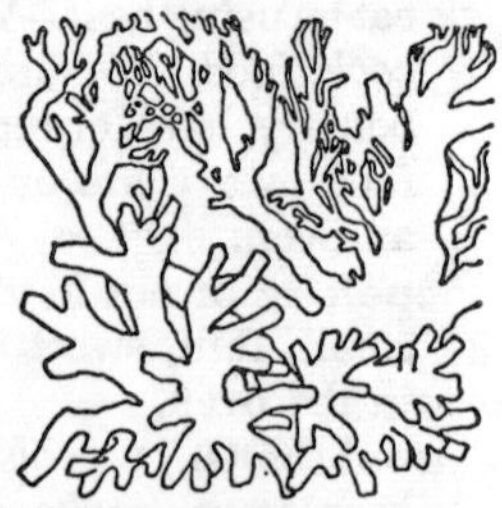

cord (KORD) *n. cords.* 1. A heavy string or thin rope.—We tied up the package with *cord.* —Bob put a new *cord* on his kite.

2. A stringlike structure in the body.—*Cords* join the muscles to the bones.

3. A pile of wood eight feet long, four feet wide, and four feet high.

core (KOR) *n. cores.* The seedy center part of apples, pears, and some other fruits.—We do not eat the *core.*

cork (KORK) *n. corks* and *adj.* 1. The bark of a *cork* oak tree. *Cork* is light and stretchy. It does not soak up water. Because it floats, it is used for life preservers.
2. A piece of cork shaped to fit the opening of a bottle.
—*v. corks, corked, corking.* Put the cork or stopper in.—Father *corked* the bottle.

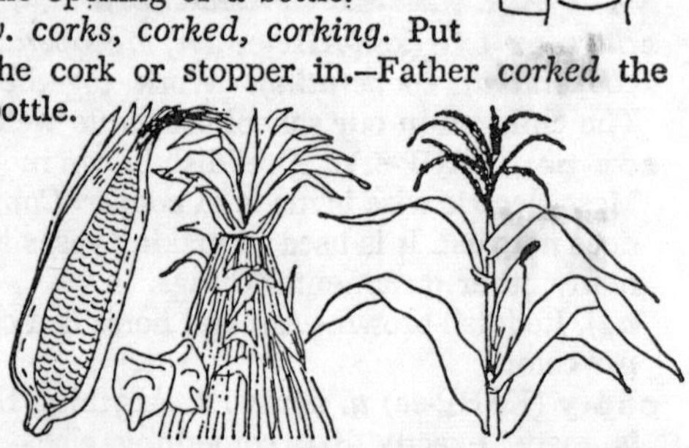

corn (KORN) *n.* 1. A tall plant that bears a large grain on cobs, or ears. The kernels of *corn* grow on a *corn*cob. *Corn* on the cob is called an ear of *corn. Corn* is ground into *corn*meal, from which *corn*bread and other foods are made.
2. In some countries, oats and wheat are called *corn.*
3. A kernel of any grain.—Birds eat *corn.*

cor·ner (KOR-ner) *n. corners.* 1. A point where two straight surfaces, such as walls, meet.—A cupboard stands in the *corner.*
2. Where streets come together.—Bob met me at the street *corner.*—There is a grocery store on the *corner.*
3. A secret place.—The children hid the peanuts for the hunt in every *corner* of the house.
—*v. corners, cornered, cornering.* Force into a position where one cannot get out.—The dogs *cornered* the fox.

cor·net (kor-NET) *n. cornets.* A musical instrument something like a trumpet, made of bent brass tubes.

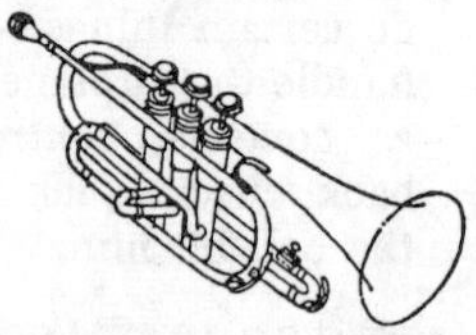

corn·starch (KORN-stahrch) *n.* A fine starchy flour made from corn. *Cornstarch* is used to thicken gravy, soups, puddings, cream pies, etc.

cor·po·ral (KOR-pə-rəl *or* KORP-rəl) *n. corporals.* A soldier in the army ranking below sergeant and above private first class.

corps (KOR) *n. sing.* and *pl.* A number of people who have been trained to do certain things as a group under a leader.—John belongs to the bugle *corps* of the Boy Scouts.—In our school there is a large *corps* of teachers under the direction of the principal.

corpse (KORPSS) *n. corpses.* The body of a dead person.

cor·pus·cle (KOR-puss-əl) *n. corpuscles.* A small cell which is part of the blood, lymph, etc. Red and white *corpuscles* circulate in the blood. Red *corpuscles* carry oxygen from the lungs to the rest of the body. Some white *corpuscles* fight disease-causing germs.

cor·ral (kə-RAL) *n. corrals.* A pen; a space with a fence around it.—Cattle and horses are kept in a *corral.*—Wagons placed close together are sometimes used to form a *corral.*

—*v. corrals, corralled, corralling.* Place in a corral or pen. — The cowboy *corralled* the ponies.

COSTUME

cor•rect (kə-REKT) *v. corrects, corrected, correcting.* Make right; go over to see that all is right.–I *corrected* my arithmetic problem, which was wrong.–The teacher *corrected* our spelling tests and gave them back to us so we could see our mistakes.
–*adj.* 1. Right; true.–Your answer is *correct.*–Is this the *correct* way to play the game?
2. Proper; well-mannered.–It is *correct* to thank people for their gifts to you.

cor•rec•tion (kə-REK-shən) *n. corrections.* A change that is made to make something right which was wrong.–The only *correction* made on my paper was that an "ie" was changed to an "ei" to make the word "receive" right.

cor•re•spond (kor- *or* kahr-ə-SPAHND) *v. corresponds, corresponded, corresponding.* 1. Write letters to one another.–Grandmother and I *correspond* when she is not with us.
2. Be in harmony; go together well.–The colors of the rugs, curtains, and cushions all *correspond* nicely.
3. Be like; fill the same purpose as.–The wings of an airplane *correspond* to the wings of a bird.

cor•rode (kə-ROHD) *v. corrodes, corroded, corroding.* Slowly and gradually eat away.–Rust is *corroding* the bumper on Father's car.

cor•set (KOR-sət) *n. corsets.* A tight-fitting undergarment worn around the waist and hips to support and give shape to the body. *Corsets* are sometimes called foundations. *Corsets* are worn for support by some women, and sometimes, after certain sicknesses, by men.

cos•mic (KAHZ-mik) *adj.* Having to do with the entire universe, or with the orderly nature of things.–The relationship between the sun, the earth, and the stars is a *cosmic* relationship.

cost (KAWST) *n. costs.* 1. Amount paid for, or amount for which something is selling.–The *cost* of our new chair was $65.
2. Loss or sacrifice.–The hero saved the baby at the *cost* of his own life.
–*v. costs, cost, costing.* Be priced at; be worth; be selling for.–Mother asked the clerk how much the hat *cost.* The clerk said it *cost* $11.

cos•tume (KAHSS-toom *or* -tyoom) *n. costumes.* 1. Dress or clothes worn to act parts, or to make believe that one is a different person or a person of a different time or place.–The art teacher and the sewing teacher made the *costumes* for the school play. My *costume* represented Old Mother Hubbard.
2. Clothes.–The store on the corner sells sports *costumes* and evening *costumes.*

co•sy (KOH-zee) *n.* and *adj.* Another way of spelling *cozy.*

cot (KAHT) *n. cots.* A low, narrow bed.–I slept on a *cot* at camp.

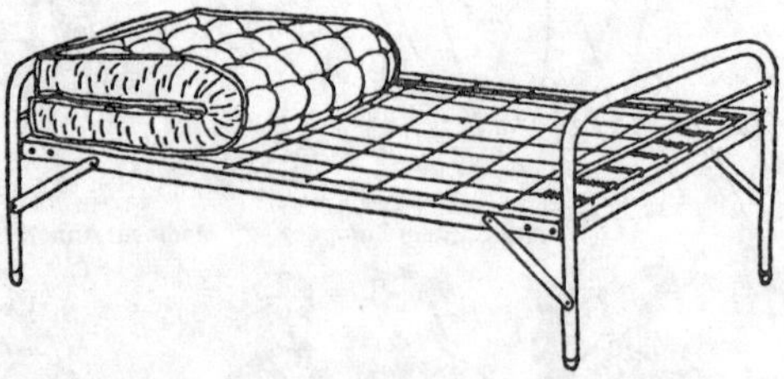

cot•tage (KAHT-ij) *n. cottages.* A small, simple house.–In the summer we go to our *cottage* at the lake.

cot•ton (KAHT-n) *n.* and *adj.* A fluffy white substance that grows around the seeds of the *cotton* plant. It is spun into threads, from which *cotton* cloth is made. *Cotton* is also cleaned and used to fill cushions and quilts, and for dressing cuts, burns, and other wounds.

couch (KOWCH) *n. couches.* A lounge, sofa, or upholstered seat for several people.–I sit on the living-room *couch* when I watch television shows.

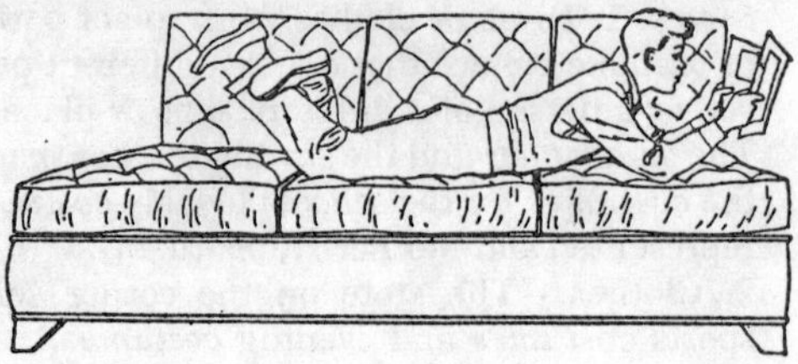

cou•gar (KOO-ger) *n. cougar* or *cougars.* A large, yellow-brown member of the cat family. *Cougars* are found both in North and South America and are also known as panthers, wildcats, pumas, or mountain lions.

cough (KAWF) *n. coughs.* A sudden, rough noise made by forcing air from the lungs through the throat; a sickness causing this.–Mary had a bad *cough,* so she stayed at home today.

–*v. coughs, coughed, coughing.* To force air from the lungs through the throat, making a sudden rough noise. A cold or a little tickling in the throat often causes people to *cough.* –One should cover the mouth with a handkerchief when *coughing.*

could (KUHD) *v.* One form of the verb *can.* –Baby *could* walk when she was a year old.–Bob *could* make a kite if only he had some paste.

could•n't (KUHD-ənt). Could not; was not able to.–Baby *couldn't* talk when she was a year old, but she can now.

coun•cil (KOWN-səl) *n. councils.* A group of people chosen to make rules and take care of other matters for a larger group of people.–The city *council* meets once a week.–A student *council* is a group of students who meet to discuss the problems of the school and try to solve them.

coun•sel (KOWN-səl) *n. counsels.* Advice.–When Robert has a problem, he usually goes to Father for *counsel.*

–*v. counsels, counseled* or *counselled, counseling* or *counselling.* Give advice or counsel (to); advise.–Father is always willing to *counsel* him.–The teacher *counseled* the children to do their homework with care.

–*counselor* or *counsellor, n. counselors* or *counsellors.*

count (KOWNT) *v. counts, counted, counting.* 1. Number, in order to add up.–The children *counted* the blocks in the box. They found out how many there were.

2. Name numbers in regular order.–When

you are angry, *count* ten before you speak. Say the numbers 1, 2, 3, 4, 5, 6, 7, 8, 9, 10 in order.
3. Put down; record.–The ball player did not touch home plate, so the run could not be *counted.*
4. Think; consider.–When the boat upset, the girl *counted* herself lucky to be able to swim.
5. Rely or depend.–If there is work to be done, you can *count* upon Bob to help.
6. Be valuable or worth while.–Every good deed you do *counts,* even little things.

count•er (KOWN-ter) *n. counters.* In a store, a long cabinet or table behind which the sales clerk stands when serving the customer.–The man put the money for the drugs on the *counter.*

coun•ter (KOWN-ter) *v. counters, countered, countering.* Oppose.–Bob wanted to see a movie. Jack *countered* with a suggestion that they both go fishing instead.
–*adj.* Opposing.–Jack made a *counter* proposal.

coun•ter•clock•wise (kown-ter-KLAHK-wyz) *adj.* and *adv.* In the opposite direction from the way a clock's hands turn.–Jack ran around the building clockwise and John ran *counterclockwise,* and they bumped into each other.

coun•ter•feit (KOWN-ter-fit) *v. counterfeits, counterfeited, counterfeiting.* Make an imitation, especially of money.–The men who *counterfeited* the ten-dollar bills are now in prison.
–*adj.* Imitation; fake.–The men were put in jail for making *counterfeit* money.

coun•try (KUN-tree) *n. countries.* 1. Land.–The *country* near the lake is sometimes covered with water.
2. A nation; one's native land; land where one was born.–"My *country,* 'tis of thee, sweet land of liberty, of thee I sing."–Pierre comes from another *country.* He comes from France.
3. Land where people do not live close together, as they do in cities and towns.–We live in town, but Grandfather lives in the *country.*–We go to the *country* for the entire summer.

coun•ty (KOWN-tee) *n. counties.* A section or division of a state. The states, such as New York, Ohio, and Indiana, are divided into smaller parts called *counties.* The people elect officers to take care of the business in their *county.*

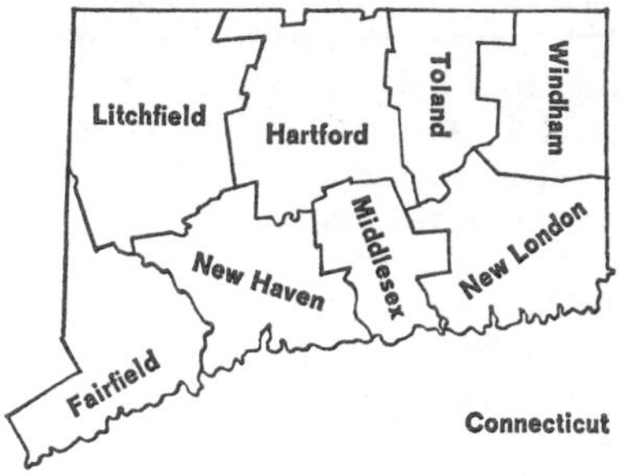

cou•pé (koo-PAY *or* KOOP) *n. coupés.* A closed automobile with only one seat, which has room for two or three people.

cou•ple (KUP-əl) *n. couples.* 1. Two of anything.–Mother bought a *couple* of vases for the mantelpiece, one for each end.
2. A boy and girl, or man and woman.–That *couple* won the dancing contest.
3. A husband and wife.–The old *couple* likes to play cards on the porch after supper.–Father and Mother are a very happy *couple.*
–*v. couples, coupled, coupling.* Join to; put together; connect.–The trailer was *coupled* to the automobile for the trip.

cou•pon (KYOO- *or* KOO-pahn) *n. coupons.* 1. A ticket or printed card showing that the holder of it is due to receive something.–For each pound of tea we buy, the grocer gives us a *coupon* which says that we are entitled to a free can to put tea in.

2. A printed form to be filled out and mailed to order something.–Father cut out and sent in the *coupon* ordering the new books.

cour•age (KER-ij) *n.; courageous, adj.; courageously, adv.* Bravery.–The people showed much *courage* when the lion got out of the cage. They did not show their fear or become excited.

course (KORSS) *n. courses.* 1. A route; a way. –The airplane got off its *course.* It no longer went in the right direction.
2. A movement forward; path. – The river leaves sand and mud in its *course.*
3. Regular happening.–To take things in their *course* means to take care of things one at a time as they come, without looking ahead to things that haven't happened yet.–We go to school in the morning as a matter of *course.*–The doctor said that the sickness would have to run its *course.*
4. Grounds.–Father plays golf on the Red Run golf *course.*
5. A series of classes or lessons.–Mother is taking an evening *course* in cooking at the high school.
6. A part of a meal which is served at one time.–Soup or fruit cup is often served for the first *course;* meat, vegetables, and salad for the next, and ice cream and cake for the last *course.*
–*Of course* means certainly or surely. – *Of course* we are going to the movies; we always go.

court (KORT) *n. courts.* 1. A hard, level place marked off for a game.–Tennis is played on a tennis *court.*

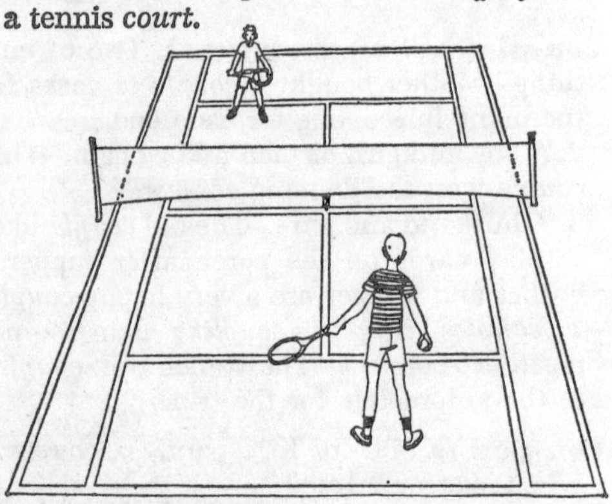

2. A yard, or the space between or nearly shut in by the walls of buildings.–Most *courts* are paved with concrete or stone.–Children who live in apartment houses often play in the *court.*

3. The place where the king, or any other ruler lives, and the people who attend him. –Cinderella went to the ball at the *court.*
4. Attentions.–The soldier who wanted a higher position paid *court* to the king. He tried to please the king, to get the king to like him.
5. A place where matters are settled according to law. The judges who have charge of the trials are also known as the *court.*–The burglar was taken into *court* to be tried for robbing the gas station.

–*v. courts, courted, courting.* 1. To pay much attention to a woman with the wish of winning her for a wife.–The prince *courted* Cinderella.
2. Invite; try to bring on.–Children who cross streets with the red traffic light *court* accidents. They risk accidents.–Jack felt it would be *courting* trouble to ask Bill if he had seen his ball.

cour·te·ous (KER-tee-əss) *adj.; courteously, adv.* Polite, kind, and thoughtful.–People always like Mary at once because she is so *courteous.*

cour·te·sy (KER-tə-see) *n. courtesies.* 1. Politeness; good manners; respect for other people's feelings.–The clerk in the store is well liked because of his *courtesy.*
2. A special attention; a kindness.–Grandmother thanked the minister for his many *courtesies,* such as sending flowers when she was sick.

court·house (KORT-howss) *n. courthouses.*
1. A building where trials of law are held.
2. A building in which county officers take care of the business of the county.

court•yard (KORT-yahrd) *n. courtyards.* A large yard, often paved, with buildings or walls all around, or nearly all around it.—Children who live in apartment houses often play in the *courtyard.*

cous•in (KUZ-ən) *n. cousins.* The children of one's aunts or uncles.—My father's sister and his brother both have children. These children are my *cousins.*—My mother's brother and her sister also have children. These children are my *cousins,* too.

cove (KOHV) *n. coves.* A small bay or inlet set off from a main body of water; a small hollow in woods or hills.—John sailed his boat into a sheltered *cove* so he would be protected from the high winds on the lake.—The Boy Scouts pitched their tent in a *cove* in the woods.

cov•er (KUV-er) *n. covers.* 1. A lid or top.—Put a *cover* on the pot when you cook potatoes.—The box has no *cover.*

2. A wrapper or jacket on the outside of a book or magazine. —Books sometimes have leather *covers,* sometimes cloth *covers,* and sometimes *covers* made of hard cardboard.

3. A blanket or spread for a bed. —Sally kicked her *covers* off because she was too hot.
4. Protection; a shelter.
—*v. covers, covered, covering.* 1. Put over the top or outside of.—To *cover* potatoes with water means to put water over them.—To *cover* the bed with a quilt means to spread a quilt over the bed.—To *cover* a book means to fit paper or other material over the outside of the book.
2. Travel over; get through.—You cannot *cover* as much ground in an hour with a horse and buggy as you can *cover* with an automobile.—The teacher said we had another lesson to *cover.*
3. Include; take in.—Mary's diary *covers* the years 1960–1961. She kept her diary during those two years.—Jack's composition on what he wants to be when he grows up *covered* many fields.
4. Hide.—The thief *covered* his tracks.

cov•er•ing (KUV-er-ing) *n. coverings.* Anything used to cover something.—Candy bars have paper *coverings.*—Quilts and blankets are bed *coverings.*—A hat is a *covering* for the head.
—*v.* One form of the verb *cover.*—Susan is *covering* her doll with a blanket.

cow (KOW) *n. cows.* 1. A large farm animal raised to give milk.—Grandfather milks the *cows* each evening.

2. Grown-up female elephants, seals, and some other large animals are known as *cows.*

cow•ard (KOW-erd) *n. cowards.* A person who is afraid or who cannot face danger.—The biggest boy in our school is a *coward.* He is afraid of anyone who really wants to fight.

cow•boy (KOW-boi) *n. cowboys.* A man who rides horses and looks after cows and other cattle on a cattle ranch.

cow•slip (KOW-slip) *n. cowslips.* A small yellow flower that grows in marshy places. The *cowslip* plant has large green leaves that are smooth and somewhat round.

coy•o•te (ky-OH-tee *or* KY-oht) *n. coyote* or *coyotes.* A kind of small wolf found on the plains of western United States.

co•zy (KOH-zee) *n. cozies.* A thick cover for a teapot.—Mother puts a *cozy* around the teapot to keep the tea hot.
—*adj. cozier, coziest.* Snug and comfortable.—The children are *cozy* in their warm beds.

crab (KRAB) *n. crabs.* 1. A sea animal that has a hard shell something like a turtle's on its back. *Crabs* have a pair of pincers with which they grab or hold on to things. Many *crabs* are good to eat.

2. An ill-tempered, complaining person.—That man is a *crab.* He is always finding fault.

crab ap·ple (KRAB ap-əl) *crab apples.* A kind of small, sour apple. *Crab apples* are very good to eat when preserved with spice and sugar.

crack (KRAK) *n. cracks.* 1. A quick, sharp, snapping or popping sound.—The horses were away at the first *crack* of the whip.
2. A thin, long opening or split.—We could see a light through the *crack* in the wall.
—*v. cracks, cracked, cracking.* 1. Snap.—The lion tamer *cracked* his whip to make the lions behave.
2. Break open.—Squirrels *crack* nuts with their teeth.
3. Split without separating into parts.—The plate *cracked,* but it didn't break into pieces.

crack·er (KRAK-er) *n. crackers.* A thin biscuit baked till it is crisp. *Crackers* are eaten with soups, salads, tomato juice, etc.

crack·le (KRAK-əl) *n. crackles.* A sharp, cracking sound.—We heard the *crackle* of the fire.
—*v. crackles, crackled, crackling.* Make a sharp, cracking sound.—Dry leaves *crackle* when you walk on them.

cra·dle (KRAY-dəl) *n. cradles.* A small baby's bed with sides and on rockers.—Mother rocks the baby to sleep in the *cradle.*

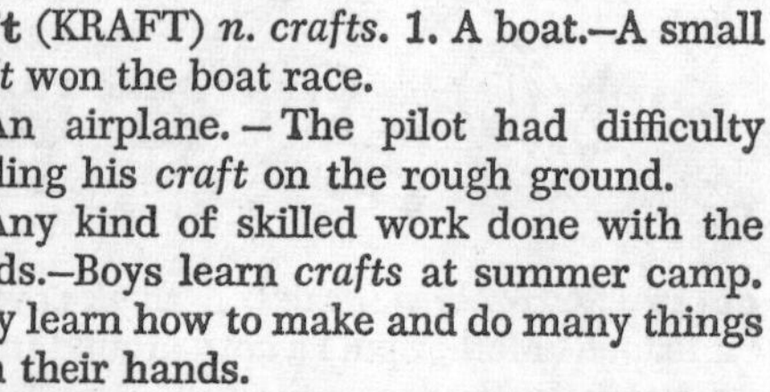

craft (KRAFT) *n. crafts.* 1. A boat.—A small *craft* won the boat race.
2. An airplane. — The pilot had difficulty landing his *craft* on the rough ground.
3. Any kind of skilled work done with the hands.—Boys learn *crafts* at summer camp. They learn how to make and do many things with their hands.
4. A trade or art.—Shoemaking is a *craft.*
5. Trickery.—The man got the horse by *craft.*

cramp (KRAMP) *n. cramps.* A sudden, painful tightening of the muscles.—A *cramp* in the leg of the runner caused him to lose the race.

cran·ber·ry (KRAN-bair-ee) *n. cranberries* and *adj.* A kind of dark red berry that grows on low bushes in damp places.—We make *cranberry* sauce, jelly, and preserves to eat with turkey, chicken, and other meats.

crane (KRAYN) *n. cranes.* 1. A large wading bird.—We saw a *crane* making a nest in the rushes in the water.

2. A machine for lifting heavy loads.—The workmen used a *crane* to lift very heavy things from the ship.

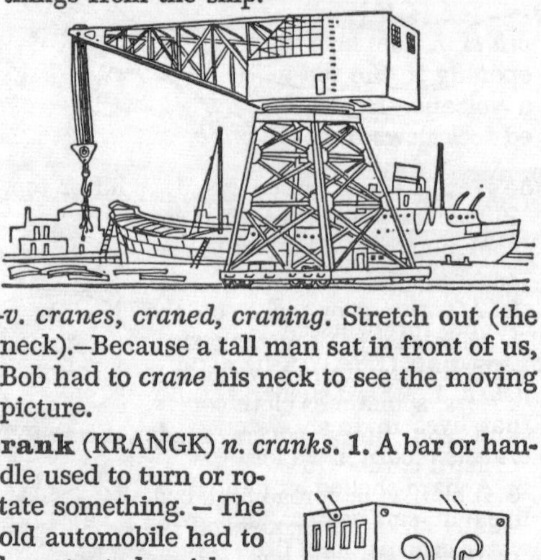

—*v. cranes, craned, craning.* Stretch out (the neck).—Because a tall man sat in front of us, Bob had to *crane* his neck to see the moving picture.

crank (KRANGK) *n. cranks.* 1. A bar or handle used to turn or rotate something. — The old automobile had to be started with a *crank.* — The organ-grinder has to turn a *crank* to make music.

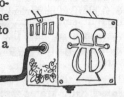

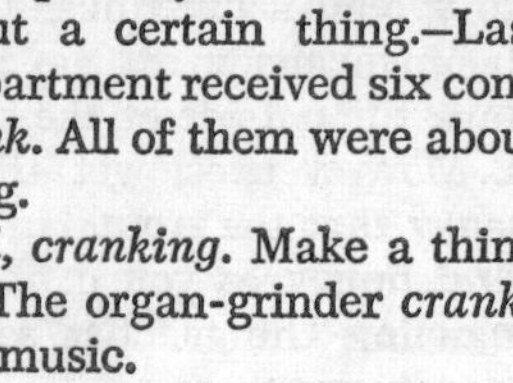

2. An odd person, especially someone who is unreasonable about a certain thing.—Last week the police department received six complaints from a *crank.* All of them were about the same silly thing.
—*v. cranks, cranked, cranking.* Make a thing go with a crank.—The organ-grinder *cranks* his organ to make music.

crank•shaft (KRANGK-shaft) *n. crankshafts.* A bar that either turns, or is turned by, a crank. A *crankshaft* passes motion from one part of a machine to another part.

crash (KRASH) *n. crashes.* 1. The loud breaking or banging noise of something falling down or striking something. – When the waiter dropped his tray of dishes, there was a loud *crash.*
2. A sudden wrecking.–Both drivers were hurt in the *crash* of their cars.
–*v. crashes, crashed, crashing.* 1. Fall down noisily.–The pans *crashed* to the floor.
2. Break (through).–The ball hit the window and *crashed* through it.
3. Be wrecked suddenly. – The airplane *crashed* after taking off.

crate (KRAYT) *n. crates.* A box or frame made of wooden slats.
–The oranges and apples were packed into *crates.*

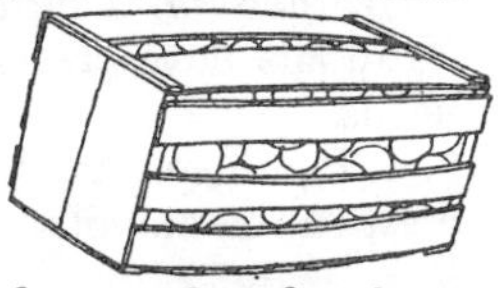

–*v. crates, crated, crating.* Pack in a box or frame.–Our furniture was *crated* before we moved.

cra•ter (KRAY-ter) *n. craters.* The hole or opening in the top of a volcano.–Hot melted rock flows from the *crater* of the volcano.

crave (KRAYV) *v. craves, craved, craving.* 1. Long for; want or need strongly.–Hungry people *crave* food.
2. Ask sincerely for; plead for. – The boy showed that he was sorry for his mistake by *craving* forgiveness.

craw•fish (KRAW-fish) *n. crawfish* or *crawfishes.* 1. A hard-shelled animal that lives in fresh water. The *crawfish* looks like a lobster.
2. A hard-shelled animal that lives in salt water. This salt-water *crawfish* is a little larger than the one that lives in fresh water.

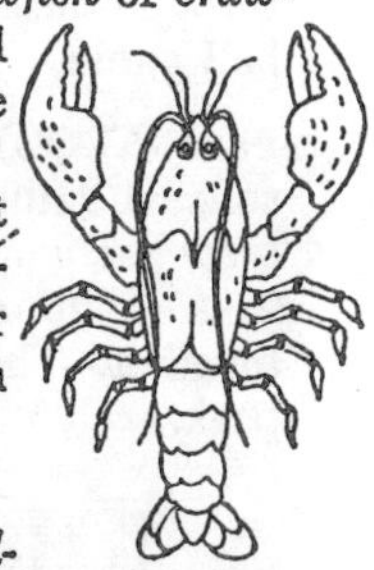

crawl (KRAWL) *v. crawls, crawled, crawling.* 1. Pull or draw the body along the ground.–Caterpillars and worms *crawl.*
2. Move about on the hands and knees.–Babies *crawl* before they learn to walk.
3. Move very slowly. – The traffic was so heavy that the cars *crawled* along the road.
–*Crawling* may mean to be covered with crawling things. – The windowpane was *crawling* with bugs.

cray•on (KRAY-ahn *or* -ən) *n. crayons.* A stick of colored wax or chalk.–We colored the pictures with *crayons.*

cra•zy (KRAY-zee) *adj. crazier, craziest.* 1. Insane; sick in mind.–The man was sent to a home for people who are *crazy.*
2. Foolish and silly.–John did a *crazy* thing this morning. He put his shirt on backwards.

creak (KREEK) *n. creaks.* Squeaking sound. –The door opened with a sharp *creak.*
–*v. creaks, creaked, creaking.* Make a squeaking sound.–Father wanted to surprise us, but the door *creaked* as he opened it.

cream (KREEM) *n. creams.* 1. A thick, yellowish fat found in milk.–We let the milk stand and the *cream* rose to the top.–Butter is made from *cream.*
2. Any soft, thick, wet substance that suggests the cream in milk.–Father uses shaving *cream* for shaving.–Mother uses cold *cream* to keep her hands soft.
3. The best part.–Bob always gets the *cream* of everything.
–*v. creams, creamed, creaming.* Make a smooth, pasty mixture by pressing together. –Mother *creams* butter, sugar, and milk to make icing for a cake.
–*adj.* A light yellowish color.–Mother wore a *cream*-colored hat.

cream•er•y (KREEM-er-ee) *n. creameries.* A place where butter, cheese, and other milk products are made or sold.

crease (KREESS) *n. creases.* 1. A fold or ridge made by folding or pressing.–The legs of men's trousers have *creases* in the front and back.–Pressing the *creases* with a hot flatiron makes them last a long time.
2. Wrinkle.–Do not lie down while wearing your new dress or you may get *creases* in it.
–*v. creases, creased, creasing.* Make a fold or wrinkle in.–The children *creased* their papers in the middle for the spelling test.

cre•ate (kree-AYT) *v. creates, created, creating.* 1. Cause.–We *created* much excitement when we dressed like ghosts.
2. Make; design; make up out of one's own mind.–Mary *created* a picture. She did not copy it; she made it up.

crea•ture (KREE-cher) *n. creatures.* An animal or person.—All *creatures* require food to keep them alive.

cre•den•tials (krə-DENCH-əlz) *n. pl.* Official documents or papers vouching for a person's character, position, or ability.—Father asked the detective to show his *credentials.*

cred•it (KRED-ət) *n. credits.* 1. A reputation for paying bills.—Our *credit* is good at the corner store. We can get groceries and pay for them later. The grocer knows we will pay.
2. Reward; favorable regard.—Jack got *credit* for writing the class motto, even though several children helped him.
3. Amount in one's favor.—Mother had $35 in the savings account. After she took out $25, she still had a $10 *credit* with the bank.
4. A person or thing that improves a reputation.—Bob is a *credit* to the ball team. He helps to give it a good name or reputation.
5. Acknowledgment.—When Father paid $10 on our grocery bill, the clerk gave him *credit.* He marked down that Father had paid $10.
—*v. credits, credited, crediting.* Believe; put trust in.—The teacher *credits* the stories of the children. She believes them.
—*Buy on credit* means to pay for something some time after it is purchased.

creed (KREED) *n. creeds.* 1. A statement of religious principles and beliefs.
2. Any set of principles, beliefs, opinions, etc.—Belief in man's goodness is part of Grandfather's *creed.*

creek (KREEK) *n. creeks.* A small stream of water. — The boys went swimming in the *creek.*

creep (KREEP) *v. creeps, crept, creeping.* 1. Move about on the hands and knees.—Most babies *creep* before they learn to walk.
2. Crawl or move along close to the ground. —The boys had to *creep* to get under the fence.
3. Grow along the ground and take roots at many places. — Vines are *creeping* all over the garden, crowding out the plants.
4. Feel shivery. — The howling of dogs at night makes Mary *creep.*
5. Move along very slowly.—Traffic was so heavy that our car could only *creep.*

crepe (KRAYP) *n. crepes.* A thin, crinkly cloth of silk, cotton, etc.—Grandmother has a new dress of black *crepe.*
—*Crepe paper* is a soft, crinkly paper. — We decorated the table for the party with *crepe paper.*

crept (KREPT) *v.* One form of the verb *creep.* —We *crept* up the stairs to surprise the other boys and girls.

cres•cent (KRESS-ənt) *n. crescents* and *adj.*
1. The moon as it appears in its first quarter.
2. Any object or arrangement in this shape. — Mother has a jeweled *crescent.* It is a gold pin.

crest (KREST) *n. crests.* 1. A topknot or tuft of feathers on a bird's head.—Cardinals have *crests* on their heads.

2. A top ridge.—As we rode along we saw the *crest* of the mountains.

3. The top edge (of a wave).—The boat rode over the *crest* of the wave coming in to the beach.

crev•ice (KREV-əss) *n. crevices.* A crack; a thin split or separation. — David peeked through the *crevice* in the fence to watch the ball game.

crew (KROO) *n. crews.* 1. The group of persons who run a train, airplane, or ship.—The *crew* has gone ashore for the evening.
2. A group of persons who do certain work together.—The city has a *crew* cleaning the park.

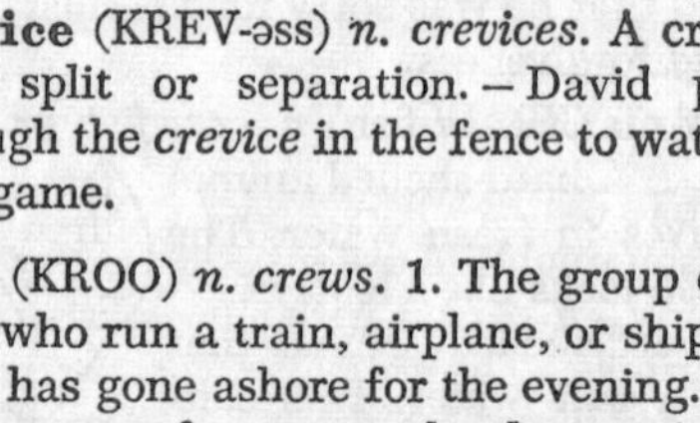

crib (KRIB) *n. cribs.* 1. A small bed with high sides.—The baby sleeps in a *crib.*

2. A large box, bin, or shed with open spaces on the sides to let air in.–Farmers keep their corn in a *crib.*

3. A manger or deep box for feed.–Horses eat from *cribs.*

crick•et (KRIK-ət) *n. crickets.* A black insect something like a grasshopper. *Crickets* make a chirping sound. They hide under large stones and logs.

cried (KRYD) *v.* One form of the verb *cry.* – The little girl *cried* when she burned her hand.–The peddler *cried,* "Apples for sale."

cries (KRYZ) *v.* One form of the verb *cry.*–Baby *cries* when she wants someone to hold her.–The newsboy *cries,* "Morning paper?"

crime (KRYM) *n. crimes.* An evil or bad act that is against the law.–The prisoner was guilty of many *crimes.*–People are punished for *crimes.*

crim•i•nal (KRIM-ə-nəl) *n. criminals.* A person who does evil and unlawful things.–The *criminal* was sent to prison for stealing.
–*adj.* Having to do with crime.–Stealing is a *criminal* act.

crim•son (KRIM-zən) *adj.* Of a bright red color.–Mary's new dress is *crimson.*–The angry man's face turned almost *crimson.*

crip•ple (KRIP-əl) *n. cripples.* A lame person; a person unable to use his body, legs, or arms properly.–A person without a leg or an arm is a *cripple.*–The *cripple* learned to do everything for himself without the help of others.

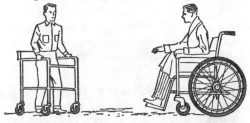

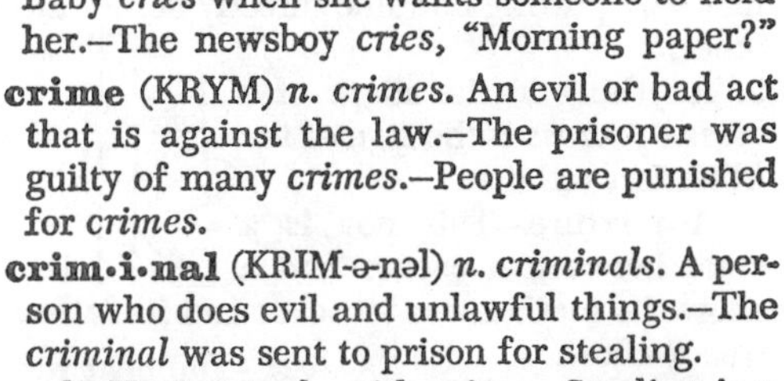

–*v. cripples, crippled, crippling.* Make lame or disabled.–The sailor was *crippled* by a fall from the mast of his ship.–The airplane hit a tree and was *crippled;* it no longer could run.

cri•sis (KRY-siss) *n. crises.* 1. An important turning point.–The company had reached a *crisis.* Business would either get better, or the company would fail.
2. The very important moment in a disease after which the patient either recovers or dies.–The doctor said Uncle John had passed the *crisis.* He would now get better fast.
3. A serious problem or trouble.–The farmer said that a *crisis* had arisen. It had not rained for so long that all his crops would soon be ruined from lack of water.

crisp (KRISP) *adj.* 1. Brittle; not soft; easily broken.–Good crackers are *crisp.*
2. Fresh; refreshing.–A walk in the *crisp* morning air will make you feel wide awake.

crit•i•cal (KRIT-ə-kəl) *adj.; critically, adv.*
1. Likely to find fault.–The teacher is *critical* of careless work. She is quick to find fault with it.
2. Serious; dangerous.–The sick woman is in *critical* condition.

crit•i•cism (KRIT-ə-siz-əm) *n. criticisms.*
1. A statement about the good or bad points or qualities of something.–Jack was pleased with the teacher's *criticism* of his composition. She said that he had spelled each word right.
2. Unfavorable comment. – When children behave badly, they often receive *criticism.*

crit•i•cize (KRIT-ə-syz) *v. criticizes, criticized, criticizing.* 1. Find fault with.–Father does not *criticize* the work we do.
2. Point out the good and bad parts of something.–The teacher will *criticize* our compositions.

croak (KROHK) *n. croaks.* A low, hoarse, throaty noise.–The *croak* of the bullfrog kept us awake.
–*v. croaks, croaked, croaking.* Make a low, hoarse, throaty noise.–Frogs *croak.*

cro•chet (kroh-SHAY) *v. crochets, crocheted, crocheting.* Do a kind of lacy handwork with a hooked needle. You *crochet* by making a series of loops, and then pulling the thread through the first loops with the hook to make more loops.

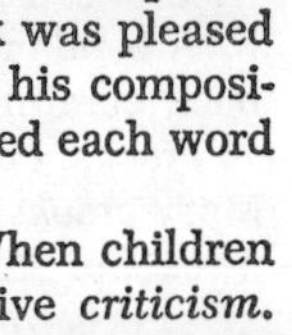

crock (KRAHK) *n. crocks.* A jar or pot made of clay and baked until hard.–Grandmother puts milk in a *crock.* – Mother keeps a cookie *crock* in the pantry.

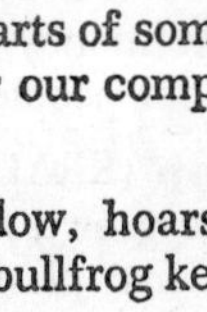

croc•o•dile (KRAHK-ə-dyl) *n. crocodiles.* A large, four-legged, flesh-eating animal that looks like an alligator but has a narrower, longer head. *Crocodiles* have scaly skins. They live in warm waters and in marshes.

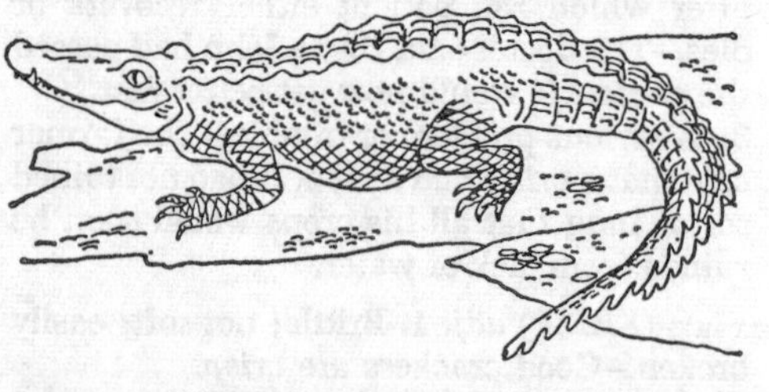

cro•cus (KROH-kəss) *n. crocuses.* A short-stemmed early spring flower, usually yellow, purple, or white. The *crocus* belongs to the iris family. The flowers stick out of the ground like little spikes. The *crocus* grows from a bulb.

crook (KRUHK) *n. crooks.* 1. A person who gets money by dishonest tricks.–The *crook* tried to sell Father a stolen car.
2. A bend or curve.–We saw a lady on horseback coming around the *crook* in the road.
–*v. crooks, crooked, crooking.* Bend or arch.–Mary *crooks* her little finger when she holds a teacup. She curls her little finger up.

crook•ed (KRUHK-id) *adj.; crookedly, adv.* 1. Not straight.–This road is *crooked.* It has many curves and twists.
2. Not honest.–The man had made much of his money in *crooked* dealings, in which other people were cheated.

crop (KRAHP) *n. crops.* 1. Food plants that are grown by people in large amounts.–The farmer plants his *crops* in the spring.

2. A harvest of anything; fruit or vegetables which are picked or reaped. – The cherry *crop* is large this year.–The cotton *crop* is poor.
3. A thick growth.–Jack has a *crop* of bright red hair.
4. A riding whip with a loop on the whipping end of it.–The horseman carried a *crop.*
5. A chicken's *crop* is one of its stomachs, in which food is digested.
–*v. crops, cropped, cropping.* 1. Bite off.–The hungry rabbits *crop* the lettuce in the garden.
2. Cut off closely.–In summer some men *crop* their hair.

cro•quet (kroh-KAY) *n.* A game played by setting wire arches in smooth ground and hitting wooden balls through them with a long-handled wooden hammer, or mallet.

cross (KRAWSS) *n. crosses.* 1. A mark [+] made by putting one line directly across another.
2. Anything in the shape of a cross.–A *cross* is the sign of the Christian religion.

3. A mixture.–This dog is a *cross* between a cocker and a chow. Its mother was a cocker and its father was a chow.
–*v. crosses, crossed, crossing.* 1. Put one across another.–The children *crossed* their fingers.
2. Go from one side to another.–Be careful when you *cross* the street.
3. Go against, or disagree with.–Bob never *crosses* Jack.
4. Put a line through, to cancel.–That answer is wrong. *Cross* it out and write the correct answer.
–*adj.* Ill-tempered.–When I am tired, I get *cross.* Nothing suits me, and I get angry easily.

cross-eyed (KRAWSS-yd) *adj.* Having eyes which turn in toward the nose, so that one cannot look straight ahead with both eyes at the same time.

cross•ing (KRAWSS-ing) *n. crossings.* 1. A place where streets cross or where a track crosses a street.–Always stop, look, and listen at railroad *crossings.*
2. A place where a street is crossed by people.–Policemen stand at *crossings* to help the children go across the street.

cross sec•tion (KRAWSS SEK-shən). 1. A section of anything as it would appear if it were cut through at right angles to its length. A *cross section* shows the inside surface of something. When you slice a banana, you make many *cross sections.*
2. Parts selected from a group, to show what the whole group is like; a sample.–The newspaper printed a *cross section* of public opinion on the new law.

crouch (KROWCH) *v. crouches, crouched, crouching.* Bend down with the back and knees; squat.–The escaped prisoner *crouched* on the bridge until the train had passed.

crow (KROH) *n. crows.* 1. A large, black bird. –*Crows* eat the farmer's corn.

2. A call or cry.–The rooster's *crow* woke us early in the morning.
–*v. crows, crowed, crowing.* 1. Call or cry. – We heard the rooster *crow* early in the morning.
2. Cry out gleefully.–Baby *crowed* with delight when Father held her on his head.
3. Boast or brag.–Ed likes to *crow* over all the things he has done and can do.

crowd (KROWD) *n. crowds.* A large group of people.–A *crowd* gathered along the street to see the parade.
–*v. crowds, crowded, crowding.* 1. Pack; cram. –Do not *crowd* the eggs into the basket. Do not press them together.
2. Push and shove.–Do not *crowd* in the line, but wait your turn.

crown (KROWN) *n. crowns.* 1. A fancy circlet or band worn on the heads of kings and queens. *Crowns* usually have many jewels in them.

2. A wreath for the head.–The children made *crowns* of daisies.
3. The center part of a hat, which sticks up. –Sally stepped on Father's hat and squashed the *crown.*
–*v. crowns, crowned, crowning.* 1. Reward.– The man's efforts were *crowned* with success.
2. Put a crown on; make king or queen.–The mayor *crowned* the girl who was voted most beautiful.

crude (KROOD) *adj.; crudely, adv.; crudeness, n.* 1. Raw; not prepared for use; impure. –*Crude* oil must be treated or refined before it is used.
2. Rough or unfinished.–Abraham Lincoln was born in a *crude* cabin.
3. Not in good taste; not pleasing to others. –Bill's manners are *crude.*

cru•el (KROO-əl) *adj.; cruelly, adv.* 1. Taking pleasure in hurting others or in seeing them hurt; without kindness or pity.–Father became angry when he saw the *cruel* man beating the horse.
2. Causing pain.–Steve's *cruel* remark hurt the stranger's feelings.

cru•el•ty (KROO-əl-tee) *n. cruelties.* Heartless treatment or act; lack of mercy.–The man was arrested for his *cruelty* to the horse.

cruise (KROOZ) *n. cruises.* A trip or journey in a boat.–Father and Mother went on a *cruise* for their vacation.
–*v. cruises, cruised, cruising.* Travel from place to place on the water.–Father and Mother *cruised* to Bermuda.

cruis•er (KROOZ-er) *n. cruisers.* 1. A large, fast warship, next in size to a battleship.–The navy has many *cruisers.*

2. A police car which patrols certain parts of a city.–A *cruiser* picked up the message from headquarters with its radio.

crumb (KRUM) *n. crumbs.* 1. A small bit of bread, cake, etc.–Sally threw *crumbs* to the birds.
2. A tiny amount.–That man was a very bad guide. He had only *crumbs* of information about the things we wanted to know.

crum•ble (KRUM-bəl) *v. crumbles, crumbled, crumbling.* Break into small crumbs or very tiny pieces.–Baby *crumbled* the cookie in her hands.

crum•ple (KRUM-pəl) *v. crumples, crumpled, crumpling.* Wrinkle or curl up; crush.–Jack *crumpled* his spelling paper in his hand and threw it into the wastepaper basket.

crunch (KRUNCH) *v. crunches, crunched, crunching.* Chew noisily with the teeth.–It is hard to eat celery or peanut brittle without *crunching* it.

crush (KRUSH) *n. crushes.* A closely packed crowd of people.–Bob and Bill went to the game together, but were separated in the *crush* going through the gates.
–*v. crushes, crushed, crushing.* 1. Break up by pressure.–The stones were *crushed* into little pebbles by the steam roller.
2. Wrinkle; wad up.–Mary tried not to *crush* her new hair ribbon when she put on her hat.–The man's hat was *crushed* when the car ran over it.
3. Defeat completely; overcome.–The army *crushed* the enemy.

crust (KRUST) *n. crusts.* 1. The pastry shell of a pie.–The *crust* of the pie burned, but the filling was all right.
2. The hard outer covering of bread.–The *crust* of bread is good to eat.
3. A thin, hard coat or covering.–There was a *crust* of ice on the snow.
–*v. crusts, crusted, crusting.* Cover with a hard film.–The syrup *crusted* with sugar.

crus·ta·cean (krəss-TAY-shən) *n. crustaceans.* Any member of a very large class of hard-shelled animals that usually live in or near water. Lobsters, shrimps, crabs, and crayfish are *crustaceans.*

crutch (KRUCH) *n. crutches.* A long prop which fits under the arm. It is moved by the arm and hand to help one walk when one's leg is lame.

cry (KRY) *n. cries.* 1. A loud call or shout. –We heard the *cry* of the boy who fell into the water.–We heard the baby's *cry.*
2. A call (of a bird or animal).–The *cry* of the robin is cheerful.
–*v. cries, cried, crying.* 1. Shed tears and make a noise showing pain or sorrow; weep; sob. –Most children *cry* when they are hurt.
2. Shout; call in a loud voice.–The workman on the roof *cried,* "Look out below!" when he dropped his hammer.

crys·tal (KRISS-tl) *n. crystals* and *adj.* 1. A clear, shiny quartz.–The water is as clear as *crystal.*
2. A glass cover on the dial of a watch.–Bob broke the *crystal* of his watch.
3. Clear, shiny glass that contains lead.– Mother has some goblets made of *crystal.*

CRUSTACEANS

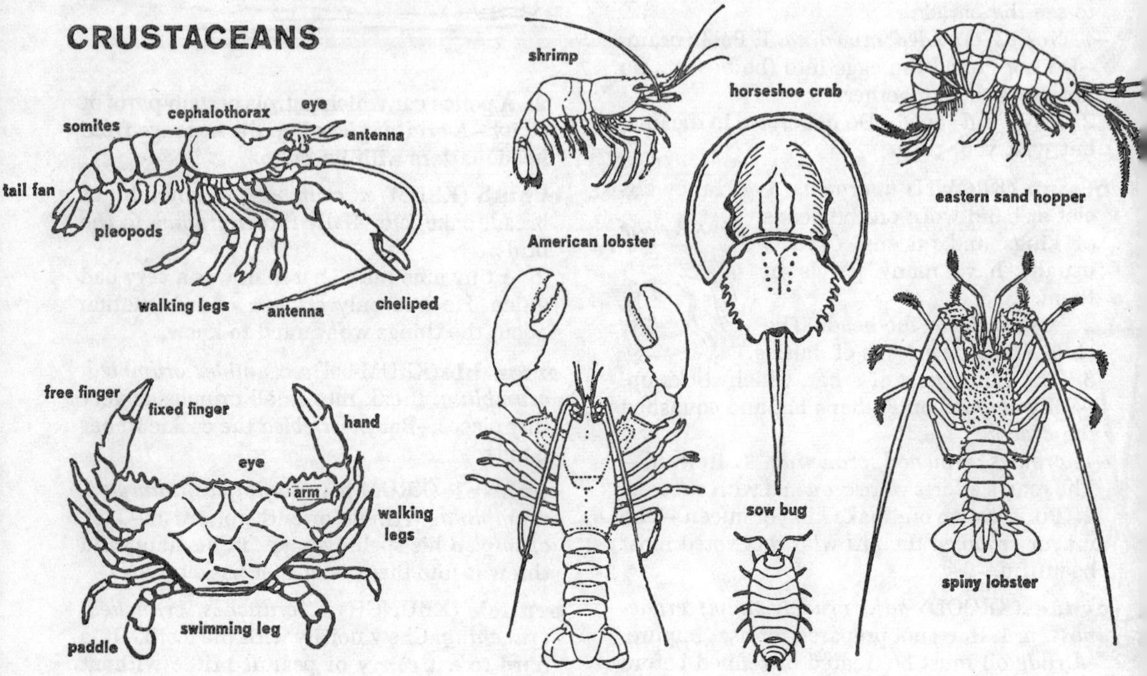

They are made of glass that is very clear and perfectly polished.
4. A body, such as a snow *crystal,* that is formed when many substances become solid. *Crystals* have flat surfaces that are evenly arranged.

cub (KUB) *n. cubs.* A young baby bear, wolf, lion, etc.–The lion *cubs* looked like large kittens.

cube (KYOOB) *n. cubes.* A solid figure that has six square sides which are all the same size.–Baby's blocks are *cubes.*

cuck•oo (KOO-koo *or* KUHK-oo) *n. cuckoos.* A small bird that has a whistling call. Some *cuckoos* do not build their own nests, but lay their eggs in the nests of other birds. Other *cuckoos* build their own nests.

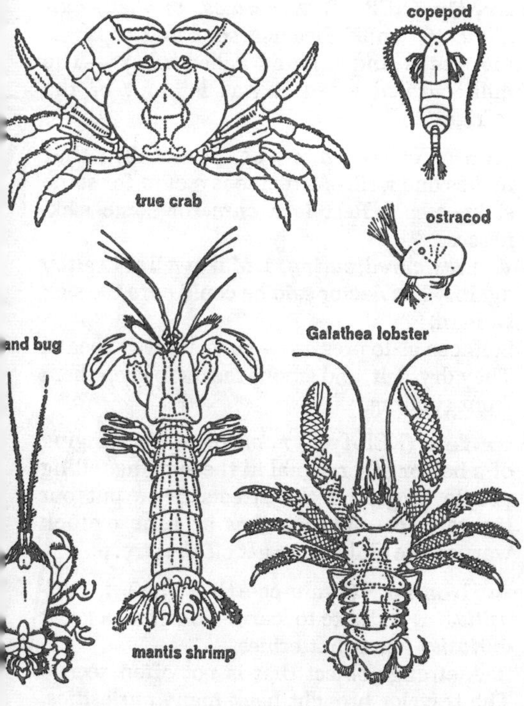

cu•cum•ber (KYOO-kum-ber) *n. cucumbers.* A long, green vegetable that grows on a vine close to the ground. The outer skin is green and the inner part, which has many seeds in it, is white. *Cucumbers* are often eaten raw in salads, as pickles, or sometimes dipped in egg and flour and then fried.

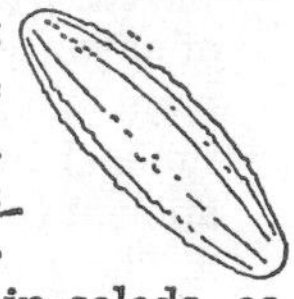

cud (KUD) *n. cuds.* A lump of food brought back from the first stomach of a cow (or other animal with two stomachs) into the mouth for chewing again.

cud•dle (KUD-l) *v. cuddles, cuddled, cuddling.* Hold closely and affectionately.–Mother *cuddles* the baby. She holds it closely.

cue (KYOO) *n. cues.* 1. (Sometimes spelled *queue)* A long, braided tail of hair hanging down in back.–John took the part of a Chinese man in the play and wore a long *cue.*

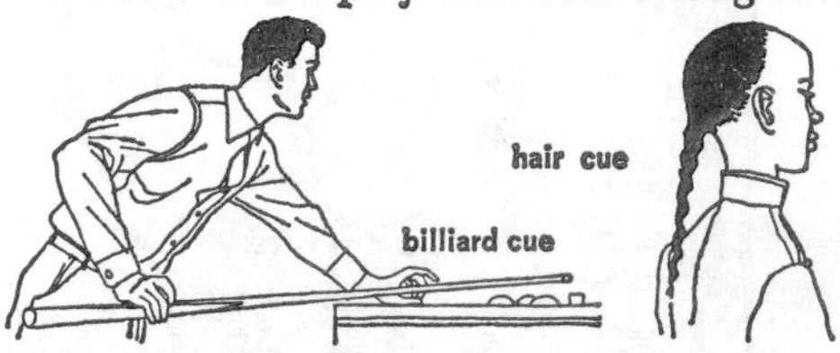

2. A long stick with a soft tip used in the game of pool or billiards to hit the ball.
3. A word or action in a play which serves as a signal to an actor.–The actor went onto the stage when he heard his *cue.*
4. A signal.–Bob went into the ball game when he got his *cue* from the coach.

cuff (KUF) *n. cuffs.* 1. A band around the lower part of a sleeve. –The *cuffs* of Father's old shirt were badly worn.
2. The part of a man's trouser leg that is turned up at the bottom. – Father asked Mother to press the *cuffs* of his trousers.

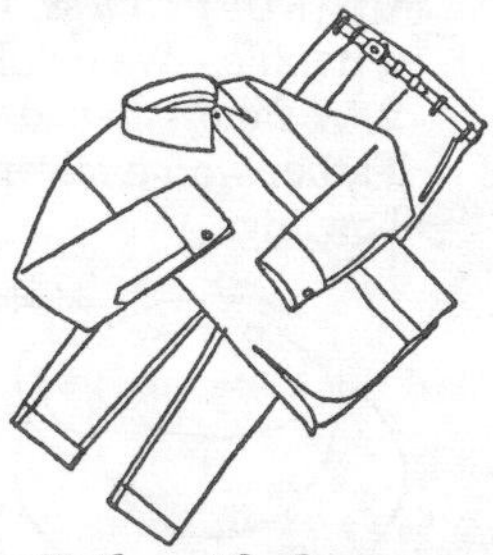

–*v. cuffs, cuffed, cuffing.* Strike with the open hand.–Grandfather *cuffed* the dog when it jumped on his suit.

cul•ti•vate (KUL-tə-vayt) *v. cultivates, cultivated, cultivating.* 1. Plant and tend a crop. –Farmers *cultivate* their crops. They help them grow. They plow the ground, make the ground rich, plant seeds, hoe out the weeds, and harvest the crops.
2. Try to improve. – Arthur *cultivates* his manners.

cul•ture (KUL-cher) *n. cultures.* 1. The state of advancement in the arts, sciences, government, etc., of a nation or people at any given time.–John is reading about the *culture* of ancient Greece.
2. The good manners, taste, refinement, etc., acquired as the result of good education.–Peter's parents value *culture* highly. They intend to send their children to college.
3. The care and preparation of land for farming, or for the raising of a particular crop.–Harry is an expert on peanut *culture.*

cu•ne•i•form (KYOO-nə-form) *adj.* Shaped like a wedge.–*Cuneiform* letters were often used in ancient writing.

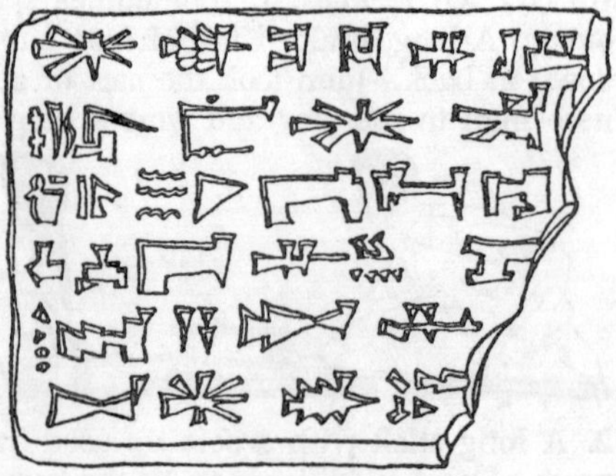

a Babylonian seal

cun•ning (KUN-ing) *adj.; cunningly, adv.* 1. Sly; tricky.–The fox is *cunning.*
2. Cute; charming.–John has a *cunning* little sister.

cup (KUP) *n. cups.* 1. A small open vessel with a handle.–We drink from a *cup.*
2. A fancy-shaped vessel given as a prize.–Father won a silver *cup* for his high score in bowling.

3. The small hole into which a golfer tries to hit the ball.–The golf player pushed the ball into the *cup.*
4. Anything shaped like a cup is often called a *cup.*–Some machines have small *cups* into which oil should be put.
5. A cupful.–Have a *cup* of coffee.
–*v. cups, cupped, cupping.* Form a cuplike shape from.–The man *cupped* his hands and lifted water from the brook.

cup•board (KUB-erd) *n. cupboards.* A cabinet or closet with shelves and drawers in it.–We keep dishes, food, linens, and silver in the *cupboard.*

cu•pid (KYOO-pid) *n. cupids.* 1. (Spelled with a capital "C.") The god of love in the stories of the Romans.
2. A picture of a baby with wings, representing love.–Mary put a *cupid* on Jack's valentine.

curb (KERB) *n. curbs.* 1. A very low stone or cement walk along the outer edge of a street.–We stood on the *curb* and waited for the bus.

2. The part of a horse's bridle that passes under the lower jaw. A *curb* is used to control the horse, to get him to do what is wanted.
–*v. curbs, curbed, curbing.* Control; check.–The city tried to *curb* the waste of water.–John tried to *curb* his anger.

curd (KERD) *n. curds.* The thick part of sour milk. When sour milk is heated, the *curd* separates from the watery part and is made into cottage cheese.

cur•dle (KERD-l) *v. curdles, curdled, curdling.* (Of milk) Become sour and separate into curds and a liquid called whey.–The milk *curdled* when it was left out of the refrigerator.

cure (KYUHR) *n. cures.* Something that makes one well.–Medicine is a *cure* for some sicknesses.–Rest is a *cure* for some sicknesses.
–*v. cures, cured, curing.* 1. Make well or healthy again.–The doctor said he could *cure* the sick woman.
2. Fix so as to preserve.–Farmers *cure* meats. They dry, salt, and smoke meats to keep them from spoiling.

cur•few (KER-fyoo) *n. curfews.* The ringing of a bell or other signal in the evening telling people to get off the streets or to put out lights, etc.–The *curfew* at nine o'clock warned the children to get off the streets.

cu•ri•os•i•ty (kyuhr-ee-AHSS-ə-tee) *n. curiosities.* 1. A desire to learn.–John has a great *curiosity* about butterflies.
2. A strange object that is not often seen.–The traveler brought back many *curiosities.*

cu•ri•ous (KYUHR-ee-əss) *adj.; curiously, adv.* 1. Eager to learn.–Jack is *curious* about raising chickens, ducks, and geese.
2. Odd.–We found several *curious* shells on the beach. They were different from the others.

curl (KERL) *n. curls.* 1. A coiled or rolled bunch of hair.–Mary has long *curls.*
2. Anything coiled in a spiral shape. – The boys twisted the wire around and around to make a *curl.*

–*v. curls, curled, curling.* 1. Roll into curls.–The hairdresser *curled* Mother's hair.
2. Wind.–Some plants *curl* around trees and bushes.

curl•y (KER-lee) *adj. curlier, curliest.* Curled up; having curls.–Baby's hair is *curly.*

cur•rant (KER-ənt) *n. currants.* 1. A small, very sour berry that grows in clusters, or bunches, on bushes. *Currants* are white or red. *Currant* jelly is made from *currants.*

2. A small, black raisin without seeds. – Grandmother put *currants* into the cookies.

cur•rent (KER-ənt) *n. currents.* 1. Something flowing in a steady stream. When we say a *current* of air, a *current* of water, or a *current* of electricity, we mean a flowing or moving of air, water, or electricity.
2. A fast stream of water moving through a slower stream. – The boy could not swim through the *current* in the middle of the river.

–*adj.* In use at present.–Mother reads *current* magazines, the ones that have just been printed.

curse (KERSS) *n. curses.* Something that causes evil or trouble.–The boy's laziness is a *curse* to him.
–*v. curses, cursed, cursing.* 1. Swear; use profane language.–Boys who *curse* at animals and people are not well liked.
2. Request that God make some harm or evil come to (a person).–The man *cursed* his enemy.

cur•tain (KER-tn) *n. curtains.* 1. A cloth covering for a window or door.–Mother hung *curtains* at the front window.

window curtain

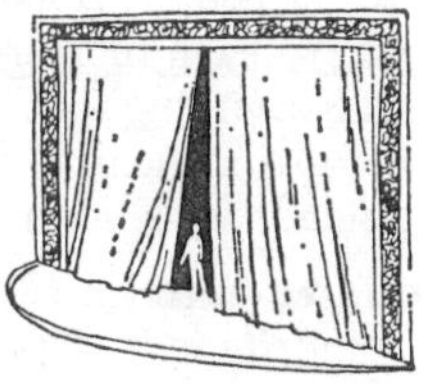

stage curtain

2. A heavy cloth covering to hide a stage from the audience.–The *curtain* on the stage of the theater opened and the play started.

curt•sy (KERT-see) *v. curtsies, curtsied, curtsying.* Make a bow, usually by bending the knees slightly and lowering the body. Women *curtsy;* men bow.–The little girl *curtsied* before the prince.

curve (KERV) *n. curves.* 1. A line that changes its direction little by little and regularly throughout its length.

2. Something which changes direction little by little; a bend.–The automobile went around the *curve* in the road.
–*v. curves, curved, curving.* Bend in a curve. –The road ahead *curved* around the lake.

cush•ion (KUHSH-ən) *n. cushions.* A pad or pillow to sit on, or to lean or rest against. –The *cushions* on the couch are filled with feathers.

–*v. cushions, cushioned, cushioning.* To furnish with a cushion.–Mother *cushioned* the chair with a pillow.–The snow drift *cushioned* Bob's fall.

cus•tard (KUSS-terd) *n. custards.* A mixture of eggs, sugar, flavoring, and milk that is baked or steamed.–Mother said we would have *custard* for dessert.

cus•to•di•an (kəss-TOH-dee-ən) *n. custodians.* Someone who is responsible for the care of something; a keeper.–The *custodian* of the museum made sure all the doors were locked before he left the building.

cus·to·dy (KUSS-tə-dee) *n. custodies.* Care; charge.–The wallet was put in the *custody* of a reliable person until its owner could be found.

cus·tom (KUSS-təm) *n. customs.* 1. Something usually done.–It is Father's *custom* to shave each morning before breakfast.
2. Something that has been done regularly so long that nearly everyone does it.–Greeting friends by shaking hands is an old *custom.*

cus·to·mar·y (KUSS-təm-air-ee) *adj.; customarily, adv.* Usual; commonly done.–It is *customary* for men to take off their hats in the house.

cus·tom·er (KUSS-təm-er) *n. customers.* One who is buying; one who often buys at a certain place.–The clerk waited on the *customer.*–Mother is a *customer* at Mr. Smith's grocery. She usually buys her groceries there.

cut (KUT) *n. cuts.* A gash made by something sharp.–Bob fell on the glass and got a *cut* on his hand.
–*v. cuts, cut, cutting.* 1. Separate into pieces, or make a cut in, with a knife or other sharp edge.–Father *cut* the meat into small pieces. –The woodmen *cut* down trees with axes.–Bob *cut* his finger with his knife.
2. Clip; make shorter.–John *cuts* the grass with a lawnmower.
3. Go quickly, by a short way.–The boys *cut* through the woods to the river.
4. Hurt keenly.–The man's cruel words *cut* John.
5. Make less or smaller.–Bob's allowance was *cut* from $2.00 to $1.50.

cute (KYOOT) *adj. cuter, cutest; cutely, adv.* 1. Charming; darling.–The baby is *cute.*
2. Smart; clever.–I don't think you can do that. It will be a *cute* trick if you can.

cut·let (KUT-lət) *n. cutlets.* A piece of meat cooked by being fried, broiled, or rolled in egg and cracker crumbs and cooked in deep fat.–Veal *cutlets* are tasty.

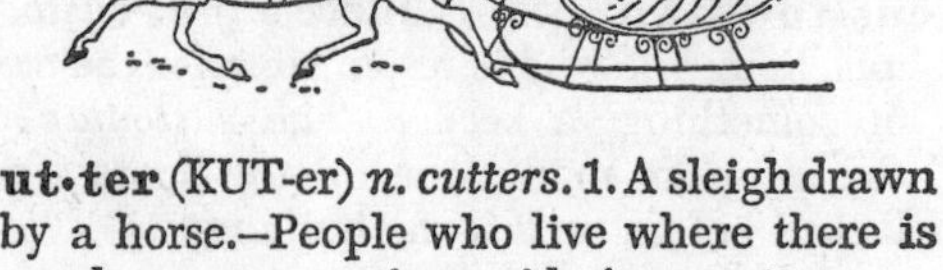

cut·ter (KUT-er) *n. cutters.* 1. A sleigh drawn by a horse.–People who live where there is much snow sometimes ride in a *cutter.*
2. A machine or tool for cutting.–We cut the vegetables into fancy shapes with a new vegetable *cutter.*
3. A kind of sailboat with one mast for sails. –The young man has a *cutter* to sail on the lake.

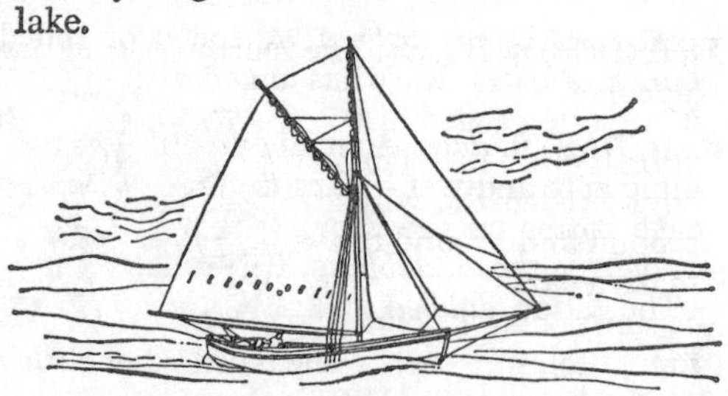

4. A small, fast boat used by the U.S. Coast Guard for patrols and rescue work.–The men

on the sinking sailboat were saved by a Coast Guard *cutter.*

cut·ting (KUT-ing) *n. cuttings.* 1. Something cut out.–We saved the newspaper *cuttings* about the ball game.
2. A part of a plant cut off for planting.–This bush grew from a *cutting.*
–*v.* One form of the verb *cut.*–Mother is *cutting* the cake now.
–*adj.* Sharp; hurting.–*Cutting* words are words that hurt one's feelings.

cy·clone (SY-klohn) *n. cyclones.* A very strong, fierce windstorm.–A *cyclone* uprooted the trees.

cyl·in·der (SIL-ən-der) *n. cylinders.* A long, round body that is hollow or solid.–The main part of a rolling pin is a *cylinder.*–An automobile motor has hollow *cylinders* in it into which solid *cylinders* called pistons fit. The pistons work up and down in the *cylinders* to make the car run.

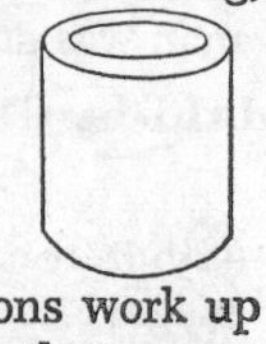

cym·bal (SIM-bəl) *n. cymbals.* A pair of *cymbals* is a pair of metal musical instruments shaped something like dinner plates. They are played by being struck together.

D d

D, d (DEE) *n. D's, d's.* The fourth letter of the alphabet.

dab (DAB) *n. dabs.* A small amount of something soft and wet.—Mary dropped a *dab* of cake batter on the floor.
—*v. dabs, dabbed, dabbing.* Pat; touch lightly. —The kitten *dabbed* at Sally's face with its paw.

dachs•hund (DAHKS-huhnd) *n. dachshunds.* A small dog with a very long body and short legs.—*Dachshunds,* originally bred in Germany, are kept as pets in the United States.

dad (DAD) *n. dads.* A father is often called *Dad* by his children.

dad•dy (DAD-ee) *n. daddies.* Some fathers are called *Daddy* by their children. — Sally often calls her father *Daddy.*

daf•fo•dil(DAF-ə-dil) *n. daffodils.* A yellow flower that blooms early in the spring. The stems and leaves of the *daffodil* are long and slender.

dag•ger (DAG-er) *n. daggers.* A short, pointed knife used as a weapon for stabbing.—The man was stabbed with a *dagger.*

dahl•ia (DAL- *or* DAHL-yə) *n. dahlias.* A bright-colored flower that blooms in the middle of summer. *Dahlias* grow from bulbs that look like sweet potatoes. The plants grow tall and bushy, and have many flowers.

dai•ly (DAY-lee) *adj* and *adv.* Every day.—The newsboy brings the paper *daily.*—Anything that takes place every day is a *daily* happening.

dain•ty (DAYNT-ee) *n. dainties.* Fancy food. —At the party we had ice cream, cookies, and many other *dainties.*
—*adj.; daintily, adv.* 1. Pleasing, delicate, and pretty.—Mary's new dress is very *dainty.* It is of thin cloth with a tiny pattern of flowers. 2. Having careful, particular little ways and tastes.—Mary has *dainty* manners.

dair•y (DAIR-ee) *n. dairies.* 1. A place where butter, cheese, and other milk products are made.

DAIRY PRODUCTS

2. A store where milk, butter, cheese, and other milk products are sold. — Uncle Jim runs a *dairy.*

dair•y cat•tle (DAIR-ee kat-l). Certain breeds of cattle that are raised especially to give milk to be used in making dairy products.

dai•sy (DAY-zee) *n. daisies.* A flower which often grows wild, with white petals and yellow centers. Garden *daisies* are pink, yellow, or white, and larger than wild ones.

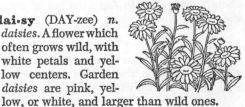

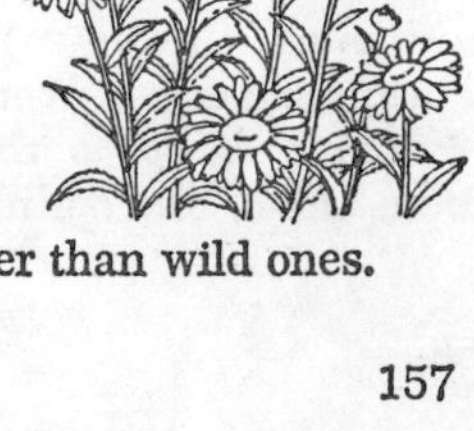

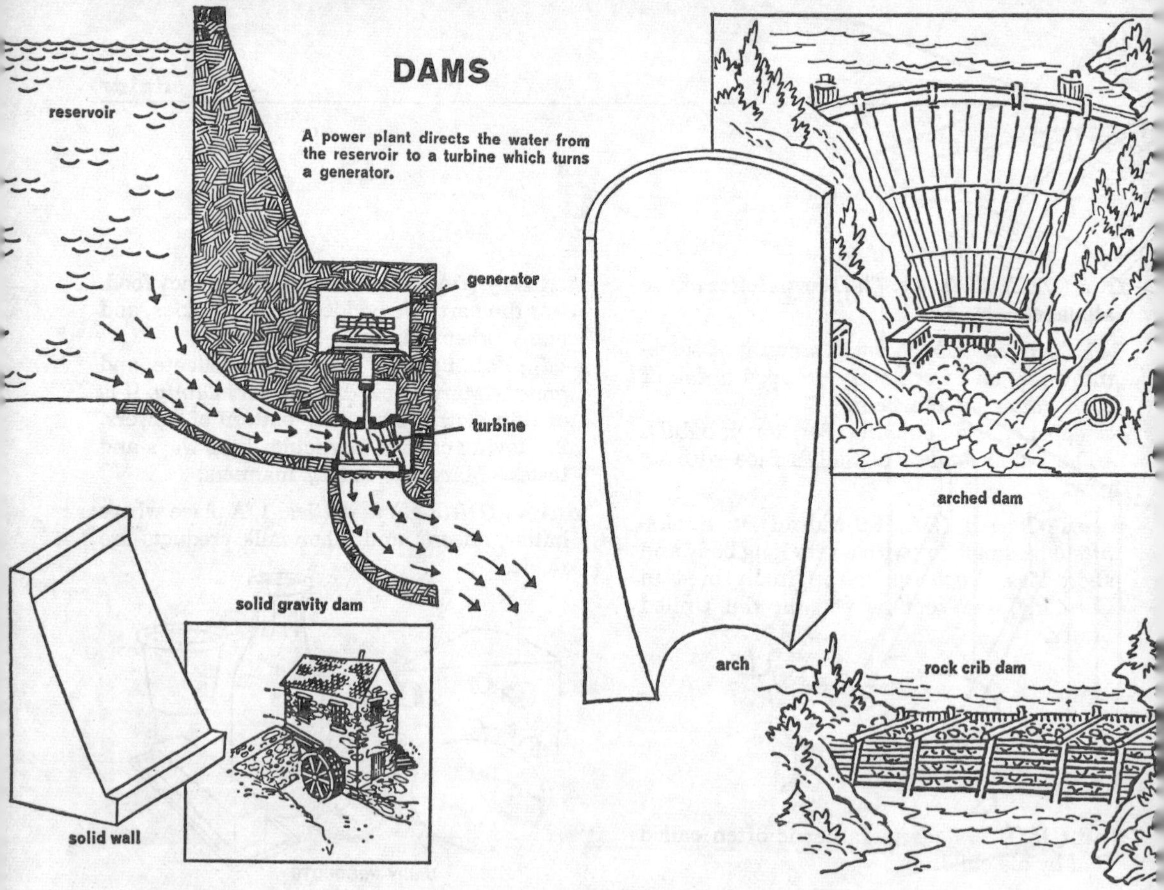

dam (DAM) *n. dams.* A wall built across a river or stream to hold the water back.—Father built a *dam* in the brook to make a swimming pool.
—*v. dams, dammed, damming.* Put a dam or wall across.—They *dammed* the river to hold back the water.

dam·age (DAM-ij) *n.* Harm; destruction.—The heavy frost did much *damage* to the farmer's crops.
—*v. damages, damaged, damaging.* Hurt; injure.—Forest fires *damage* trees and destroy much wild life.
—*Damages* means money paid to make up for harm done to someone or someone's property.—The man who was to blame for the accident on the highway had to pay the *damages* on the car.

damp (DAMP) *adj.; dampness, n.* A little wet.—The cellar is too *damp* for us to play in.—The air that blows in from the sea is raw and *damp.*

damp·en (DAMP-ən) *v. dampens, dampened, dampening.* Wet slightly; make damp.—Mother *dampens* the clothes before she irons them. She sprinkles them with water.

damp·er (DAMP-er) *n. dampers.* A metal plate in a smoke pipe or chimney which can be turned to increase or reduce the draft for the fire.—Father adjusted the *damper* in the stovepipe to make the fire burn faster.

dance (DANSS) *n. dances.* 1. A series of steps in time to a piece of music.—Mary did a little *dance* for the class.

2. A party for *dancing.*—Father and Mother went to a *dance.*
3. Music to dance by.—The band played a *dance.*
—*v. dances, danced, dancing.* 1. Take steps in time to music.—George asked me to *dance* with him.
2. Jump about in a playful way.—The lambs *danced* in the field.

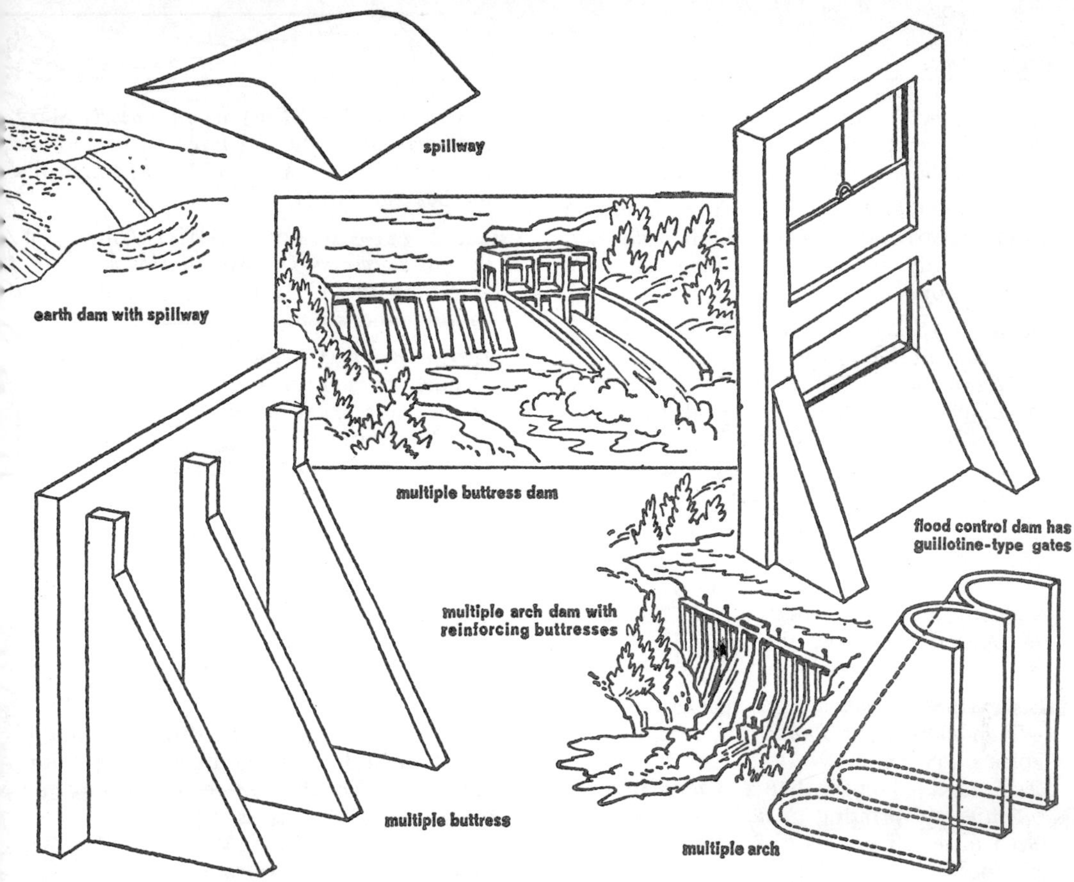

danc•er (DAN-ser) *n. dancers.* 1. A person who dances.–The older girls are good *dancers.*
2. A person whose work is dancing in public to entertain people.

dan•de•li•on (DAND-əl-y-ən) *n. dandelions.* A weed that bears thick, round, yellow flowers. – Children like to gather *dandelions* in the spring. They make chains of the hollow stems.

dan•dy (DAN-dee) *n. dandies.* A man who dresses in fancy clothes.–Ed is a *dandy.* He pays a great deal of attention to the way he looks.
–*adj.* Some people use the word *dandy* to mean fine or very good. – This is a *dandy* lunch.

dan•ger (DAYN-jer) *n. dangers.* 1. A chance or possibility that something bad or harmful will happen.–When floods come in the spring, there is great *danger.* People may be injured or lose their homes.
2. A thing that is a risk, or not safe.–An automobile with poor brakes, a driver who is careless, a sharp turn in the road, are all *dangers.* They may cause bad accidents.

dan•ger•ous (DAYN-jer-əss) *adj.; dangerously, adv.* Not safe; likely to cause harm.–It is *dangerous* to play with matches. One may get burned.

dan•gle (DANG-gəl) *v. dangles, dangled, dangling.* Hang so as to swing back and forth.–A long chain *dangled* from the back of the oil truck.

dare (DAIR) *n. dares.* A challenge to do something.–Bob would not take John's *dare* to jump off the porch roof.
–*v. dares, dared, daring.* 1. Challenge.–John *dared* Bob to jump off the roof. He challenged him to see if he would really do it.
2. Have courage enough; be brave enough.–Only the animal trainer *dared* to go into the lion's den.

dark (DAHRK) *adj. darker, darkest.* 1. Without light.–Night is *dark.*–When it is completely *dark,* one cannot see.
2. More like black than like white.–Grandmother wore a *dark* dress.
3. Deep in shade; not pale.–The living-room walls are painted *dark* yellow, not a light yellow.

dark•ness (DAHRK-nəss) *n.* Lack of light.–The sun went down, and *darkness* came.–People cannot see well in *darkness.*

dar•ling (DAHR-ling) *n. darlings.* Someone who is dearly loved.–Our baby is a *darling.*
–*adj.* Greatly loved.–Jack is Grandmother's *darling* boy.

darn (DAHRN) *n. darns.* A mended place.–One *darn* in Bob's sock was very large.
–*v. darns, darned, darning.* Make stitches back and forth to close a hole.–Mary *darned* the toe of her stocking.

dart (DAHRT) *n. darts.* A small arrow thrown by hand, not shot from a bow.–We had fun throwing *darts* at the target.

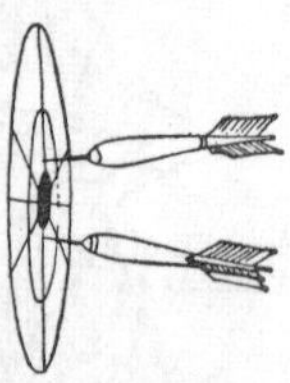

–*v. darts, darted, darting.* Run suddenly and fast.–When Father opened the door, the dog *darted* into the house.

dash (DASH) *n. dashes.* 1. A speck; a tiny bit.–Grandmother put a *dash* of ginger into the spice cake.
2. A mark [–] longer than a hyphen, used in writing and printing. A *dash* is sometimes used to set off one part of a sentence from another.
–*v. dashes, dashed, dashing.* 1. Run fast.–The horse *dashed* across the bridge.
2. Splash; throw.–The teacher *dashed* water into the face of the boy who had fainted.
3. Shatter; ruin.–A shower of rain *dashed* our hopes for the picnic.

date (DAYT) *n. dates.* 1. The exact time: day, month, and year.–The *date* for the wedding has been set for September 12 of this year.
2. Time.–Carriages were used at an earlier *date* than automobiles.
3. A small brown fruit that grows on a *date* palm tree. It has a long seed, or pit, through the middle. *Dates* are very sweet.

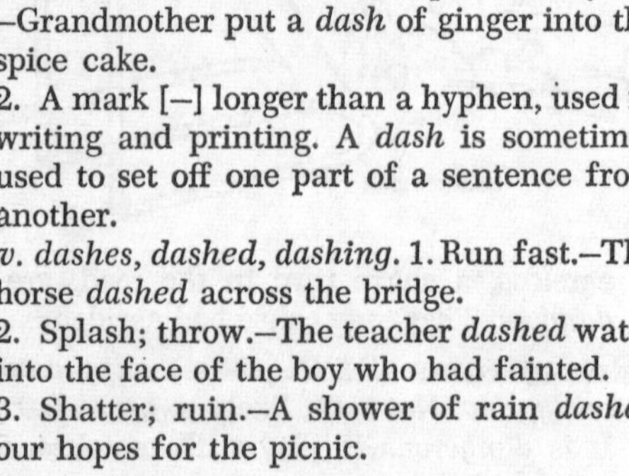

–*v. dates, dated, dating.* Write the month, day, and year on.–The teacher *dates* our report card every time she gives it to us.

daugh•ter (DAWT-er) *n. daughters.* Mary is a girl. She is the *daughter* of her mother and father. Bob is a boy. He is the son of his mother and father.

daugh•ter-in-law (DAWT-er-in-law) *n. daughters-in-law.* The wife of a person's son.–Grandmother is Father's mother. Mother is Grandmother's *daughter-in-law.*

dav•en•port (DAV-ən-port) *n. davenports.* A couch that has arms and a back. A *davenport* has springs and padding in it to make it soft.

dawn (DAWN) *n. dawns.* The time of day when it begins to get light.
–*v. dawns, dawned, dawning.* Grow light.–The morning *dawned* cool and clear.
–*Dawn on one* means come to one's mind.–It didn't *dawn on me* till after I got up that it was Saturday and there would be no school.

day (DAY) *n. days.* 1. The time from morning till night. It is dark at night and light during the *day.* The time between the rising and the setting of the sun is *day.*
2. Sometimes night and day together are called a *day.*–There are twenty-four hours in a *day.*
3. One's lifetime, or the time in which one is living.–In our *day,* airplanes have become quite common.–In our great-grandmother's *day,* people usually traveled by train.

day•break (DAY-brayk) *n. daybreaks.* Dawn; the time when it first gets light.–We arose at *daybreak.*

day•dream (DAY-dreem) *n. daydreams.* Pleasant things that one imagines dreamily.
–*v. daydreams, daydreamed, daydreaming.* Dreamily imagine pleasant things.–Mary is apt to *daydream* about being an actress while doing her arithmetic.

day•light (DAY-lyt) *n.* 1. Light that comes from the sun; the light of daytime.–We turn on electric lights after the *daylight* goes.
2. Dawn, when the darkness of night goes and the light of day comes.–The farmer gets up at *daylight.*

day•time (DAY-tym) *n. daytimes.* The time when it is light, or day.–We sleep at night and work during the *daytime.*

daze (DAYZ) *n. dazes.* A confused condition; a state of not realizing what is going on around one.–The boy walked around in a *daze* after being hit by the baseball.

–*v. dazes, dazed, dazing.* 1. Confuse; put in a condition of not knowing what to feel or what to do.–The driver of the car was *dazed* by the sight of the truck coming toward him. He couldn't think clearly.
2. Stun; make senseless.–The boy was *dazed* for a moment by the blow on his head. He didn't know what had happened.

daz•zle (DAZ-əl) *v. dazzles, dazzled, dazzling.* Make blind or confused by a sudden great brightness.–Coming from a dark room into a brightly lighted room, one is often *dazzled.*

dead (DED) *n. pl.* People no longer living. –We put flowers on the graves of our *dead.*
–*adj.* 1. Not living.–The rosebush is *dead* from lack of water.
2. Quiet and dull.–The town is very *dead* on Sundays.
–*adv.* Completely.–Father's car ran out of gas and stopped *dead.*

deaf (DEF) *adj.; deafness, n.* Having poor hearing.–The old lady is *deaf.* She cannot hear well.–Some people are so *deaf* they cannot hear at all.

deaf•en (DEF-ən) *v. deafens, deafened, deafening.* Make deaf.–The noise *deafened* Jim for a minute. He could not hear.

deal (DEEL) *n. deals.* 1. Amount.–Mother spends a great *deal* of her time taking care of the baby.
2. A bargain.–Jack asked Father if he could make a *deal* with him to mow the lawn for twenty-five cents an hour.
3. An opportunity; an arrangement offering a chance.–The teacher said she wanted to give the children a fair *deal* on the test.
–*v. deals, dealt, dealing.* 1. Hand out; give to each of several others.–Bob likes to *deal* the cards when we play.–Mother *dealt* out the cookies to the children.
2. Trade.–A grocery store *deals* in groceries. –A clothing store *deals* in clothes.–We usually *deal* at the corner grocery store.
3. Strike.–Bill *dealt* Jack a sudden blow.
–*Deal with* sometimes means to concern or be about.–This book *deals with* the life of Abraham Lincoln.
–*Deal with* can also mean treat.–The boy *deals* roughly *with* those who abuse his dog.

deal•er (DEEL-er) *n. dealers.* 1. A trader; one who buys and sells.–Mr. Smith is an automobile *dealer;* he buys and sells cars.
2. One who deals or gives out the cards to the players in a card game.

dealt (DELT) *v.* One form of the verb *deal.* –We have *dealt* with this dairyman for many years. We have traded with him.–Father *dealt* the cards to each player.

dear (DIR) *n. dears.* A pet name.–Mother often calls me "*Dear.*"
–*adj.* 1. Loved.–We have a *dear* baby at our house. She is loved by everyone.
2. Expensive.–John wanted to buy a baseball, but it was too *dear.* It cost too much.
3. When we write a letter, we put "*Dear*" before the person's name, as a polite way of beginning to write to him.–Mary started her letter, "*Dear* Grandfather."
–"*Oh, dear!*" is an exclamation some people use when they mean "How sad!" or "What a pity!"

dear•ly (DIR-lee) *adv.* 1. Greatly.–Bob loves his mother *dearly.* He is very fond of her.
2. At a high cost.–Success comes *dearly.* One has to work very hard for it.

death (DETH) *n. deaths.* The end of life.–After the *death* of Joe's dog, his father promised to get him another.–Accidents cause many *deaths.* Many people meet with *death* through accidents.

de•bate (di-BAYT) *n. debates.* 1. An argument carried on as a contest before an audience.–Our school team won the *debate* on the question: "Should the Government Own the Railroads?"
2. Any discussion for and against something. –Father took part in a *debate* over the new town water system at the meeting last night.
–*v. debates, debated, debating.* Argue for or against something.–We *debated* having a picnic on the last day of school.

debt (DET) *n. debts.* 1. Something which is owed.–The men paid all their *debts* before going out of business.
2. State of owing something.–The sick man is very much in *debt.* He owes many people money.

debt•or (DET-er) *n. debtors.* A person who is in debt; one who owes someone something.

dec•ade (DEK-ayd) *n. decades.* A group of ten, usually ten years.–Many changes have taken place during the last five *decades,* or during the last fifty years.

de•cay (dee-KAY) *n.* A slow rotting.–Tooth *decay* can often be prevented by eating the right foods.
–*v. decays, decayed, decaying.* Rot; go bad.–If an apple starts to *decay,* take it from the basket, or the others will *decay* also.

de•ceased (di-SEEST) *adj.* Dead.–The *deceased* man left his large home to his son.
–*The deceased* means the dead person.–This was the home of *the deceased.*

de•ceit (di-SEET) *n.* Untruthfulness; hiding the truth by a trick or lie.–It was *deceit* on Bill's part to sell the broken bicycle by pretending it was new.

de•ceive (di-SEEV) *v. deceives, deceived, deceiving.* Make someone believe something which is not true.–Bill tried to *deceive* his mother. He tried to make her believe that he was at Jack's house when he was really downtown.

De•cem•ber (di-SEM-ber) *n. Decembers.* The twelfth month of the year. *December* has thirty-one days.

de•cent (DEE-sənt) *adj.; decently, adv.* 1. Fair; reasonable; good enough.–Uncle Jim gets a *decent* salary now.
2. Proper; respectable; modest.–The language the angry man used wasn't *decent.*–Grandmother thinks some modern clothes are not *decent.*

de•cide (di-SYD) *v. decides, decided, deciding.* 1. Make up one's mind.–Grandfather couldn't *decide* which horse to buy, because he liked them both.–The policeman *decided* to let the man go.
2. Settle; judge.–Father will *decide* who won the argument as soon as he gets home from the office.

dec•i•mal (DESS-ə-məl) *n. decimals* and *adj.* You can write the fractions that tell tenths, hundredths, and thousandths as *decimals.* The fraction 1/10 is written .1 when written as a *decimal.* The fraction 2/100 is written .02 when written as a *decimal.* The dot is called a *decimal* point.

de•ci•sion (di-SIZH-ən) *n. decisions.* 1. What has been decided; final opinion.–The race was so close that we had to wait for the judge's *decision* to find out who had won.–I have come to the *decision* that it is better to wait for Father than to go ahead.
2. A strong, determined way of thinking or acting, without changing one's mind back and forth.–"We shall certainly go, no matter what happens," said Father, in a tone of *decision.*

deck (DEK) *n. decks.* 1. The floor of a boat.
–The boat we were on had three *decks.* Some of us were on the second *deck,* and some were on the third.

2. A pack (of playing cards).–Mother bought a new *deck* of cards.
–*v. decks, decked, decking.* Dress; array.–The children *decked* themselves out in Mother's clothes and played house.

dec•la•ra•tion (dek-lə-RAY-shən) *n. declarations.* A forceful announcement or statement.–The mayor made the *declaration* that he would definitely open the new playground next week.

de•clar•a•tive (di-KLAR-ə-tiv) *adj.* Making a statement of fact or opinion.–"John was late" is a *declarative* sentence.

de•clare (di-KLAIR) *v. declares, declared, declaring.* Say or announce positively.–When Jack came home from playing football, Mother *declared* that she had never seen such a dirty boy.–Jack and Bill have *declared* peace. They have made it known that they will not fight any more.

de•cline (di-KLYN) *n.* A slow fall or sinking.
–A *decline* in the man's health caused him to give up his job.
–*v. declines, declined, declining.* 1. Refuse; say that one cannot accept something.–Because Mary would be out of town on Joe's birthday, she *declined* the invitation to his party.
2. Become less.–Attendance at school *declined* during the bad weather.
3. Slant downward.–The roof of the house *declines* at a sharp angle.

dec•o•rate (DEK-ə-rayt) *v. decorates, decorated, decorating.* 1. Put things on to make gay and pretty; trim.–The children *decorate* the Christmas tree every year.
2. Paint and otherwise dress up a room or other place.–Mother had the living room *decorated* in blue and white.
3. Give a medal to.–The general *decorated* the soldier for bravery.

dec·o·ra·tion (dek-ə-RAY-shən) *n. decorations.* 1. The act of making pretty, or decorating.—The *decoration* of the living room cost $90.
2. Trimmings and other things used to make something gay and pretty.
3. A medal.—The soldier was very proud of his *decoration.*

dec·o·ra·tor (DEK-ə-ray-ter) *n. decorators.* A person who trims something or plans how to make it gay or pretty.—A window *decorator* arranges the displays in store windows. —Mother had an interior *decorator* plan the colors of the living room.

de·coy (di-KOI *or* DEE-koi) *n. decoys.* 1. A fake bird used to attract birds into flying close to a hunter or into a trap.—The hunter planted a duck *decoy* on the lake.

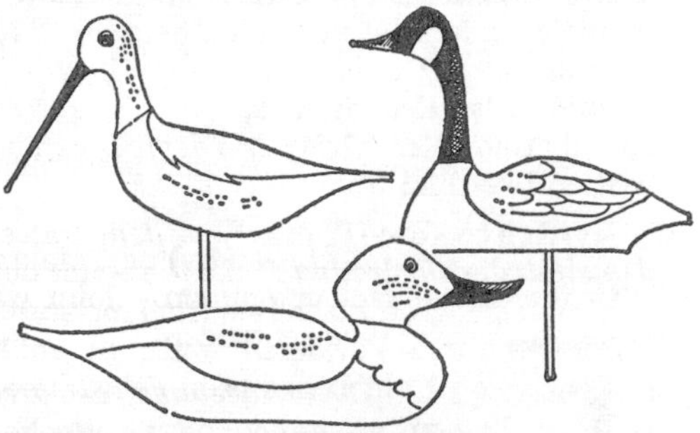

2. Any bait or lure designed to lead a person or an animal into a trap.—The police trapped the jewel thief with the aid of a *decoy.* The *decoy* was a fake necklace left on the counter.

de·crease (DEE-kreess) *n. decreases.* A reduction or cut; a lessening.—A *decrease* in the man's salary brought suffering to his family.
—(di-KREESS) *v. decreases, decreased, decreasing.* Make or become less.—The policeman told the driver to *decrease* his speed. He told him not to drive so fast.

de·cree (di-KREE) *n. decrees.* An official pronouncement, order, decision, etc., made by a person in authority.—The principal issued a *decree* extending the school year by three weeks.

ded·i·cate (DED-ə-kayt) *v. dedicates, dedicated, dedicating.* 1. The writer *dedicated* his new book of stories to all the little children in the land. He wrote it in their honor. He said in the book that it was for them.
2. Give or devote; spend for one thing.—Sometimes a doctor *dedicates* his life to the study of certain diseases. He gives his whole life to this study.

deed (DEED) *n. deeds.* 1. Act.—A good Boy Scout does one good *deed* each day.—Joe carried an old lady's bundles for her. Bob helped a lame man across the street. These were good *deeds.*
2. A written legal statement of property sold. —The man who sold us our house gave us a *deed.* The *deed* said in legal language that he had sold us the house.

deep (DEEP) *adj. deeper, deepest; deeply, adv.* 1. Going far down.—We dug a *deep* hole in the ground.
2. In distance from front to back.—Our house stands on a lot 50 feet wide and 200 feet *deep.*
3. Hard to reach, grasp, or understand; beyond the touch of something.—Father's jokes are often too *deep* for me. They are impossible for me to understand.—Mary was lost in *deep* thought.
4. Very dark.—Mary's new Easter hat is a *deep* blue.

deer (DIR) *n. sing.* and *pl.* A swift, pretty animal that lives in the woods and can run very fast. Full-grown *deer* are about as large as ponies. The male has horns called antlers. *Deer,* like cattle, chew cuds; that is, they bring back into the mouth a part of their food and chew it again.

de·feat (di-FEET) *n. defeats.* State of being beaten; failure.—After its *defeat,* the army retreated.
—*v. defeats, defeated, defeating.* Win a victory over; beat.—Our school team played ball with Central's team and *defeated* them. We won.—A small army can *defeat* a larger one if it has better weapons.

de·fect (di-FEKT *or* DEE-fekt) *n. defects.* A flaw; something wrong with a thing.—We bought the plates for very little because they had *defects* in them. They were not perfect.

de•fend (di-FEND) *v. defends, defended, defending.* 1. Protect.–The older boy *defends* the younger boy against bullies.
2. Stand up for; fight in behalf of.–Even though many people did not like the mayor's speech, Father *defended* it.
–*defender, n. defenders.*

de•fense (di-FENSS) *n. defenses.* 1. A protection.–The army was not large enough for the *defense* of the town.–The farmer's *defense* against the sun was a big straw hat.
2. Something said or done in support of a person or thing that is blamed.–Bob spoke in Jack's *defense* when Jack was accused of breaking the window.

de•fi•ance (di-FY-ənss) *n. defiances.* 1. A showing of contempt for authority; refusal to heed or obey authority.–The rebels showed their *defiance* of the king by ripping down the palace flag.
2. Open disregard of any force or opposition; challenge.–The swimmer's *defiance* of the swift current resulted in his death by drowning.

de•fi•ant (di-FY-ənt) *adj.; defiantly, adv.* Showing defiance.–The *defiant* boy refused to obey his mother.

def•i•nite (DEF-ə-nit) *adj.; definitely, adv.* Certain; clear; fixed; not confused or vague. –His plans are *definite.* He will arrive at 2:30, visit me and then John, and leave at 7:45.

def•i•ni•tion (def-ə-NI-shən) *n. definitions.* An explanation; a statement of what something means.–The teacher wrote a *definition* of the word "inhabit" on the blackboard. She wrote, "Inhabit means to live in." "To live in" is the *definition* of "inhabit."–This dictionary has many *definitions* in it.

de•fy (di-FY) *v. defies, defied, defying.* 1. Dare.–I *defy* you to tell Mother about the window I broke. I say that you are afraid to tell her.–The boy *defied* us to follow him into the empty house. He did not want us to follow him, but he dared us to.
2. Act opposite to; act against; disobey; pay no attention to.–The speeding driver was *defying* the law.
3. Be too much for.–Sometimes Mary's actions *defy* explanation. It is no use to try to explain them. They do not seem to make sense.

de•gree (di-GREE) *n. degrees.* 1. A short extent or distance; a small amount at a time.–Mr. Martin's success came by *degrees.* At first he peddled fruit from house to house. Then he worked as a clerk in a fruit market. Next, he was able to buy a fruit store of his own.–There is a *degree* of improvement in the sick man's condition today. He is a little better than he was yesterday.
2. Class or rank; standing.–Bob is a student whose work is of a high *degree* of excellence. –Dan's job is one that demands a certain *degree* of skill.
3. A title which shows that one has finished certain work or certain courses satisfactorily. –When people finish college, they are given *degrees.* Mr. Jones has a master's *degree.* It takes about five years of study after high school to get a master's *degree.* It takes three years more to get a doctor's *degree.*
4. A unit of measure.–Circles are measured at their centers by *degrees.* There are 360 *degrees* in any circle, no matter how big around it is.–Heat is measured by *degrees* on a thermometer. Thirty-two *degrees* can be written like this: 32°.

de•hy•drate (dee-HY-drayt) *v. dehydrates, dehydrated, dehydrating.* Take the water out of; make free from moisture. – Powdered milk is milk which has been *dehydrated.*

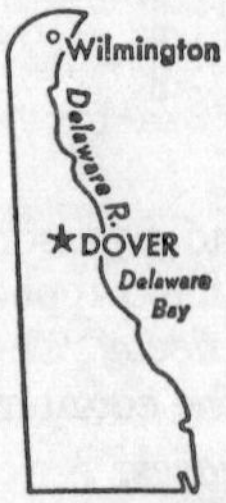

Del•a•ware (DEL-ə-wair) *n.* The second smallest state in the United States. *Delaware* is located on the east coast. Its land is flat and favorable for farming and raising apples and peaches.

de•lay (di-LAY) *n. delays.* Waiting or putting something off.–When Father was sick, we called a doctor without *delay.* We called right away.
–*v. delays, delayed, delaying.* 1. Hold up; cause to be stopped for a while.–The rain *delayed* the ball game one hour.
2. Slow up; cause to be late.–The heavy rain washed away the bridge, and we were *delayed* getting home.
3. Stop; waste time.–Mother told Bob not to *delay* on his way to school.

del•e•gate (DEL-ə-gayt *or* gət) *n. delegates.* A representative; someone to act for other people.–The United States sent *delegates* to the United Nations meeting.
–(DEL-ə-gayt) *v. delegates, delegated, delegating.* Give out (responsibility); pass over to another to do.–Mother *delegated* part of the work to Mary.

del•e•ga•tion (del-ə-GAY-shən) *n. delegations.* 1. Giving something such as power or responsibility to someone.–The *delegation* of various duties to the officers of the club is covered in the club's constitution.
2. A group of persons selected to represent other people, as in a hearing, convention, etc. A *delegation* may also consist of one person. –The school sent a *delegation* to the national students' conference.

de•lete (di-LEET) *v. deletes, deleted, deleting.* 1. Take out; remove.–John *deleted* a paragraph from his editorial so that it would be short enough to fit into the paper.
2. Cross out; put a line through.–Jan's paper was very messy. Each time she misspelled a word, she *deleted* it and then wrote the correct spelling after it.

del•i•cate (DEL-ə-kət) *adj.; delicately, adv.* 1. Easily damaged; not strong.–The girl is a very *delicate* child.–Orchids are *delicate* flowers.
2. Fine; not coarse.–The threads in the lace shawl were *delicate.*
3. Pleasingly mild or light; soft.–The pudding had a *delicate* flavor. It was pleasing to taste.–Mary's new dress is a *delicate* blue.

del•i•ca•tes•sen (del-i-kə-TESS-ən) *n. delicatessens.* A store that sells food which is already prepared, cooked, or ready to serve, such as baked ham, potato salad, relishes.–The *delicatessen* around the block is open late.

de•li•cious (di-LISH-əss) *adj.; deliciously, adv.* 1. Very tasty; very good to eat.–This is a *delicious* apple. It tastes very good.
2. Highly pleasing.–The roses have a *delicious* fragrance.

de•light (di-LYT) *n. delights.* Something that pleases.–The old man's cats were his greatest *delight.*
–*v. delights, delighted, delighting.* Make happy; please.–Mickey Mouse *delights* the boys and girls.

de•light•ful (di-LYT-fuhl) *adj.; delightfully, adv.* Giving pleasure.–Aunt Emma's visit to our house was *delightful.* It gave happiness and pleasure to everyone.

de•lir•i•ous (di-LIR-ee-əss) *adj.; deliriously, adv.* 1. Temporarily out of control of one's senses; raving; talking wildly, etc.–The woman was so sick that for a while she was *delirious.*
2. Wildly excited or aroused.–The city was *delirious* with joy when the home team won the pennant.

de•liv•er (di-LIV-er) *v. delivers, delivered, delivering.* 1. Bring and give.–The newsboy *delivers* papers. He takes them to people's houses and leaves them there.
2. Set free.–The boy *delivered* the bird from the cage. He let the bird out.

de•liv•er•y (di-LIV-er-ee) *n. deliveries.* 1. Bringing and giving.–The *delivery* of the package caused excitement among the children.
2. A round of delivering.–We have two *deliveries* of mail each day. The postman makes two trips a day to leave mail.

del•ta (DEL-tə) *n. deltas.* The earth that is left piled up by a river where it flows into the ocean. A *delta* is usually shaped like a triangle.

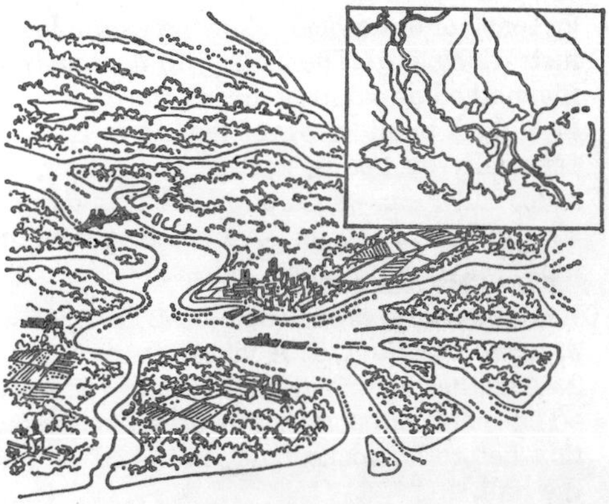

de•mand (di-MAND) *n. demands.* A desire to have.–There is a great *demand* for gasoline.
–*v. demands, demanded, demanding.* 1. Insist; ask with the power to force obedience.–The policeman *demanded* that we tell him whether the dog had a license. He had a right to know.
2. Ask for or need.–The hungry kitten *demanded* her food.–This problem *demands* attention.

de•moc•ra•cy (di-MAHK-rə-see) *n. democracies.* A nation in which the people freely elect those who govern and make the laws, and in which the law gives everyone the same rights and privileges.–The United States is a *democracy.*

dem•o•crat (DEM-ə-krat) *n. democrats.* 1. A person who believes that the government of a country should be run by and for the people; one who believes in democracy.
2. (Spelled with a capital "D.") A member of the Democratic Party, one of the two main political parties in the United States.

dem•o•crat•ic (dem-ə-KRAT-ik) *adj.; democratically, adv.* 1. Having to do with democracy, as a *democratic* government.
2. Believing in the idea that people are equal; fair; just.–Our teacher is very *democratic*. She treats all her students fairly and does not favor anyone.

de•mol•ish (di-MAHL-ish) *v. demolishes, demolished, demolishing.* Destroy by completely taking apart; tear down.–The workmen are *demolishing* the old building to make way for a new one.

dem•on•strate (DEM-ən-strayt) *v. demonstrates, demonstrated, demonstrating.* 1. Prove; show; make clear by explanation and reasoning.–The speaker *demonstrated* that his point of view was correct.
2. Teach or describe by showing examples, illustrations, etc.–The artist will *demonstrate* his method of painting during the class.
3. Make a public show of feeling or opinion, especially by taking part in a meeting, parade, rally, etc.–A group of citizens *demonstrated* before the mayor's office to demand more playgrounds for children.

dem•on•stra•tion (dem-ən-STRAY-shən) *n. demonstrations.* 1. A visual example.
2. A gathering or parade to honor someone. –The man's supporters put on a *demonstration* before he spoke. They marched around the hall.

den (DEN) *n. dens.* 1. A small room furnished for a man.–Father goes to his *den* when he wants to study, read, or be alone.
2. The place where a wild animal lives.–The lion lives in a *den.*
3. The place where criminals meet and make plans.–The thieves met at their *den* to plan the robbery.

de•nom•i•na•tion (di-nahm-ə-NAY-shən) *n. denominations.* 1. A religious group bearing a certain name and being different in some way from other religious groups.–Presbyterians and Baptists are two *denominations* of the Protestant religion.
2. A name; a title of a group of related things. – Chemistry, biology, and physics come under the *denomination* of science.
3. A unit that is part of a series of units.– Pennies, dimes, and one-dollar bills are *denominations* of money. – Ounces, pounds, and tons are *denominations* of weight.

de•nom•i•na•tor (di-NAHM-ə-nay-ter) *n. denominators.* The number appearing below the line in a fraction.–In the fraction "3/5," 5 is the *denominator*.–The *denominator* tells us how many parts make up the whole. In the fraction "3/5," five parts make up the whole; "5/5" equals "1."

dense (DENSS) *adj.; denser, densest; densely, adv.* 1. Thickly set; close; heavy.–The forest is *dense.*–During the fire the smoke was so *dense* we could hardly see.
2. Not very smart.–The boy is *dense* about arithmetic.

den•si•ty (DENS-ə-tee) *n. densities.* 1. Closeness; compactness.–The *density* of the jungle trees made our trip almost impossible.
2. The ratio of the mass of a substance to its volume.–The *density* of lead is greater than that of wood. This means that lead is heavier than wood.

dent (DENT) *n. dents.* A hollow place bent in, as by a blow.–Baby hit the tin dish with a spoon and made a *dent* in it.
–*v. dents, dented, denting.* Make a hollow in. –She did not mean to *dent* the dish.

den•tal (DEN-təl) *adj.* Concerned with the teeth, or with a dentist's work.–Tom had a toothache, so he went for a *dental* examination.

den•tine (DEN-teen) *n.* The hard, bonelike material of which the main part of the tooth is formed. It consists mostly of calcium.– The outside enamel of a tooth covers the *dentine* inside.

den•tist (DEN-tist) *n. dentists.* A doctor who repairs and cares for teeth.–You should visit your *dentist* at least twice a year.

de•ny (di-NY) *v. denies, denied, denying.* Claim (a statement) is untrue.–Bob said that Joe had borrowed his baseball bat. Joe *denied* it.

de•part (di-PAHRT) *v. departs, departed, departing.* 1. Go away; leave.–The famous man made a speech of farewell before he *departed*.
2. Change.–We *departed* from our usual program. We did not do the usual things.

de•part•ment (di-PAHRT-mənt) *n. departments.* A part or division that has certain work to do.—The fire *department* is a division of the city government.—We buy shoes in the shoe *department* of a store.

de•par•ture (di-PAHR-cher) *n. departures.* A going away.—When school is over, the children make their *departure.* They leave.

de•pend (di-PEND) *v. depends, depended, depending.* 1. Be unable to do without; need; be under the care or control of.—Little babies *depend* on their mothers.
2. Put trust in.—The teacher *depends* on the children to keep the room in order.
3. Be the result of.—Success *depends* on hard work and good sense.

de•pend•a•ble (di-PEN-də-bəl) *adj.* Reliable; capable of being trusted.—John is *dependable.* If he promises to do something, you can be sure he will do it.

de•pend•ence (di-PEND-ənss) 1. State of being unable to do without.—The team's *dependence* on Chuck is very great. When Chuck plays, they win, and when he doesn't play, they lose.
2. Trust; confidence.—Spot's *dependence* on Mary pleases her. She is happy that he won't trust anyone else to feed him or to take him for walks.

de•pend•ent (di-PEN-dənt) *n. dependents.* A person who depends on another for support.—Bob and Mary are Father's *dependents.* He takes care of them.
—*adj.* 1. Having need for help or support.—Baby is *dependent* on Mother.
2. Resulting from.—Whether John passes or not is *dependent* on whether he makes up the work he missed.

de•port•ment (di-PORT-mənt) *n.* Behavior; the way one acts.—Bob's *deportment* is very good.

de•pos•it (di-PAHZ-it) *n. deposits.* 1. Money placed in a bank account.—Father made a *deposit* in the bank today.
2. A part payment offered to show that one wishes to complete a purchase. – Mother chose a coat and paid a *deposit* on it so the store would hold it for her.
—*v. deposits, deposited, depositing.* 1. Put away to keep safe.—We *deposit* money in a bank.
2. Place; lay.—The wind carried the leaves to the fence corner and *deposited* them there.

de•pot (DEE-poh) *n. depots.* 1. A railroad station.—Uncle Bill is coming on the seven o'clock train. We are going to meet him at the *depot.*

2. A room or building in which things are stored.—Milk is stored in a milk *depot.*—The army's supplies are stored in a supply *depot.*

de•press (di-PRESS) *v. depresses, depressed, depressing.* Sadden; put into low spirits.—The sad story *depressed* me. I felt unhappy about things after reading it.

depth (DEPTH) *n. depths.* How far down something goes, or how far it is from the top to the bottom.—The *depth* of the box is twelve inches. It is twelve inches deep, or twelve inches from the top to the bottom.—The *depth* of the water here is eight feet.

dep•u•ty (DEP-yə-tee) *n. deputies.* A substitute or assistant picked to do work for someone else.—The sheriff picked a *deputy* to help him keep law and order.

de•rive (di-RYV) *v. derives, derived, deriving.* 1. Get, receive, or obtain from.—Mary *derives* pleasure from music. She is very fond of music.
2. Come from.—Turpentine is *derived* from resin.

de•scend (di-SEND) *v. descends, descended, descending.* 1. Go or come down.—Baby can climb the stairs easily, but she cannot *descend.*
2. Be handed down.—The jewels *descended* from my grandmother to my mother, and finally to me.

de•scent (di-SENT) *n. descents.* A coming down.—The mountain was so steep that the men couldn't make the *descent* without holding onto ropes.

de•scribe (di-SKRYB) *v. describes, described, describing.* Give a picture of something in words.—I will *describe* something and you guess what it is. I will tell you its size, shape, and color.

de•scrip•tion (di-SKRIP-shən) *n. descriptions.* 1. An account or telling about something.—We wrote a *description* of our trip to the zoo. We told the whole story of it.
2. A telling of how something looks.—"The American flag has red and white stripes" is part of a *description* of the flag.

de•sert (di-ZERT) *v. deserts, deserted, deserting.* Go away from and leave uncared for. —The man *deserted* his family. He left them.

des•ert (DEZ-ert) *n. deserts.* A large, sandy place which has very little water and very few trees or plants.—Camels are often used to travel on the *desert.*

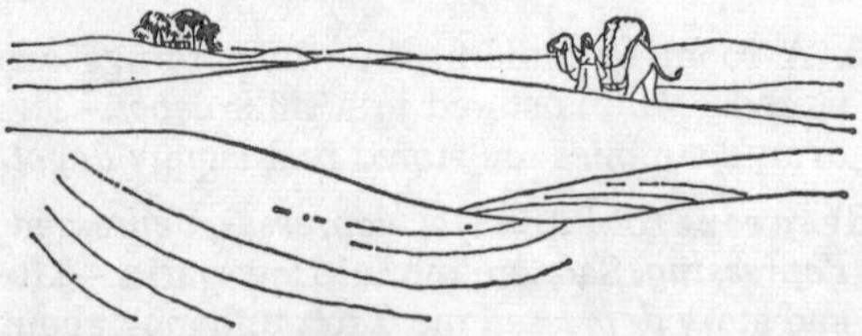

de•serve (di-ZERV) *v. deserves, deserved, deserving.* Ought to have; be worthy of.—That kind woman *deserves* a better home.—A person who steals *deserves* to be punished.

de•sign (di-ZYN) *n. designs.* 1. A sketch or pattern; a plan.—John made a *design* for the car he would like to have.
2. A pattern.—The cloth for Mother's dress has a *design* of flowers on it.

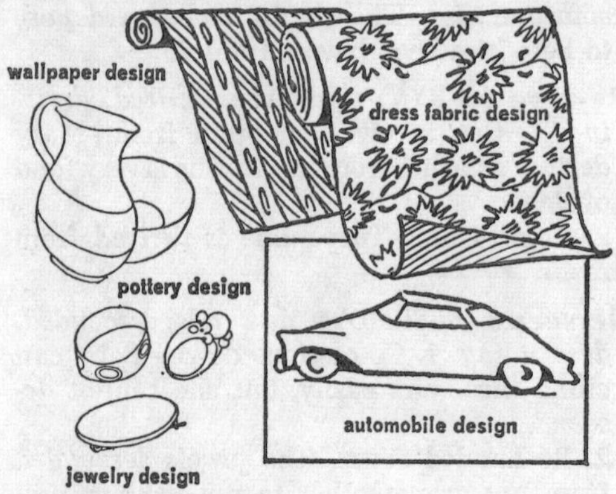

—*v. designs, designed, designing.* Think up a plan of how something is to be made, and put the plan on paper.—An engineer *designs* bridges. Some people *design* dresses, some *design* tools, and some *design* automobiles.

de•sir•a•ble (di-ZYR-ə-bəl) *adj.; desirably, adv.* Worth having; worth wanting; agreeable.—Good teeth are highly *desirable.*

de•sire (di-ZYR) *n. desires.* 1. The thing one wishes for.—Happiness is my *desire.*
2. A wish or longing (for something).—Bob has a great *desire* for ice cream.
—*v. desires, desired, desiring.* Wish for.—Some people *desire* money; others *desire* happiness.

desk (DESK) *n. desks.* A piece of furniture like a table, sometimes with drawers at the sides.—There are forty *desks* in our schoolroom. The children sit at their *desks* to write.

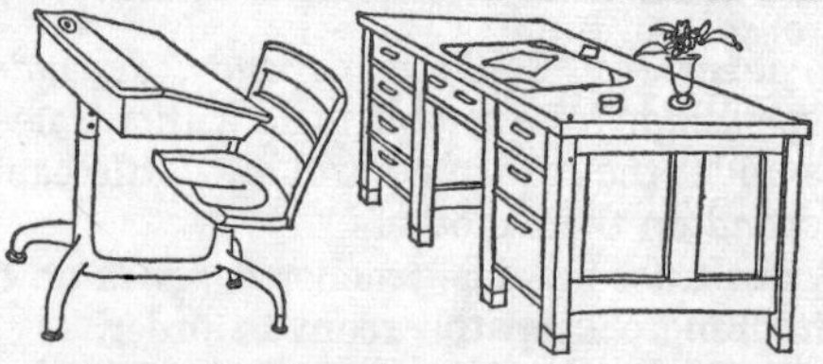

des•o•late (DESS-ə-lət) *adj.; desolately, adv.* 1. Deserted; ruined; empty of people.—The town was *desolate* after the flood. The houses were under water, and the people had fled.
2. Lonely; without company. — The shipwrecked sailor led a *desolate* life on the island.

de•spair (di-SPER) *n. despairs.* A feeling that all hope is gone.—Jack was in *despair* when he could not find his dog.
—*v. despairs, despaired, despairing.* Lose hope; give up.—The woman *despaired* of ever finding her lost money.

des•per•ate (DESS-per-it) *adj.; desperately, adv.; desperation, n.* 1. Very dangerous.—The young boy is sick with a *desperate* disease.
2. Not caring what one does any more, because one is frightened, unhappy, or without hope.—The robber was *desperate* enough to kill anyone who tried to catch him.

de•spise (di-SPYZ) *v. despises, despised, despising.* Look down on; dislike; think badly of.—Jack is very honest and *despises* people who cheat.

de•spite (di-SPYT) *prep.* In spite of.—*Despite* his good promises, Bill was late again today.

des•pot (DESS-pət) *n. despots; despotic, adj.* A ruler with absolute power who is cruel to his people; a tyrant.—*Despots* usually bring suffering and unhappiness to their countries.

des•sert (di-ZERT) *n. desserts.* The part of a meal eaten after the main part; the last course. *Dessert* is usually something sweet, like cake or ice cream or pudding.

des•ti•na•tion (dess-tə-NAY-shən) *n. destinations.* The place to which someone is going or to which something is being sent; a goal.—John hopes to reach his *destination* by nightfall.—The package was sent to its *destination* by messenger.

des·ti·ny (DESS-tə-nee) *n. destinies.* Fate; the way something is sure to end, or turn out.—It was the sailor's *destiny* to reach home again after all his hardships.

de·stroy (di-STROI) *v. destroys, destroyed, destroying.* Ruin or put an end to.—Fire *destroyed* the old woodshed.—Potato bugs *destroy* potato vines.—The sudden rain *destroyed* our fun.

de·struc·tion (di-STRUK-shən) *n.* Wrecking; great damage; a violent end.—The forest fire brought *destruction* to many trees.

de·tach (di-TACH) *v. detaches, detached, detaching.* Separate; unfasten; disconnect; part.—Mary *detached* her locket from its chain.

de·tail (di-TAYL *or* DEE-tayl) *n. details.* A small part of anything.—Sending invitations, ordering the refreshments, and decorating the table are some of the *details* of giving a party.—Tell me the *details* of your trip to Canada.

de·tain (di-TAYN) *v. detains, detained, detaining.* Keep, or make wait.—The teacher will not *detain* you after school if your work is finished.

de·tec·tive (di-TEK-tiv) *n. detectives.* A policeman or a person who tries to find out about crimes and people without their knowing that he is trying to do so.—Many famous *detectives* worked on the murder case.

de·ter·mine (di-TER-mən) *v. determines, determined, determining.* 1. Firmly decide.—John *determined* to become a pitcher on the ball team.

2. Decide upon.—Father *determined* the amount of spending money we should receive.—The weather will *determine* whether we go skating or not.

3. Find out.—Jack was asked to *determine* how much had been spent for the party.

—*determination, n.*

de·test (di-TEST) *v. detests, detested, detesting.* Have great dislike for; hate.—Susan *detests* strawberries. John likes them.

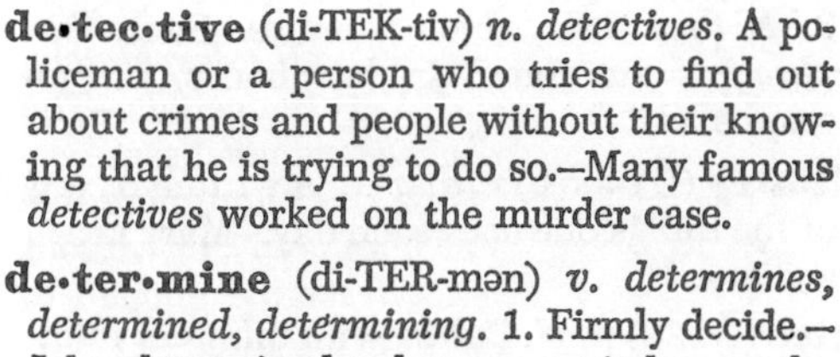

de·tour (DEE-tuhr) *n. detours.* A roundabout road or route.—We drove to Grandmother's on the *detour.* The direct road was closed off —*v. detours, detoured, detouring.* Turn onto a roundabout route.—We had to *detour* because the main road was being repaired.

de·vel·op (di-VEL-əp) *v. develops, developed, developing.* 1. Grow.—Boys *develop* into men.

2. Build; slowly make or create.—Mary *developed* her love for music by listening to it every day.—Jack *developed* a story around how he got his dog.

de·vel·op·ment (di-VEL-əp-mənt) *n. developments.* 1. Growth.—Baby's *development* in the past few months has been fast. She has learned to talk and walk.

2. New happening or result.—The doctor said to call him if there were any *developments* after taking the medicine.

de·vice (di-VYSS) *n. devices.* 1. A piece of machinery or a tool needed for certain work. —An egg beater is a *device* for beating eggs.

2. A scheme or plan, usually used to trick someone.—The burglar used an old *device* to get into the building: he posed as a deliveryman.

3. (In the plural only) Free choice or will.—The dog misbehaves when left to his own *devices.* He tears the pillows and scratches the furniture.

dev·il (DEV-əl) *n. devils.* 1. An evil spirit that is supposed to try to get people to do bad things; Satan.

2. A cruel or wicked person is sometimes called a *devil.*

de·vote (di-VOHT) *v. devotes, devoted, devoting.* Give completely.—Mary *devotes* much time to playing the piano.—The doctor *devoted* his whole life to the study of cancer.

de·vo·tion (di-VOH-shən) *n. devotions.* Great love.—Father's *devotion* to his family is one reason why he stays home every evening.—The man's *devotion* to his music made him a great musician.

de·vour (di-VOW-er) *v. devours, devoured, devouring.* 1. Eat the way an animal eats.—Children *devour* their food when they are very hungry.

2. Consume or destroy.—The fire *devoured* the whole forest.

de·vout (di-VOWT) *adj.; devoutly, adv.* Very religious; devoted to prayer.—Grandfather is *devout.* He spends a great amount of time going to church and praying.

dew (DOO *or* DYOO) *n.; dewy, adj.* Tiny drops of water which form on cold things.—At night *dew* gathers on the grass, plants, and trees.

di·ag·nose (dy-əg-NOHSS *or* -NOHZ) *v. diagnoses, diagnosed, diagnosing.* Decide what is wrong with a sick person by studying his symptoms.—When the doctor saw that Mary had broken out in red spots and that she had a fever, he *diagnosed* her illness as measles. *—diagnosis, n. diagnoses.*

di·ag·o·nal (dy-AG-ə-nəl) *adj.; diagonally, adv.* Slanting; having the direction taken by a straight line drawn between the opposite corners of a rectangle.—Mary's dress had *diagonal* stripes.

di·a·gram (DY-ə-gram) *n. diagrams.* A drawing or drawn plan of a building, piece of machinery, or anything else made after a pattern. A *diagram* is like a map, not like a picture.—Bob drew a *diagram* of the schoolroom. He drew squares to show where each seat is, where the teacher's desk is, and where the windows are.

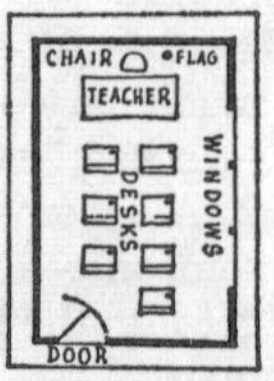

di·al (DY-əl) *n. dials.* A round plate that has numbers or letters at equal distances apart around the edge.—We turn the *dial* of a radio to get another station.—Some telephones have *dials.* You call the number you want by turning the *dial.*—The face of a watch is a *dial.*

di·a·logue (DY-ə-lawg) *n.* 1. Conversation; talk between two or more people.—The *dialogue* between the two statesmen was brief. 2. The conversations of characters in a play, book, story, etc.—Nobody enjoyed the play because the *dialogue* was dull.

di·am·e·ter (dy-AM-ə-ter) *n. diameters.* The distance from one side of a circle to the opposite side, measured through the center.

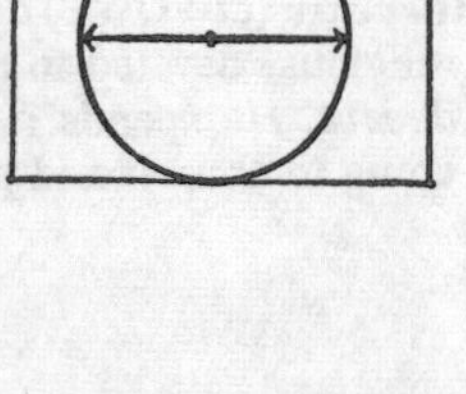

di·a·mond (DY-mənd *or* DY-ə-mənd) *n. diamonds.* 1. A bright, sparkling, clear precious stone used in rings, pins, and other jewelry.

2. A figure drawn in this shape:

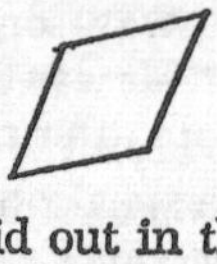

3. A baseball field, which is laid out in the shape of a *diamond.*

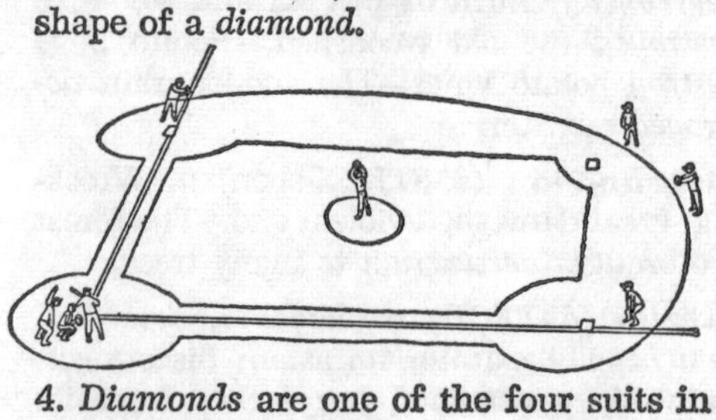

4. *Diamonds* are one of the four suits in a pack of playing cards.

di·a·phragm (DY-ə-fram) *n. diaphragms.*

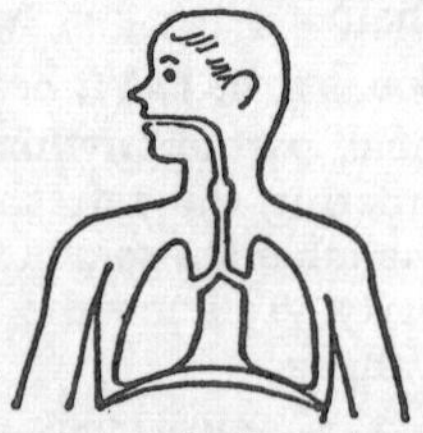

1. A curved wall of muscle and sinew. It stretches below the cavity where the lungs are. When the *diaphragm* contracts, air is sucked into the lungs. When it expands, air is pushed out of the lungs.

2. Any thin piece used as a divider.

3. A thin disk which vibrates. Such *diaphragms* are found in telephones, phonographs, etc.

di·a·ry (DY-ə-ree) *n. diaries.* A written record of the things one does each day.—Mary keeps a *diary.*

dice (DYSS) *n. pl.* Cubes, with different numbers of dots on their sides, which are tossed in playing games of chance. Just one of these cubes is called a *die.*

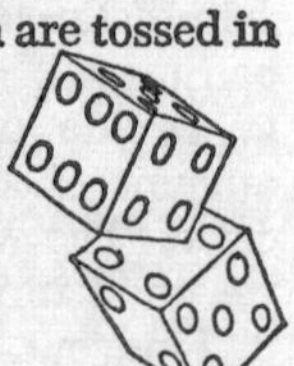

—v. dices, diced, dicing. Cut into small pieces.—The cook *diced* the chicken to make salad.

dic·tate (DIK-tayt) *v. dictates, dictated, dictating.* 1. Tell what to do, and firmly see that it is done.—Father never *dictates* our actions. He lets us do as we like.

2. Tell another what to write, word for word.—The business manager will *dictate* a letter to the clerk.

dic·ta·tion (dik-TAY-shən) *n. dictations.* 1. Speaking aloud so that one's words may be written down or recorded.—Henry was engaged in *dictation* when the telephone rang.

2. The words so taken down or recorded.—The secretary misplaced the notebook containing Henry's *dictation.*

dic·ta·tor (DIK-tay-ter *or* dik-TAY-ter) *n. dictators.* A person who rules with absolute power.—The *dictator* led his nation into war.

dic·tion (DIK-shən) *n.* The manner in which one speaks one's words. If one has good *diction,* one's words are pronounced clearly and pleasantly and are easily heard.—Tom's *diction* is poor. He is trying to improve it.

dic·tion·ar·y (DIK- shən-air-ee) *n. dictionaries.* A book of words and their meanings. The words in a *dictionary* are put in alphabetical order to help you find them easily.

did (DID) *v.* One form of the verb *do.*—I shall do my spelling this afternoon. I *did* my arithmetic this morning.

did·n't (DID-ənt). Did not.—Mother called Bob, but he *didn't* hear her.

die (DY) *v. dies, died, dying.* Stop living.—Plants *die* without water.—The hurt dog will not *die* if we care for him properly.

die·sel en·gine (DEE-zəl en-jən) *n. diesel engines.* An engine that uses hot air to ignite its fuel. The air is heated by being subjected to a very great pressure. Its temperature reaches 1,000° F. Automobile engines use sparks to ignite their fuel. *Diesel engines* do not need fire of any kind.

di·et (DY-ət) *n. diets.* The food we eat regularly.—After I was sick, the doctor put me on a special *diet.* I had to eat foods chosen especially for me.

dif·fer (DIF-er) *v. differs, differed, differing.* 1. Be not alike.—The dresses *differ* only in color. One is red and one is pink.
2. Disagree.—Mary and Jack find something to *differ* about every day.

dif·fer·ence (DIF-er-ənss *or* DIF-rənss) *n. differences.* A way or amount in which things vary, or are not the same.—The only *difference* between the two dresses is that one is red and one is pink.—The *difference* between a quarter and one dollar is seventy-five cents.

dif·fer·ent (DIF-er-ənt *or* DIF-rənt) *adj.; differently, adv.* 1. Not the same.—A pen is *different* from a pencil.
2. Separate.—Mary has been absent two *different* times. She was absent yesterday, and she was absent another time last week.

dif·fi·cult (DIF-ə-kult) *adj.* 1. Hard; not easy.—It is *difficult* to run uphill.
2. Hard to handle or manage.—Baby can be very *difficult* when she is teething.

dif·fi·cul·ty (DIF-ə-kul-tee) *n. difficulties.* 1. A hard time; trouble.—The man had much *difficulty* starting his car.
2. Cause of trouble.—The main *difficulty* in this problem is understanding the big words.
3. A dispute.—The boys settled their *difficulties* by themselves.

dig (DIG) *v. digs, dug, digging.* 1. Make a hole, especially in the ground.—Dogs like to *dig* with their front paws to bury bones.—People *dig* with shovels.
2. Make or get by digging.—Grandfather *dug* a well to get drinking water.—The fisherman *digs* bait before going fishing.
3. Scratch.—The cat may *dig* you with her claws, if you are not careful.

di·gest (də-JEST) *v. digests, digested, digesting.* Turn (food) in the stomach into a liquid so that the body can use it.—Foods will *digest* more easily if you chew them well.

di·ges·tion (də-JEST-shən) *n. digestions.* The turning of food in the stomach into a liquid so that the body can use it.—If we eat when we are too tired or upset, it may hurt our *digestion.*

dig·ni·fied (DIG-nə-fyd) *adj.* Stately; having dignity.—The woman's manner was very *dignified.* She acted as if she had much self-respect and pride.

dig·ni·ty (DIG-nə-tee) *n.* 1. Quality of having a stately or grand manner.—The woman always behaves with *dignity.* She is always calm, proud, and ladylike.
2. Worthy of respect and admiration; nobility.—The *dignity* of that man is unquestionable. He is a fine and honorable person.

dike (DYK) *n. dikes.* A high wall, usually of earth, to keep back the water from the sea or from a river.—Many *dikes* are needed along the coast of Holland.

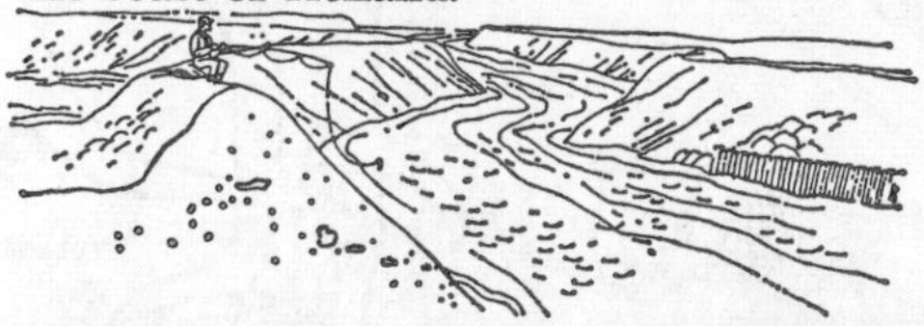

dil·i·gent (DIL-ə-jənt) *adj.; diligently, adv.; diligence, n.* Active and busy about one's work.—Bob is a *diligent* student. He studies hard.

di·lute (di- *or* dy-LOOT) *v. dilutes, diluted, diluting.* Make less powerful, or less thick. This is usually done by adding water or some other liquid. — Painters *dilute* their paints with turpentine.—Mother *diluted* the pea soup by adding water to it.

DINOSAURS

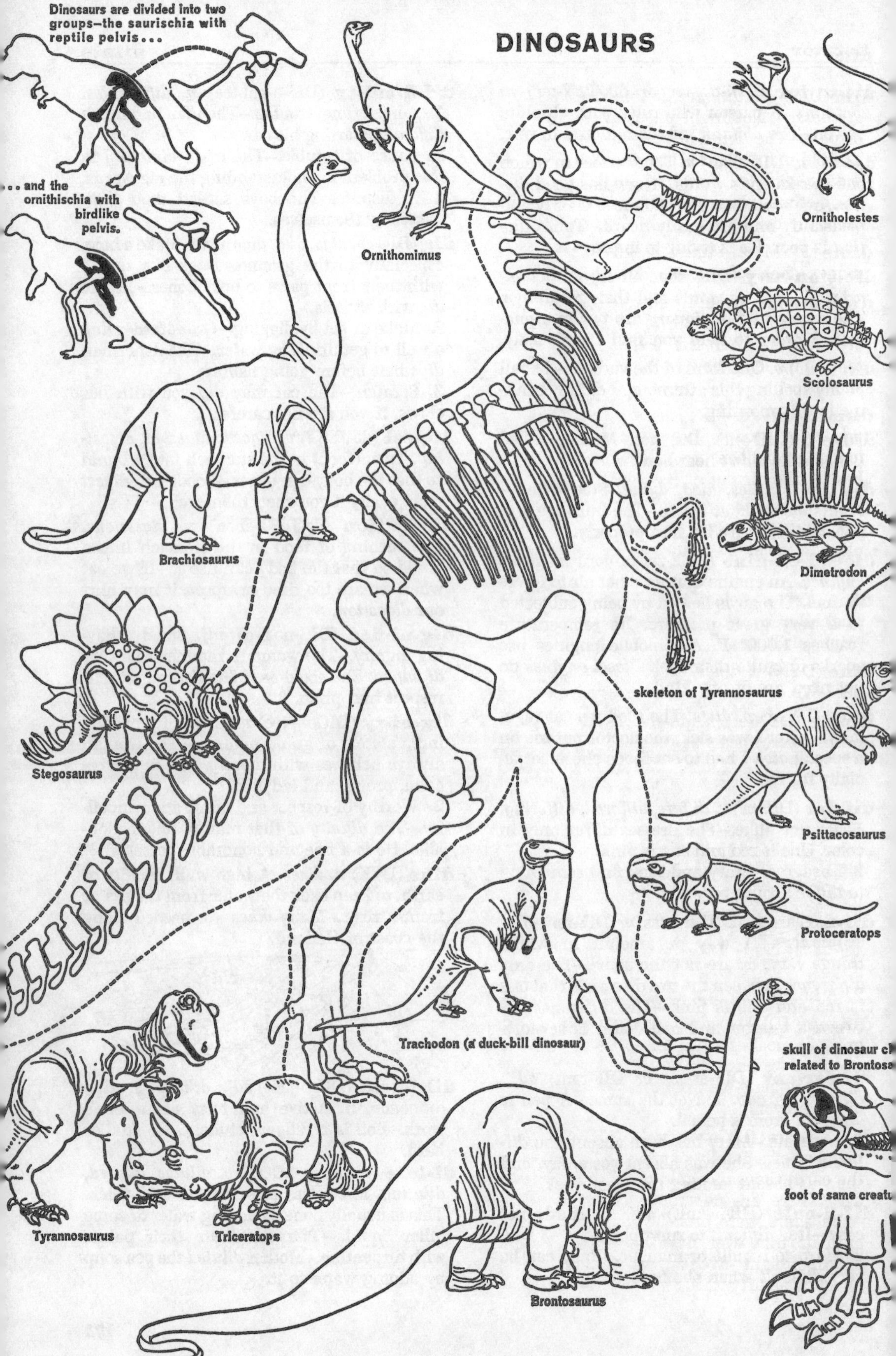

Dinosaurs are divided into two groups—the saurischia with reptile pelvis . . .
. . . and the ornithischia with birdlike pelvis.
Ornithomimus
Ornitholestes
Scolosaurus
Brachiosaurus
Dimetrodon
skeleton of Tyrannosaurus
Stegosaurus
Psittacosaurus
Protoceratops
Trachodon (a duck-bill dinosaur)
skull of dinosaur cl
related to Brontosa
foot of same creatu
Tyrannosaurus
Triceratops
Brontosaurus

dim (DIM) *adj.dimmer,dimmest; dimly,adv.; dimness, n.* Not bright and clear; faint, weak, or pale.–The lights in the town were *dim.*–The old man's sight is growing *dim.*
–v.dims, dimmed, dimming. Make less bright. –Sometimes when we drive at night, Father *dims* the car lights.

dime (DYM) *n. dimes.* A ten-cent piece of money.–Bob spent a *dime* for apples.

di•men•sion (də-MEN-shən) *n. dimensions.* Length, width, or depth.–Father took the *dimensions* for a new screen door. He measured to see how long, how wide, and how thick it should be.

di•min•ish (də-MIN-ish) *v. diminishes, diminished, diminishing.* Become smaller or less.–The balloon *diminished* in size as the boy let the air out of it.–During the winter our supply of coal *diminishes* each day.

dim•ple (DIM-pəl) *n. dimples.* A little hollow place in the flesh.–Baby has a *dimple* in each cheek.

din (DIN) *n.* A loud noise or disturbance.–The children make a great *din* when they play "Musical Chairs."

dine (DYN) *v. dines, dined, dining.* Eat dinner.–We *dine* at six o'clock every evening.

din•er (DYN-er) *n. diners.* 1. A car, on a train, where meals are served.

2. A lunchroom in a small, carlike building.

din•ner (DIN-er) *n. dinners.* 1. The biggest or main meal.–Father cannot come home at noon, so we have *dinner* at night.
2. A banquet.–We went to a *dinner* in honor of the mayor.

di•no•saur (DY-nə-sor) *n. dinosaurs.* Any member of a family of reptiles that roamed the earth thousands and thousands of years ago There are no *dinosaurs* living today. *–Dinosaurs* were probably the largest land animals that ever lived, some reaching a length of eighty-five feet, and some weighing as much as fifty tons.

dip (DIP) *n. dips.* 1. A low place or hollow.–We slowed down when we came to the *dip* in the pavement.
2. A plunge.–We went for a *dip* in the lake.
–v. dips, dipped, dipping. 1. Put into a liquid and lift out.–Grandmother used a cup to *dip* the soup from the kettle.–The artist *dips* his brush into the paint.–The rower *dips* the oars of the boat into the water.
2. Lower for a moment.–The sailor *dipped* the flag.

diph•the•ri•a (dif- *or* dip-THIR-ee-ə) *n.* A dangerous disease of the throat. *Diphtheria* is catching; one person can get it from another.

di•plo•ma (də-PLOH-mə) *n. diplomas.* A printed paper given by a school which says that one has finished the needed amount of work in that school. When a person finishes high school or college, he is given a *diploma.*

dip•lo•mat (DIP-lə-mat) *n. diplomats; diplomatic, adj.* 1. A person employed by his government to handle its affairs with other governments.–Many *diplomats* were present at the conference.
2. A person who knows how to deal with people without hurting their feelings or making them angry.–Harry handles complaints in a department store. He is a real *diplomat.*

dip•per (DIP-er) *n. dippers.* 1. A ladle or a deep, cup-shaped spoon.–We dip gravy from a bowl with a *dipper.*

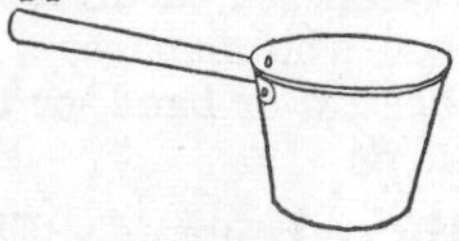

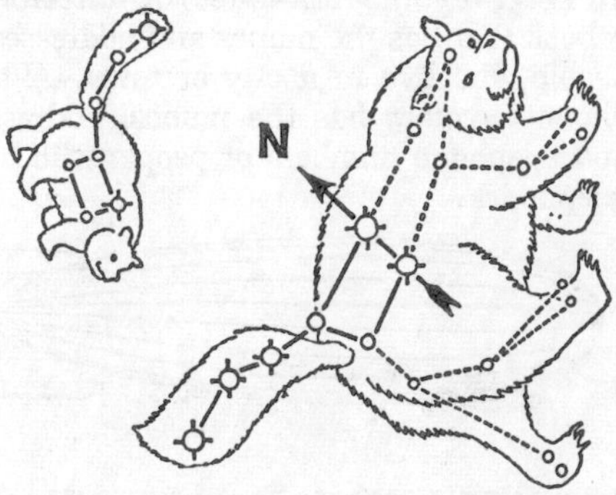

2. (Spelled with a capital "D.") A group of stars that make the form of a dipper with a long handle.–We watched the skies to see the Big *Dipper* and the Little *Dipper.*

di•rect (də-REKT) *v. directs, directed, directing.* 1. Guide; point out (the way).—The Boy Scouts will *direct* people about the city during the convention.
2. Address; put the address on.—The letter was not *directed* right, and was returned.
3. Give; turn.—The teacher asked the children to *direct* their attention to the writing on the board.
4. Order; instruct.—The fire chief *directed* his men to surround the burning building.
—*adj.* Straight; not roundabout.—Grandfather told Bob to take the *direct* road to the store. —When the teacher questioned me, I gave her a *direct* answer.

di•rect cur•rent (də-REKT KER-ənt). Electric current that flows through a wire, or through any conductor of electricity, in one direction only. *Direct current* is abbreviated *D.C.* or *d.c.* It is the opposite of alternating current, which reverses its direction.

di•rec•tion (də-REK-shən) *n. directions.* 1. Way; a point toward which one can face. North, south, east, and west are the main *directions.*—The stranger was going in the *direction* of the depot.—A compass tells us the *directions.*

2. Management or leadership.—The store is under the *direction* of a very able man.
3. Order or instruction.—The officer gives his men *directions,* and they obey them.

di•rec•tor (də-REK-ter) *n. directors.* A person who manages a business, leads an orchestra or band, or tells other people what to do.

di•rec•to•ry (də-REK-tə-ree) *n. directories.* A book that has the names and addresses of people who live in a city or town.—A telephone *directory* has the names, addresses, and telephone numbers of people who have telephones.

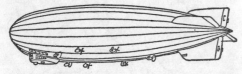

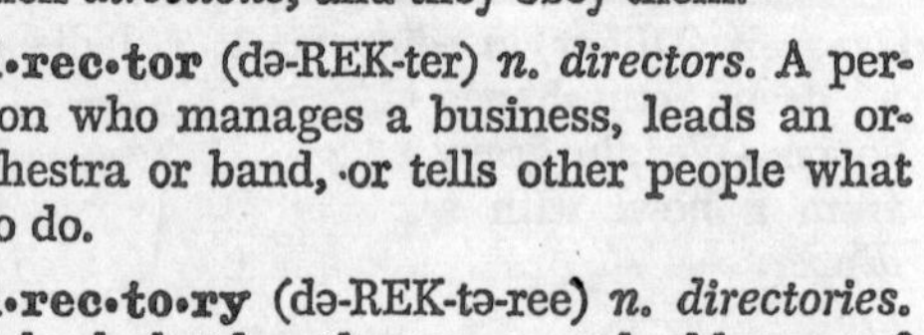

dir•i•gi•ble (DIR-ij-ə-bəl) *n. dirigibles.* An airship or large balloon. *Dirigibles* can be steered through the air, and they have motors to make them go.

dirt (DERT) *n.* 1. Earth; soil.—We put some *dirt* into the flowerpot.
2. Anything that is not clean.—Mary swept the *dirt* from the porch.

dirt•y (DER-tee) *adj. dirtier, dirtiest.* Not clean; soiled.—The child's hands were *dirty* after he made mudpies.

dis•ad•van•tage (diss-əd-VAN-tij) *n. disadvantages.* 1. Anything that makes it difficult to achieve success; a handicap.—Tom entered the race with a *disadvantage.* He had a sore leg.
2. Harm; injury; loss.—The bargain was to John's *disadvantage.* He lost money and time.

dis•a•gree (diss-ə-GREE) *v. disagrees, disagreed, disagreeing.* 1. Think differently.—Jack *disagrees* with his father about how much money a ten-year-old boy needs.
2. Be different from; be not the same or alike.—What you say now *disagrees* with what you said yesterday.
3. Quarrel.—The boys *disagreed* over whose turn it was.
4. Make sick.—Cold milk *disagrees* with the baby. It upsets her stomach.
—*disagreement, n. disagreements.*

dis•a•gree•a•ble (diss-ə-GREE-ə-bəl) *adj.* 1. Cross; easily made angry; not friendly.—Sick children are often *disagreeable.*
2. Not pleasant.—The taste and odor of some foods are *disagreeable* to some people.

dis•ap•pear (diss-ə-PIR) *v. disappears, disappeared, disappearing.* 1. Go out of sight.—We watched the airplane until it *disappeared.*
2. Stop being; go away.—Snow *disappears* in the springtime. It goes away.
—*disappearance, n. disappearances.*

dis•ap•point (diss-ə-POINT) *v. disappoints, disappointed, disappointing.* 1. Make unhappy by failing to satisfy a wish or something expected.—If Grandmother doesn't come, it will *disappoint* the children. — Mother was *disappointed* with her new dress. It was not what she expected or hoped for.
2. Fail; let down.—John promised to stop for Bob. Bob told John not to *disappoint* him by failing to keep his promise.

dis•ap•point•ment (diss-ə-POINT-mənt) *n. disappointments.* 1. Something that causes an unhappy feeling because it does not turn out as it was expected to.—It was a *disappointment* to us that Grandmother couldn't come.

2. The feeling one has when a thing that was expected to happen does not happen.–Mary's *disappointment* over not receiving the letter did not last long.

dis•ap•prove (diss-ə-PROOV) *v. disapproves, disapproved, disapproving.* Think unfavorably about; consider to be wrong.–Mother *disapproves* of too much exercise right after lunch.

dis•as•ter (di-ZA-ster) *n. disasters.* Anything that happens suddenly to bring great pain, sorrow, or suffering to people. Fires, storms, and accidents are *disasters.*

dis•card (diss-KAHRD) *v. discards, discarded, discarding.* Get rid of; throw away; cast aside something that is of no use or worn out. –Father *discarded* his torn old shoes.

dis•charge (diss-CHAHRJ) *v. discharges, discharged, discharging.* 1. Dismiss from work; let go.–When the work was done, the men were *discharged.*

2. Give off.–The boil on the man's arm *discharged* pus.

3. Shoot off or fire.–The man *discharged* the cannon as a salute.

4. Unload.–The ship *discharged* its cargo.

5. Pay.–Father always *discharges* his debts.

6. Perform or do.–Bob *discharged* his duties with care.

dis•ci•ple (di-SY-pəl) *n. disciples.* 1. A follower; a person who accepts the teachings of another and who tries to pass these teachings on to others.–The young architect became a *disciple* of Frank Lloyd Wright. He felt that Wright's designs were perfect, and he tried to build his own buildings the way Wright built his.

2. A follower of Jesus Christ; one of the twelve men who followed Him during His lifetime.

dis•ci•pline (DISS-ə-plin) *n.* Control of behavior.–*Discipline* is strict in the army. A soldier must do as he is told.

–*v. disciplines, disciplined, disciplining.* Force to obey; punish.–The teacher *disciplined* the boys for throwing chalk at each other.

dis•con•nect (diss-kə-NEKT) *v. disconnects, disconnected, disconnecting.* Separate; break the connection between; undo.–Tom *disconnected* the lamp by pulling the plug out of its socket.

dis•con•tent (diss-kən-TENT) *n.; discontented, adj.* A feeling of not being satisfied. –Bob feels no *discontent* with his new job. He is satisfied.

dis•con•tin•ue (diss-kən-TIN-yoo) *v. discontinues, discontinued, discontinuing.* Stop. –Mother told the newsboy to *discontinue* bringing the newspaper while we were away.

dis•count (DISS-kownt) *n. discounts* and *adj.* A reduction; a lessening of the price.– When Mother bought the coat, it was on sale, so she got it at a *discount.* She got it for less than its original price.

–(diss-KOWNT) *v. discounts, discounted, discounting.* Not include; not take into account.–The teacher said she would *discount* the low marks on our homework papers if we did well on the test. She would not include the low marks in our final grades.

dis•cour•age (diss-KER-ij) *v. discourages, discouraged, discouraging.* 1. Cause to lose hope.–The old woman was *discouraged* over her poor health.

2. Cause to give up a desire.–We tried to *discourage* John from going swimming when it was so cold.

dis•cour•te•ous (diss-KER-tee-əss) *adj.; discourteously, adv.; discourtesy, n.* Impolite; rude; bad-mannered. – *Discourteous* people do not make friends easily.

dis•cov•er (diss-KUV-er) *v. discovers, discovered, discovering.* Find; learn of.–Columbus *discovered* America. He found it for the first time.–Mother *discovered* that her new stove cooked things fast.

dis•cov•er•y (diss-KUV-er-ee) *n. discoveries.* 1. A finding.–The *discovery* of America was made by Columbus.

2. Something found or learned.–The scientist's *discovery* was a cure for a certain fever.

dis•cuss (diss-KUSS) *v. discusses, discussed, discussing.* Talk about; speak for and against. –Father will *discuss* the plans for the party tonight.

dis•cus•sion (diss-KUSH-ən) *n. discussions.* A serious talk.–John and Bob had a *discussion* about baseball. – At the meeting there was *discussion* about the men who were running for mayor.

dis•ease (di-ZEEZ) *n. diseases.* A sickness or illness.–Mumps, chicken pox, and measles are some common *diseases.*

dis•grace (diss-GRAYSS) *n. disgraces.* A shameful thing.–The boy's behavior in stealing the marbles was a *disgrace.* He lost the respect of his friends.

–*v. disgraces, disgraced, disgracing.* Bring shame to.–The man *disgraced* his family by stealing.

dis•guise (diss-GYZ) *n. disguises.* Things used to change appearance.–The boy's *disguise* was so good that his mother did not recognize him.
–*v. disguises, disguised, disguising.* Make up to look like some other person or thing; change something to keep it from being recognized. –Mary went to the Halloween party *disguised* as a ghost.–When Bob called Mother on the telephone, he *disguised* his voice.

dis•gust (diss-GUST) *n. disgusts.* A feeling of deep dislike.–The man's *disgust* for certain foods was caused by his sickness.
–*v. disgusts, disgusted, disgusting.* Give a feeling of strong dislike.–Bill's bad behavior at the party *disgusted* Bob.

dish (DISH) *n. dishes.* 1. A container in which food is served; a saucer, plate, etc.– The children broke so many *dishes* in washing them that Mother decided to wash them herself.

2. A combination of foods.–A woman on the radio told how to prepare a new *dish.*
3. A dish filled with something.–Mother set the *dish* of tomatoes on the table.
–*v. dishes, dished, dishing.* Serve; put in dishes.–The cook *dished* out the food.

dis•hon•est (diss-AHN-əst) *adj.; dishonestly, adv.; dishonesty, n.* Not honest; not fair. –The *dishonest* boy cheated on his spelling test. It was a *dishonest* thing to do.

dis•hon•or (diss-AHN-er) *n; dishonorable, adj.* Shame.–The man brought *dishonor* to his position when he broke the law.
–*v. dishonors, dishonored, dishonoring.* Disgrace; ruin the honor of.–Bob would not *dishonor* his school by cheating in the contest.

dis•in•fect (diss-in-FEKT) *v. disinfects, disinfected, disinfecting.* Destroy disease-producing germs with heat, chemicals, etc.–The doctor *disinfected* his instruments by boiling them.

dis•in•te•grate (diss-IN-tə-grayt) *v. disintegrates, disintegrated, disintegrating.* Fall apart; break up; go to pieces.–The curtains *disintegrated* when they were removed from the windows of the deserted house. They crumbled into dust.

dis•joint•ed (diss-JOINT-əd) *adj.; disjointedly, adv.; disjointedness, n.* 1. Out of joint; not connected at the joints.
2. Not connected; rambling; not making sense.–Bill's speech was *disjointed.* He jumped from topic to topic.

disk (DISK) *n. disks.* 1. Any round, flat plate. –The machine punched out small *disks* from large sheets of metal. The *disks* looked like coins.
2. A phonograph record.–John bought a new *disk* at the record shop.

dis•like (diss-LYK) *n. dislikes.* A feeling of not liking.–Mother has a *dislike* of rats.
–*v. dislikes, disliked, disliking.* Have an unpleasant feeling toward. – I *dislike* people who are not honest.

dis•mal (DIZ-məl) *adj.; dismally, adv.* Gloomy; unpleasant.–We had *dismal* weather all week.

dis•miss (diss-MISS) *v. dismisses, dismissed, dismissing.* 1. Let go; send away.–It is almost time to *dismiss* the music class.
2. Put out of one's mind; forget about. – When Father and Bob finished their argument, Father said they would *dismiss* the subject.
3. Discharge; fire; let go.–The automobile factory *dismissed* fifty men.

dis•o•bey (diss-ə-BAY) *v. disobeys, disobeyed, disobeying.* Refuse to follow orders as to what to do or not to do.–Do not *disobey* the traffic policeman, for you may have an accident. –*disobedience, n. disobediences.*

dis•or•der (diss-OR-der) *n. disorders.* Confusion; lack of order.–The classroom was in *disorder* after the play period.

dis•play (diss-PLAY) *n. displays.* A showing to the public.–We saw a *display* of toys in the store window.

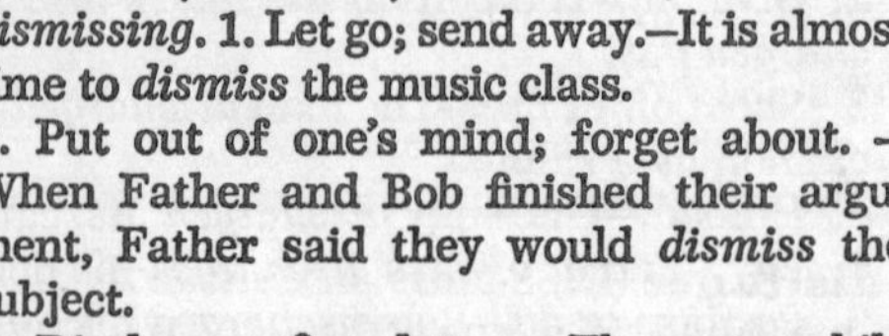

–*v. displays, displayed, displaying.* Show.–Bob *displayed* his stamp collection.

dis•pose (diss-POHZ) *v. disposes, disposed, disposing.* *Dispose of* means do away with. –Father *disposed of* the bricks by filling up the hole in the driveway with them.
–*Be disposed* means feel favorable. – The teacher *was disposed* to read us a story.

dis•po•si•tion (diss-pə-ZISH-ən) *n. dispositions.*. The way one feels and acts toward others.—Mother has a pleasant *disposition.* She is always pleasant and friendly toward people.

dis•pute (diss-PYOOT) *n. disputes.* Argument; disagreement.—The girls had a *dispute* over how to do the arithmetic problem.
—*v. disputes, disputed, disputing.* Argue against.—Bob would not *dispute* Father's word.

dis•rupt (diss-RUPT) *v. disrupts, disrupted, disrupting.* Break up.—We hope the rain will not *disrupt* our plans to go fishing.

dis•sect (di-SEKT) *v. dissects, dissected, dissecting.* 1. Cut plants or animals apart to study their insides.—The teacher *dissected* a frog so that we could look at its heart and stomach.
2. Take apart and examine closely, bit by bit.—The class *dissected* the story to try to find out why it was so scary.

dis•solve (di-ZAHLV) *v. dissolves, dissolved, dissolving.* Break up and disappear when put into a liquid.—Salt will *dissolve* in water.

dis•tance (DISS-tənss) *n. distances.* 1. Space measured in a line.—The *distance* between our house and the school is two blocks.
2. A faraway place or position.—We saw the airplane in the *distance.*

dis•tant (DISS-tənt) *adj.; distantly, adv.* 1. Far off.—England is a *distant* country.
2. Shy; not very friendly.—The new boy is *distant* because he does not know us.

dis•tinct (diss-TINGKT) *adj.; distinctly, adv.* 1. Not alike or the same.—The color green is *distinct* from both yellow and blue.
2. Plain; clear.—Mary's speech is *distinct.*

dis•tinc•tion (diss-TINGK-shən) *n. distinctions.* 1. Difference.—Mary could not understand the *distinction* between plus and minus.
2. Worth; excellence.—Our mayor is a man of *distinction.*

dis•tin•guish (diss-TING-gwish) *v. distinguishes, distinguished, distinguishing.* 1. Notice the difference.—Some people cannot *distinguish* one color from another.
2. Recognize; see.—Grandmother's writing was so dim that we could hardly *distinguish* the words.
—*Distinguished* means famous or very well-known.—The man is a *distinguished* writer.

dis•tract (diss-TRAKT) *v. distracts, distracted, distracting.* Draw attention away.—The radio *distracted* Mary from her lessons.
—*distraction, n. distractions.*

dis•tress (diss-TRESS) *n.* 1. Pain and suffering.—The man's injury caused him much *distress.*
2. Unhappiness and trouble.—The burning of the barn brought *distress* to the farmer.
3. Danger; need of help.—The pilot gave a signal saying that his airplane was in *distress.*
—*v. distresses, distressed, distressing.* Trouble.—It *distressed* me to hear that the boy was sick.

dis•trib•ute (diss-TRIB-yoot) *v. distributes, distributed, distributing.* 1. Hand out; deliver.—The teacher *distributed* the books.
2. Spread about.—Bob didn't *distribute* the butter evenly over his bread.
—*distribution, n. distributions.*

dis•trict (DISS-trikt) *n. districts.* Section; a division or part of a country.—We live in a farming *district.*

Dis•trict of Co•lum•bi•a (DISS-trikt əv kə-LUM-bee-ə). Sixty-nine square miles in eastern United States, owned by the government of the United States. It is occupied by Washington, capital of the United States, and is noted for its many beautiful views and government buildings.

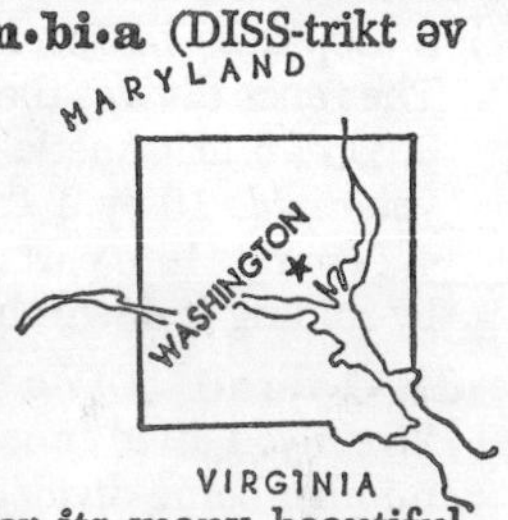

dis•turb (diss-TERB) *v. disturbs, disturbed, disturbing.* 1. Upset; bother; cause to worry.—Mother is resting. Do not *disturb* her.—The news of the accident *disturbed* Father.
2. Cause to get out of order.—The wind *disturbed* the papers on the teacher's desk.

dis•turb•ance (diss-TER-bənss) *n. disturbances.* 1. Disorder; confusion.—A *disturbance* was created when Bill brought his snake to the party.
2. Lack of balance; worry; anxiety.—The patient is suffering from a mental *disturbance.*

ditch (DICH) *n. ditches.* A long narrow hole in the ground.—The workmen dug a *ditch* at the side of the road to drain the water away.

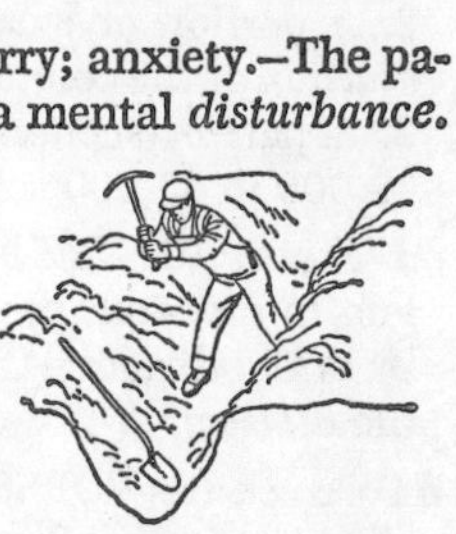

dive (DYV) *n. dives.* A plunge into water.–Joe made a beautiful *dive* from the high board.

–*v. dives, dived* or *dove, diving.* 1. Plunge or throw oneself headfirst.–The children *dive* into the water from the diving board.

2. Come down nose first.–We saw the airplane *dive.*

di•vert (di-VERT) *v. diverts, diverted, diverting.* 1. Throw off the natural course; change the direction of.

2. Change the object of a person's attention; redirect a person's attention.–Lora was crying about Mother's going out, so Gregg told her funny stories to *divert* her.

di•vide (də-VYD) *n. divides.* The ridge where water starts to drain down both sides of a mountain. The Rocky Mountains are known as the Great *Divide* because the water on the western side flows into the Pacific Ocean, and the water on the eastern side flows into the Gulf of Mexico or the Atlantic Ocean.

–*v. divides, divided, dividing.* 1. Separate into parts, portions, or shares. – Father *divided* the ice cream and gave each of us some.

2. Separate or form a boundary between.–The fence *divides* the yards.

3. Do an arithmetic problem in division.–If you *divide* 10 by 2, the answer is 5.

4. Separate into parts.–*Divide* your test paper by folding it down the middle.

div•i•dend (DIV-ə-dend) *n. dividends.* 1. When you divide one number by another, the number being divided is the *dividend.*–When you divide 10 by 2, 10 is the *dividend.*

2. A share of profits in a business paid to a person who owns stock.

di•vine (də-VYN) *adj.* Of God; holy.–To most Christians, Jesus Christ is *divine.*

di•vis•i•ble (də-VIZ-ə-bəl) *adj.* Able to be divided evenly. – Thirty is *divisible* by five. $30 \div 5 = 6$.

di•vi•sion (də-VIZH-ən) *n. divisions.* 1. Dividing one number by another, or seeing how many times one number goes into another.

2. A portion or part. – The men in Father's *division* of the company are going on a picnic.

3. A part or section of the army containing 12,000 to 15,000 soldiers.

di•vi•sor (də-VYZ-er) *n. divisors.* In a problem in division, the number that you divide by is the *divisor.*–If you divide 10 by 2, 2 is the *divisor.*

di•vorce (də-VORSS) *n. divorces.* An ending of a marriage by law.–The judge granted the married couple a *divorce.* They are no longer married.

–*v. divorces, divorced, divorcing.* Bring a marriage to an end by getting a divorce. – The woman *divorced* her husband.

diz•zy (DIZ-ee) *adj. dizzier, dizziest.* Having the feeling that one is whirling around. – Turning around fast may make you *dizzy.*

do (DOO) *v. does, did, doing.* 1. Act; carry out a plan.–Try to *do* your best every day.–The children *do* their arithmetic in the morning and their spelling in the afternoon. – Baby tries to *do* everything that we *do.*

2. Be satisfactory.–The teacher said my pencil would *do* if I didn't have a pen.

3. *Do* is sometimes used to begin questions. –*Do* you have my book?

4. *Do* may take the place of other words so that we need not say them twice.–"He writes as well as I *do*" means "He writes as well as I write."

dock (DAHK) *n. docks.* A wharf; a platform that is built along the shore, or which runs out into the water so that boats can come along the sides of it to load and unload.

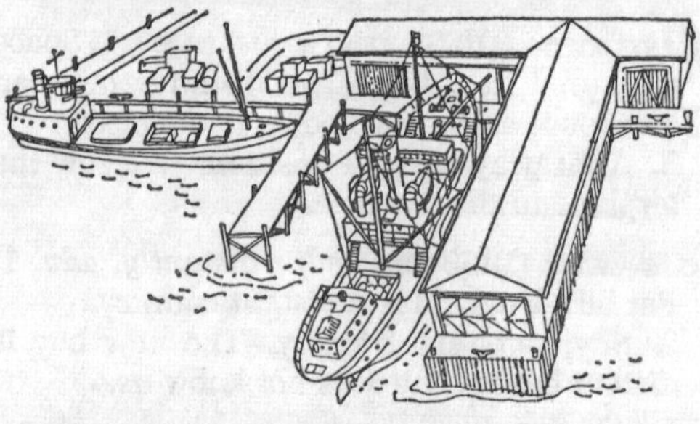

doc•tor (DAHK-ter) *n. doctors.* 1. A person who knows about sicknesses and how to treat them. Physicians and surgeons are *doctors.* A *doctor* must have a license to treat sick people.

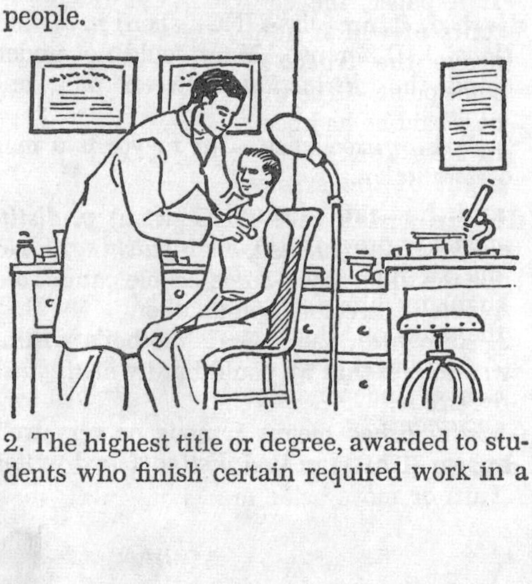

2. The highest title or degree, awarded to students who finish certain required work in a

DOGS

college or university, or to those the university wishes to honor.—Jack's uncle has completed his studies for the degree of *doctor* of philosophy.
—*v. doctors, doctored, doctoring.* Treat. — The school nurse *doctors* the children for small injuries and illnesses.

doc·u·ment (DAHK-yə-mənt) *n. documents.*
1. A paper, the contents of which help prove the truth of some point. — The witness said he had been in New York on the night of the crime, and he had *documents* to prove it. He had a ticket stub from the air line and a letter from his hostess thanking him for coming and mentioning the dates on which he was there.

2. An official piece of writing.—The Declaration of Independence is a great historical *document.*

dodge (DAHJ) *v. dodges, dodged, dodging.* Turn or move aside quickly to avoid something.—When the ball came through the window, the teacher had to *dodge* to keep from being hit.

doe (DOH) *n. does.* The female or she animal of some animals, such as the deer. — The female deer, or *doe,* does not have antlers.

does (DUZ) *v.* One form of the verb *do.*—I do my work; he *does* his.

does·n't (DUZ-ənt). Does not.—John *doesn't* like to be sick.

dog (DAWG) *n. dogs.* A four-legged animal kept as a pet or for work. Some *dogs* are smaller than cats; others are very much larger. Some *dogs* are used to tend sheep; others are used to hunt animals; and some are kept as pets.

do·ings (DOO-ingz) *n. pl.* Things that a person or people do.—The *doings* at the party were fun.

doll (DAHL) *n. dolls.* A toy that looks like a person. Children play with *dolls* and pretend that the *dolls* are people.

dol•lar (DAHL-er) *n. dollars.* A sum of money equal to 100 cents. It can be written $1. One *dollar* is equal to 100 cents, or 20 nickels, or 10 dimes, or 4 quarters, or 2 half *dollars.* Some *dollars* are made of silver and some of paper.

dol•phin (DAHL-fən) *n. dolphins.* A cousin of the whale which leaps out of the water as it swims. A *dolphin* has a long nose, a black back, and a white belly. It is usually between six and eight feet long.

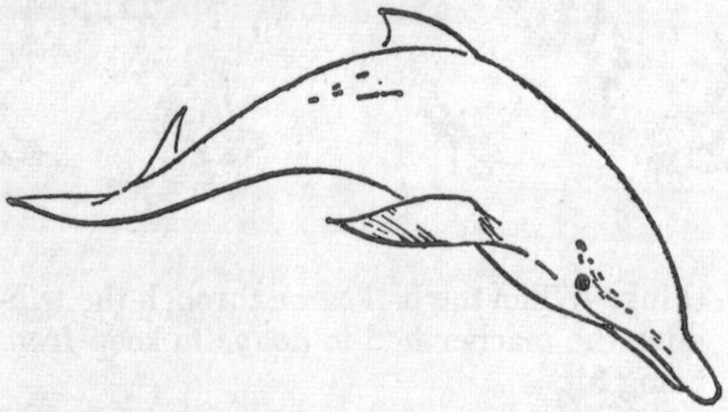

dome (DOHM) *n. domes.* A circular roof that is shaped like the one in the picture. Some churches and capitol buildings have *domes.*

do•mes•tic (də-MESS-tik) *adj.* 1. Having to do with the home or family.–Cooking, sewing, and cleaning are *domestic* tasks.
2. Belonging to the home; tame.–Animals, such as cats and dogs, that live about the home are *domestic* animals.–Farm animals are *domestic* animals.
3. Of one's own country.–Things that are made in one's country are *domestic* products.

dom•i•nate (DAHM-ə-nayt) *v. dominates, dominated, dominating.* 1. Govern; control by power or strength.–Large nations have often *dominated* smaller ones.
2. Hold a position above everybody or everything else; overshadow.–The coach believes his team will *dominate* the league. He believes it will win the most games.

do•min•ion (də-MIN-yən) *n. dominions.* 1. Supreme power, control, or authority, such as over a territory or land. – India was once under British *dominion.*
2. The lands or territories so controlled.–The king visited his *dominions* beyond the sea.

dom•i•no (DAHM-ə-noh) *n. dominoes.* One of the small brick-shaped pieces used in playing the game of *dominoes.*

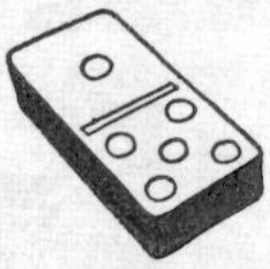

done (DUN) *v.* One form of the verb *do.*–I would have *done* my work earlier if I had known you were coming.
–*adj.* 1. Finished; completed; ended. – My arithmetic is all *done.*
2. Completely cooked.–We can't have dinner yet because the potatoes aren't *done.*

don•key (DAWNG-kee) *n. donkeys.* 1. An animal that is something like a horse with long ears. *Donkeys* are strong work animals. They are often stubborn.

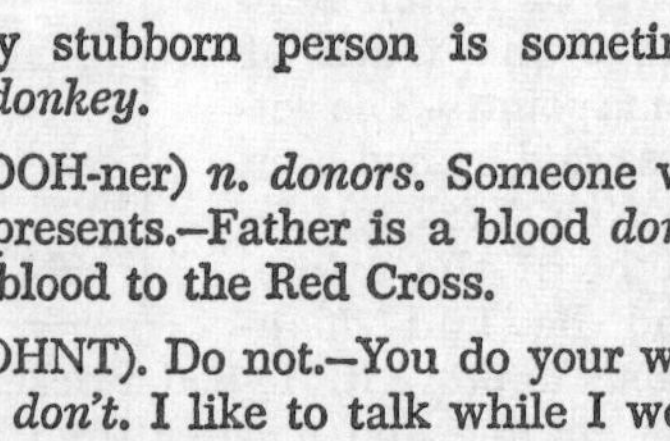

2. A very stubborn person is sometimes called a *donkey.*

do•nor (DOH-ner) *n. donors.* Someone who gives or presents.–Father is a blood *donor.* He gives blood to the Red Cross.

don't (DOHNT). Do not.–You do your work quietly. I *don't.* I like to talk while I work.

doom (DOOM) *n. dooms.* Fate, usually a bad fate.–The ship met her *doom* on the rocky island coast. She broke in two.
–*v. dooms, doomed, dooming.* Mark for a certain fate.–Those trees are *doomed* to destruction by the forest fire.

door (DOR) *n. doors.* 1. Doorway; the opening you go through into a house, or from room to room.—Mary ran to Father as soon as he came through the *door.*

2. The wooden or metal covering in a doorway which is opened or closed.—We heard a knock on the *door.*

door·way (DOR-way) *n. doorways.* The opening leading into a room or house.—We go into the house through a *doorway.*

dose (DOHSS) *n. doses.* A certain amount of medicine taken at one time.—The doctor told Mother to cut down on her *dose* when she felt better.

dot (DAHT) *n. dots.* A very small round mark. —The *dots* on Mary's green dress are white.

—*v. dots, dotted, dotting.* Put a dot or dots on.—Be sure to *dot* your i's and cross your t's.

dou·ble (DUB-əl) *v. doubles, doubled, doubling.* 1. Make twice as big or much.—John got 40 in spelling yesterday. Today he *doubled* that mark. He got 80 today.
2. Fold in two.—Mary *doubled* the napkins neatly as Mother ironed them.
—*adj.* 1. Having two instead of one.—The word "doll" has a *double* l in it. It has two l's.
2. Twice as much or many.—The farmer's hens laid ten eggs yesterday and *double* that today. They laid twenty today.

doubt (DOWT) *n. doubts.* A question in the mind as to whether something is true or not. —I have my *doubts* that Bill has a new pony.
—*v. doubts, doubted, doubting.* Be unsure about; not be able to believe.—I *doubt* if Father will be home so early.

doubt·ful (DOWT-fuhl) *adj.; doubtfully, adv.; doubtfulness, n.* Not sure; not certain. —We are *doubtful* about whether or not Tom will pass.

doubt·less (DOWT-ləss) *adv.* Surely; no doubt.—You will *doubtless* be able to tell me how to get to the station.

dough (DOH) *n.* A soft mass of flour, salt, shortening, water, and other things, which is to be baked into bread, pastry, etc.—Mary rolled the *dough* for the pie crust.

dough·nut (DOH-nut) *n. doughnuts.* A cake made of sweet bread dough and cooked in deep fat. Most *doughnuts* have a hole in the middle and are round.

dove (DUV) *n. doves.* A pigeon. Some *doves* are tame and live in barns or near houses.

down (DOWN) *n.* The soft feathers on ducks, chickens, and geese. —Mary has a pillow filled with *down.*
—*adj., adv.,* and *prep.* 1. From a higher place to a lower place.—When we took the *down* elevator, we went *down* to the main floor.— He ran *down* the hill.
2. From a time long past to a time not so long past, or the present. — These jewels were handed *down* from my great-great grandmother to us.

down·stairs (down-STAIRZ) *adj.* On the lower floor of the house.—The kitchen, living room, and dining room are *downstairs* rooms.
—*adv.* To the lower floor of the house.—We come *downstairs* when we smell breakfast cooking.

down·town (down-TOWN) *adj.* and *adv.* The part of town where most of the office buildings and stores are; the business section.—Father has a *downtown* office.—We go *downtown* to do our shopping.

down·ward (DOWN-werd) *adv.* From a higher place to a lower place.—The soap bubbles floated *downward* from the window.

down·y (DOWN-ee) *adj. downier, downiest.* Fuzzy; covered with tiny fine hairs.—Little ducks are *downy.* They have soft feathers. —Peaches are *downy.*—Baby's hair is *downy.*

doze (DOHZ) *n.* A little nap.—I took a *doze* after school.
—*v. dozes, dozed, dozing.* Sleep lightly.—The old woman sits in her chair and *dozes.*

doz·en (DUZ-ən) *n. dozens* and *adj.* A group of twelve.—Mother asked me to buy some cookies, and I bought a *dozen.*

drab (DRAB) *adj.; drabness, n.* 1. Dull in color.—Grandfather's old overcoat is *drab.*
2. Dull; not exciting.—Cinderella lived a *drab* life until she went to the ball.

draft (DRAFT) *n. drafts.* 1. A sketch or early plan.–The builder made a *draft* of the plans for the new house.–The writer made a *draft* of his new story.
2. A strong current of air.–Do not sit in a *draft,* or you may get a cold. Do not sit where the air blows right on you.
3. A current of air in a stove, chimney, etc.–On a windy day the *draft* in our chimney is strong and makes the fire burn faster.
4. A damper.–We opened the *draft* in the chimney so that the fire would get a greater supply of air.
5. The calling of people for armed service to their country.–Ed was turned down by the *draft* because of ear trouble.
–*v. drafts, drafted, drafting.* 1. Draw carefully.–The builder *drafted* the plans for Uncle Paul's house.
2. Call (a person) into service whether he wants to go or not.–Many men were *drafted* into the Army and Navy during World War II.

drag (DRAG) *v. drags, dragged, dragging.* 1. Pull along behind one.–The boy *dragged* his sweater on the ground. – The older boy *dragged* the little fellow along by the hand.
2. Go so slowly as to seem endless.–The rainy afternoon *dragged.*

drag·on (DRAG-ən) *n. dragons.* A terrible beast, told about in stories and poems of long ago, that was said to have wings and scales on its long, snakelike body.

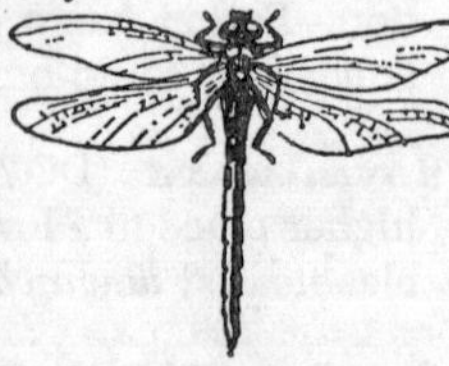

drag·on·fly (DRAG-ən-fly) *n. dragonflies.* An insect with a long, slim body and four wings that you can see through.

drain (DRAYN) *n. drains.* 1. A pipe, ditch, or gutter for carrying away water.–The ditch is a *drain* for the field.–Most roofs have *drains* that carry off rain water.

2. Something that uses up, or draws upon, continuously.–There was so much sickness in the man's family that the medical bills were a *drain* on his money.
–*v. drains, drained, draining.* 1. Pour the water off.–Mother *drains* the potatoes after they have boiled long enough.
2. Let water drip off.–Mary took the dishes from the hot water and put them into a wire basket to *drain.*
3. Use up.–The man's strength was *drained* from working both day and night.

drake (DRAYK) *n. drakes.* A male member of the duck family.

dra·ma (DRAH-mə) *n. dramas; dramatic, adj.; dramatically, adv.* 1. A play acted on the stage.–We are going to the theater to see a *drama.*
2. Any very exciting event, or series of events, which is like a play on a stage.–To Mary, all of life is one big *drama.*

dram·a·tize (DRAM-ə-TYZ) *v. dramatizes, dramatized, dramatizing.* Make a play of.–The children will *dramatize* the story of Little Red Riding Hood, and Mary will act the part of Red Riding Hood.

drank (DRANGK) *v.* One form of the verb *drink.*–Baby *drank* up all her milk.

drape (DRAYP) *v. drapes, draped, draping.* Wrap or fasten so as to hang in soft folds. – The dressmaker *draped* the cloth around Mother to plan the dress.–We *drape* windows with curtains.

dra·per·y (DRAYP-er-ee) *n. draperies.* A curtain or cloth that hangs loosely or in folds. – Father hung the window *draperies.*

draw (DRAW) *n. draws.* A tie.–Neither team won the high school football game. The score was tied. It was a *draw.*
–*v. draws, drew, drawing.* 1. Make a likeness of something by making lines with a pen, pencil, or other writing tool.–Children *draw* pictures with colored crayons.
2. Pull; attract; bring out. – The children *draw* their wagons after them.–We expect our ball game to *draw* many people to the ball field.–The man *drew* a knife from his pocket.
3. Come.–The automobile *drew* up by our side.–Dinnertime is *drawing* near.
4. Take in.–Mary *drew* a long breath of relief when her work was done.

draw·bridge (DRAW-brij) *n. drawbridges.* 1. A bridge that can be drawn up on its end so that no one can cross it. Castles and forts in ancient times were often approached or entered over *drawbridges.*
2. A bridge that can be raised or turned aside to allow tall boats to pass. *Drawbridges* are used today over many rivers.

draw·er (DROR) *n. drawers.* A boxlike part that slides in and out of cupboards, desks, tables, cabinets, etc. We keep linens, silver, papers, and other things in the *drawers* of buffets and chests.

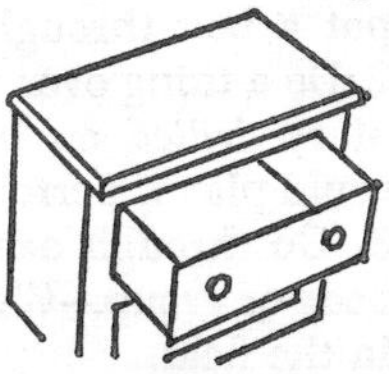

–*Drawers* are a piece of underwear to cover the legs and hips.–Grandpa wore *drawers.*

draw·ing (DRAW-ing) *n. drawings.* 1. A picture or diagram.–Bob made a pencil *drawing* of a man on a horse.
2. The art of making pictures or diagrams with lines.–In her class in *drawing,* Mary made a picture of a daffodil in a pitcher.

drawn (DRAWN) *v.* One form of the verb *draw.*–Mary had *drawn* a heart on Mother's valentine.

dread (DRED) *n.* Fear of something which may happen in the future.–Mary went toward the big dog with *dread* in her heart.
–*v. dreads, dreaded, dreading.* Be very much afraid of; look forward to with fear.–I *dread* crossing the lake in that leaky canoe.

dread·ful (DRED-fuhl) *adj.; dreadfully, adv.* Terrible.–A *dreadful* accident happened on the corner.

dream (DREEM) *n. dreams.* The thoughts, feelings, and pictures that pass through your mind while you are asleep, or a happening you imagine while awake.–Mary has *dreams* of being an actress.
–*v. dreams, dreamed* or *dreamt, dreaming.* Have a dream.–Last night I *dreamed* I kept a pet bear in the dining room.
–*dreamer, n. dreamers.*

drear·y (DRIR-ee) *adj. drearier, dreariest.* Dark; gloomy.–It was a *dreary* winter's day.

dredge (DREJ) *n. dredges.* A machine used for digging, deepening, and cleaning out ditches or channels.

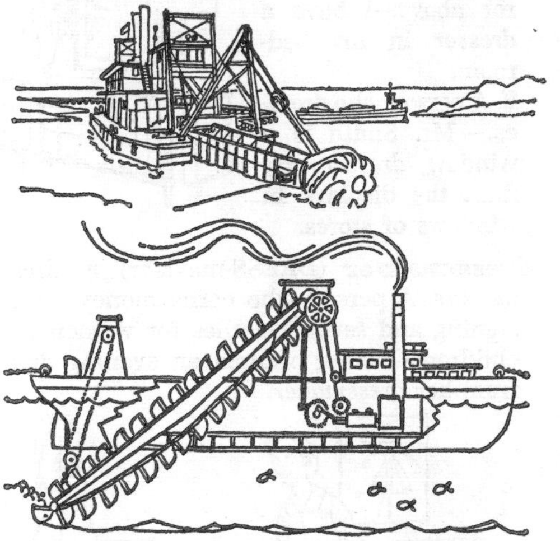

–*v. dredges, dredged, dredging.* Clean out or deepen a river, channel, etc.–The men *dredged* the river with a dredge.

drench (DRENCH) *v. drenches, drenched, drenching.* Soak through; make as wet as can be.–We were caught in the rain and our clothes were *drenched.*

dress (DRESS) *n. dresses.* A woman's or girl's outer garment or clothes.–In winter Mary wears a heavy *dress.*

–*v. dresses, dressed, dressing.* 1. Clothe; put clothes on.–Baby cannot *dress* herself yet.
2. Put bandages and medicines on.–Doctors *dress* boils, burns, sores, and other wounds.

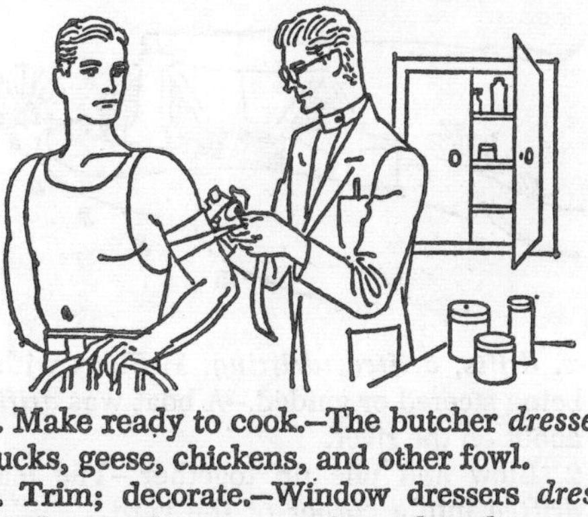

3. Make ready to cook.–The butcher *dresses* ducks, geese, chickens, and other fowl.
4. Trim; decorate.–Window dressers *dress* windows.–The curtains *dressed* up the room.

dress•er (DRESS-er) *n. dressers.* 1. A chest of drawers with a mirror above.–I have a *dresser* in my bedroom.
2. A person who dresses. – Mr. Smith is a window *dresser.* He fixes the displays in windows of stores.

dress•mak•er (DRESS-mayk-er) *n. dressmakers.* A person who earns money by designing and sewing clothes for women and children.–Mother ordered an evening dress from her *dressmaker.*

drew (DROO) *v.* One form of the verb *draw.* –Sally *drew* a picture of Father carrying a green umbrella.

dried (DRYD) *v.* One form of the verb *dry.*– Mary *dried* the dishes for Mother.

dri•er (DRY-er) *n. driers.* 1. A device to take the water out of wet clothes.–Some washing machines have *driers* on them.
2. Anything that helps to make a thing dry. –Turpentine mixed with paint serves as a *drier.* It thins the paint and makes it dry faster.

drift (DRIFT) *n. drifts.* A pile made of something, such as snow, blowing together.–Sally jumped into the *drift* of snow and got all covered up.

–v. drifts, drifted, drifting. 1. Float without being steered or guided.–A boat was *drifting* about on the river.
2. Blow and pile up together.–The leaves *drifted* into a corner of the yard.

drill (DRIL) *n. drills.* 1. A machine or tool for making holes.–Bob bored a hole through the board with a *drill.*

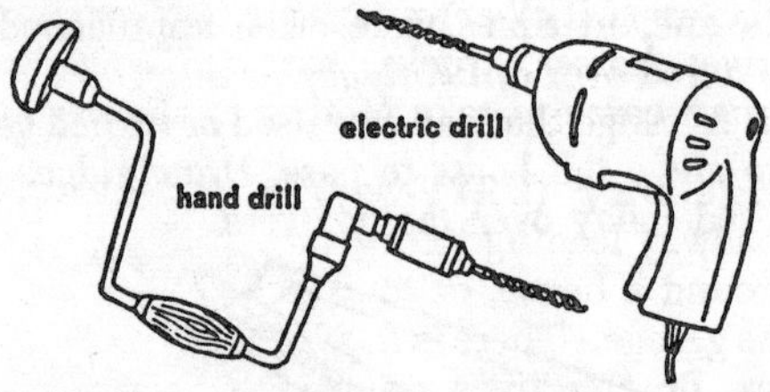

2. Practice.–We have arithmetic *drill* every morning in class.
3. Training in bodily exercises, in a group.– We watched the soldiers out on *drill.*
–v. drills, drilled, drilling. 1. Bore a hole with a drill.–The workmen *drilled* the metal to put a bolt through.
2. Do a thing over and over again; practice.– Mary *drilled* on her piano exercise till she could play it perfectly.
3. Go through exercises, or marching, in a body or group.–We watched the soldiers *drill* in the field.

drink (DRINGK) *n. drinks.* 1. A liquid food. –Ginger ale, cocoa, tea, water, and coffee are *drinks. Drinks* can be swallowed without chewing.
2. Alcoholic liquor.–The man went into the saloon to buy himself a *drink.*
–v. drinks, drank, drinking. 1. Put (liquid) into the mouth and swallow it.–Baby *drinks* milk.
2. Drink alcoholic liquor.–The unhappy man *drinks* too much.

drip (DRIP) *n. drips.* A leak.–Father stopped the *drip* in the bathtub faucet by putting in a new washer.
–v. drips, dripped, dripping. Fall drop by drop. –The rain *dripped* from the roses in the garden.

drive (DRYV) *n. drives.* 1. A ride.–We went for a *drive* into the country in our automobile.
2. A roadway.–Father parked the car in the *drive* at the side of the house.–Ed lives at 8 Lakeside *Drive.*
3. A campaign to raise money for a particular purpose.–We contributed $5 to the Community Chest *drive.*
–v. drives, drove, driving. 1. Direct, guide, or force to go.–Bob *drives* the cows to pasture for Grandfather when we are at the farm.– Jack has to *drive* himself to get up on time in the morning.
2. Steer a car and make it go. – Father is teaching Mother to *drive.*

driv•en (DRIV-ən) *v.* One form of the verb *drive.*–We had *driven* only a few miles when we ran out of gasoline.

driv•er (DRYV-er) *n. drivers.* A person who drives horses, trucks, cars, etc.–The taxi *driver* came to take Mother to the depot.

drive•way (DRYV-way) *n. driveways.* A roadway leading to or around a house, or to the garage.–There is a row of elm trees on each side of Grandmother's *driveway.*

driz•zle (DRIZ-əl) *n. drizzles.* A mistlike rain. –The *drizzle* turned into a heavy downpour.
–*v. drizzles, drizzled, drizzling.* Rain in fine drops.–It was *drizzling* when we went to school.

drom•e•dar•y (DRAHM-ə-dair-ee) *n. dromedaries.* A fast, light camel with only one hump. *Dromedaries* are used for riding. They are often called "Arabian camels."

drone (DROHN) *n. drones.* 1. A male bee. *Drones* do no work. They gather no honey. They do not sting.
2. A continual low humming sound.–We heard the *drone* of the class across the hall reciting the lesson.

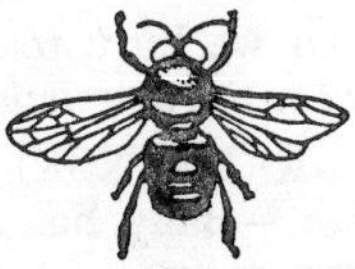

–*v. drones, droned, droning.* Make a droning or humming sound.–A bee *droned* around Grandmother's hollyhocks.

droop (DROOP) *v. droops, drooped, drooping.* Bend over, as if tired; wilt and bend over.– Flowers *droop* when they need water.

drop (DRAHP) *n. drops.* 1. A small amount of a liquid that forms a tiny round globe or ball when it falls.–A *drop* of rain fell on my nose.–The doctor told me to take ten *drops* of medicine in a glass of water.
2. A fall.–Bob hurt his ankle in his *drop* from the high wall.
3. A distance fallen; distance straight down. –The *drop* from the wall was a full twelve feet.
–*v. drops, dropped, dropping.* 1. To fall or let fall.–The pilot *dropped* five hundred feet before his parachute opened.–Do not *drop* the dish.
2. Stop; end; forget all about.–The teacher told the boys to *drop* their argument.
3. Lower or be let down.–The curtain *dropped* at the end of the play.
4. Leave out. – *Drop* the "e" in the word "make" and add "ing" to spell "making."

drove (DROHV) *n. droves.* A crowd of people, a swarm of insects, or a number of animals, moving along together.–People went to the football game in *droves.*–A *drove* of animals rushed out of the burning barn.
–*v.* One form of the verb *drive.*–We *drove* to John's house in our car.

drown (DROWN) *v. drowns, drowned, drowning.* 1. Die from having the head kept under water so that the breathing is stopped; cause to die in this way.–The black kitten would have *drowned,* but Jack saved it in time.–Bob *drowned* the rat he caught in his trap.
2. Make enough sound to keep another sound from being heard.–The radio was turned on so loud that it *drowned* out the ring of the doorbell.

drow•sy (DROW-zee) *adj. drowsier, drowsiest.* 1. Sleepy.–After supper the baby became *drowsy* and had to be put to bed.
2. Making one want to sleep. – On warm, *drowsy* days, the teacher lets us read stories in the afternoon.

drug (DRUG) *n. drugs.* 1. A medicine, or one of the things mixed together to make medicines.–Mother puts labels on all the *drugs* in the medicine cabinet.
2. A substance that dulls a person in body or mind. – The doctor gave Mother a *drug* to make her sleep after her operation.
–*v. drugs, drugged, drugging.* Give a drug to, especially one that causes sleep.–The police said the man had been *drugged* before he was robbed.

drug•gist (DRUG-ist) *n. druggists.* A person who sells medicines, or who mixes drugs to make medicines.–Mother asked the *druggist* to fill the doctor's prescription.

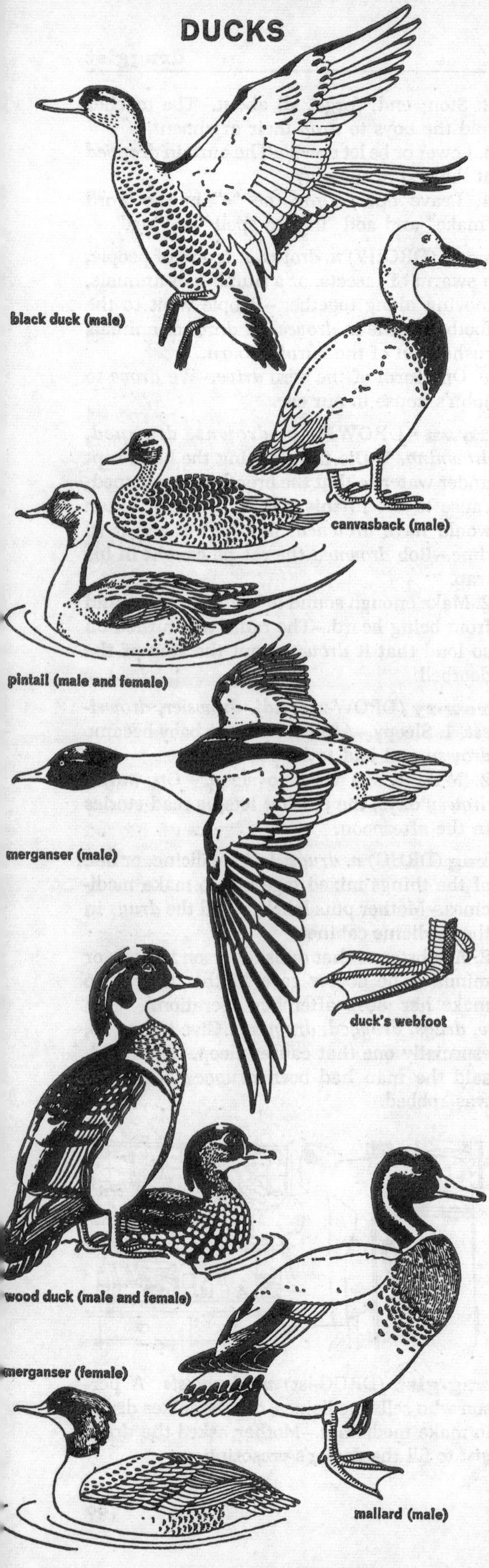

drum (DRUM) *n. drums.* 1. A hollow musical instrument that is played by beating upon the flat ends with drumsticks or with the hands. The sides of a *drum* are usually made of wood or metal. The ends are made of skins or other material stretched tightly across them.

2. Anything shaped like a drum.–Oil for automobiles sometimes comes in oil *drums.*

–*v. drums, drummed, drumming.* 1. Beat.–Baby likes to *drum* on her high chair with her spoon.

2. Get together.–We *drummed* up a lot of people to see our show.

3. Teach by continued repetition.–The teacher tries to *drum* the lessons into Bill's head.

drum·mer (DRUM-er) *n. drummers.* A person who beats a drum. – Jack is the *drummer* in the school band.

drum·stick (DRUM-stik) *n. drumsticks.* 1. One of the short sticks with which a drum is beaten.

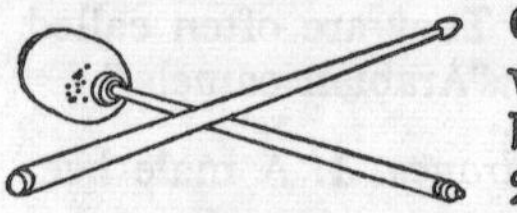

2. The leg of a fowl.–When we have roast chicken for dinner, I ask for the *drumstick.*

drunk (DRUNGK) *v.* One form of the verb *drink.* – Baby has *drunk* up her milk and wants more.

–*adj.* Having lost control of the body and mind through drinking too much alcoholic liquor. –The man who drove into the tree was *drunk.*

drunk·ard (DRUNGK-erd) *n. drunkards.* A person who makes a habit of drinking too much alcoholic liquor.–He was a *drunkard.*

dry (DRY) *v. dries, dried, drying.* 1. Take the wetness from. – Mary *dries* the dishes for Mother every day.–Mother *dries* apples and sweet corn, and puts them away for the winter.

2. Lose moisture or wetness.–The leaves have *dried* up.

–*adj. drier, driest.* 1. Not wet; without any moisture.–The sun makes the ground *dry.*

2. Thirsty.–The farmer's horses were very *dry* after plowing the field.

dry cell (DRY sell) *dry cells.* An electric cell in which the chemical producing the current is mixed with other ingredients, such as sawdust, to form a damp paste.

dry•er (DRY-er) *n. dryers.* One way to spell the noun *drier.*

duck (DUK) *n. ducks.* A flat-billed bird that swims. Ducks' feet are webbed. Oil on their feathers helps keep them on top of the water. Some ducks are tame and some are wild.–Grandfather raises *ducks* to sell and eat.
–*v. ducks, ducked, ducking.* 1. Plunge.–The boys *ducked* their heads under the water to get the sand out of their hair.
2. Dodge down quickly.–When the ball came toward me, I *ducked* so it would not hit me.

due (DOO *or* DYOO) *adj.* 1. Expected to come, or to be done or paid.–Our gas bill is *due.*–The postman is *due* any minute.
2. Just; fair; rightful.–The boys got their *due* reward for returning the money they found.
–*adv.* Directly.–If you will go *due* south, you will find the house you are looking for.

du•el (DOO- *or* DYOO-əl) *n. duels.* A fight between two people who agree on the time, place, and weapons they will use. Each person has a witness to the fight, who is called a second. – In olden times, quarrels were sometimes settled by *duels.*
–*v. duels, dueled, dueling.* Fight a duel.–The actors *dueled* on the stage.

dues (DOOZ *or* DYOOZ) *n. pl.* Money one pays for a membership.–Today Father paid his union *dues.*

du•et (doo- *or* dyoo-ET) *n. duets.* A song written for or sung by two people. *Duets* are also written for piano, violin, saxophone, and other musical instruments.

dug (DUG) *v.* One form of the verb *dig.*–The dog *dug* a hole in the ground with his front paws.

duke (DOOK *or* DYOOK) *n. dukes.* A high-ranking nobleman.–The king called in the *dukes* of the kingdom to advise him.

dull (DUL) *adj. duller, dullest; dully, adv.; dullness, n.* 1. Blunt; not sharp.–The knife is *dull;* it should be sharpened.
2. Stupid.–Some people are *dull.* They do not understand things easily.
3. Not bright or colorful.–The beggar's coat was a *dull* color.
4. Dim; not bright or cheerful.–Yesterday was a *dull* day. It wasn't clear and bright.
5. Not interesting. – The conversation was *dull.*

dumb (DUM) *adj.; dumbly, adv.; dumbness, n.* 1. Not able to speak.–There are special schools for persons who are *dumb.*–Animals are called *dumb* because they cannot talk.
2. Stupid; not smart. – There isn't a *dumb* person in this class.

dum•my (DUM-ee) *n. dummies.* 1. A very stupid person.–The boys called Mary a *dummy* because she didn't know the rules of baseball.
2. A figure made to look like a person.–The window trimmer dressed the *dummies* and put them in the store window.

3. In some card games, a player who turns his cards face up and does not play the hand. –When we played bridge, I was the *dummy* four times. I put my cards face up on the table and my partner played them.

dump (DUMP) *n. dumps.* A place set aside for throwing away trash or other things no longer wanted.–Old cans, boxes, and other rubbish are taken to the city *dump.*
–*v. dumps,. dumped, dumping.* Unload or empty a wagon, truck, etc., by tilting the load so that it will slide off; to drop off in a heap.–The truckman *dumped* the sand into the road.

dump•ling (DUMP-ling) *n. dumplings.* A small ball of dough cooked in broth or with stewed fruits.

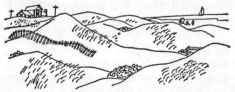

dunce (DUNSS) *n. dunces.* A person who learns very slowly.

dune (DOON *or* DYOON) *n. dunes.* A hill or ridge of sand that the wind has piled up.–There are *dunes* along the seacoast.

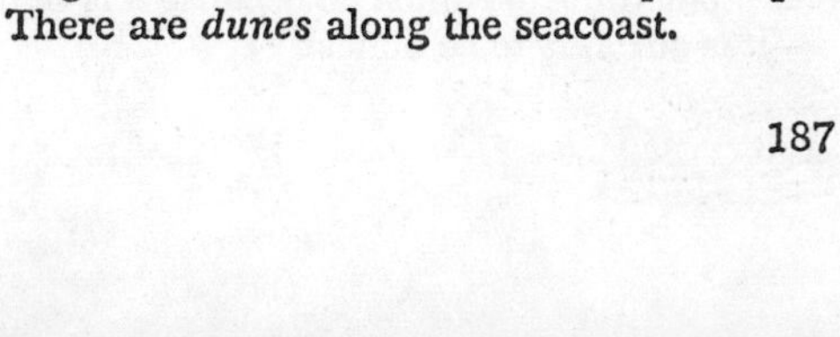

dun·geon (DUN-jən) *n. dungeons.* A dark, underground cell or room.–Prisoners are sometimes put into *dungeons.*

du·pli·cate (DOOP- *or* DYOOP-lə-kət) *n. duplicates.* A copy; something just like an original.–If you like this picture, I will get a *duplicate* of it for you.

–(DOOP- *or* DYOOP-lə-kayt) *v. duplicates, duplicated, duplicating.* Copy; make a copy of. –The teacher *duplicated* the tests so that each child might have his own copy.

du·ra·ble (DUHR- *or* DYUHR-ə-bəl) *adj.* Long-lasting; not easily worn away.–This has been a *durable* pair of shoes. They have lasted a long time.–Aluminum is more *durable* than tin.

dur·ing (DUHR- *or* DYUHR-ing) *prep.* While (something) is going on.–*During* the ball game it started to rain.–We wear heavy coats *during* the winter.

dusk (DUSK) *n.* 1. The time of evening just before dark.–The men went fishing at *dusk.* 2. Gloom and darkness.–The old woman sat in the *dusk* of her room.

dust (DUST) *n.* Dirt or another substance in very fine, dry particles; a powder.–The speeding car left a cloud of *dust* behind it.–The white *dust* on the kitchen floor is some flour that Sally spilled.

–*v. dusts, dusted, dusting.* 1. Wipe the dust from.–Mary *dusts* the furniture. She wipes off the tiny pieces of dirt.

2. Spread with a powdery stuff. – Mother *dusts* the pan with flour before putting the cake batter into it.

dust·y (DUST-ee) *adj. dustier, dustiest.* Full of, or covered with, dust or fine dirt.–The furniture is *dusty.*–The air is *dusty.*

du·ty (DOO- *or* DYOO-tee) *n. duties.* 1. A task or work that one must do.–Mother's main *duties* are cooking, keeping the house, and taking care of the children.

2. Something one must do because it is right. –It is our *duty* to be honest.

3. A tax that must be paid on things brought from one country to another.–Mother had to pay *duty* on the necklace she brought in from Canada.

dwarf (DWORF) *n. dwarfs.* 1. A person, plant, or animal that is very much smaller than others of its own kind or family. 2. In fairy tales a *dwarf* is often a small, ugly person who is strong and wicked.

dwell (DWEL) *v. dwells, dwelt* or *dwelled, dwelling.* Live; make one's home.–We *dwell* in houses.

–*Dwell on* means think hard about; talk about.–The boys *dwelt on* the subject of baseball a long time. They talked and thought about baseball.

dwell·er (DWEL-er) *n. dwellers.* One who lives in a certain place.–A person who dwells or lives in a city is a city *dweller.*–A bird that nests in the swamp is a swamp *dweller.*

dwell·ing (DWEL-ing) *n. dwellings.* Place to live; house.–We live in a two-story *dwelling.*–Their *dwelling* is a house-trailer.

dwelt (DWELT) *v.* One form of the verb *dwell.*–The princess *dwelt* in a foreign land for many years.

dye (DY) *n. dyes.* A coloring substance.–Mother dipped the dress in red *dye.*

–*v. dyes, dyed, dyeing.* Change the color of something by putting coloring into it.–Mary's dress was faded, so Mother *dyed* it red.

dy·ing (DY-ing) *v.* One form of the verb *die.* –When they pulled the cat out of the water, they thought it was *dying,* but it lived.

dy·na·mite (DY-nə-myt) *n.* A chemical that explodes with great force.–*Dynamite* is used by workmen to blow up rocks.

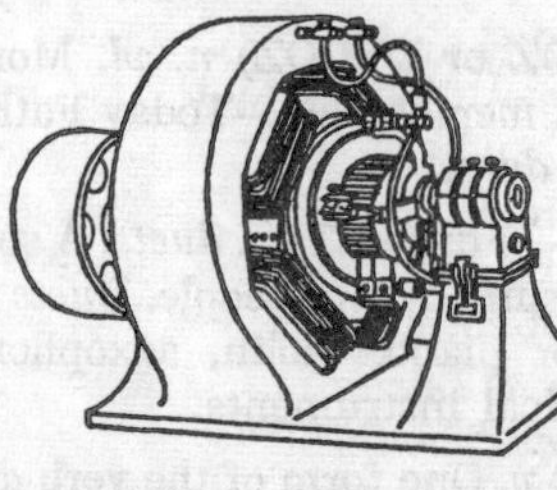

dy·na·mo (DY-nə-moh) *n. dynamos.* A machine that makes electric current by changing mechanical energy into electric energy; an electric generator.–The farm has a small *dynamo* to supply it with electricity in case the regular power supply fails.

E e

E, e (EE) *n. E's, e's.* The fifth letter of the alphabet.

each (EECH) *adj.* If you speak of every person or thing in a group as separate from the others, you say *each* person or thing.–*Each* child has a Christmas gift.

ea•ger (EE-ger) *adj.; eagerly, adv.* Wanting; having great desire.–We are *eager* to go to the farm. We are excited about going.

ea•ger•ness (EE-ger-nəss) *n.* Very great desire.–The boy had a great *eagerness* to learn about animals.

ea•gle (EE-gəl) *n. eagles.* A large bird that eats other birds and animals.–The bald *eagle* is the emblem of the United States.

ear (IR) *n. ears.* 1. The part of the body which hears sounds. Man's *ears* are on each side of his head. – Some dogs' *ears* stand up, and some lie down.

2. The ability to hear. –Bob has an *ear* for bird calls. He recognizes the call of each bird.
3. The bunch of grain on plants, such as wheat, oats, corn, etc.–Mother cooked several *ears* of corn.

ear•drum (IR-drum) *n. eardrums.* The thin membrane between the middle ear and the outer ear. The *eardrum* is very delicate and quivers when struck by sound waves.

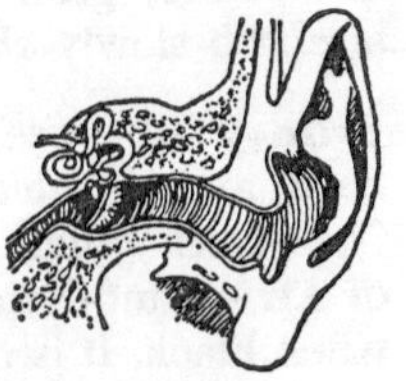

ear•ly (ER-lee) *adj. earlier, earliest.* 1. Soon to come.–Father is expecting an *early* telephone call.
2. One of the first.–One player was hurt during an *early* game. He was hurt in one of the first games of the season.
–*adv.* 1. Before the set or usual time.–Some children come to school *early;* others come late.
2. In the first part. – The newsboy comes *early* in the evening.

earn (ERN) *v. earns, earned, earning.* 1. Receive as pay.–Father *earns* eighty dollars a week.
2. Be entitled to.–Father *earns* every bit of the eighty dollars. He works hard and well enough to deserve eighty dollars a week.– She has done enough work to *earn* a rest.

ear•nest (ER-nist) *adj.; earnestly, adv.* Sincere; conscientious. – The workman is an *earnest* worker. He is sincere, and he tries to do what he is supposed to do.
–*In earnest* means serious or seriously. – Grandfather was *in earnest* when he told us not to climb the apple tree. He meant what he said.

earn•ings (ER-ningz) *n. pl.* Pay; wages or salary.–Father's *earnings* are eighty dollars a week.

earth (ERTH) *n.* 1. The world we live on. The *earth* is called a planet because it circles about the sun. The *earth* is shaped like a ball, a little flattened at the top and bottom.

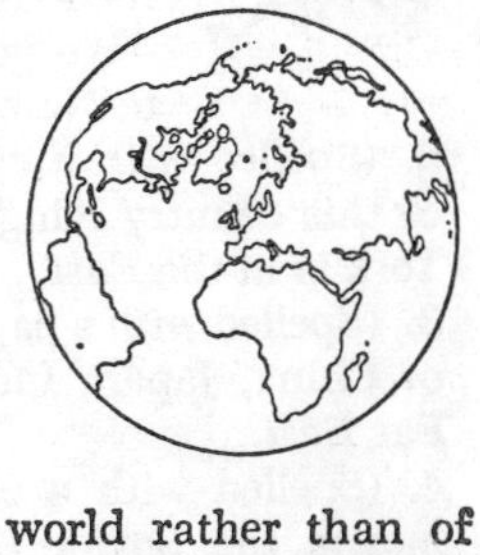

2. Ground; soil. – Plants grow in the *earth.*
–*earthly, adj.* Of the world rather than of heaven.–His mind is set on *earthly* things. He loves money, fine clothes, rich food.

earth•en (ERTH-ən) *adj.* Made of clay or baked earth. – *Earthen* jugs, pitchers, and jars are those that are made of clay, then baked until hard.

earth•quake (ERTH-kwayk) *n. earthquakes.* A shaking of a part of the earth's surface. Sudden changes inside the earth cause a shaking and sometimes an opening in the earth's surface.

earth•worm (ERTH-werm) *n. earthworms.* A long, crawling worm that lives in the ground. *Earthworms* crawl about in the ground making little tunnels which keep the soil loose.

ease (EEZ) *n.* Freedom from effort or difficulty.–Bob skates with *ease.*
–*v. eases, eased, easing.* Make comfortable; lessen (pain).–The nurse tried to *ease* the old man's pains.

ea•sel (EE-zəl) *n. easels.* A stand on which an artist places his canvas so that it is held upright while he paints a picture.

eas•i•er (EEZ-ee-er) *adj.* One form of the word *easy.* – The second problem is *easier* than the first one.

eas•i•ly (EEZ-ə-lee) *adv.* With ease; with no trouble.–The singer sings *easily.*

east (EEST) *n., adj.,* and *adv.* 1. The direction toward the sunrise.–*East* is one of the four directions, as shown in the picture. The directions help us to find places. –We go *east* from Ohio to get to New York.

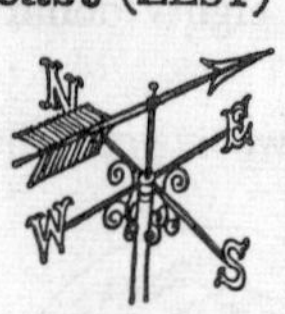

2. (Spelled with a capital "E.") The section of this country lying toward the east.–New York is in the *East.*
3. (Spelled with a capital "E".) The countries of China, Japan, India, etc., are called the Far *East.*
4. (Spelled with a capital "E.") Sometimes means the Soviet•Union and its satellite countries.

East•er (EESS-ter) *n. Easters.* The Sunday each year on which Christian peoples celebrate the rising of Christ from the grave. The date of *Easter* varies. But *Easter* always comes between March 21 and April 26.

east•ern (EESS-tern) *adj.* 1. Lying to the east. – New York, Maine, and New Jersey are some *eastern* states. They are in the *eastern* part of the United States.

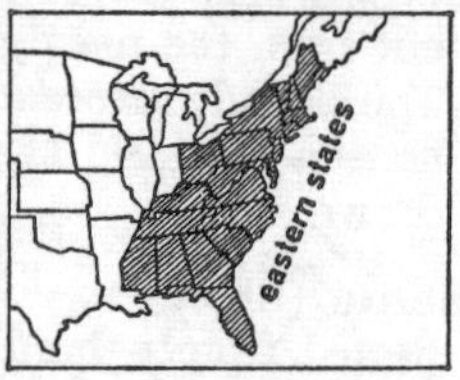

2. (Spelled with a capital "E.") Sometimes means "of the eastern United States."
3. (Spelled with a capital "E.") Sometimes means "of Asia."–Two *Eastern* religions are Buddhism and Hinduism.

east•ward (EEST-werd) *adv.* Toward the east; the direction in which the sun rises.– The auto turned *eastward.*

eas•y (EE-zee) *adj. easier, easiest.* Not hard or difficult.–Jack's work is *easy.*–The old farmer lives an *easy* life. He is comfortable; he has no cares or worries; he has enough money to buy what he needs.–The teacher is an *easy* person to get along with.

eat (EET) *v. eats, ate, eating.* 1. Take as food. – Cows *eat* grass. – People *eat* vegetables, fruits, and meats.
2. Take meals.–We expect to *eat* at the café while Mother is away.
3. Dissolve.–Acids *eat* metals. They dissolve metals and make holes in them.

eaves (EEVZ) *n. pl.* The part of a roof that sticks out beyond the walls. Metal troughs are often fastened under the *eaves* to catch and carry away rain when it falls on the roof. Otherwise, water drips from the *eaves* onto the ground

ebb (EB) *v. ebbs, ebbed, ebbing.* 1. Go back or out, as the tide returning to the sea after having come in towards the shore. – The beach becomes larger as the tide *ebbs.*
2. Decline; grow weaker. – The old man's strength slowly *ebbed.*

eb•on•y (EB-ən-ee) *n. ebonies* and *adj.* A very hard and durable, heavy wood. It comes from trees which grow in the tropical areas of Africa and Asia. *Ebony* is most valuable when black. It is used for fine cabinet work, black piano keys, handles, etc.

ec•cen•tric (ik- *or* ek-SEN-trik) *adj.* Different from the usual; odd; queer; peculiar.—The old lady is *eccentric.* She lives alone with sixteen cats and keeps her window shades drawn all day.

ech•o (EK-oh) *n. echoes.* Sound that is reflected from a hard surface.—The children called out toward the hillside and heard the *echo* of their own voices.
—*v. echoes, echoed, echoing.* Repeat; say again.—Little children *echo* the things they hear older people say

e•clipse (ee-KLIPSS) *n. eclipses.* When the moon passes between the earth and the sun, it cuts off the sunlight in some places. This is an *eclipse* of the sun.
—*v. eclipses, eclipsed, eclipsing.* 1. Cut off light from; hide.—The moon *eclipses* the sun.
2. Cast into a shadow; surpass.—John's score in the game *eclipsed* Tony's record.

e•con•o•my (i- *or* ee-KAHN-ə-mee) *n. economies.* Saving.—To practice *economy* means to save, to waste nothing, to use what one has without spending money for new things that are not really necessary.

edge (EJ) *n. edges.* 1. The outside part of something where it ends; the top or bottom or one side.—The cup fell off the *edge* of the table.—The children put lines near the *edges* of the paper.—Father stood on the *edge* of the river fishing.
2. The sharp side of a blade.—The *edge* of the knife is very sharp.
—*v. edges, edged, edging.* 1. Put a border around; decorate the edges of.—Mother *edged* her handkerchief in green.
2. Move sidewise little by little.—The doctor *edged* through the crowd to get to the man who had been hurt.

ed•i•ble (ED-i-bəl) *adj.* Suitable or safe for eating.—Early man soon learned which plants were *edible* and which were unpleasant or poisonous.

e•di•tion (i-DISH-ən) *n. editions.* Number of copies of a book or other publication printed at one time.—Many *editions* of "Tom Sawyer" have been printed.

ed•i•tor (ED-ə-ter) *n. editors; editorial, adj.* A person in charge of publishing books, newspapers, or magazines. The *editor* decides what should be printed in the book or paper, corrects mistakes, and decides how the material should be arranged or placed.

ed•i•to•ri•al (ed-ə-TOR-ee-əl) *n. editorials.* Article written by a magazine or newspaper editor, giving opinions about the news.—His *editorial* praised the action of the President.

ed•u•cate (EJ-ə-kayt) *v. educates, educated, educating.* Teach; train. — Teachers try to *educate* children in reading, writing, arithmetic, and other subjects.

ed•u•ca•tion (ej-ə-KAY-shən) *n.* 1. Teaching; training.—We go to school to get *education.*
2. Things learned.—What you know or learn through reading, through going to school, through experience, or through training, is your *education.*

eel (EEL) *n. eels.* A long, slippery, snakelike fish. Some kinds of *eels* are good to eat.

ef•fect (ə-FEKT) *n. effects.* 1. A result.—The *effect* of too much reading is tired eyes.
2. Force; being in action.—The new rule does not go into *effect* until Monday. It will not be followed until Monday.
—*v. effects, effected, effecting.* Cause; bring about.—The doctor said the medicine would *effect* a cure.

ef•fec•tive (ə-FEK-tiv) *adj.; effectively, adv.* Bringing about the result wanted. — Sometimes children are spanked to make them behave. With some children spanking is not *effective.* It doesn't make them behave.

ef•fi•cient (ə-FISH-ənt) *adj.; efficiently, adv.; efficiency, n.* Getting the best results with the least effort.—The workman is very *efficient.* He is able, and does his work well. He gets results.

ef•fort (EF-ert) *n. efforts.* Spending energy; trying hard.—Bob's success in arithmetic was brought about by *effort.*—The fighter's success is due to his *effort* to win.

egg (EG) *n. eggs.* The first stage from which birds and some other creatures grow. Hens, ducks, geese, and other birds lay *eggs. Eggs* have shells. The centers of *eggs* are yellow and the part between the center and shell is whitish. Snakes, fish, and turtles also lay *eggs.*

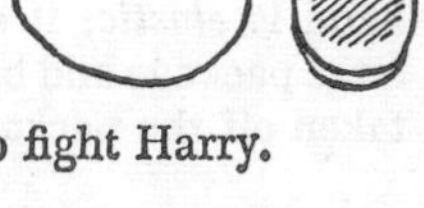

—*v. eggs, egged, egging.* Urge; encourage.—He *egged* his brother on to fight Harry.

egg·plant (EG-plant) *n. eggplants.* A widely-grown plant whose large, purple, smooth-skinned fruit is cooked and eaten as a vegetable.

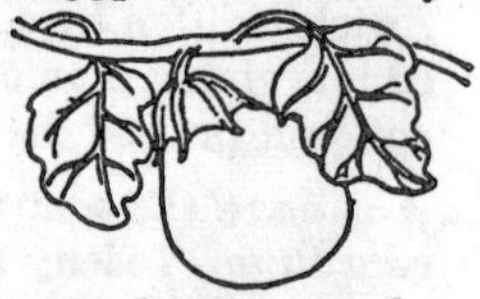

eight (AYT) *n. eights* and *adj.* The number [8] coming after 7 and before 9.–We have two thumbs and *eight* other fingers.

eight·een (AY-TEEN) *n. eighteens* and *adj.* The number [18] coming after 17 and before 19.–Eight and ten make *eighteen.*

eighth (AYTTH) *n. eighths.* One of 8 equal parts. If you cut anything into eight parts all the same size, each part is called one *eighth.* One *eighth* is written 1/8.
–*adj.* Coming in order as number 8 in a series. –August is the *eighth* month of the year.

eight·y (AYT-ee) *n. eighties* and *adj.* The number [80] coming after 79 and before 81.–Eight tens make *eighty.*

ei·ther (EE- *or* Y-ther) *adj. adv., conj.*, and *pron.* 1. One or the other of two.–Mary brought Mother two pans. Mother said *either* pan was large enough for the cake.–*Either* shut the door or open it wide.
2. Each one of two.–On *either* side of the street was a sidewalk. There was a sidewalk on both sides of the street.
3. John can't swim and Bob can't *either.*

e·lab·o·rate (ee- *or* i-LAB-ə-rayt) *v. elaborates, elaborated, elaborating.* Work out with care and detail; add details to.–He *elaborated* on his plan to surprise the boys.
–(i-LAB-ə-rit) *adj.; elaborately, adv.* Done with great care, and with attention to even the smallest details.–The artist painted an *elaborate* design.–The feast was *elaborate,* with many fine dishes and wines.

e·lapse (ee- *or* i-LAPSS) *v. elapses, elapsed, elapsing.* Go by; slip away or pass, as time passes.–Tom didn't realize how much time had *elapsed* since he had begun to work.

e·las·tic (ee- *or* i-LASS-tik) *n. elastics.* 1. A kind of ribbon containing rubber threads which allow it to stretch and snap back.–Mother put *elastic* in the tops of Bob's socks to make them stay up.
2. A rubber band.
–*adj.* Able to be stretched out and then go back to its usual length or size.–A rubber band is *elastic;* it stretches to go around a large package and becomes small again when taken off the package.

el·bow (EL-boh) *n. elbows.* 1. The joint or place where the upper and lower parts of the arm come together.–Do not put your *elbows* on the table when you eat.

2. A curved metal band used to join pipes where they turn. Plumbers use *elbows.*

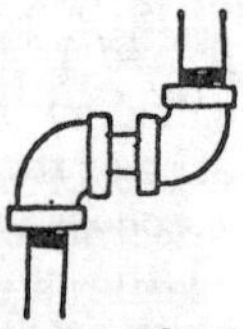

–*v. elbows, elbowed, elbowing.* Push with the elbows.–Bob *elbowed* his way through the crowd to get to the store.

eld·er (EL-der) *n. elders.* 1. A person who is older.–Bob is always respectful to his *elders.*
2. A church officer.–The *elders* of the church met last night.
–*adj.* Older of two.–Jack is the *elder* brother. He is older than his brother.

eld·er·ly (EL-der-lee) *adj.* Somewhat old.–An *elderly* gentleman knocked at the door.

eld·est (EL-dəst) *adj.* Oldest of more than two.–Mary is the *eldest* child in the large family. All the other children are younger than she is.

e·lect (ee- *or* i-LEKT) *v. elects, elected, electing.* 1. Choose by a vote.–We are going to *elect* a person to be chairman of the class.
2. Choose (without voting).–Jane was the one *elected* to carry the water.

e·lec·tion (ee- *or* i-LEK-shən) *n. elections.* 1. A choosing or being chosen, usually by vote.–After his *election,* the mayor thanked those who had voted for him.
2. The time for voting.–Our city *election* is held in November.

e·lec·tric (ee- *or* i-LEK-trik) *adj.* Operated by or having to do with electricity.–*Electric* irons are heated by electricity.–*Electric* clocks are run by electricity.

e·lec·tri·cal (ee- *or* i-LEK-trə-kəl) *adj.* Electric; having to do with or operated by electricity.–Joe is studying to be an *electrical* engineer. He will learn to design and make *electrical* things.

e·lec·tri·cian (ee- *or* i-lek-TRISH-ən) *n. electricians.* A person who repairs and installs electric tools and machines, wiring, etc.–Father called the *electrician* to come and put a new plug in the dining room.

e·lec·tric·i·ty (ee- *or* i-lek-TRISS-ə-tee) *n.* A kind of force that can be sent through wires to give light, heat, or power. *Electricity* for our use is made by machines called generators or dynamos. *Electricity* is also found in nature. Lightning is a charge of *electricity* shooting through the air.

e·lec·tro·mag·net (ee- *or* i-lek-troh-MAG-nət) *n. electromagnets.* A soft-iron bar with a coil of wire wrapped around it. When electric current is passed through the wire, the iron bar becomes magnetized; when the current is removed, the iron bar loses its magnetism. *Electromagnets* used in heavy industry can lift many times their own weight.

e·lec·tron (ee- *or* i-LEK-trahn) *n. electrons; electronic, adj.* A tiny part of an atom which carries a negative charge of electricity. Electrons are on the outer shells of atoms. They go around the protons and neutrons.

el·e·gant (EL-ə-gənt) *adj.; elegantly, adv.* Superior and refined; rich in taste and quality; fine.–The queen is *elegant.* She wears beautiful gowns and jewels, and always behaves royally.

el·e·ment (EL-ə-mənt) *n. elements.* 1. One of the simplest parts of anything.–Addition is an *element* of arithmetic.
2. One of the hundred or more substances which combine to make up all the material in the world.–Salt is a substance made up of two *elements* called sodium and chloride.
3. (In the plural) The forces which make up bad weather.–On the mountain peak in a thunderstorm, the climber was at the mercy of the *elements.*

el·e·men·ta·ry (el-ə-MEN-tə-ree *or* el-ə-MENT-ree) *adj.* 1. Concerned with the beginning stages of any subject; what one must learn before one can go on to harder things.–*Elementary* schooling is necessary to prepare pupils for high school.
2. Simple; easy.–"*Elementary,* my dear Watson" means "That's simple, my dear Watson."

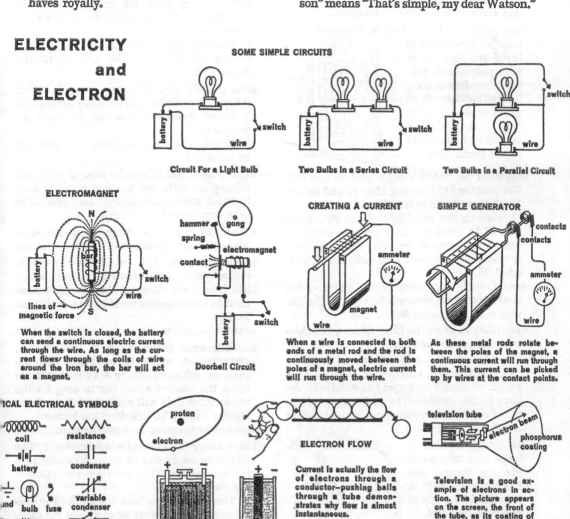

ELECTRICITY and ELECTRON

SOME SIMPLE CIRCUITS

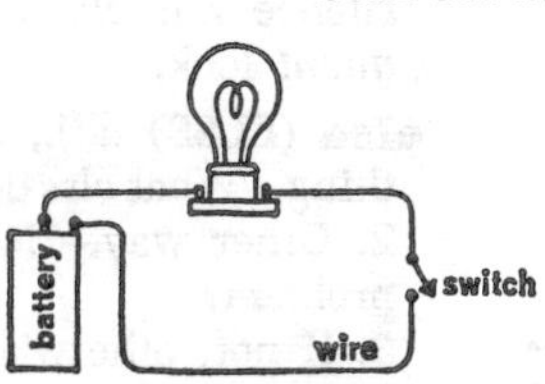

Circuit For a Light Bulb

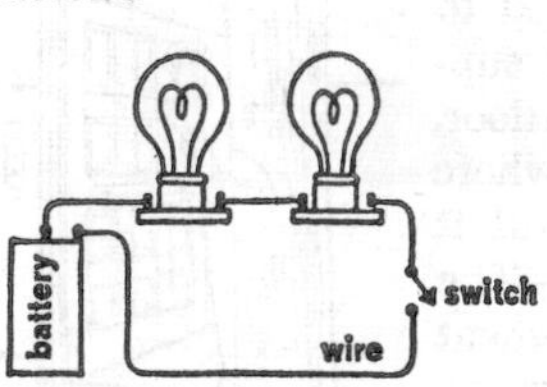

Two Bulbs in a Series Circuit

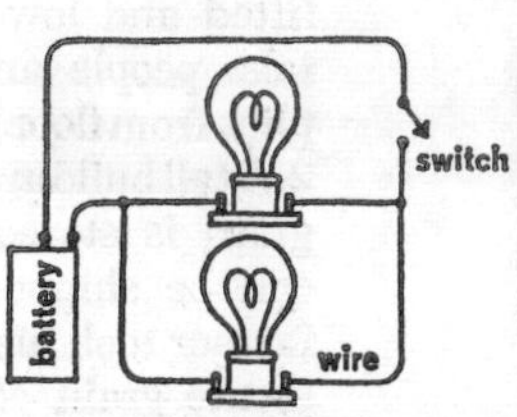

Two Bulbs in a Parallel Circuit

ELECTROMAGNET

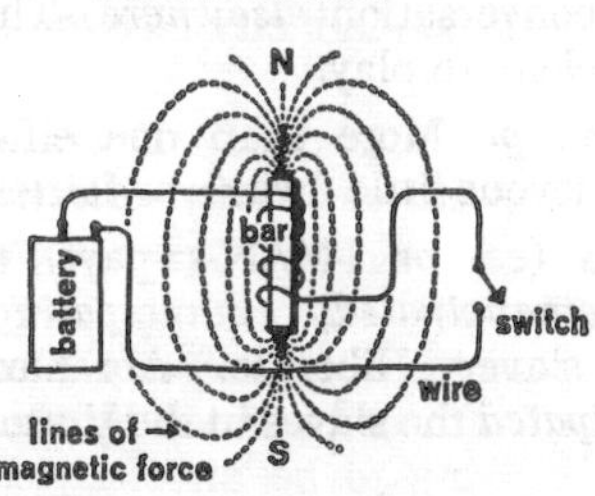

When the switch is closed, the battery can send a continuous electric current through the wire. As long as the current flows through the coils of wire around the iron bar, the bar will act as a magnet.

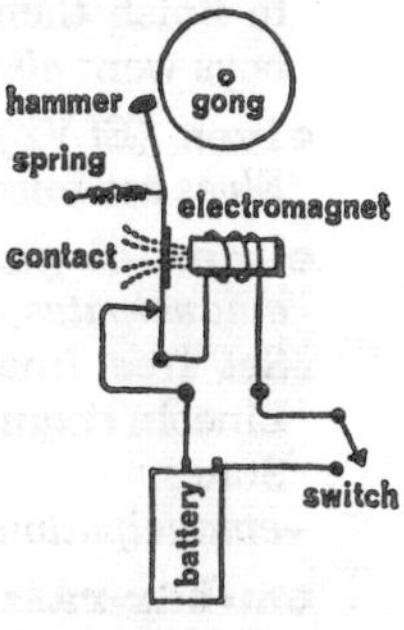

Doorbell Circuit

CREATING A CURRENT

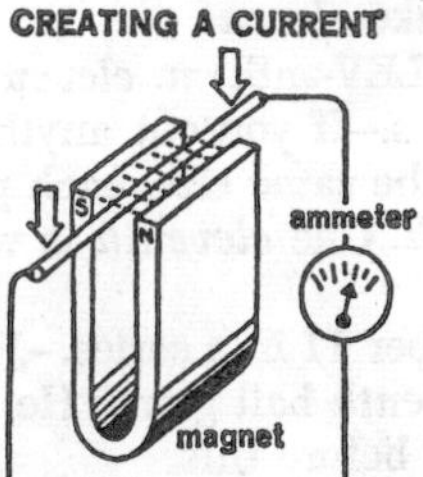

When a wire is connected to both ends of a metal rod and the rod is continuously moved between the poles of a magnet, electric current will run through the wire.

SIMPLE GENERATOR

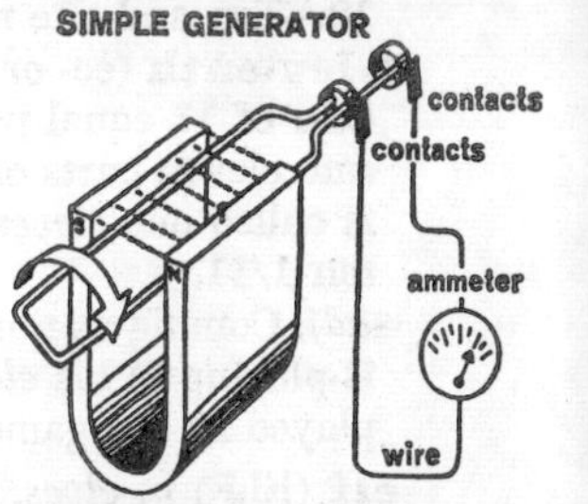

As these metal rods rotate between the poles of the magnet, a continuous current will run through them. This current can be picked up by wires at the contact points.

ICAL ELECTRICAL SYMBOLS

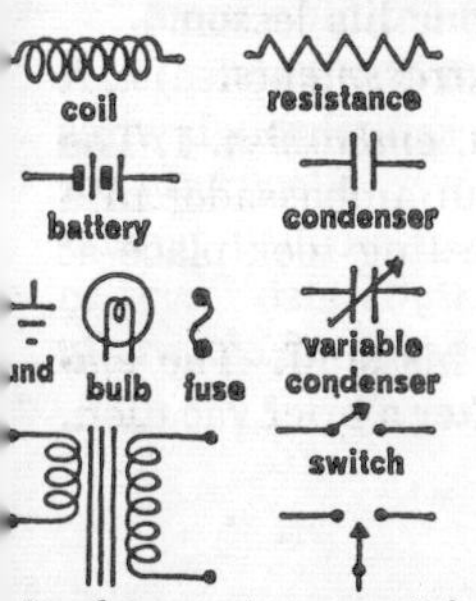

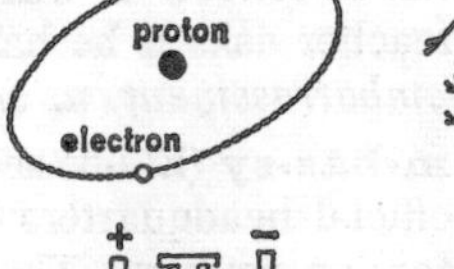

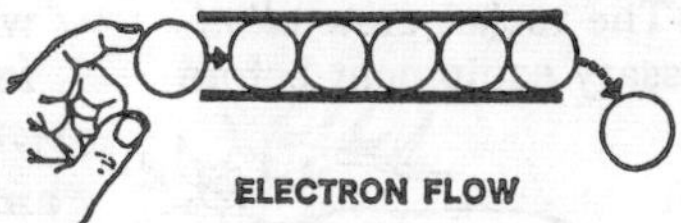

ELECTRON FLOW

Current is actually the flow of electrons through a conductor–pushing balls through a tube demonstrates why flow is almost instantaneous.

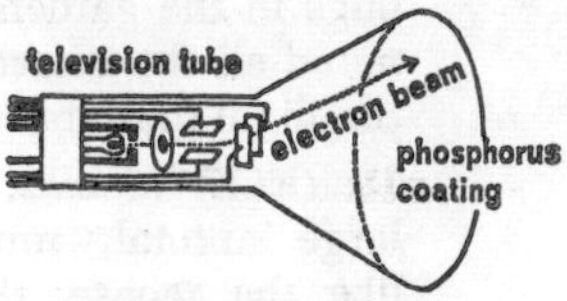

Television is a good example of electrons in action. The picture appears on the screen, the front of the tube, as its coating of phosphorus is hit by a moving beam of electrons. The beam of electrons is shot from the neck of the tube.

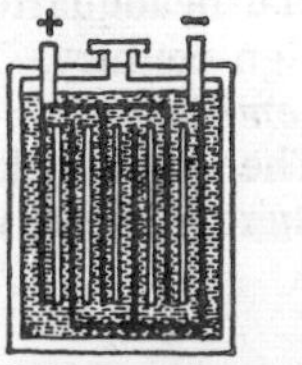

lead acid battery (car battery)

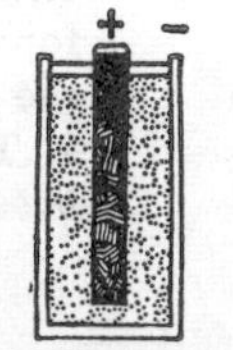

dry cell battery (flashlight battery)

el•e•phant (EL-ə-fənt) *n. elephants.* A large animal found in Africa and Asia. An *elephant* has a thick gray skin, large ears, small eyes, two ivory tusks, and a long trunk which he uses to pick up food and water.

el•e•vate (EL-ə-vayt) *v. elevates, elevated, elevating.* 1. Raise up; put at a higher place.–The car was *elevated* on the grease rack.
2. Promote or raise in rank or position.–Bob was *elevated* from clerk to manager.

el•e•va•tor (EL-ə-vayt-er) *n. elevators.* 1. A cage or room that is lifted and lowered to take people and supplies from floor to floor.
2. A tall building where grain is stored till it can be shipped.–The farmer took his wheat to the grain *elevator.*

e•lev•en (ee- *or* i-LEV-ən) *n. elevens* and *adj.* The number [11] coming after 10 and before 12.–Ten and one make *eleven.*

e•lev•enth (ee- *or* i-LEV-ənth) *n. elevenths.* One of 11 equal parts.–If you cut anything into eleven parts of the same size, each part is called one *eleventh.* One *eleventh* is written 1/11.
–*adj.* Coming as number 11 in a series.–John is playing in his *eleventh* ball game. He has played in ten games before this.

elf (ELF) *n. elves.* In fairy tales, a mischievous little dwarf or fairy.

e•lim•i•nate (ee- *or* i-LIM-ən-ayt) *v. eliminates, eliminated, eliminating.* Get rid of.–Father uses an insect spray to *eliminate* the bugs in the garden.–The rocket crew *eliminated* all the unnecessary equipment before the flight to Mars.

elk (ELK) *n. elks.* A large animal, much like the moose, that has large flat antlers. It is found mostly in northern climates.

el•lipse (i-LIPSS) *n. ellipses.* An oval or squeezed-in circle whose ends are alike.

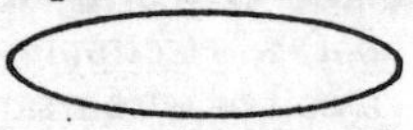

elm (ELM) *n. elms.* A large shade tree. The branches of the *elm* spread out at the top like an umbrella.

e•lon•gate (ee- *or* i-LAWNG-gayt) *v. elongates, elongated, elongating.* Make longer; stretch; extend.–A story of Kipling's tells how the elephant's child had its nose *elongated* into a trunk.

el•o•quent (EL-ə-kwənt) *adj.; eloquently, adv.* 1. Very powerful and expressive in speech.–The retiring professor made an *eloquent* farewell speech.
2. Moving; expressive; forceful.–The man's silence was *eloquent.*–She gave me an *eloquent* look.

else (ELSS) *adj., adv.,* and *conj.* 1. Other thing.–What *else* do you have in your pocket?
2. Other way.–How *else* can we work the problem?
3. If not; otherwise.–Be good; *else* you will be punished.

else•where (ELSS-hwair) *adv.* At or to another place.–The teacher told Bob and Jack to finish their conversation *elsewhere.*–The boys went *elsewhere* to play.

elves (ELVZ) *n. pl.* More than one elf.–*Elves* are mischievous little dwarfs or fairies.

e•man•ci•pate (ee- *or* i-MAN-sə-payt) *v. emancipates, emancipated, emancipating.* Set free from slavery; liberate.–Abraham Lincoln *emancipated* the slaves in the United States.
–*emancipation, n.*

em•bar•rass (em-BAR-əss) *v. embarrasses, embarrassed, embarrassing.* Make shy, uneasy, or ashamed.–Mary was *embarrassed* when the teacher asked her to sing for the whole school.–It will *embarrass* Tom if the teacher asks if he has done his lesson.
–*embarrassment, n. embarrassments.*

em•bas•sy (EM-bə-see) *n. embassies.* 1. The official headquarters of an ambassador in a foreign country.–The meeting took place at the *embassy.*
2. The ambassador and his staff.–The *embassy* returned to work after a brief vacation.

em•ber (EM-ber) *n. embers.* A small piece of wood or fuel that is burning or glowing.–The boys sat by the dying fire and watched the *embers.*

em•bez•zle (em-BEZ-əl) *v. embezzles, embezzled, embezzling.* Steal by betraying someone's confidence and trust, as an officer of a company stealing the company's funds.–The bookkeeper was arrested for having *embezzled* money from her employers.

em•blem (EM-bləm) *n. emblems.* 1. Sign; that which stands for something.–The *emblem* of the United States is an eagle.

2. A medal or badge of honor.–The man was given an *emblem* for his bravery.

em•brace (em-BRAYSS) *n. embraces.* A holding in the arms.–Father held Baby in a warm *embrace.*
–*v. embraces, embraced, embracing.* Hold in the arms to show love.–Mother *embraces* the baby.

em•broi•der (em-BROI-der) *v. embroiders, embroidered, embroidering.* 1. Decorate with fancy stitches made with a needle and thread, often colored.–Mother *embroidered* a towel for Grandmother.
2. Add imaginary details to a true account; exaggerate for effect.–He *embroidered* in telling the story of his travels.

em•broi•der•y (em-BROI-der-ee) *n. embroideries.* A kind of fancy decoration made with needle and thread.–Molly's *embroidery* is well known. She has stitched M's on all her handkerchiefs. Whenever she loses one, it is always returned.

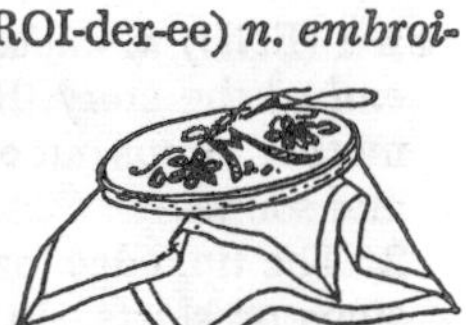

em•bry•o (EM-bree-oh) *n. embryos.* 1. An animal in the beginning stages of its development, before its birth.–A chick inside the egg is called an *embryo.*
2. A plant before it sprouts out of the seed.–An apple seed contains the *embryo* of an apple.
3. An undeveloped state.–John is very modest. Whenever he makes a suggestion he says, "This is just an *embryo* of an idea."

em•er•ald (EM-er-əld) *n. emeralds.* A valuable, bright green jewel.
–*adj.* Bright green. – The costume Ann wore in the play was *emerald* silk.

e•merge (ee- *or* i-MERJ) *v. emerges, emerged, emerging.* 1. Come out.–A deer *emerged* from the woods.
2. Come into view.–A light *emerged* from behind the house.

e•mer•gen•cy (ee- *or* i-MER-jən-see) *n. emergencies.* A sudden or unforeseen situation requiring immediate attention or action.–The flood created a serious *emergency.* People were homeless, and some were hurt and without food.

em•i•grant (EM-ə-grənt) *n. emigrants.* A person who goes from his own country to live in another country.–*Emigrants* from many countries have settled in the United States.

em•i•grate (EM-ə-grayt) *v. emigrates, emigrated, emigrating.* Go from one's own country to live in another.–Very few Americans *emigrate.*

em•i•nent (EM-ə-nənt) *adj.; eminently, adv.* Above other persons, especially in one's own field or profession; distinguished.–The science club invited an *eminent* scientist to be its guest speaker.

e•mo•tion (ee- *or* i-MOH-shən) *n. emotions.* A feeling such as anger, joy, love, or fear.–Mary is a person of strong *emotions.* She feels things deeply.

em•per•or (EM-per-er) *n. emperors.* The ruler or head of the government in an empire.

em•pha•sis (EM-fə-siss) *n.* 1. Force; stress; accent.–To put *emphasis* on a syllable of a word, you make it stand out by saying it a little more loudly than the other syllables. You accent it.
2. Special importance; stress.–The teacher put *emphasis* on learning the multiplication tables. She told the students how important it is to learn them.

em•pha•size (EM-fə-syz) *v. emphasizes, emphasized, emphasizing.* Give emphasis to; stress as important.–The teacher *emphasized* our learning the multiplication tables. –He *emphasized* the word "not."

em•phat•ic (em-FAT-ik) *adj.; emphatically, adv.* Strong; decisive; forceful; striking.–Tom gave an *emphatic* answer to the question.–The *emphatic* applause pleased the actors.

em·pire (EM-pyr) *n. empires.* A group of countries or states ruled by one government or one person.–The ancient Roman *Empire* was ruled for a time by the Caesars. It consisted of many conquered nations and peoples.

em·ploy (em-PLOI) *n.* Paid service.–At that time I was a maid in her *employ.*
–*v. employs, employed, employing.* 1. Hire and pay for working.–Automobile factories *employ* many men.
2. Use.–*Employ* the skills you have learned in playing this game.

em·ploy·ee (em-PLOI-ee *or* em-ploi-EE) *n. employees.* A person who works for pay for some other person or company.–The teacher is an *employee* of the city school system.

em·ploy·er (em-PLOI-er) *n. employers.* A person who hires others to work for him.–The man who hired Father, who gave him a job and pays him for working, is his *employer.*

emp·ty (EMP-tee) *v. empties, emptied, emptying.* Take everything out of.–I will *empty* the basket for you.
–*adj.* Having nothing in it.–The box is *empty.* It has nothing in it.

en·a·ble (in-AY-bəl) *v. enables, enabled, enabling.* Make (a person, animal, or thing) able to do something.–The boy's ability to swim *enabled* him to get to shore safely.

en·am·el (in-AM-əl) *n. enamels.* 1. A hard, shiny paint or other coating.–Some of Mother's pots and pans are *enamel*ware.–Father painted the walls of the kitchen with green paint and the woodwork with white *enamel.*
2. The hard outer covering of the teeth.
–*v. enamels, enameled, enameling.* Paint or cover with a hard, glossy coating or with a paint called enamel.–Father *enameled* the woodwork in white.

en·chant (in-CHANT) *v. enchants, enchanted, enchanting.* 1. Fill with delight and wonder.–The clowns at the circus *enchant* the children.
2. Cast a spell on by a magic charm.–The white deer was a princess whom a jealous fairy had *enchanted.*

en·cir·cle (in-SER-kəl) *v. encircles, encircled, encircling.* Surround; make a ring around.–The house was *encircled* by large maple trees.–The children *encircled* the May Queen's head with white clover.

en·close (in-KLOHZ) *v. encloses, enclosed, enclosing.* 1. Put inside something.–Bob wrote Grandfather a letter, and Mother *enclosed* it in the envelope with hers.
2. Close up; shut in by surrounding with walls, a fence, etc.–Father *enclosed* our front porch with windows and screens to make a sun room.
–*enclosure, n. enclosures.*

en·coun·ter (in-KOWN-ter) *n. encounters.* 1. A coming up against something; a meeting.–The farmer had an *encounter* with the bees while trying to get the honeycombs.
2. A battle.–The Battle of Gettysburg was a fierce *encounter.*
–*v. encounters, encountered, encountering.* Meet; come up against.–The men *encountered* trouble in digging the ditch. They struck rocks, and had much rain.

en·cour·age (in-KER-ij) *v. encourages, encouraged, encouraging.* 1. Give hope to; cheer; make eager to go on.–The doctor *encouraged* the sick man by telling him that he would be well in a few days.
2. Speak or work in favor of something.–The owner of the factory *encouraged* the men to build homes near it.

en·cy·clo·pe·di·a or **en·cy·clo·pae·di·a** (in-sy-klə-PEE-dee-ə *or* in-sy-kloh-PEE-dee-ə) *n. encyclopedias* or *encyclopaedias.* A book or a set of books that tells many facts about many things. To help you find things easily, the subjects in an *encyclopedia* are put in alphabetical order just like the words in a dictionary.–Bob looked up tropical fish in the *encyclopedia* to give the class a report about them.

end (END) *n. ends.* 1. The last part.–At the *end* of the story, Red Riding Hood's grandmother jumps out of the wolf's stomach, safe and sound.
2. The tip, edge, or side of a thing, where it stops or starts.–In my pencil, one *end* has lead in it and the other has an eraser on it.–A little table stands at the *end* of the sofa.
3. Goal; purpose.–Ed wanted money for his photography. With this *end* in view, he became a newsboy.
–*v. ends, ended, ending.* Finish.–The ball game has *ended.*

en·deav·or (in-DEV-er) *n. endeavors.* An undertaking; an effort.–Building a bridge is a big *endeavor.* It is a big thing to try to do.
–*v. endeavors, endeavored, endeavoring.* Try; make an effort.–John will *endeavor* to get his story written today.

end•ing (END-ing) *n. endings.* The last part. — Alice likes stories that have sad *endings.* –*v.* One form of the verb *end.*–The day is *ending.*

end•less (END-ləss) *adj.; endlessly, adv.* 1. Going on forever; never coming to a finish or a stop.–The lesson was so long that it seemed *endless.*
2. Without ends.–A circle is *endless* because it has no ends; it meets itself everywhere.

en•dorse (in-DORSS) *v. endorses, endorsed, endorsing.* 1. Sign one's name on the back of a note, bill, or document, as on the back of a check.–The lawyer asked his client to *endorse* his contract.
2. Show approval; give support to.–Famous people are often paid to *endorse* products for advertising purposes.

en•dow (in-DOW) *v. endows, endowed, endowing.* 1. Make (a person) rich.–Snow White was *endowed* by nature with great beauty.
2. Give money or property to an institution. –The wealthy art lover *endowed* the museum with a collection of valuable paintings.
3. Set up a permanent fund.–Mr. Cornell *endowed* a university. He arranged to have money given to the university every year.

en•dur•ance (in-DOOR-ənss *or* in-DYOOR-ənss) *n.* 1. Ability to stand something.–The boy who had been sick didn't have much *endurance.* He didn't have the strength to do anything without soon becoming tired.
2. Quality of wearing well.–Cheap shoes do not have the *endurance* of better shoes.

en•dure (in-DOOR *or* -DYOOR) *v. endures, endured, enduring.* 1. Undergo; stand.–The men traveling through the forest *endured* many hardships.
2. Last.–President Lincoln said the Civil War tested whether this nation could long *endure.*

en•e•my (EN-ə-mee) *n. enemies.* Someone or something that works against one or fights one.–Laziness is the boy's greatest *enemy.* It keeps him from doing many things he could do.–Lions and tigers are great *enemies* of other jungle animals. They kill and eat other animals.

en•er•gy (EN-er-gee) *n. energies.* A strong desire to do things; the strength to do things. –The children have so much *energy* that it keeps their teacher busy planning work for them.

en•force (in-FORSS) *v. enforces, enforced, enforcing.* See that a program, law, etc., is carried out or kept.–The police *enforce* the laws of the city. They see that the laws are obeyed.
–*enforcement, n. enforcements.*

en•gage (in-GAYJ) *v. engages, engaged, engaging.* 1. Hire.–During the harvest season, Grandfather *engages* more men to work for him.
2. Be doing; be in the act of; be busy at.–Sally was *engaged* in feeding the ants sugar when Mother called her.
3. Promise to marry.–Mother was *engaged* to Father for a whole year before they were married.

en•gage•ment (in-GAYJ-mənt) *n. engagements.* 1. An appointment.–Mother has an *engagement* with Bob's teacher. She has agreed to meet her at a certain time and place.
2. A promise to be married.–The girl told us of her *engagement* to the soldier.
3. A battle.–The armies met in a fierce *engagement.*

en•gine (EN-jən) *n. engines.* 1. A machine that makes power which will make other machinery work.–Our car has a gasoline *engine.*
2. A locomotive.–An *engine* can pull a long train of railroad cars.

en•gi•neer (en-jə-NIR) *n. engineers.* 1. A man who takes care of engines and makes them go.–Uncle Jim is a railroad *engineer.*
2. A man who designs and builds bridges, railroads, tunnels, and the like.–My uncle is an *engineer.*
–*v. engineers, engineered, engineering.* Manage; take charge of.–Bob likes to *engineer* all our school affairs.

en•grave (in-GRAYV) *v. engraves, engraved, engraving.* Carve markings on or into.–The boys *engraved* their names on the tree so that they could come back and find them there in ten years.

en•joy (in-JOI) *v. enjoys, enjoyed, enjoying.* 1. Find pleasure in; like. — We *enjoy* swimming, singing, and playing games.
2. Have the benefit or use of.—The old couple *enjoys* a steady income.
—*Enjoy oneself* means have a good time.—He *enjoyed himself* at the circus.

en•joy•a•ble (in-JOI-ə-bəl) *adj.; enjoyably, adv.* Happy; pleasant; delightful.—We had a very *enjoyable* time at the party.

en•joy•ment (in-JOI-mənt) *n. enjoyments.* Pleasure; joy; happiness.—Father gets much *enjoyment* from inventing things.

en•large (in-LAHRJ) *v. enlarges, enlarged, enlarging.* Make bigger.—Mother ordered the picture of the children *enlarged*, so she could frame it.—Father is going to have the house *enlarged* so he can have a workroom.

en•list (in-LIST) *v. enlists, enlisted, enlisting.* 1. Join; enroll.—Bob *enlisted* in the army.
2. Get the help of.—We *enlisted* the teacher's help in preparing our play.

e•nor•mous (i-NOR-məss) *adj.; enormously, adv.* Very big; much bigger than usual.—A man who weighs three hundred pounds is *enormous*.—Elephants are *enormous*.

e•nough (ee- *or* ə-NUF) *n., adj.,* and *adv.* As many or as much as needed. — Will twelve apples be *enough?* — Bob didn't run fast *enough*, so he lost the race.—I have *enough*, thank you. I do not need any more.

en•rage (in-RAYJ) *v. enrages, enraged, enraging.* Make angry.—The boys *enraged* the lion by throwing sticks at him.

en•roll (in-ROHL) *v. enrolls, enrolled, enrolling.* 1. Become a member.—Bob has *enrolled* in a Sunday school class.
2. Record on a list of membership. — Our teacher will *enroll* you in our class. She will write your name in a list or roll with the names of the other children.

en•sign (EN-sən) *n. ensigns.* An officer in the navy whose rank is the same as a second lieutenant in the army.

en•tan•gle (in-TANG-gəl) *v. entangles, entangled, entangling.* 1. Wind or mix up in.—The kitten became *entangled* in Grandmother's ball of yarn.
2. Include; make mixed up in.—The boys tried to *entangle* Bob in the trouble they had on the ball field.

en•ter (EN-ter) *v. enters, entered, entering.* 1. Go or come into.—The children *entered* the school room.
2. Record.—The teacher will *enter* your name in her roll book.
3. Become a member of.—My sister will *enter* high school this fall.
4. Cause to join.—His parents have *entered* him in a new school.

en•ter•prise (EN-ter-pryz) *n. enterprises.* 1. An undertaking or project, especially one that requires strength, courage, or energy for its success. — Father is involved in a new *enterprise*. He is going to Africa to capture lions for our zoo.
2. Determination; energy; imagination; readiness to undertake something difficult. —The pioneers showed great *enterprise* in conquering the wilderness.

en•ter•tain (en-ter-TAYN) *v. entertains, entertained, entertaining.* 1. Amuse in any way. —The children gave a play to *entertain* their parents.
2. Have as a guest. — We *entertained* the Smiths for dinner.
3. Have guests.—The Browns are *entertaining* tonight.
4. Consider.—I would never *entertain* such a thought!

en•ter•tain•ment (en-ter-TAYN-mənt) *n. entertainments.* 1. Anything that pleases, interests, or makes fun.—Reading books, watching animals at the zoo, listening to the radio, going to motion pictures, and talking to interesting people are different kinds of *entertainment*.
2. A public performance to give pleasure.— The *entertainment* at the school assembly was a puppet show.

en•thu•si•asm (in-THOOZ-ee-az-əm *or* en-THYOOZ-ee-azm) *n. enthusiasms.* Excited interest.—Bob has great *enthusiasm* for baseball.

en•thu•si•as•tic (in-thoo-zee-ASS-tik *or* en-thyoo-zee-ASS-tik) *adj.; enthusiastically, adv.* Full of eager interest; much pleased.—Bob is very *enthusiastic* about his new bicycle.

en•tire (in-TYR) *adj.; entirely, adv.* Whole; complete.—The hungry man ate an *entire* pie. —We expect to paint the *entire* house.

en•ti•tle (in-TY-təl) *v. entitles, entitled, entitling.* 1. Give the right or privilege. — The children are *entitled* to take books from the library.
2. Name; give a title.—The author *entitled* his story "The Black Witch."

en•trance (EN-trənss) *n. entrances.* 1. Door; place through which people pass to and from a building or house. – The teacher walked out of the front *entrance* of the school.

2. A coming in; an entering. – The clown's *entrance* into the ring made the children laugh.
3. A beginning; becoming a member of.–The man's *entrance* into the army surprised his family.
–(en-TRANSS) *v. entrances, entranced, entrancing.* Delight; fill with joy.–The puppet ballet *entranced* the children.

en•try (EN-tree) *n. entries.* 1. A passage or hallway through which people pass when entering or leaving a building.
2. A coming in; entering. – The musician's *entry* was a signal for all to be quiet.

e•nun•ci•ate (i-NUN-see-ayt) *v. enunciates, enunciated, enunciating.* 1. Say or pronounce words. – Please *enunciate* carefully so that you may be understood.
2. State, declare, or announce formally.–The government *enunciated* its new foreign policy.

en•vel•op (en-VEL-əp) *v. envelops, enveloped, enveloping.* Wrap.–The box was *enveloped* in papers of many colors.

en•vel•ope (EN- *or* AHN-və-lohp) *n. envelopes.* A paper cover or holder used to put letters in when you send them through the mail.

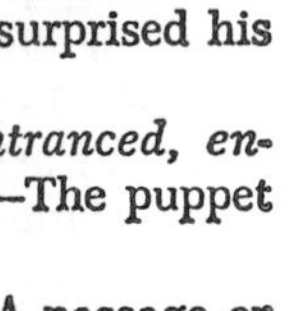

en•vi•ous (EN-vee-əss) *adj.; enviously, adv.* Wanting what another has.–Bob gets better marks in school than Bill does. Bill is *envious* of Bob. He wishes he could get marks as good as Bob's.–People with little money are often *envious* of those with much money.

en•vy (EN-vee) *n.* 1. Something which people wish they had.–Our new car is the *envy* of everyone on our street. Everyone wishes it were his.
2. The feeling of unhappiness or dislike caused by wanting something another has.–*Envy* sometimes makes people do things that are wrong.
–*v. envies, envied, envying.* Want what another has.–All the girls in the class *envy* Mary's dresses. They wish they had dresses like Mary's.

e•on (EE-ahn *or* -ən) *n. eons.* A very, very long period of time; an age.–Mankind has developed over a vast number of *eons.*

ep•i•dem•ic (ep-ə-DEM-ik) *n. epidemics.* Fast spreading of a disease to many people.–The schools will close if the *epidemic* of measles continues.

ep•i•sode (EP-ə-sohd) *n. episodes.* A connected, yet separate, event taking place within the normal course of events.–The hike was unexciting except for one *episode*: the time the rattlesnake crossed our path.

e•qual (EE-kwəl) *n. equals.* Like another in some respect.–John and Harry are *equals* in the classroom. The teacher is above them both. She can tell them what to do.–Harry is not John's *equal* in spelling this week. John got A; Harry got B.
–*v. equals, equaled, equaling.* Be of the same size, amount, worth, etc.–Five pennies *equal* one nickel.
–*adj.; equally, adv.* 1. Of the same size, worth, amount, etc. – Two pints are *equal* to one quart.–Our team is *equal* to its opponents.
2. Strong enough.–Father was so tired that he was not *equal* to walking very far.

e•qua•tor (ee-KWAY-ter) *n.* An imaginary circle around the earth halfway between the North Pole, or point farthest north on the earth, and the South Pole, or point farthest south on the earth. It is hot near the *equator.*

e•qui•lib•ri•um (ee-kwə-LIB-ree-əm) *n.* Balance; a state of even distribution between opposing forces, such as weights.–John lost his *equilibrium* when he stumbled. – The scales are not in *equilibrium.* One side is down and one side is up.

e•qui•nox (EE- *or* E-kwə-nahks) *n. equinoxes.* The moment the sun crosses the equator, occurring twice a year, about March 21 and September 23. There are the same number of hours of day as there are of night in every part of the world at the time of the *equinox.*

e•quip (i-KWIP) *v. equips, equipped, equipping.* Provide; furnish; fit out. – We must *equip* our workshop with new tools.

e•quip•ment (i-KWIP-mənt) *n.* The things with which anything is fitted out or furnished; things needed for certain uses.–The *equipment* of a factory includes machines and tools.

e·quiv·a·lent (i-KWIV-ə-lənt) *n. equivalents* and *adj.* Something equal in value, measure, meaning, force, etc., to something else.—Sixteen ounces is the *equivalent* of one pound.—"Can't" is the *equivalent* of "cannot." —Twelve inches is the *equivalent* of a foot.

e·rase (i-RAYSS) *v. erases, erased, erasing.* Rub out.—It is easier to *erase* pencil marks than ink marks.

e·ras·er (i-RAYSS-er) *n. erasers.* Anything used to rub out a mark, usually a spongy piece of rubber.—Many pencils have *erasers* on the ends.

ere (AIR) *conj.* and *prep.* Before.—*Ere* is used in old-fashioned verse and stories:

Ere day was done,
The fight was won.

e·rect (i-REKT) *v. erects, erected, erecting.* Build; set up.—The workmen will *erect* a house at the corner.—It took the men hours to *erect* the fallen telephone pole.
—*adj.* Straight; upright.—Soldiers stand *erect.*

e·rode (i-ROHD) *v. erodes, eroded, eroding.* Wear away; destroy by eating away.—Floods and rains have *eroded* the soil.—Even hard rock can be *eroded* by rain, wind, and the pounding of the sea.
—*erosion, n. erosions.*

err (AIR *or* ER) *v. errs, erred, erring.* Make a mistake.—Jack *erred* in believing that there would be no school on Friday. There was school on that day.

er·rand (AIR-ənd) *n. errands.* 1. A trip or journey taken to deliver a message or to do whatever you are sent to do.—Mary likes to run *errands* for the teacher during the arithmetic class.
2. A thing one goes to do.—Jack's *errand* was to buy a newspaper for Father.

er·ror (AIR-er) *n. errors.* A mistake.—John made one *error* in spelling; he made a mistake in spelling one word.

e·rupt (i-RUPT) *v. erupts, erupted, erupting.* Burst forth; break out.—The volcano *erupted* with smoke, fire, and molten lava.
—*eruption, n. eruptions.*

es·ca·la·tor (ESS-kə-lay-ter) *n. escalators.* A stairway built so that the stairs move up or down continuously. People are carried up or down simply by standing still on the moving stairs. Many department stores have *escalators* today.

es·cape (ə-SKAYP) *n. escapes.* Getting away, or the means used in getting away. A fire *escape* is a stairway on the side of a building, or a large metal tube big enough for a person to slide through to get out of a burning building.—The prisoner made his *escape* through a tunnel he had dug.

—*v. escapes, escaped, escaping.* 1. Get away from something; get out of; run away.—The man *escaped* from the burning building by climbing down a rope.
2. Avoid; not fall into.—All the children had the measles except Mary. She *escaped* having them.

Es·ki·mo (ESS-kə-moh) *n. Eskimos* and *adj.* One of a people who live in the northern part of North America. They are not very tall, and have a yellowish skin and straight black hair. Most of them live by hunting and fishing.

e·soph·a·gus (ee- *or* i-SAHF-ə-gəss) *n.* The passageway or tube leading from the back of the mouth to the stomach; the throat or gullet.

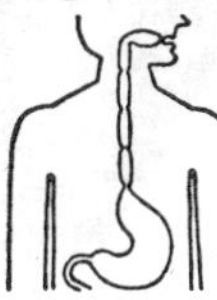

es·pe·cial (əss-PESH-əl) *adj.* Particular; outstanding; main.—Have you any *especial* reason for wanting to stay home?

es·pe·cial·ly (əss-PESH-əl-ee) *adv.* 1. Very; exceptionally. — Bob is *especially* good in spelling and arithmetic.
2. Particularly.—I *especially* like walnuts.

es·pi·o·nage (ESS-pee-ə-nahzh) *n.* Spying; the use of secret agents or spies.—Tom likes to read tales of *espionage.*

es·sen·tial (ə-SEN-shəl) *adj.; essentially, adv.; essential, n.* Necessary; needed.—Knowing the multiplication table is *essential* in working many arithmetic problems.—Wings are *essential* to airplanes.

es·tab·lish (ə-STAB-lish) *v. establishes, established, establishing.* 1. Set up; organize.—This church was *established* in 1890.
2. Settle.—Mr. Jones is well *established* in his new business. He is doing well.
3. Prove.—The suspect *established* the fact that he was in Boston when the store was robbed.

es·tab·lish·ment (əss-TAB-lish-mənt) *n. establishments.* 1. A church, school, store, house, or business organization set up for some purpose.
2. A setting up.—The *establishment* of colonies was an early step in the founding of the United States.

es·tate (əss-TAYT) *n. estates.* 1. A large piece of land with several buildings, used as a dwelling place.—That rich man has a large *estate* in the country.
2. One's entire property.—The old woman left her *estate* to a children's home.

es·ti·mate (ESS-tə-mət) *n. estimates.* Judgment; rough guess.—The agent gave us an *estimate* of how much our house would sell for. After he looked at it, he told us how much he thought it would sell for.
—(ESS-tə-mayt) *v. estimates, estimated, estimating.* Judge; guess at from what one can see.—It is hard to *estimate* the age of some people.—Bob *estimated* the height of the soldier to be six feet.

e·ter·nal (ee-TER-nəl) *adj.; eternally, adv.* Lasting forever.—The sky is *eternal.*—Mary said she was sick of the *eternal* rain. It seemed as if the rain would never stop.

e·ther (EE-ther) *n.* A drug used to make persons unconscious. Doctors often give *ether* to patients before an operation, so that the patients will feel no pain.

et·i·quette (ET-ə-ket) *n.* Manners that are expected of polite people.—It is good *etiquette* to thank people for gifts.—It is *etiquette* for boys and men to take off their hats when they go into a house.

Eu·rope (YUH-rəp) *n.; European, adj.* A continent that has more people than any other except Asia. France and Germany are two of the countries in *Europe. Europe* is divided from Asia by the Ural Mountains in Russia.

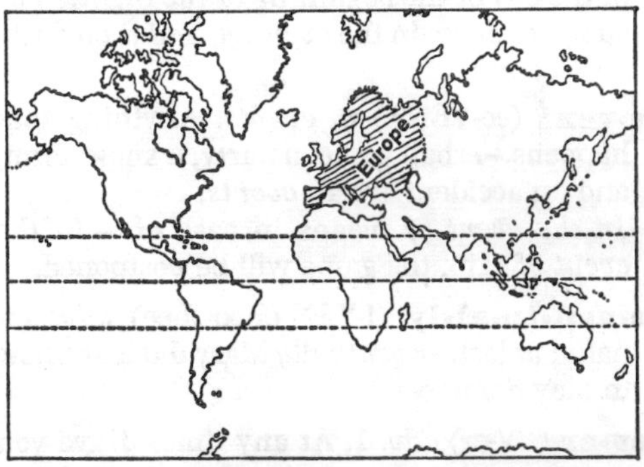

e·vade (i-VAYD) *v. evades, evaded, evading.* Dodge; avoid slyly.—The robber tried to *evade* the police by having his hair dyed. — Bill *evaded* answering the question by pretending he had not heard it.

e·val·u·ate (i-VAL-yoo-ayt) *v. evaluates, evaluated, evaluating.* Find out how much something is worth; determine the value of something.—The real estate man *evaluated* the property.
—*evaluation, n. evaluations.*

e·vap·o·rate (i-VAP-er-ayt) *v. evaporates, evaporated, evaporating.* Turn into vapor or steam.—If you boil water, it will *evaporate.* When the kettle boils dry, all the water has *evaporated.*
—*evaporation, n.*

eve (EEV) *n. eves.* 1. Evening.—It was a bitter winter's *eve.*
2. The day or evening before a special holiday.—December 25 is Christmas Day. December 24 is Christmas *Eve.*—December 31 is New Year's *Eve.*

e•ven (EE-vən) *v. evens, evened, evening.* Make equal or the same.–Bob's home run *evened* the score.–The dressmaker will *even* the hem of Mother's dress.
–*adj.; evenly, adv.* 1. Level.–Mother used an *even* cupful of flour in the cake.
2. Flat.–The ground is *even* along the river. It is not hilly or rough.
3. Regular.–The horse runs at an *even* pace. He runs at just about the same pace all the time.
4. The numbers 2, 4, 6, 8, 10, 12, 14, etc., are *even* numbers because they can be divided by two without any being left over.
–*adv.* Yet; still.–Mary spells well, but Bob spells better than Mary, and John spells *even* better than Bob.

eve•ning (EEV-ning) *n. evenings.* The end of the day or the beginning of the night.–The sun goes down in the *evening,* and then darkness comes.

e•vent (ee-VENT) *n. events.* Anything that happens.–A ball game, a party, a snowstorm, and an accident are all *events.*
–*In the event of* means in case of. – *In the event of* rain, the game will be postponed.

e•ven•tu•al•ly (i-VEN-choo-əl-ee) *adv.* Finally; at last.–*Eventually* Mary did learn how to play dominoes.

ev•er (EV-er) *adv.* 1. At any time.–Have you *ever* seen a bear?
2. Always.–That boy is *ever* ready to help.
3. By any chance; at all.–How did you *ever* manage to get away so early?
–*Ever so* means extremely or very.–I'm *ever so* grateful to you.

ev•er•green (EV-er-green) *n. evergreens.* A tree or plant that has green leaves all the year round. Pine trees and cedars are *evergreens.*

ev•er•y (EV-ree) *adj.* Each.–*Every* person in the class had a chance to talk.

ev•er•y•bod•y (EV-ree-bahd-ee) *pron.* Every person.–*Everybody* voted for Bob.

ev•er•y•day (ev-ree-DAY) *adj.* Happening or being used every day; not special.–My blue dress is my *everyday* dress.–Singing is an *everyday* event in our class.

ev•er•y•one (EV-ree-wun) *pron.* Each person.–Mary invited *everyone* in our class to her party.

ev•er•y•thing (EV-ree-thing) *pron.* All the things; each thing. – The house and *everything* in it burned down.

EVERGREENS

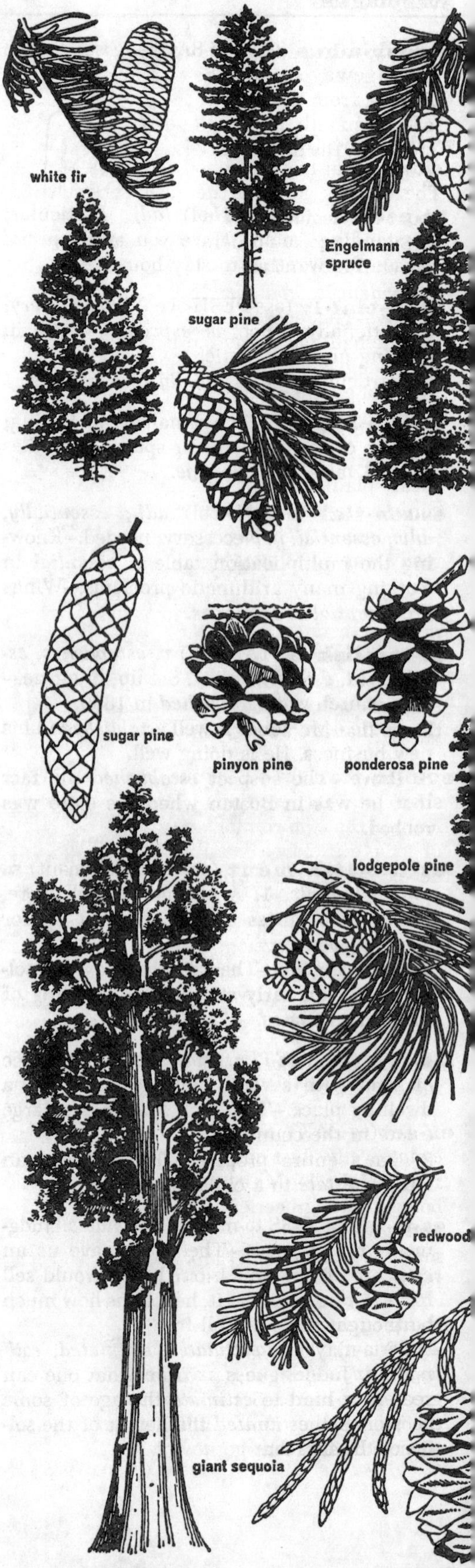

ev•er•y•where (EV-ree-hwair) *adv.* In every place; in all places.–The sun shines *everywhere.*

ev•i•dence (EV-ə-dənss) *n. evidences.* 1. A clue to what has happened or to what is so.–The witness gave all the *evidence* he could about the accident. He told what he knew.
2. Signs; proof. – There were *evidences* of jam on the boy's face.
–*v. evidences, evidenced, evidencing.* Show plainly.–The poor man's clothes *evidenced* that he had had many hardships.
–*In evidence* means showing very plainly.–The bad effects of the war were *in evidence* everywhere.

ev•i•dent (EV-ə-dənt) *adj.; evidently, adv.* Clear; plain; obvious; without possibility of confusion.–The facts in the case are *evident.* –She agreed to go, but it was *evident* that she really wanted to stay home.

e•vil (EE-vəl) *n. evils.* Wrongdoing; wickedness.–Selfishness has always been an *evil* of human nature.
–*adj.; evilly, adv.* Bad; harmful; wrong.–An *evil* person is one who has bad thoughts, does things that are wrong, and hurts feelings.

ev•o•lu•tion (ev-ə-LOO-shən *or* ev-ə-LYOO-shən) *n.* By studying fossils, scientists learned that the complex animals and plants of today developed from earlier forms. This development is called *evolution.*

e•volve (i-VAHLV) *v. evolves, evolved, evolving.* Gradually develop.–After discussing the problem for some time, the boys finally *evolved* a plan that was acceptable to everyone in the class.

ewe (YOO) *n. ewes.* A female or mother sheep.

ex•act (eg-ZAKT) *adj.; exactly, adv.* Just correct; right. – Mary bought the groceries and gave the groceryman the *exact* change for them.

ex•ag•ger•ate (eg-ZAJ-er-ayt) *v. exaggerates, exaggerated, exaggerating.* Add to; make bigger, worse, greater, or more.–Some children *exaggerate* the stories they tell. – Bill *exaggerated* the size of the fish that got away.

ex•am•i•na•tion (eg-zam-ə-NAY-shən) *n. examinations.* 1. A test. – Mary passed her spelling *examination.*
2. An inspection; a careful looking over.–The dentist made an *examination* of Bobby's teeth.

ex•am•ine (eg-ZAM-ən) *v. examines, examined, examining.* 1. Look at carefully; inspect.–The teacher *examined* the children's hands to see if they were clean.
2. Question. – The judge will *examine* the witness.

ex•am•ple (eg-ZAM-pəl) *n. examples.* 1. A model.–Bob's drawing was put on the board as an *example* of the work the class was doing.
2. A problem. – John could not work the second *example* in the arithmetic lesson.

ex•ca•vate (EKS-kə-vayt) *v. excavates, excavated, excavating.* 1. Dig; hollow out.–The workmen are *excavating* a tunnel.
2. Uncover by digging out; remove the earth and whatever else lies over something.–The members of the expedition *excavated* an ancient tomb.
3. Scoop out; dig and remove earth and rocks.–Steam shovels are used for *excavating.*
–*excavation, n. excavations.*

ex•ceed (ek-SEED) *v. exceeds, exceeded, exceeding.* Be greater than; go more than.–Automobile drivers should not *exceed* the speed limit. They should not go faster than the law allows.

ex•ceed•ing•ly (ek-SEED-ing-lee) *adv.* Very. –It is *exceedingly* warm today.

ex•cel (ek-SEL) *v. excels, excelled, excelling.* 1. Do better than.–Bob *excels* the others in his class in reading. He is better in reading than all the others.
2. Be outstanding.–Bob *excels* in reading.

ex•cel•lent (EKS-ə-lənt) *adj.; excellently, adv.; excellence, n.* Very good.–The teacher said that the children did *excellent* work.

ex•cept (ek-SEPT) *prep.* But.–John worked all the problems *except* the third one.

ex·cep·tion (ek-SEP-shən) *n. exceptions.* One left out; a different one.—The men work every day of the week except Sunday. Sunday is the *exception.*

—*Take exception* means object.—He liked the plan, but *took exception* to its timing.

ex·cess (ek-SESS) *n. excesses.* 1. More than is needed, required, or measured. — Mother had more than enough flour with which to bake the cake. She used the *excess* to make some cookies.

2. Going beyond normal limits, in such things as eating or playing.—If you eat candy to *excess,* you will probably get sick.

—(EK-sess) *adj.* Extra.—Mother used the *excess* dough for cookies.

ex·change (eks-CHAYNJ) *n. exchanges.* The central telephone office.—Mother called the telephone *exchange* to report that our neighbor's phone was out of order.

—*v. exchanges, exchanged, exchanging.* 1. Give back for another one. — Mary's shoes were too small, and she had to *exchange* them. She took them back to the store and got a larger size.

2. Trade; give back and forth.—The children *exchanged* trading cards.

ex·cite (ek-SYT) *v. excites, excited, exciting.* Awaken or stir up the feelings of (a person, etc.).—The teacher *excited* the children by telling them that she would take them to the zoo. — The doctor told the boys that they shouldn't *excite* their sick friend.

ex·cite·ment (ek-SYT-mənt) *n. excitements.* Stirred-up or active feeling.—The fire engine caused much *excitement.*—In our *excitement* we forgot to lock the door.

ex·claim (eks-KLAYM) *v. exclaims, exclaimed, exclaiming.* Cry out; speak excitedly.—When the children saw the Christmas tree, they *exclaimed* joyously.

ex·cla·ma·tion (eks-klə-MAY-shən) *n. exclamations.* A sudden cry uttered in surprise, pain, anger, etc. Help! Ouch! Oh! Hurrah! Say! Hey! and similar expressions are cries of *exclamation.*

—An *exclamation mark* [!] is a mark of punctuation placed after an exclamation, as in the examples above.

ex·cur·sion (eks-KER-zhən) *n. excursions.* A special trip taken by a group, usually for fun.—Our class is going to go on an *excursion* to the lake on the last day of school.—Last week we went on an *excursion* to the dairy to learn about making butter.

ex·cuse (eks-KYOOSS) *n. excuses.* A reason or explanation of why one has done something wrong.—If you are absent from school, you must have an *excuse.*

ex·cuse (eks-KYOOZ) *v. excuses, excused, excusing.* 1. Dismiss; let go.—The teacher will *excuse* us from school at two o'clock so we can go to the ball game.

2. Pardon; forgive. — The teacher *excused* Jack's bad manners because he was sick.

ex·e·cute (EKS-ə-kyoot) *v. executes, executed, executing.* 1. Do; perform; carry out. —The soldiers *executed* their orders.

2. Produce according to a plan or design.—The sculptor says the monument will be *executed* in bronze.

3. Put into effect, especially by legally fulfilling all necessary requirements, such as the signing of documents.—The lawyer will *execute* the dead man's will.

4. Put to death in the manner ordered by a judge or in accordance with the law.—The killer will be *executed* in the morning.

ex·ec·u·tive (eg-ZEK-yə-tiv) *n. executives* and *adj.* A manager; one who gives orders.—Father is an *executive* in the factory. He holds an *executive* position.

ex·er·cise (EKS-er-syz) *n. exercises.* 1. Activity that builds strength or skill. After Billy's

broken arm had healed, he had to do several *exercises* to make the muscles strong again. —Marjorie had *exercises* to practice on the piano.

2. A ceremony.—We went to the graduation

exercises when Mary's brother finished high school.
–*v. exercises, exercised, exercising.* 1. Use; apply.–The teacher told Jack to *exercise* more care in writing his lesson.
2. Do a thing again and again so as to make stronger and more skillful.–Mary plays the scales on the piano to *exercise* her fingers.

ex•hale (eks-HAYL) *v. exhales, exhaled, exhaling.* Breathe out. When you breathe air into your lungs, you inhale; when you breathe out air, you *exhale.*

ex•haust (eg-ZAWST) *n. exhausts.* Fumes from burnt gasoline and oil.–The *exhaust* from the car quickly filled the garage.
–*v. exhausts, exhausted, exhausting.* 1. Tire; wear out.–The race *exhausted* the boys.
2. Use up.–When the Boy Scouts had *exhausted* all their matches, they started a fire by rubbing two sticks together.
3. Blow out; give out.–The fumes from burnt gasoline are *exhausted* from a motor through a pipe.

ex•hib•it (eg-ZIB-ət) *n. exhibits.* A showing. –Each year our class has an art *exhibit.*

–*v. exhibits, exhibited, exhibiting.* Show; display.–This year Mary *exhibited* a basket she had made.

ex•hi•bi•tion (eks-ə-BISH-ən) *n. exhibitions.* A showing.–We had an *exhibition* of model airplanes at the school.

ex•ile (EG-zyl *or* EK-syl) *n. exiles.* 1. A person who is sent away from his native country.–The *exile* was lonely in the strange land.
2. State of being sent away; banishment.–The traitor was in *exile* for life.
–*v. exiles, exiled, exiling.* Send away as punishment. – The traitor was *exiled* from the country for life.

ex•ist (eg-ZIST) *v. exists, existed, existing.* 1. Live; keep alive.–The lost sailors *existed* for days without food or water.
2. Be; have reality. – Ghosts do not *exist.* They are not real.
3. Remain.–This cave has *existed* for as long as Grandfather can remember.

ex•ist•ence (eg-ZISS-tənss) *n. existences.* 1. Being; state of being real.–Some people believe in the *existence* of fairies.
2. Life; way of living.–The old lady led a peaceful *existence.*

ex•it (EKS- *or* EGZ-it) *n. exits.* 1. A way or door that takes one out of a building.–We left the church by the side *exit.*
2. Going out, especially leaving a stage after an appearance in a play. – There was great applause as Mary made her *exit* from the stage.

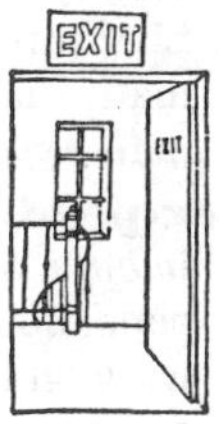

ex•pand (eks-PAND) *v. expands, expanded, expanding.* 1. Grow larger; spread out.–Yeast makes bread dough *expand.*
2. Make larger. – The storekeeper will *expand* his business.
–*expansion, n. expansions.*

ex•pect (eks-PEKT) *v. expects, expected, expecting.* 1. Look for; await.–We *expect* a letter from Mother every day.
2. Feel sure. – We *expect* that it will rain today.

ex•pec•ta•tion (eks-pek-TAY-shən) *n. expectations.* 1. Something expected.–Getting a watch for Christmas was Mary's one *expectation.*
2. Excitement of expecting, or looking forward to something.–Mary was full of *expectation.*

ex•pe•di•tion (eks-pə-DISH-ən) *n. expeditions.* 1. A trip for a particular purpose, such as discovery, war, or exploration.–Admiral Byrd went on many long *expeditions.*
2. A group of people traveling together.–The museum sent an *expedition* to the unknown jungle.

ex•pel (eks-PEL) *v. expels, expelled, expelling.* Put out; force or drive out.–When a bullet is *expelled* from a gun, it is going so fast that you cannot see it.–Jack was *expelled* from school because he would not obey the rules.

ex•pense (eks-PENSS) *n. expenses.* Cost; amount spent. – The *expense* of buying a home did not keep us from buying one.

ex•pen•sive (eks-PEN-siv) *adj.; expensively, adv.* High-priced. – Mother wanted the dress, but it was too *expensive.* It cost too much.

ex·pe·ri·ence (eks-PIR-ee-ənss) *n. experiences.* 1. Anything that happens to one.–Going to the circus was a new *experience* for Sally.
2. Practice.–Father has had much *experience* driving cars.
–*v. experiences, experienced, experiencing.* Live through; have. – We have *experienced* many happy times together.–The wounded man *experienced* much pain.

ex·per·i·ment (eks-PAIR-ə-mənt) *n. experiments.* A trial or testing to see what will happen.–Bob made an *experiment* with a wider wing on his model airplane.
–*v. experiments, experimented, experimenting.* Try out; do something to see what will happen. – Bob *experimented* with a wider wing on his model airplane.

ex·per·i·men·tal (eks-pair-ə-MEN-təl) *adj.; experimentally, adv.* 1. Based on, or having to do with, trials, tests, or experiments.–Psychology and chemistry are *experimental* sciences.
2. Used for experiments or tests.–The auto manufacturer built an *experimental* car.

ex·pert (EKS-pert) *n. experts.* A person who does something very well.–Father is an *expert* at driving a car.
–(eks-PERT *or* EKS-pert) *adj.* Highly skilled.–Father is an *expert* driver.

ex·pire (eks-PYR) *v. expires, expired, expiring.* 1. Become worthless; lose force; die.–The automobile license *expires* on January 1. After January 1 it will not be valid.
2. Breathe out.–Air *expired* from the lungs has lost its oxygen.

ex·plain (eks-PLAYN) *v. explains, explained, explaining.* 1. Tell about; make clear.–The teacher will *explain* the problem. She will try to help us understand it.
2. Tell the meaning of.–Bob *explained* the word.
3. Teach; tell.–Mother will *explain* to you how to make a bow knot.

ex·pla·na·tion (eks-plə-NAY-shən) *n. explanations.* Act of explaining, or of telling what something means or shows.–Bob's absence needed no *explanation.* Mother knew he was playing ball because his ball and bat were missing from the back porch.–Father's *explanation* of the word made its meaning clear to us.

ex·plode (eks-PLOHD) *v. explodes, exploded, exploding.* Blow up.–The lighted firecracker *exploded* with a bang.–The boy blew so much air into the balloon that it *exploded.*

ex·plore (eks-PLOR) *v. explores, explored, exploring.* 1. Travel through newly found land or land that is little known.–Admiral Byrd *explored* the region of the South Pole.
2. Examine to find something new, or out of curiosity; study.–The boys *explored* the old railroad bridge.–The committee *explored* the possibility of having a real Indian speak to the class.

ex·plor·er (eks-PLOR-er) *n. explorers.* A person who travels to find something new.–The *explorers* traveled through deep jungle, looking for the source of the river.

ex·plo·sion (eks-PLOH-zhən) *n. explosions.* A blowing up.–We heard the *explosion* of the dynamite among the rocks.

ex·port (EKS-port) *n. exports.* Something sent out of one country to be sold in another. –Automobiles are one of our most important *exports.*
–(EKS-port *or* eks-PORT) *v. exports, exported, exporting.* Send out of the country to sell.–We *export* many automobiles.

ex·pose (eks-POHZ) *v. exposes, exposed, exposing.* 1. Lay open; leave uncovered; make known.–Wet clothes will soon dry if they are *exposed* to the sun and wind.–He *exposed* the secret of the magic trick.
2. Bring into contact with.–John was *exposed* to scarlet fever, but he did not get it. –The film was *exposed* to light.

ex·po·si·tion (eks-pə-ZISH-ən) *n. expositions.* 1. A public exhibition, display, or show. –The company sent its products to the trade *exposition.*
2. A detailed explanation or discussion. –During the debate each speaker presented an *exposition* of his point of view to the audience.

ex·po·sure (eks-POH-zher) *n. exposures.* 1. Disclosing or making known for common knowledge.–*Exposure* of all the facts proved the prisoner's innocence.
2. Outlook.–The windows have a northern *exposure.*
3. Lack of protection from the weather. –The man was suffering from *exposure* after spending the night in the cold woods.
4. The process of letting light contact a photographic film.–The picture was spoiled because of too long an *exposure.*
5. The section of film used for a single picture.–The roll has enough film for eight *exposures.*

ex·press (eks-PRESS) *n.* A way of sending things.–Packages can be sent from town to town by parcel post or by *express.*
–*v. expresses, expressed, expressing.* Say, tell, or reveal in words, movements, etc.–It is hard for some people to *express* themselves. It is hard for some people to say what they want to say.–Baby *expresses* her wants through waving her hands or by crying.

ex·pres·sion (eks-PRESH-ən) *n. expressions.* 1. Way of speaking, telling, reading, etc.–Mary reads with good *expression.* She makes the meaning clear by putting force on the right words.
2. A saying, or a particular way of saying something.–"We learn to do by doing" is an old *expression.* – "That's nothing" is an *expression* Jack uses when somebody praises him for something he has done.
3. The look on a person's face.–The old man said nothing, but his *expression* was sad.

ex·tend (eks-TEND) *v. extends, extended, extending.* 1. Hold out.–The blind man *extended* his cup for pennies.
2. Spread out; go as far as.–Grandfather's farm *extends* to the corner.
3. Make longer.–The city will *extend* the bus line several miles out.
4. Offer.–We *extended* our best wishes to our teacher on her birthday.

ex·te·ri·or (eks-TIR-ee-er) *n. exteriors* and *adj.* Outside.–The man painted the *exterior* of his house.

ex·ter·nal (eks-TER-nəl) *adj.; externally, adv.* Exterior; outside.–This medicine is for *external* use only. It should be rubbed on the skin, not swallowed.

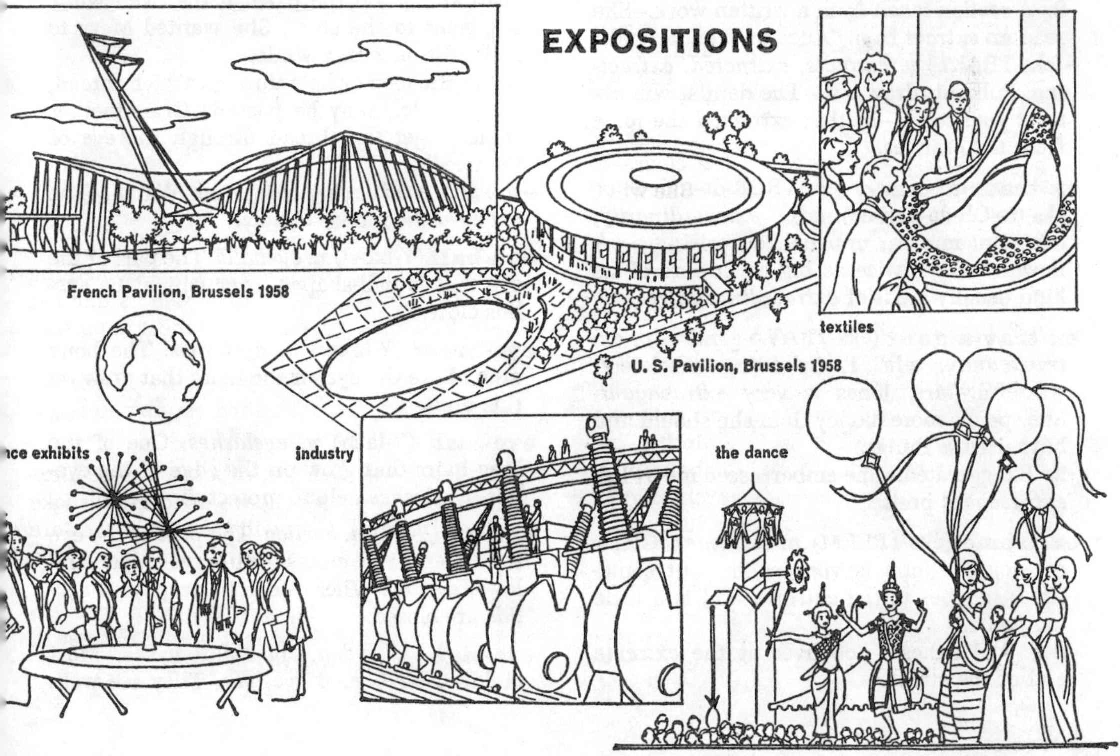

ex·tinct (eks-TINGKT) *adj.* 1. No longer in existence, like a species of plant or animal that has died out with not a single living one remaining.–The kiwi, a bird that cannot fly, is almost *extinct.* The dodo, another flightless bird, is *extinct.* There are no more living dodoes in all the world.
2. No longer working, having burned itself out.–The volcano became *extinct* many years ago. It never erupts anymore.

ex·tin·guish (eks-TING-gwish) *v. extinguishes, extinguished, extinguishing.* Put out (a light or fire).–At night we *extinguish* the light before going to bed.–The Boy Scouts *extinguished* the campfire.

ex·tol (iks-TOHL) *v. extols, extolled, extolling.* Glorify; praise highly.–The teacher *extolled* the boy who had won the national science competition.

ex·tra (EKS-trə) *n. extras.* Something in addition.–George bought a pencil for everyone in the class. He also bought several *extras.*
–*adj.* and *adv.* In addition; more than is needed; beyond the usual.–George bought a few *extra* pencils.–Mary received *extra* spending money for Christmas shopping.–Tom is *extra* tall. He is taller than most boys his age.

ex·tract (EKS-trakt) *n. extracts.* 1. A flavoring taken from fruits, vegetables, etc.–I like lemon and vanilla *extracts* in puddings.
2. A section taken from a written work.–She read an *extract* from "Alice in Wonderland."
–(eks-TRAKT) *v. extracts, extracted, extracting.* Pull out; draw out.–The dentist will *extract* your tooth.–Mother *extracted* the juice from the oranges.

ex·traor·di·nar·y (eks-TROR-də-nair-ee *or* eks-trə-OR-də-nair-ee) *adj.; extraordinarily, adv.* Uncommon; unusual; surprising. – A flower that is twice as big as flowers of its kind usually are is of *extraordinary* size.

ex·trav·a·gant (eks-TRAV-ə-gənt) *adj.; extravagantly, adv.* 1. Spending carelessly; wasteful.–Mrs. Jones is very *extravagant.* She spends more money than she should and buys useless things.
2. Exaggerated.–She embarrassed me by her *extravagant* praise.

ex·treme (eks-TREEM) *n. extremes.* Greatest degree.–John is very polite. But sometimes he goes to the *extreme* and is a little too polite.
–*adj.* 1. Farthest.–Bob lives at the *extreme* end of the street.
2. Belonging to either of the opposite ends of something; being at the limit.–I do not enjoy *extreme* weather. I do not like it when it is too cold or too hot.–The young woman wears *extreme* clothes. They are not in good taste, because they are too noticeable.

ex·treme·ly (eks-TREEM-lee) *adv.* Very; at or to the extreme.–It is *extremely* warm today.

eye (Y) *n. eyes.* 1. The part of any person or animal with which he sees.–We see with our *eyes.*

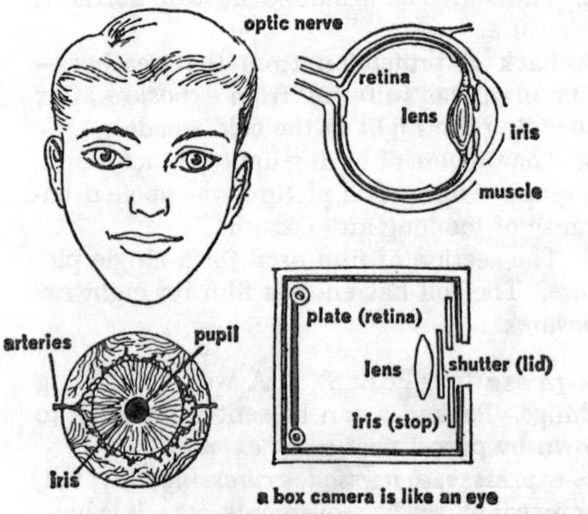

a box camera is like an eye

2. A lookout; watch.–Mother asked Mary to keep an *eye* on the cake in the oven while she went to the store. She wanted Mary to look at it once in a while.
3. A little loop or hole through which thread, a hook, etc., may be passed.–Grandmother couldn't get the thread through the *eye* of the needle.
–*v. eyes, eyed, eying* or *eyeing.* Watch.–The cat *eyed* the mouse closely.

eye·ball (Y-bawl) *n. eyeballs.* The part of the eye that is ball-shaped, over which the eyelids close.

eye·brow (Y-brow) *n. eyebrows.* The bony arch above the eye, or the hairs that grow on this arch.

eye·lash (Y-lash) *n. eyelashes.* One of the long hairs that grow on the edge of the eyelids. *Eyelashes* help to protect the eyeball.

eye·lid (Y-lid) *n. eyelids.* The part of the eye that opens and closes. You have upper and lower *eyelids.* When you are asleep, your *eyelids* are closed.

eye·sight (Y-syt) *n.* The ability to see.–Most children have good *eyesight.* They see well.

F f

F, f (EF) *n.* *F's, f's.* The sixth letter of the alphabet.

fa (FAH) *n.* The fourth tone on the scale in music. Do, re, mi, *fa*, sol, la, ti, do.

fa•ble (FAY-bəl) *n.* *fables.* A short story written to teach a lesson. Animals usually do the talking in *fables.* The story of "The Fox and the Grapes" is a *fable.*

fab•ric (FAB-rik) *n.* *fabrics.* Cloth.–Blankets are often made of a woolen *fabric.*–Some towels are made of a cotton *fabric,* and some of a linen *fabric.*

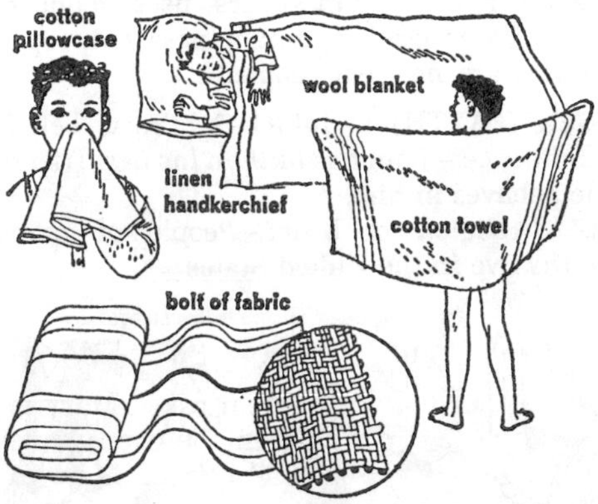

face (FAYSS) *n.* *faces.* 1. The front side of your head. Your chin, cheeks, nose, mouth, eyes, and forehead form your *face.*

2. The front, or the most important side, of anything; the surface.–The *face* of a watch is the side which shows the time. –The *face* of a building is the front.

3. Expression of the face.–The clowns made funny *faces* at the children.
–*v.* *faces, faced, facing.* 1. Look toward.–The house *faces* the north. The front of the house is toward the north.–The teacher asked the children to *face* the front of the room.
2. Meet with courage.–Ellen found it hard to *face* her brother after she lost his favorite ball.

fact (FAKT) *n.* *facts.* A thing that is true.–The man told all the *facts* of the accident. He told exactly how each thing happened.–It is a *fact* that Christmas comes on December 25.

fac•to•ry (FAK-tə-ree *or* FAK-tree) *n.* *factories.* A building where things are made.–Automobiles are made in *factories.*

fac•ul•ty (FAK-əl-tee) *n.* *faculties.* 1. A natural ability to do something; talent.–Monkeys have a *faculty* for climbing.
2. One of the physical powers of the body, such as sight or hearing.–The old man is deaf. He has lost the *faculty* of hearing.
3. The teaching staff of a school or college. –He was appointed to the Harvard College *faculty* as a professor of history.

fade (FAYD) *v.* *fades, faded, fading.* 1. Become less bright or less strong; grow fainter. –Sunlight often makes bright colors *fade.* –As they drove away, the dog's cries *faded.*
2. Wither and die.–Flowers *fade.*

Fahr•en•heit (FAR-ən-hyt) *adj.* According to, or concerned with, the scale of measurement on a thermometer whose freezing point is 32° above zero and whose boiling point is 212° above zero.

fail (FAYL) *v.* *fails, failed, failing.* 1. Not succeed.–Study hard or you are likely to *fail.*
2. Leave; not support or help.–The man's courage *failed* him when he met the tiger.
3. Get weak; grow worse. – The sick man seemed to be *failing,* and then he suddenly improved.
4. Disappoint.–The newsboy *failed* us. He did not bring the newspaper.

fail·ure (FAYL-yer) *n. failures.* 1. An event, a happening, or an effort that is not a success.—The party was a *failure* because nobody came.—After one *failure* to solve the problem, Bob tried again.
2. A person who does not succeed in life.—The old tramp was a *failure.*

faint (FAYNT) *v. faints, fainted, fainting.* Fall suddenly into unconsciousness because of sickness, shock, or other disturbance to the body.—Hunger caused the old man to *faint.*
—*adj.; faintly, adv.* 1. As if about to faint.—The heavy air in the sickroom made me feel *faint.*
2. Weak; not clear or strong in sound, looks, taste, etc.—The knock on the door was *faint.*
—The writing on the board was *faint.*

fair (FAIR) *n. fairs.* A big sale of things brought by the people who have made, grown, or prepared them.—The ladies of our church had a *fair.* They showed and sold handwork, baked goods, canned fruit, and many other things.—We went to the state *fair* and saw horses, cattle, machinery, farm products, and needlework.
—*adj. fairer, fairest; fairness, n.* 1. Honest; just.—The boy is always *fair* in playing games. He does not cheat.—An umpire must be *fair* to both sides.
2. Light.—Some people have *fair* skin and hair, and some have dark.
3. Not very bad and not very good, but just in between.—Bob got a good mark in arithmetic, but his mark in spelling was just *fair.*
4. Clear; sunny.—This is a *fair* day. The sky is clear.
5. Beautiful.—The prince loved the *fair* Cinderella.

fair·ly (FAIR-lee) *adv.* 1. Quite.—Bob gets *fairly* good marks in history. They are not too good and not too bad.
2. According to the proper rules; honestly; justly.—She distributed the prizes *fairly.*

fair·y (FAIR-ee) *n. fairies.* A small, imaginary person who, in stories, uses magic to bring happiness or unhappiness to people. *Fairies* are not real people.

faith (FAYTH) *n. faiths.* 1. Trust; belief; confidence.—John has *faith* in his new friend. He believes in him.
2. A religion or belief.—People of many *faiths* live in the United States.

faith•ful (FAYTH-fuhl) *adj.; faithfully, adv.; faithfulness, n.* 1. Loyal.–The man is Father's *faithful* friend. He can be trusted.
2. Honest.–The witness was *faithful* in describing everything he had seen.

fal•con (FAL-kən) *n. falcons.* A kind of hawk which can be trained to hunt other birds.

fall (FAWL) *n. falls.* 1. A coming down; a sinking; a drop.–The *fall* of the picture startled us all.–There was a *fall* in the sick boy's temperature. His temperature was not as high as it had been before.
2. Autumn; the time of the year just after summer.–We pick apples in the *fall.*
3. A place where water falls over rocks from a higher place to a lower place.–We paddled slowly up the river toward the *falls.*

–*v. falls, fell, falling.* 1. Drop; sink; come down.–Apples *fall* from the trees when they are ripe.
2. Become less; go down.–The number of people who are hurt in accidents is *falling.* –The temperature has *fallen* since morning.
3. Go down suddenly, so that the body is on the ground.–The man *fell* over the hose.
4. Come or arrive. – Thanksgiving always *falls* on Thursday.
5. Be captured.–The city *fell* to the enemy.
6. Be divided.–The long poem *falls* into three main parts.
–*Fall asleep* means go to sleep.The baby *fell asleep* in her carriage.
–*Fall on* or *upon* means attack.–The thief *fell on* him in the dark street.–The lion *fell upon* its prey.

fall•out (FAWL-owt) *n.* Radioactive particles in the atmosphere which result from an atomic explosion.

false•hood (FAWLSS-huhd) *n. falsehoods.* A lie; something that is not true. You have been guilty of a *falsehood.*

fal•ter (FAWL-ter) *v. falters, faltered, faltering.* 1. Stumble or hesitate in moving; waver.–After the long march, the soldiers' steps began to *falter.*
2. Stammer or hesitate in speaking.–Jane was so nervous that she *faltered* once or twice when she gave her first speech.
3. Become unsteady in purpose; lose heart. –Halfway up the mountain, the climbers *faltered.* Some were ready to go back without reaching the peak.

fame (FAYM) *n.* Well-known reputation; state of being widely known and respected.–Henry Ford had great *fame.*

fa•mil•iar (fə-MIL-yer) *adj.; familiarly, adv.* 1. Well known.–The song "America" is *familiar* to everyone in the United States.
2. Acquainted.–Bob is *familiar* with many books. He knows all about them.
3. Bold; forward.–Some people are too *familiar* with strangers.

fam•i•ly (FAM-ə-lee) *n. families.* 1. A father, a mother, and their children.
2. Children of a father and mother.–The children are called Father's and Mother's *family.*
3. A group of people related to each other.–Your whole *family* is all of your relatives: father, mother, aunts, uncles, cousins, grandparents, sisters, brothers, etc.
4. The people who live together in one house.
5. A group of plants or animals that are related.–The house cat and the tiger both belong to the cat *family.*

fam•ine (FAM-ən) *n. famines.* 1. A great shortage of food.–When there is a *famine,* many people starve.
2. A shortage.–We had a gasoline *famine.* We could not get enough gasoline.

fa•mous (FAY-məss) *adj.; famously, adv.* Well known and respected.–George Washington was a very *famous* man.

fan (FAN) *n. fans.* 1. Anything used to stir up the air. – In hot weather we keep the electric *fan* going all day. – Mother opened up her *fan* and waved it over the baby.

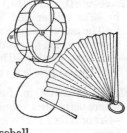

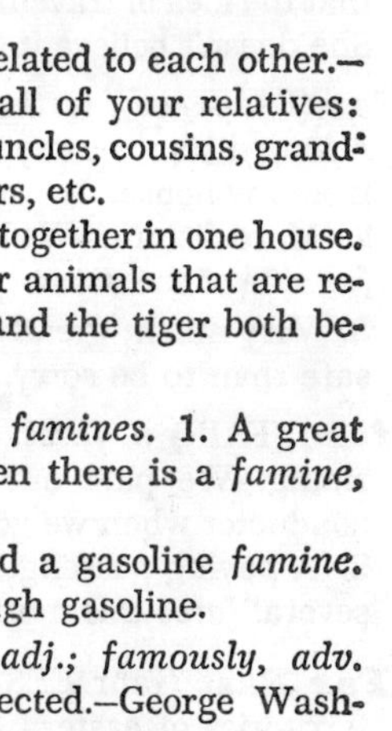

2. A person who is fond of some public entertainment. – Bob is a baseball *fan.* He is much interested in baseball.
–*v. fans, fanned, fanning.* Stir up the air, or blow air on, with a fan.–Mother *fanned* Baby to keep him cool.

fan·cy (FAN-see) *v. fancies, fancied, fancying.* 1. Imagine; picture to yourself. – Just *fancy* Grandmother skating on roller skates.
2. Like.–I *fancy* having my hair short.
–*adj.* 1. Beautifully trimmed; special.–I wear a plain dress to school and a *fancy* one on Sunday.
2. Especially choice.–We gave our teacher a basket of *fancy* fruit. It was fine fruit.

fang (FANG) *n. fangs.* A long, sharp, pointed tooth, like that of a snake, wolf, or dog.–The snake bared its *fangs.*

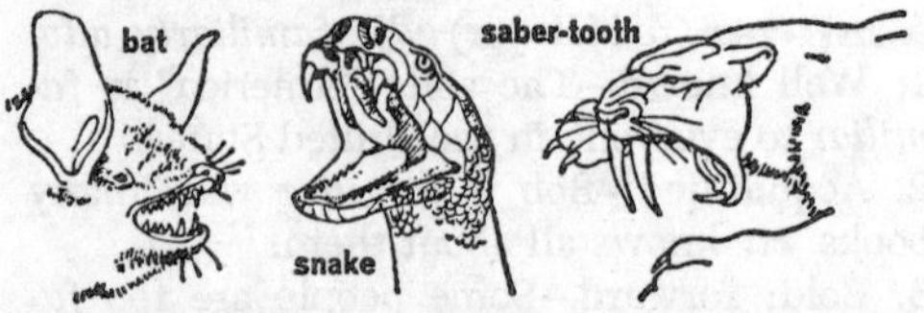

fan·ta·sy (FAN-tə-see *or* -zee) *n. fantasies; fantastic, adj.* 1. The imagination; or, the product of one's imagination.–The play was a *fantasy* for children.
2. Any wild idea or fancy.–Mother believes that the idea of traveling to Mars is a *fantasy.* She doesn't believe it can be done.

far (FAHR) *adj. farther, farthest* and *adv.* 1. A long distance away.–It is not *far* to school from my house.
2. More distant.–We hung the picture on the *far* side of the room.
3. Very much; greatly.–It is *far* better to be safe than to be sorry.

fare (FAIR) *n. fares.* 1. Money charged for riding.–We paid our *fare* to the streetcar conductor when we got off the car.
2. A paying passenger.–The taxi driver had several *fares* this morning.

Far East (fahr EEST). The countries and territories of eastern and southeastern Asia. –China, Japan, Korea, and the Philippine Islands are in the *Far East.*

fare·well (fair-WEL) *n. farewells.* 1. Good-by.–The soldier said *farewell* to his mother.
2. The act of going away.–Bob did not look forward to his *farewell* to the school.
–*adj.* Last; parting.–The teacher gave a *farewell* speech just before he retired.

farm (FAHRM) *n. farms.* A piece of land where plants and animals are grown for food. –Grandfather raises grain and cattle on his *farm.*
–*v. farms, farmed, farming.* Raise crops and animals on a farm. – Grandfather likes to *farm.*

farm·er (FAHRM-er) *n. farmers.* A person who lives on a farm and makes his living from it.

farm·house (FAHRM-howss) *n. farmhouses.* A house in which people live on a farm.

farm·yard (FAHRM-yahrd) *n. farmyards.* The yard or space around the barns and other farm buildings on a farm.

far-off (FAHR-awf) *adj.* At a great distance; far away.–China is a *far-off* country.

far·ther (FAHR-ther) *adj.* and *adv.* One form of the word *far.* – Bob walked four blocks and Bill walked seven blocks. Bill walked *farther* than Bob.

far·thest (FAHR-thəst) *adj.* and *adv.* One form of the word *far.* – Bob walked four blocks, Bill walked seven, and Jack walked eight. Jack walked *farthest* of all.

fas·ci·nate (FASS-ə-nayt) *v. fascinates, fascinated, fascinating.* Hold the attention of. –The beautiful music *fascinates* Mother. It greatly interests her and completely holds her attention.
–*fascination, n. fascinations.*

fash·ion (FASH-ən) *n. fashions.* 1. A style. –It is the *fashion* to wear long hair.
2. Way; manner. – She is behaving in a strange *fashion* these days.
–*v. fashions, fashioned, fashioning.* Shape; form; make.–Mary *fashioned* a bowl from clay.

fash·ion·a·ble (FASH-ən-ə-bəl) *adj.; fashionably, adv.* In style; in fashion.–It is *fashionable* to wear the hair in curls.

fast (FAST) *n. fasts.* A period of time passed without food.–The man's *fast* was a week long.
–*v. fasts, fasted, fasting.* Go without food.– The man *fasted* for a week.
–*adj. faster, fastest.* 1. Ahead. – Since our clock was ten minutes *fast,* we were ten minutes early for our appointment.
2. Quick.–We made a *fast* trip to the store.
3. Firm; firmly set.–If the color of your dress is *fast,* it will not fade or run when washed.– He is a *fast* friend of mine.
–*adv.* 1. Quickly; swiftly.–The car goes *fast.*
2. Firmly; tightly.–I will sew the button *fast* to your dress.
3. Deeply; completely.–He was so *fast* asleep, we could not wake him.

FARM

fas·ten (FASS-ən) *v. fastens, fastened, fastening.* 1. Lock or latch; make tight.–I will *fasten* the door.
2. Tie.–I will *fasten* your shoes.
3. Attach. – I will *fasten* a letter to the package.–Don't try to *fasten* the blame on me.

fat (FAT) *n. fats.* An oily substance, especially in meat.–The *fat* in meat looks white. In chickens it is yellow.–Milk has *fat* in it; when separated from the rest of the milk, this *fat,* called cream, makes butter.
–*adj. fatter, fattest.* 1. Having much flesh on the body.–Some children are thin; others are *fat.*
2. Full.–The rich man had a *fat* pocketbook.

fa·tal (FAY-təl) *adj.; fatally, adv.* 1. Causing death.–The accident was not *fatal* to the dog. It did not kill him.
2. Causing ruin.–The frost was *fatal* to the fruit. It ruined it.
3. Fateful; serious; important.–At last the *fatal* day came when the winner of the contest was announced.

fa·ther (FAHTH-er) *n. fathers.* 1. The man parent.–Your mother and *father* are your parents.
2. God is called *Father.*
3. A priest in a church is called *Father.*
–*v. fathers, fathered, fathering.* Care for as a father.–Uncle Jim has *fathered* the boys for many years.

fa·ther-in-law (FAHTH-er-ən-law) *n. fathers-in-law.* The father of one's wife or husband.–When a man marries, his wife's father becomes his *father-in-law.* When a woman marries, her husband's father becomes her *father-in-law.*

fa·tigue (fə-TEEG) *n.; fatigued, adj.* Tiredness or weariness, especially that resulting from work.–The ditch diggers are suffering from *fatigue.*

fau·cet (FAW-sit) *n. faucets.* A spout or valve to control the flow of water. – We turned the handle of the *faucet* and the water rushed out into the sink.

fault (FAWLT) *n. faults.* 1. Something wrong.–Bob's greatest *fault* is talking too much.
2. A mistake.–It was Jack's *fault* that the bicycle was left out in the rain.
–*At fault* means to blame.–The man driving the small car was *at fault* in the accident.

fault·less (FAWLT-ləss) *adj.; faultlessly, adv.* Perfect. – The musician's performance was *faultless.*

faul·ty (FAWL-tee) *adj. faultier, faultiest; faultily, adv.* Imperfect; having faults.–The flute was *faulty* when we bought it; the note F did not sound.

fa·vor (FAY-ver) *n. favors.* 1. A gift.–Each child received a *favor* at the party.
2. A kindness; a kind act.–Our neighbors do us many *favors.*
3. Liking; pleasure. – The king looked upon his soldiers with *favor.*
–*v. favors, favored, favoring.* 1. Help; do a kindness for.–Will you *favor* us by letting us use your telephone?–The teacher *favored* us with a story.
2. Approve; prefer. – The children *favored* having the party after school.
3. Show extra kindness and attention to.–Mary thought Grandfather *favored* Bob. She thought he paid more attention to Bob than to her.

fa·vor·a·ble (FAY-ver-ə-bəl) *adj.; favorably, adv.* Agreeable; desirable; good. – If the weather is *favorable,* we will go to the park tomorrow.–When Bob asked Father for extra money, Father's answer was not *favorable.* He said no.

fa·vor·ite (FAY-və-rət) *n. favorites.* The one best liked.–Bob is the *favorite* of his father.
–*adj.* Best liked.–Blue is a *favorite* color of many people.

fawn (FAWN) *n. fawns.* A young deer. –As we were walking through the woods, we saw a *fawn.*
–*adj.* Light brown. – Mother bought a *fawn* coat.

fear (FIR) *n. fears.* The feeling you have when you are scared or afraid.
–*v. fears, feared, fearing.* Be frightened of.– Some girls *fear* mice.

fear·ful (FIR-fuhl) *adj.; fearfully, adv.* 1. Dreadful; frightening. – A *fearful* animal came out of the woods.
2. Afraid; frightened.–I am *fearful* of windstorms.

fear·less (FIR-ləss) *adj.; fearlessly, adv.* Not afraid of anything.–The soldiers were *fearless.*

feast (FEEST) *n. feasts.* A rich meal; a big dinner. – On Thanksgiving Day we have a *feast.*

–*v. feasts, feasted, feasting.* Eat a lot; eat a big or elaborate meal.–The men *feasted.*
–*Feast on* means to get pleasure or delight from seeing, hearing, doing, or eating something.–Mary *feasted on* the music at the concert.–We *feast on* turkey on Thanksgiving.

feat (FEET) *n. feats.* A great thing to do; a deed or act which takes skill or courage.–Swimming across the swift stream is a difficult *feat.*

feath•er (FETH-er) *n. feathers.* One of the light parts of the covering of a bird. *Feathers* are soft and light. They are used in pillows.

feath•er•y (FETH-er-ee) *adj.* Light and fluffy like feathers.–Milkweed blossoms are *feathery.*

fea•ture (FEE-cher) *n. features.* 1. Any one part of your face, like your chin or nose.
2. A point or quality.–The teacher said there were many good *features* in Bob's drawings.
3. A part.–The main *features* of the program were a play and a song.
–*v. features, featured, featuring.* Present as most important.–The store is *featuring* raincoats in its sale today.

Feb•ru•a•ry (FEB-yə-wair-ee *or* FEB-roo-air-ee) *n. Februaries.* The second month of the year.–George Washington's birthday is in *February.*

fed (FED) *v.* One form of the verb *feed.*–The mother robin *fed* worms to the baby robins.

fed•er•al (FED-er-əl) *adj.; federally, adv.* National; concerning a union of states.–The states of the United States are united under one government called the *Federal* Government.

fee (FEE) *n. fees.* Money paid for something done for you, or for the right to do something. –Doctors, lawyers, dentists, etc., charge a *fee* for their work.–That library charges a *fee* of two cents a day for the use of a book.

fee•ble (FEE-bəl) *adj. feebler, feeblest; feebly, adv.* Weak.–The old woman is too *feeble* to walk very far.

feed (FEED) *n. feeds.* Food for farm animals. –Grandfather bought a bag of chicken *feed.*
–*v. feeds, fed, feeding.* 1. Give food to. – Mother will *feed* the baby his breakfast.
2. Put into. – Father *feeds* gasoline to the motor by pushing on the accelerator.

feel (FEEL) *v. feels, felt, feeling.* 1. Notice by touching, handling, or being touched.–When you touch things, they may *feel* soft or hard, smooth or rough, warm or cold.
2. Have a condition of mind.–We *feel* happy, sad, angry, afraid, etc.
3. Believe.–Bob *feels* that his team will win.
4. Hunt by touching.–Mary *felt* in her desk to find her pencil.

feel•er (FEEL-er) *n. feelers.* One of a pair of long, stiff, hairlike arms that an insect uses to feel with.–A rabbit has *feelers,* too. They are his whiskers.

feel•ing (FEEL-ing) *n. feelings.* 1. A sensation.–When the ball hit me on the head, I had a dizzy *feeling.*
2. An emotion, or sense of pleasure, anger, etc.–The child had a *feeling* of happiness when her father got home.
3. Opinion; judgment.–What is your *feeling* about Mary's ability to run the fair? Do you think she can do it?
4. (In the plural) The boys hurt the girl's *feelings* when they told her she was ugly.

feet (FEET) *n. pl.* More than one *foot.* – A centipede has many *feet.*–In the table of measurement three *feet* make one yard.

fell (FEL) *v.* One form of the verb *fall.*–Jack *fell* down.

fel•low (FEL-oh) *n. fellows.* A word often used for a man or boy, or sometimes an animal.–Four of the *fellows* came to see Jack when he was sick.–One of the fish Bob caught was really a big *fellow.*
–*adj.* Belonging to the same group.–A *fellow* student came home with Dick.

felt (FELT) *n. felts* and *adj.* A kind of stiff, smooth cloth made of pressed wool, hair, and fur.–Father's hat is made of *felt.*
–*v.* One form of the verb *feel.*–We *felt* the sand blowing in our faces.

fe•male (FEE-mayl) *n. females* and *adj.* A woman, girl, or she animal. – Men and boys are males; women and girls are *females.* – Hens and cows are *females.*

fem•i•nine (FEM-ə-nən) *adj.* Belonging to or relating to women; like a woman. – High-heeled shoes and dresses are *feminine* belongings. They are worn by women.

fence (FENSS) *n. fences.* A wall or barrier put up to keep things apart, or to keep people or animals in or out.

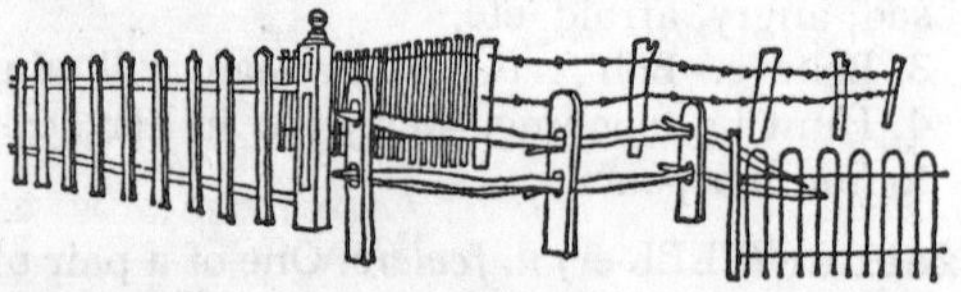

–v. fences, fenced, fencing. Put a fence around.–The farmer *fenced* in his pasture to keep his cattle from getting out.

fend•er (FEN-der) *n. fenders.* **1.** A guard placed over the wheel of a vehicle to keep dirt from being thrown up when the vehicle is moving.

2. A metal guard set in front of a fireplace.

fer•ment (fer-MENT) *v. ferments, fermented, fermenting.* Cause a gradual chemical change in a substance, usually accompanied by bubbling and hissing.–Vinegar is sometimes made by *fermenting* wine.

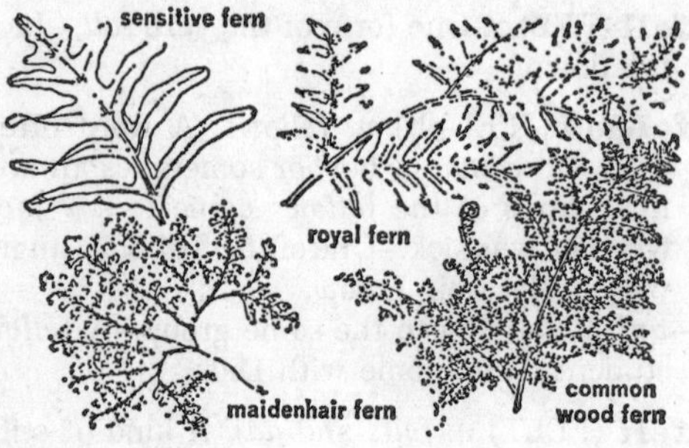

fern (FERN) *n. ferns.* A kind of leafy plant that does not have flowers. Some *ferns* grow best in shady places.

fer•ry (FAIR-ee) *n. ferries.* A boat that carries people and vehicles across a lake or river.

–v. ferries, ferried, ferrying. Carry on a ferry or other boat.–Father *ferried* the family to the island in a rowboat.

fer•tile (FER-təl) *adj.* **1.** Rich; productive.–The land on Grandfather's farm is very *fertile.* It produces good crops.

2. Able to produce.–A *fertile* seed is one that is able to grow into a plant that will bear fruit and seeds.–Hans Christian Andersen had a *fertile* imagination. It enabled him to write many stories.

fer•ti•lize (FER-təl-yz) *v. fertilizes, fertilized, fertilizing.* Make (soil) richer by adding something to it.–If the land is not rich enough to make things grow, it must be *fertilized.*

fer•ti•liz•er (FER-təl-yz-er) *n. fertilizers.* Anything put on the ground to make it rich so that crops will grow.–Manure is a *fertilizer.*

fes•ti•val (FESS-tə-vəl) *n. festivals.* A time for merrymaking, celebrating, and feasting. –Christmas is a *festival.* It is the time for celebrating the birth of Christ.

fes•tive (FESS-tiv) *adj.; festively, adv.; festivity, n.* Fit for a feast; gay; merry; joyful.–Thanksgiving is a *festive* holiday.

fetch (FECH) *v. fetches, fetched, fetching.* Get and bring back.–Jack and Jill went up the hill to *fetch* a pail of water.

feud (FYOOD) *n. feuds.* A long-standing quarrel between two persons, families, or groups of people, often with active fighting taking place between the quarreling sides.–There has been a *feud* between those families for years. They are always fighting.–Mother had a long *feud* with a department store over a bill for something she didn't receive.

feu•dal•ism (FYOOD-əl-iz-əm) *n.* The system which existed in Europe during the Middle Ages, in which lords held or owned land as a gift from the king. These lords ruled the peasants who farmed the land as their subjects, or vassals.

fe•ver (FEE-ver) *n. fevers.* 1. Unusual warmth or high temperature of the body caused by illness. Normal body temperature is about 98.6°. A body temperature higher than that is called a *fever.*
2. An excited condition.–The children were in a *fever* over the circus.

fe•ver•ish (FEE-ver-ish) *adj.; feverishly, adv.* 1. Having a fever; running a high temperature.–The baby is *feverish.* She has a fever.
2. Nervously excited.–The cattle were *feverish* during the storm.

few (FYOO) *adj. fewer, fewest.* Not many; a small number.–We ate only a *few* nuts.

fi•ber or **fi•bre** (FY-ber) *n. fibers* or *fibres.* A threadlike or hairlike part of wool, cotton, or similar material.–*Fibers* are twisted or spun into yarn or thread.

fic•tion (FIK-shən) *n.* A writing about imaginary happenings; a story or stories.–Mary likes to read *fiction.*

fid•dle (FID-əl) *n. fiddles.* A violin.–Father plays the *fiddle* in the orchestra.

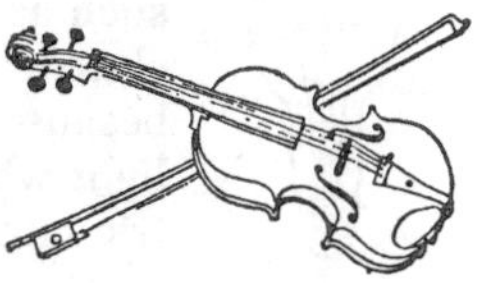

–*v. fiddles, fiddled, fiddling.* 1. Play the violin.–Father *fiddles* while the children dance.
2. Move about restlessly; toy; play.–Stop *fiddling* and get to work.–Don't *fiddle* with the pencil. You distract me.

fid•dler (FID-ler) *n. fiddlers.* A violinist; one who plays the fiddle or violin.

fidg•et (FIJ-it) *v. fidgets, fidgeted, fidgeting.* Squirm and move nervously. – The teacher told the children not to *fidget* so much.

fidg•et•y (FIJ-ə-tee) *adj.* Restless; nervous.–When Bob has to stay in the house, he becomes *fidgety.*

field (FEELD) *n. fields.* 1. A piece of open land.–This is a grassy *field* where cows feed. – The farmer plants grain in large *fields.*

2. A special piece of ground marked off for a game.–The baseball team ran out onto the *field.*
3. Area, of many kinds, as, an ice *field* in the Arctic; a *field* of battle; the gold *fields* of South Africa.–A magnetic *field* is the area around a magnet in which the magnetism works.–Bob will go into the *field* of biology. He will become a biologist.

fierce (FEERSS) *adj. fiercer, fiercest; fiercely, adv.* Savage; wild; untamed; cruel.–Tigers are *fierce.*–The man had a *fierce* temper.

fi•es•ta (fee-ESS-tə) *n. fiestas.* A carnival-type religious holiday; a saint's day; any gay holiday.–People danced in the streets during the *fiesta.*

FIESTA

fife (FYF) *n. fifes.* A small, flutelike musical instrument that makes a shrill, whistling sound.–We listened to the *fife* and drums.

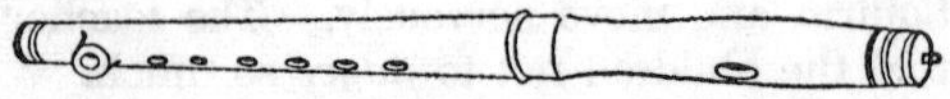

fif·teen (fif-TEEN) *n. fifteens* and *adj.* The number [15] coming after 14 and before 16. –Ten and five make *fifteen.*

fif·teenth (fif-TEENTH) *n. fifteenths.* One of 15 equal parts.–If you divide anything into fifteen parts, all the same size, each part is one *fifteenth.* It may be written 1/15.
–*adj.* Coming as number 15 in a series.–My name was *fifteenth* on the list.

fifth (FIFTH) *n. fifths.* One of 5 equal parts. –If you divide anything into five parts, all the same size, each part is one *fifth.* It may be written 1/5.
–*adj.* Coming as number 5 in a series.–May is the *fifth* month of the year.

fif·ti·eth (FIF-tee-əth) *n. fiftieths.* One of 50 equal parts.–If you divide anything into fifty equal parts, each part is called one *fiftieth.* It is also written 1/50.
–*adj.* Coming as number 50 in a series.–Today is Aunt Ellen's *fiftieth* birthday. She is fifty years old.

fif·ty (FIF-tee) *n. fifties* and *adj.* The number [50] coming after 49 and before 51.–Five tens are *fifty.*

fig (FIG) *n. figs.* A small pear-shaped fruit that grows in some warm countries. It has many tiny round seeds in it. *Figs* may be eaten fresh or dried. They may also be stewed like prunes.

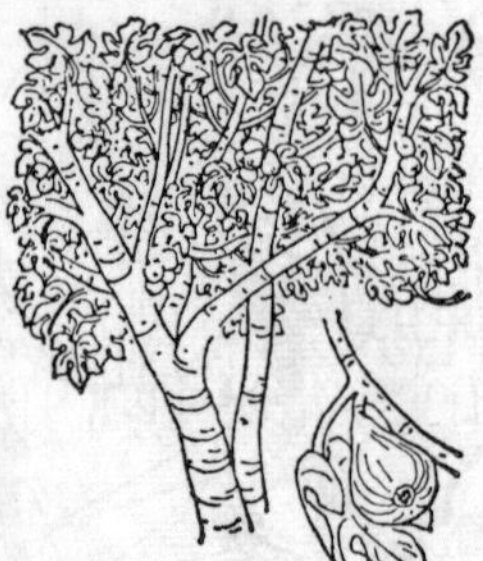

fight (FYT) *n. fights.* A struggle against someone or something.–Give money to help the *fight* against disease.
–*v. fights, fought, fighting.* Try to win over someone or something by hurting or weakening him. – Dogs *fight* over bones. – Some children *fight* with one another.–Armies *fight* with guns, tanks, airplanes, bombs, and other weapons.

fight·er (FYT-er) *n. fighters.* Someone who fights.–Two *fighters* will have a boxing contest to see who is the champion.
–A *fighter plane* is a small, fast airplane built for attacking bombers and other planes.

fig·ure (FIG-yer) *n. figures.* 1. A sign that stands for a number.–1, 2, 3, 4, 5, 6, 7, 8, 9, 0 are *figures.*
2. A shape or form.–A circle, a square, and a triangle are *figures.*–We saw the *figure* of a black cat sitting on the back fence.–The *figures* in my dress are small moons and stars.
3. A person or character.–The clown is an important *figure* in the circus.
4. A diagram in a book.–*Figure* 3 shows the working of the heart in the human body.
–*v. figures, figured, figuring.* 1. Find out something by working with numbers.–Bob tried to *figure* the cost of his new ball, bat, and glove. He wrote down how much each cost, and added the numbers.
2. Play a part; enter into; be included.–Getting Mary on his side *figured* largely in Jack's plans for winning the game.
–*Figure out* means understand.–Bob couldn't *figure out* how he was going to pay for the things he wanted with the money he had.

fil·a·ment (FIL-ə-mənt) *n. filaments.* Any delicate, threadlike structure, such as the fine wire inside an electric bulb.–The bulb lights because the *filament* gives off light when it is heated by electric current.

fil·bert (FIL-bert) *n. filberts.* A nut that belongs to the hazelnut family.

file (FYL) *n. files.* 1. A cabinet or a system for keeping papers in a certain order so they can be found easily.–The clerk put the letters in the *file.*

2. A line or row.–Our teacher told us to walk in single *file.*
3. A long piece of steel with ridges across it. –Mother smoothed off her broken fingernail with a *file.*

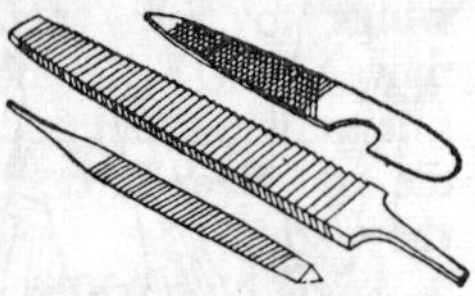

–*v. files, filed, filing.* 1. Put in order or in a file.

–Mother *files* her bills according to the date.
2. Walk in line.–The children *filed* out of the school building during the fire drill. They marched out in a row, one behind the other.
3. Make smooth or smaller by rubbing with a file.–Mother *files* her fingernails before she polishes them.

Fil•i•pi•no (fil-ə-PEE-noh) *n.* and *adj.* A person born in the Philippine Islands.

fill (FIL) *n.* All that can be held or desired.–For once Bob had his *fill* of ice cream.
–*v. fills, filled, filling.* 1. Put as much into something as it will hold.–Mother will *fill* the pitcher with milk.
2. Take up all the room or time.–Smoke *filled* the air.–Tears *filled* Baby's eyes.–The doctor said his time was *filled* with appointments.
3. Give what is called for; serve.–The grocer will *fill* your order. He will get you all the things you want.
4. Take or occupy.–Jack went to see about a position as newsboy, but it had been *filled.*
5. Become full.–The boat had a hole in it, and it soon *filled* with water.
6. Plug; stop up–The dentist *filled* the cavity in my tooth.

fill•ing (FIL-ing) *n. fillings.* Material used to fill a space.–The dentist put a *filling* in the hole in my tooth.–Mother put lemon *filling* between the layers of the cake.

film (FILM) *n. films.* 1. A thin coating or layer.–It was cold enough last night to form a *film* of ice on the water.
2. A material which is sensitive to light and is used for taking photographs. – We got a roll of *film* for our camera.

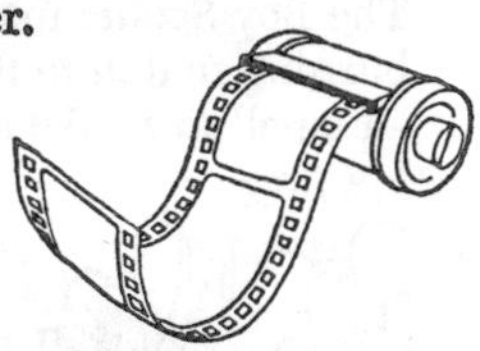

3. A motion picture.–We saw a *film* last night.
–*v. films, filmed, filming.* Make (a moving picture).–It takes a long time to *film* a motion picture.

filth•y (FILTH-ee) *adj. filthier, filthiest; filth, n.* Very dirty.–The man had not washed his hands for a long time, and they were *filthy.*

fin (FIN) *n. fins.* One of the little flaps which a fish moves in swimming. Birds have wings to help them move about. Fish have *fins* to help them paddle and steer through the water.

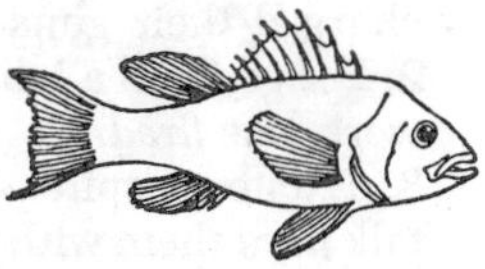

2. Something which looks or functions like a fin.–The airplane has a *fin* on its tail.

fi•nal (FY-nəl) *adj.; finally, adv.* Last; closing.
–This is the *final* game of the baseball series.
–The teacher said a few *final* words and then told us to go home.
–The *finals* means the last, decisive game or games of a contest.–The winner of the tennis *finals* received a gold cup.

fi•nal•ly (FY-nəl-ee) *adv.* At last.–*Finally* I have my work done.

fi•nance (fə-NANSS *or* FY-nanss) *v. finances, financed, financing.* Pay for.–I can go to the movie if Mother will *finance* me. I can go if she will give me the money for it.–Father will *finance* Bob's college education. He will pay for it.

fi•nan•cial (fə- *or* fy-NAN-shəl) *adj.; financially, adv.* Relating to money.–Ed reads the *financial* section of the newspaper, the part which tells about money matters.

finch (FINCH) *n. finches.* A kind of small songbird. A sparrow is one kind of *finch.*

find (FYND) *n. finds.* Something found.–Bob thought the terrier was a good *find.* It was just the sweet-natured dog he had been looking for.
–*v. finds, found, finding.* 1. Come upon; discover where a thing is.–Did you ever *find* a four-leaf clover?–Mary lost her ring in the grass and it took a long time to *find* it.
2. See; discover; learn.–I *find* that you have been absent twice, according to the records. –Did you *find* anything of interest in that book?
3. Reach a decision.–After studying the case, the judge *found* the accused man innocent.

fine (FYN) *n. fines.* Money paid as a punishment.–The policeman gave the man a ticket for driving too fast. The man had to pay a *fine.*
–*v. fines, fined, fining.* Make (someone) pay money as a punishment.–The judge *fined* the man five dollars.
–*adj. finer, finest.* 1. Beautiful; good; excellent.–Mother has a *fine* new dress.–Mary is a *fine* musician.
2. Not coarse.–Sugar is *fine,* but salt is *finer.* Salt has smaller grains.
3. Narrow.–My fountain pen has a *fine* point. It makes a thin line.
4. Clear and sunny.–If the day is *fine,* we shall go sailing tomorrow.

fin·ger (FING-ger) *n. fingers.* 1. We have *fingers* on each hand. The thumb is shorter and thicker than the other *fingers.* We pick things up, turn pages, tie knots, point things out, write, and do many other things with the *fingers.*

2. Anything that is like a finger on the hand. –Mary couldn't get her fingers into the *fingers* of her glove.
–*v. fingers, fingered, fingering.* Touch or handle lightly.–The grocer does not like you to *finger* the fruit.

fin·ish (FIN-ish) *n. finishes.* 1. An end.–One horse dropped out of the race before the *finish.*
2. A surface.–Father sanded the rough board so that it had a smooth, even *finish.*
–*v. finishes, finished, finishing.* 1. Complete; become complete; come to the end of.–Mother expects to *finish* reading the book today.–The story running in the newspaper *finished* today.
2. Give a certain kind of surface to.–Bob made a letter box and *finished* it with varnish.

fiord or **fjord** (FYORD) *n. fiords* or *fjords.* A long, narrow finger of sea, bounded by high cliffs. *Fiords* are found along the coasts of Norway.

fir (FER) *n. firs.* A tree belonging to the pine tree family. *Firs* have cones on them.

fire (FYR) *n. fires.* Something burning.–The Boy Scouts made a *fire.* They touched a burning match to the paper to make it burn. –I smell *fire.*–We saw the fire engine at the big *fire.*

–*v. fires, fired, firing.* 1. Shoot.–The soldiers *fired* at the enemy. They aimed and discharged their guns.
2. Let go from a job.–The man who did poor work was *fired.*
3. Excite; inspire.–The team captain's pep talk *fired* them with determination to do their best.
4. Bake in intense heat.–Ed *fired* the clay bowl in a kiln to make it hard.

fire·arm (FYR-ahrm) *n. firearms.* A gun, revolver, or the like.–Soldiers use *firearms* and other weapons to destroy the enemy.

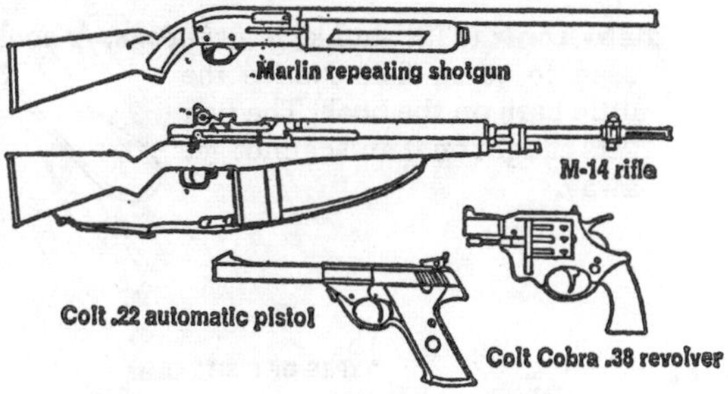

fire·crack·er (FYR-krak-er) *n. firecrackers.* A cylinder made of rolled paper with gunpowder inside. It blows up and makes a loud noise when lighted with a match.

fire es·cape (FYR ə-skayp) *fire escapes.* An outside stairway or ladder used for escape when there is a fire in the building.–The men left the burning building by the *fire escape.*

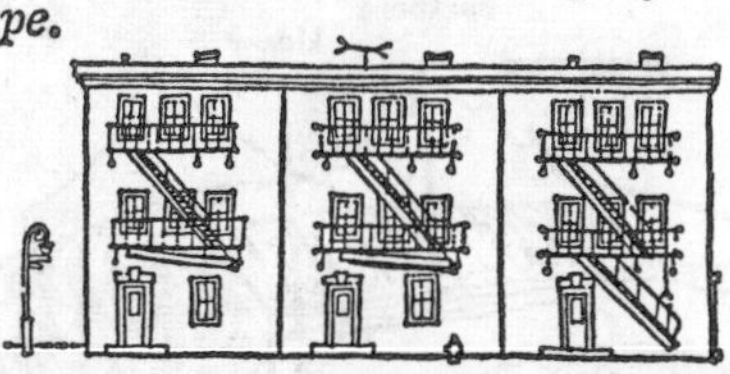

fire·fly (FYR-fly) *n. fireflies.* A small insect that produces a flashing yellowish light which can be seen at night.–We sat on the porch in the evening and watched the *fireflies* in the garden.

fire·light (FYR-lyt) *n.* Light given off by a fire.–The Boy Scouts sat in the *firelight* and told stories.

fire·man (FYR-mən) *n. firemen.* 1. A man whose duty it is to put out fires.–The *firemen* arrived on their engine at the burning store.

2. A man on a railroad steam engine who takes care of the fire; a man whose job it is to take care of any fire.

fire·place (FYR-playss) *n. fireplaces.* An open place built of stone or brick for a fire.–The children hung their stockings in front of the *fireplace.* – We cooked at a *fireplace* on the picnic grounds.

fire·proof (FYR-proof) *v. fireproofs, fireproofed, fireproofing.* Make so as not to catch fire, or not to catch fire easily.–Our house has been *fireproofed.* It will not burn easily.
–*adj.* Made resistant to fire.–Many buildings today are *fireproof.*

fire·works (FYR-werkss) *n. pl.* Firecrackers and other things that make colored lights and loud noises when they explode. – On the Fourth of July we went to see the *fireworks.*

firm (FERM) *n. firms.* A business company. –There is a law *firm* opening up for business in that building.
–*adj. firmer, firmest; firmly, adv.* 1. Solid; not shaking or moving.–Father set the flagpole in cement to make it stand *firm.*
2. Solid; not liquid or soft.–Mother put the gelatin in the icebox to make it *firm.*
3. Strong; steady; not changing back and forth; decided.–Father spoke in a *firm* voice when he said no.–Jack is *firm* in his belief that Spot is the smartest and most beautiful dog in the world.

fir·ma·ment (FER-mə-mənt) *n.* The sky; the great covering arch of the heavens.–The stars shone brightly in the *firmament.*

first (FERST) *adj.* and *adv.* 1. Coming as number 1; before or in front of others.–The *first* day of the week is Sunday. It comes before all the rest.–The *first* person in the row collects the pencils. The person who sits in the seat ahead of all the others in the row collects the pencils.–When Bob and Ned raced to the ball park, Bob got there *first.*
2. Before doing something else; rather.–"I'd die *first,*" Mary said when I asked her not to tell my secret to anyone.
–*At first* means in the beginning.–*At first* Father had only a few men working for him; now he has many.

fish (FISH) *n. fish* or *fishes.* A cold-blooded animal that lives in water and gets oxygen from the water it breathes through its gills. Most *fish* are covered with scales. Some *fish* are good to eat.
—*v. fishes, fished, fishing.* 1. Try to catch fish. —I like to *fish.*
2. Look (in something).—She *fished* in the drawer for a safety pin.

fish•er•man (FISH-er-mən) *n. fishermen.* A man who catches fish for a living; or, sometimes, a man who fishes just for fun.

fish•hook (FISH-huhk) *n. fishhooks.* A hook used to catch fish. Notice the little barb on the hook. The fish gets caught on it and cannot get away.

FISH

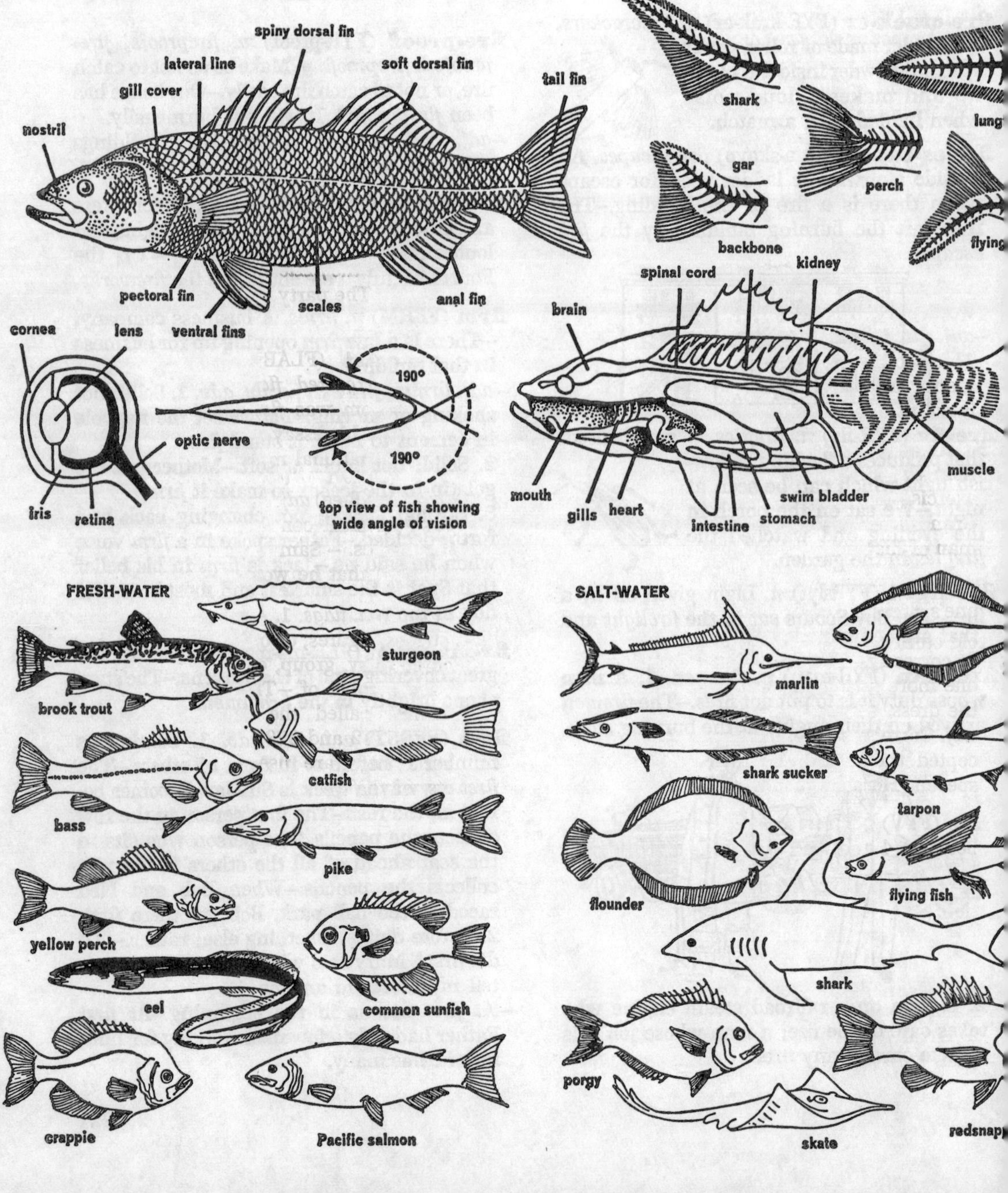

fis·sion (FISH-ən) *n.* A splitting.–The destructive force of the atom bomb is due to atomic *fission.* Tremendous energy is released when the atoms split.

fis·sure (FISH-er) *n. fissures.* An opening; a split.–John stuck his hand into the *fissure* in the rock and drew out the knife that he had hidden there.

fist (FIST) *n. fists.* The hand closed tightly into a ball. You make a *fist* by bending your fingers inward as hard as they will go.

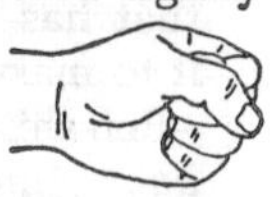

fit (FIT) *n. fits.* 1. A kind of violent sickness that comes on very suddenly. Dogs sometimes have fits.
2. A short spell.–The baby had a *fit* of crying in the middle of the night.
–*v. fits, fitted, fitting.* 1. Be the right size for. –Jack's shoes were too small. They did not *fit.*
2. Arrange or fix in a particular way.–Bob tried to *fit* the parts of the puzzle together. He tried to make them go together right.
3. Be suitable for.–The word does not *fit* in that sentence. You need a more accurate word.
–*adj. fitter, fittest.* 1. Right; proper; suitable.–This book is not *fit* for this class. The stories are for smaller children.–Mary says her coat is not *fit* to be seen on the street.

fit·ness (FIT-nəss) *n.* Good physical condition; the kind of strength that comes from exercise and training.–The doctor said that Grandfather's *fitness* is extraordinary for a man of his age.

fit·ting (FIT-ing) *n. fittings.* A meeting with one's dressmaker or tailor to try on clothes that are being made or altered to see if they fit correctly.–The dressmaker said that after one more *fitting* she would be able to finish the dress.
–*adj.* Correct; suitable; right.–When Jerry accepted the award, he made a very *fitting* speech. He said just what he should have.

five (FYV) *n. fives* and *adj.* The number [5] between 4 and 6.–Three and two make *five.*

fix (FIKS) *n. fixes.* Trouble, or a difficult position.

"Now the clock is striking six.
I am in an awful *fix.*"

–*v. fixes, fixed, fixing.* 1. Make right again.–Father *fixed* the flat tire. He mended it.
2. Arrange; prepare; put something a certain way. – Mary *fixed* Mother's birthday package. She put little white bows on it. Jane *fixed* dinner.
3. Set firmly.–Father *fixed* the flagpole in cement.–Mary wrote the history dates down to *fix* them in her mind.
4. Set; decide upon. – I will buy your dog when you *fix* a price for him.
5. Direct toward.–Bob *fixed* his attention on his work.
6. Keep from changing.–When Mother dyed the old curtains, she put vinegar in the dye to *fix* it, so it would not fade.

fix·ture (FIKS-cher) *n. fixtures.* Anything that is put in place to be left there for a long time.–A bathtub, a washbowl, a toilet seat, and towel racks are bathroom *fixtures.* Some schoolroom *fixtures* are desks, blackboards, and cupboards.

fizz (FIZ) *v. fizzes, fizzed, fizzing.* Bubble up; make a hissing sound.–When we opened the bottle of soda, it started to *fizz.*

fiz·zle (FIZ-əl) *n. fizzles.* 1. Hissing.–Jim loves to hear the *fizzle* of his soft drink.
2. Failure.–The party was really a *fizzle.* No one came.

flab·ber·gast (FLAB-er-gast) *v. flabbergasts, flabbergasted, flabbergasting.* Amaze; astonish.–Tom was *flabbergasted* when he learned that his essay was going to be published in a national magazine.

flab·by (FLAB-ee) *adj. flabbier, flabbiest.* Not in good physical condition; not fit; having limp muscles. – Sam does exercises every morning so that he won't become *flabby.*

flag (FLAG) *n. flags.* 1. A square of cloth that has stripes, figures, or other designs to show which country, group, or other organization it is the symbol of.–The American *flag* is sometimes called the Stars and Stripes. See pages 322 and 323.
2. Some *flags* are used for signals.–Boy Scouts wave *flags* to send messages.
3. A piece of brightly colored cloth used to attract attention.–The phone company puts red *flags* on poles that stick out of the back of their trucks.
–*v. flags, flagged, flagging.* 1. To give a signal to by waving a flag.–The watchman *flagged* down the train. He waved a flag to signal the train to stop.
2. Droop; grow weak.–The children's pace *flagged* as they neared the end of their long hike.

flake (FLAYK) *n. flakes.* A very small, thin piece of anything.—Each little piece of snow is a *flake.*—Soap shavings are *flakes.*

—*v. flakes, flaked, flaking.* Break off in thin, flat pieces.—The bark on the tree *flaked* off.

flame (FLAYM) *n. flames.* A blaze; the colored part of fire.—We smelled smoke, but we could not tell where the fire was until we saw the *flame* rise above the roof.—When you light the gas on the stove, it makes a *flame.*

—*v. flames, flamed, flaming.* Make flames or grow bright like flame.—Color *flamed* in the boy's face as the teacher praised him.

fla·min·go (flə-MING-goh) *n. flamingos* or *flamingoes.* A large water bird with a very long neck and legs. Its feathers are pinkish, and its flat bill hooks downward.

flank (FLANGK) *n. flanks.* The side of the body between the ribs and the hipbone.—He patted the horse on the *flank.*

—*v. flanks, flanked, flanking.* Be on either side of.—Members of his staff *flanked* the general.

flan·nel (FLAN-əl) *n. flannels.* A soft woolen cloth.—Father often wears a suit of gray *flannel.*

flap (FLAP) *n. flaps.* A part that folds over.—The *flap* on Bob's pocket buttons to the pocket.—To seal an envelope, moisten the *flap* and press it down.

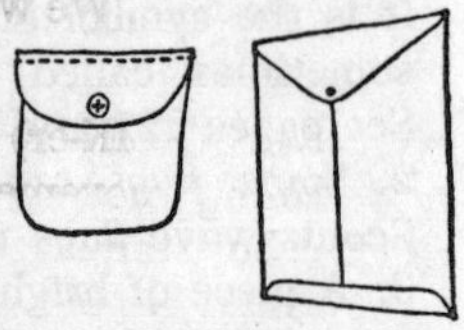

—*v. flaps, flapped, flapping.* Wave up and down or back and forth.—Birds *flap* their wings when they fly.—The clothes hanging on the clothesline *flap* in the wind.

flash (FLASH) *n. flashes.* 1. A light that comes on suddenly and lasts a very short time.—Fireflies, or lightning bugs, make *flashes.*

2. A short time.—We will be back in a *flash.*—The accident happened in just a *flash.*

3. A quick, sudden feeling.—Jack recognized his lost dog with a *flash* of joy.

—*v. flashes, flashed, flashing.* 1. Shine quickly or suddenly.—The boys *flashed* light from the sun into the room with a mirror.—The taxi driver *flashed* his spotlight on the house numbers.

2. Dart; dash.—A cat *flashed* across the road.

flash·light (FLASH-lyt) *n. flashlights.* 1. A small electric light that has a battery in it to make it light up.—Bob shined his *flashlight* into the dark room.

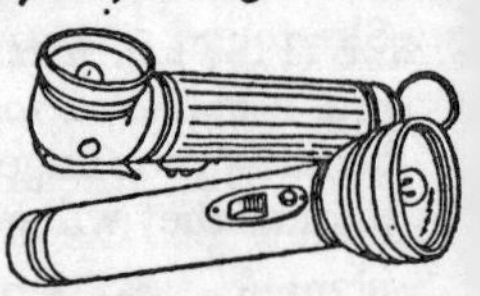

2. A light used to take pictures indoors or at night.—The newspaper reporters used *flashlights* to take pictures of the wedding.

flask (FLASK) *n. flasks.* A bottle that has a small neck or opening.—Soldiers carry water in a *flask,* or canteen.

flat (FLAT) *n. flats.* 1. An apartment.—We live in the lower *flat,* or the rooms on the lower floor of the house.

2. In music, a tone or note a half step lower than that named, indicated by the sign ♭.

—*adj. flatter, flattest; flatly, adv.* 1. Level; even.—The land is *flat* here.

2. Spread out.—It spoils a new book to open it out, face down, *flat* on a table.

3. Low.—Pansies look better in a *flat* bowl than they do in a high vase.

4. In music, lower by a half step.—E *flat* in music is a half tone lower than E.

5. Tasteless.—Soup cooked without salt is *flat.*

—*adv.* In music, a little lower than or below the true tone.—One violin sounds *flat.*

flat·ten (FLAT-n) *v. flattens, flattened, flattening.* Make or become flat.—Ironing *flattens* the clothes.—The wind *flattened* the corn stalks.

flat·ter (FLAT-er) *v. flatters, flattered, flattering.* 1. Praise more than is deserved.—Dad *flatters* me. He calls me beautiful.

2. Make to seem nicer than is really the case.—This picture doesn't *flatter* Mary. It doesn't make her look prettier than she really is.

fla·vor (FLAY-ver) *n. flavors.* Taste.—I like the *flavor* of this cake.

—*v. flavors, flavored, flavoring.* Season; add something to give a certain taste.—Grandmother *flavored* the icing with lemon.

fla•vor•ing (FLAY-ver-ing) *n. flavorings.* Anything added to foods to make them taste like the thing added.–Onions, spices, vanilla, and many other strong-tasting foods are *flavorings.*

flaw (FLAW) *n. flaws.* An error; a fault; something wrong.–Mother did not buy the pitcher, because it had a *flaw* in it. – The teacher found a *flaw* in our figuring of the problem. She found a mistake.

flax (FLAKS) *n.* and *adj.* The threadlike stems of the *flax* plant, a tall, slender plant that has blue flowers. Linen thread is made from *flax.*

flax•en (FLAKS-ən) *adj.* Pale yellow, like flax fibers.–The girl has *flaxen* hair.

flea (FLEE) *n. fleas.* A small insect that jumps. *Fleas* suck the blood of some furry animals and of people.– Our dog has *fleas.*

fled (FLED) *v.* One form of the verb *flee.*– The burglar *fled* through the open second-story window.

fledg•ling or **fledge•ling** (FLEJ-ling) *n. fledglings* or *fledgelings.* 1. A young bird that has just learned how to fly.–The *fledgling* spread its wings and flew out of its nest.
2. A young and inexperienced person. – David hopes to be a famous reporter some day. Right now he is a *fledgling.*

flee (FLEE) *v. flees, fled, fleeing.* Run away; escape; get away quickly.–We saw a burglar *fleeing* from the gas station.

fleece (FLEESS) *n.* The woolly coat of an animal. – The farmer clipped the *fleece* from the sheep's back.
–*v. fleeces, fleeced, fleecing.* 1. Cut the wool from.–He *fleeces* his sheep once a year.
2. Cheat. – The dishonest salesman *fleeced* Uncle Mike of all his savings.

fleet (FLEET) *n. fleets.* 1. A company of boats or ships moving together or under one commander.–We watched the *fleet* move down the river.–The United States *fleet* sails the oceans.
2. Any group or team of moving vehicles.– We saw a *fleet* of trucks on the highway. There were many trucks moving together.

–*adj. fleeter, fleetest.* Swift.–An animal or person who is *fleet* of foot is one who moves fast.

flesh (FLESH) *n.* 1. The part of your body that covers the bones. *Flesh* is meat. We eat the *flesh* of cows, lambs, and certain other animals.
2. The parts of fruits and vegetables that you eat.–The *flesh* of the peach is juicy.
3. Kindred; a relative.–A person who is one of your own *flesh* is a person who is related to you, one of your own family.

flesh•y (FLESH-ee) *adj. fleshier, fleshiest.* Plump.–Mother thinks Father is too *fleshy.*

flew (FLOO) *v.* One form of the verb *fly.*–The bird *flew* to her nest with a worm for her babies.

flex•i•ble (FLEKS-ə-bəl) *adj.; flexibly, adv.; flexibility, n.* 1. Bending easily without breaking.–The wire was so *flexible* that Bob could roll it into a ball.
2. Capable of being changed. – Our plans were *flexible.* We were willing to accept other suggestions.

flick•er (FLIK-er) *n. flickers.* 1. A quick, trembling movement. –The boy stared at me without a *flicker* of an eyelash.
2. One of the largest birds of the woodpecker family. The underparts of a *flicker's* wings are red or golden. *Flickers* live chiefly on ants.
–*v. flickers, flickered, flickering.* Flutter or move quickly.–The fire *flickered* a few times and then went out.

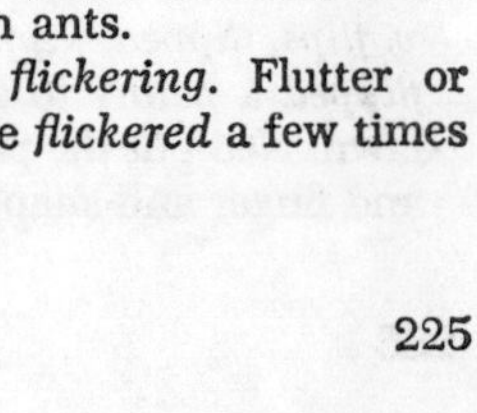

fli·er (FLY-er) *n. fliers.* Anything that flies.–Birds and insects that have wings are *fliers.* –Aviators are *fliers.* They fly airplanes.

flies (FLYZ) *n. pl.* More than one *fly.*–*Flies* carry diseases.
–*v.* One form of the verb *fly.*–Bob *flies* his kite on windy days. – The bird *flies* home with worms for its young.

flight (FLYT) *n. flights.* 1. Movement through the air.–Bob shot the arrow and then watched its *flight.*
2. A distance flown.–It is a long *flight* from Canada to England.
3. A flock of birds. – A *flight* of geese just passed over our town.

4. A set of steps, or stairway.–We went up two *flights* to get to our classroom.
5. Act of fleeing.–The policeman put the burglar to *flight.* He made him start running away.

flim·sy (FLIM-zee) *adj. flimsier, flimsiest; flimsily, adv.* Soft, thin, and not very strong. –The cloth in Mary's dress is *flimsy.*–Tissue paper is *flimsy.* It tears easily.

flinch (FLINCH) *v. flinches, flinched, flinching.* Draw back suddenly in fear of being hurt.–When the man started to hit the horse, it *flinched.*

fling (FLING) *n. flings.* 1. A Scottish dance.–Scottish people dance the Highland *fling.*
2. A time given up to complete enjoyment of oneself without any duties.–The boys are having their *fling* now during their vacation.
–*v. flings, flung, flinging.* Throw or toss. – Jack likes to *fling* darts at a target.–She *flung* herself on the bed.

flint (FLINT) *n. flints.* A very hard stone also known as "quartz." – The Boy Scouts lighted a fire with a spark made by rubbing *flint* against a piece of steel.

flip (FLIP) *n. flips.* A throw.–On the first *flip* the coin landed tails up.
–*v. flips, flipped, flipping.* Toss.–Ned and Bob *flipped* a penny to see who would mow the lawn. Ned put the penny between his thumb and finger and snapped it into the air.

flip·per (FLIP-er) *n. flippers.* A fin of a fish or seal, or the foreleg of a turtle. *Flippers* are like paddles. They help water animals to swim.

flit (FLIT) *v. flits, flitted, flitting.* Dart; fly; move swiftly and lightly.–Mary *flitted* across the hall in her long party dress.–A butterfly *flitted* through the window.

float (FLOHT) *n. floats.* 1. Anything that stays on top of the water or other liquid, such as a raft.–The fisherman uses a cork *float,* or bob, on his fishline to support the hook in the water and keep it from going all the way to the bottom. The *float* goes up and down when a fish is biting.
2. A decorated platform which is drawn by a car, or a horse.–One store had several *floats* in the parade.
–*v. floats, floated, floating.* 1. Stay at the top of a liquid.–Some soaps *float.* They do not sink.–Wood *floats* in water.

2. Make float.–He *floated* his toy sailboat in the bath.
3. Drift.–The toy balloon *floated* through the air.

flock (FLAHK) *n. flocks.* A group.–We speak of a crowd of people, a herd of cattle, and a *flock* of sheep or birds.

–*v. flocks, flocked, flocking.* Gather; come in groups. – A crowd of people *flocked* to the schoolhouse to hear the speaker.

flog (FLAHG) *v. flogs, flogged, flogging.* Whip; beat.–The cruel groom *flogged* the horse.

flood (FLUD) *n. floods.* 1. Too much water.–A river sometimes rises and flows over its banks, causing a *flood* on either side of it.–The Mississippi *flood* made many people homeless.

2. Anything that comes in great numbers or quantities, such as a *flood* of callers, a *flood* of sunlight, or a *flood* of angry words.
—*v. floods, flooded, flooding.* 1. Flow over; cover with water.—The long, heavy rains *flooded* the countryside.

2. Fill to overflowing.—When Mary was sick, her friends *flooded* her room with flowers.

floor (FLOR) *n. floors.* 1. Just as the ceiling is the top of the room, the *floor* is the bottom.—The table stands on the *floor.*—I dropped my hat on the *floor.*

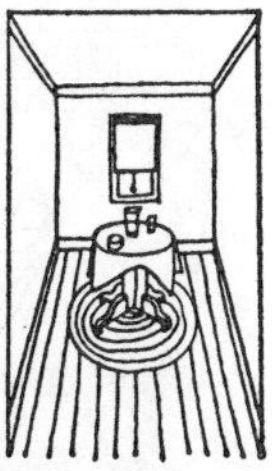

2. A story or level of a building.—We live on the first *floor* of the house.—Shoes can be bought on the third *floor* of the store.
3. Right to speak in a meeting.—Don't interrupt Mary. She has the *floor.*
—*v. floors, floored, flooring.* 1. Make a floor.—We *floored* the garage with bricks.
2. Cause to fall to the floor. — One fighter *floored* the other.

flop (FLAHP) *v. flops, flopped, flopping.* 1. Drop down. — Father was so tired after the race that he *flopped* onto the bed without undressing. He threw himself heavily onto the bed.
2. Toss or throw the body from side to side.—The fish *flopped* about in the net.

Flor·i·da (FLAWR-ə-də) *n.* A flat peninsular state on the southeastern coast of the United States, popular as a resort. Citrus fruits and vegetables are raised the year round. *Florida* ships sugar, fruit, tobacco, lumber, and fertilizer to other parts of the world.

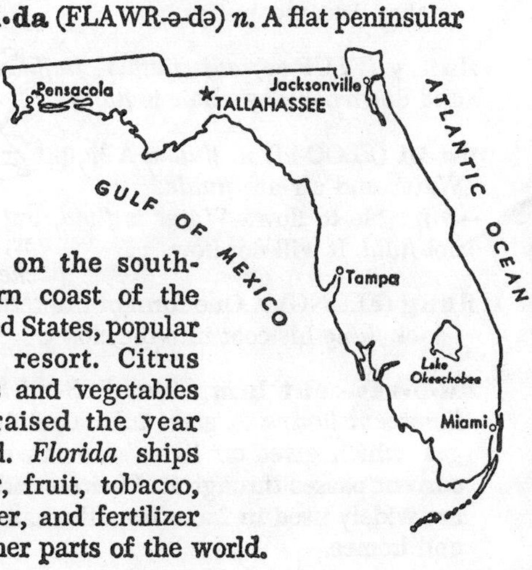

flo·rist (FLAWR- *or* FLOR-ist) *n. florists.* A person who sells and sometimes also raises flowers.

floss (FLAWSS) *n.* 1. A soft silk thread that is not twisted.—Mother is embroidering my woolen dress with silk *floss.*
2. The silky threads on the ears of corn, the fluffy part of dandelion seeds, and other silky parts of plants.

floun·der (FLOWN-der) *n. flounder* or *flounders.* A *flounder* is a fish, about a foot long, used for food.

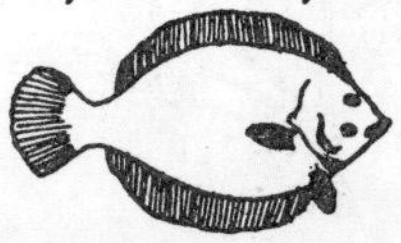

—*v. flounders, floundered, floundering.* 1. Flop about helplessly.—Jack *floundered* about in the water after he fell in.
2. Be awkward or helpless; hesitate.—When the teacher asked Bob the difficult question, he *floundered.*

flour (FLOW-er) *n. flours.* A powdery substance made from a ground grain, such as wheat, rye, or barley.—Bread is made from *flour.*

flour·ish (FLER-ish) *v. flourishes, flourished, flourishing.* 1. Thrive.—The flowers in Grandmother's garden *flourish.* The flowers in Grandmother's garden are strong and healthy.
2. Prosper.—Father's new business is *flourishing.* It is very successful.

flow (FLOH) *n.* 1. A stream.—There is a big *flow* of oil coming from the oil well.
2. A smooth, steady motion. — He speaks well. He has a wonderful *flow* of words.—The baby was lulled by the *flow* of the music.
—*v. flows, flowed, flowing.* 1. Run; pour; go along as a liquid. — Water *flows* from the spring.
2. Move like a stream of water.—Many people are *flowing* through the gates to see the circus.
3. Ripple; wave.—Arabs wear robes that *flow* as the men walk.

FLOWERS

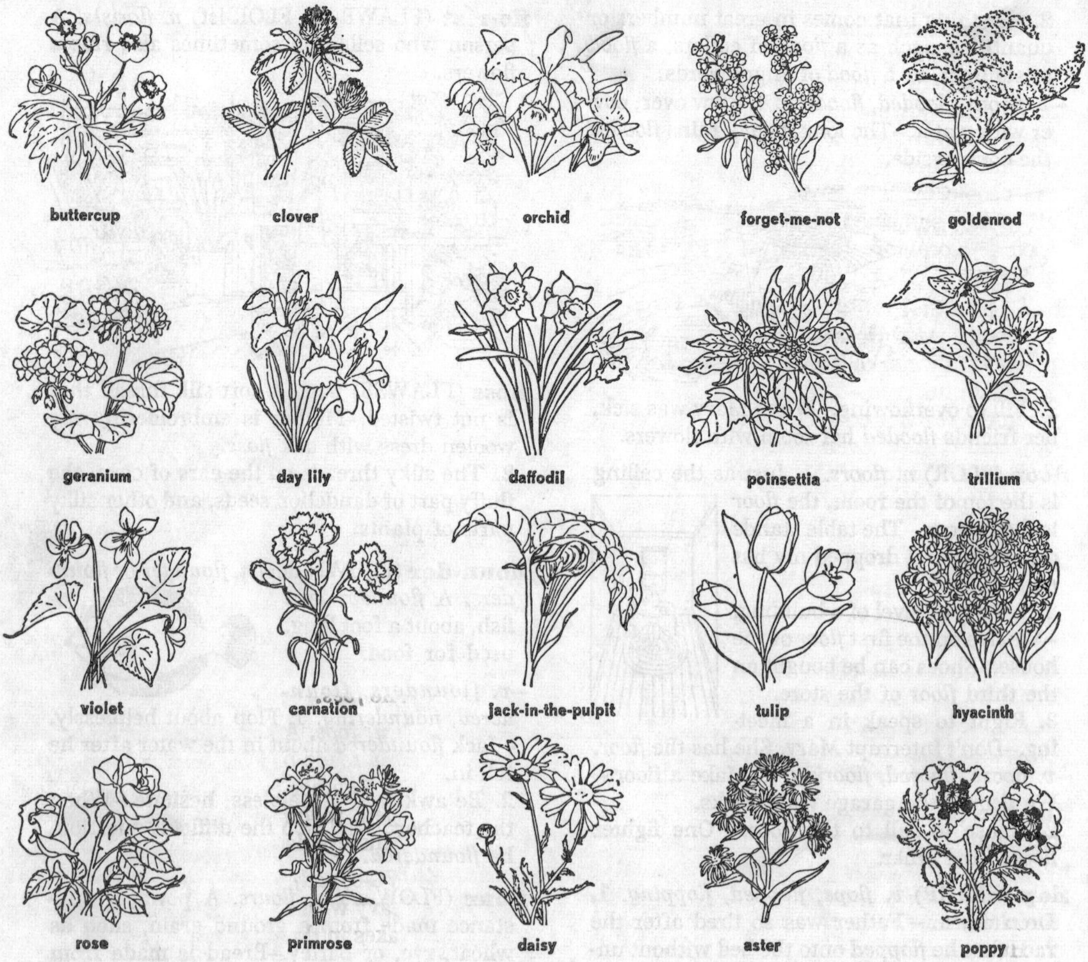

flow•er (FLOW-er) *n. flowers.* The blossom of any plant. *Flowers* are of many colors and shapes. The seeds of a plant are produced in the *flowers.*
–*v. flowers, flowered, flowering.* 1. Produce flowers.–This plant does not *flower* until late in the fall.
2. Thrive.–Knighthood *flowered* in the Middle Ages.

flown (FLOHN) *v.* One form of the verb *fly.* –The flier has *flown* many miles in his airplane.

flu•ent (FLOO-ənt) *adj.; fluently, adv.; fluency, n.* Having a smooth, easy, graceful flow in speech or writing.–Father speaks *fluent* Spanish. He speaks the language easily and well.

fluff (FLUF) *n. fluffs.* Any soft, light substance, such as soft feathers, or bits of cotton or wool.
–*v. fluffs, fluffed, fluffing.* Make puffy and soft. – Grandmother *fluffs* up the pillows when she makes the bed. She shakes them so they become puffy.

fluff•y (FLUF-ee) *adj. fluffier, fluffiest.* Soft and downy.–Baby's hair is *fluffy.*

flu•id (FLOO-id) *n. fluids.* A liquid or gas.– Water and air are *fluids.*
–*adj.* Able to flow.–Water is *fluid,* but ice is not *fluid.* It will not flow.

flung (FLUNG) *v.* One form of the verb *fling.* –Jack *flung* his coat into the closet.

flu•o•res•cent lamp (flu-RESS-ənt LAMP) *florescent lamps.* A glass tube containing a gas which gives off light when an electric current passes through it. *Fluorescent lamps* are widely used in factories, offices, schools, and homes.

flu•or•o•scope (FLUHR-ə-skohp) *n. fluoroscopes.* An instrument used for examining the insides of people or objects by viewing their shadows on a special screen while the people or objects are being subjected to X-rays.—The doctor used a *fluoroscope* to examine the patient's abdomen.

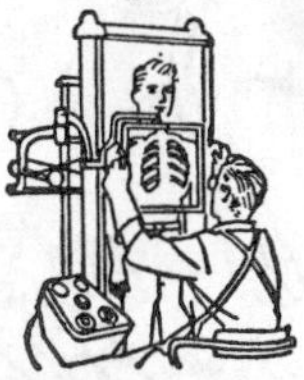

flush (FLUSH) *v. flushes, flushed, flushing.* 1. Flood; pour over. — Father *flushed* the porch with water to get the dust off.
2. Blush; turn red.—The girl's cheeks *flushed* when the teacher called on her.
—*adj.* and *adv.* 1. Even; level. — The milk is *flush* with the top of the glass.
2. Well provided.—Bob is *flush* with money today.

flute (FLOOT) *n. flutes.* A musical instrument made of a tube that is closed at one end and has holes in the side. The holes are covered with the fingers and with keys to make the different tones of the scale. The sound is made by blowing across a hole in the side at the closed end.

flut•ter (FLUT-er) *n. flutters.* A state of excitement.—The crowd was in a *flutter.*
—*v. flutters, fluttered, fluttering.* 1. Move rapidly back and forth.—The clothes *flutter* on the clothesline.
2. Hurry excitedly. — Mary *fluttered* about getting ready for school.

fly (FLY) *n. flies.* 1. In baseball, a hit ball that goes high in the air.—Bob hit a long *fly* to the left fielder.
2. A kind of insect with two wings. *Flies* spread diseases.
3. A fishing bait made to look like an insect.—The fisherman used a handmade *fly* to catch the trout.

—*v. flies, flew, flying.* 1. Move through the air. —Birds and insects are able to *fly* by moving their wings.
2. Wave freely in the air.—The clothes on the clothesline *fly* in the wind.—The flag is *flying* over the schoolhouse.
3. Cause to fly.—Jack *flew* his model airplane.

fly•er (FLY-er) *n. flyers.* One way of spelling the noun *flier,* meaning a person or thing that flies.

foam (FOHM) *n. foams.* A mass of tiny bubbles.—When she poured the ginger ale, the *foam* went over the top of the glass.
—*v. foams, foamed, foaming.* Make tiny bubbles.—Many drinks *foam.*—The sea *foams* during storms.

foam•y (FOHM-ee) *adj. foamier, foamiest.* Filled with bubbles.—Sometimes water along the edge of a lake is *foamy.*—Some drinks are *foamier* than others.

fo•cus (FOH-kəss) *v. focuses, focused, focusing.* 1. Concentrate on one spot, thing, subject, etc.—Please *focus* your attention on one thing at a time.
2. Bring into clear view, especially by bringing light rays together at one point, as through a person's eyes or through lenses. —The camera lens *focused* the image near the center of the film.
—*focus, n. focuses.*

fod•der (FAHD-er) *n.* Dried feed, such as hay or corn, for farm animals.—Horses and cattle eat *fodder.*

foe (FOH) *n. foes.* An enemy.—Bob has many friends, but no *foes.*

fog (FAWG) *n. fogs.* A cloud lying near the ground. *Fog* is made of tiny drops of water floating close together in the air.
—*v. fogs, fogged, fogging.* Make misty.—The mist *fogged* his eyeglasses.

fog•gy (FAWG-ee) *adj. foggier, foggiest; foggily, adv.* Heavy with fog; misty.—It is often *foggy* near lakes in the morning.

foil (FOIL) *n. foils.* 1. A light sword used for fencing.

2. A very thin sheet of metal.—Candy is often wrapped in a *foil* called tin*foil.*
—*v. foils, foiled, foiling.* Upset; keep from success.—The policeman *foiled* the robber's plans. He kept the robber from carrying out his plans.

fold (FOHLD) *n. folds.* 1. A crease or place where something is bent double.—To make a *fold* in cloth means to double the cloth back on itself.
2. A pen for sheep.—Sheep are kept in a *fold.*
—*v. folds, folded, folding.* 1. Bend so that the surfaces lie together.—Do not *fold* your spelling papers.
2. Clasp together.—*Fold* your arms and sit up straight. Put one arm over the other and keep them close together.

FOOD

fold·er (FOHLD-er) *n. folders.* 1. A holder made of folded paper or cardboard.–The children made a *folder* to keep their drawings in.
2. A booklet made of a sheet of paper folded many times.–Father got a *folder* telling about vacation trips.

fo·li·age (FOH-lee-ij *or* FOHL-yij) *n.* The leaves of trees and plants.–The *foliage* turns different colors in the fall.

folk (FOHK) *n. folk* or *folks.* 1. People.–Our neighbors are friendly *folks.*–Country *folk* often have favorite family remedies for illness.
2. Relatives. – Grandmother's *folks* came from Ireland.

folk dance (FOHK danss) *folk dances.* 1. A dance made up by the common people and handed down through the generations.
2. The music for a folk dance.

folk song (FOHK sawng) *folk songs.* A song made up by the common people and handed down through the generations.–We learned the *folk songs* of the Scottish people.

fol·low (FAHL-oh) *v. follows, followed, following.* 1. Come after, in order.–Page 10 *follows* page 9.
2. Go along behind; pursue.–Bob's dog *followed* him to school.
3. Go along. – *Follow* this street until you come to the corner.
4. Do according to. – *Follow* the directions at the top of the page.
5. Give attention to.–*Follow* me now while I tell you the story.
6. Be the result of.–Success *follows* hard work.

fol·low·er (FAHL-oh-er) *n. followers.* 1. A person who follows the leadership of another. –Little John was one of Robin Hood's *followers.*
2. A person who acts according to some teaching.–He is a *follower* of the Christian religion.

fol·low·ing (FAHL-oh-ing) *n. followings.* A group of people who are followers.–The leader has a large *following.*
–*v.* One form of the verb *follow.*–The dog is *following* me.
–*adj.* Next.–The *following* story will be about a dog.–Bob will read this story and Mary will read the one *following.*

fol·ly (FAHL-ee) *n. follies.* Foolishness; unwise action.–People who do unwise things usually pay for their *folly.*

fond (FAHND) *adj. fonder, fondest; fondly, adv.* 1. Loving; full of love.–Father is *fond* of his children.
2. Filled with interest or liking.–Bob is *fond* of baseball.

fon•dle (FAHN-dl) *v. fondles, fondled, fondling.* Handle with love; pet.–Sally *fondles* her kitten gently.

fond•ness (FAHND-nəss) *n.* Liking; love.–Mary has a great *fondness* for music.

food (FOOD) *n. foods.* Something to eat or drink.–Vegetables, meats, fruits, nuts, and milk are *foods*.–The restaurant served good *food*.

fool (FOOL) *n. fools.* 1. A person who is very unwise.–The man is a *fool*. He does things that are not sensible.
2. A clown; a person who amuses and entertains people by acting funny.
–*v. fools, fooled, fooling.* To trick.–We *fooled* Bob on the first of April. We tricked him into believing there was no school on that day.

fool•ish (FOOL-ish) *adj.; foolishly, adv.* Not wise; not sensible.–It is *foolish* to stay in swimming too long.

fool•ish•ness (FOOL-ish-nəss) *n.* 1. Silly behavior.–The teacher told the children to stop their *foolishness*.
2. Action that is not wise.–The boy's *foolishness* got him into trouble.

foot (FUHT) *n. feet.* 1. The part of the body on which a person or animal stands and walks. – We have five toes on each *foot*. – Dogs have four *feet*.

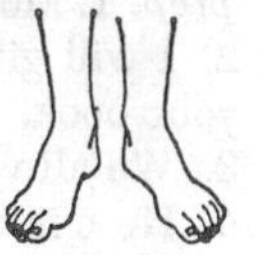

2. The bottom; the lowest part. –Bob stood at the *foot* of the stairs and called to his mother upstairs.

3. A measurement of length.– Twelve inches are equal to one *foot*. –There are three *feet* in a yard.

–*v. foots, footed, footing.* Pay; be responsible for.–We are going to the show and Father will *foot* the bill.

foot•ball (FUHT-bawl) *n. footballs.* 1. A game played between two teams of eleven men with an oval-shaped, leather-covered ball.

2. The ball used in the game of football.

foot•note (FUHT-noht) *n. footnotes.* A note at the bottom of a page. It gives additional information. – Bob read the *footnote*. The *footnote* told where to find the directions for making the kite described on that page.

foot•path (FUHT-path) *n. footpaths.* A path or narrow way for people walking.–The children walked on the *footpath*.

foot•print (FUHT-print) *n. footprints.* The track or mark made by a foot.–We saw the man's *footprints* in the snow.

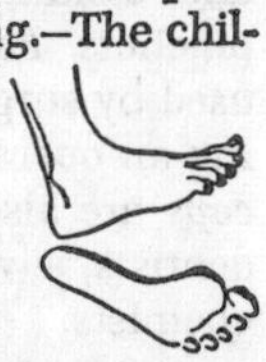

foot•step (FUHT-step) *n. footsteps.* The sound or noise made by one's feet when walking or stepping along.–We heard a man's *footsteps* in the hall.

foot•stool (FUHT-stool) *n. footstools.* A low stool for the feet. – Father sat with his feet on the *footstool* and smoked his pipe.

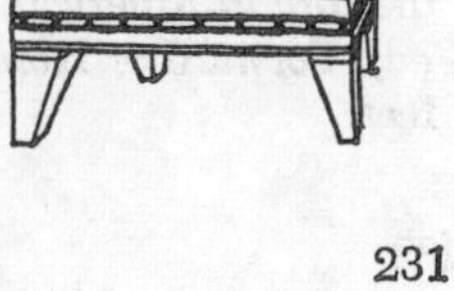

for (FOR) *conj.* Because; since.–I know that she has the book, *for* I saw it.
–*prep.* 1. Mother left *for* Chicago today.
2. I will give you my knife in exchange *for* your book.
3. We all voted *for* Mary.
4. Here is a gift *for* you.
5. Since you worked so hard, you may have an hour *for* rest.
6. We looked *for* Father's hat.
7. Mary has a great fondness *for* music.
8. A mark of "B" is good *for* her; that is as well as she can do.
9. Milk is good *for* you; it makes you strong.
10. Father rode on the train *for* a whole day. –Baby slept *for* hours.
11. Will you do something *for* me?

for•bade (fer-BAD *or* for-BAYD) *v.* One form of the verb *forbid.*–The policeman *forbade* the man to drive up the one-way street.

for•bid (fer- *or* for-BID) *v. forbids, forbade, forbidding.* Refuse to allow.–I *forbid* you to leave town today.–Father *forbids* us to play in the street.

force (FORSS) *n. forces.* 1. Strength.–The water runs with much *force.*
2. A thing that causes a change in motion.–A ball that is thrown into the air is pulled to earth by the *force* of gravity.
3. A body of men formed for a certain purpose.–The police *force* marched in the parade.
–*v. forces, forced, forcing.* 1. Make; compel.–The officer *forced* the thief to surrender.
2. Make something go or move by strength. –We *forced* the top off the box to get the balls and bats inside.

for•ceps (FOR-səpss) *n. sing.* and *pl.* An instrument for seizing and holding things; pinchers. *Forceps* are used by surgeons during an operation. *Forceps* are also used by dentists, jewelers, and chemists.

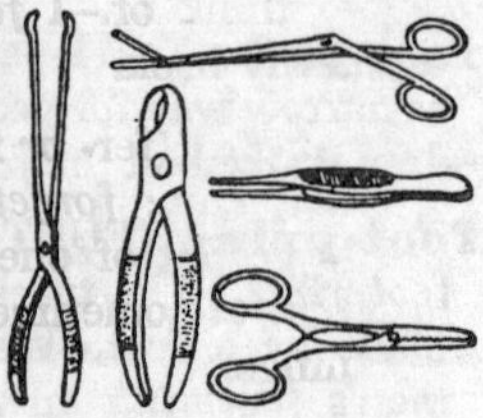

ford (FORD) *n. fords.* Shallow place in a stream where one may cross by walking through it.–They crossed the river at the *ford.*
–*v. fords, forded, fording.* Cross at a shallow place by wading.–The boys *forded* the stream.

fore (FOR) *n.* Front.–That year he came to the *fore* in American politics.
–*adj.* Forward or front.–A horse has two *fore* feet.
–A golf player calls "*fore*" when he wishes to warn people that they are in danger of being hit by a ball.

fore•arm (FOR-ahrm) *n. forearms.* The part of the arm below the elbow and above the hand.

fore•cast (FOR-kast) *n. forecasts.* A telling of what will happen; a prediction.–We heard the weather *forecast* on the radio today. It told us ahead of time what kind of weather we were going to have.
–*v. forecasts, forecast, forecasting.* Tell ahead of time; predict.–The weatherman *forecasts* the weather.

fore•fa•ther (FOR-fah<u>th</u>-er) *n. forefathers.* A person from whom one is descended; ancestor.–Your father, mother, and your grandparents are some of your *forefathers.*

fore•fin•ger (FOR-fing-ger) *n. forefingers.* The finger next to the thumb.

fore•head (FOR- *or* FAHR-əd *or* hed) *n. foreheads.* The part of the face between the eyes and scalp.–Bob wears his cap pulled down over his *forehead.*

for•eign (FOR- *or* FAHR-ən) *adj.* Of a country other than one's own.–The priest speaks several *foreign* languages. He speaks the language of several countries besides his own.

for•eign•er (FOR- *or* FAHR-ən-er) *n. foreigners.* A person in a country where he is not a citizen, or a person of a foreign country. –An American is a *foreigner* when he is in Europe.

fore•man (FOR-mən) *n. foremen.* A boss of a certain number of workers; a supervisor.–Bob's uncle is a *foreman* in the factory. He is boss of many workmen.

fore•most (FOR-mohst) *adj.* and *adv.* Main; chief; first; most important.–The *foremost* reason we did not go was that it was raining. –He was considered the village's *foremost* citizen.–He fell head *foremost.*

fore•noon (FOR-noon) *n. forenoons.* The morning; the part of the day before noon.

fore•see (for-SEE) *v. foresees, foresaw, foreseeing* Know ahead of time.–Bob *foresaw* that his team would lose, but he played his best anyway.

fore•sight (FOR-syt) *n.* Concern or thought for the time to come, based on being able to tell what will probably happen.—Young men who have *foresight* save money now so they can live on it when they are old.

for•est (FOR- *or* FAHR-əst) *n. forests.* Woods; land that is thickly covered with trees.—Wild animals live in the *forest.*

for•est•er (FOR- *or* FAHR-əss-ter) *n. foresters.* A man who takes care of a forest or woods.

fore•tell (for-TEL) *v. foretells, foretold, foretelling.* Forecast; tell ahead of time.—Grandfather said he could not *foretell* what the weather would be tomorrow.

fore•thought (FOR-thawt) *n.* Thinking or planning ahead of time.—The boy's *forethought* kept the train from being wrecked. When he saw that the bridge was washed out, he ran back and waved a flag to stop the train. He thought what to do to prevent an accident.

fore•told (for-TOHLD) *v.* One form of the verb *foretell.*—The wise man *foretold* many of the things that have since happened.

for•ev•er (fer- *or* for-EV-er) *adv.* 1. For all time to come.—The snow will not last *forever.*
2. Always.—She is *forever* complaining.—Our kitten is *forever* getting lost.

for•feit (FOR-fət) *n. forfeits.* Something given up or paid as a penalty.—Repeated speeding resulted in the *forfeit* of his driver's license.
—*v. forfeits, forfeited, forfeiting.* Give up.—In this game you have to *forfeit* something every time you do not guess the right answer.

for•gave (fer- *or* for-GAYV) *v.* One form of the verb *forgive.*—The gardener *forgave* the tardy boy for running across the newly planted lawn.

forge (FORJ) *n. forges.* The fireplace in which a blacksmith heats metal.

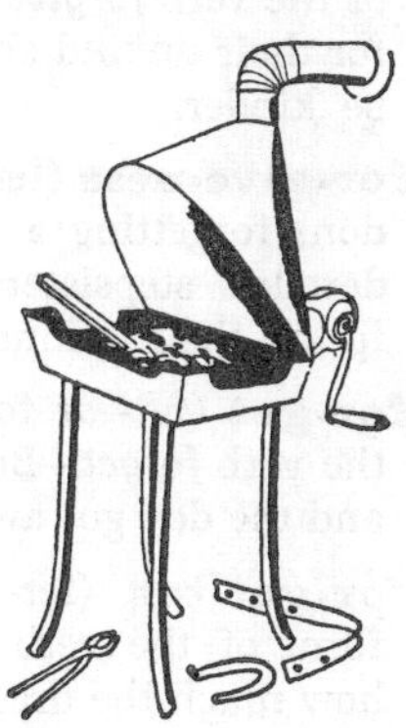

—*v. forges, forged, forging.* 1. Soften with heat and hammer into shape.—A blacksmith *forges* horseshoes. He shapes hot iron to fit the horse's hoofs.
2. Make or write falsely; counterfeit.—The man *forged* Mr. Smith's signature on a check.
3. Move with great difficulty, but steadily.—The army *forged* ahead.

forg•er (FORJ-er) *n. forgers.* A person who signs someone else's name to checks or papers, or who makes false things and pretends they are real.

for•ger•y (FORJ-er-ee) *n. forgeries.* 1. The signing of another person's name to checks or other papers; the imitation of someone else's writing or painting for the purpose of cheating.
2. The making of anything that is false and pretending that it is real; also, the thing so made.—This five dollar bill is a *forgery.* It is a counterfeit.

for•get (fer- *or* for-GET) *v. forgets, forgot, forgetting.* 1. Not think of something which one was supposed to think of at a certain time.—Do not *forget* to wear your rubbers. Remember to wear them.
2. Be unable to remember a thing one is trying to think of.—I *forget* who it was that found my book.

for•get•ful (fer- *or* for-GET-fuhl) *adj.; forgetfully, adv.; forgetfulness, n.* Apt to let things go out of one's mind.—Grandmother is *forgetful* sometimes. She doesn't remember things.

for•get-me-not (fer- *or* for-GET-mee-naht) *n. forget-me-nots.* A small blue flower that grows on low plants. *Forget-me-nots* stand for friendship.

for•give (fer- *or* for-GIV) *v. forgives, forgave, forgiving.* Excuse; pardon.—I will *forgive* you for not coming if you will promise to come another time.

for·giv·en (fer- *or* for-GIV-ən) *v.* One form of the verb *forgive.*—The boys were *forgiven* for their unkind acts when they promised to be kinder.

for·give·ness (fer- *or* for-GIV-nəss) *n.* Pardon; forgetting a wrong done to one.—Cinderella's stepsisters begged her *forgiveness* for all their unkindness to her.

for·got (fer- *or* for-GAHT) *v.* One form of the verb *forget.*—Bob *forgot* to close the gate and the dog got away.

for·got·ten (fer- *or* for-GAHT-n) *v.* One form of the verb *forget.*—I have *forgotten* how much the dress cost.

fork (FORK) *n. forks.* 1. A table utensil with several long points, for picking up solid food. We eat meat, vegetables, salad, and pie with a *fork.*

2. A place where something splits out into two or more directions.—We came to a *fork* in the road, and didn't know which turn to take.
—*v. forks, forked, forking.* 1. Split in different directions. — The road *forks* by the farmhouse.
2. Take up with a fork.—The farmer *forked* the hay onto the wagon. He lifted it onto the wagon with a forklike tool called a pitchfork.

for·lorn (fer- *or* for-LORN) *adj.; forlornly, adv.* Lonely; pitiful; left all alone and uncared for.—The empty house looked *forlorn.*—The old woman looked *forlorn* sitting by the dying fire with her cat.

form (FORM) *n. forms.* 1. Shape.—What is the *form* of your new scarf, square or three-cornered?
2. Shape; condition.—The fighter is in *form* for the championship fight.
3. A kind.—Sand is a *form* of earth.
4. Rules of polite society.—The party was carried out according to *form.*—It is good *form* to thank people for gifts.
5. A way of presenting something, or arranging it.—I have heard the story told in the *form* of a poem.—There is a standard *form* for beginning a letter.
6. A sheet of paper on which to provide information.—Have you applied for a license yet? Or have you forgotten to fill out the *form?*
—*v. forms, formed, forming.* 1. Make; take the shape of.—We *formed* a circle around the player who stood in the middle. — Cream *forms* butter when beaten or churned.
2. Come or bring into shape; develop; grow. —Buds are *forming* on the trees.—John has *formed* the habit of brushing his teeth twice a day.

for·mal (FOR-məl) *adj.; formally, adv.* 1. Stiff; not homey, friendly, and easy. — The big room seemed very *formal* when we went in. We were afraid to make ourselves comfortable in it.
2. According to form, or the rules of polite society.—The party was *formal.* It was all carefully planned, and the guests wore evening clothes.

for·ma·tion (for-MAY-shən) *n. formations.*
1. The making or forming of something.—The *formation* of a dramatic club pleased the drama students.
2. Something made or formed.—Tornadoes are always accompanied by funnel-shaped cloud *formations.*
3. An arrangement of military forces, such as soldiers or ships.—The fighter planes flew in *formation.* They flew in a group, with one leading.

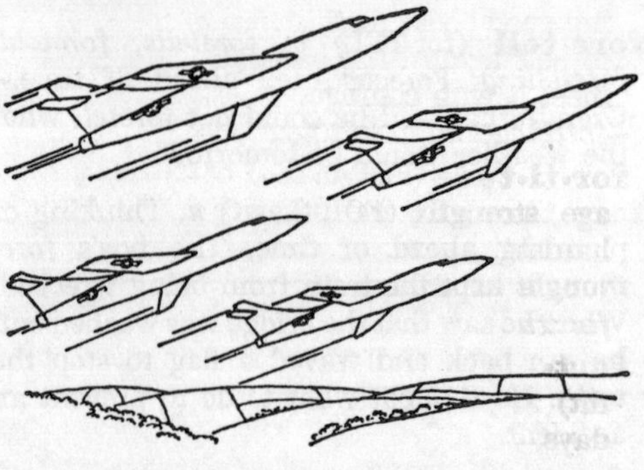

for·mer (FOR-mer) *adj.; formerly, adv.* Having happened or been in the past.—Miss Smith is a *former* teacher of mine. She was once my teacher, but she isn't now.—In *former* years means in time gone by.

for·mu·la (FOR-myə-lə) *n. formulas.* 1. A prescription or recipe. — The druggist prepared the *formula.*—Mother uses a *formula* for the special milk Baby drinks.
2. A special combination of words or symbols used to express a rule, fact, or principle. —The chemical *formula* for water is H_2O, meaning two parts of hydrogen to one of oxygen.

for·sake (fer- *or* for-SAYK) *v. forsakes, forsook, forsaking.* Leave; go away from.—Bob would not *forsake* his duty for pleasure.—Ellen would not *forsake* her pet kitten.

for·sak·en (fer- *or* for-SAYK-ən) *v.* One form of the verb *forsake.*–The people have *forsaken* the town. They have left it.
–*adj.* Lonely; left all alone.–The old house looks *forsaken.* It looks as if everyone has left it for good.

fort (FORT) *n. forts.* A place with strong walls, furnished with guns to repel attacks.

forth (FORTH) *adv.* Forward.–Mother rocked the baby back and *forth.*–Bill stepped *forth* from behind the bush and called to Ed.

for·ti·eth (FOR-tee-əth) *n. fortieths.* One of 40 equal parts.–If a piece of farmland is divided into forty equal parts, each piece will take up one *fortieth* of the farm. In figures it is written 1/40.
–*adj.* Coming as number 40 in a series.–This is Uncle Jim's *fortieth* birthday. Last year he celebrated his thirty-ninth birthday. Next year he will be forty-one.

for·ti·fy (FOR-tə-fy) *v. fortifies, fortified, fortifying.* 1. Strengthen militarily, by building forts, establishing gun positions, etc.–The army *fortified* the coastline.
2. Make stronger.–Father believes that reading good books *fortifies* the mind.–I *fortified* myself against the bad news by deciding to meet it with courage.
–*fortification, n. fortifications.*

for·ti·tude (FOR-tə-tood *or* -tyood) *n.* Courage, strength, and patience in facing up to hardship, pain, or danger.–Those on the jungle expedition were men of daring and *fortitude.*

fort·night (FORT-nyt. In England, FAWT-nit) *n. fortnights.* Two weeks, or fourteen days.

for·tress (FORT-rəss) *n. fortresses.* A fort, building, or place that can be defended against an enemy.–The soldiers built a *fortress* by the river.

for·tu·nate (FOR-chə-nət) *adj.; fortunately, adv.* Lucky.–Bob was fortunate to find the book he had lost.

for·tune (FOR-chən) *n. fortunes.* 1. Money; property; wealth.–The rich man left his *fortune* to the college he had gone to.–Father says Mr. Brown is worth a *fortune;* he says Mr. Brown is rich.–The youngest son made his clothes into a bundle and went out into the world to seek his *fortune.*
2. Luck.–It was my good *fortune* to find Mary at home when I called.
3. What is going to happen to one in the future.–The gypsy told us our *fortunes* by reading our palms.

FORTS AND FORTRESSES

Fort Boone, Kentucky

13th century fortress, Italy

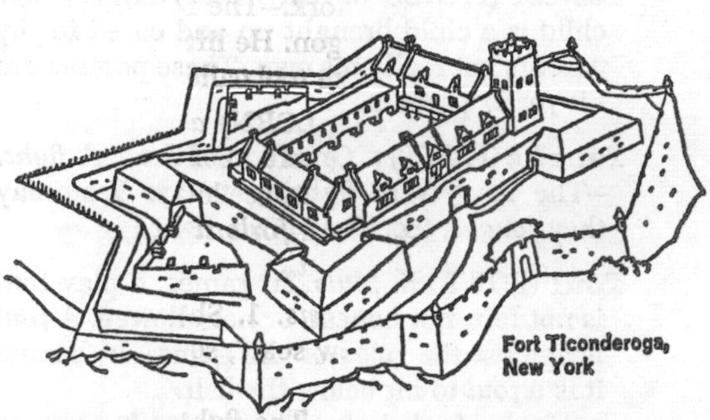
Fort Ticonderoga, New York

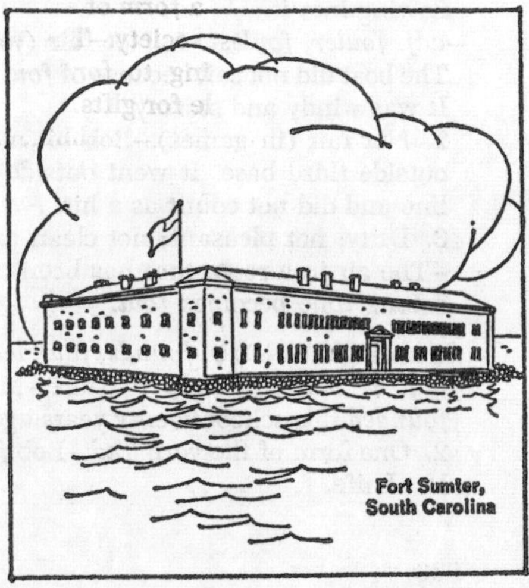
Fort Sumter, South Carolina

for·ty (FOR-tee) *n. forties* and *adj.* The number [40] coming after 39 and before 41.–Four tens make *forty.*

for·ward (FOR-werd) *v. forwards, forwarded, forwarding.* Send on.–If a letter comes for you after you have gone, we will *forward* it.
–*adj.* and *adv.* 1. Bold; anxious to be noticed.–Some children are very *forward,* and others are shy.
2. Front; or toward the front.–She went to the *forward* part of the ship. She went *forward.*

fos·sil (FAHSS-əl) *n. fossils.* A trace of a plant or animal that has been preserved in the earth, usually in rock or sand. The trace may be a part of the thing itself, like a bone; or a hardened part of the thing, like a petrified egg; or a model of the thing cast in the

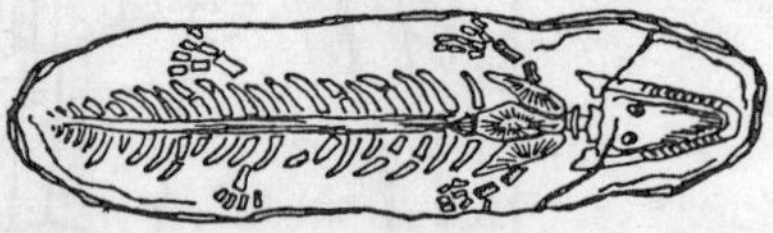

surrounding rock; or a print of the thing, like a bird track.

fos·ter (FAWSS- *or* FAHSS-ter) *adj.* A *foster* child is a child brought up and cared for by parents not really his own. These parents are his *foster* parents.

fought (FAWT) *v.* One form of the verb *fight.* –The boys were fighting today. Yesterday they *fought,* too. They often fight.

foul (FOWL) *n. fouls.* In games, a play that is not fair, not honest, or not allowed. A *foul* is against the rules of the game.–In boxing it is a *foul* to hit below the belt.
–*v. fouls, fouled, fouling.* Make impure or filthy.–The river water was *fouled* by waste flowing into it.
–*adj. fouler, foulest.* 1. Not fair (weather).–The boat did not sail because of *foul* weather. It was windy and stormy.
2. Not fair (in games).–Bob hit a *foul* ball outside third base. It went outside the base line and did not count as a hit.
3. Dirty; not pleasant; not clean and fresh. –The air in a room that has been closed for a long time becomes *foul.*

found (FOWND) *v. founds, founded, founding.* 1. Start, or help to start.–Mr. Smith *founded* this school twenty years ago.
2. One form of the verb *find.*–Bob *found* his lost knife.

foun·da·tion (fown-DAY-shən) *n. foundations.* 1. A base; the part on which something stands. – The *foundation* of our house is made of concrete.

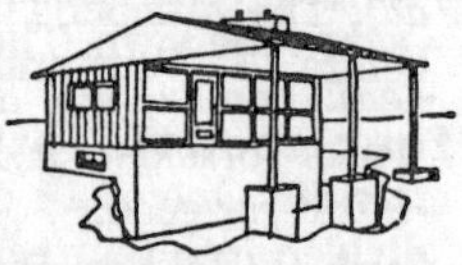

2. Basis.–A successful life usually requires a *foundation* of good schooling.

found·er (FOWN-der) *n. founders.* A person who starts or helps to start something. – George Washington was one of the *founders* of our country.

foun·dry (FOWN-dree) *n. foundries.* A building where melted iron, steel, or other materials are molded into different shapes and allowed to harden.

foun·tain (FOWNT-n) *n. fountains.* 1. A place where water is made to spurt upward, as from a pipe.–Children at school drink from a drinking *fountain.*–The men built a *fountain* in the park. The water piped into the *fountain* is thrown high up into the air and then drops back.

2. Place to get drinks. –The children went to the soda *fountain* after school.

foun·tain pen (FOWNT-n PEN) *fountain pens.* A writing pen in which there is a small sack filled with ink. As you write, the sack lets ink down to the point of the pen.

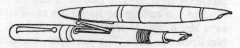

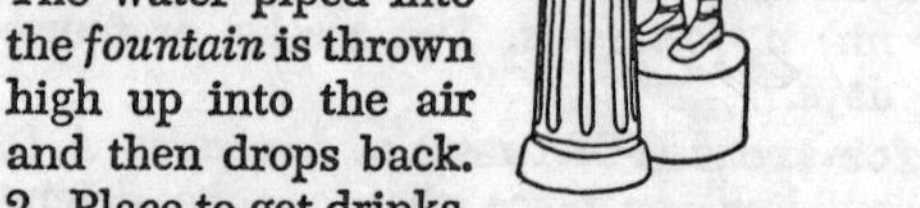

four (FOR) *n. fours* and *adj.* The number [4] coming after 3 and before 5.–Two and two make *four.*

four·score (FOR-SKOR) *n.* and *adj.* Eighty, or four times twenty.–*Fourscore* years are eighty years.

four·teen (FOR-TEEN) *n. fourteens* and *adj.* The number [14] coming after 13 and before 15.–Four and ten make *fourteen.*

four·teenth (FOR-TEENTH) *n. fourteenths.* One of 14 equal parts.–If a cake is divided into fourteen equal parts, each part is one *fourteenth.* In figures it is written 1/14.
–*adj.* Coming as number 14 in a series.–Today is my *fourteenth* birthday. I am fourteen years old.

fourth (FORTH) *n. fourths.* One of 4 equal parts.–Father ate a *fourth* of the pie. He ate one of the four equal parts into which it was cut. In figures it is written 1/4.
–*adj.* Coming as number 4 in a series.–This is Baby's *fourth* birthday. It is the next birthday after her third.

fowl (FOWL) *n. fowl* or *fowls.* A bird or chicken.–Birds that are eaten, such as geese, ducks, and pigeons, are *fowl.*

fox (FAHKS) *n. fox* or *foxes.* An animal that belongs to the dog family. *Foxes* are sly. Their fur is used for coats, collars, and trimming. Some fur is red, the color of red hair, and some is dark, with bits of silver.

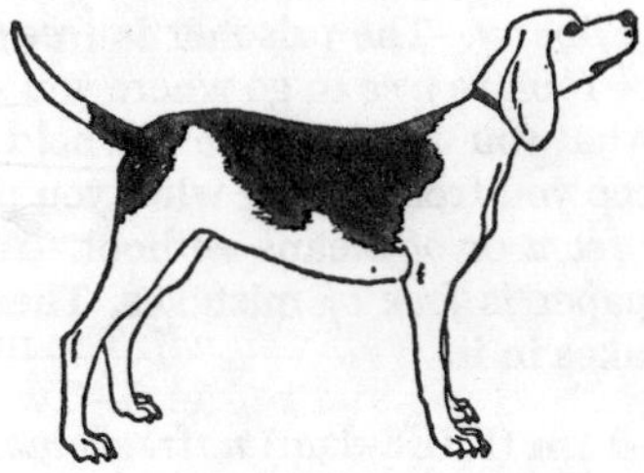

fox·hound (FAHKS-hownd) *n. foxhounds.* A dog trained to hunt foxes.–Ed uses a *foxhound* when he hunts foxes.

fox ter·ri·er (fahks TAIR-ee-er) *fox terriers.* A kind of dog. Some *fox terriers* have smooth hair, and others have rough or wiry hair.

foy·er (FOI-yay *or* -er) *n. foyers.* 1. A lobby or entrance hall, especially that of a theater.–The audience came out to the *foyer* between the acts of the play.
2. An entrance hall in a house or an apartment.–The clothes closet is in the *foyer* of our apartment.

frac·tion (FRAK-shən) *n. fractions.* A part of anything. All of anything is a whole. A part of it is a *fraction* of it.–A slice of an apple is just a *fraction* of an apple.–Mary gives a small *fraction* of her time to her arithmetic.
–*Fractions* are written in figures like this: 1/2, 1/5, 2/3, 1/6.

frac·ture (FRAK-cher) *n. fractures.* A break or a crack. – The old woman is suffering from a *fracture* of the leg.
–*v. fractures, fractured, fracturing.* Break; crack.–She fell on the ice and *fractured* a bone in one of her legs.

frag·ile (FRAJ-əl) *adj.* Delicate; not strong and sturdy.–Window glass, dishes, and mirrors are *fragile.* They break easily.–The old man has a *fragile* constitution.

frag·ment (FRAG-mənt) *n. fragments.* A small part or broken-off piece of anything.–A *fragment* of stone fell from the top of the wall.–When Baby dropped the stick of candy, it broke into small *fragments.*

fra·grance (FRAY-grənss) *n. fragrances.* A pleasant smell or odor.–The *fragrance* of the lilacs came through the open window.

fra·grant (FRAY-grənt) *adj.; fragrantly, adv.* Smelling sweet, like perfume. – Lilacs and lilies of the valley are *fragrant.*

frail (FRAYL) *adj. frailer, frailest.* 1. Apt to get sick easily; not able to stand much discomfort or hardship; not strong.–Old people often become *frail.* They lose their strength and become weaker.
2. Easily broken or torn.–Fine lace is *frail.*

frame (FRAYM) *n. frames.* 1. The skeleton, or part of anything that gives it shape and around which it is built.—Grandfather built a *frame* for the beans to grow up.—The *frame* of a house makes the shape of the house. The *frame* is made of strong timbers.

The *frame* usually does not show from the outside, but is covered by the walls.—The skeleton, made up of all the bones of the body, is a person's *frame*.

2. A border.—The *frame* on the mirror is gold.

—*v. frames, framed, framing.* 1. Put, or place, in a frame.—Mother *framed* the mirror herself. She put the frame on it herself.

2. Form; make.—The boys are *framing* some plans for starting a club.

3. Make an innocent person appear guilty of a crime.—John Smith said in court he had been *framed* for a crime that another man committed.

—*Frame of mind* means mood.—If Mother is in a good *frame of mind*, she will let us make candy.

franc (FRANGK) *n. francs.* A unit of money, used especially in France, Switzerland, and Belgium.

frank (FRANGK) *adj. franker, frankest; frankly, adv.; frankness, n.* Honest and direct in talking.—Father is very *frank* in talking to people. He says just what he thinks.

frank•furt•er (FRANGK-fert-er) *n. frankfurters.* A roll of spiced meat, shaped like a sausage, and pressed into a skin; often called a "hot dog."

fran•tic (FRAN-tik) *adj.; frantically, adv.* Excited; wild with upset feelings.—The lost child was *frantic*.—The sick man was *frantic* with pain.

fra•ter•nal (frə-TER-nəl) *adj.* 1. Relating to or like brothers.—Dick and Bob are almost as close as brothers. There is a *fraternal* bond between them.

2. Made up of members who have banded together for a common purpose.—A labor union is a *fraternal* organization.

fra•ter•ni•ty (frə-TER-nə-tee) *n. fraternities.* 1. A club or society, especially of male students in a college or university.—Tom belongs to a college *fraternity*.

2. A brotherhood or group of men belonging to the same profession or having common interests.—Dr. Jones belongs to the medical *fraternity*.

3. Brotherhood.—The French Revolution had as its motto, "Liberty, equality, *fraternity!*"

fraud (FRAWD) *n. frauds.* 1. Cheating.—The man's *fraud* in selling rotten apples was discovered.

2. A person who cheats or deceives others.—That man selling furs is a *fraud*. He is not honest. He makes believe that poor furs are good ones.

3. Something which deceives or cheats people.—The fancy fruit basket turned out to be a *fraud*. There was very little fruit in it.

fray (FRAY) *n. frays.* A loud quarrel or fight.—When Bob saw the boys having a snowball fight, he entered the *fray*.

—*v. frays, frayed, fraying.* Wear out into separate threads.—Grandfather *frayed* his coat collar with long wear. It is worn and raveled where it has rubbed against his neck.

freak (FREEK) *n. freaks.* An extremely unusual thing or happening.—A rabbit with three ears would be a *freak*. It would be odd, strange, not like others.

freck•le (FREK-əl) *n. freckles.* A tan spot on the skin.—Jack has red hair, and *freckles* all over his nose.—The sun makes *freckles* come out on one's face, arms, or body.

—*v. freckles, freckled, freckling.* Break out with freckles.—Some people tan in the sun, but do not *freckle*.

free (FREE) *v. frees, freed, freeing.* Turn loose; set at liberty.—Bob will *free* the turtle from the box. He will let it loose to go where it wants to go.

—*adj. freer, freest.* 1. Costing nothing.—Come to the show with me. I have been given *free* tickets.

2. At liberty.—The prisoner is *free* from jail now.—You are *free* to go where you want and say what you want; no one will hold you back or keep you from saying what you please.

—*Free from* or *of* means without.—Your spelling paper is *free of* mistakes. There are no mistakes in it.

free•dom (FREE-dəm) *n. freedoms.* Liberty; right to believe and act as one pleases.—Bob gave the turtle his *freedom*. He set him loose; he let him go.—We enjoy our *freedom* in this great land of ours.

freeze (FREEZ) *v. freezes, froze, freezing.* 1. Turn to ice.–Water will *freeze* when it gets cold enough.
2. Make so cold that it becomes solid.–The children helped to *freeze* the ice cream. They turned the crank of the freezer till the mixture of the cream and sugar was *frozen* almost solid.
–*freezer, n. freezers.*

freight (FRAYT) *n.* 1. Any goods sent from one place to another.–Some trains and ships carry more *freight* than others.–A *freight* train carries all kinds of goods from place to place.
2. The cost of shipping goods.–Father paid the *freight* on our new piano. He paid the money charged for sending it by train.

freight·er (FRAYT-er) *n. freighters.* A boat carrying freight or goods.–We saw a big *freighter* going down the river.

fren·zy (FREN-zee) *n. frenzies.* Fury; a fit of rage or great excitement.–The driver was in a *frenzy* because someone ran into his car. He was excited and angry.

fre·quent (free-KWENT) *v. frequents, frequented, frequenting.* Visit often.–He *frequents* the drugstore. He likes to buy sodas there after school.
–(FREE-kwənt) *adj.; frequently, adv.* Coming often, or close together in time.–Mother has *frequent* headaches. She has them often.

fresh (FRESH) *adj. fresher, freshest; freshly, adv.* 1. Newly gotten, gathered, made, drawn; clean.–I drank a glass of *fresh* water from the spring.–These beets are *fresh* from the garden.–These cookies are *fresh* from the oven.–Baby wore a *fresh* dress today.
2. Rested and well.–A good night's rest will make you feel *fresh.*
3. Not salty.–The water in the ocean is salty. The water in lakes and rivers is usually *fresh.*

fresh·man (FRESH-mən) *n. freshmen.* A student in the first year of high school or college.–This is my brother's first year in college. He is a *freshman.* He was a *freshman* in high school four years ago.

fret (FRET) *v. frets, fretted, fretting.* 1. Become disturbed and restless.–When Father is late for dinner, we all *fret* about him. We worry and get uneasy.
2. Complain; get cross.–When Mary has to get up early in the morning, she *frets.*

fret·ful (FRET-fuhl) *adj.; fretfully, adv.* Restless, nervous, and irritable.–Children become *fretful* when they are sleepy.

fri·ar (FRY-er) *n. friars.* A man belonging to a religious order of the Roman Catholic Church.

fric·tion (FRIK-shən) *n.* 1. If you rub smooth boards together, they slide back and forth easily. If you rub rough boards together, they do not slide so easily because the roughness makes the rubbing hard. This action against the rubbing, or the thing that makes it hard to slide the rough boards against each other, is called *friction. Friction* causes heat.–Sliding down a slide on the playground causes *friction.*–Rubbing a match on a matchbox causes *friction.* The heat made by the *friction* causes the match to light.–*Friction* between the tires on a car and the pavement keeps the car from skidding.
2. Quarreling; trouble.–There is *friction* between the neighbors. They annoy each other and do not get along well together.

Fri·day (FRY-dee) *n. Fridays.* The day after Thursday. *Friday* is the sixth day of the week.

fried (FRYD) *v.* One form of the verb *fry.*–Mother *fried* the bacon in a frying pan.–The bacon *fried* while we ate our cereal.

friend (FREND) *n. friends.* 1. A person who likes another person and associates with him.–Mary and Ruth are close *friends.* They know each other very well. They are fond of each other.
2. A person who believes in a group, organization, idea, etc., and gives it help.–The man is a *friend* of the poor. He helps them.

friend•less (FREND-ləss) *adj.* Without friends; all alone.–The poor boy found himself *friendless* in the strange city.

friend•ly (FREND-lee) *adj. friendlier, friendliest.* Like a friend; warm in manner; ready to be nice to others.–The girl is *friendly* toward me. She is like a friend. She acts as if she wants to help me and know me well.

friend•ship (FREND-ship) *n. friendships.* The feeling of knowing and liking which friends have between them.–Bob and John are friends. Their *friendship* started when they were in kindergarten.

fright (FRYT) *n. frights.* 1. Fear.–The fire at the zoo caused *fright* among the animals. They were frightened.–You gave me quite a *fright* when you almost fell out of the tree.
2. A horrible sight.–Mary told Father that she is a *fright* in her last year's coat.

fright•en (FRYT-ən) *v. frightens, frightened, frightening.* Scare. – When the telephone rang suddenly, it *frightened* me.

fright•ful (FRYT-fuhl) *adj.; frightfully, adv.* Horrible; terrible; awful. – We saw a *frightful* accident.

frig•id (FRIJ-id) *adj.* 1. Very cold.–Meat is kept in a *frigid* place.
2. Unfriendly; very cold in manner.–She gave me a *frigid* look.

frill (FRIL) *n. frills; frilly, adj.* A fancy ruffle. – Mother wears a *frill* on the front of her dress.

fringe (FRINJ) *n. fringes.* An edging made of heavy cord twisted and tied together, or just of loose-hanging long threads. – Our window shades have a *fringe* across the bottom.

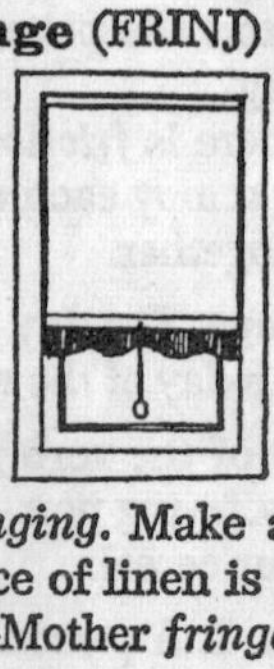

–*v. fringes, fringed, fringing.* Make a fringe on.–The edge of a piece of linen is sometimes raveled to *fringe* it.–Mother *fringed* the napkins.

frisk (FRISK) *v. frisks, frisked, frisking.* Romp and play happily.–We watched the baby lambs *frisk* about in the field. They ran and played.

frisk•y (FRISK-ee) *adj.* Playful.–Sally's kitten is *frisky.*

frit•ter (FRIT-er) *n. fritters.* A small cake with corn, bananas, pineapple, or other foods in it. It is fried in deep fat.
–*v. fritters, frittered, frittering.* Waste here and there; use up in silly ways.–Mary *frittered* away her whole morning trying to curl her hair.

fro (FROH) *adv.* From, meaning forward. – The wind blew the branches to and *fro,* backward and forward.

frock (FRAHK) *n. frocks.* Dress. – Mary had a new *frock* for Easter.

frog (FRAWG) *n. frogs.* 1. A small animal that lives in or near the water. *Frogs* have no tails and their feet are webbed like ducks' feet to help them swim. Tadpoles grow to be *frogs.*
2. A fastener made of fancy braid and buttons.–The suits worn by the boys in the band are fastened with *frogs.*

frol•ic (FRAHL-ik) *n. frolics.* A party; a time set aside for fun.–We are having a school *frolic.*
–*v. frolics, frolicked, frolicking.* Romp and frisk.–The little lambs *frolic* about the field.

from (FRUM) *prep.* 1. The opposite of to.–I have a letter *from* Rose. She sent it to me.–It is miles *from* here to the park.–The boys took the nuts *from* the basket.–Five minutes *from* now we will be on our way home.–Sally knows her letters *from* a to z.–Some flowers grow *from* seeds, and some grow *from* bulbs.
2. By; according to.–We can not tell *from* the description who the man is.
3. *From* is used to show a difference.–It is not hard to tell blue *from* yellow.

frond (FRAHND) *n. fronds.* A fern leaf; a single stem with rows of green leaflets growing along it, or a single leaflet.–The bouquet of roses was wrapped in fern *fronds.*

front (FRUNT) *n. fronts.* The forward part; the side facing forward. – The *front* of the house faces the street.–He was at the *front* of the line.
–*In front of* means ahead of or before.–Bob sits *in front of* Jack.

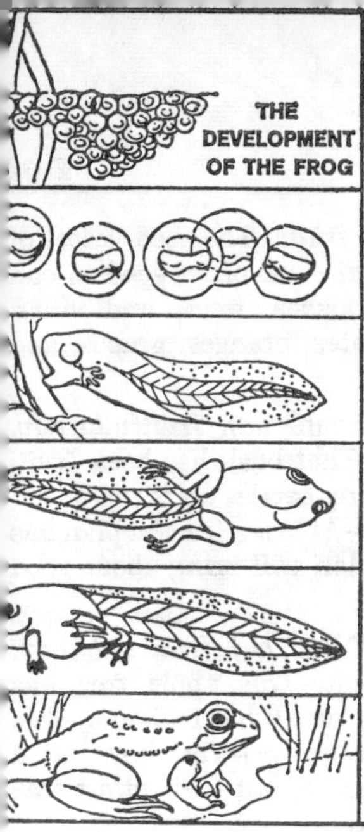

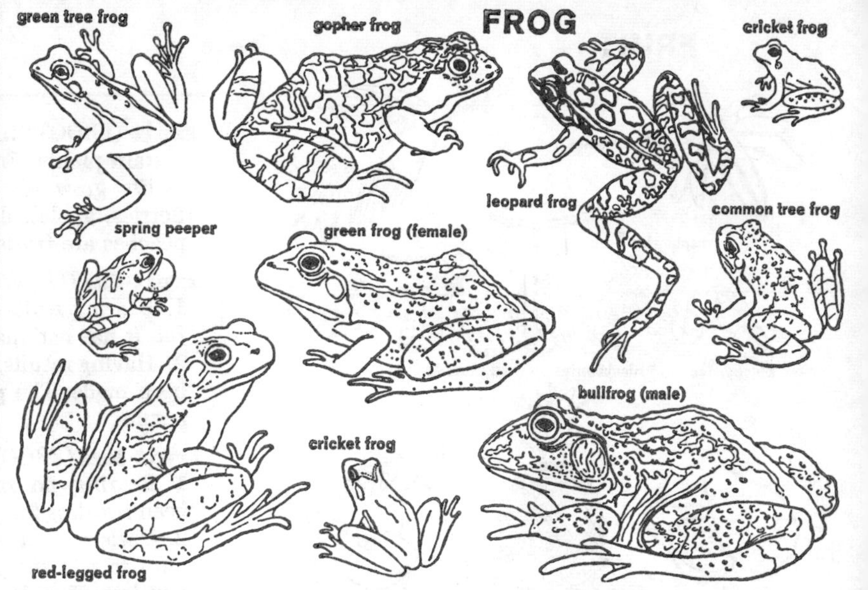

fron•tier (frun-TEER *or* FRUN-teer) *n. frontiers.* 1. The boundary line between countries; the border. – Soldiers were stationed along the *frontiers* of the nation.
2. The area or border beyond which little or nothing is known, such as in science and geography. – Man is now reaching out toward the *frontiers* of space.–The wilderness stretched beyond the *frontier.*

frost (FRAWST) *n. frosts.* 1. Frozen dew.–We saw *frost* on the grass this morning.
2. Frozen moisture.–There was *frost* on the windowpane. We could not see through it.

–*v. frosts, frosted, frosting.* Cover with icing. –Mother will *frost* Mary's birthday cake with white frosting.

frost•bite (FRAWST-byt) *n.* The injury that comes from freezing of the flesh.–The Arctic explorer got a bad case of *frostbite.*

frost•bit•ten (FRAWST-bit-n) *adj.* Injured by freezing.–Because the dog waded through the ice and snow all night, his feet were *frostbitten.*

frost•ed (FRAWST-id) *adj.* 1. Covered with frost or with something such as icing that looks like frost.–The windows are *frosted.* –Mary's birthday cake was *frosted.*
2. Frozen.–All the plants were *frosted* this morning.

frost•ing (FRAWST-ing) *n. frostings.* 1. A sugary covering for cake; icing. –I like chocolate *frosting* on cakes.

2. A dull finish that looks like frost.–This electric light bulb makes a softer light because of the *frosting* on the glass.

frost•y (FRAWST-ee) *adj. frostier, frostiest.*
1. Cold enough for frost.–It is *frosty* today. It is cold.
2. Covered with frost.–The windows are so *frosty* that we can't see out.
3. Cold; unfriendly.–We got home late and received a *frosty* welcome.

froth (FRAWTH) *n.; frothy, adj.* Foam; liquid filled with tiny bubbles. – The bubbles that rise on root beer and other drinks after they have been poured make *froth.*

frown (FROWN) *n. frowns.* A scowl; a wrinkling of the brow.–The man's *frown* showed he was not pleased.
–*v. frowns, frowned, frowning.* 1. Wrinkle up the forehead.–When the sun shines in my eyes, I *frown.*
2. Wrinkle up the forehead to show that one is angry or not pleased.–Father *frowned* at the man's cruelty to his dog.

froze (FROHZ) *v.* One form of the verb *freeze.*–We *froze* ice cream in the refrigerator.

fro•zen (FROHZ-ən) *v.* One form of the verb *freeze.*–We could not skate on the lake, because the water had not *frozen.*

FRUIT

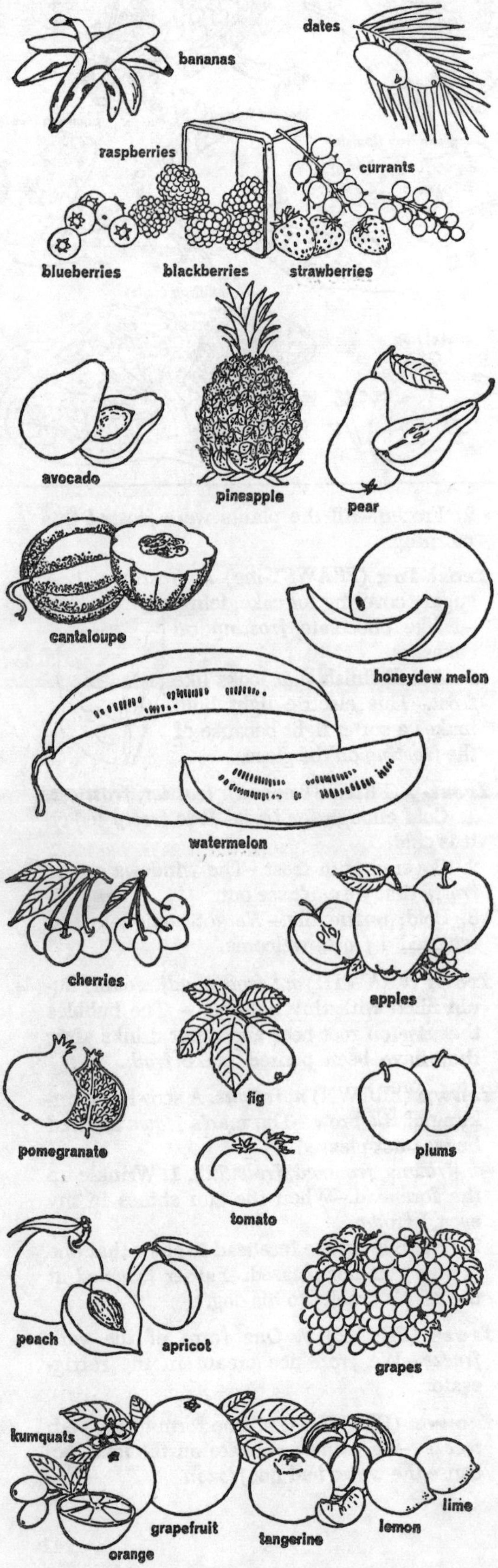

fruit (FROOT) *n. fruits.* The seed vessel of certain plants. *Fruits* are often good to eat. *Fruits* grow on bushes, trees, and vines. Berries, apples, dates, oranges, grapes, and peaches are *fruits.*

fruit•ful (FROOT-fuhl) *adj.; fruitfully, adv.* 1. Bearing fruit.–That bush has been *fruitful.* It has had many berries on it.
2. Having results.–At last a *fruitful* plan has been made. The plan will bring about good results.

fruit•less (FROOT-ləss) *adj.; fruitlessly, adv.* 1. Bearing no fruit.–This apple tree has been *fruitless* for years. It has had no apples.
2. Useless; not effective.–The boys tried hard to win the game, but their effort was *fruitless.* They lost.

fry (FRY) *v. fries, fried, frying.* Cook in grease. –We *fry* potatoes when we cook them in a little butter or fat in a skillet or pan on top of the stove.

fudge (FUJ) *n.* A soft candy made with sugar, milk, butter, and flavoring.–On Sunday evening Mother lets us make *fudge.*

fu•el (FYOO-əl) *n. fuels.* Something used for burning. Coal, oil, wood, coke, or any other material that is burned to keep houses warm, to run machines, or for other useful fires is *fuel.*

fu•gi•tive (FYOO-jə-tiv) *n. fugitives.* A person escaping or running away.–The man who robbed the bank is a *fugitive.* He is trying to escape being captured.

ful•crum (FUHL-krəm) *n. fulcrums.* The support on which a lever rests or turns while lifting or moving an object.–The farmer used a lever and *fulcrum* to move the heavy rock.

ful•fill or **ful•fil** (fuhl-FIL) *v. fulfills* or *fulfils, fulfilled, fulfilling.* 1. Keep; carry out.–Mary always *fulfills* her promises.
2. Satisfy.–Bob can *fulfill* the wishes of the boys and girls by winning the race.
3. Do to satisfaction.–The soldier *fulfilled* his duties. He did satisfactorily the things that he was supposed to do.
–*fulfillment* or *fulfilment, n.*

full (FUHL) *adj. fuller, fullest.* 1. Able to hold no more.–The pitcher is *full* of milk.–We ate until we were *full.*
2. Complete; entire.–We had a *full* week of vacation.
3. Well filled out; plump.–The buds on the trees are *full.*

ful•ly (FUHL-ee) *adv.* Completely; wholly.—Father *fully* understands the directions for making the model airplane. He understands all of them very well.

fum•ble (FUM-bəl) *n. fumbles.* A dropping of the ball in football.—Bob's team had two *fumbles.* They lost the ball two times by dropping it.
—*v. fumbles, fumbled, fumbling.* 1. Drop.—The football player *fumbled* the ball.
2. Feel clumsily.—Bob *fumbled* in his pocket for his pencil.

fume (FYOOM) *n. fumes.* Strong-smelling smoke or vapor.—We smelled the *fumes* from Grandfather's pipe.—You can smell the *fumes* from gasoline and ether.

fun (FUN) *n.* 1. Happy play; pleasure.—We had *fun* at the circus.
2. Entertainment; amusement.—The clowns added to the *fun* for the children.
—*Make fun of* means to ridicule or tease.—The boys *made fun of* the boy riding the girl's bicycle.

func•tion (FUNGK-shən) *n. functions.* 1. Use; work.—It is the *function* of a watch to keep time.
2. A ceremony or gathering.—The teachers were expected to attend school *functions* such as band concerts, P.T.A. meetings, and social affairs.
—*v. functions, functioned, functioning.* Work; operate; run.—Bob's watch *functions* perfectly. It never gains or loses.

fund (FUND) *n. funds.* A supply of anything, especially of money. — Father and Mother have a $100 Christmas *fund.* They have put away $100 for Christmas.—Bob has a *fund* of good ideas for giving holiday parties.
—*Funds* means money.—College boys often write home for *funds.*

fu•ner•al (FYOO-ner-əl) *n. funerals.* The service with which a person is buried. After a person dies, friends gather at his home or a church or the cemetery for the *funeral.* They hold a service of prayers and speeches to pay him honor.

fun•gus (FUNG-gəss) *n. fungi.* A plant that grows without light. A *fungus* does not have a green color like most plants. Toadstools, mushrooms, and molds are *fungi.*

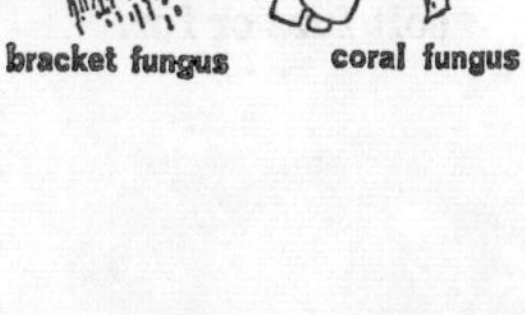

fun•nel (FUN-əl) *n. funnels.* 1. A cone-shaped container, open at the top and having a spout or tube at the bottom. It is used for pouring things into a narrow opening, such as the top of a bottle.—The man at the gas station puts oil in the car through a *funnel.*

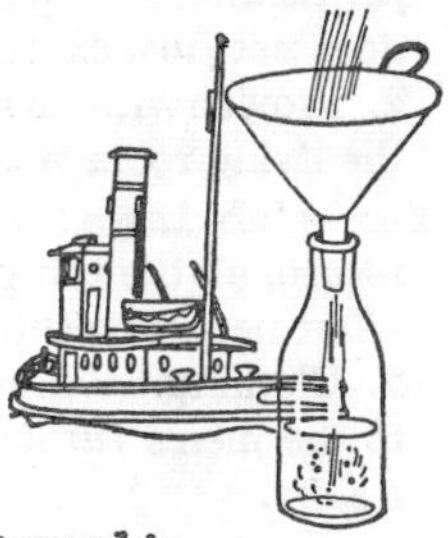

2. A smokestack on a steamship.

fun•ny (FUN-ee) *adj. funnier, funniest.* 1. Causing laughter; humorous.—A *funny* story is one that makes you laugh, or amuses you.
2. Strange; odd; curious.—It is *funny* that I have not heard from Father.

fur (FER) *n. furs* and *adj.* 1. The hairy covering of some animals.—Beavers, cats, rabbits, and many other animals are covered with *fur.*
2. The pelt or skin of an animal which has fur.—*Furs* are often used for coats.

fu•ri•ous (FYUHR-ee-əss) *adj.; furiously, adv.* 1. Very angry.—Grandfather was *furious* when he discovered that he had been cheated.
2. Fierce and strong. — There is a *furious* wind blowing over the lake.

fur•lough (FER-loh) *n. furloughs.* A short vacation or leave of absence. — The soldier came home for a ten-day *furlough.*

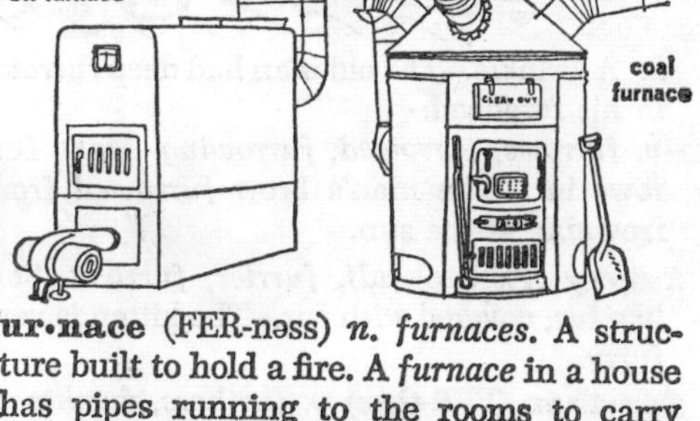

fur•nace (FER-nəss) *n. furnaces.* A structure built to hold a fire. A *furnace* in a house has pipes running to the rooms to carry steam, hot water, or hot air to heat the house. In foundries, fires are made in large *furnaces* to heat and melt metal.

fur·nish (FER-nish) *v. furnishes, furnished, furnishing.* 1. Supply or provide.–Our school does not *furnish* pencils for the children.
2. Provide with furniture.–Mother *furnished* the living room with new furniture.

fur·nish·ings (FER-nish-ingz) *n. pl.* 1. Furniture; all the things needed to outfit a room. –Our new *furnishings* are mostly in blue.
2. Clothing.–While in the store, Father went to the men's *furnishings* department to buy a shirt.

fur·ni·ture (FER-ni-cher) *n.* Chairs, tables, beds, etc., used in a house, an office, etc. – Mother bought a table and other *furniture* for the new house.

fur·ri·er (FER-ee-er) *n. furriers.* A person who makes or sells fur coats and other things made of fur.

fur·row (FER-oh) *n. furrows.* 1. A little ditch or groove made in the earth by a plow.

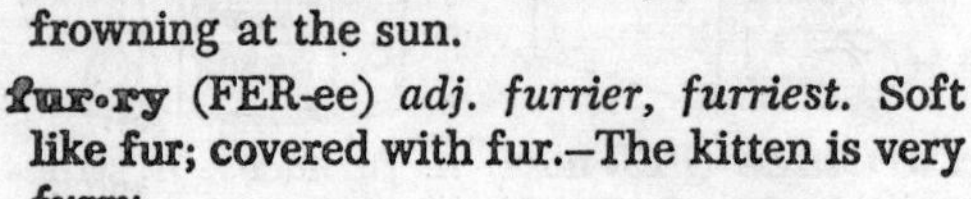

2. A wrinkle.–The old man had deep *furrows* in his forehead.
–*v. furrows, furrowed, furrowing.* Make furrows in. – The man's brow *furrowed* from frowning at the sun.

fur·ry (FER-ee) *adj. furrier, furriest.* Soft like fur; covered with fur.–The kitten is very *furry.*

fur·ther (FER-ther) *v. furthers, furthered, furthering.* Help forward.–Our plans were *furthered* by a gift of money.
–*adj.* and *adv.* 1. A greater distance; farther. –The door is *further* down the hall than the window.
2. More. – We had *further* surprises when Grandfather came.

fur·thest (FER-thəst) *adj.* and *adv.* Lying at the greatest distance.–The *furthest* of the three runners is Bob. He has run *furthest.*

fu·ry (FYUHR-ee) *n. furies.* 1. Rage; anger.– The lions at the zoo were in a *fury.* They were very angry.
2. Fierceness.–The *fury* of the storm had gone before it reached the town.

fuse (FYOOZ) *n. fuses.* 1. The string which burns down to set off an explosive.–The men lighted the *fuse* on the stick of dynamite and then ran to safety.

2. In a system of electric wiring, a piece of metal which melts if too much current goes through the wires, making the wires too hot. When the *fuse* melts, it cuts off the electricity.
–*v. fuses, fused, fusing.* 1. Join or blend, especially metals, by heating and melting together.
2. Join together or combine. – Goodness, honesty, and love of life were all *fused* in Grandfather's character.
–*fusion, n. fusions.*

fu·se·lage (FYOOSS- *or* FYOOZ-ə-lahzh *or* -lij) *n. fuselages.* The body of an airplane; the structure to which the wings and tail section are attached. The passengers, crew, and cargo usually go in the *fuselage.*

fuss (FUSS) *n. fusses.* An unnecessary worry or bother.–Grandfather makes a *fuss* over little troubles.
–*v. fusses, fussed, fussing.* Fret; worry.–He *fusses* over little troubles.

fuss·y (FUSS-ee) *adj. fussier, fussiest.* Too particular; apt to fret.–Some people are *fussy* about what they eat.

fu·ture (FYOO-cher) *n.* and *adj.* The time that is to come.–In the *future,* rocket ships may be used to travel in space to distant planets.

fuzz (FUZ) *n.* Soft down or hair.–The little duck is covered with *fuzz.*–Peaches are covered with *fuzz.*

fuzz·y (FUZ-ee) *adj. fuzzier, fuzziest.* Covered with fuzz; soft as fuzz.–A *fuzzy* little kitten came to the door. It was covered with soft fuzz or fur.

G g

G, g (JEE) *n. G's, g's.* The seventh letter of the alphabet.

ga•ble (GAY-bəl) *n. gables.* An end of a pointed roof and the triangular piece of wall enclosed by its two sides.–The house in the picture has two *gables.*

gadg•et (GAJ-it) *n. gadgets.* An unusual or tricky tool of any kind. A fork with a bottle opener at the top is a *gadget.*

gai•e•ty or **gay•e•ty** (GAY-ə-tee) *n. gaieties* or *gayeties.* Happy fun; jolliness.–There was much *gaiety* at the party.

gai•ly (GAY-lee) *adv.* Merrily; happily.–On May Day the children danced *gaily* around the Maypole.

gain (GAYN) *n. gains.* 1. An increase.–The school had a *gain* in attendance from 500 to 553.
2. Profit.–If he is not careful, the desire for *gain* can lead a businessman into dishonest practices.
–*v. gains, gained, gaining.* 1. Get ahead.–Our clock *gains.* It runs too fast.
2. Have or get more.–If you buy a pencil for five cents and sell it for seven cents, you *gain* two cents.
3. Move forward.–The football team *gained* eight yards.
4. Get; win.–The team expects to *gain* the pennant this year.
5. Earn.–The pilot *gained* fame by flying around the world.
6. Improve in health.–Grandfather has *gained* so much this week that he can soon go home from the hospital.
7. Arrive at; reach.–By running all the way he *gained* the station in time for the train.
–*Gains* means profits.–After a month on his newspaper route John felt well satisfied with his *gains.*

gait (GAYT) *n. gaits.* A manner of movement, such as walking or running.–The horse has a smooth, graceful *gait.*

gal•ax•y (GAL-ək-see) *n. galaxies.* 1. (Usually spelled with a capital "G.") The great mass of stars and heavenly bodies known as the Milky Way.–The *Galaxy* looked like a mass of tiny pinpoints that clear night.
2. Any great mass of stars.–There are countless *galaxies* in our universe.

gale (GAYL) *n. gales.* 1. A strong wind. – A *gale* drove the ship far out to sea.
2. A roar; a loud burst.–*Gales* of laughter were heard through the open windows.

gal•lant (gə-LAHNT *or* GAL-ənt) *adj.; gallantly, adv.; gallantry, n.* 1. Polite to ladies; courteous. – Uncle Jim is very *gallant.* He pays every courtesy to ladies.
2. (GAL-ənt) Noble; brave; fine.–The soldier is *gallant.* He is brave and loyal.

gal•ler•y (GAL-er-ee *or* GAL-ree) *n. galleries.* 1. A building or room for displaying works of art.–Pictures and statues are shown in the art *gallery.*

2. The highest floor of seats in a theater.–The whole family had to sit in the *gallery* at the movies.

gal•lon (GAL-ən) *n. gallons.* A measurement of liquids.–Four quarts make one *gallon.*

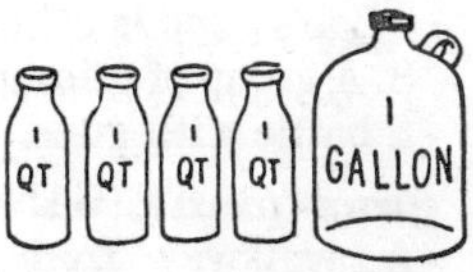

gal•lop (GAL-əp) *n. gallops.* 1. A fast leaping gait, usually of a horse. When a horse moves at a *gallop,* all four feet are off the ground at once during each bound.–The horse's *gallop* was comfortable for Mary.
2. A ride at a gallop.–Let's go for a *gallop.*
–*v. gallops, galloped, galloping.* Run at a gallop. – The horse *galloped* down the street.

ga•losh•es (gə-LAHSH-əz) *n. pl.* A pair of overshoes to protect the feet in bad weather.

gam•ble (GAM-bəl) *n. gambles.* A great risk. —Buying land along the marsh is a *gamble.* The land may become worthless.
—*v. gambles, gambled, gambling.* 1. Play games for money.—Father does not *gamble.*
2. Take risks; take a risk.—He says the wooden bridge is safe for a car, but I wouldn't *gamble* on it.

gam•bler (GAM-bler) *n. gamblers.* A person who plays games for money, or who bets on things regularly.—The *gambler* lost a hundred dollars on the race.

game (GAYM) *n. games.* 1. A kind of playing that is done according to rules.—Baseball, dominoes, checkers, and hide-and-seek are *games.*
2. An outfit or set of equipment for playing a game.—You can get many *games* at a dime store.
3. Wild animals that are hunted.—There is less *game* in this country than there once was.
—*adj.* 1. Wild.—*Game* birds are birds that are hunted for fun or for food.
2. Brave; daring.—I asked him to dive off the high board at the pool with me. He was *game* and we did it without mishap.

gan•der (GAN-der) *n. ganders.* A male or he goose.

gang (GANG) *n. gangs.* 1. A group of workmen.—A *gang* is repairing the street.
2. A group of people who go about together. —Bob's *gang* is going to gather walnuts.
3. A group of criminals.—The rival *gangs* had a battle with guns.

gang•plank (GANG-plangk) *n. gangplanks.* A walkway from a ship to the shore.—The sailors walked across the *gangplank* to the dock. — When all the people have left or gone onto the boat, the *gangplank* is taken up.

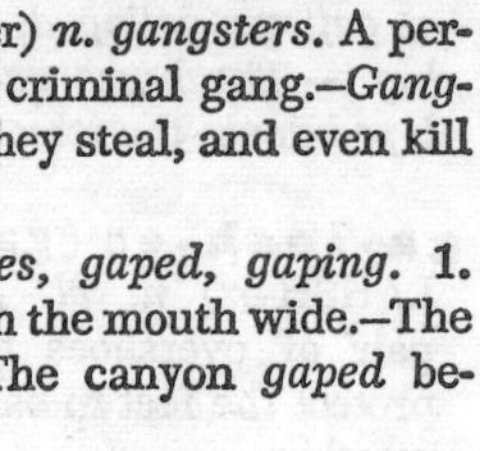

gang•ster (GANG-ster) *n. gangsters.* A person who belongs to a criminal gang.—*Gangsters* do bad things. They steal, and even kill people.

gape (GAYP) *v. gapes, gaped, gaping.* 1. Yawn; open wide; open the mouth wide.—The sleepy boy *gaped.*— The canyon *gaped* before us.
2. Stare with open mouth.—We *gaped* at the huge elephant.

ga•rage (gə-RAHZH *or* -RAHJ) *n. garages.* 1. A building to keep cars in. Some *garages* are built back of houses; others join the houses.—At night we keep our car in the *garage.*

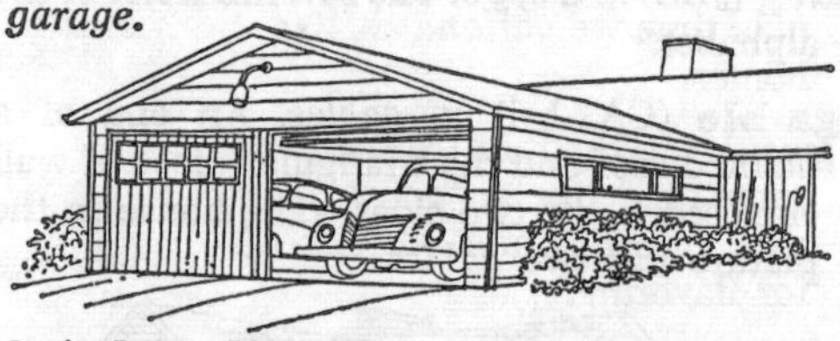

2. A shop where cars are stored or repaired. —When Father's car needs to be repaired or fixed, he takes it to a *garage.*

gar•bage (GAHR-bij) *n.* and *adj.* Waste food; food that is spoiled. Potato peelings, corn husks, meat bones, etc., are *garbage.* In cities, *garbage* is collected from *garbage* cans and burned or buried. In the country, people must dispose of *garbage* themselves.

gar•den (GAHRD-n) *n. gardens.* 1. A piece of ground where flowers or vegetables are grown.—Bob has a vegetable *garden* and Mary has a flower *garden.*

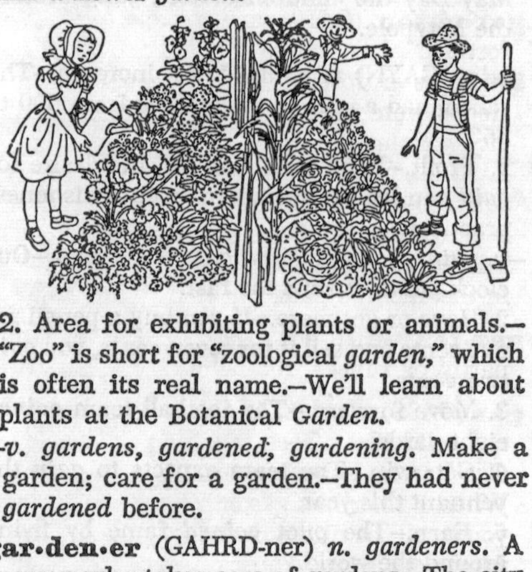

2. Area for exhibiting plants or animals.— "Zoo" is short for "zoological *garden,*" which is often its real name.—We'll learn about plants at the Botanical *Garden.*
—*v. gardens, gardened, gardening.* Make a garden; care for a garden.—They had never *gardened* before.

gar•den•er (GAHRD-ner) *n. gardeners.* A person who takes care of gardens.—The city hires a *gardener* to care for the flowers in the park.

gar•gle (GAHR-gəl) *n. gargles.* A liquid for bathing the throat.—Salt water is a good *gargle.*
—*v. gargles, gargled, gargling.* Bathe the throat by holding liquid in the back of the mouth and blowing through the liquid.—When Mother's throat was sore, the doctor told her to *gargle* with salt water.

gar•land (GAHR-lənd) *n. garlands.* A wreath.

—On May Day we crowned the May queen with a *garland* of daisies.

—*v. garlands, garlanded, garlanding.* Decorate with wreaths.—At Christmas time we *garland* the front doors of our homes.

gar•lic (GAHR-lik) *n.* A plant something like an onion. It is used in soups and other foods for flavoring.

gar•ment (GAHR-mənt) *n. garments.* A piece of clothing.—Coats, dresses, and suits are *garments.*

gar•ret (GAR-ət) *n. garrets.* An attic; the part of a house under a peaked roof. *Garrets* usually are not plastered or finished.

gar•ri•son (GAR-ə-sən) *n. garrisons.* 1. A fortified place where soldiers are stationed, such as a fort or a military base.—More troops were sent to the *garrison* when the city was threatened.

2. The soldiers stationed there.—The *garrison* was on special duty.

—*v. garrisons, garrisoned, garrisoning.* Station soldiers (in a place) for defense.—The village in the enemy's path was quickly *garrisoned.*

gar•ter (GAHR-ter) *n. garters.* A band, made partly of rubber, for holding up stockings.

gas (GASS) *n. gases.* 1. Any substance that is not solid like a rock, nor liquid like water. *Gas* has no shape or form.—Air is a *gas.*—When Father has gasoline put into the car, you smell the fumes from the gasoline. These fumes are a *gas.* You cannot see it but you can smell it.—Mother cooks by a *gas* that burns easily. It is poisonous if it escapes into the air.

2. Gasoline is often called *gas* for short.

—*v. gases, gassed, gassing.* Poison with gas.—Bob's grandfather was *gassed* in the first World War, but he recovered.

gas•e•ous (GASS-ee-əss) *adj.* Of gas; like gas.—There was a *gaseous* odor in the room.

gash (GASH) *n. gashes.* A long, deep cut.—Bob fell and cut a *gash* in his leg.

—*v. gashes, gashed, gashing.* Make a long, deep cut.—A sharp rock *gashed* Bob's knee.

gas•o•line (gass-ə-LEEN *or* GASS-ə-leen) *n. gasolines.* A liquid used for running automobiles and other engines. *Gasoline* catches fire easily and burns very fast. Its fumes will explode.

gasp (GASP) *v. gasps, gasped, gasping.* 1. Pant; breathe fast and heavily.—The boys *gasped* after running across the field.

2. Draw in a sudden breath.—The boy *gasped* when he was pushed into the cold water of the river.

gate (GAYT) *n. gates.* The part of a fence or wall that opens and closes like a door. —Someone left the *gate* open and the dog ran out of the yard into the street.

gath•er (GATH-er) *v. gathers, gathered, gathering.* 1. Pick up and put together; collect.—We *gather* violets in the spring.

2. Come together.—A large crowd of people *gathered* on the corner to watch the parade.

3. Sew in folds.—The sleeves of Mary's dress are *gathered* at the top.

4. Understand.—From what you say, I *gather* that you had a very good time.

gauze (GAWZ) *n. gauzes.* A very thin cloth. *Gauze* is so thin you can see through it. It is often used to cover sores or injuries.

gave (GAYV) *v.* One form of the verb *give.*—Grandfather *gave* Bob a white rabbit to take home.

gav•el (GAV-əl) *n. gavels.* The mallet or hammer used by the chairman of a meeting, or a judge in court, to signal for order or attention.—The judge rapped his *gavel* and asked everyone to stop talking and pay attention.

gay (GAY) *adj. gayer, gayest; gaily* or *gayly, adv.* 1. Jolly; merry.—We had a *gay* time at the party. We had lots of fun.

2. Bright and cheerful.—Mary's new dress is very *gay.* It has bright colors in it.

gaze (GAYZ) *n. gazes.* A steady look.—The boy's *gaze* rested upon the new bicycle.

—*v. gazes, gazed, gazing.* Look long and steadily.—The little girl *gazed* at the doll in the window.

ga•zelle (gə-ZEL) *n. gazelles.* A small antelope that runs very fast. A *gazelle* is something like a deer.

gear (GEER) *n. gears.* 1. A set of equipment, clothing, or the like.—The sailor took all his *gear* aboard the ship in a canvas bag.—Grandfather keeps all the *gear* for mowing and reaping in the barn.
2. A wheel with cogs or teeth on the edge to fit into the teeth on another similar wheel. Cars and trucks have *gears.*
—*In gear* means with the teeth of the gears fitted together so that one turns the other.—When Father put the car *in gear,* the motor began turning the wheels.

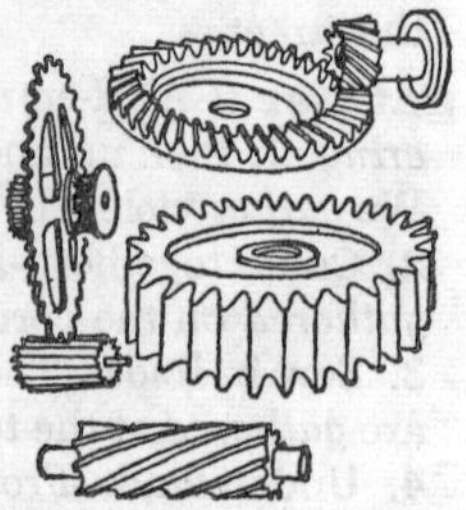

geese (GEESS) *n. pl.* More than one *goose. Geese* are large birds with long necks. They make a honking noise.

Gei•ger count•er (GY-ger KOWN-ter) *Geiger counters.* An instrument used for discovering the presence of radioactivity and for measuring its strength.—The *Geiger counter* revealed large amounts of radioactivity in the area of the atomic explosion.

gel•a•tin (JEL-ə-tin) *n. gelatins.* A jellylike substance from which glue is made. *Gelatin* is also used in making desserts to eat. *Gelatin* is made from the hoofs and bones of animals.

gem (JEM) *n. gems.* 1. A precious stone.—Rubies, diamonds, sapphires, and emeralds are *gems.*
2. A particularly valuable or outstanding thing.—The *gem* of all the pictures is the one of the old man smoking his pipe. It is the most beautiful and the best.

gen•er•al (JEN-er-əl) *n. generals.* One of the highest officers in an army. He has charge of many men.—General Patton was a United States *general.*
—*adj.* 1. Happening or existing all over.—The rain was quite *general.* It rained all around, not just in one place.
2. Whole; entire; not special; covering everything or everybody.—The exhibit is open to the *general* public. It is open to all people who wish to go.—Bob is going to take a *general* course in high school. He is not going to specialize in any one subject.
3. Rough; not clear.—Mother doesn't know exactly how the sweater should be made, but she has a *general* idea.

gen•er•al•ly (JEN-er-əl-ee) *adv.* 1. Usually; most of the time.—*Generally* Mary gets better marks than Jack.
2. Widely; all over.—Although it has not been publicly announced, it is *generally* known that the mayor will not seek re-election.

gen•er•ate (JEN-er-ayt) *v. generates, generated, generating.* Bring into being; produce. —A dynamo *generates* electricity.—Wide reading *generates* thought.

gen•er•a•tion (jen-ə-RAY-shən) *n. generations.* 1. Bringing into being; producing.—Waterfalls can be used for the *generation* of electric power.
2. The people born during the same period of time, as during World War II. — Tom's parents belong to the *generation* of the 1920's. Tom belongs to the *generation* of the 1950's.
3. The time interval between a father's birth date and that of his child, estimated to be about thirty years.—Two *generations* ago, in the early 1900's, air travel was unknown to the world.
4. One stage in the line of descent of people, animals, or plants.—Sam can trace his family line back four *generations,* or back to his great great-grandfather.

gen•er•a•tor (JEN-ə-ray-ter) *n. generators.* 1. A person or thing that brings something into being.—Einstein was the *generator* of new ideas about time and space.
2. A machine for producing electric power, gas, etc.; a dynamo.—The electricity was cut off when the *generator* broke down.

gen•er•os•i•ty (jen-er-AHSS-ə-tee) *n. generosities.* 1. Willingness to share; unselfishness. —The hospital was endowed through Mr. Jones' *generosity.*
2. Unselfish gift or deed.—Mr. Jones' many *generosities* will be long remembered in his home town.

gen•er•ous (JEN-er-əss) *adj.; generously, adv.* 1. Willing and glad to share things with others.—Jack is very *generous.* He gives some of his cookies to the other boys at lunch, and lends them his bicycle.
2. Large.—We had *generous* servings of ice cream at the party.
3. Good; kind; not bearing hard feelings toward others.—It is *generous* of you to overlook my mistake.

ge•ni•al (JEEN-yəl) *adj.; genially, adv.; geniality, n.* Warm and pleasant; hearty.—Grandfather has a *genial* manner.

gen•ius (JEEN-yəss) *n. geniuses.* 1. A person who has remarkable natural ability. A great musician, a great inventor, or a great poet is a *genius.*
2. A special ability that very few people have. —Grandmother believes that Mary has a *genius* for playing the piano.

gen•tian (JEN-shən) *n. gentians.* A plant that has blue flowers. *Gentians* often grow in the mountains.

gen•tle (JEN-tl) *adj. gentler, gentlest; gentleness, n.* Soft; soothing; mild; not sharp or sudden.—A *gentle* breeze is blowing from the lake.—The old man is very *gentle* in manner. —If the sides of a hill slant gradually, little by little, we say the hill has a *gentle* slope.

gen•tle•man (JENT-l-mən) *n. gentlemen.* A man who acts honorably, considerately, and politely to others.—Mr. Jones is a *gentleman.* He is a courteous, well-bred man.

gen•tly (JENT-lee) *adv.* 1. In a careful, soft, or tender way.—The boys handled the kitten *gently.*—The snow falls *gently* on the roof.—We told him the sad news *gently.*
2. Gradually.—They planted the trees on the *gently* sloping hillside.

gen•u•ine (JEN-yoo-ən) *adj.; genuinely, adv.* 1. Real; not imitation.—This coat is *genuine* mink.
2. True; honest; sincere.—Bob's friendship is *genuine.*

ge•og•ra•phy (jee-AHG-rə-fee) *n. geographies.* 1. The study of the earth and life upon it. When we study *geography,* we study about the earth and its people, its animals, its mountains and valleys, its rivers, oceans, and other waters, its climate, and its products.
2. A book about geography.

ge•ol•o•gist (jee-AHL-ə-jist) *n. geologists.* A person who studies the history of the earth, its rocks and minerals.

ge•ol•o•gy (jee-AHL-ə-jee) *n.* The scientific study of the earth and its history, especially through the study of rocks and minerals.—*Geology* is of interest to oil and mining companies. It helps them locate valuable natural resources.

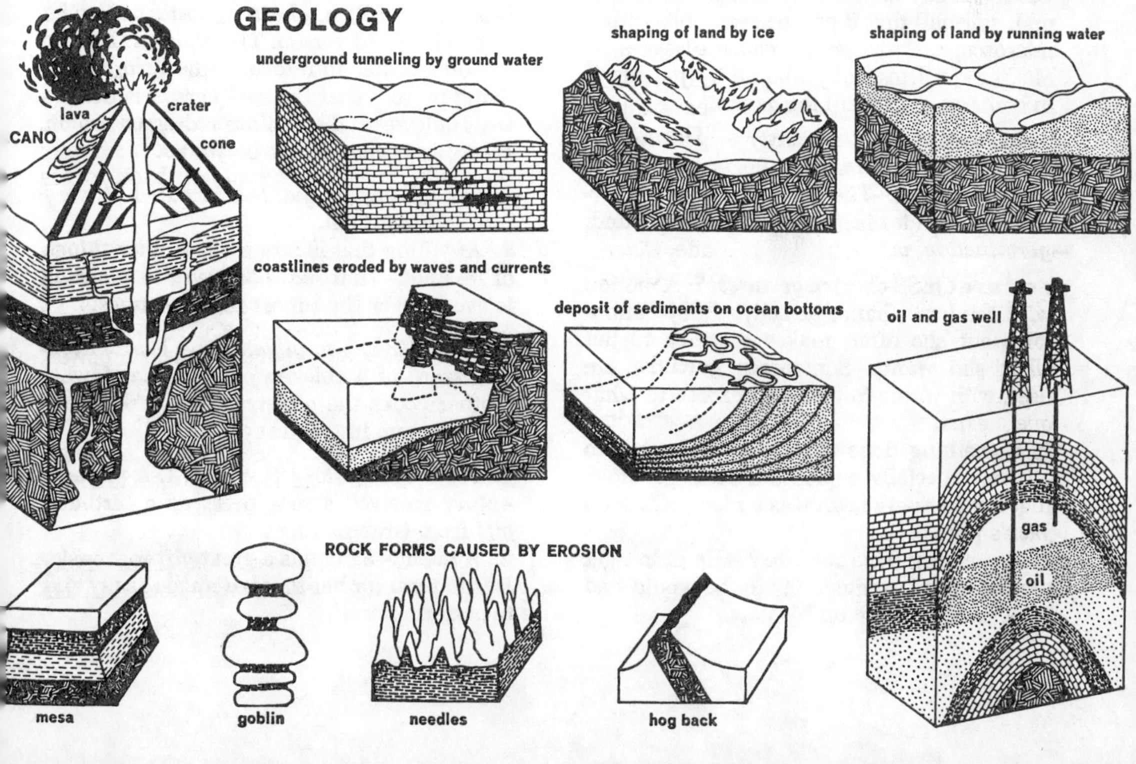

ge•om•e•try (jee-AHM-ə-tree) *n.; geometrical, adj.* The branch of mathematics that deals with the relationships and measurements of angles, lines, surfaces, and solid objects. *Geometry* is used by engineers, architects, and surveyors.

Geor•gette (jor-JET) *n.* A thin silk or rayon crepe cloth that you can partly see through. —Mother has a new dancing dress made of *Georgette.*

Geor•gia (JOR-jə) *n.* The largest state in the United States east of the Mississippi River, located on the east coast. *Georgia* is two-thirds covered with forests, and is important for its cotton, peanut, and peach crops, and for its mining and manufacturing industries.

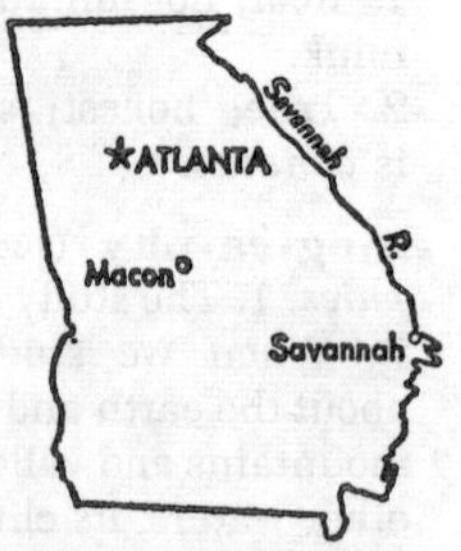

ge•ra•ni•um (jə-RAY-nee-əm) *n. geraniums.* A flowering plant. Some *geraniums* are wild, and some are grown and cared for by people. The flowers are red, white, or salmon color. They are often planted in porch boxes.

germ (JERM) *n. germs.* A tiny plant or animal, so small that it can be seen only with a microscope. Some *germs* cause diseases. —Mother sterilizes Baby's bottle by putting it in boiling water to kill the *germs.*

ger•mi•nate (JER-mə-nayt) *v. germinates, germinated, germinating.* Begin to develop or grow; sprout.—The plant has begun to *germinate.*—An idea is *germinating* in my mind. —*germination, n.*

ges•ture (JESS-cher) *n. gestures.* 1. A motion with the head, hand, or body.—Baby cannot talk, but she often makes *gestures* to tell what she wants.—Sometimes *gestures* are used with words to give extra force to what one means.
2. Something done to express a feeling to others, especially a pleasant feeling.—Mowing the old man's lawn was a nice *gesture* on Jack's part.
3. Something done for effect.—He didn't get me the book I wanted. Saying he would had been just a *gesture* on his part.

get (GET) *v. gets, got, getting.* 1. Receive; take.—I *get* a new pair of shoes about every six months.—Go and *get* your book and we'll read.—Did you *get* a letter today?—Bob *gets* his allowance from Father.
2. Earn.—I *get* two dollars a week for mowing lawns.
3. Arrive; reach.—When we *get* home, I shall change my shoes.
4. Become; grow.—We *get* cold when the window is open wide.—Baby is *getting* big.
5. Persuade.—We could not *get* Mother to read to us till we had done our homework.
—To *get* something done means to do or finish something. —When we *get* the dishes washed, we can play
—To *get* something done can also mean to have it done by someone else. — Mother went to *get* the car fixed.

gey•ser (GY-zer) *n. geysers.* A hot spring which from time to time throws out water, mud, or steam in the form of a gushing fountain.

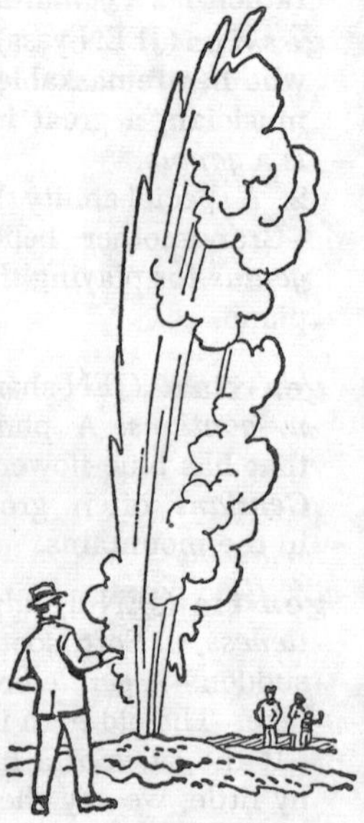

ghost (GOHST) *n. ghosts; ghostly, adj.* The spirit of a dead person. The *ghost* is thought by some people to return in the form of the living person after the real person is dead.—On Halloween the children dressed up in sheets and pretended to be *ghosts.*

gi•ant (JY-ənt) *n. giants* and *adj.* 1. A very large, strong man.
2. Anything that is larger than other things of its kind.—That redwood tree is a *giant.* It is even larger than most redwood trees.

gib•let (JIB-lət) *n. giblets.* The heart, liver, or gizzard of a chicken or any other fowl.—Mother cooks the *giblets* of the turkey and cuts them up in the gravy.

gift (GIFT) *n. gifts; gifted, adj.* 1. A present. —Mary received a new dress as a birthday *gift* from Grandmother.
2. A talent.—Sally has a great *gift* for music. It is natural for her to learn music easily and to perform it well.

gi·gan·tic (jy-GAN-tik) *adj.* Very large.—The fisherman caught a *gigantic* fish. It was nearly as big as he was.

gig·gle (GIG-əl) *n. giggles.* A tittering laugh. —We heard a *giggle* coming from the corner of the room.
—*v. giggles, giggled, giggling.* Laugh in a silly, jerky way. — Some children *giggle* at anything.

gild (GILD) *v. gilds, gilded, gilding.* Put a thin coating of gold over.—Mother's good dinner plates are *gilded* around the edges.

gill (GIL) *n. gills.* The organ used by fish for breathing under water.

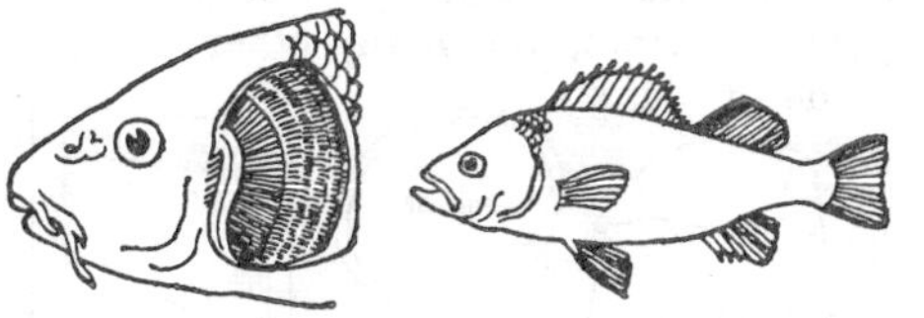

gill (JIL) *n. gills.* One fourth of a pint, or half a cup, in liquid measure. — The chemist poured a *gill* of alcohol into a container.

gilt (GILT) *n.* A thin outer coating of gold.—The *gilt* on the frame is becoming tarnished.
—*adj.* Gold-painted. — The picture has a *gilt* frame.

gin (JIN) *n. gins.* 1. A kind of alcoholic liquor. — *Gin* is sometimes mixed with other liquids to make a cocktail.
2. A cotton *gin* is a machine for taking the seeds out of cotton.

gin·ger (JIN-jer) *n.* and *adj.* 1. The dried, ground roots of the *ginger* plant, used as a spice in cooking, in medicines, and in ginger ale.

2. A candy made from the *ginger* root by sugaring, or by packing in syrup.

gin·ger·bread (JIN-jer-bred) *n.* A molasses cake in which ginger is used for flavor.

gi·raffe (jə-RAF) *n. giraffes.* A very tall, yellowish, spotted animal. It has very long front legs and a long neck. *Giraffes* can eat leaves from tall trees. When they eat from the ground, they either get down as a person does when he kneels, or spread their front feet far apart. *Giraffes* come from Africa.

girl (GERL) *n. girls.* A young woman; a female child, usually called a little *girl.*—Mother is a woman. Mary is a little *girl* of five. Jane is a *girl* of sixteen.

give (GIV) *v. gives, gave, giving.* 1. I will *give* you some flowers. I will make you a present of them. I will hand them to you and you may keep them.—Boy Scouts *give* first aid to those who need it.—Mother *gives* her children much attention. She pays lots of attention to them.—We will come if Mother *gives* her consent, if she says we may.
2. Produce; make. — Cows *give* milk. — Fire *gives* heat.
3. Feed.—Grandfather *gives* his horse hay.
4. Have; arrange.—The children are *giving* a party.
5. Cause; make for.—Our cat *gives* us lots of trouble.—Reading *gives* pleasure.
6. Yield; move as a result of force.—Father tried to move the big rock, but it wouldn't *give* an inch.
—*Give up* can mean stop trying.—Mary could not guess the answer, but she would not *give up.*
—*Give up* can also mean sacrifice or do without.—Alice *gave up* candy for Lent.

giv·en (GIV-ən) *v.* One form of the verb *give.* —We have *given* magazines to the hospital.
—*adj.* 1. Already arranged or understood.—The boys arrived at the *given* time. They arrived at the time that had been set or named.
2. Inclined.—Mary is *given* to temper tantrums. She has them often.

giz•zard (GIZ-erd) *n. gizzards.* A second stomach which birds have. In the *gizzard,* food is ground up very small.

gla•cier (GLAY-sher) *n. glaciers.* A whole field of ice that moves slowly down a mountainside. The snow on the mountain packs down tightly and freezes to form the field of ice.

glad (GLAD) *adj. gladder, gladdest; gladly, adv.* Happy; pleased.–We are *glad* Mother is home.

glade (GLAYD) *n. glades.* An open space in the woods where there are no trees. – The children picked daisies in the *glade.*

glad•i•o•lus (glad-ee-OH-ləss) *n. gladioli* or *gladioluses.* A flower of various colors that grows on a long stem. The buds near the bottom of the stem blossom first, then the others. *Gladioli* grow from bulbs.

glad•ness (GLAD-nəss) *n.* Joy; happiness.–Christmas is a time of *gladness.*

glam•our or **glam•or** (GLAM-er) *n.; glamourous* or *glamorous, adj.* Magic; enchantment; a charm that is not as great as it seems.–Jean was attracted by the *glamour* of a movie star's life. She didn't realize that most movie stars work very hard.

glance (GLANSS) *n. glances.* A short look. –Bill shot a *glance* at the teacher to see if she was watching him.
–*v. glances, glanced, glancing.* 1. Look quickly.–We just *glanced* at the picture. We looked at it for just a moment.
2. Bounce off in a slanting direction.–The stones hit the wall and *glanced* off.

gland (GLAND) *n. glands.* An organ of a person's body. *Glands* make things that the body needs. Saliva, the liquid in the mouth which helps digest the food, is made by *glands.*

glare (GLAIR) *n. glares.* 1. Angry look or stare.–Bob saw the *glare* on the lion's face.
2. Strong, blinding light.–Jack moved his seat away from the *glare* of the sun.
–*v. glares, glared, glaring.* 1. Stare angrily.– The boy *glared* at me.
2. Shine blindingly.–The light *glares* on my paper.

glass (GLASS) *n. glasses* and *adj.* 1. A hard material that you can see through. Windowpanes, mirrors, and many other things are made of *glass.*

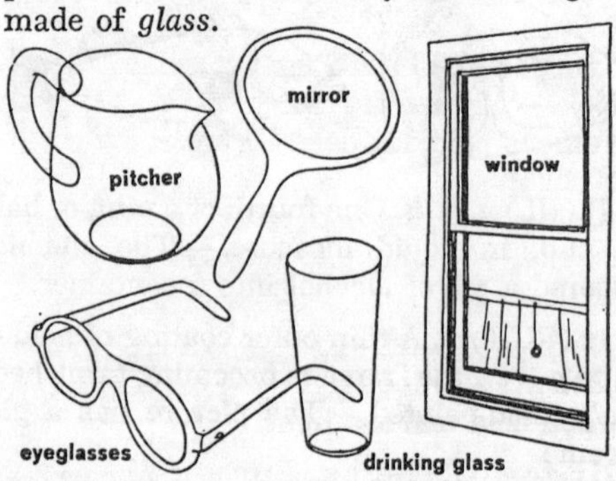

2. A drinking container made of glass; the amount of a liquid that a *glass* will hold.– Mary drank a *glass* of milk.
3. *Glasses,* or eye*glasses,* are round pieces of glass, ground to different thicknesses and fastened to a frame. People who have something wrong with their eyes can see better when wearing *glasses.*

glass•ful (GLASS-fuhl) *n. glassfuls.* As much as can be put into a glass. – Mary drank a *glassful* of milk.

glaze (GLAYZ) *n. glazes.* A smooth, shiny finish.–The vase has a nice *glaze.*–Varnish is a *glaze.*
–*v. glazes, glazed, glazing.* Cover with a glassy sheet of something.–The freezing rain *glazed* the windshield with ice.

gleam (GLEEM) *n. gleams.* A beam or flash. –A *gleam* of light comes from the island lighthouse.
–*v. gleams, gleamed, gleaming.* Shine. – A light *gleams* in the window.

glee (GLEE) *n.; gleeful, adj.; gleefully, adv.* Joy; happiness; delight. – The children shouted with *glee* when the clown appeared.

glide (GLYD) *v. glides, glided, gliding.* Move smoothly and silently.–The river *glides* gently to the sea.

glid·er (GLYD-er) *n. gliders.* An airplane that has no motor. A *glider* is kept up and carried along by the air or wind.

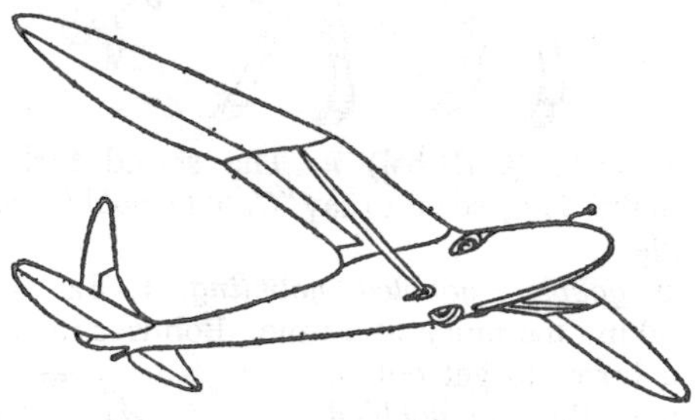

glimpse (GLIMPSS) *n. glimpses.* A short look. – Mother let us have a *glimpse* at Father's birthday cake before she put it out of sight.
–*v. glimpses, glimpsed, glimpsing.* Get a quick look at.–We only *glimpsed* the President as he drove by.

glis·ten (GLISS-ən) *v. glistens, glistened, glistening.* Shine brightly.–Diamonds *glisten* when held under a light.

glit·ter (GLIT-er) *n.* Brightness; sparkling. –The *glitter* of the jewels in the display was dazzling.
–*v. glitters, glittered, glittering.* Sparkle brightly.–The snow *glitters* in the sunlight.

globe (GLOHB) *n. globes; global, adj.* 1. A ball; any solid object that is round. – The earth is a *globe.*

2. A map of the world made on a ball or sphere. – Mary found China on the *globe.*

gloom (GLOOM) *n.* 1. Sadness; a hopeless feeling.–A feeling of *gloom* came over the old man.
2. Darkness.–*Gloom* was everywhere about us as we entered the cave.

gloom·y (GLOOM-ee) *adj. gloomier, gloomiest; gloomily, adv.* 1. Dark and dreary.–Before the rain came, the sky was very *gloomy.*
2. Not hopeful; sad.–Aunt Ellen is *gloomy* about the future. She believes all the worst things will probably happen.

glo·ri·fy (GLOR-ə-fy) *v. glorifies, glorified, glorifying.* 1. Praise; see as being splendid. –The champion was *glorified* by his admirers.
2. Adore; worship; exalt.–The church congregation is *glorifying* God by singing hymns.

glo·ri·ous (GLOR-ee-əss) *adj.; gloriously, adv.* 1. Brilliant and shining.–It is a *glorious* day. The sun is shining and it is very bright.
2. Excellent; fine in every way.–We had a *glorious* time at the party.
3. Full of glory; magnificent.–The hero received a *glorious* welcome.

glo·ry (GLOR-ee) *n. glories.* 1. The praise and honor given a person for doing some great thing.–The soldier won great *glory.*
2. Brightness; great show; splendor. – The king arrived in all his *glory.*
–*v. glories, gloried, glorying.* Take delight and great pride.–Grandmother *glories* in Jack's good work at school.

gloss (GLAWSS *or* GLAHSS) *n.; glossy, adj.* A bright finish.–The maid put a *gloss* on the furniture by using furniture polish.

glos·sa·ry (GLAWSS- *or* GLAHSS-ə-ree) *n. glossaries.* A list of difficult words and phrases, with explanations, usually found at the end of the book in which they appear.– Scientific books often have *glossaries.*

gloss·y (GLAWSS- *or* GLAHSS-ee) *adj. glossier, glossiest.* Shiny.–The waxed furniture is *glossy.*–The kitten has *glossy* fur.

glove (GLUV) *n. gloves.* We wear *gloves* on our hands to keep them warm. A *glove* has a place for each finger and the thumb.

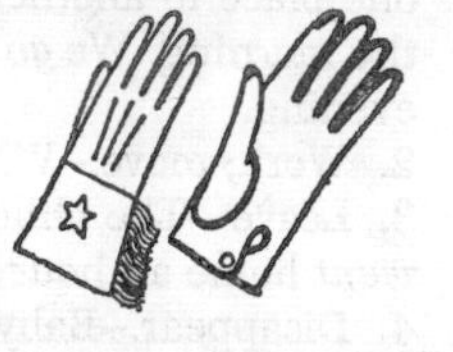

glow (GLOH) *n. glows.* 1. The light and color made by something burning or fiery.–We sat by the dying fire and watched the *glow* of the coals.
2. A warm shine.–A *glow* came into his eyes.
–*v. glows, glowed, glowing.* 1. Shine with heat.–The fire *glows.*
2. Brighten.–The child's face *glowed* when he saw Santa Claus. His face shone with eagerness and excitement.

glue (GLOO) *n. glues.* A sticky substance made from gelatin. Gelatin is made by boiling the bones and other waste parts of animals.–Bob used *glue* to fasten the parts of his airplane together.
–*v. glues, glued, gluing.* Stick on with glue.– Father *glued* the leg to the chair.

glum (GLUM) *adj. glummer, glummest; glumly, adv.* Quiet, gloomy, and sad.–Jack is *glum* because he did not get a good mark in arithmetic.

glut•ton (GLUT-n) *n. gluttons; gluttonous, adj.* A person who eats too much and too fast.–*Gluttons* seem to be afraid that they will not get their share.

glyc•er•in or **glyc•er•ine** (GLISS-er-ən) *n.* A clear, thick, sweet liquid made from fats and oils. It is used in making medicines and explosives.

gnarled (NAHRLD) *adj.* Knotty; rugged; twisted.–The *gnarled* old tree was struck by lightning. – The fisherman's hands were *gnarled* and weather-beaten.

gnash (NASH) *v. gnashes, gnashed, gnashing.* Hit (the teeth) fiercely together, making a sound.–The dragon *gnashed* his teeth when he saw the knight approaching with drawn sword.

gnat (NAT) *n. gnats.* A small insect that has two wings and long feelers.

gnaw (NAW) *v. gnaws, gnawed, gnawing.* Chew at.–Dogs like to *gnaw* the meat from bones. They bite or pick it off little by little with their teeth.

go (GOH) *v. goes, went, going.* 1. Move from one place to another.–We come to school in the morning. We *go* home from school in the evening.

2. Work; move.–What makes the engine *go*?

3. Leave.–The children were here, but they *went* home an hour ago.

4. Disappear.–Baby's milk is all *gone*. None is left.

5. Belong.–Your hat *goes* in the hall closet.

6. Attend regularly.–Do you *go* to school?

goal (GOHL) *n. goals.* 1. The line or place that players try to reach to make points for their team or to win the game.–He made a *goal* and won the game for his team.

2. Any place one tries to reach.–The holy city of Mecca is the *goal* of many Mohammedan pilgrims.

3. The thing one wants most.–The man's *goal* is to be a good citizen.

goat (GOHT) *n. goats.* An animal about the size of a sheep, with horns and a beard. *Goats'* milk is good to drink.

gob•ble (GAH-bəl) *n.* The sound turkeys make. They seem to say *"Gobble, gobble, gobble."*

–*v. gobbles, gobbled, gobbling.* 1. Eat fast, taking too much at a time.–Bob was in such a hurry to get out to play that he *gobbled* his lunch.

2. Make a turkey's gurgling sort of cry.–The turkeys *gobbled*.

gob•bler (GAHB-ler) *n. gobblers.* A male or he turkey.

gob•let (GAHB-lət) *n. goblets.* A drinking glass. A *goblet* has a long stem and a flat base.

gob•lin (GAHB-lən) *n. goblins.* An ugly, mischievous elf. *Goblins* are written about in fairy tales.

God (GAHD) *n.* People of many religions believe that *God* is the maker and ruler of all things.

god (GAHD) *n. gods.* A male spirit that is worshiped. Some primitive people believe that there are many *gods*.

god•dess (GAHD-əss) *n. goddesses.* A woman god; any female spirit that is worshiped.

goes (GOHZ) *v.* One form of the verb *go*.–Father *goes* to work in the morning.

go•ing (GOH-ing) *v.* One form of the verb *go*.–Never get off the train while it is *going*. –The watch is *going*.

gold (GOHLD) *n.* 1. A precious yellow metal. *Gold* comes from mines. It is used in making watches, rings, chains, and other jewelry. Some coins used to be made of *gold*.

2. Much money. – The miser counted his *gold* every night by the light of a candle.
–*adj.* 1. Made of gold.–I have a *gold* ring.
2. A deep, rich yellow color.–Mother has a *gold* suit.

gold·en (GOHL-dən) *adj.* Made of gold; of the yellow color of gold.–Baby has *golden* curls.–The king had *golden* plates.

gold·en·rod (GOHL-dən-rahd) *n.* A plant that blossoms in late summer. Its golden-yellow flowers grow on tall stems that have leaves all along them.

gold·finch (GOHLD-finch) *n. goldfinches.* A small yellow bird with bits of black on it. The *goldfinch* sings beautifully and is often called a wild canary.

gold·fish (GOHLD-fish) *n. goldfish* or *goldfishes.* A small gold-colored fish. – The children feed the *goldfish* in the fish bowl each day.

golf (GAHLF) *n.* A game played on a large outdoor course. *Golf* is played with a small

plastic ball with rubber inside it. The ball is hit with one of a number of clubs.

gon·do·la (GAHN-də-lə) *n. gondolas.* 1. A small boat, pointed at each end, used on nar-

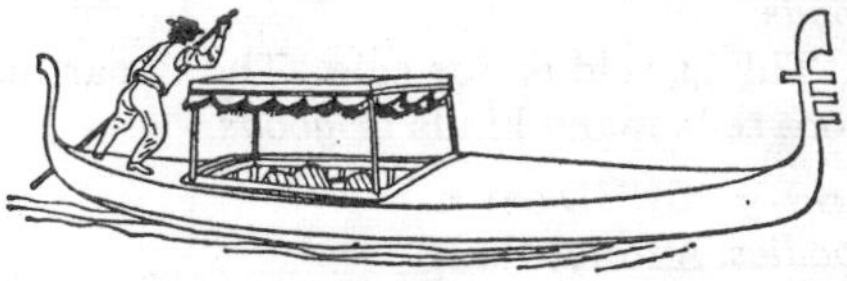

row canals. The *gondolas* of Venice, in Italy, are famous.
2. A kind of open railway car for carrying coal, stone, etc.

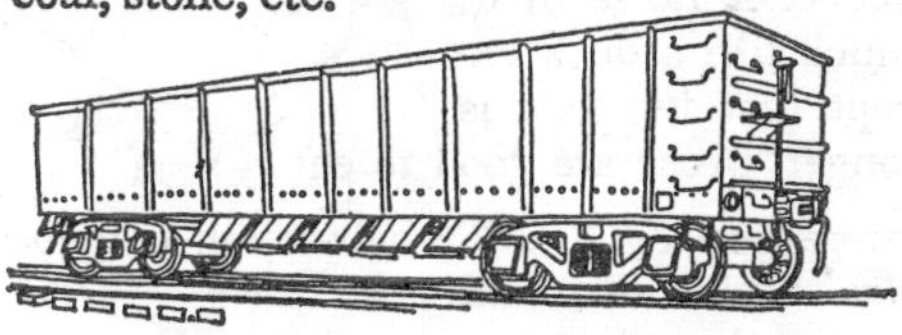

3. A car that hangs below a dirigible to carry passengers and crew.

gone (GAWN) *v.* One form of the verb *go.*–Bob put his hat in the hall but now it is *gone.*
–The family has *gone* away for the summer.

gong (GAWNG) *n. gongs.* A round, curved piece of metal which rings when struck.–The fireman rang the fire *gong.*

good (GUHD) *n.* Benefit.–We gave the money for the *good* of all the family.
–*adj. better, best.* 1. Well-behaved.–Some children are bad; others are *good.*
2. Desirable; excellent; fine.–Some boys do poor work, but Bob's work is *good.*–This is my *good* hat.
3. Full.–The peddler gave us a *good* basket of apples.
4. Pleasant.–This is a *good* day.
5. Kind.–It was *good* of you to call.
6. Real; not artificial.–Mother's diamond is *good.*
7. Giving satisfaction.–This is a *good* book.

good-by or **good-bye** (guhd-BY) *n. good-bys* or *good-byes* and *interj.* A customary thing to say when parting. It is a wish of good fortune for those who are leaving.

good-na·tured (guhd-NAY-cherd) *adj.; good-naturedly, adv.* Pleasant; easy to get along with.–Grandmother is *good-natured;* she doesn't care how much noise we make.

good·ness (GUHD-nəss) *n.* Honesty and kindness. – The old woman is known and liked for her *goodness.*
–*interj.* An expression of surprise.–*Goodness,* how he can run!

goods (GUHDZ) *n. pl.* 1. Household property. – Tables, chairs, and other furniture are *goods.*
2. Things sold or for sale.–The department store sells many kinds of *goods.*

good•y (GUHD-ee) *n. goodies.* A fancy thing to eat. Candy and cookies are *goodies.*

goose (GOOSS) *n. geese.* A large bird, much like a duck except that its neck is longer. *Geese* are good to eat.

goose•ber•ry (GOOSS-bair-ee) *n. gooseberries.* A kind of round berry that is very sour. *Gooseberries* are red or yellow when ripe. The green berries are used in pies.

go•pher (GOH-fer) *n. gophers.* A small animal that is much like a rat. – *Gophers* dig long, tunnel-like holes in the ground to live in.

gorge (GORJ) *n. gorges.* A narrow valley or passageway.–We passed through a *gorge* between the mountains.

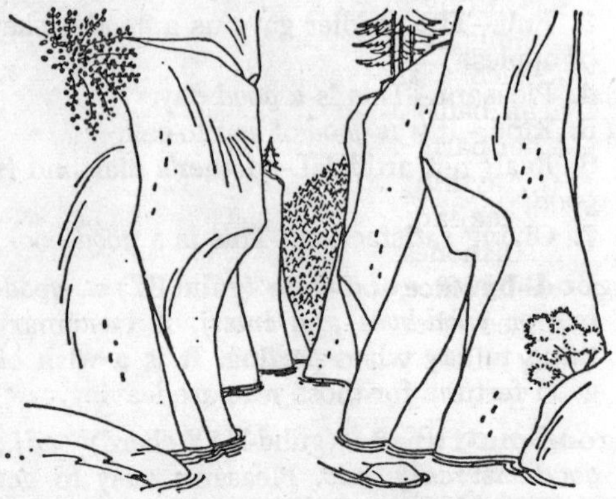

–*v. gorges, gorged, gorging.* Eat too much.– It is not polite to *gorge* oneself.

gor•geous (GOR-jəss) *adj.; gorgeously, adv.* Splendidly colored; beautiful and magnificent.–The leaves on the trees in autumn are *gorgeous.*–The man was wearing a *gorgeous* costume.

go•ril•la (gə-RIL-ə) *n. gorillas.* A huge, man-like ape. *Gorillas* are strong and fierce.

gos•sip (GAHSS-əp) *n. gossips.* 1. Conversation, sometimes (but not always) unkind or too revealing, about others' private affairs.– I don't believe that mean story about Mary. It sounds like mere *gossip.* – Martha and I had a pleasant *gossip* at the store.
2. A person who talks indiscreetly and too much about people's private affairs.–The woman was not well-liked because she was a *gossip.*
–*v. gossips, gossiped, gossiping.* Talk about other people, either pleasantly, or carelessly and unwisely. – Martha and I *gossiped* for a while. – People were *gossiping* about the man's gambling. Sometimes they exaggerated the facts.

got (GAHT) *v.* One form of the verb *get.*– Father *got* home late last night.

got•ten (GAHT-n) *v.* One form of the verb *get.*–It has *gotten* very cold.

gourd (GORD) *n. gourds.* A fruit that has a hard rind and grows on a vine. – *Gourds* are of many shapes and colors.

gov•ern (GUV-ern) *v. governs, governed, governing.* Manage; control; rule.–The mayor and the council *govern* the town.–The speed at which we may drive is *governed* by law.–Everybody must learn to *govern* his temper.

gov•ern•ment (GUV-ern-mənt) *n. governments.* 1. The group of persons elected or appointed to govern or rule a country.–The *government* runs the postal service.
2. The way a country is controlled or managed.–The *government* of the United States is based on the Constitution.

gov•er•nor (GUV-er-ner) *n. governors.* 1. A man at the head of the government of a state or territory.

2. A device that controls speed.–Our new car has a *governor* on the engine. The *governor* keeps it from going too fast.

gown (GOWN) *n. gowns.* 1. A dress. – Mother has a new party *gown.*
2. A long, loose garment.–Bill and his classmates wore caps and *gowns* when they graduated from high school.

grab (GRAB) *v. grabs, grabbed, grabbing.* Snatch; take hold of suddenly.–Bob *grabbed* his coat from the chair and hurried away.

grace (GRAYSS) *n. graces.* 1. Beautiful, easy movement.–Mary dances with *grace.*
2. Favorable regard.–Bob got in Mother's good *graces* by helping to wash the dishes.
3. A prayer of thanks for food.–Father said *grace* when the family sat down at the table.

grace•ful (GRAYSS-fuhl) *adj.; gracefully, adv.* 1. Beautiful and easy in movement.– The dancers are *graceful.*
2. Beautiful in form. – The pitcher has a *graceful* shape.

gra•cious (GRAY-shəss) *adj.; graciously, adv.* Kind and pleasant. – Grandmother is very *gracious* to her guests.

grack•le (GRAK-l) *n. grackles.* 1. Any of various blackish birds, such as the myna bird of India and Asia, or American blackbirds and starlings.
2. The purple *grackle,* about a foot long and blackish purple in color, is quite common in the United States east of the Allegheny Mountains.

grade (GRAYD) *n. grades.* 1. A class.–Mary is in the third *grade.*
2. Quality.–Mother buys the best *grade* of meats.
3. A slope.–The hill has quite a *grade* to it.
4. Mark.–I got a good *grade* in spelling.
–*v. grades, graded, grading.* 1. Mark; correct; score.–We always *grade* each other's spelling papers.
2. Smooth.–The men are *grading* the road.
3. Classify or separate. – The pupils were *graded* according to age and ability.

grad•u•al (GRAJ-oo-əl) *adj.; gradually, adv.* Happening or occurring little by little, or slowly and continuously. – The hill has a *gradual* slope.–She noticed a *gradual* change for the better in Joe's health.

grad•u•ate (GRAJ-oo-ət) *n. graduates.* A person who has satisfactorily finished the work of a school.–Father is a *graduate* of a large college.
–(GRAJ-oo-ayt) *v. graduates, graduated, graduating.* Leave (a school) upon the satisfactory finishing of one's studies.–Tom *graduated* from high school last June.

grad•u•a•tion (graj-oo-AY-shən) *n. graduations.* 1. Leaving (a school) after satisfactorily finishing one's studies.–After *graduation* from high school, Tom went to college.
2. The special exercises or ceremony of leaving a school.–We expect to attend the *graduation* of Bill's class.

graft (GRAFT) *n. grafts.* 1. Taking a part of one tree or plant and making it live as a part of another tree or plant.–The farmer performed a *graft* on the old apple tree. He made a slot in the trunk of the tree and fixed a new branch into it.

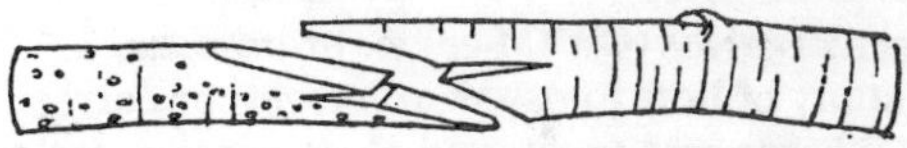

2. Cutting skin or bone from one place and joining it to another.–The surgeon performed a skin *graft* on the man who had been badly burned. He took the skin from other parts of the burned man's body.
3. Anything so grafted.–The branch bearing the larger apples on that tree is a *graft.*
4. Dishonest dealing, often by persons in public office, for private gain.–The mayor resigned when the *graft* and corruption in the city offices were revealed.
–*v. grafts, grafted, grafting.* 1. Perform a graft. – The farmer *grafted* branches from stronger trees to his weaker fruit trees to improve the yield of his orchard.–The surgeon removed the diseased part of the bone and *grafted* healthy bone to it.
2. Obtain money or favors by dishonest means, such as bribery.–The city meat inspector was found to be *grafting.* He accepted money for grading meat higher than its real quality.

grain (GRAYN) *n. grains.* 1. The edible seeds of certain plants. Wheat, corn, barley, and oats are *grains.*

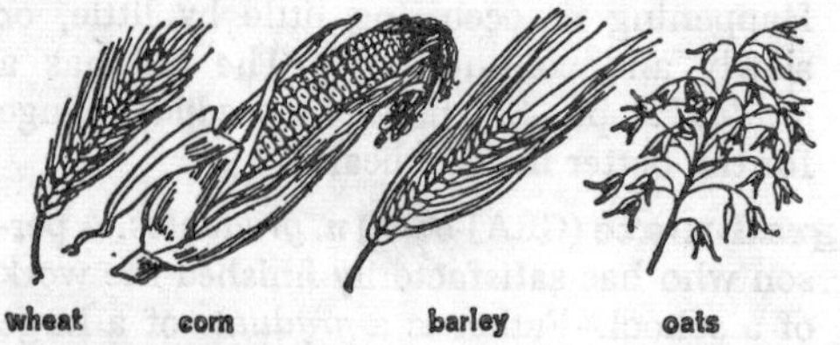

2. A plant that bears an edible seed, such as wheat or rye.
3. A tiny piece.—Father got a *grain* of sand in his eye.
4. The fibers of wood; their direction.—The *grain* in pine boards is easy to see.—The *grain* of the wood goes up and down a tree. You may saw it with the *grain* (up and down) or against the *grain* (across).

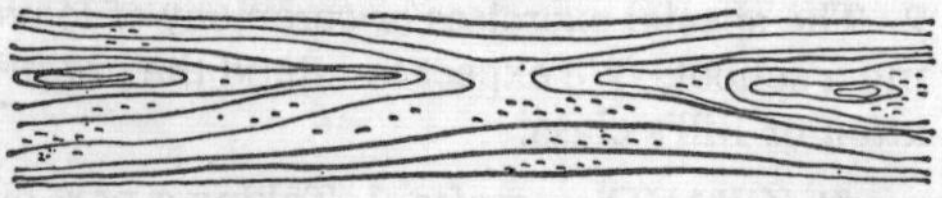

5. Feel or consistency.—Mother's cake had a nice *grain.* It was fine, not coarse.

gram (GRAM) *n. grams.* A small unit of weight. One thousand *grams* are equal to one kilogram, and one kilogram weighs only a little more than two pounds.

gram·mar (GRAM-er) *n. grammars.* 1. The study of how to use words together correctly. —Nouns and verbs and their correct use are part of the study of *grammar.*
2. Using the rules of grammar.—"The boy ain't there" is incorrect *grammar.* The correct contraction for "is not" is "isn't."—In the upper grades of elementary school all the children make a special study of *grammar.*
3. A text book about grammar.

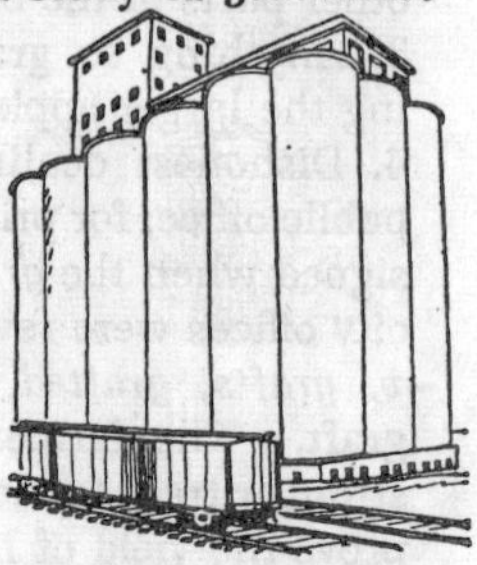

gran·a·ry (GRAN- *or* GRAYN-er-ee) *n. granaries.* A building for storing grain.—Farmers often keep their grain in a building called a *granary.*

grand (GRAND) *adj. grander, grandest; grandly, adv.* 1. Large and splendid.—The rich man lives in a *grand* house.
2. Main.—The *grand* ballroom of the mansion dated back to Colonial times.
3. Complete. — The *grand* total of profits from the fair was six hundred dollars.

grand·child (GRAN-chyld) *n. grandchildren.* A child of one's son or daughter.

grand·daugh·ter (GRAN-daw-ter) *n. granddaughters.* A daughter of one's son or daughter.

grand·fa·ther (GRAN-fahth-er) *n. grandfathers.* The father of one's parent.—My father's father and my mother's father are my *grandfathers.*

grand·ma (GRAN-mah) *n. grandmas.* A grandmother.

grand·moth·er (GRAN-muth-er) *n. grandmothers.* The mother of one's parent.—My father's mother and my mother's mother are my *grandmothers.*

grand·pa (GRAN-pah) *n. grandpas.* A grandfather.

grand·par·ent (GRAN-par-əntss) *n. grandparents.* A parent of one's father or mother. —Your grandfathers and grandmothers are your *grandparents.*

grand·son (GRAN-sun) *n. grandsons.* The son of one's son or daughter.

grand·stand (GRAN-stand) *n. grandstands.* The main stand or place with seats where people sit during games or other events.—We sat in the *grandstand* at the baseball game.

gran·ite (GRAN-ət) *n.* A very hard, gray rock.—Many monuments and buildings are made of *granite.*

grant (GRANT) *v. grants, granted, granting.* 1. Allow; give.—The fairy *granted* the prince his wish.
2. Admit; agree.—I *grant* that I have made a mistake.

grape (GRAYP) *n. grapes.* A fruit that grows in bunches on grapevines. *Grapes* are green, red, or purple. They are good to eat.

grape·fruit (GRAYP-froot) *n. grapefruits.* A large, sour fruit something like an orange but yellow and larger. *Grapefruit* is good to eat for breakfast.

grape•vine (GRAYP-vyn) *n. grapevines.* A vine on which grapes grow.

graph (GRAF) *n. graphs.* A *graph* is a set of lines or blocks that shows how two or more changing things are related.

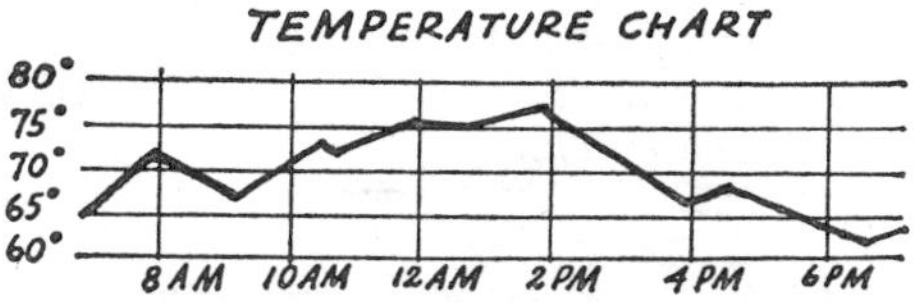

grasp (GRASP) *n. grasps.* A hold or clasp.—The man's tight *grasp* on my arm made it hurt.
—*v. grasps, grasped, grasping.* 1. Take hold firmly.—The man *grasped* the side of the boat and held on tightly.—The baby *grasped* her father's hand.
2. Understand; learn.—Bob *grasps* arithmetic quickly.

grass (GRASS) *n. grasses.* 1. Long, narrow, green leaves or blades that grow close together. – The yard is covered with green *grass.* Cows like to eat *grass.* —Bob mows the *grass.*

2. The plants that bear grains, such as rye, wheat, and oats. Plants having long, slender stalks, like the bamboo and sugar cane, are also *grasses.*

grass•hop•per (GRASS-hahp-er) *n. grasshoppers.* A kind of insect that jumps or hops long distances. *Grasshoppers* eat plants. Sometimes they eat up the farmers' crops.

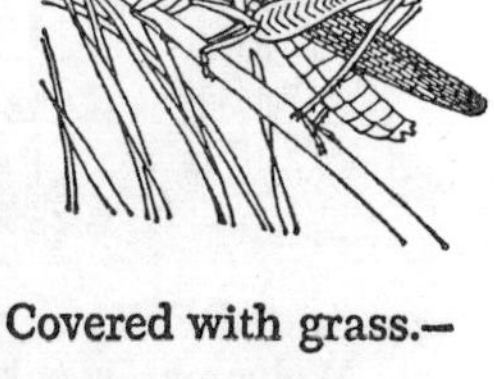

grass•y (GRASS-ee) *adj. grassier, grassiest.* Covered with grass.—The field is *grassy.*

grate (GRAYT) *n. grates.* A container or a framework made of iron bars.—The coal in a furnace rests on a *grate,* through which the ashes fall.
—*v. grates, grated, grating.* 1. Rub against a prickly piece of metal to cut into small bits.—Mother *grates* such foods as cheese, horseradish, and coconut.
2. Make a harsh sound.—Rough, dry things *grate* when they are rubbed together. – A piece of metal dragged along the sidewalk *grates* on the concrete.
3. Have an irritating effect. – That noise *grates* on my nerves.

grate•ful (GRAYT-fuhl) *adj.; gratefully, adv.* Thankful; appreciative; glad of something.—We are *grateful* for our homes and for having enough to eat.

grat•i•tude (GRAT-ə-tood *or* -tyood) *n.* Appreciation; thankfulness; gladness for something given to or done for one.—Bob expressed his *gratitude* for the gifts.

grave (GRAYV) *n. graves.* A hole in the ground for burying a person or animal that is dead.—The boys dug a *grave* for their dog that had died.
—*adj. graver, gravest; gravely, adv.* Thoughtful; serious.—The old woman had a *grave* look on her face. She was thinking about something important.

grav•el (GRAV-əl) *n. gravels.* Stone broken into small pieces; pebbles.—We drove off the pavement and down a side road covered with *gravel.*

grave•stone (GRAYV-stohn) *n. gravestones.* A stone tablet or marker put over a grave. The name of the person buried in the grave and the dates of his birth and his death are usually engraved on the *gravestone.*

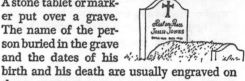

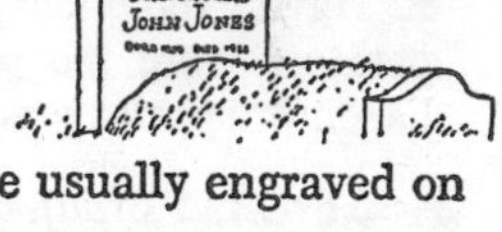

grave•yard (GRAYV-yahrd) *n. graveyards.* A cemetery; a large yard where the dead are buried.

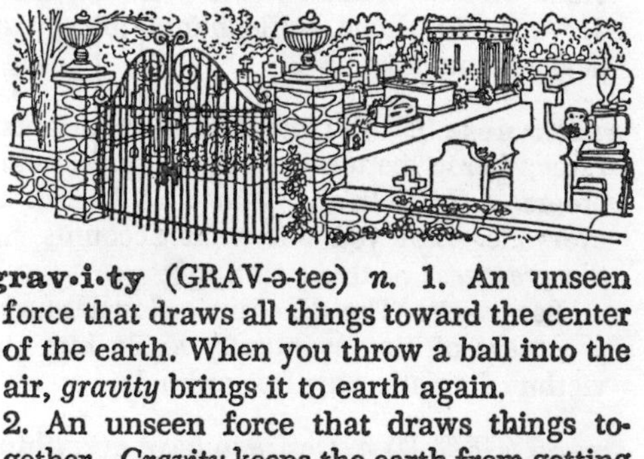

grav•i•ty (GRAV-ə-tee) *n.* 1. An unseen force that draws all things toward the center of the earth. When you throw a ball into the air, *gravity* brings it to earth again.
2. An unseen force that draws things together.—*Gravity* keeps the earth from getting farther from the sun. – *Gravity* keeps the moon close to the earth.
3. Seriousness.—The *gravity* of war is known

gra·vy (GRAY-vee) *n. gravies.* The fat and juice that cook out of meats and fowls. Sometimes flour or other thickening and milk or water are added to this juice to make a thick *gravy.*

gray (GRAY) *n. grays.* A color that is a mixture of black and white.
–*adj. grayer, grayest.* 1. Of the color of gray.–Some rabbits are *gray.*–Grandmother's hair is *gray.* When she was younger, her hair was brown.
2. Dismal.–What a *gray* day!–*Grayish* means somewhat gray.

graze (GRAYZ) *v. grazes, grazed, grazing.* 1. Eat grass from the ground where it grows.–The cows *graze* in the pasture.
2. Brush or barely touch in passing.–The flying ball just *grazed* my head. It just touched my head lightly as it went by me.
3. Rub the skin from.–Baby fell on the gravel path and *grazed* her knee.

grease (GREESS) *n. greases.* An oil or fat. Butter, lard, and olive oil are *greases.*
–(GREESS *or* GREEZ) *v. greases, greased, greasing.* Put grease on.–Father *greased* his car. He put grease on all the parts that rub together.

greas·y (GREESS- *or* GREEZ-ee) *adj. greasier, greasiest.* 1. Covered with grease.–The workman's hands are *greasy.*
2. Having too much fat or oil in it.–The fried potatoes were too *greasy.*–Father likes his bacon crisp, not *greasy.*

great (GRAYT) *adj. greater, greatest; greatly, adv.* 1. Much more than usual.–There was a *great* snowfall last week.
2. Important; outstanding; famous and honored.–Thomas Edison was a *great* inventor.
3. Very big; huge.–Elephants are *great,* heavy animals.

great·ness (GRAYT-nəss) *n.* 1. Importance; fame; being better and finer than many others.–Lincoln's *greatness* is known to everyone.–Can you tell what accounts for the *greatness* of this painting?
2. Largeness.–The dinosaur's slowness and *greatness* of size eventually made him the victim of smaller, swifter animals.

greed (GREED) *n.* Desire to have everything for oneself, or more than one needs.–The man had few friends because of his *greed* for money.

greed·y (GREED-ee) *adj. greedier, greediest; greedily, adv.* 1. Wanting to eat more than one's share, and as fast as possible, as if it were going to disappear.–Don't be *greedy.* Eat slowly and wait to be offered a second helping.
2. Wanting too much for oneself.–The miser is *greedy.* All he thinks about is how to get more money for himself.

green (GREEN) *n. greens.* 1. The color of grass.–We have chosen *green* as the color for this room.
2. A smooth piece of ground covered with very short grass.–The man playing golf hit the ball onto the *green.*–They danced on the village *green.*

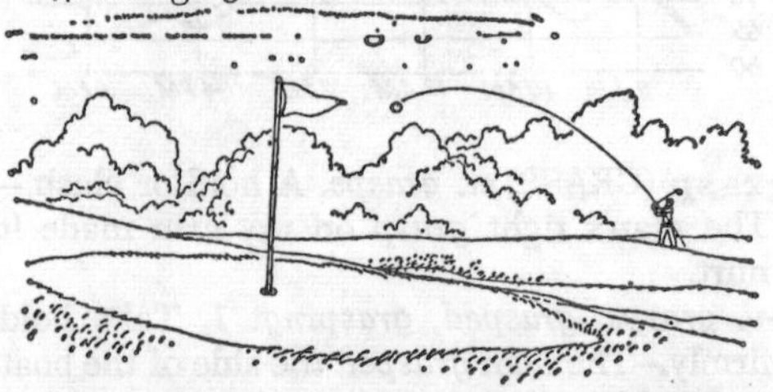

–*adj. greener, greenest.* 1. Of the color green.–Most leaves are *green* in the summer. They turn yellow, red, and brown in the fall.
2. Not ripe.–We could not eat the melon, because it was still *green.*
3. New; not experienced.–Bob is *green* at playing tennis. He doesn't know much about it.
–*Greenish* means somewhat green.

green·house (GREEN-howss) *n. greenhouses.* A hothouse. We buy flowers at a *greenhouse.* A *greenhouse* is built of glass to protect the plants and to let in sunshine to help keep them warm and make them grow.

greet (GREET) *v. greets, greeted, greeting.* 1. Welcome; speak to someone on seeing him. We *greet* people when we meet them by saying "Good morning," "Hello," or "Good evening," or by shaking hands.–His election was *greeted* with cheers.
2. Meet; appear to.–A sorry sight *greeted* her at home; the vase lay broken on the floor.

greet•ing (GREET-ing) *n. greetings* and *adj.* 1. A welcome.–We give Father a warm *greeting* when he comes home at night.
2. A message of good wishes.–Grandmother sent me a birthday *greeting*.–The drugstore sells cards of *greeting*, or *greeting* cards, for wishing people happiness on special days.
3. An opening statement.–"Dear John" is the *greeting* in a letter to John.

grew (GROO) *v.* One form of the verb *grow*. –The plant *grew* fast in the rich earth.

grey•hound (GRAY-hownd) *n. greyhounds*. A tall, lean dog, noted for its speed and keen eyesight. *Greyhounds* were bred for racing in ancient Egypt and are still raised for that purpose in many countries.

grid•dle (GRID-l) *n. griddles*. A flat metal plate for cooking. It is something like a skillet without sides.–Grandmother fried bacon and eggs on a *griddle*.

grid•dle•cake (GRID-l-kayk) *n. griddlecakes*. A pancake that is cooked on a griddle on top of the stove.

grid•i•ron (GRID-y-ern) *n. gridirons*. 1. A cooking utensil made of parallel iron bars. Steaks, chops, and other meats are laid on *gridirons* over open flames to broil.
2. A football field.–The football team is practicing on the *gridiron*.

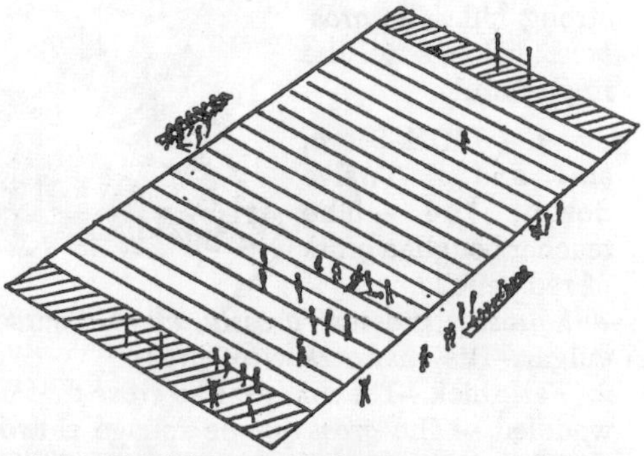

grief (GREEF) *n. griefs*. Sorrow; sadness.–Much *grief* has come to the family. They have had all kinds of bad fortune.

grieve (GREEV) *v. grieves, grieved, grieving*. 1. Make unhappy and troubled.–The bad boy *grieves* his mother.
2. Feel sad. – Do not *grieve* over the lost money.–Jim *grieved* over the disappearance of his dog.
–*grievance, n. grievances*.

grill (GRIL) *n.* 1. A gridiron; bars for cooking over direct flame.
2. Meat so cooked.–He ordered a mixed *grill* –chops, steak, and liver–for lunch.
3. A dining room which mostly serves grilled foods.–We ate in the *grill* at the hotel.
4. (Also spelled *grille*.) Any flat covering made of bars or having a series of openings. –To fix the radiator Father had to remove the *grill*.–Father polished the *grill* on the front of the car.
–*v. grills, grilled, grilling* 1. Broil; cook by a direct flame. – We *grill* meat by holding it right over a fire to cook it.
2. Question for a long time without stopping. –The police *grilled* the suspected man for hours.

grim (GRIM) *adj. grimmer, grimmest; grimly, adv.* 1. Solemn and stern; forbidding; unyielding.–Father was *grim* when Jack confessed that he had lost the ten dollars.–The castle looked *grim* under the threatening thunderclouds.
2. Very unpleasant and depressing; frightful.–The accident was a *grim* sight.

grime (GRYM) *n.* Dirt rubbed or ground into a thing. – Bob's hands were covered with *grime* after playing ball.

grin (GRIN) *n. grins*. A big smile. – A *grin* spread over Jack's face when he saw the strawberry shortcake.
–*v. grins, grinned, grinning*. Smile broadly, showing the teeth.–The man *grins* because he is so happy.

grind (GRYND) *n. grinds*. Hard work. – Climbing the hill was a steady *grind*.
–*v. grinds, ground, grinding*. 1. Crush or cut very fine.–The grocer *grinds* the coffee. He puts it into a mill which cuts it into tiny pieces.
2. Rub against a rough stone.–Father sharpens knives by *grinding* them.
3. Make or work by turning a handle.–The organ-grinder *grinds* out music by turning a handle on the organ.
4. Rub together and make a grating sound.–Baby sometimes *grinds* her teeth. She thinks it sounds funny.

grind•stone (GRYN-stohn) *n. grindstones.* A flat, rough stone turned by a motor or by hand to sharpen tools and knives.

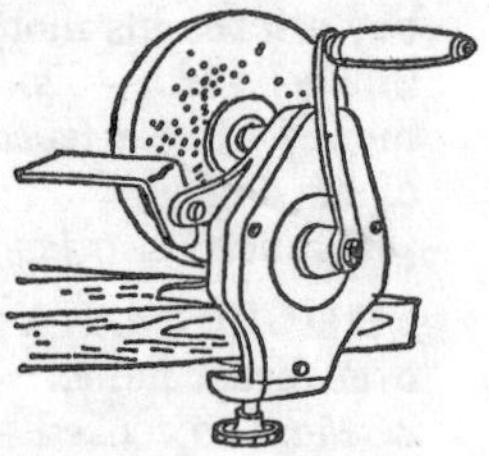

grip (GRIP) *n. grips.* 1. A tight grasp. – Sally keeps a *grip* on Father's hair when he carries her on his shoulder.
2. A suitcase or handbag.–Father packed his *grip* quickly and hurried for the train.
3. Control; power.–The dictator held the nation in an iron *grip.*
—*v. grips, gripped, gripping.* Take hold of and hold tightly.–The frightened child *gripped* his father's hand.

grippe (GRIP) *n.* A cold and fever, often with aches all over the body.–The doctor says that Jack has the *grippe.*

gris•tle (GRISS-əl) *n.* A hard, white, stretchy substance found in meat. People do not eat the *gristle.* They cannot chew it.

grit (GRIT) *n. grits; gritty, adj.* 1. Very small hard particles, especially of sand.–The wind blew some *grit* into my eyes.
2. Courage.–Bob nearly lost his *grit* when he saw the bear.
—*v. grits, gritted, gritting.* Grind; grate.–Baby *grits* her teeth together.

griz•zled (GRIZ-əld) *adj.* Somewhat gray.–The elderly man has thick, *grizzled* hair.

griz•zly (GRIZ-lee) *n. grizzlies* and *adj.* A big, fierce brown bear. There are many *grizzlies* in the western part of our country. They are also called *grizzly* bears.

groan (GROHN) *n. groans.* A low sound of pain or suffering.–The wounded man sank down with a *groan.*
—*v. groans, groaned, groaning.* Moan; make a low sound of pain or suffering. – The sick woman *groans* at times.

gro•cer (GROH-ser) *n. grocers.* A man in charge of a grocery store.

gro•cer•y (GROH-ser-ee) *n. groceries.* A store where foods are sold.–Mother sent Bob to the *grocery* for bread.

—*Groceries* are foods bought at a grocery.–Oranges, coffee, crackers, and a jar of peanut butter are all *groceries.*

groom (GROOM) *n. grooms.* 1. A man who cares for horses.–Grandfather has a *groom* at his stable.
2. A bridegroom; a man who has just been or is about to be married.
—*v. grooms, groomed, grooming.* 1. Care for (a horse).–The groom spends time daily *grooming* the horses. He feeds them and brushes them.
2. Care for; make neat.–Jane *grooms* her hair carefully. She brushes it, combs it, and has it washed and cut often.

groove (GROOV) *n. grooves.* A hollow trough cut in a surface.–There is a *groove* on your desk to lay your pencils in.–Father put *grooves* in the drainboard so that the water would run down them into the sink.

grope (GROHP) *v. gropes, groped, groping.* Feel around in the dark with the hands.–Father *groped* in the closet for his hat.

gros•beak (GROHSS-beek) *n. grosbeaks.* A bird with a large, strong bill. The *grosbeak* belongs to the finch family.

gross (GROHSS) *n. sing.* and *pl.* Twelve dozen; 144. – The teacher bought a *gross* of red pencils.
—*adj. grosser, grossest; grossly, adv.* 1. Coarse; vulgar.–His manners were *gross.*
2. Fat; thick.–The man was so *gross* that he waddled. – The *gross* jungle foliage slowed their progress.
3. Large; obvious.–Your arithmetic answer shows you've made a *gross* error somewhere.

4. Total.–The arithmetic problem asked us to find the man's *gross* earnings, his earnings before any expenses were taken out.

grouch (GROWCH) *n. grouches.* 1. A person who grumbles and sulks a good deal.–The old man is a *grouch.* He becomes angry easily and often sulks.
2. A bad mood. – Jack always gets over a *grouch* quickly.

grouch·y (GROWCH-ee) *adj. grouchier, grouchiest.* Grumbling, cross, and untalkative. A *grouchy* person is one who becomes angry and sulks or will not talk.

ground (GROWND) *n. grounds.* 1. The soil; the surface of the earth.–We plant seeds in the *ground.*
2. Land set aside for a particular purpose.–We play on the play*ground.*–We picnic on picnic *grounds.*
3. Land around a house.–Trees, shrubs, and flowers have been planted on the *grounds* around the rich man's house.
4. A reason; evidence; basis.–The man had absolutely no *ground* for accusing Jack of stealing.
5. The small, hard, dark brown grains left in the pot after the coffee has been poured.–Mary emptied the *grounds* from the coffeepot.
–*v. grounds, grounded, grounding.* 1. Force to stay on the ground.–All the airplanes had been *grounded.* They could not fly because of bad weather.
2. Run aground.–The boat *grounded* on a sand bar.
3. One form of the verb *grind.*–The flour was *ground* at the mill.
–*adj.* On a level with the ground.–We live on the *ground* floor.

ground hog (GROWND hawg) *ground hogs.* A woodchuck, which is a small, grayish-brown animal that burrows in the ground. It sleeps all winter in a hole it digs.

group (GROOP) *n. groups.* 1. A number of persons or things all of one kind, put together.–Children form *groups* of three and four to play.–Several pictures hung together on the wall make a *group.*
2. A small crowd or collection.–A *group* of people stood on the corner.
–*v. groups, grouped, grouping.* 1. Put into groups.–The teacher *grouped* the children according to age.
2. Form a group. – The children *grouped* around the teacher.

grouse (GROWSS) *n. sing.* and *pl.* A game bird that looks something like a chicken. Some types of *grouse* are called partridges. Hunters hunt them as sport or for food.

grove (GROHV) *n. groves.* A group of trees. –We can see a beautiful *grove* at the bottom of the hill.

grow (GROH) *v. grows, grew, growing.* 1. Get bigger. – Children *grow.* – Plants *grow.* –The city has *grown* since we moved here.
2. Become; get.–The sky *grew* black during the storm.–Alice has *grown* thinner.
3. Raise.–We *grow* vegetables and flowers in our garden.

growl (GROWL) *n. growls.* A deep, throaty, fierce sound. – We heard the *growl* of the watchdog.
–*v. growls, growled, growling.* 1. Make a deep, throaty, frightening sound. – Dogs *growl* when they are angry.
2. Talk grouchily; complain and grumble.–People sometimes *growl* at bad luck.

grown (GROHN) *v.* One form of the verb *grow.*–Baby has *grown* a great deal this year. She has gotten much bigger.
–*Full-grown* means finished getting bigger. –These plants are *full-grown.* They are as large as they will get.

grown·up (GROHN-up) *n. grownups.* An adult; a man or woman.–Mary is very anxious to become a *grownup,* so that she can do just as she pleases.
–*grown-up, adj.* No longer growing; no longer a child.–Father and Mother are *grown-up.* They are adult.–You are a *grown-up* young man now. You must earn your own living.

growth (GROHTH) *n. growths.* 1. The amount a person, a plant, an animal, or anything will grow or has grown.–Bob doesn't have his full *growth* yet. He has not grown as much as he will.
2. Crop; amount grown.–The soldier had a thick *growth* of whiskers.

grub (GRUB) *n. grubs.* An insect in its early, short, thick, wormlike form. When the *grub* has gone through several stages of growth, it becomes a beetle or some other insect.

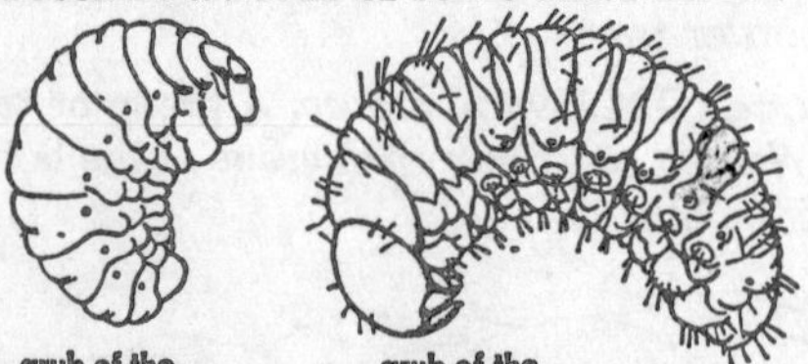

grub of the common bean weevil — grub of the strawberry root weevil

grudge (GRUJ) *n. grudges.* Hard feeling; dislike because of a special reason. – The prisoner said the policeman had a *grudge* against him. He believed the policeman was holding something against him, and that he was being accused unfairly.
–*v. grudges, grudged, grudging.* Not liking to give something one has to give.–The employer *grudged* the man the money he earned. He paid him, but he didn't want to pay him.

gru•el (GROO-əl) *n.* A thick, liquid food frequently fed to sick people and to babies. *Gruel* is made by boiling meal or oatmeal in milk or water.

gruff (GRUF) *adj., gruffly, adv.* 1. Rough, harsh, or deep in sound.–Grandfather sometimes talks in a *gruff* voice when he is trying hard not to laugh.
2. Rude; rough; harsh.–The man's *gruff* manner made me decide to ask someone else for directions.

grum•ble (GRUM-bəl) *v. grumbles, grumbled, grumbling.* Find fault or complain in a low voice. – Some children *grumble* about everything they have to do.
–*grumble, n. grumbles.*

grump•y (GRUMP-ee) *adj. grumpier, grumpiest.* Cross and gruff; not satisfied; bad-tempered.–Baby gets *grumpy* when she is sleepy.

grunt (GRUNT) *n. grunts.* A deep, quick noise made in the throat.–We heard the *grunts* of the pigs when Grandfather was feeding them.
–*v. grunts, grunted, grunting.* Make a deep, quick noise in the throat.–Dogs bark, roosters crow, and pigs *grunt.*

guar•an•tee (gar-ən-TEE) *n. guarantees.* A promise to make good if something or someone does not bring satisfaction.–The jeweler gave us a *guarantee* on the watch.
–*v. guarantees, guaranteed, guaranteeing.* 1. Promise that something will be satisfactory. –The jeweler *guaranteed* that the watch would run for a year. He would replace or fix it if it didn't.
2. Promise to do something.–Grandfather borrowed some money from the bank. Father *guaranteed* to repay it if Grandfather did not.
3. Insure.–My insurance policy *guarantees* me payment for fire damage to my house.

guard (GAHRD) *n. guards.* 1. A person, group, or device that defends or protects things, or that prevents things from happening: as, a coast *guard*, a *guard* in a basketball game, a *guard* in a jail, or a life*guard* at the beach.–He wore an arm *guard* in archery to prevent the bowstring from rubbing his wrist.
2. A group of soldiers for use as protection or in a ceremony.–They change the *guard* at the palace every few hours.–At the wedding of the soldier the *guard* of honor crossed swords to make an arch.
3. Watch.–The policeman kept *guard* over the prisoner.
–*v. guards, guarded, guarding.* 1. Watch over; protect.–The dog *guarded* the baby while Mother went into the store.–Soldiers *guarded* the storehouse.
2. Be careful.–The teacher told us to *guard* against catching cold. She wanted us to take care of ourselves so that we would not catch cold.
–*On guard* means ready to defend against danger or harm at any moment.

guard•i•an (GAHRD-ee-ən) *n. guardians.* One who has the care of someone or something.–Fathers and mothers are the *guardians* of their children. They take care of them. –The orphan's uncle is her *guardian.* He is the person who was named by law to care for her till she is old enough to look after herself.

guer•ril•la or **gue•ril•la** (gə-RIL-ə) *n. guerrillas* or *guerillas.* Fighters, not part of a regular army, who attack in small bands, often by night in country that is hilly, mountainous, or easy to hide in.–*Guerrillas* attacked the farms at night. They slept by day.
–*adj. Guerrilla* warfare is warfare carried on by guerrillas. *Guerrilla* fighters use sabotage, attacks on homes, and snipe-shots at individuals to gain their ends. They avoid encounters with large numbers of the enemy.

guess (GESS) *n. guesses.* 1. Something thought or decided without much basis.–I'll make a *guess* that it won't rain tomorrow.
2. A chance or turn to guess.–In this game each person has three *guesses.*
–*v. guesses, guessed, guessing.* 1. Say what something is, or decide about something, without knowing much about it and on the chance of being right.–Bob described an object and we *guessed* what it was. We told what we thought or believed it to be without seeing the object or having him name it.
2. Believe; suppose.–How cold do you think it is? I don't know, but I *guess* it must be nearly zero.–I *guess* it will be all right for you to take that book.

guest (GEST) *n. guests.* 1. A visitor; a person invited.–Mother is expecting *guests* for dinner.–Bob invited many *guests* to his party.
2. A person living at a hotel or other place with rooms for hire.–When staying in the city, Father was a *guest* at a small hotel.

guide (GYD) *n. guides.* One who shows the way, as through wilderness or through a museum.–When our parents came to the school to visit, Bob was a *guide.* He showed them the way through the different rooms.
–*v. guides, guided, guiding.* Show the way; lead; direct.–We will go through the woods if you will *guide* us.–The teacher *guides* us in our work.

guild (GILD) *n. guilds.* A group or society of persons having common interests or a common trade or profession organized for mutual benefit. *Guilds* known as craft *guilds* existed throughout Europe during the Middle Ages. There was a merchants' *guild,* a carpenters' *guild,* and the like.–The Newspaper *Guild* is a trade union for reporters and other employees of newspapers.

guil•lo•tine (GIL-ə-teen) *n. guillotines.* An apparatus or machine for cutting off a person's head. A heavy blade slides down the grooves of two vertical posts and through the victim's neck, which rests on a block beneath. The *guillotine* came into use in France at the time of the French Revolution.
–*v. guillotines, guillotined, guillotining.* Execute on the guillotine.–Queen Marie Antoinette of France was *guillotined* by the revolutionists.

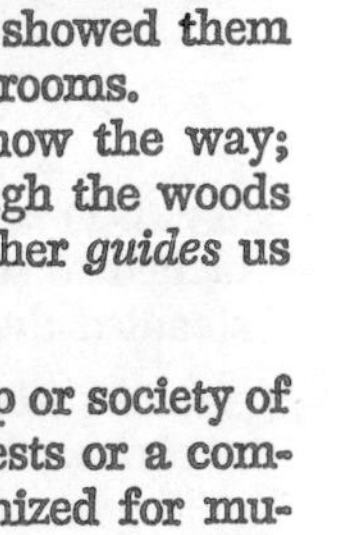

guilt (GILT) *n. guilts.* Having done wrong; deserving blame for a crime or bad act.–Jack had a feeling of *guilt* after taking the cover of the old man's garbage pail for a shield.

guilt•y (GIL-tee) *adj. guiltier, guiltiest; guiltily, adv.* 1. At fault or to blame for a crime or wrong done.–The jury found the man *guilty.* It decided that the man had done wrong and should be punished.
2. Ashamed; conscious of guilt.–Bob said he felt *guilty* for telling a lie, and asked to be forgiven.

guin•ea hen (GIN-ee hen) *guinea hens.* A fowl often seen on farms. *Guinea hens* are purplish-gray with white spots. They can fly quite high and roost high up in trees. They are very noisy when excited.

guin•ea pig (GIN-ee pig) *guinea pigs.* A tiny animal that looks a little like a rat.

Guinea pigs are used by scientists in experiments to study diseases and see how medicines act.

gui•tar (gi-TAHR) *n. guitars.* A musical instrument with strings. The strings are picked with the fingers to make music.

gulf (GULF) *n. gulfs.* A large bay that extends far into the land. The *Gulf* of California is a part of the Pacific Ocean. The *Gulf* of Mexico is a part of the Atlantic Ocean.

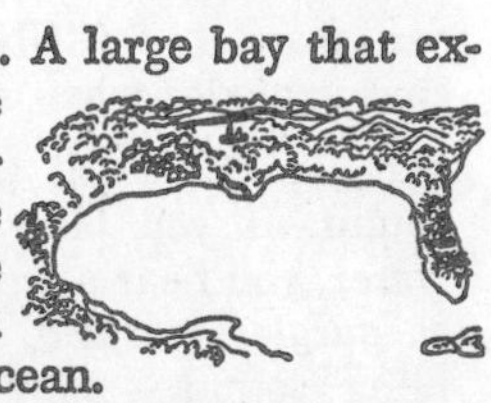

gull (GUL) *n. gulls.* A large, web-footed sea bird. *Gulls* are gray or white. *Gulls* often follow a boat and eat bits of food thrown from it. They eat fish, also. They are also known as sea *gulls.*

gul·ly (GUL-ee) *n. gullies.* Small ditch.—It rained so hard that the water running down the hillside cut a *gully.*

gulp (GULP) *n. gulps.* A loud, hard swallow. —The thirsty boy drank the cool water in *gulps.*
—*v. gulps, gulped, gulping.* Swallow hard and loudly.—Bob was in such a hurry to play ball that he *gulped* his food. He filled his mouth very full and swallowed his food without chewing it well.

gum (GUM) *n. gums; gummy, adj.* 1. A sticky juice that comes out of some trees. It hardens when air gets to it.
2. Chewing *gum,* which is made from gums and flavorings.
3. The fleshy part of one's mouth that covers the roots of one's teeth. One's teeth are partly covered by the *gums.*
—*v. gums, gummed, gumming.* Make sticky with gum or anything else that is sticky.—Postage stamps are *gummed* on the back for sticking them on envelopes.

gun (GUN) *n. guns.* A weapon used for shooting bullets, shells, rockets, and the like. Cannons and rifles are *guns.*

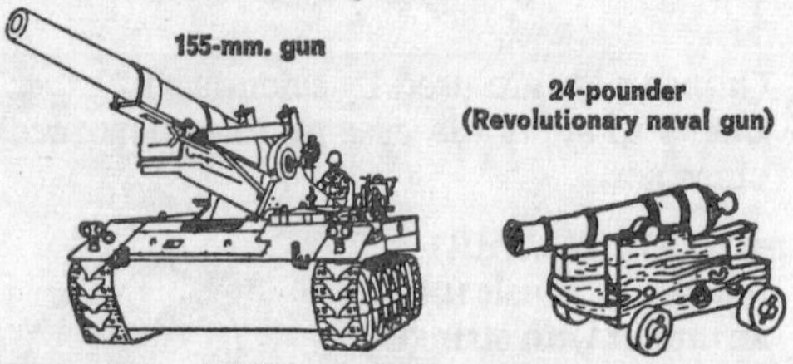

gun·ner (GUN-er) *n. gunners.* One who shoots a gun.—My brother was a *gunner* on a bombing plane during the war.

gun·pow·der (GUN-pow-der) *n.* A powder that explodes when struck or lighted.

gur·gle (GER-gəl) *n. gurgles.* A bubbling sound.—If you blow through a straw into water, you hear a *gurgle.*
—*v. gurgles, gurgled, gurgling.* Make a bubbling sound.—Baby *gurgles* when she is pleased and interested in something.

gush (GUSH) *n. gushes.* A sudden outpouring.—Water poured out in one big *gush.*—Her excitement caused her words to pour forth in a *gush.*
—*v. gushes, gushed, gushing.* 1. Rush out suddenly.—When the water pipe burst, water *gushed* out.
2. Exaggerate one's affection or praise.—I never liked Mrs. Jones. One moment she is *gushing* over us and the next she is scolding us for no reason.

gust (GUST) *n. gusts; gusty, adj.* A sudden rush or blast of air or wind.—There was a big *gust* of wind, and the boat turned over.—A *gust* of wind whirled the dust around in a circle.

gut·ter (GUT-er) *n. gutters.* 1. An eaves trough. *Gutters* are small grooves or open pipes made of metal or wood and fastened to the lower edges of a roof to carry away the rain water from the roof.

2. A ditch or trough along the side of a road to carry away water.

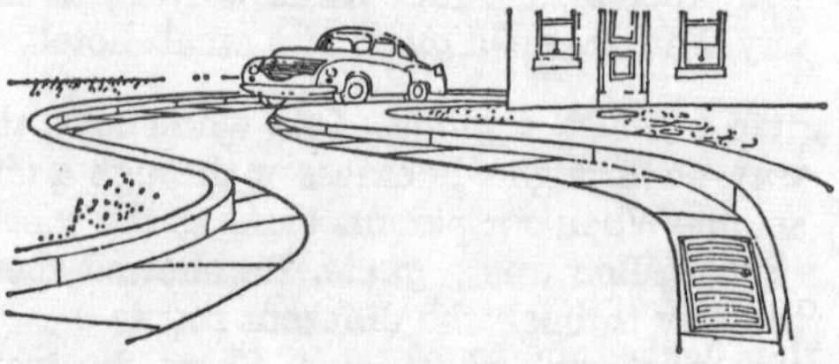

guy (GY) *n. guys* and *adj.* A rope or wire attached to something to steady it.—The boys steadied their tent with *guy* ropes.

gym·na·si·um (jim-NAY-zee-əm) *n. gymnasiums.* A building or room in which people exercise and try to build up their bodies. Basketball, indoor tennis, and other games are played in *gymnasiums.* Such a room is often known as a "gym."

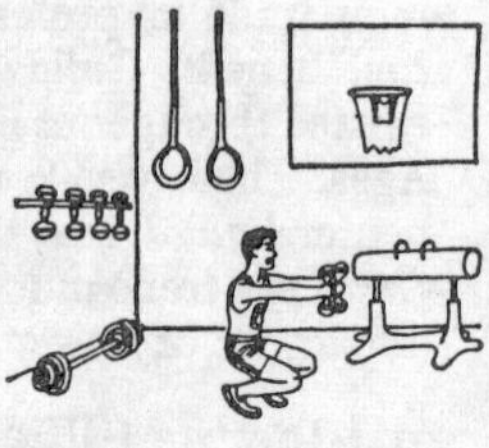

gyp·sum (JIP-səm) *n.* A common white mineral which can form either masses or crystals. It is used to make fertilizers, plaster of Paris, glass, and many other things. *Gypsum* is very soft and can be partially dissolved in water.

gyp·sy or **gip·sy** (JIP-see) *n. gypsies* or *gipsies.* A member of a tribe of people who wander about. They make their living telling fortunes, mending pots, and doing odd jobs. *Gypsies* probably came originally from India, a country in Asia.

Hh

H, h (AYCH) *n. H's, h's.* The eighth letter of the alphabet.

ha (HAH) *interj.* An exclamation of joy or surprise.–*Ha!* We won.

hab·it (HAB-it) *n. habits.* A custom; the usual thing to do; a regular practice.–The children formed the *habit* of brushing their teeth twice a day.

hab·i·tat (HAB-ə-tat) *n. habitats.* The place where an animal or person usually lives or where a plant is usually found.–A deer's *habitat* is the forest.

hack (HAK) *n. hacks.* 1. A carriage drawn by horses and hired out with a driver.
2. A taxicab.

–*v. hacks, hacked, hacking.* 1. Cut or chop roughly. – Father *hacked* the board in two with the dull hatchet.
2. Cough dryly.–Bob had a cold and *hacked* continually in class.

had (HAD) *v.* One form of the verb *have.*–If I *had* a pet, I would take care of it.–Yesterday I *had* three dollars.

had·dock (HAD-ək) *n. haddock* or *haddocks.* A large fish caught in the ocean for food.

had·n't (HAD-nt). Had not. – I *hadn't* been home long before it started to rain.

hail (HAYL) *n. hails.* 1. Frozen raindrops.–The *hail* beat loudly on the tin roof.
2. A shower of anything solid.–When the strong wind blew, there was a *hail* of acorns from the tree.
3. A call.–We heard the *hail* of the man on the boat.
4. Salute.–*Hail* to the king!
–*v. hails, hailed, hailing.* 1. Have a fall of hail. –It *hailed* when we had the big thunder storm.
2. Call to.–Father *hailed* the taxi driver.
3. Greet.–The class *hailed* the sick boy when he came to the window.
4. Come; be.–I *hail* from the South.

hail·stone (HAYL-stohn) *n. hailstones.* A frozen raindrop; a small piece of hard ice that sometimes falls during a thunderstorm.

hair (HAIR) *n. hairs.* 1. The strands or a single one of the strands that grow on the head.–Mary's *hair* covers her ears.

2. *Hair* grows on parts of the body other than the head, and many animals are covered with *hair.*

hair·y (HAIR-ee) *adj. hairier, hairiest.* Covered with hair.–The man's arms are *hairy.*

half (HAF) *n. halves.* One of two equal parts. If you divide anything into two parts the same size, each part is one *half.*–One *half* is written 1/2.
–*adj.* and *adv.* The glass is *half* full of milk. It can hold twice as much milk as it has in it now.–Dinner is only *half* cooked.

half broth·er (HAF bru<u>th</u>-er) *half brothers.* A brother by one parent only.–John and Tom have the same mother, but their fathers are different persons. John and Tom are *half brothers.*

half sis·ter (HAF siss-ter) *half sisters.* A sister by one parent only.–Jane and Ruth have the same mother, but their fathers are different persons. Jane and Ruth are *half sisters.*

half·way (HAF-WAY) *adj.* and *adv.* 1. Half of the distance.–The *halfway* point between the two cities is at Eagle Corners.–Mary's belt will only go *halfway* around Mother's waist.
2. As far as the middle.–Bob has read *halfway* through the book.

hall (HAWL) *n. halls.* 1. A small room or passageway at the entrance of a building or connecting different rooms in a building.—We walk through a *hall* to our room.

2. A large room where meetings are held.—The lecture was given in a *hall* downtown.

Hal•low•een (hal-oh-WEEN) *n.* The night of the last day of October.—Children celebrate *Halloween* by dressing up in funny costumes.

ha•lo (HAY-loh) *n. halos.* 1. A circle or ring of light occasionally seen around the sun or moon. *Halos* are caused by very small ice crystals in the earth's atmosphere.

2. The ring of radiance around the head of an angel, saint, or holy person in pictures. It is used to show holiness.

halt (HAWLT) *n. halts.* A full stop.—The car came to a *halt.*

—*v. halts, halted, halting.* 1. Come to a stop.—The officer told the boy to *halt.*

2. Bring to a stop.—The officer *halted* the boy.

hal•ter (HAWLT-er) *n. halters.* 1. A strap or rope used to lead a horse.—I led the horse by the *halter.*

2. A woman's sunback blouse, sleeveless and held up by a strap or ribbon around the neck.

halves (HAVZ) *n. pl.* More than one *half.*—A whole apple divided into two equal parts is in two *halves.*

ham (HAM) *n. hams.* 1. The upper part of a hog's back leg, either fresh or salted and smoked, eaten as meat.

2. Operator of an amateur radio station.

ham•burg•er (HAM-berg-er) *n. hamburgers.* 1. Ground beef or steak.—Mother bought two pounds of *hamburger* at the butcher's.

2. A round, flat patty of chopped meat, broiled or fried; usually served on a bun or roll.

ham•let (HAM-lət) *n. hamlets.* A small village, often made up of only a few houses.—The traveler stopped at a tiny *hamlet* for refreshment.

ham•mer (HAM-er) *n. hammers.* A tool for pounding, or for driving nails. The head is metal and the handle is usually of wood. A *hammer* with a wooden head is a mallet.

—*v. hammers, hammered, hammering.* Pound with a hammer.—Mother has a bowl made of metal which has been *hammered* into shape.

ham•mock (HAM-ək) *n. hammocks.* A swinging couch hung by ropes at each end.—Sailors on some ships sleep in *hammocks.*

ham•per (HAMP-er) *n. hampers.* A large basket with a cover.—Mother keeps the soiled clothes in a *hamper.*—We carried our food in the picnic *hamper.*

—*v. hampers, hampered, hampering.* Make difficult.—Bad weather *hampers* airplane travel.—The broken heel on her shoe *hampered* her walking.

hand (HAND) *n. hands.* 1. The part of the body at the end of the arm, used for grasping and holding. We have two *hands.* Fingers are part of the *hand.*

2. A worker.—Grandfather has several hired *hands* on the farm.

3. One of the pointers on the face of a clock. —The *hands* of the clock show the time.

4. A unit of measure equal to four inches.—The horse is fifteen *hands* high. He is sixty inches high.

5. Side.—On the one *hand,* Bob did not want to go to school; on the other *hand,* he knew he should go.

6. Share; part.—I had no *hand* in the decision.

7. One round of a card game.—Who dealt the last *hand?*

8. Cards held by one player.—I have a poor *hand;* I have all low cards.

9. Handwriting.—She writes in a clear *hand.*

—*v. hands, handed, handing.* Give with the hand.—Bob *hands* out the papers to each one in the class.—Please *hand* me the butter.

—*In hand* means under control.—The firemen had the fire *in hand* by the time we arrived.

hand•bag (HAND- *or* HAN-bag) *n. handbags.* A bag small enough to carry in the hand.–Mother carries her money in her *handbag.*

hand•book (HAND- *or* HAN-buhk) *n. handbooks.* A small book containing information; a guidebook or manual.–The television repairman consulted his *handbook* before repairing the set.

hand•cuff (HAND- *or* HAN-cuf) *n. handcuffs.* One of a pair of metal bracelets fastened together with a chain. They are locked about the wrists of prisoners to keep them from running away.

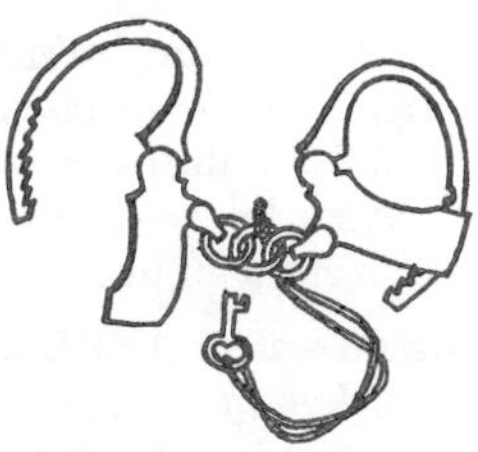

–*v. handcuffs, handcuffed, handcuffing.* Put handcuffs on.–The policeman *handcuffed* the two prisoners he had just captured.

hand•ful (HAND- *or* HAN-fuhl) *n. handfuls.* 1. As much as can be held in the hand.–Grandmother threw a *handful* of crumbs to the birds.
2. Very few.–There was just a *handful* of people at church this morning.

hand•i•cap (HAN-dee-cap) *n. handicaps.* 1. Anything that hinders one.–A sore thumb is a *handicap* to a person when he tries to write.
2. An official advantage or disadvantage in a contest.–Bob offered Bill a *handicap* of five yards in the race. He offered to start five yards behind Bill.
–*v. handicaps, handicapped, handicapping.* Hinder.–John's sore thumb *handicapped* him in writing.

hand•i•craft (HAN-dee-kraft) *n. handicrafts.* 1. Ability or skill in working with the hands.–The blind man's *handicraft* is remarkable. He can weave beautiful baskets out of straw.
2. Any occupation or art requiring such skill. –Clay modeling is a *handicraft.*

hand•ker•chief (HANGK-er-chif *or* -cheef) *n. handkerchiefs.* A small square of cloth used for wiping the face or the nose.

han•dle (HAND-əl) *n. handles.* A part of an object by which it is held.–Cups, pitchers, and pans have *handles.*–Father turned the *handle* of the car door.

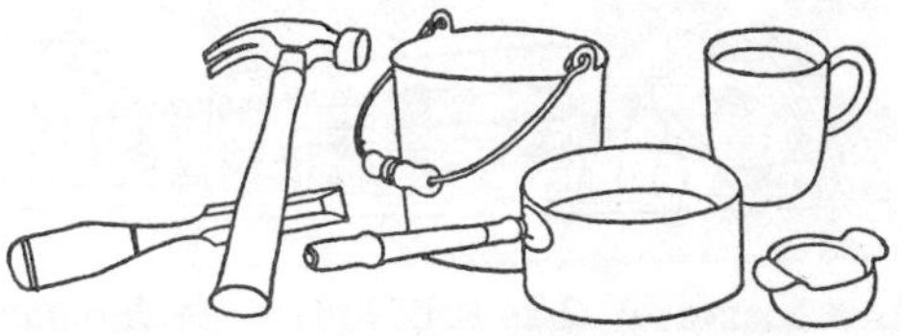

–*v. handles, handled, handling.* 1. Hold and feel with the hands.–The grocer asked us not to *handle* the fruit.
2. Manage.–Father is a good foreman. He knows how to *handle* the men who work for him.
3. Buy and sell.–Our grocer *handles* only the very best foods.

hand•some (HANT- *or* HAN-səm) *adj. handsomer, handsomest; handsomely, adv.* 1. Very good-looking.–Father is *handsome* in his new suit.
2. Generous and large; large and fine.–The man offered a *handsome* amount of money for the house.

hand•writ•ing (HAND-ryt-ing) *n. handwritings.* Writing done with a pen or pencil held in the hand.–Mary's *handwriting* is easy to read.

hand•y (HAN-dee) *adj. handier, handiest; handily, adv.* 1. Skillful.–Father is *handy* with the hammer and saw. He uses them easily and well.
2. Convenient.–Mother keeps the salt in a *handy* place.

hang (HANG) *n.* A knack.–Mary doesn't get the *hang* of knitting. She can't seem to do it.
–*v. hangs, hung, hanging.* 1. Fasten at one or more points and let fall loosely. – Mother *hangs* the clothes on the clothesline to dry.–Children *hang* their stockings on the mantel at Christmas.
2. Droop.–The hot sun made the flowers *hang* down.
3. Decorate with hanging things.–The room was *hung* with Christmas bells, wreaths, and holly.
–*v. hangs, hanged, hanging.* 1. Kill by hanging with a rope around the neck.–The murderer was *hanged.*
2. Die by hanging with a rope around the neck.–The murderer was told he would *hang* for his crime.

hang·ar (HANG-ər) *n. hangars.* A building or shed to keep airplanes in.

hap·haz·ard (hap-HAZ-ərd) *adj.; haphazardly, adv.* Aimless.–The child does his work in a *haphazard* way.

hap·pen (HAP-ən) *v. happens, happened, happening.* 1. Take place.–An accident *happened* just as we reached the corner.
2. Do something or occur by chance.–I *happened* to hear the music as I was passing by.
3. Go wrong.–Something has *happened* to Father's car. It will not run.

hap·pen·ing (HAP-ən-ing) *n. happenings.* An event; a thing that happens.–If a space ship landed on Grandfather's farm, it would be an unusual *happening.*

hap·pi·ness (HAP-ee-nəss) *n. happinesses.* Joy and gladness.–The children brought *happiness* to their parents.

hap·py (HAP-ee) *adj. happier, happiest; happily, adv.* 1. Pleased and glad.–The children are *happy* when they are playing.
2. Lucky; fortunate.–It was a *happy* chance that Bob found the quarter.

hap·py-go-luck·y (HAP-ee-goh-LUK-ee) *adj.* Carefree; without worries.–Mary is a *happy-go-lucky* person. Nothing worries her.

har·bor (HAHR-bər) *n. harbors.* A sheltered body of water where ships and boats may go for safety from storms and waves; a port.

–*v. harbors, harbored, harboring.* 1. Shelter; protect.–If you let a criminal hide from the police in your house you would be said to be *harboring* him illegally.
2. Hold; bear in one's mind.–She *harbored* a grudge against Lucy.

hard (HAHRD) *adj. harder, hardest* and *adv.* 1. Solid; not soft; not easy to bend or dent.–Stones are *hard.*–A *hard* object does not give or change shape when you touch it.
2. Firm; not liquid.–Gelatin becomes *hard* when chilled.
3. Difficult; not simple. – Some arithmetic problems are *harder* than others.
4. Determined.–Bob is a *hard* worker. He works steadily and does his best.
5. With all or most of one's strength or skill. –Bob tries *hard* to make good grades.–He gave the rope a *hard* pull.
6. Rough. – The hunters had a *hard* trip through the woods.
7. Full of trouble and suffering.–Times are *hard* when many men are out of work.
8. Strict and severe.–The man was a *hard* master. He treated those under him without mercy.
9. Containing minerals. – *Hard* water does not make soap suds easily.
10. Containing much alcohol. – One must have a license to sell *hard* liquors.–Whiskey is a *hard* liquor.

hard·en (HAHRD-n) *v. hardens, hardened, hardening.* Make or become hard.–Mother put the ice cream in the freezer to *harden.*–The sun *hardened* the clay.

hard·ly (HAHRD-lee) *adv.* 1. Scarcely; only just; barely.–We *hardly* had enough cake for everyone.–It is *hardly* ten o'clock.
2. Not likely.–Since Bob has to work, he will *hardly* be able to attend the party.

hard·ship (HAHRD-ship) *n. hardships.* Something that is difficult to stand or endure. –The explorers experienced many *hardships* before they reached their goal.

hard·ware (HAHRD-wair) *n.* Articles made of metal, such as nails, wire, and tools.–We bought *hardware* for the new house.

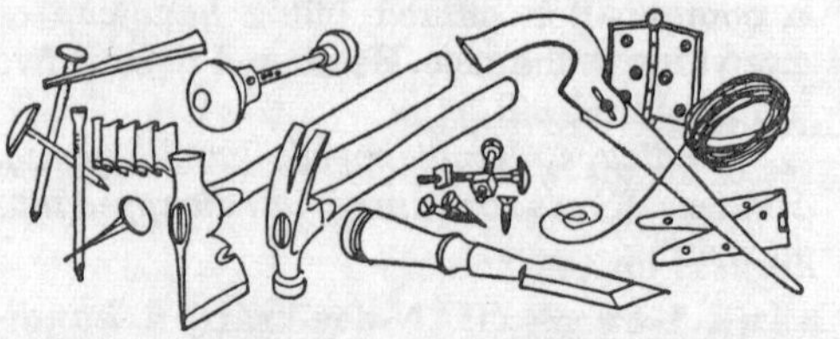

har·dy (HAHRD-ee) *adj. hardier, hardiest.* Strong and healthy.–Some plants are *hardy.* They are not easily destroyed.

hare (HAIR) *n. hares.* A gray or brown animal very much like a rabbit, but larger. A *hare* can run very fast.

hark (HAHRK) *v.* Listen!–*Hark!* I hear footsteps.

harm (HAHRM) *n. harms.* Injury or damage.–Mother tries to keep the baby safe from *harm.*
–*v. harms, harmed, harming.* Hurt.–The dog will not *harm* you.

harm•ful (HAHRM-fuhl) *adj.; harmfully, adv.* Damaging; causing harm. – Freezing weather is *harmful* to plants.–Some snakes are *harmful.*

harm•less (HAHRM-ləss) *adj.; harmlessly, adv.* Not dangerous.–Most snakes are *harmless.*

har•mon•i•ca (hahr-MAHN-ə-kə) *n. harmonicas.* A small, flat musical instrument played by blowing out and drawing in air through a row of holes. It is sometimes called a mouth organ.

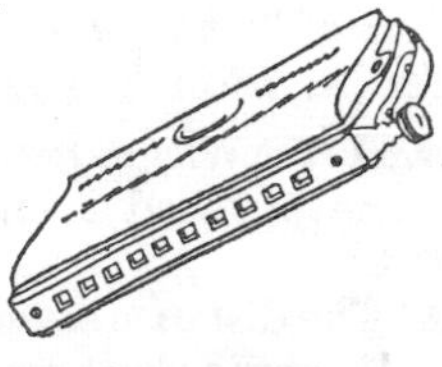

har•mo•nize (HAHR-ma-nyz) *v. harmonizes, harmonized, harmonizing.* Look or sound well together.–The colors of Mother's dress and hat *harmonize.* – The musical notes C and G *harmonize* well.

har•mo•ny (HAHR-mən-ee) *n.* 1. Peace and friendship.–If children live in *harmony* at home, they are apt to get along well together in school, too.
2. A beautiful combination of color or sound. –There is *harmony* in the colors of the rainbow. The colors go well together.–Beautiful *harmony* can be created by the sounding of more than one musical note at a time.

har•ness (HAHR-nəss) *n. harnesses.* 1. The set of straps with which a horse is hitched to a wagon, plow, etc.–Grandfather put the *harness* on the horse.

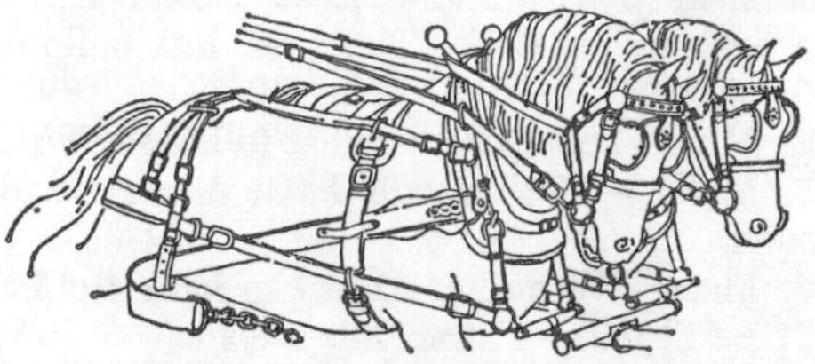

2. Straps like a horse's harness used to hold a baby in a carriage or at the end of a leash in walking.
–*v. harnesses, harnessed, harnessing.* Put a harness on.–The farmer *harnessed* the horse and hitched it to the wagon.

harp (HAHRP) *n. harps.* A large, stringed musical instrument that stands on the floor and is played with the fingers of both hands.

har•poon (HAHR-poon) *n. harpoons.* A spear with barbs that stick backward from the point. –*Harpoons* are used for catching whales and large fish.

–*v. harpoons, harpooned, harpooning.* Pierce with a harpoon.–The man stood up in the boat and *harpooned* the large fish.

harp•si•chord (HAHRP-si-kord) *n. harpsichords.* A musical instrument with a keyboard like that of a piano. Its sound is similar to that of a harp. It was developed before the piano.

har•row (HAR-oh) *n. harrows.* A piece of farm equipment used to smooth and crumble soil. In its simplest form a *harrow* is a frame set with rows of metal hooks, spikes, or disks. Some *harrows* have several such frames set side by side or at angles.

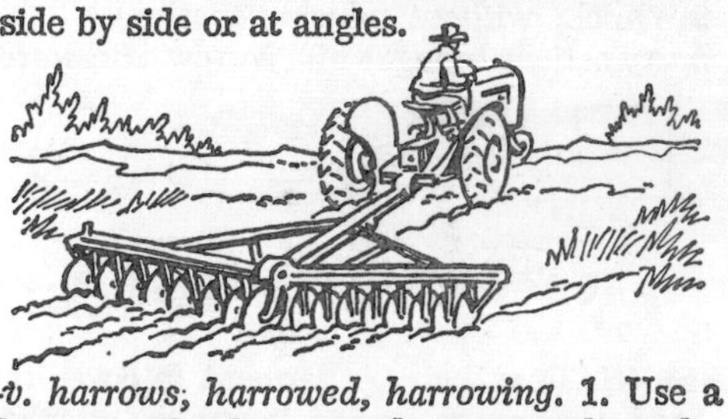

–*v. harrows, harrowed, harrowing.* 1. Use a harrow.–The farmer is *harrowing* the soil.
2. Torment; wound; hurt. – Please do not *harrow* us by telling us the terrible details of the accident.

harsh (HAHRSH) *adj. harsher, harshest; harshly, adv.* 1. Rough; grating or coarse.–The man's voice was *harsh.*–The stone felt *harsh* to the touch.
2. Severe.–The officer was *harsh* with his men. He treated them without mercy.

har•vest (HAHR-vəst) *n. harvests.* 1. Crop. –There was a large *harvest* of potatoes this year.
2. The time of gathering crops.–*Harvest* is in the fall or late summer.
–*v. harvests, harvested, harvesting.* Gather.–The farmer *harvests* his grain, fruit, and other crops.

har•vest•er (HAHR-vəst-er) *n. harvesters.* A person or a machine that gathers grain and other crops.

has (HAZ) *v.* One form of the verb *have.*—Mother *has* a new hat.

hash (HASH) *n. hashes.* 1. A food made by chopping and cooking meat, onions, potatoes, and other foods together.
2. A mess; a confusion.—Little Jane has made a *hash* of the silver drawer. She's mixed up knives, forks, and spoons.

has•n't (HAZ-ənt). Has not.—Father *hasn't* come home yet.

haste (HAYST) *n.* A great hurry.—Grandmother left in *haste* when she got the letter from home.

has•ten (HAYSS-ən) *v. hastens, hastened, hastening.* Hurry.—Our teacher told us to *hasten* home. She *hastened* us on our way.

hast•i•ly (HAYSS-tə-lee) *adv.* 1. Quickly and a little carelessly.—Bob wrote his paper *hastily* and then went home.
2. Quickly; before thinking.—Do not speak *hastily.*

hast•y (HAYSS-tee) *adj.* 1. Quickly made.—Mother cooked a *hasty* lunch.
2. Quick; without pausing to think.—Bob's *hasty* actions brought him sorrow afterward.

hat (HAT) *n. hats.* A garment to cover the head. *Hats* are made of felt, straw, and other materials.—Mother wears a *hat* when she goes to town.

hatch (HACH) *n. hatches.* An opening in the deck of a ship.—The sailor came up through the *hatch.*

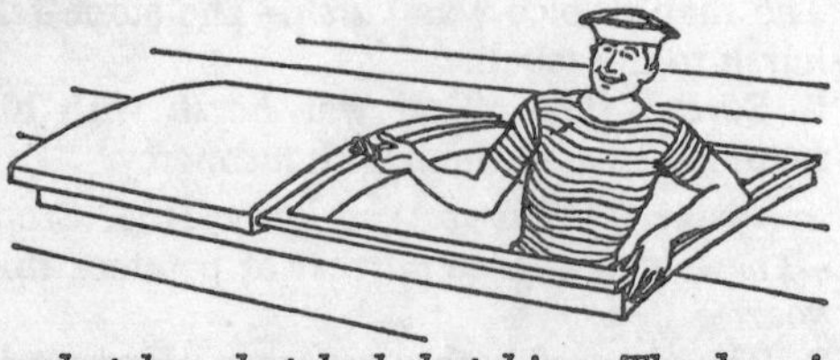

—*v. hatches, hatched, hatching.* The hen is patiently sitting on her eggs. She is *hatching* her chicks.—The mother robin sits on eggs in the nest until they *hatch,* until the baby robins come out of the shell.

hatch•et (HACH-ət) *n. hatchets.* A small chopping tool with a short handle. You can pound with one end of the head of a *hatchet* and chop with the other. You use it with one hand.

hate (HAYT) *n. hates.* Bitter dislike.—Our dog has great *hate* for cats.
—*v. hates, hated, hating.* Dislike very much.—Bill *hates* working.

ha•tred (HAY-trəd) *n. hatreds.* A feeling of great dislike.—There is *hatred* between those men. They hate each other.

haugh•ty (HAW-tee) *adj. haughtier, haughtiest; haughtily, adv.* Having contempt for others while thinking too highly of oneself.—The girl's *haughty* attitude made it difficult for her to make friends.

haul (HAWL) *n. hauls.* 1. Amount gathered.—The boy had a big *haul* of hickory nuts today.
2. The distance covered in moving an object.—It is only a short *haul* from the farm to town.
—*v. hauls, hauled, hauling.* 1. Pull.—The dog *hauled* the sled over the snow.
2. Carry from place to place in a vehicle.—The man *hauls* sand for a living.

haunch (HAWNCH) *n. haunches.* The upper part of an animal's hind legs.—Animals sit on their *haunches.*

haunt (HAWNT) *n. haunts.* A place one spends much time in.—The old shack is the favorite *haunt* of the boys.
—*v. haunts, haunted, haunting.* 1. Visit often.—The boys *haunt* the old shack in the woods.
2. *Haunt* is used in connection with ghosts.—Ghosts *haunt* that house.

have (HAV) *v. has, had, having.* 1. Own; possess; keep with one.—I *have* a ball.—I *have* a book in my desk.—The store *has* balloons for sale.
2. Must.—People *have* to eat to keep alive.
3. Make.—Mother will *have* dinner ready soon.
4. Meet.—We do not expect to *have* trouble.
5. Be ill with.—Father *has* a cold.
6. Take.—Will you *have* an apple?
7. Hold.—We will *have* a contest.
8. *Have* is used with verbs.—They *have* gone.—He *has* gone.
9. Cause to.—*Have* the store deliver it to me.
10. Allow.—I won't *have* the boys walking through the kitchen with muddy feet.

Ha·wai·i (hə-WY-ee *or* hə-WAH-yə) *n.* The fiftieth state to be admitted to the union of the United States. *Hawaii,* also called the Hawaiian Islands, is made up of a chain of islands in the Pacific Ocean. *Hawaii* is also the name of the largest island in the chain.

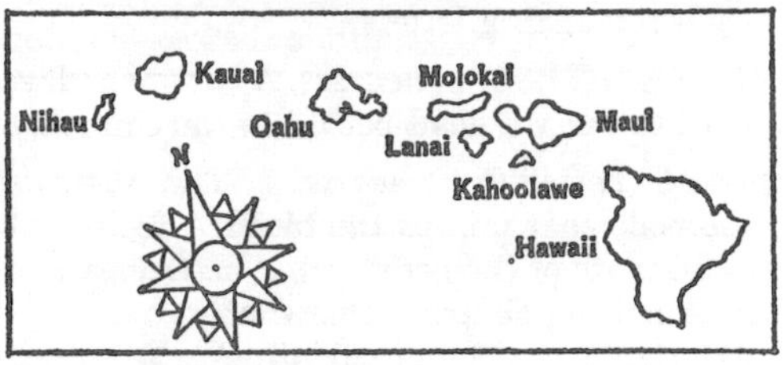

Ha·wai·ian (hə-WY-ən *or* hə-WAH-yən) *n. Hawaiians.* 1. A person born, or living, in Hawaii.
2. The language native Hawaiians speak.
–*adj.* Having to do with Hawaii.–It is a *Hawaiian* custom to greet visitors with garlands of flowers.

hawk (HAWK) *n. hawks.* A large, strong bird that lives by eating other birds and animals. *Hawks* have strong, hooked bills.

haw·thorn (HAW-thorn) *n. hawthorns.* A kind of bush or tree that has red berries and long thorns on it.

hay (HAY) *n.* Grass dried for use as food. In winter the farmer feeds his cattle *hay.*

hay·cock (HAY-kahk) *n. haycocks.* A small stack or pile of hay.–Little Boy Blue was under the *haycock,* fast asleep.

hay fe·ver (HAY fee-ver). Sneezing, watering of the eyes, and other discomfort caused by breathing the fine pollen of certain plants.–Every year, in August, Mary gets *hay fever* from ragweed.

hay·stack (HAY-stak) *n. haystacks.* A pile of hay.–The farmer has a *haystack* in the field.

haz·ard (HAZ-erd) *n. hazards.* 1. A danger or risk.–Papers placed near a furnace are a fire *hazard.* They are in danger of catching fire.
2. Something in the way that obstructs.–Golf courses have *hazards* to make the game harder.

haze (HAYZ) *n.; hazy, adj.* Mist or smoke in the air which makes it difficult for one to see. –We could not see the hill because of the *haze.*

H-bomb (AYCH-bahm) *n. H-bombs.* Hydrogen bomb; one in which the hydrogen atom is used to create a nuclear explosion. The *H-bomb* is many times more powerful than the first atom bomb.

he (HEE) *pron.* A word used instead of the name of a boy, a man, or a male animal.–Father came home. *He* was tired.

head (HED) *n. heads.* 1. The upper part of the body, containing the ears, eyes, nose, and mouth. – Hair grows on the *head.*–Your face is part of your *head.*

2. The top part; anything like the head in shape or position.–Mother bought a *head* of lettuce.–The carpenter hit the nail on the *head* with the *head* of the hammer.–We sleep with our *heads* at the *head* of the bed.
3. Front.–The clown was at the *head* of the circus parade.
4. A leader; a manager.–The principal is the *head* of our school.
5. The place where a boil or other infection opens.–The boil on Mary's arm came to a *head.*
6. Ability to understand.–Father has a good *head* for mechanics. It is not hard for him to learn about machinery.
7. Self-control.–All of the children kept their *heads* during the fire drill.
8. One or more of a group.–Grandfather sold five *head* of cattle last week.
–*v. heads, headed, heading.* 1. Lead; be ahead of.–She *headed* the list of scholarship contestants. She was ahead of all others.
2. Write an introduction, or heading.–Did you *head* your spelling paper correctly?
3. Go toward.–The hunters *headed* north.
–*adj.* First or leading.–Miss Smith was *head* counselor at camp last summer.

head·ache (HED-ayk) *n. headaches.* An ache or pain in the head.

head·light (HED-lyt) *n. headlights.* A light at the front of a vehicle such as an automobile, a bicycle, or a locomotive on a train.

head·line (HED-lyn) *n. headlines.* A few words in large print over an article in a newspaper. They tell what the article is about.

head·quar·ters (HED-kwor-terz) *n. sing.* and *pl.* 1. The base from which a military commander issues orders; the place where a commanding officer lives.–The captain received a change of orders from *headquarters.* –The general's *headquarters* were at Versailles.
2. Any main base of operations.–The mayor's *headquarters* is City Hall.

heal (HEEL) *v. heals, healed, healing.* Make or get well.–The sore on Mother's arm has *healed* now.–There's nothing wrong with him that fresh air and good food won't *heal.*

health (HELTH) *n.* The condition of one's body.–If you are well, you are in good *health.* If you are sick, you are in poor *health.*

health·ful (HELTH-fuhl) *adj.; healthfully, adv.* Good for the health.–The climate in this country is *healthful.*

health·y (HELTH-ee) *adj. healthier, healthiest; healthily, adv.* In good condition; not ill. –Bob is a *healthy* boy. He almost never gets sick.

heap (HEEP) *n. heaps.* A pile or stack.–We saw a *heap* of gravel by the roadside.
–*v. heaps, heaped, heaping.* Pile.–After Father cut the grass, the children *heaped* it into a large pile.

hear (HIR) *v. hears, heard, hearing.* 1. Notice a sound with the ears.–We see with our eyes, and *hear* with our ears.–Did you *hear* the radio program?
2. Learn by hearing or reading.–I *heard* that she was very sick.–What do you *hear* from your brother in Africa? Have you had a letter lately?

hear·ing (HIR-ing) *n.* 1. The ability to notice sounds with the ears.–Grandfather's *hearing* is not as good as it was when he was younger.
2. A chance to say what one has to say and be heard.–The boy asked the teacher to give him a *hearing* before punishing him.
3. The distance one can hear a sound.–The boys were talking within our *hearing.*
4. Learning by hearing or reading.–I like *hearing* from my brother in Africa. He writes such interesting letters.

hearse (HERSS) *n. hearses.* A car or carriage used to carry a dead person to the cemetery.

heart (HAHRT) *n. hearts.* 1. The organ of the body that pumps the blood to all parts of the body.

2. Anything shaped somewhat like the heart.–Some valentine cards have *hearts* on them.
3. Feelings.–The man has a kind *heart.* He has a kind feeling toward people and animals.
4. Courage. – Grandfather didn't have the *heart* to tell Bob that he had to go home.
5. The middle part of anything.–The store is in the *heart* of the town.–The boys like the *heart* of the watermelon.
6. The most important part.–The motor is the *heart* of an automobile.
–*By heart* means from memory.–The children learned the poem *by heart.*

hearth (HAHRTH) *n. hearths.* The floor of a fireplace or the bricks or stone in front of it. –We sat by the *hearth* and told stories.

heart·y (HAHR-tee) *adj. heartier, heartiest; heartily, adv.*
1. Sincere.–Bob gave Jack a *hearty* wish for a happy birthday.
2. Big and cheerful.–Father has a *hearty* laugh.
3. Strong and healthy.–The old woman is quite *hearty.*
4. Big and satisfying.–We ate a *hearty* meal on Thanksgiving.

heat (HEET) *n. heats.* 1. Warmth; the opposite of cold. *Heat* is a form of energy. It can be felt but not seen. The sun gives off *heat.*
2. Excitement.–In the *heat* of battle men do many things they would not do in everyday life.–In the *heat* of anger he said things he later regretted.
–*v. heats, heated, heating.* Make or become warm or hot.–Electricity *heats* Mother's iron. –The iron *heats* slowly.

heat·er (HEET-er) *n. heaters.* Something used to make a room, car, etc., warm. Furnaces are *heaters.* Some cars have *heaters.*

hea•then (HEE-thən) *n. heathens* and *adj.* 1. A person who does not believe in the one God of the Bible; a person who is not a Jew, Christian, or Mohammedan.
2. A person who worships idols.

heave (HEEV) *v. heaves, heaved* or *hove, heaving.* 1. Lift or raise with effort.–The man *heaved* the bundle to his shoulder.
2. Cast; throw; toss.–John *heaved* the football to Hugh, and Hugh made the touchdown.
3. Breathe very heavily, with a rising and falling of the chest. –After being pulled from the water, the boy lay *heaving* on the ground.
4. Rise and fall heavily.–The ground *heaved* during the earthquake.
5. Utter with effort. The man *heaved* a sigh of relief.
6. Haul; pull with effort.–The sailors finally *heaved* the anchor out of the water.
–*heave, n. heaves.*

heav•en (HE-vən) *n. heavens.* 1. The space above the earth; the sky.–Airplanes fly in the *heavens.*
2. (Sometimes written with a capital "H.") A place where God is said to dwell, where there is perfect happiness and peace forever; sometimes it means God himself.–Many people believe that they will go to *heaven* when they die.–May *Heaven* bless you!
3. A state of great happiness.–Mary is in *heaven* when she is reading.

heav•en•ly (HE-vən-lee) *adj.* 1. Being in the sky.–The moon and stars are *heavenly* bodies.
2. Sacred; having to do with God's heaven.–Angels are *heavenly* messengers.
3. Beautiful and delightful.

heav•i•ly (HE-və-lee) *adv.* In a heavy fashion.–The man walked *heavily.*

heav•y (HE-vee) *adj. heavier, heaviest.* 1. Weighing much; not easy to move or lift.–
2. Very large or great.–There was a *heavy* snowfall last night.–Traffic was so *heavy* that we had to drive slowly. There were many cars and other vehicles on the road.
3. Bulky; weighty; thick.
4. Unhappy; sad.–The old man has a *heavy* heart. He is weighed down with troubles.

He•brew (HEE-broo) *n. Hebrews.* 1. A Jew.
2. The ancient language of the Jews; the language of Israel.
–*adj.* Jewish.

he'd (HEED). A short way of writing the words "he had" or "he would."–He said *he'd* cut the grass.

hedge (HEJ) *n. hedges.* A row of bushes or shrubs used as a fence.–We have a *hedge* around our yard.

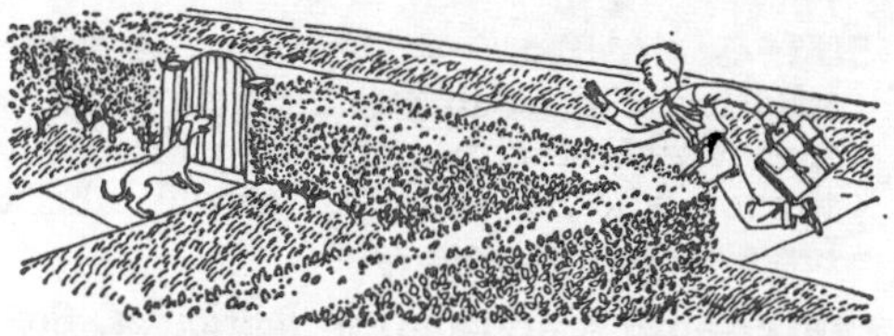

–*v. hedges, hedged, hedging.* 1. Surround.–The policemen *hedged* about the man to protect him from the crowd.
2. Avoid giving a frank or plain answer.–Bill tried to *hedge* when the teacher asked him about the broken window.

hedge•hog (HEJ-hawg) *n. hedgehogs.* 1. In America, a porcupine.–*Hedgehogs* are covered with stiff, pointed quills. These quills protect them.
2. The Old World *hedgehog,* a similar, but actually unrelated animal.

heed (HEED) *n.* Attention; notice; thought.–Bill paid no *heed* to his mother's call.
–*v. heeds, heeded, heeding.* Pay attention to.–The boy did not *heed* the directions given him, so he became lost.

heel (HEEL) *n. heels.* 1. The rounded part at the back of your foot just below your ankle.
2. The part of your stocking or other footwear that fits over the heel.–Bob's shoe rubbed a hole in the *heel* of his sock.
3. The leather or rubber part fastened to the bottom of your shoe just below your heel.–Mother wears shoes with high *heels,* and Mary wears shoes with low *heels.*

heif•er (HEF-er) *n. heifers.* A young cow that has not had a calf.

height (HYT) *n. heights.* 1. How high anything is from the ground or from a given place.–Bob's *height* is 4 feet 6 inches. He is that tall.–The *height* of that mountain is 12,500 feet.
2. Peak; topmost point.–The writer was at the *height* of his career when he was forty years old. He was doing better work then than at any other time in his life.
3. A mountain, cliff, or other very high place.–The eagle flew to its nest on a stony *height.*

heir (AIR) *n. heirs.* The person who has a right to another's property, money, or title when that person dies.

heir•ess (AIR-əss) *n. heiresses.* A woman who has a right to another's property and money when that person dies, particularly a woman who has inherited or will inherit a large amount of money.

heir•loom (AIR-loom) *n. heirlooms.* Something valuable that has been handed down from person to person for many years, in one family.–Mother's locket is an *heirloom.* It once belonged to her great-grandmother, then to her grandmother, then to her own mother. Now it is hers.

held (HELD) *v.* One form of the verb *hold.*–Bob *held* the ball. He got it and kept it.–Mother *held* Baby's hand.

hel•i•cop•ter (HEL-ə-kahp-ter) *n. helicopters.* An aircraft with horizontal overhead propellers. These propellers enable the craft to rise straight up in the air, to hover in one place, and to descend straight down. *Helicopters* are often used for rescue work.

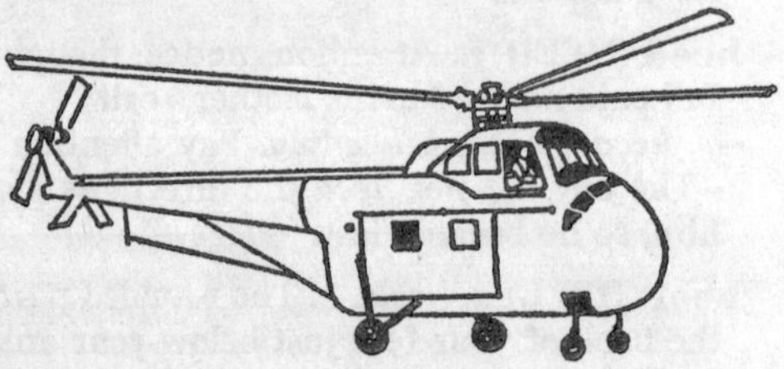

he•li•um (HEE-li-əm *or* HEE-lee-əm) *n.* One of the lightest gases known. It is colorless, odorless, and does not burn. *Helium* is often used to inflate airships and balloons.

hell (HEL) *n. hells.* 1. The place where many people think that evil persons are sent to be punished after they die.
2. Any miserable place or condition.–Life for the people in London during the air raids of World War II is said to have been *hell.*

he'll (HEEL). A short form for *he will* or *he shall.*–*He'll* go to school tomorrow.–*He'll* return at once.

hel•lo (he-LOH) *n. hellos* and *interj.* A friendly greeting.–Mary said a bright *hello* to me.

helm (HELM) *n. helms.* 1. The wheel or handle that is used to steer a boat.
2. Any position of command.–With Lincoln at the *helm,* the Union was safely steered through the Civil War.

hel•met (HEL-mət) *n. helmets.* A covering worn to protect the head. Football players, soldiers, and deep-sea divers wear *helmets.* Knights wore *helmets* in battle.

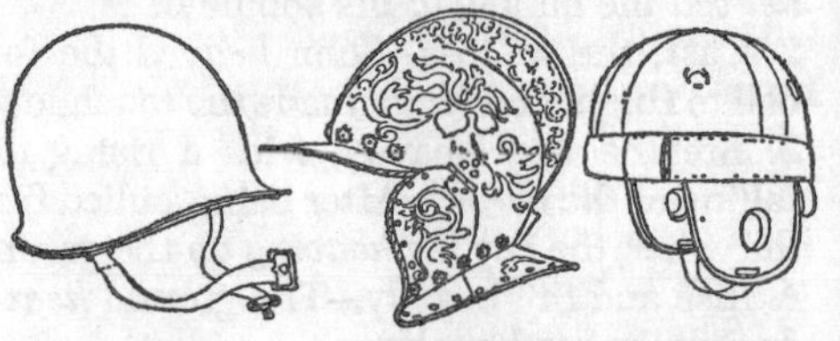

modern soldier's helmet — medieval knight's helmet — football helmet

help (HELP) *n. helps.* 1. An aid; something or someone that assists in a task or problem. –Jack was a *help* to Father in painting the house.–Her calling at that moment was a *help* in brightening my day.
2. Relief.–The medicine proved a *help* in her illness.
–*v. helps, helped, helping.* 1. Do something to make a person's work or efforts easier; give aid to.–Mary *helped* Mother get dinner by setting the table.–Bob *helped* Father get his work done by mowing the lawn.–Quiet and rest *helped* Mother's headache.
2. Avoid; keep oneself from doing something, or prevent something from happening.–Bob could not *help* being late, because the bus was late.
–*Help to* means give or serve.–Mother *helped* us *to* some potatoes.

help•er (HEL-per) *n. helpers.* A person who does things for another.–Mary is our teacher's *helper.* She passes out pencils for the teacher.

help•ful (HELP-fuhl) *adj.; helpfully, adv.* Useful.–Bob is *helpful* about the farm. He does things to help.

help•ing (HELP-ing) *n. helpings.* 1. A serving.–Judy had a second *helping* of ice cream.
2. Assisting.–*Helping* at home is good training for the future.
–*v.* A form of the verb *help.*–Mary is *helping* Mother.

help•less (HELP-ləss) *adj.; helplessly, adv.; helplessness, n.* 1. Not able to do anything for oneself.–Sickness made the old sea captain *helpless.*
2. Not able (to do something).–The firemen, with their small hose, were *helpless* in the face of the great fire.

hem (HEM) *n. hems.* A folded edge on a dress, sleeve, coat, etc. A *hem* is made by folding back the material and sewing it along the edge.—Mary's new dress was too long, so Mother put a wider *hem* on the bottom of the skirt to shorten it.
—*v. hems, hemmed, hemming.* Make a hem in.—Mother *hemmed* the dress.

hem·i·sphere (HEM-is-fir) *n. hemispheres.* 1. Half of a ball or globe. A sphere is a ball or globe. A *hemisphere* is half of one.
2. The earth can be divided into Northern and Southern *Hemispheres,* or into Eastern and Western *Hemispheres.*

hem·lock (HEM-lahk) *n. hemlocks.* 1. A kind of evergreen tree. *Hemlocks* have needles instead of flat, broad leaves.
2. A poisonous plant related to the carrot.

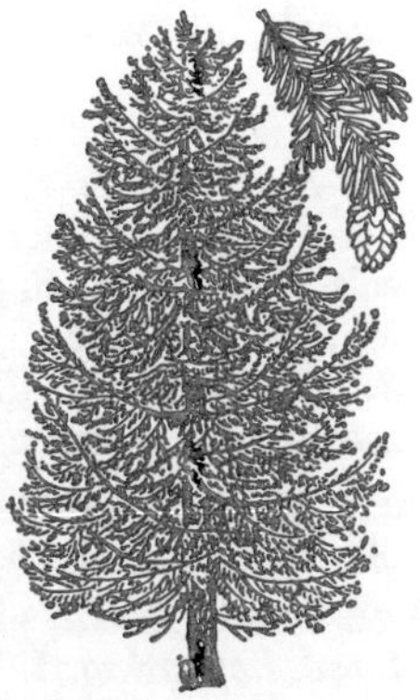

hemp (HEMP) *n.* A plant that has a very tough stem. The fibers or threadlike parts of *hemp* are made into rope or coarse cloth called burlap. Some large bags for grain and potatoes are made from this useful coarse cloth.

hem·stitch (HEM-stich) *n. hemstitches.* A fancy stitch often used in hemming towels and other linens.
—*v. hemstitches, hemstitched, hemstitching.* Make such a fancy stitch.—Mother *hemstitched* Mary's dress.

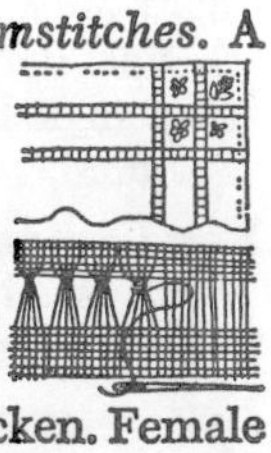

hen (HEN) *n. hens.* A female chicken. Female birds and other female fowls are called *hens,* too. *Hens* lay eggs.

her (HER) *adj.* Belonging to a girl or woman or female animal.—Mary brought *her* doll. It belonged to Mary.—Mother lost *her* purse.
—*pron. Her* stands for the name of a woman or a girl, or any female animal.—The cat hid, and Mother could not find *her.*—A woman knocked at the door, and Mother let *her* in.

her·ald (HAIR-əld) *n. heralds.* 1. Person who makes an announcement.—The king's *herald* announced the news of the royal wedding.
2. Person or thing which comes before and brings news of what is coming.—Black clouds are *heralds* of the storm.—The king's *herald* bade the village make ready for his arrival.
—*v. heralds, heralded, heralding.* Proclaim or announce; bring news in advance of something.—Church bells rang throughout the nation *heralding* the prince's marriage.—The returning birds *herald* the coming of spring.

herb (ERB *or* HERB) *n. herbs.* 1. A plant that has no wood in its stem and dies down to the roots when the season is over.—She is studying the trees and *herbs* of this region.
2. A plant whose leaves or stems are used for medicines or for seasoning foods.—Mint is an *herb* used to flavor tea, candy, and meats.

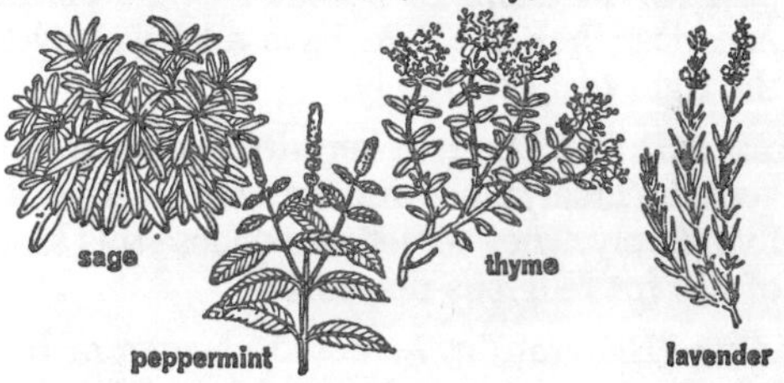

her·biv·o·rous (her-BIV-er-əss) *adj.* Plant-eating. — Sheep and cattle are *herbivorous* animals.

herd (HERD) *n. herds.* A large number of cattle or other animals that are all together.—A few cows would not be a *herd.* Twenty-five cows would be a *herd.*

—*v. herds, herded, herding.* Drive together in a group. — The shepherd *herds* his sheep. He keeps them together while they move from place to place.

herds·man (HERDZ-mən) *n. herdsmen.* A man who takes care of a herd of cattle or other animals.

here (HIR) *adv.* 1. In or at this place.—Who sits *here*?
2. To this place.—Send the boy *here.*
3. Present.—The children said "*Here*" when the teacher called their names.

here•aft•er (hir-AF-ter) *adv.* From now on; in the future.—You were nearly hurt; *hereafter,* be more careful.

he•red•i•tar•y (hi-RED-ə-tair-ee) *adj.; heredity, n.* 1. Passed, or able to be passed, from a parent to a child, or from ancestors to their descendants.—Red hair is *hereditary* in Bob's family.
2. Held by inheritance.—The king's title and throne are *hereditary.*

here's (HIRZ). Here is.—*Here's* your coat.

her•it•age (HAIR-ə-tij) *n.* Ideas, tastes, or customs passed on from ancestors to descendants.—The book "Little Women" is part of our literary *heritage.* Our parents read it, and we read it. It is something we all share in.
2. A right; something that has been passed down to us and that we are entitled to possess.—Freedom of speech is part of the American *heritage.* We have all been given the right to speak freely.

her•mit (HER-mət) *n. hermits.* A person who goes to a lonely place and lives alone. *Hermits* live simply. They sometimes choose this kind of life for religious reasons.

he•ro (HEE-roh) *n. heroes.* 1. A man or boy who has done a very brave thing.—The man who saved the drowning boy was a *hero.*
2. A man whom one respects and wants to be like.—Lincoln and Washington are two of our national *heroes.*
3. The man or boy who takes the leading or most important part in a book or play.—Tom Sawyer is the *hero* of a book by Mark Twain.

he•ro•ic (hi-ROH-ik) *adj.; heroically, adv.* Brave. – The man who saved the drowning boy was *heroic.*

her•o•in (HAIR-oh-in) *n.* A white pain-relieving drug made from morphine. Since it is dangerous and habit-forming, it may not be grown or brought into the United States.

her•o•ine (HAIR-oh-in) *n. heroines.* 1. A woman or girl who does a very brave thing. —Mary is a *heroine.* She helped rescue a child from a burning building.
2. A woman whom one respects and wants to be like.—Miss Jasper is our *heroine.* We wish we were like her.
3. The woman or girl who is the leading or most important character in a book or play.—Jo is the *heroine* of "Little Women," by Louisa May Alcott.

her•o•ism (HAIR-oh-iz-əm) *n.* Courage and brave deeds; saving or helping others without thinking of one's own safety.—The man who saved the drowning boy showed great *heroism.*

her•on (HAIR-ən) *n. herons.* A wading bird that lives in marshes or near the water. It has very long legs and a long, pointed bill.

her•ring (HAIR-ing) *n. herrings.* A small fish caught in great numbers for food.

hers (HERZ) *pron.* Belonging to a woman or a girl or a female animal.—Grandmother gave Mary a cat. It belongs to Mary now. It is *hers.*

her•self (her-SELF) *pron.* 1. Sally dressed *herself* this morning. She put on her own clothes.
2. *Herself* is used to make a statement stronger.—Mary made the cake *herself;* nobody helped her.—Mother *herself* sometimes puts salt instead of sugar in the cocoa. Even Mother does that.
3. Her usual self.—Sally was not *herself* this morning. She was cross and cranky.

he's (HEEZ). He is.—Grandfather is getting old. *He's* sixty-eight years old today.

hes•i•tate (HEZ-ə-tayt) *v. hesitates, hesitated, hesitating.* 1. Wait, as if not sure how to go on.—The boy *hesitates* when he speaks. He speaks slowly, with little pauses between his words.
2. Feel doubt about doing something.—I *hesitate* to do his work for him. I'm not sure that I should.

hes•i•ta•tion (hez-ə-TAY-shən) *n. hesitations.* A slight pause or stop, as a *hesitation* in one's speech or actions.

hex•a•gon (HEKS-ə-gahn) *n. hexagons; hexagonal, adj.* A geometric shape having six sides and six angles.—Each of the floor tiles in the bathroom is a *hexagon.*—Jim was amazed when he read that all snowflakes are in the shape of a *hexagon.*

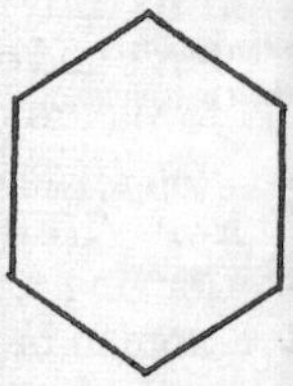

hey (HAY) *interj.* A word or cry often used to show that a person is pleased or surprised, or to call one's attention to something.—*Hey!* Bring back my umbrella.

hi•ber•nate (HY-ber-nayt) *v. hibernates, hibernated, hibernating.* Spend the winter sleeping.—Bears *hibernate.* They eat a lot and store up fat, and then go into caves and sleep until spring.

hic•cup (HIK-up) *n. hiccups.* A jerky gulp made when the muscles that control our breathing do not work properly.
—*v. hiccups, hiccuped, hiccuping.* Make a hiccup.—Sally *hiccuped* after drinking her milk too fast.

hick•o•ry (HIK-ə-ree) *n. hickories* and *adj.* A nut-bearing tree with very hard wood. The nuts of the *hickory* are used in candy and cake. The wood of the *hickory* tree is used for canes, for ball bats, and for handles on hammers.

hide (HYD) *n. hides.* The skin, especially of an animal. — Bags and belts are made of animals' *hides.*—Father has a belt of cow*hide.*
—*v. hides, hid, hiding.* 1. Put or go out of sight, or where it is hard to be found.—We have to *hide* sharp things from Baby.—Jack *hid* behind the tree.
2. Keep secret.—Bob tried to *hide* his mistake.
3. Keep from being seen.—The clouds *hid* the sun.—The sun was *hidden* by the clouds.

hid•e•ous (HID-ee-əss) *adj.; hideously, adv.* Very, very ugly; horrible; frightful. — The witch had a *hideous* face.

hi•er•o•glyph•ic (hy-ər-ə-GLIF-ik *or* hy-rə-GLIF-ik) *n. hieroglyphics.* 1. A picture character, such as a bird, snake, or cat, in the writing system of ancient Egypt. *Hieroglyphics* stood first for whole words or ideas and later became signs for sounds. They are the ancestors of modern alphabets.
2. A picture character in any language, such as that of certain American Indians.

high (HY) *adj. higher, highest* and *adv.* 1. Tall; far above the ground.—Bob stands 4 feet 6 inches *high.*—The jet airplane flies very *high.*
2. First; excellent.—He is a man of *high* standing in the town. He is very respected.
3. Costly; dear.—We pay a *high* rent. We pay more rent than is usually paid, or than should be paid, for a house like ours.
4. In music a *high* tone is one that is far up the scale.—On the piano, the keys at the right end give out *high* tones.—Most women have *higher* voices than men. They can sing *higher* tones.
5. Much above average; strong; powerful.—Glass melts at a *high* temperature.—The *high* wind blew sand in their eyes.

HIEROGLYPHICS

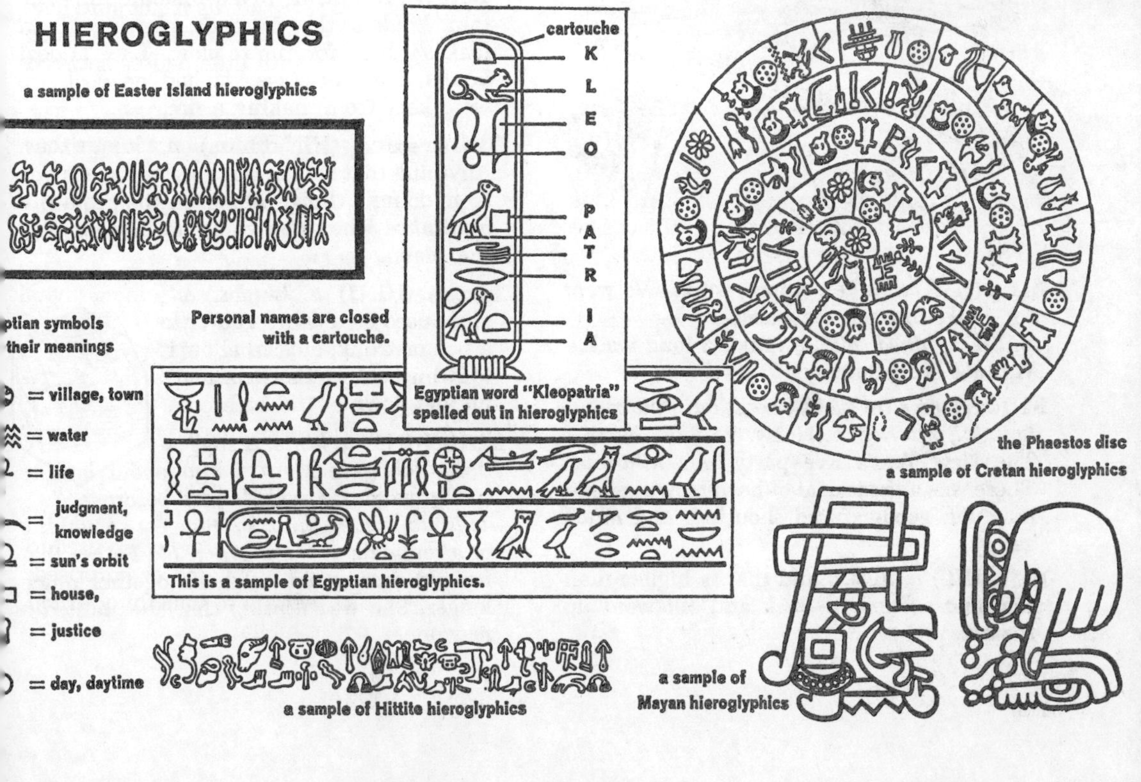

high-fi•del•i•ty (HY-fi-DEL-ə-tee) *adj.* (Often called "hi-fi.") Reproducing sounds by radio or phonograph so that they are very close to the original sound. The better the sound reproduction, the more complicated the *high-fidelity* radio or phonograph is likely to be.

high-fre•quen•cy (HY-FREE-kwən-see) *adj.* Recurring rapidly, used especially to describe a certain group of radio and television waves.

high•land (HY-lənd) *n. highlands.* High or hilly country.

High•ness (HY-nəss) *n. Highnesses.* "Your *Highness,*" "Her *Highness,*" and "His *Highness*" are titles of honor used when speaking to or about kings, queens, princes, princesses, and other royal people.

high school (HY skool) *high schools.* The school above grade school and junior high school; usually, the tenth, eleventh, and twelfth grades. After boys and girls finish grade school, they go to junior high school or to *high school.* Most junior high schools are made up of the seventh, eighth, and ninth grades. Where there is a grade school which ends with the eighth grade, and no junior high school, *high school* includes the ninth grade.

high•way (HY-way) *n. highways.* A main road.–Automobiles travel on *highways.*

hike (HYK) *n. hikes.* A long walk.–We went for a *hike* through the woods.
–*v. hikes, hiked,. hiking.* Take a long walk.–We *hike* every Sunday.

hi•lar•i•ous (hi-LAIR-ee-əss) *adj.; hilariously, adv.; hilarity, n.* Noisy, gay, or merry.–The New Year's Eve party was *hilarious.* There was a great deal of horn-blowing, loud laughter, good-natured shouting, and much gaiety.

hill (HIL) *n. hills.* Land that is higher than the land around it.–Jack and Jill went up the *hill.*

hill•side (HIL-syd) *n. hillsides.* The side of a hill.–Sally slid down the *hillside* where the mud was smooth and slippery.

hill•top (HIL-tahp) *n. hilltops.* The top of a hill.

hill•y (HIL-ee) *adj. hillier, hilliest.* With many hills.–This country is *hilly.* The land goes up and down.

hilt (HILT) *n. hilts.* The handle of a sword, dagger, or other weapon with a blade.

him (HIM) *pron.* A boy, man, or male animal. – Father wanted a new tie, so Bob gave *him* one.–Jack looked for his dog, but could not find *him.*

him•self (him-SELF) *pron.* 1. *Himself* is used to make a statement stronger.–The mayor *himself* visited our class today.
2. Jack seated *himself* at his desk to draw a plan of his new boat.
3. His usual self.–When John gets well and is *himself* again we'll see if he can jump as far as you can.

hind (HYND) *adj.* Back.–The *hind* legs of a dog are the legs at the back.–Rabbits have very long *hind* legs which help them take big jumps.

hin•der (HIN-der) *v. hinders, hindered, hindering.* Prevent, or make difficult for.–The rain *hinders* the farmer's plowing. Rain makes it hard for him to plow.–Lack of coal *hindered* us. Because we had no coal, we were kept from making a fire.

hin•drance (HIN-drənss) *n. hindrances.* Anything that gets in one's way or keeps one from doing a thing.–Music on the radio is a *hindrance* when one wants to read or play the piano.

hinge (HINJ) *n. hinges.* A jointed metal piece used on a door, a cover to a box or trunk, etc., to allow it to swing back and forth or move up and down.

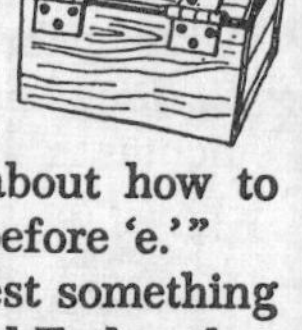

hint (HINT) *n. hints.* A suggestion.–Bob gave Mary a *hint* about how to spell a word. He said, "Use 'i' before 'e.'"
–*v. hints, hinted, hinting.* Suggest something in a roundabout way.–Mary told Father that her old coat would not hold together much longer. She was *hinting* that she wanted a new one.

hip (HIP) *n. hips.* A part of the human body. The *hips* are on both sides, just below the waistline. – The teacher told us to put our hands on our *hips* to do the deep-breathing exercise.

hip•po•pot•a•mus (hip-ə-PAHT-ə-məss) *n. hippopotamuses.* A big animal, with popping eyes and an ugly face, that lives near and in the rivers in Africa. It eats water plants. The *hippopotamus* has skin that looks like heavy leather.

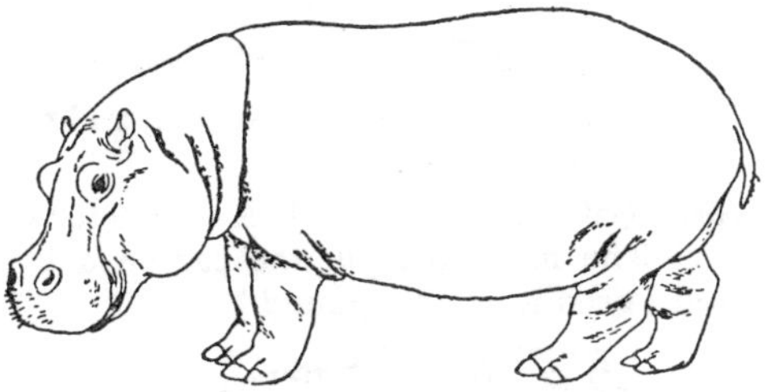

hire (HY-er) *v. hires, hired, hiring.* 1. Rent, or borrow for money.–For ten dollars, Father *hired* a trailer to move some furniture.
2. Buy the work of; pay a person for work done for one.–Many men were *hired* at the factory. They were given jobs and will be paid for working there.

his (HIZ) *adj.* Belonging to a boy, man, or male animal.–Jack's dog, Spot, came home with *his* tail between *his* legs.
–*pron. His* stands for the name of a man, boy, or male animal.–Bob has a new baseball. It is *his*.

hiss (HISS) *n. hisses.* A sound like *ssss*.–We could tell by the *hiss* of the kettle that the water was boiling.
–*v. hisses, hissed, hissing.* Make a sound like *sss*.–The radiator is *hissing*.–Geese *hiss*.

his•tor•ic (hiss-TAWR-ik *or* hiss-TOR-ik) *adj.* Well-known or famous in history.–The Gettysburg battlefield is a *historic* spot.

his•tor•i•cal (hiss-TAWR-ə-kəl *or* hiss-TOR-ə-kəl) *adj.; historically, adv.* 1. Connected with history.–He wrote *historical* books.
2. True; not legendary.–The story of Pocahontas is a *historical* one.

his•to•ry (HISS-tə-ree) *n. histories.* 1. The story or step-by-step record of everything known about what people have done since the days when the first records were kept. Boys and girls study *history* in school.
2. A story or account of the past.–Father asked the man to tell his *history*, to tell about his life.

hit (HIT) *n. hits.* 1. A blow.–The fighter landed a good *hit* on the jaw.
2. A great success.–The play which has been running for years is a great *hit*.
3. In baseball, a ball hit so that no one catches it and the runner reaches base safely. –Jack got three *hits* in the game.
–*v. hits, hit, hitting.* 1. Strike; give a blow; come up against with force.–An automobile *hit* the tree.–The bad boy *hit* the baby.–Baby rolled the ball and it *hit* Father's shoe.
2. Bring sudden trouble on.–The family was hard *hit* when their home burned.
–*Hit upon* means suddenly find something or a way of getting something done.–The boys *hit upon* a way to solve the problem.

hitch (HICH) *n. hitches.* 1. Something that prevents or gets in the way.–The rain put a *hitch* in our plans to go to the ball game.
2. A knot that can be undone easily.–The boys in the boat took a *hitch* around the post with a rope.
–*v. hitches, hitched, hitching.* Tie or fasten, as with a harness. –The man *hitched* his horses to the plow.

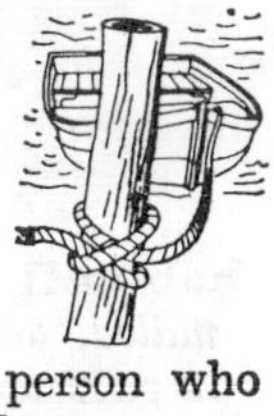

hit•ter (HIT-er) *n. hitters.* A person who hits.–The ball player is a good *hitter*.

hive (HYV) *n. hives.* 1. A box or a small house in which bees live. The queen bee is put into the *hive*, and all the other bees follow.
2. A great number of bees all together in one box or beehive.

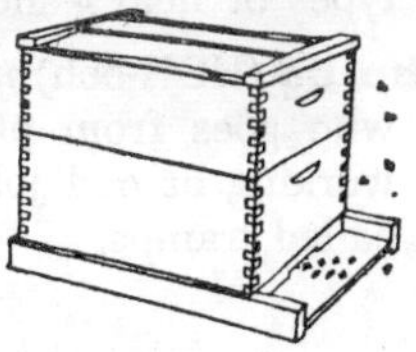

3. A place where many people work busily together.–The kitchen is a regular *hive* just before dinner.

hoard (HORD) *n. hoards.* A store or secret supply.–We found the squirrel's *hoard* of nuts.
–*v. hoards, hoarded, hoarding.* Store away or save up things secretly.–Some people *hoard* food, some *hoard* money.–Some animals *hoard* food for the winter.

hoarse (HORSS) *adj. hoarser, hoarsest; hoarsely, adv.; hoarseness, n.* 1. Deep and rough in sound.–When you have a cold, your voice may be *hoarse*.
2. Having a hoarse voice.–Bob shouted at the football game until he was *hoarse*.

hob•ble (HAHB-əl) *n. hobbles.* 1. A limping walk.–The lame man moved with a *hobble.*
2. A device to keep horses from moving away. *Hobbles* are usually made of leather or rope.
–*v. hobbles, hobbled, hobbling.* 1. Limp or walk as though crippled.–The man hurt his leg and *hobbled* around for a week afterward.
2. Tie the legs together.–The cowboys *hobbled* their horses for the night.

hob•by (HAHB-ee) *n. hobbies.* Something a person likes to do that is not his everyday work.–Mary's *hobby* is collecting unusual buttons.–Bob's *hobby* is making model airplanes.

hob•by•horse (HAHB-ee-horss) *n. hobbyhorses.* A wooden horse; a rocking horse.–Little children like to ride on *hobbyhorses.*

hob•nail (HAHB-nayl) *n. hobnails; hobnailed, adj.* A short, large-headed nail used to protect the heels and soles of certain types of heavy shoes.

ho•bo (HOH-boh) *n. hobos.* A homeless man who goes from place to place, sometimes working at odd jobs. *Hobos* are sometimes called tramps.

hock•ey (HAHK-ee) *n.* A game played on ice or on a field by two teams. In ice *hockey* there are six players on a team. In field *hockey* there are eleven players on a team. Each player has a hockey stick. He uses it to hit a disk or a ball into a net or goal.

hoe (HOH) *n. hoes.* A garden tool with a long handle and a broad blade.–The farmer uses a *hoe* to weed his garden, dig potatoes, and loosen the soil about the plants.
–*v. hoes, hoed, hoeing.* Dig with a hoe.–Bob helps *hoe* the garden.

hog (HAWG) *n. hogs.* 1. A pig, particularly a large pig.

2. A person who is greedy, selfish, and dirty is sometimes called a *hog.*

hoist (HOIST) *n. hoists.* 1. A device for lifting.–The mechanic put the car on a *hoist* and raised it off the ground.

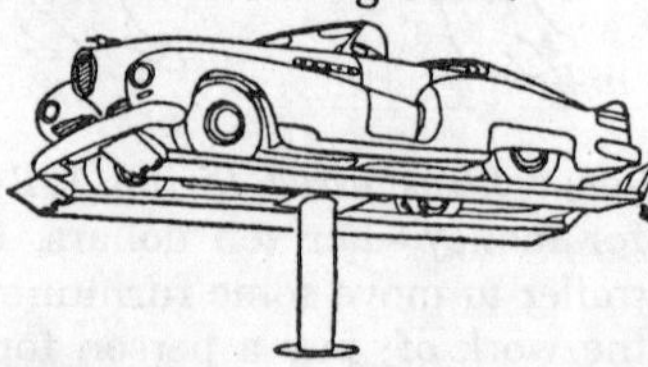

2. A lifting up; a boost.–Give the bag a *hoist.*
–*v. hoists, hoisted, hoisting.* Raise or lift up.–The Boy Scouts *hoisted* the flag to the top of the flagpole.

hold (HOHLD) *n. holds.* 1. A grasp.–Do not lift the baby until you have a good *hold* on her.
2. Power.–He has some kind of a *hold* over her. Perhaps he knows a secret of hers and she is afraid of him.
3. The part of a ship where the cargo is carried. – The barrels were stacked in the *hold.*

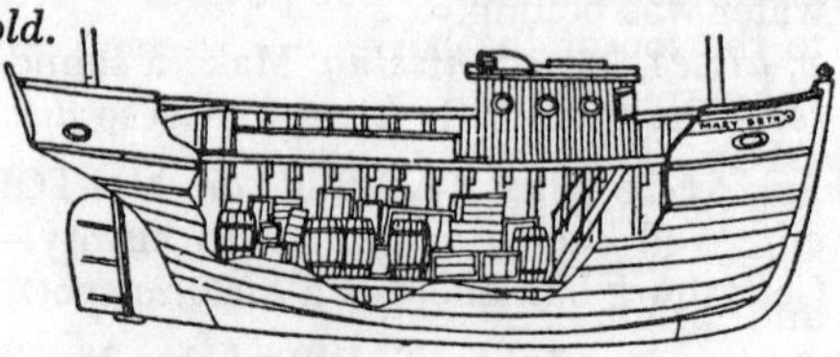

–*v. holds, held, holding.* 1. Get something into one's hands and keep it there.–I will *hold* your book while you put on your coat.
2. Be able to have inside; contain.–This bottle *holds* one pint of milk. You can put one pint of milk in it and it will be full.
3. Fasten.–A nail *holds* the boards together. –Glue *holds* the papers together.–Buttons *hold* the sides of my coat together.
4. Have.–The football team will *hold* a meeting today.–He *holds* a high opinion of us.

5. Own; have.–Grandfather *holds* some land in the country.
6. Keep.–The lost-and-found office will *hold* your umbrella until you call for it.

hold•er (HOHLD-er) *n. holders.* A person or a thing that holds something.–Candlesticks are *holders* for candles.–Pot *holders* are used to lift hot pots and pans.

hole (HOHL) *n. holes.* 1. An opening.–A *hole* in your shoe is a place where leather has worn away and left an open space.
2. A hollow space in anything.–The boys dug a *hole* where they believed the pirate treasure was buried.–The rabbit ran into his *hole*.–The golfer played the ninth *hole*. He hit his ball until it went into the ninth *hole* on the course.

hol•i•day (HAHL-ə-day) *n. holidays.* 1. A day when we play and do the things we want to do, or a special day in memory of a certain event.–New Year's Day and the Fourth of July are *holidays* in the United States. They are days we all celebrate.
2. A vacation.–We go to Grandmother's for our Christmas *holiday*.–Bill decided to spend the *holiday* picking apples.

hol•low (HAH-loh) *n. hollows.* 1. A hole.–The squirrel popped into a *hollow* in the tree.
2. A little valley.–We picked violets in the *hollow*.
–*v. hollows, hollowed, hollowing.* Dig out the inside of.–Jack *hollowed* out the log to make a canoe.
–*adj. hollower, hollowest; hollowly, adv.* 1. Not solid; empty in the middle.–A brick is solid. A stovepipe is *hollow;* it has a hole running through the center.–Balloons are *hollow*.
2. Empty-sounding.–Bob put his head down to the top of the barrel and called out. His voice sounded *hollow*, like an echo.

hol•ly (HAH-lee) *n. hollies.* An evergreen tree or bush that has shiny, prickly leaves and bright red berries on it.–The children hung a wreath of *holly* on the door at Christmas time.

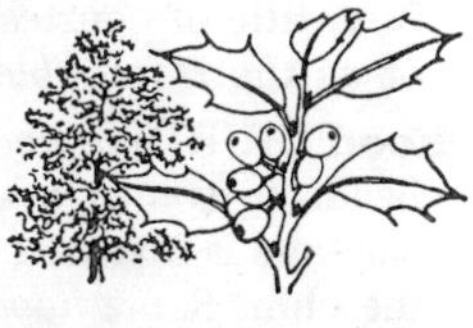

hol•ly•hock (HAH-lee-hahk) *n. hollyhocks.* A tall flower which comes in many colors. *Hollyhocks* grow along a long stem. The plant has large, fuzzy leaves.

hol•ster (HOHL-ster) *n. holsters.* A leather holder for a pistol, worn on a belt over the shoulder or around the waist. The *holster* is shaped somewhat like a pistol.–The policeman carries his gun in his *holster*.

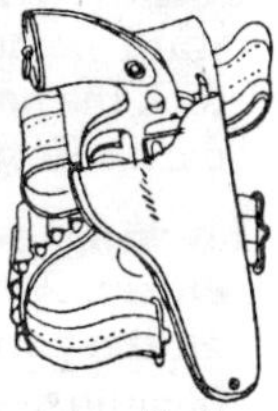

ho•ly (HOHL-ee) *adj. holier, holiest.* Good; sacred; belonging to God.–Saints are *holy* people.–A place of worship is a *holy* place.

home (HOHM) *n. homes* and *adj.* 1. The place one comes from.–My *home* was Paris, France. It is the place where I was born.
2. The place where one lives.–My present *home* is at 37 Main Street, in Newtown.
3. A building run for people who need special care of some kind.–The blind man lives in a *home* for the blind.
4. The home plate or the goal in many games. –The baseball player reached *home* safely. –The children made the tree stump *home* in their game of hide-and-seek.

home e•co•nom•ics (hohm ee-kə-NAHM-iks *or* ek-ə-NAHM-iks). The art and science of running a home; the study of how to buy food and clothing and how to cook, sew, and decorate.–The girls are studying *home economics* in high school to prepare them for the time when they will be housewives and mothers.

home•ly (HOHM-lee) *adj. homelier, homeliest.* 1. Not nice looking; ugly.–Beautiful Cinderella had *homely* stepsisters.
2. Plain and simple.–Hash is a *homely* dish.

home•made (hohm-MAYD) *adj.* Made in the home.–Did you buy this cake at the bakery, or is it *homemade*?

home•sick (HOHM-sik) *adj.; homesickness, n.* Lonely for home; missing home very badly. –After Bob had been away from home a week, he became *homesick*.

home•stead (HOHM-sted) *n. homesteads* and *adj.* 1. A house or farmhouse with its surrounding buildings.
2. A piece of public land acquired as a homestead under the United States *homestead* laws. These laws require settling on the land for a fixed period of time and cultivating it before ownership may be obtained.
–*v. homesteads, homesteaded, homesteading.* To get or occupy a homestead under the homestead laws.–Many people, called "homesteaders," went West to *homestead* when the original law was passed in 1862.

home•ward (HOHM-werd) *adj.* and *adv.* Toward home; in the direction of home.–Bob took the *homeward* path when it began to get dark.–He turned *homeward.*

ho•mog•e•nize (hə-MAHJ-ə-nyz) *v. homogenizes, homogenized, homogenizing.* Make all the parts more or less alike by mixing or blending.–Milk is *homogenized* by a blending process that spreads the cream evenly and permanently through the milk.

hom•o•nym (HAHM-ə-nim) *n. homonyms.* A word pronounced like another word but having a different meaning and, often, a different spelling. The following pairs of words are *homonyms*: him and hymn; see and sea; made and maid.

hone (HOHN) *n. hones.* A fine stone for sharpening knives, tools, and razors.–Father sharpened the knife on a *hone.*
–*v. hones, honed, honing.* Sharpen on a fine stone.–Father *honed* the knife.

hon•est (AHN-əst) *adj.; honestly, adv.* Just; fair; telling the truth; not cheating.–Abraham Lincoln was an *honest* man. He was truthful; he didn't cheat or steal. He was fair with all people.

hon•es•ty (AHN-əs-tee) *n.* Fairness and truthfulness in all one says and does.–*Honesty* pays.

hon•ey (HUN-ee) *n.* 1. A sweet, sticky, syrup-like yellow liquid made by bees. They make it from a sweet liquid called nectar, which they gather from flowers.
2. The sweet liquid which bees gather from flowers; nectar.
3. A pet name.–Mother calls Baby *"honey."*

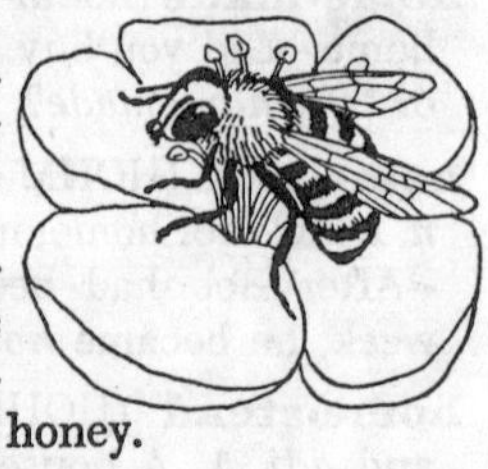

hon•ey•bee (HUN-ee-bee) *n. honeybees.* The kind of bee that gathers nectar and makes honey.

hon•ey•comb (HUN-ee-kohm) *n. honeycombs.* A great number of little hollow boxes or compartments of wax fastened together. *Honeycombs* are made by bees. Bees store honey in the *honeycomb.*

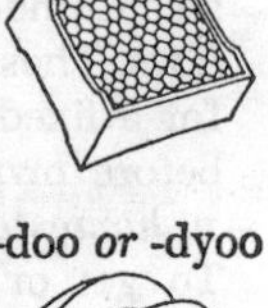

hon•ey•dew mel•on (HUN-ee-doo *or* -dyoo mel-ən) *honeydew melons.* A sweet melon that tastes something like a muskmelon. It has a smooth, white or greenish skin.

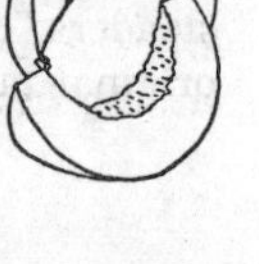

hon•ey•moon (HUN-ee-moon) *n. honeymoons.* A vacation taken by a couple after their marriage.
–*v. honeymoons, honeymooned, honeymooning.* Go on such a trip.–The couple expect to *honeymoon* in the mountains.

hon•ey•suck•le (HUN-ee-suk-əl) *n. honeysuckles.* A climbing vine that has sweet-smelling blossoms on it.

honk (HAWNGK) *n. honks.* 1. The cry that a wild goose makes.
2. Any sound like the wild goose's cry.–We heard the *honk* of the horn on the automobile.
–*v. honks, honked, honking.* Make such a sound.–Father will *honk* the horn when he is ready to go.

hon•or (AHN-er) *n. honors.* 1. High character and reputation, or name.–"He was a man of *honor*" means that he was honest, fair, and upright, and deserved to be thought well of.
2. A credit; something to be proud of.–Mary is an *honor* to her class.
3. "Your *Honor*" and "his *Honor*" are titles given certain officials, such as a mayor or judge.
4. Prize; award; recognition of merit.–Joan took most of the *honors* at the high school graduation.
–*v. honors, honored, honoring.* Show respect for.–The men removed their hats to *honor* the flag.
–*Do honor to* means to show respect and admiration for.–They *did honor to* the explorer in presenting him with a medal

hon•or•a•ble (AHN-er-ə-bəl) *adj.; honorably, adv.* 1. Worthy of honor, of respect, of being thought well of.–Abraham Lincoln was an *honorable* man.
2. A title of courtesy.–The mayor is spoken of as the *Honorable* John Smith.

hood (HUHD) *n. hoods.* 1. A covering for the head. It comes over the ears and is fastened under the chin. Some *hoods* are attached to a coat or cloak.
–Little Red Riding Hood's *hood* was fastened to her cape.
2. A covering over the motor of an automobile.–Father lifted the *hood* of the car to see why the motor would not start.

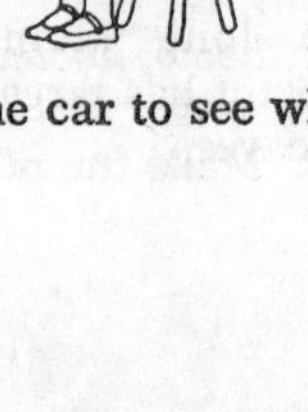

3. Any covering that is like a hood.–There was a *hood* over the stove to prevent heat and grease from damaging the kitchen walls and ceiling.

hoof (HOOF) *n. hoofs.* A covering of horn on the feet of horses, cattle, pigs, and some other animals. *Hoofs* protect an animal's feet as shoes protect ours.

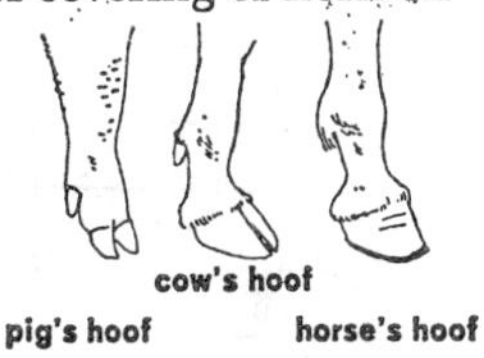

hook (HUHK) *n. hooks.* A piece of metal that is curved or turned back at one end so that it will catch or hold things.–A fish*hook* is used to catch fish.–*Hooks* and eyes, or metal loops, are often used in place of buttons to fasten a dress.–Coats are hung on clothes *hooks.*

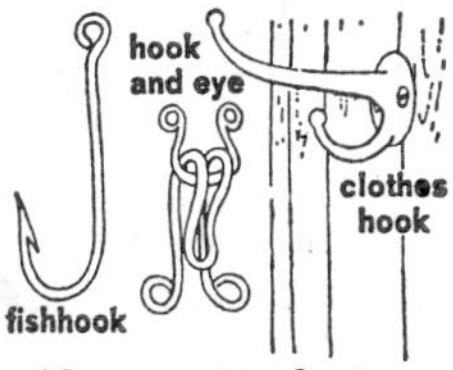

–*v. hooks, hooked, hooking.* 1. Fasten or catch on a hook.–The fisherman *hooked* a fish.–Mary *hooked* the door to keep it closed.
2. Make (usually a rug) with a hook.–Colonial Americans *hooked* attractive rugs.

hooked (HUHKT) *adj.* 1. Curved at the end like a hook.–The handle on Grandfather's cane is *hooked.*
2. Done with a hook.–*Hooked* rugs are made by pulling narrow strips of cloth or yarn through a coarse cloth with a hook. The rug is smooth on one side and has loops on the other.

hoop (HOOP) *n. hoops.* 1. A circle or band of wire, metal, or wood.–*Hoops* are used around wooden buckets, barrels, and kegs to hold them together.–*Hoops* are used as toys, too.
2. A wire or wooden frame used by women in olden times to make their skirts stand out around them.

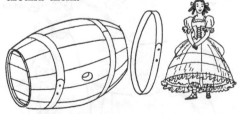

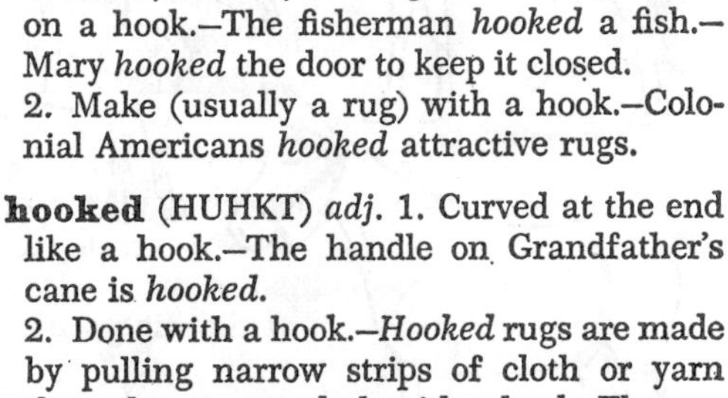

hoot (HOOT) *n. hoots.* The call or cry of an owl.
–*v. hoots, hooted, hooting.* 1. Give the call of an owl.
2. Make fun of; mock.–The crowd *hooted* at the speaker. They called out to him scornfully to show that they did not like the things he said.–Jack *hooted* at Mary's fear of the roller coaster.

hop (HAHP) *n. hops.* A jump.–The rabbit took a *hop* and disappeared into his hole.
–*v. hops, hopped, hopping.* Move by leaps or jumps.–The frog *hops.*–Birds *hop.* They spring along with both feet off the ground at once.–Children like to *hop* on one foot while they hold up the other foot.

hope (HOHP) *n. hopes.* 1. A desire or wish that something will happen.–Our one *hope* is that Father will be well soon.
2. Person or thing that gives hope.–John is the *hope* of the football team. He is such a good player that he may help the team to win.
–*v. hopes, hoped, hoping.* 1. Want something to happen.–We *hope* Father will be well soon.
2. Expect.–Mother *hopes* to be home by noon.

hope•ful (HOHP-fuhl) *adj.; hopefully, adv.* Believing that a thing will work out right; thinking a good thing will happen.–The doctor is very *hopeful* about the sick baby. He feels sure that the baby will get well soon.

hope•less (HOHP-ləss) *adj.; hopelessly, adv.* 1. Without much chance of turning out right.–Building a fire with wet wood is almost *hopeless.*–The boys made a *hopeless* attempt to move the big rock.
2. Thinking things will turn out badly.–Bill feels *hopeless* about passing the test. He is sure he will not pass.

hop•scotch (HAHP-skahch) *n.* A game in which children hop from square to square and try not to touch the lines between the squares.

horde (HORD) *n. hordes.* A crowd; a large group.–A *horde* of baseball fans stormed the box office for World Series tickets.

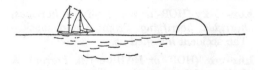

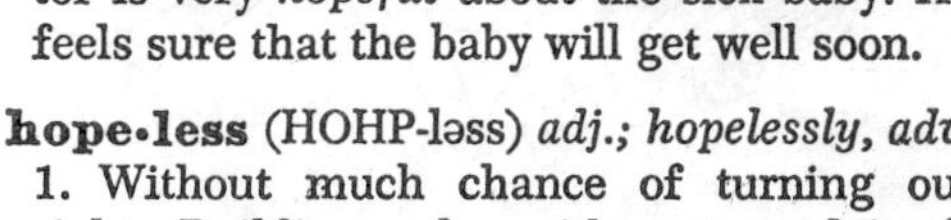

ho•ri•zon (hə-RY-zən) *n. horizons.* The line where the sky seems to meet the earth or the sea.–The sun seems to come up in the morning from behind the *horizon* and to sink below the *horizon* at night.–Jack saw a boat on the *horizon.*

hor·i·zon·tal (hor- *or* hahr-ə-ZAHN-təl) *adj.; horizontally, adv.* A line that runs straight up and down is a vertical line. A line that runs straight across is a *horizontal* line.—A telephone pole stands in a vertical position, and the pieces of wood across the top are in a *horizontal* position.—The lines across your writing paper are *horizontal* lines.

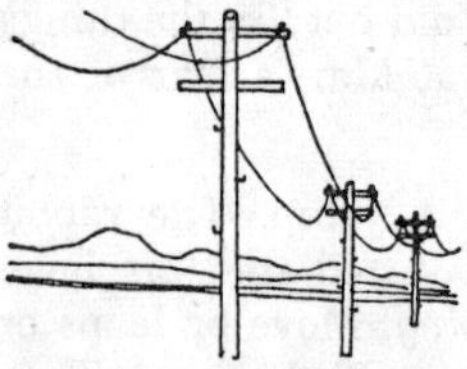

horn (HORN) *n. horns.* 1. A hard, bonelike thing that grows on the heads of cattle, goats, sheep, deer, and some other animals. Animals' *horns* were often scraped and made into drinking *horns*, powder *horns*, and other containers.

2. A musical instrument played by being blown through.

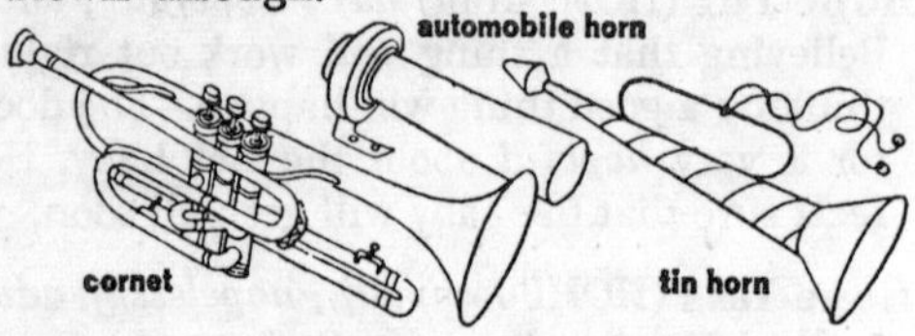

hor·net (HORN-ət) *n. hornets.* An insect with a severe sting. *Hornets* are not bees. They are wasps. They do not make honey.

hor·ri·ble (HOR- *or* HAHR-ə-bəl) *adj.; horribly, adv.* Terrible; frightful.—We saw a *horrible* fire that burned many homes. — We saw a *horrible* accident at the corner.

hor·rid (HOR- *or* HAHR-əd) *adj.; horridly, adv.; horridness, n.* Dreadful or terrible.—Dragons in fairy stories were *horrid* beasts that breathed fire.—Skunks give off a *horrid* smell.

hor·ri·fy (HOR- *or* HAHR-ə-fy) *v. horrifies, horrified, horrifying.* Frighten and shock.—The accident *horrified* us.

hor·ror (HOR- *or* HAHR-er) *n. horrors.* A feeling of fear, shock, or great disgust. – I have a *horror* of fire. I am very much afraid of it.—Mother has a *horror* of mice.

horse (HORSS) *n. horses.* 1. A large, hoofed animal used for working or for riding.—The farmer uses *horses* to pull heavy loads.—Bob rides on the *horse's* back.

HORSE

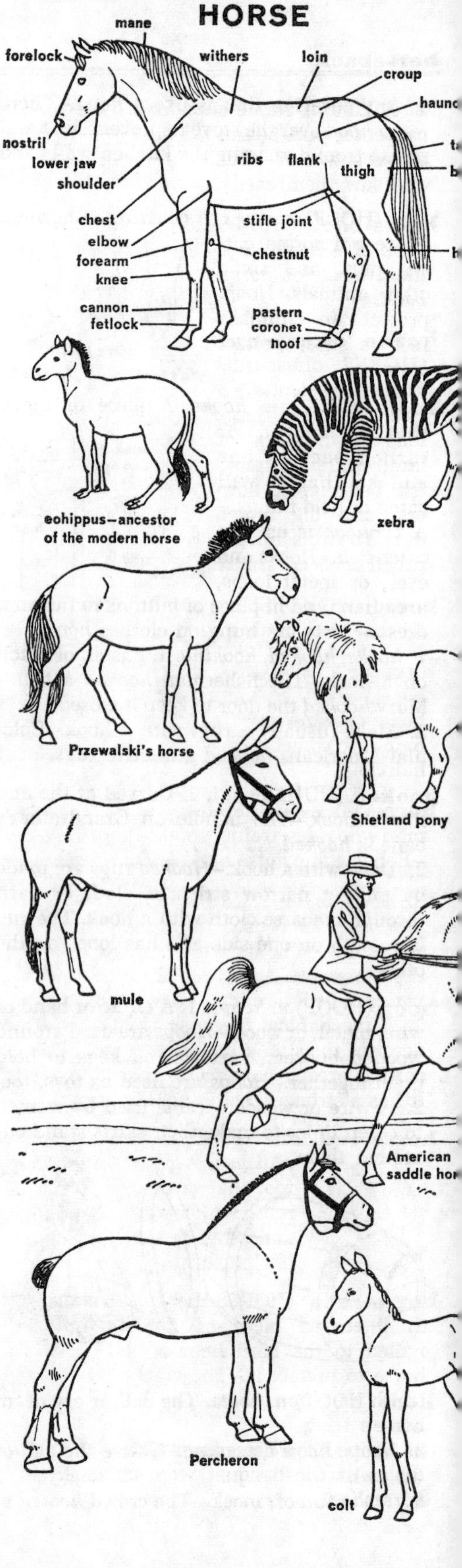

2. A kind of frame supported by legs.–The carpenter puts boards across saw*horses* so he can saw them easily.

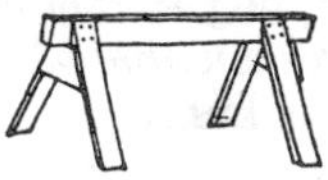

horse•back (HORSS-bak) *n.* and *adv.* The back of a horse.–Bob likes to ride on *horseback.*

horse chest•nut (HORSS chess-nut) *horse chestnuts.* A tree that has large leaves, clusters of large white and pinkish bell-shaped flowers, and big brown nuts. The nuts are also called *horse chestnuts.*

horse•fly (HORSS-fly) *n. horseflies.* A large fly that bites cattle and horses.

horse•hair (HORSS-hair) *n. horsehairs.* The hairs from a horse's mane or tail. These hairs are sometimes woven into cloth called haircloth.

horse•man (HORSS-mən) *n. horsemen.* A man who rides, trains, or takes care of horses. –Bob is a fine *horseman.* He rides well.

horse•pow•er (HORSS-pow-er) *n.* 1. The power or force used by a horse in pulling something.–The farmer hitched his horse to the bumper of the car and by sheer *horsepower* pulled the car out of the ditch.
2. A mechanical measure of power used to describe the strength of an engine.–The new car has greater *horsepower* than the old one. It has a stronger, better-quality engine.

horse-rad•ish (HORSS-rad-ish) *n. horseradishes.* A plant with a large root that is ground to make a relish which is eaten with meats and other foods. It tastes hot, like mustard.

horse•shoe (HORSS-shoo) *n. horseshoes.* 1. A curved piece of metal nailed to the hard hoof of a horse to protect it.–The blacksmith put *horseshoes* on the horse's feet.
2. Shape like a horseshoe.–The tables at the banquet were arranged in a *horseshoe.*

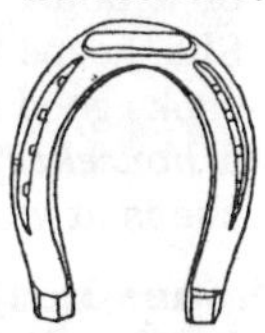

horse•wom•an (HORSS-wuh-mən) *n. horsewomen.* A woman who rides horseback.–Mary is a good *horsewoman.*

hose (HOHZ) *n. hoses.* A long tube, usually of rubber or plastic, through which liquid can flow. – Bob used the *hose* to sprinkle the lawn.
–*v. hoses, hosed, hosing.* Use a hose for sprinkling with water. –John *hosed* the lawn every dry evening.

hose (HOHZ) *n. sing.* and *pl.* 1. A stocking or stockings.–Mary has new *hose.*
2. Tights; long close-fitting breeches or pants.–The brownie in the play wore *hose.*

ho•sier•y (HOH-zher-ee) *n.* Stockings.–The shop sells *hosiery.*

hos•pi•ta•ble (HAHSS-pit-ə-bəl) *adj.; hospitably, adv.* Friendly toward company; enjoying entertaining people.–Grandmother is very *hospitable.* She loves to have guests.

hos•pi•tal (HAHSS-pit-əl) *n. hospitals.* A place where sick and injured people are cared for.–When Father was very sick, the doctor sent him to the *hospital.*

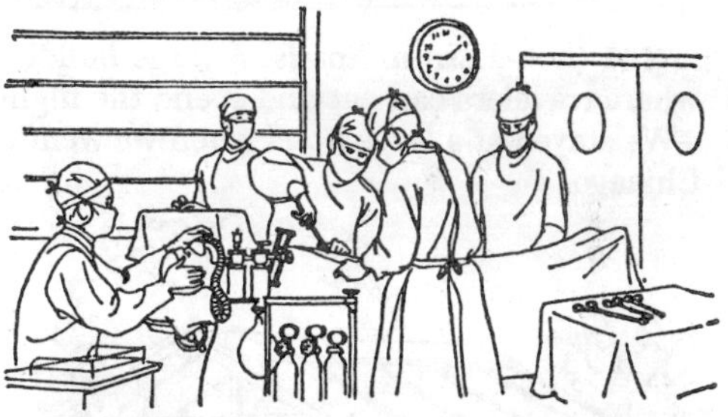

hos•pi•tal•i•ty (hahss-pə-TAL-ə-tee) *n.* Warm welcome and friendly entertainment. –We were shown much *hospitality* when we visited in the country. Everyone was kind and friendly toward us.

host (HOHST) *n. hosts.* 1. A man or boy who entertains a guest.–Bob was a fine *host* at his birthday party. He made everyone feel at home and have a good time.
2. A man who keeps an inn or hotel.
3. A great many.–Father has a *host* of friends.

hos•tage (HAHST-əj) *n. hostages.* A person who is held by an enemy as a guarantee that a promise or an agreement will be carried out. When the promise is kept, he is returned. Soldiers are often taken as *hostages.*

host•ess (HOHST-əss) *n. hostesses.* 1. A girl or woman who entertains guests.—Mary was a friendly *hostess* at her birthday party.
2. A woman who welcomes guests in a public restaurant, a club, a hotel, or some other such place.
3. A woman who helps passengers on an airplane.—Anne would like to be an airline *hostess* when she grows up.

hos•tile (HAHSS-təl) *adj.* Not friendly; like an enemy.—Jack told Sally they might meet *hostile* Indians on their walk in the woods.

hot (HAHT) *adj. hotter, hottest; hotly, adv.* 1. Very warm.—Ice and snow are cold. Fire is *hot*.—Things get *hot* when put over a fire.
2. Sharp; burning; biting to the taste.—Pepper, horse-radish, and mustard are *hot*.
3. Fiery; quick; excitable.—The boy has a *hot* temper. He becomes angry easily.

ho•tel (hoh-TEL) *n. hotels.* A large building where travelers can eat and spend the night. —We stayed at a large *hotel* when we went to Chicago.

hot•house (HAHT-howss) *n. hothouses.* A building whose roof (and usually sides) are of glass. The glass lets sunlight in. Plants and flowers are raised in *hothouses*. In winter, a *hothouse* is heated to keep the plants warm.

hound (HOWND) *n. hounds.* A kind of hunting dog.—Grandfather uses a *hound* when he goes hunting.

hour (OW-er) *n. hours.* 1. Time is measured by years, months, weeks, days, *hours*, minutes, and seconds. There are sixty minutes in an *hour* and twenty-four *hours* in a day.
2. The time for a certain thing.—Children study during school *hours*.—Father's working *hours* are from nine to five.
3. The time.—I shall call for you at an early *hour*.—The clock struck the *hour* of twelve.

hour•ly (OW-er-lee) *adj.* and *adv.* Happening once every hour, or every sixty minutes.—Our clock strikes *hourly*.—Buses stop at our corner *hourly*.

house (HOWSS) *n. houses.* 1. A building in which people live.—Our *house* is made of bricks.
2. Any building or shelter used for a special purpose.—We have school in a school*house*. —We keep the dog in a dog*house*.
3. Audience.—We had a full *house* for the Christmas play. All the seats were taken.
4. A group of lawmakers.—In the United States Congress, we have a *House* of Representatives, a group of elected men who meet to help make our laws. The upper *house* is called the Senate.
—(HOWZ) *v. houses, housed, housing.* Provide shelter for.—We *housed* the puppy while the Smiths were away.

house•hold (HOWSS-hohld) *n. households.* All the people who live together in one house. —There are seven people in our *household*. —*adj.* Having to do with home and family.—*Household* furnishings are the things it takes to furnish a home.—*Household* duties are the duties one has in keeping house.

house•keep•er (HOWSS-keep-er) *n. housekeepers.* The person who keeps or takes care of a house.—Mother is a good *housekeeper*. She keeps our home neat and clean, and cooks good meals for us.—Mrs. Jones employs a *housekeeper* to look after her home while she is at work.

house•keep•ing (HOWSS-keep-ing) *n.* Caring for the home or the house.—*Housekeeping* keeps Mother busy.

HOUSES

ander's hut
Indian adobe house
thatched cottage
half-timber house
igloo
African hut
pioneer sod hut
mansion
modern house
Alpine chalet
Arab tent
n cliff dwellings
Roman house
log cabin
Chinese houseboat
lake dwelling
East Indian grass-roofed house
medieval château

house•wife (HOWSS-wyf) *n. housewives.* A woman who takes care of the house, buys the food and clothing, and cooks the food.–Mother is a *housewife.* She is the manager of our house.

hov•er (HUV-er) *v. hovers, hovered, hovering.* 1. Stay suspended in the air over a place or object.–Helicopters *hovered* over the ship. –Hawks *hovered* over the henhouse.
2. Stay close to.–We *hover* about the fireplace in the wintertime.

how (HOW) *adv.* 1. In what way.–*How* did you make the cake?–Tell me *how* you came. Did you walk or ride?
2. What amount.–*How* old are you?–*How* far is it to school?–*How* much candy have you?
3. In what condition.–*How* are you today? What is the state of your health?
4. Why; for what reason.–*How* is it that we do not have school today?
5. What.–*How* about going to the movies?

how•ev•er (how-EV-er) *adv.* and *conj.* 1. Nevertheless.–The sky looks clear; *however,* I shall take an umbrella just in case it should rain.
2. In any kind of way.–You may do the work *however* you want to. You may do it in whatever way you want.
3. How much.–*However* cold it is outside, it will be warm indoors with the new furnace.

howl (HOWL) *n. howls.* A long, deep cry or wail.–We heard the *howl* of the hungry dog. –Grandfather told of hearing the *howl* of wolves.–There was a long *howl* when our team lost.
–*v. howls, howled, howling.* Give a long, deep cry; make a wailing noise.–Dogs sometimes *howl* when they hear bells ringing.–The winter wind *howled* around the house.

hub (HUB) *n. hubs.* 1. The center part of a wheel, where it fits over the axle.
2. Center.–The assembly hall was the *hub* of activity when the boys were practicing their play.

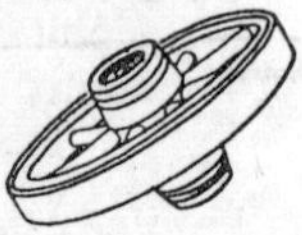

huck•le•ber•ry (HUK-əl-bair-ee) *n. huckleberries.* A small, smooth, dark blue berry, smaller than a blueberry. –*Huckleberries* are good to eat.

hud•dle (HUD-l) *n. huddles.* A little group close together.–The football players went into a *huddle* to get the signal for the next play.

–*v. huddles, huddled, huddling.* 1. Crowd close together.–The little chickens *huddle* under the hen's wings to get warm.
2. Hunch; curl oneself close.–The wet child *huddled* by the fire.

hue (HYOO) *n. hues.* A color, or shade of a color.–Dark red, light red, and pink are all *hues* of red.

huff (HUF) *n.* A spell of anger.–The boy is in a *huff* because he was not asked to the party.

hug (HUG) *n. hugs.* A tight hold with the arms.–Mother gave Bob a loving hug.
–*v. hugs, hugged, hugging.* 1. Hold tightly in the arms. Mother *hugs* the baby lovingly.
2. Keep close to.–The old man *hugs* the high buildings to keep out of the wind.

huge (HYOOJ) *adj. huger, hugest; hugely, adv.* Very large.–An elephant is a *huge* animal.

hull (HUL) *n. hulls.* 1. The covering of a seed.–The long green pods that peas grow in are known as *hulls.*
2. The body of a boat or ship.
–Ships and boats are made with steel or wood *hulls.*

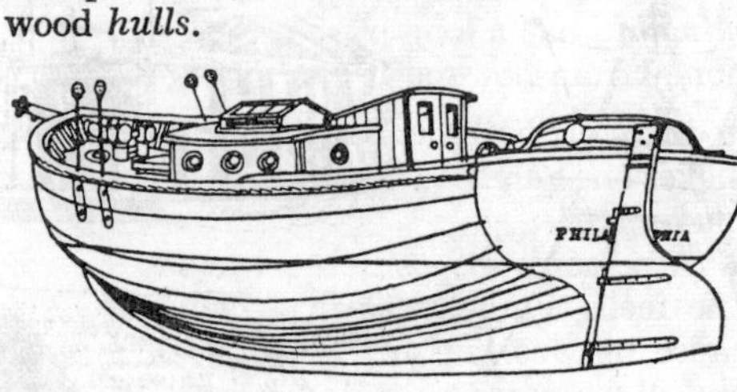

–*v. hulls, hulled, hulling.* Remove or take the hull from.–Mother is *hulling* peas.

hum (HUM) *n. hums.* The sound of the voice when the lips are closed; or any similar sound.–Keep your lips closed and say the letter "m." The sound you make is a *hum.*
–*v. hums, hummed, humming.* 1. Sing with the lips closed.–The boys will sing the words to the song, and the girls will *hum.*
2. Make a hum.–Hundreds of bees *hummed* about the hive.

hu•man (HYOO-mən) *n. humans.* A person. –The god in the legend disguised himself as a *human.*
–*adj.* Of or like people.–Men, women, and children are *human* beings.–Sally said that to cry sometimes is just *human* nature.

hu•mane (hyoo-MAYN) *adj.; humanely, adv.* Kind and sympathetic.–The old man is very *humane;* he wouldn't hurt anyone or anything.

hum•ble (HUM-bəl) *adj. humbler, humblest; humbly, adv.* 1. Feeling no pride; modest.–A person who is not proud, who does not think highly of himself, is *humble.*
2. Not grand; simple and poor.–The poor man loved his *humble* home.
3. Unimportant; low.–The man has a *humble* job.

hu•mid (HYOO-mid) *adj.; humidity, n.* Moist; damp.–The day was hot and *humid.* There was a lot of moisture in the air.–*Humid* days are usually uncomfortable.

hu•mil•i•ate (hyoo-MIL-ee-ayt) *v. humiliates, humiliated, humiliating.* Shame; lower (a person's) pride or self-respect in public.–The supervisor *humiliated* the shop assistant when he scolded her in front of a customer.

hum•ming•bird (HUM-ing-berd) *n. hummingbirds.* A tiny, bright-colored bird that flutters its wings so fast when flying that they make a humming sound. A *hummingbird* has a long bill with which it sucks honey from flowers. It can fly backward.

hu•mor (HYOO-mer) *n.* 1. Something that makes one laugh.–The clown amused us with his *humor.*
2. A person's disposition or mood; the way one feels.–Father was in a bad *humor* because he was late for work. He was angry and ill-tempered.
–*v. humors, humored, humoring.* Agree with; give in to (someone's wishes) in every way.–Mother *humors* Sally when she is sick. She lets Sally have her way.

hu•mor•ous (HYOO-mer-əss) *adj.; humorously, adv.* 1. Funny.–Bob's jokes are always *humorous.*
2. Loving fun and laughter.–Bob is very *humorous.*

hump (HUMP) *n. humps.* A lump; a raised place.–Camels have *humps* on their backs.–The house stood on a *hump* of land. It stood on a small hill.

hu•mus (HYOO-məss) *n.* A dark mixture of decaying vegetable and animal matter used to enrich and fertilize the soil.–Father added the *humus* he made from last year's dead leaves to the soil in his garden.

hunch (HUNCH) *n. hunches.* A feeling one has about something for no particular reason.–I have a *hunch* that our team will win.
–*v. hunches, hunched, hunching.* Bend.–The boy *hunched* over in his seat, and the teacher told him to sit up.

hunch•back (HUNCH-bak) *n. hunchbacks.* A person with a curved spine which makes a hump on his back.

hun•dred (HUN-drəd) *n. hundreds* and *adj.* The number [100] coming after 99 and before 101.–Twenty-five and seventy-five make one *hundred.*

hun•dredth (HUN-drədth) *n. hundredths.* One of 100 equal parts.–If anything is divided into a hundred parts all the same size, each part is one *hundredth.*–One *hundredth* may be written 1/100 or .01.
–*adj.* Coming as number 100 in a series.–We have had ninety-nine days of school. Today is the *hundredth* day, or the day after the ninety-ninth.

hung (HUNG) *v.* One form of the verb *hang.* –The children *hung* up their stockings last Christmas.

hun•ger (HUNG-ger) *n.* 1. The feeling of needing or wanting food.–Bob's *hunger* made him eat too fast.
2. Any need or want.–She felt a strong *hunger* for the sight of her family.
–*v. hungers, hungered, hungering. Hunger for* means want.–People *hunger for* peace.

hun•gry (HUNG-gree) *adj. hungrier, hungriest; hungrily, adv.* Wanting food.–The baby is *hungry.* She wants something to eat.
–*Hungry for* means wanting. – The child is *hungry for* a playmate.

hunt (HUNT) *n. hunts.* A trip made to catch or kill a person or animal. – The men have gone on a deer *hunt* today. They have gone to find and kill deer.–The policemen went out on a *hunt* for the escaped murderer.
–*v. hunts, hunted, hunting.* 1. Go out to find and catch or shoot a person or animal.–The hunter *hunts* rabbits and kills them for food.
2. Look (for); try to find.–Grandmother lost her thimble, and we had to *hunt* for it.

hunt·er (HUN-ter) *n. hunters.* A person who hunts and kills animals for food or sport.

hur·dle (HERD-l) *n. hurdles.* Barrier to be jumped over in an obstacle race.
–*v. hurdles, hurdled, hurdling.* 1. Leap over, especially while running.–The runners *hurdled* the barriers one after another.
2. Overcome or master an obstacle or difficulty.–Jack didn't have enough money to get a bicycle, but he *hurdled* that problem by working after school.

hurl (HERL) *v. hurls, hurled, hurling.* Throw hard.–The boys *hurled* snowballs at each other.

hur·rah (her-RAW) *n. hurrahs* and *interj.* A cheer, or cry of joy or success.–*Hurrah* for the winner!–The *hurrahs* drowned out the boos.

hur·ri·cane (HER-ə-kayn) *n. hurricanes.* A very strong windstorm. In a *hurricane* the wind blows seventy-five miles or more an hour.–The *hurricane* blew down trees and houses.

hur·ry (HER-ee) *n.; hurried, adj.; hurriedly, adv.* Quick action, or an intention to act quickly.–Mother is in a *hurry* to go.
–*v. hurries, hurried, hurrying.* 1. Act or move quickly.–Father had to *hurry* to get to work on time.
2. Send or take quickly.–We *hurried* the injured boy to the doctor.
3. Do hastily and carelessly.–The teacher told Bob not to *hurry* his work.

hurt (HERT) *n. hurts.* Something that causes pain. – Wounds, such as cuts, burns, or bruises, are *hurts.*

HUNTING

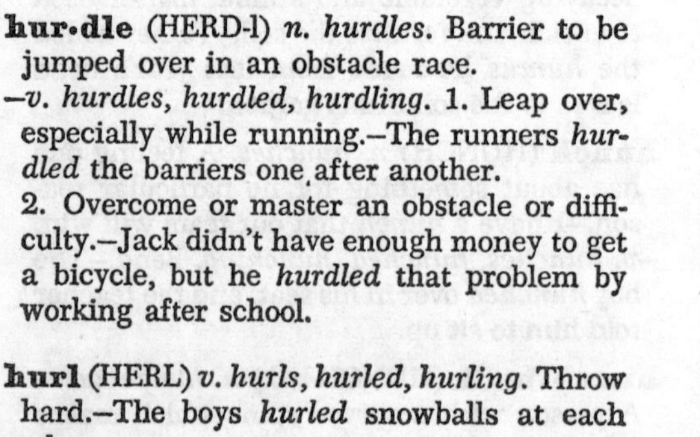

rhinoceros hunting, Africa

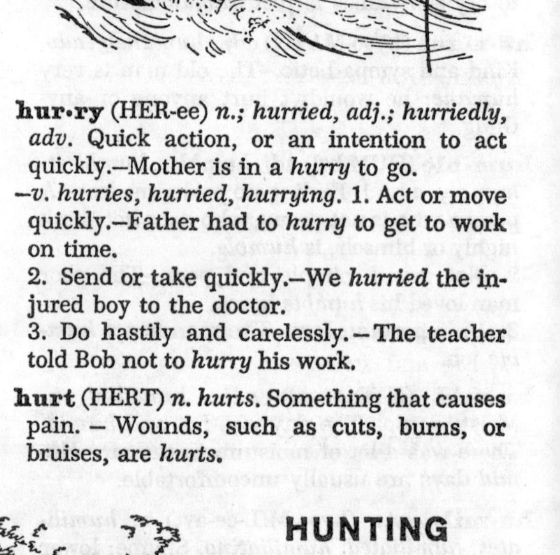

pheasant hunting, England

tiger hunting, India

–*v. hurts, hurt, hurting.* 1. Cause pain or suffering to.–The bee's sting *hurt* the boy.
2. Harm or damage.–The frost did not *hurt* the fruit.
3. Be painful.–John's head *hurts.* He has a pain in his head.

hus•band (HUZ-bənd) *n. husbands.* A married man; the man a woman is married to. –Father is Mother's *husband.*

hush (HUSH) *n. hushes.* A silence; a stillness. – A *hush* came over the crowd as the mayor rose to speak.
–*v. hushes, hushed, hushing.* 1. Be still; stop making noise.–*Hush!* Don't wake the baby.
2. Make quiet. – She *hushed* the children near the sickroom.

husk (HUSK) *n. husks.* The outer covering of corn and other grains.
–*v. husks, husked, husking.* Remove the husks from. – The farmer *husks* his corn.

husk•y (HUSK-ee) *n. huskies.* A dog used to pull a sled in the Far North.
–*adj. huskier, huskiest; huskily, adv.*
1. Big and strong. – The fighter is *husky.*
2. Hoarse; low and rasping.–Bob yelled so much that his voice became *husky.*

deer hunting, U.S.A.

hunting for small animals with a falcon–Europe, 14th century

hus•tle (HUS-əl) *n. hustles.* A rush; a hurry. –We went to school in a *hustle.*
–*v. hustles, hustled, hustling.* 1. Rush; move, send, or take quickly. – We *hustled* the injured boy to the doctor.
2. Push roughly. – Bob *hustled* through the crowd to get to his seat.
3. Hurry; move quickly.–Mother told us to *hustle* to school.

hut (HUT) *n. huts.* A small, roughly made house.–The hunters lived in the woods in a small *hut.*

hutch (HUCH) *n. hutches.* 1. A coop or cage for small animals.–Tom built a *hutch* for his white rabbit.
2. A small hut.–The fisherman's *hutch* was swept away by the storm.

hy•a•cinth (HY-ə-sinth) *n. hyacinths.* A flowering plant that grows from a bulb and blossoms in the spring. The flower has a very sweet scent.

hy•brid (HY-brid) *n. hybrids* and *adj.* 1. A plant or animal bred from two different but related plants or animals. Only *hybrids* of fairly closely related plants or animals are successful.–The mule is a *hybrid* of a horse and an ass.
2. Anything of mixed origin.–The idea is a *hybrid* based on the suggestions of many people.

hy•drant (HY-drənt) *n. hydrants.* A large water pipe with a valve to control the flow of water. – Fire engines usually get water from *hydrants* to fight fires.–When the *hydrant* is open, water spurts into the street.

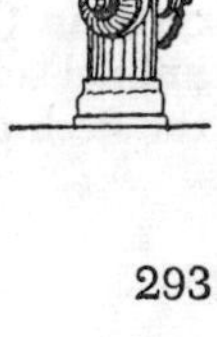

hy•dro•gen (HY-drə-jən) *n.* A colorless, odorless gas which catches fire easily. *Hydrogen* is the lightest gas known to man.–Water is a combination of *hydrogen* and oxygen.

hy•dro•gen bomb (HY-drə-jən bahm) *hydrogen bombs.* A very powerful bomb in which the hydrogen atom is used to create a nuclear explosion.

hy•dro•pho•bi•a (hy-drə-FOH-bi-ə *or* hy-drə-FOH-bee-ə) *n.* A deadly disease of dogs and other animals; rabies. A person bitten by an animal should see a doctor immediately to prevent any possibility of getting *hydrophobia* or another infection.

hy•dro•plane (HY-drə-playn) *n. hydroplanes.* 1. A plane that can land on and take off from water; a seaplane.

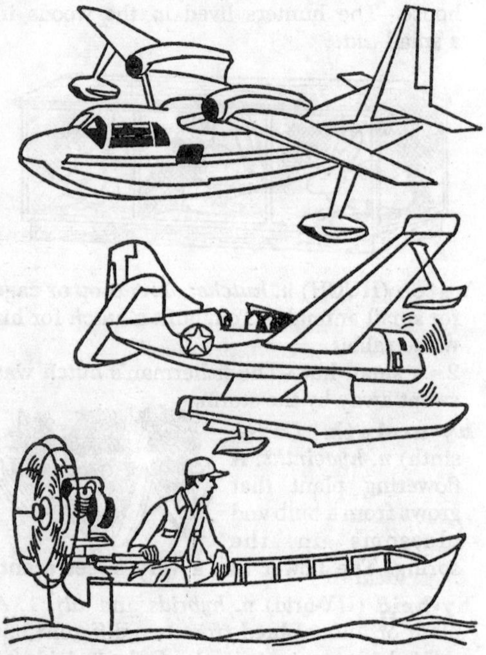

2. A high-speed, high-powered motorboat that glides or planes along the surface of the water.

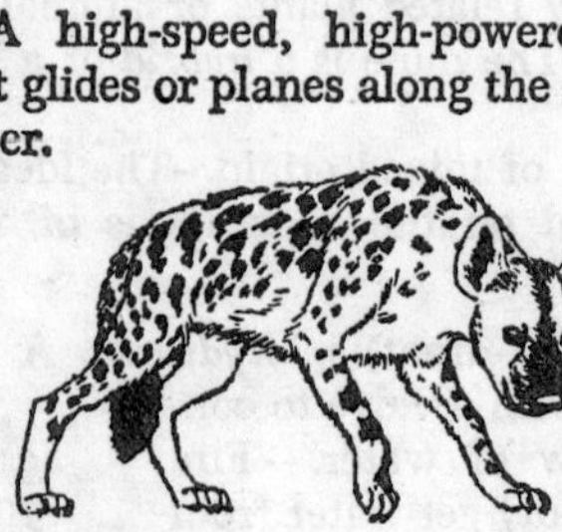

hy•e•na (hy-EE-nə) *n. hyenas.* A large wild animal something like a dog. The *hyena* eats the flesh of other animals.

hy•giene (HY-jeen) *n.* The science of keeping well and strong. – In school, we study *hygiene.*

hy•grom•e•ter (hy-GRAHM-ə-ter) *n. hygrometers.* An instrument for measuring humidity, or the amount of moisture in the air.

hymn (HIM) *n. hymns.* A song of praise.–We sing *hymns* in praise of God.

hy•phen (HY-fən) *n. hyphens.* A small mark (-) used to connect two words that are used as one word or to break a word at the end of a line.–Good-by is written with a *hyphen.* –A *hyphen* is about half as long as a dash.

hyp•no•tize (HIP-nə-tyz) *v. hypnotizes, hypnotized, hypnotizing.* Put (a person) into a state something like sleep, in which he has little control over what he says, and will usually answer any questions. It is used by doctors on patients who are mentally ill. –*hypnotism, n.*

hyp•o•crite (HIP-ə-krit) *n. hypocrites.* A person who pretends to be something that he is not, or who says things he doesn't really think or feel.–When the bully said he was sorry he had hit the little boy, he was being a *hypocrite.*

hy•po•der•mic (hy-pə-DER-mik) *n. hypodermics* and *adj.* 1. The medical instrument used by doctors for giving injections, or "shots."–The doctor filled a *hypodermic* and gave Tom his polio shot.
2. The medicine given through a hypodermic.–The *hypodermic* will protect Tom from polio.
3. The injection itself.–The *hypodermic* did not hurt.

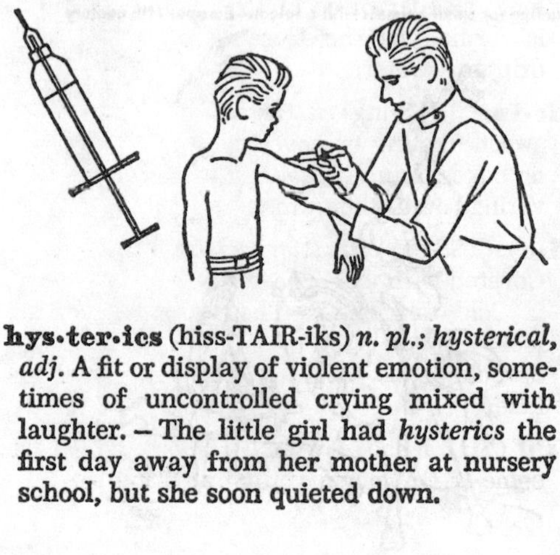

hys•ter•ics (hiss-TAIR-iks) *n. pl.; hysterical, adj.* A fit or display of violent emotion, sometimes of uncontrolled crying mixed with laughter. – The little girl had *hysterics* the first day away from her mother at nursery school, but she soon quieted down.

I i

I, i (Y) *n. I's, i's.* The ninth letter of the alphabet.

I (Y) *pron.* A word used to mean oneself.–When you speak about yourself, you say *I*.–*I* like to read. Don't you?–Jack and *I* went skating yesterday.

ice (YSS) *n. ices* and *adj.* 1. Frozen water.–*Ice* is hard and keeps foods cold.
2. A kind of flavored frozen dessert.–Mother likes orange *ice*.
–*v. ices, iced, icing.* 1. Cover with icing or frosting.–The baker *iced* the cake.
2. Make cold with ice.–Mother *iced* the lemonade.

ice•berg (YSS-berg) *n. icebergs.* A very large piece of ice that floats in the sea. Most of an *iceberg* is below the surface of the water.

ice cream (YSS-kreem) *ice creams.* A frozen dessert made of cream, milk, eggs, sugar, and flavoring.

i•ci•cle (YSS-i-kl) *n. icicles.* A long, slender piece of ice that is formed by the freezing of dripping water.

ic•ing (YSS-ing) *n. icings.* A sweet frosting or covering put on cakes. *Icing* is made of butter, sugar, flavoring, and other things.

i•cy (YSS-ee) *adj. icier, iciest; icily, adv.* 1. Covered with ice.–The street is *icy*.
2. Cold; unfriendly.–The man gave us an *icy* look.
3. Cold as ice.–The *icy* wind came from the lake.

I'd (YD). I had; I would; I should.–*I'd* have come if *I'd* known you wanted me to.

I•da•ho (Y-də-hoh) *n.* A state in northwestern United States known for its rich lead and silver mines, its lumbering industry, and farming. *Idaho* ranks second among the states in raising potatoes.

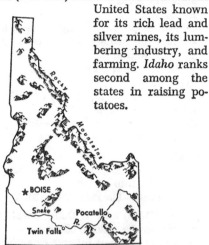

i•de•a (y-DEE-ə) *n. ideas.* A thought; a plan; a belief.–I have no *idea* how to bake a cake.–I had an *idea* that Jack wouldn't come.–Bob has the *idea* of becoming a doctor.

i•de•al (y-DEEL) *n. ideals.* A model; something thought of as perfect.–George Washington is Bob's *ideal*. Bob would like to be like Washington.–Honesty and doing one's best were two *ideals* the teacher tried to encourage in her pupils.
–*adj.; ideally, adv.* Exactly right.–This is an *ideal* spot from which to see the races.–This is an *ideal* day for a picnic.

i•den•ti•cal (y-DENT-i-kəl) *adj.; identically, adv.* 1. Just alike.–The writing on the two papers is *identical*, so they must have been written by the same person.
2. Same.–That is the *identical* bracelet I lost two years ago. It is the bracelet that I lost.

i•den•ti•fy (y-DENT-i-fy) *v. identifies, identified, identifying.* 1. Make known to be a certain person or thing.–The policeman told the man to *identify* himself. He told the man to tell who he was.
2. Recognize; know as a certain one.–You may have the dog if you can *identify* it among the others. Then I'll know it's yours.
–*identification, n. identifications.*

id·i·ot (ID-ee-ət) *n. idiots.* A weak-minded person who cannot take care of himself.—An *idiot* cannot learn to read.

i·dle (YD-l) *v. idles, idled, idling.* 1. Do nothing; waste time.—Why are you *idling* when there is so much to be done?

2. Run without being in gear.—Father stopped the car at the traffic light and let the motor *idle*.

—*adj. idler, idlest.* 1. Doing nothing; not busy. —While the machines were being repaired, the men were *idle*.

2. Lazy.—The *idle* man would rather go hungry than work.

3. Useless.—It is *idle* to cry over things that have already happened.

—*Idle away* means to waste.—Bob *idled away* his time, so he had to study after school.

i·dle·ness (YD-l-nəss) *n.* 1. Condition of being without anything to do.—*Idleness* often leads boys into mischief.

2. Laziness.—The man lives a life of *idleness*.

i·dly (YD-lee) *adv.* 1. Doing nothing.—Mary sat *idly* in the rocking chair.

2. Slowly; without interest or enthusiasm.—Bob *idly* turned the pages of the magazine, looking at the pictures.

i·dol (YD-l) *n. idols.* 1. An image of a god.—*Idols* were often decorated with jewels.

2. A person who is very much admired.—The baseball hero is an *idol* of many boys.

if (IF) *conj.* 1. Whether.—I do not know *if* the train has gone.

2. Though.—Even *if* it rains, we shall play ball.

ig·loo (IG-loo) *n. igloos.* An Eskimo's house. It is made of snow and ice blocks.

ig·ne·ous rock (IG-nee-əss rahk) *igneous rocks.* Rock made from once melted minerals that have cooled either inside or on the surface of the earth. Some *igneous rocks* have crystals; others haven't.

ig·nite (ig-NYT) *v. ignites, ignited, igniting.* 1. Set fire to.—Bob *ignited* the waste paper in the stove with a match.

2. Take fire; begin to burn.—Dry paper *ignites* more easily than wet paper.

ig·ni·tion (ig-NISH-ən) *n. ignitions.* 1. Setting or catching on fire.—A special lighter fluid helps the *ignition* of the charcoal in our grill for outdoor cooking.

2. The mechanical means of igniting the fuel mixture in certain kinds of engines; the process itself.—Father had the *ignition* of his car checked at the service station.—The *ignition* failed and the car would not start.

ig·no·rance (IG-ner-ənss) *n.* State of not having knowledge (of); not knowing about. —Our *ignorance* of the lesson was due to our having been absent.

ig·no·rant (IG-ner-ənt) *adj.; ignorantly, adv.* Without knowledge.—An *ignorant* person is one who doesn't know much.

ig·nore (ig-NOR) *v. ignores, ignored, ignoring.* Not to notice or pay attention to.—The ball player *ignored* the boos of the crowd. He paid no attention to them.

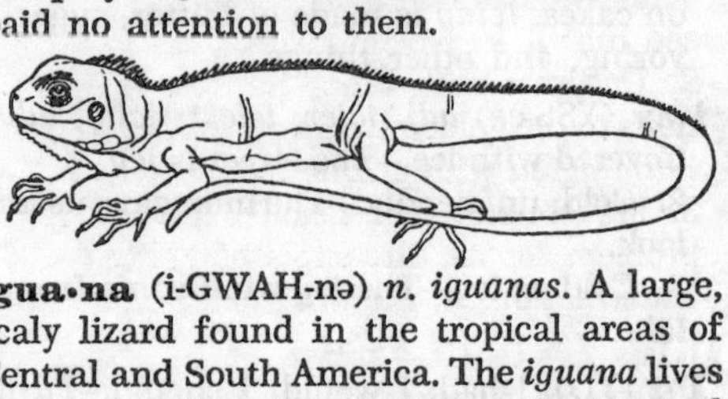

i·gua·na (i-GWAH-nə) *n. iguanas.* A large, scaly lizard found in the tropical areas of Central and South America. The *iguana* lives in trees and feeds mainly on leaves and fruits. It may grow to be five or six feet long.

ill (IL) *adj.* 1. Having something wrong with the body; sick.–Baby has the measles. She is *ill.*
2. Bad; evil; harmful.–If you do *ill* deeds, you must expect to be punished.
–*adv.* In an ill manner; badly; poorly.–A job *ill* done may be better not done at all.

I'll (YL). I will or I shall.–*I'll* go to town tomorrow if I finish my work in time.

il·le·gal (i-LEE-gəl) *adj.; illegally, adv.* Against the law.–Driving on the wrong side of the street is *illegal.*

il·leg·i·ble (i-LEJ-ə-bəl) *adj.; illegibly, adv.* Not able to be read.–The boy's writing is *illegible.*

Il·li·nois (il-ə-NOI) *n.* A leading manufacturing, farming, and mining state in north central United States. It is the flattest state and is the second-largest corn-raising state. Much coal, as well as many hogs, cattle, sheep, and soybeans come from *Illinois.*

il·lit·er·a·cy (i-LIT-er-ə-see) *n.* Inability to read or write; lack of education or learning.–There is little *illiteracy* in the United States, where most of us go to school.

il·lit·er·ate (i-LIT-er-ət) *adj.; illiterately, adv.* Unable to read or write.–Many Africans and Asians are *illiterate* because there are not enough schools in Africa and Asia to educate everyone.

ill·ness (IL-nəss) *n. illnesses.* Sickness; poor health.–Grandmother's *illness* kept her at home on Christmas day.

il·lu·mi·nate (i-LOOM-ə-nayt *or* il-YOOM-ə-nayt) *v. illuminates, illuminated, illuminating.* 1. Light up; make bright with lights.–When we came nearer the church, we could see that it had been *illuminated.*
2. Decorate with fancy figures.–The invitations to the golden wedding anniversary were *illuminated* with golden letters.
3. Make clear.–The teacher *illuminated* the problem for us. She explained it to us.
–*illumination, n. illuminations.*

il·lus·trate (IL-ə-strayt *or* i-LUSS-trayt) *v. illustrates, illustrated, illustrating.* 1. Show. The teacher will *illustrate* how to make a box. She will make each step clear to us by doing it herself.
2. Decorate or make clear with pictures.–Some authors *illustrate* their own books.

il·lus·tra·tion (il-ə-STRAY-shən) *n. illustrations.* 1. A picture that helps to explain.–Children like storybooks with *illustrations* of the important happenings.
2. An explanation.–The teacher gave an *illustration* of how to make a paper box.

I'm (YM). I am.–*I'm* ten years old today.

im·age (IM-ij) *n. images.* 1. A likeness.–A photograph of you is an *image* of you because it looks like you.
2. A picture in the mind.–The boy had an *image* of the airplane he was going to build.
3. A statue; an idol.–In olden times, some people worshiped *images.*

im·ag·i·nar·y (im-AJ-in-air-ee) *adj.* Existing only in the mind; not real.–Little Susie has an *imaginary* playmate. Her playmate isn't real.

im·ag·i·na·tion (im-aj-in-AY-shən) *n. imaginations.* 1. The power to picture things in the mind.–Some children have great *imaginations.* They picture many things that they have never seen.
2. Ability to create new ideas or things.–Artists and inventors must have *imagination.*

im·ag·ine (i-MAJ-in) *v. imagines, imagined, imagining.* 1. Picture in the mind.–Bob *imagines* that he will be a baseball hero.
2. Suppose.–I *imagine* she'd like supper early, since she's going to a movie.

im·i·tate (IM-ə-tayt) *v. imitates, imitated, imitating.* 1. Act like.–The children tried to *imitate* their teacher.
2. Make something just like something else. –Bob can *imitate* bird calls. He can make the sound of a bird call by whistling.

im·i·ta·tion (im-ə-TAY-shən) *n. imitations.* 1. A copying.–Bob gave an *imitation* of the song of a canary.
2. Something made to look like something else.–This is not a real diamond, but an *imitation* of one. It is made of glass and cut to look like a diamond.
–*adj.* Not original or real; copied.–This jewel is an *imitation* diamond.

im·ma·ture (im-ə-TYOOR *or* -CHUHR) *adj.; immaturity, n.* 1. Not fully developed or mature.–Children are *immature.*
2. Not yet ripe.–This is an *immature* tomato. It is still small and green.

im·me·di·ate (i-MEE-dee-ət) *adj.* 1. Coming right away.–We received an *immediate* answer to our letter.
2. Close; near.–My father and mother are my most *immediate* living relatives.

im·me·di·ate·ly (i-MEE-dee-ət-lee) *adv.* Right away.–The fire engine came *immediately* after getting our call.–Mary sang a song *immediately* after the dance.

im·mense (i-MENSS) *adj.; immensely, adv.* Very large; huge.–The rich man has an *immense* amount of money.

im·mi·grant (IM-ə-grənt) *n. immigrants.* A person from a foreign land coming into a country to live there.–If you should go to live in England, you would be an *immigrant* there.

im·mi·grate (IM-ə-grayt) *v. immigrates, immigrated, immigrating.* Come from a foreign land into a country to live there.–Many people *immigrate* into the United States.
–*immigration, n. immigrations.*

im·mune (i-MYOON) *adj.* 1. *Immune to* means not affected by or able to ignore.–The little boy is *immune to* his sister's teasing. It doesn't bother him at all.
2. *Immune to* also means protected against infection from.–After being vaccinated, a person is *immune to* smallpox for a number of years. He cannot get smallpox.
3. *Immune from* means safe, protected, or free from.–This fort is *immune from* attack.
–Mary seems to be *immune from* criticism. She never seems to do anything wrong.

imp (IMP) *n. imps; impish, adj.* 1. A mischievous child.–The boy is a little *imp.* He loves to tease and play jokes.
2. In fairy stories, a small, mischief-making fairy.

im·par·tial (im-PAHR-shəl) *adj.; impartially, adv.* Showing no favor for one side against another; fair.–Father tries to be *impartial* when he is asked to settle a quarrel between the children.

im·pa·tient (im-PAY-shənt) *adj.; impatiently, adv.; impatience, n.* Cross; anxious and uneasy; unable to wait quietly. – Mother sometimes becomes *impatient* when we are late getting ready for breakfast.

im·peach (im-PEECH) *v. impeaches, impeached, impeaching.* Formally accuse a public official with a charge of wrongdoing in office before a group who can dismiss him from his job if they find him guilty of the charge.

im·per·a·tive (im-PAIR-ə-tiv) *adj.; imperatively, adv.* 1. Absolutely necessary; not to be escaped.–It is *imperative* to get the fire under control. Otherwise the next building will burn down.
2. Commanding, or having the quality of an order.–Though the policeman asked politely if he might use the phone, his tone was *imperative.*
–An *imperative sentence* is one that commands or urges. Some examples are: Don't do that! Come here! Step down, please. Think before you speak.

im·per·fect (im-PER-fikt) *adj.; imperfectly, adv.* Not perfect; having flaws, faults, or mistakes.–John's spelling paper was *imperfect.* He had made two mistakes.

im·per·son·al (im-PER-sən-əl) *adj.; impersonally, adv.* Without reference to any one person in particular.–"May the best man win!" is an *impersonal* remark.–The teacher's request that the class be quiet was *impersonal.* She wasn't referring to anyone in particular.

im·ple·ment (IM-plə-mənt) *n. implements.* A tool; something used for a certain job.–A harrow is a farm *implement.*

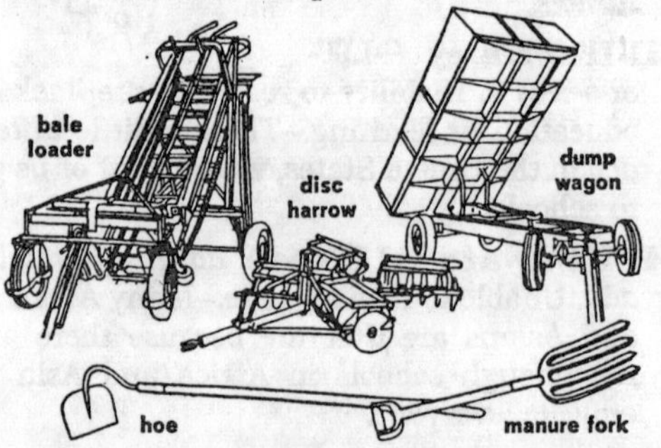

im·plore (im-PLOR) *v. implores, implored, imploring.* Ask urgently; beg.–She *implored* the teacher to let her take the examination over again.

im·ply (im-PLY) *v. implies, implied, implying.* Mean something without actually saying it; suggest.–Mother *implied* that she was annoyed at our lateness. But all she asked was why we hadn't started home sooner.

im·po·lite (im-pə-LYT) *adj.; impolitely, adv.* Not polite; not courteous.–It is *impolite* to talk when someone else is talking.

im·port (IM-port) *n. imports.* Something brought into one country from another.–Foods, clothing, and other articles brought into our country are *imports.*

–(im-PORT) *v. imports, imported, importing.* Bring into a country.–Americans *import* coffee from South America.

im•por•tance (im-PORT-ənss) *n.* To say that something is of *importance* means that it matters very much.–It is of *importance* to spell correctly.–The *importance* of a thing is the reason why it matters.–The *importance* of being careful with fire is that you may be burned if you are not careful.

im•por•tant (im-PORT-ənt) *adj.; importantly, adv.* 1. Mattering a great deal; having great meaning or value.–Good habits and manners are *important.* They mean much to people.
2. Having much power and influence.–The school principal is an *important* person in our town.

im•pos•si•ble (im-PAHSS-ə-bəl) *adj.; impossibly, adv.; impossibility, n.* Not possible; not able to happen or be done.–It is *impossible* for me to sing well when I have a cold.

im•press (im-PRESS) *v. impresses, impressed, impressing.* 1. Mark; stamp; press on or in.–The rabbit *impressed* his footprints in the snow.
2. Strongly fix in the mind.–Mary repeated the poem so many times that it was *impressed* upon her mind. She knew it well.
3. Have an effect on someone's mind.–He *impressed* me as a good worker. It seemed to me that he was a good worker.

im•pres•sion (im-PRESH-ən) *n. impressions.* 1. A print; a mark pressed in.–The rabbit left the *impression* of its feet in the snow.
2. An effect on someone's thoughts.–Mary wanted to make a good *impression* on her new teacher. She wanted the teacher to think well of her.
3. An idea; a belief.–It is my *impression* that Bob is at his grandmother's. Possibly he is not.

im•prob•a•ble (im-PRAHB-ə-bəl) *adj.* Not likely to happen or to be true; unlikely.–It is *improbable* that the world will end tomorrow.

im•prop•er (im-PRAHP-er) *adj.; improperly, adv.* Not proper; wrong; not suitable.–Mother said it was *improper* of me to wear my bathing suit at dinner. – Shouting in church is *improper* behavior.
–An *improper fraction* is one in which the denominator is smaller than the numerator; a fraction greater than 1. 8/3 and 7/2 are *improper fractions.*

im•prove (im-PROOV) *v. improves, improved, improving.* 1. Make better.–You can *improve* your piano playing by practicing.
2. Get better.–Grandmother is *improving* each day. Her health is getting better.
3. Make good use of.–The children *improve* their spare time by reading.

im•prove•ment (im-PROOV-mənt) *n. improvements.* 1. Anything that makes a thing better.–Grandmother has made many *improvements* in her kitchen; she has a new stove, a new sink, and a new light.
2. A making or getting better.–Bob's handwriting shows much *improvement.* It is better than it was.

im•pu•dent (IM-pyoo-dənt) *adj.; impudently, adv.; impudence, n.* Forward; saucy; not polite; bold. – The *impudent* boy threw a snowball at the teacher.

im•pulse (IM-pulss) *n. impulses; impulsive, adj.; impulsively, adv.* 1. A sudden desire to do something.–Bob had an *impulse* to throw the ball over the roof.–Dick acted on *impulse.* He acted without thinking about his action ahead of time.
2. A driving force or thrust producing motion.–The *impulse* of the blow of the hammer drove the nail into the wood.

im•pure (im-PYOOR) *adj.* Not pure, clean, or refined.–Do not drink *impure* water. It may make you sick.

in (IN) *adv.* and *prep.* 1. Bob has his hand *in* his pocket.
2. There are thirty days *in* June.
3. Uncle Jim is *in* training for the army.
4. The dog lived *in* fear of the cat.
5. Come *in* the house!
6. The doctor isn't *in.* He is not *in* his office.
7. The door closed and we were locked *in.*
8. A car turned *in* at the driveway.
9. I'll be there *in* a minute.

in•ac•cu•rate (in-AK-yə-rət) *adj.; inaccurately, adv.; inaccuracy, n.* Not accurate; incorrect; in error.–It is *inaccurate* to say that Mary is never late. She was late last Friday.

in•au•gu•ra•tion (in-awg-yə-RAY-shən) *n. inaugurations.* 1. The ceremony of installing someone in office.–The *inauguration* of the President now takes place on the January twentieth following his election.
2. A formal beginning.–The local paper reported the *inauguration* of a suburban bus service.
3. Ceremonial opening.–The mayor spoke at the *inauguration* of the new town swimming pool.

in•can•des•cent (in-kən-DESS-ənt) *adj.* White, or glowing with intense heat; brilliant.–The flame of the blowtorch was *incandescent.*

–An *incandescent lamp* is one that produces light when an electric current heats the filament inside the bulb.

in•cense (IN-senss) *n.* A substance that has a sweet, fragrant odor when burned.–We burn *incense* to make a room smell sweet or fragrant.

–(in-SENSS) *v. incenses, incensed, incensing.* Anger greatly.–Cruelty *incenses* my grandfather.

in•cen•tive (in-SEN-tiv) *n. incentives.* Something which encourages (one) to effort or action; a stimulant.–The possibility of getting an increase in wages is an *incentive* to hard work.

inch (INCH) *n. inches.* A measurement of length.–Twelve *inches* make a foot.–We measure ribbon by the yard, the foot, and the *inch.*

–*v. inches, inched, inching.* Move or progress very slowly.–We *inched* along the icy path.

–*Inch by inch* means slowly.–We are getting to the top of the hill *inch by inch.*

in•ci•dent (IN-sə-dənt) *n. incidents; incidental, adj.* A happening; something that happens.–John lost his balance and fell into the brook. Mary thought the *incident* was very funny.

in•cin•er•a•tor (in-SIN-ə-ray-ter) *n. incinerators.* A furnace used to burn garbage or rubbish. Many apartment buildings have *incinerators* for the convenience of the tenants.

in•ci•sor (in-SY-zer) *n. incisors.* A tooth used for cutting, especially one of the front teeth in human beings.

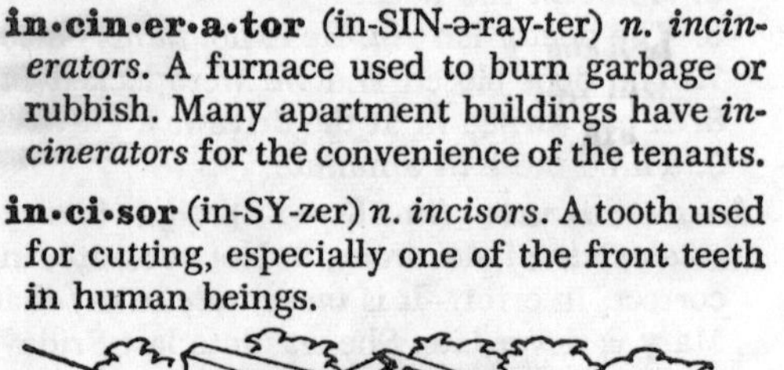

in•cline (IN-klyn) *n. inclines.* A slope or slant.–The car went up the *incline* slowly.

–(in-KLYN) *v. inclines, inclined, inclining.* 1. Bow; bend over.–Grandfather *inclined* his head forward in order to hear.

2. Have a tendency.–Father *inclined* to believe the man. It seemed that Father would believe him.

3. Slope; slant.–The road *inclined* gradually to the valley.

in•close (in-KLOHZ) *v.* Another way of spelling the word *enclose.*

in•clude (in-KLOOD) *v. includes, included, including.* 1. Contain; cover.–The price of my piano lessons *includes* the teacher's pay, books, and the use of the piano.

2. Take count of.–There are five people here, *including* Mary.

in•cog•ni•to (in-kahg-NEE-toh) *adj.* and *adv.* Passing unrecognized; disguised as someone else.–The prince decided to be *incognito* on the trip, so he traveled under the name of Mr. Jones, and no one recognized him.

in•come (IN-kum) *n. incomes.* The money that one gets for work, for rent, or for interest.–Father's *income* is seven thousand dollars a year.

in•com•plete (in-kəm-PLEET) *adj.; incompletely, adv.* Not complete; unfinished; missing some part.–The newspaper was *incomplete.* Two pages were missing.

in•con•sist•ent (in-kən-SISS-tənt) *adj.; inconsistently, adv.* Not consistent; not in harmony or agreement with itself or something else; not logical.–The man's latest statement was *inconsistent* with his earlier one. At first he said he didn't know Harry Brown. Then he said he did.

in•cor•po•rate (in-KOR-pə-rayt) *v. incorporates, incorporated, incorporating.* Include something as part of something else; combine or blend into one; closely unite.–The teacher *incorporated* the students' suggestions in her plan for a picnic.

–*incorporation, n. incorporations.*

in•cor•rect (in-kə-REKT) *adj.; incorrectly, adv.* Wrong; in error; not correct or right.–Mike said that the dance would be on Wednesday, but he was *incorrect.* The dance was planned for Thursday.

in•crease (IN-kreess) *n. increases.* The amount or degree by which something is made or becomes larger in size, number, speed, amount, etc.–Father got an *increase* of ten dollars per week in his pay.

–(in-KREESS) *v. increases, increased, increasing.* Make or become greater.–Father's pay was *increased* to eighty-five dollars per week.

–You can *increase* your speed in writing if you practice enough.

in•cu•ba•tor (IN-kyə-bay-ter) *n. incubators.* 1. A device for hatching eggs without having a hen sit on them. Eggs are placed in the *incubator,* which is kept at just the right temperature to make the eggs hatch.

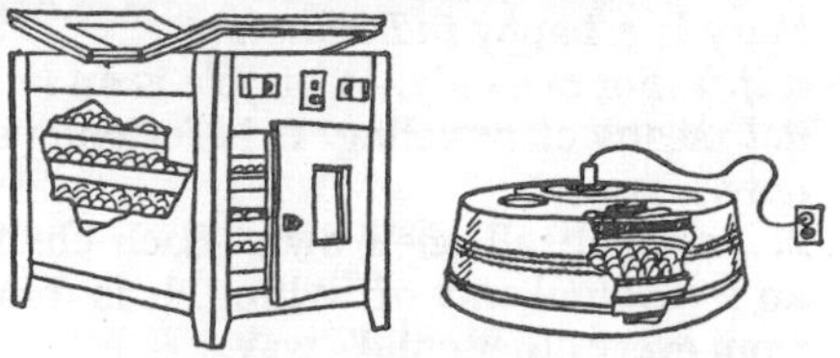

2. A special kind of box that very tiny babies are sometimes kept in when they are first born. It keeps them warm all the time.

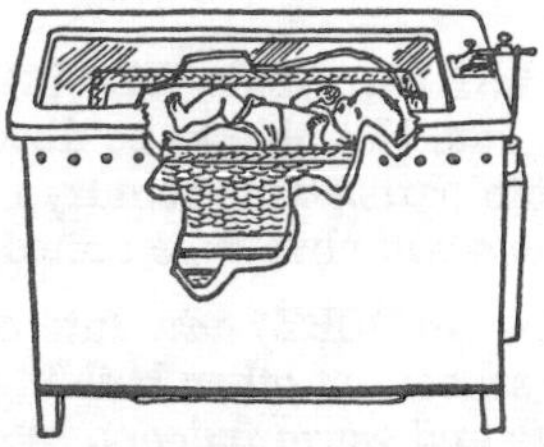

in•debt•ed (in-DET-id) *adj.* Owing money or gratitude (to someone); under obligation. –The nation is *indebted* to its great leaders. –I am *indebted* to Mr. Brown for his many kindnesses to me.

in•deed (in-DEED) *adv.* Really; in truth.– *Indeed,* I will not be ten years old until my next birthday.–Yes, *indeed,* I should like very much to come.

in•def•i•nite (in-DEF-ə-nit) *adj.; indefinitely, adv.* 1. Not definite; vague; not certain.– The family's vacation plans were *indefinite.* They were not sure when or where they would go.
2. Without exact limit.–An *indefinite* number of men will be needed for the job. We are not sure how many it will take.–Jack will be away for an *indefinite* length of time.
–The *indefinite article* is either of the words "a" or "an." An *indefinite article* is used to show that the noun before which it appears is not a special one, but any one of that kind: a boy, an hour, an idea, a cat, an author.

in•del•i•ble (in-DEL-ə-bəl) *adj.; indelibly, adv.* 1. Impossible to erase, wash out, or remove; permanent; fixed.–The paint spots on Jane's dress seem to be *indelible.* Mother cannot get them out.
2. Making marks that are permanent or hard to remove.–Bob wrote his name on the back of his shirt with an *indelible* pencil.

in•dent (in-DENT) *v. indents, indented, indenting.* 1. Notch; put a notch or hole in.– Caves *indent* that mountain.
2. Set in from a line or margin.–We *indent* the first line of each paragraph in a story. We start it farther in from the left margin than the other lines.

in•de•pend•ence (in-də-PEND-ənss) *n.* Freedom from the control or help of others.– John will get his *independence* from his family when he is twenty-one years old.–The United States won its *independence* from England long ago.

in•de•pend•ent (in-də-PEND-ənt) *adj.; independently, adv.* 1. Free from the control or help of others.–A person who can do things for himself without help from others is *independent.*
2. Having no help from others; having enough money to care for oneself.–Harry is *independent* now; he has a job and doesn't need money from his parents.
3. Separate; not dependent on or influenced by others.–Harry has an *independent* income.–John has an *independent* mind. He thinks for himself.

in•dex (IN-deks) *n. indexes.* A list that names in alphabetical order the things that are written about in a book and tells the pages on which they may be found. An *index* comes at the end of a book.
–*v. indexes, indexed, indexing.* Prepare an index (for).–The author is *indexing* his book.
–The *index finger* is the one next to the thumb.

In•di•an•a (in-dee-AN-ə) *n.* A flat state in the corn belt in north central United States. *Indiana* produces coal and building stone, hogs and cattle. It manufactures airplane and automobile parts and farm equipment, and has the greatest steel mill in the country.

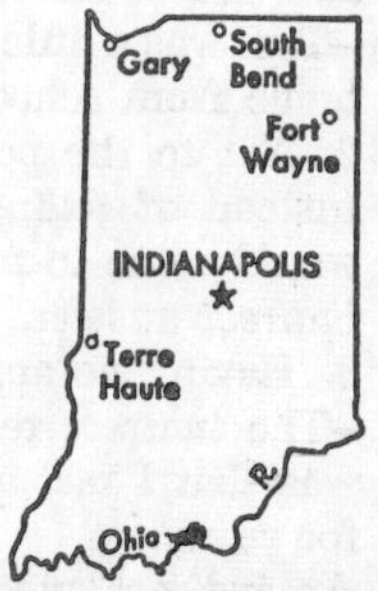

in•di•cate (IN-də-kayt) *v. indicates, indicated, indicating.* 1. Show; point out.–The hands on the clock *indicate* the time.–The hunting dog *indicated* the path the hunter should follow.
2. Make known.–Smoke in the room *indicated* to us that there was a fire.
3. Be a sign of; show that something will happen.–Dark clouds *indicate* a storm.

in•di•ca•tion (in-də-KAY-shən) *n. indications.* 1. Act of indicating, or of being indicated.—The *indication* of rain made us cancel the picnic.
2. Something that indicates.—Fever is an *indication* of illness. It shows that one is ill.

in•dif•fer•ence (in-DIF-er-ənss) *n.; indifferent, adj.* Lack of interest or concern; not caring one way or another.—Harry's *indifference* to everything since his pet died is sad to see.—Whether or not the newspaper carries its bridge column is a matter of *indifference* to those who don't play bridge.

in•di•ges•tion (in-də-JEST-chən) *n.* A condition in the stomach that occurs when food is not being digested properly. When the stomach digests food, it changes it so that the body can use it. When one has *indigestion,* the stomach is not changing the food properly for use. *Indigestion* causes discomfort.

in•dig•nant (in-DIG-nənt) *adj.; indignantly, adv.* Angry at a wrong done.—Bob was *indignant* because he was treated meanly and unfairly.

in•dig•na•tion (in-dəg-NAY-shən) *n.* Anger at, or strong disagreement with, something that has been done; strong belief that something is wrong.—The unjust law aroused the *indignation* of the citizens.

in•di•go (IN-də-goh) *n. indigos* or *indigoes.* A plant from which a blue dye or a blue coloring is made.
—*adj.* Of a deep, violet-blue color.

in•di•rect (in-də-REKT) *adj.; indirectly, adv.* 1. Not direct; roundabout; not straight. —Tom was a little late today because he came home from school by an *indirect* route.
2. Not to the point; not straightforward.—Instead of telling me whether or not she would come to my party, Jane gave me an *indirect* answer.
3. Having no apparent or clear connection. —The *indirect* result of my trip downtown was that I met an old friend I hadn't seen for years.
—An *indirect quotation* is one that does not repeat the exact words of the original statement.—"Bob said that he was coming" is an *indirect quotation.* Bob actually said, "I am coming."

in•dis•tinct (in-də-STINKT) *adj.; indistinctly, adv.* Not clear; not easily understood, seen, or heard.—The voices on the radio were *indistinct.*—The fog on the lake made the boat *indistinct.*—The teacher had explained the problem, but Bob's memory of what she said was *indistinct.* He wasn't sure of it any more.

in•di•vid•u•al (in-də-VIJ-oo-əl) *n. individuals.* One person, one thing, or one animal.—Mary is a happy *individual.*
—*adj.* 1. For one only.—A bicycle is an *individual* means of traveling. It is for one person only.
2. Personal; all one's own.—Each child has an *individual* way of writing. It is different from every other child's way.

in•di•vid•u•al•ly (in-də-VIJ-oo-əl-ee) *adv.* One at a time; each by himself.—Each child sang *individually,* and then they all sang together.

in•di•vis•i•ble (in-də-VIZ-ə-bəl) *adj.; indivisibly, adv.* Not able to be divided or separated into parts.—This country is *indivisible.* The states will always be united.

in•doors (in-DORZ) *adv.* Into or inside the house, school, or other building.—It is cold outdoors and warm *indoors.*

in•duce (in-DOOSS *or* -DYOOSS) *v. induces, induced, inducing.* 1. Persuade; get (some-

INDUSTRY

making paper from wood chips

one) to do something.–Bob tried to *induce* John to go skating. He tried to get him to go.
2. Bring on; cause.–Too little sleep *induces* a tired feeling. It causes a tired feeling.

in•dus•tri•al (in-DUSS-tree-əl) *adj.; industrially, adv.* Having to do with manufacturing; relating to factories and the making of things to be sold.–Detroit is an *industrial* city. It has many industries, with many men working there.

in•dus•tri•ous (in-DUSS-tree-əss) *adj.; industriously, adv.* Hard-working.–Bob is very *industrious.* He is always hard at work.

in•dus•try (IN-də-stree) *n. industries.* 1. A kind of manufacturing.–The automobile *industry* is the business of making automobiles. –The woolen *industry* is the business of making woolen yarns, blankets, etc.
2. All businesses taken together.–American *industry* grew rapidly during the war.
3. Hard work.–*Industry* will bring one good marks in school.

in•ef•fi•cien•cy (in-ə-FISH-ən-see) *n. inefficiencies; inefficient, adj.; inefficiently, adv.* Inability to do things quickly or well; wasting time and energy at one's work.–The man's *inefficiency* caused him to lose his job.

in•ex•pen•sive (in-iks-PEN-siv) *adj.; inexpensively, adv.* Cheap; not costing much.–Mary's play clothes are *inexpensive.* They cost little.

in•ex•pe•ri•ence (in-iks-PIR-i-ənss) *n.; inexperienced, adj.* Lack of experience; lack of the knowledge and skill which come from actually having done or experienced something.–John could not get a job as a radio announcer because of his *inexperience.*

in•fant (IN-fənt) *n. infants.* A baby, especially a very young baby.

–*adj.* 1. Having to do with babies.–Mother likes to make *infant* clothing. She likes to make clothes for babies.
2. Started only a short time ago.–Our baseball club is an *infant* club.

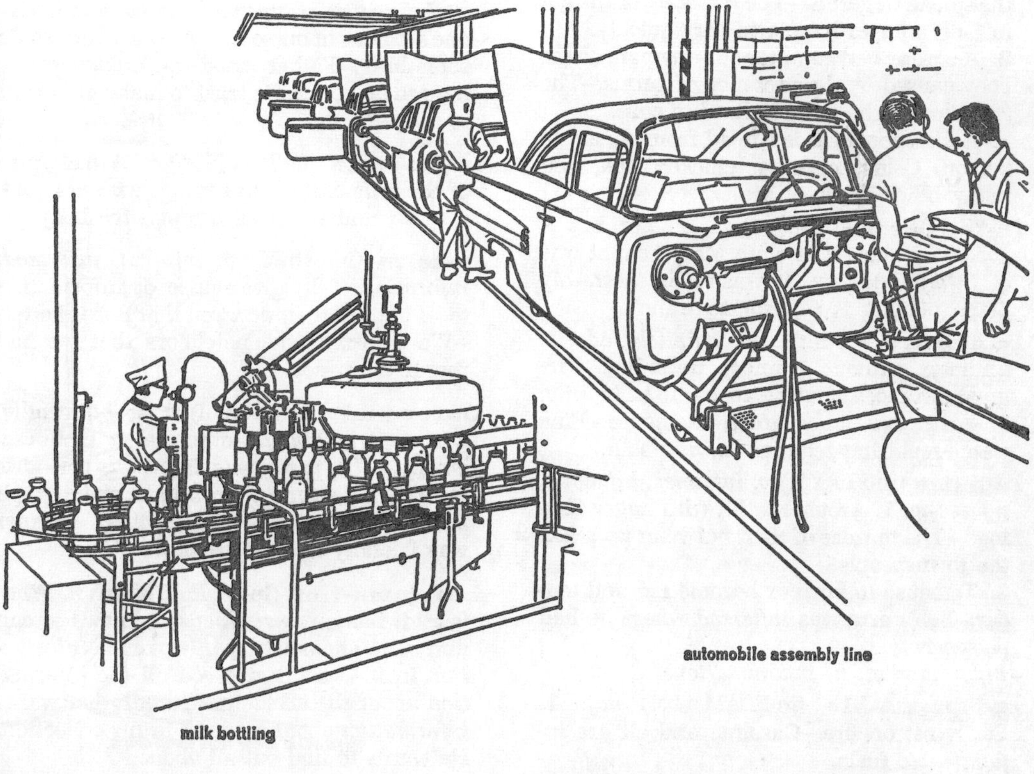

automobile assembly line

milk bottling

in·fan·try (IN-fən-tree) *n.* The branch of an army that fights on foot; the soldiers in this branch.–The hill was defended by a regiment of *infantry.*

in·fect (in-FEKT) *v. infects, infected, infecting.* 1. Make ill or diseased by spreading or adding to the germs that cause disease.–If you have a cold, sneeze into your handkerchief, so that you will not *infect* others.
2. Spread (a feeling) to.–John's enthusiasm for starting a newspaper *infected* the whole class. Everyone wanted to help him.

in·fec·tion (in-FEK-shən) *n. infections; infectious, adj.* 1. The causing of a disease by the spread of germs.–The *infection* of the cut in Sally's finger happened very quickly.
2. A sick or bad condition of any part of the body caused by the presence of germs.–The *infection* in the cut was hard to cure.
3. A disease which is spread from person to person. Colds, measles, chicken pox, and many other diseases are *infections.*

in·fe·ri·or (in-FIR-ee-er) *adj.* Poorer; not as good as others.–The cloth Mary bought was of *inferior* quality. It wasn't the best.–My piano playing is *inferior* to Anne's.

in·fi·nite (IN-fə-nit) *adj.; infinitely, adv.* 1. Endless; without bounds; unlimited.–The great distances of space appear to be *infinite.*
2. Vast; extremely great; immense.–Fine watch-repairing requires *infinite* skill.

in·flame (in-FLAYM) *v. inflames, inflamed, inflaming.* 1. Arouse, or fill with angry feelings.–The murder of their neighbor *inflamed* the townspeople.
2. To cause to burn or become red and tender.–Bob's arm was *inflamed* where he had poison ivy.
–*inflammation, n. inflammations.*

in·flam·ma·ble (in-FLAM-ə-bəl) *adj.* 1. Easily set on fire.–Gasoline and oil are *inflammable* fuels.
2. Easily excited; easily aroused or angered. –People with *inflammable* tempers should avoid arguments.

in·flate (in-FLAYT) *v. inflates, inflated, inflating.* 1. Put air into.–Father stopped at a gas station to *inflate* the spare tire.–*Inflating* the tire made it swell or puff up.
2. Swell out.–Bob *inflated* his chest when he marched in the parade.
3. Exaggerate.–Bob considerably *inflated* his own part in the rescue when he told us about it.
–*inflation, n. inflations.*

in·flict (in-FLIKT) *v. inflicts, inflicted, inflicting.* Bring (something cruel or very unpleasant) upon (someone).–Jack loves animals too much ever to *inflict* pain on one.
–*infliction, n. inflictions.*

in·flu·ence (IN-floo-ənss) *n. influences.* 1. Power, persuasion, or ability to cause something to happen.–Mother's presence has a soothing *influence* on the children. Just by being around, she makes them feel quiet and peaceful.
2. Person with this power.–John is a poor *influence* on Dick. He causes Dick to be late to school.
–*v. influences, influenced, influencing.* Use one's power upon someone to get him to do something.–Father tried to *influence* the man to do better. He tried to make him want to do better.

in·flu·en·za (in-floo-EN-zə) *n.* A bad form of the grippe. *Influenza* brings with it a cold, a fever, and aches all through the body.

in·form (in-FORM) *v. informs, informed, informing.* Tell; give notice or information to.–I phoned to *inform* you that Bob is better. –We *informed* the neighbors that we had found their dog.

in·for·mal (in-FOR-məl) *adj.; informally, adv.; informality, n.* Not formal; without ceremony.–The party was *informal;* the girls wore their daytime dresses and a phonograph provided the music.–The teacher's manner was friendly and *informal.*

in·for·ma·tion (in-fer-MAY-shən) *n.* What is told; facts; news; what one knows or can find out.–The newspaper has much *information* in it.–I shall give you all the *information* about the accident.–Grandfather wants *information* about a stamp in his collection. He wants to find out all about it.

in•gre•di•ent (in-GREE-dee-ənt) *n. ingredients.* One of the parts of a mixture, a combination, or a compound.–The *ingredients* of Mother's soup were vegetables, chicken, salt, pepper, and water.

in•hab•it (in-HAB-it) *v. inhabits, inhabited, inhabiting.* Live in.–Many wild animals *inhabit* the woods.–Eskimos *inhabit* the north countries.–Many people *inhabit* the city.

in•hab•it•ant (in-HAB-ə-tənt) *n. inhabitants.* A dweller; one who lives in a certain place.–Deer are *inhabitants* of the woods. They live there.–Most of the *inhabitants* of this town are miners.

in•hale (in-HAYL) *v. inhales, inhaled, inhaling.* Take into the lungs.–We *inhale* air when we breathe in. We exhale air when we breathe out.

in•her•it (in-HAIR-it) *v. inherits, inherited, inheriting.* 1. Have at birth from one's ancestors.–Mary *inherits* her curly hair from her mother. Her mother has curly hair.
2. Get money or property rightfully from someone after that person is dead.–Father *inherited* a house and lot from his brother who died.

in•her•it•ance (in-HAIR-ə-tənss) *n. inheritances.* Something that you rightfully receive from someone who has died.–Mother's *inheritance* from her aunt was a diamond ring.

in•hu•man (in-HYOO-mən) *adj.; inhumanly, adv.* Cruel; having no pity or kind feeling at all.–The man is *inhuman.* He is as cruel as a beast.

in•i•tial (in-ISH-əl) *n. initials.* The letter with which a name begins.–Mary's handkerchief has her first *initial* on it. It has an M on it.

–*v. initials, initialed, initialing.*
1. Put initials on.–Mother had Father's Bible *initialed.* She had his initials put on it.
2. Sign by writing one's initials on.–John Smith *initialed* his note J. S.
–*adj.* The first or beginning.–Bob is going to the *initial* meeting of his baseball club. It is their first meeting.

in•i•ti•a•tion (in-ish-ee-AY-shən) *n. initiations.* 1. The formal ceremonies by which someone is made a member of a club or other organization.–The details of the *initiation* were known only to members of the college fraternity.
2. Actual admission to membership.–A regular meeting of the club was held after the *initiation* of new members.
3. An introduction or beginning.–The *initiation* of a program of low-cost housing was the first step toward clearing away the city slums.

in•jure (IN-jer) *v. injures, injured, injuring.* 1. Harm; damage.–Frost will *injure* the fruit.–The boy was *injured* in the accident.
2. To *injure* a person is to do wrong to him. –The older boys *injured* David's feelings by leaving him behind.

in•ju•ri•ous (in-JYUH-ree-əss) *adj.; injuriously, adv.* Harmful.–A very hot iron is *injurious* to silk. It damages the silk.

in•ju•ry (IN-jer-ee) *n. injuries.* 1. A hurt.–The auto race ended without an *injury* to any of the cars or drivers.
2. An act which is unfair or unkind to another.–To tell a lie about a person is to do him an *injury.*

ink (INK) *n. inks.* A liquid used with a pen for writing.–*Ink* can be red, blue, black, green, or purple.
–*v. inks, inked, inking.* Cover with ink, or mark with ink.–Jack *inked* the pencil lines on his plan of the boat.

ink•well (INK-wel) *n. inkwells.* A container for ink.–Bob filled the *inkwells* in the desks with ink.

in•land (IN-lənd) *adj.* and *adv.* In or toward the inner part of a country.–The explorers came to the country by boat and went *inland* on horseback. They made an *inland* journey.

in•mate (IN-mayt) *n. inmates.* A person who has been put in a prison, a home for old people, a hospital, or other big institution.–The *inmates* of the prison were frightened when fire broke out.

inn (IN) *n. inns.* A house where travelers stop to eat and rest for the night.–The travelers stopped at an *inn* in the mountains.

INSECTS

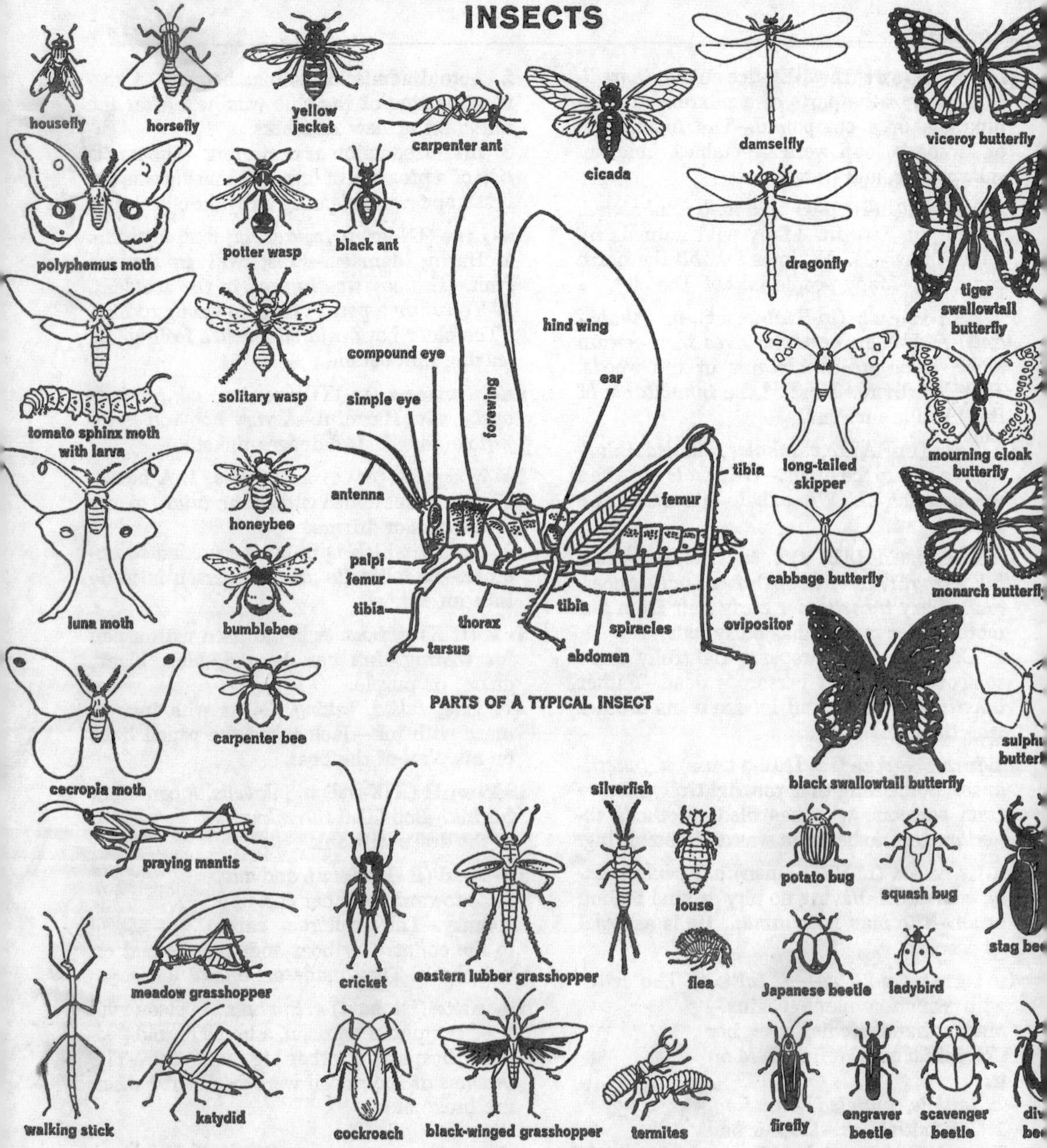

in•ner (IN-er) *adj.* 1. Inside; farther away from the sides.—Father always carries his wallet in an *inner* pocket, not in an outside pocket.
2. Of the mind or spirit; private.—Her *inner* happiness showed itself in her cheerful smile.

in•ning (IN-ing) *n. innings.* In baseball, one team bats until three men are out, then the other team has a turn or chance to bat. When both teams have had a chance to bat, an *inning* has been played.—Bob hit a home run in the last half of the last *inning.*

in•no•cent (IN-ə-sənt) *adj.; innocently, adv.; innocence, n.* 1. Not guilty.—The man was *innocent* of the crime. He had not committed it, nor had he anything to do with it.
2. Pure; knowing nothing wrong.—Little babies are *innocent.*
3. Harmless.—Playing ball is *innocent* sport. —It was an *innocent* mistake.

in•nu•mer•a•ble (i-NYOO-mer-ə-bəl) *adj.; innumerably, adv.* Too many to be counted; numberless.—There were *innumerable* people at the beach on that beautiful Sunday.

in•oc•u•late (i-NAHK-yə-layt) *v. inoculates, inoculated, inoculating.* Give a disease in mild form to a person or animal to prevent a more serious attack.–The doctor *inoculated* the baby against whooping cough.
–*inoculation, n. inoculations.*

in•quire (in-KWYR) *v. inquires, inquired, inquiring.* Ask about; find out about.–Mother sent me to *inquire* about the accident.

in•quir•y (in-KWYR-ee *or* IN-kwə-ree) *n. inquiries.* 1. A question.–We received many *inquiries* about the house we have to sell.
2. An investigation; a looking into.–The police are making an *inquiry* into the cause of the accident.

in•sane (in-SAYN) *adj.; insanely, adv.* 1. Mentally sick; not able to think of things as they are; not able to reason properly.–Doctors can help *insane* people get well.
2. Foolish and silly.–The ten-year-old boy had the *insane* idea of running away to join the army.

in•sect (IN-sekt) *n. insects.* A tiny animal with six jointed legs and, in most cases, wings. *Insects'* bodies have three parts or sections. Ants and bees are *insects.*

in•sert (in-SERT) *v. inserts, inserted, inserting.* Put in.–Mary spelled the word "sweet" with one "e," and later *inserted* another "e" to correct it.–Mother *inserted* a piece of cloth in the back of Bob's coat to make it bigger.

in•side (in-SYD) *n. insides, adj., adv.,* and *prep.* 1. The side that is in, not out.–The *inside* of Bob's coat is lined with fur.–The *inside* of the cupboard is painted red; the outside is painted white.
2. To or on the inside of.–Mother put her money *inside* her purse.–We went *inside* to eat.
3. Privately known; secret.–Bill told Jack he had *inside* information about the arithmetic marks.

in•sig•ni•a (in-SIG-nee-ə) *n. pl.* Badges or special emblems worn by soldiers or other people to show their rank or branch of service, or to show that they have done something outstanding.

in•sist (in-SIST) *v. insists, insisted, insisting.* Make a point of wanting a thing done and seeing that it is done.–Mother *insists* that we wear our overshoes when it rains. She tells us to wear them, and she doesn't change her mind about it.

INSIGNIA

in·sol·u·ble (in-SAHL-yə-bəl) *adj.* 1. Not capable of being dissolved.–Sugar can be dissolved in water, but oil can not be. Oil is *insoluble* in water.
2. Impossible to solve or explain.–The case of the missing person seemed *insoluble.* No one could discover how or why the man disappeared.

in·spect (in-SPEKT) *v. inspects, inspected, inspecting.* Look closely and carefully at, to be sure it is as it should be.–Our teacher *inspects* our hands each morning to see if they are clean.–Father *inspects* tools at the factory. He examines them to see if they are in good condition.

in·spec·tion (in-SPEK-shən) *n. inspections.* A close looking over, to be sure that things are as they should be.–The soldiers lined up for morning *inspection.*–The *inspection* of airplanes before they fly is very important.

in·spec·tor (in-SPEKT-er) *n. inspectors.* A person who looks over or examines things to see that they are as they should be.–Father is an *inspector* of tools in a tool factory. He looks at the tools to see if they are as they should be in every way.

in·spi·ra·tion (in-sper-AY-shən) *n. inspirations.* 1. A deep and strong desire to do something, especially something new and different.–Sally had an *inspiration* to write a poem.
2. A good influence.–Mary's music teacher is her *inspiration.* She makes Mary want to play well.

in·spire (in-SPYR) *v. inspires, inspired, inspiring.* Fill with good and uplifted feelings, and a desire to do fine things.–The minister's sermon *inspired* Grandmother. – Mother hopes the concert will *inspire* Jack to become a violinist.

in·stall (in-STAWL) *v. installs, installed, installing.* 1. Set up or fix in place.–We had a new oil burner *installed* in our home.
2. Put formally into office.–The officers of our club will be *installed* tonight.
–*installation, n. installations.*

in·stall·ment or **in·stal·ment** (in-STAWL-mənt) *n. installments* or *instalments.* One of several parts of something that goes on over a period of time.–Mary is reading the second *installment* of the magazine story.–Our car cost nineteen hundred dollars. We paid for it in *installments* of a hundred dollars a month.

in·stant (IN-stənt) *n. instants.* A moment.–Come here this *instant!*
–*adj.* Happening right away.–The poison for rats brings *instant* death. The rats die at once after eating it.

in·stant·ly (IN-stənt-lee) *adv.* At once; without any delay.–Come here *instantly!*

in·stead (in-STED) *adv.* In place (of).–Some people eat margarine *instead* of butter.–Bob came *instead* of Mary.–Joan went to church *instead* of coming here.

in·step (IN-step) *n. insteps.* The upper part of your foot between the toes and the ankle. –The *instep* of your shoe is the part that covers the *instep* of your foot.

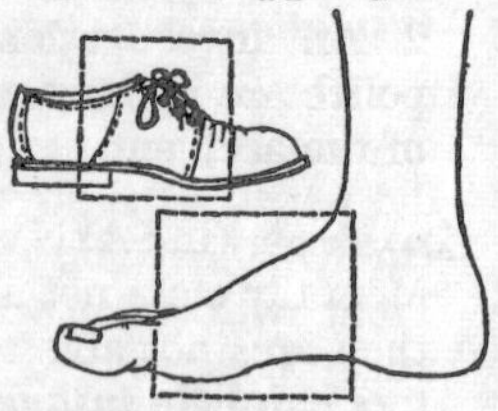

in·stinct (IN-stinkt) *n. instincts; instinctive, adj.; instinctively, adv.* 1. A natural way of behaving, used mostly when speaking of animals.–Squirrels bury nuts by *instinct.*
2. A natural talent or bent.–Even though Ellen has never studied art, she seems to have an *instinct* for design and color.

in·sti·tu·tion (in-stə-TOO-shən *or* in-stə-TYOO-shən) *n. institutions.* 1. An organization or society of any kind. There are *institutions* of learning, *institutions* for the diseased, *institutions* for orphans, etc.
2. A custom.–Father thinks marriage is a good *institution.*
3. Setting up or founding.–The children have benefited by the *institution* of a school library.

in·struct (in-STRUKT) *v. instructs, instructed, instructing.* 1. Teach.–Our teacher *instructs* us in reading.
2. Give an order to; direct.–Father *instructed* the men to dig the ditch wider.

in·struc·tion (in-STRUK-shən) *n. instructions.* 1. Teaching.–The teacher gives free *instruction* in knitting.
2. Direction.–Mother read the *instructions* for making the sweater.

in·struc·tor (in-STRUKT-er) *n. instructors.* One who teaches or instructs.–Miss King is our *instructor* in arithmetic.

in·stru·ment (IN-strə-mənt) *n. instruments.* 1. A tool; something used to work with.–Dentists use many special *instruments.*–A screwdriver is an *instrument* for putting in screws.

2. A music-making device.–Violins, violas, pianos, and cellos are musical *instruments*.
3. A means.–John, who had seen Ruth take the cookies against Mother's orders, was the *instrument* of Ruth's undoing.

in•su•late (IN-sə-layt) *v. insulates, insulated, insulating.* Protect against loss of heat or transfer of electricity.–Many homes are *insulated*. A material is placed inside the walls to keep the heat in.–Electric wires are *insulated* to prevent injury to people and damage to buildings. They are wrapped with tape, rubber, or other covering.
–*insulation, n. insulations.*

in•sult (IN-sult) *n. insults.* A very rude act or remark, meant to offend.–The children did not like the boy's *insults*.
–(in-SULT) *v. insults, insulted, insulting.* Treat with great scorn and rudeness.–The angry boy *insulted* the other children. He said rude things to them.

in•sur•ance (in-SHUHR-ənss) *n.* and *adj.* An amount of money paid for protection against loss in case of accident, fire, theft, death, damage by storm, or whatever misfortune the *insurance* is to cover. A person agrees to pay an *insurance* company a certain amount of money at regular times. The company, in turn, agrees to pay the person a certain amount in case the misfortune the *insurance* is arranged to cover should happen. The amount you pay to the company is called *insurance* or premium. The amount you receive from the company is called *insurance* or indemnity.–We pay $27.50 a year for fire *insurance*. When our garage burned, the *insurance* company paid us *insurance* of $450.

in•sure (in-SHUHR) *v. insures, insured, insuring.* Protect by insurance; arrange to pay an insurance company a certain amount of money so that, if harm comes to someone or something, the insurance company will pay back a larger amount of money.–Mother *insured* her fur coat.–Our garage was *insured* for $450.

in•tact (in-TAKT) *adj.* Not injured; not touched; whole.–When the girl dropped the box of glasses, the glasses, surprisingly, remained *intact*. Not a single one was broken.

in•teg•ri•ty (in-TEG-rə-tee) *n.* 1. Quality of being honest and upright even when it is easy to do the wrong thing and get away with it.–Tom is a boy of *integrity* He took the ten dollars he found to the police so that the owner might claim the money.
2. Completeness.–The exploring party maintained its *integrity* through many misfortunes. No one left it.

in•tel•lect (IN-tə-lekt) *n. intellects; intellectual, adj.* 1. The power of reasoning, thinking, knowing, or understanding.–Man uses his *intellect* to understand problems and to solve them.
2. Intelligence or mental ability.–A scholar is a man of *intellect*.
3. A person having high intelligence or great mental ability.–Albert Einstein, the famous scientist, was one of the great *intellects* of the twentieth century.

in•tel•li•gence (in-TEL-ə-jənss) *n.* 1. Ability to learn or understand things.–The bright boy has high *intelligence*.
2. Information; knowledge. – On receiving the *intelligence* that his wife was ill, Mr. Jones flew home.–The general received the *intelligence* from agents abroad that the enemy was about to attack.

in•tel•li•gent (in-TEL-ə-jənt) *adj.; intelligently, adv.* Able to understand and learn.–It was *intelligent* of Spot to learn how to open the door with his paw.

in•tend (in-TEND) *v. intends, intended, intending.* 1. Plan; mean.–Bob *intends* to go to Grandmother's on Saturday if it doesn't rain.
2. Do a thing purposely; mean to do a thing.
–Mary did not *intend* to hurt your feelings.

in•tense (in-TENSS) *adj.; intensely, adv.* 1. Very great; deep; very strong.–The injured man suffered *intense* pain.–The hunters in the north felt the *intense* cold.
2. Strongly interested; giving much attention.–Bob is an *intense* worker. He is eager and serious about his work.

in•tent (in-TENT) *adj.; intently, adv.* Deeply interested; giving strict attention.–Mary was so *intent* on her practicing that she did not hear Jack come up behind her.

in•ten•tion (in-TEN-shən) *n. intentions; intentional, adj.; intentionally, adv.* A purpose.
–Bob accidentally broke a glass. It was not his *intention* to break it.

in•ter•cept (in-ter-SEPT) *v. intercepts, intercepted, intercepting.* 1. Seize before arrival at a destination, especially along the way.–The message was *intercepted* by the enemy. It never reached our headquarters.
2. Halt; block; check.–The police *intercepted* everyone attempting to leave the office building after the robbery.

in•ter•est (IN-ter-əst) *n. interests.* 1. A desire to know about a thing.—The class took a great *interest* in their teacher's getting married.—Mary has no *interest* in arithmetic. She would just as soon never hear about it.
2. Advantage; benefit.—It is in your *interest* to listen when your teacher explains a problem.—A lawyer looked after our legal *interests* when we bought the property. He made sure we were treated fairly and honestly.
3. A share; a part.—Father owns an *interest* in Grandfather's farm.
4. Money paid for the use of money.—Father paid six dollars per year *interest* on a hundred dollars which he borrowed from the bank.
—*v. interests, interested, interesting.* Get the attention of.—The story of Huckleberry Finn *interests* most boys. They want to know all about it.

in•ter•est•ing (IN-trəst-ing) *adj.; interestingly, adv.* Holding one's thought and attention.—Bob is reading an *interesting* story. It makes him anxious to know what will happen next.

in•ter•fere (in-ter-FIR) *v. interferes, interfered, interfering.* 1. Try to do another person's work or handle his affairs when he wants to take care of them himself; meddle.—Mother never *interferes* with other people's business. She does not try to help unless people need help and want it.
2. Prevent by coming at the same time or being in the same place.—The deep snow *interfered* with our plans to go ice skating.
—*interference, n. interferences.*

in•te•ri•or (in-TIR-ee-er) *n. interiors* and *adj.* The inside; the inner part.—The *interior* of a country is the part near the middle, the part away from the border or coastline.—The *interior* of our house is cool, even on a hot day.

in•ter•jec•tion (in-ter-JEK-shən) *n. interjections.* 1. Something inserted or added in between, usually in speaking.—The classroom discussion was interrupted occasionally by *interjections* from the teacher. She asked us a number of questions.
2. An exclamation or sudden cry, such as: Oh! Hurrah! Ouch!

in•ter•mis•sion (in-ter-MISH-ən) *n. intermissions.* 1. The interval during which activity or action stops; a pause, like that between the acts of a play.—During the *intermission* we all went back to stand in the theater lobby.
2. Temporary halt; interruption.—The clock has been ticking for years without *intermission.* It has never stopped.

in•ter•nal (in-TER-nəl) *adj.; internally, adv.* Inside; having to do with the insides.—When it says on a medicine bottle "Not for *internal* use," it means one should not swallow it.

in•ter•na•tion•al (in-ter-NASH-ən-əl) *adj.; internationally, adv.* Concerned with relations between, or among, two or more nations.—The United Nations is an *international* organization.—*International* law is the group of laws agreed to by many nations to govern relations between them.

in•ter•plan•e•tar•y (in-ter-PLAN-ə-tair-ee) *adj.* Between planets; having to do with the regions of the planets.—Advances in science are bringing man closer and closer to *interplanetary* travel. — Travelers through space will ride in *interplanetary* vehicles, or spaceships.

in•ter•pret (in-TER-prət) *v. interprets, interpreted, interpreting.* 1. Give the meaning of; explain.—Bob tried to *interpret* the sentence for the class. He tried to tell what it meant.
2. Translate; put into a different language.—What the man said in French had to be *interpreted* in English so that we could understand it.
3. Show the meaning of something for others.—A musician *interprets* music. He tries to bring out for his hearers the feeling or meaning the composer wanted brought out.

in•ter•rog•a•tive (in-tə-RAHG-ə-tiv) *n. interrogatives.* A word used in asking questions, such as who? or what?
—*adj.* Expressing a question.—"Are you coming?" is an *interrogative* sentence. It asks a question.

in•ter•rupt (in-tə-RUPT) *v. interrupts, interrupted, interrupting.* Do something that suddenly stops or hinders what is being done or happening; break in on.—While I was talking on the telephone, someone else who wanted to use the phone *interrupted* me.—It is not polite to *interrupt* someone who is talking.—A rainstorm *interrupted* the picnic.

in•ter•rup•tion (in-tə-RUP-shən) *n. interruptions.* A sudden breaking in on or stopping; a remark or happening which breaks into something already going on.—The storm caused an *interruption* in the ball game.—Your *interruptions*, Joan, make it very hard to understand what Betty is telling us.

in•ter•sect (in-ter-SEKT) *v. intersects, intersected, intersecting.* Cut across; divide by crossing or passing through.—Johnson Avenue *intersects* Maple Street a block from my house. It crosses Maple Street there.

in•ter•sec•tion (in-ter-SEK-shən) *n. intersections.* The act or place of cutting across, or intersecting.—There is a traffic light at the *intersection* of Johnson Avenue and Maple Street. It is a busy *intersection.*

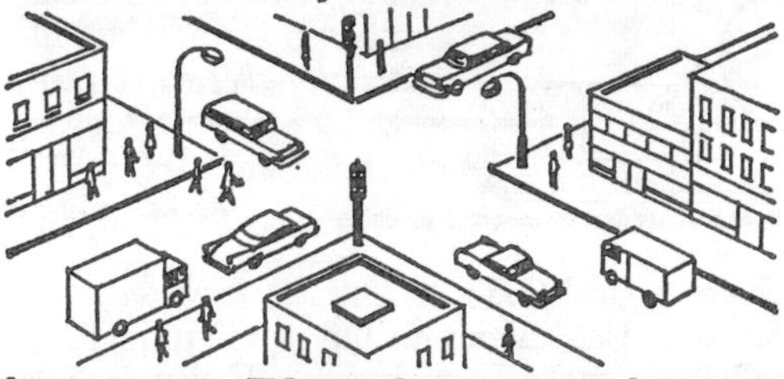

in•ter•val (IN-ter-vəl) *n. intervals.* 1. A space in between, or a length of time in between.—The chairs were set around the room at *intervals* of about three feet.—The doctor's appointments were spaced at *intervals* of fifteen minutes.
2. In music, the distance between two notes in the scale.

in•ter•view (IN-ter-vyoo) *v. interviews, interviewed, interviewing.* Meet and talk face to face with someone, usually for the purpose of getting information.—The television news reporter *interviewed* the senator about the new tax law. He asked the senator questions which brought out new facts and the senator's own opinion as to what should be done.
—*interview, n. interviews.*

in•tes•tine (in-TESS-tən) *n. intestines.* The bowels; the tubelike part of the body's alimentary canal which help to change the food one eats so that the body can use it. The *intestines* also pass out the waste which cannot be used by the body.

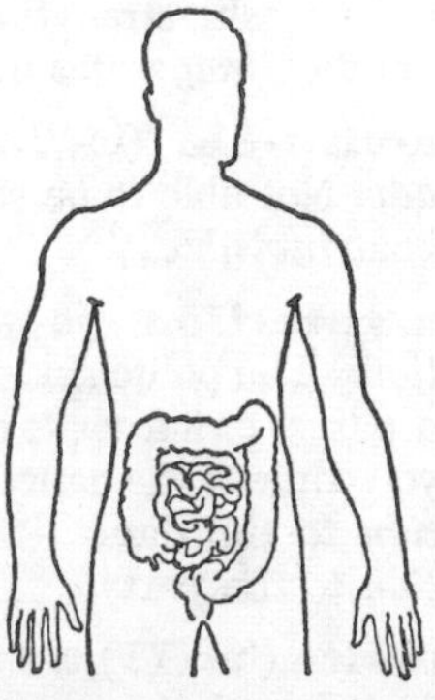

in•ti•mate (IN-tə-mət) *adj.; intimately, adv.* Very close and familiar.—Ruth is Mary's *intimate* friend. They know each other very well.
—(IN-tə-mayt) *v. intimates, intimated, intimating.* Hint.—The teacher *intimated* that she knew John's absence hadn't been caused by sickness. She asked if he had enjoyed the ball game.

in•to (IN-too) *prep.* 1. Toward and in; to the inside of.—The children went *into* the house when it began to rain.
2. *Into* describes a change from one kind of thing to another.—Churning changes cream *into* butter.—Spring passed *into* summer.

in•tol•er•ant (in-TAHL-er-ənt) *adj.; intolerantly, adv.; intolerance, n.* Not tolerant; unwilling to let others think or practice anything that differs from one's own thoughts or practices; impatient of or unkind about any difference, such as those of race or way of speaking.—Getting to know more about people often helps those who are *intolerant* to change their views.

in•tox•i•cate (in-TAHKS-ə-kayt) *v. intoxicates, intoxicated, intoxicating.* 1. Make drunk with alcohol.—Drinking too much whiskey will *intoxicate* one.
2. Make very excited.—The sense of freedom so *intoxicated* the released prisoner that he forgot where he was going and lost his way.
—*intoxication, n.*

in•tro•duce (in-trə-DOOSS *or* -DYOOSS) *v. introduces, introduced, introducing.* 1. Present; bring one person to another so that they will get to know one another.—Bob *introduced* his mother to the new teacher.
2. Bring in.—The new witness *introduced* more facts about the accident.—Firecrackers were first *introduced* into the United States from China.
3. Bring to notice.—The dancers are *introducing* a new kind of dance.
4. Begin.—The minister *introduced* his sermon with a quotation from the Bible.

in•tro•duc•tion (in-trə-DUK-shən) *n. introductions.* 1. The act of making things known to people, or of making people known to each other.—I will give you a letter of *introduction* to my friend in France.—Before the *introduction* of electric lights, people used lamps, candles, or gas lights.
2. The beginning or first part.—The *introduction* to the book told about the writer.

in•trude (in-TROOD) *v. intrudes, intruded, intruding.* 1. Force or push (something) in or upon.—The stranger *intruded* his views in the discussion of plans which had nothing to do with him.
2. Go where one is not invited, welcome, or wanted.—I am sorry to have entered your office when you were talking to someone else. I didn't mean to *intrude.*
—*intrusion, n. intrusions.*

INVENTIONS

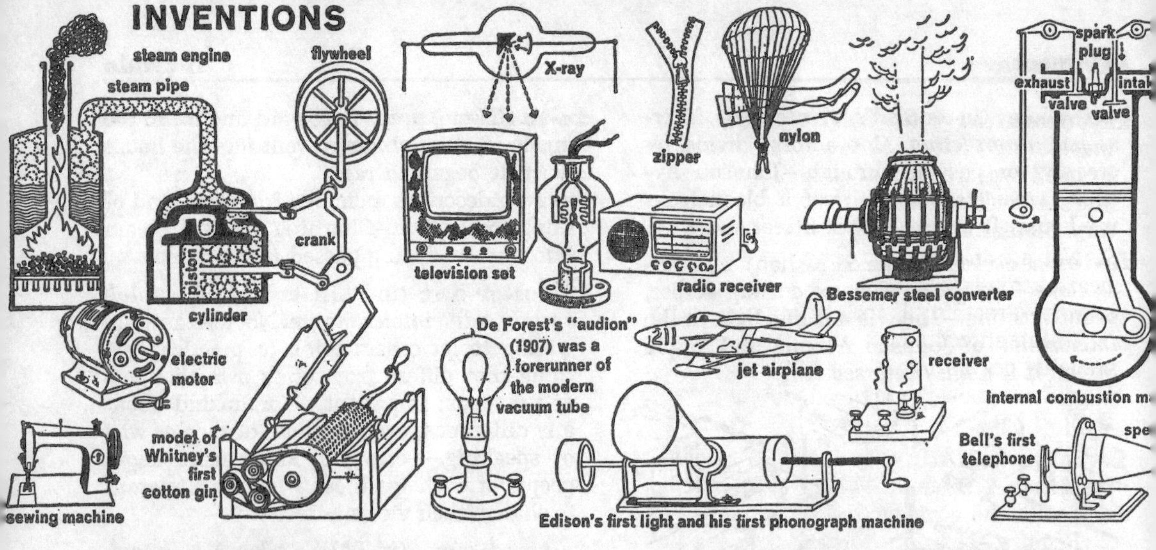

in•vade (in-VAYD) *v. invades, invaded, invading.* 1. Go in by force and take over.–The enemy *invaded* the country.
2. Interfere with; meddle with.–Do not *invade* the rights of others.
–*invasion, n. invasions.*

in•va•lid (IN-və-lid) *n. invalids.* A sick person; one who needs to be cared for.–The old man was a helpless *invalid* after he lost the use of his legs.

in•vent (in-VENT) *v. invents, invented, inventing.* 1. Plan and make something that has never been made before.–Alexander Bell *invented* the telephone.
2. Imagine; make up in the mind.–Writers *invent* stories.

in•ven•tion (in-VEN-shən) *n. inventions.*
1. Something planned and made for the first time, by skill and imagination; something invented or imagined.–The tractor is a wonderful *invention* for the farmer.
2. Inventing; thinking up and making.–The *invention* of radio took many years.

in•ven•tor (in-VENT-er) *n. inventors.* A person who thinks up and makes new things.–Thomas Edison, who invented the electric light, was an *inventor.*

in•ven•to•ry (IN-vən-tor-ee) *n. inventories.*
1. A list of goods, property, or merchandise including information such as price, value, quality, and quantity.–An *inventory* of his merchandise was made by the storekeeper before and after the sale.
2. All the things so listed.–The merchant's *inventory* was much smaller after his sale. He had few goods left.

in•ver•te•brate (in-VER-tə-brit *or* -brayt) *n. invertebrates.* An animal without a backbone. Worms and insects are *invertebrates.*

in•vest (in-VEST) *v. invests, invested, investing.* Use money to buy something that will help make more money.–If you *invest* seventy-five dollars in certain Government bonds, each will earn twenty-five dollars for you in about nine years. You will get a hundred dollars for each bond.–She *invested* in a plot of ground. She bought it and hoped to be able to sell it later at a higher price.
–*investment, n. investments.*

in•ves•ti•gate (in-VESS-tə-gayt) *v. investigates, investigated, investigating.* Look into; examine; find out about.–Father *investigated* the noise in the attic to find out what made it.
–*investigation, n. investigations.*

in•vig•or•ate (in-VIG-ə-rayt) *v. invigorates, invigorated, invigorating.* Give energy or life to; refresh; strengthen.–A cool swim on a hot day *invigorates* most people.

in•vis•i•ble (in-VIZ-ə-bəl) *adj.; invisibly, adv.* Not able to be seen.–The fog made the boat *invisible.*

in•vi•ta•tion (in-və-TAY-shən) *n. invitations.* The polite asking of someone to attend a party, pay a visit, or do something.–"Will you come to the dance with me?" is an *invitation* to the dance.–She received an *invitation* to the party.

in•vite (in-VYT) *v. invites, invited, inviting.*
1. Ask someone to come to a party or to visit; politely ask someone to do something.–Bob will *invite* his teacher to the party.–Dick *invited* us to tell him what we thought of his plan.
2. Call for; give cause for.–Jack's bad behavior *invited* punishment from his father.
3. Tempt.–On hot summer days the sight of the pool *invites* us to swim.

in•vol•un•tar•y (in-VAHL-ən-tair-ee) *adj.; involuntarily, adv.* 1. Not voluntary; not done by one's own free will or choice; unwilling.–Jim's attendance at the party was *involuntary.* Mother almost had to drag him.
2. Not possible to control by the will.–Your heartbeat is *involuntary.* You cannot stop or start it.–Breathing is mostly *involuntary.*
3. Unintentional; not on purpose.–Tom's stepping on the man's toe was *involuntary.* He did not know the man was there when he stepped back.

in•volve (in-VAHLV) *v. involves, involved, involving.* 1. Include.–Three cars were *involved* in the accident.
2. Require.–Learning to play the piano *involves* many hours of practice.
3. Occupy (oneself); absorb (oneself).–John *involved* himself so deeply in his work that he forgot his appointment.
4. Mix up; entangle.–I do not want to *involve* Bob in my argument with Jack.

i•o•dine (Y-ə-dyn) *n.* A kind of dark brown medicine used on cuts and sores to kill disease germs.

i•on•o•sphere (y-AHN-əss-fir) *n.* The outer layers of the earth's atmosphere, beyond the stratosphere. The height of these layers from the earth varies at different times. The *ionosphere* extends several hundred miles above the earth's surface. It makes long-distance radio communication possible by reflecting radio waves back to earth.

I•o•wa (Y-oh-wə) *n.* A farming state in midwestern United States, important for raising corn and other grain, poultry, and cattle. *Iowa* is important also for its manufacturing of farm tools and its river shipping.

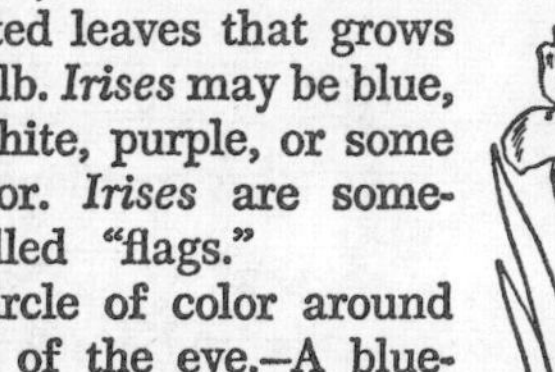

i•ris (Y-rəss) *n. irises.* 1. A flower with long, flat, pointed leaves that grows from a bulb. *Irises* may be blue, yellow, white, purple, or some other color. *Irises* are sometimes called "flags."
2. The circle of color around the pupil of the eye.–A blue-eyed person has blue *irises.*

i•ron (Y-ern) *n. irons.* 1. A hard metal from which steel is made.
2. A device for pressing cloth, usually heated by electricity. –Mother uses an *iron* for pressing our clothes.

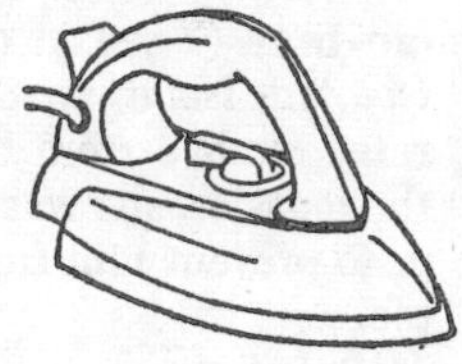

–*v. irons, ironed, ironing.* Press with an iron.–Mother *irons* our good clothes and linens.
–*adj.* 1. Made of iron.–We painted the old *iron* bedstead.
2. Strong; tough.–The aviator has *iron* nerves; he can stand almost anything.

ir•ra•di•ate (i-RAY-dee-ayt) *v. irradiates, irradiated, irradiating.* 1. Cast rays of light upon; illuminate; brighten.–Powerful searchlights *irradiated* the dark sky.
2. Treat by exposing to rays, such as X-rays or ultraviolet rays.–The doctor *irradiated* his patient's back with an ultraviolet lamp.

ir•reg•u•lar (i-REG-yə-ler) *adj.; irregularly, adv.; irregularity, n.* 1. Not even or straight; not evenly spaced.–The coastline of the lake is *irregular.*
2. Not in the usual or proper order or way; not according to the rule.–Father usually comes home at six o'clock, but tonight he came at seven. This was *irregular.*

ir•ri•gate (IR-ə-gayt) *v. irrigates, irrigated, irrigating.* Bring water to land by a system of ditches or pipes.–In dry parts of the country, farmers *irrigate* the land.
–*irrigation, n.*

ir•ri•tate (IR-ə-tayt) *v. irritates, irritated, irritating.* 1. Make nervous or angry.–Noise *irritates* Grandmother.
2. Cause to be sore.–Harsh soap *irritates* the baby's skin.
–*irritation, n. irritations.*

is (IZ) *v.* One form of the verb *be.*–Father *is* home.–Winter *is* coming.–The rose *is* red.

is•land (Y-lənd) *n. islands.* 1. A piece of land that has water all around it.–Ireland is an *island* near England.
2. Anything like an island. – The policeman stands on an *island* at the intersection and guides the traffic.

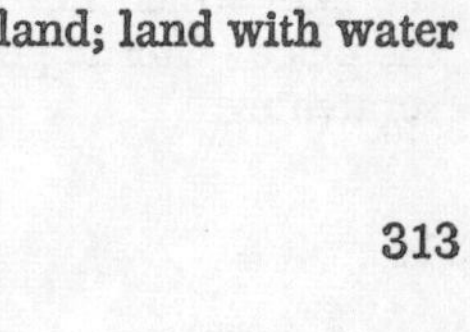

isle (YL) *n. isles.* An island; land with water all around it.

is•n't (IZ-ənt). Is not.–It *isn't* time to go yet.

i•so•late (Y-sə-layt *or* ISS-ə-layt) *v. isolates, isolated, isolating.* Set or keep apart; separate; remove from others.–When Jane had the measles, she was *isolated* from her brother to prevent him from catching the measles too.
–*isolation, n.*

is•sue (ISH-oo) *n. issues.* 1. A single printing.–His picture is in the latest *issue* of the magazine, the April *issue.*
2. A point on which people have different opinions.–Taxes will be an *issue* in the coming election.
–*v. issues, issued, issuing.* 1. Publish.–The Rescue Committee *issued* a pamphlet on its work.–The book will be *issued* in the fall.
2. Result.–A fight often *issues* from angry words.
3. Give out; pass out.–The teacher will *issue* books to us.–The general *issued* a command.
4. Come out.–Smoke *issued* from the chimneys.

isth•mus (ISS-məss) *n. isthmuses.* A narrow strip of land that connects two larger pieces of land.–The *Isthmus* of Panama connects South and Central America.

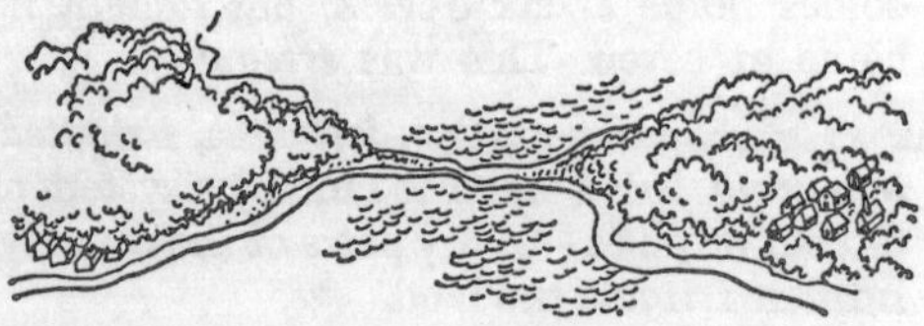

it (IT) *pron.* 1. A word used in speaking about a place, an animal, or a thing.–The snow fell fast. *It* covered the fields.–The cow is in the yard. *It* may eat all the grass.–The city is large. *It* has many beautiful parks.
2. *It* is used to tell about the weather or the general condition of any place.–*It* is raining. –*It* is hot in here.
3. *It* is time to go to bed.–*It* is not good for you to stay up late.

i•tal•ics (i-TAL-iks) *n. pl.* Any of many styles of printing type in which the letters are slanted up to the right: *This sentence is printed in italics. Italics* are often used for emphasis, or to set certain words, phrases, or sentences apart from others.

itch (ICH) *n. itches.* 1. A prickly feeling of the skin which makes one want to scratch the place.–Our dog must have an *itch.* He is scratching.
2. A disease that makes spots break out on the body.–The old beggar had the *itch.*
–*v. itches, itched, itching.* Have a prickly feeling of the skin which makes one want to scratch or rub the place.–My mosquito bite *itches.*

i•tem (Y-təm) *n. items.* 1. A separate article or thing in a list or group.–Apples, bread, and sugar are *items* on Mother's shopping list.
2. A bit of news.–Father read in the newspaper a short *item* about the fires.

i•tin•er•ar•y (y-TIN-ə-rair-ee) *n. itineraries.* 1. A route, plan, or outline of a journey.–The President's *itinerary* in Asia included India and Pakistan.
2. An account or record of a journey.–Reading her *itinerary* makes us wish we had been on the trip with her.

its (ITSS) *adj.* A word used to show that something belongs to or is a part of a thing or animal.–The bird sings. *Its* song is beautiful. –The flower is beautiful. *Its* fragrance is sweet.–The idea is not new. *Its* appeal is age-old.

it's (ITSS). It is.–*It's* raining.

it•self (it-SELF) *pron.* 1. A word used in certain cases to refer to a thing or animal.–The cat licks *itself* with its tongue.–The road curves around and crosses *itself.*
2. A word used to emphasize the word it refers to.–The box *itself* weighs a pound without anything in it.

I've (YV). I have.–*I've* traveled all over the United States.

i•vo•ry (YV-ree *or* YV-er-ee) *n. ivories* and *adj.* The substance of which tusks of the elephant and walrus are made. *Ivory* is very hard and has a whitish color. Piano keys are often made of *ivory.*

i•vy (Y-vee) *n. ivies.* A climbing plant with green leaves and no flowers.

J j

J, j (JAY) *n. J's, j's.* The tenth letter of the alphabet.

jab (JAB) *n. jabs.* A poke, punch, or stab.—Someone gave me a sharp *jab* in the back. —*v. jabs, jabbed, jabbing.* Stick into; punch; stab.—Someone *jabbed* me in the back with a pencil.

jab•ber (JA-ber) *v. jabbers, jabbered, jabbering.* Chatter; talk fast and indistinctly.—Mary told Bob that she could not understand him because he was *jabbering.*

jack (JAK) *n. jacks.* 1. A cranking device used for lifting heavy things. — Father put the *jack* under the bumper to raise the car.

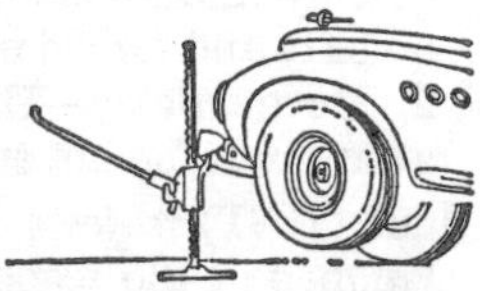

2. A nickname for John. — *Jack's* real name is John.
3. (In the plural) A game played with small, six-pronged pieces and a ball.—Children like to play *jacks.*
4. A playing card with the picture of a young man on it.—The *jacks* in a deck of cards are also called knaves.

—*v. jacks, jacked, jacking.* Lift with a jack.—It is not hard to *jack* up a heavy car with a jack.

jack•al (JAK-awl) *n. jackal* or *jackals.* A wild, doglike animal that eats other animals.

jack•et (JAK-it) *n. jackets.* 1. A short coat.—Mary wears a long coat, but Ruth wears a *jacket.*
2. Any outside covering. — When we have baked potatoes, Father eats the *jacket.*

jack•knife (JAK-nyf) *n. jackknives.* 1. A large folding knife.—Bob carries a *jackknife* in his pocket.
2. A forward dive during which the diver touches his feet with his hands and then straightens out before entering the water.

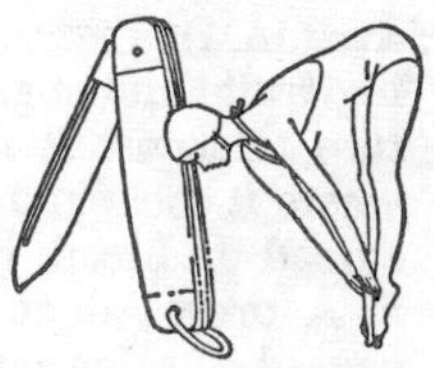

jack-o'-lan•tern (JAK-ə-lan-tern) *n. jack-o'-lanterns.* A hollowed-out pumpkin with a face cut into it and a light inside.—On Halloween the children make *jack-o'-lanterns.*

jack rab•bit (JAK rab-ət) *jack rabbits.* A kind of hare that looks like a long-legged, long-eared rabbit.

jack•straws (JAK-strawz) *n.* A game of picking up small sticks one at a time from a jumbled pile without disturbing the rest of the sticks in the pile.

jade (JAYD) *n. jades.* A kind of green stone used in making jewelry.—Mary has a necklace of *jade.*
—*adj.* The color of jade.—Mother has a *jade* dress.

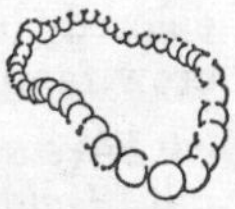

jag•ged (JAG-gid) *adj.* Having points sticking out; having rough edges.—Bob scraped his leg on a *jagged* stone.—Mary got a *jagged* tear in her stocking when she walked through the bushes.

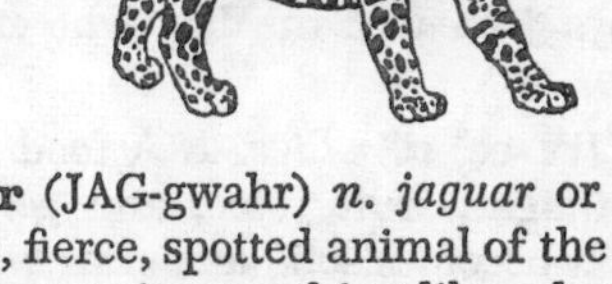

jag•uar (JAG-gwahr) *n. jaguar* or *jaguars.* A large, fierce, spotted animal of the cat family. A *jaguar* is something like a leopard.

jail (JAYL) *n. jails.* A place where prisoners are kept for small crimes, or until their trials for larger crimes.—The burglar was put in *jail* until time for his trial.

jail•er (JAYL-er) *n. jailers.* The man who has charge of a jail.

jam (JAM) *n. jams.* 1. A sweet made by cooking fruits and sugar together until the mixture thickens. It is then poured into jars, where it cools and becomes thick enough to spread on bread, put on salads, etc.
2. A crowded condition.—The accident caused a traffic *jam.*
—*v. jams, jammed, jamming.* 1. Crowd into.—A large crowd *jammed* the ball park.
2. Crush.—Bob *jammed* his finger in the door. It got caught and was bruised.

jan•i•tor (JAN-ə-ter) *n. janitors.* A caretaker of a public building or other large building.—The school *janitor* keeps our building clean.

Jan•u•ar•y (JAN-yoo-air-ee) *n. Januarys.* The first month of the year. *January* has thirty-one days.

jar (JAHR) *n. jars.* A small container with a wide opening.—Mother cans fruit in glass *jars.*
—*v. jars, jarred, jarring.* Shake; jolt.—The thunder *jarred* the whole house.

jaw (JAW) *n. jaws.* The lower part of the face.—Your *jaw* is hinged so that you can open your mouth.

jay (JAY) *n. jays.* A medium-sized, bright-colored bird of the crow family.

jeal•ous (JEL-əss) *adj.; jealously, adv.; jealousy, n.* Feeling unhappy and angry toward someone who has something which you believe you should have.—Mary is *jealous* of Baby. She feels that Baby gets all the love and attention that was once given to her.—Dick is *jealous* of Bob because Bob got a higher mark in spelling.

jeer (JIR) *n. jeers.* A mocking remark.—The *jeers* of the boys made Tom uncomfortable.
—*v. jeers, jeered, jeering.* Make fun of.—The bad boys *jeered* at the boy who made the mistake.

jel•ly (JEL-ee) *n. jellies.* 1. A food made by boiling sugar, fruit juice, and gelatine together. It becomes solid and clear when cool.—Mother makes grape *jelly* by boiling grape-juice, sugar, and gelatine together. The *jelly* will stand up in shape when taken from the glass.
2. Any jellylike substance.

jel•ly•fish (JEL-ee-fish) *n. jellyfish* or *jellyfishes.* A sea animal that has a jellylike body. Most *jellyfish* have long, stringy tentacles. A *jellyfish* does not have a backbone.

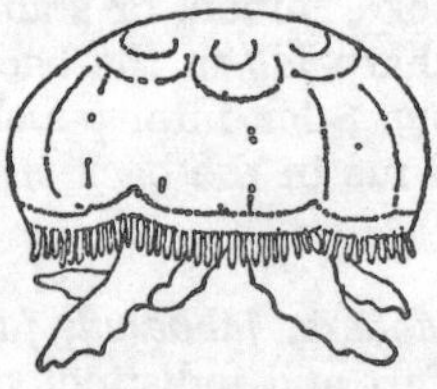

scyphozoan

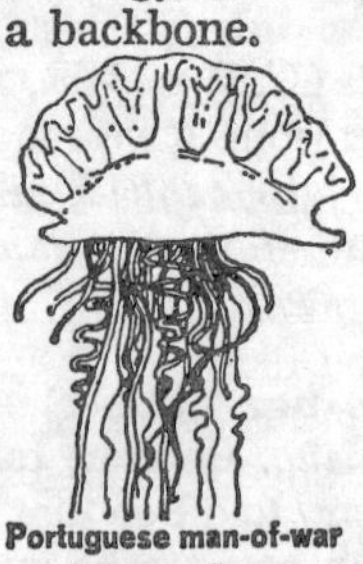

Portuguese man-of-war

jerk (JERK) *n. jerks.* A sudden, short movement.—The train stopped with a *jerk.*
—*v. jerks, jerked, jerking.* 1. Cause to jolt quickly and suddenly. —The car stopped quickly and *jerked* my head.
2. Move quickly.—The baby *jerked* her hand away from the hot stove.

jest (JEST) *n. jests.* A joke; fun.—The class laughed at the teacher's *jest.*
—*v. jests, jested, jesting.* Make a joke.—The clown *jests* about his big feet.

Je•sus (JEE-zəss) *n.* The founder of the Christian religion. You can read about *Jesus* in the New Testament of the Bible.

jet (JET) *n. jets.* 1. A shiny black substance.—The buttons on Mother's dress are made of *jet.*—*Jet*-black means solidly black.
2. A gush of liquid or gas.—Sally ran under the *jet* of water from the hose.
—Some special uses of this word are:
1. A *jet engine* is an engine which achieves a forward driving power from jets of hot air and gases that are shot out through the rear of the engine. These gases are produced by burning fuel.
2. A *jet plane* is a plane powered by a jet engine.
3. *Jet-propelled* means driven by a jet engine.
4. *Jet propulsion* is shooting gas out of the back of something with such force that the thing is pushed forward.

Jew (JOO) *n. Jews.* 1. A descendant of the people who were led to Israel by Moses.
2. A person of the Jewish religion.

jew•el (JYOO-əl) *n. jewels.* A precious stone, such as a diamond, pearl, or ruby.—The rich woman wears many *jewels.*

jew·el·er or **jew·el·ler** (JYOO-əl-er) *n. jewelers* or *jewellers.* A person who makes jewelry; one who sells jewels.

jew·el·ry (JYOO-əl-ree) *n.* Brooches, rings, and other ornaments, often set with precious or pretty stones.

Jew·ish (JOO-ish) *adj.* Of the Jews.

jig (JIG) *n. jigs.* A kind of lively dance.

jig saw (JIG saw) *jig saws.* A sawing machine. You can guide your piece of wood against the moving blade and cut any shape you like.
–*jigsaw, adj.* A *jigsaw* puzzle is a puzzle with strangely shaped pieces that were cut by a jig saw.

jin·gle (JIN-gəl) *n. jingles.* 1. A tinkling sound.–We heard the *jingle* of the bells.
2. A rhyme.–Our teacher reads *jingles* to us. "Jack and Jill went up the hill" is a *jingle.*
–*v. jingles, jingled, jingling.* Make something ring or tinkle.–Bob *jingled* his pennies.

jin·rik·i·sha or **jin·rick·sha** (jin-RIK-shaw) *n. jinrikishas* or *jinrickshas.* A small, hooded, two-wheeled carriage which a man pulls. *Jinrikishas* are used for public transportation in certain Asiatic countries.

job (JAHB) *n. jobs.* 1. Regular work. – My brother has a *job* as an office boy. He is paid to help around an office.
2. Piece of work. – Repairing the streets is a big *job.*

JETS

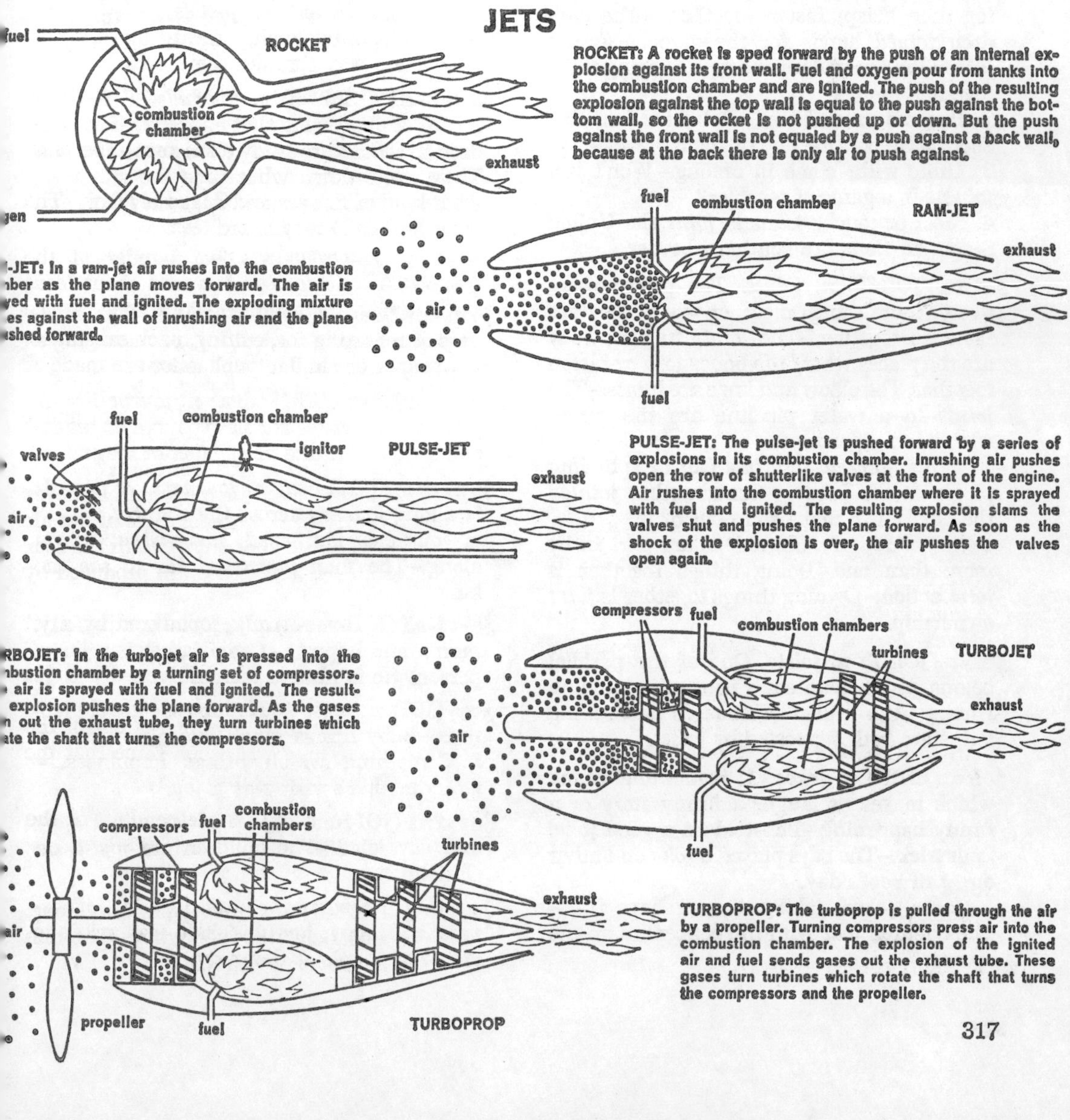

ROCKET: A rocket is sped forward by the push of an internal explosion against its front wall. Fuel and oxygen pour from tanks into the combustion chamber and are ignited. The push of the resulting explosion against the top wall is equal to the push against the bottom wall, so the rocket is not pushed up or down. But the push against the front wall is not equaled by a push against a back wall, because at the back there is only air to push against.

-JET: In a ram-jet air rushes into the combustion nber as the plane moves forward. The air is yed with fuel and ignited. The exploding mixture es against the wall of inrushing air and the plane shed forward.

PULSE-JET: The pulse-jet is pushed forward by a series of explosions in its combustion chamber. Inrushing air pushes open the row of shutterlike valves at the front of the engine. Air rushes into the combustion chamber where it is sprayed with fuel and ignited. The resulting explosion slams the valves shut and pushes the plane forward. As soon as the shock of the explosion is over, the air pushes the valves open again.

RBOJET: In the turbojet air is pressed into the nbustion chamber by a turning set of compressors. air is sprayed with fuel and ignited. The result- explosion pushes the plane forward. As the gases n out the exhaust tube, they turn turbines which ate the shaft that turns the compressors.

TURBOPROP: The turboprop is pulled through the air by a propeller. Turning compressors press air into the combustion chamber. The explosion of the ignited air and fuel sends gases out the exhaust tube. These gases turn turbines which rotate the shaft that turns the compressors and the propeller.

jock•ey (JAH-kee) *n. jockeys.* A person paid to ride a horse in a horse race. *Jockeys* usually do not weigh very much.

jog (JAHG) *v. jogs, jogged, jogging.* 1. Nudge or push.–Someone *jogged* me in the ribs with his elbow.
2. Arouse; awaken.–The teacher *jogged* my memory about the work that was not done. She reminded me that it was not done.
3. Go forward with a bobbing movement.–The milkman's horse *jogs* along.

join (JOIN) *v. joins, joined, joining.* 1. Fix together; clasp; fasten together. – The children *joined* hands for the game. – Father *joined* the two ends of the rope by tying them together.
2. Become a member of.–Bob *joined* the Boy Scouts. He became one of them.
3. Unite with; come in among.–Won't you *join* us in a game of marbles?
4. Meet or touch.–Canada *joins* the United States on Canada's southern border.

joint (JOINT) *n. joints.* The place where two or more things meet, or where they are fastened together.–The *joints* in your body are the places where the bones join or fasten together. The elbow and knee are *joints*.–The *joints* in a water pipeline are the places where two pipes meet.
–*v. joints, jointed, jointing.* Cut or split into pieces at the joints. – Grandmother *jointed* the chicken to make soup out of it.
–*adj.; jointly, adv.* Shared; taken part in by more than one.–Doing things together is *joint* action.–Owning things together is *joint* ownership.

joist (JOIST) *n. joists.* One of the parallel beams which span each floor of a building from wall to wall. Floor boards and ceiling strips are both supported by *joists*.

joke (JOHK) *n. jokes.* 1. Something funny which makes us laugh; a funny story or a funny happening.–Bob told us a good *joke*.
2. A trick.–The boys played a *joke* on Father on April Fool's day.
–*v. jokes, joked, joking.* Tease; have fun.–The children *joke* with the policeman on the corner.

jok•er (JOHK-er) *n. jokers.* 1. A person who tells jokes, plays tricks, and teases people.
2. An extra playing card used in some card games.

jol•ly (JAH-lee) *adj. jollier, jolliest.* Happy and gay. – Jack is a *jolly* fellow. He laughs and plays and has fun.

jolt (JOHLT) *n. jolts.* Jerk.–The train stopped with a sudden *jolt*.
–*v. jolts, jolted, jolting.* Bounce roughly.–The car with a flat tire *jolted* along.

jon•quil (JAHN-kwil) *n. jonquils.* An early spring flower. *Jonquils* are white and yellow, have a pleasant odor, and grow from bulbs.

jos•tle (JAHSS-əl) *v. jostles, jostled, jostling.* Push; crowd; shove. – Bill *jostled* his way through the crowd.

jour•nal (JERN-əl) *n. journals.* 1. A daily record of everything that happens.–The children in the nature-study class kept a *journal*. They wrote down what time the sun rose, what kind of flowers and bugs they saw, and what bird calls they heard.
2. A daily newspaper; any newspaper or magazine.

jour•nal•ism (JERN-l-iz-əm) *n.* The business of reporting for, editing, or managing a newspaper or similar publication.

jour•nal•ist (JERN-ə-list) *n. journalists.* A person who writes for newspapers or magazines; an editor of a newspaper or magazine.

jour•ney (JER-nee) *n. journeys.* A trip.–It is a long *journey* across the country.
–*v. journeys, journeyed, journeying.* Travel along.–The men *journeyed* far to see the king.

jo•vi•al (JOH-vee-əl) *adj.; jovially, adv.* Jolly, merry, and happy. – Grandfather is a *jovial* person. He is always joking.

joy (JOI) *n. joys.* 1. Happiness; great gladness.–Baby brings much *joy* to the family.
2. Something which brings happiness. – Grandmother's visit was a *joy*.

joy•ful (JOI-fuhl) *adj.; joyfully, adv.* Happy and gay; glad.–The children are *joyful* on Christmas.

joy•ous (JOI-əss) *adj.; joyously, adv.; joyousness, n.* Happy; joyful.–There was a *joyous* crowd of people at the party.

ju•bi•lee (JOO-bə-lee) *n. jubilees.* A time of rejoicing and gaiety. A *jubilee* is sometimes set to celebrate some particular event or anniversary.–The people held a week of *jubilee* in honor of the young king's twenty-first birthday.

judge (JUJ) *n. judges.* 1. A person who is elected or appointed to hear all the facts about crimes or other law cases. He then decides what should be done to settle the case, or what punishment should be given.
2. A person who examines anything and decides how good or bad it is.–Let the teacher be the *judge* of the drawings.
–*v. judges, judged, judging.* Decide about the quality of a thing.–The teacher will *judge* your handwriting. She will say whether it is good.

judg•ment (JUJ-mənt) *n. judgments.* 1. Ability or intelligence about deciding what to do.–Mary showed good *judgment* in calling the doctor right away.
2. Opinion; final decision.–The teacher gave her *judgment* of the plans for the party. She liked them.
3. A court's decision.–The judge will pronounce his *judgment* when all the witnesses have been heard.

jug (JUG) *n. jugs.* A heavy pitcher or container for holding water or other liquids. – Mother buys vinegar in a *jug.*

jug•gle (JUG-əl) *v. juggles, juggled, juggling.* Do tricks which require much practice. –Bob can *juggle* five balls at once. He can keep them in the air without letting them drop to the floor.

jug•gler (JUG-ler) *n. jugglers.* A person who amuses people by doing tricks, such as keeping five or six balls moving in the air without dropping them.

jug•u•lar (JUG-yə-ler) *adj.* Part of the neck or throat. A *jugular* vein is a vein that goes through the neck carrying blood from the brain back to the heart.

juice (JOOSS) *n. juices.* The watery or liquid part of fruits, vegetables, or meat.–We drink tomato *juice* and orange *juice.*–Grandmother poured the *juice* off the roast beef to make gravy.

juic•y (JOOSS-ee) *adj. juicier, juiciest.* Containing or having much juice; not dry.–The orange was so *juicy* that it squirted when Mary squeezed it.

ju•jit•su (joo-JIT-soo) *n.* The art of combat in which the opponent's own strength and weight are turned against him. No weapons are used. The art of *jujitsu,* originally developed in China, was improved and further developed by the Japanese.

Ju•ly (juh-LY) *n. Julys.* The seventh month of the year.–*July* has thirty-one days.

jum•ble (JUM-bəl) *n. jumbles.* A mess; confused heap. – The things were not in their right places. They were in a *jumble.*
–*v. jumbles, jumbled, jumbling.* Mix up.–The things in Mother's sewing basket were *jumbled* up.

jump (JUMP) *n. jumps.* A leap or start.–Mother gave a great *jump* when she saw the mouse.
–*v. jumps, jumped, jumping.* 1. Leap; raise or throw oneself through the air without using the hands to help.–The cow *jumped* over the moon. – Frogs *jump.* – The boy *jumped* off the diving board.
2. Jerk suddenly. – Father *jumped* when Sally said "Boo!"

junc•tion (JUNK-shən) *n. junctions.* 1. The place where railroad lines meet or cross.–We met at the railroad *junction.*

2. The meeting place of highways, rivers, etc.–Turn left at the *junction* of the roads.

June (JOON) *n. Junes.* The sixth month of the year.–*June* has thirty days.

jun•gle (JUNG-gəl) *n. jungles.* Land, mostly in hot countries, which is covered by trees, vines, and bushes growing so close together that it is hard to get through them. It rains often in a *jungle.* Apes, tigers, and other wild animals live in *jungles.*

jun•ior (JOON-yer) *n. juniors* and *adj.* 1. A person younger than another.–Bill is Bob's *junior* by several years. He is several years younger.
2. A person who is in his third year in high school or college.

ju•ni•per (JOON-ə-per) *n. junipers.* An evergreen tree or shrub of the pine family. It bears blue berrylike fruit.

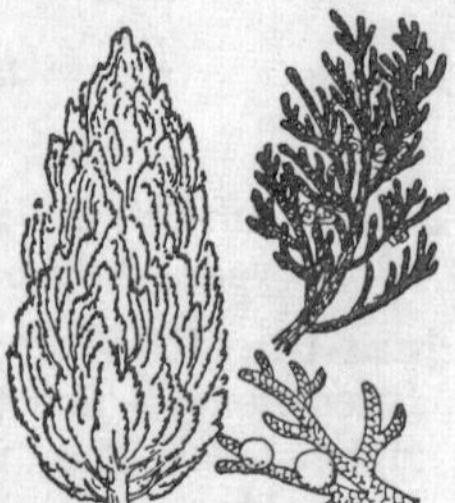

junk (JUNK) *n. junks.* 1. A Chinese sailboat.

2. Old iron, cans, paper, broken furniture, and other things that are considered useless. –The empty lot was full of *junk.*

Ju•pi•ter (JOO-pə-ter) *n.* 1. A god the ancient Romans believed was the supreme ruler of the heavens.–The Roman god *Jupiter* was known as Zeus to the ancient Greeks.
2. The largest planet known to man. *Jupiter* is the second brightest planet in our heavens and fifth away from our sun.

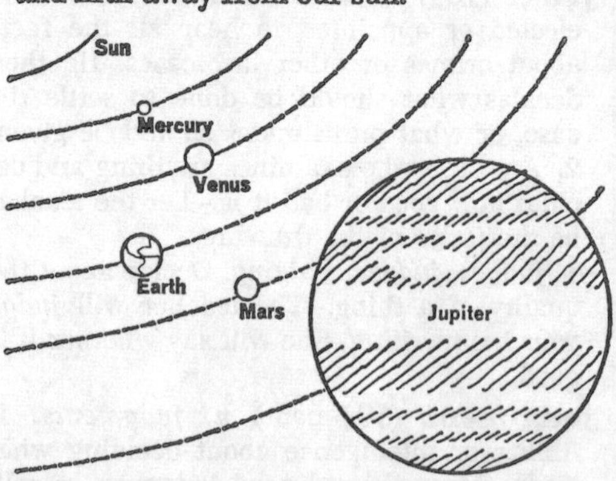

ju•ry (JUHR-ee) *n. juries.* A group of people who listen to cases in court and then decide whether the person on trial is innocent or guilty.

just (JUST) *adj.; justly, adv.* Fair.–The bad boy received *just* punishment.
–*adv.* 1. Perfectly.–These shoes *just* fit. They are exactly the right size.
2. Very recently.–I cannot eat anything; I have *just* had dinner.
3. By only a moment. – You *just* missed Mary; she left a few minutes ago.

jus•tice (JUST-əss) *n. justices.* 1. Fairness; honesty; what is right.–Bob said that there was no *justice* in the way he was treated.
2. A judge.

jus•ti•fy (JUST-ə-fy) *v. justifies, justified, justifying.* Give or be a reason for being fair or right.–Bill could not *justify* his behavior. He could not prove that he was right.–The heavy rain *justifies* your coming late. It is a fair reason for your coming late.

jut (JUT) *v. juts, jutted, jutting.* Stick out or stand out.–Jack tore his sweater on a sharp rock that *jutted* out of the cliff.

jute (JOOT) *n.* A plant from which we get a heavy fiber or thread which is also called *jute.* Ropes, burlap bags, and coarse cloth are made from *jute.*

ju•ve•nile (JOO-və-nəl *or* -nyl) *adj.* Young or youthful; suitable for young boys and girls.– A person who acts or plays youthful roles is a *juvenile* actor.–The public library has many *juvenile* books.

UNIFORMS

Roman Empire A.D. 400
England 1415
Germany 1520
France 1630
Spain 1710
France 1743
England 1758
United Colonies 1775
Sweden 1779
France 1796
Prussia 1813
United States 1862
Confederate States 1864
Canada 1885
Belgium 1914
can City 1930
Germany 1943
Russia 1948
Argentina 1950
United States 1960

FLAGS OF MANY NATIONS

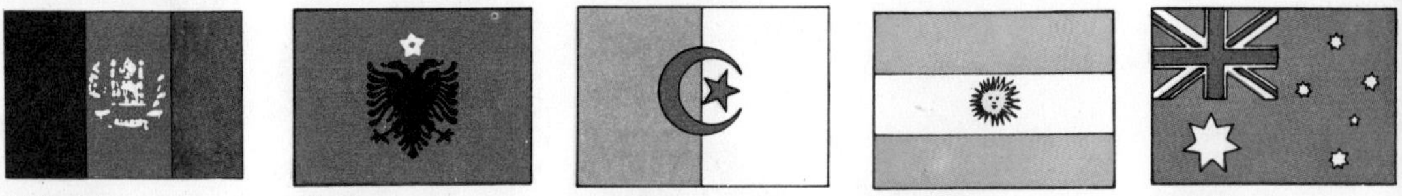

Afghanistan Albania Algeria Argentina Australia

Austria Belgium Bolivia Brazil Bulgaria

Burma Byelorussian SSR Cambodia Canada Ceylon

Chile China Colombia Costa Rica Cuba

Czechoslovakia Denmark Dominican Republic Ecuador El Salvador

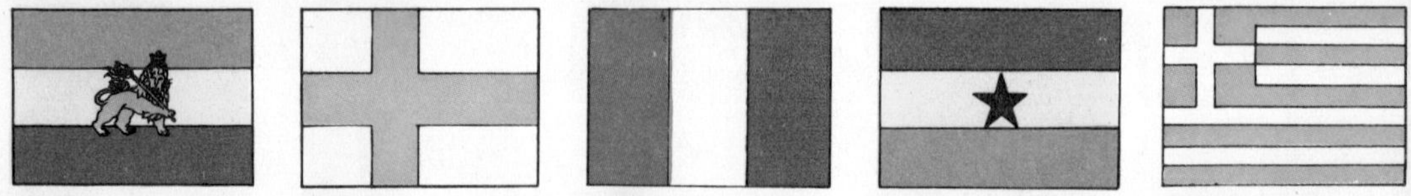

Ethiopia Finland France Ghana Greece

Guatemala Guinea Haiti Honduras Hungary

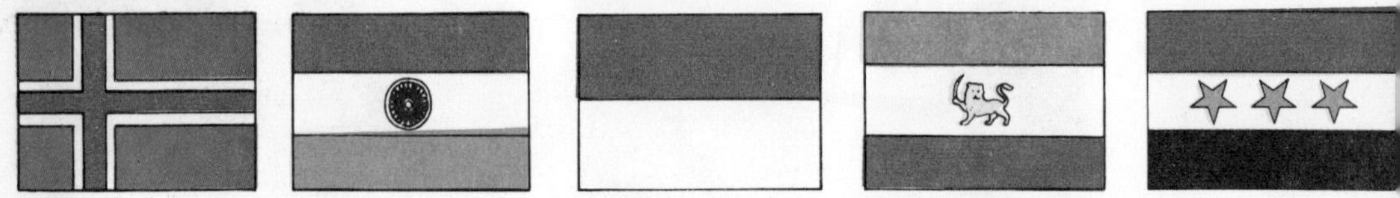

Iceland India Indonesia Iran Iraq

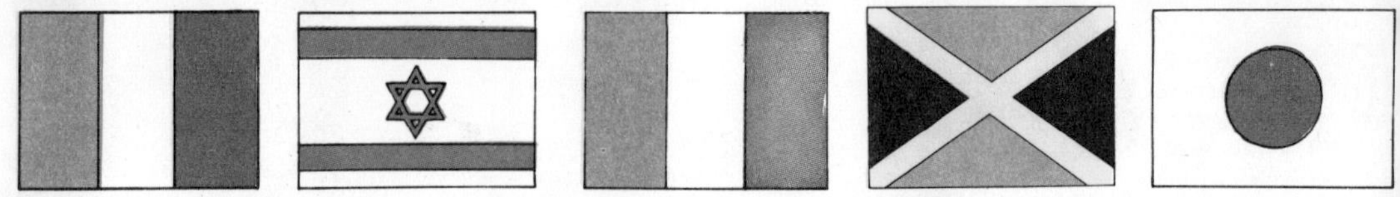

Ireland Israel Italy Jamaica Japan

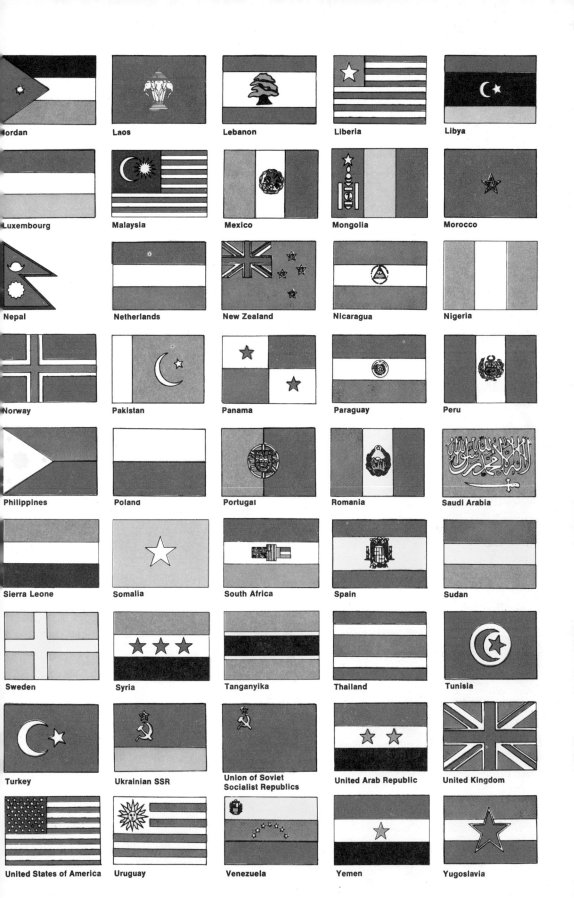

Jordan — Laos — Lebanon — Liberia — Libya

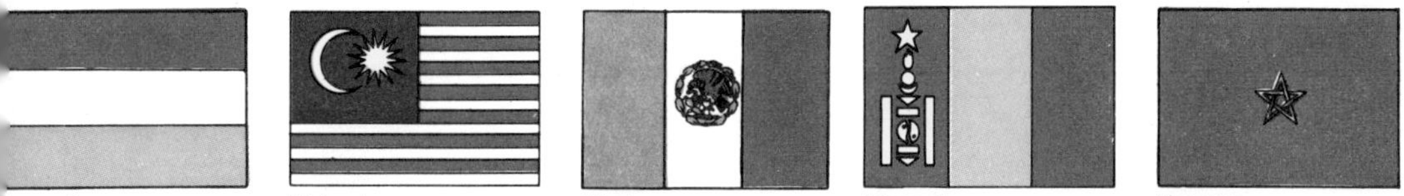

Luxembourg — Malaysia — Mexico — Mongolia — Morocco

Nepal — Netherlands — New Zealand — Nicaragua — Nigeria

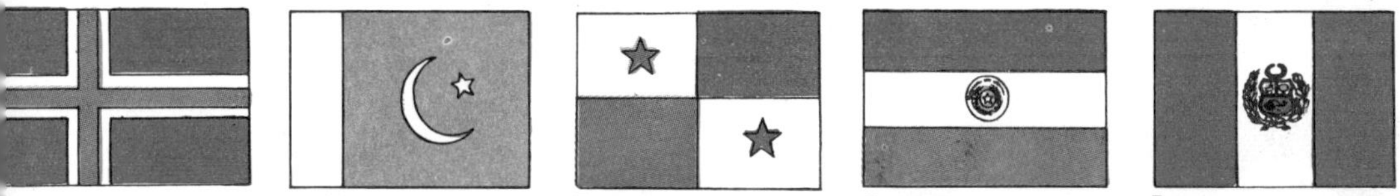

Norway — Pakistan — Panama — Paraguay — Peru

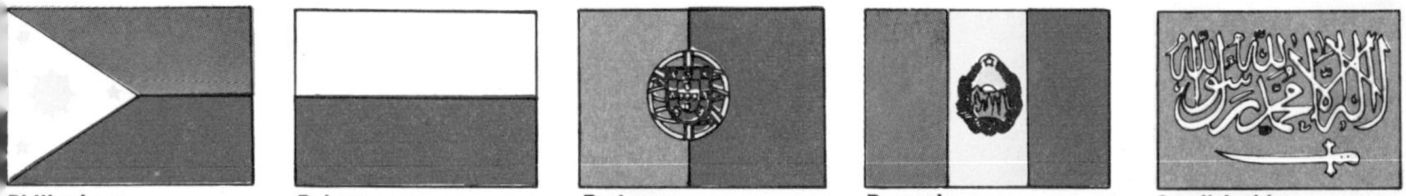

Philippines — Poland — Portugal — Romania — Saudi Arabia

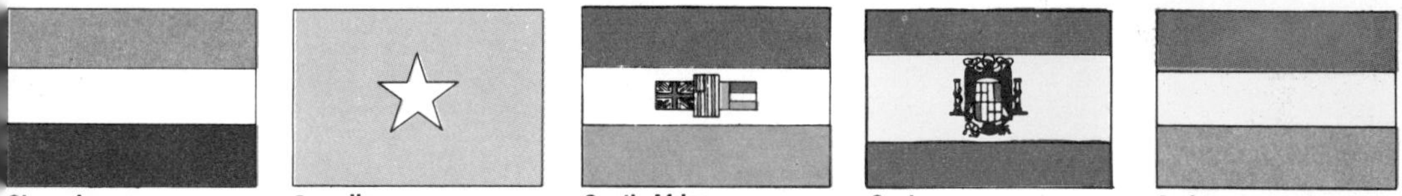

Sierra Leone — Somalia — South Africa — Spain — Sudan

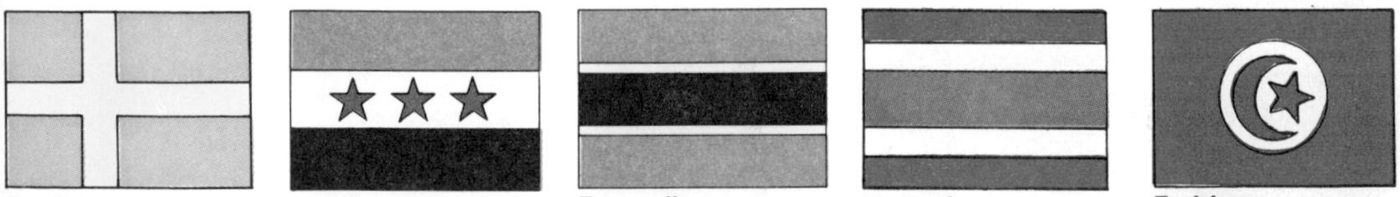

Sweden — Syria — Tanganyika — Thailand — Tunisia

Turkey — Ukrainian SSR — Union of Soviet Socialist Republics — United Arab Republic — United Kingdom

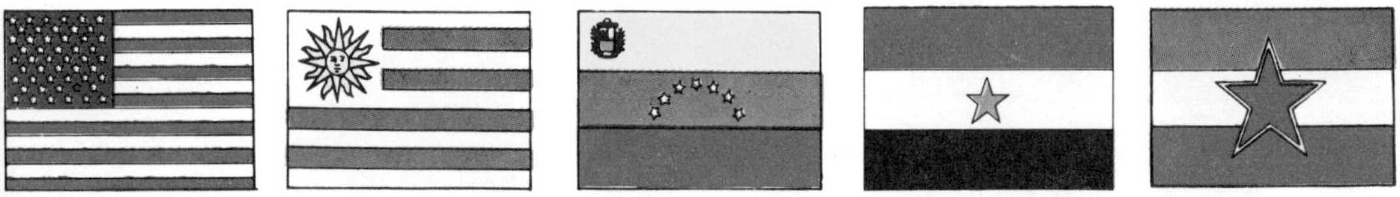

United States of America — Uruguay — Venezuela — Yemen — Yugoslavia

AIRPLANES

WORLD WAR I

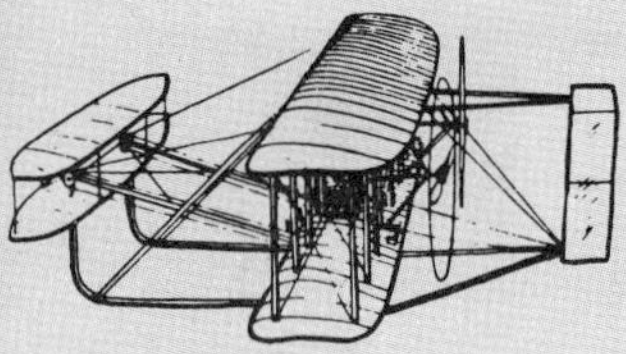

Curtiss Flier

Spad biplane

Fokker triplane

FOLLOWING WORLD WAR I (1930's)

Lindbergh's Ryan

Supermarine racer

Dornier DOX2

WORLD WAR II

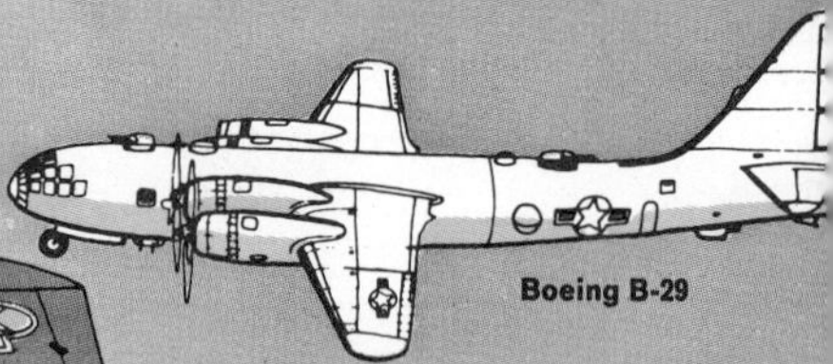

Boeing B-29

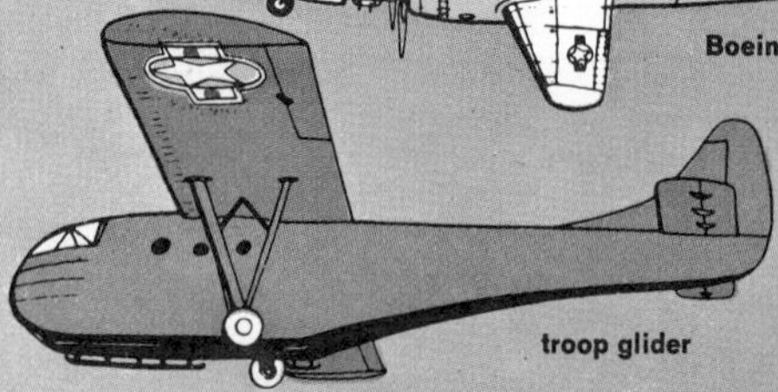

troop glider

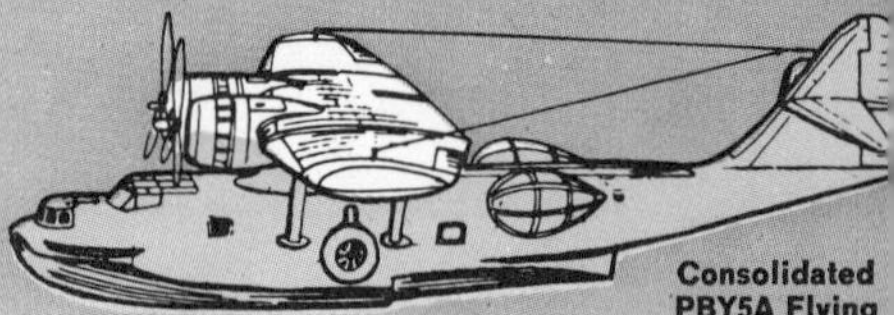

Consolidated PBY5A Flying Boat

Mustang P-51

SINCE WORLD WAR II

Piper Cub

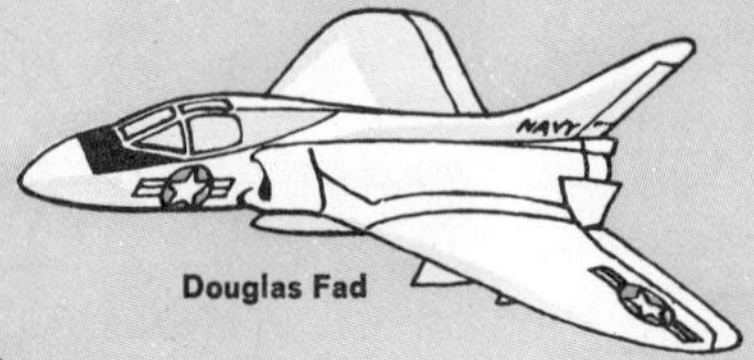

Douglas Fad

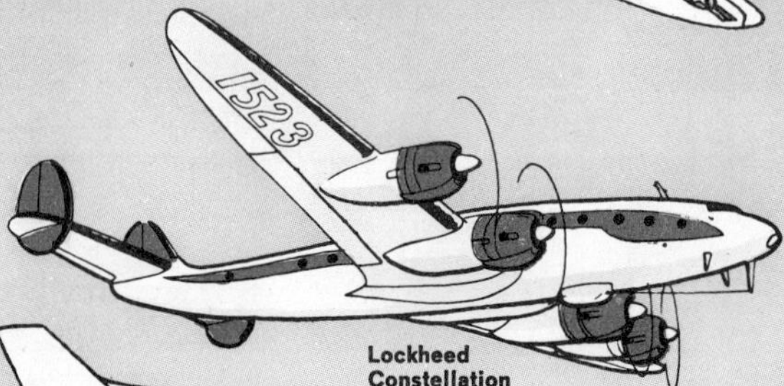

Lockheed Constellation

Boeing 707 jet

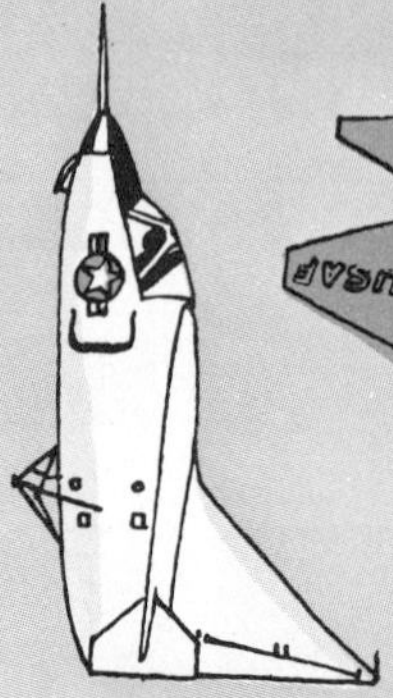

Ryan X-13 (VTOL)

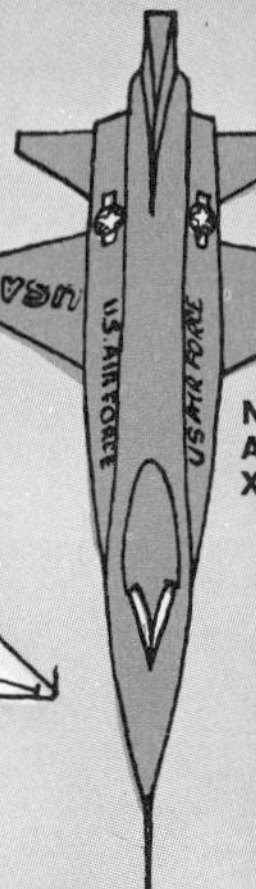

Ne
Ar
X-

Hiller X-18 (VTOL)

BOATS

tugboat
single man racing shell
basket boat
canoe
outrigger
kayak
motorboat
rowboat
sea sled
log raft
outboard motorboat
Viking ship
rboard sailboat
galley
Chinese junk
caravel
side-wheeler
river boat
PACKET BOAT COMPANY
SOUTHERN BELLE

PARTS OF A BIRD
back
rump
tail
secondaries
crown
bill
coverts
primaries
throat
back
breast
rump
side
tail
feet
BIRDS
Robin
Wren
Redheaded Woodpecker
Song Sparrow
Cedar Waxwing
Jay
Chickadee
Oriole
Hummingbird
Cardinal
Redwing
Kingfisher
Meadowlark
Whip-poor-will
Bobwhite
Sparrow Hawk
Eagle
Goldfinch
Macaw
Barn Owl
Penguin
Great Blue Heron
Stork
Ostrich
Sandpiper
Toucan
Puffin
Swan
Flamingo
Gull
Tern
Turkey
Mallard
Cormorant
Pelican
Pigeon
Mourning Dove
FEET OF SOME BIRDS COMPARED
Owl
Robin
Yellowlegs
Ptarmigan
Coot
Duck
Woodpecker
Pheasant

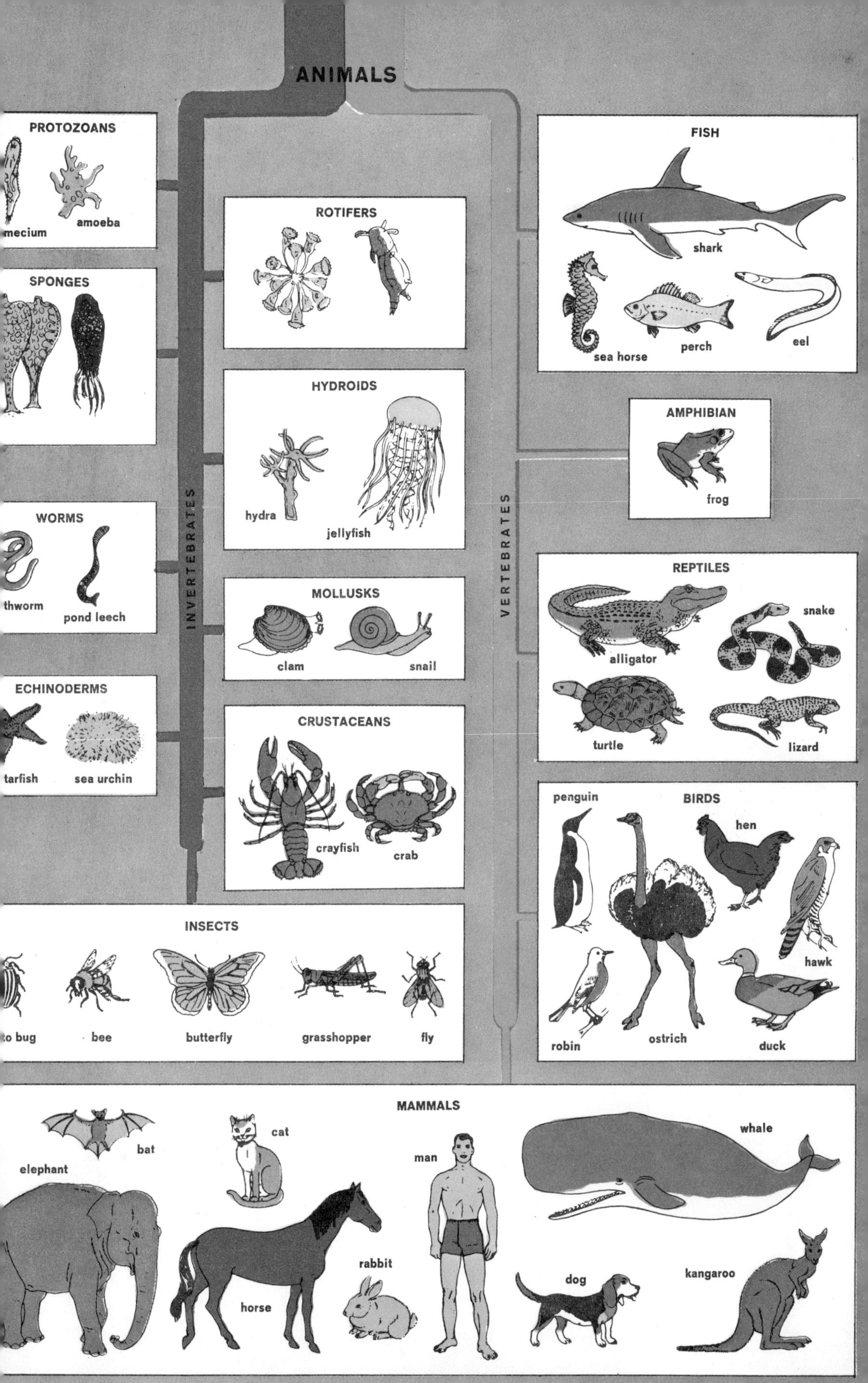
ANIMALS
INVERTEBRATES
VERTEBRATES
PROTOZOANS
mecium
amoeba
SPONGES
WORMS
thworm
pond leech
ECHINODERMS
tarfish
sea urchin
ROTIFERS
HYDROIDS
hydra
jellyfish
MOLLUSKS
clam
snail
CRUSTACEANS
crayfish
crab
INSECTS
o bug
bee
butterfly
grasshopper
fly
FISH
shark
sea horse
perch
eel
AMPHIBIAN
frog
REPTILES
alligator
snake
turtle
lizard
BIRDS
penguin
hen
hawk
robin
ostrich
duck
MAMMALS
bat
elephant
cat
man
whale
horse
rabbit
dog
kangaroo

TREES

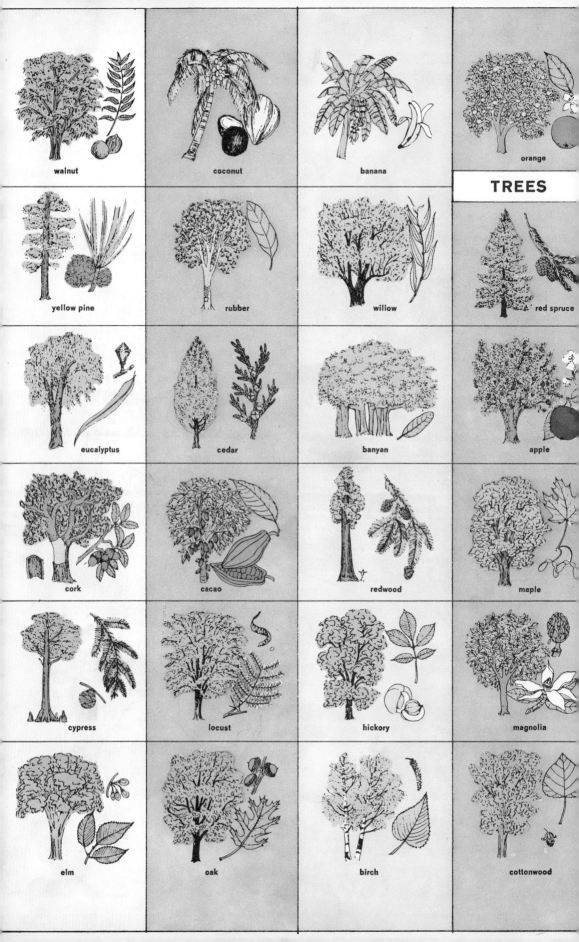

walnut

coconut

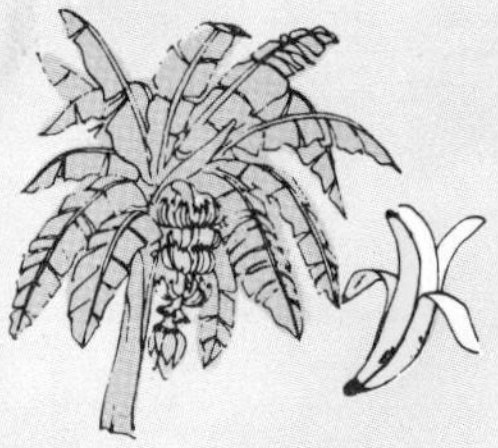
banana

orange

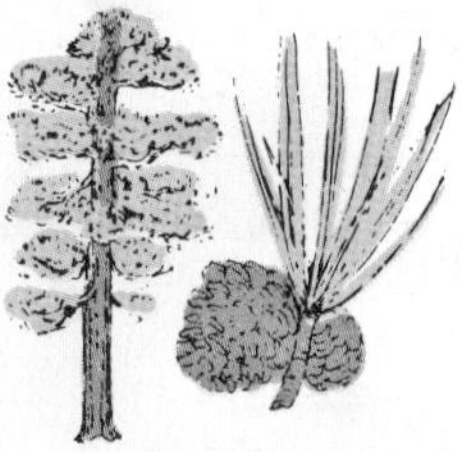
yellow pine

rubber

willow

red spruce

eucalyptus

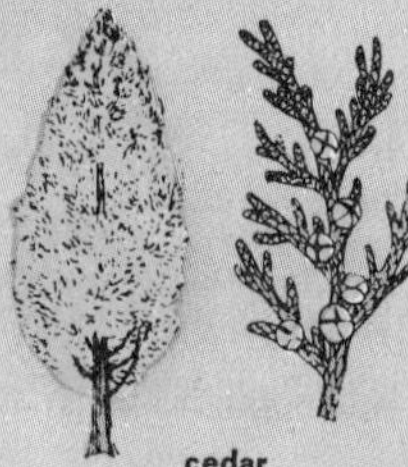
cedar

banyan

apple

cork

cacao

redwood

maple

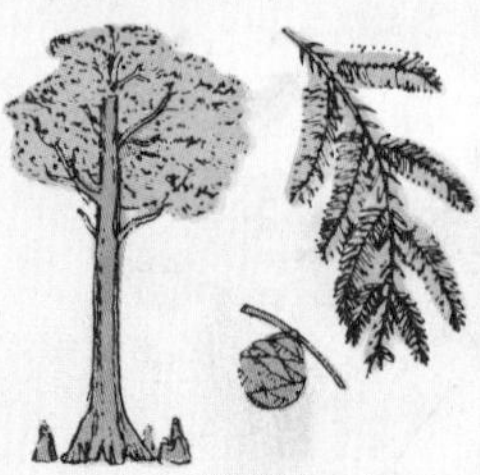
cypress

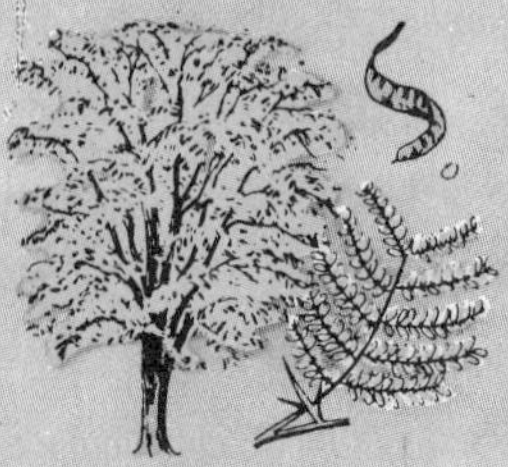
locust

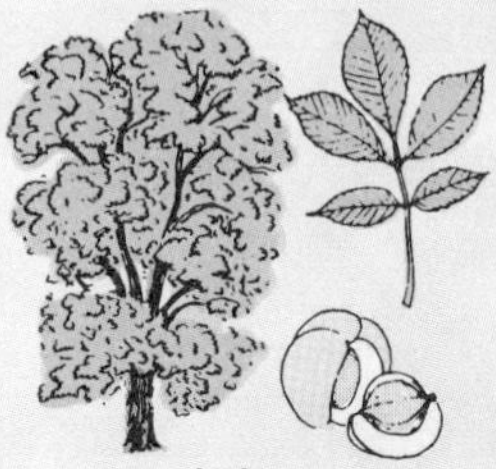
hickory

magnolia

elm

oak

birch

cottonwood

K k

K, k (KAY) *n. K's, k's.* The eleventh letter of the alphabet.

ka•lei•do•scope (kə-LY-də-skohp) *n. kaleidoscopes.* A tube containing two mirrors and many tiny bits of colored glass. You look through a hole at one end and watch the pattern change as you turn the *kaleidoscope.*

kan•ga•roo (kang-gə-ROO) *n. kangaroos.* A large animal that lives in Australia. It has short front legs, very strong back legs, and a long, thick tail. The *kangaroo* leaps something like a rabbit. He can go very fast. The mother carries her baby *kangaroo* in a pouch or pocket on the underside of her body.

Kan•sas (KAN-zəss) *n.* A flat, agricultural state in central United States. It leads all other states in raising wheat, ranks high in livestock, and has large oil and coal centers.

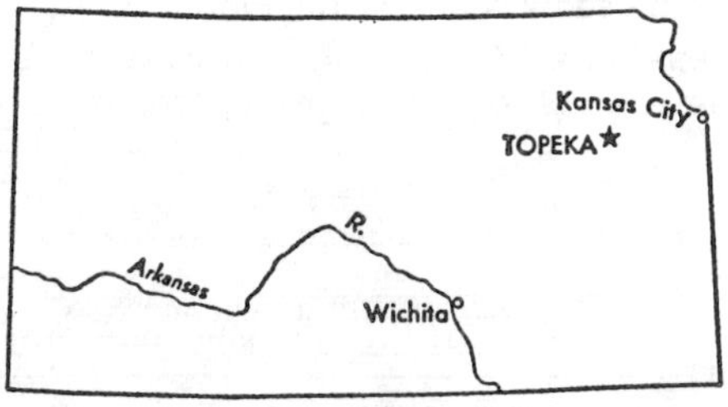

ka•ty•did (KAY-tee-did) *n. katydids.* A green insect that looks like a grasshopper. *Katydids* live in trees. They seem to call out in a shrill voice, "Katy did, Katy didn't."

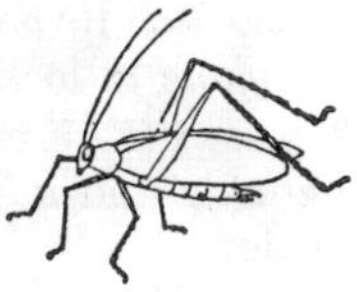

kay•ak (KY-ak) *n. kayaks.* A small boat, pointed at both ends, and covered over the top except for a hole or cockpit in the middle for a person to sit in. The Eskimos were the first to make *kayaks,* using sealskins stretched over a wooden frame.

keel (KEEL) *n. keels.* A long piece of wood or metal that goes along the bottom of a ship or boat from end to end.

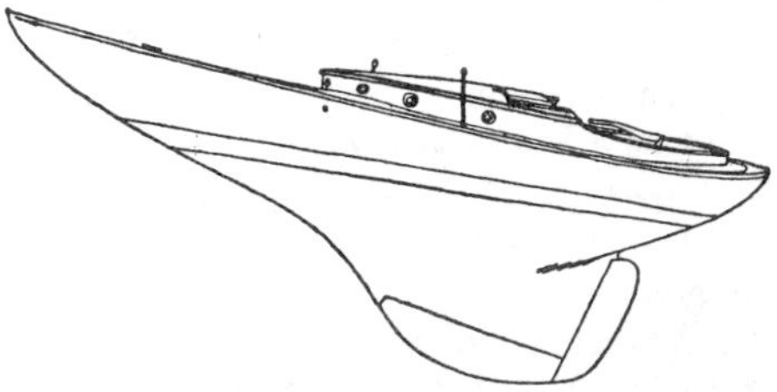

–v. keels, keeled, keeling. Turn (over).–The girl *keeled* over and fainted from the intense heat.

keen (KEEN) *adj.; keenly, adv.* 1. Sharp.–Father uses a *keen* razor blade when he shaves.
2. Sharp and biting.–The wind was *keen* as they hurried along the lake shore.
3. Quick; bright.–Bob has a *keen* mind.
4. Interested; anxious to do a thing.–The children are *keen* about reading. They are eager to read.

keep (KEEP) *n.* One's room and meals.–The man who lives at our house pays for his *keep.*
–v. keeps, kept, keeping. 1. To have for one's own as long as one wants.–Grandmother gave me a basket to *keep.*
2. Take care of regularly; maintain.–Mother *keeps* house.–Bill *keeps* rabbits.–Can you *keep* a secret?
3. Hold for a time.–I will *keep* your key until you come home.–Bob could not *keep* a straight face when he told the joke.
4. Stay.–*Keep* to the right side of the street.
5. Continue; not stop.–*Keep* trying; go on trying.
6. Celebrate; observe; show respect for.–We *keep* Christmas by going to church.
7. Put regularly; have a place for.–I *keep* the back door key in the kitchen drawer.
8. Last; stay fresh.–We must eat the peaches soon because they won't *keep.*

keep·er (KEEP-er) *n. keepers.* A person who keeps or takes care of persons or things.–A *keeper* at a zoo takes care of the animals.

keep·ing (KEEP-ing) *n.* 1. Care.–Mother left the children in the neighbor's *keeping* while she went to the store.
2. Observing; celebrating.–Grandmother believes in the *keeping* of the Sabbath.
3. Harmony; going well with.–That color is not in *keeping* with a green and yellow color scheme.

keep·sake (KEEP-sayk) *n. keepsakes.* Something to keep and remember someone by.–Grandmother gave Mary her locket and chain as a *keepsake.*

keg (KEG) *n. kegs.* A small barrel holding up to ten gallons. – Grandfather sent us a *keg* of vinegar.

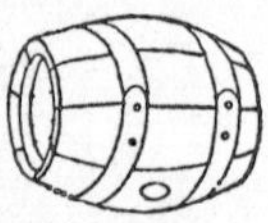

ken·nel (KEN-əl) *n. kennels.* 1. A dog's house.–Spot sleeps in a *kennel.*
2. A place where dogs are raised, or fed and taken care of for a small amount of money.–When we go away from home, we leave Spot at a *kennel.*

Ken·tuck·y (kən-TUK-ee) *n.* A mountainous state in south central United States, sometimes called the Blue Grass State. It is known for its many farm products, its coal mines, and the thoroughbred horses it raises. It ranks second among the states in tobacco raising.

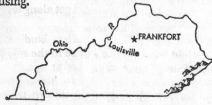

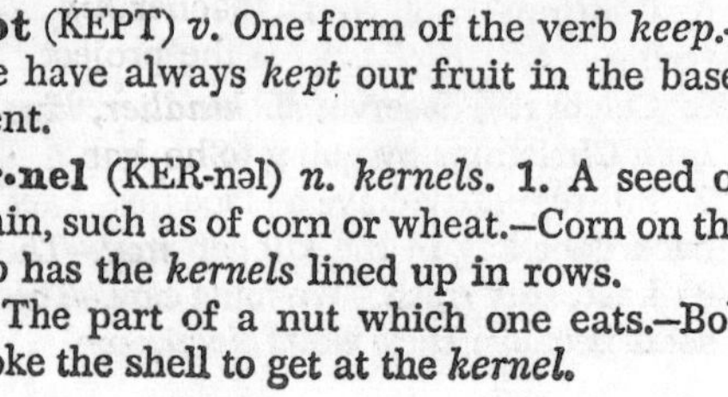

kept (KEPT) *v.* One form of the verb *keep.*–We have always *kept* our fruit in the basement.

ker·nel (KER-nəl) *n. kernels.* 1. A seed or grain, such as of corn or wheat.–Corn on the cob has the *kernels* lined up in rows.
2. The part of a nut which one eats.–Bob broke the shell to get at the *kernel.*

ker·o·sene (KAIR-ə-seen) *n.* A kind of oil burned in lamps and in stoves for cooking or heating.

ketch·up (KECH-əp) *n.* Catsup; a sauce made from tomatoes, vinegar, sugar, spices, and other things.

ket·tle (KET-l) *n. kettles.* A covered metal cooking pot. A tea *kettle* has a spout and is used for heating water.

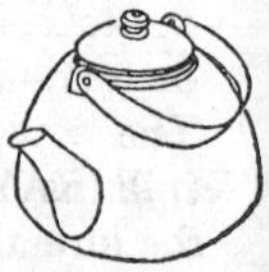

ket·tle·drum (KET-l-drum) *n. kettledrums.* A drum shaped like a kettle, usually made of copper or brass, with parchment stretched across the top. A *kettledrum* is the only kind of drum that can be tuned.

key (KEE) *n. keys.* 1. A piece of metal cut or shaped to fit a lock. We lock and unlock doors with *keys.*
2. The part of a problem that must be understood or worked out before the solution to the problem can be found.

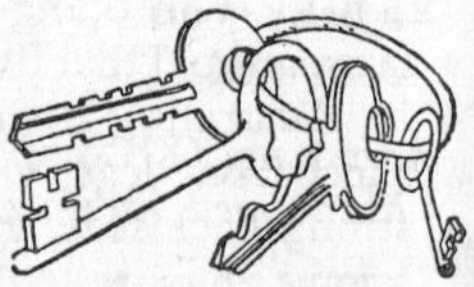

3. A list of answers.–The teacher gave us a *key* so that we could mark our own papers.
4. Any part one presses or strikes to make something work.–A piano has black and white *keys* that one strikes to make tones or music.–Some horns have *keys.*–Typewriters and adding machines have *keys.*
5. In music, the note which is "do" in a particular piece of music. A song in which the note C is "do" is written in the *key* of C.
6. A low piece of land mostly or entirely surrounded by water, as the Florida *Keys.*

key·board (KEE-bord) *n. keyboards.* A row or rows of keys on a piano, typewriter, etc.

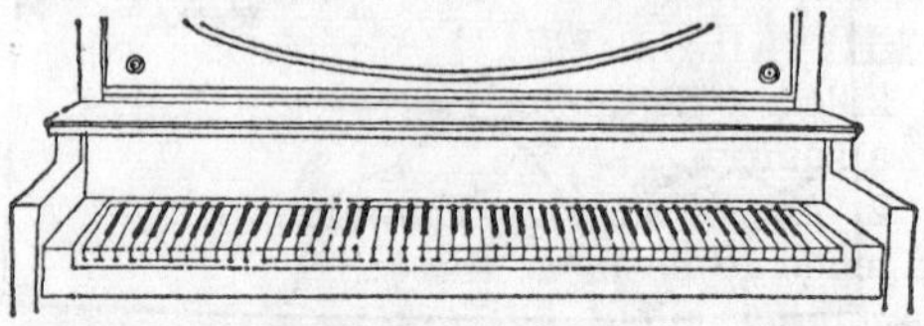

key·hole (KEE-hohl) *n. keyholes.* The hole in a lock into which the key is put.–Bob turned the key in the *keyhole* to lock the door.

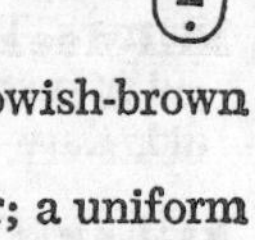

khak·i (KAK-ee *or* KAH-kee) *n. khakis* and *adj.* 1. A dull, yellowish-brown color.
2. A cotton material of this color; a uniform of this color.–The soldier was dressed in *khaki.*–He was glad to exchange his *khaki* uniform for a gray flannel suit when he finished his army service.

kick (KIK) *n. kicks.* 1. A blow with one or two feet.–Jim gave the football a hard *kick.*
2. A thrill; entertainment.–People get a *kick* out of watching acrobats doing dangerous feats.–John gets a *kick* out of watching the kitten play.
–*v. kicks, kicked, kicking.* 1. Hit with the foot or feet.–Bob *kicks* the football a long way.–The cow *kicked* Grandfather while he was milking her.
2. Jerk the feet.–Baby *kicks* when she lies on her back.–In swimming we *kick* with the feet and paddle with the hands.

kid (KID) *n. kids.* 1. A baby goat.
2. Thin, soft leather made from the skin of a baby goat.
3. A child.

kid•nap (KID-nap) *v. kidnaps, kidnaped* or *kidnapped, kidnaping* or *kidnapping.* Steal a child or a person, often for ransom.–The rich man's baby was *kidnaped.*

kid•nap•er or **kid•nap•per** (KID-nap-er) *n. kidnapers* or *kidnappers.* A person who kidnaps, or steals another person.–The police desperately hunted the *kidnaper,* fearing he would harm the child.

kid•ney (KID-nee) *n. kidneys.* An organ of the body. The heart pumps blood to all parts of the body. The work of the *kidneys* is to separate waste matter from the blood. This waste passes from the body as urine.

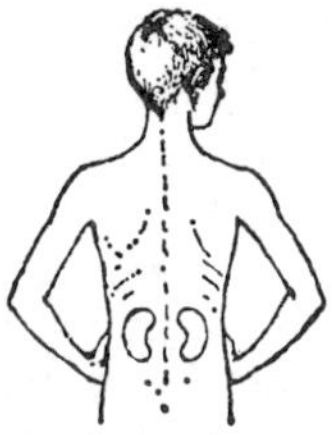

kill (KIL) *n. kills.* 1. Game that has been killed.–The hunter's *kill* was two rabbits and a squirrel.
2. Act of killing.–The other hunters hastened to be in at the *kill.*
–*v. kills, killed, killing.* Cause to die; injure so as to cause death.–Grandfather *killed* a big rat.–Father was afraid the frost would *kill* the flowers.

kill•deer (KIL-dir) *n. killdeer* or *killdeers.* A small bird; a plover. It is named for the sound of its cry.

kill•er (KIL-er) *n. killers.* A person or an animal that kills or puts to death other persons or animals.–The hawk is a *killer.* It kills chickens.

kiln (KIL *or* KILN) *n. kilns.* An oven or furnace for hardening and baking bricks, tile, pottery, and similar objects.

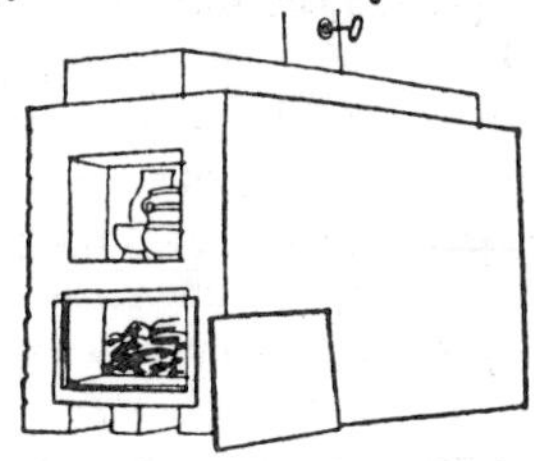

kil•o•watt (KIL-ə-waht) *n. kilowatts.* A unit of electrical power equal to 1000 watts. A family is usually billed by the electric company for the number of *kilowatts* it has used.

kilt (KILT) *n. kilts.* A short, pleated skirt that comes to the knees. Men in the highlands of Scotland often wear *kilts.*

ki•mo•no (kə-MOHN-ə) *n. kimonos.* A loose gown originally worn by both men and women in Japan. A *kimono* usually has wide, flowing sleeves and a wide sash.

kin (KIN) *n. pl.* and *adj.* The people related to a person.–Your aunts, uncles, brothers, sisters, mother, father, and other relatives are your *kin.*

kind (KYND) *n. kinds.* A sort or type.–What *kind* of dog does Jack have? Is it a spaniel, a terrier, or a collie?–What *kind* of dress did you get? Is it a party dress or a school dress, and what does it look like?
–*adj. kinder, kindest; kindly, adv.* Good to others.–When Mother was sick, our neighbors were very *kind* to us.

kin•der•gar•ten (KIND-er-gahr-tən) *n. kindergartens.* A school or class for young children, usually five years old. Children learn to work and play and get along together in *kindergarten.*

kin•dle (KIND-l) *v. kindles, kindled, kindling.* 1. Set fire to.–The fire in the stove had gone out, so Father *kindled* it again.
2. Catch fire.–The dry grass *kindled* from a lighted cigarette that was thrown there.
3. Inspire; arouse.–The teacher *kindled* the children's enthusiasm for the project.

kind•ly (KYND-lee) *adj. kindlier, kindliest.* Kind; friendly; pleasant.–She has a *kindly* face.
–*adv.* In a kind or pleasant way.–The girl spoke *kindly* to the lost little boy.–The children took *kindly* to their new home.

kin•dred (KIND-rid) *n. pl.* and *adj.* One's relatives; the people who are related to a person.—Your father, grandfather, mother, sisters, brothers, are some of your *kindred.*

king (KING) *n. kings.* 1. A ruler.—In the United States the President is at the head of the government. In some countries a *king* is at the head of the government.
2. A playing card; a piece in chess and checkers.

king•dom (KING-dəm) *n. kingdoms.* 1. A country that is ruled by a king or queen.
2. In nature, everything on and in earth belongs to one of three groups: an animal group, a vegetable group, or a mineral group. Each group is called a *kingdom;* for example, the animal *kingdom.* Man is a member of the animal *kingdom.*

king•fish•er (KING-fish-er) *n. kingfishers.* A bright blue bird with a crested head, a short tail, and a long, straight bill. *Kingfishers* eat fish.

kink (KINGK) *n. kinks; kinky, adj.* 1. A twist, curl, or tangle.—When the kitten played with the ball of yarn, the yarn became full of *kinks.*
2. A stiffness.—Father had a *kink* in his neck and could not turn his head.

kiss (KISS) *n. kisses.* 1. A touch of the lips to show love.—Mother gave the baby a *kiss.*
2. A kind of candy.—She unwrapped the foil from the chocolate *kiss.*
—*v. kisses, kissed, kissing.* Touch with the lips. —Mother *kissed* the baby.

kit (KIT) *n. kits.* A set of instruments, tools, or equipment of any kind, sometimes fitted into a case.—Father has a *kit* of tools.—We gave John a metal-working *kit.*

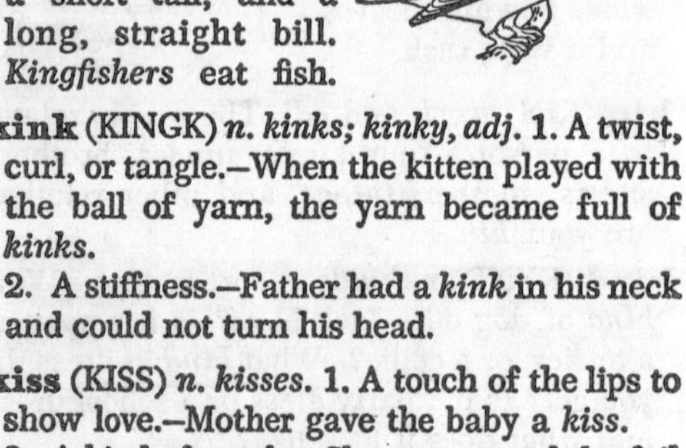

kitch•en (KICH-in) *n. kitchens.* A room where food is prepared and cooked.

kite (KYT) *n. kites.* 1. A frame of wooden sticks with a string stretched around the edges, covered with paper, and with a long string tied to the middle. A long tail of cloth is added for balance. *Kites* are made to be flown in the air.
2. A bird of the hawk family.

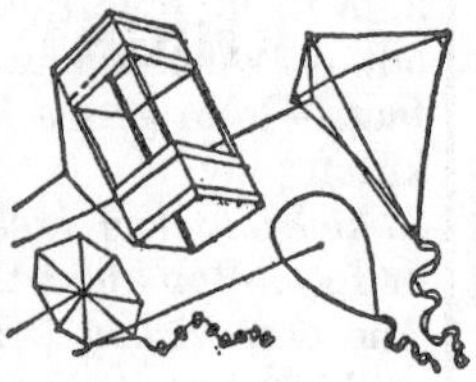

kit•ten (KIT-n) *n. kittens.* A baby cat.

kit•ty (KIT-ee) *n. kitties.* A kitten; a little cat.

knack (NAK) *n. knacks.* 1. A natural ability. —Some children have a *knack* for painting pictures. They learn quickly how to paint.
2. A special skill.—Playing jacks is easy, once you get the *knack* of it.

knap•sack (NAP-sak) *n. knapsacks.* A leather or canvas bag or case for carrying clothes, food, etc., as on a hike. It is carried strapped to the back. Boy Scouts and soldiers carry *knapsacks.*

knave (NAYV) *n. knaves.* 1. A man who is tricky, or not honest; a rascal.—The man said that some *knave* had stolen his horse.
2. In cards, a jack.

knead (NEED) *v. kneads, kneaded, kneading.* Work over or mix with the hands.—Grandmother *kneads* the bread dough with her hands.

knee (NEE) *n. knees.* A joint in the leg. It joins the upper and lower parts of the leg.

knee•cap (NEE-kap) *n. kneecaps.* A flat, oval bone which protects the front of the knee joint.

kneel (NEEL) *v. kneels, knelt* or *kneeled, kneeling.* Get or be down on the knees.—Bob trained his pony to *kneel* down.—She *knelt* on the ground to look into the cave.

knell (NEL) *n. knells.* The sound or ringing of a bell used to tell that someone has died; the slow ringing of a bell.

knelt (NELT) *v.* One form of the verb *kneel.* —We *knelt* and prayed.

knew (NOO *or* NYOO) *v.* One form of the verb *know.*—John *knew* how to drive the car when he was sixteen.

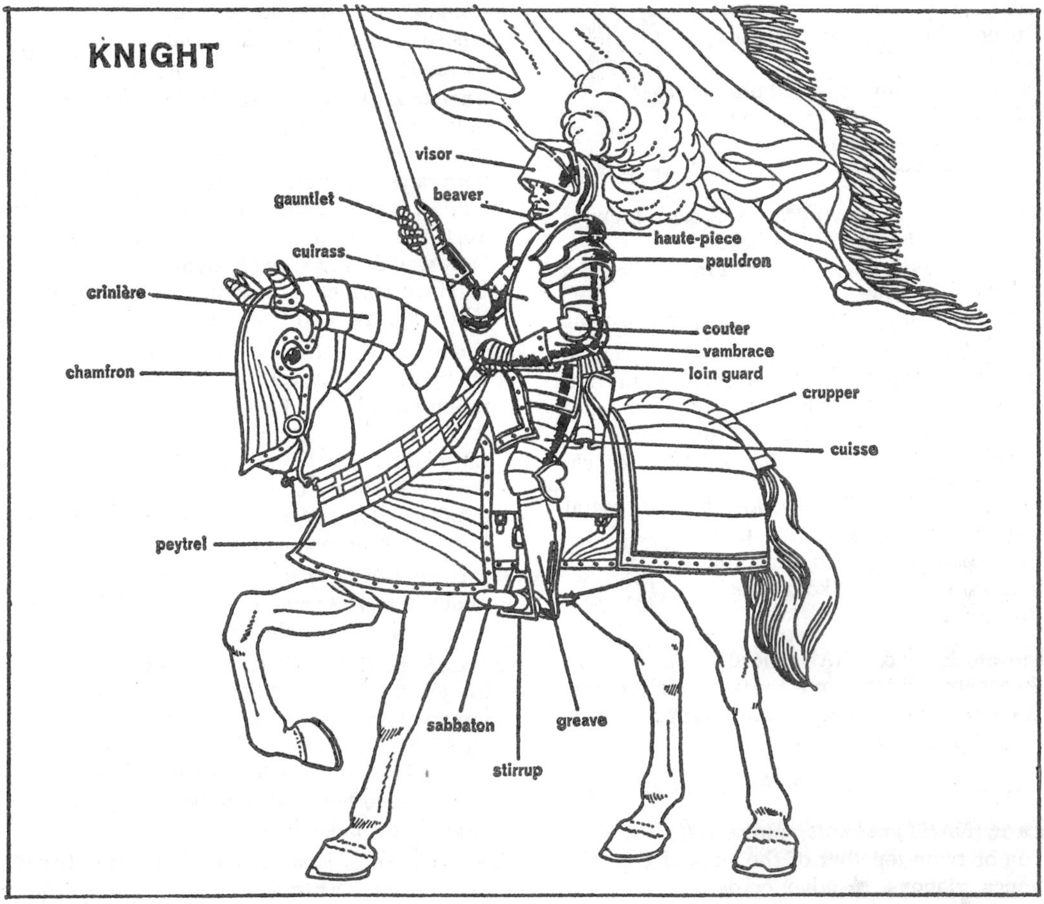

knife (NYF) *n. knives.* 1. A sharp blade of steel, silver, glass, or other hard substance fastened to a handle. It is used for cutting.

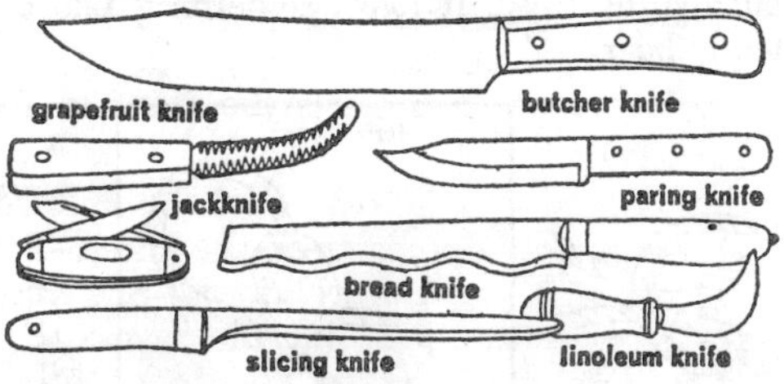

2. A blade like that used on a farm tool, a lawn mower, and other cutting instruments.

knight (NYT) *n. knights; knightly, adj.* 1. In times long ago, a man who was taught all about fighting and weapons and was given a high military rank. A *knight* promised to be brave, courteous, and faithful.
2. Nowadays, in England, a man is given the title of *knight* because of some service to his country. A *knight* is addressed as "Sir." For instance, when Arthur Brown becomes Sir Arthur Brown, he is addressed as "Sir Arthur."
–*v. knights, knighted, knighting.* Make a knight.–The king *knighted* Robin Hood.

knit (NIT) *v. knits, knitted* or *knit, knitting.* 1. Make locked loop stitches on two or more long needles.–Mother *knits* sweaters for the children.
2. Draw close and grow together.–Broken bones *knit*, or heal. – Frequent letters *knit* family bonds when relatives are separated.

knives (NYVZ) *n. pl.* More than one *knife*.–Mother has many *knives* and forks.

knob (NAHB) *n. knobs; knobby, adj.* 1. A handle to turn. – Someone turned the *knob,* and the door opened.

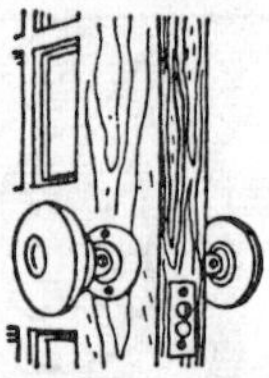

2. A little lump or raised place. –There was a little *knob* on the side of the tree where a branch had once been.

knock (NAHK) *n. knocks.* 1. A hard blow.–I received a *knock* on the head.
2. A rap with the knuckles; a tap.–I heard a *knock* at the door.
–*v. knocks, knocked, knocking.* 1. Hit or give something a hard blow.–One fighter tried to *knock* the other one down. He tried to hit him so he would fall.–When Baby is angry, she *knocks* her head against her high chair.
2. Rap.–If there is no doorbell, just *knock.*

knock•er (NAHK-er) *n. knockers.* A metal tongue or ring fastened to a door with hinges so that you can swing it to make a knocking sound.

knock•kneed (NAHK-need) *adj.* Having kneecaps which tend to face each other. Sometimes the knees touch when a *knock-kneed* person walks.

knoll (NOHL) *n. knolls.* A small, round hill.

knot (NAHT) *n. knots; knotty, adj.* 1. A looping or tying together of the ends of threads, ropes, ribbons, or other cords.
2. A hard part in wood formed at the place where a branch has grown out from the tree.
3. A measure of the speed of a boat.–One *knot* is a little over 6,080 feet per hour.
4. A group.–A little *knot* of people stood at the corner.
5. A tangle.–The kitten played with the ball of yarn and got it into a *knot.*

knot•hole (NAHT-hohl) *n. knotholes.* A hole in a board where a knot has fallen out.

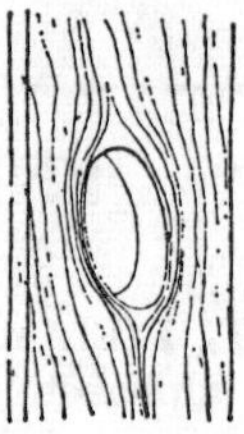

know (NOH) *v. knows, knew, knowing.* 1. Understand; be able.–Tom *knows* how to swim.
2. Be acquainted or familiar with (a person, place, language, etc.).–Do you *know* Mary?–Ed *knows* New York well; he has lived there a long time.–How well do you *know* French?
3. Have correct information.–Do you *know* when the train will be here?

knowl•edge (NAHL-ij) *n.* 1. The things that we know; all that we have learned.–Jack has much *knowledge* of boats.
2. All that man knows.–Scientists advance the frontiers of *knowledge.*
3. The knowing of something.–Mary made a cake without Mother's *knowledge.* Mother knew nothing about it.

known (NOHN) *v.* One form of the verb *know.*–I have *known* ever since I was in the second grade that the world is round.

knuck•le (NUK-əl) *n. knuckles.* 1. One of the joints of your hands.–Your fingers join your hand at the *knuckles.*

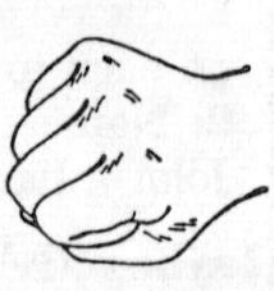

2. The knee or ankle joint of an animal.–Mother boiled a beef *knuckle* to make soup.

ko•a•la (koh-AH-lə) *n. koalas.* A gray, furry Australian animal without a tail. The *koala* has a pouch in which to carry its young. It climbs trees, and feeds mostly on the leaves and buds of eucalyptus trees. It looks something like a teddy bear.

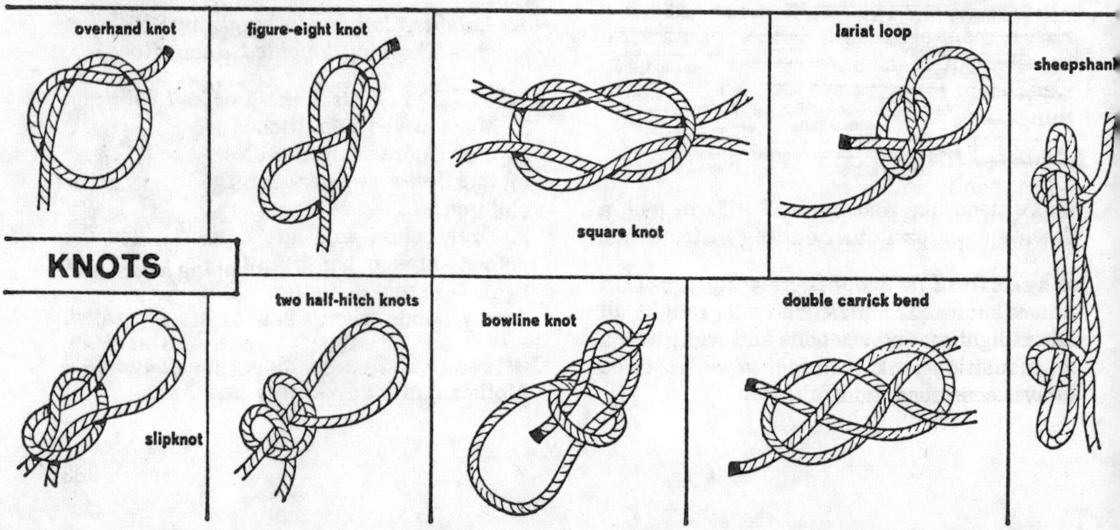

Ll

L, l (EL) *n. L's, l's.* The twelfth letter of the alphabet.

la (LAH) *n.* The sixth tone of a musical scale. –Do, re, me, fa, sol, *la,* ti, do.

la•bel (LAY-bəl) *n. labels.* A tag or small piece of paper, cardboard, or cloth fastened to a garment, bottle, or something else, to tell something about it.–The doctor put a

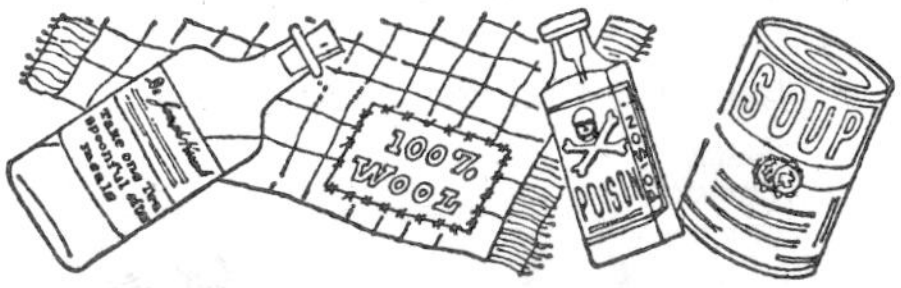

label on the medicine bottle. It read "Take one teaspoonful after meals."–The *label* on my scarf says "100% wool."–Read the *label* before you use the medicine.
–*v. label, labels, labeled.* 1. Put labels on.–Mother will *label* the gifts. She will put a tag on each to tell whom it is for.
2. Name or call.–We don't want to *label* John a liar without positive evidence.

la•bor (LAY-ber) *n.* 1. Workers.–*Labor* is hard to get on a farm.
2. Workers as a body; workers who belong to unions.–Organized *labor* will support John Brown in the election.
3. Work done or to be done.–Building roads is hard *labor.*
–*v. labors, labored, laboring.* 1. Work.–The farmer *labors* in the fields.
2. Move slowly, with difficulty.–The fat man *labored* up the hill.

lab•o•ra•to•ry (LAB-rə-tor-ee) *n. laboratories.* A room or building where experiments are tried out. A scientist uses a *laboratory* to experiment in, to try to find out more about things.

la•bor•er (LAY-ber-er) *n. laborers.* A worker. –The man is a *laborer* in a factory.–A man who can do heavy work for which he does not need special training is a *laborer.*

la•bo•ri•ous (lə-BOR-ee-əss) *adj.; laboriously, adv.* 1. Requiring much, or hard, work.–Ditch-digging is a very *laborious* occupation.
2. Industrious; hard-working.–Edward is a *laborious* worker.

lace (LAYSS) *n. laces.* 1. A cord for tying the parts of a thing together.–Our shoes are held together with shoe*laces.*

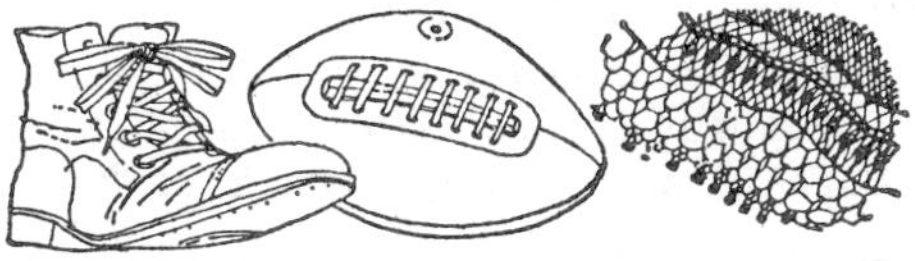

2. An openwork trimming used on dresses, towels, table covers, and other such materials.
–*v. laces, laced, lacing.* Fasten with laces.–Baby cannot *lace* her shoes.–Bob uses a leather lace to *lace* up his football.

lack (LAK) *n. lacks.* Absence; not being or happening.–*Lack* of rain caused the plants to dry up.
–*v. lacks, lacked, lacking.* Be without; have none.–We cannot go to the show, because we *lack* the money.

lac•quer (LAK-er) *n. lacquers.* A kind of varnish that dries quickly. *Lacquer* comes from a Japanese tree.
–*v. lacquers, lacquered, lacquering.* Put lacquer on.–Bob *lacquered* the table he made.

la•cy (LAY-see) *adj. lacier, laciest.* Delicate; like fine lace.–The leaf shadows made a *lacy* pattern on the floor.

lad (LAD) *n. lads.* A boy.–My brother Jack is a small *lad.*

lad•der (LAD-er) *n. ladders.* A set of wood or metal steps made by fastening round or flat pieces, called rungs, to two long side pieces. *Ladders* are used to climb on.–The painter uses a *ladder* to climb up when he paints a house.

lad•en (LAYD-n) *adj.* Loaded; weighed down.–The pirate ship was *laden* with treasure.–Mother came home from shopping *laden* with packages.

la•dies (LAYD-eez) *n. pl.* More than one *lady.* –The speaker said, "Good evening, *ladies* and gentlemen."

la·dle (LAYD-l) *n. ladles.* 1. A deep, cup-like spoon with a long handle.–Mother dipped up the soup with a *ladle.*

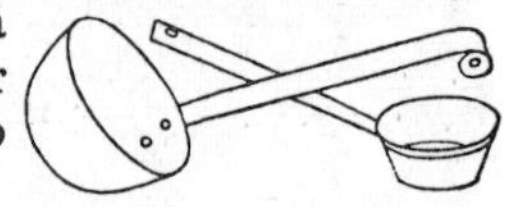

–*v. ladles, ladled, ladling.* Dip up with a ladle. –Grandmother *ladled* the milk.

la·dy (LAY-dee) *n. ladies.* 1. A well-bred woman; a woman with fine manners.
2. The woman who is the head of a household.–Mother is the *lady* of the house.
3. (Usually spelled with a capital "L.") In England, a woman of a certain rank.

la·dy·bug (LAY-dee-bug) *n. ladybugs.* A small, reddish-brown beetle. It has black spots on its smooth, rounded back.

la·dy's-slip·per (LAY-deez-slip-er) *n. lady's-slippers.* A yellow, pink, or white flower of the orchid family, shaped something like a slipper. *Lady's-slippers* grow wild in the woods.

lag (LAG) *n. lags.* Slowness; falling behind.–There is a *lag* in the store's deliveries this week. Deliveries are slow.
–*v. lags, lagged, lagging.* Fall behind; get behind.–The wounded soldier *lagged* behind the others.

la·goon (lə-GOON) *n. lagoons.* A shallow lake or pond, usually near, or connecting with, the sea.

laid (LAYD) *v.* One form of the verb *lay.*–Bob *laid* the book on the table.–The hens have *laid* eggs every day for a week.

lain (LAYN) *v.* One form of the verb *lie.*–The tired dog has *lain* on the rug all morning. He likes to lie there.

lair (LAIR) *n. lairs.* A den.–Lions and other wild beasts rest and sleep in their *lairs.*

lake (LAYK) *n. lakes.* A large body of water with land all around it.

lamb (LAM) *n. lambs.* A baby sheep. The flesh or meat of a *lamb* is good to eat.

lame (LAYM) *adj. lamer, lamest; lamely, adv.*
1. Crippled; not able to walk without limping or showing that the legs have been injured.–The boy who was hurt by the automobile will be *lame* for a time.
2. Sore and stiff.–Father has a *lame* back from lifting the heavy table.
3. Weak.–A *lame* excuse is one that is poor or not easy to believe.

la·ment (lə-MENT) *v. laments, lamented, lamenting.* Mourn; sorrow; weep.–The family deeply *laments* Grandfather's death.
–*lament, n. laments.*

lamp (LAMP) *n. lamps.* A device for making light. A kerosene *lamp* makes light by burning kerosene. An electric *lamp* makes light by heating a tiny wire white hot.

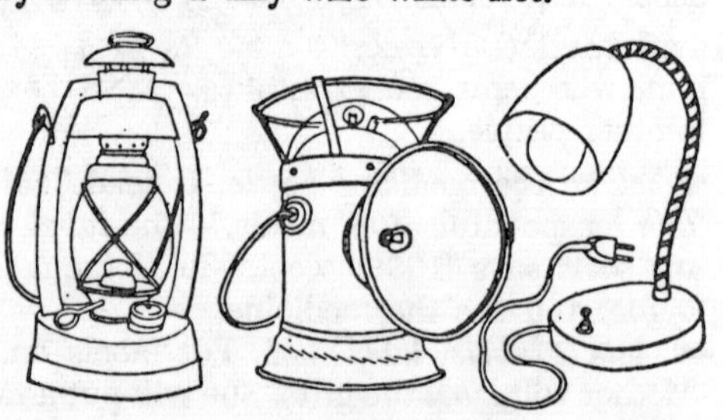

lance (LANSS) *n. lances.* 1. A sharp instrument used by a doctor to open an infection.
2. A spear; one who carries such a weapon. –Soldiers who carried *lances* were called "*lances*" or "lancers."

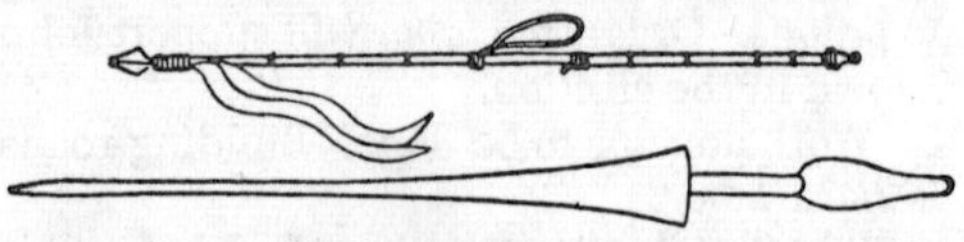

–*v. lances, lanced, lancing.* Open with a sharp instrument.–The doctor *lanced* the boil on the boy's arm to release the pus.

land (LAND) *n. lands.* 1. The solid part of the earth; ground.–About one third of the earth's surface is *land;* two thirds is covered with water.
2. Ground; soil. – Most of the *land* on the farm is good for growing crops.
3. A country or territory. – We study about many *lands* in geography class.
–*v. lands, landed, landing.* 1. Come to the land from air or water.–The sailors *landed* safely at the dock.–The airplane *landed* on Grandfather's farm.
2. Arrive.–We *landed* in the city after dark.
3. Catch (a fish or sea animal).–The fisherman *landed* a big fish.

land·ing (LAND-ing) *n. landings.* 1. A coming to the ground.–The airplane made a safe *landing.*

2. A place for boats to land. – The fisherman brought his boat to the *landing.*
3. A platform part of the way up a set of stairs.–The toy bear fell down the stairs as far as the *landing.*

land·la·dy (LAND-lay-dee) *n. landladies.* 1. A woman who rents rooms, houses, or property to others.
2. A woman who owns a house in which people rent rooms.

land·lord (LAND-lord) *n. landlords.* 1. A man who rents rooms, houses, or property to other people.
2. A man who keeps a hotel or other place where people pay to live and eat.

land·mark (LAND-mahrk) *n. landmarks.* 1. Any object that can be easily seen and is used as a guide in traveling. – The tall chimney is a *landmark* that shows you are entering the town.
2. A happening that marks off or distinguishes a period of history.–The invention of the airplane is a *landmark* in the history of travel.

land·scape (LAND-skayp) *n. landscapes.* 1. A view of land.–We stood on a high hill and admired the *landscape* below.
2. A picture of a view. – The *landscape* showed a river winding through the valley.
–*v. landscapes, landscaped, landscaping.* Improve land by planting and tending trees, grass, shrubs, and flowers.–We *landscaped* our lawn.

lane (LAYN) *n. lanes.* 1. A path or narrow road between fences or hedges.

2. A route; a set course. – Ships follow certain *lanes* in going across the ocean.
3. A section of a road marked off by lines on the pavement.–We drive in the right *lane* on the highway.

lan·guage (LANG-wij) *n. languages.* 1. Speech; spoken or written words.–We exchange ideas by means of *language.*
2. The set of words used by a large group of people in talking and writing.–In Spain, the people speak the Spanish *language.*
3. Any means of communication.–Sign *language* is communication by making motions with the hands and body.

lank (LANGK) *adj. lanker, lankest.* Tall and thin or slender.–The man was long and *lank.* –The *lank* pine trees towered above them.

lank·y (LANGK-ee) *adj. lankier, lankiest.* Tall and thin.–Abraham Lincoln's *lanky* figure is familiar to us from pictures.

lan·o·lin (LAN-ə-lin) *n.* A substance obtained from wool fat, used in creams and lotions for soothing and softening the skin and hair.

lan·tern (LAN-tern) *n. lanterns.* A case with glass sides used for carrying or holding a light. A *lantern* has an arched handle to carry it by.

lap (LAP) n. *laps.* 1. A flap.–The *lap* on a jacket is the part that folds over to button.
2. The front part of the body from the waist to the knees when a person is sitting down. –The baby likes to sit on Mother's *lap.*
3. One turn around a racecourse.–Bob's car won the first *lap* of the race.
4. Stage in a trip or journey.–Philadelphia to New York was the last *lap* in our auto trip from Los Angeles.
–*v. laps, lapped, lapping.* 1. Lick; take with the tongue.–The dog *lapped* up the milk we put in the feeding pan.
2. Slap gently.–The waves *lapped* against the side of the boat.
3. When two flat things lie together one may *lap* over the other.–Mother doesn't like the table so crowded that one place mat *laps* over the next.

la·pel (lə-PEL) *n. lapels.* The front part of a coat that folds back.–Father often wears a flower in the buttonhole of his *lapel.*

lapse (LAPSS) *n. lapses.* 1. A slight error; a falling away from the usual standard.–Jane's *lapse* in the spelling test was due to her lack of sleep.
2. Gradual passing; interval.–After a *lapse* of time I saw him again.
–*v. lapses, lapsed, lapsing.* 1. Slip or fall gradually backward; fall away from a former standard.–John had stopped biting his nails, but now he has *lapsed* into the habit again.
2. Return to a former condition.–For a moment a light glowed in one window, then the house *lapsed* into darkness.
3. End or stop because one has not met requirements to continue (something).–Father paid his insurance premium on time so that the insurance would not *lapse.*

lar•ce•ny (LAHR-sə-nee) *n.* Theft; the illegal taking of someone else's property without his consent.–The thief was sent to jail for having committed *larceny.*

larch (LAHRCH) *n.* *larches.* A kind of pine tree with very hard wood.

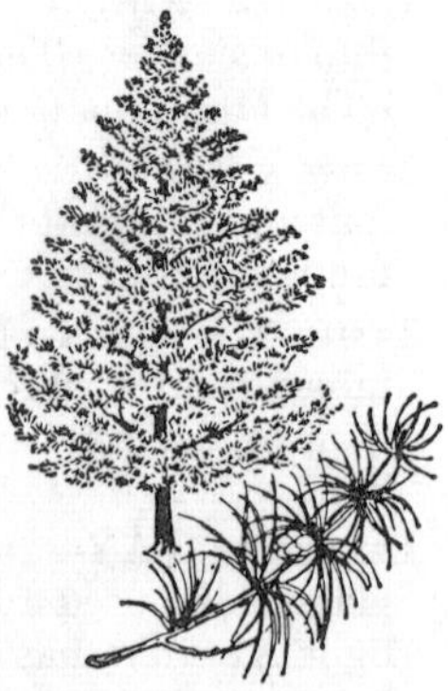

lard (LAHRD) *n.* The melted-down and refined fat of pigs. *Lard* is used in cooking.

lard•er (LAHR-der) *n. larders.* A storeroom for food; a place where food is kept; a pantry. – The ship's *larder* was well stocked with food for the long voyage.

large (LAHRJ) *adj. larger, largest.* Big; of great size.–Cats are small. Elephants are *large.*

–*At large* means free, not held under control. –The lion that escaped is still *at large.*

large•ly (LAHRJ-lee) *adv.* Mostly; chiefly.– The troubles she tells us about are *largely* imaginary.

lar•i•at (LAR-ee-ət) *n. lariats.* A lasso; a rope with a sliding loop.–The cowboy ropes cattle with his *lariat.*

lark (LAHRK) *n. larks.* 1. A songbird.–Meadow *larks* are about the size of robins. They build nests on the ground.

2. A good time or a joke is sometimes called a *lark.*

lark•spur (LAHRK-sper) *n. larkspurs.* A tall slender plant that has blue, pink, white, or purplish blossoms along the top of the stem.

lar•va (LAHR-və) *n. larvae.* An insect in its first, wormlike stage as it comes from the egg. Caterpillars are *larvae.*

lar•yn•gi•tis (lar-ən-JY-tiss) *n.* An inflammation or swelling of the larynx, which is the organ that produces the voice. A person suffering from *laryngitis* often loses his voice temporarily.

lar•ynx (LAR-ingks) *n. larynxes* or *larynges.* The upper part of the windpipe, containing the vocal cords. The *larynx* in human beings, as well as in many other animals, is the organ of voice.

lash (LASH) *n. lashes.* 1. One of the little hairs along the edges of the eyelids.

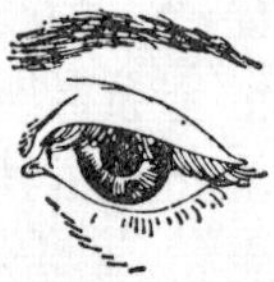

2. A whip, or the flexible part of a whip.

–*v. lashes, lashed, lashing.* 1. Beat at.–The waves *lashed* the shore.

2. Beat or whip.–The fleeing bandit *lashed* his horse to make it run faster.

3. Tie with a rope (used most often of tying something on a ship or boat).–As the storm began, the seamen *lashed* the hatch cover to the hatch so that it would not be swept away.

lass (LASS) *n. lasses.* A girl.–Betty is a tiny *lass.*

las•so (LASS-oh) *n. lassos* or *lassoes.* A long rope with a slip loop at one end.–The cowboy ropes cattle with his *lasso.*

–*v. lassoes, lassoed, lassoing.* Catch with a lasso.–Bob would like to *lasso* horses.

last (LAST) *n. lasts.* A mold shaped like a foot.–The cobbler puts shoes on a *last* to mend them.

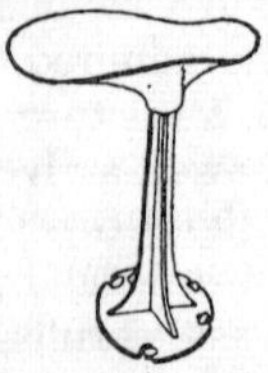

–*v. lasts, lasted, lasting.* 1. Keep on; continue. – The storm will not *last* long.

2. Hold out.–Our supply of water must *last* until we reach home.

–*adj.* and *adv.* 1. Final; coming at the end.– Sunday is the first day of the week. Saturday is the *last* day of the week. It comes *last.*

2. The latest.–I saw him *last* week.

last•ly (LAST-lee) *adv.* Finally; at the end. – Firstly, it is too far away; secondly, we haven't time; and *lastly,* I don't want to go.

latch (LACH) *n. latches.* A fastener used to hold a door or gate closed. –"Lift the *latch* and come in!"

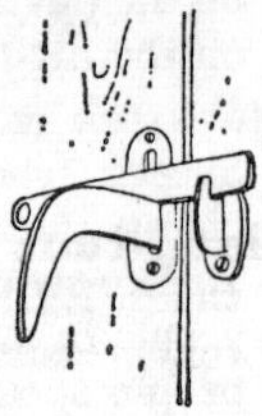

–*v. latches, latched, latching.* Lock; fasten with a latch. – Grandfather *latched* the barn door after the horse was stolen.

late (LAYT) *adj. later, latest* or *last* and *adv.*
1. Tardy; after the proper time.–Bob was *late* for school.
2. Near the end.–Mary came home *late* in the week.
3. Recent; that has just happened.–The *late* news came over the radio.
4. *Late* is used in speaking of a person who has died recently. – The *late* Franklin D. Roosevelt was President of the United States.

late•ly (LAYT-lee) *adv.* A short time ago; recently.–I have been very busy *lately.*

lat•er•al (LAT-er-əl) *adj.; laterally, adv.* Sideways; of, at, from, or toward the side. –The football player made a *lateral* pass.

lath (LATH) *n. laths.* A thin, narrow, rough strip of wood. Plaster sticks to *laths.*–The carpenter nailed *laths* onto the walls.

lathe (LAYTH) *n. lathes.* A machine to which a piece of wood or metal is fastened to be turned for shaping.–Father made Bob a baseball bat on his *lathe.*

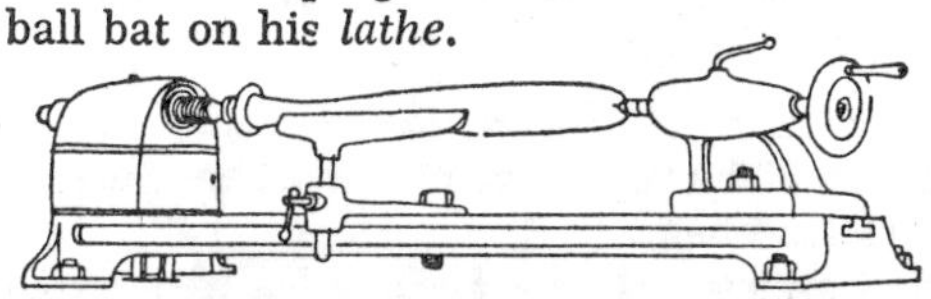

lath•er (LATH-er) *n.* Foam, such as soapsuds, or the sweat of an animal.–Father puts *lather* on his face before shaving.–The horse was in a *lather* after the race.
–*v. lathers, lathered, lathering.* Cover with foam.–Father *lathers* his face with shaving cream.

Lat•in (LAT-n) *n. Latins* and *adj.* 1. The language of the ancient Romans. Greek and *Latin* are known as classical languages. Ancient plays, poems, and other writings in these languages are called classics.
2. A citizen or native of a country such as Italy, Spain, France, or Argentina where the language used is closely descended from that of the ancient Romans.

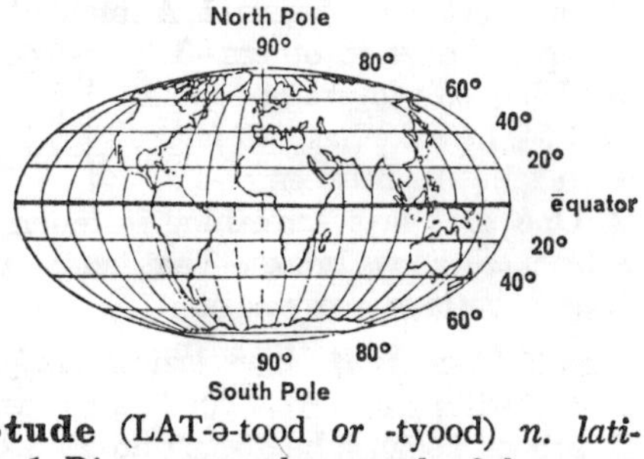

lat•i•tude (LAT-ə-tood *or* -tyood) *n. latitudes.* 1. Distance north or south of the equator, measured in degrees on the curved surface of the earth. Lines of *latitude* appear on a map as horizontal lines.–One degree of *latitude* on the earth's surface equals almost seventy miles. Therefore, ten degrees north *latitude* is an imaginary line nearly seven hundred miles north of the equator.
2. A region or geographic location. – Palm trees grow in warm *latitudes.* They grow in *latitudes* near the equator.
3. Freedom from narrow rules or limits.–People living in a democracy are allowed great *latitude* in speech.

lat•ter (LAT-er) *adj.* 1. Coming later; the second of two.–Bob read "Tom Sawyer" and "Little Women." The former was written by Mark Twain, and the *latter* was written by Louisa May Alcott.
2. Later; toward the end.–Mother will be home the *latter* part of the week.

lat•tice (LAT-əss) *n. lattices.* A framework of crossed wooden or metal pieces.–Mother trained the rose bushes to climb the *lattice.*

laugh (LAF) *n. laughs.* The sound of merriment made with the voice. – Mary gave a short *laugh* when she heard the story.
–*v. laughs, laughed, laughing.* Make sounds of merriment with the voice.–A funny joke makes you *laugh.*

laugh•ter (LAF-ter) *n.* Act of laughing; the sounds made by laughing.–We heard *laughter* in the next room.

launch (LAWNCH) *n. launches.* A power boat that is frequently used to carry people and supplies between a ship and the shore.

–*v. launches, launched, launching.* 1. Set (a ship) afloat; start (something) off.–The ship was named when it was *launched.* – John *launched* his model plane.
2. Start.–The city is going to *launch* a drive to clean up the streets.

laun•der (LAWN-der) *v. launders, laundered, laundering.* Wash. – On Monday Mother *launders* our clothes.

laun•dress (LAWN-drəss) *n. laundresses.* A woman who washes and irons clothes.–Our neighbor hires a *laundress.*

laun•dry (LAWN-dree) *n. laundries.* 1. A room where clothes are washed.–The *laundry* is in the basement in our house.

2. A building where clothes and linens are washed for many people.
3. Clothes to be washed.–Our *laundry* is kept in a large hamper.

laun•dry•man (LAWN-dree-mən) *n. laundrymen.* A man who works for a laundry.–The *laundryman* delivered our laundry.

lau•rel (LAWR-əl) *n. laurels* and *adj.* 1. An evergreen shrub or tree that has smooth, stiff leaves. Some *laurels* have blossoms.

2. An honor or recognized success. Laurel leaves were once used to make wreaths to crown heroes and great poets.–Bob won his *laurels* in baseball.

la•va (LAH- or LA-və) *n.* Melted rock that comes out of a volcano.–Volcanoes throw out hot *lava* when they erupt.

lav•a•to•ry (LAV-ə-tor-ee) *n. lavatories.* 1. A bowl or basin used in washing the hands and face.
2. A room used for washing oneself.

lav•en•der (LAV-ən-der) *n. lavenders.* A plant with long woolly leaves and small, pale purple flowers which are sweet-smelling. Dried *lavender* is often used to make clothing and clothes cabinets smell sweet.

–*adj.* A light purple color. –Grandmother has a *lavender* dress.

law (LAW) *n. laws.* 1. One of a set of rules made to control people's actions or behavior. The *laws* protect us from those who wish to do harm.
2. Any rule, such as the *laws* of a game, a *law* of grammar, the *law* of gravity.
3. The profession of a lawyer.–Tom is studying *law.* He will become a lawyer.

law•ful (LAW-fuhl) *adj.; lawfully, adv.* According to the laws; allowed by law.–It is *lawful* to cross the street when the light is green.

lawn (LAWN) *n. lawns.* A grass-covered plot of ground, usually kept closely cut.–Bob mowed the *lawn* around his house.

law•yer (LOI-yer) *n. lawyers.* A person trained and licensed to handle all matters having to do with the laws.–Father hired a *lawyer* to draw up the lease for the house. The *lawyer* wrote the lease so it would be right according to the law.

lax (LAKS) *adj. laxer, laxest; laxly, adv.* 1. Loose.–The rope became *lax* when the knot was loosened.
2. Careless.–Do not become *lax* about your homework.

lax•a•tive (LAKS-ə-tiv) *n. laxatives.* A medicine to make the bowels move.–Never take a *laxative* unless you are told to.

lay (LAY) *v. lays, laid, laying.* 1. Place or put in a flat position.–*Lay* your gloves in the drawer.
2. Produce and give out (eggs).–Hens *lay* eggs.
3. Put or place (used in many ways).–The clerk said she would *lay* the dress away for Mother.–The carpenter came to *lay* the floor.
4. Prepare.–Mother *laid* plans for the party.
5. One form of the verb *lie.*–Yesterday, the baby *lay* in her crib all day.

lay•er (LAY-er) *n. layers.* 1. A thickness; one flat piece next to others.–The road has two *layers* of cement on it.–The cake has two *layers* with icing in between.

2. One that lays something.–A brick*layer* lays bricks.–That hen is a good *layer.* She lays many eggs.

la•zy (LAY-zee) *adj. lazier, laziest; lazily, adv.* 1. Not willing to work.–The *lazy* boy will fail in school, because he doesn't do his work.
2. Slow-moving; weary-acting.–The boy walked down the street in a *lazy* way.

lead (LEED) *n. leads.* 1. Clue; hint.–I have a *lead* on where to buy exactly the chair we are looking for.–The detectives are following a new *lead* in solving the robbery.
2. Amount ahead; place ahead.–Our team has a *lead* of two games.–The brown horse took the *lead* in the race.
3. Example.–Following Jane's *lead,* I took the path to the left.
4. Turn to play first in a game of cards.–It's my *lead.* I throw a ten of clubs.
5. Leash.–She took the dog out on his *lead.*
–*v. leads, led, leading.* 1. Guide; show the way. –I will *lead* you to the place where the road turns off.
2. Have the highest record; be first.–The left fielder *leads* the team in batting home runs.
3. Direct.–Our teacher *leads* the singing each morning.
4. Play first, in card games.–It's your turn to *lead.* What card will you *lead?*
5. Tend or help to bring about.–Paying attention in class *leads* to good grades.
6. Spend or pass.–She *leads* a very busy life.

lead (LED) *n. leads.* 1. A heavy, bluish-gray metal. *Lead* is used to make some water pipes, bullets, and many things that need to be heavy or must not rust.
2. A black substance used in pencils.–The *lead* in this pencil is too hard.

lead•er (LEED-er) *n. leaders.* A person who leads, goes ahead, directs, or guides others, or shows how to do things.–The band *leader* directs the band.

leaf (LEEF) *n. leaves.* 1. One of the flat, usually green parts that grow on trees, plants, and bushes.

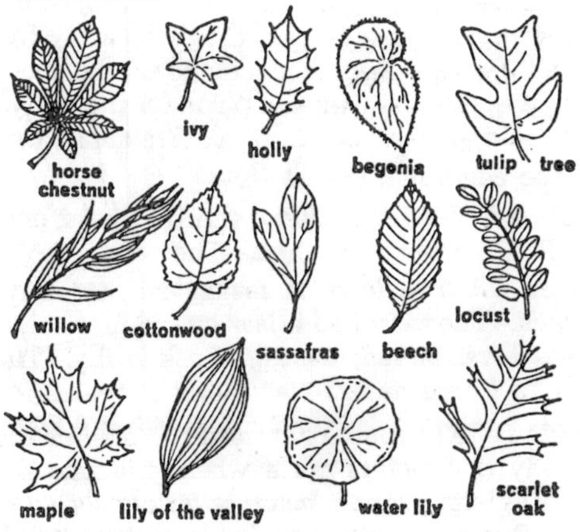

2. A thin sheet.–One *leaf* of the book was torn out.–Gold *leaf* is a very thin sheet of gold used for decorating or gilding.
3. A board used to make a table larger.–When we have guests for dinner, Mother puts an extra *leaf* in the table.

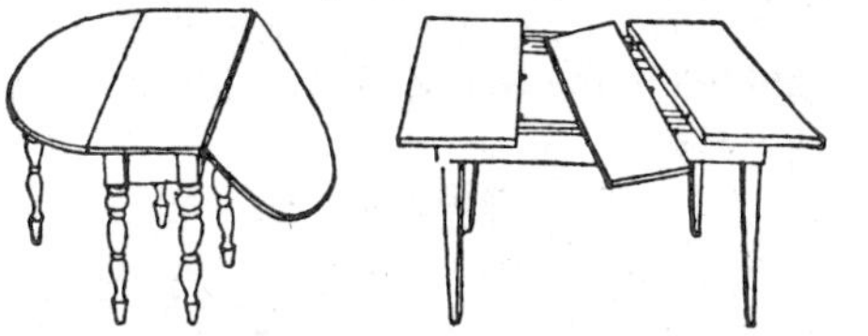

leaf•let (LEEF-lət) *n. leaflets.* 1. A small, young leaf.–A hickory tree has many *leaflets* growing off each stem.
2. A folder; a folded page of printed material.–Father received a *leaflet* on gardening.

leaf•y (LEEF-ee) *adj. leafier, leafiest.* Having leaves; of the material of a leaf.–Spinach is a green, *leafy* vegetable.

league (LEEG) *n. leagues.* A union of individuals, nations, peoples, teams, etc., joined together by a set of rules for a particular purpose.–The New York Yankees are a baseball team belonging to the American *League.*–My mother belongs to the *League* of Women Voters.

leak (LEEK) *n. leaks.* An accidental crack or hole that lets a gas, liquid, powder, etc., in or out of something.–Father found a *leak* in the water pipe.
–*v. leaks, leaked, leaking.* 1. Come out through a small opening.–The water was *leaking* through the leak in the pipe.
2. Be spread about by chance (as news).–The news of the party *leaked* out.

leak•y (LEEK-ee) *adj. leakier, leakiest.* Having leaks.–The boat is *leaky.* It has cracks in it which let the water in.

lean (LEEN) *n.* The red part of meat that is made up of muscle.–Jack Sprat would eat no fat, his wife would eat no *lean.*
–*v. leans, leaned, leaning.* 1. Rest against slantingly.–The ladder *leans* against the wall.
2. Be at an angle; slant.–The tree *leaned* with the wind.
3. Bend.–Mother *leaned* over to pick up the baby's toys.
4. Depend; rely.–Boys *lean* upon their parents for support until they can take care of themselves.
–*adj. leaner, leanest.* 1. Not fat; thin.–The dog that had not had enough to eat was *lean* and hungry.
2. Poor; producing very little wealth.–The farmer had a *lean* year last year; he had a poor harvest.

lean·to (LEEN-too) *n. lean-tos.* A crude shelter with a single downward-sloping roof, built against trees or posts.–The Boy Scouts built a *lean-to* to sleep in when they were camping in the woods. They built the *lean-to* from branches.

leap (LEEP) *n. leaps.* A jump; a springing up.–The horse made a high *leap.*
–*v. leaps, leaped, leaping.* Jump.–The horse *leaped* over the fence.

leap·frog (LEEP-frahg) *n.* A game in which one person leaps over others bent over in a row.

leap year (LEEP yir) *leap years.* The year in every four that has 366 days instead of 365. In *leap year,* February has 29 days instead of 28.

learn (LERN) *v. learns, learned, learning.* Come to know.–In school we *learn* to read, write, and do arithmetic.–Ted *learned* that his brother was very ill.

lease (LEESS) *n. leases.* A written agreement to occupy a property for a stated time for a stated amount of rent money.
–*v. leases, leased, leasing.* Rent under a written agreement.–We *lease* the house from a friend of Father's.

leash (LEESH) *n. leashes.* A leather strap fastened to an animal's collar or harness.–Bob leads his dog with a *leash.*

–*v. leashes, leashed, leashing.*–Put or keep on a leash.–The law in this community says you must *leash* your dog rather than let him go about loose.

least (LEEST) *n.* Smallest in amount or size. –Mary has twenty-five cents, Bob has twenty cents, and Baby has ten cents, the *least* of all.
–*adj.* and *adv.* Very small; very little.–Move the picture the *least* bit to the right.
–*At least* means not less than.–One should have *at least* eight hours of sleep a night.
–*At least* also means in any case or anyhow.– If you won't stay for supper, *at least* come in and say hello.

leath·er (LETH-er) *n. leathers.* The prepared hide or skin of certain animals. The hair is removed and the hide is soaked in a special liquid to make *leather* of it. Shoes, suitcases, and many other things are made of *leather.*

leave (LEEV) *n. leaves.* 1. Permission.–The teacher gave us *leave* to play ball.
2. Permission to be away; time away from duty.–The soldiers had a short *leave.*
–*v. leaves, left, leaving.* 1. Go away.–The teacher had to *leave* before the class was over.
2. Allow to stay.–Do not *leave* your hat on the table.–*Leave* your bundles here while you shop.
3. Let go till later.–I shall *leave* practicing the piano until after the party.

leaves (LEEVZ) *n. pl.* More than one *leaf.*– The *leaves* are falling.

lec·ture (LEK-cher) *n. lectures.* A speech; a talk about a definite subject.–The teacher will give a *lecture* on life in France at the meeting tonight.
–*v. lectures, lectured, lecturing.* 1. Give a talk or lecture.–The teacher will *lecture* tonight.
2. Scold.–Mother *lectures* me every time I forget to wash my hands before eating.

lec·tur·er (LEK-cher-er) *n. lecturers.* Person who gives a lecture.–The *lecturer* at the museum talked on "Eastern American Wildflowers."

led (LED) *v.* One form of the verb *lead.*–Bob *led* the horse to the barn.

ledge (LEJ) *n. ledges.* 1. A narrow shelf.– Mother put the plates on the *ledge* around the dining room.
2. A narrow, shelflike formation of rock.– The eagle had a nest on the *ledge* high up on the cliff.

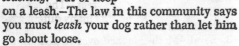

leer (LIR) *n. leers.* A mean, evil, sideways look.–The man had a *leer* on his face.
–*v. leers, leered, leering.* Look evilly.–The man *leered* at us.

left (LEFT) *n.* At or toward the side of the body that points north when you face the rising sun.–John's house is on our *left.*
–*v.* One form of the verb *leave.*–Father *left* early this morning.
–*adj.* On the left.–Mary writes with her *left* hand. Most people write with their right.

left-hand (LEFT-HAND) *adj.* On the left side.—John's house is the *left-hand* one of the two as you face them.

left-handed (LEFT-han-dəd) *adj.* A *left-handed* person is one who does things more easily with his left than with his right hand.

leg (LEG) *n. legs.* 1. One of the lower limbs of the human body. Your feet are at the lower end of your *legs,* and your body is at the upper end. We walk by means of our *legs.*

2. One of the limbs of an animal. Cows, cats, dogs, and horses have four feet and four *legs.*

3. A long, slim part of a piece of furniture, on which it stands. Most tables and chairs have four *legs.*

4. A part of clothing.—John put his right foot into the right *leg* of his trousers.

le•gal (LEE-gəl) *adj.; legally, adv.* Lawful; right according to the rules of the country.—In the United States it is *legal* to drive on the right side of the street. It is not *legal* to drive on the left side unless you are on a one-way street.

leg•end (LEJ-ənd) *n. legends.* A story of the past, which may not be true, but many people believe to be so.—The adventures of Robin Hood are *legends.*

leg•ging (LEG-ing) *n. leggings.* Long, heavy coverings for the legs. Children wear *leggings* in the winter.

leg•i•ble (LEJ-ə-bəl) *adj.; legibly, adv.* Readable, or easily read.—Mother's writing is *legible.*

le•gion (LEE-jən) *n. legions.* 1. An army; any armed force.—Reinforcements were sent to aid the *legions* fighting the enemy.

2. Any great number of people, animals, or things.—Movie stars often have *legions* of fans.

leg•is•la•tion (lej-iss-LAY-shən) *n.* 1. The making of law.—The Senate and the House of Representatives have the power of *legislation.*

2. The laws made.

leg•is•la•tor (LEJ-iss-lay-ter) *n. legislators.* One of a group of people who make the laws of the country or of a state. Senators and Representatives who are elected by the people are lawmakers, or *legislators.*

leg•is•la•ture (LEJ-əss-lay-cher) *n. legislatures.* A group of people who are elected to make laws.—The New York State *Legislature* makes special laws for the state just as Congress does for the whole country.

lei•sure (LEEZH-er) *n.* and *adj.* The free time you have after your work is done.—Joan uses her *leisure* for her hobbies.—Harry spent his *leisure* hours reading.

lei•sure•ly (LEEZH-er-lee) *adj.* and *adv.* Without hurry.—Joe had a *leisurely* visit with his grandmother. — Mary walked *leisurely* through the woods.

lem•on (LEM-ən) *n. lemons.* 1. A sour, juicy fruit that has a pale yellow skin. The juice of *lemons* is used in drinks, in pies, for flavoring, and for many other purposes.

—*adj.* A light yellow; the color of the fruit.

lem•on•ade (LEM-ən-ayd) *n. lemonades.* A drink, served cold or hot, made of lemon juice, water, and sugar.

lend (LEND) *v. lends, lent, lending.* 1. Let someone else use a thing belonging to one.—Will you *lend* me your pencil? I *lent* you mine last week.

2. Give.—Boy Scouts willingly *lend* help to old people.

3. Make a loan (of money).—Banks *lend* money for interest as part of their regular business.

length (LENGTH) *n. lengths.* 1. How long a thing is; how long a thing lasts.—The *length* of the boat is thirty-six feet.—The *length* of the show depends on how many different acts there are.

2. A *length* of material is a piece of material from a roll.

length•en (LENGTH-ən) *v. lengthens, lengthened, lengthening.* Make or grow longer.—Mother had to *lengthen* Mary's dress.—The shadows *lengthened* more and more as the day wore on.

length•y (LENGTH-ee) *adj. lengthier, lengthiest; lengthily, adv.* Long.—Bob gave a *lengthy* talk on snakes.

le•ni•ent (LEEN-nyənt *or* LEE-nee-ənt) *adj.; leniently, adv.* 1. Not strict or harsh.–John's parents are *lenient* with him when he makes mistakes. They try to teach him with kindness.
2. Merciful.–The judge was *lenient* with the prisoner because it was the prisoner's first offense. He dismissed him with a warning.

lens (LENZ) *n. lenses.* 1. A specially shaped piece of glass used in eyeglasses, cameras, field glasses, and the like. *Lenses* are usually so made as to make things look larger.

2. The part of the eye which focuses light rays upon the retina. If you look up the word "eye," you will find a picture that shows the *lens.*

Lent (LENT) *n.* A forty-day period just before Easter, set aside for fasting and for worship. Many Christian people keep *Lent.*

lent (LENT) *v.* One form of the verb *lend.*–I *lent* you my book yesterday.

leop•ard (LEP-erd) *n. leopards.* A large animal of the cat family. It has a yellowish color with black spots. *Leopards* are very fierce. *Leopards* come from Asia and Africa.

less (LESS) *adj.* and *adv.* Not so much; smaller in amount.–We have *less* money today than we had last week, because we spent some.–Ann asked her brother to walk *less* quickly. She couldn't keep up with him.
–*prep.* Minus.–Three *less* two is one.

les•son (LESS-ən) *n. lessons.* 1. Something learned or taught.–The teacher taught a *lesson* in geography.–Have you learned your *lessons?*
2. The amount to be learned at a time.–There were ten words in the first spelling *lesson.*
3. A reading from the Bible during church.

lest (LEST) *conj.* In order not to; so that (something) won't happen.–Don't run, *lest* you fall.

let (LET) *v. lets, let, letting.* 1. Allow; permit.–*Let* me help you with your work.
2. Rent; hire out.–We have trailers to *let.*

let's (LETSS). Let us.–*Let's* go to the beach and have a picnic.

let•ter (LET-er) *n. letters.* 1. A symbol used for a sound.–There are twenty-six *letters* in the English alphabet. A, b, c, d, e, f, g are the first seven *letters.*
2. A written message; a note.–We write *letters* to our friends and relatives. We put our *letters* in envelopes and send them through the mail.

let•ter•ing (LET-er-ing) *n.* Letters or words printed, painted, pasted, or drawn.–The *lettering* on the poster is done in green.

let•tuce (LET-əss) *n.* A leafy garden plant used in salads. Some *lettuce* grows in heads like cabbage, and some grows just as large leaves.

leu•ke•mi•a (loo-KEE-mee-ə) *n.* A blood disease. A person suffering from *leukemia* has more white blood cells and fewer red blood cells than a healthy person has.

lev•ee (LEV-ee) *n. levees.* A bank built along a river.–*Levees* are built to keep the water from overflowing and flooding the land.

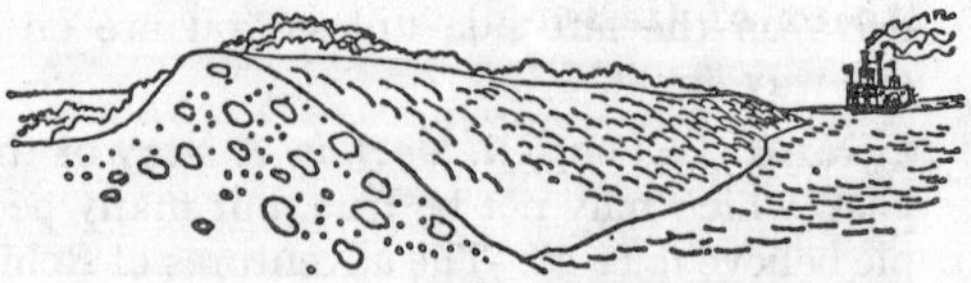

lev•el (LEV-əl) *n. levels.* 1. The point to which a thing rises or reaches; height.–Jack comes to the *level* of Father's shoulders.–New York City is only a few feet above sea *level.*
2. Stage or rank.–A king and a president are at about the same *level.*–John is an able student; he shows a high *level* of achievement.
3. An instrument for telling whether a table, floor, or any flat surface is horizontal.–The carpenter used his *level* on the new shelf for the bookcase.
–*v. levels, leveled* or *levelled, leveling* or *levelling.* 1. Make smooth and flat.–Bob *leveled* the dirt with his rake.
2. Raise to a level for shooting.–The policeman *leveled* his gun at the intruder.
–*adj.* 1. Flat and even everywhere.–The bowling alley must be *level* so that the balls will roll smoothly.
2. Sensible; not easily excited.–Bob has a *level* head.–Joan has a *level* disposition.

le•ver (LEV ər) *n. levers.* 1. A bar used to lift and move objects.

2. Part of a machine that one lifts, pulls, or pushes.—To buy a candy bar from this machine, insert your coin and pull the *lever.*

lev•y (LEV-ee) *n. levies.* 1. Money collected by law; a tax.—The government often puts *levies* on imported goods to protect home industries from foreign competition.

—*v. levies, levied, levying.*—Put on or collect (a tax or fine).—The government *levied* a new sales tax.

li•a•ble (LY-ə-bəl) *adj.* 1. Likely; apt.—You are *liable* to take cold if you get your feet wet.—You are *liable* to have an accident unless you cross the street with the green light.

2. Responsible.—The sign read, "We are not *liable* for lost hats and coats."

li•ar (LY-er) *n. liars.* A person who tells things he knows are not true but that he wants people to believe are true.

lib•er•al (LIB-er-əl) *adj.; liberally, adv.* 1. Generous; plentiful.—Father gave us *liberal* servings of ice cream.

2. Broad in outlook; not set in one's ways of thought.—He is a *liberal* thinker. He accepts new ideas easily.

lib•er•ate (LIB-er-ayt) *v. liberates, liberated, liberating.* Set free. — Father *liberated* the lamb that was caught in the fence.

lib•er•ty (LIB-er-tee) *n. liberties.* Freedom.—Patrick Henry, a great American, said, "Give me *liberty* or give me death."

li•brar•i•an (ly-BRAIR-ee-ən) *n. librarians.* A person who has charge of a library or a collection of books.

li•brar•y (LY-brair-ee) *n. libraries.* A place where many books are kept; a room or building with many books, which can be borrowed. —We get books to read from our town's public *library.*—Many schools have *libraries.*—Many homes have private *libraries.*

lice (LYSS) *n. pl.* More than one *louse. Lice* are small, flat, wingless insects which live on the heads and bodies of unsanitary people and animals. Chickens and birds pick *lice* off their bodies with their bills.

li•cense or **li•cence** (LYSS-ənss) *n. licenses* or *licences.* A written order giving one the legal right to do something.—Father has a driver's *license.* — In this country one must have a *license* to fish, to hunt, to marry, and to do many other things.

li•chen (LY-kən) *n. lichens.* A small leafless, stemless plant which grows on rocks, logs, trees, etc. *Lichens* grow in waste regions in all parts of the world and are of a variety of shapes and colors. Some provide food for men and animals.

lick (LIK) *n. licks.* 1. A small amount.—John didn't do a *lick* of work this morning.

2. A stroke with the tongue.—The mother cat gave her kitten a *lick.*

—*v. licks, licked, licking.* 1. Rub or stroke with the tongue.—The dog *licked* the milk from his pan.—Cows *lick* large pieces of rock salt.

2. People sometimes say *lick* when they mean whip or beat.—Bob would like to *lick* the bully at school.

3. To move like a lapping tongue.—Flames *licked* furiously at the walls of the burning house.

lic•o•rice (LIK-rish *or* LIK-ə-riss) *n. licorices.* A plant whose dried roots are used in making medicines and as flavoring for a sweet, black candy.

lid (LID) *n. lids.* 1. A cover or top.—Mother puts a *lid* on the kettle when she cooks potatoes for dinner.

2. An eye*lid,* or the covering of one's eye.

lie (LY) *n. lies.* A statement that is not true.—*Lies* usually get the liars into trouble.

—*v. lies, lied, lying.* Tell a thing that you know is not true.—Do not *lie.*

lie (LY) *v. lies, lay, lying.* 1. Stretch the body out flat.–We *lie* down to sleep.
2. Rest; stay in the same flat position without moving.–The rug *lies* on the floor.
3. Be at; be located.–The city *lies* at the foot of the mountains.
4. Be; prove to be.–The reason for that error *lies* in carelessness.

lieu·ten·ant (loo- *or* lyoo-TEN-ənt) *n. lieutenants.* An officer in the army whose rank is next below that of captain; an officer in the navy whose rank is next below that of lieutenant commander.

life (LYF) *n. lives.* 1. Living, growing, and producing more of the same kind. Plants, animals, and people have *life*. The earth and the rocks do not have *life*.
2. The period during which a person, animal, or plant is alive.–Grandfather lived in this house all his *life*.
3. A person.–The guard saved many *lives*.
4. A way of living.–*Life* in Japan is different from *life* in England.
5. The story of a person during the time he was alive.–Bob read a *life* of Thomas Edison.
6. Energy; vigor; interest.–After a hard day's work, the boys couldn't put much *life* into their ball game.
7. Period of existence.–The boys' secret club had a short *life*.

life·boat (LYF-boht) *n. lifeboats.* A small boat carried on a ship to save the passengers if the ship sinks. *Lifeboats* are also kept on some beaches.

life·guard (LYF-gahrd) *n. lifeguards.* An expert swimmer who is hired to watch bathers in the water at a beach or pool and help them in case of accident.

life pre·serv·er (LYF pri-zerv-er) *life preservers.* A life belt; a ring of cork which will float and hold up a person who is in danger of drowning.

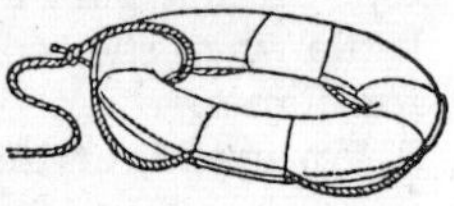

lift (LIFT) *n. lifts.* 1 Help.–The boy gave the farmer a *lift* with his work.
2. A free ride.–The driver gave Bob a *lift*.
3. Something which raises things up.–An elevator is sometimes called a *lift*.
4. A feeling of happiness or encouragement. –The teacher's praise gave Mary a *lift*.
–*v. lifts, lifted, lifting.* 1. Put up higher; go up higher; raise or rise.–Father *lifted* the baby into her high chair.–The truckman *lifted* the basket up to the truck.–Jack's low spirits *lifted* as soon as his lost puppy was found.

lig·a·ment (LIG-ə-mənt) *n. ligaments.* A strong band of fibers, or threadlike body tissues, that holds bones of the body together.

light (LYT) *n. lights.* 1. The opposite of dark. –At night it is dark; in the daytime it is *light*. –The sun gives *light*.

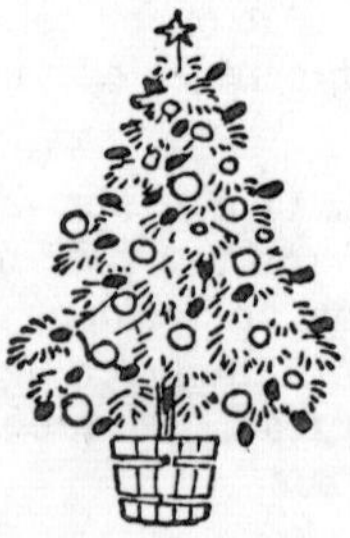

2. Anything that gives light.–The *lights* on the Christmas tree were blue, white, and red.
3. Brightness.–The *light* in Mrs. Smith's eyes told Joan she was welcome.
4. Public knowledge; knowledge of any kind. –More and more facts of the true story came to *light*.–We need more *light* on the subject to be able to discuss it intelligently.
–*v. lights, lighted* or *lit, lighting.* 1. Take or cause to take fire.–Matches *light* when they are struck.–Father *lit* his pipe.
2. Turn on the lights of.–A little girl *lighted* the Christmas tree.
3. Make light; brighten.–A smile *lit* up the baby's face when he saw his mother.
4. Come down; land or fall (on).–Marjorie's eye *lighted* on just the hat she wanted.–The crow *lighted* on the fence post.
–*adj. lighter, lightest; lightly, adv.* 1. Pale.–Mother wore a dark blue dress and Mary wore a *light* blue dress.
2. Bright.–It's too *light* to read sitting in the sunshine.
3. Not heavy.–Father's basket was heavy, but Bob's was *light*.
4. Cheerful; gay.–The dentist was in a *light* mood today.

light·en (LYT-n) *v. lightens, lightened, lightening.* 1. Lessen; make lighter.–Many people helping will *lighten* the work for all.

2. Make or grow lighter.–Mix white with the paint to *lighten* the shade.
3. Become cheerful.–The sad boy's face *lightened* when he heard the good news.

light•heart•ed (LYT-hahr-təd) *adj.; light-heartedly, adv.* Cheerful and gay.–Jack is always *lighthearted* on Saturday night when his friends drop by.

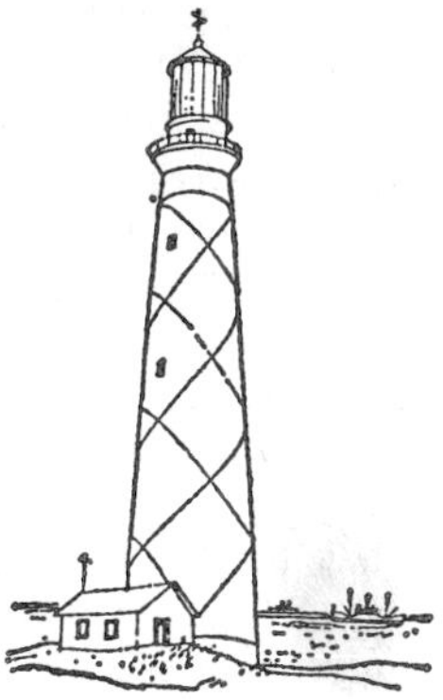

light•house (LYT-howss) *n. lighthouses.* A tower built in the sea or along the shore from which a bright light shines. Ships are guided by the light beaming from the *lighthouse.*

light•ning (LYT-ning) *n.* Light caused in the sky by a flash of electricity. *Lightning* is usually followed by thunder.

light•ning rod (LYT-ning rahd) *lightning rods.* A rod of metal planned to take lightning into the ground, thus preventing it from damaging the building. – The farmer's barn has *lightning rods* on it.

light-year (LYT-yir) *n. light-years.* The unit used in measuring distances between stars; the distance covered by a ray of light traveling for one year. One *light-year* is equal to about six trillion (6,000,000,000,000) miles.

lig•nite (LIG-nyt) *n.* A variety of coal, woody-looking and not completely developed, usually dark brown in color; brown coal.–The world's greatest producer of *lignite,* or brown coal, is Germany.

lik•a•ble or **like•a•ble** (LYK-ə-bəl) *adj.* Pleasant and friendly, so that one is liked by everybody.–Mary is a very *likable* person.

like (LYK) *n. likes.* 1. A thing enjoyed.–We all have our *likes* and dislikes.
2. An equal.–Mary enjoys cookies, candies, and the *like.*
–*v. likes, liked, liking.* Enjoy; be pleased by; get pleasure from.–I *like* ice cream.–I *like* to play baseball.
–*adj., adv., conj.,* and *prep.* 1. Much the same as.–Sally's dress is *like* mine.
2. In a similar manner or to a similar degree. –David swims *like* a fish.
3. As if there would be.–It looks *like* rain.
4. Inclined for.–He feels *like* swimming.
5. What one would expect of.–It's just *like* George to be late. He is often late.

like•ly (LYK-lee) *adj. likelier, likeliest.* 1. Probable.–It isn't *likely* that Father will be home early today. He isn't apt to be.
2. Promising.–Is this a *likely* place to look for her?
–*adv.* Probably.–We very *likely* will have our house painted soon. We are apt to.

like•ness (LYK-nəss) *n. likenesses.* 1. Sameness; being alike.–There was much *likeness* between the twins.
2. Appearance; dress; shape.–Sue appeared in the play in the *likeness* of a brownie.
3. One's portrait or picture.–A *likeness* of Grandmother as a young girl hangs over the mantel.

like•wise (LYK-wyz) *adv.* 1. The exact same thing.–The man jumped into the water holding his nose and the boy did *likewise.*
2. Also; too.–Jack must go to bed early, and Bob *likewise.*

lik•ing (LYK-ing) *n. likings.* Enjoyment of; pleasure in.–The artist has a *liking* for painting landscapes.

li•lac (LY-lak) *n. lilacs.* A purple or white flower that grows in clusters on bushes.–Mary picked some white *lilacs.*
–*adj.* Pinkish-purple, the color of the purple lilac.–Mother has a *lilac* blouse.

lil•y (LIL-ee) *n. lilies.* A plant of many varieties that grows from a bulb. The flowers of the *lily* are cone-shaped on the under side. Easter *lilies* are white and blossom at Easter time. Tiger *lilies* are orange.

lil•y of the val•ley (lil-ee əv thə VAL-ee) *lilies of the valley.* A flower that grows from a bulb. The fragrant white flowers are like little bells growing along a stem.

limb (LIM) *n. limbs.* 1. An arm or leg.–The man broke no *limbs* in the accident.

2. Branch.–We had a swing tied to the *limb* of the tree.

lim•ber (LIM-ber) *v. limbers, limbered, limbering.* Make flexible or easy to bend; loosen (up).–The prize fighter *limbered* up his muscles before the fight by doing exercises.
–*adj.* Bending easily; flexible.–Grandpa still plays tennis. He is *limber* for his age.

lime (LYM) *n. limes.* 1. A white powder made by heating limestone, which is a certain kind of stone. *Lime* is used in whitewash. Farmers sometimes use *lime* on soil to make it less sour or acid.

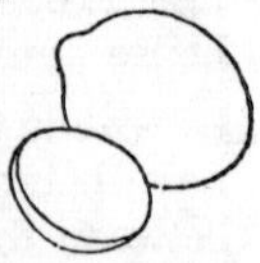

2. A small, sour, light-green, lemonlike fruit that grows on a tree.

lim•er•ick (LIM-er-ik) *n. limericks.* A nonsense verse of five lines in which the first, second, and fifth lines rhyme with each other, as do the shorter third and fourth lines. A typical *limerick* begins: "There was a young lady of Stowe, Who decided to walk in the snow . . ."

lime•stone (LYM-stohn) *n. limestones.* A rock from which lime is made.

lim•it (LIM-it) *n. limits.* 1. A boundary line; a line that shows where a thing ends; a stated amount or number.–We walked as far as the city *limits.*
2. As far as a person or thing can go or do.–The rope was stretched to its *limit.*–She pushed to the *limit* of her strength but she could not budge the rock.
–*v. limits, limited, limiting.* Keep within a certain amount or number.–Mother *limits* herself to three cups of coffee a day.

lim•it•ed (LIM-it-id) *adj.* Held within a certain number, a certain kind, or the like.–A *limited* train makes only so many stops.

lim•ou•sine (LIM-ə-zeen *or* lim-ə-ZEEN) *n. limousines.* 1. An automobile in which the chauffeur or driver sits in the open, with the

back section for the passengers enclosed.
2. Any luxurious, chauffeur-driven car.

limp (LIMP) *n. limps.* A hobbling or lame step.–He walks with a *limp.*
–*v. limps, limped, limping.* Put more weight on one foot than on the other in walking.–The crippled man *limps.*
–*adj. limper, limpest; limply, adv.* Drooping; having lost stiffness.–The flowers have gone without water so long that they are *limp.*–Mother said she was so tired she felt *limp.*

lin•den (LIN-dən) *n. lindens.* A shade tree with heart-shaped leaves and fragrant, yellowish flowers; the American basswood. The wood of the *linden* is fine-grained.

line (LYN) *n. lines.* 1. A slender rope, cord, or wire such as a telephone *line,* a fishing *line,* or a chalk *line,* used for measuring and leveling by bricklayers.
2. A long straight or curved mark made by a pencil, a piece of chalk, a paintbrush, or the like.–Our writing paper has *lines* across it.
3. A row.–A long *line* of people waited to get tickets.

4. A boundary; edge. – We walked to the city *line.*
5. A line of writing or printing.–Read the first *line* of the story again.
6. Business.–My father's *line* is painting.
7. A system of railroads, buses, or other transportation.–The New York Central *lines* go to Chicago.
8. Course.–The soldier died in the *line* of duty.
–*v. lines, lined, lining.* 1. Make lines on.–The children were told to *line* their papers for the spelling test.
2. Cover the sides or insides of. – People *lined* the street. People stood all along the edge of the street. – Mother *lined* Father's coat with gray silk.

lin•e•ar (LIN-ee-er) *adj.* 1. Having to do with, or consisting of, lines.–There was a *linear* design on the pretty paper napkins. The design was made with lines.
2. Having to do with length. *Linear* measure includes inches, feet, yards, and miles.

lin•en (LIN-ən) *n. linens* and *adj.* 1. Cloth or thread made from flax or from hemp.
2. Tablecloths, towels, doilies, sheets, pillowcases, and other household cloths.

lin•er (LYN-er) *n. liners.* 1. A large passenger steamship.–Mary wants to go to France some day on an ocean *liner.*

2. A hit ball that flies through the air very fast and close to the ground.–The batter hit a *liner* to the shortstop.

lin•ger (LING-ger) *v. lingers, lingered, lingering.* Be slow; delay.–Mother told Bob not to *linger* on his way to school.

lin•i•ment (LIN-ə-mənt) *n. liniments.* A liquid medicine that is rubbed on.–Grandfather rubbed *liniment* on his sore wrist.

lin•ing (LYN-ing) *n. linings.* An inside covering. – The tailor sewed the *lining* into Father's coat. – The *lining* in Mary's purse is blue.

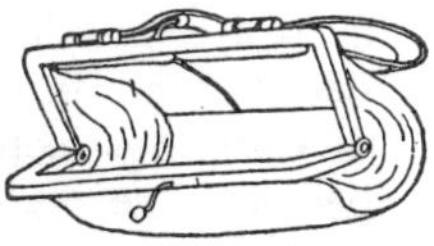

link (LINGK) *n. links.* 1. One of the rings that form a chain when joined together.–A chain is made of *links.*
2. Anything that joins other things together to make a complete thing.–Facts that join together to make a complete story are *links.*

–*v. links, linked, linking.* Connect.–The detectives *linked* a noted thief with the bank robbery. They felt he had done it.

li•no•le•um (lə-NOH-lee-əm) *n. linoleums* and *adj.* A kind of hard floor covering. It has a rough cloth back, covered with a mixture of linseed oil and ground cork. *Linoleum* has different kinds of patterns on it, like rugs. It has a hard, shiny surface and is easily washed. *Linoleum* flooring is often used in kitchens.

lin•seed (LIN-seed) *n.* The seeds of flax. Oil made from *linseed* is used in some paint.

lint (LINT) *n.* 1. Tiny bits of thread.–Much *lint* collects on Father's blue suit.
2. The soft, downy bits that come off linen. –*Lint* used to be made into bandages.

li•on (LY-ən) *n. lions.* A large, yellowish, flesh-eating animal of the cat family. *Lions* live in rocky places in tropical Africa.

li•on•ess (LY-ən-əss) *n. lionesses.* A female lion.

lip (LIP) *n. lips.* 1. Either of the two edges of your mouth. Your *lips* move when you open your mouth to speak, sing, or eat. When you whistle, you pucker up your *lips.*
2. The part of a pitcher or other vessel that bends out so that liquids will pour out in a narrow stream.

liq•uid (LIK-wid) *n. liquids.* Not solid, and not a gas.–Water and milk are *liquids.* They flow easily.–Many medicines are *liquids.*

liq•uor (LIK-er) *n. liquors.* 1. Wines, whiskey, or other drinks that contain alcohol.
2. The juice or watery part of anything.

lisle (LYL) *n.* and *adj.* A hard-twisted cotton thread. Stockings are sometimes made of *lisle.*

lisp (LISP) *n. lisps.* A person with a *lisp* says the "th" sound for the sounds of s and z.– To say "The thun thines brightly" for "The sun shines brightly" is to talk with a *lisp.*
–*v. lisps, lisped, lisping.* Talk with a lisp.– Babies sometimes *lisp,* but they usually outgrow it later on.

list (LIST) *n. lists.* A row or column of words or numbers. – Our teacher wrote a *list* of spelling words on the blackboard.
–*v. lists, listed, listing.* 1. Write in a row or column.–Mother *listed* the groceries she expected to buy.
2. (Of a ship) Lean to one side; float unevenly.–The ship *listed* badly to port after the collision.

lis•ten (LISS-ən) *v. listens, listened, listening.* Try to hear; pay attention so that one hears.–The teacher told us to *listen* to what she had to say.–We *listen* to the radio, to birds singing, and to people talking.

lis•ten•er (LISS-ən-er) *n. listeners.* A person who listens or tries to hear.–Bob is a good talker and also a good *listener.*

lit (LIT) *v.* One form of the verb *light.*–During the storm, Father *lit* the candle.

lit•er•al (LIT-er-əl) *adj.; literally, adv.* 1. According to the exact meaning of the words. –In a *literal* sense, the sentence "Mr. Brown's door is always open" would mean just what it says. Such a statement, however, often means "Mr. Brown is always willing to see people who want to see him," and is not to be taken *literally.*
2. According to the facts; without exaggeration.–The newspaper gave a *literal* account of the fire.

lit•er•ar•y (LIT-er-air-ee) *adj.* Connected with written works, like poetry, novels, and stories.–Writing books is *literary* work.

lit•er•a•ture (LIT-er-ə-cher *or* LIT-rə-choor) *n. literatures.* Poems, stories, and other writings.–In school we study *literature.*

lit•mus pa•per (LIT-məss pay-per) *litmus papers.* Paper treated with a chemical dye that causes the paper to turn red when it touches acid and blue when it touches alkali. *Litmus paper* is widely used by chemists in testing for the presence of acids or alkalis.

lit•ter (LIT-er) *n. litters.* 1. A curtained couch which rests on shafts. It is used for carrying a person of rank or importance.
2. A stretcher or frame used to carry sick or wounded people.

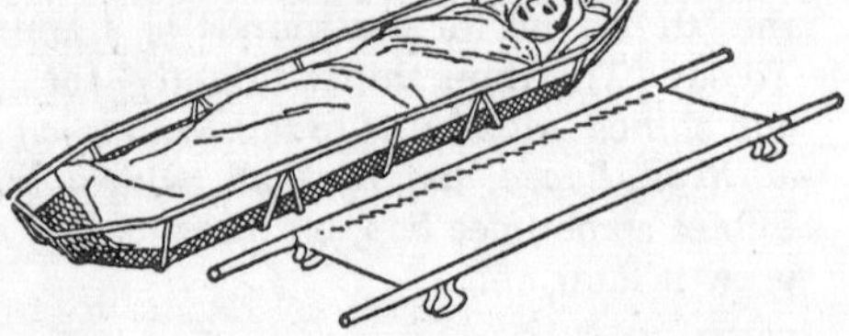

3. The number born to one animal at one time.–Our dog had a *litter* of four puppies.
4. The hay or straw used for bedding for animals.
5. A mess; little bits scattered all over.–The children cut out pictures and made a *litter* all over the floor.
–*v. litters, littered, littering.* Leave things scattered about.–Mother told us we could get lunch if we would be careful not to *litter* the kitchen.

lit•tle (LIT-l) *adj. littler* or *less* or *lesser, littlest* or *least.* 1. Small.–Elephants are big, but ants are *little.*
2. A small amount of.–Mother takes a *little* sugar in her tea.
3. Slight.–Baby still has a *little* cold.

live (LIV) *v. lives, lived, living.* 1. Have life; grow and produce others of the same kind. –Plants, animals, and people *live.*
2. Continue to live.–The man *lived* to be very old.
3. Get a living, or money to get food, clothing, and homes.–Men must work in order to *live.*
4. Dwell; have one's home.–We have *lived* in this house many years. We have made our home here.
5. Feed (on); be kept alive by.–Cattle *live* upon grass.
6. Go through life.–The old man *lives* in ease.
7. Act; behave.–The man *lives* as he believes. He does the things he believes in.
–(LYV) *adj.* 1. Alive; not dead.–Only a few *live* trees were left after the fire.
2. Burning.–The Boy Scouts poured water on the *live* coals of the fire before they left the camp.
3. Not yet exploded.–Stand back! That is a *live* firecracker.
4. Carrying electricity.–After the storm, the people were warned that many *live* wires were down.
5. Having much energy.–Bob is a really *live* newsboy.

live•li•hood (LYV-lee-huhd) *n. livelihoods.* A way of earning money to support life; the money so earned.–Father's grocery business is his *livelihood.*–Fred repairs television sets for his *livelihood.*

live•ly (LYV-lee) *adj. livelier, liveliest.* 1. Active; full of life.–Mary's lamb is *lively.*
2. Gay.–The band played *lively* music.
3. Exciting.–We saw a *lively* television show last night.

liv•er (LIV-er) *n. livers.* An organ of the body. Its work is to make bile (a yellowish, bitter liquid) which helps to change the food one eats so that the body can use it.–The *livers* of many animals are used as food.

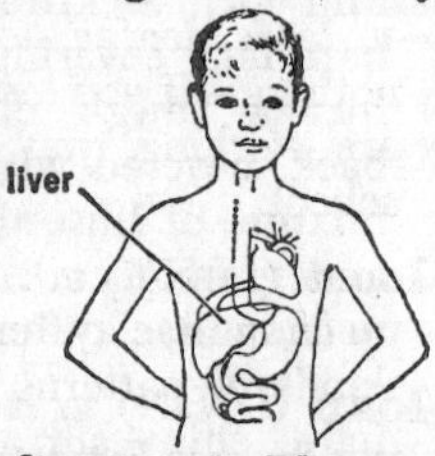

liv•er•y (LIV-er-ee) *n. liveries.* 1. The special clothes or uniforms worn by the servants of very rich persons.–The castle servants wore scarlet and gold *livery.*
2. The keeping and care of horses for money; the business of renting horses and carriages; a stable for this purpose.–You rarely see a *livery* in this age of automobiles.

live•stock (LYV-stahk) *n. sing.* and *pl.* Cattle, horses, pigs, and other farm animals.–The farmer sold his *livestock.*

liz•ard (LIZ-erd) *n. lizards.* A four-legged, snakelike animal. *Lizards* have long, scaly bodies, long tails, and short legs.

lla•ma (LAH-mə) *n. llamas.* A large, long-haired animal used in South America to carry loads.

load (LOHD) *n. loads.* 1. Anything that is carried.–The truck is carrying a *load* of dirt.
2. A charge of powder or a cartridge.–The gun had no *load* in it.
–*v. loads, loaded, loading.* 1. Put a load on.–The men *loaded* the truck with stones.
2. Fill (a gun) with cartridges.–The policeman *loaded* his pistol.

load•stone or **lode•stone** (LOHD-stohn) *n. loadstones* or *lodestones.* A stone or a substance that is able to attract iron as a magnet does.

loaf (LOHF) *n. loaves.* 1. A large piece of bread baked in one piece. –Mother bought two *loaves* of bread and sliced them to make sandwiches.
2. Something baked in one piece shaped like a loaf of bread.–We had a meat *loaf* for dinner.

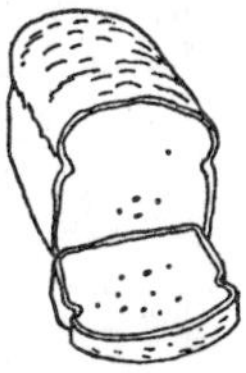

–*v. loafs, loafed, loafing.* Spend time doing nothing.–If you *loaf* while the other children are working, you will have to work after school.

loam (LOHM) *n.* A kind of rich earth made up of sand, clay, and decayed plants.

loan (LOHN) *n. loans.* 1. A lending; a giving for use for a time.–The farmer gave us the *loan* of his cart.
2. Something lent. – Father got a *loan* of money from the bank to start his business.
–*v. loans, loaned, loaning.* Lend.–The bank *loaned* Father two thousand dollars.

loath (LOHTH) *adj.* Not willing.–Bob was *loath* to tell a lie.

loathe (LOHTH) *v. loathes, loathed, loathing.* Feel disgust or strong dislike for; despise. –Mother *loathes* people who are dishonest.
–*loathing, n. loathings.*

loath•some (LOHTH-səm) *adj.* Making one feel loathing; disgusting.–Rotten eggs have a *loathsome* odor.

loaves (LOHVZ) *n. pl.* More than one *loaf.* –The baker bakes many *loaves* of bread each day.

lob•by (LAH-bee) *n. lobbies.* An outer hall or entrance room.–Smoking is permitted in the *lobby* of the theater.
–*v. lobbies, lobbied, lobbying.* Try to influence members of a legislative body.–A group of dairymen were *lobbying* against a proposed tax on milk. They talked to many members of the lawmaking body and tried to convince them that they should not vote for the milk tax.

lobe (LOHB) *n. lobes.* A rounded section or part.–Mother wears earrings on the *lobes* of her ears.

lob•ster (LAHB-ster) *n. lobsters.* A large shellfish found in the sea. It has two large claws and four pairs of legs. *Lobsters* are good to eat.

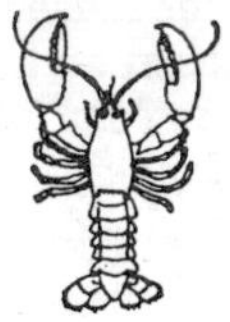

lo•cal (LOH-kəl) *adj.; locally, adv.* 1. Having to do with one certain place.–*Local* laws are those that are made in a place and apply only to that place. –A *local* theater is one nearby.–A *local* infection is one that stays in one part of the body and does not spread to other parts.
2. A *local* train stops at all the stations on the line.

lo•cal•i•ty (loh-KAL-ə-tee) *n. localities.* A place; a certain area.–Bob lives in a different *locality* from Bill.

lo•cate (LOH-kayt) *v. locates, located, locating.* 1. Find; discover the position or location of.–Jack lost his knife and did not *locate* it for a week.–The air force *located* the marooned sailors on the iceberg and rescued them.
2. Put or stand in a place.–Mr. Brown decided to *locate* his hardware store on Maple Street.

lo•ca•tion (loh-KAY-shən) *n. locations.* 1. Place where something is or happens.–The *location* of the castle is on a high hill.
2. Act of locating.–The *location* of our ships by the enemy made our admiral change his battle plans.

lock (LAHK) *n. locks.* 1. An enclosed section of a river or canal in which the water can be raised or lowered so that boats can pass through it to a different level.

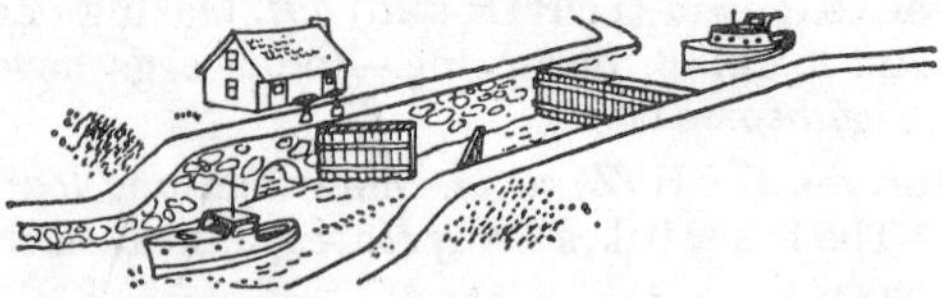

2. A curl; a few short lengths of curly hair. –A *lock* hung down on the baby's forehead.

3. A fastening for doors, drawers, etc., that cannot be opened without a key or a combination of turns. – Grandfather had a new *lock* put on the barn door.

–*v. locks, locked, locking.* 1. Fasten with a lock.–We *lock* our doors at night.

2. Put in a locked place.–The farmer *locked* the horse in the barn. He put the horse in the barn and locked the door.

3. Join. – The girls *locked* arms and walked down the street.

lock•er (LAHK-er) *n. lockers.* A small closet or cupboard that can be locked. – Many schools have *lockers* in which the pupils keep their coats.

lock•et (LAHK-it) *n. lockets.* A small case for holding pictures. *Lockets* are worn on chains that fasten about the neck.

lock•jaw (LAHK-jaw) *n.* A form of blood poisoning in which the jaws become tightly locked; a form of tetanus, a disease that enters the body through wounds.

lock•smith (LAHK-smith) *n. locksmiths.* A person who is skilled in making or repairing locks and keys and earns his living in this way.

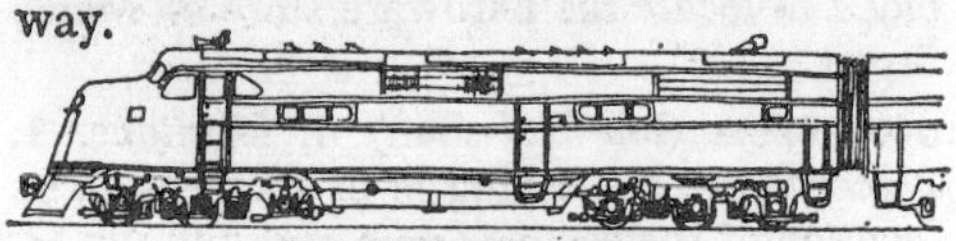

Santa Fe diesel locomotive

lo•co•mo•tive (loh-kə-MOH-tiv) *n. locomotives.* A railroad engine, or any engine, that moves by its own power.

lo•cust (LOH-kəst) *n. locusts.* 1. A kind of grasshopper insect. – *Locusts* often destroy farmers' crops.

2. A tree that bears clusters of sweet-smelling flowers that look like small sweet peas.

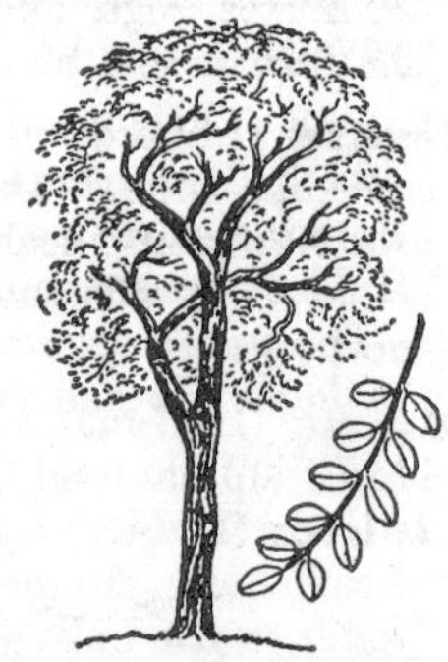

lodge (LAHJ) *n. lodges.* 1. A sportsmen's house in the woods.–Father stayed at a small *lodge* in the woods while hunting.

2. A men's club.–Father goes to the meeting of his *lodge* on Thursday nights.

–*v. lodges, lodged, lodging.* 1. Live. – We *lodged* in a tourist cabin for a week.

2. Land and become stuck.–A piece of dirt *lodged* in my eye.

lodg•ing (LAHJ-ing) *n. lodgings.* 1. A room to live in for a while.–You can get *lodging* at Mrs. Jones's house.

2. *Lodgings* means a room or rooms rented in a house, rather than a hotel.

loft (LAWFT) *n. lofts.* 1. The part of a barn under the roof.–Pigeons made a nest in the barn *loft*.

2. An attic.–Grandmother has an interesting trunk in the *loft*.

loft•y (LAWF-tee) *adj. loftier, loftiest; loftily, adv.* 1. Extremely high; towering. – Mount McKinley, the highest mountain in North America, has a *lofty* peak.

2. Majestic; imposing; exalted. – The Declaration of Independence and the Constitution of the United States express *lofty* ideals and principles.

3. Haughty; proud; dignified.–The prince's manner was *lofty*.

log (LAWG) *n. logs.* 1. A daily record of a ship's voyage.

2. An instrument to measure the speed of, or distance traveled by, a ship.

3. All or part of the trunk or a large branch of a tree after it has been cut down.–Abraham Lincoln lived in a cabin made of *logs*.

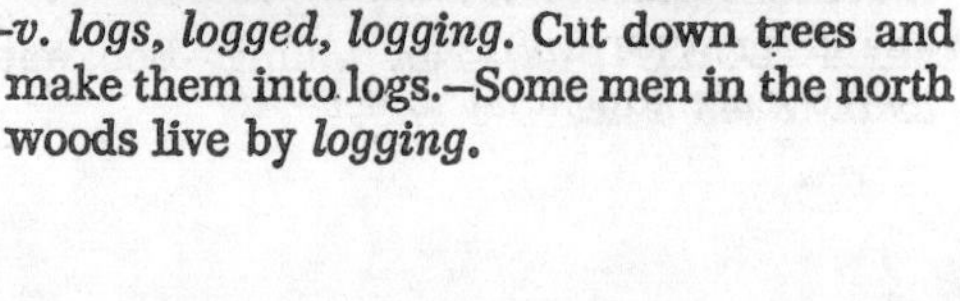

–*v. logs, logged, logging.* Cut down trees and make them into logs.–Some men in the north woods live by *logging*.

log•book (LAWG-buhk) *n. logbooks.* A book in which is kept the daily record of a ship's voyage.

log•ic (LAHJ-ik) *n.; logical, adj.; logically, adv.* 1. The science of reasoning and sound thinking.–I took a course in *logic.*
2. Good sense; sound and reliable thinking. –The man's argument showed a great deal of *logic.* He had good reasons for what he believed.

loi•ter (LOI-ter) *v. loiters, loitered, loitering.* Loaf; hang around doing nothing.–Do not *loiter* in the halls.

loll (LAHL) *v. lolls, lolled, lolling.* Lie lazily. –Sit up. Do not *loll* about in your seat.

lol•li•pop (LAH-lee-pahp) *n. lollipops.* A large lump of hard candy on a stick which serves as a handle.

lone (LOHN) *adj.* 1. Alone; without company or contact with others.–A *lone* wolf is one that does not travel with the pack.
2. Single.–The man had a *lone* dime.

lone•li•ness (LOHN-lee-nəss) *n.* The feeling you have when you are all alone and want to be with other people.

lone•ly (LOHN-lee) *adj. lonelier, loneliest.* 1. Having few people.–This is a *lonely* part of the country.
2. Sad from being alone.–Mary felt *lonely* when the other children were in school.

lone•some (LOHN-səm) *adj.* 1. Lonely; sad from being alone.–The soldier was *lonesome* when he thought of home.
2. Having few people.–This is a *lonesome* part of the country.

long (LAWNG) *adj. longer, longest* and *adv.* 1. Having a great distance from one end to the other.–Bob's pencil is *long;* Mary's is short.–It will be a *long* trip.
2. In length; from end to end.–The ruler is one foot *long.*
3. Extended in time; an extended time.– Winter seemed *long* this year.–How *long* will you be away?–She is *long* getting back.
–v. longs, longed, longing. Wish sadly.–The sick man *longs* to go home.

long•hand (LAWNG-hand) *n.* Writing by hand in the usual fashion; not shorthand or typewriting. –We learn *longhand* in school.

A Golden Book

long•horn (LAWNG-horn) *n. longhorns.* 1. One of a breed of cattle with long horns.
2. A Texas *longhorn,* a special breed of cattle. There are not many of these cattle left.

long•ing (LAWNG-ing) *n. longings.* A strong desire or wish.–Bob had a *longing* to go to the camp.

lon•gi•tude (LAHN-jə-tood *or* -tyood) *n. longitudes.* Distance east or west measured in degrees on the curved surface of the earth. Lines of *longitude,* known as meridians, appear on a map as vertical lines drawn between the North and South Poles. Position in *longitude* is given in degrees west from the "zero meridian," which is the line of *longitude* that passes through Greenwich, England.

look (LUHK) *n. looks.* 1. Appearance.–From the *look* of the cabin, no one lives in it.
2. A stare; the act of looking or watching.– The stranger gave us a long *look.*
–v. looks, looked, looking. 1. Notice by seeing; turn the eyes toward to see.–*Look* at the sunset.
2. Appear to the sight.–The snow *looks* beautiful on the trees.
3. Appear; seem.–It *looks* as though we are late.
4. Search.–Father is *looking* for his lost pen.
5. Face.–Our cottage *looks* toward the sea.

look•ing glass (LUHK-ing glass) *looking glasses.* A mirror; a glass that reflects an image. – Mother looks into a *looking glass* when she fixes her hair.

look•out (LUHK-owt) *n. lookouts.* 1. A state of watchfulness. –A person watching for something to happen is on the *lookout.*
2. A place from which one watches.–The policeman's *lookout* is a high tower.
3. A watchman; a person watching.–The *lookout* saw the train coming.

loom (LOOM) *n. looms.* A machine for weaving threads into cloth. –Jane's great-grandmother made cloth for her family's clothes on her *loom.*

–v. looms, loomed, looming. 1. Weave on a loom.–The rug was *loomed* in Turkey.
2. Appear.–An airplane *loomed* out of the clouds.–A ship *loomed* over the horizon.

loop (LOOP) *n. loops.* A figure formed by something turned to cross itself. A pencil line, a rope, or a thread, when curved around so that it closes or crosses, forms a *loop.*

–*v. loops, looped, looping.* Enclose with a loop.–Bob *looped* the rope over the post.

loose (LOOSS) *adj. looser, loosest; loosely, adv.* 1. Not firm or snug; not tight.–My shoe is *loose.*–The gravel on the road is *loose.*
2. Not fastened.–One end of the dog's leash is *loose.*
3. Free.–Bob's pony got *loose* and ran away.
4. Not enclosed in a package.

loos•en (LOOSS-ən) *v. loosens, loosened, loosening.* Make loose or less tight.–The boy ate so much that he had to *loosen* his belt.

loot (LOOT) *n.* Stolen goods.–The robbers took their *loot* with them.
–*v. loots, looted, looting.* Rob.–The robbers *looted* the store.

lope (LOHP) *v. lopes, loped, loping.* Run with long, easy steps.–See the horse *lope.*

lop•sid•ed (LAHP-sy-dəd) *adj.* Crooked; uneven.–Mary's drawing of the chair is *lopsided.*

lord (LORD) *n. lords.* 1. A ruler; a master.–The man is *lord* of all he owns.
2. In England, a man of noble birth.

Lord (LORD) *n.* God or Jesus Christ.

lose (LOOZ) *v. loses, lost, losing.* 1. Accidentally drop or leave something where one cannot find it; fail to keep; allow to disappear by chance.–If you *lose* your pencil, you will have to use a pen.
2. Have taken away or destroyed. – The farmer *lost* his fruit because of the storm.
3. Be defeated in. – Unless everyone plays well, we may *lose* the ball game.
4. Waste.–We *lost* no time in getting home.
5. Wander from. – Hansel and Gretel *lost* their way.
–*Be lost* means not be able to find one's way.–Hansel and Gretel *were lost* in the woods. They did not know how to get home.

los•er (LOOZ-er) *n. losers.* 1. A defeated person or side.–We were the *losers* in the game.
2. One who has lost something.–Who is the *loser* of this pencil? Who lost it?

loss (LAWSS) *n. losses.* 1. Destruction.–The storm caused great *loss* of property.
2. Failing to keep; a losing; end of having.–The *loss* of his dog made Bob unhappy.
3. Thing lost.–Among our *losses* in the fire were some old family portraits.
4. Defeat.–The *loss* of the ball game put our team in last place.

lost (LAWST) *v.* One form of the verb *lose.*–Mary *lost* her books.–We *lost* the ball game.

lot (LAHT) *n. lots.* 1. A piece of ground or land.–Our house stands on a small *lot.*
2. Something used to make a decision by chance.–We drew *lots* to see who would go to the store for Mother.
3. A group or collection.–This *lot* of coconuts came by train.

lo•tion (LOH-shən) *n. lotions.* A liquid preparation for the skin, used for purposes of health or beauty.–Mother uses hand *lotion* after she does the dishes.

lot•ter•y (LAHT-er-ee) *n. lotteries.* A plan for giving out prizes by chance.–We had a *lottery* to raise money for the club. We sold many tickets, then drew a number which won a prize for the person whose ticket had that number on it.

loud (LOWD) *adj. louder, loudest; loudly, adv.* 1. Of great sound; not soft or quiet.–The door blew shut with a *loud* noise.
2. Showy; bright in color.–Bob's new suit is *loud.*

loud•speak•er (LOWD-SPEEK-er) *n. loudspeakers.* A machine or device which makes sounds louder so that they can be heard more easily.–We heard the radio program over the *loudspeaker* in the school auditorium.

Lou•i•si•an•a (loo-eez-ee-AN-ə *or* looz-ee-AN-ə) *n.* A state in southern United States along the Mississippi River. It has valuable timberlands, trading centers, mines, and gas and oil wells. Sugar cane, rice, strawberries, and vegetables are raised abundantly there.

lounge (LOWNJ) *n. lounges.* 1. A couch; a bed; a sofa.
2. A room where a person can sit or lie around and feel comfortable.

–*v. lounges, lounged, lounging.* Lie or sit lazily.–We *lounged* in the living room.

louse (LOWSS) *n. lice.* A small, flat insect that lives on the bodies of animals, plants, or, sometimes, human beings.

lov•a•ble (LUV-ə-bəl) *adj.; lovably, adv.* Inviting love; attractive.–We have a *lovable* baby. She is easy to love.

love (LUV) *n. loves.* A feeling of deep liking; a pleasant feeling resulting from liking something or someone very much.–Mother has a great *love* for Baby.–John has a *love* of sailing.
–v. loves, loved, loving. 1. Have this feeling for.–Mother *loves* the baby.
2. Like; enjoy.–I *love* reading. I get pleasure from it.

love•ly (LUV-lee) *adj. lovelier, loveliest.* 1. Beautiful.–Mother has a *lovely* new hat.
2. Likable; winning. – Grandmother has a *lovely* way of explaining things to us.

low (LOH) *v. lows, lowed, lowing.* Call softly; moo. – We heard the cattle *lowing* in the distance.
–adj. lower, lowest. 1. Near the ground.–Trees are tall, but bushes are *low.*
2. Mean. – It was a *low* trick to hide the baby's toys.
3. Weak; in poor health.–The sick man is very *low.*
4. Small.–Mary bought a dress for a very *low* price.
5. Almost used up.–Our sugar supply is *low.*
6. Of deep pitch; toward the bottom of the scale.–The girls sang the high notes, and the boys sang the *low* notes.

low•er (LOH-er) *v. lowers, lowered, lowering.* 1. Pull down; let down.–Mother *lowered* the shades to keep out the sun.
2. Make less; reduce. – Rents have been raised, not *lowered.*
–adj. Not as high.–The water in the lake is *lower* than it was last year.

low•land (LOH-lənd) *n. lowlands.* Land that is not as high as the land around it.

low•ly (LOH-lee) *adj. lowlier, lowliest.* Unimportant.–The man is in a *lowly* position.

loy•al (LOI-əl) *adj.; loyally, adv.* Faithful; unchanging in devotion. – Mary is a *loyal* friend. You can always count on her.

lu•bri•cate (LOOB- *or* LYOOB-ri-kayt) *v. lubricates, lubricated, lubricating.* Put oil or grease on to make something work smoothly. –Father had our car *lubricated* so that it would run smoothly.
–lubrication, n. lubrications.

luck (LUK) *n.* Chance, especially good fortune.–It was just by *luck* that I found the money.–It was bad *luck* for the team when the quarterback sprained his ankle.

luck•y (LUK-ee) *adj. luckier, luckiest; luckily, adv.* Fortunate; having good luck.–The sailor was *lucky* to reach shore in the storm.

lug (LUG) *v. lugs, lugged, lugging.* Drag; carry with difficulty.–Bob's dog *lugged* a big boot into the living room.

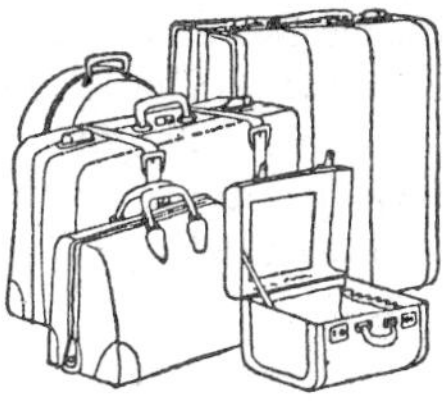

lug•gage (LUG-ij) *n.* Trunks and bags. – Mother packed our *luggage.*

luke•warm (look- *or* lyook-WORM) *adj.* 1. Of medium warmth; a little warm.–Baby drinks milk that is *lukewarm;* it is neither too cool nor too hot.
2. Having slight enthusiasm or interest. – Father was only *lukewarm* toward the plan.

lull (LUL) *n. lulls.* A period of quiet or lack of activity.–After the crash, there was a *lull.*
–v. lulls, lulled, lulling. Quiet; soothe or hush to sleep.–Mother *lulled* the child to sleep.

lull•a•by (LUL-ə-by) *n. lullabies.* A song sung softly to put a baby to sleep.

lum•ber (LUM-ber) *n.* Wood cut into planks, boards, etc.–Trees are cut down for *lumber.*

–v. lumbers, lumbered, lumbering. 1. Cut lumber.–Bob is *lumbering* in Canada.
2. Move awkwardly and noisily.–The wagon *lumbered* up the hill.

lum•ber•man (LUM-ber-mən) *n. lumbermen.* 1. A man who cuts down trees and gets logs ready to cut into boards, planks, etc.
2. A man who buys and sells lumber, or gets lumber ready to sell.

lu•mi•nous (LOO- *or* LYOO-mə-nəss) *adj.; luminously, adv.* Brilliant; shining; giving off light. – Many watches and clocks have *luminous* hands and dials which can be seen in the dark.

lump (LUMP) *n. lumps.* 1. A mass or a bit of anything that has no particular shape.–A *lump* of dirt fell off the truck.

2. A hump; a swelling; a raised place; a bump.–Baby fell off the bed and got a *lump* on her head.

–*v. lumps, lumped, lumping.* 1. Put together into one.–The children *lumped* their savings together to buy a present for Mother.

2. Form lumps.–The gravy *lumped* because it was not stirred well.

–*adj.* In a lump; in one lot.–Mr. Smith offered a *lump* sum of fifty dollars rather than an hourly rate for the job.

lu•nar (LOO- *or* LYOO-ner) *adj.* Having to do with, or like, the moon.–A *lunar* month is shorter than a calendar month. The latter is based on the movements of the sun.

lu•na•tic (LOON- *or* LYOON-ə-tik) *n. lunatics.* An insane person; a person whose mind is sick. Sometimes we call a person a *lunatic* when he is not sick, but just odd.

lunch (LUNCH) *n. lunches.* A light meal.–We eat *lunch* at noon.

–*v. lunches, lunched, lunching.* Eat lunch.–We *lunched* at the restaurant today.

lunch•eon (LUNCH-ən) *n. luncheons.* A lunch; a light meal served for guests around noon.–Mother invited some friends in for *luncheon.*

lung (LUNG) *n. lungs.* One of the pair of organs in the chest that take in fresh air for the body to use.

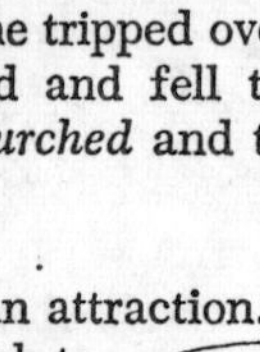

lurch (LERCH) *v. lurches, lurched, lurching.* Stagger or roll from side to side; move suddenly and sharply.–As Jane tripped over the wire, she *lurched* forward and fell to the ground.–The small boat *lurched* and tossed in the storm.

–*lurch, n. lurches.*

lure (LUHR) *n. lures.* 1. An attraction.–The *lure* of the movies drew Bob to town.

2. Something to tempt a fish.–Father has many bright-colored *lures* in his fishing kit.

–*v. lures, lured, luring.* Tempt by offering bait.–The boys *lured* the rabbit into the barn by holding out a carrot.

lurk (LERK) *v. lurks, lurked, lurking.* Hide; wait unseen and unheard. – The hunters *lurked* in the bushes, waiting to see the rabbit come out.

lus•ter (LUSS-ter) *n.* Brightness; shininess.–The maid polished the furniture to a high *luster.*

lute (LOOT *or* LYOOT) *n. lutes.* A stringed musical instrument that was widely used in the sixteenth and seventeenth centuries.

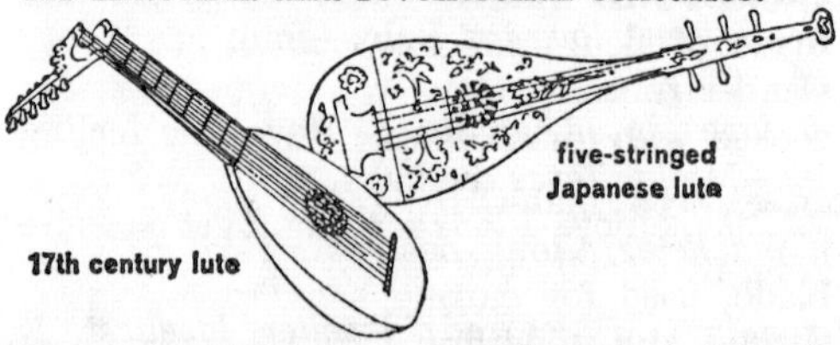

lux•u•ry (LUK-sher-ee) *n. luxuries.* 1. Rich comfort; condition of having much that is pleasant but not necessary to have.–The rich man lives in *luxury.*

2. Something which one has just for the pleasure of having it and not because it is needed.–Mother said a piano would be a *luxury* for our family, since no one could play it.

lye (LY) *n.* A substance used in making soap and for cleaning. *Lye* is a deadly poison.

ly•ing (LY-ing) *n.* The telling of falsehoods. –*Lying* about something doesn't change it.

lymph (LIMF) *n.* An almost colorless liquid found in the tissues of the body. *Lymph,* which is similar to blood, lacks red blood cells.

lynx (LINGKS) *n. lynx* or *lynxes.* A wildcat with long legs and a short tail.

lyre (LYR) *n. lyres.* A stringed musical instrument that was played by people long, long ago, particularly in ancient Greece.

lyr•ic (LIR-ik) *n. lyrics; lyrical, adj.* 1. A short poem that expresses some strong personal feeling of the writer.

2. A poem written to be set to music. The words for a song are the *lyrics.*

Mm

M, m (EM) *n. M's, m's.* The thirteenth letter of the alphabet.

ma (MAH) *n. mas.* Some children call their mothers *Ma.*

mac•a•ro•ni (ma-kə-ROH-nee) *n.* A food made of flour and water dried into long, slender tubes. – Have you eaten *macaroni* cooked with tomatoes and cheese?

ma•che•te (mah-CHAY-tay *or* mə-SHET-ee) *n. machetes.* A long, heavy knife with a broad blade, used for cutting sugar cane, vines, shrubs, and underbrush, in such places as Cuba, Haiti, and the West Indies. The *machete* is sometimes used as a weapon.

ma•chine (mə-SHEEN) *n. machines.* Something planned and built to do certain work more quickly and better than people could do it. Some *machines,* such as carpet sweepers, are simple and are worked by hand. Others, such as airplanes and printing presses, are large and are run by burning fuel or by electricity.

ma•chine gun (mə-SHEEN gun) *machine guns.* A gun that fires bullets automatically and very rapidly as long as the trigger is pressed.

M-60 hand machine gun (mounted)

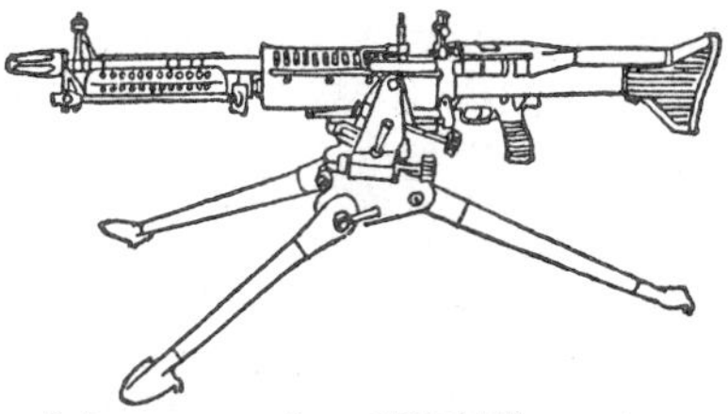

ma•chin•er•y (mə-SHEEN-ə-ree) *n.* 1. A group of machines.–Some of the *machinery* in the plant has broken down.
2. The parts of a machine.–Our vacuum cleaner has stopped working. Father thinks that something must be wrong with the *machinery.*

ma•chin•ist (mə-SHEEN-ist) *n. machinists.* Someone who makes or runs machines, or keeps them in working order.

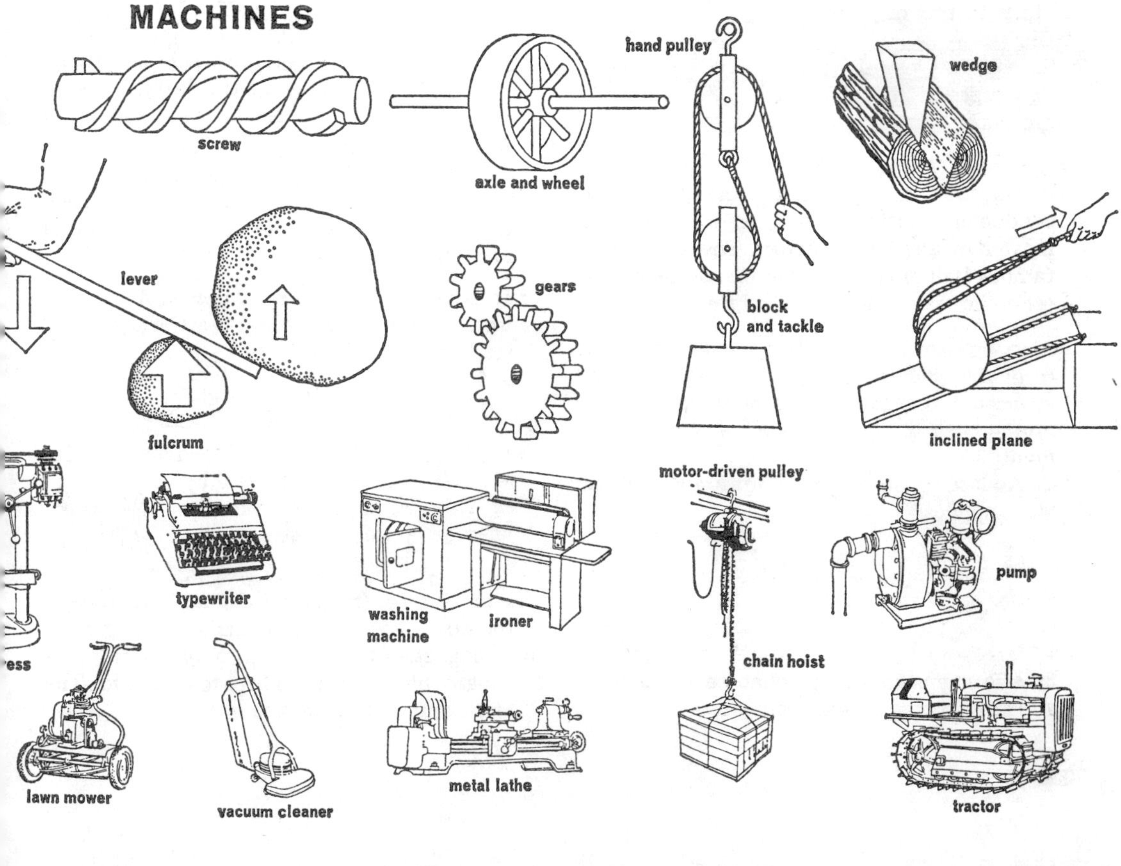

mack•er•el (MAK-er-əl *or* MAK-rəl) *n. mackerel* or *mackerels.* A medium-sized ocean fish that is good to eat.

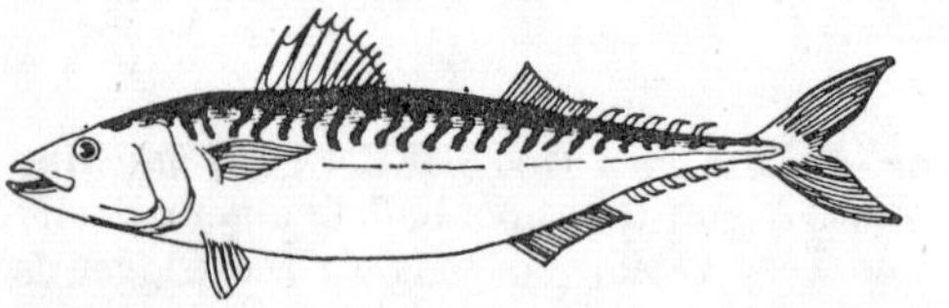

mad (MAD) *adj. madder, maddest; madly, adv.; madness, n.* 1. Crazy or insane.–The miser went *mad* when he lost his money.
2. Wild and foolish.–Mary has a *mad* desire to be a movie actress.
3. Some people say *mad* when they mean angry.–Jack was *mad* at Bill for taking his bicycle without asking for it.
4. Some people say *mad* when they mean delighted with something. – Mary is *mad* about her new dress.
5. Having the disease of rabies, or hydrophobia.–If one is bitten by a *mad* dog, he should go to a doctor at once.

mad•am (MAD-əm) *n.* A polite name for a woman.–The clerk said to Mother, "May I help you, *madam?*"

made (MAYD) *v.* One form of the verb *make.* –Sally *made* a valentine for Father.

Ma•don•na (mə-DAHN-ə) *n.* 1. The Virgin Mary, mother of Jesus Christ.
2. A statue, painting, or picture of the Virgin Mary.

maes•tro (MYSS-troh) *n. maestros.* A noted or respected orchestra conductor, music teacher, or composer; a master in any art. – Arturo Toscanini, the famous Italian *maestro,* was one of the greatest orchestra conductors of all time.

mag•a•zine (mag-ə-ZEEN) *n. magazines.* 1. A publication, usually paper-covered, that comes out at regular times. Some *magazines* are published once a week, some once a month.
2. A place for storing ammunition and other war supplies.

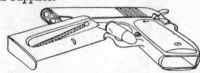

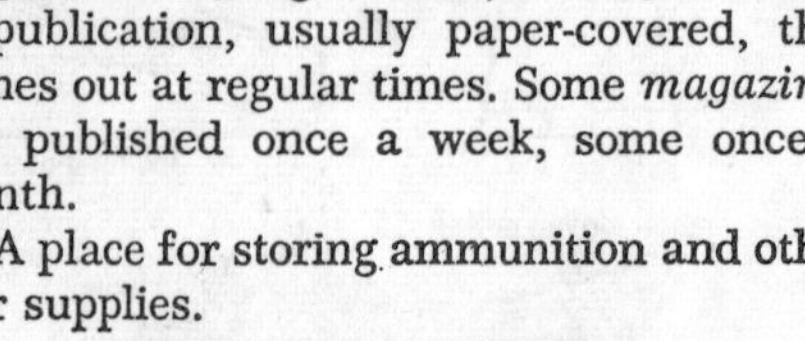

3. The compartment or chamber of a gun which holds the cartridges.

mag•got (MAG-ət) *n. maggots.* The worm-like first stage of development of some insects. Some *maggots* turn into flies.

mag•ic (MAJ-ik) *n.; magic* or *magical, adj.; magically, adv.* Things happening by mysterious powers; also, the pretended art of producing effects by mysterious powers. – In olden times, people believed in *magic.*–In the story, the fairy godmother used *magic* to turn the pumpkin into a coach.

ma•gi•cian (mə-JI-shən) *n. magicians.* 1. A man who does tricks that mystify or puzzle people.–The *magician* pulled a rabbit out of Father's hat.
2. In olden times, a man believed to have magic powers.–The *magician* gave the king a sword which would cut through stone.

mag•is•trate (MAJ-is-trayt) *n. magistrates.* 1. An officer of the government having the power to apply and enforce the law.–The governor is the chief *magistrate* of a state.
2. A minor judge. – The police *magistrate* fined the driver for speeding.

mag•ma (MAG-mə) *n. magmata.* Melted rock, either in fluid form or in paste, that originates deep within the earth.–Lava, the fluid rock which flows from a volcano in eruption, is a form of *magma.*

mag•nan•i•mous (mag-NAN-ə-məss) *adj.* Very generous towards others; giving others more than you expect from them. – David gave his favorite toy to the little boy who didn't have any toys. It was a *magnanimous* thing for him to have done.–It was *magnanimous* of Ted to forgive the child who smashed his toy. Ted was sorry that his toy had been broken, but he told the child that it didn't matter.

mag•net (MAG-nət) *n. magnets.* A piece of iron or stone that pulls or attracts iron or steel objects toward it.

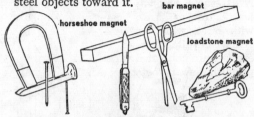

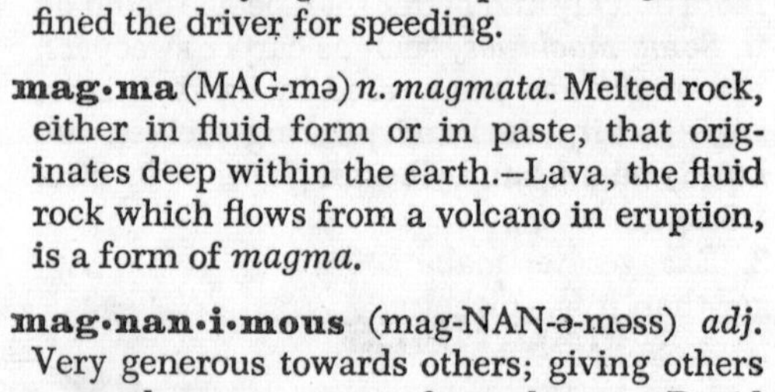

mag•net•ic (mag-NET-ik) *adj.* 1. Having the powers or properties of, or dealing with, a magnet.–Anything with *magnetic* force is capable of attracting things to it, as a magnet attracts iron and steel.

2. Capable of being attracted by a magnet, or of becoming magnetized.–Iron is *magnetic.*
3. Attractive; charming.–The movie star's *magnetic* personality draws large audiences to her pictures.

mag•net•ism (MAG-nə-tiz-əm) *n.* 1. The power of a magnet; the quality of being magnetic.
2. The power to charm or attract others.–The child felt the teacher's *magnetism.*

mag•net•ize (MAG-nə-tyz) *v. magnetizes, magnetized, magnetizing.* 1. Make magnetic; give the powers and properties of a magnet to something.–An electromagnet is *magnetized* through the use of electricity.
2. Charm. – The storyteller *magnetized* the children with his beautiful tale.

mag•nif•i•cent (mag-NIF-ə-sənt) *adj.; magnificently, adv.; magnificence, n.* 1. Grand and splendid. – The opera house is *magnificent.*
2. Beautiful and brilliant.–We watched the *magnificent* sunset.

mag•ni•fy (MAG-nə-fy) *v. magnifies, magnified, magnifying.* 1. Cause to look larger. –Grandmother's eyeglasses *magnify* things.
2. Exaggerate; make something sound bigger than it is.–Fishermen sometimes *magnify* the size of the fish they catch.

mag•ni•tude (MAG-nə-tood *or* -tyood) *n.* 1. Size.–The *magnitude* of the gift was unknown.
2. Greatness, either in size or importance. –It is practically impossible to describe the *magnitude* of the universe.

mag•no•li•a (mag-NOHL-yə) *n. magnolias.* A tree or shrub with large white or yellowish-white flowers. Certain cultivated varieties have pink or purplish flowers before the leaves appear.

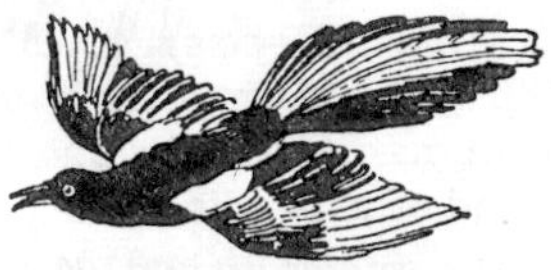

mag•pie (MAG-py) *n. magpies.* A black-and-white bird known for its noisy chattering.

ma•hog•a•ny (mə-HAHG-ə-nee) *n.* A tree found in hot countries. Its hard, reddish-brown wood is used for making furniture.

maid (MAYD) *n. maids.* 1. A girl or woman who does housework in someone else's house, for pay.
2. A young woman who is not married.

maid•en (MAY-dən) *n. maidens.* A girl or young woman who is not married.
–*adj.* First (trip, voyage, etc.).–Father went on the ship's *maiden* voyage. It was the ship's first trip.

maid of hon•or (mayd əv AHN-er). In a wedding ceremony, the unmarried principal attendant of the bride. If married, this attendant is called a "matron of honor." The *maid of honor* is a witness to the wedding.

mail (MAYL) *n. mails.* Letters, cards, packages, and other things sent through the post office.–Sally received a great deal of *mail* on her birthday.
–*v. mails, mailed, mailing.* Drop into a mailbox, or send through the post office. – Bob went to the corner to *mail* the letter.

mail•bag (MAYL-bag) *n. mailbags.* A leather or canvas bag used for carrying mail.

mail•box (MAYL-bahks) *n. mailboxes.* A box in a post office or building, on a house, or on a street, where mail is put by the sender or by the mailman.

mail•man (MAYL-man) *n. mailmen.* A man who delivers mail from the post office, and picks up mail from mailboxes.

maim (MAYM) *v. maims, maimed, maiming.* Hurt badly, so as to cripple.–If you play in the street, a car may strike you and *maim* you.

main (MAYN) *n. mains.* 1. Ocean or sea.–The pirates went sailing over the rough and rolling *main.*

2. A large pipe. – When the water *main* burst, water ran all over the street.–Gas for cooking often comes through gas *mains.*

–*adj.* Chief or most important.–We eat our *main* meal at noon. We eat dinner at noon. –The *main* purpose of Mother's trip downtown was to buy a new dress.

Maine (MAYN) *n.* A mountainous state on the rocky eastern coast of the United States, largely bounded by Canada. *Maine* is over half wooded. The state is important for its wood and wood pulp, for its farm products, especially potatoes, for its paper and cotton mills, and for its shoe factories.

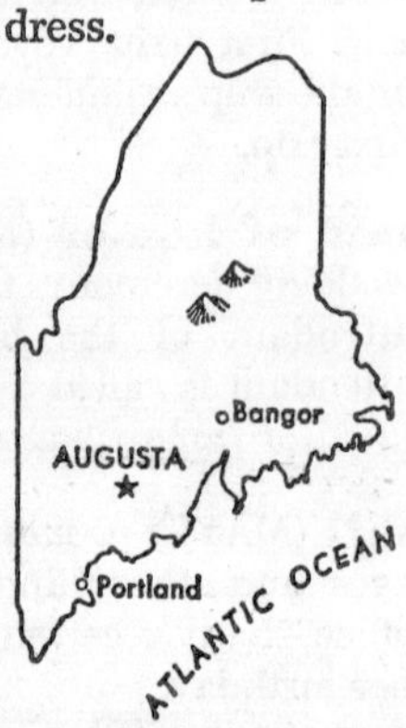

main·land (MAYN-lənd) *n.* A large body of land.–When we lived on the island for the summer, we had to row to the *mainland* to buy food.

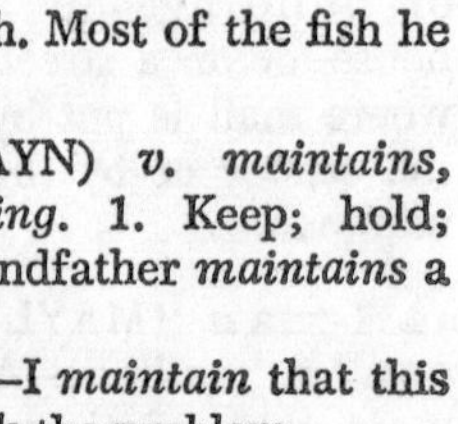

main·ly (MAYN-lee) *adv.* Chiefly or mostly. – The fisherman's catch was *mainly* perch. Most of the fish he caught were perch.

main·tain (mayn-TAYN) *v. maintains, maintained, maintaining.* 1. Keep; hold; have and support.–Grandfather *maintains* a large farm.

2. Insist; say strongly.–I *maintain* that this is the right way to work the problem.

maize (MAYZ) *n.* The kind of corn grown originally in America.

–*adj.* Deep yellow; of the color of corn. – Mother's Easter suit is *maize.*

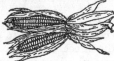

maj·es·ty (MAJ-ə-stee) *n. majesties; majestic, adj.* 1. Stateliness, dignity, and grandeur. –The music of the hymn had great *majesty.*

2. *Your Majesty* is a title used in speaking to kings and queens.

3. *His Majesty* and *Her Majesty* are titles used in speaking of kings and queens.

ma·jor (MAY-jer) *n. majors.* An army officer whose rank is just above that of captain.

–*adj.* 1. Greater.–We spent the *major* part of our vacation at Grandmother's.

2. In music, the *major* scale is one of the two principal scales.

ma·jor·i·ty (mə-JAHR-ə-tee *or* mə-JAWR-ə-tee) *n. majorities.* 1. Greater number; most. –The *majority* of children in town go to our school.

2. More than half.–Bob received a *majority* of the votes for captain of the team.

3. More (in number) than any other.–Bob won by a *majority* of five. He received five more votes than anyone else.

make (MAYK) *n. makes.* A kind or sort. – Father's new car is of a different *make* from the old one.

–*v. makes, made, making.* 1. Build; construct; prepare.–Many boys like to *make* model airplanes.–Most girls would rather *make* candy.

2. Cause.–Mary never *makes* trouble for her teacher.

3. Cause to become.–The furnace *makes* the house warm.

4. Be or become.–Bob will *make* a good captain.–Kind people *make* friends easily.

5. Be; amount to.–Ten and five *make* fifteen.

6. Earn. – Jack *makes* ten dollars a week from his newspaper route.

7. Force or compel.–If Baby does not want to eat, Mother does not *make* her.

–*Make believe* means pretend.–Mary likes to *make believe* she is an actress.

–*Make a difference* means matter.–Does it *make any difference* where you go to school?

mak·er (MAYK-er) *n. makers.* 1. A person who makes something.–The shop of the toy*maker* was bright and sunny.

2. Something which makes something else. –At New Year's, people sound horns, rattles, and other noise*makers.*

ma·lar·i·a (mə-LAIR-ee-ə) *n.* A disease causing chills, high fever, and sweating. It is given to human beings by the bite of a particular kind of mosquito.

male (MAYL) *n. males* and *adj.* A man, boy, or he animal.–A rooster is a *male;* a hen is a female.

mal·lard (MAL-erd) *n. mallard* or *mallards.* A kind of wild duck.

mal·let (MAL-ət) *n. mallets.* A wooden hammer.–Jack used a *mallet* to shape the copper bowl.–We use *mallets* with long handles to hit the balls in croquet.

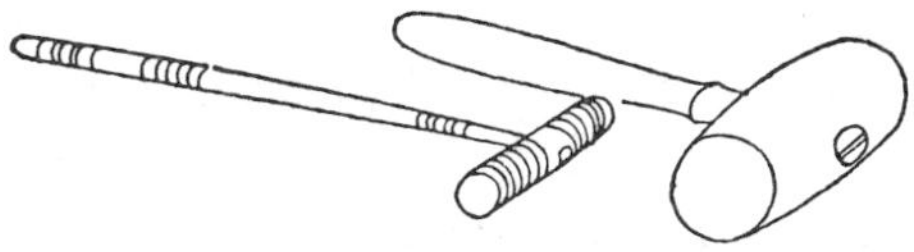

mal·nu·tri·tion (mal-noo-TRISH-ən *or* mal-nyoo-TRISH-ən) *n.* Lack of the proper food to maintain health; poor nourishment. –If you ate nothing but candy all the time, you would soon begin to suffer seriously from *malnutrition.*

malt (MAWLT) *n. malts.* Barley or other grain that has been soaked in water until it sprouts, or begins to grow. *Malt* is used in making some kinds of drinks.

mam·ma (MAH-mə) *n. mammas.* A child's word for mother.

mam·mal (MAM-əl) *n. mammals.* One of the order, or group, of animals that have warm blood and feed their young at the breast. Man is a *mammal.* Cats, dogs, bears, and whales are other examples of *mammals.* Fish, birds, and insects are some of the animals that are not *mammals.*

mam·moth (MAM-əth) *n. mammoths.* A kind of hairy elephant with long tusks that lived long, long ago.

–*adj.* 1. Huge; very, very large.–The "Queen Mary" is a *mammoth* ship.

2. Tremendous; very great.–It was a *mammoth* task to rebuild the bombed city.

man (MAN) *n. men.* 1. A full-grown male person.–Boys grow up to be *men.*

2. *Man* sometimes means the human race.– *Man* has invented many wonderful things.

–*v. mans, manned, manning.* Provide with men to operate.–The ship was *manned* by a crew of fifty.

MAMMALS

EXISTING MAMMALS

EXTINCT MAMMALS

man•age (MAN-ij) *v. manages, managed, managing.* 1. Control; handle; do things with.–Jack *managed* the horse well at the county fair.
2. Run or carry on a business for someone.–Father *manages* a shoe store.
3. Find a way; be able.–Mother *manages* to give us lunch and feed the baby at the same time.
4. Get along. – Jack will *manage* on the money he has earned.

man•age•ment (MAN-ij-mənt) *n. managements.* 1. Direction; control; way of running a thing.–With careful *management,* you can make your money last all week.
2. The managers; people in control. – Ed spoke to the *management* of the restaurant about the mistake in his check.

man•ag•er (MAN-ə-jer) *n. managers.* A person in charge.–Father is the *manager* of a shoe store.

man•do•lin (MAN-də-lin) *n. mandolins.* A musical instrument with strings stretched over a sound box. We play a *mandolin* by picking the strings with a flat pick.

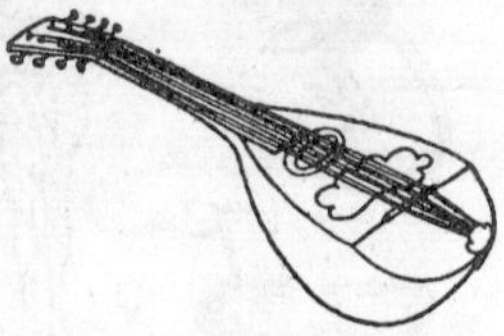

mane (MAYN) *n. manes.* The long hair that grows on the head and neck of some animals. – My horse's *mane* streams in the wind when we gallop.

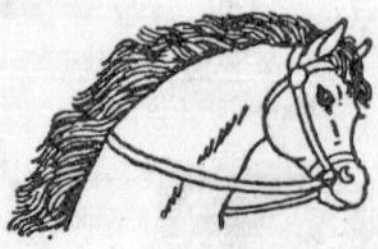

ma•neu•ver (mə-NOO-ver *or* mə-NYOO-ver) *n. maneuvers.* A planned movement.–We went to the bay to watch the *maneuvers* of the yachts.–It proved a clever *maneuver* to buy the property.
–*v. maneuvers, maneuvered, maneuvering.* 1. Make a series of planned moves.–The yacht *maneuvered* to get in the right position for the start of the race.
2. Scheme.–Mary always *maneuvers* to sit near the teacher.

man•ger (MAYN-jer) *n. mangers.* An open box from which horses and cows eat.

man•gle (MANG-gəl) *n. mangles.* A machine with rollers that irons such things as sheets, linens, and clothing.

–*v. mangles, mangled, mangling.* Crush and tear.–A careful machinist like Mr. Block would never catch his hand in a machine and *mangle* his fingers.

man•i•cure (MAN-ə-kyuhr) *n. manicures.* A cleaning, filing, and polishing of the fingernails.–Sometimes Mother gives Mary a *manicure.*
–*v. manicures, manicured, manicuring.* Clean, file, and polish the fingernails.–Mother *manicures* her nails.
–*manicurist, n. manicurists.*

ma•nip•u•late (mə-NIP-yə-layt) *v. manipulates, manipulated, manipulating.* 1. Handle, operate, treat, or work, especially with skill. –Tom *manipulates* the sails of his boat like a sailor.
2. Manage or control cleverly, often with intent to cheat or deceive.–The dishonest politician tried to *manipulate* the election in order to win.
–*manipulation, n. manipulations.*

man•kind (man-KYND) *n.* All people, as a group; human beings; the human race.–All *mankind* desires peace.

man•ner (MAN-er) *n. manners.* 1. A way.–The children treat the kitten in a gentle *manner.*
2. (In the plural) *Manners* means ways of doing things.–Sally has good *manners.* She is polite to her guests.–Bob has bad *manners.* He eats with his knife and leaves his spoon in his cup.

man•sion (MAN-shən) *n. mansions.* A large, beautiful house.–The rich family lives in a *mansion.*

man•tel (MAN-tl) *n. mantels.* A shelf above a fireplace.—We hung our stockings from the *mantel.*

man•tle (MAN-tl) *n. mantles.* 1. A loose cloak without sleeves. — King Arthur's knights wore *mantles.*
2. Any smooth covering. — A *mantle* of snow covered the ground on Christmas morning.

man•u•al (MAN-yoo-əl) *n. manuals.* 1. A handbook of directions.—Mary received a *manual* telling how to make the marionettes.
2. A book telling how to use another book. —The teacher has a reading *manual* It tells how to use the reader.
—*adj.* Done with the hands.—Hoeing the garden is *manual* work.

man•u•fac•ture (man-yə-FAK-cher) *n.* Making in factories.—The *manufacture* of automobiles is a big business.
—*v. manufactures, manufactured, manufacturing.* Make in factories in great numbers. — They *manufacture* many automobiles in Detroit, Michigan.

man•u•fac•tur•er (man-yə-FAK-cher-er) *n. manufacturers.* A person who owns a factory where goods are manufactured.—The *manufacturer* supplies Father with shoes for his shoe store.

ma•nure (mə-NUHR *or* -NYUHR) *n.* Animal waste from the barn.—The farmer spreads *manure* over his fields. *Manure* helps the crops grow.

man•u•script (MAN-yə-skript) *n. manuscripts.* A book or article written by hand or on a typewriter; a piece of writing not in published form.

man•y (MEN-ee) *n.* A large number.—Father is one of the *many* who watch football games on television.—She knew *many* of the answers.
—*adj. more, most.* A great number of.—*Many* people were at the game.
—*pron.* A large number of people or things.— Some people stayed at home, but *many* came.

map (MAP) *n. maps.* A drawing of all or a part of the earth. On a *map* the cities are often represented by dots, and the rivers by lines.

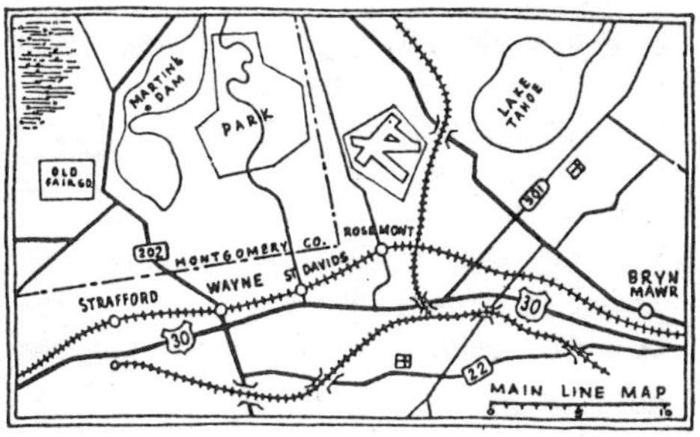

—*v. maps, mapped, mapping.* 1. Make a map of.—Some parts of the world have never been *mapped.*
2. Plan.—Each day we *map* out our work.

ma•ple (MAY-pəl) *n. maples* and *adj.* A large shade tree. *Maple* syrup and sugar are made from the sap of one kind of *maple.* Furniture is made from the light-colored wood of another kind.

mar (MAHR) *v. mars, marred, marring.* Spoil; ruin. — The teacher asked us not to *mar* the tops of our desks by writing or scratching on them.

mar•ble (MAHR-bəl) *n. marbles.* 1. A hard stone, often white, used for statues and big buildings.
2. A small ball, usually of glass, with which you can play games.—Do you ever play with *marbles?*

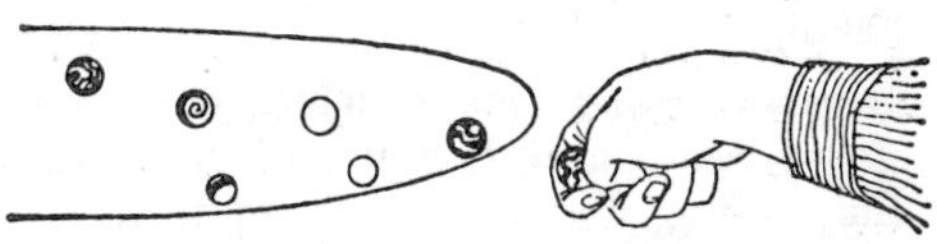

march (MAHRCH) *n. marches.* Music to walk in time to.—The school band played a *march* in the parade.
—*v. marches, marched, marching.* Walk in time, taking steps of the same length.—Jack's uncle taught the boys to *march.*

March (MAHRCH) *n. Marches.* The third month of the year. *March* has thirty-one days.

mare (MAIR) *n. mares.* A female or she horse. —Uncle Paul's *mare* won the big race.

mar•ga•rine (MAHR-jə-rin) *n. margarines.* A food made of fats and vegetable oils.–We sometimes spread *margarine* on our bread instead of butter.

mar•gin (MAHR-jin) *n. margins.* A blank border around a printed or written page.–When Mary writes a composition, she leaves a *margin* on her paper.

mar•i•gold (MAR-ə-gohld) *n. marigolds.* A flower with many yellow, red, or orange petals.

ma•rim•ba (mə-RIM-bə) *n. marimbas.* A musical instrument made of a series of wooden bars of different sizes laid on a frame and designed to produce different musical tones when struck by small hammers or sticks.–*Marimbas* are often used in South American dance orchestras.

ma•rine (mə-REEN) *n. marines.* A soldier in the U.S. *Marine* Corps. He can fight on land and at sea.

–*adj.* Of or belonging to the sea. – Fish are *marine* animals.

mar•i•ner (MAR-ə-ner) *n. mariners.* A seaman or sailor. – The *mariner* was glad to be on his ship again.

mar•i•o•nette (mar-ee-ə-NET) *n. marionettes.* A doll or little figure which moves by the pulling of strings fastened to its arms and legs.–Mary made the *marionette* dance across the stage.

mar•i•time (MAR-ə-tym) *adj.* 1. Having to do with the sea, boats, shipping, etc. – Bob likes to read *maritime* stories.

2. Living or located by, near, or on the sea. –Sailors and fishermen usually live in *maritime* cities. They usually live in cities along the coast.

mark (MAHRK) *n. marks.* 1. A target or object aimed at.–The hunter's shot hit the *mark.*

2. A scar.–The deep cut on Father's thumb left a *mark.*

3. A sign or indication.–France presented the United States with the Statue of Liberty as a *mark* of friendship.

4. A line, cross, or any written figure.–The children made chalk *marks* on the sidewalk.

5. A grade.–Jack got a high *mark* in arithmetic, though his *mark* in spelling was C.

–*v. marks, marked, marking.* 1. Indicate.–Bob *marked* with a large stone the place where he found the strange flowers.

2. Put a tag or name on.–On Christmas Eve we wrap and *mark* the presents.

3. Put a grade on.–The teacher let us exchange our spelling papers and *mark* them ourselves.

–*Mark my words* means "Listen to what I'm saying; it's the truth."–*Mark my words,* Jack will be a great man some day.

mar•ket (MAHR-kit) *n. markets.* 1. A place where goods are traded, bought, or sold. – Mother goes to the fruit *market* to buy watermelon.

2. A demand.–There is a great *market* for sugar in this country.

–*v. markets, marketed, marketing.* 1. Shop for food.–Mother *markets* on Saturday.

2. Sell. – Grandfather *markets* his cattle in the city.

mar•ma•lade (MAHR-mə-layd) *n.* A kind of preserve eaten on bread. Orange *marmalade* is made of sugar, oranges, and orange peelings.–We have *marmalade* on our toast at breakfast.

ma•roon (mə-ROON) *v. maroons, marooned, marooning.* Put (a person) on a lonely island, or some such desolate place, and leave him there.—The captain threatened to *maroon* the stowaway on an island.
—*adj.* Of a dark red color.—Mother has a *maroon* suit.

mar•riage (MAR-ij) *n. marriages.* 1. The ceremony by which a man and a woman become husband and wife. – The bride wore white for her *marriage.*
2. Life together as husband and wife.—My parents' *marriage* is a very happy one.

mar•row (MAR-oh) *n.* The soft substance found inside most bones.—The ghost story frightened her to the *marrow* of her bones.

mar•ry (MAR-ee) *v. marries, married, marrying.* 1. Take as husband or wife.—Jean will *marry* John.
2. Become husband and wife. – They will *marry* in June.
3. Make husband and wife.—The Reverend Frank Brown will *marry* Jean and John.

Mars (MAHRZ) *n.* 1. The god of war worshiped in ancient Rome.
2. The fourth planet from the sun in our solar system. *Mars* is known as the "red planet" because of its reddish appearance.

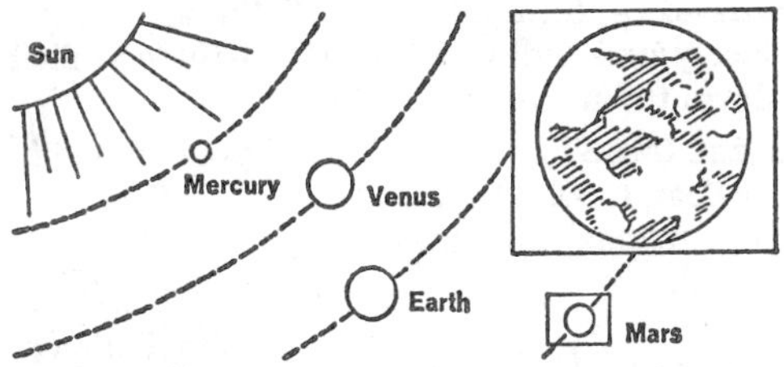

marsh (MAHRSH) *n. marshes.* A swamp or lowland partly covered by water.—Cattails grow in the *marsh.*

mar•shal (MAHRSH-əl) *n. marshals.* 1. A high officer of the court; a police officer; in some countries, a high army officer.
2. An officer who makes arrangements for special events, such as parades.
—*v. marshals, marshaled, marshaling.* Call together and place in order.—The general *marshaled* his forces for the attack.

marsh•mal•low (MAHRSH-mel-oh) *n. marshmallows.* A kind of soft, white candy covered with powdered sugar. – We toasted *marshmallows* over the campfire when we visited the Boy Scout camp.

mar•tin (MAHR-tn) *n. martins.* A bird something like a swallow.

mar•tyr (MAHR-ter) *n. martyrs.* A person who dies or undergoes great hardship for something he believes in rather than give up his belief.

mar•vel (MAHR-vəl) *n. marvels.* A wonder; a wonderful thing.—Electricity is one of the *marvels* of the world today.
—*v. marvels, marveled, marveling.* Wonder.—We stopped to *marvel* at the beauty of the waterfall.

mar•vel•ous (MAHR-vəl-əss) *adj.; marvelously, adv.* Amazing and wonderful.—The magician did some *marvelous* tricks.—The view from the top of the mountain was *marvelous.*

Mar•y•land (MAIR-ə-lənd) *n.* A state on the east coast of the United States in which farming, fishing, and the manufacture of clothing and many other articles are important industries.

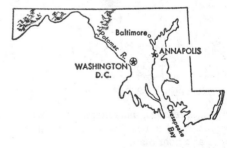

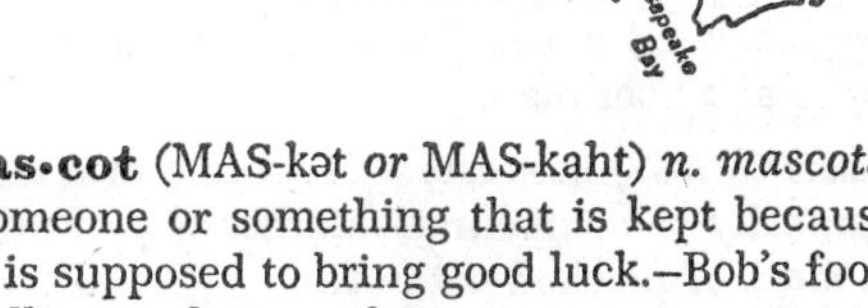

mas•cot (MAS-kət *or* MAS-kaht) *n. mascots.* Someone or something that is kept because it is supposed to bring good luck.—Bob's football team has a white mouse as a *mascot.* Fred's team has a billy goat.

mas•cu•line (MASS-kyə-lin) *adj.* 1. Strong and manly.—Jack's voice is very *masculine.*
2. Mannish; like a man's.—Sue doesn't wear slacks because she thinks they are too *masculine* for girls.

mash (MASH) *n.* A mixture containing boiled grain or bran, used as a food for farm animals.
–*v. mashes, mashed, mashing.* Crush or beat. –Mary helps Mother *mash* the potatoes.

mask (MASK) *n. masks.* A covering to hide the face and disguise the person wearing it.– A false face is a *mask.*

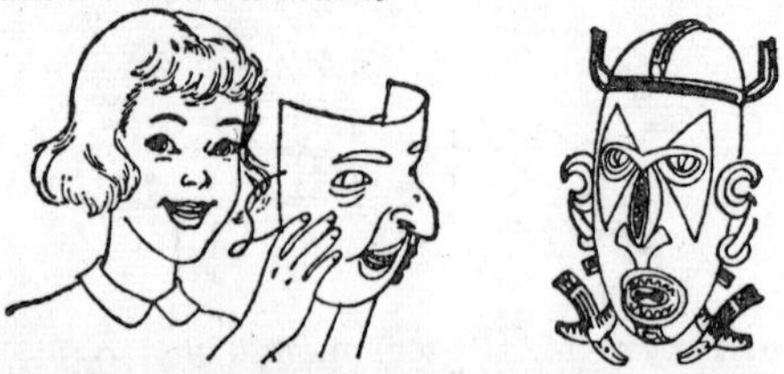

–*v. masks, masked, masking.* 1. Wear a mask. –Mary *masked* for the Halloween party.
2. Hide by covering or concealing.–Jack tried to *mask* his feelings.

ma•son (MAY-sən) *n. masons.* A person who builds with stone or brick.–Father hired a *mason* to build a stone wall around our house.

mas•quer•ade (mask-ə-RAYD) *n. masquerades.* A party at which people wear masks or disguises.

–*v. masquerades, masqueraded, masquerading.* Pretend to be.–The rich miser *masquerades* as a poor man.

mass (MASS) *n. masses.* 1. A lump or a large quantity of something.–Mother gave Father a *mass* of mashed potatoes.
2. The greater number; majority.–The *mass* of people voted for a new park.
3. (Spelled with a capital "M.") A service in the Roman Catholic Church.
-*v. masses, massed, massing.* Put together or collect.–The flags were *massed* at the head of the parade.

Mas•sa•chu•setts (mass-ə-CHYOO-sətss) *n.* A state on the east coast of the United States. *Massachusetts* is important for its many educational institutions and printing and publishing houses. Important also are its manufacturing of shoes, rubber goods, cloth, and leather goods, and its fishing industries.

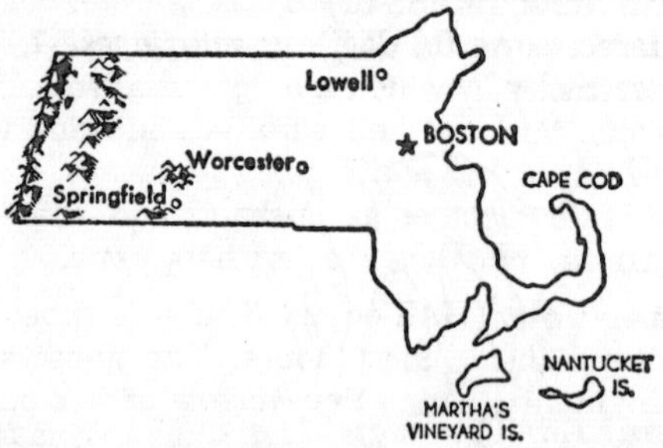

mas•sa•cre (MASS-ə-ker) *n. massacres.* A cruel killing of many people.
–*v. massacres, massacred, massacring.* Kill without pity.–The savages *massacred* their prisoners.

mas•sage (mə-SAHZH) *v. massages, massaged, massaging.* Treat the muscles and joints of the body by rubbing, patting, and kneading, to remove stiffness, stimulate blood circulation, and improve general physical condition.–The athlete was *massaged* after the game.

mas•sive (MASS-iv) *adj.* Solid and large; heavy and bulky.–A *massive* boulder rolled down the mountain.

mast (MAST) *n. masts.* A tall pole on a ship or boat, to which sails and ropes are fastened.

mas•ter (MAST-er) *n. masters.* 1. A person who rules or controls. –In olden times, a king was the real *master* of his country. Everyone had to do as he said.
2. An expert; one who knows all about a certain subject.–Mary's music teacher is a *master* of his subject.
3. (Spelled with a capital "M.") A title of respect for a boy.–Jay's father is called Mr. Ray Smith. Jay is called *Master* Jay Smith.
4. A man schoolteacher.
–*v. masters, mastered, mastering.* 1. Overcome or control.–Bob has learned to *master* his temper.
2. Thoroughly learn.–Sally has *mastered* the alphabet.

mas•ter•piece (MASS-ter-peess) *n. masterpieces.* Something done with exceptional skill, taste, art, and craftsmanship; an extraordinary example of art or skill.–The art museum in our city contains many *masterpieces.*

mas•tiff (MASS-tif) *n. mastiffs.* A kind of large, powerful dog. A *mastiff* makes a good watchdog.

mat (MAT) *n. mats.* 1. A small rug.–Mother keeps a *mat* at the door for us to wipe our feet on.
2. A pad.–Small *mats* are placed under hot dishes to protect the table.
3. A piece of cardboard forming a border around a picture.–Bob pasted his picture on a blue *mat.*
–*v. mats, matted, matting.* Tangle and stick together.–Mud has *matted* the puppy's fur.

match (MACH) *n. matches.* 1. A little stick of wood or cardboard tipped with a material that makes a flame when the tip is scratched against a rough or chemically prepared surface.–Father lights his pipe with a *match.*

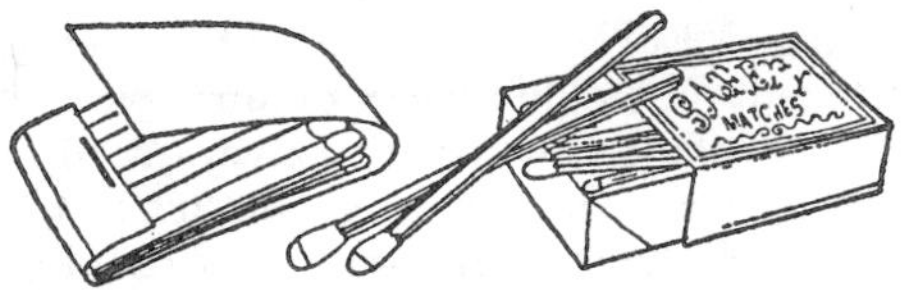

2. A contest.–Our team won the spelling *match.*
3. An equal; one as good as.–Jack is a good runner, but he is no *match* for Bob.
4. A well-suited pair.–Father and Mother are a good *match.*
–*v. matches, matched, matching.* 1. Find or make something just like another.–Mother could not *match* the material of Mary's dress.
2. Be the same as, especially in color.–Sally's hair ribbon *matches* her dress. They are both light blue.

mate (MAYT) *n. mates.* 1. One of a pair.–Bob cannot find the *mate* to his blue sock.
2. A husband or wife.
3. On a ship, an officer who ranks just below the captain.
–*v. mates, mated, mating.* Pair off in couples. –Birds *mate* in the spring.

ma•te•ri•al (mə-TIR-yəl) *n. materials.* 1. The substance from which something is made.–Cement is the *material* used to lay sidewalks.
2. Cloth. – Mary's dress is made of finely woven *material.*

math•e•mat•ics (math-ə-MA-tiks) *n.* The study of numbers and measurements.–Arithmetic is one kind of *mathematics.*

mat•i•nee (mat-n-AY) *n. matinees.* An afternoon show.–The theater on our street has a *matinee* for children.

mat•ri•mo•ny (MAT-rə-moh-nee) *n.* Marriage.–The minister joined the young couple in holy *matrimony.*

ma•tron (MAY-trən) *n. matrons.* 1. A married woman, especially a mother or an older person.–The girls asked two *matrons* to be chaperones at the school's Saturday night dance.
2. A woman in charge of children, girls, or other women in a camp, dormitory, school, institution, or prison.–The playground *matron* organized a number of games for the children.

mat•ter (MAT-er) *n. matters.* 1. Trouble.–What is the *matter* with Bob?
2. A topic; a question; a subject.–The meeting will be short, since we have only a few *matters* to talk about.
3. It is only a *matter* of one week before Mary will be well enough to go out.
4. The substance that things are made of.–The world of *matter* is the physical world of things.
–*v. matters, mattered, mattering.* Make a difference.–Does it *matter* to you if we cannot come?

mat•tress (MAT-rəss) *n. mattresses.* A large, thick pad used to sleep on. Some *mattresses* have springs in them.

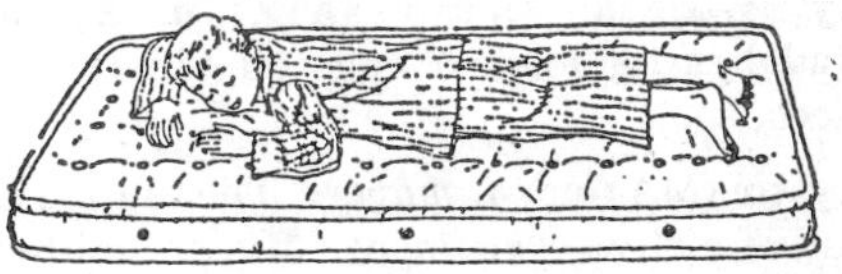

ma•ture (ma-TOOR *or* -TYOOR) *v. matures, matured, maturing.* 1. Become adult or grow up.–We grow wiser as we *mature.*
2. Ripen.–Peaches *mature* in late summer.
–*adj.* Adult; grown-up.–Bob showed *mature* judgment in calling the doctor promptly.
–*maturity, n.*

maul (MAWL) *n. mauls.* A heavy hammer.—The carpenter used a *maul* to pound the posts into the ground.
—*v. mauls, mauled, mauling.* Handle roughly.—If you *maul* your pets, they will not be happy.

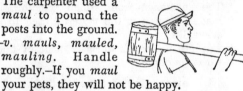

mau·so·le·um (maw-sə-LEE-əm) *n. mausoleums.* A large, stately, and magnificent tomb or burial place.—The Taj Mahal, a white marble *mausoleum* in India, is probably the most beautiful tomb in the world.

max·im (MAK-sim) *n. maxims.* A short statement of principle or general truth; a brief rule of conduct; a proverb; a saying.—"Don't count your chickens before they are hatched" and "A rolling stone gathers no moss" are *maxims.*

max·i·mum (MAK-sə-məm) *adj.* 1. Most or greatest number of.—The *maximum* number of points that you can get on this test is 100.
2. Highest.—Thirty miles an hour is the *maximum* legal speed in this city.

May (MAY) *n. Mays.* The fifth month of the year. *May* has thirty-one days.

may (MAY) *v. might.* 1. Be allowed or permitted.—*May* I have an apple?
2. Possibly will.—It *may* be too late for the matinee.
3. Let it be that.—*May* you have a merry Christmas! I hope you do!

may·on·naise (may-ə-NAYZ) *n.* A thick salad dressing made of eggs, oil, vinegar, and spices.

may·or (MAY-er) *n. mayors.* The man at the head of a city government.—*Mayor* Smith appointed a new chief of police.

maze (MAYZ) *n. mazes.* 1. A bewildering arrangement of paths or passageways.—Tom was confused by the *maze* of halls in the building. He had trouble finding his way out.
2. Confusion.—Father spent the evening sorting out a *maze* of bills and papers.

me (MEE) *pron.* A word used to refer to oneself.—When you speak of yourself, you use the words I and *me.*—Let *me* do the work.—Give it to *me.*

mead·ow (ME-doh) *n. meadows.* A grassy field.—The children pick wild flowers in the *meadow.*

mead·ow lark (ME-doh lahrk) *meadow larks.* A songbird about the size of a robin and having a yellow breast with black and white markings. *Meadow larks* build their nests on the ground.

mea·ger or **mea·gre** (MEE-ger) *adj.; meagerly, adv.; meagerness, n.* Poor; thin; scanty; barely enough.—Jack's wages are *meager;* he can hardly pay for his lunches.

meal (MEEL) *n. meals.* 1. An amount of food prepared to be eaten at one time.—We eat three *meals* a day.
2. Ground grain.—The miller ground the corn into *meal.*

mean (MEEN) *v. means, meant, meaning.* 1. Intend.—Bob didn't *mean* to hurt you.
2. Be intended to say or convey.—A dictionary tells you what words *mean.*—Strike *means* hit.—Bob didn't know what the word *meant.*
—*adj. meaner, meanest; meanly, adv.* 1. Spiteful and unkind.—Jack felt sorry for his *mean* remarks.
2. Selfish and stingy.—The man was too *mean* to pay for the work.
3. Poor.—The prince found Cinderella wearing *mean* clothing.
—*Means* sometimes means a person, thing, or way by which or through which something is accomplished.—A car is a *means* of transportation.—Our team won by fair *means.*

mean·ing (MEEN-ing) *n. meanings.* A thought; intended idea.—I do not understand the *meaning* of your question. I do not know what you are asking me.

mean·time (MEEN-tym) *adv.* The time during some named activity; at the same time.—Father walked to the store. *Meantime,* Jack washed the car.

mean•while (MEEN-hwyl) *adv.* Meantime; the time during some named activity.–Red Riding Hood walked on. *Meanwhile,* the wolf ran to Grandmother's house.

mea•sles (MEE-zəlz) *n.* A disease or sickness which makes a person break out in red spots.

meas•ure (MEZH-er) *n. measures.* 1. A degree or amount.–Mary has already met with a *measure* of success in singing.

2. In music, the notes and rests between two bars.

–*v. measures, measured, measuring.* Find the size, amount, or degree of something.–When we *measure* milk we find out how many pints or quarts of it there are.–Father *measured* the board and found that it was fifteen feet long.

–*Measure off* means mark to certain measurements or size.–The boys *measured off* the football field.

–*Measure up* means come up to some standard.–Bob *measured up* to the teacher's opinion of him. He was as good as she thought he was.

meas•ure•ment (MEZH-er-mənt) *n. measurements.* 1. A finding out of the size or amount of anything.–The *measurement* of the board required the use of a ruler.

2. A size or dimension measured.–The *measurements* of the board were 8 inches by 4 inches by 2 inches.

meat (MEET) *n. meats.* 1. Animal flesh (other than that of fish and fowl) that can be eaten. –We usually eat *meat* for dinner.

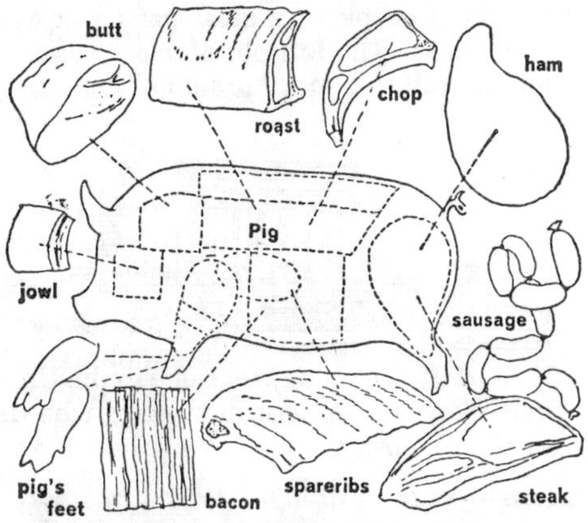

2. The part of a nut that can be eaten.–Bob cracked the nut and picked out the *meat.*

me•chan•ic (mə-KAN-ik) *n. mechanics.* A person who makes or repairs machinery.–A *mechanic* repaired Father's car.

me•chan•i•cal (mə-KAN-ə-kəl) *adj.* Having to do with machinery or tools.–Dick likes *mechanical* things. He wants to study to be an engineer.

med•al (MED-l) *n. medals.* A badge given to someone as a reward for an outstanding act.–The soldier received a *medal* for bravery.

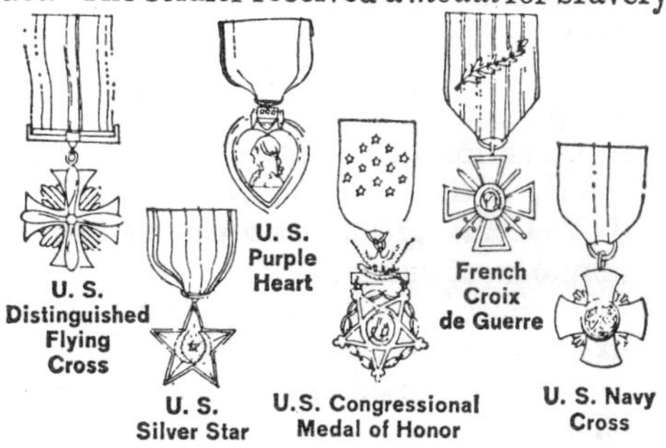

med•dle (MED-l) *v. meddles, meddled, meddling.* Interfere with someone else's doings; pry; snoop; ask curiously.–Do not *meddle* in your neighbor's affairs.

med•i•cal (MED-ə-kəl) *adj.; medically, adv.* Having to do with medicine and the treatment of sickness.–Uncle Jim went to *medical* school to learn to be a doctor.

med•i•cine (MED-ə-sən) *n. medicines.* 1. Something taken to make one well. *Medicines* may be pills, tablets, powders, or liquids.–The doctor gave Mother a bottle of *medicine* to treat her cough.

2. The science of how to treat sick people.–Uncle Jim studied *medicine* at medical school.

me•di•o•cre (MEE-dee-oh-ker *or* mee-dee-OH-ker) *adj.* Ordinary; not particularly good or bad; commonplace.–The performance was *mediocre.*

med•i•tate (MED-ə-tayt) *v. meditates, meditated, meditating.* 1. Reflect; think deeply and quietly.–Grandmother often *meditates* in church.

2. Consider; plan; intend.–Father is *meditating* a trip to California for our vacation.

me•di•um (MEED-ee-əm) *adj.* In between. –The mother bear was the *medium*-sized bear. She was neither the largest nor the smallest.

me•dul•la (mi-DUL-ə) *n. medullae.* The soft section at the rear base of the brain. It connects with the spinal cord.

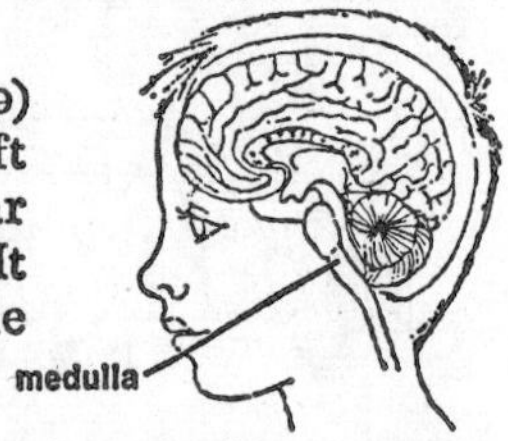

meek (MEEK) *adj. meeker, meekest; meekly, adv.* 1. Mild in manner; tame.–Lambs are *meek* animals.
2. Lacking confidence; timid.–The man's attitude was *meek* and apologetic.

meet (MEET) *v. meets, met, meeting.* 1. Come upon.–I did not expect to *meet* you here.
2. Come or get together.–We shall *meet* at my house.
3. Come together; join.–The roads *meet* at the top of the hill.
4. Welcome; greet.–We are going to the station to *meet* Father.
5. Be introduced to; get to know.–I would like to *meet* the new teacher.
6. Pay; make good.–Father always *meets* his bills.

meet•ing (MEET-ing) *n. meetings.* 1. A gathering together; an assembly.–We had a *meeting* of all the players this noon.
2. A coming together.–The *meeting* of the armies took place this morning.

meg•a•phone (MEG-ə-fohn) *n. megaphones.* A funnel-shaped instrument, such as a horn, that is used to make the voice sound louder.–The chief used a *megaphone* to give orders to the firemen fighting the blaze.

mel•an•chol•y (MEL-ən-kahl-ee) *adj.* Sad. –Jack is never *melancholy.* He is always happy.

mel•low (MEL-oh) *adj.; mellowly, adv.* 1. Soft and ripe.–*Mellow* pears hung on Grandfather's trees.
2. Rich and soft.–We heard the *mellow* song of a bird.

mel•o•dy (MEL-ə-dee) *n. melodies.* A tune.–The song has a beautiful *melody.*–Can you hum the *melody* of that song?

mel•on (ME-lən) *n. melons.* A large juicy fruit that grows on a vine. *Melons* have a heavy rind.–Water*melons* are red inside.

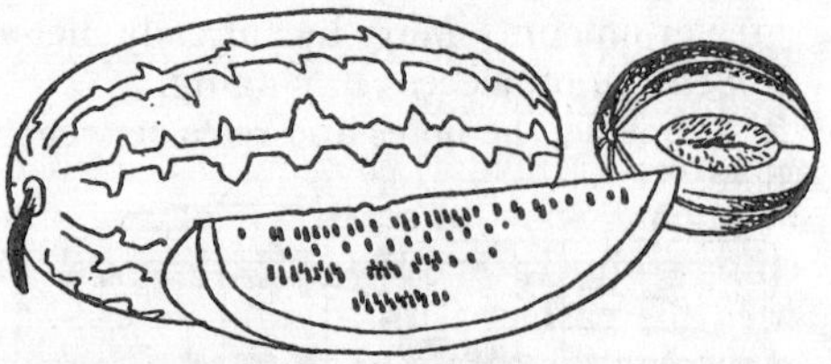

melt (MELT) *v. melts, melted, melting.* 1. Become liquid.–When some hard or solid substances get warm, they *melt.*–When ice *melts,* it becomes liquid.
2. Dissolve.–Sugar *melts* in water.
3. Disappear little by little.–The clouds *melted* away.
4. Soften.–The old man's anger *melted* when he saw the boy's unhappiness.

mem•ber (MEM-ber) *n. members.* One who belongs to an organization or group.–Bob is a *member* of the Boy Scouts.

mem•ber•ship (MEM-ber-ship) *n. memberships.* 1. Being a member of a group.–Bob enjoys his *membership* in the Boy Scouts.
2. All the members of a group.–The boys enlarged their club's *membership* by inviting several new boys to join.

mem•brane (MEM-brayn) *n. membranes.* Any soft, thin, flexible layer of animal or plant tissue.

me•mo•ri•al (mə-MOR-ee-əl) *n. memorials.* Something, often a building or monument, to remind people of a great person or event of the past.–The Lincoln *Memorial* is a *memorial* built to honor Abraham Lincoln.

–*Memorial* Day is a day set aside in the United States to honor American soldiers who died for their country.

mem•o•rize (MEM-ə-ryz) *v. memorizes, memorized, memorizing.* Learn by heart; learn to repeat exactly.–We *memorize* poems in literature class.

mem•o•ry (MEM-ə-ree) *n. memories.* 1. The ability to bring to mind something that happened in the past.–Grandmother has a good *memory.*
2. Something remembered.–Jack has pleasant *memories* of the summers he has spent in the country.

men (MEN) *n. pl.* More than one *man.*–Two *men* were in the car.

men•ace (MEN-iss) *v. menaces, menaced, menacing.* Show, or act in, a hostile or threatening manner; threaten.–The criminal *menaced* the cashier with a gun.–The storm is *menacing* the safety of everyone aboard the small boat.

me•nag•er•ie (mə-NAJ-ə-ree) *n. menageries.* A place where wild animals are kept in cages so that people can see them.–At the circus we visited the *menagerie* to see the lions and tigers.

mend (MEND) *n. mends.* A place that has been repaired.–The *mend* looks very neat.
–*v. mends, mended, mending.* 1. Repair; put in proper condition.–Mary tore a hole in her sweater and had to *mend* it.
2. Get better or improve.–Grandmother has been sick, but now she is *mending.*

men•tal (MEN-tl) *adj.; mentally, adv.* Of the mind; having to do with thinking.–Bill is physically stronger than Jack, but Jack has better *mental* powers. Jack thinks faster and more clearly than Bill does.

men•tion (MEN-shən) *n. mentions.* A notice; a speaking of.–I saw a *mention* of you in the school paper.
–*v. mentions, mentioned, mentioning.* Speak of.–*Mention* your special interests to your teacher.

men•u (MEN-yoo) *n. menus.* A list of foods being served.–Mother looked at the *menu* in the restaurant and chose a cheese sandwich.

mer•ce•nar•y (MER-sə-nair-ee) *adj.* Doing things only for money or reward.–*Mercenary* soldiers hire themselves out to fight for pay in a foreign army.

mer•chan•dise (MER-chən-dyss) *n.* Goods or articles for sale.–The stores have a large stock of *merchandise* before Christmas

mer•chant (MER-chənt) *n. merchants.* A person whose business is to buy and sell goods.
–*adj.* Engaged in carrying goods.–*Merchant* ships carry goods to different countries of the world.

mer•chant ma•rine (mer-chənt mə-REEN). All the ships of one country that carry goods and passengers to and from different countries.

mer•ci•less (MER-si-ləss) *adj.; mercilessly, adv.* Heartless; without mercy.–The *merciless* king condemned all of his prisoners to death.

mer•cu•ry (MERK-yə-ree) *n.* 1. A heavy, silver-white, liquid metal. It is used in some thermometers; it expands and rises in the tube as it gets warmer, and contracts and falls as it cools off.
2. (Spelled with a capital "M.") An ancient Roman god. *Mercury* was believed to be the messenger of the gods.
3. (Spelled with a capital "M.") The nearest known planet to the sun and the smallest in our solar system. The planet *Mercury* has a diameter of about 3,000 miles.

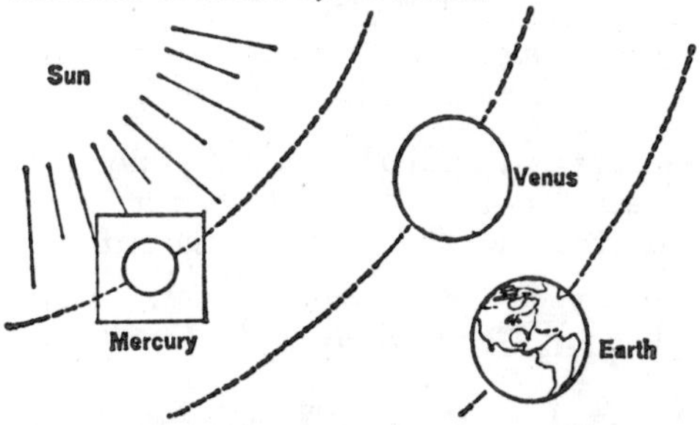

mer•cy (MERSS-ee) *n. mercies.* 1. Pity.–The gentle princess had *mercy* on the prisoner and set him free.
2. A kindness.–On Thanksgiving, the Pilgrims thanked God for his *mercies.*

mere (MIR) *adj. merest.* Only; nothing more than.–It is *mere* foolishness to run into danger.

mere•ly (MIR-lee) *adv.* Only; simply.–Bob *merely* wanted to be helpful.–This is *merely* a suggestion; you may do as you wish.

merge (MERJ) *v. merges, merged, merging.* Combine; come together and unite.–Two lanes of traffic *merge* into one at the bridge. –Two banks in our town *merged* last week. Now there is one big bank instead of the two smaller ones.

me•rid•i•an (mə-RID-ee-ən) *n. meridians.* A line of longitude; any imaginary circle around the earth that passes through the North and South Poles. *Meridians* appear on a map as vertical lines and are marked with degrees of longitude which show how far each line is from Greenwich, England.

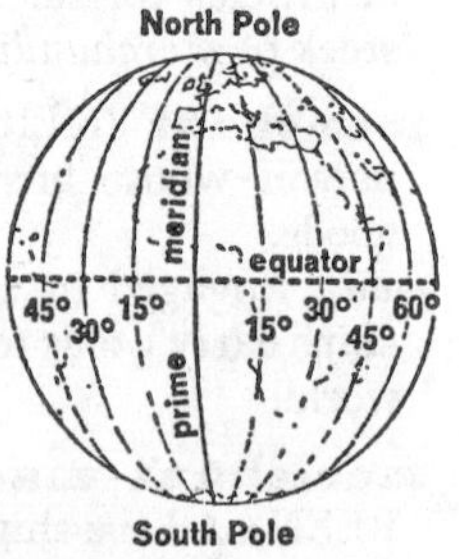

mer•it (MAIR-it) *n. merits.* A good quality.–Bob's essay has many *merits* and few faults. –*v. merits, merited, meriting.* Deserve.–Bob's work *merits* the highest praise.

mer•maid (MER-mayd) *n. mermaids.* A sea maiden told about in fairy tales. *Mermaids* were supposed to have the form of a woman down to the waist and the form of a fish from the waist down.

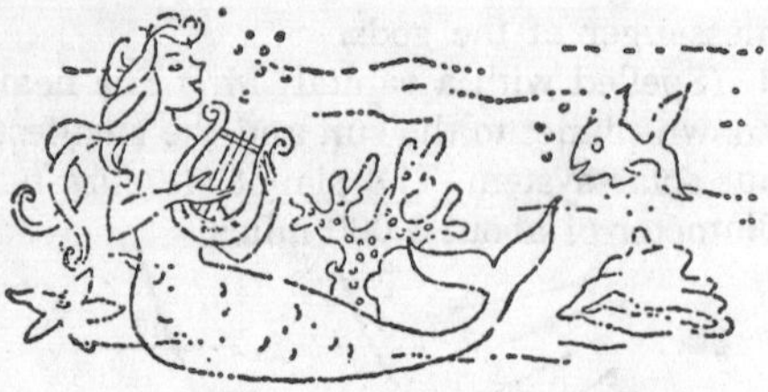

mer•ri•ly (MAIR-ə-lee) *adv.* Joyfully; gaily; cheerfully.–Sally laughed *merrily* as she watched the kitten play with the string.

mer•ry (MAIR-ee) *adj. merrier, merriest.* Happy; gay; joyful.–A *merry* Christmas to you!

mer•ry-go-round (MAIR-ee-goh-rownd) *n. merry-go-rounds.* A round platform with a ring of hobbyhorses or other animals on which children can ride. Music plays as the *merry-go-round* turns.

me•sa (MAY-sə) *n. mesas.* A steep-sided hill with a flat top.–The cowboys met at the *mesa* near the ranch.

mesh (MESH) *n. meshes.* 1. One of the holes or open spaces in a net.–Small fish can get through the *meshes* in a fisherman's net.
2. Openwork or net. –Mary pinned a rose in the *mesh* of her lace costume.

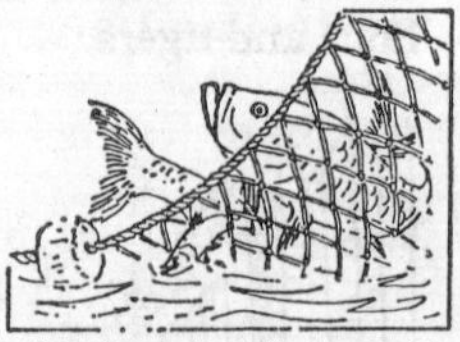

mess (MESS) *n. messes.* 1. An untidy condition.–The careless campers left the picnic grounds in a *mess.* They left papers all over.
2. Trouble.–If you do not do your work daily, you will be in a *mess* before the test.
3. A meal or meals, in the army or navy.–Soldiers eat *mess* together in a large hall.
–*v. messes, messed, messing.* Upset.–Try not to *mess* up your room after Mother has cleaned it.

mes•sage (MESS-ij) *n. messages.* 1. Word; information. *Messages* can be sent by radio, mail, phone, etc.–Bob sent his mother a *message* that he would be late for dinner.
2. A formal speech.–Did you hear the President's *message* on the radio?

mes•sen•ger (MESS-ən-jer) *n. messengers.* One who carries messages from one person to another.–The telegraph company has many *messengers* to deliver telegrams.

met (MET) *v.* One form of the verb *meet.*–I *met* Mary on my way to the store.

met•al (MET-l) *n. metals.* A hard, shiny substance that usually comes from ore mined from the earth. Iron, gold, silver, and copper are *metals.* All *metals* are conductors of heat and electricity.

me•te•or (MEE-tee-er) *n. meteors.* A shooting star.–Mary made a wish when she saw the *meteor* flash across the sky.

ETEOR AND METEORITE

meteor crater, Arizona

A large iron meteorite found in Greenland. It weighs over 36 tons.

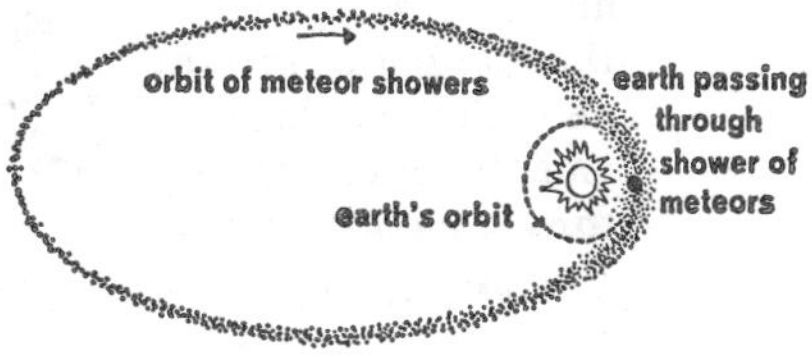

me•te•or•ite (MEE-tee-ə-ryt) *n. meteorites.* Any mass of metal or stone that has fallen to earth from outer space. *Meteorites* range in size from pebbles to gigantic masses weighing over 100,000 pounds.

me•te•or•ol•o•gy (mee-tee-ə-RAHL-ə-jee) *n.* The science or study of the atmosphere with regard to weather.

me•ter (MEE-ter) *n. meters.* A machine which measures without help, all by itself. –A gas *meter* tells the amount of gas you use.–An electric *meter* tells the amount of electricity you use.

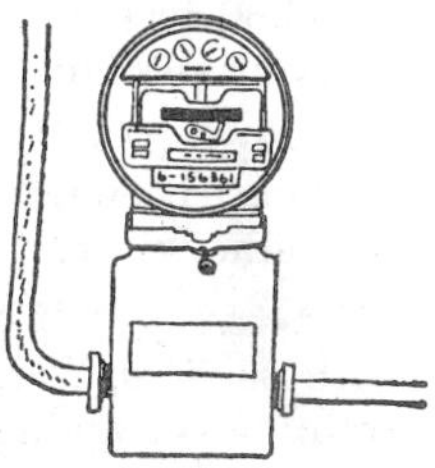

meth•od (METH-əd) *n. methods; methodical, adj.* 1. A way of doing something.–Mother has one *method* of making piecrust and Grandmother has another *method.*
2. An orderly system for doing something.–If you have a *method* for doing your homework, you get it done faster.

met•ric sys•tem (MET-rik SISS-təm) A system of weights and measures based on counting by ten. The meter is the unit of length and the gram is the unit of weight.

me•trop•o•lis (mə-TRAHP-ə-ləss) *n. metropolises.* The most important city of a state, area, or nation.–Paris is the *metropolis* of France.

mez•za•nine (MEZ-ə-neen) *n. mezzanines.* A half story or balcony between the first and second floors of a building. In theaters, the *mezzanine* is usually between the orchestra and the first balcony.–We sat in the *mezzanine* when we saw the play.

mi•ca (MY-kə) n. A heat-resistant mineral that divides easily into thin layers. *Mica* is often used in lanterns, furnace windows, protective coverings, insulating materials, and radar equipment.

mice (MYSS) *n. pl.* More than one *mouse.*–White *mice* are often kept as pets.

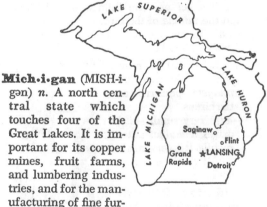

Mich•i•gan (MISH-i-gən) *n.* A north central state which touches four of the Great Lakes. It is important for its copper mines, fruit farms, and lumbering industries, and for the manufacturing of fine furniture, drugs, automobiles, and many other products.

mi•crobe (MY-krohb) *n. microbes.* A living organism so tiny that it cannot be seen with the naked eye; a germ. Some *microbes* cause diseases, such as pneumonia, diphtheria, and typhoid fever.

mi•cro•phone (MY-krə-fohn) *n. microphones.* An instrument used for sending sounds, as in a radio broadcast, or for increasing sounds, as in a loudspeaker system.–The announcer moved up to the *microphone* before he read the latest news.

mi•cro•scope (MY-krə-skohp) *n. microscopes.* A strong magnifying instrument which makes things look many times larger than they actually are. Many things that cannot be seen at all with the eyes alone can be seen clearly through a *microscope.*

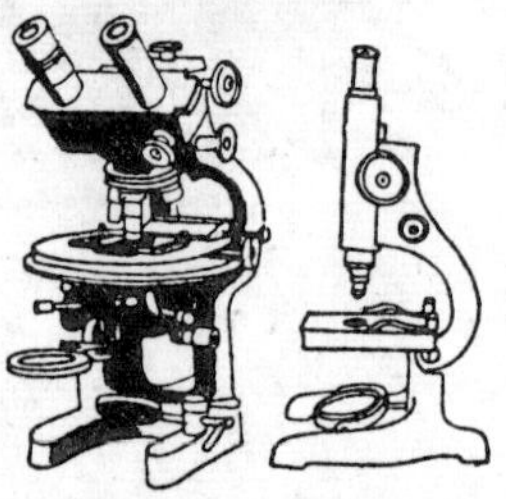

mid (MID) *adj. midmost.* Middle; halfway between the beginning and the end of anything.–In *mid*winter it is very cold.–*Mid*night is 12 o'clock at night.

mid•day (MID-day) *n. middays.* Noon, or the middle of the day. – We eat lunch at *midday.*

mid•dle (MID-l) *n. middles.* 1. The part or point that is the same distance from each end or side.–The teacher told us to fold our papers evenly so there would be a crease down the *middle.*

2. The center.–The child who is "it" stands in the *middle* of the circle.

–*adj.* Medium. – The mother bear was the *middle*-sized bear.

midg•et (MIJ-it) *n. midgets.* A very tiny person. – We saw the *midgets* perform at the circus.

–*adj.* Very small. – Ed drives a *midget* automobile. It is very much smaller than most cars.

mid•night (MID-nyt) *n. midnights.* The middle of the night, or 12 o'clock at night. A new day begins at *midnight.*

mid•ship•man (MID-ship-mən) *n. midshipmen.* A young man studying to be an officer in the navy; a cadet at the U. S. Naval Academy.

midst (MIDST) *n.* Middle.–Mother was in the *midst* of her housework when the bell rang.

mid•sum•mer (mid-SUM-er) *n.* The middle of the summer.–Today it was as hot as *midsummer.*

mid•win•ter (mid-WIN-ter) *n.* The middle of the winter.–In *midwinter* it is usually very cold.

might (MYT) *n.* Strength.–Jack tried with all his *might* to lift the huge stone.

–*v.* One form of the verb *may.*–Bob *might* have won the race if he had not stumbled.–The teacher said that we *might* have a spelling bee if we wanted to.

might•y (MYT-ee) *adj. mightier, mightiest; mightily, adv.* Very strong.–An elephant is a *mighty* animal.

mi•grate (MY-grayt) *v. migrates, migrated, migrating.* 1. Go to another place to live.–Many settlers *migrated* to California.

2. Travel to another place.–Birds *migrate* north in the spring, and south in the fall. They fly from one part of the country to another part.

mild (MYLD) *adj. milder, mildest; mildly, adv.; mildness, n.* 1. Warm and gentle.–A *mild* wind blew in from the sea.

2. Not strong-tasting.–Father smokes *mild* cigars.

3. Kind; gentle.–Bob has a *mild* disposition.

mil•dew (MIL-doo *or* -dyoo) *n.* A kind of mold, or fungus, that sometimes appears on things left in a damp place.

mile (MYL) *n. miles.* A unit of measure equal to 5,280 feet. Long distances are measured by *miles.*–We live thirty *miles* from Chicago.

mile•age (MYL-ij) *n.* The number of miles that have been traveled.–What is the *mileage* on Father's car?

mil•i•tar•y (MIL-ə-tair-ee) *adj.* Having to do with soldiers, war, and the army.–*Military* training is training given to soldiers.

mi•li•tia (mə-LISH-ə) *n. militias.* An army that receives military training, but is called for active service only during emergencies. –The *militia* was called out to help stop the riot.

milk (MILK) *n. milks.* 1. A white liquid food produced by animal mothers to feed their young. Most of the *milk* that we drink comes from cows.

2. The white juice of a coconut.

–*v. milks, milked, milking.* Take milk from (an animal).–Grandfather *milks* the cows.

milk•man (MILK-man) *n. milkmen.* A man who sells or delivers milk.

milk•weed (MILK-weed) *n. milkweeds.* A weed that has a sticky, white juice in it. The pods of *milkweed* are filled with feathery seeds.

Milk•y Way (mil-kee WAY). The band of stars forming the faint path of light which can be seen stretching across the sky at night. The *Milky Way* contains countless numbers of distant stars.

mill (MIL) *n. mills.* 1. A machine for grinding coffee, corn, or other grains or seeds.
2. A building where grain is ground by a machine.–Grandfather takes his wheat to the *mill.*
3. A factory.–There are many steel *mills* in Pittsburgh.
–*v. mills, milled, milling.* 1. Grind.–The miller *mills* the grain.
2. Move about in a disorderly way. – The angry crowd *milled* about the jail.
3. Notch; groove. – The edges of dimes and some other coins are *milled.*

mill•er (MIL-er) *n. millers.* A person who owns or works at a mill.–The *miller* grinds the grain.

mil•lion (MIL-yən) *n. millions.* One thousand thousands.
100 is one hundred.
1,000 is one thousand.
1,000,000 is one thousand thousands, or one *million.*

mil•lion•aire (mil-yən-AIR) *n. millionaires.* A very rich person, one who has at least one million dollars.

mim•ic (MIM-ik) *n. mimics.* One who can do things that others do, in exactly the same way.–Jack is a good *mimic.* He can imitate birds, animals, and different people. He can make his voice sound like theirs.
–*v. mimics, mimicked, mimicking.* Imitate, particularly in fun.–Jack sometimes *mimics* his friends by doing things just as they do them.

mince (MINSS) *v. minces, minced, mincing.* Chop up.–Mother *minced* the onion.

mince•meat (MINSS-meet) *n.* A mixture of ground meat, fruits, spices, sugar, and fat. Mince pies are filled with *mincemeat.*

mind (MYND) *n. minds.* 1. The part of a person that thinks, feels, knows, and guides his actions. If you have a good *mind,* you are intelligent and can learn much.
–*v. minds, minded, minding.* 1. Obey.–Bob *minds* his mother. He does what she asks him to do.
2. Object.–I do not *mind* if you turn on the television set while I read. It does not bother me.
3. Take care of.–Mary has to *mind* the baby while Mother is downtown.
4. Pay attention to.–*Mind* the traffic signals when you cross the street.
–*On one's mind* means in one's thoughts.– Mary forgot about her homework because she had the movies *on her mind.*

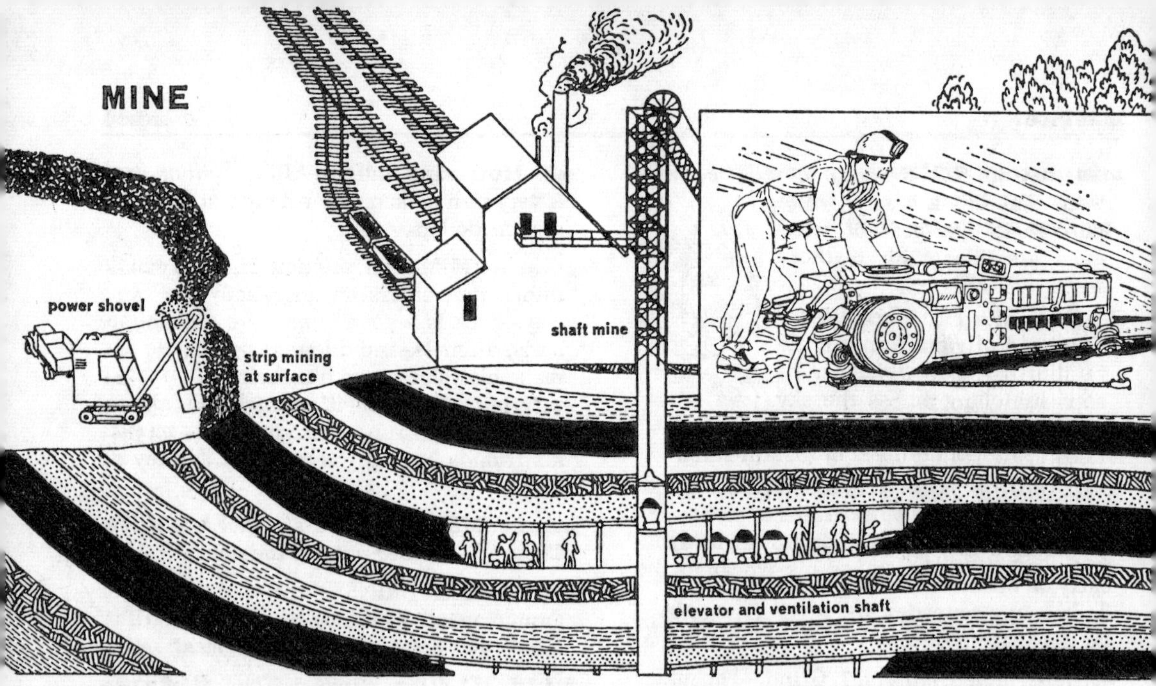

mine (MYN) *n. mines.* 1. A large hole or tunnel dug into the earth, from which ores or other minerals are taken. Coal and diamonds come from *mines.*
2. A bomb which blows up when it is touched or disturbed. *Mines* are placed under water to blow up enemy ships during war. Land *mines* are buried in the ground or hidden in buildings in time of war.

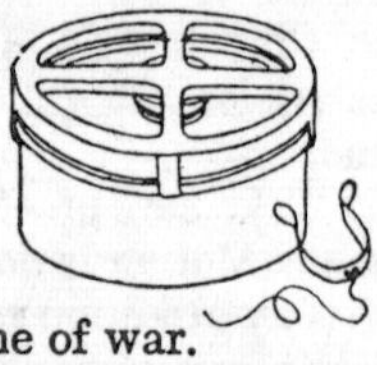

–*v. mines, mined, mining.* 1. Take out or dig from a mine.–The men *mine* copper from the copper mine.
2. Lay or plant mines in warfare. – Submarines *mined* the harbor.
–*pron.* Belonging to me.–This hat is *mine,* not Jack's. I own it.

min•er (MYN-er) *n. miners.* A man who works in a mine. *Miners* go underground to dig out ores, coal, and other minerals.

min•er•al (MIN-er-əl) *n. minerals.* 1. A substance, such as iron, salt, or gold, that is taken from the earth. Most *minerals* are solids.
2. Anything that is not animal or vegetable. is *mineral.*

min•gle (MING-gəl) *v. mingles, mingled, mingling.* Mix.–After the meeting, the mayor *mingled* with the crowd.

min•i•a•ture (MIN-ə-cher *or* MIN-ee-ə-cher) *n. miniatures.* 1. A very small portrait, or other picture.–Inside Mary's locket is a *miniature* of Grandmother as a young girl.
2. A small copy of something.–Mother has a real stove, and Jane has a *miniature* to play with.
–*adj.* Tiny.–Father made a set of *miniature* furniture for Jane's dollhouse.

min•i•mum (MIN-ə-məm) *adj.* The least amount or the smallest number of anything. –The *minimum* age for entering school in our town is five and a half.

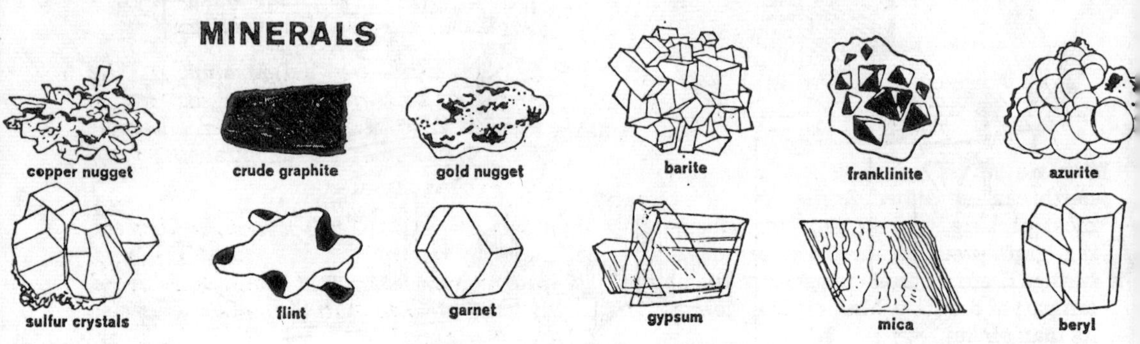

min·is·ter (MIN-iss-ter) *n. ministers.* 1. A pastor, preacher, or clergyman.—Our *minister* lives next to the church.

2. A person who goes to a foreign country to carry on business for his government.
3. In many countries, the head of a particular department of the government is called a *minister.*
—*v. ministers, ministered, ministering.* Serve; look after; attend to.—We had a nurse to *minister* to Grandmother's needs while she was ill last year.

mink (MINGK) *n. mink* or *minks.* A small furry animal that lives in and around the water. Coats made of the brown fur of *minks* are very valuable.

Min·ne·so·ta (min-ə-SOH-tə) *n.* A state in north central United States, important for meat packing, trading, dairying, stock raising, grain products, and furniture manufacturing. There are iron-ore mines in the northern part of the state. *Minnesota* is famous for its many lakes.

min·now (MIN-oh) *n. minnows.* A very small fish that lives in fresh water. *Minnows* are used for bait to catch larger fish.

mi·nor (MY-ner) *n. minors.* A person who is less than 21 years old is a *minor.*
—*adj.* Less important. — 1. Our teacher knows even the *minor* details of George Washington's life, such as what he ate for breakfast and dinner.
2. In music, the *minor* scale is one of the two principal scales. The other is the major scale. A piece written in a *minor* key is one in which the *minor* scale is used.

mi·nor·i·ty (mə-NOR-ə-tee *or* mə-NAHR-ə-tee) *n. minorities* and *adj.* The smaller group or number of persons or things; the number that is less than half of the whole.—The children who didn't want to go to the circus were in the *minority.* Most of the children wanted to go.

min·strel (MIN-strəl) *n. minstrels.* 1. An entertainer, usually blacked to look like a Negro, who sings Negro songs and tells jokes.
2. In olden times, a musician who traveled from place to place, playing and singing songs for people.

mint (MINT) *n. mints.* 1. A pleasant-smelling plant. The juice of its leaves is used as flavoring. A candy that is so flavored is often called a *mint.* Pepper*mint* and spear*mint* are kinds of *mint* often used to flavor candy and chewing gum.

2. A place where coins are made.—Pennies are made at the *mint.*
3. Great amount (of money). — Uncle Joe made a *mint* of money from his business. It has made him rich.
—*v. mints, minted, minting.* Make coins. — Many pennies are *minted* every year.

min·u·end (MIN-yoo-end) *n. minuends.* The number from which another number is taken, in subtraction.—Here is an example: 85 (*minuend*) minus 40 (subtrahend) = 45 (remainder).

min·u·et (min-yoo-ET) *n. minuets.* A slow, dignified dance. – In the time of George Washington, ladies and gentlemen danced the *minuet.*—The music for a *minuet* is also called a *minuet.*

mi•nus (MY-nəss) *adj.* Without.—After the sudden wind had passed, Father found that he was *minus* his hat. His hat was gone.
—*prep.* Less.—Six *minus* two is four. Two taken away from six leaves four.

min•ute (MIN-ət) *n. minutes.* 1. A measure of time which equals 60 seconds. Sixty *minutes* make one hour.—There are sixty *minutes* from six o'clock to seven o'clock.
2. A very short time.—Dinner will be ready in a *minute.*
3. (In the plural) A record of what business took place.—Bob kept the *minutes* of the meeting. He wrote down everything that was discussed at the meeting.

mi•nute (mə-NOOT *or* -NYOOT) *adj.; minutely, adv.; minuteness, n.* 1. Very small.—The doctor removed a *minute* splinter of steel from Father's finger.
2. Including every little fact about a thing.—Mary described the play to Sally in *minute* detail.

mir•a•cle (MIR-ə-kl) *n. miracles.* 1. A wonderful thing that happens which cannot be explained by the laws of nature. If the water in a river suddenly turned and flowed uphill, it would be a *miracle.*
2. An extraordinary happening. – It was a *miracle* that no one was hurt in the wreck.

mi•rage (mə-RAHZH) *n. mirages.* Something one thinks he sees in a certain place but which is not really there at all. *Mirages* are often seen in hot desert areas where layers of heated air reflect images of distant objects.

mire (MYR) *n. mires.* Mud.—Father's car got stuck in the deep *mire.*

mir•ror (MIR-er) *n. mirrors.* A looking glass; a glass in which you can see yourself.—Father looks into a *mirror* while he shaves.

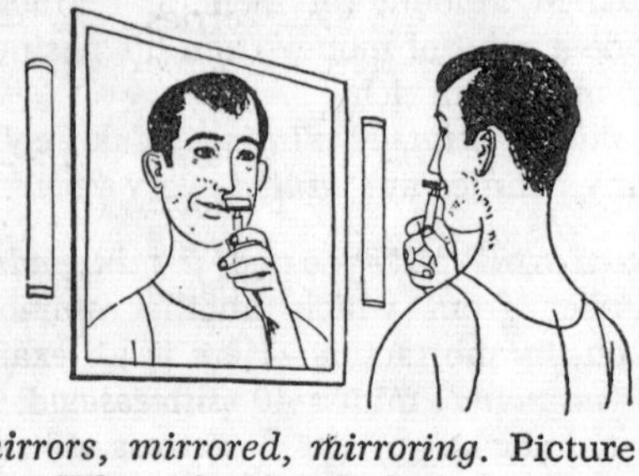

—*v. mirrors, mirrored, mirroring.* Picture or reflect.—When the dog looked down at the stream, the water *mirrored* his image, and he thought he saw another dog.

mirth (MERTH) *n.* Merry laughter and fun. —The clown caused much *mirth* at the circus.

mis•cel•la•ne•ous (miss-əl-AY-nee-əss) *adj.* Of many different kinds.—The teacher's desk is covered with *miscellaneous* things, such as marbles, flowers, books, pencils, and bean shooters.

mis•chief (MISS-chəf) *n. mischiefs.* 1. Trouble or damage caused by someone.—Letting air out of auto tires for fun is *mischief.*
2. A person who annoys others by making jokes in talk or actions.—Sally is a little *mischief.*
3. A person who causes harm or trouble.

mis•chie•vous (MISS-chə-vəss) *adj.; mischievously, adv.; mischievousness, n.* Apt to play pranks and tricks on people.—Ed is a *mischievous* person.

mi•ser (MY-zer) *n. misers.* A person who loves money and saves it just for the sake of having it.—King Midas was a *miser.*

mis•er•a•ble (MIZ-er-ə-bəl) *adj.; miserably, adv.* 1. Unhappy.—The wet, lost puppy looked so *miserable* that Mother said we might keep him.
2. Bad or unpleasant.—The weather was so *miserable* that we were glad to play indoors.

mis•er•y (MIZ-er-ee) *n. miseries.* 1. Suffering and unhappiness.—War causes terrible *misery.*
2. Wretched surroundings.—Many families live in *misery* in time of war.

mis•for•tune (miss-FOR-chən) *n. misfortunes.* 1. Bad luck.—I had the *misfortune* to lose my bracelet.
2. Unlucky happening or accident. – The storybook hero met with many *misfortunes* before he found the magic city.

Miss (MISS) *n. Misses.* A title given to a girl or woman who is not married.—My teacher's name is *Miss* Smith.

miss (MISS) *v. misses, missed, missing.* 1. Fail to do something.—Bob *missed* the first ball. He failed to hit it.—I went to meet Father at the station, but I *missed* him. I didn't find him.
2. Fail to catch.—The traveler *missed* the boat. He was too late to get on the boat before it sailed.
3. Lose.—Mary *missed* only one day of school all year. She was absent only one day.
4. Feel lonely for.—We *miss* Mother when she goes away. We wish that she were with us.
5. Notice an absence; see that someone is gone.—Baby *misses* Mother as soon as she leaves the room.

mis•sile (MISS-əl) *n. missiles.* Anything that can be hurled, shot, thrown, or launched, such as a rock, bullet, or rocket.–A guided *missile* is a rocket that can be controlled and directed in flight.

U.S. Army Guided Missiles

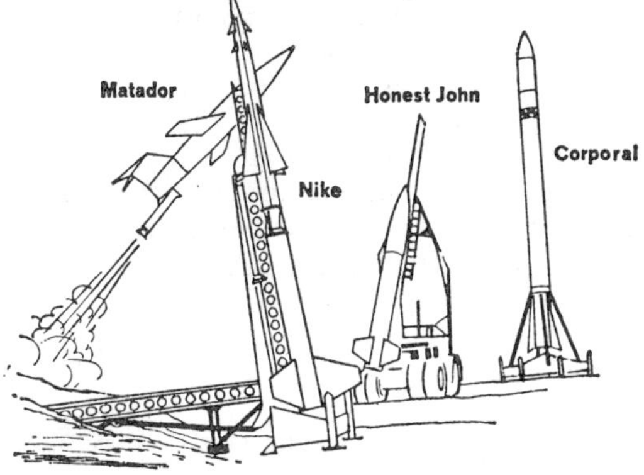

miss•ing (MISS-ing) *adj.* Gone; no longer in place.–Mary counted her books and found that one was *missing.* She had had six books. Now she has only five.

mis•sion (MISH-ən) *n. missions.* 1. One or more persons sent somewhere for a particular purpose.–The government sent a *mission* to England to discuss trade relations.
2. The purpose for which the person or group is sent.–The *mission* was accomplished.
3. The base or headquarters of a group of missionaries. – The missionaries built their *mission* at the edge of the jungle.
4. The missionaries themselves. – The *mission* conducts classes for the natives.
5. A calling in life; a duty or obligation one takes on.–A priest's *mission* is devotion to God.

mis•sion•ar•y (MISH-ə-nair-ee) *n. missionaries.* A person sent to urge others to adopt the religious beliefs and teachings of his church.–*Missionaries* have traveled to many parts of the world to instruct others in their faith.

Mis•sis•sip•pi (miss-ə-SIP-ee) *n.* A state in south central United States. *Mississippi* is bordered on the west by the river bearing the same name. Half the state is covered with timber, but farming is the leading industry.

Mis•sou•ri (mə-ZUH-ree) *n.* A scenic state along the Mississippi River in central United States, noted for cattle raising, meat packing, and for the great variety of its farming. The great river, the *Missouri,* which crosses the state, is almost 3,000 miles long.

mis•spell (miss-SPEL) *v. misspells, misspelled, misspelling.* Spell wrong.–Look up your words in the dictionary so you will not *misspell* them.

mist (MIST) *n. mists.* 1. Fog.–The air is sometimes filled with *mist* before sunrise. Very fine drops of water in the air make it look gray.
2. A fine rain.–A *mist* is falling.
–*v. mists, misted, misting.* Cloud.–The sky *misted* over.

mis•take (miss-TAYK) *n. mistakes.* 1. An error.–Mary made one *mistake* in the spelling test. She spelled one word the wrong way.
2. A bad idea.–It is a *mistake* to start to school too late. It is the wrong thing to do.
–*v. mistakes, mistook, mistaking.* Mix up; confuse.–Our teacher often *mistakes* one of the twins for the other. She often thinks Ted is Bill. She calls them by the wrong names.

mis•tak•en (miss-TAYK-ən) *adj.; mistakenly, adv.* Wrong.–Bob was *mistaken* about the score of the football game. He thought the score was 19 to 7. It was really 18 to 7.

Mis•ter (MISS-ter) *n.* A title used before a man's name. It is usually written *Mr.*–Our postman's name is *Mr.* Brown.

mis•tle•toe (MISS-əl-toh) *n.* An evergreen plant that has white berries that look like wax. *Mistletoe* lives on or clings to trees. It does not grow from the ground. We hang *mistletoe* in the doorway at Christmas time. Anyone who stands under the *mistletoe* is kissed.

mis•tress (MISS-trəss) *n. mistresses.* A woman who is in charge, as a *mistress* of a household.–A school*mistress* is a schoolteacher.

mist•y (MIST-ee) *adj.; mistily, adv.; mistiness, n.* 1. Foggy.–It is a *misty* morning.
2. Covered with mist.–The windshield of Father's car is *misty.*

mite (MYT) *n. mites.* 1. Anything very small; a tiny amount.
2. A very small child.–Baby is just a *mite.*

mitt (MIT) *n. mitts.* 1. A glove with short, open fingers.
2. A padded glove to catch a ball in.–Bob got a baseball *mitt* for Christmas.

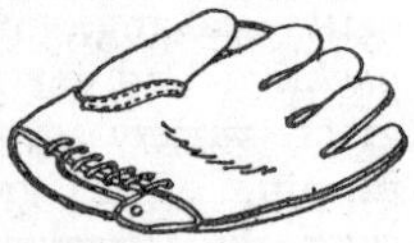

mit·ten (MIT-n) *n. mittens.* A covering for the hand that has a part for the thumb by itself and another part for all the other fingers.

mix (MIKS) *v. mixes, mixed, mixing.* 1. Stir together.–We make hot chocolate by *mixing* hot milk and cocoa.
2. Join; mingle.–The stranger did not *mix* with the other people at the party. He wasn't friendly.
3. Confuse.–Sally *mixes* up her words when she talks too fast.

mix·er (MIKS-er) *n. mixers.* 1. A device that mixes things. – Mother has an electric *mixer* to beat the batter for her when she makes a cake.

2. A person who mixes.–Mary is a good *mixer.* She gets along well with any group of people.

mix·ture (MIKS-cher) *n. mixtures.* Anything made by mixing or stirring several things together.–Fudge is a *mixture* of sugar, chocolate, and milk.

moan (MOHN) *n. moans.* A low, sad sound; a sound of pain. – The wounded trooper's *moans* stopped when the doctor had dressed his injury.
–*v. moans, moaned, moaning.* 1. Make sad sounds.–In the winter the wind *moans* in the trees.
2. Complain. – The grouchy man *moans* about everything.

moat (MOHT) *n. moats.* A large ditch dug

around a castle, a fort, or a town, to protect it from enemies.

mob (MAHB) *n. mobs.* Many people gathered together who are so excited that they will do things without thinking.
–*v. mobs, mobbed, mobbing.* Gather angrily about.–The boys *mobbed* the umpire when he called the player out.

mo·bile (MOH-bəl *or* MOH-beel) *adj.* 1. Movable; capable of being easily moved.–Although the piano is big, it is *mobile* because it is on wheels.
2. Easily changed, as a facial expression or mood.–The clown twisted his *mobile* face into all sorts of funny expressions.

moc·ca·sin (MAHK-ə-sən) *n. moccasins.* 1. A soft leather shoe or sandal. –American Indians wore *moccasins* sewed by hand from pieces of leather.

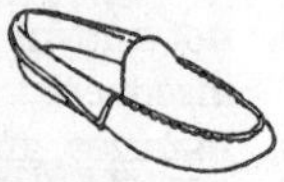

2. A water *moccasin* is a kind of poisonous snake.

mock (MAHK) *v. mocks, mocked, mocking.* 1. Make fun of.–The actor *mocks* famous people by doing things the way they do them, only in a humorous way.
2. Imitate.–Jack can *mock* the songs of birds.
–*adj.* Make-believe.–A *mock* bullfight is not real.

mode (MOHD) *n. modes.* 1. A way or manner. –People of different parts of the world have different *modes* of life. They have different customs and habits.
2. The way a thing is being done at a certain time; the fashion.–The *mode* of wearing the hair was quite different when Mother was a girl.

mod·el (MAHD-l) *n. models.* 1. A pattern from which something is made.–*Models* for statues are often made of clay and then copied in stone or metal.
2. A style.–Ed's car is a late *model.*
3. A person in a store who wears clothes owned by the store to show customers.
4. A person who poses for an artist or a photographer.
–*v. models, modeled, modeling.* Shape or make.–Mary *modeled* an ashtray out of clay for Father.
–*adj.* 1. Worth trying to be like. – Bob is a *model* student.
2. A small copy.–Tom makes *model* airplanes.

mod•er•ate (MAHD-er-ət) *adj.; moderately, adv.* 1. Medium.–Jack's father gets a *moderate* salary. It is neither large nor small.
2. Not extreme; neither very much nor very little. – Mother likes *moderate* styles. She doesn't like clothes to be very noticeable.–Jack drank a *moderate* amount of milk. He drank enough, but not a lot.

mod•er•a•tor (MAHD-er-ay-ter) *n. moderators.* A person who guides discussions or debates and whose job it is to keep things running smoothly. – The *moderator* called for order when the discussion became too heated.

mod•ern (MAHD-ern) *adj.* 1. Existing now; not known in earlier times; recently made or discovered. – Air conditioners, nuclear submarines, and television sets are some *modern* inventions.
2. Having the ideas, the manners, and the habits that most people of today have.

mod•est (MAHD-əst) *adj.; modestly, adv.; modesty, n.* Not vain or conceited; not thinking too highly of oneself.–Bob is *modest.* He doesn't brag even when he does things well.

mod•i•fy (MAHD-ə-fy) *v. modifies, modified, modifying.* 1. Describe or add to the meaning of.–One word sometimes *modifies* another. "We live in a white house." The word white *modifies,* or describes, the house spoken of.
2. Change.–Jack decided to *modify* the design of his model airplane. He decided to give it one set of wings instead of two.
3. Lessen or reduce.–When Mother saw that John was really sorry for his bad behavior, she *modified* his punishment.

Mo•ham•med•an (moh-HAM-ə-dən) *n. Mohammedans.* A follower of Mohammed, or a believer in the Moslem religion that was founded by Mohammed. *Mohammedans* believe in, and live by, the Koran, the sacred scripture of the Moslem religion.

moist (MOIST) *adj.* Damp; slightly wet. – Grandmother keeps the soil around her ferns *moist.*

mois•ten (MOISS-ən) *v. moistens, moistened, moistening.* Dampen; make slightly wet. – Mother *moistens* the clothes before she irons them.

mois•ture (MOISS-cher) *n.* Dampness or wetness.–The *moisture* in the cellar caused mildew to form on the things stored there.

mo•lar (MOH-ler) *n. molars.* Any of the broad teeth in the back of the mouth.

mo•las•ses (mə-LASS-əz) *n.* A thick, dark syrup that comes from sugar cane. *Molasses* tastes sweet and slightly bitter.

mold (MOHLD) *n. molds.* 1. A hollow shape or form in which liquids or soft substances are placed and left until they become firm.–Mother put the gelatin dessert in a *mold* to cool.

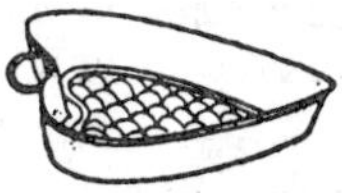

2. A fuzzy white or greenish growth.–*Mold* often forms on the top of fruit, bread, or other foods that have been in a damp place for a long time.
–*v. molds, molded, molding.* Shape.–Mary *molded* a rabbit from clay.

mold•ing (MOHLD-ing) *n. moldings.* A strip

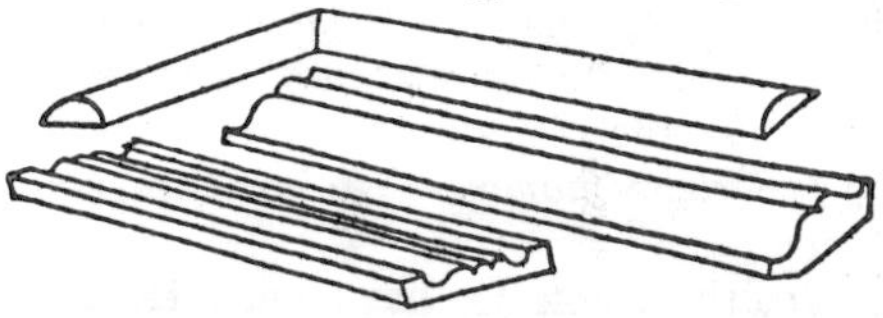

or band used for decorating.–Our room has a *molding* around the top of the wall.

mole (MOHL) *n. moles.* 1. A spot on the skin. Most *moles* are brown.
2. A little, soft, furry animal that lives under the ground and digs tunnels. *Moles* cannot see well.

mol•e•cule (MAHL-ə-kyool) *n. molecules.* 1. The tiniest particle of matter into which a substance can be broken without chemically changing it.–Most *molecules* are so small that they cannot be seen even under a microscope.
2. Any tiny particle. – After Mother finished cleaning, not a *molecule* of dust could be seen in the house.

mol•lusk (MAHL-əsk) *n. mollusks.* An animal belonging to a large family of animals usually having hard shells, soft bodies, and no backbones. Clams, oysters, snails, and mussels are *mollusks.*

molt (MOHLT) *v. molts, molted, molting.* Shed or lose the hair, feathers, or outer skin. Birds *molt.*

mol•ten (MOHL-tn) *adj.* Melted, especially by intense heat.–The workman poured the *molten* iron into a mold.

mo•ment (MOH-mənt) *n. moments.* A very short time.–My work will be finished in a *moment.*

mo•men•tum (moh-MEN-təm) *n.* The force possessed by a moving object which keeps the object moving; a moving body's speed of motion.–The stone gained *momentum* as it rolled down the hill.

mon•arch (MAHN-ark) *n. monarchs.* A ruler, such as a king or queen.

mon•as•ter•y (MAHN-ə-stair-ee) *n. monasteries.* The house or group of buildings in which monks live away from other people.–The *monastery* is quiet and peaceful.

Mon•day (MUN-dee) *n. Mondays.* The day after Sunday. *Monday* is the second day of the week.–Our school week starts on *Monday.*

mon•ey (MUN-ee) *n. moneys.* **1.** Coins and pieces of paper made by the government and having a definite value according to the law. –Pennies, nickels, dimes, and dollar bills are American *money.* – We buy things with *money.*
2. Wealth.–Uncle Joe has *money.* He is very rich.

mon•grel (MAHNG-grəl) *n. mongrels.* A dog with parents of different breeds.–Jack's dog is a *mongrel.* He is part terrier and part bulldog.

mon•i•tor (MAHN-ə-ter) *n. monitors.* Someone chosen to help and to see that certain things are done.–The teacher told the *monitors* to pass out the books.

monk (MUNGK) *n. monks.* A man who belongs to a religious group of men who live by themselves, usually in a building called a monastery.

mon•key (MUNG-kee) *n. monkeys.* A tree-climbing animal with a long tail, and paws that look something like a man's hands.–The children watched the *monkeys* at the zoo.

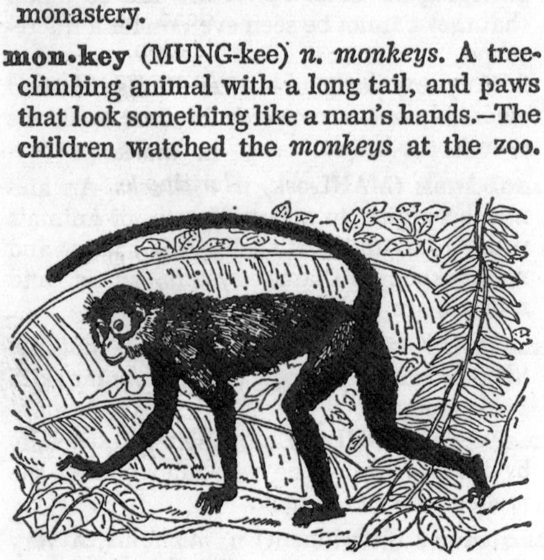

–*v. monkeys, monkeyed, monkeying.* Play or fool.–It is dangerous to *monkey* with fire.

mon•o•gram (MAHN-ə-gram) *n. monograms.* Initials put together to make a design. – Mother embroidered Tom's *monogram* on his handkerchief.

mon•o•plane (MAHN-ə-playn) *n. monoplanes.* An airplane with only one set of wings.

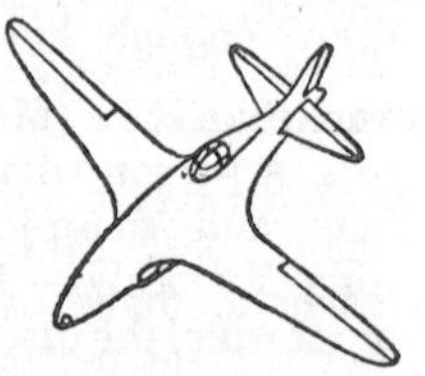

mo•nop•o•ly (mə-NAHP-ə-lee) *n. monopolies.* **1.** The sole ownership or control of something.–Bob seems to have a *monopoly* on home runs today. He is the only one who has hit a home run today.
2. The sole control of a product or service in a particular area; the company or companies having such control, or the product or service that is so controlled.

mon•o•tone (MAHN-ə-tohn) *n. monotones; monotonous, adj.* An unchanging tone of voice.–The boy recited in a *monotone.* His tone of voice was always the same.

mon•soon (mahn-SOON) *n. monsoons.* **1.** A seasonal wind of the Indian Ocean and southern Asia. The *monsoon* blows from the northeast during the cold months of the year and from the southwest during the warm months.
2. The rainy season in India which accompanies the southwest wind.

mon•ster (MAHN-ster) *n. monsters.* **1.** A very large or unusual animal.–A dog as big as a horse would be a *monster.*
2. A very cruel and dreadful animal or person.–The dragons in fairy tales are *monsters.* –Bluebeard was a *monster.*

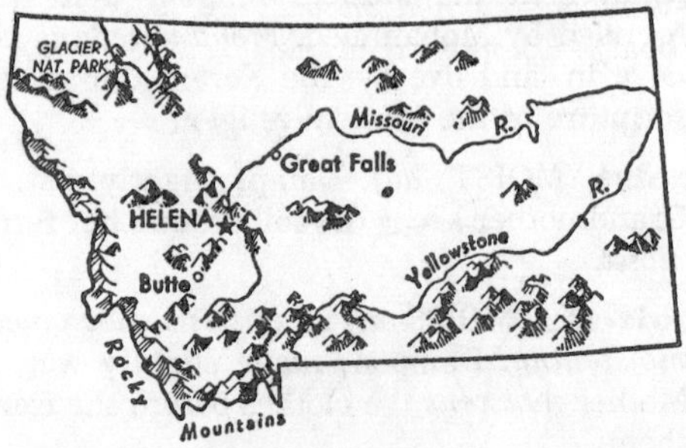

Mon•tan•a (mahn-TAN-ə) *n.* A state, half mountains and half plains, in western United States, in which is found one of the richest copper mines in the world. Lumbering, mixed farming, and sheep raising are *Montana's* important industries.

month (MUNTH) *n. months.* A measure of time. Twelve *months* make a year.

month•ly (MUNTH-lee) *n. monthlies.* A publication put out once each month.–Some magazines are *monthlies.*
–*adj.* and *adv.* Once each month.–We have a *monthly* visit from Grandmother. She comes to see us once a month.–We pay our rent *monthly.*

mon•u•ment (MAHN-yə-mənt) *n. monuments.* Something built or set aside to make people remember a great person or happening.–The Washington *Monument* was built in honor of George Washington.

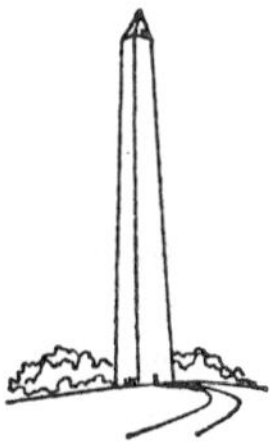

mood (MOOD) *n. moods.* The way one feels in one's mind: happy, sad, merry, etc.–Baby is in a playful *mood.*

moon (MOON) *n. moons.* The *moon* is a heavenly body nearer the earth than any of the stars or planets. It goes around the earth. The *moon* appears to shine because the sun is shining on it.

crescent moon quarter moon gibbous moon full moon

moon•light (MOON-lyt) *n.* Light from the moon.–Sometimes the *moonlight* shines in our bedroom window
–*adj.* Bright with light from the moon.–We went swimming on a *moonlight* night.

moor (MUHR) *n. moors.* A stretch of waste land, especially in England or Scotland.
–*v. moors, moored, mooring.* Fasten or tie (a boat).–Ed *moored* his boat to the dock.

moose (MOOSS) *n. sing.* and *pl.* A large animal of the deer family. *Moose* are found in the northern United States and in Canada.–The hunter shot three *moose.*

mop (MAHP) *n. mops.* A sponge or bunch of pieces of yarn tied together at one end and fastened to a handle to use for cleaning.
–*v. mops, mopped, mopping.* Wash with a mop.–Mother *mops* the floor twice a week.

mor•al (MOR-əl) *n. morals.* 1. The lesson of a story or fable.–The *moral* of the story is: Don't ask for help unless you really need it. 2. An idea of right and wrong.–A person's *morals* are his beliefs as to what is right and what is wrong.
–*adj.* Concerned with right and wrong.–A *moral* person is a good person, one who lives by the standards of right and wrong set up by civilized people.

mo•rale (mə-RAL) *n.* The way people feel about the life they are leading.–If the *morale* of a school is high, it means that the students are interested, satisfied, and proud of their school.

more (MOR) *n.* and *adj.* A larger amount or number.–Two pounds is *more* than one pound.–Bob ate *more* apples than I did. He ate three and I ate two.–Please don't give me any *more.*
–*adv.* To a greater extent or degree.–Bob writes *more* easily than Bill.

more•o•ver (mor-OH-ver) *adv.* Further; besides; in addition to what has been said.–Mary didn't wish to go to the show; *moreover,* she didn't have enough money.

morgue (MORG) *n. morgues.* A place where the bodies of unknown dead persons are taken and held for identification.–The body found in the river this morning was taken to the *morgue.*

morn•ing (MORN-ing) *n. mornings.* The first half of the day.–*Morning* ends at 12 o'clock noon.

morn•ing-glo•ry (MORN-ing-glor-ee) *n. morning-glories.* A climbing vine with flowers of many colors that blossom in the morning.

mor•sel (MOR-səl) *n. morsels.* A tiny piece.–Not even a *morsel* of food was left after the hungry children had finished eating.

mor•tal (MOR-tl) *n. mortals.* A human being.–*Mortals* cannot know everything.
–*adj.; mortally, adv.* 1. Certain to die some day.–All men are *mortal.* No one can live forever.
2. Causing death. – Saint George gave the dragon a *mortal* wound.

mor•tar (MOR-ter) *n. mortars.* 1. A mixture of cement, lime, sand, and water.–Bricks used in building houses are held together with *mortar.*

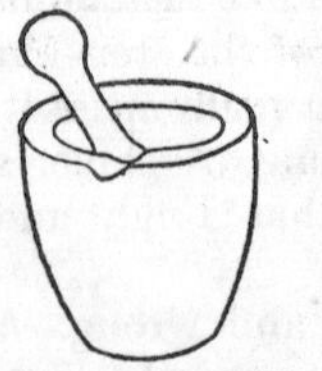

2. A strong bowl in which to pound materials into a powder. –The druggist uses a *mortar.*

mort•gage (MOR-gij) *n. mortgages.* A written agreement to give up one's property if money borrowed is not paid back when it is due.

mo•sa•ic (moh-ZAY-ik) *n. mosaics.* A design, pattern, or picture that has been made by fitting together small pieces of colored stone, glass, etc., in some other material, often mortar. *Mosaics* are widely used for decorating walls, floors, and furniture.

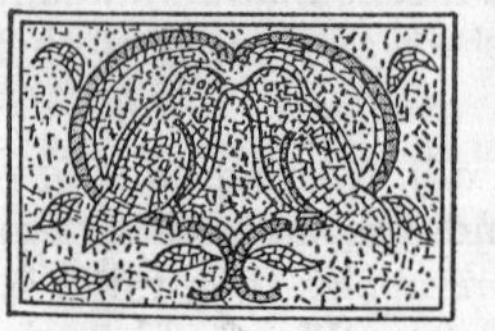

Mos•lem (MAHZ-ləm) *n. Moslems.* A Mohammedan.
–*adj.* Of or concerning the religion founded by the prophet Mohammed.

mos•qui•to (mə-SKEE-toh) *n. mosquitoes.* A small flying insect. The female *mosquito* bites.

moss (MAWSS) *n. mosses.* A mass of tiny, green plants. *Moss* grows on trees, rocks, and the ground. It is soft and velvety.

moss•y (MAWSS-ee) *adj. mossier, mossiest.* Covered with moss.–The ground under the trees is *mossy.*

most (MOHST) *n.* and *adj.* 1. The greatest number or amount.–Bob worked harder than *most* and he solved the *most* problems.
2. Almost all; more than half.–Baby drank *most* of her milk.
–*adv.* To the greatest extent or degree.–Bill runs quickly, Jack runs more quickly than Bill, and Bob runs *most* quickly of all.

most•ly (MOHST-lee) *adv.* Almost all; chiefly.–The stories in Sally's book are *mostly* fairy tales.

mo•tel (moh-TEL) *n. motels.* A hotel for travelers going by car, usually a group of cottages or cabins along a main road. *Motels* provide space for parking cars and rooms for sleeping.–We stopped at many *motels* during our car trip across the country.

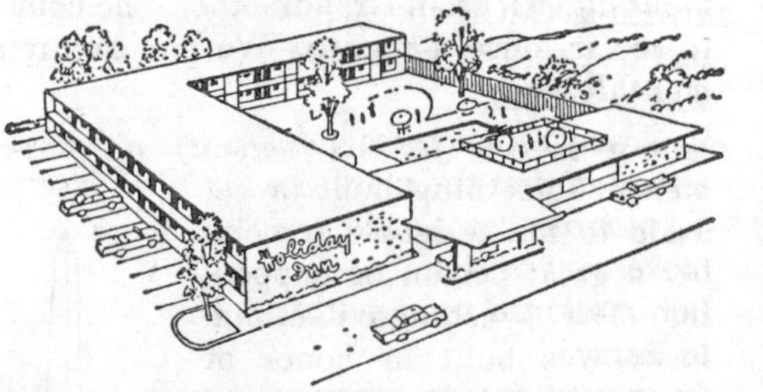

moth (MAWTH) *n. moths.* An insect that looks something like a butterfly. The tiny worms from which some *moths* come eat holes in woolen things.

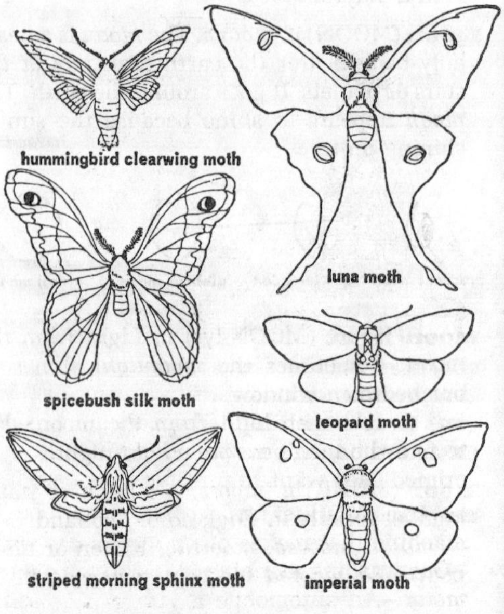

moth•er (MUTH-er) *n. mothers.* 1. A woman who has a child or children.–Your parents are your *mother* and father.
2. Any female animal that has young.–The calf gets milk from its *mother.*
–*v. mothers, mothered, mothering.* Care for.–Mary likes to *mother* baby.

moth•er-in-law (MUTH-er-in-law) *n. mothers-in-law.* The mother of one's husband or one's wife.–Grandmother is Father's mother. She is Mother's *mother-in-law.*

moth•er•ly (MUTH-er-lee) *adj.* Like a mother; kind and sympathetic.–Our teacher is *motherly.*

moth•er-of-pearl (MUTH-er-əv-PERL) *n.* The hard, shiny, and sparkling inner lining of various shells, such as those of pearl oysters and mussels. *Mother-of-pearl* is used for jewelry, buttons, handles, and many other decorative articles.

mo•tion (MOH-shən) *n. motions.* 1. Movement.–Every *motion* that the dancer made was beautiful.

2. A suggestion to be voted on.–Mary made a *motion* that the class should have a party.

–*v. motions, motioned, motioning.* Make a movement or signal to show what is meant.–Bob *motioned* to us with his hand to tell us to hurry.

–*In motion* means moving.–Never open the door of a car that is *in motion.*

mo•tion•less (MOH-shən-ləss) *adj.* Without moving.–The dog will fall down and lie *motionless* when Jack orders him to play dead.

mo•tion pic•ture (moh-shən PIK-cher) *motion pictures.* A movie; a series of pictures that appear to move when projected or shown rapidly, one after the other, on a screen.

mo•tive (MOH-tiv) *n. motives.* An inner feeling, reason, or thought which causes someone to do something.–The police are trying to find the man's *motive* for committing the crime. They want to find out why he did it.

mo•tor (MOH-ter) *n. motors.* An engine; a machine that makes other machinery work. –Our washing machine is run by an electric *motor.*–An automobile is run by a gasoline *motor.*

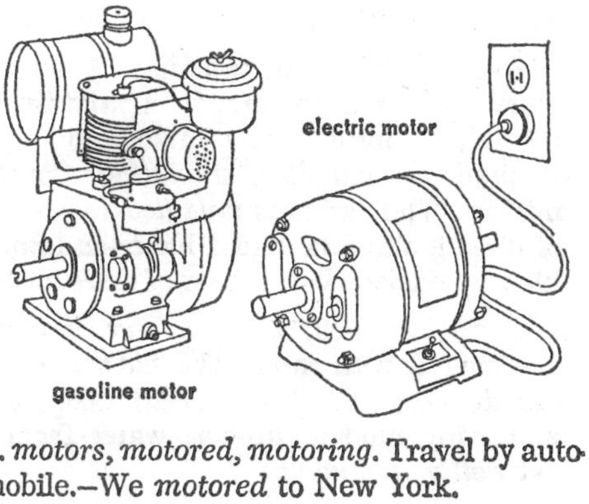

–*v. motors, motored, motoring.* Travel by automobile.–We *motored* to New York.

mo•tor•boat (MOH-ter-boht) *n. motorboats.* A boat run by a motor.

mo•tor•cy•cle (MOH-ter-sy-kəl) *n. motorcycles.* A heavy bicycle run by a motor.–Mr. Jones, the policeman, rides a *motorcycle.*

mo•tor•ist (MOH-ter-ist) *n. motorists.* A person traveling in an automobile.–On Sunday, there are many *motorists* on the road.

mo•tor•man (MOH-ter-mən) *n. motormen.* A person who drives a trolley car, a subway train, or any other electrically driven vehicle.

mot•to (MAH-toh) *n. mottoes* or *mottos.* A short saying to guide one's actions.–Bob's *motto* is, "If at first you don't succeed, try, try again."

mound (MOWND) *n. mounds.* 1. A small round pile or hump.–Sally made a *mound* of sand in the sand pile.

2. In baseball, the place from which the pitcher throws.

mount (MOWNT) *n. mounts.* 1. A horse to ride.–Ed's *mount* was a beautiful black horse.

2. A mountain.–*Mount* Everest is the tallest mountain in the world.

–*v. mounts, mounted, mounting.* 1. Climb up or upon.–Sally *mounted* the stairs to go to bed.–Ed *mounted* his horse and rode off.

2. Set or fix something on something else, usually for display or study.–Jane *mounted* her picture on gold paper for the art show.

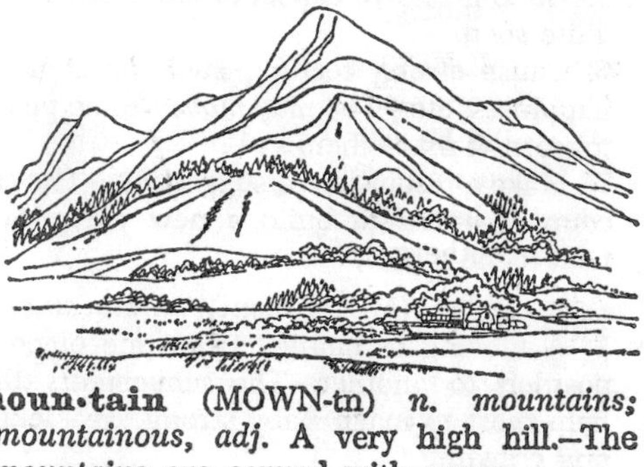

moun•tain (MOWN-tn) *n. mountains; mountainous, adj.* A very high hill.–The *mountains* are capped with snow.

mount·ing (MOWN-ting) *n. mountings.* Anything upon which something is set or fixed.–Bob's butterflies were pinned on a black velvet *mounting.*

mourn (MORN) *v. mourns, mourned, mourning.* Grieve or sorrow for.–The people *mourned* the death of Abraham Lincoln.

mouse (MOWSS) *n. mice.* A little animal, usually gray but sometimes brownish-gray or even white, that lives in people's houses, in barns, or in the fields or woods.

mous·tache (MUSS-tash *or* mə-STASH) *n.* Another way of spelling *mustache.*

mouth (MOWTH) *n. mouths.* 1. The opening in a person's face through which he eats, speaks, or makes sounds.–Your tongue and teeth are in your *mouth.*
2. The *mouth* of a cave is the opening where one enters.–The *mouth* of a river is the part where the river flows into the sea.

mouth·ful (MOWTH-fuhl) *n. mouthfuls.* As much as the mouth will hold.–Jack could not answer the telephone, because he had a *mouthful* of cake.

mov·a·ble (MOOV-ə-bəl) *adj.* Able to be moved.–Most furniture is *movable.* It can be taken from place to place.

move (MOOV) *v. moves, moved, moving.* 1. Change the position of.–Father *moved* the sofa.
2. Change position.–When Jack's dog plays dead, he lies without *moving.*
3. Go; be in motion.–Sally's turtle *moves* slowly.
4. Set in motion.–The water in the river *moves* the logs.
5. Go to live.–We expect to *move* to the city quite soon.
6. Cause strong feeling, such as sadness, happiness, etc.–The play *moved* some people to tears. It made them sad.
7. Make a resolution or suggestion.–The city council *moved* to build a new playground next to the school.

move·ment (MOOV-mənt) *n. movements.* 1. A moving or change from one place or position to another.–The *movements* that help most to make Baby strong are kicking and crawling.
2. A united effort by many people to bring about a certain thing.–There is a *movement* in town to get more playgrounds.
3. Part of a long musical composition.–Most symphonies have four *movements.*

mov·ie (MOOV-ee) *n. movies.* A motion picture.–Mary likes the *movies.*

mov·ing pic·ture (moov-ing PIK-cher) *moving pictures.* A motion picture, or a series of pictures that appear to move when shown rapidly, one after the other, on a screen.

mow (MOH) *v. mows, mowed, mowing.* Cut down.–Bob will *mow* the grass with the lawn mower.

mow·er (MOH-er) *n. mowers.* A machine for cutting hay, grass, weeds, or the like.

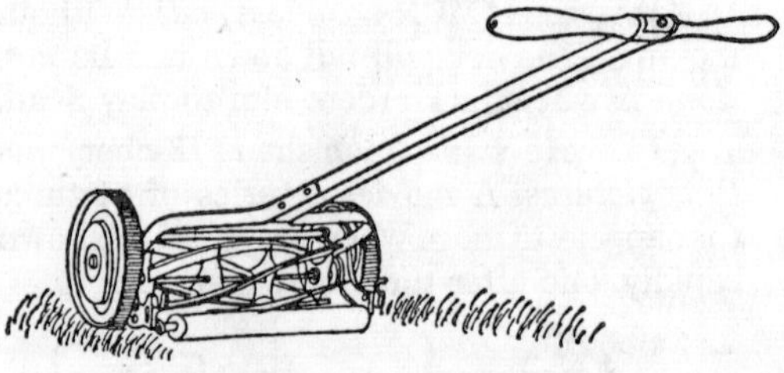

much (MUCH) *n.* and *adj. more, most.* 1. A great quantity or amount.–Please don't give me *much.*–*Much* milk is sold in our town each day.
–*adv.* To a great degree.–John is *much* stronger than Paul.
–*Too much* means more than is needed.–Some people talk *too much.*
–*How much* means what amount.–*How much* allowance do you get?

mu·cous mem·brane (MYOO-kəss MEM-brayn) *mucous membranes.* The tissue that lines the inner surface of the eyelid, the nose, the throat, and the other passages of the body which need lubrication.

mud (MUD) *n.* Wet, sticky earth.–Our car got stuck in the *mud.*

mud·dle (MUD-l) *n. muddles.* A mess. –Mary got her arithmetic in a *muddle.* She got it all confused and mixed up.
–*v. muddles, muddled, muddling.* Confuse; mix up.–The darkness *muddled* Jack's sense of direction and he had a hard time finding his way home.

mud·dy (MUD-ee) *adj. muddier, muddiest.* 1. Covered with mud.–The cat's feet were *muddy.*
2. Having mud in it.–The water from the old well was *muddy.*

muff (MUF) *n. muffs.* A soft tube made of fur or other warm material into which women put their hands to keep them warm.

–*v. muffs, muffed, muffing.* 1. Fail to catch.–The catcher *muffed* the ball and lost the game.
2. Do anything badly; miss an opportunity. –Bill *muffed* his chance to make the team by not coming to practice.

muf•fin (MUF-ən) *n. muffins.* A small cup-shaped cake.

muf•fle (MUF-əl) *v. muffles, muffled, muffling.* Cover up to silence or make quieter. –Mother *muffled* the telephone so that it would not wake the baby if it rang.

muf•fler (MUF-ler) *n. mufflers.* 1. A scarf.–Grandfather wears a woolen *muffler* about his neck to keep it warm in the winter.

2. Something that deadens sounds. – The automobile has a *muffler* to make the motor sound quieter.

mug (MUG) *n. mugs.* A tall, heavy drinking cup with a handle. *Mugs* are usually made of metal, earthenware, or heavy china.–Father likes his coffee in a *mug.*

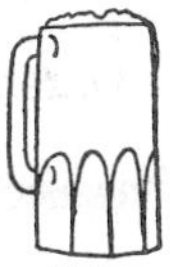

mul•ber•ry (MUL-bair-ee) *n. mulberries.* 1. A tree that has dark purple berries on it called *mulberries.*

2. A dark, reddish-blue color.

mulch (MULCH) *v. mulches, mulched, mulching.* Spread a mixture of earth, straw, leaves, wood shavings, etc., on the ground around plants, trees, shrubs, or bushes.–The farmer *mulched* his plants to protect their roots from too much cold and to keep the soil around them damp.

mule (MYOOL) *n. mules.* 1. An animal which is half horse and half donkey. *Mules* are used as work animals.

2. A flat house slipper without any covering for the heel.
3. A spinning machine.

mul•ti•pli•cand (mul-tə-plə-KAND) *n. multiplicands.* In arithmetic, the number that is multiplied by another number.–In 2 times 6 equals 12, 6 is the *multiplicand.*

mul•ti•pli•ca•tion (mul-tə-plə-KAY-shən) *n.* A short way of adding.–6 times 2 equals 12. This is *multiplication,* or a short way of adding six 2's together.

mul•ti•pli•er (MUL-tə-ply-er) *n.* In multiplication, the number which one multiplies by.–When you multiply 2 times 6 it equals 12. The *multiplier* is 2.

mul•ti•ply (MUL-tə-ply) *v. multiplies, multiplied, multiplying.* 1. Find the product of by multiplication.–2 *multiplied* by 6 equals 12.
2. Increase in number.–Rabbits *multiply* fast. They have baby rabbits often and in large numbers.

mul•ti•tude (MUL-tə-tood *or* -tyood) *n. multitudes.* A very great number (of persons or things).–A *multitude* of people came to the last game of the year. Every seat in the stands was taken.

mum (MUM) *adj.* Silent.–The captured spy kept *mum.* He did not tell anything.

mum•ble (MUM-bəl) *v. mumbles, mumbled, mumbling.* Speak so that it is hard to be understood; speak with the mouth partly closed. –The toothless old man *mumbles.* He doesn't talk clearly.

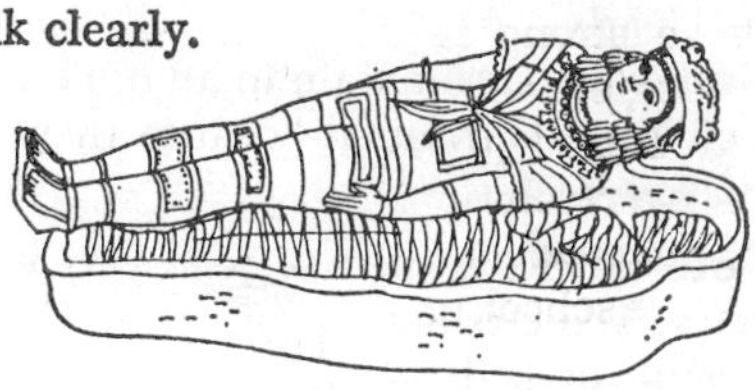

mum•my (MUM-ee) *n. mummies.* The dead body of a person that has been preserved, or kept from decaying.–Many *mummies* are found in Egypt.

mumps (MUMPSS) *n. pl.* A disease which causes glands in the face and neck to swell. –Do not go to school if you have the *mumps.* Other children may get the *mumps* if you go near them.

munch (MUNCH) *v. munches, munched, munching.* Chew.–Bob likes to *munch* an apple while he takes a walk.

mu•nic•i•pal (myoo-NISS-ə-pəl) *adj.* Having to do with the laws or affairs of a city or town.–The *municipal* buildings, the buildings in which city business is carried on, are on Main Street.

mu•ni•tions (myoo-NISH-ənz) *n. pl.* Guns, bombs, and other materials used in war.

mu•ral (MYUHR-əl) *n. murals.* A painting made on a wall.–The art teacher decorated her office with a *mural.* She painted a picture on one of the walls of her office.

mur•der (MER-der) *n. murders.* The unlawful killing of a person.
–*v. murders, murdered, murdering.* Kill unlawfully.–The gangster *murdered* the man he had robbed.

mur•der•er (MER-der-er) *n. murderers.* One who kills unlawfully. – The *murderer* said that he had planned the killing of his victim beforehand.

mur•mur (MER-mer) *n. murmurs.* A soft, low sound; soft, low talking.–We could hear the *murmur* of the running brook outside the tent.
–*v. murmurs, murmured, murmuring.* 1. Talk too low to be understood.–Do not *murmur;* speak clearly.
2. Grumble and complain in an undertone.– The children *murmured* because they could not have a recess.

mus•cle (MUSS-əl) *n. muscles.* The cordlike tissues in the body of a person or animal that move the body and the parts of the body. Exercise makes the *muscles* strong.

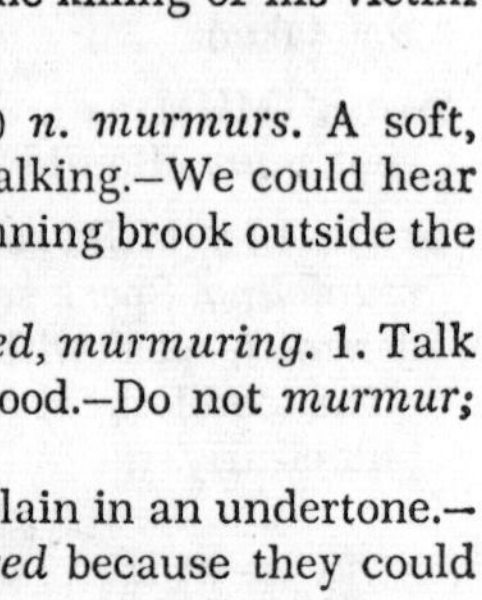

mu•se•um (myoo-ZEE-əm) *n. museums.* A building where interesting objects of art or science, such as paintings, machines, and stuffed animals, are arranged so that the public can see them.–We saw a mummy at the *Museum* of Natural History.

mush (MUSH) *n.; mushy, adj.* **1.** Boiled cornmeal.–*Mush* is good to eat.
2. Anything that is soft and thick and wet.– Mother cooked the apples to a *mush* to make applesauce.

mush•room (MUSH-room) *n. mushrooms.* A pale, spongy plant that grows close to the ground. Some *mushrooms* are good to eat, and some that grow wild are poisonous.

mu•sic (MYOO-zik) *n.* 1. Pleasing sounds made by singing voices or musical instruments.–Pianos, violins, and many other instruments make *music.*
2. Written notes or signs which, when played or sung, make pleasing sounds.

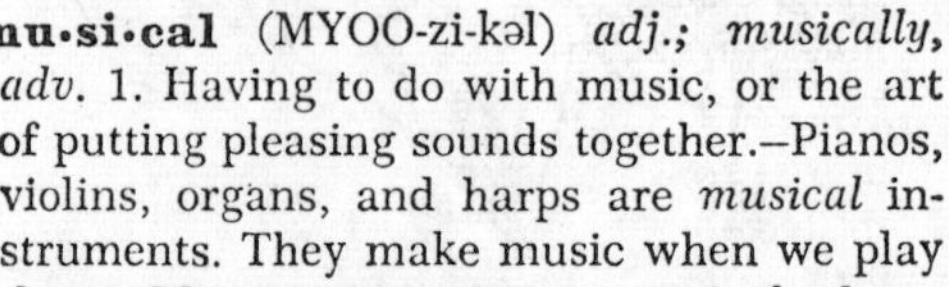

3. Any sounds that are pleasing to listen to. –We camped where we could hear the *music* of the waterfall.

mu•si•cal (MYOO-zi-kəl) *adj.; musically, adv.* 1. Having to do with music, or the art of putting pleasing sounds together.–Pianos, violins, organs, and harps are *musical* instruments. They make music when we play them.–Mary is receiving a *musical* education. She takes piano lessons and singing lessons.
2. Fond of music, or having a talent for music.–Mary is *musical.* She enjoys music. Learning music is easy for her.
3. Sweet and pleasant (of sounds).–The wind in the pine trees makes a *musical* sound.

mu·si·cian (myoo-ZISH-ən) *n. musicians.* A person who sings, or plays some musical instrument; also, one who earns his living by making music.

mus·ket (MUSS-kət) *n. muskets.* An old-fashioned gun, light enough to be fired from the shoulder.

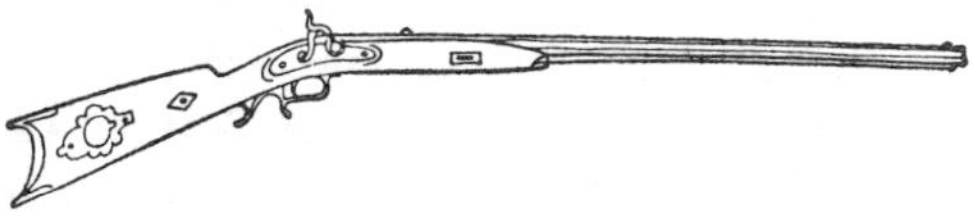

musk·mel·on (MUSK-mel-ən) *n. muskmelons.* A fruit of the melon family. *Muskmelons* have rough, thick rinds, and sweet, juicy, pinkish fruit.–We eat *muskmelons* for breakfast.

musk·rat (MUSK-rat) *n. muskrat* or *muskrats.* A water rat about the size of a cat. *Muskrats* are brown and have long tails.–Mother has a coat made of the furs of *muskrats.*

mus·lin (MUZ-lən) *n. muslins.* A cotton cloth. It may be fine and thin, or coarse. Sheets and pillow cases are made of *muslin.* Thin *muslin* is often used for dresses.

muss (MUSS) *v. musses, mussed, mussing.* Make untidy; upset.–Sally likes to *muss* Father's hair.

mus·sel (MUSS-əl) *n. mussels.* A common salt-water or fresh-water shellfish resembling a small clam. *Mussels* are used as food and as fish bait. They are generally found in very large numbers attached to rocks or stretched out on sandbanks called *mussel*-beds.

must (MUST) *v.* 1. Have to; be obliged or required to.–Most people *must* work in order to live.
2. Should.–We *must* hurry.
3. Surely or certainly is, am, or are.–Your mother *must* be happy over your good marks.

mus·tache or **mous·tache** (MUSS-tash *or* mə-STASH) *n. mustaches* or *moustaches.* The hair that grows just above a man's mouth.

mus·tard (MUSS-terd) *n.* A plant that has hard seeds which are ground and used for seasoning. The ground seeds mixed with vinegar make a dressing that is good to eat on frankfurters.

must·n't (MUSS-ənt). Must not. –You *mustn't* cross the street when the traffic light is red.

mus·ty (MUSS-tee) *adj. mustier, mustiest.* Moldy; having an odor or taste like that of something rotting.–The old house which had been closed up for a long time smelled *musty.*

mute (MYOOT) *n. mutes.* A person who is not able to talk.
–*adj.; mutely, adv.* Silent.–The witness remained *mute.* He didn't say a word.

mu·ti·ny (MYOO-tə-nee) *n. mutinies.* Revolt or open rebellion against lawful authority, especially by soldiers or seamen against their commanding officers. – The ship's captain charged the sailors with *mutiny* because they refused to obey his orders.

mut·ter (MUT-er) *v. mutters, muttered, muttering.* Speak in a low voice that cannot be understood.–As the angry boy went away, we heard him *muttering* to himself.

mut·ton (MUT-n) *n.* The flesh or meat of a sheep.–We had *mutton* for dinner.

mu·tu·al (MYOO-choo-əl) *adj.* 1. Having the quality of exchange, or of a balanced give and take of feelings, benefits, help, or the like, between two or more persons, groups, etc.–The two nations agreed upon a *mutual* assistance pact. Each nation agreed to come to the aid of the other in emergencies.
2. Having the same relation, one to another. –John and Henry have a *mutual* friend in Bob. Bob is John's friend as well as Henry's friend.

muz·zle (MUZ-əl) *n. muzzles.* 1. The nose and jaws of an animal.
2. A covering made of straps for the nose and jaws. –Jack puts a *muzzle* on his dog to keep him from biting people.
3. End or mouth (of a gun).–The man looked into the *muzzle* of the gun without flinching.
–*v. muzzles, muzzled, muzzling.* Put a muzzle on.–Jack *muzzles* his dog before taking him for a walk.

my (MY) *adj.* Of or belonging to me. The word shows that something belongs to me.–This is *my* kitten. She belongs to me. I am her owner.

myr·tle (MER-tl) *n. myrtles.* 1. A crawling evergreen plant that has shiny green leaves and blue-and-white flowers.

2. An evergreen shrub that has white or blue flowers and berries which are used in medicines. Oil made from the leaves is also used in medicines.

my·self (my-SELF) *pron.* My very self; me.–I can dress *myself*.–I have enough money to pay for *myself* at the movies.–I *myself* can work this problem, even though I am not good at arithmetic.

mys·te·ri·ous (miss-TIR-ee-əss) *adj.; mysteriously, adv.* Strange and not understood; hard to explain.–The loss of the teacher's glasses is very *mysterious*. Nobody can tell how they disappeared.–Mother saw a *mysterious* man watching our house. She did not know who he was or why he was there.

mys·ter·y (MISS-ter-ee) *n. mysteries.* 1. A deep secret or problem.–What could have happened to the lost ball was a *mystery* to Bill.
2. A detective story; a tale of strange events which are explained in the end.–Father likes to read *mysteries*.

myth (MITH) *n. myths.* A very old legend or story, often an attempt to explain natural events, like the weather and the seasons. – Long ago people explained the rising and setting of the sun by a *myth* that the sun god, Apollo, drove his horses across the sky each day.

my·thol·o·gy (mith-AHL-ə-jee) *n. mythologies.* The myths or stories of a people. – Greek *mythology* is all the myths of the Greeks.–Roman *mythology* is all the myths of the Romans.

MYTHOLOGY

N n

N, n (EN) *n. N's, n's.* The fourteenth letter of the alphabet.

nab (NAB) *v. nabs, nabbed, nabbing.* Suddenly catch or seize.—The policeman *nabbed* the thief as he ran out the door.

nag (NAG) *v. nags, nagged, nagging.* 1. Continually scold and find fault with.—Some parents *nag* their children.
2. A horse, especially a worn-out one.—The old *nag* could hardly pull the wagon.

nail (NAYL) *n. nails.* 1. One of the hard scales on the ends of your fingers and toes. —Finger*nails* protect the ends of your fingers and help you to pick up small things.
2. A slender, smooth piece of metal, pointed at one end and flat at the other.—*Nails* are pounded into boards to hold them together.
—*v. nails, nailed, nailing.* Fasten by hammering nails into.—Father *nailed* the top of the box on.

na•ked (NAY-kid) *adj.; nakedly, adv; nakedness, n.* Unclothed; bare. — Baby walked into the living room *naked.* She had nothing on.

name (NAYM) *n. names.* 1. The word a person or a thing is known by.—The *name* of the thing you sleep in is a bed.—The *name* of the things you wear on your feet is shoes.—Spot is the *name* of Jack's dog.—Jack's *name* is Jack.—Chicago is the *name* of a city.
2. A reputation.—The mayor made a good *name* for himself. He did good things for the people. People spoke well of him.—The dishonest boy made a bad *name* for himself. People spoke badly of him.
—*v. names, named, naming.* 1. Give a name to. —Jack *named* his dog Spot.
2. Mention or say.—The man told Jack to *name* the amount of money he wanted for his bicycle.
3. Choose or appoint. — The class *named* Mary for the part of Snow White.
4. Mention by name. — The school paper *named* the honor students.

name•sake (NAYM-sayk) *n. namesakes.* A person or thing named for another.—George Washington has many *namesakes.* There are many persons called by his name, George Washington.

nap (NAP) *n. naps.* 1. A short sleep.—Baby takes a *nap* each afternoon.
2. The short, woolly thread-ends that stand up like hairs on rugs and woolen cloth.—Baby likes to dig her toes into the soft *nap* on the rug.
—*v. naps, napped, napping.* Take a short nap. —Grandmother was *napping* in her rocker.

naph•tha (NAP- *or* NAF-thə) *n.* A colorless, inflammable liquid used as a cleaning fluid or a fuel. *Naphtha* is made from coal tar, shale, petroleum, or wood.

nap•kin (NAP-kin) *n. napkins.* A square or oblong piece of cloth or paper which is used at the table to wipe your mouth and fingers while eating.—You should keep your *napkin* in your lap while at the table.

nar•cis•sus (nahr-SISS-əss) *n. narcissuses* or *narcissi.* A fragrant yellow and white flower that blossoms early in the spring. *Narcissuses* grow from bulbs instead of seeds.

nar•cot•ic (nahr-KAH-tik) *n. narcotics.* A pain-relieving or sleep-inducing drug, such as morphine or opium. — *Narcotics* should be taken only under doctor's orders.—The doctor gave the badly wounded man a *narcotic* to ease his pain.

nar•rate (na-RAYT *or* NAR-ayt) *v. narrates, narrated, narrating.* Tell, as a story; relate. —The children listened quietly as the old sea captain *narrated* the story of his last trip. —*narration, n. narrations.*

nar•ra•tor (NAR-ay-ter) *n. narrators.* A person who tells a story.—When Father showed Mary the movies of our trip, John asked if he could be *narrator.* He wanted to tell Mary the story of the trip.

nar·row (NAR-oh) *v. narrows, narrowed, narrowing.* Become less wide.—The mountain road *narrows* between the cliffs.
—*adj.* 1. Not far across; not wide.—We went in single file down the *narrow* lane because it was not wide enough for two.
2. Close.—The child playing in the street had a *narrow* escape. He was nearly hit by a bus. —We are ahead in the game by a *narrow* margin. Our score is 18 and their score is 16.
—*Narrow-minded* means not able to see or understand things beyond the little that one already knows or believes.—The *narrow-minded* man would not listen to other people's ideas.

na·sal (NAY-zəl) *adj.* Having to do with the nose.—*Nasal* diseases are diseases of the nose. —*Nasal* tones are tones that are made through the nose.

nas·tur·tium (nə-STER-shəm) *n. nasturtiums.* A plant that has yellow and reddish-orange flowers and round, shiny leaves.

nas·ty (NAST-ee) *adj. nastier, nastiest.* 1. So dirty that it displeases people.—*Nasty* thoughts are evil thoughts, thoughts that are neither good nor proper.
2. Unpleasant. — The picnic was called off because of the *nasty* weather.

na·tion (NAY-shən) *n. nations.* A country in which the people live under one government. The people of a *nation* usually speak a common language and have similar customs.—Sweden is a *nation.* The people speak the same language and have one government.

na·tion·al (NASH-ə-nəl) *n. nationals.* A citizen of a nation.—Jack's uncle who lives in Canada is a Canadian *national.*
—*adj.; nationally, adv.* Anything that belongs to or is related to a nation.—The *national* anthem of the United States is "The Star-Spangled Banner." It is the country's song.

na·tion·al·i·ty (nash-ə-NAL-ə-tee) *n. nationalities.* Marie is French. Her *nationality* is French. She lives in France.—Of what *nationality* are you? To what nation do you belong?

na·tive (NAY-tiv) *n. natives.* 1. A person is a *native* of the place in which he was born.—Bob is a *native* of the United States. He was born in the United States.—Jack is a *native* of Juneau, Alaska. He was born there.
2. A person living in an uncivilized place is sometimes spoken of as a *native.*
—*adj.* Having had one's beginning or origin in a certain place.—Plants and animals are *native* to the place in which they were first found.—The zebra is *native* to Africa.

nat·u·ral (NACH-er-əl) *adj.; naturalness, n.* 1. In the original state; not changed. —Mother has a table of *natural* wood. The wood has not been painted or changed in any way.
2. Coming as a matter of course, without teaching or training.—It is *natural* for Mary to sing. It is easy for her.
3. To be expected.—It is *natural* that Jack should want to do everything that Bob can do.

nat·u·ral·ist (NACH-er-əl-ist) *n. naturalists.* A person who makes a study of plants and animals.

nat·u·ral·ize (NACH-ə-rə-lyz) *v. naturalizes, naturalized, naturalizing.* Give a person from a foreign country the rights of citizenship in another country after he has lived up to certain rules.—Jack's grandfather was *naturalized* in 1920. He was born in Europe, and became an American citizen in 1920.

nat·u·ral·ly (NACH-ə-rəl-ee) *adv.* 1. By nature.—Tom is *naturally* good at arithmetic. Arithmetic has always been easy for him.
2. Without affecting or pretending anything.—Sally talks *naturally.* She doesn't try to copy or imitate anyone.
3. Of course.—It started to snow, so *naturally* we wore our rubbers.

na·ture (NAY-cher) *n. natures.* 1. The whole world that we live in.—We live our whole life in *nature.*
2. Those parts of the world that have not been changed by man, especially the outdoors and its animal life.—Bob is fond of *nature.* He likes the woods and fields, the wild animals, the moon, the stars, and the sky.
3. All the traits that make a person or thing do certain things or behave in a certain way. —It is the *nature* of fish to swim.
4. Disposition or temper.—Ned has a gentle *nature.*

naught (NAWT) *n. naughts.* 1. A zero [0].—Put a *naught* after 1 and you have ten [10].
2. Nothing. — Bob's suggestion was all for *naught,* because Jack did not follow it.

naugh·ty (NAW-tee) *adj. naughtier, naughtiest; naughtily, adv.; naughtiness, n.* Bad in little ways; mischievous.—Do not be *naughty.* Mind your mother.

nau•se•ate (NAWZ- *or* NAWSH-ee-ayt) *v. nauseates, nauseated, nauseating.* Make sick at the stomach.–Do not eat too much candy. It may *nauseate* you.

nau•ti•cal (NAW-tə-kəl) *adj.* Having to do with the sea, with ships, seamen, or navigation. – The young sailors completed their *nautical* studies at the naval academy.

na•val (NAYV-əl) *adj.* Having to do with the navy.–*Naval* officers are officers in the navy.

na•vel (NAYV-əl) *n. navels.* The small hollow in the middle of the abdomen or belly.

nav•i•gate (NAV-ə-gayt) *v. navigates, navigated, navigating.* 1. Steer or manage a boat, ship, or airplane.–Jack *navigated* the canoe down the river very expertly.
2. Sail over.–The captain *navigates* the seas.
3. Use a compass and other instruments to tell where a ship or airplane is at a certain time.–Airplanes that fly across the ocean carry an officer whose duty is to *navigate.*
–*navigation, n.*

nav•i•ga•tor (NAV-ə-gay-ter) *n. navigators.* An officer on a ship or airplane who keeps track of where the craft is.

na•vy (NAY-vee) *n. navies.* An armed sea force which defends a nation. Warships, submarines, and airplanes are a *navy's* chief weapons.

nay (NAY) *n. nays* and *adv.* No.–*Nay* is an old-fashioned word used in stories and poems.

near (NIR) *v. nears, neared, nearing.* Get close to.–As we *neared* the station, the train came in.
–*adj. nearer, nearest* and *adv.* 1. Not far away from; close to.–Grandmother's house is *near* ours.
2. Not far off in time.–The opening of school is *near.* – It is too *near* dinner to have ice cream.
3. Closely related. – Only *near* relatives attended the wedding.

near•ly (NIR-lee) *adv.* Almost.–It is *nearly* three o'clock. It is a few minutes to three.

neat (NEET) *adj. neater, neatest; neatly, adv.* 1. Clean and tidy.–Mother's cupboards are always *neat.*
2. Fond of order; orderly in personal habits. –Father is a *neat* person. He likes to keep all his things in place.

neat•ness (NEET-nəss) *n.* Cleanliness; orderliness; tidiness.

Ne•bras•ka (nə-BRASS-kə) *n.* A state in central United States in which farming, hog and cattle raising, and meat packing are some of the important industries.

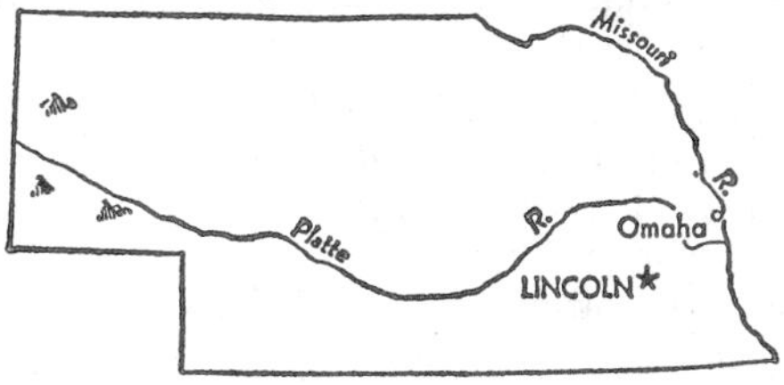

neb•u•la (NEB-yuh-lə) *n. nebulas* or *nebulae.* A shiny, cloudlike mass far away in the sky. It is made up of gas or a collection of stars. If you look through a powerful telescope, you can see hundreds of *nebulas* out in the sky.

nec•es•sar•y (NESS-ə-sair-ee) *adj.; necessarily, adv.* Needed; required.–Sleep is *necessary* for good health.

ne•ces•si•ty (nə-SESS-ə-tee) *n. necessities.* A need; something we cannot do without.–Food and drink are *necessities* of life.

neck (NEK) *n. necks.* 1. The part of the body that joins the head to the body.
2. The part of a piece of clothing that fits around the neck.–The *neck* of Bob's shirt is too tight.

neck•lace (NEK-ləss) *n. necklaces.* An ornament worn about the neck. –Gold and silver chains, and strings of pearls or beads, are *necklaces.*

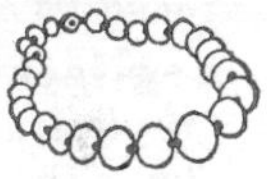

neck•tie (NEK-ty) *n. neckties.* A band of cloth worn about the neck and tied in front.–Father's *necktie* is new.

nec•tar (NEK-ter) *n. nectars.* 1. Any sweet, delicious drink. The ancient Greeks and Romans called the drink of the gods *nectar.*
2. A sweet juice that comes from flowers.–The bees take *nectar* from flowers and make honey from it.

need (NEED) *n. needs.* 1. Something required or needed.–The hermit's *needs* are few.
2. Poverty; lack of necessities.–Many families are in great *need.*
–*v. needs, needed, needing.* 1. Must have.–We *need* milk for dinner.
2. Have to; be required.–Do you *need* to spend so much time on your work?
3. Ought to have.–Mary *needs* a new skirt.

nee•dle (NEED-l) *n. needles.* 1. A slender piece of steel, pointed at one end, and with an eye, or hole, in the other end for thread to go through. A *needle* is used for sewing.
2. Anything like a sewing needle in shape or use.–A knitting *needle* is very long so that the material which has been knitted can be held on it.–Pine *needles* are the tiny, long green leaves which grow on pine trees.
3. An indicator or pointer. – The *needle* on a compass points north.–The *needle* on a speedometer shows how fast the car goes.

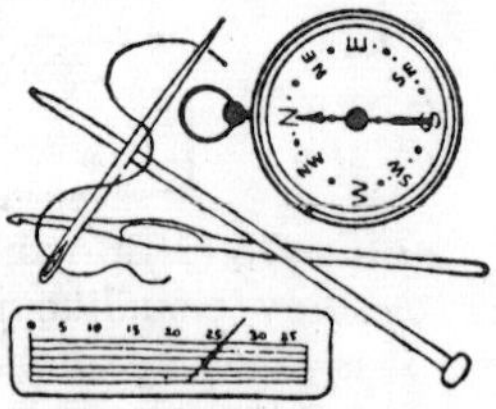

need•less (NEED-ləss) *adj.; needlessly, adv.* Unnecessary. – *Needless* to say, Jack was happy to find his dog.

need•n't (NEED-nt). Need not.–You *needn't* wait for me if you are in a hurry.

need•y (NEED-ee) *adj. needier, neediest.* Poor; in need of many things.–Every Thanksgiving we take food to *needy* families.

neg•a•tive (NEG-ə-tiv) *n. negatives; negatively, adv.* 1. Saying or meaning no.–Mother's answer was in the *negative.* She said no.
2. An image, usually on a camera film, in which light areas are dark, and dark ones are light.–I will have a print made from this *negative.*

neg•lect (nə-GLEKT) *n.; neglectful, adj.; neglectfully, adv.* Lack of care.–The ragged lawn shows *neglect.*
–*v. neglects, neglected, neglecting.* 1. Fail to take care of; pay no attention to.–If you *neglect* your dog, he may get sick.
2. Fail.–Do not *neglect* to brush your teeth twice a day.

neg•li•gent (NEG-lə-jənt) *adj.; negligently, adv.* Guilty of neglect; careless; inattentive or indifferent to what one should be doing right.–Harry failed his examination because he was *negligent* about his studies.

ne•go•ti•ate (ni-GOH-shee-ayt) *v. negotiates, negotiated, negotiating.* 1. Discuss or talk over; try to come to terms, reach an agreement, or settle a dispute.–The captain of the basketball team and the captain of the track team are *negotiating* for the use of the gym. They are deciding together when each team will have the gym to practice in.
2. Transfer or sell, especially as a business. –Stock brokers *negotiate* stocks and bonds.
–*negotiation, n. negotiations.*

Ne•gro (NEE-groh) *n. Negroes.* A person of the black race, originally from Africa.

neigh (NAY) *n. neighs.* The call or cry of a horse.–Have you ever heard the *neigh* of a horse?
–*v. neighs, neighed, neighing.* Make the sound that horses make. – I heard Grandfather's horses *neigh.*

neigh•bor (NAY-ber) *n. neighbors.* A person who lives next door or nearby. – Father is talking over the back fence with the *neighbors.*

neigh•bor•hood (NAY-ber-huhd) *n. neighborhoods.* 1. A part of a town or section.–In our *neighborhood,* all the children play together.
2. Surrounding area.–We live in the *neighborhood* of the school. The school is just around the corner.

nei•ther (NEE- *or* NY-ther) *adj.* and *conj.* 1. Not one or the other; not either.–*Neither* Jack nor Mary heard Mother call. Jack didn't hear her and Mary didn't hear her.
2. And not; nor. – Jack didn't hear her; *neither* did Mary.

ne•on (NEE-ahn) *n.* and *adj.* A gas found in small amounts in the air around the earth. When *neon* is electrically charged it gives off a reddish glow. *Neon* lights are vacuum tubes containing *neon* and small amounts of other gases.

neph•ew (NEF-yoo) *n. nephews.* A son of one's brother or sister.–Father's and Mother's *nephews* are our cousins.

Nep•tune (NEP-toon *or* -tyoon) *n.* 1. The ancient Roman god of the sea. The Greeks called him Poseidon.
2. The fourth largest planet, and eighth in order of distance from the sun. *Neptune,* whose diameter is about 33,000 miles, can be seen only with the aid of a telescope.

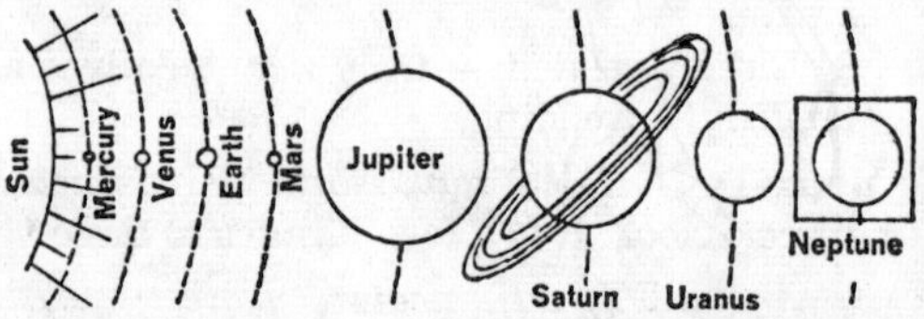

nerve (NERV) *n. nerves.* 1. One of the little threadlike bands that join the brain and the spinal cord with all the other parts of the body The *nerves* control the actions of the body.
2. Courage.–The firemen needed *nerve* to go into the burning house.

nerv•ous (NERV-əss) *adj.; nervously, adv.; nervousness, n.* 1. Restless; uneasy; upset.–Mother grew *nervous* as the time came for Mary to appear on the stage.
2. Having to do with the nerves.–Your brain, spinal cord, and nerves are your *nervous* system.

nest (NEST) *n. nests.* 1. The home of a bird, or of certain other creatures.–Birds build *nests* in which they lay eggs and raise their young. – We found the *nest* of a mouse in the cellar.

2. A cozy place to rest and sleep.–Our kitten has a *nest* in a basket.
3. A group of things that fit together.–Mother has a *nest* of tables in the living room.
–*v. nests, nested, nesting.* Make a nest. – Robins *nest* in the spring.

nes•tle (NESS-əl) *v. nestles, nestled, nestling.* 1. Snuggle.–The little kittens *nestled* against their mother.
2. Cuddle; hold close and tenderly.–The policeman picked up the hurt dog and *nestled* it in his arms.

net (NET) *n. nets.* 1. A web made by tying pieces of cord, string, or other material across each other and together in such a way that meshes or holes of the same size are made.–Ed caught the fish in a *net.*–Mother wears a hair *net.*
2. An openwork cloth.–Mary's party dress is made of *net.*

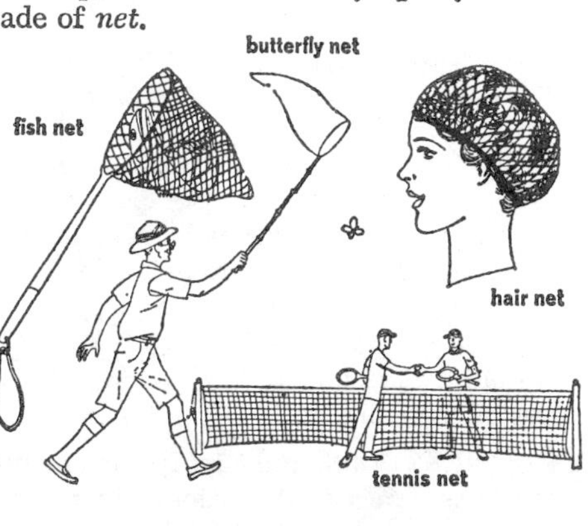

3. A trap.–The rabbit was caught in a *net.*
–*v. nets, netted, netting.* Catch in a net. – Bob is *netting* butterflies.
–*adj.* Amount remaining after necessary amounts are taken out.–The *net* profit on the apples was 49 cents. They cost Jim $1.10 a box and he sold them for $1.59.

net•tle (NET-l) *n. nettles.* A plant that has little hairlike stickers on it that sting when one touches them.
–*v. nettles, nettled, nettling.* Irritate; provoke; anger. – Mary was *nettled* at Jack's mimicking her.

net•work (NET-werk) *n. networks.* 1. A system of lines that cross or weave in and out. –A net is a *network.*
2. A group of radio or television stations linked together so that the same program can be heard, or seen, over all of them.–We heard the program over a national *network.*

neu•tral (NOO- *or* NYOO-trəl) *n. neutrals.* 1. A country that is not on either side in a fight or struggle.–Switzerland was a *neutral* in World War II.
2. When the gears of a car are in *neutral,* the engine can run without turning the wheels.
–*adj.* 1. Not on either side in a fight or struggle.–Jack and Tom each wanted the last piece of cake. Mother said they'd have to decide who would get it themselves. Mother was *neutral.*
2. Grayish, or of a not distinct hue.–Ruth likes to wear *neutral* colors.

neu•tron (NOO- *or* NYOO-trahn) *n. neutrons.* A tiny particle with no electric charge. It is about equal in mass to the proton, which is a positively charged particle. *Neutrons* and protons make up the nucleus of an atom.

Ne•vad•a (nə-VA-də *or* nə-VAH-də) *n.* A very dry, mountainous state in western United States. *Nevada* is often called the "Sagebrush State." In the irrigated regions, farming and stock raising are important occupations. Valuable gold and silver mines are found in *Nevada,* and many other metals are waiting to be mined. *Nevada* has the world's tallest dam, the Hoover Dam on the Colorado River.

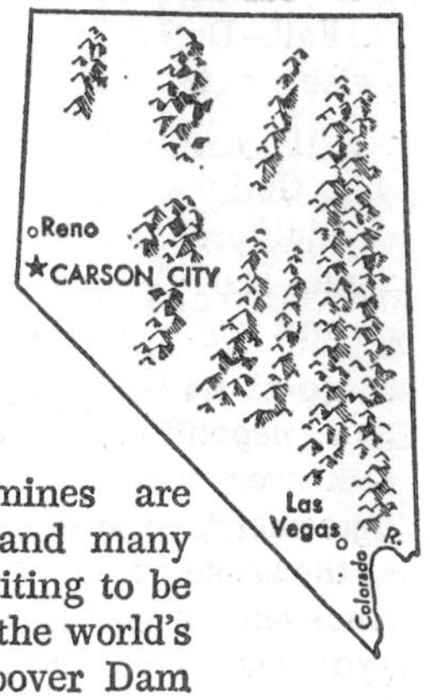

nev•er (NE-ver) *adv.* Not at any time.–Bob would *never* tell tales on anyone.–Mary has *never* been late.

nev•er•the•less (ne-ver-tha-LESS) *conj.* However; in spite of that.–Bob's hands were sore; *nevertheless,* he held on to the rope.

new (NOO *or* NYOO) *adj. newer, newest; newly, adv.; newness, n.* 1. Not known or found before; not old.–Father has a *new* idea for making paper.–Our house is *new;* it was just built.–Mother has a *new* dress. She has just bought it.

2. Different.–Father has a *new* bookkeeper.

3. Fresh.–Jack had *new* hope when he heard that his lost dog had been seen.

4. Not usual for; never done before.–Working at night is *new* to Father.

new•com•er (NOO- *or* NYOO-kum-er) *n. newcomers.* Someone who has just come.–There is a *newcomer* in our class. He has just come into our class.

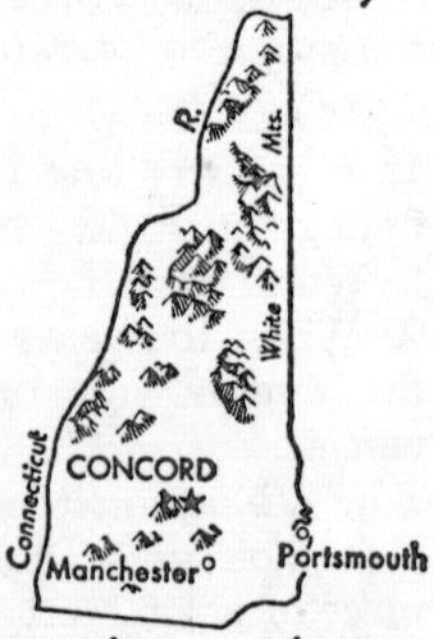

New Hamp•shire (noo *or* nyoo HAMP-sher) *n.* A rugged, mountainous state in northeastern United States, popular as a vacation spot in summer and a skiing spot in winter. Manufacturing cloth, leather goods, and paper are among its important industries.

New Jer•sey (noo *or* nyoo JER-zee) *n.* A state on the northeastern coast of the United States, known for its truck, dairy, and poultry farms, pottery making, its manufacturing, especially of silk products, and its vacation spots.

New Mex•i•co (noo *or* nyoo MEKS-ə-koh) *n.* A state in southwestern United States, much of which is desert land, with the scenic Rocky Mountains in the west. The bright sunshine and dry, mild climate make *New Mexico* a health resort.

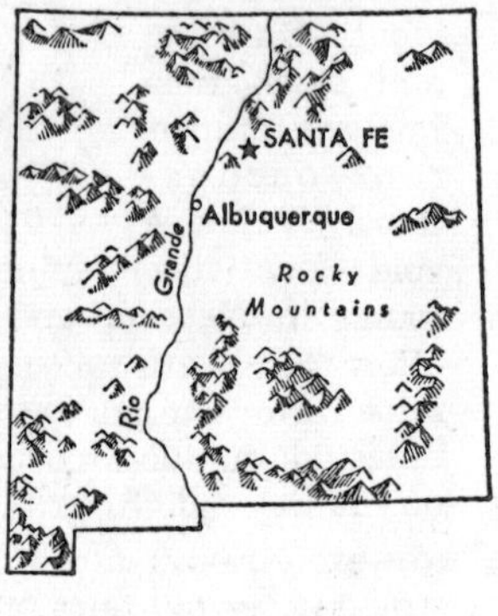

news (NOOZ *or* NYOOZ) *n.* A report of something that has happened.–We read the newspaper to learn the *news,* to find out what has happened.–The *news* that you had moved was a surprise to me.

news•boy (NOOZ- *or* NYOOZ-boi) *n. newsboys.* A boy who sells newspapers.

news•pa•per (NOOZ- *or* NYOOZ-pay-per) *n. newspapers.* A large sheet or sheets of paper printed and sold regularly. It tells people what is happening in the world and what they can buy at the stores, and gives other information and entertainment.

New Year's Day (NOO *or* NYOO YIRZ DAY). January 1st. It is the first day of a new year.

New York (noo *or* nyoo YORK) *n.* A state in eastern United States, with beautiful lakes and forest-covered mountains, important for farming, manufacturing, production of granite, marble, and other building materials, for its colleges, and for the United States Military Academy. It is known also for New York City. One of the world's largest cities, this is the world's busiest port and its financial center, and the center of the garment and publishing industries of the country.

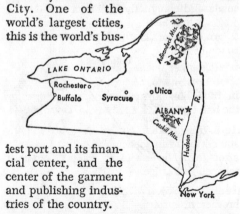

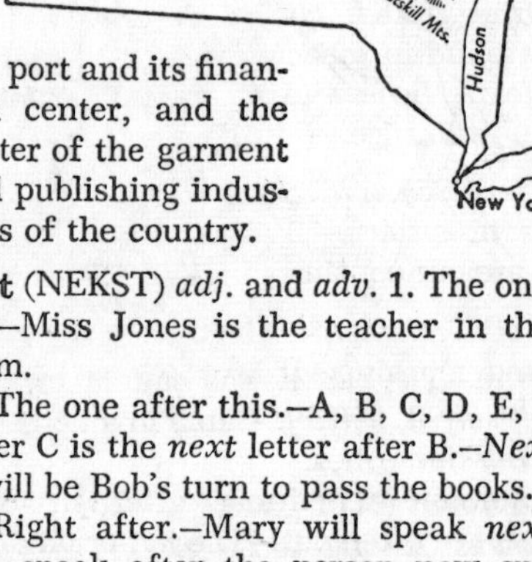

next (NEKST) *adj.* and *adv.* 1. The one nearest.–Miss Jones is the teacher in the *next* room.

2. The one after this.–A, B, C, D, E, F. The letter C is the *next* letter after B.–*Next* time it will be Bob's turn to pass the books.

3. Right after.–Mary will speak *next.* She will speak after the person now speaking finishes.

nice (NYSS) *adj. nicer, nicest; nicely, adv.* 1. Agreeable; pleasant.—This is a *nice* day.—Our neighbors are *nice* people.
2. Very careful and particular; neat.—Bob is a *nice* worker. He works carefully and neatly.

niche (NICH) *n. niches.* 1. A hollowed-out place in a wall. It is usually a long semicircle, arched at the top. Statues, vases, and things like that are put in *niches.* —The *niche* was dimly lighted by a small lamp.

2. A place or job ideally suited to a person or thing. — John finally found a *niche* for himself with the railroad.

nick (NIK) *n. nicks.* A cut; a notch. — The thoughtless boy made *nicks* in the post with his knife.—Mary dropped her plate and made a *nick* in it. She broke off a small piece of the china.
—*v. nicks, nicked, nicking.* Make a small cut in.—Bob *nicked* the table with his knife.

nick•el (NIK-əl) *n. nickels* and *adj.* 1. A metal that looks something like silver.
2. A piece of money equal to 5 cents. It is a coin made of copper and covered with nickel.

nick•name (NIK-naym) *n. nicknames.* A friendly name by which someone is called.—Robert's *nickname* is Bob.
—*v. nicknames, nicknamed, nicknaming.* Give another name to, besides the real name, just in fun.—The boys *nicknamed* everyone on the ball team. Jack's nickname is Skinny.

nic•o•tine (NIK-ə-teen) *n.* A poisonous substance found in tobacco. *Nicotine* is named after Jean Nicot who, in 1560, introduced tobacco to France.

niece (NEESS) *n. nieces.* A daughter of one's brother or sister. — Father's and Mother's *nieces* are our cousins.

night (NYT) *n. nights.* The time between evening and morning.—It is dark at *night,* and sometimes the moon shines.

night•gown (NYT-gown) *n. nightgowns.* A long, loose garment worn by some people at night when they sleep.

night•in•gale (NYT-n-gayl) *n. nightingales.* A European bird somewhat like a brown thrush. The male bird is known for his sweet singing, both night and day.

night•ly (NYT-lee) *adj.* and *adv.* Happening at night or every night. — The owl hoots *nightly* in the forest outside the lakeside cottage. It hoots every night.

night•shirt (NYT-shert) *n. nightshirts.* A long shirt which some persons wear to sleep in.

nim•ble (NIM-bəl) *adj. nimbler, nimblest; nimbly, adv.; nimbleness, n.* 1. Quick and lively.—Jack be *nimble,* Jack be quick.—Grandfather is very *nimble* for a man his age.
2. Keen; alert.—Tom has a *nimble* mind. He understands things quickly.

nine (NYN) *n. nines* and *adj.* 1. The number [9] coming after 8 and before 10.—Four and five make *nine.*
2. A baseball team.—Our *nine* won the ball game 3 to 2.

nine•teen (nyn-TEEN) *n. nineteens* and *adj.* The number [19] coming after 18 and before 20.—Nine and ten make *nineteen.*

nine•teenth (nyn-TEENTH) *n. nineteenths.* One of 19 equal parts.—If you divide anything into nineteen parts all the same size, each part is one *nineteenth.* It may be written 1/19.
—*adj.* Coming as number 19 in a series.—The *nineteenth* page of a book is the page after page 18.

nine•ti•eth (NYN-tee-əth) *n. ninetieths.* One of 90 equal parts.—If you divide anything into ninety parts all the same size, each part is one *ninetieth.* It may be written 1/90.
—*adj.* Coming as number 90 in a series.—The old woman just had her *ninetieth* birthday. Last year she had her eighty-ninth birthday.

nine•ty (NYN-tee) *n. nineties* and *adj.* The number [90] coming after 89 and before 91. —Forty and fifty make *ninety.*

ninth (NYNTH) *n. ninths.* One of 9 equal parts.—If you divide anything into nine parts all the same size, each part is one *ninth.* It may be written 1/9.
—*adj.* Coming as number 9 in a series.—Your *ninth* birthday is the one after your eighth.

nip (NIP) *n. nips*. A pinch or a bite. – The puppy gave Baby a *nip* when she pulled its tail.
–*v. nips, nipped, nipping.* 1. Pinch or bite.– The frisky puppy *nipped* playfully at the cuffs of Father's trousers.
2. Hurt or injure, especially by cold.–The heavy frost we had last night *nipped* our flowers.

nip•ple (NIP-əl) *n. nipples.* 1. The small part of a mother's breast from which a baby draws or sucks milk.
2. The rubber top on a baby's bottle, through which the baby sucks milk.

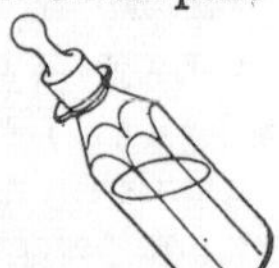

ni•trate (NY-trayt) *n. nitrates.* A chemical salt. With hydrogen it forms nitric acid. *Nitrates* have three parts of oxygen to every part of nitrogen. *Nitrates* are used in many things such as fertilizers, explosives, and medicines.

ni•tro•gen (NYT-rə-jən) *n.* One of the gases in the air we breathe. The air is a mixture of gases which we cannot see.

ni•tro•glyc•er•in or **ni•tro•glyc•er•ine** (ny-troh-GLIS-ə-rin) *n.* A highly explosive, oily liquid. *Nitroglycerin* is used in the manufacture of dynamite and certain rocket fuels.

no (NOH) *n. noes, adj.*, and *adv.* 1. The opposite of yes.–When Mother asked the children if they wanted some more ice cream, Sally said, "Yes, I want some." Mary said, "*No*, I cannot eat any more."
2. Not any.–Mary wants *no* more ice cream. She has had enough.

no•bil•i•ty (noh-BIL-ə-tee) *n. nobilities.* 1. Great or high character.–Abraham Lincoln was a man of great *nobility*.
2. A special, privileged class of people.– Dukes, barons, and earls are people of the *nobility*.

no•ble (NOH-bəl) *n. nobles.* A person of the nobility.–The prince invited many *nobles* to the tournament.
–*adj. nobler, noblest.* 1. Great and good.– Abraham Lincoln was a *noble* man.
2. Like or relating to a person who holds a high position in certain countries, such as a duke, baron, or count.–Some people in England are of *noble* birth.

no•bly (NOH-blee) *adv.* Splendidly; as a noble person would.–The soldier served *nobly*. He served with honor.

no•bod•y (NOH-bah-dee) *n. nobodies* and *pron.* 1. No one; not even one person. – *Nobody* heard the bell ring.–*Nobody* was late today.
2. An unimportant person.–In a few years, the man who had begun as a mere *nobody* was a famous actor.

noc•tur•nal (nahk-TER-nl) *adj.* 1. Having to do with, or happening during, the night.– Doctors often make *nocturnal* visits to sick people.
2. Awake and active during the night.–The owl and the bat are *nocturnal* creatures.

nod (NAHD) *n. nods.* A bend of the head.– Mother gave Mary a *nod*.
–*v. nods, nodded, nodding.* 1. Say yes by bending or bowing the head forward and downward, or moving it up and down.–When Mary asked if she might go, Mother *nodded*.
2. Let the head fall forward as though one were going to sleep.–Grandmother sat in her chair and *nodded*.

node (NOHD) *n. nodes.* A bump, lump, knot, or swelling.–*Nodes* often appear at the joints of plant stems or at spots where leaves will grow.

No•el (noh-EL) *n. Noels.* 1. Christmas.
2. (Usually not spelled with a capital "N.") A carol; a Christmas song.
–*interj.* (Usually not spelled with a capital "N.") Joy.–The angels sang, *"Noel, noel."* They were singing "joy, joy."

noise (NOIZ) *n. noises.* Loud, harsh sounds.– We heard a *noise* in the basement. It was the *noise* made by a falling lawn mower.
–*v. noises, noised, noising.* Tell everywhere.– It was *noised* abroad that the prince would marry the owner of the glass slipper.

nois•y (NOIZ-ee) *adj. noisier, noisiest; noisily, adv.; noisiness, n.* Making many noises or loud, mixed-up sounds; not quiet.–The teacher told the children that they were too *noisy*. –The old car is a *noisy* one.

no•mad (NOH-mad) *n. nomads.* A person who belongs to a tribe or group of people who have no permanent homes. They go from place to place to find food and water for their cattle and sheep.

nom•i•nate (NAHM-ə-nayt) *v. nominates, nominated, nominating.* Name a person to run for an office.–Mary was *nominated* for class secretary.

nom•i•na•tion (nahm-ə-NAY-shən) *n. nominations.* A suggestion of someone to run for an office.–Mary accepted the *nomination* for the office of secretary. She was willing to be voted on for the office.

non•con•duc•tor (nahn-kən-DUK-ter) *n. nonconductors.* A substance or material through which electricity, heat, sound, etc., cannot be passed or transmitted; an insulator.–Asbestos is a *nonconductor* of heat.

none (NUN) *pron.* Not any.–*None* of the cookies are left.
–*adv.* Not at all.–Sally is *none* the worse for having jumped into the snowbank.

non•sense (NAHN-senss) *n.; nonsensical, adj.* Talk and actions that are foolish, or that mean nothing.–It is *nonsense* to say that the moon is made of green cheese.

noo•dle (NOO-dl) *n. noodles.* A food made of flour, eggs, water, and salt. *Noodles* are rolled very thin and cut into long strips. They are often cooked in beef or chicken broth.

nook (NUHK) *n. nooks.* 1. A small sheltered place.–We had a picnic in a shady *nook* near the river.
2. A little room open on one side to a larger room.–We have our breakfast in the breakfast *nook.*

noon (NOON) *n. noons.* Twelve o'clock in the daytime; the middle of the day.–We come home for lunch at *noon.*

noose (NOOSS) *n. nooses.* A loop in a rope with a slip knot tied in it. When you pull the end of the rope through the knot, the loop becomes smaller and tighter.–The cowboy caught the steer with a *noose.*

nor (NOR) *conj.* Neither Jack *nor* Mary heard Mother call. Jack did not hear and Mary did not hear. They were too busy playing tag.

nor•mal (NOR-məl) *adj.; normally, adv.* 1. Average.–Jack's weight is *normal.* He weighs as much as most boys of his age.
2. Usual.–At eleven o'clock Mother began to worry. She said it wasn't *normal* for Jack to stay out so late.

north (NORTH) *n.* (Spelled with a capital "N.") The northern part of the country.–Winter is cold in the *North.*
–*adj.* and *adv.* 1. A direction.–If you face toward the sun as it comes up in the morning, your left shoulder will be pointing *north* and your right shoulder will be pointing south.

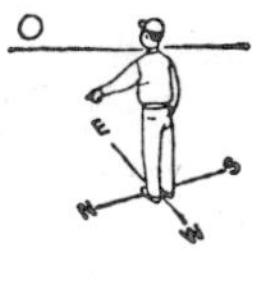

2. Toward the north.–The birds fly *north* in the spring.
3. Blowing from the north.–The *north* wind shall blow and we shall have snow and what will the robin do then?

North Car•o•li•na (north kar-ə-LYN-ə) *n.* A state on the east coast of the United States. Mt. Mitchell, 6,684 ft. high, the highest mountain in eastern United States, is in *North Carolina.* Lumbering, farming, and cotton and tobacco raising are the state's chief industries.

North Da•ko•ta (north də-KOH-tə) *n.* A state in north central United States which leads all the states in the production of spring

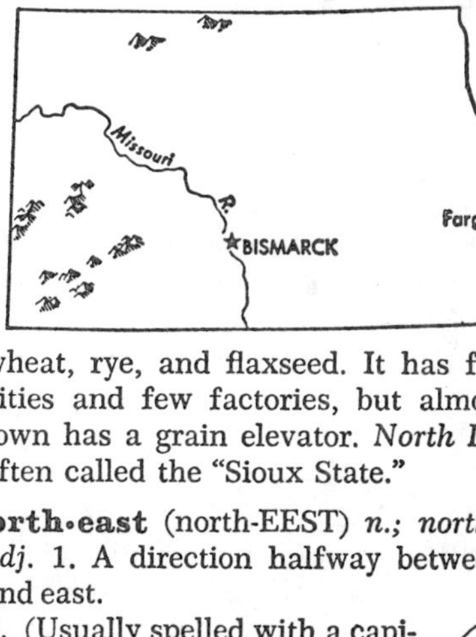

wheat, rye, and flaxseed. It has few large cities and few factories, but almost every town has a grain elevator. *North Dakota* is often called the "Sioux State."

north•east (north-EEST) *n.; northeastern, adj.* 1. A direction halfway between north and east.
2. (Usually spelled with a capital "N.") The part that lies north and east from the middle of a country or region. – The state of New York is in the *Northeast.*
–*adj.* In a direction halfway between north and east.

north•ern (NORTH-ern) *adj.* The part lying on the north side, or farthest to the north.–The United States is in the *northern* part of the Western Hemisphere. It lies between the equator and the North Pole.

north•ern lights (NOR-thern lytss). Another name for the *aurora borealis.*

north·ward (NORTH-werd) *adv.* Toward the north.–Birds fly *northward* in the spring.

north·west (north-WEST) *n.; northwestern, adj.* 1. A direction halfway between north and west.

2. (Usually spelled with a capital "N.") The part that lies north and west from the middle of a country or region.–The state of Montana is in the *Northwest.*

–adj. In a direction halfway between north and west.

nose (NOHZ) *n. noses.* 1. The part of the face or head of a person or animal that is just above the mouth. – You breathe and smell through your *nose.*

2. A sense of smell.–Jack's dog has a good *nose.* He can trace squirrels, rabbits, and many other creatures just by smelling their tracks.

3. The front tip, as the *nose* of an airplane.

–v. noses, nosed, nosing. 1. Push with nose first.–The boat *nosed* into the harbor.

2. Search or pry.–Jack *nosed* around in the deserted house.

nos·tril (NAHSS-trəl) *n. nostrils.* One of the two openings in the nose.–We breathe through the *nostrils.*

not (NAHT) *adv. Not* makes the word it goes with say just the opposite.–Baby is *not* awake. She is asleep. Asleep is the opposite of awake.

notch (NAHCH) *n. notches.* A V-shaped cut. –The sun set in the *notch* between the high Western hills.

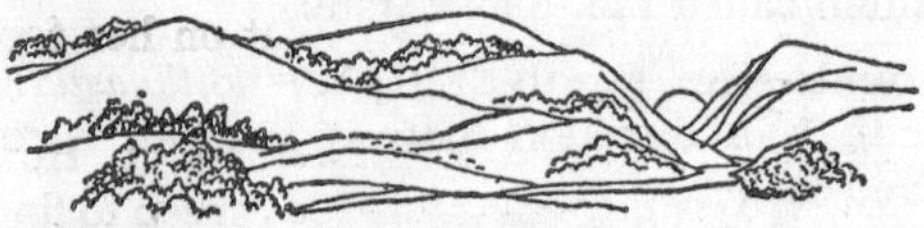

–v. notches, notched, notching. Make V-shaped cuts in.–Mother *notched* the seams of Mary's dress so that the cloth would not separate into threads.

note (NOHT) *n. notes.* 1. A short written message; a few written words.–Bob left a *note* telling his mother that he would be home late.

2. A few words to serve as a reminder.–Father was afraid he would forget the appointment, so he made a *note* of it.

3. A short explanation, usually at the bottom of a page.–Mary didn't know what the word meant, so she read the *note* at the bottom of the page.

4. A musical tone.–The song ended on the *note* of C.

5. A sign used in written music to represent a tone.–Father can play the piano, but he cannot read *notes.*

6. Well-known reputation.–Mayor Johnson is a man of *note* in our town.

–v. notes, noted, noting. Notice.–Jack *noted* that the footprints had been made by someone wearing rubbers.

note·book (NOHT-buhk) *n. notebooks.* A blank book of writing paper in which to write down things to be remembered or to be referred to.

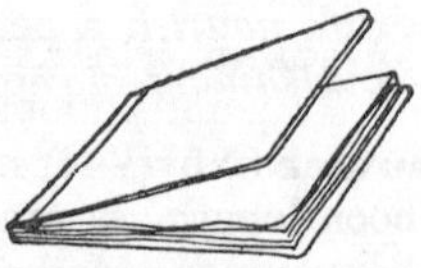

not·ed (NOHT-id) *adj.* Well-known or famous. – Paul's uncle is a *noted* baseball player.

noth·ing (NUTH-ing) *n.* 1. Not a thing.–The old woman looked in the cupboard, but she found *nothing* there.

2. Zero [0].–Four taken from four leaves *nothing.*

no·tice (NOH-təss) *n. notices.* 1. A warning. –The whistle blew to give *notice* that there was a fire.

2. An announcement, printed or spoken.–The *notice* said that there would be no school on Friday.

3. Attention.–The guide called to our *notice* the black bear standing on the rock up on the hill.

4. A word in advance.–Father gave the store where he works *notice* that he could not work there any longer.

–v. notices, noticed, noticing. See.–I *notice* that you have on a new dress.

no·tice·a·ble (NOH-təss-ə-bəl) *adj.; noticeably, adv.* Easy to see, hear, feel, smell, or the like.–The blue patch on Bob's gray shirt was quite *noticeable.* It could be seen easily.

no·ti·fy (NOH-tə-fy) *v. notifies, notified, notifying.* Give notice to; tell officially; let know. –The school board *notified* the principal that school would close for a week at Christmas time.

no·tion (NOH-shən) *n. notions.* 1. An idea, or what one thinks.–I have a *notion* that we can work the problem this way.

2. (In the plural) Any of various small articles, such as thread, buttons, etc.–The peddler came to the door selling *notions.*

no•to•ri•ous (noh-TOR-ee-əs) *adj.; notoriously, adv.* Well-known for bad deeds or qualities.–The *notorious* gangster was arrested during the night.

noun (NOWN) *n. nouns.* A word used to name a person, place, thing, or quality.–Words such as Susan, room, France, door, stone, and darkness are *nouns.*

nour•ish (NER-ish) *v. nourishes, nourished, nourishing.* Feed; give (a living thing) whatever it needs to keep alive and grow.–Sun, soil, and water *nourish* the plants.–Food and drink *nourish* a person.
–*nourishment, n. nourishments.*

nov•el (NAHV-əl) *n. novels.* A long story of book length. A *novel* is not a story of true happenings.–Mother is reading a *novel.*
–*adj.* New and unusual.–Jack had a *novel* idea for saving money.

nov•el•ty (NAHV-əl-tee) *n. novelties* and *adj.* 1. Anything new or unusual.–It was a *novelty* for Bob to stay up until midnight.
2. An unusual trinket, toy, or game.–The little store sold stationery and *novelties.*

No•vem•ber (noh-VEM-ber) *n. Novembers.* The eleventh month of the year. *November* has thirty days.

nov•ice (NAHV-iss) *n. novices.* 1. One who is new at something; a beginner.–Tom is a *novice* at tennis. He is just learning the game.
2. When a person wants to enter a religious order, he is given a trial period before he takes his vows. During that period he is called a *novice.*

now (NOW) *n.* and *adv.* 1. The present time. –Father should be home by *now.*
2. At this time; at the present time.–I shall leave *now* in order not to be late.
3. As it is.–You took too long to dress; *now* you will be late.
–*Now that* means since or seeing that.–*Now that* it is raining, we cannot play outdoors.

no•where (NOH-hwair) *adv.* Not any place at all.–There is *nowhere* Mary would rather be than at the movies.

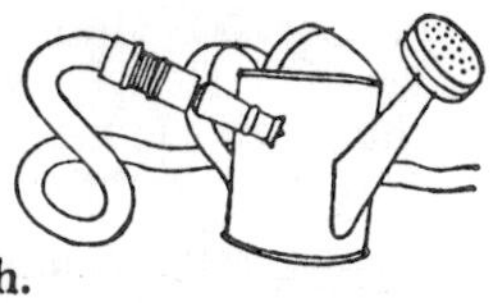

noz•zle (NAHZ-əl) *n. nozzles.* A metal pipe or tip on the end of a hose or container for liquid to come through.

nu•cle•ar en•er•gy (NOO- *or* NYOO-klee-er EN-er-jee). Another name for *atomic energy.*

nu•cle•us (NOO- *or* NYOO-klee-əss) *n. nucleuses* or *nuclei; nuclear, adj.* 1. A central part around which other parts are gathered in atoms and in plant and animal cells.

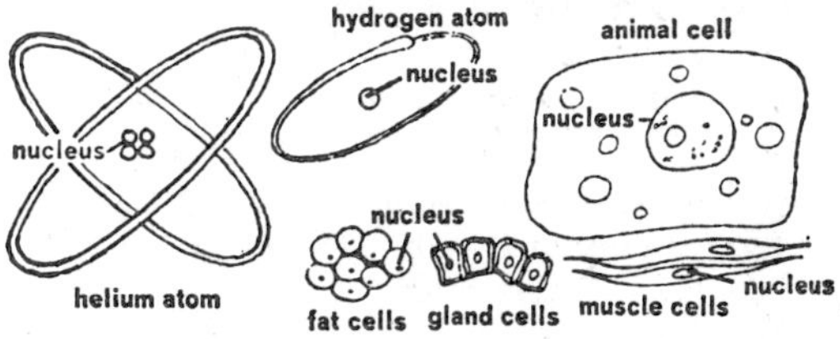

2. Anything other things gather around and depend on.–Tom, Jim, and Paul form the *nucleus* of our jazz band. Without them we couldn't play good jazz.
3. Any foundation or beginning.–The author's idea led him to write a novel. The idea was the *nucleus* of the novel.

nude (NOOD *or* NYOOD) *adj.* Naked.–We are *nude* when we get into the bathtub.

nudge (NUJ) *n. nudges.* A light push. – Bob gave Jack a little *nudge.*
–*v. nudges, nudged, nudging.* Lightly touch.–Bob *nudged* Jack to let him know that it was his turn to spell.

nug•get (NUG-ət) *n. nuggets.* A lump.–The miner found a *nugget* of gold.

nui•sance (NOO- *or* NYOO-sənss) *n. nuisances.* A person, thing, animal, etc, that bothers others or makes trouble. – When Mary would not sit still at the table, Father said she was being a *nuisance.*

numb (NUM) *v. numbs, numbed, numbing.* Make without feeling; stop feeling in.–The cold *numbed* the boy's fingers so that he could not write.
–*adj.* Without feeling.–Mary sat on her foot so long that it got *numb.*

num•ber (NUM-ber) *n. numbers.* 1. How many.–The farmer counted his sheep to find out their *number.*
2. Numeral; unit.–1, 2, 3, 4, 5, 6, 7, 8, 9, 0 and any combination of these are *numbers.*
3. Quite a few; a large quantity.–A *number* of children were playing in the yard.–The bees swarmed in great *numbers.* There were many of them.
4. An issue of a publication.–The last *number* of the Boy Scout magazine tells how to care for the flag.
–*v. numbers, numbered, numbering.* 1. Count; give a number to.–The children *numbered* their spelling words.
2. Amount to.–The stripes in the flag *number* thirteen.

nu•mer•al (NOO- *or* NYOO-mer-əl) *n. numerals.* A word or figure that stands for a number. Two, 7, 85, and III are *numerals.*

nu•mer•a•tor (NOO- *or* NYOO-mə-ray-ter) *n. numerators.* The number (or part) of a fraction that appears above the line. In the fraction 4/9, 4 is the *numerator.*

nu•mer•ous (NOO- *or* NYOO-mer-əss) *adj.* Large in number.–We received Christmas cards too *numerous* to count.

nun (NUN) *n. nuns.* A woman who belongs to a religious organization of women who give their entire lives to religious work.

nurse (NERSS) *n. nurses.* 1. A trained person who works in a hospital or home taking care of the sick, of babies, or of old people. –Ellen wants to be a *nurse.*

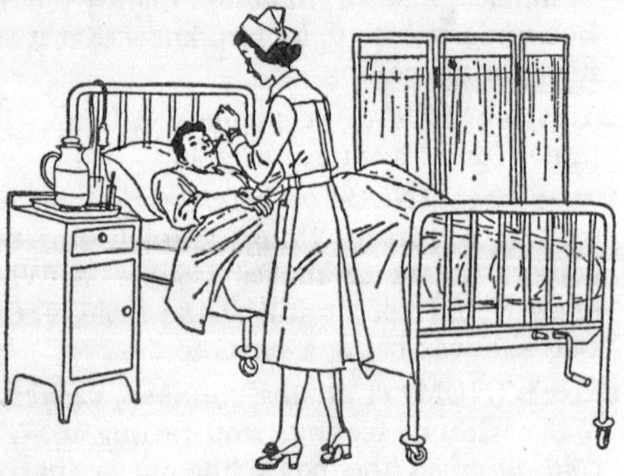

2. A *nurse*maid; a woman who takes care of children and babies for someone else.–Our neighbor has a *nurse* to care for the children when she is away.
–*v. nurses, nursed, nursing.* Take care of.–Bob *nursed* the sick puppy back to health.

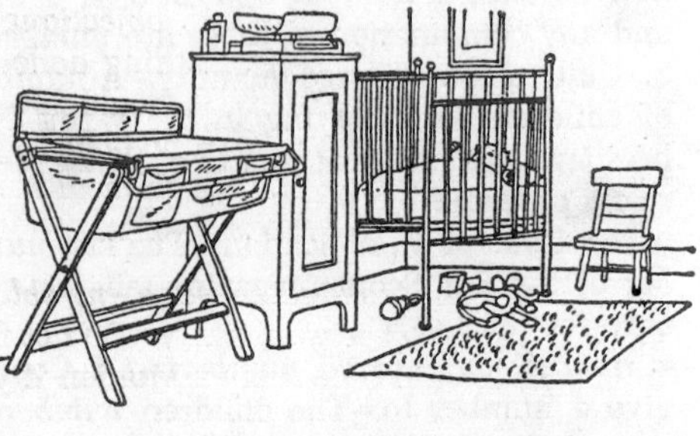

nurs•er•y (NERSS-ə-ree) *n. nurseries.* 1. A room for small children.–The children are in the *nursery* playing with their toys.
2. A kindergarten or other place where many small children are cared for.–Mothers who work often leave their children at a *nursery* during the day.
3. A place where trees and plants are raised and sold for replanting.–Father bought our shrubs at a *nursery.*

nut (NUT) *n. nuts.* 1. The fruit of certain trees. *Nuts* are covered with hard shells to protect the kernels that are inside.
2. A piece of metal that has a threaded hole through it which fits on a bolt.

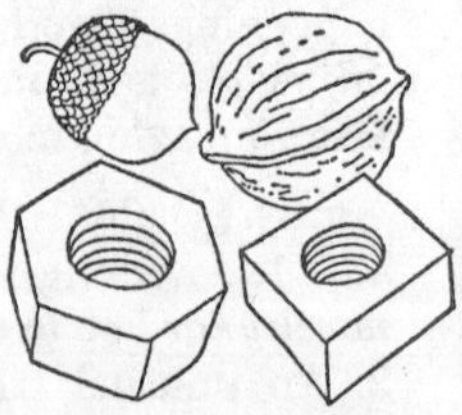

nut•hatch (NUT-hach) *n. nuthatches.* A small bird which eats nuts and insects.

nut•meg (NUT-meg) *n. nutmegs.* The seed of a tree which grows in the East and West Indies and in South America. *Nutmeg* is ground and used as a flavoring.

nu•tri•tion (noo- *or* nyoo-TRISH-ən) *n.; nutritious, adj.* 1. Food or nourishment.–Proper *nutrition* is important for good health.
2. The act or process of absorbing food.–We are going to study plant *nutrition* and learn what plants use for food and how they use it.

nut•shell (NUT-shel) *n. nutshells.* 1. The hard shell or covering of a nut.–Some *nutshells* are easier to crack than others.
2. A brief outline.–That's the story in a *nutshell.*

ny•lon (NY-lahn) *n.* A very strong and long-lasting material. *Nylon* is used to make such things as clothes, cord, parachutes, stockings, and toothbrush bristles.

nymph (NIMF) *n. nymphs.* A beautiful goddess who was supposed, in olden times, to live in forests, mountains, or rivers. *Nymphs* were the goddesses of nature.

O o

O, o (OH) *n. O's, o's.* The fifteenth letter of the alphabet.

oak (OHK) *n. oaks.* A kind of tree that has very hard wood and large, wide leaves. The

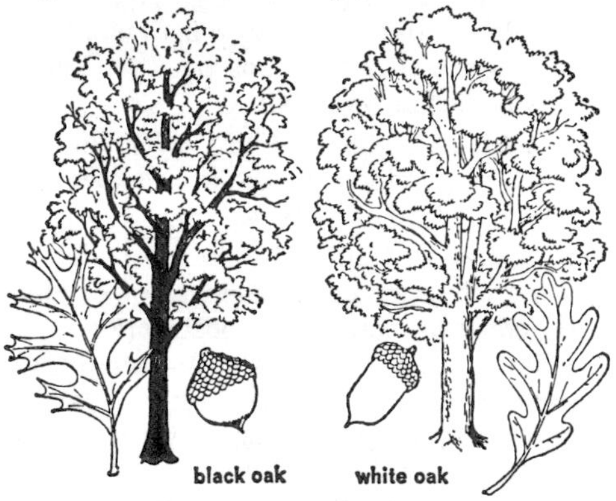

seeds of the *oak* are called acorns. The wood is used for furniture, buildings, and many other things.

oar (OR) *n. oars.* A long wooden pole that is flat like a paddle at the end that goes in the water. We row a boat with a pair of *oars.*

o•a•sis (oh-AY-səss) *n. oases.* A place in the desert where there is water, and where plants

grow.—Travelers in the desert often stop at an *oasis.*

oat (OHT) *n. oats.* A kind of grass that produces seed, or grain, which is used for food. *Oat*meal is made from *oats.*

oath (OHTH) *n. oaths.* 1. A promise made with God as the witness, to tell the truth.
2. *Oath* can mean a swear word or curse.

oat•meal (OHT-meel) *n.* Ground oats, made into a meal. Cooked *oatmeal* is good to eat for breakfast.

o•be•di•ence (oh-BEE-dee-ənss) *n.* Doing the things one is told to do.—Bob is teaching his dog *obedience;* he is teaching the dog to come when he is called.

o•be•di•ent (oh-BEE-dee-ənt) *adj.; obediently, adv.* Doing what one is told.—Jack's dog is *obedient;* he does what Jack tells him to do.

ob•e•lisk (AHB-ə-lisk) *n. obelisks.* A four-sided pillar or shaft, tapering towards the top, and ending in a pyramid.—*Obelisks* often stood in pairs before the temples of ancient Egypt.

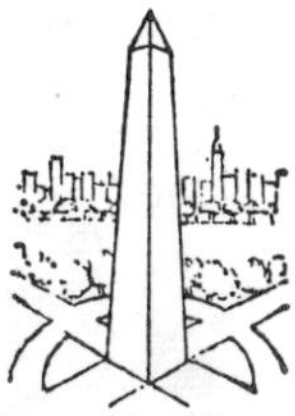

o•bey (oh-BAY) *v. obeys, obeyed, obeying.* Do what one is told; mind. — Always *obey* your mother. Do the things she tells you to do.

o•bit•u•ar•y (oh-BICH-oo-air-ee) *n. obituaries.* An announcement or notice of a person's death, often accompanied by a brief account of the person's life. — Newspapers print *obituaries.*

ob•ject (AHB-jəkt) *n. objects.* 1. A thing that one can see or feel. Clocks, books, pins, and anything else you can touch are *objects.*
2. Purpose or aim.—The *object* of this book is to tell you what words mean and show you how to use them.
—(əb-JEKT) *v. objects, objected, objecting.* Not approve; not want a thing done.—Mother *objects* to our going swimming alone.

ob•jec•tion (əb-JEK-shən) *n. objections.* A reason for not wanting something done, or for not liking something.—I should like to look at your book, if you have no *objection.*—Mary's *objection* to taking cough medicine is that she does not like the taste of it.

ob•li•ga•tion (ahb-lə-GAY-shən) *n. obligations.* 1. A duty; a responsibility.—Do not feel any *obligation* to accept my invitation if you do not wish to do so.
2. A debt.—Mother felt under *obligation* to the neighbors for minding the baby. She wanted to do something for them in return.

o•blige (ə-BLYJ) *v. obliges, obliged, obliging.* 1. Do a favor (for).—"Will you lend me a pencil?" "I should be glad to *oblige* you if I had an extra one."
2. Force or compel.—Because of the snowstorm, we were *obliged* to stay at home.

ob•lique (ə-BLEEK) *adj.; obliquely, adv.* Slanting; sloping; inclined.—The cottage roof was *oblique*. It was a slanting roof.

ob•long (AHB-lawng) *n. oblongs.* A figure that is longer than it is wide. — Our living room is an *oblong*.

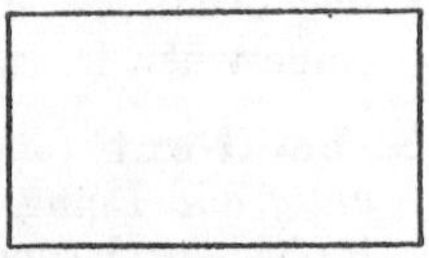

—*adj.* Being longer than wide.—Most books are *oblong*.—A football is *oblong*.

o•boe (OH-boh) *n. oboes.* A musical instrument that is played by blowing into it through two reeds that are held between the lips.

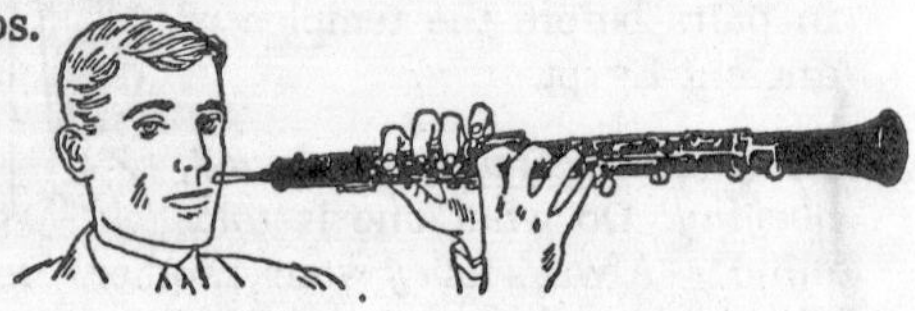

ob•scure (əb-SKYUHR) *v. obscures, obscured, obscuring.* Make unclear, unnoticeable, dim, or indistinct; hide; darken.—The trees *obscure* our house. It is hard to see our house from the road because of all the trees in front of it.—Heavy smoke *obscured* the sky.

ob•ser•va•tion (ahb-zer-VAY-shən) *n. observations.* 1. Act of observing.—The doctor kept his patient under close *observation*.—Our *observation* of Halloween was fun.
2. That which is observed. — The teacher's *observation* was that Jack had finished the test quickly.
3. The fact of being seen.—The spy was very careful to avoid *observation*.

ob•serv•a•to•ry (əb-ZER-və-tor-ee) *n. observatories.* 1. A special place or building that has telescopes and scientific instruments for observing heavenly bodies, such as the stars and planets. — There is a very famous *observatory* on Mount Palomar, in California.

2. Any building, place, or structure offering an unusual view.—The Empire State Building in New York City, the world's tallest building, has an *observatory* at the top.

ob•serve (əb-ZERV) *v. observes, observed, observing.* 1. See or notice.—The teacher *observed* that Jack had finished the test and told him to look it over.
2. Obey or follow.—Always be sure to *observe* the safety rules.
3. Celebrate.—We *observe* Christmas by having a tree and exchanging gifts.
4. Watch and study.—If you *observe* a drop of water under a microscope, you may see tiny bodies moving in it.

ob•so•lete (ahb-sə-LEET) *adj.* No longer used; old-fashioned.—Bows and arrows are *obsolete* weapons of war.

ob•sta•cle (AHB-stə-kəl) *n. obstacles.* Anything which stands in the way of or hinders progress or action; an obstruction. — The hikers found many *obstacles* on the steep path. There were fallen logs and boulders, and many rough places where it was hard to walk.

ob•sti•nate (AHB-stən-ət) *adj.; obstinately, adv.* Stubborn; refusing to give in to others, or to do what others wish.—The donkey is *obstinate*. He won't go when we want him to.

ob•struct (əb-STRUKT) *v. obstructs, obstructed, obstructing.* Block.—A wrecked car *obstructed* the traffic. It made it difficult for the traffic to pass.
—*obstruction, n. obstructions.*

ob•tain (əb-TAYN) *v. obtains, obtained, obtaining.* Get.—Bob went to the supply closet to *obtain* some colored chalk.

ob•vi•ous (AHB-vee-əss) *adj.; obviously, adv.* Easily seen, noticed, or understood; evident; plain.—It is *obvious* that it has to be cold before it will snow.—The answer to that question is *obvious*. It is easy to know what the answer is.

oc•ca•sion (ə-KAY-zhən) *n. occasions.* 1. A time.—The class play was the *occasion* of Mother's first visit to our school.
2. A reason.—It was the first time she ever had *occasion* to come.
3. A special happening.—A play is always a great *occasion* to Mary.

oc•ca•sion•al (ə-KAY-zhən-əl) *adj.; occasionally, adv.* Happening once in a while.—We make an *occasional* visit to the country.

Oc•ci•dent (AHK-sə-dənt) *n.; Occidental, adj.* The countries of Europe and the Western Hemisphere; the West.—England and France are parts of the *Occident*.

oc•cu•pant (AHK-yuh-pənt) *n. occupants.* A person or tenant who is in possession of, or occupies, a house, building, apartment, etc.—The new *occupants* will move into the office at the beginning of the month.

oc•cu•pa•tion (ahk-yuh-PAY-shən) *n. occupations.* 1. Business or work.—Father's *occupation* is selling shoes.
2. What one is doing.—Mother was sweeping the floor, but she paused in her *occupation* to listen to us.

oc•cu•py (AHK-yuh-py) *v. occupies, occupied, occupying.* 1. Take up (time or space).—Reading *occupies* most of my spare time.—This desk *occupies* too much space.
2. Live or be in.—A different family *occupies* the house next door now.
3. Take over; take possession of.—The medical convention *occupied* two floors of the big hotel.

oc•cur (ə-KER) *v. occurs, occurred, occurring.* 1. Take place or happen.—The monument marks the place where the battle *occurred.*
2. Come to one's mind.—It didn't *occur* to Mary that she could help Mother by dressing the baby. She didn't think of it.
3. Be found.—The word "God" *occurs* often in the Bible.
—occurrence, n. occurrences.

o•cean (OH-shən) *n. oceans.* 1. The sea, or large body of salt water, that covers the greater part of the earth.
2. Any of the five large parts, known as *oceans,* into which this sea is divided.—The Atlantic *Ocean* is east and the Pacific *Ocean* west of the United States.

o•ce•lot (AH-sə-lət) *n. ocelot* or *ocelots.* A black-spotted wildcat found in the southwestern United States and South America. The *ocelot* grows to a length of about three to three and a half feet, is a good climber, and usually lives in forests.

o'clock (ə-KLAHK). By the clock. — School starts at nine *o'clock.*

OCCUPATIONS

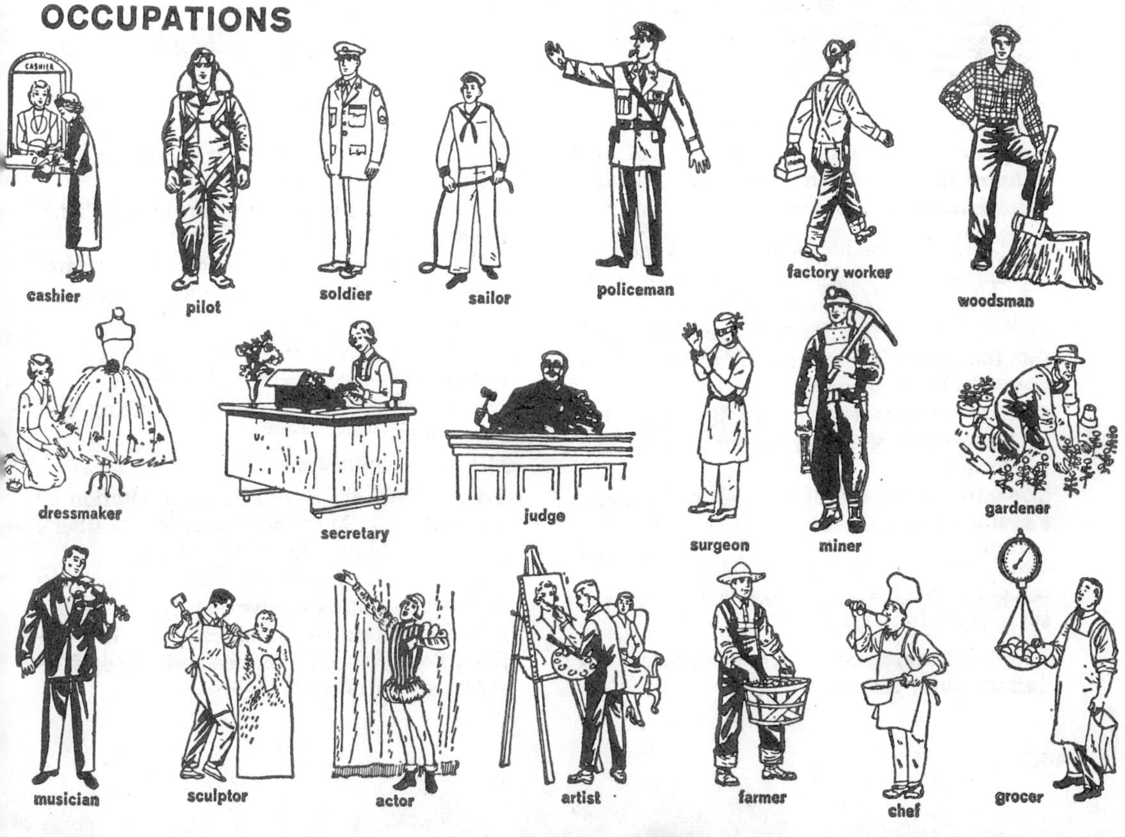

oc•ta•gon (AHK-tə-gahn *or* -gən) *n. octagons; octagonal, adj.* A plane, or flat, figure having eight sides and eight angles.—Automobile traffic "stop" signs are made in the shape of an *octagon.*

oc•tave (AHK-tiv) *n. octaves.* In music, the space between one note and the eighth note up or down from it.—From C to C or from

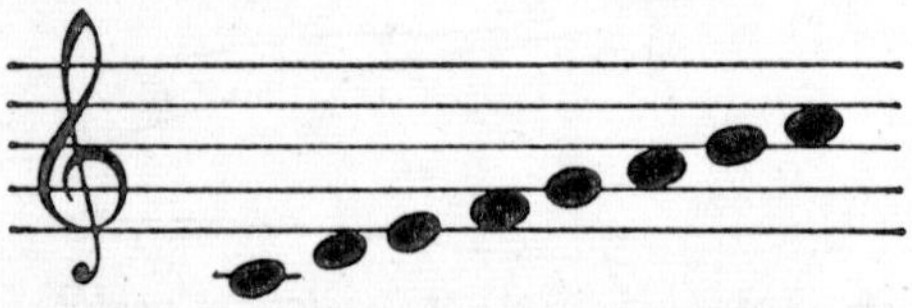

G to G is an *octave.*—Mary's fingers are long enough now to reach an *octave* on the piano.

Oc•to•ber (ahk-TOH-ber) *n. Octobers.* The tenth month of the year. *October* has thirty-one days. Halloween comes on *October* 31.

oc•to•pus (AHK-tə-pəss) *n. octopuses* or *octopi.* A sea animal that has eight arms. Along these arms are suckers which make it possible for the *octopus* to take hold of things.

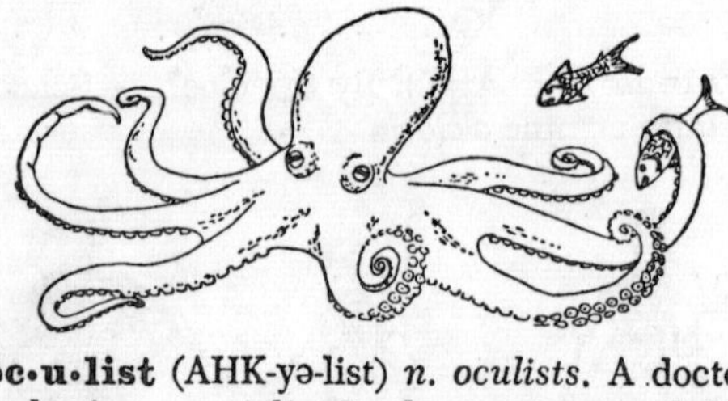

oc•u•list (AHK-yə-list) *n. oculists.* A doctor who is a specialist in the treatment of diseases of the eye.—Mother went to an *oculist* to have her eyes examined.

odd (AHD) *adj. odder, oddest; oddly, adv.* 1. Not able to be divided evenly by the number 2. —Four is an even number. It can be divided by two with no fraction left over. Two goes into four twice. Three is an *odd* number. Two goes into three once, with one left over.

2. Extra; not matching.—All Bob can ever find are *odd* socks. They do not go with any of the others.

3. Strange or queer; unusual.—It would seem *odd* if men wore dresses.

ode (OHD) *n. odes.* A poem expressing lofty or noble thoughts or feelings. *Odes* are often sung or set to music.

o•dor (OH-der) *n. odors.* A smell or scent.—A daffodil has a pleasant *odor.*

o'er (OR). Over. *O'er* is often used in poetry.—

"*O'er* hills, *o'er* dells,
Sweet evening bells."

of (UV) *prep.* 1. About or dealing with.—This is the story *of* Snow White and the Seven Dwarfs.

2. From.—Pittsburgh is west *of* New York. —Mary and Jack made a game *of* their homework.

3. Made from.—The prince wore a coat *of* flame-colored satin.

4. Who has; that has.—Bob is a boy *of* great ability.—This is a place *of* great beauty.

5. About. — We were glad *of* the warm weather for Easter.

6. In; belonging to. — The children *of* the neighborhood are going on a picnic.

7. Among.—Some *of* us should help clean up after the party.

8. Concerning; about.—If you cannot speak well *of* other people, do not speak *of* them at all.

off (AWF) *adj., adv.,* and *prep.* 1. From.—Spot jumped *off* the bed when he saw Mother.

2. Away.—The pigeon flew *off* when Sally tried to pick him up.—My birthday is two days *off.*

3. Away from.—Grandmother lives *off* the main highway.—Mary often gets *off* the question in giving her answer.

4. From one's body.—Bob took *off* his gloves. He removed them.

5. Father cleaned *off* a shelf for his tools. He removed everything from it.

6. Free.—Father took the afternoon *off* to take us to the beach.

7. Not in place; not on as it should be.—The knob is *off* that door.

8. So that it is not working or running.—Turn the water *off.*

9. Not what it should be; not up to standard. —Our star pitcher had an *off* day, and pitched badly.

of•fend (ə-FEND) *v. offends, offended, offending.* Displease or hurt the feelings of.—Do not *offend* other people by using bad language.

—*offense, n. offenses.*

of•fer (AWF-er) *n. offers.* An invitation or suggestion. — Mr. Smith accepted Father's *offer* to drive downtown with him.

—*v. offers, offered, offering.* Volunteer or show that one is willing to give.—Mary *offered* her help in making the sandwiches. — Jack *offered* Bob fifty cents for the ball. He said he would give fifty cents for it.

of•fice (AWF-əss) *n. offices.* 1. A place in which a business or profession is carried on. –We went to the doctor's *office* to get Grandmother's health checked.–Mother went to the *office* of the gas company to pay her gas bill.–Father's *office* is downtown.

2. A position of public or social duty.–Mayor Johnson has held his *office* for three years.–Everyone was pleased when Mary was elected to the *office* of class secretary.

of•fi•cer (AWF-ə-ser) *n. officers.* 1. A man in the army, navy, or air force who directs or tells other men what to do.–A captain is an *officer.*
2. A policeman.–The *officer* stopped the traffic while the children crossed the street.
3. A person who holds an office, or has charge of a certain job, in a business, a club, or an organization of any kind.–Mary is one of the *officers* of her school class. She is the secretary.

of•fi•cial (ə-FISH-əl) *n. officials.* Anyone holding an office or a public position.–The Secretary of State is a high government *official.*
–*adj.; officially, adv.* By order; according to the rules; done by someone who has authority.–It is not *official* that there will be no school tomorrow; it is just talk.

of•ten (AWF-ən) *adv.* Frequently.–We *often* go to see Grandmother.

o•gre (OH-ger) *n. ogres.* 1. A storybook giant or monster who eats people. *Ogres* are found in many fairy tales and folk legends.
2. A cruel person is sometimes called an *ogre.*

oh (OH) *interj.* 1. An exclamation, or a word that expresses a sudden feeling, such as surprise or interest, or makes the words that follow it more emphatic.–*Oh!* It's you. I didn't hear you.–*Oh,* no! I wouldn't think of going alone.–*Oh,* how wonderful!
2. *Oh* used by itself may express understanding or a question.–"This is the way to work the problem," said Jack. *"Oh,"* said Mary.

O•hi•o (oh-HY-oh) *n.* A high-ranking industrial state in north central United States, known for its colleges, its manufacturing of iron, steel, petroleum products, and rubber tires, and its shipping and mixed farming. A river, the *Ohio,* forms the long, curving boundary of the state, and is one of the most important rivers in the country for transportation of freight. In the early days, settlers came down the river to *Ohio* on flatboats.

oil (OIL) *n. oils.* Grease or fat that comes from plants, animals, or minerals. Some *oils* burn, and are used instead of coal for fuel. Gasoline is made from *oil. Oil* is used to lubricate machines. Castor *oil* is medicine. Olive *oil* is a food. *Oil* floats on top of water.
–*v. oils, oiled, oiling.* 1. Rub oil on.–Mother *oiled* the furniture to make it shiny.
2. Put oil on or in.–Father *oiled* the hinge.

oil•cloth (OIL-klawth) *n. oilcloths.* A heavy cloth that has been treated with a shiny paint or oil.–Mother put *oilcloth* on the cupboard shelves instead of paper.

oil•y (OIL-ee) *adj. oilier, oiliest.* Greasy, or covered with oil.–Father's hands are *oily* from oiling the hinge.

oint•ment (OINT-mənt) *n. ointments.* A salve or a liquid made of oils and medicines. –The doctor gave Mother an *ointment* to put on Baby's mosquito bites.

O•kla•ho•ma (ohk-lə-HOH-mə) *n.* A leading oil state in south central United States. The manufacture of oil products, and cattle and cotton raising are its chief industries.

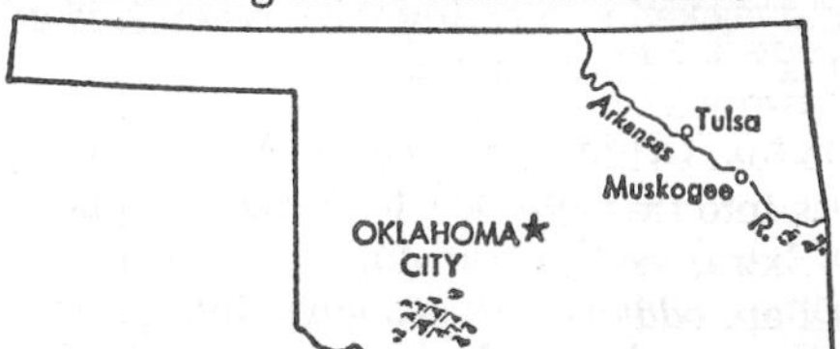

o•kra (OH-krə) *n.* A plant, or its pod, widely grown in tropical or warm climates. It is often used in soups and stews. – *Okra* is known as "gumbo" in the southern states.

old (OHLD) *adj. older, oldest.* 1. Not young. –Grandfather is *old.* He has lived a long time.
2. Not new.–*Old* shoes are more comfortable for walking.
3. Of age.–Mary is eleven years *old.*
4. Having come down to us from times long past.–It is an *old* custom for a wife to wear a wedding ring.
5. Former.–Our *old* house stood on a high hill. The house we live in now is in a valley.

old•en (OHLD-ən) *adj.* Long past.–In *olden* times, people believed that the earth was flat.

old-fash•ioned (ohld-FASH-ənd) *adj.* 1. Doing and thinking as people did long ago. – Grandmother wears *old-fashioned* dresses.
2. Out of date or out of style.–Grandmother's velvet hat is *old-fashioned.* Women don't wear hats like that any more.

o•le•o•mar•ga•rine (oh-lee-oh-MAHR-jə-rin) *n.* A substance made from vegetable oils and animal fats. It is used as a substitute for butter.

ol•ive (AHL-iv) *n. olives.* The fruit of a tree of the same name. Ripe *olives* are a dark purplish-brown color. Unripe *olives* are a soft green color. Both kinds are good to eat.
–*adj.* Greenish-yellow. –I have an *olive* skirt.

ol•ive oil (AHL-iv oil) *olive oils.* An oil made from olives. It is used in salad dressings and in cooking.

om•e•let or **om•e•lette** (AHM-lət *or* AHM-ə-lət) *n. omelets* or *omelettes.* A mixture of eggs, milk or water, and seasoning, beaten and cooked in a frying pan. When it is done, it is folded over and served.

o•men (OH-mən) *n. omens.* A sign, event, or occurrence supposed to foretell happenings of the future; a warning signal of things to come. *Omens* are usually interpreted as either good or bad.–Some people think that finding a four-leaf clover is an *omen* of good luck.

om•i•nous (AHM-ə-nəss) *adj.; ominously, adv.* Threatening; seeming to foretell evil; having the quality of a bad omen.–The sky looks *ominous.* It looks as though it may rain and spoil our hike.

o•mit (oh-MIT) *v. omits, omitted, omitting.* Leave out; skip over.–Our teacher told us to *omit* the first page of problems and start on the second page.

on (AHN) *adj., adv.,* and *prep.* 1. *On* is usually used with other words to tell where, when, how, and the like.–Where is the clock? The clock is *on* the shelf.–Grandfather is coming *on* Sunday.–When you go to school, be *on* time.–Grandmother went to sleep with her glasses *on.*–The President spoke to us *on* the radio.–Keep *on* trying, and you will succeed at last.–The Scout troop marched *on* in spite of the snow.
2. So that it works or runs.–Turn *on* the light so we can see.–Is the motor *on* or off? It is running?

once (WUNSS) *n., adv.,* and *conj.* 1. One time.–Mary has been in a boat only *once.*– May I go this *once?*
2. At one time in the past.–The poor man *once* had much money.
3. After.–It is easy to multiply, *once* you learn your multiplication tables.
–*At once* means right away.–Mother told us to come home *at once* when school was over.
–*At once* also means at the same time.–All the horses in the race started *at once.*

one (WUN) *n., adj.,* and *pron.* 1. The number written as the figure 1.
2. A single.–I have *one* dollar.–Only *one* boy was late.–There are seven days in the week. Monday is *one* day.
3. A person.–The *one* sitting in the front seat is Mary.
4. Each person.–*One* must eat to keep alive.
5. The same.–The boats were all sailing in *one* direction.
6. United.–We are *one* in purpose.
7. Some.–Grandmother will be here *one* day this week.
8. *One* is sometimes used instead of the name of a thing that has been mentioned before.–Mother looked at many hats, and then bought the *one* she had seen first.

one•self (wun-SELF) *pron.* One's own personal being. – Always to think of *oneself* before others is selfish.

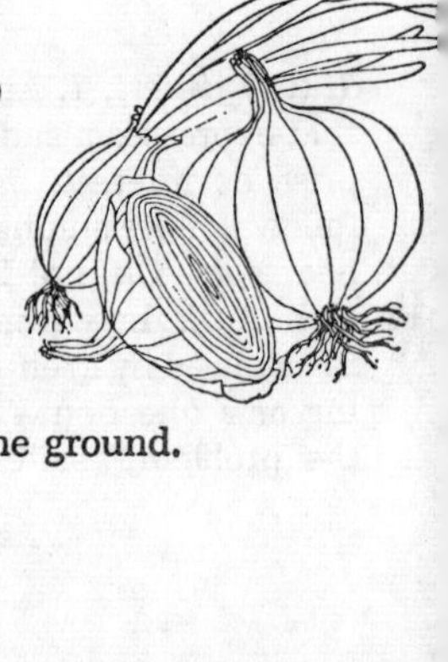

on•ion (UN-yən) *n. onions.* A bulblike vegetable that grows in the ground.

on•ly (OHN-lee) *adj., adv.,* and *conj.* 1. One; single.–Bob lost his *only* sweater.
2. Just; no more than.–It is *only* a little way to the store.–The car holds *only* three people.
3. Merely.–It is *only* I.
4. Except that.–I would go, *only* I have to study.

on•to (AHN-too) *prep.* Upon; on top of.–The farmer and his son pitched the hay *onto* the wagon.

on•ward (AHN-werd) *adj.* and *adv.* Forward. –The Boy Scouts marched *onward.*

ooze (OOZ) *v. oozes, oozed, oozing.* Leak slowly.–The blackberry juice *oozed* out of the crust of the pie.

o•pal (OH-pəl) *n. opals.* A precious stone with a milky background. It is marked with colors that change in the light. Some rare opals have a black background.

o•paque (oh-PAYK) *adj.* 1. Not permitting light to pass through; not transparent.–You can see what is outside a window because glass is transparent. You cannot see what is outside a closed door because wood is *opaque.*
2. Not bright; not reflecting light; dull; dark. –The furniture had an *opaque* finish.

o•pen (OH-pən) *v. opens, opened, opening.* 1. Change from a shut position.–Father *opened* the door so our guests could come in.
2. Take apart so as to expose or show the contents.–Mother *opened* the package.
3. Spread out.–It must be raining out, for people are *opening* their umbrellas. – That flower will *open* soon.
4. Begin business. – A new grocery store *opened* at the corner.–This store *opens* at nine every morning.
–*adj.* 1. Not shut or closed.–Mother left the door *open* so we could get in.
2. Not covered.–A lifeboat is an *open* boat.
3. Not set; able to be changed.–A person with an *open* mind will listen to new ideas.

o•pen•er (OH-pən-er) *n. openers.* Something used to open cans, jars, and bottles.–Mary opened the ginger ale with a bottle *opener.*

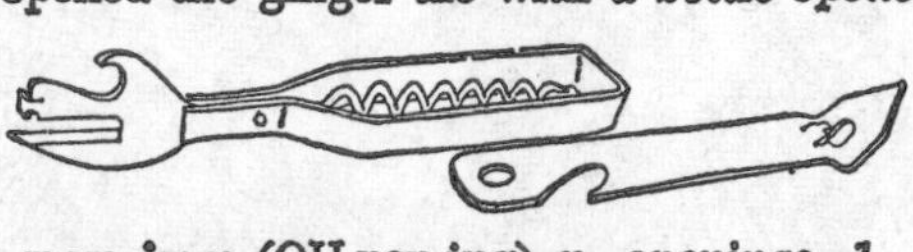

o•pen•ing (OH-pən-ing) *n. openings.* 1. A hole or open space.–We saw the sun through an *opening* in the clouds.
2. A position or job to be filled.–The storekeeper said there was an *opening* for a delivery boy.
3. A chance.–Mary waited for an *opening* to ask if she might go to the movies.
4. Beginning.–At the *opening* of the story, the king is in his castle.
5. First showing.–Father and Mother are going to the *opening* of the new play.

op•er•a (AHP-er-ə) *n. operas.* A play in which the actors sing instead of speak, and are accompanied by an orchestra.

op•er•ate (AHP-er-ayt) *v. operates, operated, operating.* 1. Work or make run.–Can you *operate* a sewing machine?
2. Keep working or running.–Many factories *operate* night and day.
3. Cut into the body in order to remove or treat an injured or diseased part.–The doctor *operated* on Mary; he took out her appendix.

op•er•a•tion (ahp-er-AY-shən) *n. operations.* 1. The act of cutting into the body to remove or treat an injured or diseased part.–The doctor did an *operation* on the man's foot.
2. An act or process.–Mary was engaged in the *operation* of putting on her galoshes.
3. A movement.–The paper told about the military *operations* of our troops.
4. The way a thing works or acts.–Father likes the *operation* of his new car.

op•er•a•tor (AHP-er-ay-ter) *n. operators.* A person who operates or runs a machine.–A telephone *operator* works a switchboard.

op•er•et•ta (ahp-ə-RET-ə) *n. operettas.* A short opera, especially with gay, light music and a simple, amusing plot.

o•pin•ion (ə-PIN-yən) *n. opinions.* 1. A belief or way of thinking.–It is my *opinion* that you could work the problem this way.
2. A judgment or estimation. – Mary likes people to have a good *opinion* of her. She likes them to think well of her.

o•pi•um (OH-pee-əm) *n.* A powerful drug that relieves pain and induces sleep. *Opium* is a narcotic. It is obtained from the dried juice of certain poppy plants.

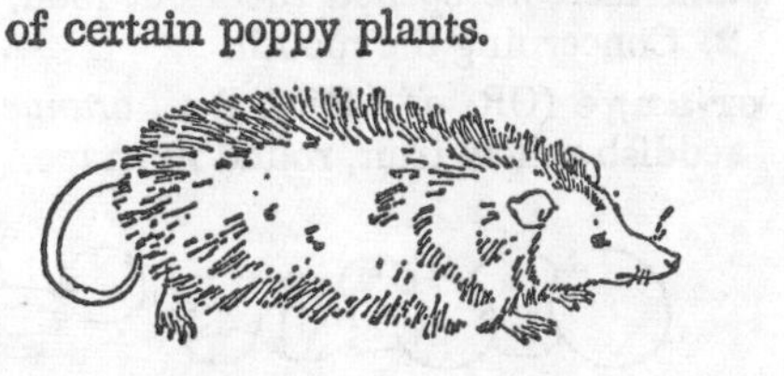

o•pos•sum (ə-PAHSS-əm) *n. oppossum* or *oppossums.* A small American animal that has grayish fur and a long skinny tail. *Opossums* pretend to be dead when they are threatened.

op·po·nent (ə-POH-nənt) *n. opponents.* A person on the other side of a contest, struggle, argument, or game; a rival.–The champion fighter defeated his *opponent* in the boxing match.

op·por·tu·ni·ty (ahp-er-TOO-nə-tee *or* ahp-er-TYOO-nə-tee) *n. opportunities.* 1. A suitable time or chance.–There was no *opportunity* to ask the teacher about the party, because she was too busy.–We have an *opportunity* to ride to school every day.
2. The chance to better oneself.–Many people who migrated to this country thought of it as the land of *opportunity.*

op·pose (ə-POHZ) *v. opposes, opposed, opposing.* Be against; disagree with.–Mary *opposed* Bob's suggestion. She didn't think it was a good idea.
–*opposition, n. oppositions.*

op·po·site (AHP-ə-zət) *n. opposites.* Something that is as different as possible from, or just the reverse of, something else.–Black and white are *opposites.*
–*adj., adv.,* and *prep.* 1. As different as possible. – Up is *opposite* from down. – Bob and Jack were on *opposite* sides of the debate.
2. Facing.–The teacher told the partners to stand *opposite* each other.–I live *opposite* the school.

op·ti·mist (AHP-tə-mist) *n. optimists; optimistic, adj.; optimistically, adv.* A person who always looks on the bright side of things, and believes that everything will end well. –Mother told John he was an *optimist* to think the rain would soon stop.

or (OR) *conj.* 1. A word used to connect words or groups of words that offer a choice.–Will you have milk *or* hot chocolate?
2. *Or* is used to introduce words that explain something that was said before.–This is a mug, *or* cup, to drink from.

o·ral (OR-əl) *adj.; orally, adv.* 1. Spoken.–We had an *oral* spelling test. We spoke the words, and then we spelled them out loud.
2. Concerning the mouth.

or·ange (OR- *or* AHR-inj) *n. oranges.* 1. A reddish-yellow fruit, round in shape.

2. A bright color that can be made by mixing red and yellow; the color of an orange.
–*adj.* Of the color orange.–Janet wore an *orange* ribbon in her hair.

o·rang·u·tan or **o·rang·ou·tang** (ə-RANG-uh-tan) *n. orangutans* or *orangoutangs.* A reddish, manlike ape found in Sumatra and Borneo. The *orangutan* has small ears and very long arms. *Orangutans* live in trees.

o·ra·tion (or-AY-shən) *n. orations.* A dignified, carefully prepared speech, especially one given on a special or notable occasion: –The minister gave an *oration* at the dedication ceremony for the new church.

or·a·tor (OR-ə-ter) *n. orators.* A person who gives an oration; a public speaker, especially one with much skill.–People in the audience listened intently when the *orator* spoke.

orb (ORB) *n. orbs.* A globe, sphere, or ball, especially one of the round heavenly bodies such as the moon or sun.–The eye or eyeball is sometimes called an *orb.*

or·bit (OR-bət) *n. orbits.* 1. The path followed by a heavenly body or space vehicle as it spins around another heavenly body.– The moon travels in its *orbit* around the earth once in about 29½ days.

2. The area under control or influence.–Before 1776, the thirteen American colonies were within the *orbit* of the British empire.
–*v. orbits, orbited, orbiting.* Move in an orbit. –The first American satellite, Explorer I, began to *orbit* on January 31, 1958.

or·chard (OR-cherd) *n. orchards.* 1. A piece of ground where fruit trees are grown.–We like to play in Grandfather's *orchard.*

2. The fruit trees in an orchard. – Grandfather has a large peach *orchard.* He has many peach trees growing together.

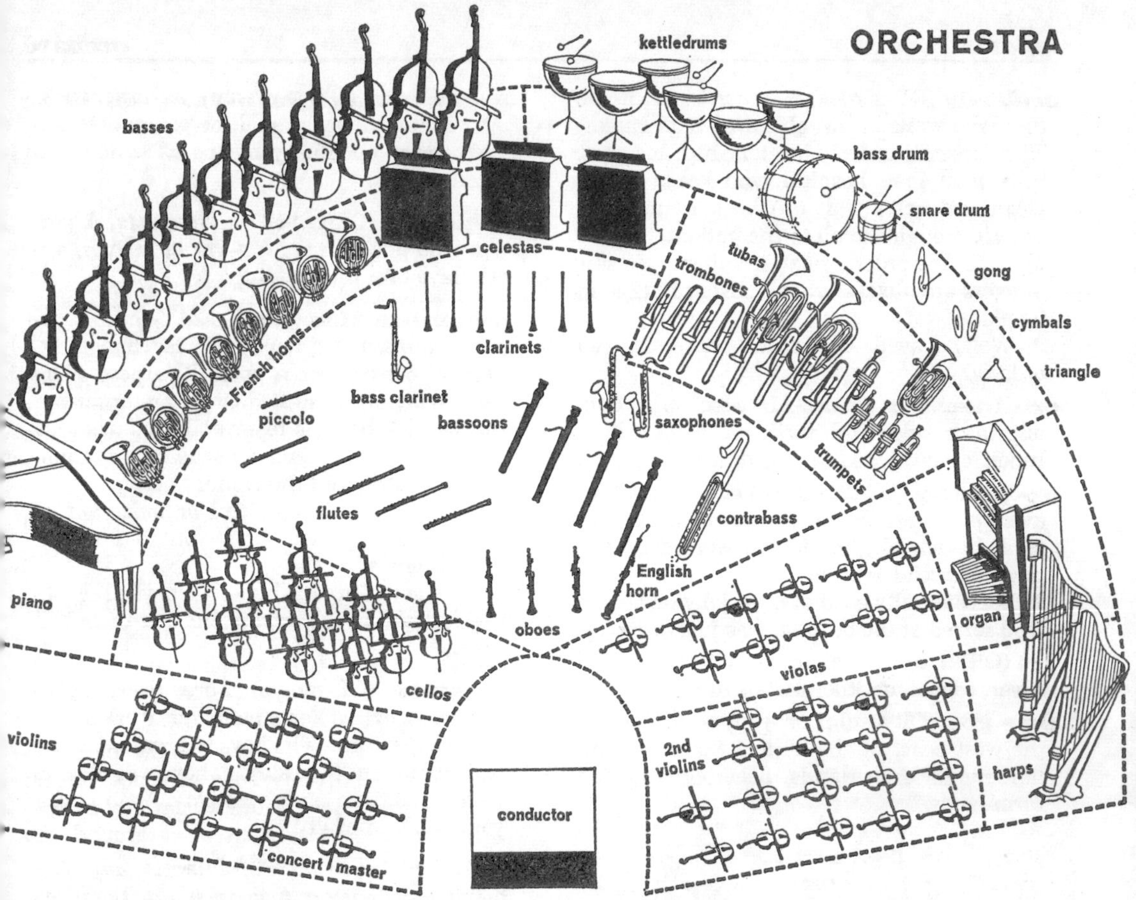

or·ches·tra (OR-kəss-trə) *n. orchestras.* 1. A group of people who play musical instruments together.—Mary plays the violin in the school *orchestra.*
2. The seats on the main floor of a theater.—We sat in the *orchestra* to see the play.

or·chid (OR-kəd) *n. orchids.* A large flower, with one petal often longer than the other two.

—*adj.* Lavender or light purple.—Grandmother has an *orchid* dress.

or·deal (OR-deel *or* or-DEEL) *n. ordeals.* 1. An ancient method of determining guilt or innocence by having the accused person pass some very difficult, painful, or dangerous test. Failure was a sign of guilt; success, a sign of innocence.
2. Any painful experience or difficult test.—The long, hot trip was an *ordeal.*

or·der (OR-der) *n. orders.* 1. The way in which things happen, or the way they follow one another.—The days of the week come in this *order:* Sunday, Monday, Tuesday, Wednesday, Thursday, Friday, Saturday.
2. Condition.—Jack found the bicycle in good *order,* so he bought it.
3. Social peace; lawful conduct.—Policemen keep *order.* They see that traffic rules and other laws are obeyed.
4. Attention.—The teacher called the class to *order.* She asked us to stop talking and get ready for our lesson.
5. An instruction or command.—The police received *orders* to arrest the suspects in the bank robbery.
6. A request for goods one wants.—Father sent in an *order* for sixty pairs of shoes for his store.
—*v. orders, ordered, ordering.* 1. Give an order for goods.—Mother *ordered* the meat for dinner. She told the butcher to send it.
2. Direct; command.—The biggest boy in the class often *orders* the smaller boys around. He tells them what to do.
—*In order* means in a neat arrangement.—After the party, the children put the room *in order.* They put things back in their right places.
—*In order to* means for the purpose of.—People must eat *in order to* live.

or·der·ly (OR-der-lee) *n. orderlies.* 1. A soldier who waits on an officer of high rank.–The general's *orderly* brought him his coat.
2. A man in a hospital who keeps things clean and helps wait on the patients.–The *orderly* brought lunch to the patient.
–*adj.* 1. In order; neat.–Mother's dresser drawers are always *orderly.* Everything is in its place.
2. Well-behaved.–The crowd was quiet and *orderly.*

or·di·nar·i·ly (or-din-AIR-ə-lee) *adv.* Usually; as a rule.–*Ordinarily* we have a light lunch at noon and a hot dinner at night.

or·di·nar·y (OR-din-air-ee) *adj.* 1. Usual or average.–In *ordinary* cases no one is excused from homework; but if you were sick, you have a special reason.
2. Not especially good or especially bad.–The food served at the hospital was just *ordinary.*

ore (OR) *n. ores.* Rock or earth that has iron, silver, copper, or other metals in it.

Or·e·gon (OR-ə-gahn *or* -gən) *n.* A state on the west coast of the United States, important for its timberlands, fisheries, and rich farm lands.

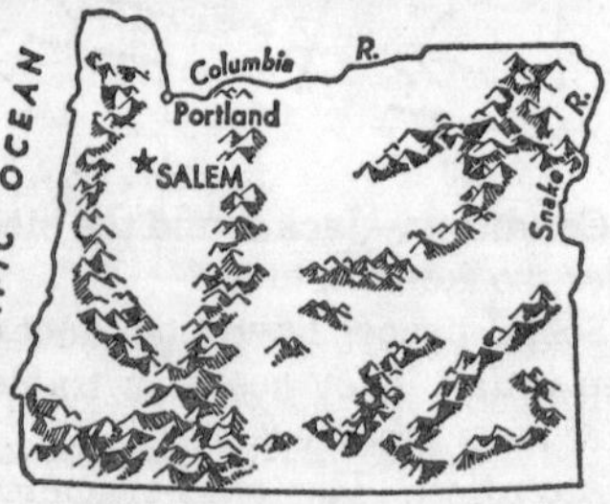

or·gan (OR-gən) *n. organs.* 1. A musical instrument played from a set of keyboards called a console. Many churches have pipe *organs,* in which the tones are made by air blowing into big pipes.

2. A part of the body which does certain work.–The heart is an *organ.* It pumps blood to all parts of the body.–The stomach, lungs, and liver are *organs.*

or·gan·ism (OR-gə-niz-əm) *n. organisms.* Any living plant, animal, or person. *Organisms* carry on life by means of various related organs.

or·gan·ist (OR-gən-ist) *n. organists.* A person who plays an organ.–The church *organist* played for the wedding.

or·gan·i·za·tion (or-gən-ə-ZAY-shən) *n. organizations.* 1. A group of people who join together to work for a special purpose.–The Boy Scouts and the Red Cross are *organizations.*–Dick belongs to several *organizations* at school. He is a member of the History Club, the orchestra, and the Honor Society.
2. Planning. – Thoughtful *organization* of your homework will help you to finish it more quickly.
3. The act of organizing.–The boys are looking forward to the *organization* of their ball team.

or·gan·ize (OR-gən-yz) *v. organizes, organized, organizing.* Form plans for; work out in advance; set up.–The boys will *organize* the ball team on Saturday. They will decide which positions each will play. – *Organize* your work carefully.

O·ri·ent (OR-ee-ənt) *n.; Oriental, adj.* The countries of eastern Asia, including the near-by islands; the East.–China and Japan are parts of the *Orient.*

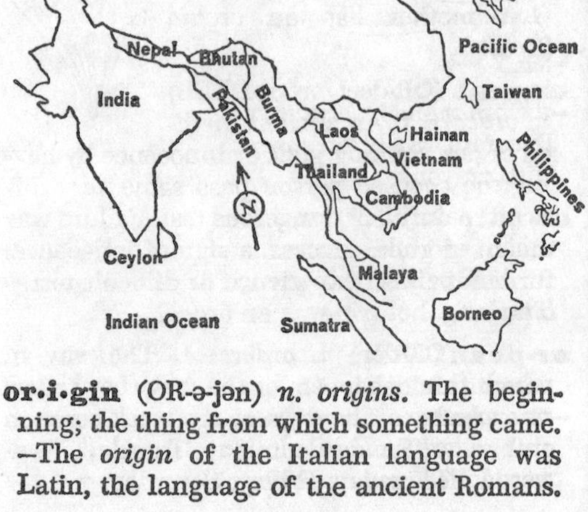

or·i·gin (OR-ə-jən) *n. origins.* The beginning; the thing from which something came. –The *origin* of the Italian language was Latin, the language of the ancient Romans.

o·rig·i·nal (ə-RIJ-ə-nəl) *n. originals.* The first one, or the one from which the others were copied.–This copy of my story is the *original,* so it may have some spelling mistakes in it.–The paintings in the museum are *originals.* They are not copies.
–*adj.; originally, adv.* 1. New.–Sally has many *original* ideas. She thinks of things that no one else has ever thought of.
2. First.–My *original* idea wasn't very good. Now I have a better idea.

o·rig·i·nate (ə-RIJ-ə-nayt) *v. originates, originated, originating.* 1. Bring into existence; start something new; invent.–The boys planned to *originate* a club. They planned to start a new club of their own.
2. Begin; come about; arise.–Does anyone know how the wheel *originated?*

o·ri·ole (OR-ee-ohl) *n. orioles.* An orange-and-black songbird. *Orioles* build their basketlike nests so that they hang down from the tree branch and swing in the wind.

or·na·ment (OR-nə-mənt) *n. ornaments.* Something that decorates other things – Beads, fancy trimmings, earrings, and bracelets are *ornaments* which make one look prettier. – Candlesticks, vases, and the like are *ornaments* that make the house look prettier.

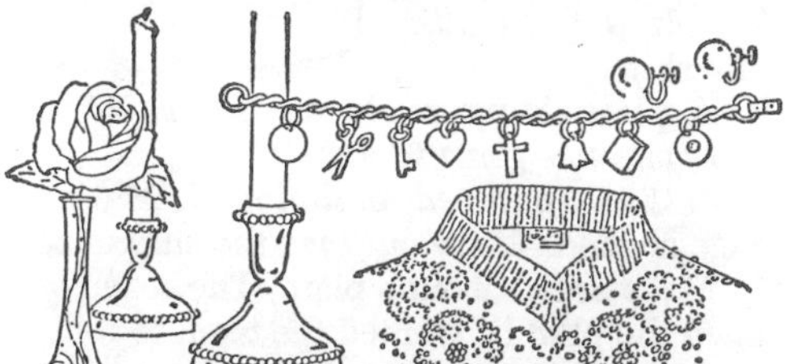

–*v. ornaments, ornamented, ornamenting.* Decorate.–Sally *ornamented* her homework with crayons.

or·nate (or-NAYT) *adj.; ornately, adv.* Very much adorned; elaborately decorated.–The furnishings of the old mansion were very *ornate.*

or·phan (OR-fən) *n. orphans.* A child whose parents are dead.
–*v. orphans, orphaned, orphaning.* Leave an orphan. – The accident in which his parents were killed *orphaned* the child.

or·phan·age (OR-fən-ij) *n. orphanages.* A home for orphans.–Some children whose parents are dead and who have no relatives to take care of them live in *orphanages.*

os·trich (AWSS-trich) *n. ostriches.* A very large bird with beautiful plumes, or large

fluffy feathers. *Ostriches* do not fly, but they run fast.

oth·er (UTH-er) *adj.* 1. A different one; another.–I will read the book some *other* time; I am too busy now. I must read this *other* book first.
2. More; besides this.–We have no *other* work, so we can go out and play.
3. Second.–Every *other* child standing in line was a boy. The children stood in this order: Mary, Bob, Ruth, Jack, Ellen, Harry.
–*pron. others.* 1. The one remaining.–Tom put on one boot and then the *other.*
2. A different one.–It was not this boy who threw the ball, but the *other.* It was not Jack; it was Bill.

ot·ter (AHT-er) *n. otters.* An animal that lives in and around the water. It feeds on fish. *Otters* are playful, and sometimes they build mud slides to coast down.

ouch (OWCH) *interj.* A word used to show that a person is in pain or that something hurts him.–*Ouch!* I burned my finger on the hot stove.

ought (AWT) *v.* 1. Should.–You *ought* to get up earlier so you can get to school on time. It is your duty to do so.
2. Be likely.–It *ought* to be warmer inside. It probably is warmer inside.

ounce (OWNSS) *n. ounces.* 1. A unit of dry measure.–Milk is measured by the pint or quart. Meat, sugar, butter, and many other things are measured by the pound and the *ounce*. There are sixteen *ounces* in a pound. 2. A tiny bit.–Bob hasn't an *ounce* of selfishness in him.

our (OWR) *adj.* Belonging to us, as *our* dog, *our* house, *our* toys. They all belong to us. We own them.

ours (OWRZ) *pron.* Something belonging to us.–The dog is *ours*. He belongs to us. We own him.

our•selves (owr-SELVZ) *pron.* We, or us; not somebody else. – When we *ourselves* heard the noise in the cellar, we understood why Tim was frightened.–The teacher told us to read the next question to *ourselves* and then tell her the answer.

out (OWT) *adj.* and *adv.* 1. Outside.–Father let the dog *out*.

2. Not at home.–We are sorry that we were *out* when you came to see us.

3. Not burning or not lighted.–The light in the hall is *out*.

4. No longer actively in the game.–After three strikes, the batter is *out*.

5. No longer a secret.–The news of the wedding is *out*. It is known.

6. Aloud.–The parrot cried *out*.

7. Till finished.–Mother let the baby sleep herself *out*. She let the baby sleep until she woke up by herself.

8. To others.–The farmer lets *out* part of his farm. He rents it.

9. From the others.–The teacher told us to pick *out* the books we wanted to read.

10. No longer having any.–We are *out* of milk. We don't have any more.

out•break (OWT-brayk) *n. outbreaks.* Beginning or start of something violent, as war or a riot.–Uncle Tom was in London at the *outbreak* of World War II.

out•burst (OWT-berst) *n. outbursts.* A sudden bursting forth.–When the dog walked into the classroom, there was an *outburst* of laughter.

out•cast (OWT-kast) *n. outcasts.* A person from whom everyone has turned away.–The boy who had cheated found himself an *outcast*. People would not associate with him.

out•come (OWT-kum) *n. outcomes.* A result. –What was the *outcome* of the ball game? Who won?

out•cry (OWT-kry) *n. outcries.* A sudden cry or scream.–We heard Mother's *outcry* when she saw the mouse.

out•doors (OWT-dorz) *adv.* Outside the house; out in the open air.–On clear days we play *outdoors*.

out•er (OWT-er) *adj.* Outside.–Mary took the *outer* wrapping off the package, but left the inner wrapping on till Christmas.

out•fit (OWT-fit) *n. outfits.* 1. Clothes.–Mary put on her Easter *outfit*.

2. Equipment or supplies.–The carpenter's *outfit* is a kit of tools and a ladder which he uses in his work.

–*v. outfits, outfitted, outfitting.* Equip or supply.–The Boy Scouts *outfitted* the camp. They brought along all the things they needed for living there.

out•grow (OWT-GROH) *v. outgrows, outgrew, outgrowing.* Grow too large or too old for.–Mother bought Mary a coat that was a little too large for her so that she would not *outgrow* it right away.–Bob gave away the story books he had *outgrown*.

out•ing (OWT-ing) *n. outings.* A short outdoor pleasure trip.–On Sunday we are going for an *outing* up the river.

out•line (OWT-lyn) *n. outlines.* 1. The line made by the outer edges of an object, showing its shape. – Bob drew the *outline* of a ship.

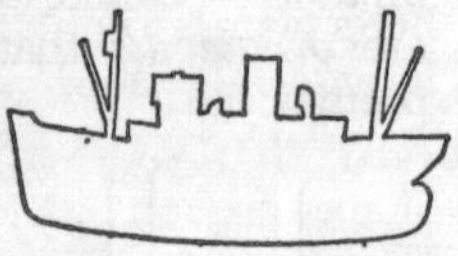

2. A plan.–Mary made an *outline* of the story she was going to write.

–*v. outlines, outlined, outlining.* 1. Make an edge around.–Mary *outlined* the ship in red. 2. Make or tell about a plan.–The coach *outlined* the plan he wanted the team to follow.

out-of-doors (owt-əv-DORZ) *adv.* Outside the house or in the open air.–We play *out-of-doors* in summer more than we do in winter.

out•put (OWT-puht) *n. outputs.* The number made or produced.–The *output* of airplanes in the factory is fifteen each week.

out•rage (OWT-rayj) *n. outrages; outrageous, adj.* A shameful deed; a serious violation of someone's rights; an act or insult that offends.–The criminal committed an *outrage* by beating and robbing the old man.

out•side (owt-SYD) *n., adj., adv.,* and *prep.* 1. The side that is out.–The house is plastered inside. It has bricks on the *outside*.–

Mother's pocketbook is leather on the *outside* and cloth on the inside.
2. Farthest from the center.–Jack was running in the *outside* lane of the track.
3. Outdoors.–Children like to play *outside.*
4. Near, but not in; beyond the limits of.–Bob waited for Jack *outside* the school.

out•stand•ing (owt-STAND-ing) *adj.* Best or most important.–Bob is the *outstanding* athlete in his class.

out•ward (OWT-werd) *adj.* and *adv.; outwardly, adv.* 1. Away from the middle or toward the outside. – The girls in the circle stepped toward the middle, and the boys stepped *outward,* so that a double circle was formed.
2. Outer.–Sometimes Bob's *outward* manner seems rough, but he doesn't mean it. He is really kind and gentle.

out•weigh (owt-WAY) *v. outweighs, outweighed, outweighing.* 1. Be greater than.–The importance of doing your homework *outweighs* the pleasure of going to the movies.
2. Weigh more than. – The champion *outweighs* the challenger. He is heavier than the fighter who is challenging him.

out•wit (owt-WIT) *v. outwits, outwitted, outwitting.* Beat or defeat by clever tricks.–The opposing football team had bigger boys than Bob's team, so Bob's team had to *outwit* them in order to win.

o•val (OH-vəl) *adj.* Shaped like an egg. – Mary has an *oval* face. –The picture of Grandmother as a bride hangs in an *oval* frame.

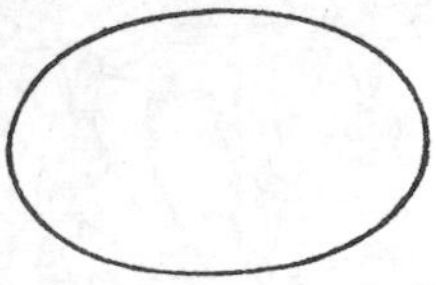

ov•en (UV-ən) *n. ovens.* 1. The closed part of a kitchen stove in which cake, bread, and pies are baked and meat is roasted.

modern oven

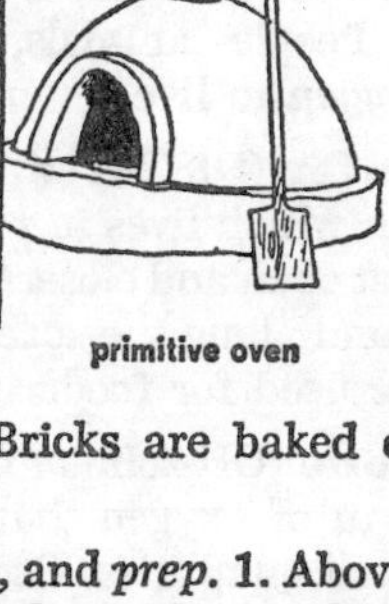
primitive oven

2. A furnace or kiln.–Bricks are baked or hardened in an *oven.*

o•ver (OH-ver) *adj., adv.,* and *prep.* 1. Above. –An awning was stretched *over* the speaker's platform.
2. Along or upon.–The wind blew the snow *over* Grandfather's fields.
3. Across the top of.–Mother ran the vacuum cleaner *over* the rug.
4. Across.–Bob tried to jump *over* the ditch. –Mary has gone *over* to Ruth's house.
5. During.–We stayed home *over* the holidays.
6. Down from the top, on the outside.–Mother put so much milk in the pitcher that it ran *over.*
7. Upon or on top of.–Father put leaves *over* the flowers to keep them from freezing.–Mother put the tablecloth *over* the table.
8. Ended.–The snowstorm should be *over* by night.
9. About.–Mother was laughing *over* the playfulness of the kitten.
10. More than.–*Over* three hundred children go to our school.
11. Down.–Spot knocked the lamp *over.*
12. The other side up. – Mother turned the tablecloth *over.*
13. More than was used.–We had several apples left *over.* There were several we didn't eat.
14. Again.–Mary did the problem twice *over* and got the same answer both times.
15. Upon.–A smile came *over* the baby's face when Mother walked in.

o•ver•alls (OH-ver-awlz) *n. pl.* Loose trousers with a bib, or front piece, attached, worn to keep one clean while working or playing.

o•ver•board (OH-ver-bord) *adv.* Over the side of a ship into the water. – Mary threw some food *overboard* for the ducks.

o•ver•coat (OH-ver-koht) *n. overcoats.* A heavy coat which is worn as an outer garment to keep one warm.

o•ver•come (oh-ver-KUM) *v. overcomes, overcame, overcoming.* 1. Get the better of someone or something; conquer.–John *overcame* his opponent in the boxing match.–If you try very hard, you can *overcome* bad habits.
2. Make unconscious.–The rescue squad revived the fireman who was *overcome* by smoke.
–To *be overcome* means to be made helpless, or be conquered.–Our team *was overcome* by the Wildcats.–The swimmer *was overcome* by the waves, and had to be rescued by the lifeguard.

o·ver·do (oh-ver-DOO) *v. overdoes, overdid, overdoing.* 1. Work too hard and become very tired.–Father told Mother not to *overdo.* 2. Carry too far.–Mabel often *overdoes* her teasing.

o·ver·eat (oh-ver-EET) *v. overeats, overate, overeating.* Eat too much.–Do not *overeat,* or you may get sick.

o·ver·haul (oh-ver-HAWL) *v. overhauls, overhauled, overhauling.* Check the condition of and repair completely.–Father had his car *overhauled* before we took our trip.

o·ver·head (oh-ver-HED) *adj.* and *adv.* 1. Raised; over the head.–Some trains run on an *overhead* track. The track is high above the street.
2. Above.–The stars shine *overhead.*–The ceiling is *overhead.*

o·ver·hear (oh-ver-HIR) *v. overhears, overheard, overhearing.* Hear something that one is not supposed to. – Mary *overheard* Mother telling Father about her birthday party.

o·ver·joyed (oh-ver-JOID) *adj.* Delighted.–The children were *overjoyed* with their gifts.

o·ver·lap (oh-ver-LAP) *v. overlaps, overlapped, overlapping.* Lie partly over another. –A fish's scales *overlap.*–The parts of a pine cone *overlap.*–Shingles on a house *overlap.*

o·ver·shoe (OH-ver-shoo) *n. overshoes.* A rubber shoe or a cloth shoe with a rubber sole which is worn over one's regular shoes to keep them dry.

o·ver·take (oh-ver-TAYK) *v. overtakes, overtook, overtaking.* 1. Catch up with.–Sally ran to *overtake* Mary, who was going out the door.
2. Come upon.–Darkness has *overtaken* us, and we can not see where we are going.

o·ver·time (OH-ver-tym) *n., adj.,* and *adv.* Past one's usual quitting or stopping time.–Father stayed late and worked *overtime.*

o·ver·turn (oh-ver-TERN) *v. overturns, overturned, overturning.* Upset.–Sally's kitten *overturned* Father's inkwell.

o·ver·weight (OH-ver-wayt) *adj.* Weighing too much for a person of one's age and height.–Ed is *overweight.*

o·ver·whelm (oh-ver-HWELM) *v. overwhelms, overwhelmed, overwhelming.* Completely crush; overcome.–The football team *overwhelmed* its rival in the last game.

o·ver·work (oh-ver-WERK) *v. overworks, overworked, overworking.* Work too hard or too long.–The doctor told Grandfather not to *overwork.*

owe (OH) *v. owes, owed, owing.* Have to pay. –Jack bought the ball from Bob but still *owes* him for it.–If I borrow a dime from you, I will *owe* you a dime.

owl (OWL) *n. owls.* A large bird that has large eyes and sharp claws. *Owls* eat mice and other small animals. *Owls* fly mostly by night, and make a hooting cry.

own (OHN) *v. owns, owned, owning.* Have. –I *own* a bicycle. It belongs to me.
–*adj.* Belonging to oneself or itself.–Is that your *own* pencil? Is it yours and nobody else's?–This bicycle is my *own.* It is my property.

own·er (OH-ner) *n. owners.* The person to whom a thing belongs.–Father is the *owner* of this store.

ox (AHKS) *n. oxen.* A full-grown male animal of the cattle kind adapted for use as a work animal for plowing, pulling loads, and other heavy jobs.

oxen (AHKS-ən) *n. pl.* More than one *ox.*

ox·y·gen (AHKS-ə-jən) *n.* A gas which you cannot see, taste, or smell. Air has *oxygen* in it. People, animals, and plants must have *oxygen* to live.

oys·ter (OIST-er) *n. oysters.* A kind of shellfish which lives in rough shells that open and close. *Oysters* are found along the seacoast. They are used for food.

o·zone (OH-zohn *or* oh-ZOHN) *n.* 1. A bluish form of oxygen that is found in the air in small quantities. *Ozone* is used as a sterilizing agent and as a bleaching agent.
2. Pure, fresh air is sometimes called *ozone.*

P p

P, p (PEE) *n. P's, p's.* The sixteenth letter of the alphabet.

pa (PAH) *n.* A name sometimes used instead of papa or father.

pace (PAYSS) *n. paces.* 1. A person's step; the way one walks.–Father walks with a rapid *pace.*
2. The length of a step.–A man's *pace* is about 2½ feet.
3. The rate at which a thing is done.–The men are working at a fast *pace.*
–*v. paces, paced, pacing.* 1. Measure by stepping along.–The boys *paced* off the distances for the baseball diamond.
2. Walk.–He *paced* up and down the hall while he waited for his appointment.

pac•i•fy (PASS-ə-fy) *v. pacifies, pacified, pacifying.* Make peaceful; soothe; calm.–The salesman tried to *pacify* the angry customer.

pack (PAK) *n. packs.* 1. A bundle of food, blankets, etc., carried by a hiker.–Jack set out on the hike with a *pack* on his back.

2. A deck (of playing cards).–Father bought a new *pack* of cards.
3. A number of animals that travel together.–The hunter saw a *pack* of wolves.
–*v. packs, packed, packing.* 1. Put away carefully.–Mother *packed* the china in a barrel.
2. Fill.–Father *packed* the suitcase.

pack•age (PAK-ij) *n. packages.* A bundle or parcel; something wrapped and tied or sealed.

pact (PAKT) *n. pacts.* An agreement.–The two nations signed a trade *pact.*

pad (PAD) *n. pads.* 1. A kind of cover or flat cushion with a soft filling.–Mother puts a *pad* under the tablecloth to protect the table.

2. A small tablet of paper.–Mother keeps a *pad* on the door to write her grocery list on.
3. The little cushions on the bottoms of the paws of dogs, cats, and some other animals.
4. The leaf of a water lily.
–*v. pads, padded, padding.* 1. Cover with a pad or pads.–Mother *padded* the kitchen chairs by fastening pads to the seats.
2. Stuff with a filling.–When Mother made the cushions, she *padded* them with soft cotton.
3. Walk softly. – The dog *padded* across Mother's clean kitchen floor.

pad•dle (PAD-l) *n. paddles.* 1. A stick, flattened at the end, which is pulled through the water to make a boat move.
2. A flat stick. – Rugs are often dusted by beating them with a *paddle.*

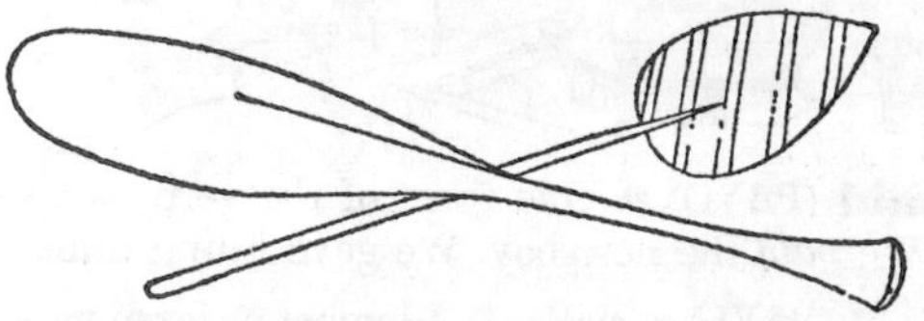

–*v. paddles, paddled, paddling.* Make move with a paddle. – Bob *paddled* the canoe across the lake.

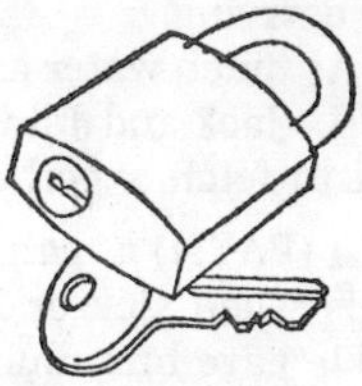

pad•lock (PAD-lahk) *n. padlocks.* A lock that can be put on and taken off.

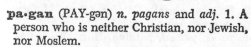

pa•gan (PAY-gən) *n. pagans* and *adj.* 1. A person who is neither Christian, nor Jewish, nor Moslem.
2. A person who worships idols or who believes in many gods.–The missionaries tried their best to convert the *pagans* to Christianity.
3. A person who doesn't believe in any god.

page (PAYJ) *n. pages.* 1. One side of a leaf of paper in a book, magazine, etc.–This is *page* 445 in this book.
2. A boy who serves at a royal court.–The *page* found Cinderella's glass slipper on the stair.
3. A young person who carries messages.
–*v. pages, paged, paging.* Call.–The bellboy at the hotel was *paging* Mr. Smith.

pag•eant (PAJ-ənt) *n. pageants.* 1. A performance or entertainment in which a story is told in a series of scenes.–On February 12, the eighth grade gave a *pageant* of the life of Abraham Lincoln.
2. Any colorful spectacle or show.–In the water *pageant* the swimmers held red balloons while they swam.

pa•go•da (pə-GOH-də) *n. pagodas.* A structure used for temples and memorials in China, India, Japan, and other Eastern countries. It is tall and round, with many levels, each level narrower than the one below. In China *pagodas* have projecting roofs at each level.

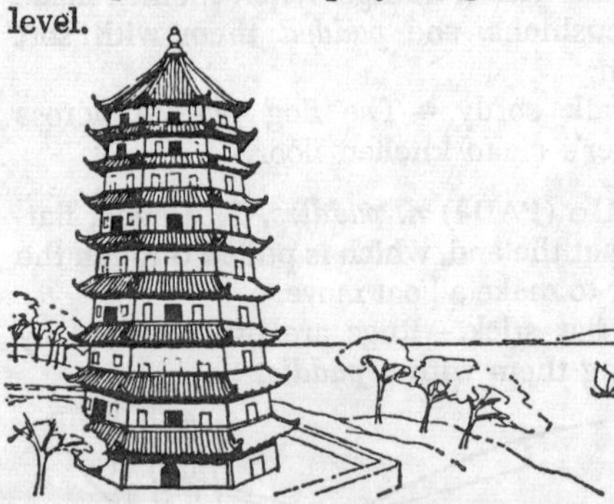

paid (PAYD) *v.* One form of the verb *pay.*–We *paid* the newsboy. We gave him a dime.

pail (PAYL) *n. pails.* 1. A bucket or large vessel with a handle over the top for carrying.
2. As much water as a pail will hold.–Jack and Jill went up the hill to fetch a *pail* of water.

pain (PAYN) *n. pains.* 1. The hurt which one feels when sick or injured.–Jack's sprained ankle gave him much *pain.*
2. (In the plural) Careful effort.–Mother takes great *pains* to please.
–*v. pains, pained, paining.* Hurt.–Bob's finger still *pained* him a little after the splinter was removed.

pain•ful (PAYN-fuhl) *adj.; painfully, adv.* Causing or having pain.–Father said it was not *painful* to have his tooth pulled.

paint (PAYNT) *n. paints.* A kind of coloring mixture that can be spread on a surface to color and, sometimes, to protect it. *Paint* is liquid when it is put on, but dries hard.
–*v. paints, painted, painting.* 1. Spread paint on; cover with paint.–Father *painted* the shutters blue.
2. Make (a picture) with paint.–Sally *painted* a picture of Mother.

paint•er (PAYN-ter) *n. painters.* 1. An artist; a person who paints pictures.

2. A person who paints buildings and other things for a living.

paint•ing (PAYNT-ing) *n. paintings.* A painted picture.–We saw many *paintings* and drawings in the art museum.

pair (PAIR) *n. pairs.* 1. Two things of a kind that go together, such as a *pair* of boots.
2. Anything such as scissors, pliers, and trousers made of two parts joined together, as a *pair* of scissors, a *pair* of pliers, a *pair* of trousers.
3. A couple; a set of two.–Father and Mother are a happy *pair.*–I have a *pair* of rabbits.
–*v. pairs, paired, pairing.* Group in twos.–The children *paired* off to play London Bridge.

pa•ja•mas (pə-JAHM-əz) *n. pl.* A suit worn to sleep in. *Pajamas* are usually in two pieces.

pal•ace (PAL-əss) *n. palaces.* A large, grand house in which kings and queens live.

pal•ate (PAL-ət) *n. palates.* 1. The roof of the mouth. The hard *palate* is the bony part in front; the soft *palate* is the fleshy part in back.
2. Taste, or the sense of taste.–The magnificent feast was fit for a king's *palate.*

pale (PAYL) *adj. paler, palest.* 1. Very white, or colorless. – The frightened boy's face turned *pale.*
2. Light.–Mary's new dress is *pale* blue.

PALEONTOLOGY

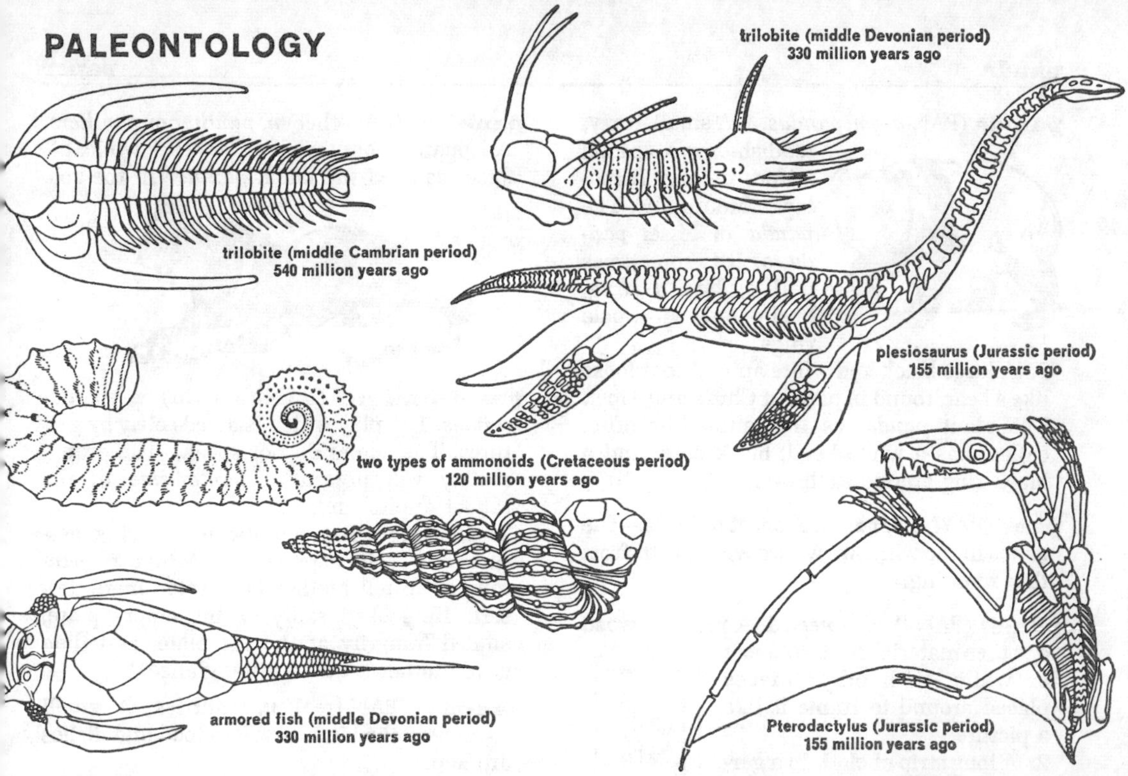

pa·le·on·tol·o·gy (pay-lee-ən-TAHL-ə-jee) *n.* The science or study of ancient plant and animal forms in relation to the geological periods in which they lived. *Paleontology* deals with fossils.

pal·ette (PAL-ət) *n. palettes.* A thin, flat oval or oblong piece of wood with a thumb hole at one end for holding it. An artist keeps and mixes his paints on his *palette* while he is painting.

pal·let (PAL-ət) *n. pallets.* A bed or sleeping mat made of straw; any poor bed.–The beggar slept on a ragged *pallet.*

palm (PAHM) *n. palms.* 1. The inside of the hand between the wrist and the fingers. 2. A tree that grows in very warm regions. The leaves of the *palm* are long and flat, and grow in bunches near the top of the tree.–Dates grow on date *palms,* coconuts on coconut *palms.*

pam·pas (PAM-pəz) *n. pl.* A flat, grassy plain that ranges down southeastern South America and covers a major part of Argentina.

pam·phlet (PAM-flət) *n. pamphlets.* A booklet; a thin little book, usually having a paper cover.

pan (PAN) *n. pans.* An open metal vessel used in cooking.–Mother bakes pies in a pie *pan.*

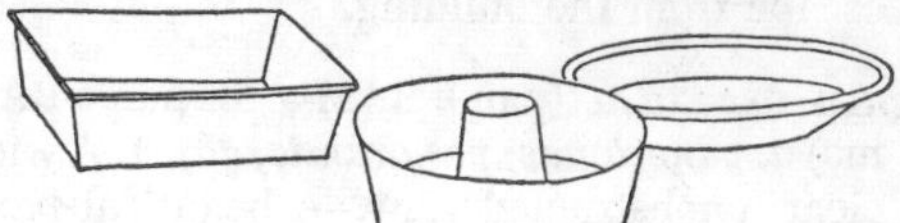

pan·cake (PAN-kayk) *n. pancakes* and *adj.* A thin, flat cake made of batter and fried on a griddle or skillet.–Mother makes *pancakes* every Saturday.

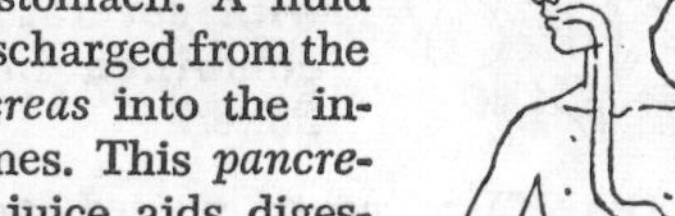

pan·cre·as (PAN- *or* PANG-kree-əss) *n.; pancreatic, adj.* A large gland which is near the stomach. A fluid is discharged from the *pancreas* into the intestines. This *pancreatic* juice aids digestion. Certain cells of the *pancreas* also produce insulin.

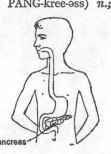

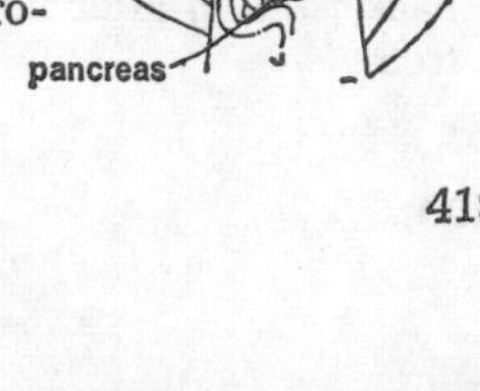

pan•da (PAN-də) *n. pandas.* 1. A small, furry, reddish-brown animal found in the Himalayan Mountains. The *panda,* or lesser *panda,* as it is sometimes called, has a long, bushy tail with pale rings.

2. A large black and white animal that looks like a bear, found in parts of China and Tibet. The giant *panda,* as this animal is often called, has a white head, black ears, and a black ring around each eye.

pane (PAYN) *n. panes.* A sheet of glass.–The *panes* in the windows were covered with frost this morning.

pan•el (PAN-l) *n. panels.* 1. A piece of wood or other material set into doors or walls, with other pieces placed around to frame it like a picture.

2. A long strip of cloth in a garment. – Mary's new skirt has *panels* in the front and in the back.

pan•ic (PAN-ik) *n. panics.* Wild behavior caused by fear.–The fire caused a *panic* among the people. Everyone rushed for the door at once in a frantic attempt to escape from the building.

pan•o•ram•a (pan-ə-RAM-ə *or* pan-ə-RAH-mə) *n. panoramas; panoramic, adj.* 1. A wide, clear, unobstructed view.–A beautiful *panorama* of the valley could be seen from the mountaintop.

2. A broad picture shown section by section in a continuous display. – The audience watched the vast *panorama* of the Grand Canyon unfold as the picture was projected upon the screen.

pan•sy (PAN-zee) *n. pansies.* A flower with broad petals that grows on a low plant. *Pansies* are of many beautiful colors, often with several colors combined in each flower.

pant (PANT) *v. pants, panted, panting.* Breathe hard and quickly.–The dog came back *panting* after he chased the cat up the tree.

pan•ther (PAN-ther) *n. panther* or *panthers.* A leopard, mountain lion, or other wildcat.–Jack watched the black *panther* in the zoo.

pan•to•mime (PAN-tə-mym) *n. pantomimes.* 1. A play which is acted solely by gestures. The actors do not speak.–The drama society will present a *pantomime* in the school auditorium.

2. Showing what you mean by using gestures and facial expressions.–John used *pantomime* to tell Mother he wanted more dessert. He looked sadly at his empty plate, smiled hungrily at the pie plate, and then gave Mother a questioning glance.

pan•try (PAN-tree) *n. pantries.* A small room near the kitchen where food and dishes are kept.

pants (PANTSS) *n. pl.* 1. Trousers.–Bob has on long *pants.*

2. A short lower undergarment; drawers.

pa•pa (PAH-pah) *n. papas.* A child's word for father.

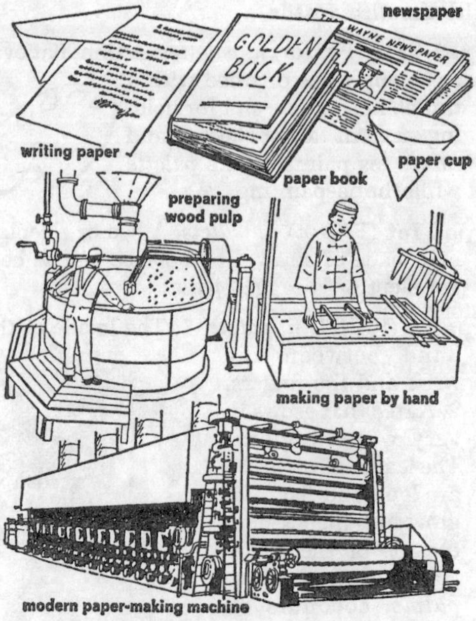

pa•per (PAY-per) *n. papers* and *adj.* 1. A material made in thin sheets from ground wood or rags.–The pages of this book are *paper.*

2. A newspaper.–We get the daily *paper.*
3. A composition.–Bob read his *paper* to the class.
4. A printed or written legal agreement.–Father bought a new house and got the *papers* saying it was his.
–*v. papers, papered, papering.* Put wallpaper on.–The paper hanger *papered* the walls.

pa•poose (pa-POOSS) *n. papooses.* An American Indian baby.–Indian mothers used to carry their *papooses* on their backs.

pa•py•rus (pə-PY-rəss) *n.* 1. A tall water plant which grows in Egypt and in Ethiopia.
2. A paperlike sheet made from this plant which the people of the ancient Middle East wrote on.

par (PAHR) *n.* 1. A condition of equality; an even basis or level.–Frank plays tennis on a *par* with Bob. The two play equally well. Neither one plays better than the other.
2. The number of strokes required to play a perfect hole or round of golf.–Joe took four strokes on the eighth hole, which was *par.*

par•a•ble (PAR-ə-bəl) *n. parables.* A short story which illustrates a moral or lesson without explaining it.–Jesus used *parables* in his teaching.

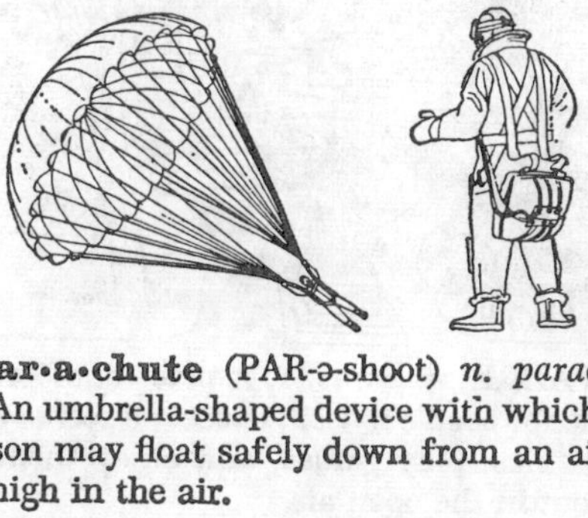

par•a•chute (PAR-ə-shoot) *n. parachutes.* An umbrella-shaped device with which a person may float safely down from an airplane high in the air.

pa•rade (pə-RAYD) *n. parades.* A marching forward of people, vehicles, or animals just for show.

–*v. parades, paraded, parading.* 1. March in formation.–The soldiers *paraded* through the city.
2. Display or show off. – Bob *paraded* his model airplanes before the pilot.

par•a•dise (PAR-ə-dyss) *n.* 1. Heaven.
2. (Spelled with a capital "P.") The garden of Eden.–Adam and Eve originally lived in *Paradise.*
3. Any joyful place.–A resort area is often called a vacation *paradise.*

par•af•fin (PAR-ə-fin) *n.* A white wax.–Mother always seals the jelly jars with *paraffin.*

par•a•graph (PAR-ə-graf) *n. paragraphs.* A group of sentences telling about one thing. –Mary's composition was made up of four *paragraphs.*

par•a•keet (PAR-ə-keet) *n. parakeets.* A small slender parrot with a long pointed tail. – Many people keep *parakeets* as pets.

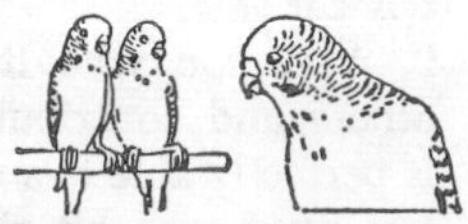

par•al•lel (PAR-ə-lel) *adj.* Being the same distance apart throughout. – The opposite sides of your desk are *parallel.* – Railroad tracks are *parallel.* They are the same distance apart throughout their entire length.

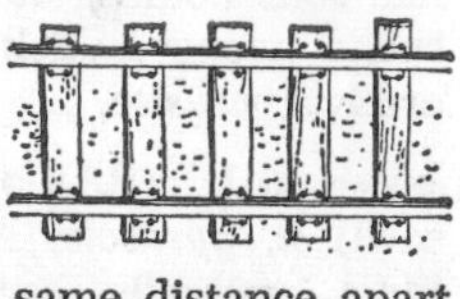

pa•ral•y•sis (pə-RAL-ə-səss) *n. paralyses.* 1. Loss of the ability to move or feel in some part of the body.–The soldier has *paralysis* in one leg.
2. Condition of being unable to move or act. –The snowstorm caused a *paralysis* of traffic on the highway. None of the motorists could make their cars move through the snow.

par•a•lyze (PAR-ə-lyz) *v. paralyzes, paralyzed, paralyzing.* 1. Make unable to move or feel.–The soldier's leg is *paralyzed.* He can't move it.
2. Make inactive or helpless.–The traffic was *paralyzed* by the snowstorm.

par•a•me•ci•um (par-ə-MEE-shee-əm *or* par-ə-MEE-see-əm) *n. paramecia.* A tiny, one-celled animal that is shaped like a bedroom slipper. The *paramecium* is covered with hairlike threads called "cilia." By moving its cilia, a *paramecium* can swim forward or backward. *Paramecia* live in fresh water.

par•a•pet (PAR-ə-pet) *n. parapets.* 1. A wall that soldiers stand behind for protection.–As the rebels approached, the castle guards fired at them from behind the *parapet.*
2. A low wall along a balcony, bridge, or some other such place, which keeps people from falling over the edge.

par•a•pher•nal•ia (par-ə-fə-NAYL-yə) *n.* 1. Personal belongings.–The campers gathered together their *paraphernalia* and put it all into the truck.
2. Equipment or special materials.–The fire destroyed all of the *paraphernalia* that the family had stored in the warehouse. Bicycles, trunks, and suitcases were all burned.

par•a•site (PAR-ə-syt) *n. parasites; parasitic, adj.* 1. A plant or animal that depends on another plant or animal for its food or protection. The plant or animal it depends on is called a "host." The *parasite* lives either in or on its host. It gives nothing in return for what it gets.
2. A person who lives at the expense of others and contributes nothing, though he is perfectly able to support himself.–Richard has lived with his rich uncle for years and has done nothing but spend money. Richard is a *parasite.*

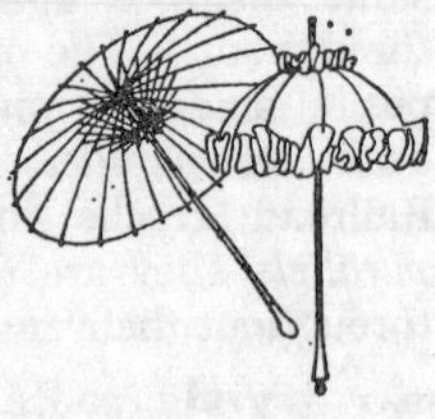

par•a•sol (PAR-ə-sawl) *n. parasols.* A fancy umbrella carried by women for protection from the sun.

par•a•troop•er (PAR-ə-troo-per) *n. paratroopers.* A soldier trained to use a parachute in jumping from a high-flying plane. *Paratroopers* are valuable because they can enter any area quickly.

par•cel (PAHR-səl) *n. parcels.* A package or bundle.–Father got a *parcel* in the mail today.

parch (PAHRCH) *v. parches, parched, parching.* Make hot and dry.–The baking sun *parched* the earth.

parch•ment (PAHRCH-mənt) *n. parchments.* The dried skin of goats, sheep, or other animals, treated so that it can be written on.–Ancient *parchments* were found in a cave.

par•don (PAHR-dn) *n. pardons.* Forgiveness.–Mary said, "I beg your *pardon,*" when she interrupted Father.
–*v. pardons, pardoned, pardoning.* 1. Excuse or forgive.–When Mary bumps into someone, she says, "*Pardon* me."
2. Release from punishment.–The prisoner was *pardoned* for good behavior.

pare (PAIR) *v. pares, pared, paring.* Peel.–Mary helped Mother *pare* the potatoes.

par•ent (PAIR-ənt) *n. parents.* A mother or father.–Either of your *parents* may sign your report card.

pa•ren•the•sis (pə-REN-thə-səss) *n. parentheses.* 1. Either of two marks ( ) used to set off certain words from the rest of a sentence. *Parentheses* are sometimes put around words in a sentence to explain something that has been said just before.–Monday (the second day of the week) is a school day.
2. The phrase enclosed in parentheses.–(The second day of the week) is a *parenthesis.*

par•ing (PAIR-ing) *n. parings.* A peel or skin.–The potato *parings* were fed to the pigs.

par•ish (PAR-ish) *n. parishes.* 1. A church district under the spiritual guidance of a clergyman or priest.–The young pastor was sent to his first *parish,* the church and district to which he would minister.
2. The members of a church.–The priest canvassed his *parish* for people to serve on the new church committee.
3. The people living in the area of a church. – The whole *parish* was excited about the wedding.
4. Any county in the state of Louisiana.

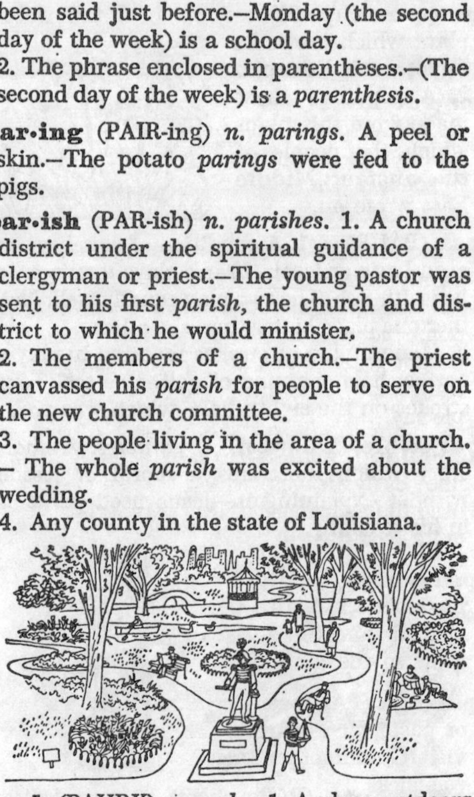

park (PAHRK) *n. parks.* 1. A place outdoors set aside for people to visit, to see the scenery, have picnics, play games, and enjoy themselves out in the open air.

2. A camp or other place where cars may be parked. – We once stayed overnight in a trailer *park.*
–*v. parks, parked, parking.* Put an automobile in a certain place and leave it there.–Every driver should know that it is unlawful to *park* too near a fire hydrant.

par•ka (PAHR-kə) *n. parkas.* A warm, hooded jacket or coat that is worn in very cold weather.–Tom wore a *parka* when he went skiing.

par•lia•ment (PAHR-lə-mənt) *n. parliaments.* (Sometimes spelled with a capital "P.") A lawmaking assembly; a legislature, especially that of Great Britain.–The British *Parliament* is divided into the House of Commons and the House of Lords.

par•lor (PAHR-ler) *n. parlors.* 1. A room for receiving guests; a living room.–We sat in Grandmother's *parlor* when the company came.
2. A room used for a certain business, such as hairdressing.–Mother has her hair waved at the beauty *parlor.*

pa•ro•chi•al (pə-ROH-kee-əl) *adj.* Having to do with a parish or a religious body.–Many children in the United States attend *parochial* schools. They attend schools that are supported by a church.

par•rot (PAR-ət) *n. parrots.* A kind of brilliantly colored bird with a hooked bill. Some *parrots* can be taught to imitate the things they hear people say.

pars•ley (PAHRSS-lee) *n.* A plant that has fine curly leaves which are used to flavor foods and to decorate food dishes.

pars•nip (PAHRSS-nip) *n. parsnips.* A white vegetable shaped something like a carrot. *Parsnips* grow in the ground.

par•son (PAHR-sən) *n. parsons.* A minister or pastor of a church.–The *parson* came to visit Grandmother once a week when she was sick.

par•son•age (PAHR-sən-ij) *n. parsonages.* A minister's home provided by his church. The *parsonage* is often next door to the church.

part (PAHRT) *n. parts.* 1. A piece or amount less than the whole.–Baby ate *part* of an orange.
2. A share.–Bob always does his *part* to keep the house neat.
3. A role in a play.–Mary was given the *part* of Snow White in the play.
4. A side.–The twins always take Jack's *part* in a quarrel.
5. A section.–We live in a hilly *part* of the country.
6. A dividing line.–The *part* in Bill's hair is on the left.
7. A piece.–When Bob put the clock back together, he had one *part* left over.
8. A voice.–There are several *parts* in this song. Mary sings the alto, or lower *part.*
9. Each of the equal pieces into which a thing can be divided.–A fifth *part* of a pie is one of five equal pieces.
–*v. parts, parted, parting.* 1. Make separate; force apart.–Jack *parted* the fighting dogs as quickly as possible.
2. Go away from one another; separate.–Bob and Jack *parted* when they reached the corner.
3. Make a dividing line.–Bill *parts* his hair on the side.
–*Part with* means give up.–Little girls do not like to *part with* their dolls.

par•tial (PAHR-shəl) *adj.; partially, adv.* 1. Prejudiced; likely to favor one side.–The umpire wasn't *partial* to either team.
2. Likely to prefer.–I have always been *partial* to the color green.
3. Part.–Father made a *partial* payment on our car. He paid part of the amount owed.

par•tic•i•pate (pahr-TISS-ə-payt) *v. participates, participated, participating.* Take part; share or join with others.–All the children *participated* in the spelling bee.

par•tic•u•lar (pahr-TIK-yə-ler) *adj.; particularly, adv.* 1. Very careful; fussy.–Mother is *particular* about the baby's food.
2. Special or outstanding.–There is one *particular* point I must warn you about.
3. Certain.–On this *particular* morning the sun shone warm and bright.

par•ti•tion (pahr-TISH-ən) *n. partitions.* An inside wall that separates rooms or compartments.

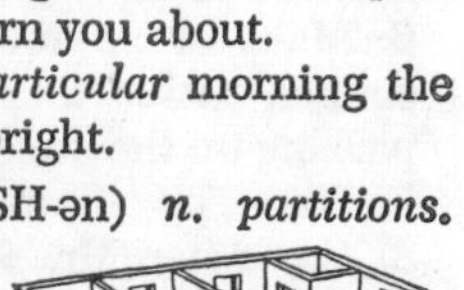

part•ly (PAHRT-lee) *adv.* Less than the whole; not completely.–The house is *partly* finished. There is still work to be done on it.

part•ner (PAHRT-ner) *n. partners.* 1. One of several persons who play on a side in a game.
2. One of several owners of one thing.–Two men are *partners* in owning the store.
3. A person with whom one is paired for a dance, or a game.–Mary and Bob were *partners* in the last dance.

par•ty (PAHR-tee) *n. parties.* 1. A group entertainment.–We had a *party* at school for our class.
2. A group of people who work together to try to elect certain persons to office. – The most important *parties* in the United States are the Republican *Party* and the Democratic *Party.*
3. One of the people involved in something. –He was a *party* to our plan. He knew all about our plan, and even helped us work it out.

pass (PASS) *n. passes.* 1. A path or narrow road. – We walked through the mountain *pass.*

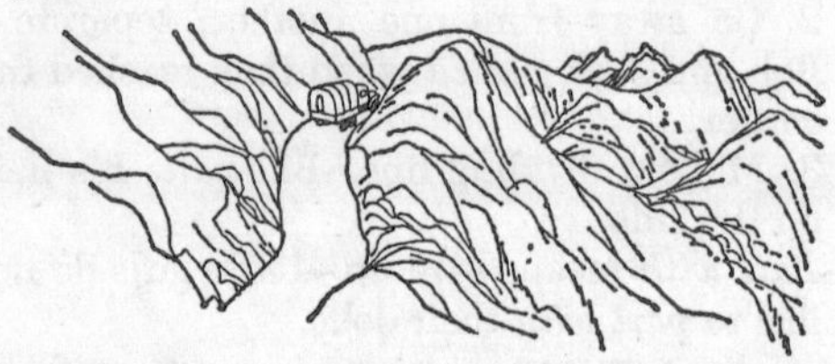

2. A written permit. – The children must have a *pass* to go through the halls.
3. A free ticket.–The owner of the ball club gave Bob and Jack *passes* to the Saturday afternoon ball game.
–*v. passes, passed, passing.* 1. Go by, or move past.–We saw the parade *pass* the school.
2. Hand.–The teacher asked us to *pass* our papers in.–*Pass* me the salt, please.
3. Be mistaken.–When Mary is dressed in Jack's clothes, she could *pass* for a boy.
4. Spend.–Bob *passed* the time reading.
5. Finish the work of a school grade or course and succeed in an examination on it.–Everyone in our class *passed* the test.
6. Make or approve (a law). – The town council *passed* a law that forbids overnight parking on the streets.
7. Die.–The old man *passed* away.
8. Go.–After Mr. Smith's death, his estate *passed* to his nephew.–The circus *passed* on to another town.

pas•sage (PASS-ij) *n. passages.* 1. Movement or travel from one place to another.–The ship had a stormy *passage* to New York.
2. A tunnel, hall, or other place through which one can pass from place to place.–We walked through the *passage* to the train.

3. Approval of a law, resolution, etc.–*Passage* of a law against overnight parking was urged by the mayor.
4. Section from a book or piece of writing.–The teacher read a *passage* from "Moby Dick" to the class.

pas•sen•ger (PASS-ən-jer) *n. passengers.* A person traveling on a plane, train, streetcar, bus, boat, car, etc.

pas•sion (PASH-ən) *n. passions; passionate, adj.* 1. Great love; strong desire.–Jack has a real *passion* for golf.
2. The thing loved or desired.–Golf is Jack's *passion.*
3. Violent rage or anger.–The man's *passion* was hard to control.
4. Any strong feeling or emotion.–Joy and sorrow are *passions.*

pass•port (PASS-port) *n. passports.* A special document given to a citizen by his country which gives him the right to travel in other countries.

past (PAST) *n.* 1. Time gone by.–In the *past* we started to school at 8:30 in the morning; now we go at 9:00.
2. One's life up to now.–Grandfather told us stories of his *past.*
–*adj.* Already gone by.–In *past* years we have always gone to Grandmother's for Thanksgiving; this year she is visiting us.
–*adv.* By.–Mary ran *past* in a great hurry.
–*prep.* 1. After.–It is ten *past* nine.
2. Beyond.–John is so sleepy that he's *past* caring what we do.–Ellen's house is *past* the post office.
3. By.–Dan ran *past* the house.

paste (PAYST) *n. pastes.* 1. A soft substance used for sticking things together.–Mary used *paste* to stick the pictures in her scrapbook.
2. Any soft, moist, doughy substance.–We brush our teeth with tooth *paste.*
–*v. pastes, pasted, pasting.* Stick with paste. –Mary *pasted* the picture in her scrapbook.

paste•board (PAYST-bord) *n.* A material made in stiff sheets by pasting paper together, or by pressing into sheets ground-up paper mixed with a special paste.

pas•tel (pass-TEL *or* PASS-tel) *n. pastels* and *adj.* 1. A type of drawing crayon made from a paste of ground colors. *Pastels* produce the effect of colored chalk.
2. A drawing made by using such crayons.—All the paintings and drawings, including the *pastels,* are for sale.
3. A pale, soft shade of any color.—Jane favored *pastels* for her summer dresses.

pas•teur•ize (PASS-cher-yz) *v. pasteurizes, pasteurized, pasteurizing.* Treat with heat to kill harmful germs.—The dairyman *pasteurized* the milk before he sold it.

pas•time (PASS-tym) *n. pastimes.* A game or pleasant activity.—Bob's favorite *pastime* is building model airplanes.

pas•tor (PASS-ter) *n. pastors.* A minister or a priest who has charge of a church.

pas•try (PAYSS-tree) *n. pastries.* Food, such as pies or tarts, made of rich dough.—The bakery window displayed many *pastries.*

pas•ture (PASS-cher) *n. pastures.* 1. A grassy field where cattle feed.—Bob drove Grandfather's cow to the *pasture.*
2. Grass or other plants which cattle eat.—The *pasture* is very good this year.

pat (PAT) *n. pats.* 1. A light touch; a light, friendly tap with the whole hand.—Sally gave the dog a *pat.*
2. A small cake or piece.—The waiter brought a *pat* of butter.
—*v. pats, patted, patting.* Touch gently; give a pat to.—Sally likes to *pat* the dog.

patch (PACH) *n. patches.* 1. A piece of cloth sewn over a hole or tear in cloth.—Mother sewed a *patch* on Jack's old trousers.
2. Any piece of material, such as cloth or sheet metal, used to cover a hole, crack, injury, or damage.—The workman put a *patch* on the leaking metal roof.

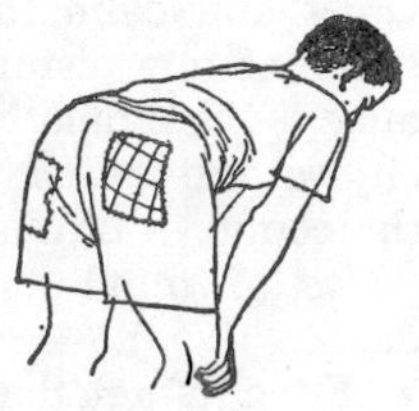

3. A piece of land.—Grandfather has a small vegetable *patch* planted with onions.
4. An area in a larger area.—Jenny's horse has a *patch* of white on his side.—There is a *patch* of daisies in that field.
—*v. patches, patched, patching.* 1. Put a patch on.—Mother *patched* Jack's torn sleeve.
2. Fix up; make right.—Jack and Bill have *patched* up their troubles.

pat•ent (PAT-nt) *n. patents.* A written paper from the government which gives an inventor, and no one else, the right to make and sell his invention for a certain number of years.
—*v. patents, patented, patenting.* Receive a patent for.—Father *patented* his new shoe-repairing machine last month.

path (PATH) *n. paths.* 1. A narrow trail or track worn by animals or people walking, or made for animals or people to walk on.

2. A course. – We were able to follow the satellite's *path* across the sky with the naked eye.

pa•thet•ic (pə-THET-ik) *adj.; pathetically, adv.* Arousing a feeling of pity or sympathy.—The crying boy, who had just lost his dog, was a *pathetic* sight.

pa•tience (PAY-shənss) *n.* The ability to be calm or to stand discomfort or other annoyance without complaining.—We do not realize how much *patience* Mother has with us.

pa•tient (PAY-shənt) *n. patients.* A person in the care of a doctor.—Our doctor has two other *patients* living in this block.
—*adj.; patiently, adv.* 1. Calm; not bothered.—Our teacher is very *patient* with us when we ask questions. She does not become disturbed or irritated with us.
2. Able to wait calmly for results. – John realized that he had to be *patient* when he built the radio set from an instruction manual. It was a long, hard job.

pa•ti•o (PAHT- *or* PAT-ee-oh) *n. patios.* 1. An interior courtyard, especially one exposed to the sky.—Houses in Spain and Latin America often have *patios.*
2. Any outdoor terrace or living area. – Mother invited her guests to relax on the *patio.*

pa•tri•arch (PAY-tree-ahrk) *n. patriarchs.* The father, head, and ruler of a family or tribe, especially in the Bible.–In the Bible, Isaac was a *patriarch.*

pa•tri•ot (PAY-tree-ət) *n. patriots.* A person who shows great love for his country. –Thomas Jefferson was an early American *patriot.*

pa•tri•ot•ic (pay-tree-AHT-ik) *adj.; patriotically, adv.* Showing great love for one's country.–Abraham Lincoln was *patriotic.* He worked for the good of the people of his country.

pa•trol (pə-TROHL) *n. patrols.* A guard or guards who go over a certain route again and again to watch and keep order.–Police *patrols* watch the highways.
–*v. patrols, patrolled, patrolling.* Watch; go back and forth along and keep a watch over. –The soldiers *patrolled* the border of the country.

pat•ter (PAT-er) *n.* A gentle tapping.–We heard the *patter* of little feet upstairs.
–*v. patters, pattered, pattering.* Tap lightly.–The rain is *pattering* on the windowpanes.

pat•tern (PAT-ern) *n. patterns.* 1. A form or guide to follow in cutting out or building something.–Mother bought a *pattern* to make Mary a dress.

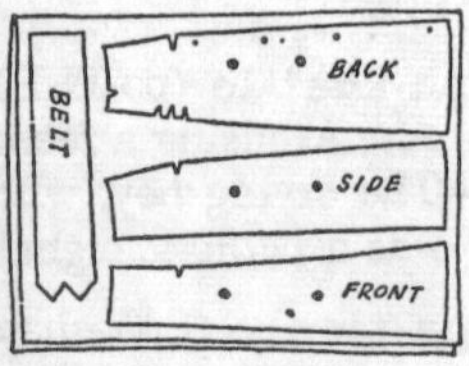

2. A design or figure. –The cloth for Mary's dress had a leaf *pattern.*
3. An ideal or an example.–Bob is a *pattern* for the other boys to follow.
–*v. patterns, patterned, patterning.* Model; copy.–Harry *patterned* his model airplane on the diagram in the instruction book.

pat•ty (PAT-ee) *n. patties.* A cup-shaped shell made of dough and baked.

pau•per (PAW-per) *n. paupers.* A very poor person.–The man said that he could not buy food because he was a *pauper.*

pause (PAWZ) *n. pauses.* A short stop or wait.–Mary waited for a *pause* in the conversation to ask if she might go to the movies.
–*v. pauses, paused, pausing.* Stop for a moment.–Mother *paused* to think before she began the letter to the teacher.

pave (PAYV) *v. paves, paved, paving.* Cover with pavement.–The workmen are *paving* the dirt road with concrete.

pave•ment (PAYV-mənt) *n. pavements.* The hard surface of concrete, asphalt, or other substance covering roads and walks.

pa•vil•ion (pə-VIL-yən) *n. pavilions.* 1. A low building with open sides.–We ate our lunch in the picnic *pavilion.*

2. A large tent.

paw (PAW) *n. paws.* A foot of an animal that has claws.–The kitten batted the ball with her *paw.*
–*v. paws, pawed, pawing.* 1. Scrape with the paws or feet.–The horse *pawed* the ground nervously.
2. Handle roughly.–Do not *paw* the baby chicks.

pay (PAY) *n.* Salary or wages.–Jack's *pay* from his paper route is ten dollars a week.
–*v. pays, paid, paying.* 1. Give money in exchange. We *pay* for work done for us by others or for things which we buy.–Jack *paid* a dime for the ice cream.
2. Offer; give.–Our teacher told us to *pay* attention to what she said.
3. Be worth while.–Honesty *pays.*
4. Suffer a penalty.–She *paid* for her quarrel with the taxi company by having to walk the long way home.

pay•ment (PAY-mənt) *n. payments.* An amount of money paid. – Father makes a *payment* on the new car every month.

pea (PEE) *n. peas.* A small, round, green seed. It is eaten as a vegetable. *Peas* grow in pods on vines.

peace (PEESS) *n.* 1. Quiet and calm; absence of any disturbance. – Grandmother enjoys the *peace* of the country.–Life is happiest when one has *peace* of mind and interesting things to do.
2. Friendly relations with other countries or other people.–All people of good will want *peace.*
3. Not at war.–The country of Switzerland remained at *peace* during World War II.

4. The end of war.–The warring nations finally made *peace* with each other.

peace•ful (PEESS-fuhl) *adj.; peacefully, adv.* Quiet and calm; undisturbed. – After the storm, it was *peaceful* again in the garden.

peach (PEECH) *n. peaches.* A round, juicy fruit with a fuzzy, reddish-yellow skin. In the middle of the *peach* is a rough stone, or pit. *Peaches* grow on trees.
–*adj.* Yellowish-pink. – Mary has a pair of *peach* pajamas.

pea•cock (PEE-kahk) *n. peacocks.* A bird with beautiful green feathers spotted with other colors. The *peacock* spreads out his long tail fèathers like a fan.

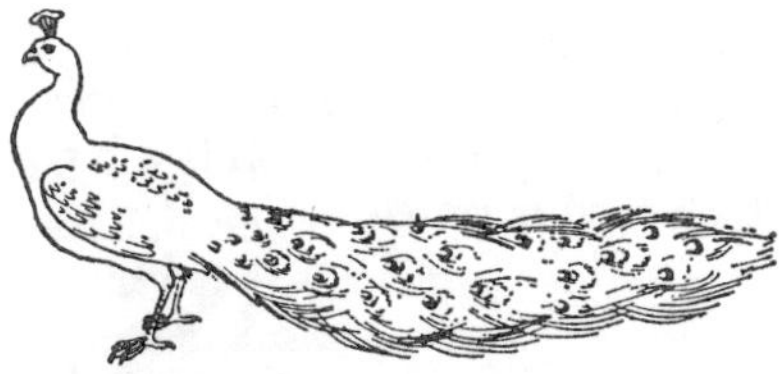

peak (PEEK) *n. peaks.* The very top point.–There is a weather vane on the *peak* of the schoolhouse.–The *peak* of the mountain is covered with snow

peal (PEEL) *n. peals.* A long, lóud ringing.–We heard the *peal* of the church bells.
–*v. peals, pealed, pealing.* Sound loudly and repeatedly.–The bells *pealed* clearly.–Thunder *pealed* in the distance.

pea•nut (PEE-nut) *n. peanuts.* A nutlike seed that is contained in a thin, soft shell. There are usually two *peanuts* in one shell. *Peanuts* grow in the ground and are good to eat.

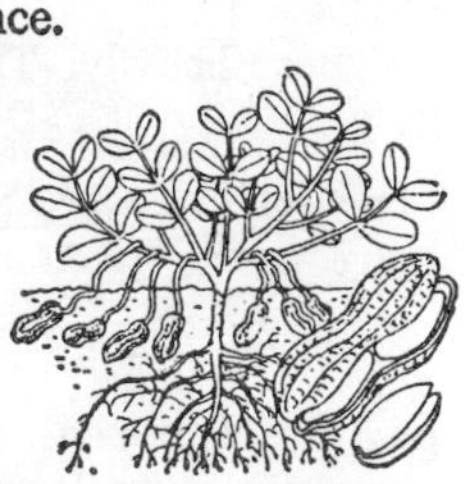

pear (PAIR) *n. pears.* Juicy, sweet fruit. When ripe, some *pears* are yellow, some are green, and some are brown. *Pears* have cores like apples.

pearl (PERL) *n. pearls. Pearls* are formed in the shells of some oysters around a grain of sand that gets into the shell. They are bluish, pinkish, or creamy white, and are used in necklaces and other jewelry.

peas•ant (PEZ-ənt) *n. peasants.* In Europe, a person who worked the soil as a farmer or a laborer was often called a *peasant.*

peat (PEET) *n.* and *adj.* A dark brown material composed mainly of decayed or partially rotted water plants, including rushes, reeds, and mosses. *Peat,* dried and cut into blocks, is used for fuel.
–*Peat moss* is the name given to any moss plant from which peat is made. Dried *peat moss* is often used to fertilize soil.

peb•ble (PEB-əl) *n. pebbles.* A small, round stone.–Sally picked up *pebbles* on the beach.

pe•can (pi-KAHN *or* -KAN) *n. pècans.* A smooth, oval nut with a brown shell. *Pecans* grow on trees.

peck (PEK) *n. pecks.* A measure of dry material, especially of vegetables. Four *pecks* make one bushel.
–*v. pecks, pecked, pecking.* Nip with the beak. – The hen *pecked* Bob.

pec•tin (PEK-tin) *n. pectins.* A chemical substance, easily dissolved in boiling water, which is present in all fruits from which jellies can be made.–Jelly- and jam-makers sometimes add *pectin* to the fruits they are using to make them set, or jell, better.

pe•cul•iar (pi-KYOOL-yer) *adj.; peculiarly, adv.* 1. Odd or strange.–Jack could tell that this was the boy they were looking for by his *peculiar* clothes.
2. Belonging to one thing or one class of things.–Feathers are *peculiar* to birds. Only birds have feathers.

ped•al (PED-l) *n. pedals.* A lever worked by the foot.–Father put his foot on the brake *pedal* to slow down the car.

–*v. pedals, pedaled* or *pedalled, pedaling* or *pedalling.* Push pedals to move a vehicle.–Sally likes to *pedal* her tricycle along the sidewalk.

ped•dle (PED-l) *v. peddles, peddled, peddling.* Carry about and sell.–The old man *peddles* shoelaces to make a living. He goes from house to house selling shoelaces.

ped•dler (PED-ler) *n. peddlers.* A person who goes along the streets or from house to house selling things.–The old *peddler* had shoelaces for sale.

ped•es•tal (PED-əss-təl) *n. pedestals.* A base for something to stand on.–The little bronze statue on Father's desk stands on a *pedestal.*

pe•des•tri•an (pə-DESS-tree-ən) *n. pedestrians.* A person who travels or goes on foot; a walker. – *Pedestrians* should cross streets only at the corners, and only with the green light.

pe•di•a•tri•cian (pee-dee-ə-TRISH-ən) *n. pediatricians.* A medical doctor who specializes in the care of children and the treatment of children's diseases.

ped•i•gree (PED-ə-gree) *n. pedigrees; pedigreed, adj.* Ancestry; the record of a breed from a long time past up to the present.–Grandfather's dog has a fine *pedigree.*

pe•dom•e•ter (pi-DAHM-ə-ter) *n. pedometers.* An instrument used to measure distance traveled in walking by counting the number of steps taken.–The Scoutmaster took along a *pedometer* to measure the distance of the hike.

peek (PEEK) *n.* A peep; a quick, sly look.–Mary took a *peek* at the parcel.
–*v. peeks, peeked, peeking.* Peep; take a quick, sly look.–Mother told Mary not to *peek* while she opened the parcel.

peel (PEEL) *n. peels.* The outer skin or rind of some fruits and vegetables.–Banana *peels* are yellow when ripe.
–*v. peels, peeled, peeling.* 1. Take off the outer skin.–We *peel* bananas before we eat them. 2. Flake off.–My skin began to *peel* a few days after I got a sunburn.

peep (PEEP) *n. peeps.* 1. A quick look; a peek. –Mother took a *peep* at the cake in the oven. 2. The cry of a bird or baby chicken.
–*v. peeps, peeped, peeping.* Peek; look slyly.–The boys *peeped* through a hole in the fence to watch the ball game.

peer (PIR) *n. peers.* 1. An equal.–Babe Ruth has no *peer* in baseball history. He hit more home runs than any other baseball player. 2. In Britain, a person of noble rank.
–*v. peers, peered, peering.* Look long and hard. –Grandmother *peered* at the picture.

pee•vish (PEE-vish) *adj.; peevishly, adv.* Cross; easily made angry.–Baby is sometimes *peevish* when she is cutting teeth.

peg (PEG) *n. pegs.* A small, round piece of wood or metal that fits into a hole or goes into the ground.
–*v. pegs, pegged, pegging.* Fasten with a peg.–Father *pegged* our tent to the ground.

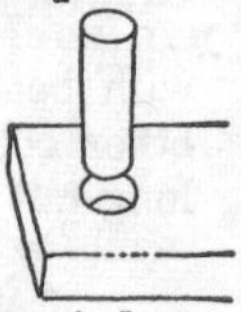

pel•i•can (PEL-ə-kən) *n. pelicans.* A large water bird. Beneath its bill is a big pouch in which food is stored.

pel•let (PEL-it) *n. pellets.* Any small ball, as of medicine, snow, earth, food, etc.–The moth balls Mother uses for protecting woolens in summer are strong-smelling *pellets* of camphor.

pelt (PELT) *n. pelts.* The hide of an animal, especially a fur-bearing animal.
–*v. pelts, pelted, pelting.* 1. Throw things at. – The boys *pelted* the girls with snowballs.
2. Beat heavily.–The rain *pelted* down.

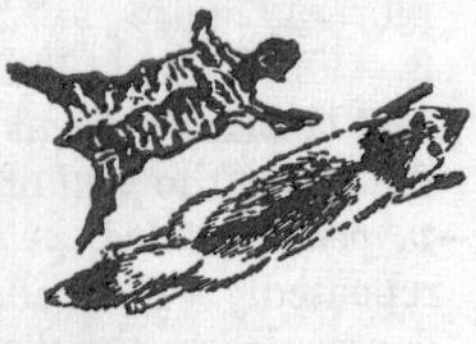

pen (PEN) *n. pens.* 1. A small enclosed space in which animals are kept.–The pig is in the pig*pen.*

2. An instrument with which we write in ink.

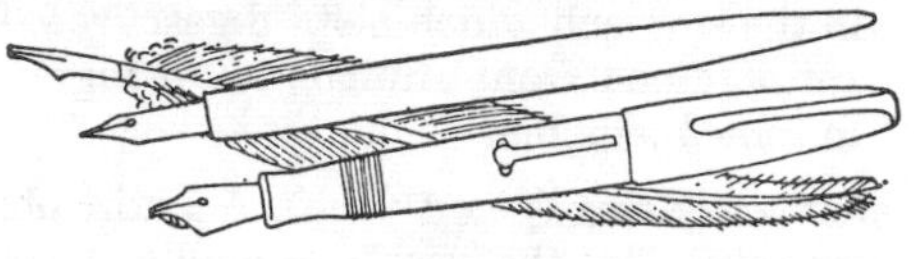

–*v. pens, penned, penning.* 1. Shut in a pen.–The farmer *penned* his pigs.
2. Shut in, as if in a pen.–The boys caught the rabbit by coming from all sides and *penning* him in.
3. Write.–Mother *penned* a letter to Helen.

pe·nal·ize (PEE-nəl-yz) *v. penalizes, penalized, penalizing.* Set a penalty on; punish; require a penalty for.–The referee *penalized* the basketball player for committing a foul. –Certain crimes are *penalized* by imprisonment.

pen·al·ty (PEN-əl-tee) *n. penalties.* A punishment.–The lawful *penalty* for stealing is a fine or imprisonment.

pen·cil (PEN-səl) *n. pencils.* A small stick of wood or metal that has a long thin piece of "lead," or graphite, through the middle, and sometimes an eraser at one end.

pen·du·lum (PEN-jə-ləm) *n. pendulums.* A weight that is hung so that it can swing back and forth.–Mr. Smith's grandfather clock has a brass *pendulum* that you can see through the glass door.

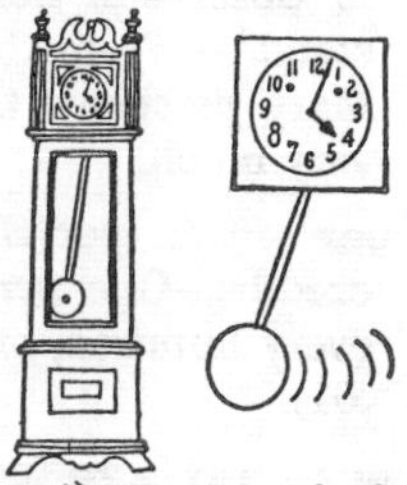

pen·e·trate (PEN-ə-trayt) *v. penetrates, penetrated, penetrating.* 1. Pierce; pass into; enter.–A nail *penetrated* Tom's shoe.
2. Pass through; force a way into.–The explorers plan to *penetrate* the jungle.
3. Understand.–The problem was so difficult that John could not *penetrate* it.
4. Spread throughout. – The flood waters *penetrated* the entire valley.

pen·guin (PEN-gwin) *n. penguins.* A sea bird that can swim, but cannot fly. *Penguins* live near the South Pole, where it is very cold.

pen·i·cil·lin (pen-ə-SIL-in) *n.* A powerful antibiotic, or germ-attacking drug, made from a fungus called penicillium. *Penicillin* is used to treat many kinds of infections.

pen·in·su·la (pə-NIN-sə-lə) *n. peninsulas.* A narrow strip of land that sticks far out into the water.–Italy is a *peninsula.*

pen·i·ten·tia·ry (pen-ə-TEN-chə-ree) *n. penitentiaries.* A prison; a place where people are kept to punish them for breaking the law.

pen·knife (PEN-nyf) *n. penknives.* A small knife with folding blades that can be carried in the pocket.

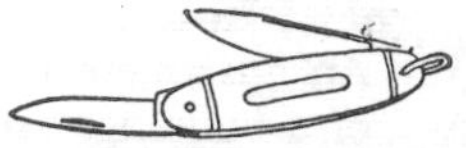

pen·man·ship (PEN-mən-ship) *n.* Handwriting; the skill of writing by hand.–We learn to write in our class on *penmanship.*

pen·nant (PEN-ənt) *n. pennants.* A long, narrow flag, usually pointed at one end.

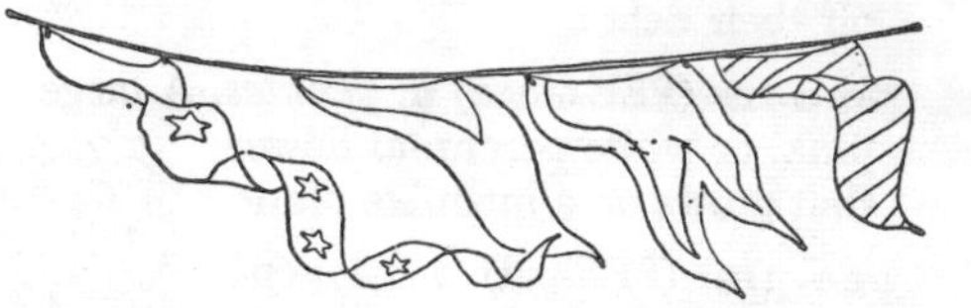

Penn·syl·va·ni·a (pen-sil-VAYN-yə) *n.* A state in mid-eastern United States, in which is mined one third of the coal in the U.S. It is a leading state in agriculture, shipbuilding, and the manufacture of locomotives. Much of our money has been minted in *Pennsylvania.*

pen·ny (PEN-ee) *n. pennies.* 1. A one-cent coin.
2. A copper coin of Great Britain, worth between one and two cents.

pen·sion (PEN-shən) *n. pensions.* A sum of money paid regularly to a person to support him when he is unable to work because of injury or has retired in old age.–Mr. Wilson used to be a night watchman. Now he gets a *pension* from the city of eighty-five dollars a month.

pen•ta•gon (PEN-tə-gahn) *n. pentagons.* A plane, or flat, figure having five sides and five angles.–The building which contains most of the United States Defense Department offices, in Arlington, Virginia, has a floor plan in the shape of a *pentagon* and is often called the *Pentagon.*

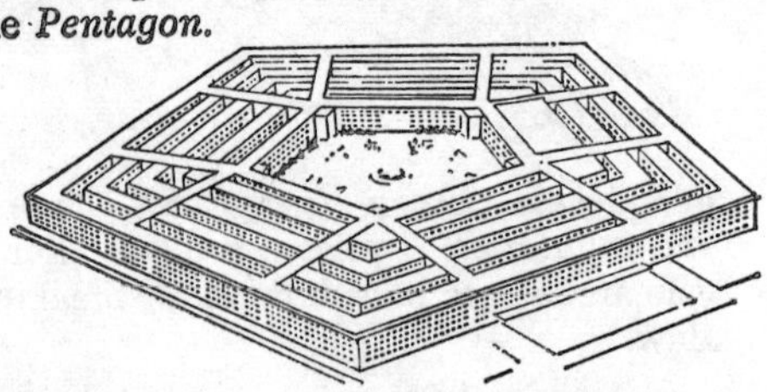

pent•house (PENT-howss) *n. penthouses.* An apartment or dwelling place on the top of a building, usually with an outdoor area where people can sit.

pe•on (PEE-ahn) *n. peons.* A laborer or unskilled worker in Spanish American countries. At one time, *peons* were forced to work for an employer until they were able to pay off their debts.

pe•o•ny (PEE-ə-nee) *n. peonies.* A large red, pink, or white perennial flower that grows on a bushlike plant.

peo•ple (PEE-pəl) *n.* 1. (*pl. people*) Human beings; men, women, boys, and girls.– Many *people* were at the circus.
2. (*pl. peoples*) A race; all the citizens of a country or a part of a country.– All the *peoples* of the earth want freedom.

pep•per (PEP-er) *n. peppers.* 1. A plant whose small red or black berries or seeds have a hot, stinging taste. These seeds are called *pepper* when ground and used as a seasoning on foods.
2. A kind of green or red vegetable used in salads and as a seasoning. Some varieties are hot to the taste, some mild.
–*v. peppers, peppered, peppering.* Put pepper on.–Mother salted and *peppered* the meat she was cooking for dinner.

pep•per•mint (PEP-er-mint) *n. peppermints.* 1. An herb or plant from which a pleasant-smelling oil is made that is used as a flavoring.
2. A candy that is so flavored.

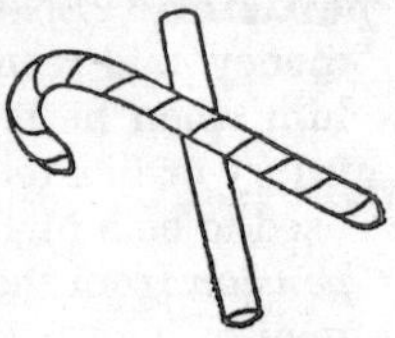

pep•sin (PEP-sin) *n.* A substance produced in the stomach which helps digest food. *Pepsin* obtained from animals is an ingredient in some medicines

per an•num (per AN-əm). A Latin phrase meaning "by the year"; annually; yearly.– Income taxes are calculated on earnings *per annum.*

per cap•i•ta (per KAP-ə-tə). A Latin phrase meaning "by heads"; for each individual; per person. *Per capita* income or expenditure is found by dividing the total for all people of a group by the number of people in it to get an average for each "head." If ten people have a total yearly income of $24,000, the *per capita* yearly income is $2,400 for each, though some may actually have more and some less. – The *per capita* income in the United States is one of the highest for any country in the world.

per•ceive (per-SEEV) *v. perceives, perceived, perceiving.* 1. Gain knowledge or discover through the senses; see, feel, taste, hear, or smell.–Harry *perceived* that there was sea food in the casserole, but he could not tell what kind.
2. Observe or notice with the mind; understand. – From the way John spoke of Bill, Mary *perceived* that John did not like Bill very much.

per cent (per SENT). Per hundred; hundredths.–One *per cent* [1%] is one out of every hundred, or one hundredth (1/100 or .01).

per•cent•age (per-SENT-ij) *n. percentages.* Per cent of the whole.–A large *percentage* of students was absent; 60% were absent.

perch (PERCH) *n. perches.* 1. A stick or bar on which a bird sits.
2. A high seat of any kind.–From his *perch* on the fence, Jack could watch the ball game.

3. A small fresh-water fish that is good to eat.

–*v. perches, perched, perching.* Sit. – Sally likes to *perch* on the fence.

per•co•la•tor (PER-kə-lay-ter) *n. percolators.* A kind of coffee pot in which water shoots up through a tube and drains back through the ground coffee.

per•cus•sion in•stru•ment (per-KUSH-ən IN-stru-mənt) *percussion instruments.* A musical instrument played by striking. Drums, bells, and cymbals are examples of *percussion instruments.*

per•en•ni•al (per-EN-ee-əl) *n. perennials* and *adj.* A flowering plant that lives from year to year.–Peonies and irises are *perennials.* They bloom every year.

per•fect (per-FEKT) *v. perfects, perfected, perfecting.* Remove all mistakes or faults from.–Bob and Jack are working to *perfect* their model airplane.
–(PER-fikt) *adj.* Completely without faults.–Bob's arithmetic paper was *perfect.* He didn't make a single mistake on it.

per•fect•ly (PER-fikt-lee) *adv.* Completely or entirely.–It is *perfectly* all right for you to go to the movies if you finish your work first.

per•fo•rate (PER-fə-rayt) *v. perforates, perforated, perforating.* Make small holes through something. – Sheets of postage stamps are *perforated* so that they can be torn apart easily.

per•form (per-FORM) *v. performs, performed, performing.* 1. Do.–The boys *performed* their work well.–The dog *performed* the trick at his master's signal.
2. Entertain an audience.–Actors *perform* on the stage.

per•form•ance (per-FORM-ənss) *n. performances.* 1. A show at a theater.–There will be two *performances* of the play tonight.
2. An action or deed.–Jack's *performance* in the play was very good. He did well.

per•form•er (per-FORM-er) *n. performers.* A person who entertains, as by acting, playing an instrument, singing, or dancing.

per•fume (PER-fyoom) *n. perfumes.* 1. A sweet-smelling liquid made from oils that are pressed from plants or obtained from certain animals.–Mother puts a drop of *perfume* behind her ears when she goes out.
2. A sweet odor.–We could smell the *perfume* of flowers in the garden.
–(per-FYOOM) *v. perfumes, perfumed, perfuming.* Make fragrant. – The flowers *perfumed* the air.

per•haps (per-HAPSS) *adv.* Maybe; possibly.–*Perhaps* Father will be home early today.

per•il (PAIR-əl) *n. perils.* Danger.–The ship was in *peril* because of the storm.

per•im•e•ter (pə-RIM-ə-ter) *n. perimeters.* 1. The border of a figure; the circumference of a circle.–The children were told not to go beyond the *perimeter* of the play area.
2. The measure of a perimeter.–Our lot has a *perimeter* of seventy-two feet.

pe•ri•od (PIR-ee-əd) *n. periods.* 1. A dot [.] used in writing and printing. We put a *period* after every sentence and after abbreviations such as Mr., Mrs., Dr.
2. A division of time.–We have reading during the first *period* of school.

per•i•scope (PAIR-ə-skohp) *n. periscopes.* A curved tube which contains mirrors so arranged that one can look into the lower end of the tube and see what is in front of the upper end. *Periscopes* are used in submarines to see what is happening above the surface of the water.

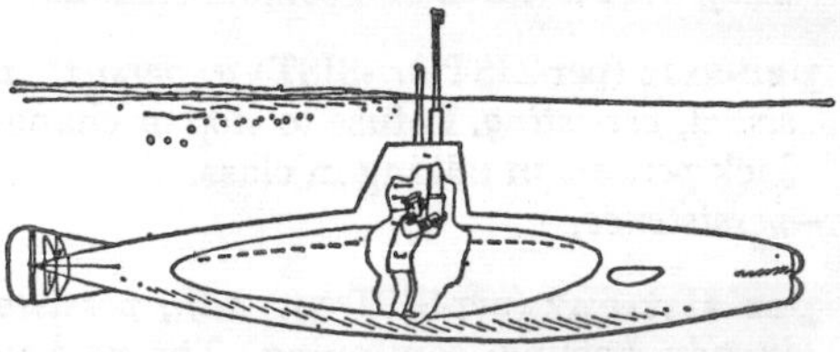

per•ish (PAIR-ish) *v. perishes, perished, perishing.* Die.–Some plants *perish* in winter.

per•ish•a•ble (PAIR-ish-ə-bəl) *adj.* Liable to to become rotten.–Milk and butter are *perishable;* they will spoil unless kept cold.

per•ma•nent (PER-mə-nənt) *adj.; permanently, adv.; permanence, n.* Unchanging; long-lasting; never needing to be replaced.–The dentist put a *permanent* filling in Father's tooth after the temporary one had fallen out.–This is our *permanent* home. We have lived here a long time, and do not intend to move.

per•mis•sion (per-MISH-ən) *n. permissions.* Leave or consent.–The teacher gave Bob *permission* to go to the library. She said he might go right away.

per•mit (PER-mit) *n. permits.* A license, or written permission.–Father has a *permit* to hunt.
–(per-MIT) *v. permits, permitted, permitting.* Allow.–Will you *permit* me to use your pen?

per•pen•dic•u•lar (per-pən-DIK-yə-ler) *adj.; perpendicularly, adv.* 1. In a straight upward position; upright; exactly vertical.–The cliff near the sea rose in a *perpendicular* line.
2. At right angles; one line standing upright on another.–A square has four right angles made by its four *perpendicular* sides.

per•pet•u•al (per-PECH-oo-əl) *adj.; perpetually, adv.* Lasting for all time; never stopping; continuous.–The never-ending flow of water over the falls makes a *perpetual* roar.

per•plex (per-PLEKS) *v. perplexes, perplexed, perplexing.* Confuse; make uncertain about a plan, act, or thought; bewilder; puzzle.–The result of the experiment *perplexed* the scientists. They didn't know what to do next.

per•se•cute (PER-sə-kyoot) *v. persecutes, persecuted, persecuting.* Harm often and unjustly; pick on.–In olden times, people were often *persecuted* because of their beliefs. They were tortured and sometimes killed.

per•sist (per-ZIST *or* -SIST) *v. persists, persisted, persisting.* Refuse to stop or change.–Jack *persists* in talking in class.
–persistence, n.

per•sist•ent (per-SIST-ənt) *adj.; persistently, adv.* Lasting; continuing.–The *persistent* cold finally forced the man to buy a new overcoat.

per•son (PER-sən) *n. persons* or *people.* A human being. – Every *person* should be treated fairly.

per•son•al (PER-sən-əl) *adj.* 1. Private.–Father takes care of his *personal* mail, and his secretary answers his business letters.
2. In person.–Jean made a *personal* request to the teacher today. She spoke to the teacher herself.
3. Of the body.–One's *personal* appearance is the way one looks.

per•son•al•i•ty (per-sən-AL-ə-tee) *n. personalities.* The traits of a person all together; a person's ways and manners.–Mary has a charming *personality.* People like her.

per•son•al•ly (PER-sən-əl-ee) *adv.* 1. In person.–Mother called on our teacher *personally* and asked her for supper.
2. In one's own interest.–*Personally,* I would rather have the picnic in the afternoon.

per•spec•tive (per-SPEK-tiv) *n. perspectives. Perspective* is a way of drawing or painting things so that their relationships in size and space are easy to see.

This picture is not in perspective.

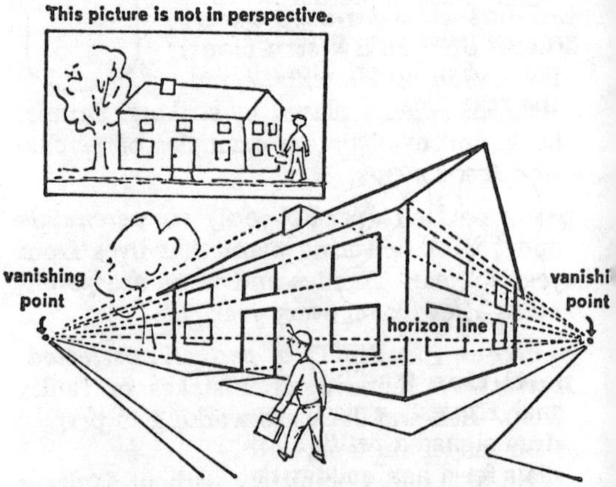

This picture is in perspective.

per•spi•ra•tion (perss-per-AY-shən) *n.* Sweat.–In hot weather, *perspiration* comes out of the skin in large quantities, and often forms large drops.

per•spire (per-SPYR) *v. perspires, perspired, perspiring.* Sweat.–When we *perspire,* drops of water come through the tiny openings of the skin.

per•suade (per-SWAYD) *v. persuades, persuaded, persuading.* Convince by urging; get someone to believe or do something.–At first Father didn't want to go swimming, but we *persuaded* him to come with us.

per•sua•sion (per-SWAY-zhən) *n. persuasions.* The act of persuading.–Bob is good at *persuasion.* He is good at getting people to do things willingly.

per•tain (per-TAYN) *v. pertains, pertained, pertaining.* Relate; have to do with.

pes•si•mist (PESS-ə-mist) *n. pessimists; pessimistic, adj.* A person who sees only the gloomy side of things; one who believes that things are more likely to end in failure than in success, or that evil will triumph over good.–Even though the sun was shining, the *pessimist* said that it would probably rain before the day was over.

pest (PEST) *n. pests.* 1. A nuisance; something or someone who makes trouble.–Bill is a *pest;* he annoys others.
2. Something that causes destruction. – Grasshoppers are *pests.* They destroy many crops.

pet (PET) *n. pets.* 1. An animal kept to love and play with.–Bob's *pet* is a little puppy.
2. Someone who is specially favored.–Jack called Mary a teacher's *pet.*
–*v. pets, petted, petting.* Pat or stroke lovingly. –Sally likes to *pet* her kitten.

pet•al (PET-l) *n. petals.* The colored leaflike parts of a flower.–Rose *petals* fall off when the rose dies.

pe•ti•tion (pə-TISH-ən) *n. petitions.* A formal request, usually written.–All the children signed a *petition* asking the school officials for a half holiday the day of the parade.
–*v. petitions, petitioned, petitioning.* Formally request, usually in writing.–The children *petitioned* the school officials for a half holiday and the request was granted.

pet•ri•fy (PET-rə-fy) *v. petrifies, petrified, petrifying.* 1. Change into stone; harden or give a stony quality to.–In Arizona there is an area of trees that have been *petrified* by nature. It is called the Petrified Forest.
2. Paralyze or freeze with fear.–Mother was *petrified* by the sound of the scream until she realized it had only come from the television set.

pe•tro•le•um (pə-TROH-lee-əm) *n.* The crude oil found in the ground. *Petroleum* is made into kerosene, gasoline, oils, and a great many other products.

pet•ty (PET-ee) *adj. pettier, pettiest.* Small, mean, or unimportant.–The story about the quarrel between the neighbors was just *petty* gossip.

pet•ty of•fi•cer (PET-ee AWF-is-er) *petty officers.* The lowest-ranking officers in the navy, ranking below ensign and warrant officer.

pe•tu•ni•a (pə-TOON-yə *or* pə-TYOON-yə) *n. petunias.* A plant that has many pink, purple, or white blossoms.

pew (PYOO) *n. pews.* A bench or long seat with a high back, used in churches.

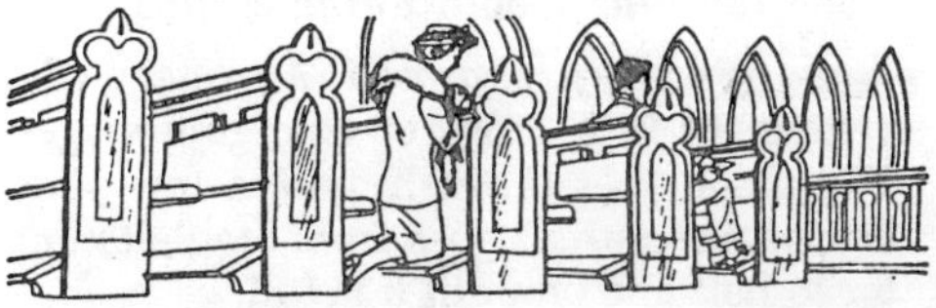

pe•wee (PEE-wee) *n. pewees.* A kind of phoebe that has gray stripes or bars on its wings. The little wood *pewee* says its own name when it calls.

pew•ter (PYOO-ter) *n.* and *adj.* A metal made from tin and lead. *Pewter* usually has more tin than lead in it. It was used in the early days of our country for tableware and eating utensils.

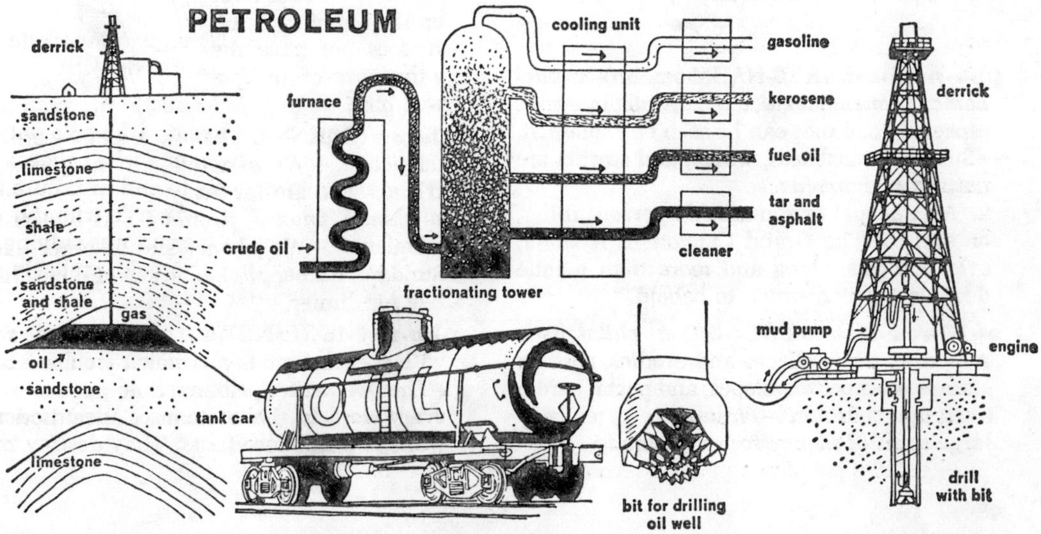

phan·tom (FAN-təm) *n. phantoms.* A ghost; an imaginary likeness of something which a person thinks is real.–In the darkness the dead tree looked like an old woman, but it was only a *phantom.*

Phar·aoh (FAIR-oh) *n. Pharaohs.* A ruler in ancient Egypt. The right to be the *Pharaoh* passed from father to son.

phar·ma·cist (FAHR-mə-sist) *n. pharmacists.* Druggist.–The *pharmacist* mixes different drugs together to make medicines.

phar·ma·cy (FAHR-mə-see) *n. pharmacies.* 1. A drugstore.–The doctor sends a prescription to a *pharmacy* to have medicine made according to his directions.
2. The study of preparing medicine.–The druggist understands *pharmacy.*

phar·ynx (FAR-ingks) *n. pharynges* or *pharynxes.* The part of the alimentary canal that leads from the mouth to the esophagus.

phase (FAYZ) *n. phases.* 1. Any stage of development in a series of changing stages.–The moon goes through quite a few *phases* during a month. It goes from cradle to quarter to half and on until it is full.
2. A part or side of a subject.–The teacher asked the class to examine all *phases* of the question. She said that when they had studied every part of the question, they would be able to answer it.

pheas·ant (FEZ-ənt) *n. pheasants.* A long-tailed game bird. Its feathers are brilliantly colored. Men hunt *pheasants* for food and for sport.

phe·nom·e·non (fi-NAHM-ə-nahn) *n. phenomena; phenomenal, adj.* 1. A fact or event, especially one that can be seen or explained. –Sunshine, darkness, winds, and storms are natural *phenomena.*
2. An unusual or remarkable person, thing, or event. – The Grand Canyon in Arizona, over 200 miles long and more than a mile deep, is a *phenomenon* to behold.

phi·lat·e·list (fi-LAT-ə-list) *n. philatelists.* A person who collects and studies postage stamps, stamped envelopes, and postal cards; a stamp collector. – *Philatelists* often pay large sums of money for rare stamps.

phi·los·o·pher (fi-LAHSS-ə-fer) *n. philosophers; philosophical* or *philosophic, adj.* 1. A person who studies or teaches philosophy; a person who loves and admires wisdom.
2. A person who accepts the hardships of life with calmness, reason, and wisdom.–When Jim said that he did not mind not having a football uniform as the rest of the boys did, Mother said he was a *philosopher.*

phi·los·o·phy (fi-LAHSS-ə-fee) *n. philosophies.* 1. The search for truth and wisdom.–*Philosophy* is concerned with investigating and trying to understand the principles of human nature, behavior, and reality.
2. A set of guiding principles.–Father's *philosophy* is that truth and dignity are the two most important things in the world.
3. A calm and reasonable acceptance of life as it is.–Grandfather always has been able to adjust to hardships and difficulties because of his *philosophy.*

phlox (FLAHKS) *n. phloxes.* A plant that has large clusters of flowers growing on a tall stem. *Phlox* is white, pink, or of mixed colors.

pho·bi·a (FOH-bee-ə) *n. phobias.* Fear or dread of something, especially without good reason. – Aunt Isabel has a *phobia* about mice. She ran out of the room when Johnny tried to show her his pet mouse.

phoe·be (FEE-bee) *n. phoebes.* A small gray bird sometimes called a pewee. A *phoebe* has a dark topknot or crest on the top of its head. It does not have the wing bars of the pewee bird.

phone (FOHN) *n. phones.* A short word for tele*phone.* – We can talk on the *phone* to friends who are far away.
–*v. phones, phoned, phoning.* Talk to over the telephone. – We *phone* Grandmother every Sunday.–Father *phoned* to say he'd be a little late for dinner.

pho·net·ic (fə-NET-ik) *adj.* Having to do with speech sounds and how they are made. –The *phonetic* spellings that appear after every word in this dictionary show how the word is pronounced.

pho•no•graph (FOH-nə-graf) *n. phonographs.* A machine used to make records of sounds, or to play back sounds from records. –The teacher had Mary's song recorded. The record was then played on a *phonograph,* and Mary heard herself sing.

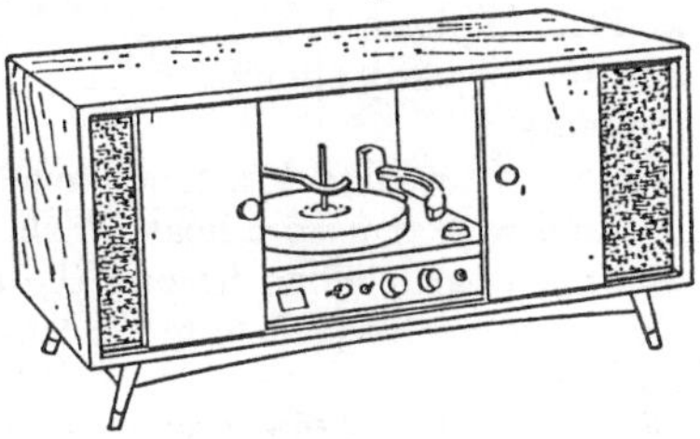

phos•pho•rus (FAHSS-fer-əss) *n.* A poisonous, waxy, chemical element. It has a yellow form that burns easily, shines in the dark, and has an unpleasant smell. There is, also, a red form which does not burn as easily and does not smell as bad. *Phosphorus* is used in fertilizers, in matches, in medicines, and in many other products.

pho•to (FOH-toh) *n. photos.* A short word for *photo*graph.–For Christmas I gave Grandmother a *photo* of myself holding my puppy.

pho•to•graph (FOH-tə-graf) *n. photographs.* A picture made with a camera. A *photograph* is made by light striking a specially prepared film or plate.–Bob brought his camera to school to take a *photograph* of our class.
–*v. photographs, photographed, photographing.* Make a photograph of. – Bob *photographed* our class with his camera.

pho•tog•ra•pher (fə-TAHG-rə-fer) *n. photographers.* A person who takes pictures with a camera.–The *photographer* came to our house to take pictures of Baby.

pho•tog•ra•phy (fə-TAHG-rə-fee) *n.* The art, skill, or business of making pictures with a camera.

pho•to•syn•the•sis (foh-toh-SIN-thə-siss) *n.* The process by which green plants produce sugar and starch from water and carbon dioxide, using sunlight as a source of energy. Only green plants, or those containing chlorophyll, are capable of *photosynthesis.*

phrase (FRAYZ) *n. phrases.* A group of words which go together. Sometimes a *phrase* is used like one word.–"The drawing class is fun." "The drawing class" is a *phrase.*
–*v. phrases, phrased, phrasing.* Divide into phrases.–In reading, it helps you to get the meaning if you *phrase* correctly, or put the words into their right groups.

PHOTOGRAPHY

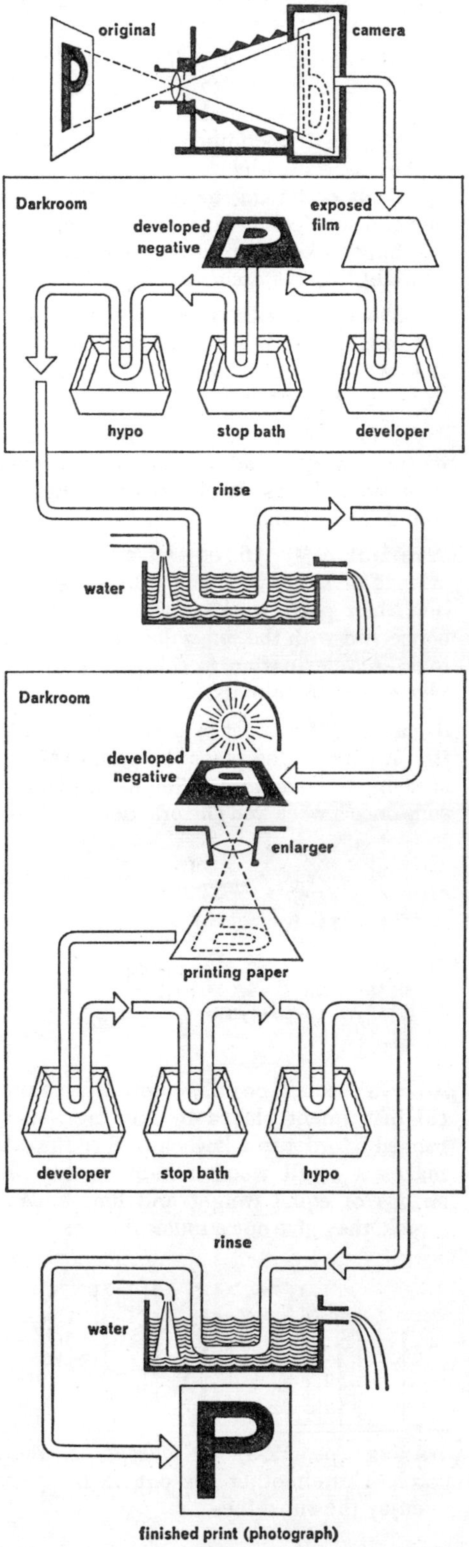

phys•ic (FIZ-ik) *n. physics.* A medicine that makes the bowels move.—Castor oil is used as a *physic.*

phys•i•cal (FIZ-ik-əl) *adj.; physically, adv.* 1. About or having to do with the body.—The doctor gave the children a *physical* examination. He examined their bodies to see if they were healthy.
2. About or having to do with things that one can see, feel, hear, taste, or smell. Natural things, like mountains, wind, rivers, and sunlight, are *physical.*

phy•si•cian (fə-ZISH-ən) *n. physicians.* A doctor of medicine.—When Grandmother was sick, we called a *physician.*—Walter is studying to be a *physician.*

phys•ics (FIZ-iks) *n.* The science or study of matter, energy, and motion. *Physics* deals with such things as electricity, light, heat, sound, and atoms.

phys•i•ol•o•gy (fiz-ee-AHL-ə-jee) *n.* The science or study of living things, especially how their parts work.—A medical doctor is concerned with the *physiology* of human beings.—A veterinarian is concerned with the *physiology* of animals.

pi•an•ist (PEE-ən-ist *or* pee-AN-ist) *n. pianists.* A person who plays the piano.—Mary is studying to be a *pianist.* She takes piano lessons once a week and she practices every day.

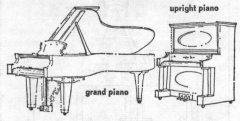

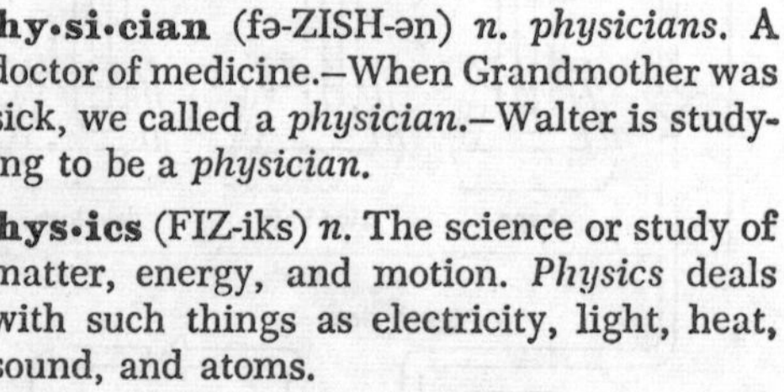

pi•an•o (pee-AN-oh) *n. pianos.* A large musical instrument played by striking keys arranged in order in a keyboard. Striking a key makes a small wooden hammer hit three strings of equal weight and length. When struck, they give out a musical tone.

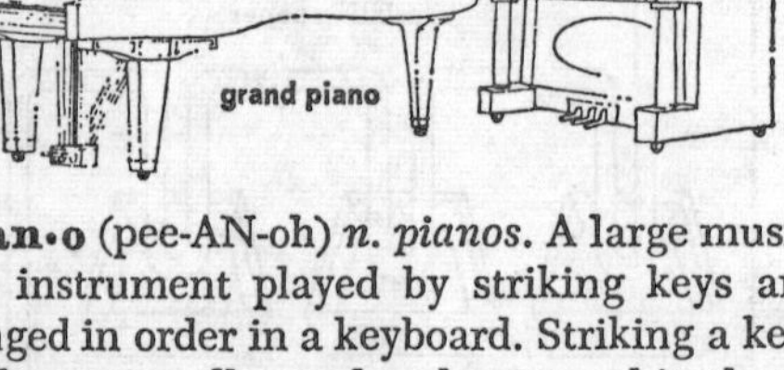

pi•az•za (pee-AZ-ə) *n. piazzas.* A roofed porch.—Grandmother sits out on the *piazza* to enjoy the sunshine.

pic•co•lo (PIK-ə-loh) *n. piccolos.* A small flute. A *piccolo* is played by blowing into a hole on one side of it.

pick (PIK) *n. picks.* 1. A choice.—We arrived at the theater early enough to have our *pick* of the seats.
2. A sharp, pointed tool fastened to a handle.—The road worker used a heavy *pick* to loosen the hard earth when he dug the ditch.—Mother used an ice *pick* to break ice for the lemonade.
—*v. picks, picked, picking.* 1. Choose or select.—Mother finally *picked* a green dress, after looking at several others.
2. Lift.—Mother *picked* up Baby to dress her.
3. Pluck, gather, or pull.—Sally likes to *pick* the flowers.—Mother *picked* the hulls off the strawberries.
4. Remove small pieces from.—It is not polite to *pick* one's teeth.—Grandmother gave Sally a chicken wing to *pick.*
5. Dig with a pick.—The men *picked* a hole in the ice.
6. Gather.—The sled *picked* up speed as it coasted down the hill. It went faster and faster.
7. Learn without studying.—Mary *picked* up some French words from her music teacher.
8. Improve or recover.—The dry plant began to *pick* up after Grandmother watered it.
9. Start or cause.—Bill *picked* a fight with Jack. Bill started the fight.
10. Open without a key.—The burglar *picked* the lock with a hairpin.

pick•ax or **pick•axe** (PIK-aks) *n. pickaxes.* A pick, or long-handled tool, with a heavy head that has a point at one end and a blade at the other.—The workman used a *pickax* to break the hard earth.

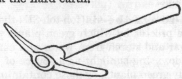

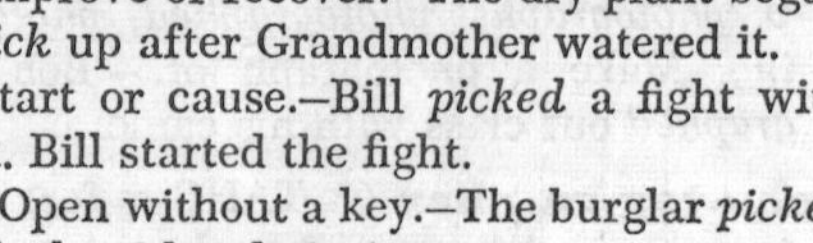

pick•et (PIK-it) *n. pickets.* 1. A pointed stake.—Grandmother's garden has a white fence made of *pickets.*
2. A soldier on guard at a certain place; a sentry or sentinel.—When the attack started, the *pickets* gave the alarm.

3. A worker on strike who marches outside the place of work to keep other workers from going in to work or to keep customers from buying at the place.
–*v. pickets, picketed, picketing.* March as a picket or surround with pickets.–The union men on strike were *picketing* the factory.

pick•le (PIK-əl) *n. pickles.* A vegetable or fruit preserved in vinegar or salt water. – Most *pickles* are made from cucumbers.
–*v. pickles, pickled, pickling.* Preserve in vinegar or salt water, usually with spices.–Mother *pickles* beets, peppers, and many other vegetables.

pick•pock•et (PIK-pahk-it) *n. pickpockets.* A person who steals things out of another person's pockets.–The city police captured a *pickpocket.*

pic•nic (PIK-nik) *n. picnics.* An outdoor party with food.–The teacher and the children went for a *picnic.*
–*v. picnics, picnicked, picnicking.* Take food on an outdoor party; go on a picnic.–We *picnicked* in the woods.

pic•ture (PIK-cher) *n. pictures.* A painting, drawing, or photograph of something.–A *picture* of Abraham Lincoln hangs on the wall.

–*v. pictures, pictured, picturing.* See in the mind; imagine.–Mary said she could not *picture* Bob as a cowboy.

pic•tur•esque (pik-cher-ESK) *adj.* Having the quality of a picture; interesting and colorful; fit for a picture. A *picturesque* sunset is a sunset so beautiful it looks like a picture.

pie (PY) *n. pies.* A baked pastry shell filled with fruit, meat, or sweets.–Mother baked a blackberry *pie.*

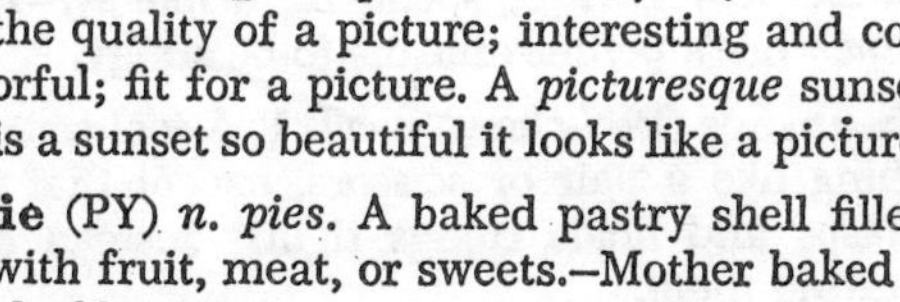

piece (PEESS) *n. pieces.* 1. A part; a bit; a scrap; a chunk.–Mary gave Bob a *piece* of paper.–Please give me a *piece* of cake.
2. One thing of its kind.–A *piece* of poetry is a poem.–A *piece* of music is a song or other complete work of music.
3. An instance; an example. – Losing his money was a *piece* of bad luck for the boy.
–*v. pieces, pieced, piecing.* Put together from small pieces. – Grandmother likes to *piece* quilts from small scraps of cloth.

pier (PIR) *n. piers.* A dock; a landing place for boats and ships.

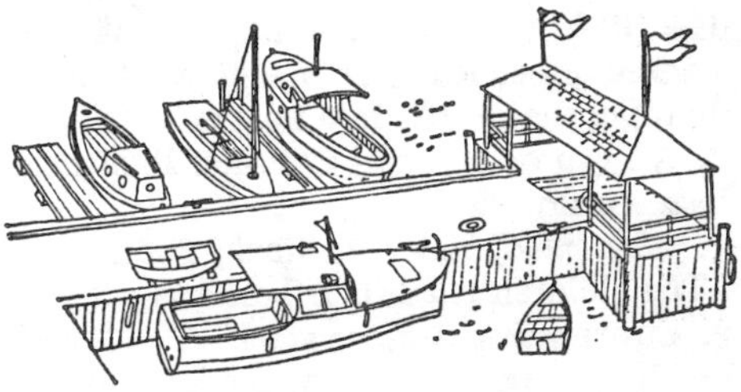

pierce (PIRSS) *v. pierces, pierced, piercing.* 1. Go or thrust through or into.–The chimney *pierces* the roof.–The arrow *pierced* the tree.
2. Stab; make a hole in.–Mother *pierced* the apple with a knife.

pig (PIG) *n. pigs.* 1. A hog, especially a young hog.–Pork is meat from *pigs.*

2. Name sometimes applied to a very greedy or dirty person.

pi•geon (PI-jin) *n. pigeons.* A large bird of the same kind as a dove. – Many *pigeons* live in the city park.

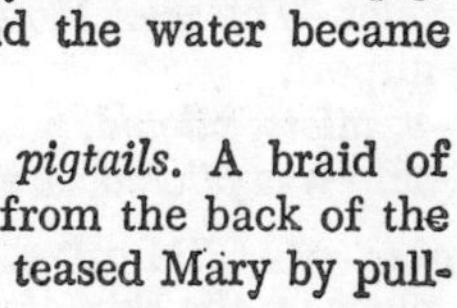

pig•ment (PIG-mənt) *n. pigments.* A substance which gives color to such things as paint, skin, hair; coloring matter. Anything lacking color lacks *pigment.*–John added yellow and blue *pigment* to the water and the water became green.

pig•tail (PIG-tayl) *n. pigtails.* A braid of hair that hangs down from the back of the head.–Sometimes Jack teased Mary by pulling her *pigtails.*

pike (PYK) *n. pikes.* 1. A long, fresh-water fish with a pointed head.

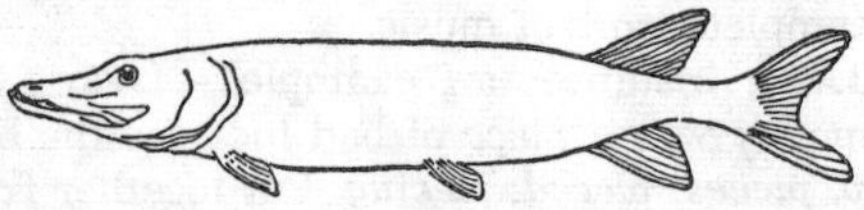

2. A road with a toll gate, or gate where money is collected for use of the road. Many roads that once had toll gates are still called *pikes.*

pile (PYL) *n. piles.* 1. A number of things stacked or heaped up in one place.–The children put their books in a neat *pile.*
2. A heap or mound.–Children like to play in the sand *pile.*
–*v. piles, piled, piling.* 1. Stack; put in a pile. –The children *piled* their books together.
2. Cover with a heap or stack.–The floor beneath the Christmas tree was *piled* with gifts.

pil·grim (PIL-grəm) *n. pilgrims.* 1. A wanderer; a traveler.
2. A person traveling to worship at a religious shrine.–Many *pilgrims* go to Rome each year.
3. (Usually spelled with a capital "P.") One of the English people who came to America in 1620 and built the Massachusetts town called Plymouth.

pill (PIL) *n. pills.* A medicine made into a small ball. Most *pills* are swallowed whole. –The doctor gave Father some *pills.*

pil·lar (PIL-er) *n. pillars.* A heavy post that supports a roof or ceiling.–The roof of the porch is held up by *pillars.*

pil·low (PIL-oh) *n. pillows.* A bag filled with feathers, cotton, or some other soft material, used to rest one's head on when lying down.

pi·lot (PY-lət) *n. pilots.* A person who guides or steers a ship or aircraft.–The ship was met near the harbor and taken into port by a *pilot.*–The *pilot* landed skillfully at the new airport.
–*v. pilots, piloted, piloting.* Guide; steer.–The ship was *piloted* safely through the storm.

pim·ple (PIM-pəl) *n. pimples.* A small, raised place on the skin often filled with pus.

pin (PIN) *n. pins.* 1. A piece of metal or wood shaped so that it can be used to fasten things together. There are safety *pins,* straight *pins,* hair*pins,* clothes*pins,* and other kinds of *pins* for different uses.

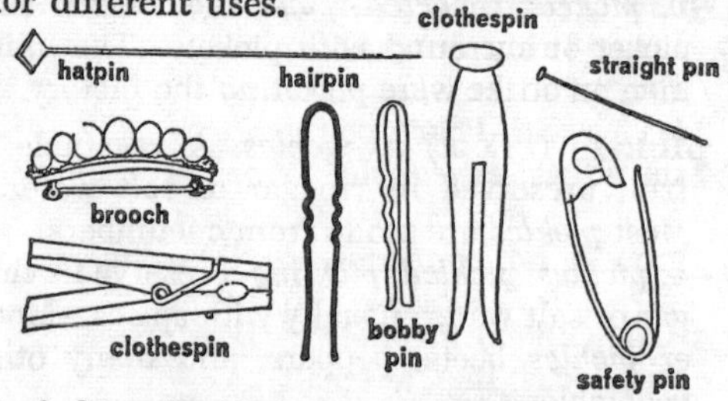

2. A brooch.–Father gave Mother a pearl *pin* for Christmas.
3. A peg.–The boys made a box and fastened it together with wooden *pins.*
4. A wooden piece shaped something like a large bottle.–The game of bowling is played with a bowling ball and ten*pins.*
–*v. pins, pinned, pinning.* Fasten with a pin. –The teacher *pinned* a flower on Mary's coat.

pin·a·fore (PIN-ə-for) *n. pinafores.* An apron made like a low-necked dress without sleeves.–The little girl wore a *pinafore* to keep her new dress clean.

pin·cers (PIN-serz) *n. pl.* Pinchers.

pinch (PINCH) *n. pinches.* A tiny bit.– Mother put a *pinch* of salt into the batter, as much as she could take between the ends of her thumb and first finger.
–*v. pinches, pinched, pinching.* 1. Squeeze between the fingers.–Aunt Ellen *pinched* Baby's cheek.
2. Catch and crush slightly.–Baby pushed the drawer shut and *pinched* her fingers in it. The drawer pressed against her fingers.
3. Be very saving; spend little money.–To *pinch* one's pennies means to be stingy.

pinch·ers (PIN-cherz) *n. pl.* 1. A tool something like a pair of scissors, except that it clasps and holds things tightly instead of cutting them.

2. The claws of crabs, lobsters, and the like. The crab or lobster grabs and pinches with its *pinchers.*

pine (PYN) *n. pines.* An evergreen tree that has long needles for leaves, and cones for seeds. We use the wood of *pine* trees for building.

pine•ap•ple (PYN-ap-əl) *n. pineapples.* A large juicy fruit that has a rough outer skin, and stiff leaves with sharp points along the edges. *Pineapples* grow on a plant, not on a tree. They grow in hot countries.

pink (PINK) *n. pinks.* A flower that smells and looks like a small carnation.–Grandmother has *pinks* in her garden.
–*v. pinks, pinked, pinking.* Notch; cut in little notches along the edges. – The seams of Mary's dress were *pinked* so they wouldn't fray off in threads.
–*adj. pinker, pinkest.* Light red.–Mary has a new *pink* dress.

pin•na•cle (PIN-ə-kəl) *n. pinnacles.* 1. The highest point; the summit.–He is at the *pinnacle* of his career.
2. A towering peak; a high, pointed rock formation.–The *pinnacle* rose thousands of feet into the air.
3. Any high, pointed structure.–Spires, turrets, and steeples are *pinnacles.*

pint (PYNT) *n. pints.* A unit of liquid measure. Milk is measured by the quart, by the *pint,* and by the half *pint.* It takes two *pints* to make a quart.

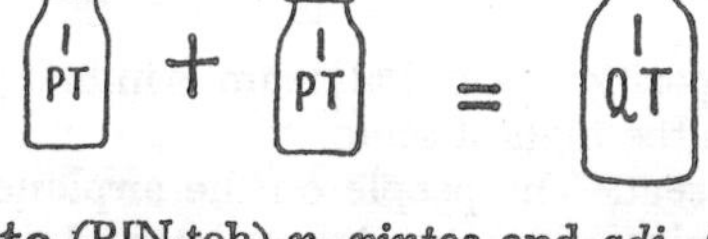

pin•to (PIN-toh) *n. pintos* and *adj.* A black and white horse; a horse having patches of color.

pi•o•neer (py-ə-NIR) *n. pioneers* and *adj.* 1. A person who does something before anyone else does it; one who prepares the way so that others may follow.–Thomas Edison was a *pioneer* in the use of electricity. He started to use it for things it had never been used for before.
2. An early settler; a person who goes to a country or part of a country that has not been lived in before.–Many *pioneers* traveled to California in covered wagons.

pi•ous (PY-əss) *adj.; piously, adv.* Religious; devoted to God.–Our neighbor is a very *pious* man. He spends most of his time in church, studying and praying.

pipe (PYP) *n. pipes.* 1. A smoking device with a small bowl and stem. The bowl is filled with tobacco, which is lit, and the smoker draws the smoke through the stem.

2. A metal tube through which such things as water and gas can move or flow.

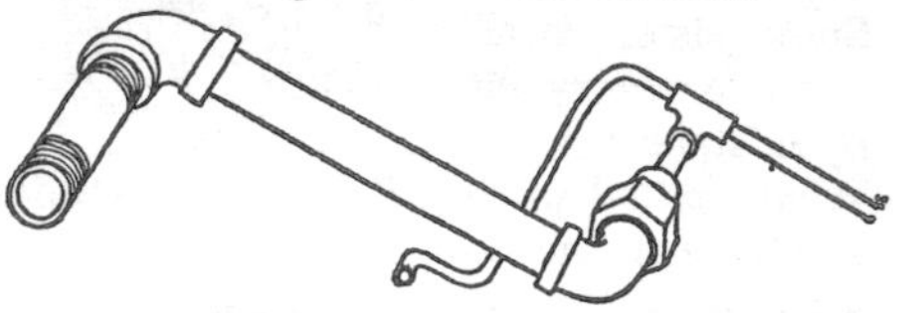

3. A tube.–The music of some organs comes out through *pipes.*
4. A musical instrument played by blowing into it.

–*v. pipes, piped, piping.* Move or convey by pipes.–The farmer *piped* water to his crops.

pi•rate (PY-rət) *n. pirates.* A robber on the seas. In olden times, *pirates* had their own ships, and used to stop and rob other ships.

pis•til (PISS-tl) *n. pistils.* One of the slender little stalks inside the cup of a flower. Insects or the wind bring yellow powder called pollen from other flowers to the *pistils.* With the help of this pollen, seeds develop down inside the *pistils.*

pis•tol (PISS-tl) *n. pistols.* A small hand gun. A revolver is one kind of *pistol.*

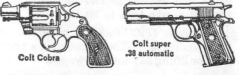

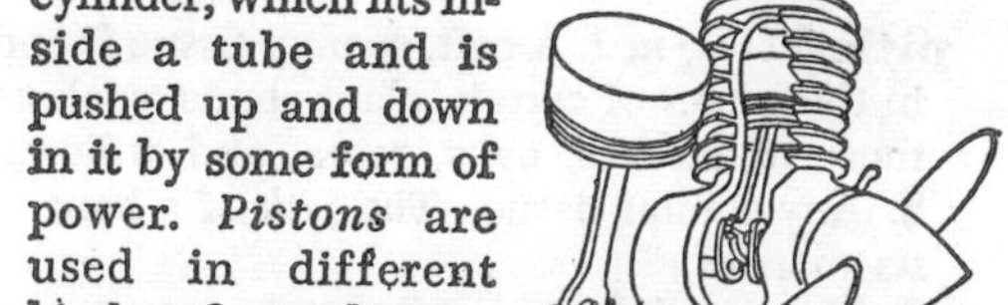

pis•ton (PISS-tən) *n. pistons.* A round piece, shaped like a solid cylinder, which fits inside a tube and is pushed up and down in it by some form of power. *Pistons* are used in different kinds of machinery. There is a *piston* in each cylinder of an automobile engine.

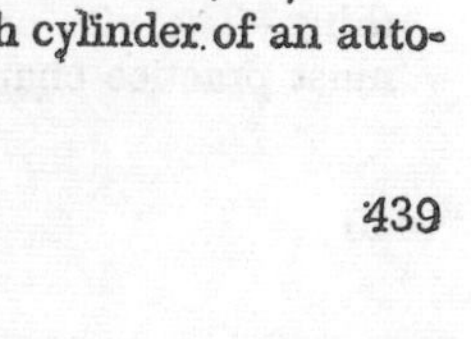

pit (PIT) *n. pits.* 1. A deep hole.–Miners go down into the *pit* to dig coal.

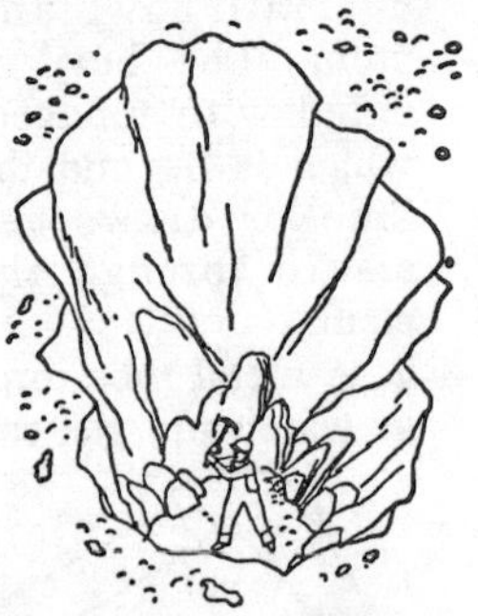

2. Any small hole on a surface. – Chicken pox may leave little *pits* on the skin.
3. The seed or stone of a fruit. – Sue's sister swallowed a cherry *pit* by mistake.
–*v. pits, pitted, pitting.* Put holes in.–Chicken pox may *pit* the skin.

pitch (PICH) *n. pitches* and *adj.* 1. A certain point. – Mary's excitement at the theater reached its highest *pitch* just before the curtain went up.
2. A tone; the highness or depth of a sound. –The singing teacher gives us the *pitch* with her *pitch*pipe.
3. A thick, black, tarlike substance used on the cracks in road pavements, to mend leaks in boats, and for other similar repairs.
–*v. pitches, pitched, pitching.* 1. Rock violently.–The ship *pitched* in the storm.
2. Throw; toss.–The boy *pitched* his hat into the car.
3. Put up; erect.–The campers *pitched* their tent for the night.

pitch•blende (PICH-blend) *n.* A dark brownish-black mineral. Uranium and radium are obtained from *pitchblende.*

pitch•er (PICH-er) *n. pitchers.* 1. A container used for pouring out liquids. The lip on a *pitcher* makes pouring easy.

2. The player in a baseball game who throws the ball to the batter, who tries to hit it.

pitch•fork (PICH-fork) *n. pitchforks.* A long-handled fork.–The farmer uses a *pitchfork* for lifting hay onto the wagon.

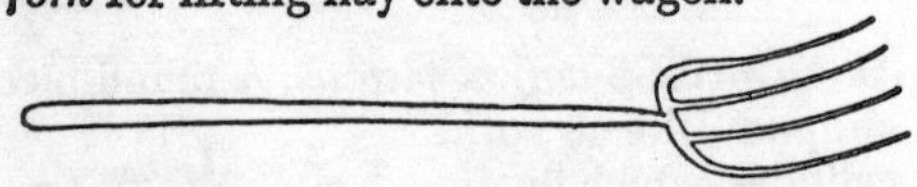

pith (PITH) *n.* 1. A soft, spongy tissue found in the center of certain plant stems, such as those of birches, oaks, roses, and willows.
2. Any similar tissue.–The *pith* of a bone is its marrow.
3. The most important or vital part of anything.–The *pith* of his lecture was that we must practice charity daily.

pit•i•ful (PIT-ə-fuhl) *adj.; pitifully, adv.* Making one feel pity; sad; piteous. – The crippled old horse was a *pitiful* sight.

pi•tu•i•tar•y gland (pi-TOO-ə-tair-ee *or* pi-TYOO-ə-tair-ee gland) *pituitary glands.* A small, two-lobed, oval gland located at the base of the brain. The *pituitary gland* is believed to influence bone growth, blood pressure, and the actions of certain muscles.

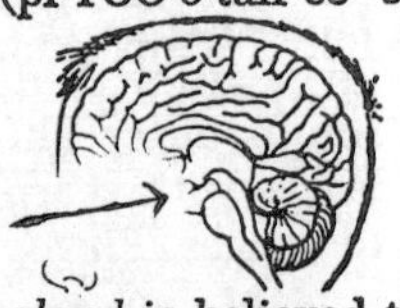

pit•y (PIT-ee) *n.* A feeling of how sad someone else's trouble is.–The stranger did not want *pity.* He didn't want people to feel sorry for him.
–*v. pities, pitied, pitying.* Feel sorry for or sympathize with someone who has trouble.– We *pity* people who are crippled or blind, or who have other misfortunes.

piv•ot (PIV-ət) *v. pivots, pivoted, pivoting.* Turn or swing (on).–A door *pivots* on a hinge. –A person *pivots* on his heel.

place (PLAYSS) *n. places.* 1. Where someone or something belongs, or usually is. – The children stood in their *places.* They stood where they usually stand. – Your home or house is your *place* of residence.–A building where people work is their *place* of business.
2. A city, town, country, or other region or location.–The teacher asked us to find several *places* on the map
3. A part; a spot.–One *place* in the apple was rotten.
4. A position.–Our ball team is in first *place.* It has the highest score.
5. A seat.–The people on the airplane took their *places* and the airplane started.
6. A duty.–It is a father's *place* to care for his family.
7. A job; work.–Bob has a *place* for the summer in the drugstore.
8. A home.–Every summer my parents rent a *place* at the seashore.
–*v. places, placed, placing.* 1. Put. – Father *placed* the gifts under the Christmas tree.
2. Find a job for.–The school helped *place* Bob in the drugstore for the summer.

plack•et (PLAK-it) *n. plackets.* The opening in a skirt or dress that makes it easy to pull over the head. Some *plackets* close with zippers, others have snaps.

pla·gi·a·rize (PLAY-jer-yz) *v. plagiarizes, plagiarized, plagiarizing.* 1. Present another's work as one's own. Someone who *plagiarizes* copies another's writings or work of art line for line.–The teacher realized that parts of Billy's composition had been copied word for word from the encyclopedia. She told Billy that she was giving him a failing mark because he had *plagiarized.*
2. Copy another's ideas and present them as one's own.–John *plagiarized* the plot for his story. He didn't make it up himself, but he took it from a play he'd seen.
–*plagiarism, n.*

plague (PLAYG) *n. plagues.* 1. A very contagious and deadly disease; an epidemic.–It has been estimated that about 25 million persons died in Europe during the *plagues* of the fourteenth century, known as the period of the Black Death.
2. Something which causes great suffering. –Floods, famine, and disease are *plagues.*

plaid (PLAD) *n. plaids* and *adj.* A pattern of stripes arranged to form checks or squares as they cross each other.–Mary has a *plaid* suit.

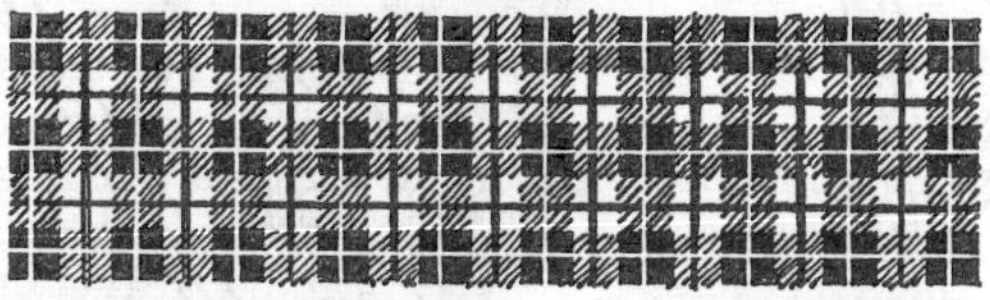

plain (PLAYN) *n. plains.* A stretch of flat, level country.–Many cattle feed on the grassy *plains* of the West.
–*adj. plainer, plainest; plainly, adv.* 1. Clear; easy to understand, see, hear.–The teacher made the directions very *plain.*–The light in the house was quite *plain* from the road. –The noise in the cellar was *plain* to us all.
2. Simple; ordinary. – Mary wore a *plain* dress, one without trimming.–We eat *plain* food. It isn't fancy or rich.–The people living in this town are very *plain* people. They are not rich or elegant.
3. Not good-looking.–That boy is *plain,* but honest and good.
4. Frank and honest.–After the fight on the playground, the teacher gave us a *plain* talk. She said just what she thought.

plain·tive (PLAYN-tiv) *adj.; plaintively, adv.* Sad; mournful; melancholy; showing sorrow.–The first night the new puppy was left alone in the kitchen, his *plaintive* cries kept the whole family awake.–The boy sang a *plaintive* song as he strummed his guitar.

plait (PLAT *or* PLAYT) *n. plaits.* A braid.–This girl has *plaits* of hair.
–*v. plaits, plaited, plaiting.* Make into a braid. – The children *plaited* the straw to make two baskets.

plan (PLAN) *n. plans.* 1. An idea worked out for what one is going to do. – We have made *plans* for Christmas. We know what we are going to do, where we are going, and what gifts we shall buy.
2. A drawing.–Father has the *plans* for our new home. The *plans* show just where and how large each room, window, door, and closet will be.

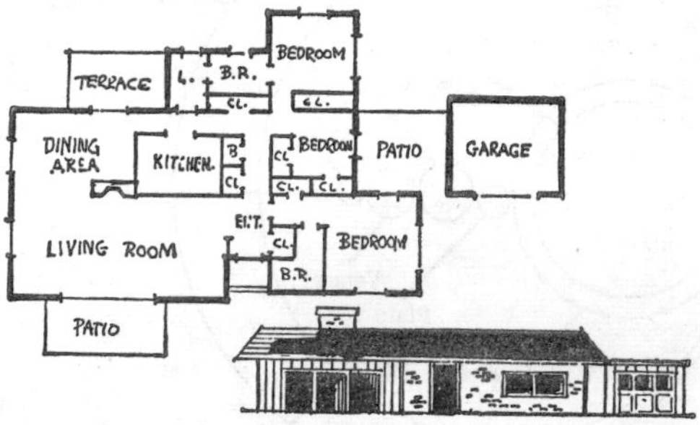

–*v. plans, planned, planning.* Work out in advance; think up a way of doing something. –The boys *plan* their work. Before they start their work, they decide how it should be done, which things should be done first, second, and so on, and what things will be needed.

plane (PLAYN) *n. planes.* 1. A tool with a sharp blade used to smooth wood and metal.–The door was too large, so the carpenter used a *plane* to shave off a little of the wood to make the door fit the frame.

2. An air*plane* is often called a *plane.*

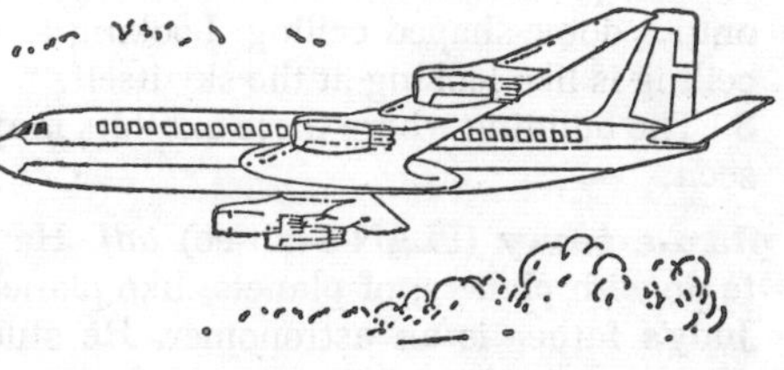

–*v. planes, planed, planing.* Make smooth with a plane.–Father *planed* the edge of the box.
–*adj.* Flat.–The top of a table, or desk, is a *plane* surface.

PLANET

AVERAGE DISTANCES OF THE PLANETS FROM THE SUN

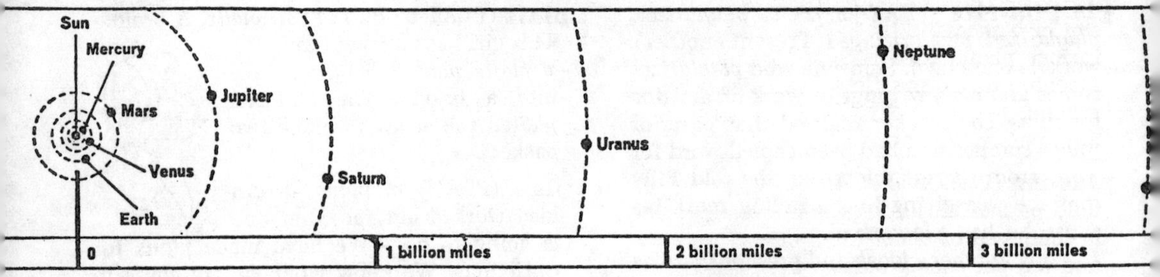

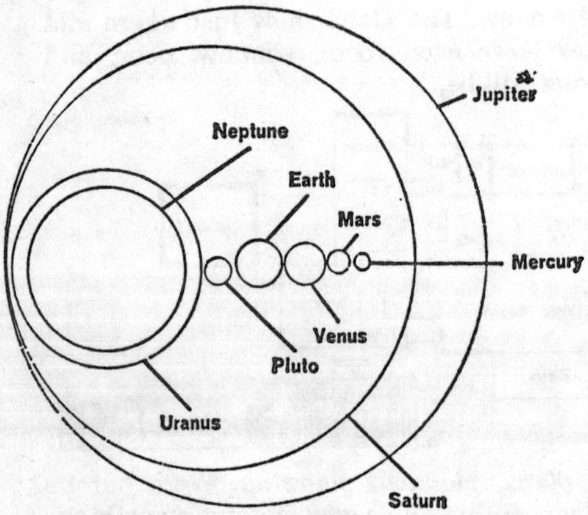

COMPARATIVE SIZES OF THE PLANETS

PLANETARIUM

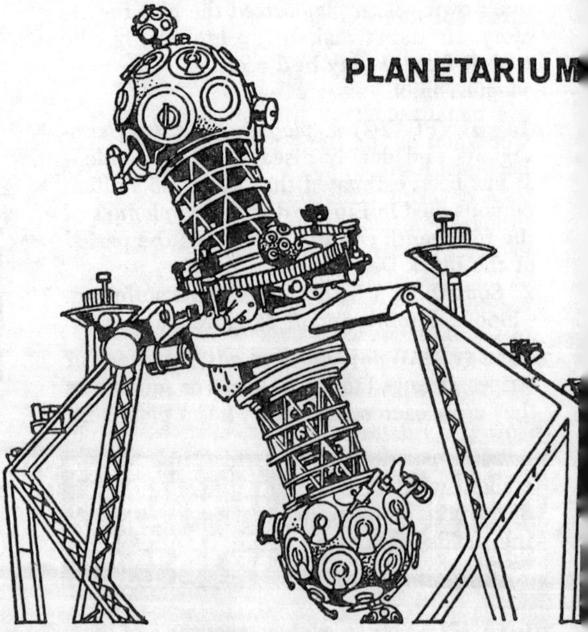

plan•et (PLAN-ət) *n. planets.* A large solid body that revolves around our sun or another star.–Mars is a *planet.*

plan•e•tar•i•um (plan-ə-TAIR-ee-əm) *n. planetariums.* 1. A model of the sun, moons, planets, and other heavenly bodies, showing them in their orbits.
2. A machine which projects the sun, moons, planets, and other heavenly bodies onto a dome-shaped ceiling. Looking at this ceiling is like looking at the sky itself.
3. The building where these exhibits may be seen.

plan•e•tar•y (PLAN-ə-tair-ee) *adj.* Having to do with planets; of planets; like planets.–Judy's father is an astronomer. He studies *planetary* motion.

plan•et•oid (PLAN-ə-toid) *n. planetoids.* A heavenly body that is like a planet; a small planet; an asteroid.–Many *planetoids* circle in orbits between the two planets Mars and Jupiter.

plank (PLANGK) *n. planks.* A wide, flat board or piece of lumber.–The bridge was made of *planks.*

plant (PLANT) *n. plants.* 1. A tree, shrub, grass, flower, vegetable, grain, or other living thing that grows in the earth, water, or air. Animals are not *plants.*
2. A factory with machinery and tools for making things.–Bill's father works in an automobile *plant.*
–*v. plants, planted, planting.* 1. Put into the ground to grow.–If you *plant* flower seeds in the spring, and take care of them, you will have flowers in the summer.
2. Set firmly.–The dog *planted* himself in front of the stove. He put himself down in front of the stove and stayed there.

plan•ta•tion (plan-TAY-shən) *n. plantations.* A large farm on which cotton, sugar, or other large crops are raised and cared for by workers who live on the farm.–There are many *plantations* in the South.

plant·er (PLANT-er) *n. planters.* 1. A person or a machine that plants seeds. — The farmer plants corn with a corn *planter,* a machine that drops the corn seeds into the ground.
2. A person who owns or runs a plantation.

plas·ma (PLAZ-mə) *n.* The almost colorless fluid part of blood or lymph.—Blood *plasma* is composed of about ninety per cent water and ten per cent proteins, salts, sugar, and other substances.

plas·ter (PLAST-er) *n. plasters.* 1. A mixture of lime, sand, and water. The walls in houses are usually covered with *plaster. Plaster* is wet when put on the walls. When it dries, it becomes hard.
2. A covering with some sort of medicine or preparation inside, used to ease pain.—Father put a *plaster* on his sore arm.
—*v. plasters, plastered, plastering.* 1. Put plaster on.—We saw a man *plastering* the walls of the new house.
2. Cover thickly.—After the rain, our car was *plastered* with mud.

plas·ter of Par·is (PLAS-ter əv PAR-iss). A white powdered substance which forms a cement when it is mixed with water. *Plaster of Paris* hardens quickly. It is used for making molds and casts.

plas·tic (PLAS-tik) *n. plastics* and *adj.* Any of many substances which can be molded or shaped when they are hot and which harden as they cool.—*Plastics* are often used instead of wood, metal, or glass in the manufacture of such things as toys, tools, frames, handles, and decorative materials.

plate (PLAYT) *n. plates.* 1. A flat dish that has slightly turned-up edges.—We eat from *plates.*

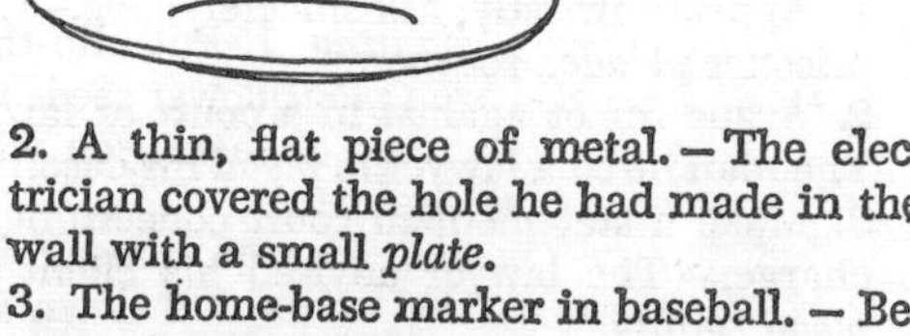

2. A thin, flat piece of metal. — The electrician covered the hole he had made in the wall with a small *plate.*
3. The home-base marker in baseball. — Because the catcher's foot was off the *plate,* the runner was safe.
—*v. plates, plated, plating.* Cover with a thin coat of a substance different from that of which the article is made.—Mother told the jeweler to *plate* the cup with silver.

PLANTS

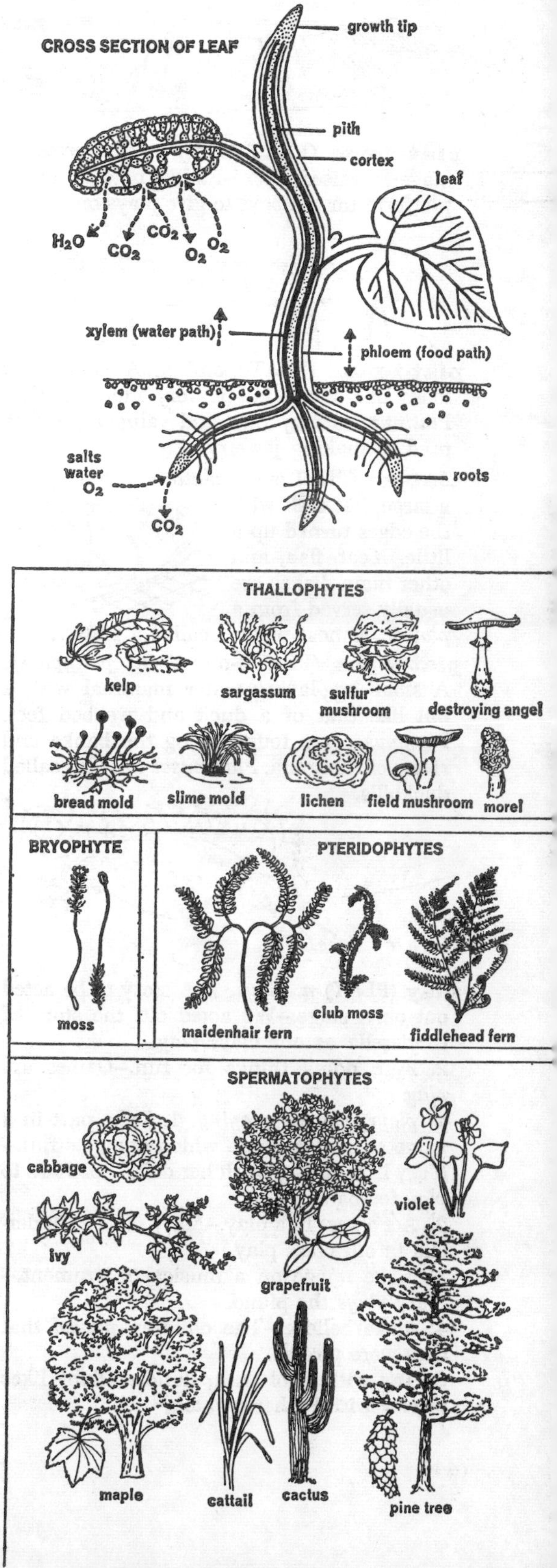

pla·teau (pla-TOH) *n. plateaus.* A high, flat-topped stretch of land.

plat·form (PLAT-form) *n. platforms.* A stage; a raised floor.–Father made a small *platform* for the boys to give plays on.

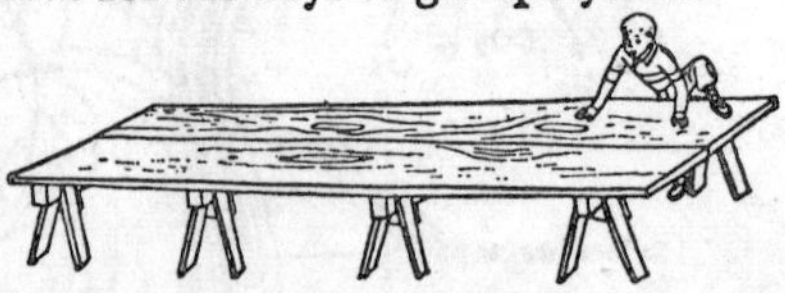

plat·i·num (PLAT-n-əm) *n.* A metal that looks like silver, but is very much harder. *Platinum* is very rare and valuable, and is used in making jewelry.

plat·ter (PLAT-er) *n. platters.* A long plate; a large, flat dish with the edges turned up a little. Meat, fish, and other main dishes are usually served from a *platter.* A meat plate is called a *platter.*

plat·y·pus (PLAT-ə-puhss) *n. platypuses.* A small egg-laying water mammal with a bill like that of a duck and webbed feet. *Platypuses* are found along the banks and rivers of Australia. *Platypuses* are also called duckbills.

play (PLAY) *n. plays.* 1. A story to be acted out on a stage.–We acted out the story of Cinderella as our class *play.*

2. Fun; doing things for fun.–Games are *play.*

–*v. plays, played, playing.* 1. Take part in a game or activity from which one gets fun.–Mary likes to *play* with her doll.–Bob likes to *play* football.

2. Act a part in a play.–Mary *played* Cinderella in our class play.

3. Make music on a musical instrument.–Mary *plays* the piano.

4. Make believe.–The children *played* that they were pirates.

5. Toy with; fool with; handle.–Baby likes to *play* with Father's watch.

play·er (PLAY-er) *n. players.* One who plays. –Babe Ruth was a ball *player.* He played baseball.–Bobby Jones was a golf *player.* He played golf. – Mary is a good piano *player.*

play·ful (PLAY-fuhl) *adj.; playfully, adv.; playfulness, n.* Full of fun.–Bob's dog is very *playful.*

play·ground (PLAY-grownd) *n. playgrounds.* A piece of ground set aside for games. – Children play on the *playground* next to the school.

play·house (PLAY-howss) *n. playhouses.* 1. A small house for children to play in. – Father built a *playhouse* for Sally in the back yard.

2. A theater.–We saw the play at the new *playhouse.*

play·mate (PLAY-mayt) *n. playmates.* A child who plays with another. – Mary and Jane have been *playmates* since they were babies.

play·thing (PLAY-thing) *n. playthings.* Something to play with; a toy.–The children sent many of their *playthings* to other children who had none.

pla·za (PLAH- *or* PLA-zə) *n. plazas.* An open public area or square in a city or town.–The *plaza* was gaily decorated for the holiday. There were ribbons strung on the lampposts around it and there was a platform in the middle where the band played.

plead (PLEED) *v. pleads, pleaded, pleading.* 1. Appeal earnestly; ask sincerely; beg.–The prisoner *pleaded* for mercy.

2. Argue for or against in a court of law.–The man hired a lawyer to *plead* his case.

3. Make a statement in court concerning a charge. – The lawyer advised his client to *plead* "guilty."

pleas·ant (PLEZ-ənt) *adj.; pleasantly, adv.; pleasantness, n.* 1. Joyful; delightful.–We went for a *pleasant* ride. It gave us much pleasure.

2. Fair and bright.–Today is certainly a

pleasant day. The sun is shining, and it isn't too cold or too hot.
3. Friendly and agreeable.–Grandmother is a very *pleasant* person.

please (PLEEZ) *v. pleases, pleased, pleasing.*
1. Give enjoyment to. – The clowns at the circus *please* the children. They bring pleasure to the children.
2. Choose; wish.–The teacher told the children they might do as they *pleased* for a while. They might do anything they wanted to do.
3. Most people say *please* when they want to ask something politely.–When Mary asks for things, she says *please.* – *Please,* may I sit here?
4. Satisfy. – The grocer tries to *please* us when we buy food at his store.

pleas•ure (PLEZH-er) *n. pleasures.* 1. Joy; delight.–It was a *pleasure* to receive so many letters from my friends.
2. Amusement. – The sick man's greatest *pleasure* is in reading his books.

pleat (PLEET) *n. pleats.* A pressed fold. – Mary has a new skirt with *pleats.*

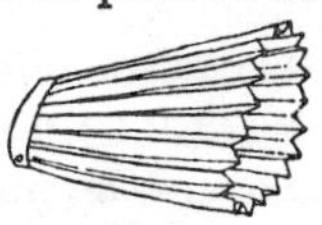

–*v. pleats, pleated, pleating.* Make pleats in.–Mother *pleated* the skirt with a hot iron.

pledge (PLEJ) *n. pledges.* A promise; word of honor.–I give my *pledge* that I will be loyal to the flag.
–*v. pledges, pledged, pledging.* Promise; swear.–I *pledge* allegiance to the flag.–Father *pledged* fifty dollars to the Community Chest. He promised to give that much money.

plen•ti•ful (PLEN-tə-fuhl) *adj.; plentifully, adv.* In great quantities.–Peaches are *plentiful* this year. There are many, all that people want.

plen•ty (PLEN-tee) *n.* 1. Enough; all that is needed.–There isn't much paper, but we have *plenty* to finish the work.
2. A great deal; an abundance.–The farmer's crops were large because there was *plenty* of sunshine and rain.–On the first Thanksgiving Day the Pilgrims gave thanks for peace and *plenty.*–In times of *plenty,* save for poorer days.

pli•a•ble (PLY-ə-bəl) *adj.* 1. Easily bent or twisted; flexible.–Copper wire is *pliable.*
2. Easily influenced; adaptable.–The young man is *pliable.* He will do anything you tell him to, even if it's something silly.

pli•ers (PLY-erz) *n. pl.* A tool used to hold, turn, cut, or bend wire or other materials. – Father used the *pliers* to hold the bolt while he tightened the nut.

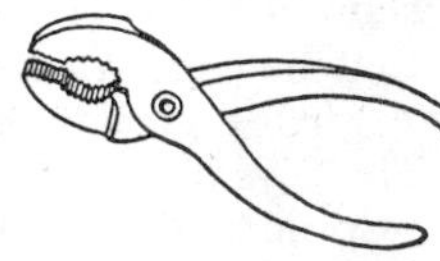

plight (PLYT) *n. plights.* A very difficult, sad, or unfortunate situation.–When Father lost the keys to his car, he was in a sorry *plight.*

plod (PLAHD) *v. plods, plodded, plodding.* Walk with slow, heavy steps.–We heard the tired horse *plodding* along the road toward the farmyard.

plot (PLAHT) *n. plots.* 1. A small piece of ground; a lot.–Father gave Mary a *plot* in the corner of the garden so that she might raise flowers.–Some land near the city has been divided up into *plots* for new, moderately-priced houses.
2. A secret plan, usually a wicked one.–The bandits had a *plot* to kill their own leader.
3. A plan of action.–Stories and plays have *plots.* The *plot* is what happens in the story or play.
4. A sketch; a drawing.–The boys made a *plot* of the baseball field.
–*v. plots, plotted, plotting.* 1. Map out.–They *plotted* the baseball field. They marked off the positions of the bases, the base paths, home plate, and the pitcher's mound.
2. Plan to do something secretly.–The spies *plotted* to destroy the bridge.

plow or **plough** (PLOW) *n. plows* or *ploughs.* A farm tool with a sharp blade, used to turn over the earth so that the farmer can plant or sow seeds. *Plows* are pulled by horses or oxen, or worked by tractors.

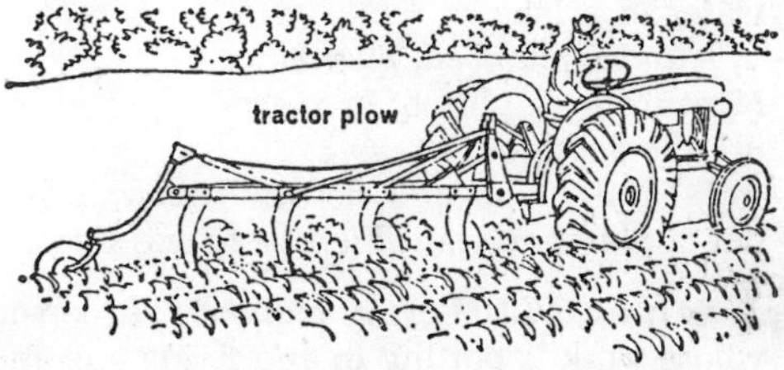

–*v. plows* or *ploughs, plowed* or *ploughed, plowing* or *ploughing.* 1. Turn over the earth in.–The farmer *plows* his fields early in the spring.
2. Make a path by pushing.–We *plowed* our way through the crowd at the Fourth of July parade.

pluck (PLUK) *n.* Courage; bravery.–Harry showed *pluck* by getting back on the horse that had thrown him.
–*v. plucks, plucked, plucking.* Pick; pull off.–The boys *plucked* apples from the apple tree. –Grandfather killed a chicken and *plucked* its feathers.

pluck·y (PLUK-ee) *adj. pluckier, pluckiest; pluckily, adv.* Brave; courageous. – It was *plucky* of Mary to defend the little girl whom the others were teasing.

plug (PLUG) *n. plugs.* 1. A piece of wood, metal, or other substance pushed tightly into a hole to stop it up.
2. An electrical connection.–Mother put the *plug* into the outlet to connect the vacuum cleaner so it would run.
–*v. plugs, plugged, plugging.* Stop up.–Father *plugged* the hole in the pipe with a rag.

plum (PLUM) *n. plums.* 1. A fruit that grows on a tree. *Plums* are red, green, purple, or yellow. They are good to eat.
2. A raisin, when used for cooking, as in a pudding.
–*adj.* A purplish-blue color. – Mother has a *plum* dress.

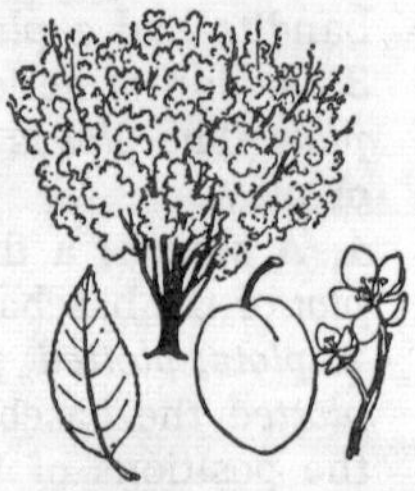

plum·age (PLOOM-ij) *n.* A coat of feathers. –Our parakeet's *plumage* is green, blue, and yellow.

plumb (PLUM) *n. plumbs.* A weight fastened to a cord. – The mason used a *plumb* to see if the wall was straight.–A *plumb* is also used to measure the depth of water in a lake.
–*v. plumbs, plumbed, plumbing.* Measure by a plumb, or measure the depth of.
–*adj.* Straight up and down.–The wall was out of *plumb*. It leaned a little to one side.

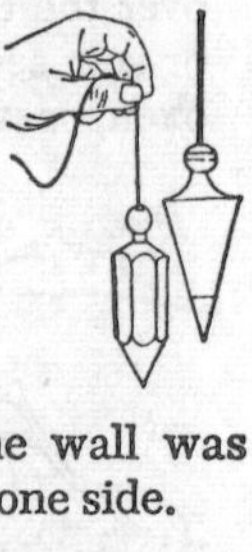

plumb·er (PLUM-er) *n. plumbers.* A person whose work is putting in and fixing gas and water pipes, bathroom fixtures, kitchen sinks. –A *plumber* put in our new hot-water heater.

plumb·ing (PLUM-ing) *n.* 1. Fixing and putting in pipes, bathroom fixtures, kitchen sinks, etc.; what a plumber does.
2. A system of water pipes and drain pipes. –The *plumbing* in our bathroom needs repair.

plume (PLOOM) *n. plumes; plumed, adj.* A fine, beautiful, and fluffy feather, like those used to trim hats.

plump (PLUMP) *adj. plumper, plumpest.* Chubby; rather fat.–Our baby is *plump*.

plun·der (PLUN-der) *n.* 1. Stolen goods.–The *plunder* was recovered from the robbers' camp.
2. Looting; robbing on a large scale.–Pirates made a profession of *plunder*.
–*v. plunders, plundered, plundering.* Rob, especially in groups.–The pirates *plundered* the town. They stole everything they wanted from the people.

plunge (PLUNJ) *n. plunges.* 1. A dive; a quick swim.–Bob took a *plunge* in the lake.
2. A sudden dip or descent.–The stock market took a *plunge* in 1929.
–*v. plunges, plunged, plunging.* 1. Dive.–The boys *plunged* into the water for a swim.
2. Push (into something).–Baby *plunged* her hand into the glass of milk.
3. Rush.–The children *plunged* out of the classroom when the bell rang.

plu·ral (PLUHR-əl) *n. plurals* and *adj.* More than one.–The word "baby" means one baby. The word "babies" means more than one baby. "Babies" is the *plural* of the word "baby."

plus (PLUSS) *adj.* Somewhat more; somewhat higher.–Mary had B minus in arithmetic, but Bob had B *plus*.
–*conj.* 1. Added to. – Five *plus* two equals seven. Five with two added to it equals seven. The sign + stands for *plus*. It means to add.
2. And.–The doctor said that some sunshine *plus* a little rest would make Grandmother feel better.

plush (PLUSH) *n.* A heavy cloth something like velvet, but softer. – The cushions in Father's chair are covered with *plush*.

Plu·to (PLOO-toh) *n.* 1. The ancient Greek god of the dead and the lower world. *Pluto,* also known as Hades, was supposed to be without pity or mercy.
2. The most distant planet in our solar system. *Pluto,* discovered in 1930, is ninth in order of distance from the sun.

plu·to·ni·um (ploo-TOH-nee-əm) *n.* A radioactive element first isolated in 1940 in experiments with uranium. *Plutonium* has been used in the atomic bomb and in other devices that use atomic energy.

ply (PLY) *v. plies, plied, plying.* 1. Make use of; work at or with.–The carpenter *plies* his trade to support his family.
2. Supply with, often and repeatedly.–The furnace must be *plied* with fuel to heat the building.
3. Travel back and forth regularly, usually over a set route.–The old steamboat has been *plying* the river from end to end for years.
4. Press someone (with something).–The detective *plied* the suspected holdup man with questions.

ply•wood (PLY-wuhd) *n.* Board made by gluing together thin layers of wood under heat and pressure. *Plywood* is generally much stronger than ordinary wood of the same thickness. *Plywood* is often used in the construction of furniture.

pneu•mat•ic (noo- *or* nyoo-MAT-ik) *adj.* Having to do with air; worked by air; filled with air.–The workman is using a *pneumatic* drill.–Automobiles have *pneumatic* tires.

pneu•mo•ni•a (noo- *or* nyoo-MOH-nyə *or* -ni-ə) *n.* A disease that affects the lungs.

poach (POHCH) *v. poaches, poached, poaching.* 1. Prepare eggs by breaking into boiling water and cooking till the yolks and whites are set.–The nurse *poached* an egg for Grandmother.
2. Trespass on someone's property in order to hunt or fish illegally.–He was *poaching* and had killed a fine deer when the police caught him.

pock•et (PAHK-it) *n. pockets* and *adj.* 1. A bag sewed into or onto one's coat, dress, or other clothing.–Boys carry marbles in their *pockets*.–Men carry money and papers in their *pockets*.
2. Any small bag that is attached to something to hold small articles.–Father's golf bag has a *pocket* for golf balls.
3. A hole in the ground where minerals are found.
–*v. pockets, pocketed, pocketing.* Put into one's pocket.–The man *pocketed* the money.

pock•et•book (PAHK-it-buhk) *n. pocketbooks.* 1. A purse, often made of leather, used for carrying money. It is small enough to go into one's pocket.

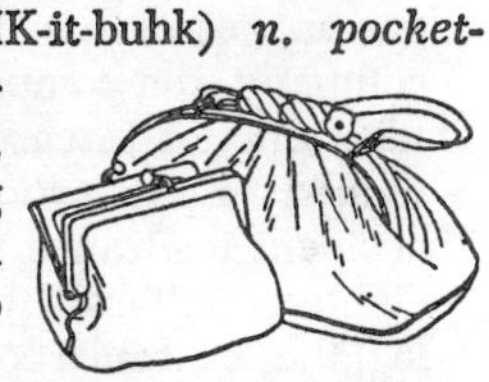

2. A lady's handbag is often called a *pocketbook.*

pod (PAHD) *n. pods.* The seed case of a plant. Peas and lima beans grow in *pods.*

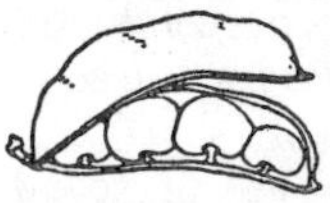

po•em (POH-əm) *n. poems.* A piece of poetry; a rhythmic and usually rhymed piece of writing. A *poem* is usually serious in intention, as contrasted with light verse or rhyme.

po•et (POH-ət) *n. poets.* A person who writes poetry.–Robert Louis Stevenson was a famous children's *poet.* He wrote poems for children.

po•et•ic (poh-ET-ik) *adj.; poetically, adv.* 1. Of poetry.–A ballad is a *poetic* form. It is one kind of poetry.
2. Like poetry; in beautiful language. –Grandmother found the minister's sermon on loving one's neighbor very *poetic.*

po•et•ry (POH-ə-tree) *n.* Writing which has a certain rhythm, often in lines that rhyme. *Poetry* is arranged in lines to show its rhythm. *Poetry* is most often intended to describe a serious mood or an experience or to tell a story which could not be conveyed so well in any other way. Light verse or nonsense rhymes are not usually considered *poetry.*

point (POINT) *n. points.* 1. A narrow tip; a sharp end.–The pin has a flat head at one end and a sharp *point* at the other.–The town was on a *point* of land reaching into the sea.
2. A use; a reason.–Jack sees no *point* in practicing on his violin because he expects to be a great baseball player.
3. The meaning or idea in something spoken or written.–Mother did not see the *point* of Father's joke.
4. A characteristic, or thing which makes something the way it is.–The good *points* in Bob's composition were the interesting story and the simple way it was written.
5. A place.–We stopped at different *points* along the road to buy food and gasoline.
6. A time or condition when a certain thing happens.–I was just on the *point* of leaving when you came.–The boiling *point* of water is 212 degrees Fahrenheit.
7. A dot or period.–If you forget to put in a decimal *point,* your answer will be wrong.
8. A unit of score in a game.–Jim's opponent gained a *point* in tennis when Jim hit the ball out of the court.
–*v. points, pointed, pointing.* 1. Show or indicate, as with the first finger.–Mary *pointed* out all the places of interest to Grandmother.
2. Aim.–The policeman *pointed* his gun at the robber.

poise (POIZ) *n.* 1. Bearing; manner of holding or conducting oneself.—Mary has fine *poise* for one so young. She is graceful and at ease.
2. Ease of social manner.—John addressed his fellow students with great *poise.*
—*v. poises, poised, poising:* Balance in a certain position.—The dancer *poised* on her toes.

poi·son (POI-zən) *n. poisons.* A substance which injures the body. A drug which is a deadly *poison* is one which may cause death.
—*v. poisons, poisoned, poisoning.* Give poison to.—Father *poisoned* the rats by putting rat poison in the cellar.

poi·son i·vy (poi-zən Y-vee). A shiny, three-leafed plant that causes an itchy, red, swollen rash on many people who touch it.

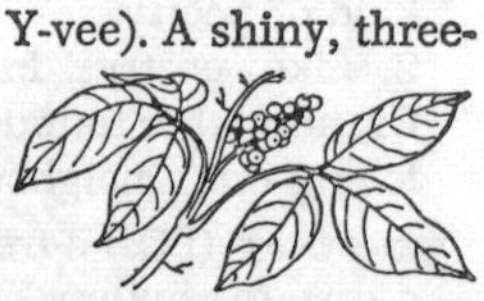

poi·son·ous (POI-zən-əss) *adj.; poisonously, adv.* Very dangerous to the body; containing something which poisons.—Some wild mushrooms are *poisonous.* They may kill a person who eats them.

poke (POHK) *n. pokes.* A push; a dig.—Bob gave Bill a *poke* to let him know the teacher was watching him.
—*v. pokes, poked, poking.* Stick; dig; push.—Baby *poked* her finger into the paint to see what it felt like.

pok·er (POH-ker) *n. pokers.* A long metal rod or stick for poking at or stirring up a fire.

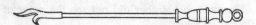

po·ker (POH-ker) *n.* A kind of card game sometimes played for money.

po·lar (POH-ler) *adj.* Having to do with the North or the South Pole; arctic or antarctic.—Admiral Byrd made many *polar* expeditions.

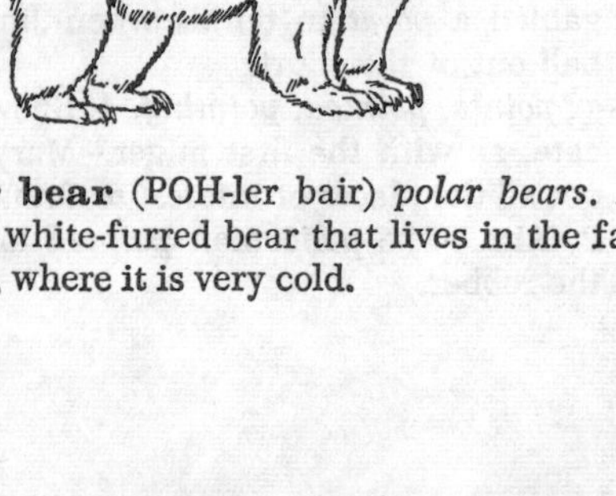

po·lar bear (POH-ler bair) *polar bears.* A fierce, white-furred bear that lives in the far North, where it is very cold.

pole (POHL) *n. poles.* 1. A long stick.—The keeper at the zoo used a *pole* to push the meat into the lion's cage.
2. (Sometimes spelled with a capital "P.") Either end of the earth's axis, which is the imaginary line going down the center of the earth and on which the earth turns; the North *Pole* or the South *Pole.*

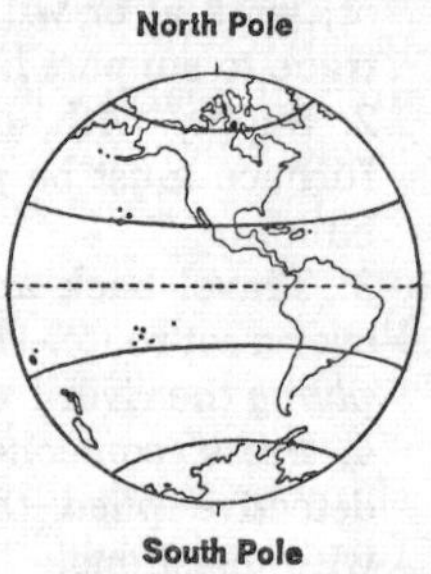

3. One of two places on a magnet or electric battery where opposite forces are strongest. Each magnet or battery has a positive *pole* and a negative *pole.*
4. "Their ideas are *poles* apart" means "Their ideas are a great distance apart."

pole·star (POHL-stahr) *n.* The North Star, found above the North Pole. The *polestar* was once an important guide for men at sea.

po·lice (pə-LEESS) *n.* A group of men hired to keep law and order.
—*v. polices, policed, policing.* 1. Keep peace and order in.—The policemen *policed* the city.
2. Clean up.—John was asked to *police* the school playground.

po·lice·man (pə-LEESS-mən) *n. policemen.* A member of the police department. *Policemen* help to keep order and protect us from people who break the laws.

pol·i·cy (PAHL-ə-see) *n. policies.* 1. A plan of action.—It is our *policy* to treat everyone the same.
2. An insurance *policy* is a written agreement that one has with an insurance company. If one makes certain regular payments to the company, the company will pay back a certain amount in case of certain misfortunes named in the *policy.*—Grandfather had an accident insurance *policy* for which he paid eighteen dollars a year. When he broke his leg, the insurance company paid him twenty-five dollars a week for the month he could not work.

po•li•o (POH-lee-oh) *n. Polio* is the short word for *polio*myelitis, a disease which often paralyzes its victims, who are mostly children. It is also known as infantile paralysis. Doctors now give people shots and pills to keep them from getting *polio.*

pol•ish (PAHL-ish) *n. polishes.* A substance that is rubbed or painted onto something to make it bright and smooth.
–*v. polishes, polished, polishing.* 1. Make shiny or smooth by rubbing.–We *polish* the furniture by rubbing it with furniture polish.
2. Improve by working over.–If you *polish* your story a little, it will be a good one.

po•lite (pə-LYT) *adj.; politely, adv.* Having good manners.–It is *polite* to thank a person who does something for you.

po•lite•ness (pə-LYT-nəss) *n.* Courtesy; a showing of good manners.–Mary is well liked for her *politeness.* She is always pleasant and thoughtful of others.

po•lit•i•cal (pə-LIT-ə-kəl) *adj.; politically, adv.* Having to do with politics or government.–A *political* party is a group of people organized to elect certain people to public office and get certain laws passed.

pol•i•ti•cian (pahl-ə-TISH-ən) *n. politicians.* A person who spends much time in working for the success of a political party in elections.

pol•i•tics (PAHL-ə-tiks) *n.* The business of governing a community, city, state, or nation. The business of getting people elected and appointed to public office is also *politics.*

pol•len (PAHL-ən) *n.* The dusty yellow material that is found in flowers. The flowers use it in making the seeds that will grow into new plants.

pol•li•wog or **pol•ly•wog** (PAHL-ee-wahg) *n. polliwogs* or *pollywogs.* An undeveloped frog or toad; a tadpole. *Polliwogs* begin life in the water, as swimming animals. Later they grow legs, lose their tails and gills, and venture out on land. Then they are *polliwogs* no longer.

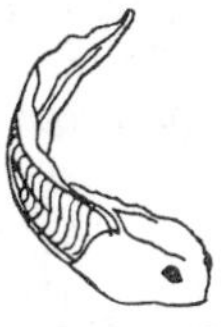

polls (POHLZ) *n. pl.* A voting place.–At election time, Father and Mother go to the *polls* to vote.

pol•lute (pə-LOOT *or* -LYOOT) *v. pollutes, polluted, polluting.* Make unclean; foul.–The waste from the factory was dumped in the river and *polluted* the water.

po•lo (POH-loh) *n.* A game played by players on horseback. The players, using long mallets, try to hit a small wooden ball through the opposing team's goal.

pol•y•gon (PAHL-i-gahn) *n. polygons.* A geometric shape with more than four sides and four angles. Some *polygons* are the five-sided pentagon, the six-sided hexagon, and the eight-sided octagon.

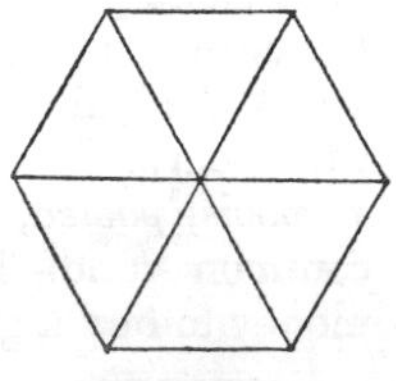

pomp (PAHMP) *n.; pompous, adj.* Great splendor; a display of wealth and magnificence.–The princess was married with *pomp.*

pond (PAHND) *n. ponds.* A pool; a little lake. –Children like to sail their boats on the *pond.*

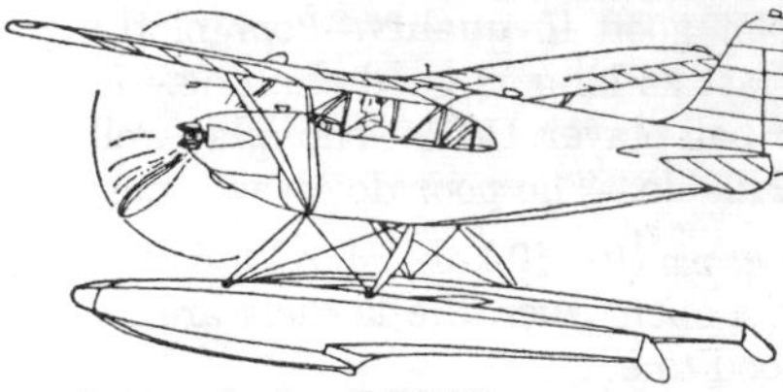

pon•toon (pahn-TOON) *n. pontoons.* 1. A float placed under the wing of a seaplane. Seaplanes have *pontoons* so that they can land on the water.
2. A kind of float that looks like a flat-bottomed boat. *Pontoons* are used to hold up rafts or temporary docks, bridges, and other such structures.
3. A floating raft or dock.

po•ny (POH-nee) *n. ponies.* A small horse.–Children like to ride the *ponies* at the park.

poo•dle (POO-dl) *n. poodles.* A kind of curly-haired dog, intelligent, and easy to train.

pool (POOL) *n. pools.*
1. Any small body of still water.—The boys have gone to the park *pool* to sail their boats.
2. A large tank filled with water.—In summer we often go to the swimming *pool.*

3. A game played on a large table with rubber cushions on all sides. The players try to knock the balls into pockets with long sticks called cues.
—*v. pools, pooled, pooling.* Put together in a common fund.—The children *pooled* their money to buy a gift for Mother.

poor (PUHR) *n. pl.* People who have very little.—Every Christmas we give food to the *poor.*
—*adj. poorer, poorest; poorly, adv.* 1. Having little property and money.—*Poor* people often cannot buy enough to eat.
2. Not good in quality.—*Poor* clothing will not last as long as good clothing.—John is a *poor* ball player. He does not play well.
3. Pitiable.—The *poor* dog was hungry.

pop•corn (PAHP-korn) *n.* A kind of corn that bursts open when the kernels are heated. It is good to eat.

pope (POHP) *n. popes.* The head of the Roman Catholic Church. When you use the word as a title or name, you spell *Pope* with a capital "P."

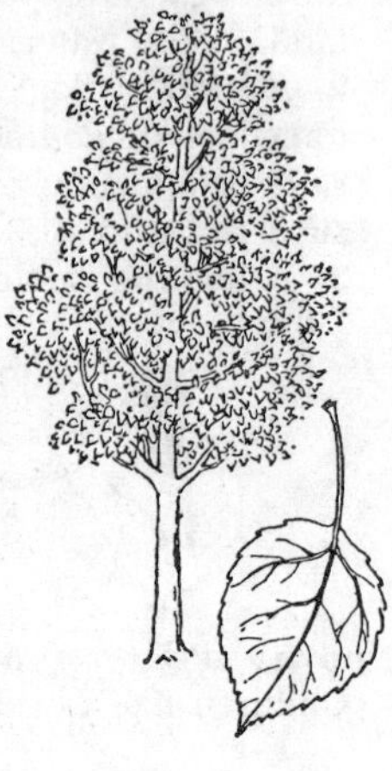

pop•gun (PAHP-gun) *n. popguns.* A small toy gun that shoots corks.—Boys like to play with *popguns.*

pop•lar (PAHP-ler) *n. poplars.* A tall, slim tree with shiny, heart-shaped leaves that tremble in even the slightest breeze. *Poplars* grow fast.

pop•py (PAHP-ee) *n. poppies.* One of a large group of flowers of different colors, especially the red *poppy. Poppy*-seeds are often sprinkled on bread and rolls.

pop•u•lar (PÁHP-yə-ler) *adj.; popularly, adv.; popularity, n.*
1. Well known and liked.—Bob is *popular* in school.
2. Representing the people; of the people.—The United States has a *popular* government.

pop•u•la•tion (pahp-yə-LAY-shən) *n. populations.* The number of people living in a community, town, city, or other area.—The *population* of this city is ten thousand.

por•ce•lain (POR-sə-lin *or* PORSS-lin) *n. porcelains.* Fine, glossy earthenware; china. —Our new dishes are made of *porcelain.*

porch (PORCH) *n. porches.* A covered entrance to a house or other building.

por•cu•pine (POR-kyə-pyn) *n. porcupines.* A small animal that has sharp quills or spines mixed in with its hair. These quills protect it.

pore (POR) *n. pores.* One of many tiny holes in a surface.—There are *pores* in skin.
—*v. pores, pored, poring.* Study thoroughly.—Bob is *poring* over a book.

pork (PORK) *n.* The meat of a pig.

po•rous (POR-əss) *adj.* 1. Full of very little holes.—The skin of human beings is *porous.*
2. Capable of absorbing fluid or of letting fluid pass through.—Sponges are *porous.*

por•poise (POR-pəss) *n. porpoises.* A cousin of the whale. It looks very much like a dolphin but has a short nose.

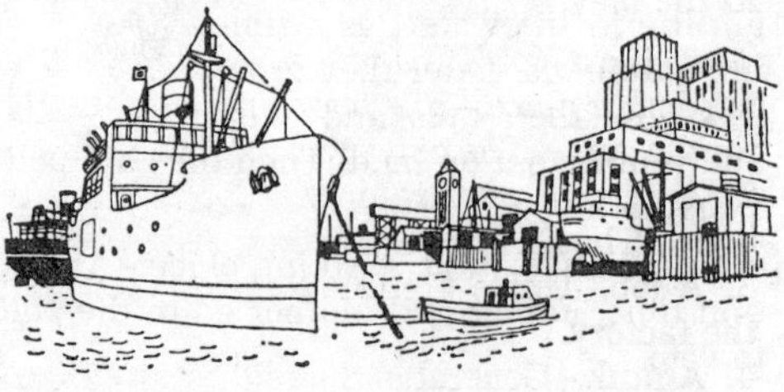

port (PORT) *n. ports* and *adj.* 1. A harbor; a place where ships may load and unload.
2. To or on the left side of a ship.—The cargo shifted to *port* and made the ship tilt.

port•a•ble (PORT-ə-bəl) *adj.* Able to be carried.—Mary has a *portable* typewriter. It is small, and can be easily carried in a case.

por•ter (POR-ter) *n. porters.* 1. A man paid for carrying baggage.—At the depot, the *porter* took our baggage.
2. A man who cleans, moves furniture, and does other such jobs in a building.—The manager called the *porter* to clean up the spilled ink.
3. A man who helps passengers on a train.—The sleeping car *porter* made up the beds.

port•fo•li•o (port-FOH-lee-oh) *n. portfolios.* A light case for carrying papers and pictures.—When Father has had a busy day at the office, he brings work home at night in his *portfolio.*

port•hole (PORT-hohl) *n. portholes.* An opening in the side of a ship to let in light and air. *Portholes* are usually round.

por•tion (POR-shən) *n. portions.* A part or share.—Bob ate a small *portion* of the food.—My *portion* of the money was only fifty cents.
—*v. portions, portioned, portioning.* Divide and give.—John *portioned* out the candy.

por•trait (POR-trayt *or* -trit) *n. portraits* and *adj.* A picture of a particular person.—The artist painted a *portrait* of Ann.

por•tray (por-TRAY) *v. portrays, portrayed, portraying.* Picture by drawing, painting, acting, or describing in words.—Bob *portrayed* the part of a prince in the play.

po•si•tion (pə-ZISH-ən) *n. positions.* 1. A particular place.—The teams got into *position* for the game. The players took their *positions.*
2. A certain posture or way of holding the body.—The ball player got into *position* to bat.
3. A job.—Uncle Tom has a new *position* in the factory.
4. A rank.—General is the highest *position* in the army.
5. A way of thinking.—Mother's *position* on the question is different from Father's. She disagrees with him.

pos•i•tive (PAHZ-ə-tiv) *adj.; positively, adv.* 1. Very sure; certain.—I am *positive* that I heard the bell ring.
2. Not negative.—She gave us a *positive* answer. She said yes to what we asked of her.
—The magnet has a *positive* pole and a negative pole.

pos•se (PAHSS-ee) *n. posses.* A force of men called together by an officer such as a sheriff to help him keep law and order.—A *posse* was formed to capture the outlaw.

pos•sess (pə-ZESS) *v. possesses, possessed, possessing.* 1. Have; own.—This house is all that I *possess.*—John *possesses* great courage.
2. Occupy.—The enemy *possessed* the fort.

pos•ses•sion (pə-ZESH-ən) *n. possessions.* 1. The papers are in my *possession.* I have them.
2. Ownership.—The house passed into Father's *possession* when the papers were signed.
3. Something owned.—Poor people do not have many *possessions.*

pos•ses•sive (pə-ZESS-iv) *adj.; possessively, adv.* 1. Showing ownership.—Words such as "theirs," "yours," "hers," and "mine" are *possessive* pronouns.
2. Showing a desire to hold on to or to own.
—Mary is very *possessive* about her favorite doll. She won't let anyone else play with it.

pos•si•bil•i•ty (pahss-ə-BIL-ə-tee) *n. possibilities.* Something that can happen or be done.—Lindbergh proved that flying a plane across the Atlantic, nonstop and alone, was a *possibility.*

pos•si•ble (PAHSS-ə-bəl) *adj.* 1. Able to happen or be done.—It is *possible* to talk by telephone to a person thousands of miles away.
2. That might be usable or suitable for.—Jack found a *possible* new member for the club.—Jim explored for *possible* camping areas.

pos•si•bly (PAHSS-ə-blee) *adv.* 1. Perhaps; maybe.—*Possibly* Father will come on the next train.
2. Within the limits of what can happen or be done.—Bob cannot *possibly* get here in time for lunch.

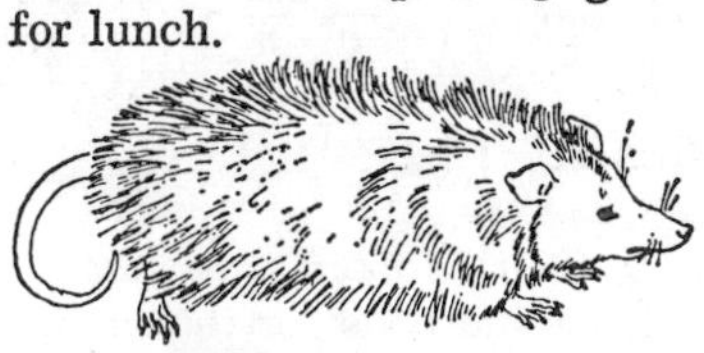

pos•sum (PAHSS-əm) *n. possums.* An opossum; a small grayish animal with sharp teeth and a long skinny tail. *Possums* live in trees.

post (POHST) *n. posts.* 1. An upright rod or column of wood or metal set in the ground to hold something up.—Telephone *posts* hold up telephone wires.

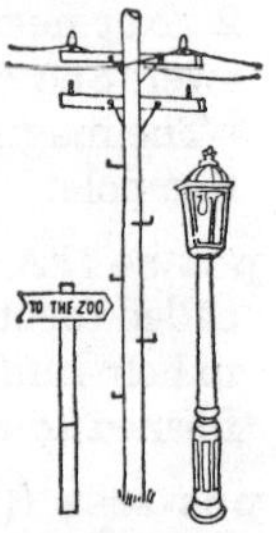

2. A place where a person is supposed to be when on duty. —The Safety Patrol boys are at their *posts* when school is out.
3. A job.—Mary obtained a *post* as bank clerk.
4. A kind of store in places where few people live, at which people may trade or buy things. —The trappers trade furs for food at the *post.*
5. Mail.—He sent the package by parcel *post.*
—*v. posts, posted, posting.* 1. Mail.—Mary will *post* your letter on the way to school.
2. Put up so that people can see.—The names of the honor students were *posted* on the bulletin board.

post·age (POHSS-tij) *n.* The charge for mailing things.—Mary did not mail the package because she didn't have the *postage.* The *postage* on the package was thirty-seven cents, and Mary only had twenty-five cents with her.

post·al (POHSS-tl) *adj.* Having to do with the mail.—*Postal* service is the delivering and collecting of mail.

post card (POHST kahrd) *post cards.* A small card that may be sent through the mail. —It costs less to send a *post card* than it does to send a letter.

post·er (POHSS-ter) *n. posters.* A sign.—A *poster* about the Red Cross was placed in the window of the store.

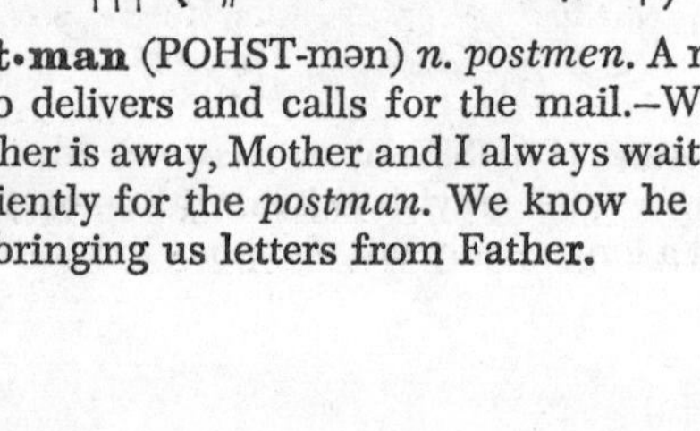

post·man (POHST-mən) *n. postmen.* A man who delivers and calls for the mail.—When Father is away, Mother and I always wait impatiently for the *postman.* We know he will be bringing us letters from Father.

post·mark (POHST-mahrk) *n. postmarks.* A mark put on a letter or package to tell the date and place where it was mailed.

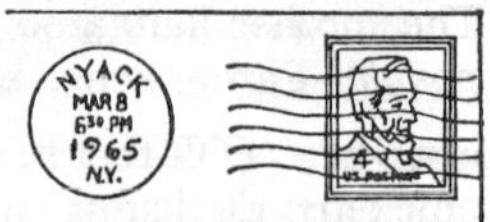

post·mas·ter (POHST-mass-ter) *n. postmasters.* A man in charge of a post office or post offices.

post of·fice (POHST awf-əss) *post offices.* A place where letters and packages are mailed, and received to be sorted for delivery, and where postage stamps are sold.

post·pone (pohst-POHN) *v. postpones, postponed, postponing.* Put off; make a later date for.—Do not *postpone* caring for your teeth.—Let's *postpone* the party until next week. —*postponement, n. postponements.*

post·script (POHSS-skript) *n. postscripts.* A short message written at the end of a letter after the writer's name has been signed. The letters P.S. stand for *postscript.*

pos·ture (PAHSS-cher) *n. postures.* The position of the body; how the body is held.—Children learn good *posture* in health class.

pot (PAHT) *n. pots.* A round vessel used for cooking, serving foods, or other uses.—*Pots* are made of metal, glass, or pottery.
—*v. pots, potted, potting.* Put in a pot.—Mother has *potted* the plants she has in the house.

po·ta·to (pə-TAY-toh) *n. potatoes.* A vegetable whose fleshy root is one of the most important foods in many parts of the world.

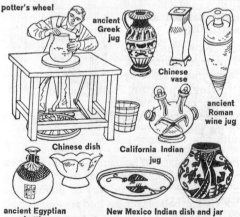

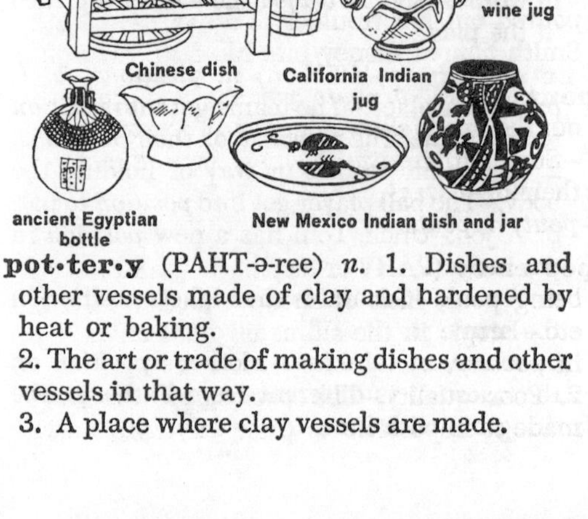

pot·ter·y (PAHT-ə-ree) *n.* 1. Dishes and other vessels made of clay and hardened by heat or baking.
2. The art or trade of making dishes and other vessels in that way.
3. A place where clay vessels are made.

pouch (POWCH) *n. pouches.* A bag or sack.–The mother kangaroo carries her baby in a *pouch.*–Father keeps his tobacco in a *pouch.*

poul·try (POHL-tree) *n.* Birds, especially chickens, ducks, or turkeys, that are raised for food.

pounce (POWNSS) *v. pounces, pounced, pouncing.* Jump suddenly.–The cat *pounced* on the dog from above.
–*pounce, n. pounces.*

pound (POWND) *n. pounds.* 1. A measurement of weight. There are sixteen ounces in a *pound.*–Meat is measured in *pounds.*–I weigh sixty-five *pounds.* How heavy are you? How much do you weigh?
2. In Great Britain, a sum of money worth a little less than three dollars.
3. A place where lost or homeless animals are cared for.–Stray dogs are taken to the *pound* by the dogcatcher.
–*v. pounds, pounded, pounding.* 1. Hit; strike; beat.–*Pound* on the door so that the deaf woman will hear you.
2. Beat heavily.–The waves *pounded* against the rocks.–Indian women *pounded* corn into flour.

pour (POR) *v. pours, poured, pouring.* 1. Make a liquid flow in a steady stream.–To *pour* from a pitcher, you tilt the pitcher until the liquid flows out.
2. Flow in a stream. – When you tilt the pitcher, the liquid *pours* out.
3. Let anything flow in great quantity.–Ann *poured* out her troubles to Mrs. Jones.–Mr. Smith *poured* money into his new business.

pout (POWT) *v. pouts, pouted, pouting.* Push out the lips to show anger or disappointment. –Some children *pout* when they cannot get their own ways.
–*pout, n. pouts.*

pov·er·ty (PAHV-er-tee) *n.* 1. Condition of being poor; lack of money, food, clothing, etc.–People in the slums of great cities live in *poverty.*
2. Poor quality.–The *poverty* of the land made it impossible to grow anything on it.

pow·der (POW-der) *n. powders.* Anything that is in fine grains like dust.–Baking *powder* is a white, dustlike substance used in baking.
–*v. powders, powdered, powdering.* 1. Grind or reduce to a powder.–Grain is *powdered* by grinding to make it into flour.
2. Dust or sprinkle with powder.–Mother *powders* Baby's skin after Baby's bath.

pow·er (POW-er) *n. powers.* 1. Strength or ability to do work; force.–It takes *power* to lift heavy things.–The motor of our car has a great deal of *power.*–Our country has *power* in international affairs.–Electric *power* may be created by water *power.*
2. Ability.–The doctor does all that is in his *power* for his patients.
3. The right.–The judge in the contest has the *power* to say who won and who lost.
4. A powerful nation.–America is a great *power* in the world.

pow·er·ful (POW-er-fuhl) *adj.; powerfully, adv.* 1. Having great strength.–A machine which can lift heavy things is *powerful.*
2. Having great authority.–The governor is the most *powerful* official in the state.

pow·er·less (POW-er-ləss) *adj.* Helpless.–The men were *powerless* to prevent the large rock from falling.

prac·ti·cal (PRAK-tə-kəl) *adj.; practicality, n.* 1. Useful.–Mary's new dress is very *practical.* She can wear it for many different occasions.–The man had many *practical* ideas.
2. Able to do many things well; good at making ideas work out.–Mother is a very *practical* person. She can understand and handle most situations.

prac·tice (PRAK-tiss) *n. practices.* 1. Something regularly or commonly done.–It is the *practice* to exchange gifts at Christmas time.
2. Doing something over and over again to perfect it.–Regular *practice* is the only way to learn to play a musical instrument.
3. The business of a professional person.–The doctor has a large *practice.* He has many patients.
4. Use.–The new plan was put into *practice.*
–or *practise, v. practices* or *practises, practiced* or *practised, practicing* or *practising.* 1. Do a thing over and over, until one does it well.–Mary *practices* playing the piano.
2. Work in a profession.–A doctor *practices* medicine.
3. Do or observe regularly.–John *practices* economy. He never spends much money.

prai·rie (PRAIR-ee) *n. prairies.* A plain where grass grows, but trees do not.–Cattle graze on the *prairie.*

prai·rie schoon·er (PRAIR-ee skoo-ner) *prairie schooners.* A canvas-covered wagon with a rounded top. The pioneers crossed the western plains of the United States in *prairie schooners.*

praise (PRAYZ) *n. praises.* A favorable comment; a statement that something is good.–Our work in spelling receives much *praise.* –*v. praises, praised, praising.* 1. Speak well of. –Our teacher *praises* our work in spelling.
2. *Praise* the Lord means worship the Lord.

prance (PRANSS) *v. prances, pranced, prancing.* Move proudly with high steps.–Horses in the circus parade *prance.*

prank (PRANGK) *n. pranks.* A trick.–The children play *pranks* on people at Halloween.

pray (PRAY) *v. prays, prayed, praying.* 1. Ask from God; speak to God.–Children *pray* to God to bless their loved ones.
2. Ask earnestly.–The princess said, "Set me free, I *pray* you."

prayer (PRAIR) *n. prayers.* What one says when speaking to God.–The minister said a *prayer.*

preach (PREECH) *v. preaches, preached, preaching.* 1. Make a speech or sermon about a religious subject.–In church, the minister *preaches.*
2. Speak earnestly about.–Mother *preaches* honesty to us every day.

preach·er (PREECH-er) *n. preachers.* A minister; a person who preaches in church.

pre·am·ble (PREE-am-bəl) *n. preambles.* An introductory statement; a preface which tells the purpose of whatever follows it. The *preamble* to the United States Constitution tells what areas of government the Constitution will cover.

pre·cau·tion (pri-KAW-shən) *n. precautions.* 1. Caution or care exercised beforehand.–Observing the rules of good health is a *precaution* against illness.
2. Anything done beforehand to prevent misfortune or to insure success.–Father had his car brakes checked at the garage as a safety *precaution.*

pre·cede (pree-SEED) *v. precedes, preceded, preceding.* Come before.–Monday *precedes* Tuesday.

pre·ced·ing (pree-SEE-ding) *adj.* Coming before; previous.–On the *preceding* day, we had packed to go.

pre·cept (PREE-sept) *n. precepts.* A rule of conduct.–Father says that everyone should base his actions on a well-reasoned set of *precepts.* He feels that one's life should be guided by rules of conduct.

pre·cinct (PREE-singkt) *n. precincts.* 1. An area or district of a city, especially a police or election district.
2. An area within certain fixed boundaries.–Visitors are not permitted within the hospital *precincts* after nine o'clock at night.

pre·cious (PRESH-əss) *adj.* 1. Valuable.–*Precious* stones or jewels are very expensive.
2. Loved; dear.–Children are very *precious* to their parents.

prec·i·pice (PRESS-ə-piss) *n. precipices.* A high, steep cliff.

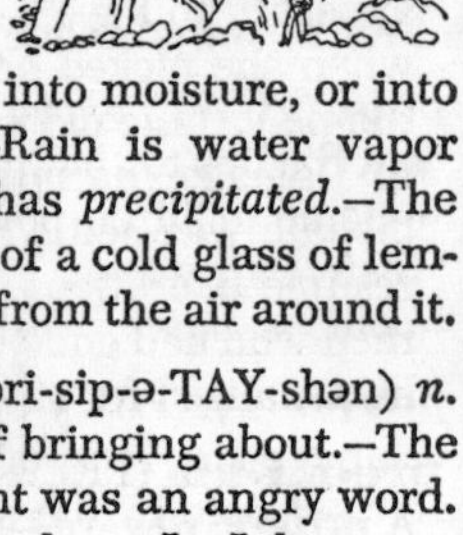

pre·cip·i·tate (pri-SIP-ə-tayt) *v. precipitates, precipitated, precipitating.* 1. Bring about suddenly or unexpectedly.–A small quarrel sometimes *precipitates* a big fight.
2. Change from vapor into moisture, or into rain, snow, or sleet.–Rain is water vapor (from a cloud) which has *precipitated.*–The wetness on the outside of a cold glass of lemonade has *precipitated* from the air around it.

pre·cip·i·ta·tion (pri-sip-ə-TAY-shən) *n. precipitations.* 1. Act of bringing about.–The *precipitation* of the fight was an angry word.
2. Rain, snow, hail, or sleet.–In July a *precipitation* of one and a quarter inches was recorded.

pre•cise (pri-SYSS) *adj.; precisely, adv.* 1. Accurate and careful.–Mother is very *precise* about her work.
2. Exact.–Father speaks very *precise* English. He wants to make his meaning clear.

pred•i•cate (PRED-ə-kit) *n. predicates.* The part of a sentence that tells what the subject does or is.–The boys play ball. The words "play ball" form the *predicate* of the sentence. They tell what the boys do.

pre•dict (pri-DIKT) *v. predicts, predicted, predicting.* Tell beforehand.–The farmer *predicted* that the grain would be ripe next month.
–*prediction, n. predictions.*

pref•ace (PREF-iss) *n. prefaces.* An introduction to something spoken or written.–As a *preface* to his talk, the lecturer told an amusing story.–Something about the author's life is in the *preface* of the book.
–*v. prefaces, prefaced, prefacing.*–Introduce something spoken or written.–He *prefaced* his talk with an amusing story.

pre•fer (pri-FER) *v. prefers, preferred, preferring.* Like better.–I *prefer* swimming to hockey.

pre•fix (PREE-fiks) *n. prefixes.* Letters or syllables put before a word to make a new word. –In the word "unfasten," "un-" is a *prefix.*

pre•his•tor•ic (pree-hiss-TOR-ik *or* pree-hiss-TAHR-ik) *adj.* Having to do with, or belonging to, a period before history was written or recorded.–The dinosaur was a *prehistoric* animal.

prej•u•dice (PREJ-ə-diss) *n. prejudices; prejudiced, adj.* 1. An opinion, favorable or unfavorable, formed in advance without good reason.–My aunt had a *prejudice* against Canadians, because she had once known a Canadian she didn't like. We thought it very foolish of her.–Mrs. Smith appeared to have a *prejudice* in Jane's favor when she picked her for the leading part in the play. Jane did not do well in the tryouts.
2. Damage; harm; injury.–When the labor dispute was settled, the company agreed to resume operations without *prejudice* to the men who had gone on strike. They would not be penalized for striking.

pre•mi•um (PREE-mee-əm) *n. premiums.* 1. A prize; a reward.–As a *premium* for buying that soap, you get a free bath towel.
2. A payment for insurance.–Father pays monthly *premiums* on his insurance.

pre•paid (pree-PAYD) *adj.* Paid for beforehand.–The package was *prepaid.*

prep•a•ra•tion (prep-ə-RAY-shən) *n. preparations.* 1. A thing or things done to get ready.–The *preparations* for the picnic are almost finished.–High school is often a *preparation* for college.
2. Something mixed or prepared.–A *preparation* may be a medicine, a food, or anything that is gotten ready for some special use.

pre•pare (pri-PAIR) *v. prepares, prepared, preparing.* 1. Get ready.–Mary *prepares* to go to school early.
2. Make ready. – Mother *prepares* Baby's breakfast.

prep•o•si•tion (prep-ə-ZISH-ən) *n. prepositions.* A connective word showing relationship. In the phrases "playing in the park," "safe among friends," and "made of steel," the words "in," "among," and "of" are *prepositions.*

pre•scribe (pri-SKRYB) *v. prescribes, prescribed, prescribing.* Order the use of; suggest as a cure, treatment, or procedure; advise.–The doctor *prescribed* a new medicine for the baby. He wrote out an order for us to take to the druggist.–Father *prescribed* less television and an earlier bedtime as one remedy for Bob's low grades.

pre•scrip•tion (pri-SKRIP-shən) *n. prescriptions.* 1. An order or direction, usually written by a doctor, giving a druggist an order for pills or medicine for a certain person.–The doctor wrote a *prescription* for my cough.
2. The medicine itself.–Did the drugstore deliver the *prescription?*

pres•ence (PREZ-ənss) *n.* 1. State or condition of being in a place or of being present.–The clown's *presence* at the circus meant fun for the children.
2. Place where someone is.–It is rude and thoughtless to gossip about someone in his *presence.*–He was ushered into the queen's *presence.*

pres•ent (PREZ-ənt) *n. presents.* 1. A gift.–Baby received a *present* on her birthday.
2. This time; the time in which we are living now; this moment.–In history class we study what man has done from times long past right up to the *present.*
–*adj.* 1. Existing or happening at this moment; now.–Mary isn't home at the *present* time. She isn't home now.
2. On hand; here.–All the children in the class are *present* today. None are absent.

PRESSES

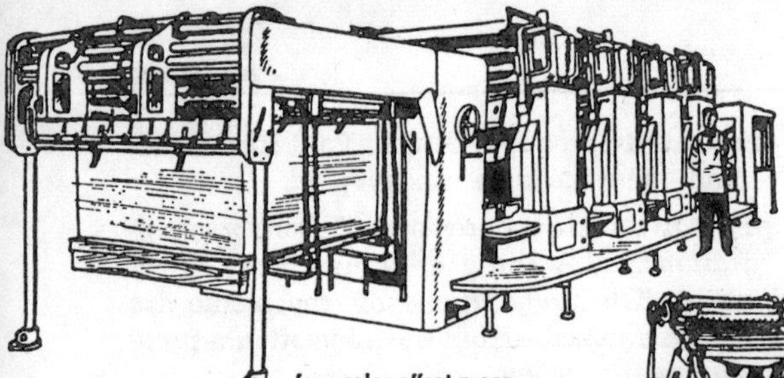

four-color offset press

platen press

early printing press

pre•sent (pri-ZENT) *v. presents, presented, presenting.* 1. Introduce.–Mary *presented* her friend to the teacher.
2. Send in; give.–The dentist *presented* his bill for the work he had done.–The class *presented* a play.–Jim *presented* his idea to the class.
3. Show; have.–Mary *presents* a neat appearance.
–When a soldier *presents arms,* he brings his gun up in front of him with the trigger away from his body and the barrel of the gun pointing upward.

pres•ent•ly (PREZ-ənt-lee) *adv.* Before long; soon. – Mother said that Father would be home *presently.*

pre•serve (pri-ZERV) *n. preserves.* 1. A kind of jelly with the whole fruit left in.–Strawberries and sugar boiled together make strawberry *preserve* or *preserves.*
2. Place where wild animals are protected.–Hunters are not allowed in the game *preserve.*
–*v. preserves, preserved, preserving.* 1. Keep from spoiling; save.–Mother cans fruits and vegetables to *preserve* them.
2. Keep up; keep in good repair.–The government is *preserving* the Colonial mansion as a museum.
3. Protect from harm or extinction.–An effort is now being made to *preserve* the animals of Africa from being entirely killed off by hunters.

pre•side (pri-ZYD) *v. presides, presided, presiding.* Have charge (of a meeting or group). –Bob will *preside* at the class meeting.

pres•i•dent (PREZ-ə-dənt) *n. presidents.* 1. The chief officer of a business firm, a union, a club, or other organization.
2. (Sometimes spelled with a capital "P.") The head of the government in a republic, such as the *President* of the United States.

press (PRESS) *n. presses.* 1. A printing machine.–City newspapers are printed on big *presses.*
2. Any machine that works by squeezing or pressing.
3. Newspapers. – The story of the accident will be printed in the morning *press.*
4. Reporters.–The *press* turned out in full force for the society wedding.
5. Pressure; push.–Mr. Smith couldn't come because of the *press* of work at his office.
–*v. presses, pressed, pressing.* 1. Push.–*Press* the button and the elevator will stop.
2. Hug.–Father *pressed* the lost child to him.
3. Urge; ask.–Because the money was due, Father *pressed* the man to pay it.
4. Push with all one's weight and force.–Bob *pressed* against the door to open it.
5. Iron.–Mother *pressed* my dress.
6. Squeeze. – Grapes are *pressed* to make wine.

pres•sure (PRESH-er) *n. pressures.* 1. A pressing against or on; the pushing force of surrounding things.–The eggs were broken by the *pressure* of other groceries.
2. The pressing of demands upon one. – Working under *pressure* to hurry or to do better than others is not easy.
3. A physical sense of tightness and discomfort.–Sinus trouble brings a feeling of *pressure* or pain around nose and eyes.

pre•sume (pri-ZOOM *or* -ZYOOM) *v. presumes, presumed, presuming.* 1. Suppose.–I *presume* you asked your mother if you might go.
2. Dare.–The boy *presumed* to ask his teacher to give the class a holiday.
–*presumption, n. presumptions.*

pre•tend (pri-TEND) *v. pretends, pretended, pretending.* 1. Make believe.–The opossum *pretends* that he is dead to fool his enemies.–
2. Claim.–Bob doesn't *pretend* to be a good speller.

pret•ty (PRIT-ee) *adj. prettier, prettiest; prettily, adv.* Quite beautiful.–Baby is *pretty.*
–*adv.* Rather; fairly.–It is *pretty* cold today.

pre•vent (pri-VENT) *v. prevents; prevented, preventing.* 1. Stop.–The work of the fireman *prevented* the fire from spreading.
2. Keep from happening.–Bob's quick thinking *prevented* an accident.
3. Hinder; interfere. – Father said nothing would *prevent* him from calling.
–*prevention, n. preventions.*

pre•vi•ous (PREE-vee-əss) *adj.; previously, adv.* Just before; earlier.–You will find pictures of presses on the *previous* page, on the page before this.

prey (PRAY) *n.* 1. Any animal that is caught by another animal for food.–Chickens are the *prey* of hawks.
2. Victim or victims.–Poor people are sometimes the *prey* of moneylenders who charge high interest.
–*v. preys, preyed, preying.* 1. Use (another animal) for food.–Hawks *prey* upon chickens and field mice.
2. Make a victim, or victims, of.–Moneylenders may *prey* upon poor people.
–*Prey upon* also means be a constant threat to in any way; feed on; gnaw. – The old woman's illness *preys upon* her mind; it worries her and does her harm.

price (PRYSS) *n. prices.* 1. The amount of money a thing costs.–The *price* of my shoes was five dollars.
2. Cost of any kind.–Illness is often the *price* of overeating.
–*v. prices, priced, pricing.* 1. Ask the price of. –Father *priced* the watermelons. The man told him they were sixty-five cents each.
2. Set a price on.–The man *priced* the bicycle at thirty dollars. That was the amount he wanted for it.

price•less (PRYSS-ləss) *adj.* So valuable that a price can hardly be set.–Many great and famous paintings are *priceless.*

prick (PRIK) *n. pricks.* 1. Sticking, or the feeling of being stuck, with something sharp and slender.–The *prick* of the needle hurt.
2. A little hole made by something sharp.– The *prick* on Mother's finger shows.
3. A hurt, as of conscience or regret.–A *prick* of conscience kept Mary from taking a piece of cake while Mother was out.
–*v. pricks, pricked, pricking.* 1. Make a little hole in with a pin, needle, or similar type of pointed instrument; stick.–Mother *pricked* her finger with the needle.
2. Hurt or bother emotionally.–Mary's conscience *pricked* her.
3. Point (upward).–Fido *pricked* up his ears at the sound of footsteps.

pride (PRYD) *n.* 1. A feeling of happiness at being thought well of, or having something one has done, or owns, thought well of.– Mother takes *pride* in keeping our house neat and clean.
2. A thing one is proud of.–Grandfather's garden is his *pride* and joy.
3. High opinion of oneself; respect for oneself.–Jack's *pride* wouldn't let him admit his fault.
–*v. prides, prided, priding.* Grandmother *prides* herself on her cookies. She thinks they are very good.

priest (PREEST) *n. priests.* A minister or clergyman in the Roman Catholic church, the Episcopal church, and certain other religious groups.

pri•ma•ry (PRY-mair-ee) *n. primaries.* Election to choose one of several people in the same party to be a candidate.
–*adj.; primarily, adv.* 1. First in time or first in order.–The *primary* grades in school are the first grades above the kindergarten.
2. Main; most important.–The *primary* reason that Mother visited the school was to meet Mary's new teacher. – The *primary* colors are red, yellow, and blue. They form the basis for mixing other colors.

prime min•is•ter (prym MIN-iss-ter) *prime ministers.* The chief official of the government in many countries.

prim•er (PRIM-er) *n. primers.* A first book.– Children learn to read from a *primer.* After the *primer,* they try the first reader.

prim•i•tive (PRIM-ə-tiv) *adj.* Referring to, or like, people or things of the earliest times on the earth; crude and simple; ancient.–The cave men were *primitive* people. They lived a rough and simple life. – *Primitive* dishes were made of clay. – When the boys go camping, they live in a *primitive* way.

prim•rose (PRIM-rohz) *n. primroses.* A plant that has yellow and pink flowers.

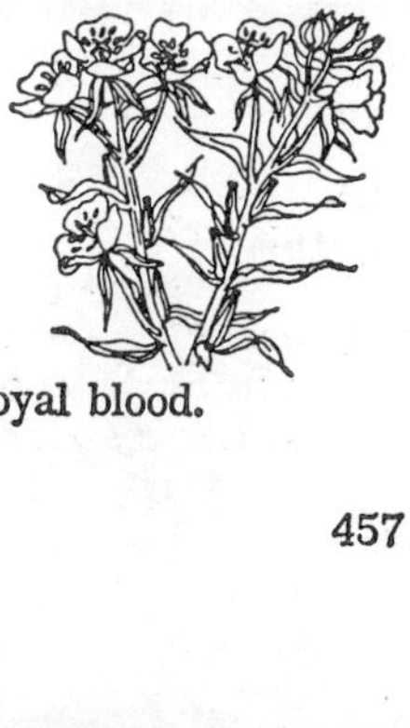

prince (PRINSS) *n. princes.* 1. The son of a king, or the son of a king's son.
2. A nobleman of the highest rank, having royal blood.

prin•cess (PRIN-səss) *n. princesses.* The daughter of a king or queen or of their son, or the wife of a prince.

prin•ci•pal (PRIN-sə-pəl) *n. principals.* 1. The head of a school.
2. An amount of money which a person owns and puts into a business or a bank so that it will earn more money for him.
–adj.; principally, adv. Chief; main.–One of the *principal* reasons for going to school is to gain knowledge and learn how to use it.

prin•ci•ple (PRIN-sə-pəl) *n. principles.* 1. One of the rules or beliefs by which people live.–Treating people as you would like to have them treat you is a good *principle.*
2. Uprightness. – Mr. Smith is a man of *principle.*
3. The idea on which something is based; a truth or fact which makes it possible to do many things.–Bob explained to the class the *principles* by which a radio works.

print (PRINT) *n. prints.* 1. A line or a mark made by pressing one thing against another, as foot*prints* in the sand, or finger*prints* on the furniture.–No two people have finger*prints* exactly alike.

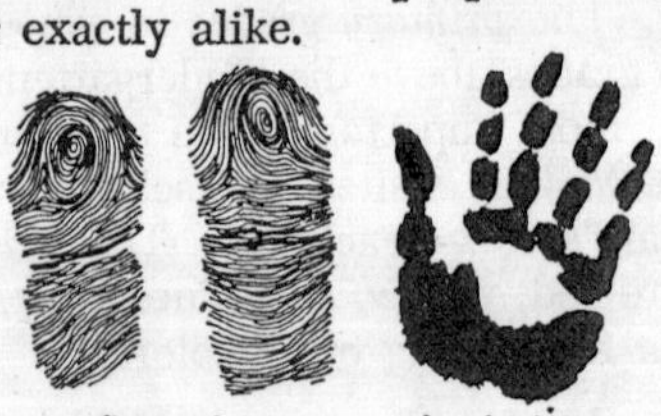

2. A finished photograph is a *print* from the negative.
3. A mechanically reproduced copy.
4. Words stamped on paper by a printing press.–I have trouble reading fine *print.*
5. A material covered with a design.–That material is a pretty *print.*
–v. prints, printed, printing. 1. Mark by pressing.–Printing presses *print* books. They stamp the letters and pictures onto the pages in ink.
2. A photograph is said to be *printed* when it is put on paper so that you can see it.
3. Form letters the way they appear in books and newspapers, instead of the way they are made in handwriting.–Little children sometimes learn to *print* their names before they learn to write them.

print•er (PRIN-ter) *n. printers.* A person whose work is printing, or setting up type to be printed.

pri•or (PRY-er) *adj.* Coming, being, or happening before something else.

prism (PRIZ-əm) *n. prisms.* A bar of glass or crystal, usually triangular, which bends and separates white light into rainbow colors: red, orange, yellow, green, blue, indigo, and violet.

pris•on (PRIZ-ən) *n. prisons.* A place where people are kept as prisoners to punish them for breaking the law.–The robbers were sent to *prison.*

pris•on•er (PRIZ-ə-ner *or* PRIZ-ner) *n. prisoners.* A person or animal that is held captive or kept shut up against his wishes.–A robin shut up in a cage is a *prisoner.–Prisoners* in a penitentiary have to work.

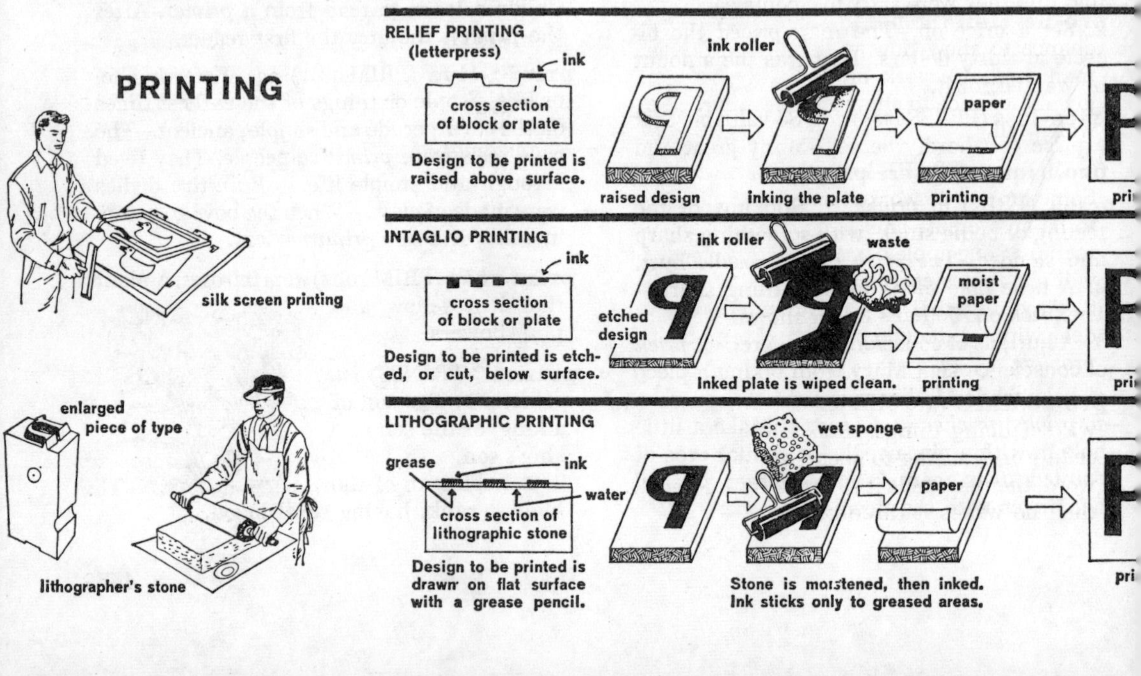

pri•va•cy (PRY-və-see) *n.* 1. The condition of being private or separated from other people.–Hedges or fences between houses insure *privacy* for neighbors who prefer it.
2. Secrecy.–The men discussed their plans in *privacy.*

pri•vate (PRY-vət) *n. privates.* A soldier who holds the lowest rank.–My brother is a *private* in the army.
–adj.; privately, adv. 1. Not for everyone, but only for a certain person or persons. – Our teacher had a *private* talk with Mother. No one else was there to listen.
2. Secret.–What I have to tell you is *private.* It is between us alone.
3. Holding no public office, like that of mayor or governor.–Father is a *private* citizen.

priv•i•lege (PRIV-ə-lij) *n. privileges.* The right to do a special thing.–Our teacher gave us the *privilege* of going home for our books. She let us go.

prize (PRYZ) *n. prizes.* A gift won by doing something better, or by being luckier, than other people.–The teacher gave a pencil as a *prize* to the person who could name the greatest number of flowers.–Bob won a *prize* at the party when he drew the lucky number from the hat.
–v. prizes, prized, prizing. Value highly.–We *prize* this picture. It is worth much to us.
–adj. Fit to win a prize; most valuable.–This lily is Grandmother's *prize* flower.

prob•a•ble (PRAHB-ə-bəl) *adj.; probably, adv.* Likely; likely to happen.–Sickness is the *probable* reason for Mary's absence from school.–Rain is *probable* today.

pro•ba•tion (proh-BAY-shən) *n.* A trial, or chance to show how well one can do.–The man went to work on *probation.* He was given a chance to show that he could do the work well.

prob•lem (PRAHB-ləm) *n. problems.* 1. Something to be worked out; a hard question to be answered.–This is a *problem* in arithmetic: If one apple costs a nickel, how much will six apples cost?
2. Anything that is hard to understand or deal with.–A naughty child sometimes is a *problem.*

pro•ce•dure (prə-SEE-jer) *n. procedures.* A way of doing things.–Bob follows this *procedure* in learning to spell: first he says the word, then he spells it to himself three times, then he writes it three times.

pro•ceed (prə-SEED) *v. proceeds, proceeded, proceeding.* 1. Move forward.–The old man *proceeded* down the road. He went on.
2. Get along according to plans.–Bob and Father are *proceeding* with their model airplanes. They are building six of them.
3. Come forth. – The wedding party *proceeded* from the church.

pro•ceed•ing (prə-SEE-ding) *n. proceedings.* Action; activity; things said or done.–Mary gave a report of the *proceedings* at the meeting.

pro•ceeds (PROH-seedz) *n. pl.* Money received for something; profit.–The *proceeds* from the fair were three hundred dollars.

proc•ess (PRAHSS-ess) *n. processes.* Plan or method. – What *process* is used in making jelly? What steps are taken in making it? What is done first, second, third, and so on?
–v. processes, processed, processing. Treat something in a special way.–Manufacturers *process* cheese to make it easy to spread or use in a sandwich.

pro•ces•sion (prə-SESH-ən) *n. processions.* The moving forward of persons or things in an orderly way.–A circus parade is a *procession.* – Children marching along in a line make a *procession.*

pro•claim (proh-KLAYM) *v. proclaims, proclaimed, proclaiming.* Announce or declare publicly. – The President *proclaimed* a national day of mourning for the dead hero.
–proclamation, n. proclamations.

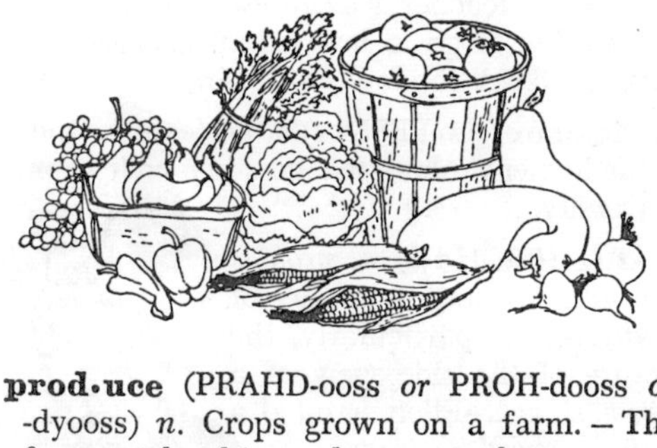

prod•uce (PRAHD-ooss *or* PROH-dooss *or* -dyooss) *n.* Crops grown on a farm. – The farmer takes his *produce* to market.

pro·duce (prə-DOOSS *or* -DYOOSS) *v. produces, produced, producing.* 1. Show or exhibit something.–The children *produced* a play. They put it on for others to see.–Mary *produced* the pieces of glass as proof that the vase was broken.
2. Make or manufacture; create.–Factories *produce* thousands of automobiles a week.
3. Grow or cause to grow.–Seeds *produce* plants.–Farmers *produce* crops.
4. Cause; bring about.–When Mary works at anything she usually *produces* results.

pro·duc·er (prə-DOO-ser *or* prə-DYOO-ser) *n. producers.* 1. A person who makes or grows things to sell.–The man is a *producer* of corn.
2. A person who produces a moving picture or play.–Uncle Robert is a *producer*. His business is having plays shown on a stage.

prod·uct (PRAHD-ukt) *n. products.* 1. A thing that is grown or made.–Cars are manufactured *products*.–Foods are *products* of the farms.
2. In a problem in multiplication, the answer you get by multiplying two or more numbers together. $2 \times 9 = 18$. The answer, 18, is the *product* of 2 times 9.

pro·duc·tion (prə-DUK-shən) *n. productions.* 1. The act of producing or making something. – *Production* is better in well-lighted factories. More goods are made in less time.
2. Anything produced or brought out, especially something literary or artistic. – The movie we saw last night was a fine *production*.

pro·fan·i·ty (prə-FAN-ə-tee) *n. profanities; profane, adj.* Language used in contempt of God; swearing.

pro·fes·sion (prə-FESH-ən) *n. professions; professional, adj.* A kind of work or occupation for which people must have a special education.–The work of a doctor, dentist, minister, or teacher is a *profession*.–William is planning to go to law school because he hopes to enter the law *profession*.

pro·fes·sor (prə-FESS-er) *n. professors.* One of the higher-ranking teachers in a college or university.

pro·file (PROH-fyl) *n. profiles* and *adj.* An outline picture of anything; or, particularly, the picture of the side view of a person's face.–Ellen painted a *profile* view of Tommy.

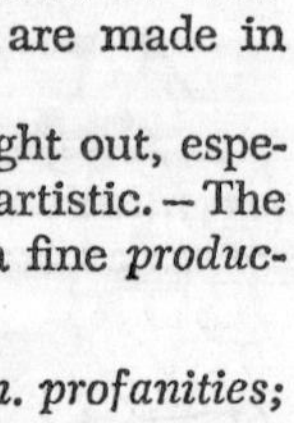

prof·it (PRAHF-it) *n. profits.* 1. A gain; money made.–Jack's *profit* from selling papers last week was $1.25. That was the amount of money he had left after all his expenses were paid.
2. Benefit, use, or good.–What *profit* is there in working till you are overtired?
–*v. profits, profited, profiting.* 1. Gain money from business.–Mr. Smith *profits* enormously, considering how little money he has to put into his business.
2. Benefit. – You will *profit* from listening closely in class.

pro·found (prə-FOWND) *adj.; profoundly, adv.* 1. Having deep meaning or understanding; scholarly. – *Profound* books require careful reading.
2. Intense; deep; extreme.–The parents expressed *profound* gratitude when their lost child was returned to them.

pro·gram (PROH-gram) *n. programs.* 1. A list of the things that are going to happen.–A *program* for the concert told what was to be played and by whom.
2. A plan of action.–The President explained his farm *program*.
3. A performance.–The parents enjoyed the assembly *program*.

prog·ress (PRAHG-rəss *or* PROH-gress) *n.* 1. Movement forward.–A turtle makes slow *progress*.
2. Improvement; movement forward.–Have you made any *progress* in your work?

pro·gress (prə-GRESS) *v. progresses, progressed, progressing.* Go forward; advance.–Jim *progressed* quickly in school.

pro·gres·sive (prə-GRESS-iv) *adj.; progressively, adv.* 1. Favoring improvements and movement forward.–A *progressive* city makes improvements and carries out new ideas.
2. Happening step by step.–His *progressive* loss of weight showed that something was seriously wrong.

pro·hib·it (proh-HIB-it) *v. prohibits, prohibited, prohibiting.* Not allow by law; forbid. –The sign said "Smoking *Prohibited*."
–*prohibition, n. prohibitions.*

proj·ect (PRAHJ-ekt) *n. projects.* A plan or design for something that is to be done; an idea all worked out.–Building a houseboat is Father's summertime *project*.

pro·ject (prə-JEKT) *v. projects, projected, projecting.* 1. Point forward; stick out.–The porch roof *projects* a little to keep the rain from blowing into the porch.

2. Cast or throw upon a flat surface.–Father *projected* the shadow of his hand onto the wall in the shape of a donkey's head.

pro•jec•tion (prə-JEK-shən) *n. projections.* 1. A part that juts out.–Jack stood on the rocky *projection* high above the valley.
2. The projecting of something onto a flat surface.–The film's *projection* was not clear.

pro•jec•tor (prə-JEK-ter) *n. projectors.* An apparatus or machine used to throw still or moving pictures on a screen.

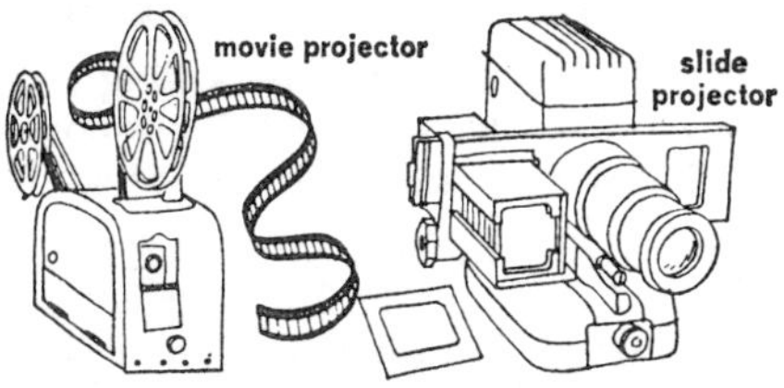

pro•long (prə-LAWNG) *v. prolongs, prolonged, prolonging.* Make longer; increase in length.–The teacher said she would not *prolong* her talk, but would leave time for us to ask questions.

prom•i•nent (PRAHM-ə-nənt) *adj.; prominently, adv.* 1. Sticking out; standing out.–A long nose is a *prominent* nose.
2. Well-known; noted.–A group of *prominent* businessmen is trying to get the city to build the playground.

prom•ise (PRAHM-iss) *n. promises.* 1. A person's statement or word that he will surely do something.–Bob gave me his *promise* to be here at nine o'clock.
2. Something which shows hope of future success.–She shows *promise* in ballet.
–*v. promises, promised, promising.* 1. Make a promise.–Bob *promised* to be here at nine.
2. Seem likely.–This *promises* to be a hot summer.

pro•mote (prə-MOHT) *v. promotes, promoted, promoting.* 1. Raise in rank, position, grade.–Bob was *promoted* from the fourth grade to the fifth.
2. Help to happen successfully.–The boys are *promoting* the Red Cross drive by giving a benefit baseball game.
–*promotion, n. promotions.*

prompt (PRAHMPT) *v. prompts, prompted, prompting.* 1. Cause; lead.–The good weather *prompted* us to go outside.
2. Remind. – The teacher *prompted* Mary when she forgot her lines in the play.
–*adj.* On time.–Bob is always *prompt.*

prong (PRAWNG) *n. prongs.* A pointed projection, as on a fork or antler.–The fish was caught on one of the hook's two *prongs.*

pro•noun (PROH-nown) *n. pronouns.* A word used instead of the name of something or someone.–The word "you" is a *pronoun* used instead of your name.–The word "he" is a *pronoun* used in speaking of a man or a boy.

pro•nounce (prə-NOWNSS) *v. pronounces, pronounced, pronouncing.* 1. Speak the sounds of.–The word "quay" is *pronounced* just like the word "key."
2. Declare officially.–The jury *pronounced* the man innocent.

pro•nun•ci•a•tion (prə-nun-see-AY-shən) *n. pronunciations.* The sound of a spoken word; the act of speaking sounds.–The *pronunciation* of the word "quay" is the same as the *pronunciation* of the word "key."

proof (PROOF) *n. proofs.* That which shows the truth of something.–Bob offered *proof* that he had been in Washington. He showed a photograph of himself in front of the Capitol.
–*adj.* Safe or protected (against something).–This coat is *proof* against water. Water will not come through it. It is water*proof.*

prop (PRAHP) *n. props.* A stick or the like that leans against something to hold the thing up.

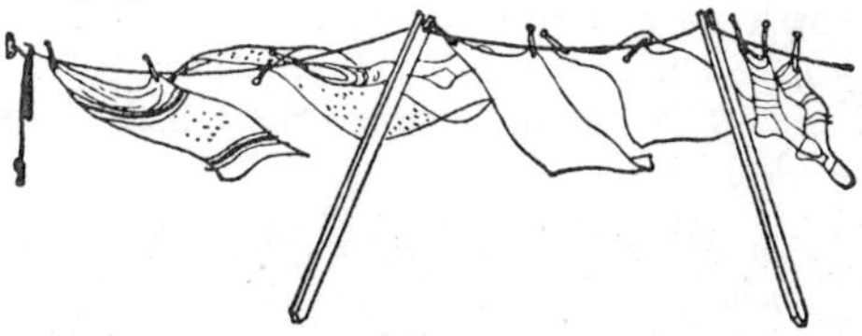

–*v. props, propped, propping.* Hold up or support with a prop or props.–Father *propped* up the fence with poles until he could have time to repair it.

prop•a•gan•da (prahp-ə-GAN-də) *n.* 1. A systematic and organized effort to spread ideas and opinions for the purposes of a person or group.–Among the tools of the dictator's *propaganda* were the nation's strictly censored books, magazines, and newspapers.
2. The ideas and opinions spread.–It is important to learn to distinguish truth from *propaganda* in reading anything.

pro•pel (prə-PEL) *v. propels, propelled, propelling.* Drive, push, or force forward; cause to move ahead.–I wonder what *propels* the human cannon balls at the circus.–Huge propellers *propel* the plane.

pro•pel•ler (prə-PEL-er) *n. propellers.* A device with curved blades that whirl around. *Propellers* are turned by engines and are used on boats and aircraft. The whirling blades push the water or air and thus make the boat or aircraft move.

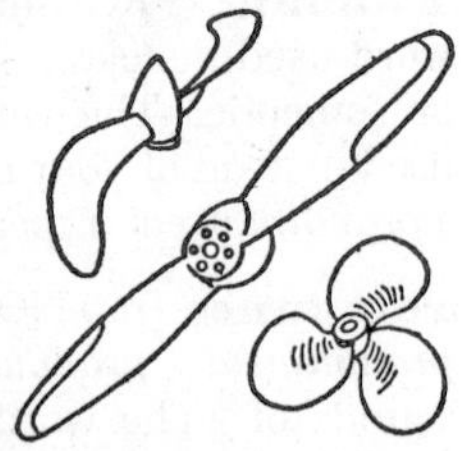

prop•er (PRAHP-er) *adj.; properly, adv.* According to rule; correct.–It is *proper* to drive on the right side of the street.
–A *proper noun* is the name of a certain person, place, or thing. *Proper nouns* always begin with capital letters.–Chicago, Mary, and America are *proper nouns.*

prop•er•ty (PRAHP-er-tee) *n. properties.* 1. That which is owned, especially land and buildings.–The *property* along the river has been worth more since the park was made.–The bicycle is Bob's *property.* It belongs to him.
2. Special quality of something.–Among the *properties* of glass is the *property* of being transparent.
3. Item used in a play, such as a letter, a handkerchief, a glass.

proph•e•sy (PRAHF-ə-sy) *v. prophesies, prophesied, prophesying.* Predict; tell beforehand.–The old man *prophesied* that there would be a war.

proph•et (PRAHF-ət) *n. prophets.* 1. A person who predicts the future.–Bob was a good weather *prophet.* He said it would snow, and it did.
2. A man who speaks for God.–Jeremiah and Paul are two of the *prophets* in the Bible.

pro•por•tion (prə-POR-shən) *n. proportions.* 1. A part.–A great *proportion* of the earth's surface is under water.
2. The relation between parts.–A normal person's body grows in proper *proportions.* The size of each part is properly related to the size of the whole body.
3. Numerical relation. – The *proportion* of boys to girls in our school is two to one. There are twice as many boys as girls.

pro•pose (prə-POHZ) *v. proposes, proposed, proposing.* 1. Suggest; put forward as a thing to do.–Bob *proposed* that the class have a picnic.
2. Ask to marry.–The young man *proposed* to the young woman.
–*proposal, n. proposals.*

prop•o•si•tion (prahp-ə-ZISH-ən) *n. propositions.* Something suggested or proposed.

pro•pri•e•tor (prə-PRY-ə-ter) *n. proprietors.* The owner and manager of a business.–The *proprietor* of the store gave us a box of candy.

prose (PROHZ) *n.* Ordinary writing (not in the form of poetry or verse). *Prose* does not have the rhythm and rhyme of poetry.

pros•e•cute (PRAHSS-ə-kyoot) *v. prosecutes, prosecuted, prosecuting.* Take to a law court; bring to trial.–The man was *prosecuted* for stealing the car.

pros•pect (PRAHSS-pekt) *n. prospects.* 1. Something looked forward to.–The *prospect* of getting a better job pleased Father.
2. A view. – The *prospect* from our front porch is very beautiful.
3. A person who may be suitable for a purpose or respond to a request.–David may be a *prospect* for our club.

pros•pec•tor (PRAHSS-pek-ter) *n. prospectors.* A person who seeks gold, oil, diamonds, and such things by searching for them in various regions.–The old *prospector* found a pocket of gold in the hills.

pros•per (PRAHSS-per) *v. prospers, prospered, prospering.* Do well; be successful.–Uncle Jim's new store is *prospering.*

pros•per•i•ty (prahss-PAIR-ə-tee) *n.* Good fortune; wealthy condition.–A man who has a good job and all he needs for comfortable living has *prosperity.*

pros•per•ous (PRAHSS-per-əss) *adj.; prosperously, adv.* Successful; well off. – The *prosperous* businessman gave a great deal of money to the playground fund.

pro•tect (prə-TEKT) *v. protects, protected, protecting.* 1. Guard; keep from danger.–The policemen *protect* us from criminals.
2. Shelter; keep from discomfort.–A raincoat *protects* you from the rain.

pro•tec•tion (prə-TEK-shən) *n.* 1. Keeping from danger.–The job of the Safety Patrol is the *protection* of children from traffic.
2. That which keeps from harm, or protects.
–A raincoat is a *protection* against rain.

pro•te•in (PROH-teen or PROH-tee-ən) *n. proteins.* A substance vital to all living animal and plant cells.–*Proteins* are found in milk, eggs, meat, and fish.

pro•test (prə-TEST) *v. protests, protested, protesting.* 1. Speak against; object.–The boy *protested* his low mark. He was sure he had done better, and said so.
2. Declare strongly.–The prisoner *protested* his innocence.

Prot•es•tant (PRAHT-iss-tənt) *n. Protestants* and *adj.* A member of any Christian church or sect other than the Roman Catholic and Greek Orthodox Churches.

pro•to•plasm (PROH-tə-plaz-əm) *n.* The living matter in all animal and plant cells. *Protoplasm,* seen under a microscope, has a colorless and jellylike appearance.

pro•trac•tor (proh-TRAK-ter) *n. protractors.* An instrument used for measuring angles and for drawing them accurately. *Protractors* are used by engineers, architects, mathematicians, and others.

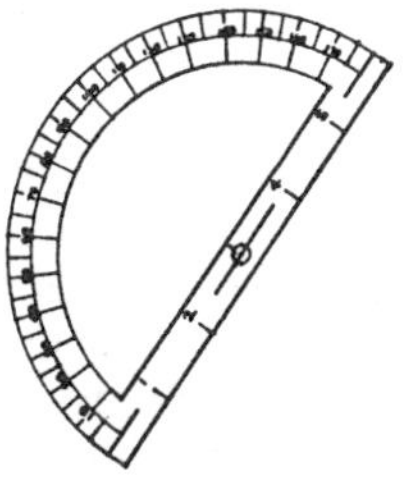

proud (PROWD) *adj. prouder, proudest; proudly, adv.* 1. Having a high regard for oneself or one's family, possessions, etc.–The boy was too *proud* to borrow carfare.
2. Conceited; having too high an opinion of oneself.–The *proud* boy annoyed others because he boasted a great deal.

prove (PROOV) *v. proves, proved, proving.* 1. Make certain the truth of.–The photograph of Bob in front of the Capitol *proved* that he had been in Washington.
2. Test and find as hoped for or believed to be. –Jane *proved* her subtraction answer by addition.–John *proved* himself in the game.

prov•erb (PRAHV-erb) *n. proverbs.* An old saying that gives advice.–"A stitch in time saves nine" is a *proverb.*

pro•vide (prə-VYD) *v. provides, provided, providing.* 1. Supply.–I will *provide* the ice cream if you will *provide* the cake.
2. Give as a condition. – The rules *provide* that no one over ten may enter the contest.
3. Prepare (for a situation) beforehand.– Father has *provided* for his old age.

prov•ince (PRAHV-inss) *n. provinces.* 1. A large division of a country.–Ontario is one of the *provinces* of Canada.

2. A section of a country far from the main city.–People from the *provinces* attended the great fair in the capital city.

pro•vi•sion (prə-VIZH-ən) *n. provisions.* 1. A given condition.–One of the *provisions* of the rules is that no one over ten may enter the contest.
2. A preparing; a making ready ahead of time.–The town had made *provision* for a heavy snowfall, and the plows started to work as soon as the storm began.
3. (In the plural) A supply, usually of things to eat and drink.–The campers have plenty of *provisions.*

pro•voke (prə-VOHK) *v. provokes, provoked, provoking.* 1. Bring on; be the cause of.– Harsh words *provoke* anger.
2. Annoy; make angry.–Bob's bad behavior *provoked* the teacher.

prow (PROW) *n. prows.* The very front part of a ship, plane, or airship.–The *prow* of the ship cut through the water.

prowl (PROWL) *v. prowls, prowled, prowling.* 1. Rove or wander about looking for food.–The hungry dog *prowled* about the alley.
2. Sneak about. – The man *prowled* about looking for something to steal.

pru•dence (PROO-dənss) *n.; prudent, adj.; prudently, adv.* Wise carefulness.–Bob shows *prudence.* He is not at all reckless.

prune (PROON) *n. prunes.* A kind of dried plum.
–*v. prunes, pruned, pruning.* Cut off (parts of plants). – The farmer *prunes* the dead branches of his trees.

pry (PRY) *v. pries, pried, prying.* 1. Try to find out about other people's affairs.–Nobody likes a person who is always *prying.*
2. Force with something used as a lever. – Mother *pried* the top off the jar with a knife.

psalm (SAHM) *n. psalms.* 1. A sacred song or poem.
2. (Spelled with a capital "P.") One of the poems in a part of the Bible known as "The Book of *Psalms.*"

psy•chi•a•trist (sy-KY-ə-trist) *n. psychiatrists.* A medical doctor who specializes in psychiatry, or the treatment of mental difficulties and diseases.

psy•chi•a•try (sy-KY-ə-tree) *n.* The science or practice of treating diseases, difficulties, or disorders of the mind.

psy•chol•o•gist (sy-KAHL-ə-jist) *n. psychologists.* A person who specializes in psychology, or the study of the mind.

psy•chol•o•gy (sy-KAHL-ə-jee) *n.* The science or study of the mind. *Psychology* deals with the mental functions of higher animals, especially those of human beings.

pub•lic (PUB-lik) *n.* The people as a whole. –The mayor of the city asked the *public* not to waste food.
–*adj.; publicly, adv.* 1. Of or for all the people. –A *public* park is open to everyone.
2. Governmental.–The mayor holds *public* office.

pub•li•ca•tion (pub-lə-KAY-shən) *n. publications.* 1. The act of telling or announcing something to the public, as in a newspaper or magazine.–This news is for *publication.*
2. A book, magazine, or paper printed to sell to the public.
3. The printing and sale to the public of a book, magazine, or similar printed matter.

pub•lic•i•ty (pub-LISS-ə-tee) *n.* Condition of being noticed by the people; public notice. –The flyer received much *publicity* through radio, television, and newspapers. People heard much about him.

pub•lish (PUB-lish) *v. publishes, published, publishing.* 1. Make known to the public.– The newspaper *published* the news of the accident on the day after it happened.
2. Make up and print books, magazines, etc., to sell to the public.

pub•lish•er (PUB-lish-er) *n. publishers.* A man or a company whose business is making up, printing, and selling books, magazines, newspapers, and other such publications.

pud•ding (PUHD-ing) *n. puddings.* A sweet, soft dessert, such as cornstarch *pudding,* tapioca *pudding,* or bread *pudding.*

pud•dle (PUD-l) *n. puddles.* A small pool of water.–Mary fell into a mud *puddle* and got her dress muddy.

pueb•lo (PWEB-loh) *n. pueblos.* An Indian village of the southwestern United States, especially one of those in New Mexico or Arizona. The houses in a *pueblo* are usually built of stone or adobe.

pug (PUG) *n. pugs* and *adj.* A small, tan, short-haired dog that has a turned-up nose and a curly tail.

pull (PUHL) *n. pulls.*
1. A drawing towards. –The man gave a *pull* on the string and it broke.
2. A strenuous climb.–The old car had a hard *pull* up the hill.
–*v. pulls, pulled, pulling.* 1. Use force to move or draw toward one; drag.–The horse *pulled* the cart up the hill.–Father *pulled* a dollar from his pocket.
2. Move.–The train *pulled* out of the station.

pul•let (PUHL-ət) *n. pullets.* A young hen.

pul•ley (PUHL-ee) *n. pulleys.* A wheel with the rim hollowed out so that a rope or chain can run on it without slipping off. *Pulleys,* usually several together, are used to lift heavy objects.

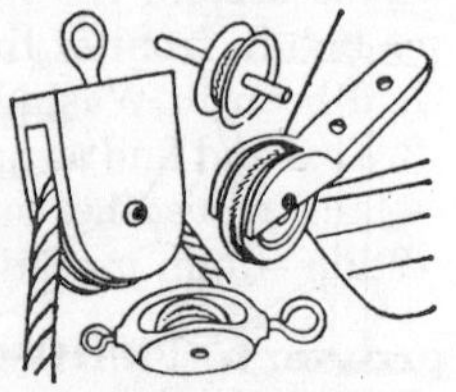

Pull•man (PUHL-mən) *n. Pullmans* and *adj.* A railroad car with berths which can be made up at night for people to sleep in.

pulp (PULP) *n.; pulpy, adj.* 1. The soft, juicy part of fruit.
2. Paper, wood, cloth, or anything else ground up very fine and mixed with enough water to make a paste.

pul•pit (PUHL-pit) *n. pulpits.* A platform where a minister stands to preach.

pulse (PULSS) *n. pulses.* 1. Beating of the heart.–The nurse listened to the boy's *pulse.*
2. Any regular beating or throbbing like that of the heart.–The boys heard the *pulse* of the motor in the steamship.
–*v. pulses, pulsed, pulsing.* Beat regularly, as a heart.–The machines *pulsed* steadily in the great factory.

pu•ma (PYOO-mə) *n. pumas.* A large American wildcat, also called a mountain lion.

pump (PUMP) *n. pumps.* 1. A machine for forcing liquid or gas through a pipe or hose from one place to another.–The car drew up to the gasoline *pump.*

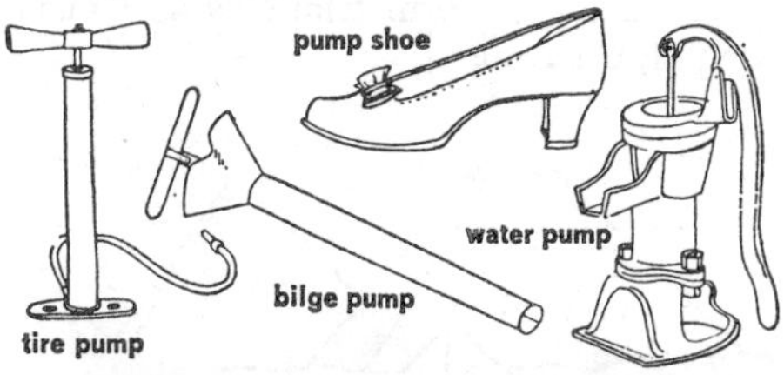

2. A kind of low shoe without laces.–Many girls wear *pumps* to dance in.
–*v. pumps, pumped, pumping.* 1. Fill with a pump.–Bob *pumped* up his bicycle tires.
2. Move, as by a pump.–One's heart *pumps* blood to all parts of the body.
3. Question (a person) continuously to draw out a secret.–Mary had a secret, but the others could not *pump* it out of her.

pump•kin (PUMP- *or* PUNG-kin) *n. pumpkins.* A large yellow fruit that grows on a vine on the ground.

punch (PUNCH) *n. punches.* 1. A blow.–One boxer gave the other a *punch* in the nose.
2. A drink made by mixing fruit juices and other liquids.
3. A tool used to make holes.–Mary made holes in the paper with a paper *punch.*
–*v. punches, punched, punching.* Hit; strike.–One boxer *punched* the other.

punc•tu•al (PUNGK-choo-əl) *adj.; punctually, adv.* Exactly on time; prompt; not late.–Tom is always *punctual* for his appointments. He never keeps anyone waiting.

punc•tu•ate (PUNGK-choo-ayt) *v. punctuates, punctuated, punctuating.* Divide up with commas, periods, question marks, etc., to make for easier reading and understanding.–The teacher told us to *punctuate* our stories.

punc•tu•a•tion (pungk-choo-AY-shən) *n.* Dividing up with marks such as the period and the comma, to make for easier reading and understanding.–Mary made three mistakes in *punctuation.*

pun•ish (PUN-ish) *v. punishes, punished, punishing.* Bring pain or unpleasantness to a person for some wrong done.–Some parents *punish* their children by spanking them.

pun•ish•ment (PUN-ish-mənt) *n. punishments.* The act of giving pain or taking away pleasure from one who has done wrong. –Spanking children is *punishment.*–Taking away a person's freedom is *punishment.*

punt (PUNT) *n. punts.* A kick of a football made by holding the ball out, dropping it, and kicking it before it touches the ground.–Our fullback made a long *punt.*
–*v. punts, punted, punting.* Kicking a football in this manner.

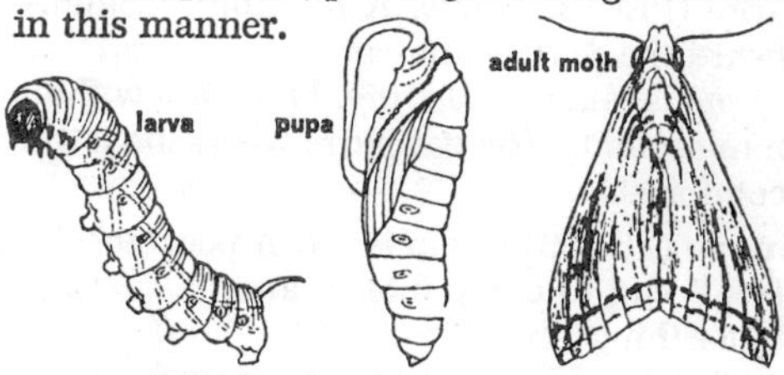

pu•pa (PYOO-pə) *n. pupae* or *pupas.* The stage through which some insects pass between the larva and the fully grown form. *Pupas* are often found in cocoons.

pu·pil (PYOO-pəl) *n. pupils.* 1. A boy or girl who is in school or studying under a teacher. –There are thirty *pupils* in our class.
2. The dark center of the eye.

pup·pet (PUP-it) *n. puppets.* A doll moved by strings or by hand on a tiny stage.

pup·py (PUP-ee) *n. puppies.* Some baby animals, especially baby dogs and foxes, are called *puppies* or pups. –Father bought a new *puppy* for Sally.

pur·chase (PER-chəss) *n. purchases.* Anything bought.–Mother's *purchase* was a dress.
–*v. purchases, purchased, purchasing.* Buy.–Mother went shopping to *purchase* a dress.

pure (PYUHR) *adj.; purely, adv.* 1. Clean and clear; not mixed with dirt or other unwanted things.–This water is *pure.*
2. Only; not including anything else.–The joke was played in *pure* fun, in fun only.

pu·ri·fy (PYUHR-ə-fy) *v. purifies, purified, purifying.* Make pure or clean.–The city *purifies* our drinking water.

pur·ple (PER-pəl) *n.* and *adj.* A dark, rich color that can be made by mixing red and blue together.–Some flowers, such as violets, are *purple.*

pur·pose (PER-pəss) *n. purposes; purposely, adv.* 1. An aim.–What is your *purpose* in going to school?
2. Deliberate intention.–You dropped your handkerchief on *purpose.* You meant to.

purr (PER) *n. purrs.* A humming sound.–I heard the *purr* of the cat.
–*v. purrs, purred, purring.* Make a low, humming sound.–The cat *purrs* when she is very comfortable.

purse (PERSS) *n. purses.* 1. A pocketbook; a small bag to carry money and other things in.
2. A sum of money put up as a prize in such events as boxing and horse racing. – The men fought for a *purse* of $10,000.

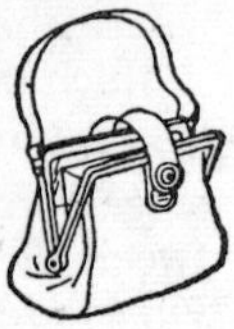

–*v. purses, pursed, pursing.* Pucker up.–When Baby cries, she *purses* her lips.

pur·sue (per-SOO *or* -SYOO) *v. pursues, pursued, pursuing.* Chase.–The policeman *pursued* the speeding automobile.

pur·suit (per-SOOT *or* -SYOOT) *n. pursuits.* 1. A chase.–The policeman is in *pursuit* of the speeding automobile.
2. Work; occupation.–What is your father's *pursuit?*

pus (PUSS) *n.* The yellowish-white matter that is found in boils and some other sores.

push (PUHSH) *n. pushes.* A shove.–We gave the car a *push* to see if we could start it.
–*v. pushes, pushed, pushing.* 1. Use force to move something away from one.–The boys *pushed* the automobile to start it.
2. Shove. – The policeman *pushed* through the crowd.

put (PUHT) *v. puts, put, putting.* 1. Place; lay.–*Put* the basket on the table.
2. Cause to change in place, feeling, or condition.–Mother *put* the cat out.

putt·er (PUT-er) *n. putters.* A golf club used for knocking the ball into the hole.
–*v. putters, puttered, puttering.* Keep busy but not get very much done.–Father *putters* in the garden on summer evenings.

puz·zle (PUZ-əl) *n. puzzles.* A problem to be worked out.–There is a crossword *puzzle* in the paper every morning.
–*v. puzzles, puzzled, puzzling.* Confuse.–The teacher was *puzzled* over the girl's behavior. The girl's behavior *puzzled* the teacher. She didn't know what to think about it.

pyr·a·mid (PIR-ə-mid) *n. pyramids.* 1. Any object that has a flat bottom and three or more sides that form triangles and meet at one point on top.

2. The massive structures built in ancient Egypt and used for tombs. The three great *pyramids* near Cairo are usually referred to as the *Pyramids,* spelled with a capital "P."

Q q

Q, q (KYOO) *n. Q's, q's.* The seventeenth letter of the alphabet.

quack (KWAK) *n. quacks.* 1. The cry of a duck.–A sheep says "Baa, baa." A duck says "*Quack, quack.*"
2. A person who fools others by pretending to know much about something about which he knows little or nothing.–The doctor who gave the sick old lady sugar pills was not a real doctor. He was a *quack.*
–*v quacks, quacked, quacking.* Make a sound like a duck.–The duck *quacked* loudly when Bill chased it.

quad·rant (KWAHD-rənt) *n. quadrants.* 1. One of the four quarters of a circle; an arc of ninety degrees.
2. An instrument used in navigation and astronomy. A *quadrant* is used to measure heights.

qua·drille (kwə- *or* kə-DRIL) *n. quadrilles.*
1. A square dance with four couples. The couples form a square and follow the directions of a person who calls out the different kinds of steps.
2. The music for such a dance.

quad·ru·ped (KWAHD-ruh-ped) *n. quadrupeds.* An animal with four feet. Horses, dogs, cattle, sheep, and many other animals are *quadrupeds.*

quad·ru·ple (KWAHD-roo-pəl) *n. quadruples.* An amount that is four times as great as another.–Eight is the *quadruple* of two. Eight is four times two.
–*adj.* 1. Four times as much, or four times as many.
2. Made up of four.–It is supposed to be good luck to find a *quadruple-* or four-leaved clover.

quad·ru·plet (kwahd-ROOP-lit) *n. quadruplets.* One of four children born to one mother at the same time.–Mrs. Ralph Jones had *quadruplets.*

quail (KWAYL) *n. quails.* A plump game bird sometimes called a bobwhite.–Father hunts *quail.*
–*v. quails, quailed, quailing.* Shrink with fear and dread.–Jack *quailed* at the thought of swimming the icy creek.

quaint (KWAYNT) *adj.; quaintly, adv.; quaintness, n.* Odd, strange, or old-fashioned, but interesting and charming.–Grandmother has a *quaint* velvet jacket like those worn years ago.

quake (KWAYK) *v. quakes, quaked, quaking.* Tremble; shake.–Mary *quaked* with excitement as the time drew near for her party.

Quak·er (KWAY-ker) *n. Quakers.* A member of the Society of Friends, a Christian religious group.

qual·i·fy (KWAHL-ə-fy) *v. qualifies, qualified, qualifying.* Be able or well suited.–Mary's teacher believes Mary is *qualified* to enter the musical contest.
–*qualification, n. qualifications.*

qual·i·ty (KWAHL-ə-tee) *n. qualities.* 1. Grade or degree of excellence.–A good *quality* of shoe leather will wear better than a poor *quality.*
2. Characteristic.–Jack's best *qualities* are honesty and truthfulness.
3. Merit or good value.–Mother would rather buy one dress of good *quality* than three dresses of poor material.

quan·ti·ty (KWAHN-tə-tee) *n. quantities.* 1. Amount.–The United States imports a large *quantity* of coffee.
2. A large number.–Grandmother baked *quantities* of cookies for the holidays.

quar·an·tine (KWOR- *or* KWAHR-ən-teen) *n.* A ship is in *quarantine* in the harbor. No one is allowed to leave until doctors make sure that the people on it have no disease which might be spread to others on land.
–*v. quarantines, quarantined, quarantining.* Keep away from others because of illness.–The children who had scarlet fever were *quarantined.*

quar•rel (KWOR- *or* KWAHR-əl) *n. quarrels; quarrelsome, adj.* Dispute or disagreement.–Jack and Bill are friends again after their *quarrel.*
–*v. quarrels, quarreled, quarreling.* 1. Disagree or argue angrily.–The boys *quarreled* over the bicycle.
2. Find fault. – Jack is always *quarreling* with the decisions of the umpire.

quar•ry (KWOR- *or* KWAHR-ee) *n. quarries.* 1. A place in the ground from which stone is dug.–There are many marble *quarries* in the state of Vermont.

2. A hunted bird or animal. – The dogs growled as if they knew they would find their *quarry* in the tree. And sure enough, the raccoon they were hunting was clinging to the highest branch.
–*v. quarries, quarried, quarrying.* Dig from a quarry.–Marble is *quarried* in Vermont.

quart (KWORT) *n. quarts.* A unit for the measurement of liquids.–Milk and other liquids are measured by the space they fill. Two pints make a *quart.* Four *quarts* make a gallon.

quar•ter (KWOR-ter) *n. quarters.* 1. One of four equal parts; one fourth.–If you divide a pie into four equal parts, each part is one fourth, or one *quarter.*

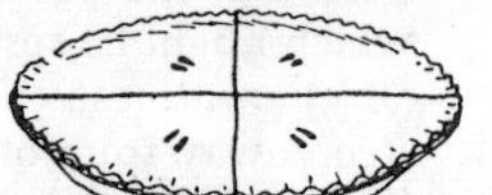

2. A section or region.–We visited the French *quarter* of the city.
3. Each of the four monthly phases of the moon. They are called: new moon, first *quarter,* full moon, and last, or fourth, *quarter.*
4. (In the plural) A place to live.–The troops moved into new *quarters.*
–*v. quarters, quartered, quartering.* 1. Provide living space for.–After the flood, many families were *quartered* in hotels.
2. Divide into four equal parts. – Mother *quartered* the orange for Sally.

quar•ter•ly (KWOR-ter-lee) *n. quarterlies.* A magazine published four times a year.
–*adj.* and *adv.* Happening or being done four times a year, or every three months.–Some people pay their income taxes *quarterly.*

quar•tet (kwor-TET) *n. quartets.* 1. A group of four persons or four things.–Four persons who sing together or play musical instruments together are a *quartet.*

2. A piece of music written for four voices or instruments.–Four boys sang a *quartet.*

quartz (KWORTSS) *n.* A kind of mineral that is made up of very hard crystals. *Quartz* is colorless, pink, yellow, brown, green, or purple.

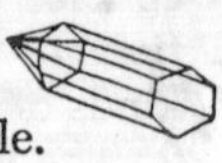

quay (KEE) *n. quays.* A wharf or landing place where boats can load and unload.–The merchant went down to the *quay* every day to watch for his ship.

queen (KWEEN) *n. queens; queenly, adj.* 1. A woman ruler, or the wife of a king.

2. A girl or woman who is chosen to be the most important one at some special event, or one who is very popular. – Mary was chosen *Queen* of the May.
3. A fully developed female bee or ant. – The *queen* insect lays the eggs.
4. A playing card that has the picture of a queen on it.

queer (KWIR) *adj. queerer, queerest; queerly, adv.; queerness, n.* Peculiar or strange; odd.–The man had a *queer* feeling of uneasiness as he stepped through the doorway of the old house.

quench (KWENCH) *v. quenches, quenched, quenching.* Extinguish or put out; put an end to.–Cool water will *quench* your thirst better than soda pop.–Rain *quenched* the forest fire.

que•ry (KWIR-ee) *n. queries.* A question.–"Where are you going?" is a *query.*
–*v. queries, queried, querying.* Inquire; ask a question. – "What is your name?" *queried* Sally.

quest (KWEST) *n. quests.* 1. A search or hunt for something.–The hunters went into the forest in *quest* of deer.
2. A search undertaken as a mission by a knight.–Sir George vowed to kill the dragon and set out in *quest* of the beast right away.

ques•tion (KWESS-chən) *n. questions.* 1. A sentence that asks something. – Sally asks many *questions,* because there are many things she wants to know.
2. Subject or problem.–At the meeting tonight, the people will discuss the *question* of improving the playgrounds.
3. A doubt or uncertainty.–If there is any *question* of the safety of the ice, do not go skating.
–*v. questions, questioned, questioning.* 1. Ask. –The teacher *questioned* us about the lost book.
2. Be uncertain of, or doubt.–No one can *question* Jack's honesty.

ques•tion•naire (kwess-chən-AIR) *n. questionnaires.* A list of questions designed to find out something specific, such as why you buy a certain brand of soap or what kind of TV programs you prefer.

queue (KYOO) *n. queues.* 1. A long braid of hair that hangs down the back. For this meaning, this word is also spelled "cue."
2. A waiting line, as at a store counter or ticket booth.–When a good movie is in town, people often have to stand in *queues* to get tickets.

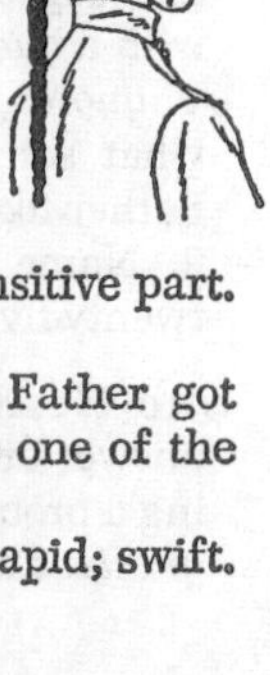

quick (KWIK) *n.* 1. Deep and sensitive part. –Mary bit her nails to the *quick.*
2. People who are alive.–When Father got over his cold, he said he felt like one of the *quick* again; he felt really alive.
–*adj. quicker, quickest.* 1. Fast or rapid; swift. –The magician was so *quick* that we could not follow his movements.
2. Hasty or unthinking.–Jack's worst fault is his *quick* temper.

quick•en (KWIK-ən) *v. quickens, quickened, quickening.* 1. Hasten or move faster; hurry. –Jack *quickened* his steps as the rain began to fall.
2. Arouse or excite.–The man's story *quickened* Ed's interest in him.

quick•ly (KWIK-lee) *adv.* Fast; hastily; with speed; rapidly.–We must pack *quickly* if we hope to catch the train.

quick•ness (KWIK-nəss) *n.* Speed; swiftness.–Bob's *quickness* in the football game surprised the other team.

quick•sand (KWIK-sand) *n. quicksands.* A very deep mass of soft, wet sand that is dangerous because a man or animal can sink into it completely, quickly, and easily.

quick•sil•ver (KWIK-sil-ver) *n.* Mercury, a silver-white metal. *Quicksilver,* or mercury, is the only metal that is fluid at normal temperatures. It is used in thermometers because it expands when it is heated and so moves up the glass tube.

qui•et (KWY-ət) *n.* Stillness and peace.–The *quiet* of the country is restful to Grandmother after a week in the city.
–*v. quiets, quieted, quieting.* Silence and soothe, or calm down.–The teacher *quieted* the excited boy.
–*adj. quieter, quietest; quietly, adv.* 1. Silent and still; calm.–The garden was so *quiet* that we could hear the bees humming.
2. Motionless.–There was no breeze, and the leaves were *quiet.*
3. Restful and peaceful.–We spent a *quiet* day in the country.
4. Gentle; mild.–Mother has a *quiet* manner.
5. Not bright or flashy.–Grandmother wore a *quiet* lavender dress.

qui•et•ness (KWY-ət-nəss) *n.* Stillness; calmness.–The *quietness* in the country is restful to Grandmother.

quill (KWIL) *n. quills.* 1. A large, stiff feather taken from the wing or tail of a goose, duck, or other fowl.
2. A pen made from a sharpened feather.–In the picture in our classroom, Columbus is drawing a map with a *quill.*
3. A stiff hair or spine.–Porcupines' bodies are covered with *quills.*

quilt (KWILT) *n. quilts.* A stuffed or filled bed cover used for warmth. – Grandmother stuffs her patchwork *quilts* with cotton.

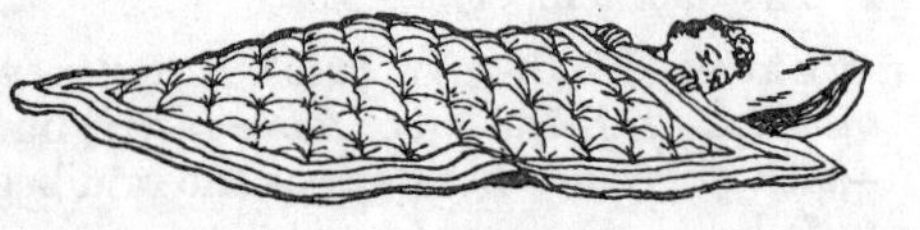

–*v. quilts, quilted, quilting.* Make a quilt; sew together, with fine stitches, two layers of cloth with something soft inside.–Mother is *quilting* a bathrobe for Sally.

quince (KWINSS) *n. quinces.* 1. A golden-yellow apple-shaped fruit that has a strong smell and a sour taste. *Quinces* are used in jelly and marmalade.
2. The shrub or small tree on which the fruit grows. The flowering *quince* has many branches, full leaves, and large white or pink flowers.

qui•nine (KWY-nyn) *n.* A bitter medicine used in treating malaria and other sicknesses.

quin•tu•plet (kwin-TUP-lət *or* kwin-TOO-plət *or* kwin-TYOO-plət) *n. quintuplets.* 1. Five things of a kind.
2. One of five animals or children born to the same mother at the same time.

quit (KWIT) *v. quits, quitted, quitting.* 1. Stop; halt.–The farmer *quits* work at eight o'clock.
2. Leave.–Bob *quit* his summer job to go back to school.

quite (KWYT) *adv.* 1. Fully; entirely; completely.–The story is not *quite* finished.
2. Truly; really.–Mary's cold is *quite* bad.
3. More than a little.–Bob was *quite* disappointed by the results of the game.
4. Very much of.–You have *quite* a suntan.

quiv•er (KWIV-er) *n. quivers.* A case for carrying arrows. – Robin Hood wore a *quiver* over his shoulder.
–*v. quivers, quivered, quivering.* Tremble or shiver gently. – The leaves *quivered* in the breeze.

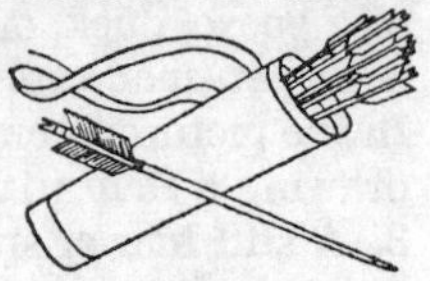

quiz (KWIZ) *n. quizzes.* A test or examination.–Our teacher gave us a *quiz* in arithmetic.
–*v. quizzes, quizzed, quizzing.* Ask questions of.–It is not polite to *quiz* others about their private affairs.
–*adj.* Bob likes to test himself on the *quiz* section in the magazine.

quoit (KWOIT) *n. quoits.* A ring of flattened metal that is used in playing a game. The game is played by pitching the metal *quoits* at a peg in the ground to see who can get the *quoit* on or nearest the peg.

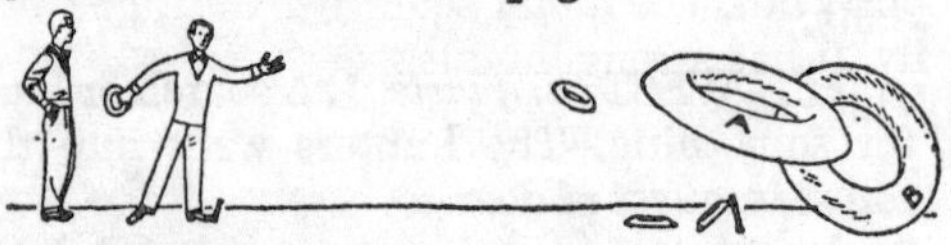

quo•rum (KWOR-əm) *n. quorums.* The minimum number of members who must be present before a meeting can be held or a vote can be taken. The rules of a club tell how many club members are needed to make a *quorum.*

quo•ta (KWOH-tə) *n. quotas.* A set share; a determined part; a certain percentage of a total.–Everyone was given ten tickets to sell. If anyone sold his *quota,* that is all ten tickets, he would be rewarded with a free ticket for himself.

quo•ta•tion (kwoh-TAY-shən) *n. quotations* and *adj.* The exact words spoken or written by one person when repeated by another person.–Bob said to him, "I would like to go to the ball game." The words in *quotation* marks are a *quotation.* The marks (". . ."), before the word I and after the word game, are *quotation* marks. They show the beginning and the end of the *quotation.*–"The Lord is my shepherd; I shall not want" is a *quotation* from the Bible.

quote (KWOHT) *n. quotes.* A quotation; the exact words spoken or written by one person and repeated by another.–Father answered with a *quote* from Shakespeare.
–*v. quotes, quoted, quoting.* 1. Repeat exactly what someone else has said or written. – Father likes to *quote* things he has read.
2. Name the price of.–The farmer *quoted* twenty-five dollars for his load of hay.

quo•tient (KWOH-shənt) *n. quotients.* The answer or number which you get after working a problem in division.–In $12 \div 3 = 4$, the *quotient* is 4.

R r

R, r (AHR) *n. R's, r's.* The eighteenth letter of the alphabet.

rab•bi (RAB-y) *n. rabbis.* A pastor of the Jewish faith.

rab•bit (RAB-it) *n. rabbits.* A small, swift animal with soft fur, long ears, and a short, puffy tail. The *rabbit* belongs to the hare family. It has strong hind legs for jumping.

ra•bies (RAY-beez) *n.* A disease which makes dogs and other animals go mad. If a person is bitten by a mad dog, he too may get *rabies.*

rac•coon or **ra•coon** (rə-KOON) *n. raccoons* or *racoons.* A small fur-bearing animal that lives in trees and moves about mostly at night.

race (RAYSS) *n. races.* 1. A contest of speed. –There are auto *races,* foot *races,* horse *races,* swimming *races,* and many other kinds.
2. A large group of people with the same skin color, kind of hair, and other common traits.

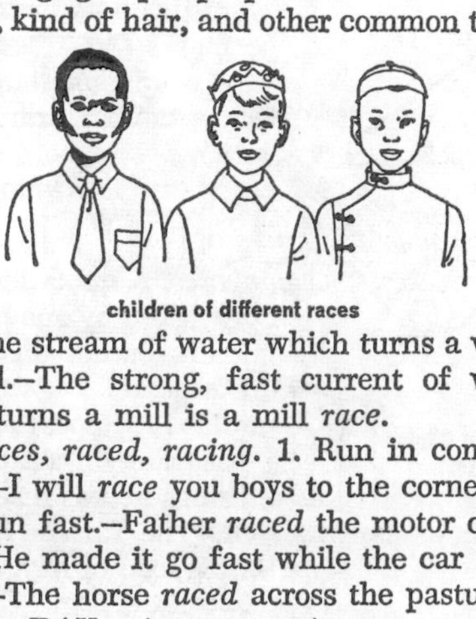

children of different races

3. The stream of water which turns a water wheel.–The strong, fast current of water that turns a mill is a mill *race.*
–*v. races, raced, racing.* 1. Run in competition.–I will *race* you boys to the corner.
2. Run fast.–Father *raced* the motor of his car. He made it go fast while the car stood still.–The horse *raced* across the pasture.

rac•er (RAY-ser) *n. racers.* A person, animal, or thing that races. An automobile, a horse, a boat, or a person that takes part in a race is a *racer.*

rack (RAK) *n. racks.* 1. A framework that is used as a holder, such as a toothbrush *rack,* a towel *rack,* a *rack* to drain dishes on, a shoe *rack,* or a hat *rack.*

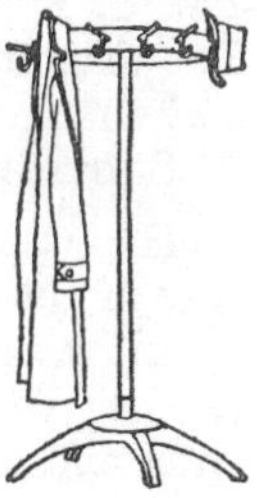

2. A box made of slats.–Grandfather puts the hay for the horses in a feed *rack.*
3. A device used long ago for torturing or hurting people by stretching their limbs.

rack•et (RAK-it) *n. rackets.* 1. A loud, confused noise.–The children made so much *racket* playing circus that Mother didn't hear the bell ring.
2. A bat with a long handle and a flat oval frame laced tightly with strong cord.–Tennis and some other games are played by hitting a ball with a *racket.*

3. A dishonest scheme or plan for getting people's money.

ra•dar (RAY-dahr) *n.* An instrument which uses radio waves for detecting standing or moving objects that can't be seen. *Radar* can determine an object's distance, speed, and direction of travel. It is a valuable aid to sea and air navigation.

ra•di•ant (RAY-dee-ənt) *adj.; radiantly, adv.* Shining; bright; brilliant and joyous.–Sally has a *radiant* smile. Her whole face lights up with joy when she smiles.

ra•di•ate (RAY-dee-ayt) *v. radiates, radiated, radiating.* 1. Send forth rays of. – The radiator *radiates* heat.–The bride's face *radiated* joy.
2. Come forth in rays.–Heat *radiating* from the hot water pipes warmed the garage.
3. Spread out from a central point.–The spokes of a wheel *radiate* from the hub.

ra•di•a•tion (ray-dee-AY-shən) *n.* 1. Sending out and spreading rays, such as those of light, heat, and electricity. – Uncontrolled atomic *radiation* can destroy all life in a wide area.
2. The rays sent out.–Thick walls of lead and concrete protect workers in atomic laboratories from dangerous *radiation.*

ra·di·a·tor (RAY-dee-ay-ter) *n. radiators.* A heater made up of tubes or pipes through which hot water or steam passes. *Radiators* are used to heat houses.

rad·i·cal (RAD-ə-kal) *n. radicals.* A person who favors extreme change or reform.
–*adj.* 1. Fundamental; going to the roots.–The teaching of math has undergone a *radical* change in recent years.
2. Extreme; favoring extreme change.

ra·di·o (RAY-dee-oh) *n. radios* and *adj.* 1. A way of sending sounds over a long distance by means of electrical waves, without connecting wires. One instrument, called the "transmitter," receives sounds and sends them out in the form of the waves. Another instrument, called the "receiver," receives the waves and changes them back into sound.
2. A *radio* transmitter.
3. A *radio* receiver.
4. A message sent by radio.
–*v. radio, radioed, radioing.* Send or despatched by radio.

ra·di·o·ac·tive (ray-dee-oh-AK-tiv) *adj.* Sending out rays from an atomic nucleus. Uranium and radium are both *radioactive* elements.

rad·ish (RAD-ish) *n. radishes.* A vegetable that grows in the ground like a carrot or a turnip. *Radishes* are round or long, red or white, and are eaten raw. Some *radishes* have a sharp taste.

ra·di·um (RAY-dee-əm) *n.* A highly radioactive metallic element. *Radium* was discovered by Professor and Madame Pierre Curie in 1898. It is used in the treatment of cancer and certain other diseases.

ra·di·us (RAY-dee-əss) *n. radii.* 1. A straight line drawn from the center of a circle or sphere to the outside rim or circumference.

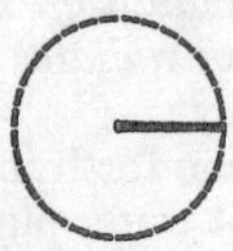

2. The length of this line.–The circle has a two-inch *radius.*
3. Area of a circle with a radius of a certain length.–In looking for the lost child the police searched the area within a *radius* of ten miles from his home.

raf·fle (RAF-əl) *n. raffles.* A way of raising money by selling chances on a prize to many people. The prize is given to the holder of the winning ticket.
–*v. raffles, raffled, raffling.* Sell by selling chances.–We *raffled* a quilt to get money for the playground. We sold it by selling chances on it.

raft (RAFT) *n. rafts.* A platform of boards, logs, etc., fastened together, which float on the water like a boat.

raft·er (RAF-ter) *n. rafters.* One of the large crosswise beams or timbers that hold up the roof of a building.

rag (RAG) *n. rags.* 1. piece of used cloth.–Mother often uses *rags* for cleaning.
2. Old, torn clothing.–At midnight, Cinderella's ball gown turned to *rags.*

rage (RAYJ) *n. rages.* 1. Wild anger.–Jack was in a *rage* over the theft of his bicycle.
2. A fashion or fad.–Hair ribbons are all the *rage.* All the girls are wearing them.
–*v. rages, raged, raging.* Act wildly. – The accused prisoner *raged* like a mad person.

rag·ged (RAG-id) *adj.* 1. Torn in pieces. –After the football game, Jack's clothes were all *ragged.*
2. Dressed in ragged clothing.–The tramp was *ragged.*
3. Rough, or not regular.–The rocks along the cliff are sharp and *ragged.*

RAILROADS

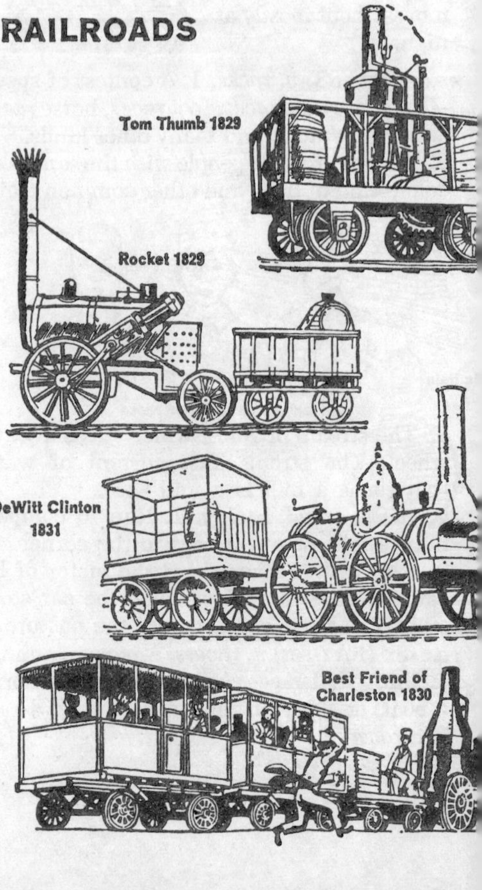

rag•weed (RAG-weed) *n. ragweeds.* A common weed. The fine pollen from its blossoms gives some people hay fever.

raid (RAYD) *n. raids.* 1. A swift attack.–The enemy airplanes made a sudden night *raid* on the city.
2. The policemen made a *raid* on the gambling club. They forced their way in and captured the gamblers.
–*v. raids, raided, raiding.* 1. Make an attack on.–The airplanes *raided* the city.
2. Break into and seize property from.–The burglars *raided* the store.

rail (RAYL) *n. rails.* 1. A slender bar of wood or metal.–Streetcars and trains run on tracks made of metal *rails.*–Some fences are made of wooden *rails.*
2. A bar in a railing.–Baby's crib has *rails* around the sides.
–*v. rails, railed, railing.* Complain or scold bitterly.–From way down the street we could hear the woman *railing* at her husband for his laziness.

rail•ing (RAY-ling) *n. railings.* An enclosure or fence made of rails.–Father put a *railing* around the porch so that the baby would not fall off.

rail•road (RAYL-rohd) *n. railroads.* 1. A track for trains, made of steel rails fastened to wooden ties with spikes.
2. A system of train tracks, trains, stations, and the body of men in charge of them.–Uncle Jim works for the *railroad.*

rail•way (RAYL-way) *n. railways.* 1. A railroad.
2. Any track made of rails for wheels to run on.

rain (RAYN) *n. rains; rainy, adj.* 1. Water which falls from clouds.–Drops of *rain* beat against my face.
2. A fall of rain.–We had a heavy *rain.*
3. A shower of anything falling like rain.–A *rain* of petals came from the apple tree.
–*v. rains, rained, raining.* 1. Fall in drops from the clouds.–It *rained* today.
2. Fall like rain.–Rice and bits of colored paper *rained* on the bride and groom.

rain•bow (RAYN-boh) *n. rainbows.* A large arch or bow of colors which often is seen in the sky opposite the sun during a light rain. It is caused by the sun shining through raindrops.–The colors of the *rainbow* are red, orange, yellow, green, blue, indigo, and violet. People used to think that rainbows were a sign of good luck.

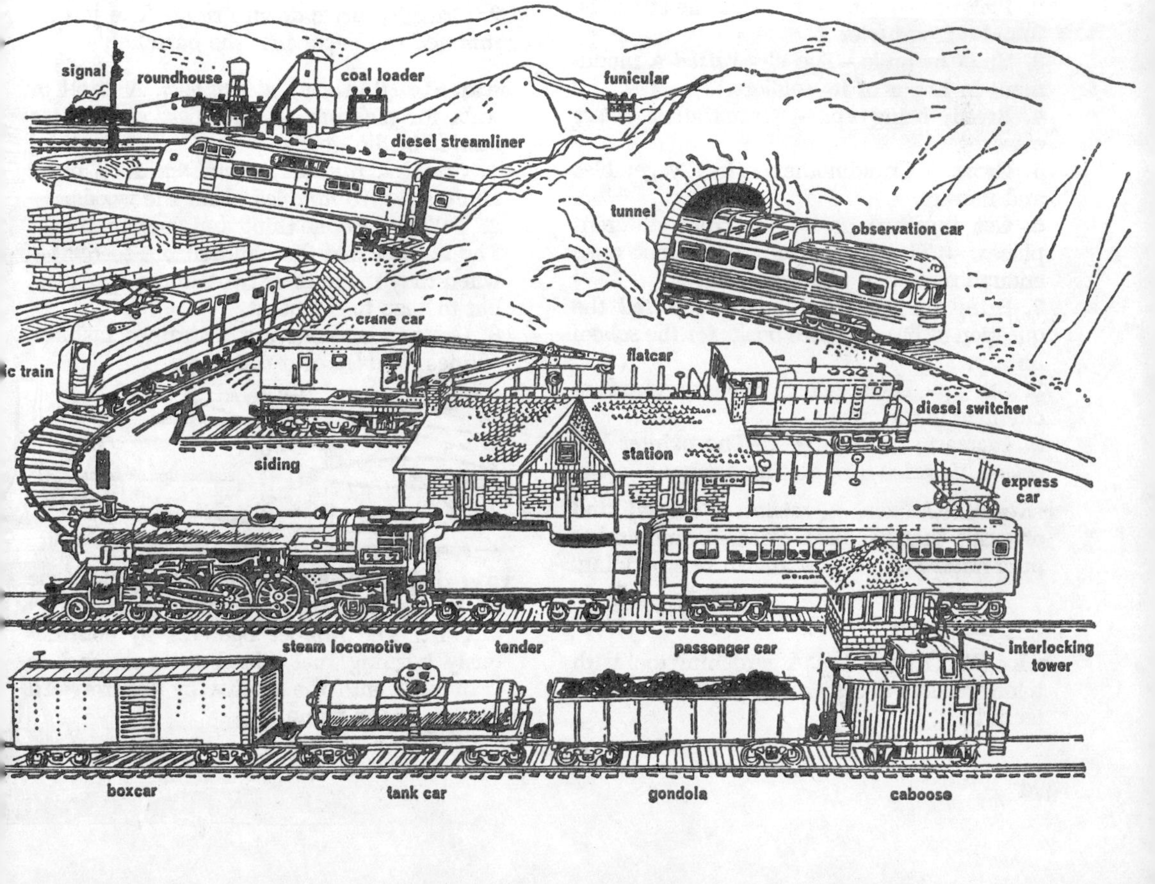

rain•coat (RAYN-koht) *n. raincoats.* A waterproof coat to keep the rain off.—When it rains, Bob wears his *raincoat.*

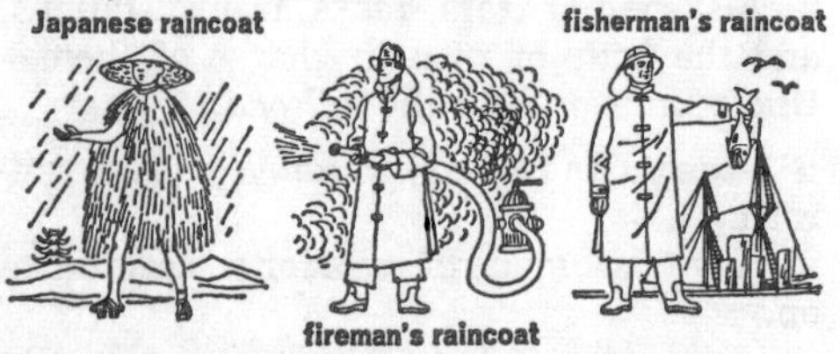

rain•drop (RAYN-drahp) *n. raindrops.* One drop of water falling from the clouds.

rain•fall (RAYN-fawl) *n. rainfalls.* 1. A shower of rain.—Today we had a heavy *rainfall.*
2. The total amount of rain that falls in a particular place during a month, year, etc.—The *rainfall* in Oregon is greater than the *rainfall* in Arizona.

rain•storm (RAYN-storm) *n. rainstorms.* A rainfall, sometimes with wind.—On our way home from school we were caught in a *rainstorm.*

raise (RAYZ) *n. raises.* Increase in wages.—Father got a *raise* of twenty dollars a week when he got his promotion.
—*v. raises, raised, raising.* 1. Lift, bring, or put up.—The witness *raised* his right hand.
2. Pick up.—When Tom *raised* the stone, he found a frog under it.
3. Erect or build.—The city *raised* a monument in honor of its soldiers.
4. Breed; bring up. — Grandfather *raises* cows.
5. Grow. — Grandmother *raises* vegetables and flowers.
6. Get together or collect from different places. — The poor family could not *raise* enough money to pay the rent.
7. Bring up for attention.—Bob *raised* the question of buying more books for the school library.
8. Stir up.—The speaker's remarks *raised* excitement in the crowd.
9. Increase; make higher.—The painter has *raised* his price for painting a room.

rai•sin (RAY-zən) *n. raisins.* A special kind of grape that has been dried.—Grandmother puts *raisins* on cookies and in rice pudding.

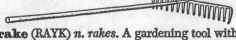

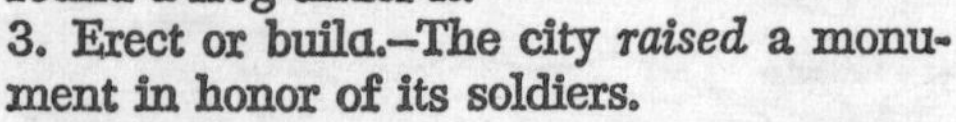

rake (RAYK) *n. rakes.* A gardening tool with a long handle and a cross rod with comblike teeth in it.
—*v. rakes, raked, raking.* 1. Comb up; gather together.—Sally likes to *rake* the leaves in the yard. She likes to use the rake.
2. Search through thoroughly.—Mary *raked* the contents of the old trunk trying to find a costume to wear.

ral•ly (RAL-ee) *n. rallies.* A large, informal meeting of people to get them enthusiastic about something.—We held a *rally* to raise money for the playground.
—*v. rallies, rallied, rallying.* 1. Start to improve or take a turn for the better.—The sick boy *rallied* after the doctor had cared for him.
2. Get together.—Bob tried to *rally* enough boys for a ball team.
3. Gather in numbers to help.—The towns-people all *rallied* to the scene of the fire.

ram (RAM) *n. rams.* 1. A male sheep.—Some *rams* have horns.

2. A machine for knocking down walls. —The battering *ram* was used in the Middle Ages for besieging castles.
—*v. rams, rammed, ramming.* 1. Strike or crash into.—An auto behind us *rammed* our car.
2. Crush or drive down firmly.—The janitor *rammed* the paper into the barrel.

ram•ble (RAM-bəl) *n. rambles.* A stroll or walk for pleasure. — The girls went for a *ramble* in the woods.
—*v. rambles, rambled, rambling.* 1. Wander aimlessly.—We *rambled* about the woods.
2. Talk first of one thing and then another.—The teacher told the children not to *ramble* when they made their two-minute speeches, but to keep to the point.
3. Grow in a wandering, untrained fashion. —Vines *rambled* over the porch.

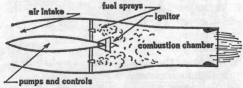

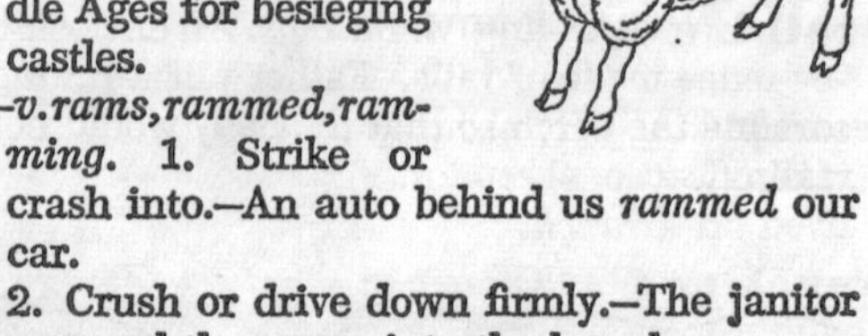

ram-jet (RAM-jet) *ram-jets.* A special type of jet engine used in certain jet-propelled aircraft. The *ram-jet* operates by continuously burning fuel mixed with air that is "rammed" into the engine by the forward motion of the plane.

ramp (RAMP) *n. ramps.* A slanting passageway joining two places, one of which is higher than the other.–We walked up the *ramp* in the stadium.

ram•page (RAM-payj) *n. rampages.* Violent behavior. – The wild bull kicked down the barn door and broke through the fence in its *rampage.*

ram•part (RAM-pahrt) *n. ramparts.* A broad, high, protecting wall made of earth, sometimes with watchtowers on the top.–Francis Scott Key watched the *ramparts* of Fort McHenry to see if the flag was still flying there as he wrote "The Star-Spangled Banner."

ram•shack•le (RAM-shak-əl) *adj.* Shaky; ready to fall apart; rickety.–The *ramshackle* hut was blown down during the storm.

ran (RAN) *v.* One form of the verb *run.*–The child *ran* to his mother.

ranch (RANCH) *n. ranches.* Large farm for raising cattle, sheep, or horses.–The cowboy lived on a *ranch.*

ranch•er (RANCH-er) *n. ranchers.* A man who works on, owns, or runs a ranch or big stock farm.

ran•dom (RAN-dəm) *adj.* Without specific plan or purpose; chance.–My seeing Bill in the store was just a *random* meeting.

–*At random* means haphazardly, or in an unorganized way.–The children ran about *at random.*

rang (RANG) *v.* One form of the verb *ring.*–The teacher *rang* the bell.

range (RAYNJ) *n. ranges.* 1. Row or chain of mountains or hills. – The Rockies are the highest mountain *range* in North America.

2. A stove to cook on. –Mother has a new electric *range.*

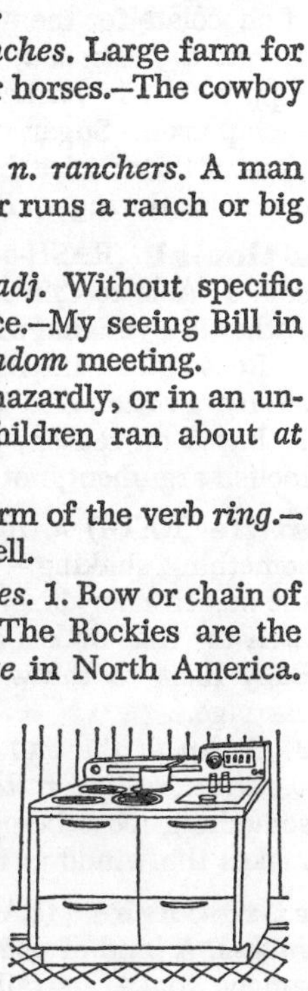

3. Reach.–The gun's *range* is a thousand yards.–Bob was careful to stay out of *range* of the angry bear.

4. Number or variety.–The books in the store covered a wide *range* of subjects.

5. Unfenced land where cattle graze, or eat grass.

–*v. ranges, ranged, ranging.* 1. Wander or roam.–In the days of the early settlers, buffaloes *ranged* the prairies.

2. Extend.–The price of baseballs *ranged* from fifty cents to four dollars.

rang•er (RAYN-jer) *n. rangers.* 1. A person whose duty is to watch over a forest and aid in putting out fires that may start.

2. A member of a group of armed men whose duty is to patrol a certain part of the country.

rank (RANGK) *n. ranks.* 1. A row.–The soldiers marched in *ranks* of four, side by side.

2. Standing or class.–A sergeant's *rank* is above that of a corporal.

–*v. ranks, ranked, ranking.* 1. Have a certain standing. – A corporal *ranks* lower than a sergeant.

2. List in order.–The students were *ranked* according to their grades.

–*adj. ranker, rankest.* Strong and disagreeable in odor and taste.–Butter and other fats that stand a long time sometimes become *rank.*

ran•sack (RAN-sak) *v. ransacks, ransacked, ransacking.* 1. Search through thoroughly.–Mother *ransacked* the clothes closets, but she couldn't find her green dress.

2. Rob or plunder. – The band of outlaws *ransacked* the town.

ran•som (RAN-səm) *n. ransoms.* Money paid to free a person who has been kidnaped or captured.–The rich man paid a *ransom* of twenty-five thousand dollars to free his son.

–*v. ransoms, ransomed, ransoming.* Pay ransom for.–The prince offered to *ransom* his men, who were prisoners of the enemy.

rap (RAP) *n. raps.* Light knock.–I heard a *rap* on my window.

–*v. raps, rapped, rapping.* 1. Tap, or hit lightly and quickly.–On Halloween the children *rapped* on the neighbors' windows.

2. Speak sharply. – The lawyer *rapped* out the questions.

rap•id (RAP-id) *adj.; rapidly, adv.* Fast or quick. – After the race, Bob could feel the *rapid* beating of his heart.

rap•ids (RAP-idz) *n. pl.* A place in a river where the water flows very fast over rocks, but not in a falls.–The boys went through the *rapids* in their canoe.

rap•ture (RAP-cher) *n. raptures.* Great joy and delight.–The family's *rapture* at their son's return was great.

rare (RAIR) *adj. rarer, rarest; rarely, adv.* 1. Seldom to be found.–This piece of china is valuable because it is so *rare.* There are very few of its kind.–The birth of quintuplets is *rare.*
2. Cooked only a short time, so as to be still juicy and pink (of meat).–Mother likes her meat well-done. Father likes it *rare.*

ras•cal (RASS-kəl) *n. rascals.* 1. Mean, wicked, tricky person.–The *rascals* who sold land they did not own were arrested as they tried to leave town.
2. Mischievous or trouble-making child or young person.–Grandmother told us Father was a *rascal* when he was a little boy.

rash (RASH) *n. rashes.* A breaking out of red spots on the skin.–A *rash* may be a sign of measles.
–adj. rasher, rashest; rashly, adv. Reckless.–It is *rash* to promise to do more than you are sure you can do.

rasp•ber•ry (RAZ-bair-ee) *n. raspberries* and *adj.* A small, seedy berry that grows on a bush. *Raspberries* are usually red, but may be black, purple, or yellow. – *Raspberry* jam has many little seeds in it.

rat (RAT) *n. rats.* An animal that looks like a large mouse. *Rats* gnaw with their sharp teeth. *Rats* are pests, and often carry diseases.

rate (RAYT) *n. rates.* 1. Amount; degree. – The plane flew at the *rate* of three hundred miles an hour. At that speed it could go three hundred miles in one hour.–The *rate* of interest on the loan will be six per cent. You will have to pay six dollars a year for each hundred dollars you borrow.
2. A price.–The theater *rates* are higher for the evening show than for the afternoon show.
3. Rank.–The hotel was first-*rate.*
–v. rates, rated, rating. 1. Set a value on.–The real-estate agent *rated* the house at ten thousand dollars.
2. Rank or consider.–Bob is generally *rated* the best student in his class.
–At any rate means anyway.*–At any rate,* we reached home before the rain started.

rath•er (RATH-er) *adv.* 1. More gladly; with more willingness.–I'd *rather* travel by train than by muleback.
2. Somewhat. – Mother is *rather* worried about Baby's cold.
3. Instead.–The bear is not dead; *rather,* it is asleep.
–Rather than means instead of.–The road runs northeast, *rather than* directly north.

rat•i•fy (RAT-ə-fy) *v. ratifies, ratified, ratifying.* Approve formally.–The Senate is expected to *ratify* the new treaty.

ra•tio (RAY-shoh *or* RAY-shee-oh) *n. ratios.* Numerical relation; proportion.–The boys in the class outnumbered the girls in the *ratio* of three to two. This means that for every three boys in the class there were two girls.

ra•tion (RASH-ən *or* RAY-shən) *n. rations.* 1. The amount of a certain article each person may have.–During the war doctors were allowed larger *rations* of gasoline than were given to men who drove their cars only for pleasure.
2. A certain amount of food allowed for each day.–The soldiers were given *rations* of chocolate for the march.
–v. rations, rationed, rationing. Give out (a supply that is limited) in fair amounts to each person.–Sugar, coffee, and gasoline are some of the articles that are *rationed* in most countries during wartime.

ra•tion•al (RASH-ən-əl) *adj.; rationally, adv.* 1. Able to think clearly and sensibly.–Father is a *rational* man.
2. Reasonable; intelligent; sensible. – John offered a *rational* excuse for his absence.
3. Based on reason; of reason. – That is a foolish argument, not a *rational* one.

rat•tle (RAT-l) *n. rattles.* 1. The sound of something shaking.–We heard the *rattle* of the screen door during the storm.
2. A toy that makes a noise when shaken.–Baby likes to throw her *rattle* out of the carriage.
3. Organ at the end of a rattlesnake's tail.
–v. rattles, rattled, rattling. Make the sound of something loose being shaken. – The wind makes the windows *rattle.*

rat•tle•snake (RAT-l-snayk) *n. rattlesnakes.* A kind of poisonous snake. Its tail has rattles, or loose rings, that make a rattling noise when the tail moves.

rav•el (RAV-əl) *v. ravels, raveled* or *ravelled, raveling* or *ravelling.* Separate or become separated into threads or yarn.–Mother hemmed the towel so that it would not *ravel.*

ra•ven (RAY-vən) *n. ravens.* A very shiny black bird somewhat like the crow, but larger.

–*adj.* Black and shiny. –Snow White had white skin, red lips, and *raven* hair.

ra•vine (rə-VEEN) *n. ravines.* A deep, narrow hollow made by running water. – We stood on the cliff and looked down into a *ravine.*

raw (RAW) *adj. rawer, rawest.* 1. Not cooked. –Cabbage can be eaten *raw.*
2. Not ready to use (of materials).–Cotton as it comes from the fields and logs as they come from the woods are *raw* materials.
3. Cold and wet (of weather).–A *raw* March wind was blowing.
4. Not trained, or not experienced.–Many *raw* sailors become seasick.
5. Sore from having the skin scraped off.–The *raw* sore on Mary's knee was caused by her falling on the sidewalk.

ray (RAY) *n. rays.* 1. Narrow beam, as of light.–A *ray* of light shone through the hole.
2. A faint sign (of hope).–Jack can always see a *ray* of hope when things look bad.
3. One of many lines extending from a center in all directions.–Sally's picture of the sun was a big circle with *rays* around it.
4. A kind of flat fish.

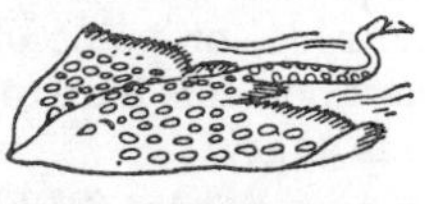

ray•on (RAY-ahn) *n.* A smooth, soft cloth woven of threads made from wood. *Rayon* looks something like silk.

raze (RAYZ) *v. razes, razed, razing.* Destroy or tear down.–The workmen *razed* the old building. They tore it down to the ground.

ra•zor (RAY-zer) *n. razors.* A sharp-bladed tool used by men for shaving. Some *razors* have folding blades; some are of a safety type in which the blade is partly covered; others have blades operated by electricity.

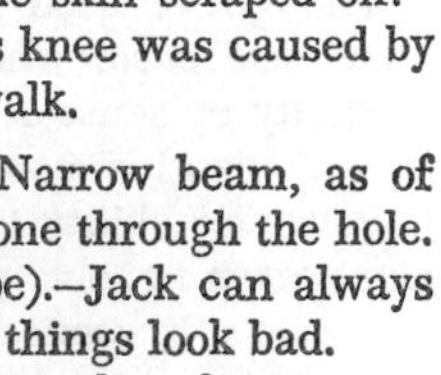

reach (REECH) *n. reaches.* 1. A stretching of the arms.–Baby made a sudden *reach* for Father's hat.
2. Range.–The frightened boy kept out of *reach* of the growling dog.
3. A long expanse, especially of water.–The steamboat pilot entered the long *reach* of rapids with caution.
–*v. reaches, reached, reaching.* 1. Thrust or push out (one's hands or arms). – Baby *reached* to Mother to be taken out of her crib.
2. Extend.–A branch of the tree *reached* to the window.
3. Get to or arrive at.–We *reached* school.
4. Impress or have influence on.–The teacher tried to *reach* Bill by appealing to his sense of fair play.

re•act (ree-AKT) *v. reacts, reacted, reacting.* 1. Act in response to something. – John *reacted* strangely to his election as class president. He didn't seem happy at all.
2. Act automatically in response to something.–When you touch a hot iron, you *react* by pulling your hand back.
3. Cause (something or someone) to act in response. – Acid *reacts* on litmus paper by turning it red.
–*reaction, n. reactions.*

read (REED) *v. reads, read, reading.* 1. Look at and get meaning from (something written or printed).–You are now *reading* this dictionary.–We may *read* by saying words aloud or by thinking of them silently.–We *read* music by singing or playing an instrument while looking at the notes.
2. Understand or get the meaning of.–When we understand a map, we can *read* it.–When we understand a speedometer on a car, we can *read* it.
3. Predict, or tell beforehand.–The weather man *reads* the weather. He tells beforehand what kind of weather we will have.
4. Show or indicate.–The gas meter *reads* ten units of gas used. – The speedometer *reads* twenty-five miles per hour.
5. Put a meaning which may not be true (into something).–He *read* jealousy into her letter, but he was mistaken. She was not jealous at all.

read (RED) *v.* One form of the verb *read.*–Have you *read* "Robinson Crusoe"?

read•er (REED-er) *n. readers.* 1. Person who reads.–Mary is quite a good *reader.* She understands books and stories that she reads.
2. A book used to teach reading.–Mary reads from the sixth-grade *reader.*

read•i•ness (RED-ee-nəss) *n.* 1. Condition of being ready or prepared.–Everything is in *readiness* for the picnic.
2. Willing promptness.–The man's *readiness* to work caused his boss to raise his salary.

read•ing (REED-ing) *n.* The act of seeing and getting the meaning of something written or printed.–*Reading* is easy for Mary, so she reads many books.

read•y (RED-ee) *adj. readier, readiest; readily, adv.* 1. Prepared. – When Father comes home, he likes to find his dinner *ready.*
2. Willing.–We are *ready* to take less money for the bicycle now that the tires are worn.
3. Quick.–Jack always has a *ready* answer in arithmetic class.
4. Right at hand, or to be had right away.–The hospital had a *ready* supply of bandages.

re•al (REE-əl) *adj.; really, adv.* Actual and true; not false, imaginary, or artificial.–Sally likes fairy tales. Mary likes stories about *real* people.
–*Real estate* is land and the buildings on it.

re•al•is•tic (ree-ə-LISS-tik) *adj.; realistically, adv.* 1. Looking very real.–The artist drew a *realistic* portrait of the man.
2. Down to earth; concerned with matters as they really are. – Harry is *realistic.* He knows what he can do and plans it well. He does not try to do what is beyond him.

re•al•i•ty (ree-AL-ə-tee) *n. realities.* What is; the truth; the way things actually are.–Mary and Jack like to tease each other, but in *reality* they are very fond of each other.

re•al•ize (REE-ə-lyz) *v. realizes, realized, realizing.* 1. Understand or know; be aware of.–Jack doesn't *realize* that his remarks sometimes hurt people's feelings.
2. Achieve, or make come true or happen.–Grandmother finally *realized* her wish when she moved back to the country.
3. Get as profit from the sale of something.–Bob *realized* five dollars on the sale of his bicycle. He sold it for five dollars more than he paid for it.

realm (RELM) *n. realms.* 1. A kingdom. – The holiday was celebrated throughout the *realm.*
2. Any region.–This story is in the *realm* of fantasy.

reap (REEP) *v. reaps, reaped, reaping.* 1. Cut and gather.–The farmer *reaps* his grain in the summer.
2. Obtain or get in return.–Give happiness to others and you will *reap* happiness.

reap•er (REEP-er) *n. reapers.* A machine for cutting grain, or a person who cuts grain.

re•ap•pear (ree-ə-PIR) *v. reappears, reappeared, reappearing.* Appear or show again; come to be seen again.–The sun went behind a cloud, and then it *reappeared.*

rear (RIR) *n.* The back or end part.–The back yard is at the *rear* of the house.–John was at the *rear* of the parade.
–*v. rears, reared, rearing.* 1. Rise.–The horse *reared* up on his hind legs.
2. Raise or bring up.–Grandmother *reared* three children.
–*adj.* Back; hind.–The *rear* wheels of the car got stuck in the soft earth.

re•ar•range (ree-ə-RAYNJ) *v. rearranges, rearranged, rearranging.* Arrange again; put in different positions. – Mother likes to *rearrange* the furniture.

rea•son (REE-zən) *n. reasons.* 1. Cause of a happening; explanation. – Can you give a *reason* for believing that the earth is round?
2. Thought or good sense.–The angry man did not use *reason* when he hit the policeman.
3. Sanity or senses.–The old miser lost his *reason* when his money was stolen.
4. Power or ability to think.–You must use your *reason* to solve problems in arithmetic.
–*v. reasons, reasoned, reasoning.* 1. Think through or solve.–Mary tried to *reason* out the problem in arithmetic.
2. Argue, or point out the other side of a question.–It is hard to *reason* with Jack when he is angry.

rea•son•a•ble (REEZ-nə-bəl) *adj.; reasonably, adv.* 1. Fair and just.–Our teacher is *reasonable* in the amount of homework she assigns us. – Mary's wish for a new dress seems *reasonable,* since she has outgrown several of her others.
2. Logical; sensible.–The answer to the problem seems too large a figure to be *reasonable.*
3. Moderate.–The price of strawberries is *reasonable* in June. They are not expensive.

reb•el (REB-əl) *n. rebels.* A person who fights against lawful control.–The *rebels* tried to overthrow the government.

re•bel (ri-BEL) *v. rebels, rebelled, rebelling.* Fight against lawful control. – Prisoners sometimes *rebel* and try to escape.

re•bel•lion (ri-BEL-yən) *n. rebellions.* 1. A rising up of people against the government or other authorities.–The discontented citizens started a *rebellion.*
2. Resistance to any authority or restriction. –John's *rebellion* against wearing a tie and jacket to class ended when he found that all the boys wore them.

re•bound (ri-BOWND) *v. rebounds, rebounded, rebounding.* Spring or bounce back. –The ball hit the wall and *rebounded.*

re•call (ri-KAWL) *v. recalls, recalled, recalling.* 1. Remember.–Bill couldn't *recall* which day he was absent.
2. Call back.–The messenger was *recalled.* He was told to come back.
3. Remove (an elected official) from office by a vote.–The mayor was *recalled* for taking bribes.

re•cede (ri-SEED) *v. recedes, receded, receding.* Move or go back; withdraw; slant backward.–The tide is *receding.*–An ape's forehead *recedes* more than a man's.

re•ceipt (ri-SEET) *n. receipts.* 1. A written statement which says that one has received something. – When the insured package came, Mother signed a *receipt* for it.
2. (In the plural) Money received. – The *receipts* from the flower show will be used to buy library books.
3. Act of receiving.–I wrote to Grandmother on *receipt* of her letter.
–*v. receipts, receipted, receipting.* Mark "Paid." –Mother asked the milkman to *receipt* his bill when she paid him.

re•ceive (ri-SEEV) *v. receives, received, receiving.* 1. Get, or have given or brought to one; accept (something offered).–We *receive* an allowance from Father each week.–We *received* a letter every week from Jack while he was at camp.–Baby *received* a bad bump when she fell.
2. Greet or welcome.–Sally likes to *receive* Mother's guests. She greets them at the door and invites them in.
3. Hold.–We left a box on the porch to *receive* the Christmas packages.
4. Have as an experience.–Mary is *receiving* a good musical education.
5. Change electric waves into sounds or pictures. – This television set doesn't *receive* Channel 8.

re•ceiv•er (ri-SEE-ver) *n. receivers.* 1. A person who gets or accepts.–Bob gave Mother a present for her birthday. Bob was the giver of the present, and Mother was the *receiver.*
2. A thing that receives. – We talk on the telephone through the mouthpiece, and we listen to or receive the message through the *receiver.*

3. A container, or something else that is used to put things in.

re•cent (REE-sənt) *adj.; recently, adv.* Happening or made not long ago. – This is a *recent* book. It was written just lately.

re•cep•ta•cle (ri-SEP-tə-kəl) *n. receptacles.* Anything which serves to hold something. –Vases, boxes, and baskets are *receptacles.*

re•cep•tion (ri-SEP-shən) *n. receptions.* 1. A party at which people are greeted by an honored guest.–After the wedding, there was a *reception.* The bride and groom received many friends.
2. Way of receiving.–They gave me a friendly *reception.* They received me in a friendly way.
3. Condition of receiving.–The *reception* on the radio is poor during a thunderstorm.

re•cep•tion•ist (ri-SEP-shən-ist) *n. receptionists.* A person who is hired by a business firm to receive visitors and clients, usually in an outer office.

re•cess (ri-SESS *or* REE-sess) *n. recesses.* 1. A nook, or hollow space.–Mother put Uncle Jim's trunk in a *recess* in the bedroom wall.
2. A short time during which work stops.–In some schools children have a *recess* in the morning and in the afternoon.
–(ri-SESS) *v. recesses, recessed, recessing.* Begin a break, recess, or holiday.–School *recessed* in June for the summer vacation.

rec•i•pe (RESS-ə-pee) *n. recipes.* A set of directions telling how a thing, especially a food dish, should be prepared. – This cake was made from a new *recipe.*

re•cit•al (ri-SYT-l) *n. recitals.* 1. A musical entertainment at which one or more persons play, sing, or dance.
2. An account or tale.–The teacher's *recital* of his travels was exciting to the children.

re•cite (ri-SYT) *v. recites, recited, reciting.* 1. Repeat or say aloud from memory.–The children can *recite* many poems.
2. Answer the teacher's questions about a lesson.–Bill, Mary, and John *recited* in social studies class today.
–*recitation, n. recitations.*

reck•less (REK-ləss) *adj.; recklessly, adv.; recklessness, n.* Very, very careless.–Do not be *reckless* while crossing the street. Do not risk being hurt.

reck•on (REK-ən) *v. reckons, reckoned, reckoning.* 1. Count up. – Jack is *reckoning* the weeks before school is out.
2. Judge or regard.–Mr. Smith is *reckoned* the best man for the job. He is thought to be the best.
–*reckoning, n. reckonings.*

re•cline (ri-KLYN) *v. reclines, reclined, reclining.* Lean back.–I like to *recline* in an easy chair and read.

rec•og•ni•tion (rek-əg-NISH-ən) *n.* 1. Being known or identified. – The books were burned beyond *recognition.*
2. Favorable attention.–The soldier received *recognition* for his bravery. He received many honors in *recognition* of his bravery.
3. Acknowledgment. – The government demanded *recognition* of its treaty rights in the use of the river.

rec•og•nize (REK-əg-nyz) *v. recognizes, recognized, recognizing.* 1. Know; identify from familiarity. – Mother didn't *recognize* my voice over the telephone.
2. Appreciate.–The teacher *recognized* the children's efforts to get their work done.
3. Admit.–Jack *recognized* it was his duty to stay home and help his mother.
4. Show favorable attention as a reward.–The country *recognized* the soldier's bravery by awarding him a medal.

rec•ol•lect (rek-ə-LEKT) *v. recollects, recollected, recollecting.* Remember.–Bob doesn't *recollect* who borrowed the book.
–*recollection, n. recollections.*

rec•om•mend (rek-ə-MEND) *v. recommends, recommended, recommending.* 1. Show favor for.–We *recommend* Mary to act as leader of her group.
2. Suggest or advise. – The doctor *recommended* that Father stay in bed several days. He advised him to do so.

rec•om•men•da•tion (rek-ə-men-DAY-shən) *n. recommendations.* A statement of praise for, or advice about, a person's work, behavior, ability, or the like. – When Jack wanted to get a job selling papers, he asked his teacher for a *recommendation.*

rec•on•cile (REK-ən-syl) *v. reconciles, reconciled, reconciling.* 1. Make up a quarrel or disagreement.–Jack and Mary had a quarrel, but they were *reconciled.*
2. Make content; satisfy.–Ted was *reconciled* to staying at home when he found that Bert was staying home, too.
3. Make agree or correspond.–The newspaper article is all mixed up. It is impossible to *reconcile* it with the facts we know.

re•con•nais•sance (ri-KAHN-ə-sənss) *n. reconnaissances.* The inspecting, observing, or examining of an area, especially for military purposes.–The plane took off on a flight of *reconnaissance.* – I will do some *reconnaissance* on possible picnic spots.

rec•ord (REK-erd) *n. records.* 1. Something written to be kept.–Bob made a *record* of all the things that happened while the teacher was away.
2. A grooved disc that gives back sounds recorded on it. – Mary played a *record* on the phonograph.

3. The things known about a person or thing. – The baseball team's *record* is five games lost and ten won.
4. The best performance.–When a racer goes faster than any other has yet gone, he breaks a *record,* and sets a new *record.*

re•cord (ri-KORD) *v. records, recorded, recording.* 1. Write down in a form that will last.–The teacher will *record* the names of the children in her class. She will write them down in her book to use later.
2. Put in a form that can be saved.–We *record* music on wax discs, records, or on tape, so that it can be played back and heard later on.
3. Show or indicate.–A speedometer on a car *records* the number of miles the car has traveled.

re•cov•er (ri-KUV-er) *v. recovers, recovered, recovering.* 1. Get back again.–Bobby *recovered* his lost dog.
2. Get well.–It will take a long time for the sick man to *recover.*
–*recovery, n. recoveries.*

re-cov•er (ree-KUV-er) *v. re-covers, re-covered, re-covering.* Put a new cover on.–We had a chair *re-covered.* We had new cloth put over it.

rec•re•a•tion (rek-ree-AY-shən) *n.* Any amusement or pastime; any game; relaxation.–Golf, tennis, strolling, swimming, and reading are all forms of *recreation.*

rec•tan•gle (REK-tang-gəl) *n. rectangles.* A plane (flat) figure that has four sides and four perfectly square corners or angles. A square is a *rectangle* with equal sides.

rec•tor (REK-ter) *n. rectors.* A clergyman in charge of a parish or church.—The *rector* is trying to raise funds for his church.

re•cu•per•ate (ri-KOO-pə-rayt *or* ri-KYOOP-er-ayt) *v. recuperates, recuperated, recuperating.* 1. Get well from an illness; recover.—Tom is *recuperating* from the measles.
2. Recover from financial losses.—The business has fully *recuperated.* Now it is earning money.
—*recuperation, n. recuperations.*

red (RED) *n. reds* and *adj.* The color of blood. —The colors of the American flag are *red,* white, and blue.
—*Reddish* means somewhat red.

Red Cross (RED KRAWSS). A world-wide organization whose purpose is to help people everywhere in time of disaster or misfortune. It cares for the sick and wounded in time of war. It gives help to those who need it during and after floods, fires, earthquakes, and other disasters. The sign of the *Red Cross* is a red cross on a white background.

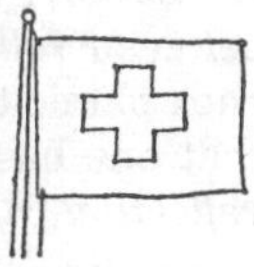

re•deem (ri-DEEM) *v. redeems, redeemed, redeeming.* 1. Get back by paying an amount owed.—The man *redeemed* his watch at the pawnshop after he found a job.
2. Make good or fulfill.—Do not make a promise you are not sure you can *redeem.*
3. Make up for.—Bill's generosity does much to *redeem* his quick temper.
4. Do well after starting badly.—After walking the first three batters, Hank *redeemed* himself by striking out the next three.

re•duce (ri-DOOSS *or* -DYOOSS) *v. reduces, reduced, reducing.* 1. Make smaller or lower. —Letting some air out of a toy balloon *reduces* its size.—Charging less money for shoes *reduces* their price.
2. Change to a different form.—A fire soon *reduced* the box to ashes.
3. Bring to a worse condition.—Mary was *reduced* to tears by Jack's teasing.—The family was *reduced* to poverty.
4. Grow thinner by dieting. — Some people often won't eat butter and potatoes because they are trying to *reduce.*
5. Change numbers to their simplest form without altering their value.—You can *reduce* 8/10 by changing it to 4/5.

re•duc•tion (ri-DUK-shən) *n. reductions.* 1. Cutting down on something; making it less. —After a *reduction* was made in the price of the bicycle, Tim was able to buy it.
2. The amount which is taken off a thing.—The price was lowered from twenty to sixteen dollars. The *reduction* was four dollars.

red-winged black•bird (RED-wingd BLAK-berd) *red-winged blackbirds.* An American blackbird that has a patch of red feathers on each wing.

red•wood (RED-wuhd) *n. redwoods.* A very large, tall tree that grows in California. Its wood is brownish-red. It belongs to the pine-tree family.

reed (REED) *n. reeds; reedy, adj.* 1. A kind of tall grass that grows in marshy places. It has hollow, jointed stems.
2. A strip or cylinder of wood, metal, or other material in the mouthpieces of some wind instruments. Clarinets, English horns, saxophones, and oboes are played with *reeds.*

reef (REEF) *n. reefs.* A ridge of rocks or sand that comes to or nearly to the top of the water in the sea.

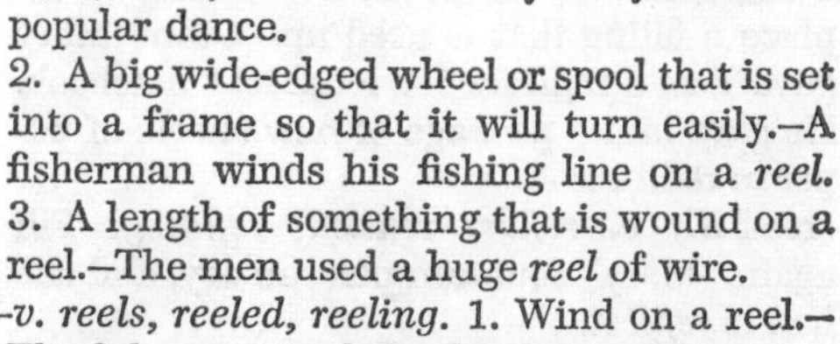

reel (REEL) *n. reels.* 1. A very lively and once-popular dance.
2. A big wide-edged wheel or spool that is set into a frame so that it will turn easily.—A fisherman winds his fishing line on a *reel.*
3. A length of something that is wound on a reel.—The men used a huge *reel* of wire.
—*v. reels, reeled, reeling.* 1. Wind on a reel.—The fisherman *reeled* in his fishing line.
2. Recite or say quickly and easily.—Jack can *reel* off his multiplication tables.
3. Whirl, or go round and round.—Bert was so sleepy that the room seemed to *reel.*
4. Sway, or move around dizzily.—The prize fighter *reeled* when he was hit.

re•en•ter (ree-EN-ter) *v. re-enters, re-entered, re-entering.* Go back in.–Mary went out and found it was raining. So she *re-entered* the house to get her umbrella.

re•fer (ri-FER) *v. refers, referred, referring.* 1. Turn to.–We *refer* to the table of contents in a book to find out on which page a story can be found.
2. Send or direct.–The teacher *referred* us to the library for other books on North and South America.
3. Speak about; call attention to.–Our teacher often *refers* to the dangers of crossing the street when the light is red.

ref•er•ee (ref-ə-REE) *n. referees.* 1. A person who acts as a judge of plays made in games and sports such as basketball, football, prize fights, and the like.–The *referee* in a baseball game is called an umpire.–The *referee* in the basketball game blows a whistle every time the ball goes out of bounds.
2. Person who decides who is right and who is wrong.–The boys asked their father to act as *referee* of the argument.
–*v. referees, refereed, refereeing.* Act as referee.–Bob *refereed* the hockey game.

ref•er•ence (REF-er-ənss) *n. references.* 1. A mention, or calling of attention.–The doctor made *reference* to the importance of good teeth. He spoke about it.
2. A person able to describe one's ability or character.–Bob gave his teacher as a *reference* in applying for the job.
3. A statement describing one's abilities or character. – Bob got a *reference* from his teacher.
4. Information to which one can refer, such as in a book or encyclopedia.–A dictionary is a work of *reference.*
5. Regard.–I am writing him in *reference* to the house he has for sale.

re•fill (REE-fil) *n. refills.* Something to replace a filling that is used up.–Grandfather gave Tom a *refill* for his loose-leaf notebook. He gave him a package of new sheets of paper to refill it.
–(ree-FIL) *v. refills, refilled, refilling.* Fill again.–Mary's fountain pen ran dry, and she had to *refill* it.

re•fine (ri-FYN) *v. refines, refined, refining.* 1. Make pure or fit for some special use.–Cotton, sugar, rubber, and other raw materials are *refined* before they are used.
2. Mother is *refined.* She is educated and kind, and has good manners.
–*refinement, n. refinements.*

re•flect (ri-FLEKT) *v. reflects, reflected, reflecting.* 1. Give back (light, heat, etc.)–A mirror *reflects* light. Polished metal *reflects* heat.–When you look into still water or into a mirror, your image, or likeness, is *reflected.*

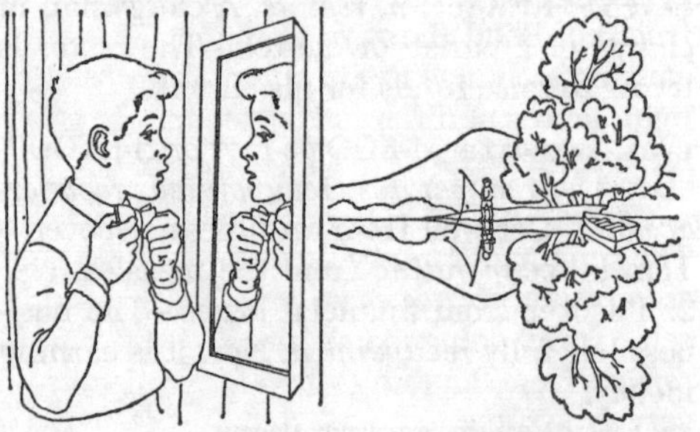

2. Throw.–Jane's politeness *reflects* credit on her parents.
3. Show the effect of; be a result of.–Jane's politeness *reflects* her parents' good training.
4. Think over carefully.–One should *reflect* on the things he reads.
–*Reflect on* also means throw blame on.–Bad behavior *reflects on* one's training. It brings back blame to one's home or school. It shows that one has had poor training or teaching.
–*reflection, n. reflections.*

re•flec•tor (ri-FLEK-ter) *n. reflectors.* That which reflects light, heat, or the like.–Automobile lights have *reflectors* to throw out the light in one direction.

re•for•est•a•tion (ree-for-iss-TAY-shən *or* ree-fahr-iss-TAY-shən) *n.* Replanting with trees. If we did not have programs of *reforestation,* we would run out of lumber, and many parts of the nation would turn into dust bowls. Trees protect areas from wind, and their roots keep the soil from washing or blowing away.

re•form (ri-FORM) *v. reforms, reformed, reforming.* 1. Improve by doing away with faults; make better.–The teacher *reformed* the mischievous pupil with kindness and understanding.–The candidate promised to *reform* the town government.
2. Correct one's own bad habits; change oneself for the better.–The judge freed the prisoner when he promised to *reform.*
–*reform, n. reforms.*

Ref•or•ma•tion (ref-er-MAY-shən) *n.* The religious movement in the sixteenth century which brought about the formation of the Protestant churches. Until then Christianity was represented in Europe only by the Catholic Church.

re•form•a•to•ry (ri-FORM-ə-tor-ee) *n. reformatories.* An institution to which young lawbreakers are sent to learn to be good citizens.–The young offender is learning a trade at the *reformatory.*

re•fract (ri-FRAKT) *v. refracts, refracted, refracting.* Bend the rays of (light, heat, etc.), causing a change in direction.–By *refracting* light, lenses of different shapes reduce or enlarge an image.

re•frain (ri-FRAYN) *n. refrains.* Chorus.–The song had a merry *refrain.*
–*v. refrains, refrained, refraining.* Keep oneself (from doing something).–Jack cannot *refrain* from laughing when Mary tries to act very grown-up.

re•fresh (ri-FRESH) *v. refreshes, refreshed, refreshing.* Make fresh again.–A swim in the lake *refreshes* one on a hot day.–Rain on a hot day *refreshes* the air.–Before the test Bob *refreshed* his memory by studying.

re•fresh•ment (ri-FRESH-mənt) *n. refreshments.* Food and drink. – Cocoa and sandwiches were the *refreshments* served at the party.

re•frig•er•ate (ri-FRIJ-ə-rayt) *v. refrigerates, refrigerated, refrigerating.* Make or keep cold.–Mother is *refrigerating* the lemonade.
–*refrigeration, n.*

re•frig•er•a•tor (ri-FRIJ-ə-ray-ter) *n. refrigerators.* A box or room for keeping foods cold. Ice is used in some boxes. Others have freezing units in them which are run by electricity or gas.

ref•uge (REF-yooj) *n. refuges.* 1. A place that is safe or protected; a shelter.–The town has a *refuge* for stray animals.
2. Protection from danger; shelter, especially from exposure to the weather. – The fleeing man is seeking *refuge.*–Never take *refuge* under a tree during a thunderstorm. Lightning may strike the tree.

ref•u•gee (REF-yuh-jee) *n. refugees.* A person who is seeking safety and protection, usually by fleeing from one country to another. –Many Jewish *refugees* came to the United States from Germany to escape persecution by the Nazi government.

re•fund (REE-fund) *n. refunds.* A sum paid back.–The store gave Mother a *refund* on the soiled dress.
–(ri-FUND) *v. refunds, refunded, refunding.* Give back.–Mother returned the soiled dress to the store and they *refunded* her money.

ref•use (REF-yooss *or* -yooz) *n.* Garbage, trash, or other waste.–After the picnic, we put the *refuse* in a trash can.

re•fuse (ri-FYOOZ) *v. refuses, refused, refusing.* Decline, or say no.–Mary *refused* to go with us, because she didn't want to walk so far.–When the hungry man asked for a dime, Father couldn't *refuse.*
–*refusal, n. refusals.*

re•gain (ri-GAYN) *v. regains, regained, regaining.* 1. Get back.–Father has *regained* his health.
2. Get back to.–The swimmers *regained* the shore just before the storm.

re•gal (REE-gəl) *adj.; regally, adv.* 1. Of royalty; of a king or queen; royal.–The *regal* procession moved slowly through the church.
2. Splendid; good enough for a king.–The rich man lived in a *regal* manner.

re•gard (ri-GAHRD) *n. regards.* 1. Respect or consideration. – Jack usually has *regard* for the rights of other people.
2. (In the plural) Good wishes.–The teacher sent mother her best *regards.*
3. A look.–The judge fixed the prisoner with a steady, earnest *regard.*
–*v. regards, regarded, regarding.* 1. Look at. –The judge *regarded* the prisoner sternly.
2. Believe to be; consider.–Bob is *regarded* as the best player on the team.
3. Think well of.–We *regard* the new mayor very highly.
–*In regard to* means about or concerning.–We received a letter *in regard to* the lost purse. The letter asked what color the purse was.

re•gat•ta (ri-GAT-ə *or* ri-GAHT-ə) *n. regattas.* A boat race, or a series of boat races (for sailboats, yachts, etc.). – The international *regatta* is a colorful event.

re•gime (rə-ZHEEM) *n. regimes.* 1. A system of government or management.—After the revolution a new *regime* was established.
2. A definite method or plan of living; a system of doing things.—The athlete's *regime* includes a morning hike and an hour more of exercise.

reg•i•ment (REJ-ə-mənt) *n. regiments.* An organized group of soldiers usually commanded by a colonel.
—*v. regiments, regimented, regimenting.* Put (persons) under strict control.—The citizens did not want to be *regimented* in any way by the government.

re•gion (REE-jən) *n. regions.* 1. Section or part of a country; part of the world.—Eskimos live in a cold *region.*
2. Part (of the body).—The ball hit Bob in the *region* of the stomach.
3. Any area.—Astronomers study distant *regions* of the sky.

reg•is•ter (REJ-iss-ter) *n. registers.* 1. A list of people's names kept for some particular purpose.—The school keeps a *register* of the names of its pupils.
2. A screened or grilled opening through which heated or cooled air comes. — Hot air comes into the room from the furnace through a *register.*

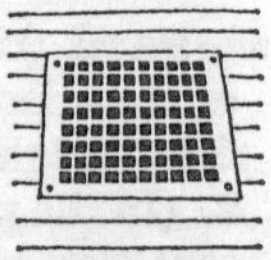

3. Range.—The *register* of one's voice is from the lowest note he can sing to the highest one he can sing.—Musical instruments have *registers,* too.
4. Something which makes a record.—The clerk rang up the price on the cash *register.*
—*v. registers, registered, registering.* 1. Have one's name recorded or put on a list.—On the first day of school, forty children *registered.*
2. Show or indicate.—Speedometers *register* the speed at which a car is going.
3. Record. — Father received a letter which had been *registered.* The postmaster had made a record to show that it had passed through the post office and had been delivered.—Mother's and Father's marriage was *registered* at the village church.
4. Express; show. — A good actor must be able to *register* joy, sorrow, fear, and many other feelings by the look on his face.

re•gret (ri-GRET) *n. regrets.* 1. Sorrow; the wish that things could be or could have been otherwise.—It was with much *regret* that Bob parted with his bicycle.
2. (In the plural) A message saying that one is sorry one cannot accept an invitation.—Mary couldn't go to the party; so she sent her *regrets.*
—*v. regrets, regretted, regretting.* Feel sorry.—I *regret* that I lost my dog.

reg•u•lar (REG-yə-ler) *n. regulars.* One who is not a substitute.—Bob is a *regular* on the ball team. He always plays.
—*adj.; regularly, adv.* 1. Even.—The shore around the lake is quite *regular.*—The teeth of the comb are *regular.* They are all the same in size and spacing.
2. Usual or customary.—The *regular* Labor Day holiday comes on the first Monday in September. It comes on the same day again and again.—The *regular* place to store a car is in a garage.
3. Belonging at all times.—Uncle Dave is a *regular* soldier in the army.
4. Usually done in a certain way and in a certain order.—Father is a man of *regular* habits. He does the same things every day at about the same time and in about the same way.
5. Real or complete.—Jack and Mary make a *regular* game of their homework.

reg•u•late (REG-yə-layt) *v. regulates, regulated, regulating.* 1. Control.—The faucet *regulates* the water that comes from it.—The thermostat *regulates* the oil burner so that the house is kept at the desired temperature.
2. Adjust the speed of.—The jeweler *regulated* my watch. He made it keep good time.
3. Organize; adjust. — Mother *regulates* her schedule so that all her work is done by the time Father gets home.
—*regulation, n. regulations.*

re•hearse (ri-HERSS) *v. rehearses, rehearsed, rehearsing.* Practice.—The actors *rehearsed* their parts for the play.
—*rehearsal, n. rehearsals.*

reign (RAYN) *n. reigns.* The length of time one ruler rules a country.—England was prosperous during the *reign* of Queen Elizabeth I.
—*v. reigns, reigned, reigning.* Rule.—The king *reigned* over his people.

rein (RAYN) *n. reins.* 1. A long strip of leather fastened to the part of a horse's bridle that goes through his mouth. A *rein* is used to guide the horse. Pull on the right *rein* and the horse will turn to the right.

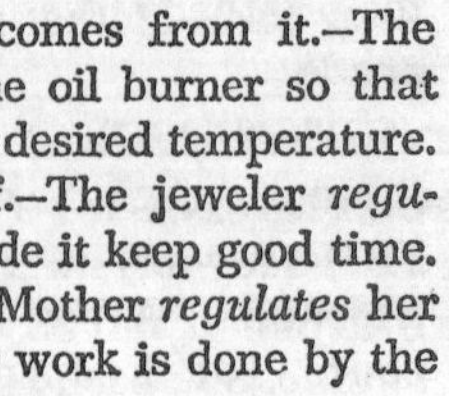

2. Control.–During Mother's absence, Grandmother took over the *reins* of the household. She managed the house.
–*v. reins, reined, reining.* 1. Pull up the reins of.–She *reined* in her horse so that he halted.
2. Restrain; check.–I *reined* in my temper as well as I could.

rein•deer (RAYN-dir) *n. sing.* and *pl.* A kind of deer with large horns or antlers. *Reindeer* live in the North, where it is cold.

re•in•force (ree-in-FORSS) *v. reinforces, reinforced, reinforcing.* Make stronger.–Mother *reinforced* the elbow of Bob's sweater by sewing an extra piece of cloth on it. – The team was *reinforced* with many new players.

re•ject (ri-JEKT) *v. rejects, rejected, rejecting.* 1. Refuse to take.–The teacher *rejected* Bill's paper because it wasn't neat.
2. Throw away or discard.–Mother *rejected* all the buns that were burned.
3. Refuse to consider.–The governor *rejected* the prisoner's plea for pardon.
–*rejection, n. rejections.*

re•joice (ri-JOISS) *v. rejoices, rejoiced, rejoicing.* Feel glad, or feel joyful.–We will *rejoice* when the baby is well again.

re•lapse (ri-LAPSS) *v. relapses, relapsed, relapsing.* Slip back into a former, and usually worse, condition or habit.–The sick man *relapsed* into unconsciousness after having been conscious for two hours.

re•late (ri-LAYT) *v. relates, related, relating.*
1. Tell.–Grandfather *related* the story of his first fishing trip.
2. Have a relation (to).–Shoes *relate* to feet.
3. Connect, or show the relations between.–The teacher asked each of us to write a composition *relating* the French and American revolutions.

re•lat•ed (ri-LAY-tid) *adj.* 1. Belonging to the same family.–Brothers are *related.* They belong to the same family.
2. Connected.–Several *related* events led to John's lateness.

re•la•tion (ri-LAY-shən) *n. relations.* 1. A telling.–The captain's *relation* of the storm at sea was thrilling.
2. Connection.–The *relation* between bread and meat is that they are foods.
3. Members of a family.–Parents, sisters, and brothers are some of one's *relations.*
4. (Often used in the plural) Dealing; condition of friendliness; day-to-day association. –My *relations* with Alice are not very good just now. We are not very friendly.–The Secretary of State conducts our foreign *relations.* He looks after the United States' association with other countries.

re•la•tion•ship (ri-LAY-shən-ship) *n. relationships.* 1. The state of being related; connection.–The doctor explained the *relationship* between germs and disease.
2. Family tie.–What is your *relationship* to Sally? I am her sister.

rel•a•tive (REL-ə-tiv) *n. relatives.* Person who is related to another; one who belongs to the same family.–Father, mother, aunts, uncles, brothers, sisters, and the like are *relatives.* They belong to one family.
–*adj.; relatively, adv.* 1. Related.–Keep your comments *relative* to what we discussed.
2. Compared; comparative. – We discussed the *relative* advantages of the two plans.
3. Depending for its meaning on a standard. –Tom told Father that he was old. Father said, "That's *relative.* Grandfather thinks that I am young."

re•lax (ri-LAKS) *v. relaxes, relaxed, relaxing.* 1. Become loose or less tense.–When you sleep, your muscles *relax.*
2. Make less rigid or strict.–During hot weather, the rules in school are *relaxed.* We can do things that we can't do at other times.

re•lay (REE-lay) *n. relays.* 1. A fresh replacement.–A *relay* of fire fighters relieved those who had been fighting the fire all night.
2. A race in which a runner carries something, runs a certain distance, and hands the thing he is carrying to another runner, who takes up the race at that point. Several sets of runners take part in the race.

–(REE-lay *or* ri-LAY) *v. relays, relayed, relaying.* Pass on from one to another.–The message was *relayed* to the general by radio, telephone, and messenger.

re•lease (ri-LEESS) *n. releases.* 1. Freedom. –The prisoner was given his *release.*
2. A statement for publication.–The school issued a news *release* about the students who had won scholarships.
–*v. releases, released, releasing.* Let go.–The woman *released* the child's hand, and he fell. –Bob took off the dog's collar and *released* him.

re•li•a•ble (ri-LY-ə-bəl) *adj.; reliably, adv.; reliability, n.* Trustworthy or dependable.–Mary is *reliable* about getting her work done on time.

rel•ic (REL-ik) *n. relics.* Things left from times long past.–Arrowheads and stone hammers are Indian *relics.*

re•lief (ri-LEEF) *n.* 1. Help; comfort; easing or removing difficulty.–Medicine brings *relief* to the sick. It helps to make them well.–The Red Cross brings *relief* to victims of floods.
2. Freedom from a task.–The sailor kept a lookout until six o'clock and then got *relief.* Another man took his place.
3. A design that stands up higher than the surface from which it is cut.

re•lieve (ri-LEEV) *v. relieves, relieved, relieving.* 1. Comfort, ease, or help.–Medicine will *relieve* the patient's pain.
2. Free from a task.–A new baseball pitcher *relieved* Bob. He freed Bob by taking his place.
3. Change the sameness of.–The whiteness of the tablecloth and dishes on the table was *relieved* by a blue bowl of yellow roses.

re•li•gion (ri-LIJ-ən) *n. religions; religious, adj.; religiously, adv.* A belief in or worship of God or gods. *Religion* is any faith or method of worship.

re•luc•tance (ri-LUK-tənss) *n.; reluctant, adj.; reluctantly, adv.* Hesitation or slowness in doing something because of not wanting to do it, but having to; unwillingness.–The father punished his son with *reluctance.*

re•ly (ri-LY) *v. relies, relied, relying.* Trust or depend.–Mother can *rely* upon Bob to take good care of Sally.
–*reliance, n.*

re•main (ri-MAYN) *v. remains, remained, remaining.* 1. Stay.–The children came, but they could not *remain* for lunch.
2. Be left over.–Only two pencils *remained* in the box when we had each taken one from it.
3. Stay (the same).–Some metals *remain* bright all the time. They never tarnish.

re•main•der (ri-MAYN-der) *n. remainders.* 1. The part that is left.–I ate part of the apple pie and Father ate the *remainder.*
2. A number found by subtracting.–If you take 4 apples from 6 apples, the *remainder* is 2 apples.

re•mark (ri-MAHRK) *n. remarks.* A statement, or something said.–The teacher made a few *remarks* about the lesson.
–*v. remarks, remarked, remarking.* Say or notice.–Sally *remarked* that Father was growing fat, but said nothing about it. Mother *remarked* to Father that he was gaining weight. She said it out loud.

re•mark•a•ble (ri-MAHR-kə-bəl) *adj.; remarkably, adv.* Worth noticing, or wonderful. –The child's manners are *remarkable* for her age.

rem•e•dy (REM-ə-dee) *n. remedies.* A relief or cure.–Medicine is a *remedy* for sickness.
–*v. remedies, remedied, remedying.* Correct, or make right.–We will *remedy* the mistake at once. We will correct it.

re•mem•ber (ri-MEM-ber) *v. remembers, remembered, remembering.* 1. Recall, or bring back to mind.–Mother can *remember* things that happened when she was a little girl.
2. Keep in mind.–*Remember* that you are invited to come. Do not forget it.
3. Show that (someone) is thought of.–The children always *remember* Mother on her birthday. They show that they love her by giving her a gift.
4. Pass greetings on.–*Remember* me to all my friends. Mention my name and give them my regards, or best wishes.

re•mem•brance (ri-MEM-brənss) *n. remembrances.* 1. Gift, keepsake, or something to remember one by.–Mary gave me a little *remembrance* for my birthday. She gave me a locket with her picture in it.
2. Memory.–They held in loving *remembrance* their grandfather who had died.

re•mind (ri-MYND) *v. reminds, reminded, reminding.* Cause to recall or remember.—*Remind* me to take an umbrella.—Mary sometimes *reminds* me of Mother.
—*reminder, n. reminders.*

rem•nant (REM-nənt) *n. remnants.* 1. A piece of cloth that is left over from a larger piece. — Mother made a doll dress from a *remnant.*
2. Leftover.—We ate the *remnants* of Sunday's dinner for our lunch on Tuesday.

re•mod•el (ree-MAHD-l) *v. remodels, remodeled* or *remodelled, remodeling* or *remodelling.* Make over.—We plan to *remodel* our barn and make it into a guest house.

re•morse (ri-MORSS) *n.; remorseful, adj.; remorsefully, adv.* Regret or sorrow for something one has done.—The child felt *remorse.* He was sorry he had stolen the pencils.

re•mote (ri-MOHT) *adj. remoter, remotest; remotely, adv.* 1. Far-off.—The explorers had visited *remote* corners of the world.—To people in South America, Russia is a *remote* country.
2. Long past; long ago.—In *remote* times people lived in caves.
3. Vague or slight.—Bob has a *remote* idea that he wants to be an engineer.

re•move (ri-MOOV) *v. removes, removed, removing.* 1. Take off.—Mary *removed* her rubbers before going into the house.
2. Take away.—*Remove* the broom from the doorway before someone trips on it.
3. Put out of.—Dishonest persons are often *removed* from their jobs.
4. End.—The medicine *removed* his pain.
5. Take out.—*Remove* the gum from your mouth.

ren•ais•sance (ren-ə-SAHNSS *or* REN-ə-sahnss) *n.* 1. New birth; revival.—There seems to be a *renaissance* of interest in poems by Longfellow. Many people seem to be reading his poems again.
2. (Spelled with a capital "R.") The period in Europe, from the fourteenth through the sixteenth centuries, marked by a great revival of interest and achievement in art, literature, science, and learning.

re•new (ri-NOO *or* -NYOO) *v. renews, renewed, renewing.* 1. Start again; continue.—I shall *renew* my subscription to the magazine.—Mary *renewed* her efforts after the teacher praised her work.
2. Make like new again.—Father *renewed* the finish on the chair by varnishing it.
—*renewal, n. renewals.*

ren•o•vate (REN-ə-vayt) *v. renovates, renovated, renovating.* Clean, repair, or make like new again.—The old house will have to be *renovated* before the family moves in.
—*renovation, n. renovations.*

rent (RENT) *n. rents.* 1. Money paid regularly for the use of a building or property.—Father pays the *rent* on the first of the month.
2. A tear; a torn place.—Bob got a *rent* in his sleeve when he caught it on a nail.
—*v. rents, rented, renting.* 1. Use a building or property for which one makes regular payments.—We *rent* our house from a real-estate company.
2. Allow a building or property to be used in return for regular payment.—Last year we *rented* our summer cottage to the Browns.

re•or•gan•ize (ree-OR-gə-nyz) *v. reorganizes, reorganized, reorganizing.* 1. Arrange differently, or according to a new plan.—Our principal *reorganized* the classes this term. He changed the hours, some of the subjects, and the method of teaching.
2. Form or get together again.—The football team will *reorganize* this fall.
—*reorganization, n. reorganizations.*

re•paid (ri-PAYD) *v.* One form of the verb *repay.*—The money you lent me will be *repaid* by the first of the month.

re•pair (ri-PAIR) *n. repairs.* 1. Necessary work on something; mending or fixing; replacement of parts.—What *repairs* will have to be made on the house before it can be lived in?
2. Condition.—If you keep your shoes in good *repair,* they will wear longer. Have them mended as soon at they need it.
—*v. repairs, repaired, repairing.* 1. Fix; mend; put back in working order.—The mechanic *repaired* the radio.
2. Make right.—Jack tried to *repair* the damage his thoughtless words had done.

re•pay (ri-PAY) *v. repays, repaid, repaying.* Pay back.—I will *repay* the money you lent me as soon as I receive my wages.

re•peal (ri-PEEL) *v. repeals, repealed, repealing.* Officially do away with or withdraw; set aside.—The unpopular law was *repealed.*

re•peat (ri-PEET) *v. repeats, repeated, repeating.* 1. Say again.—I did not quite understand. Please *repeat* what you said.
2. Do again.—Yesterday you burned your finger; be careful not to *repeat* the accident.
3. Say from memory.—Can you *repeat* the words of "The Star-Spangled Banner"?

re•pent (ri-PENT) *v. repents, repented, repenting*. Regret, or be sorry for.–If you do wrong, you are sure to *repent* it.

rep•e•ti•tion (rep-ə-TISH-ən) *n*. The act of repeating; doing or saying again. – We learn many skills through *repetition*. We learn many skills by doing them over and over again until we have mastered them. – Bob was warned that a *repetition* of his rude behavior would result in his dismissal.

re•place (ri-PLAYSS) *v. replaces, replaced, replacing*. 1. Put in place again.–*Replace* the dishes in the cupboard after you dry them.
2. Substitute another for.–Mother *replaced* the broken mirror. She bought a new one.
3. Follow; fill the position of.–The pitcher was *replaced* by a younger boy.
–*replacement, n. replacements.*

re•plen•ish (ri-PLEN-ish) *v. replenishes, replenished, replenishing*. Fill again with supplies.–Mother *replenished* the empty cupboards. She stocked them with food.

rep•li•ca (REP-lə-kə) *n. replicas*. A copy or reproduction, especially of a work of art.–Father bought a small *replica* of the famous statue for his den.

re•ply (ri-PLY) *n. replies*. An answer.–It is wiser to make no *reply* to angry words.
–*v. replies, replied, replying*. Respond; answer. –Grandmother *replies* to our letters at once.

re•port (ri-PORT) *n. reports*. 1. A story or account.–The children gave a *report* of their trip to the zoo.
2. A statement.–Each month our teacher sends home a *report* that tells of our record in school. Jack had an "A" in arithmetic on his *report*.
3. News or rumor.–We heard a *report* that school would start earlier this year.
4. A sound or an explosive noise.–The *report* of the gun startled Sally.
–*v. reports, reported, reporting*. 1. Present oneself, or go in person.–The boys *reported* for baseball practice at four o'clock.
2. Tell; give the information.–Mary *reported* that enough money had been collected by the class to buy two new books.
3. Write up in a newspaper.–Mr. Bob Smith *reports* sports news for the "Daily Sentinel."
4. Make a charge against.–If you don't stay in the playground I shall have to *report* you to the principal.

re•port•er (ri-POR-ter) *n. reporters*. A person whose job is to gather news to be printed in a newspaper.–*Reporters* hurried to the scene of the accident.

re•pose (ri-POHZ) *n*. 1. Rest; relaxation.–Mother needs some *repose* every day, because she works so hard.
2. Peace; calm.–The minister has an air of *repose* about him.
–*v. reposes, reposed, reposing*. Rest.–Baby *reposed* on Father's lap.

rep•re•sent (rep-ri-ZENT) *v. represents, represented, representing*. 1. Mean or show. –The picture Mary drew *represented* the story of Little Red Riding Hood.
2. Act the part of; pretend to be.–Two boys *represented* knights in the play. – The spy *represented* himself as an American citizen.
3. Stand for.–A red cross on a background of white *represents* the Red Cross.
4. Act for.–The Congressman we elect from this area *represents* us in Congress.

rep•re•sent•a•tive (rep-ri-ZEN-tə-tiv) *n. representatives*. 1. Someone chosen by a group to speak and act for it.–The class chose Dick as their *representative*.
2. (Sometimes spelled with a capital "R.") A member of the House of Representatives of the United States or of one of the states.

rep•ri•mand (REP-rə-mand) *v. reprimands, reprimanded, reprimanding*. Blame, especially in a formal manner; reprove sternly.–The officer was *reprimanded* for neglecting his duty.

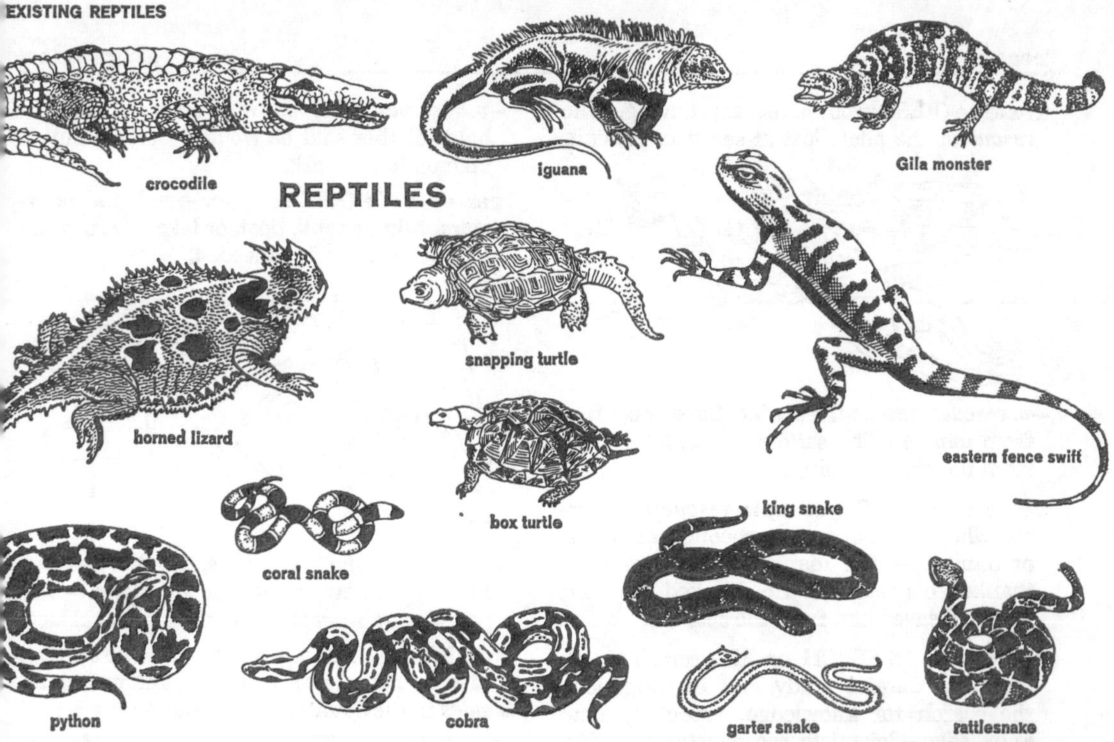

re•print (REE-print) *n. reprints.* Something printed again, usually after a lapse of time.—This book is a paperbound *reprint* of one originally issued in a hard cover.
–(ree-PRINT) *v. reprints, reprinted, reprinting.* Print again.—When all the copies of the book were sold, the publisher *reprinted* it.

re•proach (ri-PROHCH) *n. reproaches.* A blaming.—The teacher's *reproach* made us sorry that we had not done our homework.
–*v. reproaches, reproached, reproaching.* Put blame on.—The teacher *reproached* us for not doing our homework.

re•pro•duce (ree-prə-DOOSS *or* -DYOOSS) *v. reproduces, reproduced, reproducing.* 1. Produce again.—A phonograph, a tape recorder, and a radio all *reproduce* sound.
2. Make a duplicate or copy of.—Carbon paper is placed between sheets of paper to *reproduce* on the bottom sheet exactly what is written on the top sheet.
3. Bring forth offspring; bear young.
–*reproduction, n. reproductions.*

re•prove (ri-PROOV) *v. reproves, reproved, reproving.* Scold.—Father *reproved* Mary for being late.

rep•tile (REP-tyl) *n. reptiles.* A cold-blooded, animal that crawls or moves on short legs. Snakes, lizards, alligators, and turtles are *reptiles. Reptiles* have backbones.

re•pub•lic (ri-PUB-lik) *n. republics.* A nation in which the people elect or choose their rulers or representatives.—The United States is a *republic.*

re•pulse (ri-PULSS) *n. repulses.* A holding off or beating back.—The *repulse* of the outlaws was made possible by many cowboys.
–*v. repulses, repulsed, repulsing.* 1. Turn down or refuse.—The unhappy man *repulsed* all offers of friendship.
2. Beat or drive back.—The trainer *repulsed* the angry lions.

rep•u•ta•tion (rep-yə-TAY-shən) *n. reputations.* What people think and say about a person's behavior, character, or work.—Our doctor has an excellent *reputation.*

re•quest (ri-KWEST) *n. requests.* 1. A thing one asks for.—All Bob's *requests* were granted at Christmas. He was given everything he had asked for.
2. An asking (for something).—The teacher hasn't yet answered my *request* to see her.
–*v. requests, requested, requesting.* Ask.—The teacher *requested* us to work quietly.

re•quire (ri-KWYR) *v. requires, required, requiring.* 1. Have to have.—Baby *requires* much sleep.
2. Demand.—The teacher *requires* us to be on time for class.
–*requirement, n. requirements.*

res•cue (RESS-kyoo) *n. rescues.* Saving.—The *rescue* of the pilots lost at sea was difficult.

—*v. rescues, rescued, rescuing.* Save or set free from danger.—The sailors *rescued* the man from the sinking ship.

res•cu•er (RESS-kyoo-er) *n. rescuers.* A person who rescues or saves someone from harm or danger. — The man who fell overboard thanked his *rescuers.* He thanked the men who had saved him from the sea.

re•search (ri-SERCH *or* REE-serch) *n. researches.* Careful study and investigation; the search for knowledge, especially new knowledge.—Scientists are constantly doing *research.*

re•sem•blance (ri-ZEM-blənss) *n. resemblances.* A like or similar appearance.—There is a strong *resemblance* between Mother and Ann. They look very much alike.

re•sem•ble (ri-ZEM-bəl) *v. resembles, resembled, resembling.* Look somewhat like.—Our dog is so big he *resembles* a horse.

re•sent (ri-ZENT) *v. resents, resented, resenting.* Feel angry and hurt at.—Bob *resents* being called a coward.
—*resentment, n. resentments.*

re•sent•ful (ri-ZENT-fuhl) *adj.; resentfully, adv.* Showing anger and ill feeling.—Bob is *resentful* because someone called him a coward.

res•er•va•tion (rez-er-VAY-shən) *n. reservations.* 1. Anything that is held back for a special use or purpose.—Bob has a *reservation* for the ball game. A ticket for a seat is being held for him.
2. A restriction or limit.—The teacher recommended Tom without *reservations.*

re•serve (ri-ZERV) *n. reserves.* 1. Care not to be too friendly; restraint in speech or manner.—Mary answers the questions of strangers with *reserve.*
2. Extra supply for a time of need. — The teacher keeps a *reserve* of pencils in her drawer.
—*v. reserves, reserved, reserving.* Set aside or hold.—Father said he would *reserve* a day to take us to the park.

res•er•voir (REZ-er-vor *or* -vwahr) *n. reservoirs.* A huge tank, pool, or lake where water is kept for use when needed.

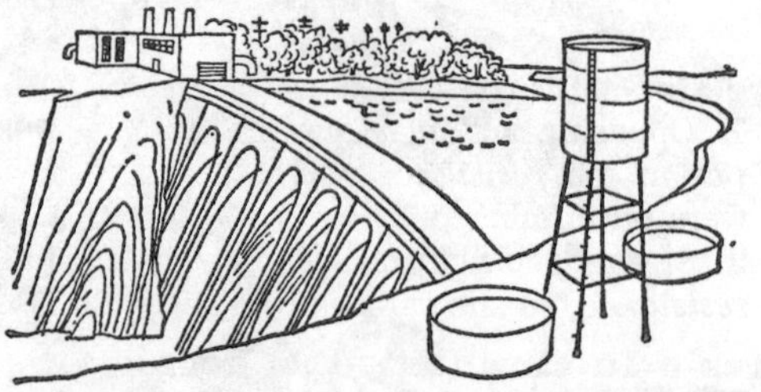

re•set (ree-SET) *v. resets, reset, resetting.* Place in a new setting, or set again. — The pearls were *reset* in a modern-style necklace.

re•side (ri-ZYD) *v. resides, resided, residing.* Live or have one's home.—Grandmother *resides* in the country.—We *reside* in town.

res•i•dence (REZ-ə-dənss) *n. residences.* A house, or place where one lives. — Alan's *residence* is on Wycoff Street.

—*Take up residence* means make one's home; go to live.—We have *taken up residence* on a farm.

res•i•dent (REZ-ə-dənt) *n. residents.* Someone who lives or makes his home in a particular place.—The *residents* of the town built a new playground for the children.

re•sign (ri-ZYN) *v. resigns, resigned, resigning.* 1. Give up.—Father *resigned* his position for a better one.
2. Make up one's mind to; submit.—Mary has *resigned* herself to spending the day at home, since it is raining too hard to go out. She knows that she must stay home.

res•ig•na•tion (rez-ig-NAY-shən) *n. resignations.* 1. The act of giving up a job or position. — John's *resignation* from the student government made a new election necessary.
2. A statement that one is resigning.—John made his *resignation* in writing.
3. Quiet patience, or quiet giving in.—Father receives bad news with *resignation.* He doesn't complain.

res•in (REZ-ən) *n.* A sticky sap that flows from such trees as the pine.–*Resin* is used in varnish and in medicines.

re•sist (ri-ZIST) *v. resists, resisted, resisting.* Fight or hold out against.–The thief did not *resist* the policeman who arrested him.–The child was not strong enough to *resist* the disease.

re•sist•ance (ri-ZISS-tənss) *n. resistances.* 1. Opposing action or power.–The outlaws put up no *resistance* when they saw they were outnumbered.
2. Strength to fight off.–The child has little *resistance,* so she catches cold easily.

res•o•lu•tion (rez-ə-LOO-shən *or* rez-ə-LYOO-shən) *n. resolutions.* 1. A decision, or something one decides to do.–Mary made a New Year's *resolution* to do better work in school.
2. A statement that something should be done. – The mayor proposed a *resolution* stating that the parks of the city should be made larger and pleasanter for the people.
3. Determination. – The President approached his new responsibilities with *resolution.*

re•solve (ri-ZAHLV) *n.* Determination; resolution.–He approached the difficult task with a *resolve* to do it well.
–*v. resolves, resolved, resolving.* 1. Decide or determine.–Bob *resolved* to eat less candy.
2. Decide by a vote.–The class *resolved* that paper in the schoolyard should be picked up by the children each afternoon.
3. Solve.–The children *resolved* the problem of litter in the schoolyard by cleaning it up each afternoon.

re•sort (ri-ZORT) *n. resorts.* 1. A place to go, especially for recreation.–In summer many people go to *resorts* for vacations.

2. What a person gets help from.–Begging was the poor old man's last *resort.*
–*v. resorts, resorted, resorting.* 1. Turn for help.–The old man *resorted* to begging in order to obtain food.
2. Turn to or make use of, when other means have failed.–When every other effort failed to keep the dog from running away, Bob finally *resorted* to tying him up.

re•source (ri-SORSS *or* REE-sorss) *n. resources.* 1. A supply of anything to be used when needed. – Our country has great *resources* of cotton, metal, timber, and other natural products.
2. Ability to meet difficult situations.–Here is a job that will test your mental *resources.*

re•spect (ri-SPEKT) *n. respects.* 1. Admiration and honor. – The children have great *respect* for their teacher.
2. Care; consideration.–The children show *respect* for their books. They take care of them.
3. A way.–In what *respect* do you disagree with Mary? In what way do you disagree with her opinion?
–*v. respects, respected, respecting.* 1. Show or feel admiration for. – The children *respect* their teacher.
2. Take care of.–The children *respect* their books.

re•spect•ful (ri-SPEKT-fuhl) *adj.; respectfully, adv.* Showing that one thinks highly of a person or thing.–Jack disagreed with the teacher's idea in a *respectful* way. He told her very politely how he thought differently.–We should handle the flag *respectfully.* We should treat it with honor.

res•pi•ra•tion (ress-pə-RAY-shən) *n.* The inhaling and exhaling of air; breathing. – *Respiration* is difficult at high altitudes because the air contains less oxygen.

res•pi•ra•tor (RESS-pə-ray-ter) *n. respirators.* A device or apparatus used to help someone to breathe.–An oxygen or gas mask is a *respirator.*

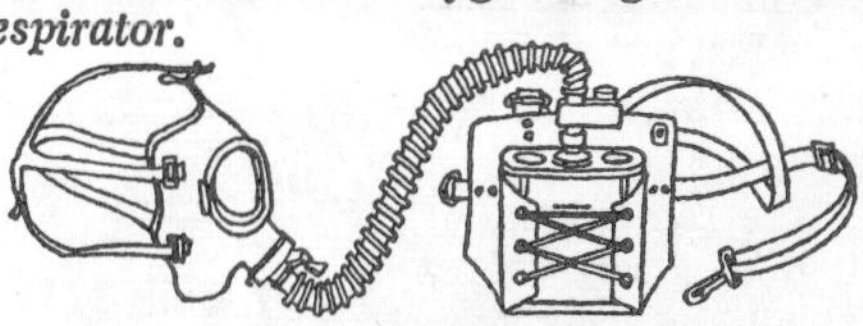

re•spir•a•to•ry (RESS-pə-rə-tor-ee) *adj.* Having to do with breathing. – Bronchitis and pneumonia are *respiratory* diseases.

res•pite (RESS-pit) *n. respites.* A time off for rest; a relief.–We had a short *respite* between classes.–We are having a *respite* from cold weather. It is warm now.

re•spond (ri-SPAHND) *v. responds, responded, responding.* 1. Answer.–Sally did not *respond* to Mother's call because she did not hear her.
2. Show effect, or react.–Some children *respond* to medicine more quickly than others. Medicine acts more quickly on some than on others.

re•sponse (ri-SPAHNSS) *n. responses.* 1. An answer.–Father is waiting for a *response* to his letter.
2. A reaction.–The child shows no *response* to the medicine.

re•spon•si•bil•i•ty (ri-spahn-sə-BIL-ə-tee) *n. responsibilities.* 1. Anything one is expected to do or attend to.–Mother's *responsibilities* are keeping the house clean, cooking, caring for the children, and helping us when we come to her.
2. Ability to carry through on obligations; trustworthiness.–John does not have much sense of *responsibility.* He just can't be depended on.

re•spon•si•ble (ri-SPAHN-sə-bəl) *adj.; responsibly, adv.* 1. Reliable.–Bob is a *responsible* person. You can always depend upon him.
2. Answerable or accountable.–The driver of the car was held *responsible* for the accident. He had to answer for it.
3. Involving important tasks.–A teacher has a very *responsible* position.

rest (REST) *n. rests.* 1. Relaxation; freedom from work or trouble. – Father must have *rest* so that he can play in the golf tournament.
2. Stillness; absence of motion. – The ball whizzed through the air and came to *rest* on the grass.
3. A pause, or sign showing a pause.–A *rest* in music is a slight pause, a short time when no note is sounded.
4. Something to lean on.–Most automobiles have arm*rests* on the doors.

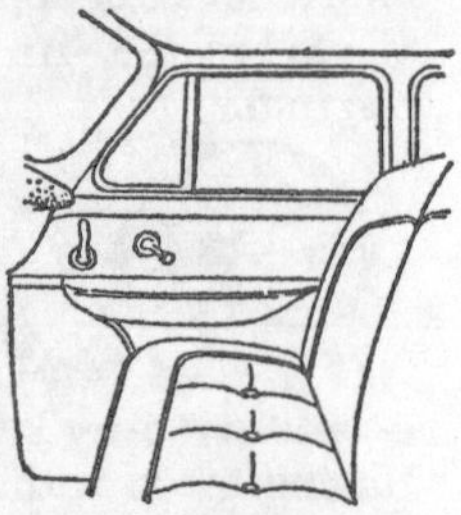

5. The remainder, or all that is left.–Mary ate all the ice cream that she wanted, and Bob ate the *rest.*
–*v. rests, rested, resting.* 1. Be still or free from work or action.–Grandfather let his horses *rest* for a time so that they would not get too tired.
2. Get over being tired.–Stop and *rest* when you are out of breath.
3. Remain.–The kitten's eyes *rested* on the mouse across the kitchen. She kept looking at the mouse.
4. Lie.–The broom *rests* against the wall.–The book *rests* upon the table.
–*Rest with* means depend upon.–The prisoner's freedom *rests with* the court.

res•tau•rant (RESS-tə-rənt) *n. restaurants.* A public place where food is served.–We stopped at a *restaurant* and ordered dinner.

rest•ful (REST-fuhl) *adj.; restfully, adv.* 1. Giving relaxation and rest.–The man had a *restful* night. It freed him from being tired.
2. Peaceful or calm; quiet.–We found a *restful* place in the hills to stay.

rest•less (REST-ləss) *adj.; restlessly, adv.* 1. Not able to keep calm or quiet.–Children in school are often *restless* in warm weather.
2. Without rest or sleep.–Father had a *restless* night because of his bad sunburn.

re•store (ri-STOR) *v. restores, restored, restoring.* 1. Renew or repair. – Bald-headed men often want to *restore* their hair. They try to grow hair again.–When the patient's health is *restored,* he will leave the hospital.
2. Put back.–The boy *restored* the stolen pen because he had a guilty conscience.

re•strain (ri-STRAYN) *v. restrains, restrained, restraining.* Hold in check or keep back.–It was hard for the rider to *restrain* the nervous horse.–The children could not *restrain* their laughter at the clown.
–*restraint, n. restraints.*

re•strict (ri-STRIKT) *v. restricts, restricted, restricting.* Keep within bounds; limit.–The hospital *restricts* the number of visitors each patient may receive.
–*restriction, n. restrictions.*

re•sult (ri-ZULT) *n. results.* A thing which happens because of something else that has happened before.–Good marks in school are a *result* of hard work.
–*v. results, resulted, resulting.* 1. Cause.–Carelessness often *results* in accidents.
2. Happen because of something.–Accidents often *result* from carelessness.

re•sume (ri-ZOOM *or* -ZYOOM) *v. resumes, resumed, resuming.* 1. Begin again; continue after a pause.–The orchestra *resumed* the concert after a brief intermission.
2. Take or occupy again.–The ballplayers are *resuming* their positions on the field.–*Resume* your seats, please.

Res•ur•rec•tion (rez-ə-REK-shən) *n.* The rising of Jesus Christ from the dead.

re•tail (REE-tayl) *adj.* Having to do with selling things in small amounts. – *Retail* stores sell goods to people who buy for their own use.

re•tain (ri-TAYN) *v. retains, retained, retaining.* 1. Hold or keep.–Some cloth does not *retain* its color when hung outdoors in the sunshine. It fades.
2. Remember. – Some children *retain* what they learn longer than others.
3. Hire for a fee.–After the accident, Father *retained* a lawyer to defend him in court.

re•tal•i•ate (ri-TAL-ee-ayt) *v. retaliates, retaliated, retaliating.* Get even, usually by paying back in a similar way.–When John pulled Mary's hair, she *retaliated* by stepping on his toes.
–*retaliation, n. retaliations.*

re•tard (ri-TAHRD) *v. retards, retarded, retarding.* Prevent progress; make (something) slow.–The boulder in the middle of the road *retarded* the flow of traffic.–Lack of sunshine *retards* the growth of many plants.

ret•i•na (RET-ə-nə) *n. retinas.* The membrane at the rear of the eyeball that receives the images seen by the eye.

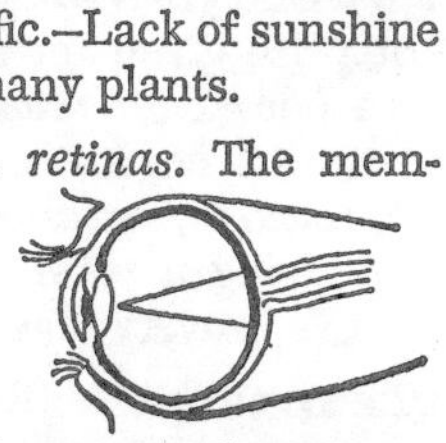

re•tire (ri-TYR) *v. retires, retired, retiring.*
1. Go to bed.–We *retire* at eight o'clock.
2. Stop working forever.–Grandfather has *retired* because he is getting old.
3. Withdraw; go away.–Father *retired* from the party because he had to get up early the next morning.
–*retirement, n. retirements.*

re•treat (ri-TREET) *n. retreats.* 1. A moving or falling back.–The beaten wolf made a quick *retreat* into the forest.
2. A place of quiet; a refuge.–Father calls the den his *retreat.* He can work there without being disturbed.
–*v. retreats, retreated, retreating.* Move or fall back.–The outlaw band was caught in the canyon and could not *retreat.*

re•trieve (ri-TREEV) *v. retrieves, retrieved, retrieving.* 1. Get back again; regain; recover.–Jack *retrieved* the ball he had dropped in the lake.
2. Find and bring back. – The hound *retrieved* the wild duck shot by the hunter.
3. Repair; make good.–Ed *retrieved* his mistake in calling Mrs. Smith "Mrs. Jones" by introducing her correctly to his friends.

re•turn (ri-TERN) *n. returns.* 1. A report.–We sat up late to see the election *returns* on television.
2. A payment back; something received in exchange for something else.–Bob's *return* for hard study was an "A" in arithmetic.–The *returns,* or amount of money made, from the puppet show were twenty dollars.
3. Coming or going back.–We welcome the *return* of the robins in spring.
–*v. returns, returned, returning.* 1. Come back. –Father will *return* after work.
2. Go back.–Mother had to *return* to the house for her key.
3. Give or send back.–*Return* your aunt's umbrella the next time you go to see her.
4. Put back.–*Return* the book to the shelf when you are through with it.
5. Pay back.–Lend me a nickel, and I will *return* it soon.
–*adj.* Used for going and coming back.–Father bought a *return* ticket to Chicago.

re•un•ion (ree-YOON-yən) *n. reunions.* Gathering or coming together again.–The students plan to hold a *reunion* each year after they graduate. They all plan to get together once each year.

re•veal (ri-VEEL) *v. reveals, revealed, revealing.* 1. Make known.–At last the truth was *revealed* to us.
2. Indicate, display, or show.–Mary's shaky voice *revealed* her nervousness.

rev•eil•le (REV-ə-lee) *n.* A military or naval signal sounded in the early morning on a bugle or drum to rouse sleeping soldiers or sailors for their duties.

re•venge (ri-VENJ) *n.* Harm or injury done to another in return for harm or injury.–When the angry man hit the mule, the mule's *revenge* was to kick the man.
–*v. revenges, revenged, revenging.* To harm or to hurt in return.–The mule *revenged* itself by kicking the man who hit it.

rev•e•nue (REV-ə-noo *or* -nyoo) *n. revenues.* Income, or money coming in.–Most of the government's *revenue* comes from taxes.

rev•er•ence (REV-rənss) *n.* Solemn respect and love.–We bow our heads in *reverence* for the soldiers who died.

Rev•er•end (REV-er-ənd) *adj.* The title of a minister or preacher of a church.–The *Reverend* Frank Smith is our minister.

re•verse (ri-VERSS) *n. reverses* and *adj.* 1. A misfortune.–During the flood, many stores and shops met with *reverses.* Their business changed from good to bad.

2. The opposite or backward direction.–To back a car out of a garage, move it in *reverse.*

3. The other side.–What is on the *reverse* of the newspaper page you want to clip?

–*v. reverses, reversed, reversing.* Turn or change to the opposite direction, position, or the like. – At first Father's answer was "No," but he *reversed* his decision. He changed it to "Yes."–The runner *reversed* his direction and ran the other way.

re•vers•i•ble (ri-VER-sə-bəl) *adj.* Able to be changed or used in an opposite manner or direction.–Mary has a *reversible* coat. She can wear it with either side out. – Father's decision proved to be *reversible.* He said that John could go after all.

re•view (ri-VYOO) *n. reviews.* 1. A going over again.–We had a *review* in spelling.

2. A report about a book, play, concert, etc.–The newspaper gave a *review* of the new book. It told what the story was about, and revealed its good and bad points.

3. An inspection.–The officer made a *review* of the troops. He looked them over to see whether they were well trained.

–*v. reviews, reviewed, reviewing.* 1. Go over again.–We did not know our lesson well, so we had to *review* it.–The judge *reviewed* the case. He examined carefully all the stories about the accident.

2. Give a report of a book, play, concert, etc. –Our teacher asked us to *review* the book.

3. Inspect.–The general *reviewed* the troops.

re•vise (ri-VYZ) *v. revises, revised, revising.* Correct, or change to improve.–After writing our stories, we had to *revise* them.

–*revision, n. revisions.*

re•vive (ri-VYV) *v. revives, revived, reviving.* 1. Bring back again.–Old movies are often *revived* on television.

2. Restore to consciousness, life, or activity; refresh.–The doctor *revived* the woman who had fainted.–A cold shower *revived* the tired athlete.

–*revival, n. revivals.*

re•volt (ri-VOHLT) *n. revolts.* Fighting against those in control.–All the prisoners joined the *revolt* against the guards.

–*v. revolts, revolted, revolting.* Fight against the government, or those in lawful control. –The prisoners *revolted* against their guards.

rev•o•lu•tion (rev-ə-LOO-shən *or* rev-əl-YOO-shən) *n. revolutions; revolutionary, adj.* 1. The complete changing of the government or rulers by people who are against the government. – In the American *Revolution,* the Americans freed themselves from England and became a separate country, with a government they made for themselves.

2. A sudden, complete change.–The use of the automobile has made a great *revolution* in people's lives. They can do things they never could do before.

3. A complete turning around of something. –The children in the circle made three *revolutions* to the right.

re•volve (ri-VAHLV) *v. revolves, revolved, revolving.* Roll or go around.–The hands on a clock *revolve.*–A merry-go-round *revolves,* too.

re•volv•er (ri-VAHL-ver) *n. revolvers.* A short, repeating gun which can be held in one hand and has a cylinder to hold the cartridges.

re•ward (ri-WORD) *n. rewards.* A payment or prize given for some special act. – The teacher gave a *reward* of five dollars for the return of her lost ring.

–*v. rewards, rewarded, rewarding.* Recognize by giving a prize or payment.–The policeman's bravery was *rewarded* with a medal.

rheu•ma•tism (ROO-mə-tiz-əm) *n.* A disease of a person's joints or muscles. *Rheumatism* causes pain, stiffness, and swelling.

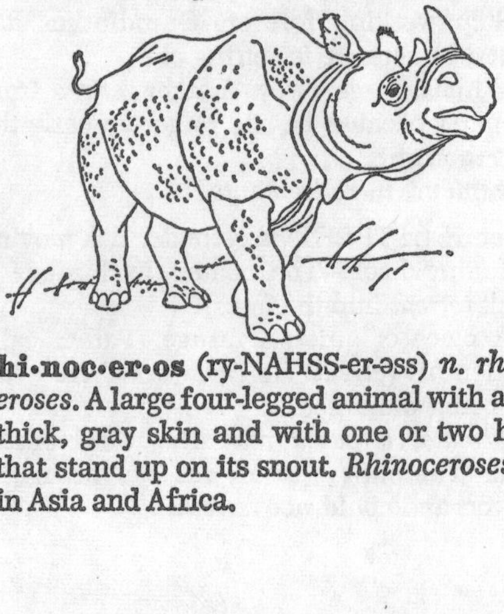

rhi•noc•er•os (ry-NAHSS-er-əss) *n. rhinoceroses.* A large four-legged animal with a very thick, gray skin and with one or two horns that stand up on its snout. *Rhinoceroses* live in Asia and Africa.

rhi•zome (RY-zohm) *n. rhizomes.* An underground plant stem that grows sideways. It takes root on its lower side, and sends up shoots from its top side. *Rhizomes* look different from real roots because they have buds and scaly leaves. Certain types of turnips and herbs have *rhizomes.*

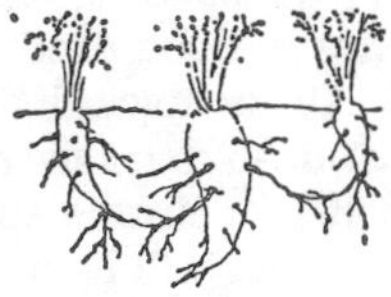

Rhode Is•land (rohd Y-lənd) *n.* A manufacturing state on the east coast of the United States. It was the first colony in the U. S. to have complete religious freedom. *Rhode Island* is the smallest of the states.

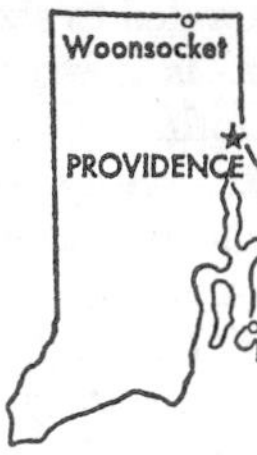

rhu•barb (ROO-bahrb) *n.* A plant with very large green leaves that grow on large stalks, or stems. The long juicy stems are stewed and used for sauce, and as a filling for pies.

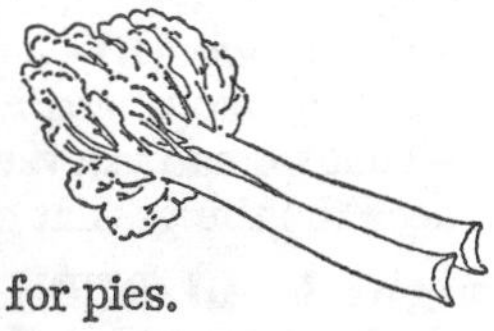

rhyme or **rime** (RYM) *n. rhymes* or *rimes.* A verse or poem in which the last words of each line sound alike.–This is a *rhyme:*

"Jack and Jill
Went up the hill."

–*v. rhymes, rhymed, rhyming.* End with the same sound.–The words "snow" and "show" *rhyme.* – Can you name two words that *rhyme?*

rhythm (RITH-əm) *n. rhythms.* The regular beat of sound or movement.–It is easy to dance to music because of its *rhythm.* The dance steps have the same regular beat as the music.

rib (RIB) *n. ribs.* 1. One of a group of bones that fasten to the spine, or backbone, and curve around to the front of the body over the chest. *Ribs* form a "box" to protect the lungs and the heart. People and many kinds of animals have *ribs.*

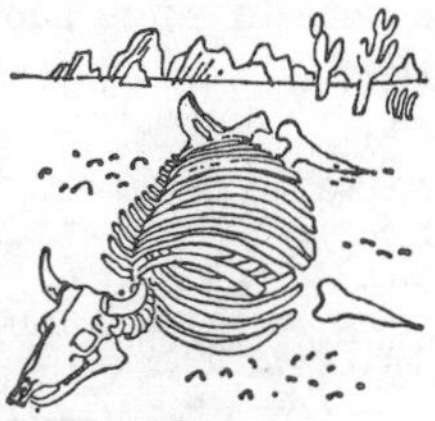

2. Anything like a person's ribs in shape or use.–The *ribs* of an umbrella are the thin metal "spokes," or rods, to which the cloth is fastened.

rib•bon (RIB-ən) *n. ribbons.* A strip or narrow band of cloth.–Ruth wears bows of *ribbon* on her braids.

rice (RYSS) *n.* A grass whose seeds are used for food. *Rice* grows in a warm climate.

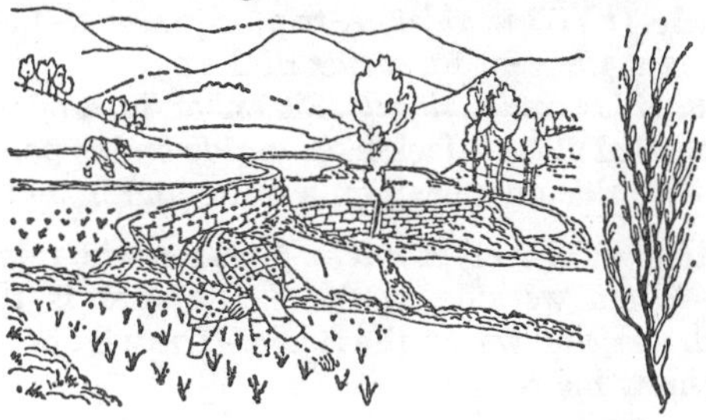

rich (RICH) *adj. richer, richest; richly, adv.; richness, n.* 1. Wealthy, or having much money, land, or the like. – The *rich* family lives in a big house with beautiful grounds.
2. Able to produce much.–A *rich* soil is soil that has plenty of food to make plants grow.
3. Having plenty. – Our country is *rich* in copper ore. It has a great supply of it.
4. Expensive or valuable.–Things that cost much, and are of the best quality, are *rich.*–The queen wore a *rich* velvet gown.
5. Nourishing or satisfying to the appetite; having much sugar, butter, etc.–The cake Mother baked was too *rich.*–*Rich* soups are very nourishing.
6. Filled with deep, pleasing shades of color and sound.–Mother's party dress is of a *rich,* warm green color.–The story of Robinson Crusoe is filled with *rich* description.

rich•es (RICH-əz) *n. pl.* Money or valuable things.–*Riches* alone could not make King Midas happy.

rich•ly (RICH-lee) *adv.* Expensively or elegantly.–The queen was *richly* dressed in velvet embroidered with emeralds.

rick•ets (RIK-itss) *n. pl.* A disease that attacks poorly fed children. Children with *rickets* suffer a softening of the bones and often become crippled.

ric•o•chet (rik-ə-SHAY) *v. ricochets, ricocheted, ricocheting.* Move in a bouncing, skipping manner, as a bullet off a wall.–Bob threw a rock which *ricocheted* off the fence.

rid (RID) *v. rids, rid, ridding.* Clear or free.–The Pied Piper *rid* the city of rats.
–*Get rid of* means become free of.–We *got rid of* our old car.

rid•den (RID-n) *v.* One form of the verb *ride.*–After we had *ridden* in the car for two days, Mother was very tired.

rid•dle (RID-l) *n. riddles.* A puzzle.–This is a *riddle:* The more you take from it, the bigger it grows. What is it? Answer: A hole.
–*v. riddles, riddled, riddling.* Pierce many holes in.–Bullets *riddled* the target.

ride (RYD) *n. rides.* A trip or journey.–Last night we went for a *ride* in the car.
–*v. rides, rode, riding.* Sit on or in, and be carried along.–Jack likes to *ride* on his pony. –We *ride* on a boat, on a train, and in a car.

rid•er (RYD-er) *n. riders.* A person who rides. –When we ride in the car, Father is the driver, and we are the *riders.*–The wild horse threw his *rider.*

ridge (RIJ) *n. ridges.* 1. A raised line or edge where two slanting surfaces meet. – The long top part of the roof on a house is a *ridge.*

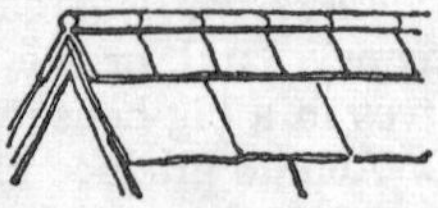

2. Any narrow, raised strip.–A heavy thread in a piece of cloth makes a *ridge.*

rid•i•cule (RID-ə-kyool) *v. ridicules, ridiculed, ridiculing.* Make fun of; mock.–Mother told the boys that it was unkind to *ridicule* the woman in the funny hat.

ri•dic•u•lous (rə-DIK-yə-ləss) *adj.; ridiculously, adv.; ridiculousness, n.* Very silly.– Men would look *ridiculous* wearing women's clothes.

ri•fle (RYF-əl) *n. rifles.* A long-barreled gun held with two hands, and with a spiral groove in the barrel. The spiral groove makes the bullet spin when it is fired, so it will go straight.

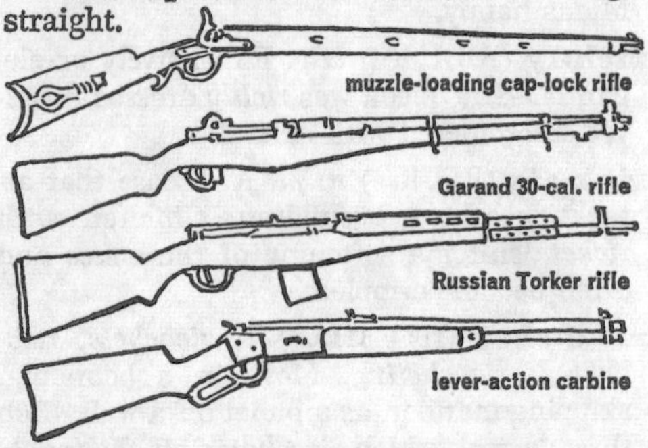

right (RYT) *n. rights.* A privilege; a lawful claim.–In the United States it is a person's *right* to go to the church he chooses.
–*v. rights, righted, righting.* 1. Correct.–Mary *righted* the misunderstanding between herself and Mother.
2. Set in the proper position. – The upset boat must be *righted* before it can be used.
–*adj.* 1. Good, proper, decent, or lawful.–*Right* is the opposite of wrong. Bad deeds are wrong. Good deeds are *right.*
2. On or toward the side opposite your left hand.–If you face south, your *right* shoulder will be pointing toward the west; your left shoulder will be pointing to the east.
3. Correct.–This clock gives the *right* time.
4. True. – John says that you have a new book. Is that *right?*
5. Intended to show, or to be worn outwards. –There is a wrong and a *right* side to this tablecloth.
6. Satisfactory. – Bob's teeth are all *right* since he had them cleaned.
7. Straight.–A *right* line is a straight line.
–*adv.* 1. Directly. – Mary looked *right* at the book and yet didn't see it.
2. Straight.–Go *right* ahead.
3. Exactly.–Tom put his toys *right* where they were supposed to go.
–*Right now* means immediately.

right•eous (RY-chəss) *adj.; righteously, adv.; righteousness, n.* Acting properly; good. –That woman is a very *righteous* person. She does the things that are good and right.

right-hand (RYT-HAND) *adj.* At or toward the hand that is on the right.–Put your book on the *right-hand* side of your desk.

right-hand•ed (RYT-han-dəd) *adj.* Mary is *right-handed.* She writes with and uses her right hand more easily and more often than her left hand.

right•ly (RYT-lee) *adv.* 1. Exactly or correctly.–I cannot *rightly* say how far it is to the city.
2. Honestly or in fairness.–Mother cannot *rightly* give more to Jack than she gives to Mary.

rig•id (RIJ-id) *adj.; rigidly, adv.* 1. Stiff and hard to bend.–Iron bars are *rigid.*
2. Unchanging, or allowing no exceptions; strict.–In some schools the rules are very *rigid.*

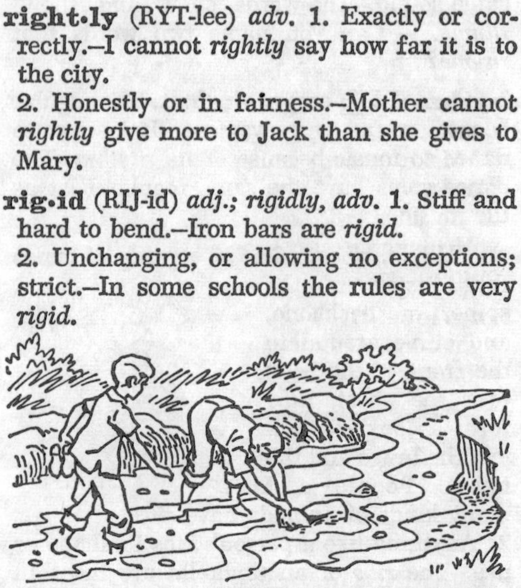

rill (RIL) *n. rills.* A little stream or river.–The boys went wading in the *rill.*

rim (RIM) *n. rims.* A border or edge.–The *rims* on Mother's eyeglasses are gold.–The *rim* of a tumbler is the top edge.

rime or **rhyme** (RYM) *n. rimes* or *rhymes.* This is a *rime,* because the ends of the lines sound alike:

"Jack and Jill
Went up the hill."

rind (RYND) *n. rinds.* The outer skin on such things as oranges, melons, squash, cucumbers, and bacon. –We eat the fruit but throw away the *rind.*

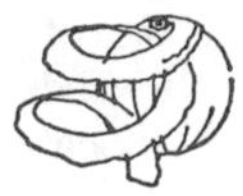

ring (RING) *n. rings.* 1. A circle. – When Father smokes his pipe, he makes *rings* of smoke in the air.

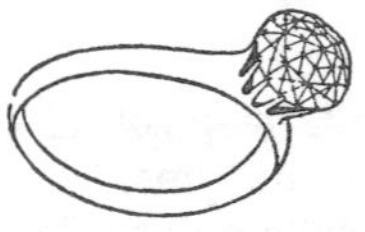

diamond ring

ring-around-the-rosy

2. A round band worn on the finger.–Mother wears a wedding *ring.*
3. Any round band.–The farmer put a *ring* in the pig's nose to keep him from digging up the ground with his nose.
4. A band or group.–A group of people who work together for bad purposes is a *ring.*–A *ring* of thieves stole the gold.
5. Sound of or like a bell.–We heard three short *rings* and knew it was Bob at the door.– The *ring* of Mary's laugh could be heard from the garden.

–*v. rings, rang, ringing.* 1. Make a sound of or like a bell.–Mary dropped the cover of the saucepan, and we could hear it *ring* as it hit the floor.
2. Make (a bell) sound.–*Ring* the doorbell, please.
3. Be filled (with sound).–The theater *rings* with laughter every time the comedian comes onto the stage.

ring·let (RING-lət) *n. ringlets.* A small, tight curl.–After a rain, Baby's hair curls in *ringlets* all over her head.

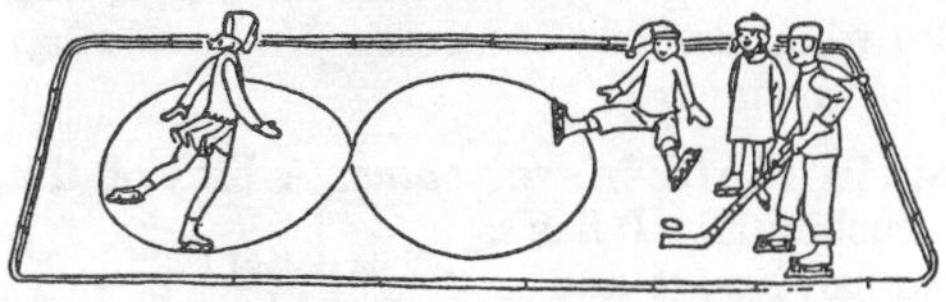

rink (RINGK) *n. rinks.* A floor, or sheet of ice, marked off or fenced in for roller skating, or ice skating.

rinse (RINSS) *v. rinses, rinsed, rinsing.* Pour water over, or dip in water, especially to wash away the soap.–Mary washed the dishes in soapsuds, and then *rinsed* them with very hot water.–Clothes that have been washed in soapy water are *rinsed* by moving them in and out of clear water again and again.

ri·ot (RY-ət) *n. riots.* Noisy quarreling and fighting by a large number of people, especially in a public place.

rip (RIP) *n. rips.* A tear or opening.–Bob had a *rip* in his coat sleeve where the threads of the seam had come out.

–*v. rips, ripped, ripping.* 1. Tear; pull apart by force.–Mother *ripped* off the bandage on her arm.–Mother *ripped* up Mary's old coat to make a coat for the baby. She cut or pulled out the threads from the seams.

rip cord (RIP kord) *rip cords.* The cord which, when pulled, opens a parachute.– The paratrooper pulled the *rip cord* to open his parachute.

ripe (RYP) *adj. riper, ripest.* Completely grown and ready to be picked for eating.– Grandfather told Bob to pick only the *ripe* cherries off the tree.

rip·en (RYP-ən) *v. ripens, ripened, ripening.* Become ripe or ready to eat.–Tomatoes *ripen* in the sun more quickly than they do in the shade.

rip·ple (RIP-əl) *n. ripples.* A tiny wave.– There isn't a *ripple* on the lake today.–When the frog jumped into the water, little *ripples* formed on the surface.

–*v. ripples, rippled, rippling.* Make little waves on.–The breeze *rippled* the lake.

rise (RYZ) *n. rises.* 1. An increase.–The *rise* in the price of milk made it hard for the large family to buy milk for their six children.
2. A slope or slant.–The steep *rise* of the roof makes it difficult to climb.

–*v. rises, rose, rising.* 1. Get up or stand up.– *Rise* before you speak in class.
2. Go or move up.–A balloon *rises* because it is lighter than air.
3. Increase. – The temperature sometimes *rises* during the daytime. The air grows warmer.
4. Slant upward. – We have made a rock garden in our backyard where the bank *rises* sharply.

risk (RISK) *n. risks.* Chance or danger.–There is no *risk* of falling if you hold on to the ladder.
–*v. risks, risked, risking.* 1. Take the chance of.–Do not *risk* crossing the street in front of a moving car.
2. Put in danger of loss or harm.–The man *risked* his life to save the child.

risk•y (RISS-kee) *adj. riskier, riskiest; riskily, adv.; riskiness, n.* Dangerous; involving chance. – It is *risky* to get too tired while swimming.

rite (RYT) *n. rites.* A solemn act or special service usually carried out according to a set form or pattern.–Marriage *rites* in our church are carried out in the same way each time a man and a woman are married.

ri•val (RY-vəl) *n. rivals.* One of two or more persons who are trying to get something only one can have.–Mary and Ruth were *rivals* in the final spelling bee. Each of them wanted to be the winner.
–*v. rivals, rivaled, rivaling.* Be a rival to.–The girls *rivaled* each other in the spelling bee.

ri•val•ry (RY-vəl-ree) *n. rivalries.* Competition between rivals.–There is *rivalry* between the boys to see who will get the higher mark.

riv•er (RIV-er) *n. rivers.* Large brook or stream.–Boats steam up and down the *river.*

riv•et (RIV-it) *n. rivets.* A metal bolt with a rounded head and without threads. A *rivet* is put through matching holes in the pieces to be fastened together, and then the small end is flattened with an automatic hammer to make another head so that the *rivet* will not come out.

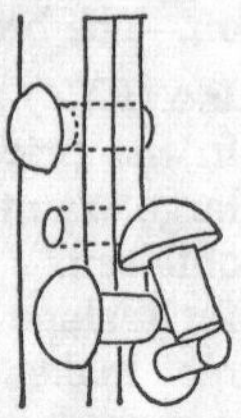

–*v. rivets, riveted, riveting.* Fasten with one or more rivets. – The workmen *riveted* the heavy steel beams together.

roach (ROHCH) *n. roaches.* A cockroach; an insect with a hard shell sometimes found in kitchens, bathrooms, and other damp places. –*Roaches* come out at night when it is dark.

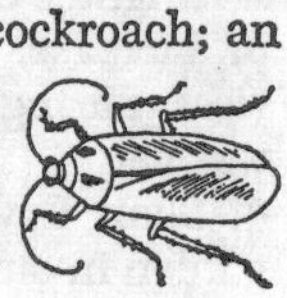

road (ROHD) *n. roads.* 1. An open way; a long, smoothed strip, often paved, on which people, cars, animals, and other things travel. *Roads* lead from one place to another.
2. A way.–Kindness is a *road* to happiness.

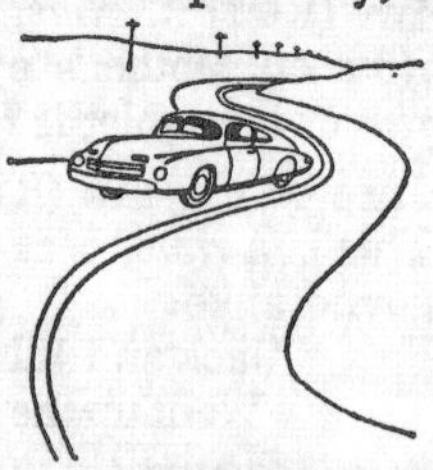

road•side (ROHD-syd) *n. roadsides.* Land at the side of a road.–The *roadside* was covered with weeds.
–*adj.* Located at the side of a road.–We buy vegetables at a *roadside* market, a market at the side of a road.

roam (ROHM) *v. roams, roamed, roaming.* Wander about.–On Sundays we like to *roam* through the woods.

roar (ROR) *n. roars.* A loud, deep sound or noise.–We heard the *roar* of the guns.
–*v. roars, roared, roaring.* Make a deep, loud sound.–The lions at the zoo *roar.*

roast (ROHST) *n. roasts.* A piece of meat to be cooked in the oven.–We ate the entire *roast* for dinner.
–*v. roasts, roasted, roasting.* Bake or cook in an oven or over live coals on an open fire.–Mother *roasted* the beef in the oven.

rob (RAHB) *v. robs, robbed, robbing.* Steal from, or force one to hand over.–The bandits *robbed* the man of his wallet and then fled.

rob•ber (RAHB-er) *n. robbers.* A person who robs or steals.–The highway *robbers* held up travelers who passed by.

rob•ber•y (RAHB-er-ee) *n. robberies.* The act of robbing or stealing. – The bank *robbery* took place at night.

robe (ROHB) *n. robes.* 1. A long, loose gown worn over other clothing. – Father has a new bath*robe.*–Men in certain offices, such as judges and ministers, wear *robes.*

2. A covering to put over the feet, legs, and lap when one sits outdoors.–We have a lap *robe* in our car.

rob•in (RAHB-in) *n. robins.* A bird of the thrush family. It has a reddish breast and is sometimes called a redbreast. – *Robins* have a cheerful song.

ro•bot (ROH-but *or* -baht) *n. robots*. 1. A machine, made to look like a man, that can walk around and do certain other things a man can do.

2. A person who acts like a machine.

ro•bust (roh-BUST *or* ROH-bust) *adj*. Strong, healthy, and sound; sturdy.–The champion is tall and *robust*.

rock (RAHK) *n. rocks*. 1. The solid material of the earth's crust, made up of minerals.–The bottom of this lake is solid *rock*.
2. A large mass of stone.–The mountain is a huge *rock*.
3. A large stone.–The boys threw *rocks* into the lake and watched them splash.
–*v. rocks, rocked, rocking*. Move to and fro and from side to side.–The boat *rocked* dangerously during the storm.–Sally *rocked* her doll to sleep in its cradle.

rock•er (RAHK-er) *n. rockers*. 1. A curved piece of wood on which the legs of a piece of furniture are set.
2. A rocking chair, or chair that moves back and forth on rockers.

rock•et (RAHK-it) *n. rockets* and *adj*. 1. A type of engine; a method of propulsion. When the fuel inside a *rocket* is lit and explodes, the explosion knocks against the walls of the *rocket* and pushes it forward. When liquid fuel is used, it is sprayed with oxygen into a combustion chamber and ignited. When solid fuel is used, the fire just eats away at the fuel.
2. A missile that uses rocket propulsion. *Rockets* are used as signals, fireworks, and weapons. Recently they have been used to send satellites into orbit.

rock•ing chair (RAHK-ing chair) *rocking chairs*. A chair on rockers.–Grandmother sits in her *rocking chair* and rocks Baby to sleep.

rock salt (RAHK sawlt). Common salt found in large, rocklike, solid masses. When pure, it is colorless and transparent. When impure, it is often yellow, red, or brown, and not transparent.

rock•y (RAHK-ee) *adj. rockier, rockiest*. Made up of rocks or covered with rocks.–The coast is very *rocky* here.

ROCKETS

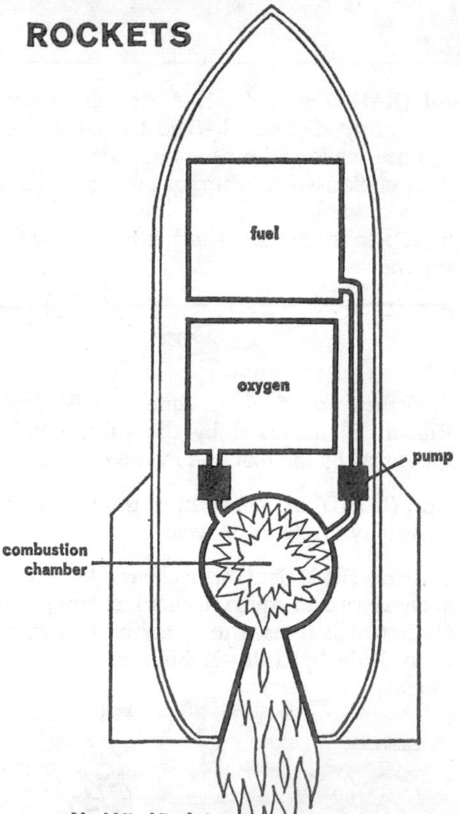

Liquid Fuel Rocket

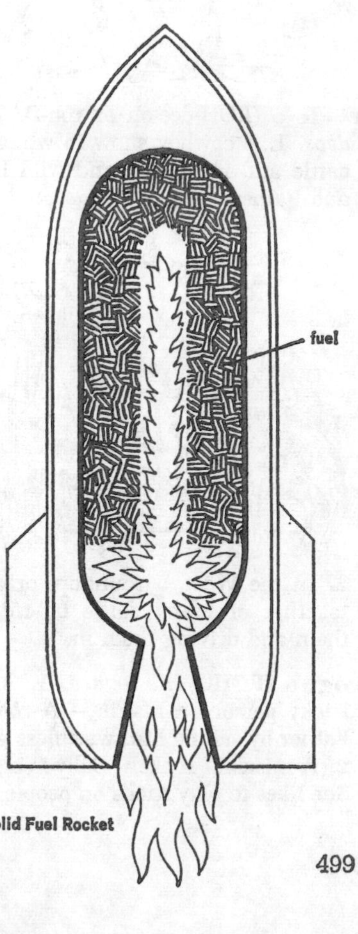

Solid Fuel Rocket

rod (RAHD) *n. rods.* 1. A straight, slender piece of wood or metal.–The doors of a prison cell are made of iron bars or *rods.*
2. A stick used to whip, or punish, a person or an animal.
3. A pole for fishing.–Father has a new fishing *rod.*

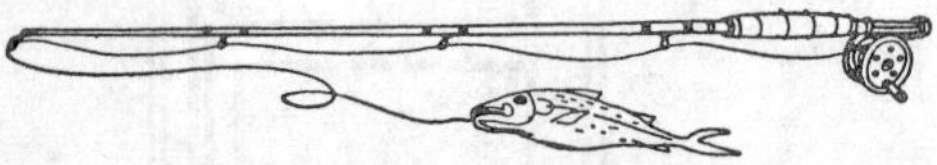

4. A measure of length equal to 16½ feet.–Ribbon is measured by the yard. Land is measured by the foot and by the *rod.*

rode (ROHD) *v.* One form of the verb *ride.*–Yesterday I *rode* my bicycle.

ro•dent (ROH-dənt) *n. rodents.* An animal, such as a rat or squirrel, that has long, sharp teeth which it uses to gnaw or bite things away little by little.–Rabbits and mice are *rodents.*

ro•de•o (ROH-dee-oh *or* roh-DAY-oh) *n. rodeos.* 1. A cowboy show in which men rope cattle and ride bulls and wild horses.–Bob and Father went to a *rodeo.*

2. In the West, a roundup, or a gathering together of many cattle by riding around them and driving them in.

rogue (ROHG) *n. rogues.* 1. A dishonest, tricky person; a rascal. – A *rogue* cheated Father by selling him worthless goods.
2. A mischief maker.–Sally is a little *rogue.* She likes to play tricks on people.

role (ROHL) *n. roles.* 1. A character or part in a show or movie played by an actor or actress. – Tim had the leading *role* in the school play. He played the part of the king.
2. Any part played in life.–Every night at suppertime, Mother plays the *role* of a cook.

roll (ROHL) *n. rolls.* 1. A continuous rumbling sound.–The prisoners heard the *roll* of the drums and the tramping of feet.–We saw a flash of lightning and heard a *roll* of thunder.
2. A list of names.–Mary checked the *roll* to see if all the children were in school.
3. Anything wound around something else, such as a *roll* of cloth, paper towels, wrapping paper, or the like.
4. Anything wound about itself. – The children made a *roll* of the clay in art class.
5. A kind of bread shaped into buns or small pieces before it is baked.–We have cinnamon *rolls* for breakfast every Sunday morning.

–*v. rolls, rolled, rolling.* 1. Turn over and over and move ahead.–The bowling ball *rolled* down the alley.
2. Wind up, or turn over and over.–The children *rolled* a snowball.–Grandmother *rolled* the yarn into a ball.–The children *rolled* up their papers and put a rubber band around them to take them home.
3. Push along on wheels or rollers.–Sally *rolled* the crippled man's wheel chair out onto the porch.
4. Flatten out with a rolling pin.–Mother *rolled* the cookie dough a quarter of an inch thick, and Mary cut out the cookies.
5. Swing from side to side.–During the storm the ship *rolled.*
6. Move continuously in a rolling, curved fashion.–The waves *rolled* in to shore.
7. Trill.–Some people *roll* their "r's" when they speak. They make their tongues vibrate against the roof of their mouth when they pronounce the letter "r."
8. Pile. – Our team *rolled* up a big score against the Rangers.

roll call (ROHL kawl) *roll calls.* A calling of names to see if anyone is absent.–After *roll call,* the teacher read us a story.

roll•er (ROHL-er) *n. rollers.* Anything that rolls, or moves along by turning over and over.–The small wheels on the legs of beds, tables, and chairs are *rollers.* – The wringer on the washing machine has two *rollers.*

roll•er skate (ROHL-er skayt) *roller skates.* A skate with rollers, or wheels, instead of a runner or blade.
–*v. roller skate, roller skated, roller skating.* Skate or glide on roller skates. – Children *roller skate* on the sidewalk.

roll•ing pin (ROHL-ing pin) *rolling pins.* A roller of wood or other material with a handle at each end. It is used to roll pie crust, to crush bread into crumbs, to roll cookie dough, and the like.

ro•mance (roh-MANSS *or* ROH-manss) *n. romances.* A poem or a story about heroes, adventure, or love.–Many people call any love story a *romance.*

Ro•man nu•mer•als (ROH-mən NOO- *or* NYOO-mer-əlz). Numbers such as I, V, X, L, C, D, and M are *Roman numerals.* I=1; V=5; X=10; L=50; C=100; D=500; and M=1,000. *Roman numerals* are often used on clocks instead of Arabic numerals.

romp (RAHMP) *n. romps.* Rough-and-tumble play.–The boys had their *romp* today.
–*v. romps, romped, romping.* Play roughly and noisily.–Jack and his dog *romp* in the yard.

roof (ROOF *or* RUHF) *n. roofs.* 1. The top covering of a building.–Our *roof* is made of green shingles.
2. Anything that is similar to a roof in position or use, such as the top of a car.

room (ROOM) *n. rooms.* 1. One of the inside divisions or parts of a building. *Rooms* are separated by walls and connected by doors. –We sleep in a bed*room.*
2. Space.–There wasn't *room* for one more thing in Mother's pocketbook.
3. Opportunity or chance.–There is *room* for advancement in Uncle Ned's business. A young man can go far.
–*v. rooms, roomed, rooming.* Live in a room in someone else's house.–Our teacher *rooms* at Mrs. Jones's house.

roost (ROOST) *n. roosts.* A perch, bar, branch, or anything else on which birds sit, stand, or rest while they sleep. The stick across a bird cage is a *roost.*
–*v. roosts, roosted, roosting.* Sit on a roost.–The canary *roosts* on his swing to sleep.

roost•er (ROOST-er) *n. roosters.* A male chicken. The mother chicken is a hen; the father chicken is a *rooster.*–The farmer's *roosters* crow early in the morning.

root (ROOT *or* RUHT) *n. roots.* 1. A part of a plant, bush, or tree that grows downward into the earth. *Roots* hold plants in place and feed them moisture and food from the soil. We eat some *roots,* such as turnips, beets, carrots, and radishes.

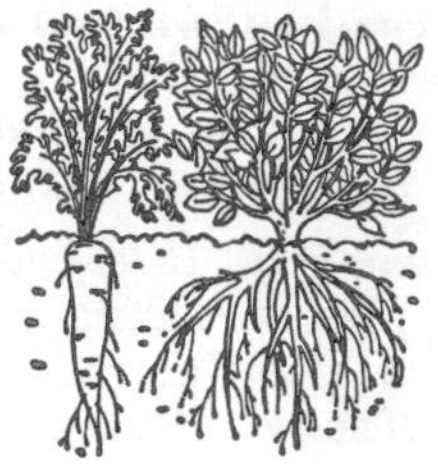

2. A part that is like the root of a plant.–Teeth have *roots* to hold them securely in place.
3. A beginning or source.–Spending all his allowance for candy was the *root* of Sam's troubles.
–*v. roots, rooted, rooting.* 1. Plant, set, or fix deeply.–The tree is well *rooted.*–It is hard to break a deeply *rooted* habit.–Bill's dislike of school is *rooted* in his lack of willingness to study.
2. Dig, pull, or remove.–The dogs *rooted* the fox out from his hiding place.–The farmer put rings in the pigs' noses so that they would not *root* up the earth.

rope (ROHP) *n. ropes.* 1. A strong, heavy cord made by twisting together several smaller cords.
2. Any large twisted strand or braid. – The children made a *rope* of dandelions to wear around their necks and heads.

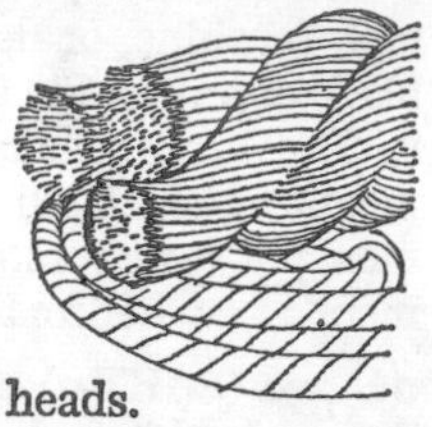

–*v. ropes, roped, roping.* 1. Separate, tie off, or divide with a rope.–A part of the street was *roped* off so that the children could play there.
2. Lasso or capture by throwing a rope around. – The cowboy *roped* the runaway horse.
3. Bind or tie with a rope.–The farmer *roped* the goat to the stake.

ro•sa•ry (ROH-zə-ree) *n. rosaries.* 1. A string of beads used to keep count in saying a number or series of prayers.
2. A group of prayers recited with this string of beads.

rose (ROHZ) *n. roses.* 1. A fragrant flower that grows on a bush. It has a prickly stem. *Roses* are red, yellow, pink, or white.
2. A deep pinkish color.
–*v.* One form of the verb *rise.*–The sun *rose* bright and hot.

ros·in (RAHZ-in) *n.* A hard brownish substance made from turpentine. *Rosin* is used on a violin bow to keep it from slipping while one plays the violin.

ros·y (ROH-zee) *adj. rosier, rosiest.* 1. Deep pink or reddish.–Baby has *rosy* cheeks.
2. Cheerful; full of promise of good things.–The days ahead of us look *rosy.*

rot (RAHT) *v. rots, rotted, rotting.* Decay; become soft and spoiled. – The potatoes remained in the wet ground so long that they *rotted.*

ro·ta·ry (ROH-tə-ree) *adj.* Rotating; turning round, as a wheel turns on its axle.–An egg beater has *rotary* parts.

ro·tate (ROH-tayt) *v. rotates, rotated, rotating.* 1. Turn around about a center or axis. –The earth *rotates* on its axis.–The wheels of a moving cart *rotate.*
2. Arrange one after the other; take in turn. –The farmer *rotates* his crops. One year he plants corn in a field, the next year he plants wheat in that field, and so on.
–*rotation, n. rotations.*

ro·tor (ROH-ter) *n. rotors.* 1. The part of a tool, machine, or device that rotates. – The blade of an electric fan is a *rotor.*
2. The arrangement of rotating blades by means of which a helicopter flies.–The workmen put a new *rotor* on the Police Department's new helicopter.

rot·ten (RAHT-n) *adj. rottener, rottenest.* 1. Decayed; soft and spoiled. – The tomatoes that were not kept in the refrigerator are *rotten.*
2. In bad condition; weak; not sound.–The boards in the front steps are *rotten,* so be careful.

ro·tun·da (roh-TUN-də) *n. rotundas.* A large round room or building, especially one with a dome.–There is a *rotunda* in the Capitol in Washington, D. C.

rouge (ROOZH) *n.* A pink or red powder or cream for coloring the skin.–Mother wears *rouge* on her cheeks.
–*v. rouges, rouged, rouging.* Put rouge on.–Mother *rouges* her cheeks.

rough (RUF) *adj. rougher, roughest; roughly, adv.; roughness, n.* 1. Uneven; irregular; not smooth or level.–Plowed ground is *rough.*–Sandpaper is *rough.*
2. Stormy; not quiet or still.–The sailors found the sea *rough.*
3. Wild and active.–Boys seem to like *rough* play. Many boys enjoy *rough* games.
4. Difficult, or filled with hard work.–Grandfather had a *rough* life when he was a boy.
5. Unpolished; not finished.–Diamonds are polished when you buy them in rings, but they are *rough* when they come from the mines.
6. Tangled; coarse.–The dog has *rough* fur.
7. Rude or ill-mannered.–The man met our offers of help with *rough* refusals.
8. Crude; not detailed or accurate. – Bob made a *rough* drawing of the model airplane he wants to build.
–*v. roughs, roughed, roughing.* 1. Rumple or tangle.–Father *roughed* up the baby's hair.
2. Make a rough outline, shape, or model of. –At first the children *roughed* out the vases they were making; then they made them smooth and true to form.
–*Rough it* means to live without the comforts of home.–The boys *roughed it* when they were camping.

rough·age (RUF-ij) *n.* Any rough or coarse material, especially certain foods that aid digestion, such as lettuce, celery, carrots, and bran. – The fragile glasses were packed in boxes filled with *roughage* to keep them from breaking. The *roughage* included strips of paper, wood shavings, and straw.

rough·en (RUF-ən) *v. roughens, roughened, roughening.* Make rough or coarse. – Cold weather *roughens* one's hands. Creams make them smooth again.

round (ROWND) *n. rounds.* 1. A regular route. – A policeman makes his *rounds* each day.
2. A dance which moves in a circle. – The Maypole dance is a *round.*

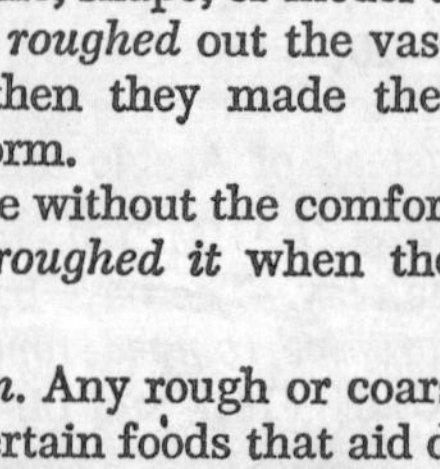

3. A number of duties, sports, pleasures, or other happenings coming one right after the other.–On our vacation we had a *round* of parties.
4. A part or period into which a fight or a game is divided.–The heavyweight champion knocked out his opponent in the third *round.*

5. Something which many people join in doing at the same time.–There was a *round* of boos when the batter struck out.
6. A song sung by a number of people beginning at different times.–Children think it is fun to sing *rounds*.
–*v. rounds, rounded, rounding.* 1. Go around. –The speeding car *rounded* the corner on two wheels.
2. Make or become circular.–Jack *rounded* the wheels of his model airplane.
–*adj.* Shaped like a ball, a circle, a wheel, or a water pipe.–Anything *round* and smooth will roll.
–*Round out* means complete. – Bob *rounded out* his story with one more paragraph.

round·a·bout (ROWND-ə-bowt) *adj.* Not straight or direct.–Because the road was being repaired, we went a *roundabout* way to the farm.

round·house (ROWND-howss) *n. roundhouses.* A round building to house railroad engines. It is built around a turning platform; the engines run onto the platform and the platform turns. In this way the engines are turned around.

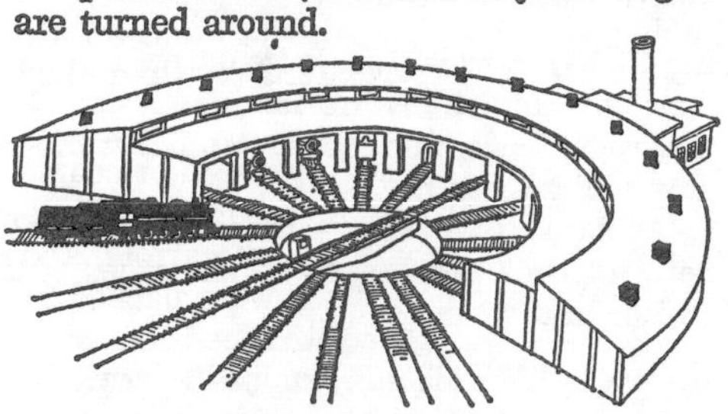

round-shoul·dered (ROWND-shohl-derd) *adj.* Having shoulders that lean forward.– The tall, thin girl is *round-shouldered*. She does not stand up straight.

round·up (ROWND-up) *n. roundups.* 1. Bringing cattle together.–The cowboys took part in the *roundup*. They brought together a large number of cattle by forming a circle around them and driving them into one herd.
2. Any gathering together of people by the efforts of others.–The police were praised for their *roundup* of gangsters in the town.

rouse (ROWZ) *v. rouses, roused, rousing.* 1. Disturb, wake up, or excite.–You may *rouse* the sleeping baby if you make too much noise.
2. Stir up or make angry.–The kidnaping *roused* the people of the town.

route (ROOT *or* ROWT) *n. routes.* A way of travel; a road or path.–What *route* did you take to the city?
–*v. routes, routed, routing.* Send along a way or road. – The policeman *routed* the cars around the washed-out bridge. He told them how to go by another way.

rou·tine (roo-TEEN) *n. routines.* A regular plan or way of doing things that is followed every time.–Mother gets her work done early because she follows a *routine*.

rove (ROHV) *v. roves, roved, roving.* Roam or wander.–The children like to *rove* in the woods.

row (ROH) *n. rows.* A line.–We sat in the first *row* of seats.–The wind destroyed a *row* of trees.
–*v. rows, rowed, rowing.* Move (a boat) with oars.–Bob *rowed* the boat to the spot where we fished.

row (ROW) *n. rows.* Noisy fight or quarrel.– The boys had a *row* over who would get the biggest piece of pie.

row·boat (ROH-boht) *n. rowboats.* A small boat moved by rowing.–The fishermen rented a *rowboat*.

roy·al (ROI-əl) *adj.; royally, adv.* Having to do with, or fit for, kings and queens.–The king and queen and their family live in the *royal* palace.–We were given a *royal* welcome.

roy·al·ty (ROI-əl-tee) *n. royalties.* 1. Kings, queens, and members of their families.–The feast was prepared for *royalty*.
2. Money paid to an inventor, author, or composer as his share of money made from the sale of his work. – Persons who write books often receive *royalties*.

rub (RUB) *v. rubs, rubbed, rubbing.* 1. Press against or together, and move back and forth. –Father's hands were so cold that he had to *rub* them together to get them warm.
2. Clean or polish by rubbing.–The maid *rubbed* the pots and pans with a cloth and scouring powder.
3. Erase.–*Rub* out the pencil marks with an eraser.

rub•ber (RUB-er) *n. rubbers.* A stretchy material made from the thick sap or juice of many plants that grow in certain warm countries; something made of this material. –Erasers, tires for cars, galoshes, water hoses, hot-water bottles, balls, and many other things are made of *rubber.*–Wear your *rubbers* when it rains.

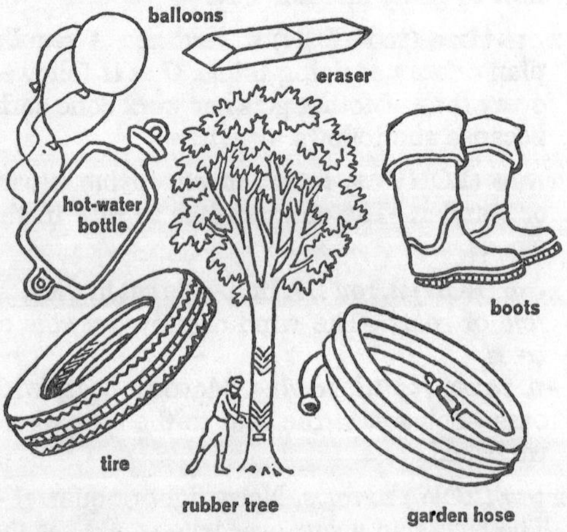

rub•bish (RUB-ish) *n.* Things to be thrown out; worthless things.–The children cleaned out the basement and put all the *rubbish* in the alley.

ru•by (ROO-bee) *n. rubies.* A deep-red precious stone.–Grandmother has a ring set with a large *ruby.*
–*adj.* Of a deep-red color.–The beautiful Snow White had coal-black hair, snow-white skin, and *ruby* lips.

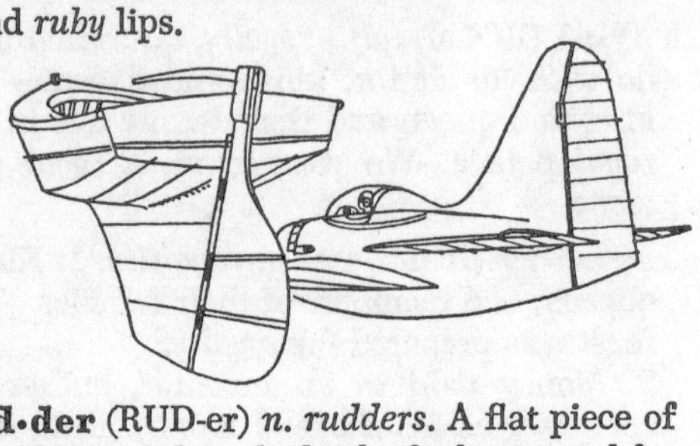

rud•der (RUD-er) *n. rudders.* A flat piece of wood or metal on the back of a boat, used for steering. Airplanes have *rudders,* too.

rude (ROOD) *adj. ruder, rudest; rudely, adv.; rudeness, n.* 1. Not polite; not courteous. – The boy was *rude;* he interrupted while his mother was talking.
2. Rough. – The boys made a *rude* boat of some old boards and a log.

ruf•fi•an (RUF-ee-ən) *n. ruffians.* A cruel, rough person.–The *ruffians* seized the salesman and beat him.

ruf•fle (RUF-əl) *n. ruffles.* A narrow piece of cloth or lace gathered at one edge and used as a trimming. – Mary's dress has *ruffles* around the hem and around the sleeves.

–*v. ruffles, ruffled, ruffling.* 1. Gather or make tiny pleats in cloth. –Mother *ruffled* the curtain borders on the sewing machine.
2. Puff out; cause to become rough or rear up.–The rooster *ruffles* his feathers when you go near him.
3. Disturb or vex. – Jack's teasing *ruffled* Mary. It made her angry.

rug (RUG) *n. rugs.* 1. A large carpet or other floor covering. *Rugs* are made of wool, cotton, rags, reeds, and grass.–Mother wants a new living-room *rug.*
2. A blanketlike robe. – Grandmother puts her *rug* over her lap when she rides with Father in the car.

rug•ged (RUG-id) *adj.; ruggedly, adv.; ruggedness, n.* 1. Uneven; rough.–The mountain country in the West is very *rugged.*
2. Rough and very simple.–Camping out is too *rugged* for Mother.
3. Strong and hardy.–Father likes to tell us how *rugged* he was when he was a boy.

ru•in (ROO-in) *n. ruins.* 1. Partly destroyed remains.–The country was in *ruins* after the storm. Buildings, trees, and other things were destroyed or damaged.–The *ruins* of some ancient buildings are still standing.
2. Useless or worthless condition. – The farmer's machines are in *ruin* from being left out in the rain so often.
3. Something which causes destruction or downfall. – Laziness and drink were the man's *ruin.*
4. Downfall or destruction. – War brought *ruin* to the country.
–*v. ruins, ruined, ruining.* Spoil or destroy.– The hailstorm *ruined* the fruit in the orchard

rule (ROOL) *n. rules.* 1. A direction telling what may and what may not be done.–The children know the *rules* of the game.
2. A flat stick, marked with evenly spaced lines, used for measuring and for drawing straight lines; a ruler.–Bob used a *rule* to measure the border on his paper and to guide his pencil in drawing the border.
3. Usual custom.–It is the *rule* to plant gardens in the spring.
–*v. rules, ruled, ruling.* 1. Mark with straight lines.–We *ruled* the paper for ten spelling words.
2. Control or govern.–The king *rules* over his country.
3. Decide.–The children *ruled* that the rules of the game should be followed carefully.

rul•er (ROOL-er) *n. rulers.* 1. A person who governs or controls.–A king is a *ruler.*
2. A flat stick marked off in inches, half inches, and so on. A *ruler* is used to measure with and to guide one's pencil in making straight lines.

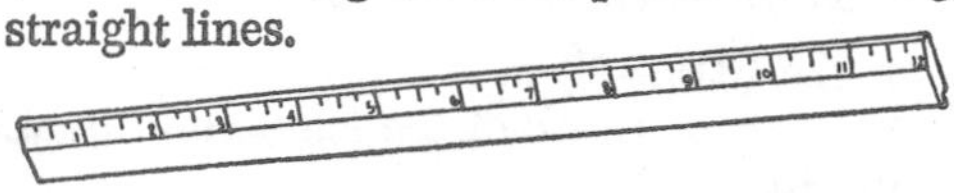

rul•ing (ROOL-ing) *n. rulings.* A judgment given by a judge or court.–It is the judge's *ruling* that the man be fined.

rum (RUM) *n. rums.* A drink containing alcohol and made from sugar cane. *Rum* is sometimes used as a flavoring in cake.

rum•ba (RUM- *or* ROOM-bə) *n. rumbas.* A dance originating among the Negroes of Cuba; an American version of the dance. The music played for the *rumba* is called by the same name.

rum•ble (RUM-bəl) *n. rumbles.* A low, heavy, rolling sound.–During the night we heard the *rumble* of thunder.
–*v. rumbles, rumbled, rumbling.* Make a low, heavy, rolling sound.–Father's old car *rumbled* as it went down the road.

rum•mage (RUM-ij) *v. rummages, rummaged, rummaging.* Look for something by moving things about haphazardly.–Father *rummaged* through the tool chest for a few nails.

ru•mor (ROO-mer) *n. rumors.* A report or story told as news without knowledge of whether it is true.–There is a *rumor* going about that the teacher is getting married.
–*v. rumors, rumored, rumoring.* Tell or spread news without knowing if it is true.–It is *rumored* that the king is sick.

rum•ple (RUM-pəl) *v. rumples, rumpled, rumpling.* 1. Wrinkle. – The baby *rumpled* the bedspread when he played on the bed.
2. Muss or tangle.–The wind *rumpled* the baby's curls.

run (RUN) *n. runs.* 1. A swift trip on foot.–Bob and his dog went for a *run* in the field.
2. A trip.–The engineer has made his last *run* on the train. He is retiring today.
3. A place where a thread has pulled out of some material; a row of raveled stitches.–Mother caught her stocking on a splinter and got a *run* in it.
4. A series of happenings.–The ball team had a *run* of bad luck.
5. A score in baseball.–The team needed two *runs* to win the game.
6. A sudden great demand. – When coffee was scarce, there was a great *run* on the stores for it.
7. A spreading.–There is a *run* of measles in the school now.
–*v. runs, ran, running.* 1. Move so fast that, at a moment in each step, all or both the legs are off the ground at the same time.–When Jack whistles, his dog *runs* to him.
2. Go or move.–The motor of the car *runs* fast and smoothly.
3. Flow.–Water *runs* from the faucet.
4. Reach or stretch out.–Our yard *runs* from the house to the corner.
5. Operate or make go.–Mary can *run* the sewing machine.
6. Thrust or push.–Do not *run* your finger into your eye.
7. Be a candidate or try to get elected. – Father would not *run* for mayor even if he were asked.
8. Become. – The sick child's temperature *ran* higher every hour.
9. Average; be usually.–The fish in this lake *run* about ten inches long.

run•a•way (RUN-ə-way) *n. runaways.* A person or animal that runs away.–A fleeing robber is a *runaway.*
–*adj.* Running out of control.–A car moving without a driver is a *runaway* car.

rung (RUNG) *n. rungs.* A round bar, usually of wood, used as a crosspiece on a ladder or between the legs of a chair or as a wheel spoke. –The painter stood on the top *rung* of the ladder.
–*v.* One form of the verb *ring.*–The bell had already *rung* when we got to school.

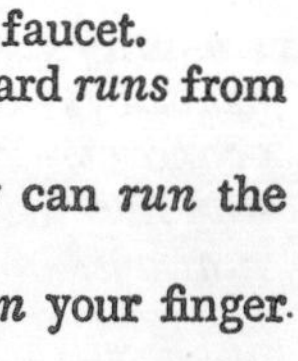

run•ner (RUN-er) *n. runners.* 1. A smooth, narrow strip on which something slides.—Sleds, ice skates, and drawers in cabinets move on *runners.*
2. Small stems that stretch along the ground and form roots from which new plants grow. —Strawberry plants have *runners.*
3. A person who runs, races, or carries messages.—An Indian *runner* stopped at the trading post with a message. — There were five *runners* in the 100-yard dash.
4. A narrow strip.—Mother put a clean *runner* of white lace on the table.—A long strip of carpet is a *runner.*

run•ning (RUN-ing) *n.* Operating.—Mother attends to the *running* of the house.—Father attends to the *running* of the car; he always drives it.
—*v.* One form of the verb *run.*—The dog is *running* after the cat.
—*adj.* 1. Flowing.—We have *running* water in the bathroom.
2. One after another, in a row.—It has rained for six days *running.*

runt (RUNT) *n. runts.* A person or animal that doesn't grow to be as large as others of the same kind.—Our dog is just a *runt,* but he can run faster than most big dogs.

run•way (RUN-way) *n. runways.* 1. A track or roadway on which something runs, slides, or moves.—The new ship slid down the *runway* into the water.—Airplanes take off from *runways.*

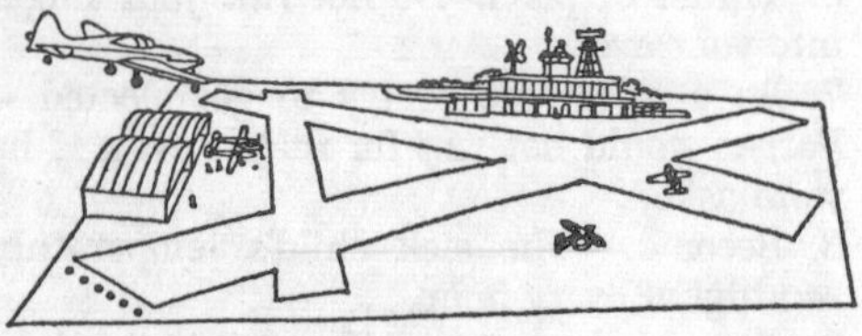

2. A path that is beaten down by animals in going to and from their feeding or drinking places.

rup•ture (RUP-cher) *v. ruptures, ruptured, rupturing.* Break; split; burst. — John *ruptured* the tiny blood vessels in his nose and had a nosebleed.

ru•ral (RUHR-əl) *adj.; rurally, adv.* Having to do with the country; living in the country.—*Rural* life is life in the country.

rush (RUSH) *n. rushes.* 1. A time of great hurrying and crowding.—We came home on the subway during the evening *rush.*
2. A sudden movement. — A *rush* of wind blew the door open.
3. A hollow reed or stem that grows in marshy or wet places.—Indians made baskets of *rushes.*
—*v. rushes, rushed, rushing.* 1. Go fast or in a hurry.—The fire truck *rushed* to the burning building.—The water *rushed* over the rocks.
2. Hurry.—Do not *rush* through your meals.
3. Attack or charge.—The football players *rushed* the players on the other team.

rust (RUST) *n.* 1. A rough, orange-brown crust that forms on iron and steel. — Unpainted iron or steel tools left out in the air or in a wet place are soon covered with *rust.*
2. A plant disease that makes spots on leaves and stems.—The wheat crop was spoiled by *rust.*
—*v. rusts, rusted, rusting.* Become covered with rust.—Your bicycle will *rust* if you leave it out all night.

rus•tic (RUSS-tik) *adj.* Rural; having to do with the country; simple and rough.—Grandfather lives in a *rustic* cottage.

rus•tle (RUSS-əl) *n.* A crackling noise.—We can hear the *rustle* of the leaves on the oak trees in autumn.
—*v. rustles, rustled, rustling.* 1. Make a crackling or whispering sound.—Mother's taffeta dress *rustles* as she walks.
2. Steal (cattle or other livestock).—A band of thieves *rustled* cattle from the ranches in the foothills.

rus•tler (RUSS-ler) *n. rustlers.* A person who steals cattle or other livestock.—The *rustler* was caught by the cowboy.

rust•y (RUST-ee) *adj. rustier, rustiest.* 1. Covered with rust.—The old saw is *rusty.*
2. Out of practice.—The musician is *rusty* because he hasn't practiced.

rut (RUT) *n. ruts.* 1. A groove or track such as one worn in the ground by the wheels of cars. — The *rut* in the road is filled with water.

2. Habit, or unchanging ways of doing things.—People who do the same work in the same way day after day may get into a *rut.*

ruth•less (ROOTH-ləss) *adj.; ruthlessly, adv.; ruthlessness, n.* Cruel and heartless; without pity or mercy.—The *ruthless* landlord put the poor family out on the street.

rye (RY) *n.* and *adj.* A grain.—Farmers grow *rye.*—*Rye* is made into flour which is used in making *rye* bread.

S s

S, s (ESS) *n. S's, s's.* The nineteenth letter of the alphabet.

Sab•bath (SAB-əth) *n. Sabbaths.* Day of rest and worship.–Sunday, the first day of the week, is the Christian *Sabbath.* – Saturday, the seventh and last day of the week, is the Jewish *Sabbath.*

sa•ber (SAY-ber) *n. sabers.* A sword with a heavy, curved blade.–Soldiers on horseback use *sabers.*

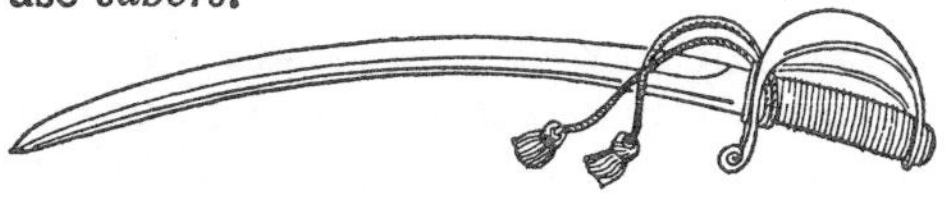

sab•o•tage (SAB-ə-tahzh) *n.* Damage or destruction of property, such as machinery and tools, especially by enemy agents during wartime, or by employees during a labor dispute.–The man who had blown up the bridge was charged with *sabotage.*

sac•cha•rin (SAK-ə-rin) *n.* An artificial sweetener; a substitute for sugar. *Saccharin* is often used by persons who are not allowed to use sugar because of illness, or who are trying to lose weight.

sack (SAK) *n. sacks.* A large bag, usually one made of burlap or other coarse material.–

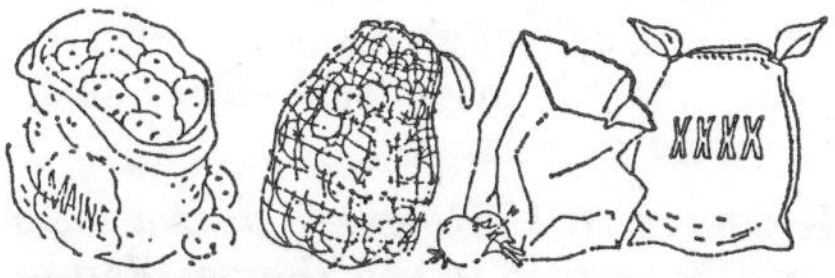

burlap sack string sack paper sack cotton sack

Sacks are used to hold potatoes, onions, wheat, and the like.

sa•cred (SAY-krid) *adj.; sacredness, n.* Holy; worthy of worship and deep respect. Things having to do with God or religion are *sacred.* –We sing *sacred* songs in Sunday school.– The name of God is *sacred.*

sac•ri•fice (SAK-rə-fyss) *n. sacrifices.* 1. Something offered to a god as a religious act. –In the Bible, Abraham killed a ram as a *sacrifice* to God.

2. A loss.–Bob sold his bicycle at a *sacrifice.*

–*v. sacrifices, sacrificed, sacrificing.* Give up.– Many soldiers have *sacrificed* their lives for our freedom.

sad (SAD) *adj. sadder, saddest; sadly, adv.; sadness, n.* 1. Having a feeling of sorrow or unhappiness.–Children are *sad* when they lose or break a toy, or when their pet dies.

2. Causing sorrow or unhappiness. – The train wreck was a *sad* accident.

sad•den (SAD-n) *v. saddens, saddened, saddening.* Make unhappy.–The loss of his dog *saddened* Jim.

sad•dle (SAD-l) *n. saddles.* A seat, usually of leather, for a person riding on a horse, bicycle, tricycle, motorcycle, or the like.– Tom sits up straight in the *saddle* on his new horse.

–*v. saddles, saddled, saddling.* 1. Put a saddle on.–The farmer *saddled* the pony for his little boy.

2. Load or burden.–The farmer *saddled* his hired man with many chores.

sad•ness (SAD-nəss) *n.* Sorrow or grief.– Much *sadness* was caused by the death of the family pet.

sa•fa•ri (sə-FAHR-ee) *n. safaris.* 1. An expedition or journey, especially for hunting.– The hunters are planning a *safari* in Africa.

2. The caravan of persons, animals, and equipment on such an expedition. – The *safari* camped near a river for the night.

safe (SAYF) *n. safes.* A steel cabinet with a lock, for keeping valuable things. – The grocer keeps his money in a *safe.*

–*adj. safer, safest; safely, adv.* Free from danger.–It is *safe* to cross the street when the light is green.–The lost child has turned up *safe* and sound at a neighbor's house.

safe•ty (SAYF-tee) *n.* Freedom from danger. –The porch has a railing around it so that the baby can play there in *safety.*

–*adj.* Giving or making sure of safety.–Father uses a *safety* razor. It is designed to protect him from cutting his skin. – Mother uses *safety* pins in dressing the baby.

safe•ty belt (SAYF-tee belt) *safety belts.* A specially designed belt fixed to each seat in an airplane. The *safety belt* is used to hold a passenger or crew member securely in his seat during take-offs, landings, and bad flying weather. *Safety belts* are also used in cars.

sag (SAG) *v. sags, sagged, sagging.* Droop or hang unevenly.–The curtain *sags* in the middle. – The tennis net is not stretched tight enough. It *sags.*

sage (SAYJ) *n.* A plant whose dried leaves are used as flavoring. – We put *sage* in chicken dressing to flavor it.

sage•brush (SAYJ-brush) *n.* A silvery-gray shrublike plant found in the western United States. *Sagebrush* grows in dry or partly dry regions. It sometimes reaches a height of twelve feet.

said (SED) *v.* One form of the verb *say.*–I *said,* "It is a nice day."

sail (SAYL) *n. sails.* 1. A large piece of heavy cloth raised over a boat so that the wind blows on it and moves the boat along.

2. A trip on a sailboat.–We went for a *sail* with Ed.

–*v. sails, sailed, sailing.* 1. Start a voyage.–The steamer *sailed* Monday.

2. Move along (of a ship).–The ship *sailed* slowly down the river.

3. Soar or move smoothly and swiftly.–The arrow *sailed* right over the top of the target. –The airplane *sailed* over the city.

4. Direct and operate (a ship or boat).–The captain and sailors *sailed* the ship.

sail•boat (SAYL-boht) *n. sailboats.* A boat moved by the wind blowing against its sails.–We went for a sail on Ed's new *sailboat.*

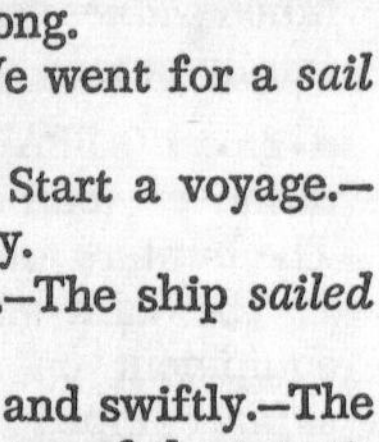

sail•or (SAY-ler) *n. sailors.* A man who sails, or works on, a boat or ship.–There were only three *sailors* in the crew of the small ship.

saint (SAYNT) *n. saints.* A holy person worthy of worship.

Saint Ber•nard (SAYNT ber-NAHRD) *Saint Bernards.* A very large, tan-and-white breed of dog. *Saint Bernard* dogs are very intelligent.

sake (SAYK) *n. sakes.* Account; cause; benefit of.–I hope the baby sleeps this afternoon, for Mother's *sake.* It will give Mother a chance to rest.–The patriots gave their lives for the *sake* of freedom.

sal•ad (SAL-əd) *n. salads.* Raw vegetables or fruits, usually served with oil and vinegar, or some other dressing.–We eat cabbage *salad,* potato *salad,* and apple and walnut *salad.* Cold eggs, meats, or fish mixed with vegetables and a dressing are *salads,* too.

sal•a•man•der (SAL-ə-man-der) *n. salamanders.* Any of various small amphibians that look very much like lizards but do not have claws or scaly skin. *Salamanders* live either on moist land or in the water.

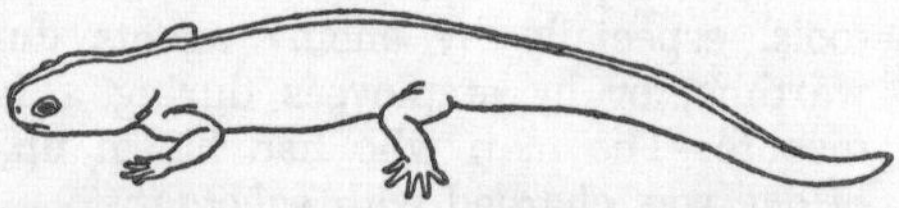

sal•a•ry (SAL-ə-ree) *n. salaries.* Money paid to a person at regular times for work done.–Fathers gets his *salary* weekly.

sale (SAYL) *n. sales.* 1. A selling of something, or an exchanging of something for money.–Bob made ten dollars on the *sale* of his bicycle.

2. A selling at prices lower than usual.–The store had a *sale* of shoes.

3. Amount of goods sold.–The Christmas *sales* were very large.

sales•man (SAYLZ-mən) *n. salesmen.* A man who is paid to sell things.–Father is a *salesman.* He sells automobiles.

sales•wom•an (SAYLZ-wuhm-ən) *n. saleswomen.* A woman who is paid to sell things. –The *saleswoman* sold me two books.

sa•li•va (sə-LY-və) *n.* The liquid that forms in the mouth and keeps it moist.–The sight of meat makes *saliva* run from the dog's mouth.

salm•on (SAM-ən) *n. sing.* and *pl.* A kind of large fish whose pink flesh is good to eat.–*Salmon* is canned for food.

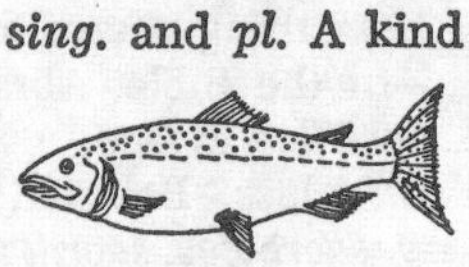

–*adj.* Yellowish-pink.–Mary's hair ribbon is a *salmon* color.

sa•loon (sə-LOON) *n. saloons.* A place where wine, beer, and other alcoholic drinks are sold and served.–The man went into a *saloon* to get a glass of beer.

salt (SAWLT) *n. salts* and *adj.* 1. A grainy white substance found in the earth and in sea water. *Salt* is used to give flavor to foods and also to preserve them, or keep them from spoiling. – Mother seasoned the vegetables with a little *salt.*

2. An old and experienced sailor. A sailor is called a *salt* because he sails the *salt* water of the sea.–The old *salt* knew many good stories.

–*v. salts, salted, salting.* 1. Put salt on or in.–Sue *salts* the water when she boils corn.

2. Provide salt for. – The farmer *salts* his cattle.

salt•cel•lar (SAWLT-sel-er) *n. saltcellars.* A small dish or other container to hold salt.–You lift the salt from a *saltcellar* with a small spoon, or shake it through a cap with little holes in it.

salt•y (SAWL-tee) *adj. saltier, saltiest.* Having much salt.–The vegetables were too *salty.*

sal•u•ta•tion (sal-yə-TAY-shən) *n. salutations.* 1. A greeting.–Shaking hands, tipping the hat, saying good morning, and saluting are all *salutations.*

2. The beginning of a letter, which addresses the person to whom one is writing.–"Dear Mother" is a *salutation.*

sa•lute (sə-LOOT) *n. salutes.* A formal greeting between officers and men in the armed forces, exchanged by raising the right hand to the forehead.–A bow or handshake is also a *salute.*

–*v. salutes, saluted, saluting.* To make a salute, or formal greeting.–The soldier *salutes* his officers. He shows respect and honor for his officers by raising his right hand to his head as if touching his hat.–Mary *saluted* the audience with a bow.

sal•vage (SAL-vij) *n. salvages.* 1. Things saved from damage.–There were several machines among the *salvage* from the burned factory. There were several machines that were not burned.

2. Money paid for saving a ship and its cargo.–The men received $10,000 in *salvage* for saving the sinking ship.

–*v. salvages, salvaged, salvaging.* Save from damage. – When the factory burned down, the men *salvaged* everything they could.

salve (SAV) *n. salves.* A kind of soft, creamy substance used as a medicine on sores, burns, and the like.–Mother rubbed *salve* on Bob's sore finger.

same (SAYM) *adj.; sameness, n.* 1. The very one; not another.–Mary wore the *same* dress to school that she wore Sunday. She did not wear a different one.

2. Just like.–Sally's pocketbook is the *same* as Mary's. It is the *same* color and the *same* style. Both are red and close with zippers.

sam•ple (SAM-pəl) *n. samples.* 1. A small part that shows what the rest is like.–This is a *sample* of my handwriting.

2. One of a number of like things used to show what all the rest are like.–This book is a *sample* copy. There are many others just like it.

–*v. samples, sampled, sampling.* Try or test.–Won't you *sample* these new cookies.

sanc•tu•ar•y (SANGK-choo-air-ee) *n. sanctuaries.* 1. A holy place.–Churches, temples, and shrines are *sanctuaries.*

2. The holiest section of a church or temple. The *sanctuary* is usually near the altar.

3. A place of refuge; a safe and protected area.–The rich old lady is having a *sanctuary* built for stray cats.

4. Protection; safety; refuge. – The fugitive sought *sanctuary* in a foreign country.

sand (SAND) *n. sands.* A large number of tiny bits of stone, often found along the shores of oceans, lakes, and rivers.–Children like to play in the white *sand* on the beach.

–*v. sands, sanded, sanding.* Scrape, polish, or smooth with sand or sandpaper. – Father *sanded* the floor before he varnished it.

san•dal (SAN-dl) *n. sandals.* 1. A shoe that is just a sole with a strap or straps to fasten it onto the foot. – Children wear *sandals* in warm weather.

2. A kind of light, open, fancy slipper.–Mother wears *sandals* when she dances.

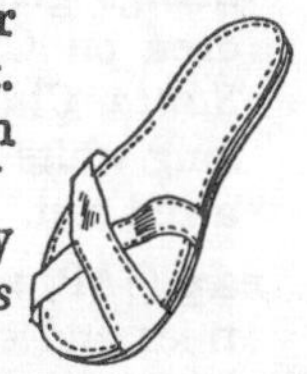

sand•bag (SAND-bag) *n. sandbags.* A bag filled with sand. *Sandbags* are used to dam flood waters, provide balloon and boat ballast, serve as defensive barriers, and to do other jobs for which bulk is necessary.

sand bar (SAND bahr) *sand bars.* A narrow ridge of sand sometimes found in coastal waters, rivers, or across the mouth of a bay. *Sand bars* are formed by the action of tides and water currents.

sand•pa•per (SAND-pay-per) *n.* A heavy paper coated on one side with a layer of sand. *Sandpaper* is used to smooth rough surfaces.

sand•pip•er (SAND-py-per) *n. sandpipers.* A rather small wading bird with long legs and a long bill.–We saw a flock of *sandpipers* at the beach.

sand•stone (SAND-stohn) *n.* A type of rock made largely of sand and held together by a natural cement, such as clay.

sand•wich (SAND- *or* SAN-wich) *n. sandwiches.* Two or more slices of bread with cheese, eggs, lettuce, jam, or other food between them. – *Sandwiches* are good to take on picnics.

–*v. sandwiches, sandwiched, sandwiching.* Squeeze (someone or something) between two other persons or things. –The little house was *sandwiched* in between two tall buildings.

sane (SAYN) *adj. saner, sanest; sanely, adv.; sanity, n.* Having good sense and a healthy mind.

sang (SANG) *v.* One form of the verb *sing.*– The children *sang* "The Star-Spangled Banner" and other songs yesterday.

san•i•tar•i•um (san-ə-TAIR-ee-əm) *n. sanitariums.* A resort or hotel in a healthful place where people go to rest or to get well after sickness.

san•i•tar•y (SAN-ə-tair-ee) *adj.* Clean and healthful.–Everything in the hospital is very *sanitary.* It is kept free from germs and all kinds of dirt.

San•ta Claus (SAN-tə klawz). The one who brings gifts to children on Christmas.– *Santa Claus* has a long white beard and a red suit.

sap (SAP) *n. saps.* A juice that flows through trees and other plants and helps them live and grow.–The *sap* of some maple trees is made into maple sugar and maple syrup.

sap•ling (SAP-ling) *n. saplings.* A young, slender tree.

sap•phire (SAF-yr) *n. sapphires.* A very costly, hard, bright blue gem.–Mother has a ring set with a *sapphire.*

–*adj.* Bright blue.–The fairy has golden hair and *sapphire* eyes. Her eyes are the color of *sapphires.*

sar•casm (SAHR-kaz-əm) *n.; sarcastic, adj.; sarcastically, adv.* Harsh, biting remarks.– The man's *sarcasm* hurt his friend's feelings.

sar•dine (sahr-DEEN) *n. sardines.* A tiny fish canned in oil, mustard, or tomato sauce. *Sardines* are good to eat.

sa•ri (SAH-ree) *n. saris.* A long, thin dress worn mostly by the women of India. A *sari* usually is made of one long piece of cotton or silk. It is worn wrapped around and draped on the body.

sash (SASH) *n. sashes.* **1.** A long wide band of cloth or ribbon worn around the waist or hips or over the shoulder. – The dancer wore a *sash.*

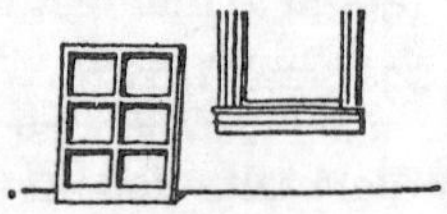

2. The part of a window that opens.

sas•sa•fras (SASS-ə-frass) *n.* and *adj.* A tree whose roots are used as flavoring and in medicine. – The roots of the *sassafras* are often used to make *sassafras* tea.

sat (SAT) *v.* One form of the verb *sit.*–Bob *sat* in his seat and read a book all morning.

satch•el (SACH-əl) *n. satchels.* A small bag with a handle.–When we went to Grandmother's, we put our clothes in a *satchel.*

sat•el•lite (SAT-ə-lyt) *n. satellites.* **1.** A heavenly body revolving around a larger heavenly body; an artificial or man-made "moon."–The planet Saturn has nine known *satellites.* The earth has one, the moon.–A number of artificial *satellites* have been placed in orbit around the earth by means of rockets fired into space. These *satellites* carry instruments and cameras which collect important information, not only about space, but about our atmosphere and the earth's surface, as well.

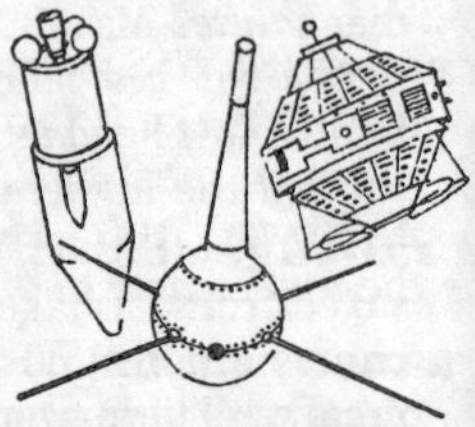

2. A country influenced or dominated by a larger neighboring country.

3. Someone attending or depending upon an important or powerful person.–The powerful lord's *satellites* swarmed about him.

sat•is•fac•tion (sat-iss-FAK-shən) *n. satisfactions.* 1. A feeling of being satisfied or contented.–Father's new car gives him much *satisfaction.*
2. Something which causes a contented feeling.–Keeping up to date on one's school work is a *satisfaction.*

sat•is•fac•to•ry (sat-iss-FAK-tə-ree) *adj.; satisfactorily, adv.* Good enough or sufficient to satisfy or please.–Jack asked the teacher if his paper were *satisfactory.*

sat•is•fy (SAT-iss-fy) *v. satisfies, satisfied, satisfying.* 1. Please.–Baby is perfectly *satisfied* with her old toys.
2. Make one feel sure; convince.–Mary *satisfied* Father that the clock was slow. She proved to him that it was slow.
3. End (a need) by filling it.–Bob *satisfied* his thirst by having a drink of water.

sat•u•rate (SACH-ə-rayt) *v. saturates, saturated, saturating.* Soak or fill completely.–The blotter was *saturated* with spilled ink.

Sat•ur•day (SAT-er-dee) *n. Saturdays.* The day after Friday. *Saturday* is the seventh day of the week.–We have no school on *Saturday.*

Sat•urn (SAT-ern) *n.* 1. The ancient Roman god of seed sowing.
2. The sixth planet away from our sun. *Saturn* is the second largest planet in our solar system.

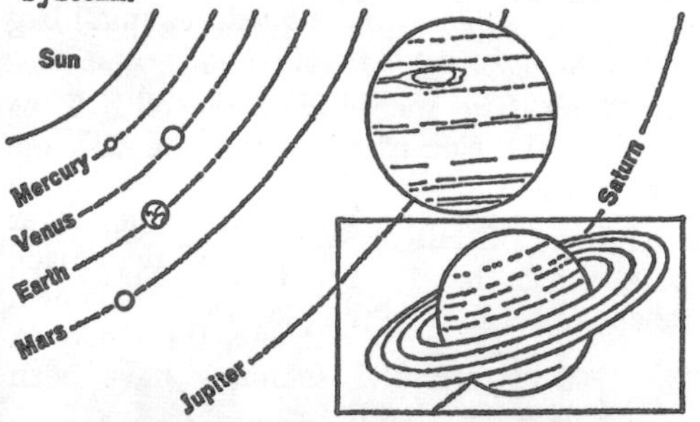

sauce (SAWSS) *n. sauces.* 1. A liquid put over food to make it tastier.–Father likes tomato *sauce* on meat loaf.
2. Stewed fruit.–Mother put lemon rind in the apple*sauce* to give it flavor.

sauce•pan (SAWSS-pan) *n. saucepans.* A metal pan with a handle, used for cooking. – Mary cooked the fudge in a *saucepan.*

sau•cer (SAWSS-er) *n. saucers.* A dish used to set a cup in.–Do not leave your spoon in your cocoa cup after stirring the sugar; lay it in the *saucer.*

sau•sage (SAW-sij) *n. sausages.* Beef, pork, or other meat prepared by grinding up and seasoning. Usually it is stuffed into a long, thin casing, like a tube.–*Sausage* is good to eat with pancakes.

sav•age (SAV-ij) *n. savages.* A person who is not civilized; one who lives a wild, simple, rough life in ignorance and superstition.–The cave men of long ago were *savages.*
–*adj.* 1. Wild or untamed.–Animals of the jungle are *savage* animals.
2. Cruel or vicious; bloodthirsty.–The *savage* king ordered the death of all his prisoners.

save (SAYV) *v. saves, saved, saving.* 1. Rescue or free from danger.–The fireman *saved* the child from the burning house.
2. Set aside; keep without using; keep for later use.–Father *saves* some money each month for our college education.
3. Lessen.–A washing machine *saves* work.
4. Prevent; avoid.–"A stitch in time *saves* nine."
5. Treat with care, or protect.–*Save* your eyes by reading only in a good light.
–*prep.* Except.–The fisherman used up all his wishes *save* one.

sav•ior (SAYV-yer) *n. saviors.* 1. One who saves.–When the man rescued Sally's kitten from the tree, Sally called him her *savior.*
2. (Spelled *Saviour* in the Bible) Jesus Christ.

saw (SAW) *n. saws.* A tool for cutting wood, metal, and the like. *Saws* are made of thin steel with sharp teeth along one edge for cutting. Some *saws* are run by electricity; some are used by hand.

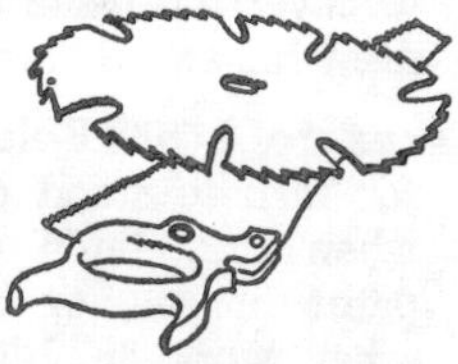

–*v. saws, sawed, sawing.* 1. Cut with a saw.–Bob *sawed* the sticks for his kite out of an old crate.
2. One form of the verb *see.*–Mary *saw* the accident last week.

saw•dust (SAW-dust) *n.* The tiny bits of wood made in sawing wood.–Sally found that her doll was stuffed with *sawdust.*

saw•horse (SAW-horss) *n. sawhorses.* A rack or frame upon which a piece of wood is placed or held while being sawed.

saw·mill (SAW-mil) *n. sawmills.* A mill or factory with machines for cutting logs into lumber or wood.

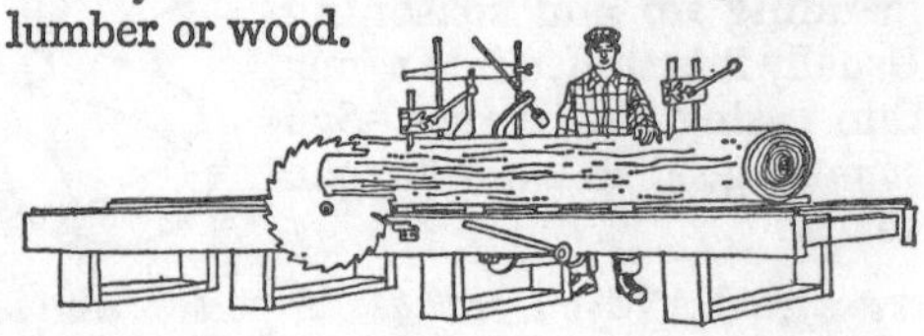

sax·o·phone (SAK-sə-fohn) *n. saxophones.* A brass musical instrument with a reed mouthpiece. You play the *saxophone* by blowing into the mouthpiece and pressing down on the keys.

say (SAY) *v. says, said, saying.* Speak words, or write words.–We *say* "Good morning" to our teacher when she comes into the room. –My book *says* that elephants live to be over one hundred years old.

say·ing (SAY-ing) *n. sayings.* A proverb, or wise words that have been handed down to us from the past. This is an old *saying:*
"Early to bed and early to rise
Makes a man healthy, wealthy, and wise."

scab (SKAB) *n. scabs.* A thin crust that forms over a sore or wound. The *scab* drops off when the sore is all healed.

scab·bard (SKAB-erd) *n. scabbards.* A case

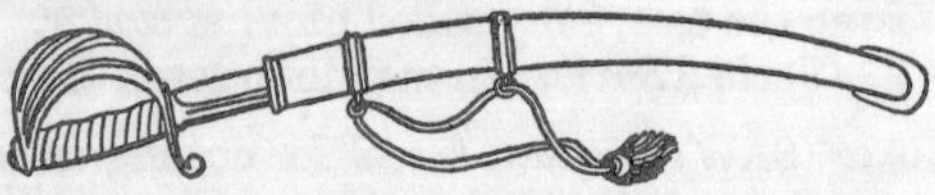

to cover the blade of a sword.–The knight drew his sword from the *scabbard.*

scaf·fold (SKAF-əld) *n. scaffolds.* A platform for men to stand on when they build or paint houses, or do other work in high places. Some *scaffolds* can be raised or lowered to the place where the workmen want to work.

scald (SKAWLD) *v. scalds, scalded, scalding.* 1. Burn with steam or hot water.–Baby *scalded* her finger when she tried to pick a carrot out of the hot soup.
2. Clean with boiling water. – *Scald* the baby's bottle before you fill it.
3. Heat until nearly boiling.–In making this pudding, you *scald* the milk and then add the sugar, eggs, and flavoring.

scale (SKAYL) *n. scales.* 1. Small, thin, horny piece something like one's fingernail.–Some fish are almost covered with *scales.*
2. Small, thin flakes of skin. – Mary's back was covered with little *scales* from her sunburn.
3. A device for weighing things. – Bob stood on the *scale* while the nurse weighed him.

4. A regular series of marks on a stick, dial, etc., used for measuring.–A ruler is a *scale.* The little lines along the edge that mark off the inches, half inches, etc., form a *scale.*–Gas meters and electric meters have *scales* which measure the amounts of gas or electricity used.
5. A series of tones in music arranged in the order of their pitch. –Mary had to practice *scales* when she took music lessons.

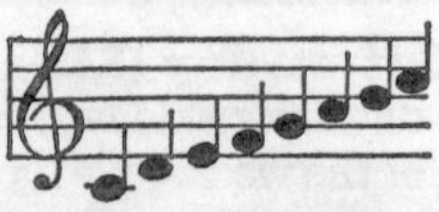

6. Small distance between places on a map or drawing compared with the real distance between the same places.–The map is drawn to *scale.* Each inch on the map stands for fifty miles of country.
–*v. scales, scaled, scaling.* 1. Scrape the scales off.–We *scale* fish before we cook them.
2. Climb.–The men *scaled* the cliff. They climbed the side of the mountain with the aid of ropes.

scal·lop (SKAHL- *or* SKAL-əp) *n. scallops.* 1. A shellfish that is good to eat. Notice the shape of its shell in the picture.

2. One of a series of curves, like the curves on a scallop's shell. – Mother embroidered *scallops* on the end of the towel.
–*v. scallops, scalloped, scalloping.* 1. Cut a pattern of repeated curves in.–Mother *scallops* the edges of many of Baby's dresses.
2. Bake in a special way with milk and crumbs.–Mother is *scalloping* the potatoes for dinner tonight.

scalp (SKALP) *n. scalps.* The skin on one's head that is covered by the hair.
–*v. scalps, scalped, scalping.* Cut off the scalp of.–Some Indians used to *scalp* the people they killed.

scam·per (SKAM-per) *v. scampers, scampered, scampering.* Run hastily.–The frightened rabbit *scampered* off when he saw us.

scan (SKAN) *v. scans, scanned, scanning.* 1. Examine closely and carefully.–The searching party *scanned* every inch of the area.
2. Look through quickly.–Some persons like to *scan* a book before buying it.
3. Examine or analyze poetry, especially with respect to its meter. – The teacher is *scanning* the poem for the class.
4. Skim over thoroughly in a set pattern.–The searchlights *scanned* the sky.

scan·dal (SKAN-dl) *n. scandals; scandalous, adj.; scandalously, adv.* 1. Disgrace or shame caused by bad actions or deeds; the action or deed itself. – The boy's bad behavior is a *scandal.*
2. Exciting and harmful gossip or talk about someone.–The discovery of bribery in the city government was the cause of a great deal of *scandal.*

scar (SKAHR) *n. scars.* 1. A lasting mark left on the body after a sore, burn, or wound has healed. – The squirrel's bite left a *scar* on Jack's wrist.
2. A mark or dent that spoils the looks of something.–The table top has many *scars* from long use.
–*v. scars, scarred, scarring.* The squirrel's bite *scarred* Jack's wrist.

scarce (SKAIRSS) *adj. scarcer, scarcest.* Hard to get; not plentiful; rare.–Butter is often *scarce* in time of war.

scar·ci·ty (SKAIR-sə-tee) *n. scarcities.* Not a big enough supply.–There is a *scarcity* of meat here. There isn't enough.

scare (SKAIR) *n. scares.* A fright.–We had a big *scare* when the house caught fire. We were afraid.
–*v. scares, scared, scaring.* Make afraid.–The noise *scared* the baby. It frightened her.

scare·crow (SKAIR-kroh) *n. scarecrows.* A figure dressed to look like a man, used to scare off crows and other birds. – The farmer put a *scarecrow* in the middle of the cornfield.

scarf (SKAHRF) *n. scarves* or *scarfs.* 1. A long woven or knitted strip of cloth worn around the neck and shoulders or over the head. – Mother knitted a *scarf* for her nephew.

2. A strip of cloth used as a cover for furniture.–Mary put a clean lace *scarf* on her dresser.

scar·let (SKAHR-lət) *n.* and *adj.* A brilliant red.–We saw the *scarlet* of the bird's feathers.

scat·ter (SKAT-er) *v. scatters, scattered, scattering.* 1. Toss or sprinkle in all directions.–The boys *scattered* food for the birds.
2. Break up and go in different directions.–The crowd *scattered* when it started to rain.
3. Drive away in all directions.–The sudden thunderstorm *scattered* the people.

scav·en·ger (SKAV-in-jer) *n. scavengers.* Any animal that feeds or lives on decaying or dead matter.–Buzzards are *scavengers.*

scene (SEEN) *n. scenes.* 1. Time and place of a story.–The *scene* of this play is summertime in the mountains.
2. A painted screen or curtain serving as background for a play.–The *scene* is a beautiful mountaintop covered with pines.
3. A division of a play.–The star of the play appears for the first time in the second *scene.*
4. A view, or thing to look at.–You can see beautiful *scenes* from the top of that hill.

5. An action which causes people to stare.–The man with the dog made a *scene* on the corner. He yelled at the dog and beat him, so that people stared.

scen·er·y (SEEN-er-ee) *n.* 1. Painted scenes for an entertainment on the stage.–The children painted their own *scenery* for their play.

2. Things to look at seen all together.–The *scenery* in the mountains is beautiful.

scent (SENT) *n. scents.* 1. An odor, fragrance, or smell.–The *scent* of fried bacon and coffee makes one hungry.
2. A trail, or a means of tracking down.–The police were thrown off the *scent* of the robber because he had changed cars.
–*v. scents, scented, scenting.* 1. Smell; notice or follow by smelling.–The dog *scented* a squirrel.
2. Give a fragrant odor to.–Roses *scented* the whole room.

scep•ter (SEP-ter) *n. scepters.* A long, fancy rod or staff carried by a ruler of a country as a sign of his power.

sched•ule (SKEJ-uhl) *n. schedules.* A list or plan of the order and time for things to happen.–The teacher wrote our *schedule* for the day on the board.
–*v. schedules, scheduled, scheduling.* Plan or arrange in a schedule.–*Schedule* your work so that we can leave early.

scheme (SKEEM) *n. schemes.* 1. A secret plan or plot.–The criminals have a *scheme* to get out of jail.
2. A planned arrangement.–Mother has a nice color *scheme* in her bedroom. She has used colors that look well together.
–*v. schemes, schemed, scheming.* Plan secretly.–The prisoners *schemed* to escape.

schol•ar (SKAHL-er) *n. scholars.* 1. A student or pupil.–We have six hundred *scholars* in our school.
2. One who has studied thoroughly and learned a great deal.–Mr. Smith is a *scholar* in history.

schol•ar•ship. (SKAHL-er-ship) *n. scholarships.* 1. Learning.–The teacher praised the bright boy for his fine *scholarship.*
2. An award, often a sum of money, given to a worthy student to help pay for additional education.–Tom received a university *scholarship* because of his brilliant school record.

school (SKOOL) *n. schools.* 1. A place for teaching and learning.–Children learn how to read in *school.*–A medical *school* is a place for teaching and learning about medicine.
2. The pupils who go to a school.–Our *school* will have a picnic on Saturday.
3. A large gathering of fish which swim together.–We saw a *school* of fish.

school•house (SKOOL-howss) *n. schoolhouses.* The building where school is held.–Our *schoolhouse* is made of white brick.–Grandfather went to school in a one-room *schoolhouse.*

schoon•er (SKOO-ner) *n. schooners.* A sailing ship with two or more masts and sails.

sci•ence (SY-ənss) *n. sciences.* 1. A way of learning about things by a planned method of seeing how things work and act, and by experimenting and testing.
2. An orderly collection of all the known facts and laws about any one kind of thing.–Botany is the *science* of plants.–Zoology is the *science* of animal life.–Mathematics is the *science* of numbers and amounts.

sci•en•tif•ic (sy-ən-TIF-ik) *adj.; scientifically, adv.* Having to do with science; like science.–John likes the *scientific* subjects in school best. His teachers all say that he has a *scientific* mind.

sci•en•tist (SY-ən-tist) *n. scientists.* A person who is learned or skilled in some science.–Charles Darwin was a great *scientist.*

scis•sors (SIZ-erz) *n. pl.* A cutting tool with two handles and two sharp blades fastened together so that the sharp blades move against each other when the handles are brought together. – Sally uses *scissors* to cut out her paper dolls.

scold (SKOHLD) *v. scolds, scolded, scolding.* Find fault with in an angry way.–The teacher *scolded* her class for being disorderly during the fire drill.

scoop (SKOOP) *n. scoops.* 1. A tool like a

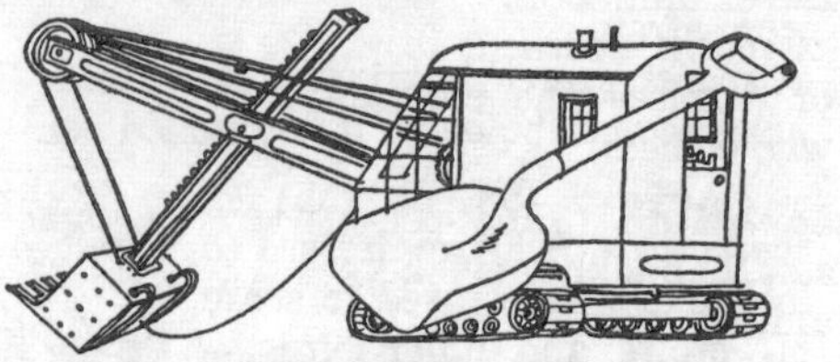

shovel, but deeper.–The man who brought the coal shoveled it with a *scoop.*

2. A big bucketlike holder which picks up sand, dirt, etc.–The men used a steam shovel with a large *scoop* to lift the sand.
3. A small shovel-shaped ladle with a short handle.–The clerk puts candy and peanuts into bags with a *scoop*.

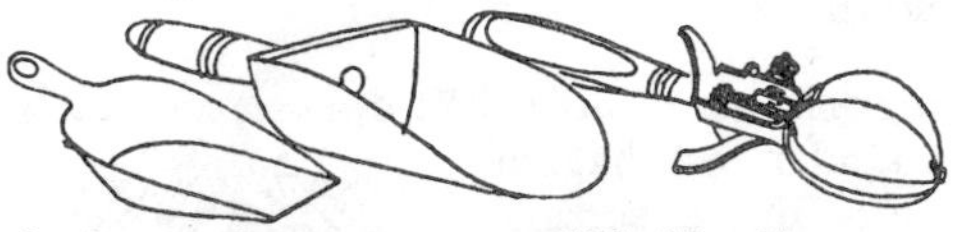

4. As much as a scoop will hold.–She put a *scoop* of peanuts into the bag.
–*v. scoops, scooped, scooping.* 1. Pick up with a scoop.–Mother *scooped* up the spilled flour.
2. Hollow or dig out.–Father *scooped* a hole in the ground to plant seeds.

scoot (SKOOT) *v. scoots, scooted, scooting.* Dart quickly.–The child *scooted* across the street.

scope (SKOHP) *n.* 1. The extent of one's mental ability.–The difficult book was beyond the *scope* of the young child.
2. Range; extent.–What is the *scope* of that field? How large is that field?–The king's power had great *scope*.

scorch (SKORCH) *v. scorches, scorched, scorching.* 1. Burn slightly.–The iron was so hot that Mother *scorched* a towel while ironing it.
2. Make dry and withered.–The hot sun has *scorched* the grass.

score (SKOR) *n. scores.* 1. The record of points made in a game.–The *score* was 5 to 1.
2. Twenty.–Four*score* years ago, Grandfather was born. Grandfather is eighty.
–*v. scores, scored, scoring.* 1. Mark. – The teacher *scored* our spelling papers.
2. Win points for the score. – Jack *scored* twice during the game.
3. Keep a record of points. – Bob was appointed to *score* the baseball game.

scorn (SKORN) *n. scorns.* Contempt; feeling of shame for.–The children looked with *scorn* at the boy who copied from someone else on the examination.
–*v. scorns, scorned, scorning.* Look down on or despise.–The children *scorned* the boy who copied.

scor•pi•on (SKOR-pee-ən) *n. scorpions.* A small, backboneless animal with a long and narrow tail that has a poisonous sting at the tip of it.

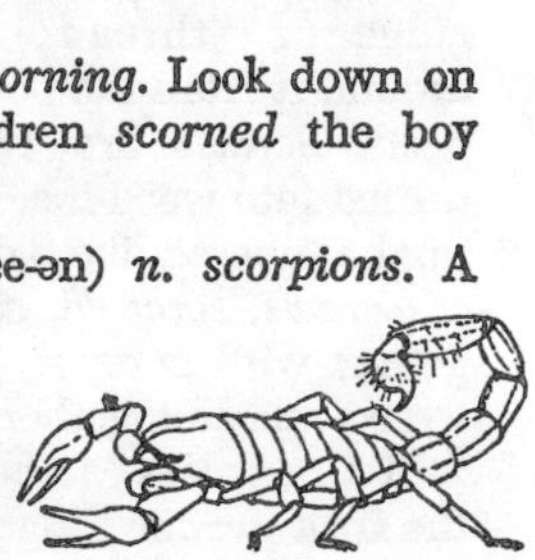

scoun•drel (SKOWN-drəl) *n. scoundrels.* A wicked person; a rascal; a villain.–The police arrested the *scoundrel* who broke the school windows.

scour (SKOWR) *v. scours, scoured, scouring.* 1. Clean; scrub the grease and dirt off. – Mother *scours* the pots and pans with steel-wool soap pads.
2. Search. – The Boy Scouts *scoured* the stores for a tent.

scout (SKOWT) *n. scouts.* 1. (Usually spelled with a capital "S.") A boy or girl who belongs to the Boy *Scouts* or the Girl *Scouts*.–Bill and Ann are *Scouts*.
2. A person who goes out looking for news of the enemy, or for other information.–Daniel Boone was a famous Indian *scout*.
–*v. scouts, scouted, scouting.* Examine; search. –The children *scouted* the town for Jack's lost dog.

scowl (SKOWL) *n. scowls.* A frown; an angry look.–Bill read his bad report card with a *scowl*.
–*v. scowls, scowled, scowling.* – Baby *scowls* when she can't have her own way.

scram•ble (SKRAM-bəl) *n. scrambles.* A hasty crowding and struggling.–There was a *scramble* for the pennies.
–*v. scrambles, scrambled, scrambling.* 1. Push, struggle, or crowd. – The children *scrambled* for the pennies.
2. Climb, crawl, or walk on hands and knees. –The Boy Scouts *scrambled* up the hillside.
3. Mix together.–Ned *scrambled* the clues to the puzzle.

scrap (SKRAP) *n. scraps.* 1. A small bit; a small piece. – The children picked up the *scraps* of paper.
2. Bits of leftover food. – We fed the *scraps* to the chickens.
–*v. scraps, scrapped, scrapping.* 1. Discard, or throw away as useless.–Jack *scrapped* the work he had done wrong and started again.
2. Quarrel or fight.–The children *scrapped* over who should be first.

scrap•book (SKRAP-buhk) *n. scrapbooks.* A book with blank pages for pasting in different kinds of clippings.–Mary made a *scrapbook* for the sick children.

scrape (SKRAYP) *n. scrapes.* 1. A harsh, grating sound.–We heard the *scrape* of the wheels of the milk wagon on the pavement.
2. Bill is always in a *scrape*. He is always in trouble because he has done something he should not have done.
–*v. scrapes, scraped, scraping.* 1. Scratch things off. – A painter *scrapes* loose paint from the house before he puts on new paint.
2. Rub.–Baby *scraped* the skin off her knee when she fell on the sidewalk.
3. Drag.–The children *scraped* their feet on the sidewalk.
4. Get together with difficulty. – The girls *scraped* together enough money to buy their mother a gift.

scratch (SKRACH) *n. scratches.* 1. Mark made by digging or scraping with anything sharp or rough.–There was a red *scratch* on Sally's arm from the kitten's claws.
2. The sound made by scraping or rubbing with something rough.–A *scratch* at the door reminded us that the dog wanted to come in.
–*v. scratches, scratched, scratching.* 1. Dig into with a sharp point.–The kitten *scratched* Sally when Sally tried to put her doll's dress on him.
2. Make a mark by digging or scraping with anything sharp or rough.–The carpenter *scratched* a line on the board with a nail.
3. Cut slightly.–Mother *scratched* her finger on a pin.
4. Rub with the fingers.–When Mary's nose itches, she *scratches* it.
5. Mark out or draw a line through.–Bob *scratched* out one word in his story that was not spelled right, and wrote it over.
6. Write poorly.–Father *scratches* his signature when he is in a hurry.

scrawl (SKRAWL) *n. scrawls.* Careless handwriting.–Father signs his name in a *scrawl* when he is in a hurry.
–*v. scrawls, scrawled, scrawling.* Scribble; write poorly. – The teacher told us not to *scrawl*, but to write neatly.

scraw·ny (SKRAW-nee) *adj. scrawnier, scrawniest.* Thin; skinny.–A *scrawny* little kitten came up to Father to be petted.

scream (SKREEM) *n. screams.* A loud, sharp outcry. – We ran to the window when we heard a *scream* in the street.
–*v. screams, screamed, screaming.* Cry out loudly and sharply.–People often *scream* when they are in pain, terror, or great grief.–The girl *screamed* when she saw the flames.

screech (SKREECH) *n. screeches.* A shrill, harsh cry or noise.–The car stopped with a *screech* of the brakes.
–*v. screeches, screeched, screeching.* Cry out or sound loudly in a shrill, harsh way.–The children *screeched* with mirth when the clown fell down on his face.

screech owl (SKREECH owl) *screech owls.* A kind of owl that has a cry like a scream, instead of a hoot.

screen (SKREEN) *n. screens* and *adj.* 1. Anything that is used to hide, cover, or protect a thing, or for sifting.–A *screen* door or a window *screen* is a frame covered with a wire netting to keep out flies, mosquitoes, and other insects.–A frame covered with a coarse

wire mesh used to sift sand, coal, and other materials is also a *screen*.–Another kind of *screen* is a frame, usually folding, that is used to cover a doorway, protect against drafts, set off part of a room, etc.–A smoke *screen* is a lot of smoke made to hide something that is going on from the enemy, like the movements of troops or ships.

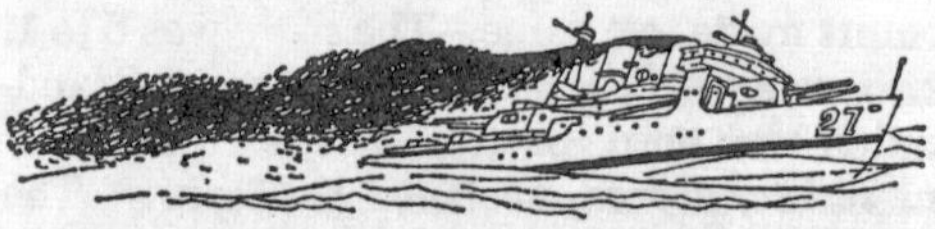

2. A white or silver curtain on which motion pictures are shown. – Mary squealed with delight when her favorite actor appeared on the *screen*.
–*v. screens, screened, screening.* Cover with a screen.–Father *screened* in the front porch for the summer.

screw (SKROO) *n. screws.* A nail with a ridge or "thread" twisting around it from the point to the head. *Screws* are twisted or turned into wood instead of being hammered like nails.

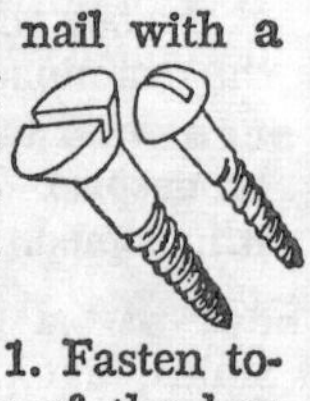

–*v. screws, screwed, screwing.* 1. Fasten together with screws.–The sides of the box were *screwed* together.
2. Turn; twist.–Mother *screwed* the cover of the fruit jar down tight.

scrib•ble (SKRIB-əl) *v. scribbles, scribbled, scribbling.* Write poorly and carelessly.–Bob *scribbled* a hasty note to Mother.

scribe (SKRYB) *n. scribes.* 1. A person, especially in olden times, who earned his living by writing or by copying writings. Before the printing press was invented, there were many *scribes.*
2. In the Bible, a scholar or teacher of the Jewish law.

scrim•mage (SKRIM-ij) *n. scrimmages.* 1. A rough-and-tumble fight. – The teacher stopped the *scrimmage* on the playground and sent the fighting boys back to study hall.
2. In a football game, the action that takes place while the ball is in play.–Tom sprained his ankle during the *scrimmage.*

script (SKRIPT) *n. scripts.* 1. Handwriting; also, a kind of printing that looks like handwriting.

All men are created equal

2. A copy of a play.–The actor forgot his part in the play and had to look at the *script* before he could go on.

scrip•ture (SKRIP-cher) *n. scriptures.* 1. (Spelled with a capital "S.") The Old and the New Testaments.–The minister read from the *Scriptures.*
2. Any sacred writing.–The *scripture* of the Moslems is called the Koran.

scroll (SKROHL) *n. scrolls.* 1. A roll of paper or other writing material.–In olden times much writing was done on *scrolls* of parchment. *Scrolls* were rolled at both ends. The reader rolled the parchment from one roll to the other instead of turning the pages as we do.
2. A design drawn to look like a partly-rolled streamer of paper. – The first page of the book of fairy tales was decorated with *scrolls.*

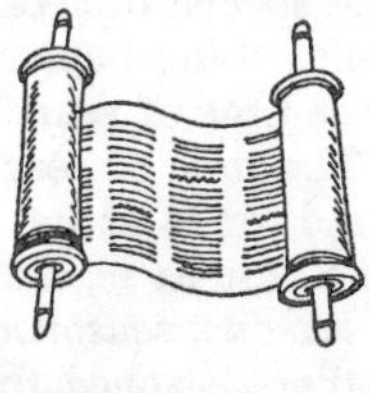

scrub (SKRUB) *n. scrubs.* Washing, or rubbing.–Jack gave his dog a good *scrub* after it had fallen in the puddle.
–*v. scrubs, scrubbed, scrubbing.* Clean by rubbing hard.–Mother *scrubbed* the floor with soapy water and a brush.

sculp•tor (SKULP-ter) *n. sculptors.* A person who carves or molds statues or other figures of stone, wood, plaster, and other materials.

sculp•ture (SKULP-cher) *n. sculptures.* The art of carving or molding statues and other figures from stone, wood, or other materials; the work so produced.–Many fine pieces of *sculpture* can be seen in an art museum.

scum (SKUM) *n.* A thin coating that forms on the top of liquids.–*Scum* often collects on shallow, still water.

scur•ry (SKER-ee) *n. scurries.* Lively running or patter.–We heard the *scurry* of Sally's feet as she tried to catch the kitten.
–*v. scurries, scurried, scurrying.* Hurry or scamper.–When the bell rang, the children *scurried* into the room.

scur•vy (SKER-vee) *n.* A disease caused by a lack of vitamin C in the diet. A person with *scurvy* usually suffers from bleeding gums, weakness, and spots on the skin. Sailors on long voyages often used to get *scurvy* because they rarely ate fruits and vegetables containing vitamin C.

scythe (SYTH) *n. scythes.* A farm tool used for cutting weeds, grain, and long grasses by hand. A *scythe* has a long handle and a long, curved blade.

sea (SEE) *n. seas.* 1. The ocean; a very large body of salt water that covers more of the earth's surface than land does.–The old salt had sailed the seven *seas.*
2. Large bodies of salt water smaller than oceans are called *seas.*–The island of Sicily is in the Mediterranean *Sea.*

3. A body of water that is rough from heavy waves. – The fishermen could not fish because of a high *sea.*

sea•coast (SEE-kohst) *n. seacoasts.* Land along the ocean or sea.–New York City is located on the eastern *seacoast* of the United States; San Francisco is on the western *seacoast.*

sea•far•ing (SEE-fair-ing) *n.* and *adj.* Working, traveling, or living on the sea or ocean.–The retired sailor misses his days of *seafaring.*

sea gull (SEE gul) *sea gulls.* A large, graceful sea bird with mostly white feathers. *Sea gulls* often follow ships and eat bits of food that are thrown from the ship. They also eat fish.

sea horse (SEE horss) *sea horses.* A fish with a head that looks like a horse's head, and a tail that curls up. The body is covered with thin bony plates. The *sea horse* is found in most warm and temperate seas around the world.

seal (SEEL) *n. seals.* 1. A sea animal that lives near the coast, especially in cold waters.

2. The fur of certain seals.–Coats and coat collars are often made of *seal.*
3. A stamping device with a raised symbol or design used for stamping letters, official papers, and the like.–Mary has a *seal* with her initials on it to close letters. She puts a little melted red wax on the envelope and then presses her *seal* against the wax. The *seal* presses her initials into the wax.

–v. seals, sealed, sealing. 1. Close tightly.–Mother *sealed* the fruit jars with paraffin.
2. Mark with a seal.–The lawyer *sealed* the will.
3. Settle or make final.–The boys shook hands to *seal* the bargain.

sea lev•el (SEE lev-əl). The surface of the sea. *Sea level* is measured from a point halfway between the average high and low tide. *Sea level* is used as the starting point in measuring altitude.

seam (SEEM) *n. seams.* A fold or line where two pieces of material join.–The *seam* of Father's coat ripped.

sea•man (SEE-mən) *n. seamen.* A sailor.

sea•port (SEE-port) *n. seaports.* A port or harbor where ships that sail the seas load and unload cargoes and passengers.

sear (SIR) *v. sears, seared, searing.* 1. Burn the surface of.–The hot stove *seared* Father's finger.
2. Cook or brown the outside of.–Mother *seared* the meat quickly in a pan with a little water in it.

search (SERCH) *n. searches.* An effort made to find something.–After a long *search* for his keys, Father found them in his pocket.
–v. searches, searched, searching. 1. Look for; try to find.–The children all *searched* for the lost purse.
2. Look through; examine. – Bob *searched* the book for the picture of the flame-snorting dragon.

search•light (SERCH-lyt) *n. searchlights.* A very strong, turning light that can throw a powerful ray of light in any direction. – A *searchlight* can be seen for many miles.

sea•shore (SEE-shor) *n. seashores.* The land along the ocean or sea.–We often go to the *seashore* for our summer vacation, so we can spend our days on the beach.

sea•sick (SEE-sik) *adj.* Sick at the stomach because of the rolling movement of a boat.–Even old sailors sometimes get *seasick* during bad storms at sea.

sea•side (SEE-syd) *n.* Seashore, or the land along the sea or ocean.–Sally likes to cover up Father with sand when we go to the *seaside.*

sea•son (SEE-zən) *n. seasons.* 1. One of the four parts into which the year is divided. Spring, summer, autumn, and winter are the four *seasons.*
2. A special time of the year in which a particular thing happens.–The planting *season* is the time of year for planting.
3. The time of year when something can be found, or is at its best.–Fresh strawberries taste best in *season.*
–v. seasons, seasoned, seasoning. 1. Flavor.–Mother *seasoned* the soup with onions and celery salt.
2. Treat or prepare for use.–Lumber to be made into furniture should first be *seasoned,* or dried thoroughly.

sea•son•ing (SEE-zən-ing) *n. seasonings.* Flavoring; something added in a small quantity to improve the taste. Salt, pepper, spices, onions, and the like are *seasonings.*

seat (SEET) *n. seats.* 1. A place in which to sit, or a thing to sit on. Chairs, benches, stools, and the like are *seats.*–The usher at the theater took us to our *seats.*

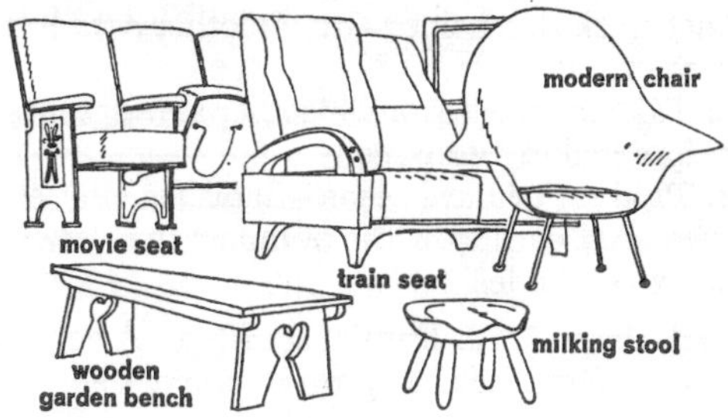

2. The part of anything that you sit on.–We have leather *seats* on our dining chairs.–Father wore a hole in the *seat* of his everyday trousers.
3. Main location or headquarters.–Detroit is the county *seat* of Wayne County. It is the principal city of that county, the city where county government is carried on.–Washington, D.C., is the *seat* of the Federal Government.
–*v. seats, seated, seating.* 1. Show to a seat or place in a seat.–The usher *seated* us in the fourth row.
2. Have enough seats for.–This room *seats* forty pupils.

sea•weed (SEE-weed) *n. seaweeds.* A kind of plant that grows in the sea.–Slippery strings of *seaweed* sometimes catch around your feet when you go swimming.

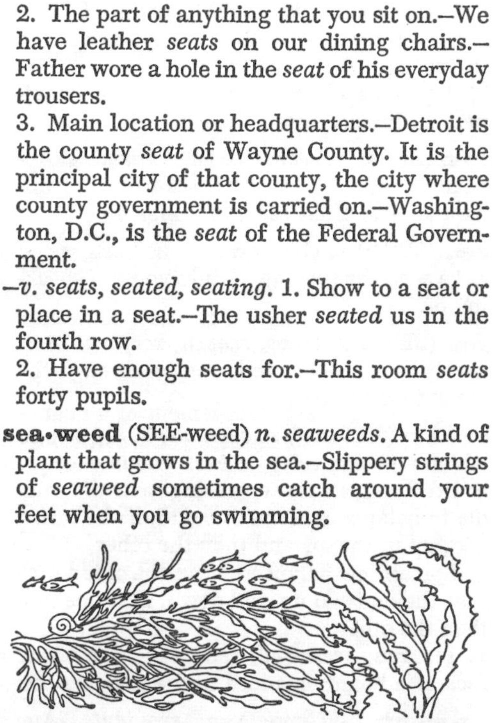

se•cede (si-SEED) *v. secedes, seceded, seceding.* Withdraw formally from a union of states, an organization, a religious or political body, etc.–The discontented group threatened to *secede* from the association.

sec•ond (SEK-ənd) *n. seconds.* 1. One of the 60 equal parts into which a minute is divided. –If you count slowly to 60, it will take you about 1 minute, or 60 *seconds.*
2. A person chosen to help a prize fighter or duelist.–The tired boxer's *second* kept urging him on.
–*adj.* 1. Directly following the first.–Sunday is the first day of the week. Monday, the day following Sunday, is the *second* day of the week.
2. One next after the first, in rank or value.–Jack won first prize, and Bob won *second* prize.
3. Like the first.–The ballplayer wanted to be a *second* Joe DiMaggio.
4. Below the first in rank or quality.–This cloth is *second* quality.
–*v. seconds, seconded, seconding.* Speak in agreement or support of.–In the class meeting, Mary made a motion to start a club, and Ruth *seconded* it.

sec•ond•hand (SEK-ənd-HAND) *adj.* Not new; used before.–We bought a *secondhand* piano.–This store sells *secondhand* goods. It buys goods from people who have been using them, and resells them to others.

se•cret (SEE-krit) *n. secrets.* Something that people are kept from knowing.–What we have for Mother's birthday is a *secret.*
–*adj.; secretly, adv.* Hidden; not known.–The man disappeared through a *secret* door.

sec•re•tar•y (SEK-rə-tair-ee) *n. secretaries.* 1. A person who writes letters, makes records, and takes care of many office duties for a person, a business, or a club.–Bob is the *secretary* for his class.
2. A kind of old-fashioned writing desk.

se•crete (si-KREET) *v. secretes, secreted, secreting.* 1. Produce and discharge, as a gland making and giving off a substance in the body.–A gland in the mouth *secretes* saliva.
2. Hide carefully; conceal.–The thief *secreted* the stolen money in a large vase.

sec•tion (SEK-shən) *n. sections.* 1. A part of anything; one of the pieces into which a thing is divided or cut. –Grapefruit and oranges are divided inside into *sections* by thin walls, or membranes.–Our class is divided into two *sections.*

2. A region.–Miners live in the mining *sections* of the country.

se•cure (si-KYUHR) *v. secures, secured, securing.* Get or obtain.–We hope to *secure* enough money to buy the new books.
–*adj.* 1. Tightly fastened.–The lock is not *secure.*
2. Free from danger or fear.–The cat had a *secure* feeling that she was safe from the dog when she was up the tree.

se•dan (sə-DAN) *n. sedans.* 1. A closed car with two seats, one in front and one in back. —Our automobile is a *sedan.*

2. (Also called a "sedan chair.") An enclosed chair carried by servants.—Long ago queens rode in *sedans.*

sed•a•tive (SED-ə-tiv) *n. sedatives.* A soothing medicine used to relieve pain and nervous excitement.—The doctor gave the sick woman a *sedative* to help her sleep.

sed•i•ment (SED-ə-mənt) *n.* The material in a liquid that settles to the bottom.—The material sometimes found at the bottom of a cup of coffee is *sediment.*

sed•i•men•ta•ry rock (sed-ə-MEN-tə-ree rahk) *sedimentary rocks.* Rock, usually in layers, made up of rock fragments and sometimes plant and animal remains that have been cemented together by heat and pressure. *Sedimentary rock* is usually formed at the bottom of a body of water, but may also form windblown sand. Shale, sandstone, and limestone are common *sedimentary rocks.*

see (SEE) *v. sees, saw, seeing.* 1. Have the power of sight.—We hear with our ears, and *see* with our eyes.
2. Notice with the eyes.—Did you *see* the dog that just passed?
3. Make certain.—*See* that the door is locked before you go to bed.
4. Go with.—Mother will *see* you to the door.
5. Visit.—We went to *see* Grandfather last week.
6. Understand.—We *saw* how to do the problem after our teacher explained it.
7. Find out.—*See* if someone is at the door.
8. Experience or live through.—That poor family has *seen* better days.

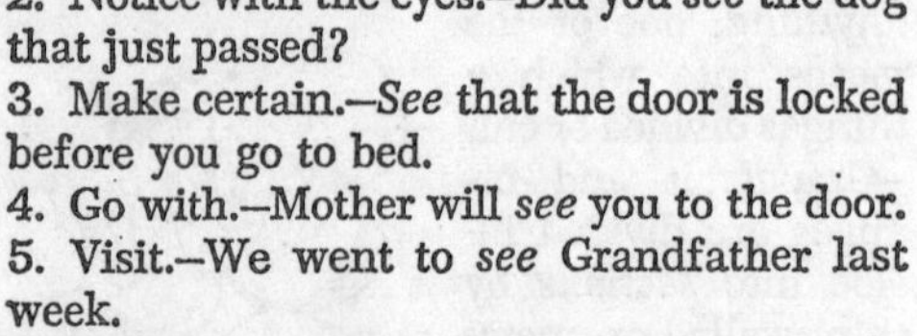

seed (SEED) *n. seeds.* The part of a plant from which another plant will grow.—Fruits have *seeds* in them.—Trees, vegetables, and flowers all grow from *seeds.*—Some *seeds* are carried by the wind.
—*v. seeds, seeded, seeding.* 1. Sow seeds in.—Last week Bob helped Grandmother *seed* her garden.
2. Take the seeds from.—Mother *seeds* grapes before making grape jelly.
3. Produce or have seeds.—Radishes and lettuce *seed* earlier in the summer than some other vegetables.

seed•ling (SEED-ling) *n. seedlings.* A young tree or plant that has grown from a seed.

seek (SEEK) *v. seeks, sought, seeking.* 1. Look for; hunt; try to find.—We are *seeking* a house to live in.
2. Try.—The old man *seeks* to give happiness to his friends.

seem (SEEM) *v. seems, seemed, seeming.* Appear to be.—The old man *seemed* very unhappy.—The child *seemed* hungry.

seen (SEEN) *v.* One form of the verb *see.*—I have *seen* the moving picture you are speaking of.

seep (SEEP) *v. seeps, seeped, seeping.* Leak slowly or ooze.—The milk *seeped* through the crack in the bottle.

see•saw (SEE-saw) *n. seesaws.* 1. A game in which a person rides on each end of a heavy board that rests on something near the middle to balance it. First one end of the board goes up in the air and then the other.
2. Something balanced near the middle so that the ends go up and down, first one and then the other.
—*v. seesaws, seesawed, seesawing.* Teeter or rock as a board balanced in the middle does.

seg•ment (SEG-mənt) *n. segments.* Any piece, section, or part of a divided or naturally separated whole.—The circle is divided into many *segments.*—Please give me a few *segments* of the tangerine.

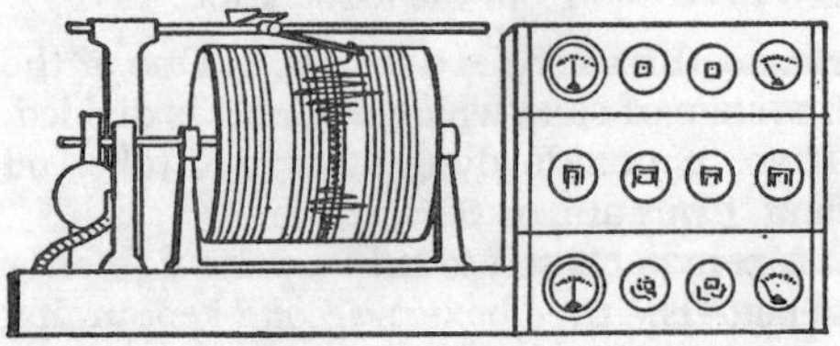

seis•mo•graph (SYZ- *or* SYSS-mə-graf) *n. seismographs.* An instrument for measuring and recording earthquakes. — The *seismograph* in California recorded an earthquake in Japan.

seize (SEEZ) *v. seizes, seized, seizing.* 1. Suddenly or violently take hold of; grab.–The frightened man *seized* a club and threw it at the wolf that was snarling at him.
2. Capture or take over.–The posse *seized* the outlaws' guns.
–*seizure, n. seizures.*

sel•dom (SEL-dəm) *adv.* Rarely, or not often. –We *seldom* see the boys, because they live too far away.

se•lect (sə-LEKT) *v. selects, selected, selecting.* Choose or pick out.–Mary likes to *select* her own dresses.
–*selection, n. selections.*

self (SELF) *n. selves.* One's own being. My*self* is I. Your*self* is you. *Self* is used with many words, as: *self*-control, meaning control of one's behavior; *self*-direction, meaning directing and guiding one's own work or actions.–Father him*self* sometimes makes mistakes in spelling.–You owe it to your*self* to do the best work you know how.

self•ish (SEL-fish) *adj.; selfishly, adv.; selfishness, n.* Too interested in oneself; without thought for others.–Bill is too *selfish* to help the class raise money to give the janitor a present.

self-re•spect (self-rə-SPEKT) *n.; self-respecting, adj.* Concern with maintaining one's own decency, honesty, and goodness.–We have *self-respect* if we are not ashamed of our own actions.

sell (SEL) *v. sells, sold, selling.* 1. Exchange for money.–The farmer *sells* chickens. He exchanges chickens for money.
2. Be exchanged.–Oranges *sell* at the corner store for sixty cents a dozen.

selves (SELVZ) *n. pl.* A form of the word *self*. Him*self* refers to one *self*, or to one boy or man alone. Them*selves* means many persons.–Mary and Sally wanted to go to town all alone, all by them*selves*.

sem•a•phore (SEM-ə-for) *n. semaphores.* 1. A system of sending signals in which the position of certain objects, such as lights or flags, gives a message.
2. An apparatus for sending such a system of signals.

sem•i•co•lon (SEM-ə-koh-lən) *n. semicolons.* A punctuation mark made by a dot with a comma under it [;]. It stands between two main parts of a sentence.–The weather was very cold; the roads were covered with ice.

sen•ate (SEN-ət) *n. senates.* 1. A group of persons elected to make the laws. Most states in the United States have *senates* to make the laws.
2. (Spelled with a capital "S.") One of two bodies of elected people making up the Congress of the United States, or one of the houses of a state legislature. The United States has a *Senate* and a House of Representatives to make laws for the country.

sen•a•tor (SEN-ət-er) *n. senators; senatorial, adj.* 1. A person elected to be a member of a senate.
2. (Spelled with a capital "S.") Title of a member of the U. S. Senate.

send (SEND) *v. sends, sent, sending.* Cause a person or thing to go or be taken from one place to another.–I will *send* your sweater to you.–Please *send* Bob home.

sen•ior (SEEN-yer) *n. seniors.* 1. An older person.–I am your *senior* by ten years. I am ten years older.
2. A person of the highest class in a college or high school.–Ed is a *senior* in college.
–*adj.* 1. The older (of two people with the same name).–Bob's father's name is Robert Smith, *Senior*. Bob's name is Robert Smith, Junior.
2. Older or higher in rank or length of service.–Mr. Miller is the *senior* member of the Miller and Black Lumber Co.–The *senior* class in high school gave a play.

sen•sa•tion (sen-SAY-shən) *n. sensations.* 1. A feeling.–Riding the merry-go-round gives Mary a dizzy *sensation*. – Standing near a radiator gives you a *sensation* of heat.
2. Great excitement.–When the lion got loose, it caused a big *sensation*.

sense (SENSS) *n. senses.* 1. Feeling.–The man who stole the money had a *sense* of guilt.
2. A quality of the body which makes us aware of things around us. The five *senses* which a person has are sight, hearing, smell, touch, and taste.
3. Judgment or intelligence.–The boy uses good *sense* in crossing the street. He knows when to cross it and when not to.
4. Meaning.–Mary couldn't get the *sense* of the sentence.
5. Idea or understanding.–The boy has a good *sense* of fairness in the games he plays.
6. (In the plural only) Mind or sanity.–A person who behaves in a strange, unreasonable way is out of his *senses*.
–*v. senses, sensed, sensing.* Feel or be aware of.–Mother *sensed* that the boy was upset.

sen•si•ble (SEN-sə-bəl) *adj.; sensibly, adv.* Wise or intelligent.—A *sensible* person is one who uses good sense or judgment.

sen•si•tive (SEN-sə-tiv) *adj.; sensitively, adv.; sensitiveness, n.* 1. Easily affected.—Mary's tooth is *sensitive* to heat. Hot tea makes it hurt.
2. Easily offended or hurt. — Johnny was *sensitive* when his two front teeth fell out. They soon grew back, and he got over it.

sent (SENT) *v.* One form of the verb *send.*—We *sent* flowers to the sick woman.

sen•tence (SEN-tənss) *n. sentences.* 1. A group of words that tells something or asks something. These are *sentences:* Mary has a new dress. Where did she get the dress?
2. A decision made by a judge as to what a person's punishment shall be for doing something not lawful.
—*v. sentences, sentenced, sentencing.* Pass official judgment on.—The judge *sentenced* the man to a year in prison.

sen•ti•nel (SEN-tə-nəl) *n. sentinels.* A guard; a sentry.—*Sentinels* were stationed at the palace gates.

sen•try (SEN-tree) *n. sentries.* A soldier who guards a place to keep away persons who have no right to be there.

se•pal (SEE-pəl) *n. sepals.* One of the leaflike parts of a flower that are found on the outside at the base of the petals. The *sepals* cover and protect the bud until it is ready to blossom; then they spread, and the flower opens.

sep•a•rate (SEP-ə-rət) *adj.* 1. Not joined or connected.—We live in *separate* houses. They are in different places, and you cannot go from one to the other without going outside.
2. Alone; just one.—A *separate* dish costs more than it would if you were to buy it as part of the whole set.
—(SEP-ə-rayt) *v. separates, separated, separating.* 1. Divide or put in different groups.—The teacher told Mary to *separate* the blue from the red crayons.
2. Keep apart or divide.—A large river *separates* the two towns.—The children were *separated* during the summer. They were no longer together.

sep•a•ra•tion (sep-ə-RAY-shən) *n. separations.* A parting or division.—The earthquake caused a *separation* of the ground.

sep•a•ra•tor (SEP-ə-ray-ter) *n. separators.* A machine which separates cream from milk. — The farmer uses a *separator* to separate the cream from the milk.

Sep•tem•ber (sep-TEM-ber) *n. Septembers.* The ninth month of the year. *September* has thirty days.

se•quel (SEE-kwəl) *n. sequels.* 1. Something that follows an earlier event; a result or consequence.—Hunger and disease were the *sequels* of the flood.
2. A new and complete story in continuation of a previous story.—The author wrote a *sequel* to his novel. He wrote another novel about the same characters.

se•quence (SEE-kwənss) *n. sequences.* 1. An order of succession, as the way one thing follows another.—The magazines are arranged in *sequence,* according to their dates.
2. A related and connected series of things or events. — A traffic signal was installed at the intersection after a *sequence* of accidents.

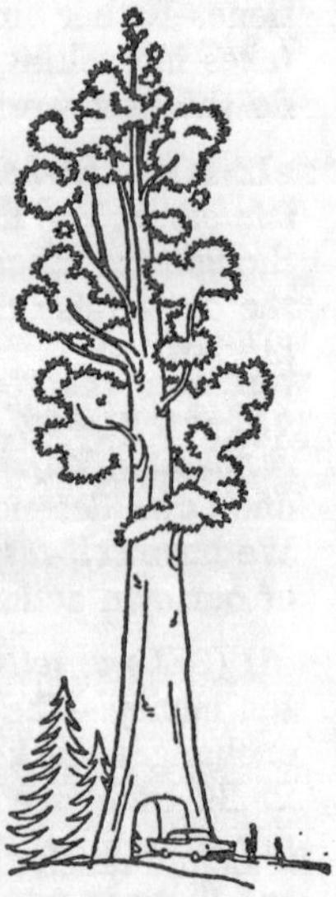

se•quoi•a (si-KWOI-ə) *n. sequoias.* A giant pine or redwood tree that grows in California. The *sequoias* are over 300 feet high and are said to be the oldest living things. Some are believed to be over 3,000 years old.

se•rene (sə-REEN) *adj.; serenely, adv.* 1. Fair and clear.—During the summer the skies are usually *serene.*
2. Quiet and calm.—The sick man spent a *serene* night. His sleep was not disturbed.

ser•geant (SAHR-jənt) *n. sergeants.* A noncommissioned officer in the army, air force, or marines. His rank is next above that of corporal, but below that of lieutenant.

se•ri•al (SIR-ee-əl) *n. serials* and *adj.* A story, movie, or radio play presented in parts.—Mother is reading a *serial* in a magazine.—Some people like to listen to the *serials* on television and radio.

se•ries (SIR-eez) *n. sing.* and *pl.* A number of like happenings one after the other, such as a *series* of baseball games, a *series* of articles about sewing, or a *series* of lessons in cooking.—Mother listened to a *series* of radio talks on how to can fruits and vegetables.

se•ri•ous (SIR-ee-əss) *adj.; seriously, adv.; seriousness, n.* 1. Dangerous or harmful.—The boy's injuries did not prove to be *serious* when they were examined.
2. Thoughtful or earnest.—The old man's face grew *serious* as he began his story.—Bob is a *serious* student.
3. Important; worthy of concern.—To Mary, becoming a movie actress is a *serious* problem.
4. Honest or in earnest.—Are you *serious* about quitting school?

ser•mon (SER-mən) *n. sermons.* 1. A religious talk.—Bob went to church and listened to the minister's *sermon*.
2. A very serious talk.—Father delivered a *sermon* to the children about getting their work done before they played.

ser•pent (SER-pənt) *n. serpents.* A snake, especially a large one.

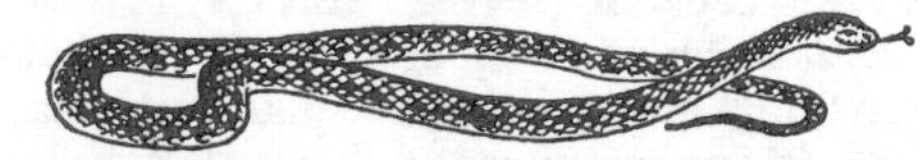

se•rum (SIR-əm) *n. serums.* 1. The liquid part of the blood. When blood thickens, the *serum* separates from the clot, or the part that gets somewhat hard.
2. Liquid taken from the blood of an animal that has had a certain disease. When this liquid is injected into a person, it may keep the person from having the disease.

serv•ant (SER-vənt) *n. servants.* 1. A person hired by others to do personal or house work.—Many *servants* work for the rich man.
2. Persons whose lives are given to serving others.—Teachers are public *servants*. They serve their city and their country by teaching boys and girls.

serve (SERV) *v. serves, served, serving.* 1. Work, help, or do good for.—A store clerk *serves* the customers.—The mayor *serves* the people of the city.
2. Be used or useful.—Boy Scouts can make two stones *serve* as a fireplace.
3. Bring food to.—The waitress *served* us. She carried our food to our table.
4. Supply or furnish.—The bakery *serves* us with bread.
5. Spend or pass (time).—The sailor *served* three years in the navy.
6. To deal with.—Having his play period taken away *served* the boy right for being tardy.
7. We *served* a notice on the family to move. We sent them a written note asking them to move.
8. Put the ball in play in certain games.—It was Mary's turn to *serve* in the championship tennis game.

serv•ice (SER-vəss) *n. services.* 1. Help or aid.—May I be of *service* to you?
2. The work one does for another.—A nurse's *services* are needed when someone is very sick.

3. A religious meeting or ceremony.—We attend *services* every Sunday.
4. A set of silver, dishes, or tableware.—Mother has a *service* for eight people. She has enough dishes for eight people.
5. Serving.—The *service* at the restaurant is good. The food is served well and promptly.
6. A military organization, as the army, navy, or air force.—Many young men are in *service* now.
7. Government work. — Postmen are in Civil *Service*. They are hired by the Government.
—*v. services, serviced, servicing.* Repair.—A man *serviced* our electric iron. He put it in working order.

ses•a•me (SESS-ə-mee) *n.* An herb growing in tropical countries. An oil similar to that obtained from olives is pressed from seeds of *sesame*. Both oil and seeds are edible.

ses•sion (SESH-ən) *n. sessions.* 1. A meeting of a class, school, court, lawmaking body, or club.—The judge looked sternly at the lawyer who was late for the first court *session* of the day.
2. A number of meetings, one after the other, by a club, court, school, etc.—The school's morning *session* is from 9 o'clock to noon.
3. A time when an organization is active.—Our school has a summer *session* and a winter *session*.

set (SET) *n. sets.* A group of articles used together.–Father has a *set* of tools.–Mother has a *set* of dishes.

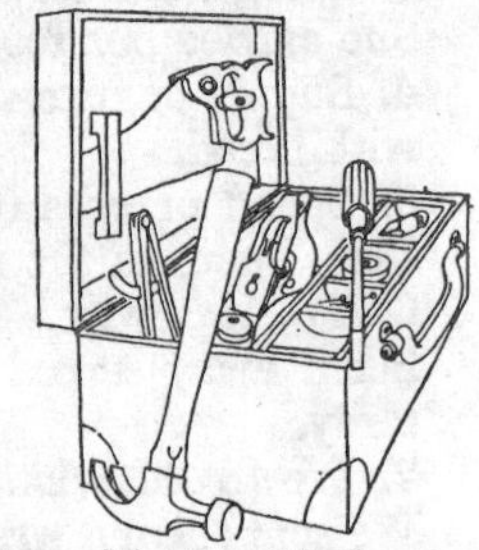

–*v. sets, set, setting.* 1. Put or place. – Mary *set* the basket on the table.

2. Put in proper condition or position.–The doctor *set* the broken bone.–Mary *set* the table for Mother.–Father *set* the alarm for five o'clock.–The men *set* the stage for the next scene of the play.

3. Put (into some condition).–The dog who was caught in the trap was *set* free.–The boys *set* the old Christmas tree on fire.

4. Get solid; take on a definite form.–Mother put the gelatin dessert in the icebox to *set.*

5. Go down (of the sun, moon, or stars).–The sun rises in the east and *sets* in the west.

6. Start or begin.–We *set* out on our trip at sunrise.

–*adj.* Established; fixed.–It is a *set* rule that we must get to school by nine o'clock.

set•ter (SET-er) *n. setters.* A hunting dog that is trained to stand very still with its tail straight out and its nose pointing toward the bird or other game which it smells.

set•tle (SET-l) *v. settles, settled, settling.* 1. Get quiet and comfortably placed and prepared.–The teacher told the children to *settle* down and study their spelling.–Bob *settled* himself in the big armchair to read his favorite book.

2. Make a permanent home, or go to live.–My uncle wants to *settle* in the country.–We *settled* in this community ten years ago.

3. Sink to the bottom.–Sand in water *settles* if the water is allowed to stand.

4. Pay.–Father *settled* the bill at the grocer's.

5. Come to rest; stop.–The golf ball rolled and then *settled* on the green.

6. Put in order; arrange.–Mother wants to *settle* her house before company comes.

7. Decide upon; agree upon.–The day for the picnic has not been *settled* upon yet.

8. End.–The teacher told the boys to *settle* their quarrel.

set•tle•ment (SET-l-mənt) *n. settlements.* 1. An agreeable ending.–After the *settlement* of the quarrel, the boys shook hands.–The two countries arranged a peaceful *settlement* of their dispute.

2. A new community or village.–A small *settlement* of French people may be found near the river.

3. A payment.–The store asked for a *settlement* of the bill.

4. A place or building in a community where help is given to the needy.

set•tler (SET-ler) *n. settlers.* One who makes his home in a new land.–The Pilgrims were among the early *settlers* in America.

sev•en (SEV-ən) *n. sevens* and *adj.* The number [7] coming after 6 and before 8.–Six and one make *seven.*

sev•en•teen (sev-ən-TEEN) *n. seventeens* and *adj.* The number [17] coming after 16 and before 18.–Ten and seven make *seventeen.*

sev•en•teenth (sev-ən-TEENTH) *n. seventeenths.* One of 17 equal parts.–If you divide anything into seventeen equal parts, each part is one *seventeenth.* It may be written 1/17.

–*adj.* Coming as number 17 in a series.–Tom is celebrating his *seventeenth* birthday.

sev•enth (SEV-ənth) *n. sevenths.* One of 7 equal parts.–If you divide anything into seven parts all the same size, each part is one *seventh.* It may be written 1/7.

–*adj.* Coming as number 7 in a series.–Billy has had six birthdays. His next one will be his *seventh.*

sev•en•ty (SEV-ən-tee) *n. seventies* and *adj.* The number [70] coming after 69 and before 71.–*Seventy* is ten more than sixty.

sev•er (SEV-er) *v. severs, severed, severing.* 1. Cut; divide; separate; part.–Jack had to *sever* the cord around the package in order to open it.

2. Cut off or break, as ties between nations.–The quarreling governments are about to *sever* relations.

sev•er•al (SEV-er-əl) *adj.* More than two, but not many.–*Several* flowers are in blossom.

se•vere (sə-VIR) *adj.; severely, adv.; severeness, n.* 1. Sharp; intense; great.–Mother had a *severe* pain in her tooth.–The poor man was shivering from the *severe* cold.
2. Hard; difficult.–Climbing the mountain was a *severe* test of the explorer's strength.
3. Strict; harsh.–Father sometimes tries to be *severe* with the children when they have disobeyed.
4. Very plain; without any trimming.–Mother's new evening dress is a *severe,* straight black gown.

sew (SOH) *v. sews, sewed, sewing.* Fasten cloth together by putting thread through it with a needle; stitch. –Mother *sews* on the sewing machine. Mary *sews* by hand.–Mother *sewed* up the rip in Father's sleeve.

sew•age (SOO- *or* SYOO-ij) *n.* Waste liquids and solids that pass through sewers.–*Sewage* is often purified and then passed into rivers to be carried off by water currents.

sew•er (SOO- *or* SYOO-er) *n. sewers.* A drain, usually underground, made of large pipes or tiles, to carry waste away from homes.–Dishwater poured into the sink is carried away by the *sewer.*

sex (SEKS) *n. sexes.* 1. Either of the two classes or divisions of living things, male or female; males or females as a group.–The club has members of both *sexes.* Both boys and girls belong to the club.
2. The differences which make a person, plant, or animal either male or female.

sex•tant (SEKS-tənt) *n. sextants.* An instrument for measuring angles, distances, and altitudes. The *sextant* is used at sea to determine latitude and longitude by measuring the heights of heavenly bodies over the horizon.

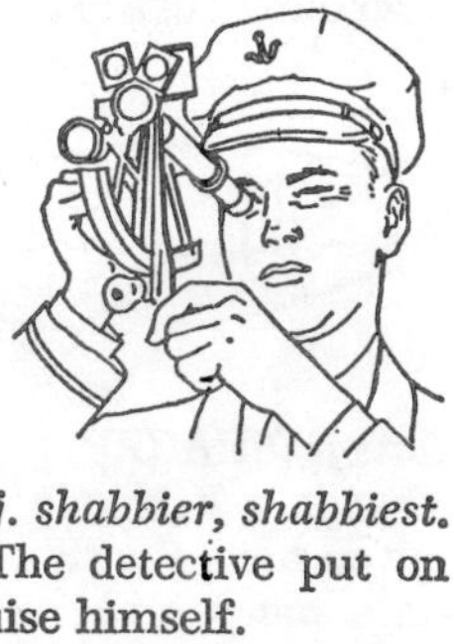

shab•by (SHAB-ee) *adj. shabbier, shabbiest.* 1. Worn and faded.–The detective put on *shabby* clothes to disguise himself.
2. Mean; not generous.–The boy's feelings were hurt because of the *shabby* way the children treated him.

shack (SHAK) *n. shacks.* A small, poorly or roughly built house.–We went into the fisherman's *shack* when we were at the shore.

shad (SHAD) *n. sing.* and *pl.* A kind of fish used for food. *Shad* are found along the eastern coast of America.

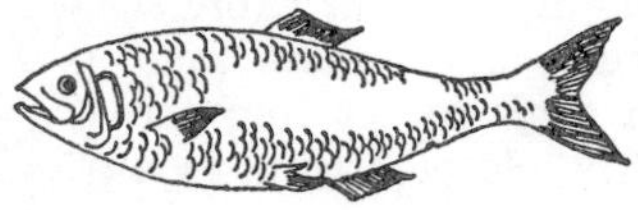

shade (SHAYD) *n. shades.* 1. A shadow or partial darkness made by something blocking the light.–We ate our picnic lunch in the *shade* of the tree.

2. Something made to shut out light.–Window *shades* cover the windows of a house.–A lamp *shade* keeps the light out of your eyes.
3. A small degree.–Bob is just a *shade* taller than Bill.
4. A tone of a color.–Mother's green dress is a lovely soft *shade.*–The sky has several different *shades* of blue.
–*v. shades, shaded, shading.* 1. Shield or partly cover.–Father *shaded* his eyes from the sun with his hands.
2. Make darker in some places than in others.–The artist *shaded* the drawing of the vase to make it look round.

shad•ow (SHAD-oh) *n. shadows.* 1. A shaded spot made by a solid body which is blocking off a light.–The *shadow* cast by the tree is longer in the morning that it is at noon, when the sun is right above it.

2. A suggestion; slight bit.–There cannot be a *shadow* of a doubt of Jack's honesty.
–*v. shadows, shadowed, shadowing:* Follow closely.–The burglar didn't know he was being *shadowed* by the detective.

shaft (SHAFT) *n. shafts.* 1. A pole, long stick, handle, or the like.–The *shaft* of the spear

was wooden, but the point was steel.–A tall *shaft* on the building supported a radio aerial.
2. A long up-and-down tunnel or opening.–The miners went down a *shaft* to get into the mine.–The elevator runs in a *shaft.*

shag·gy (SHAG-ee) *adj. shaggier, shaggiest.* Covered with long, coarse, thick, woolly hair. –Jack likes *shaggy* dogs.

shake (SHAYK) *n. shakes.* A jerk, or a quick movement up and down or to and fro.–After a few *shakes,* the salt shaker was empty.
–*v. shakes, shook, shaking.* 1. Jerk, or move up and down or to and fro quickly.–We *shake* salt out of a salt shaker.–We *shake* rugs to get the dust out of them.–The angry man *shook* his fist at the ruffian.
2. Clasp (hands).–The minister *shakes* hands with the people at the door after the service.
3. Tremble.–Mary *shook* with excitement.

shale (SHAYL) *n. shales.* A type of rock formed of thin, hardened layers of mud, clay, or silt.–*Shale* is used in making certain types of building bricks.

shall (SHAL) *v. should.* 1. Is, am, or are going to.–We *shall* see the movie tomorrow.
2. Expect or intend to.–I *shall* study my lessons before school.
3. Be required to.–He *shall* repay the money if it takes his last cent.

shal·low (SHAL-oh) *adj. shallower, shallowest.* Not deep.–Small children bathe where the water is *shallow.*

sham (SHAM) *adj.* Make-believe or pretended.–The boys had a *sham* battle.

shame (SHAYM) *n. shames.* 1. An uncomfortable feeling caused by having done something wrong or foolish.–The boy who was caught cheating felt much *shame.*
2. Disgrace or loss of respect.–The boy's bad behavior brought *shame* to the team.
3. A thing to be sorry about.–It is a *shame* that Mary didn't get to go to the play.
–*v. shames, shamed, shaming.* Cause to feel shame.–We tried to *shame* the boy for not telling the truth. We tried to make him feel bad about it.

sham·poo (sham-POO) *n. shampoos.* 1. A hair-washing.–Mother went to the beauty parlor to get a *shampoo.*
2. Soap to wash the hair with.–Some *shampoo* is liquid and comes in bottles.
–*v. shampoos, shampooed, shampooing.* Wash (hair).–Mary is *shampooing* her hair.

sham·rock (SHAM-rahk) *n. shamrocks.* A three-leaved plant that looks like a clover. It is the national emblem of Ireland.

shan·ty (SHAN-tee) *n. shanties.* A small house, or shack.–The fisherman lives in a *shanty* on the bank of the river.

shape (SHAYP) *n. shapes.* 1. A form.–The *shape* of the ball is round.–The *shape* of the box is square.

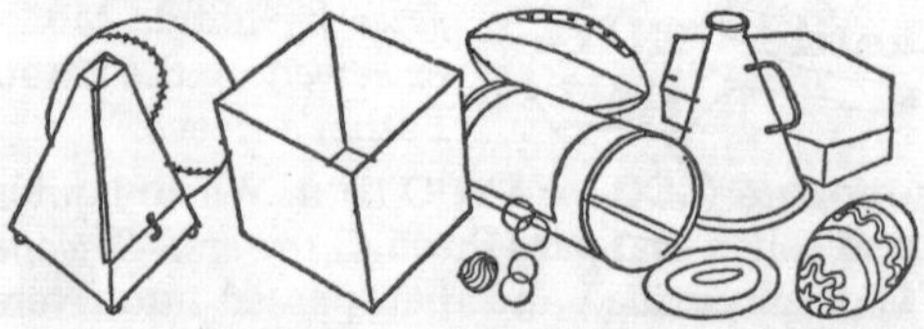

2. A figure.–We saw the *shape* of a black cat on the fence in the moonlight.
3. Order; readiness.–Mother has everything in *shape* for us to start for school.
–*v. shapes, shaped, shaping.* Mold; form.–Mary *shaped* a little bear out of clay.

share (SHAIR) *n. shares.* A part.–My *share* of the money is sixty cents.–Bob always does his *share* of the work in the garden.
–*v. shares, shared, sharing.* Divide, or allow use or enjoyment of by others; have part in. –Sally *shares* her toys with the other children.

shark (SHAHRK) *n. sharks.* A large, fierce and dangerous fish that eats other fish.

sharp (SHAHRP) *n. sharps.* A tone in music that is a half step above or higher than a given note; the sign [♯] indicating this.
–*adj. sharper, sharpest; sharply, adv.; sharpness, n.* 1. Made for cutting or piercing; not dull.–The knife is *sharp.*–The kitten's claws are *sharp.*

2. Not rounded; having a point or angle.—Mary knocked herself on the *sharp* corner of the table in the dark.—We came to a *sharp* curve in the road.
3. Biting; keen.—Vinegar has a *sharp* taste.—A *sharp* wind almost froze our faces.
4. Harsh; angry.—The teacher's *sharp* words hurt the boy's feelings.
5. Piercing.—Bob had a *sharp* pain in his stomach.
6. Quick; keen; alert.—The boy has a *sharp* mind. He is quick to solve a problem, quick to learn, quick to get a joke.—Birds have *sharp* eyes. They see well.
—*adv.* Exactly.—School starts at nine o'clock *sharp*.

sharp·en (SHAHR-pən) *v. sharpens, sharpened, sharpening.* Put a point on, or make an edge keener for cutting.—Mary *sharpened* her new pencil.—Father *sharpened* his razor this morning.

shat·ter (SHAT-er) *v. shatters, shattered, shattering.* 1. Break into many small pieces.—When the picture fell to the floor, the glass *shattered.*
2. Destroy.—The heavy snowfall *shattered* Mary's hopes for a sunny week end.

shave (SHAYV) *n. shaves.* A narrow escape.—The car almost hit the tree. It was a close *shave.*
—*v. shaves, shaved, shaving.* Cut hair off with a razor.—Father *shaves* his face every morning.

shav·ing (SHAY-ving) *n. shavings.* A thin slice or strip cut off with a knife or a carpenter's plane.—The *shavings* of wood curled up when cut off.

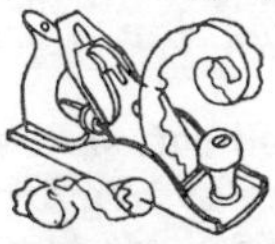

shawl (SHAWL) *n. shawls.* A square or oblong piece of material worn over the head or shoulders. — Grandmother has a wool *shawl* with fringe on the ends.

she (SHEE) *pron.* A word that stands for a girl, woman, or female animal.—Grandmother said *she* would come to see us.—The cow's name is Bessie. *She* is red and white.

sheaf (SHEEF) *n. sheaves.* A bundle of flowers, grain, arrows, or the like.

shear (SHIR) *v. shears, sheared, shearing.* Cut off.—The farmer *shears* the sheep's wool with large scissors.

shears (SHIRZ) *n. pl.* Large scissors. — The farmer uses *shears* to cut the sheep's wool.

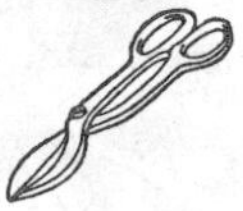

sheaves (SHEEVZ) *n. pl.* More than one *sheaf.*—The farmer tied the grain into *sheaves* after it was cut.

shed (SHED) *n. sheds.* A low, lightly built building.—The farmer keeps his tools in a *shed.*
—*v. sheds, shed, shedding.* 1. Let fall; pour out; drop.—The unhappy child *shed* tears.—The dog's hair is *shedding.*—This brush is *shedding* its bristles.
2. Give off or throw out.—The sun *sheds* light on the earth. The moon reflects light.

sheep (SHEEP) *n. sing.* and *pl.* An animal from which we get wool for clothes, flesh (mutton) to eat, and *sheep*skin for leather.

sheer (SHIR) *adj.; sheerly, adv.; sheerness, n.* 1. Thin enough to see partly through.—Mary has a pair of *sheer* silk stockings.—The living room curtains are *sheer.*
2. Complete.—Baby fell asleep in her highchair from *sheer* exhaustion.
3. Very steep; straight up and down, or almost so.—The north side of the mountain is a *sheer* cliff 3,000 feet high.

sheet (SHEET) *n. sheets.* 1. A piece of cloth big enough to cover a bed and tuck in at the sides and ends.—We sleep between two *sheets.*
2. A broad, thin piece of anything.—The teacher gave each of us a *sheet* of paper.—The ground and sidewalks were covered with a *sheet* of ice.

sheik (SHEEK) *n. sheiks.* An Arab chief or head man.—Some *sheiks* are extremely wealthy and powerful.

shelf (SHELF) *n. shelves.* A board or flat piece of metal fastened horizontally and used to set things on.—The cupboard has two *shelves* to set dishes on.

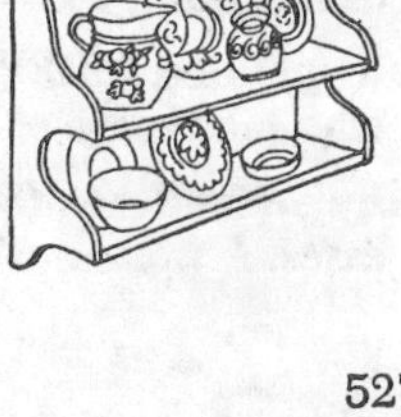

shell (SHEL) *n. shells.* 1. A hard outside covering, as on nuts, vegetables, animals, and eggs.–Walnuts, peas, turtles, ladybugs, oysters, and clams have *shells.*

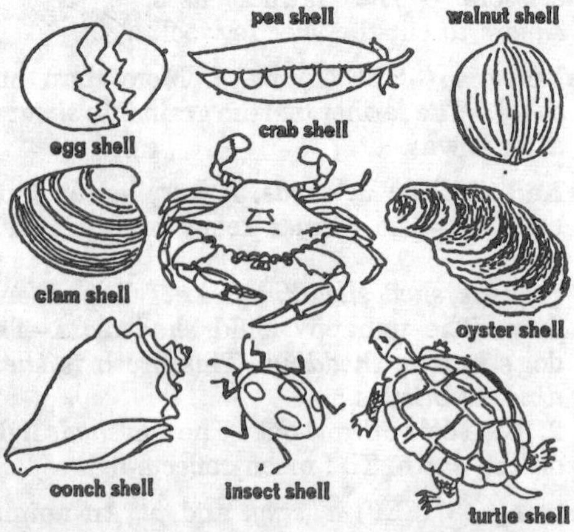

2. A crust of pastry shaped to hold a filling.–Mother made a *shell* for a lemon pie.

3. A case holding gunpowder to be fired in a gun.

4. A framework.–Only the *shell* of the house is built so far.

–*v. shells, shelled, shelling.* 1. Remove from a shell.–Mary *shelled* the peas. She took them out of the shells, or pods.

2. Fire shells at.–The soldiers *shelled* the enemy's lines until the enemy surrendered.

she'll (SHEE-əl). A short way of writing "she will."–*She'll* be here by three o'clock.

shel•lac (shə-LAK) *n. shellacs.* A clear varnishlike liquid used in finishing woods, furniture, etc.–Father put a coat of *shellac* on the bedroom floor.

shel•ter (SHEL-ter) *n. shelters.* 1. A covering that shields or protects.–An umbrella is a *shelter* from the rain.–A roof is a *shelter* from weather.

2. Protection.–We found *shelter* from the storm in the old shed.

–*v. shelters, sheltered, sheltering.* Protect or provide shelter for.–Grandfather didn't know he was *sheltering* thieves when he let the strangers sleep in the barn.

shelves (SHELVZ) *n. pl.* More than one *shelf.* –We have two cupboard *shelves* to set all the dishes on.

shep•herd (SHEP-erd) *n. shepherds.* A man who takes care of sheep.

shep•herd•ess (SHEP-er-dəss) *n. shepherdesses.* A woman who takes care of sheep.

sher•iff (SHAIR-əf) *n. sheriffs.* A man elected to enforce the law in a county.–The bank robbers were arrested by the *sheriff.*

she's (SHEEZ). A short way of writing "she is."–*She's* six years old today.

shield (SHEELD) *n. shields.* 1. Anything that protects or keeps one from harm.–The boy who stood in front of the baby to protect her from the flying stones was acting as a *shield.*

2. A large plate of metal or wood carried on the arm to protect one in battle.–The knights carried *shields.*

–*v. shields, shielded, shielding.* Protect.–Father would not *shield* the thief from the police.

shift (SHIFT) *n. shifts.* 1. A group of people who work during a certain time; also, the period of time they work.–Father now works on the day *shift.* Next month Father will work on the night *shift.*

2. A change of position.–There have been two *shifts* of the regular baseball players.

–*v. shifts, shifted, shifting.* 1. Change position.–The boy *shifted* in his seat.

2. Exchange positions of.–Mary had her slippers on the wrong feet, so she *shifted* them.

shift•less (SHIFT-ləss) *adj.; shiftlessly, adv.; shiftlessness, n.* Lazy or good-for-nothing.–Because the girl was so *shiftless,* she was not promoted.

shil•ling (SHIL-ing) *n. shillings.* An English coin. A *shilling* is worth about fourteen cents in American money.

shin (SHIN) *n. shins.* The front part of the leg below the knee.–Bob skinned his *shin* when he fell off the box.

–*v. shins, shinned, shinning.* Bob can *shin* a pole or tree. He pulls himself up by hugging the pole with his arms, then with his legs, while he reaches higher.

shine (SHYN) *n. shines.* 1. Clear or bright weather.–Rain or *shine,* the postman delivers the mail.

2. A polish.–Father gave his shoes a *shine.*

–*v. shines, shined* or *shone, shining.* 1. Send or give out light.–The sun *shines.*

2. Polish or make bright.–Mary *shined* the knives and forks for Mother.

3. Look bright; reflect light.–The furniture *shines* after Mother has waxed it.

4. Be noticeably smart or bright.–Bob *shines* in arithmetic.

shin·gle (SHING-gəl) *n. shingles.* 1. One of many thin pieces of wood, thicker at one end, that are used to cover roofs and sometimes outside walls. The thick end of one *shingle* laps over the thin end of another, to keep out water. *Shingles* made of fireproof materials are the same thickness from end to end.
2. A sign.–The new doctor has hung out his *shingle* over his office door.
–*v. shingles, shingled, shingling.* 1. Put shingles on.–Grandfather *shingled* his barn.
2. Cut (hair) quite short.–During the summer, Mary has her hair *shingled.*

shin·y (SHY-nee) *adj. shinier, shiniest.* Bright and glistening.

ship (SHIP) *n. ships.* 1. A large vessel that sails on the seas.–In olden times, *ships* were moved by wind blowing on the sails.
2. An airship.–Uncle Jim told about the time he was assigned to a new *ship* in the Air Force.
–*v. ships, shipped, shipping.* 1. Send.–We *shipped* the package by mail.
2. Go as a member of a ship's crew.–The sailor has *shipped* on the same vessel for many years.

ship·ment (SHIP-mənt) *n. shipments.* Goods sent at one time to a certain place.–We expect a *shipment* of coal today.

ship·wreck (SHIP-rek) *n. shipwrecks.* Destruction or loss of a ship.–A big windstorm at sea caused the *shipwreck.*

ship·yard (SHIP-yahrd) *n. shipyards.* Place where ships are built or repaired.

shirt (SHERT) *n. shirts.* 1. Cloth garment worn on the upper part of the body by boys.
2. Undergarment for the upper part of the body.

shiv·er (SHIV-er) *v. shivers, shivered, shivering.* Shake or quiver from cold, fright, or excitement.–The coatless boy *shivered.*

shoal (SHOHL) *n. shoals.* A place where the water is shallow, or a sand bar at such a place.–The boats were blown onto the *shoal.*

shock (SHAHK) *n. shocks.* 1. A sudden jar or blow.–The *shock* of the collision with the other car stunned Father for a few minutes.
2. Something very upsetting or disturbing.–When the man's house burned, it was a great *shock* to him.
3. The feeling caused by electricity passing through a person.–When Bob touched the broken electric wire, he got a *shock.*–An electric *shock* can be very dangerous.
–*v. shocks, shocked, shocking.* Upset, disturb, or offend.–The man's rage *shocked* us all.

shod (SHAHD) *v.* One form of the verb *shoe.* –A blacksmith *shod* the horses. He put shoes on them.

shoe (SHOO) *n. shoes.* 1. A covering for the feet.–Most *shoes* are made of leather.
2. A curved strip of iron nailed to the hoofs of certain animals, such as horses. It protects the hoof as a person's *shoe* protects his foot.
–*v. shoes, shod, shoeing.* Provide with shoes.–The blacksmith *shoes* horses. He fastens horseshoes to their hoofs.

SHIPS

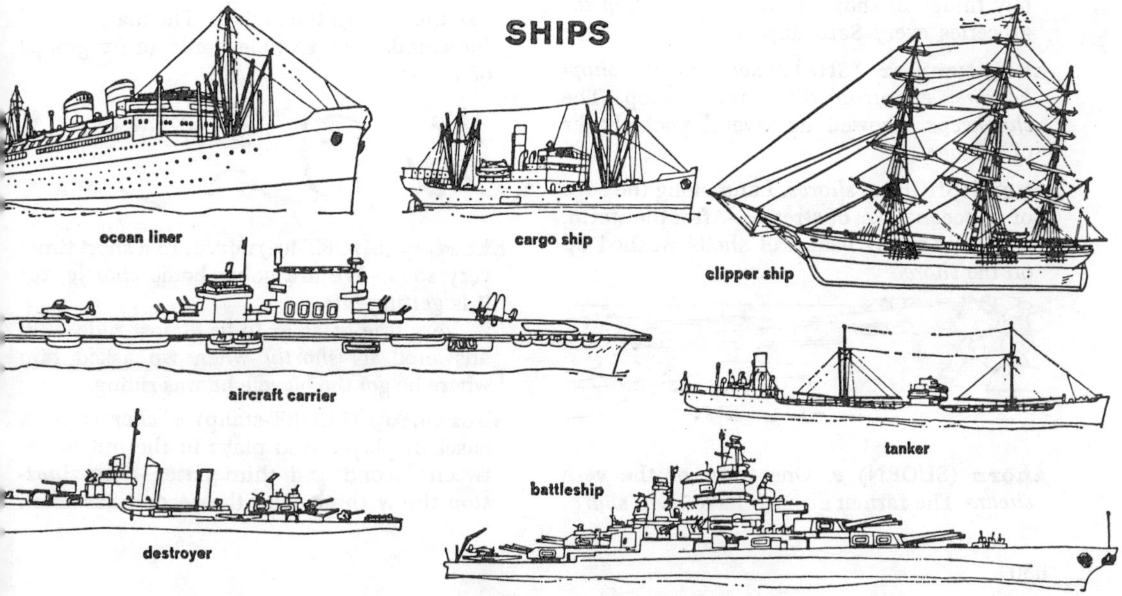

shoe·mak·er (SHOO-mayk-er) *n. shoemakers.* A person who makes or repairs shoes. – When Bob's shoes needed repair, he took them to a *shoemaker.*

shone (SHOHN) *v.* One form of the verb *shine.*–Mary rubbed the big red apple until it *shone.*

shoo (SHOO) *n. shoos.* A sound made to scare away animals.–The farmer says *"Shoo!"* when he wants to chase the chickens away.
–*v. shoos, shooed, shooing.* Scare away by shouting.–The farmer *shooed* the chickens from his porch.

shook (SHUHK) *v.* One form of the verb *shake.*–The boys *shook* the apple tree to make the apples fall.

shoot (SHOOT) *n. shoots.* A small branch.–The bush has many new *shoots,* now that spring has come.
–*v. shoots, shot, shooting.* 1. Fire (a gun).–The hunter knew just when to *shoot.*
2. Hit with an arrow or bullet.–The hunter tried to *shoot* a squirrel.
3. Move very fast.–I saw the dog *shoot* through the door after the cat.
4. Send (a ball, arrow, or the like) swiftly and with force.–The pitcher *shoots* the ball over the plate past the batter.

shop (SHAHP) *n. shops.* 1. A small store.–Mother went to the hat *shop* to buy a new hat.
2. A place where things are made.–Father works in a machine *shop.*
–*v. shops, shopped, shopping.* Look at and buy things in shops or stores.–We *shop* for groceries every Saturday.

shop·keep·er (SHAHP-kee-per) *n. shopkeepers.* A person who runs a shop.–The *shopkeeper* showed us several pocketbooks of leather.

shore (SHOR) *n. shores.* Land along the edge of an ocean, lake, or stream.–After the storm, we found many beautiful shells washed up on the *shore.*

shorn (SHORN) *v.* One form of the verb *shear.*–The farmer's sheep have been *shorn.*

short (SHORT) *adj. shorter, shortest.* 1. Not long; little in height or length.–The pencil has been sharpened so many times that it is very *short.*–A man is tall, and a little boy is *short.* – The children went for a *short* walk.

2. Having less than the right or needed amount.–We ran *short* of sugar when Mother canned the fruit.–My change from the grocer was five cents *short.*
3. So brief as to be almost rude.–Jack gave Mary a *short* answer when she asked him the same question for the third time.
–*adv.* Suddenly.–Father put on the brakes and we stopped *short.*

short·age (SHOR-tij) *n. shortages.* An amount lacking; a needed quantity; a lack.–Many persons in the world suffer from *shortages* of food and clothing.

short·cake (SHORT-kayk) *n. shortcakes.* A dessert made of biscuit dough in layers with filling and with topping of strawberries or other fresh fruit, and often with whipped cream.

short·en (SHOR-tn) *v. shortens, shortened, shortening.* Make shorter, or less long.–The sleeves in Mary's new coat were too long, so Mother had to *shorten* them.

short·en·ing (SHORT-ning) *n.* Fat used in baking to make the dough crisp, rich, and crumbly.–Butter and lard are two kinds of *shortening.*

short·hand (SHORT-hand) *n.* A system of writing words quickly by using little marks like the ones in the picture. The marks stand for sounds, or for whole words, or for groups of words.

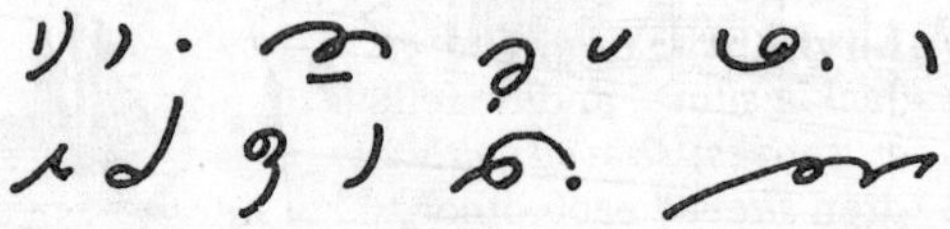

short·ly (SHORT-lee) *adv.* 1. In a short time; very soon.–We are going home *shortly,* for it is getting late.
2. Very briefly, so as to be almost rude.–Bill answered us *shortly* when we asked him where he got the bicycle he was riding.

short·stop (SHORT-stahp) *n. shortstops.* A baseball player who plays in the infield between second and third bases.–The *shortstop* threw the ball to the second baseman.

shot (SHAHT) *n. shots.* 1. The tiny balls of lead used in cartridges for shotguns.
2. The noise made when a gun is fired.–The farmer heard *shots* from the hunters' guns.
3. A marksman.–The men weren't very good *shots,* for no one hit the circle.
4. A throw, a strike, or a try at doing something.–When Father drove the golf ball a long way, he made a good *shot.*
–*v.* One form of the verb *shoot.*–The rocket *shot* through the air at 3000 miles per hour.
–The hunter *shot* the rabbit.

should (SHUHD) *v.* 1. One form of the verb *shall.*
2. Ought to.–Tom *should* drink more milk.
3. Expect to.–I told her that I *should* receive the package in time to bring it to the party.
4. Would.–I *should* have been glad to help you if you had asked me, but you didn't.

shoul•der (SHOHL-der) *n. shoulders.* 1. The part of the body to which the arms of a person or the front legs of a four-footed animal are joined.–The girl carried her purse by a strap over her *shoulder.*
2. The part of a dress or coat that fits over a person's shoulders.–The *shoulder* seam on Bob's coat is ripped apart.
–*v. shoulders, shouldered, shouldering.* 1. Take upon oneself.–The teacher was not willing to *shoulder* the responsibility of taking the children along without their parents' consent.
2. Pick up and carry on one's shoulder. – Father *shouldered* Sally and marched down the hall with her.

shout (SHOWT) *n. shouts.* Yell or loud call.– We heard the *shout* of the newsboy.
–*v. shouts, shouted, shouting.* Yell, or call out loudly.–The teacher told the children to talk softly, not to *shout.*

shove (SHUV) *n. shoves.* A push.–Bill gave Jack a *shove,* and he fell off the diving board.
–*v. shoves, shoved, shoving.* Push.–The children *shoved* each other to get into the house.

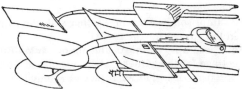

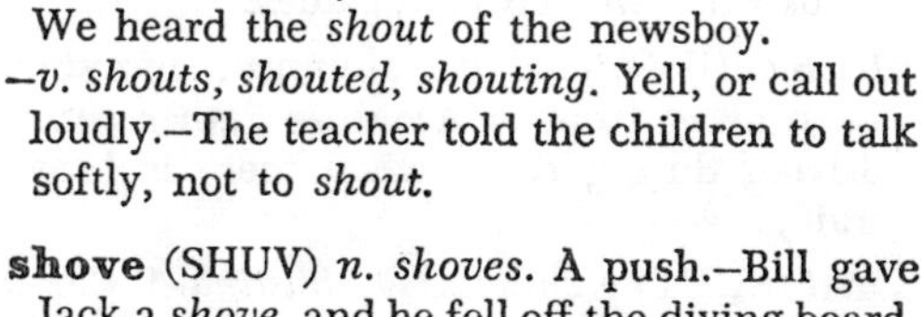

shov•el (SHUV-əl) *n. shovels.* A tool used to lift and move snow, coal, dirt, or the like.– Father uses a *shovel* to put coal into the furnace.
–*v. shovels, shoveled* or *shovelled, shoveling* or *shovelling.* Lift up with a shovel and put somewhere else.–The boys *shoveled* the snow from the sidewalks.

show (SHOH) *n. shows.* 1. A display, or a place where things are taken to be looked at and admired.–We are going to a dog *show.* The finest dogs will get prizes.
2. An entertainment.–We went to the moving picture *show.*
–*v. shows, showed, showing.* 1. Allow to look at; allow or cause to be seen.–I will *show* you my stamp collection.–Mother *showed* pleasure at the compliment.
2. Be visible.–Mother's slip was longer than her dress, so it *showed.*
3. Teach by doing.–Our teacher *showed* us how to make a kite. She taught us by letting us watch her do it first.
4. Point out to.–The clerk *showed* us where to buy stockings.

show•case (SHOH-kayss) *n. showcases.* A glass case where things are put so that they can be seen or looked at. – We saw the rings and watches in the *showcase* in the jeweler's window.

show•er (SHOW-er) *n. showers.* 1. A short rainstorm.–We had a *shower* this morning.
2. Anything that falls like a shower of rain. –A *shower* of paper came from the office windows.
3. A bath in which water is showered down from above.–Bob takes a *shower* every morning.
–*v. showers, showered, showering.* Drop, or rain down.–The children *showered* rice upon the bride and groom.–It *showered* today.

shown (SHOHN) *v.* One form of the verb *show.*–The books were *shown* to the children.

shrank (SHRANGK) *v.* One form of the verb *shrink.* – Mary's dress *shrank* when it was washed.

shred (SHRED) *n. shreds.* 1. Narrow strip or rag.–The old flag was burned because it was worn into *shreds.*
2. Bit.–Not one *shred* of food was left after the picnic.
–*v. shreds, shredded, shredding.* Cut into small strips.–Mother *shredded* the cabbage.

shrewd (SHROOD) *adj.; shrewdly, adv.* Sharp and clever; quick-witted, especially in business dealings.–Mr. Greene is a *shrewd* businessman.

shriek (SHREEK) *n. shrieks.* A scream; a loud piercing sound like one made by a whistle, or a person who is afraid, hurt, or angry.
–*v. shrieks, shrieked, shrieking.* Make this noise.–The police siren *shrieked* as it passed.

shrill (SHRIL) *v. shrills, shrilled, shrilling.* Make a high piercing sound. – The birds *shrilled* loudly. They called out in high, sharp voices.
–*adj. shriller, shrillest; shrilly, adv.*–High and piercing in tone.–Whistles and police sirens make *shrill* sounds.

shrimp (SHRIMP) *n. shrimps.* 1. A kind of small shellfish. – The meat of *shrimps* is good to eat.
2. A little person (often used scornfully). – Jack's feelings were hurt when the big boys called him a *shrimp.*

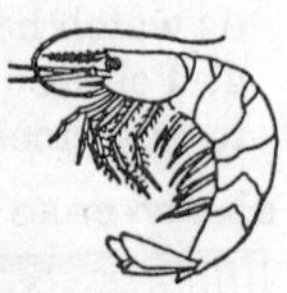

shrine (SHRYN) *n. shrines.* Any place or thing that is sacred or holy or held in reverence.–The Lincoln Memorial is a *shrine* because it is loved and held as a sacred symbol by Americans.

shrink (SHRINGK) *v. shrinks, shrank, shrinking.* 1. Become or make smaller.–If Baby's stockings *shrink* when they are washed, she will not be able to wear them.
2. Draw back or away.–The horse is so afraid that it *shrinks* every time it sees a whip.

shriv•el (SHRIV-əl) *v. shrivels, shriveled* or *shrivelled, shriveling* or *shrivelling.* Dry up; wrinkle; wither.–The apple was *shriveled.*

shrub (SHRUB) *n. shrubs.* A bush or low tree with many stems that come from the ground

instead of from a trunk, as those of most trees do.–*Shrubs* are used around houses and in gardens.

shrub•ber•y (SHRUB-ə-ree) *n. shrubberies.* A group of low bushes or shrubs.

shrug (SHRUG) *n. shrugs.* A raising of the shoulders to show that one is not sure about something, or does not care, or does not like something.
–*v. shrugs, shrugged, shrugging.* Raise the shoulders in a shrug. – When the teacher asked Bill a question, he just *shrugged* his shoulders.

shrunk (SHRUNGK) *v.* One form of the verb *shrink.*–After Mother washed Mary's dress, she found that it had *shrunk.*

shuck (SHUK) *n. shucks.* A husk or outer covering. The outer leaves or coverings on ears of corn are *shucks.*

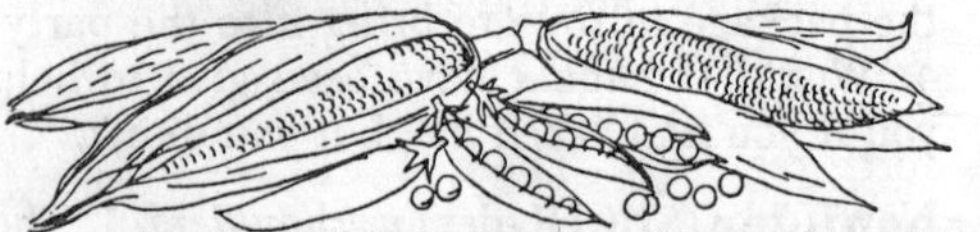

–*v. shucks, shucked, shucking.* Remove shucks from. – The children like to *shuck* corn for Mother.

shud•der (SHUD-er) *n. shudders.* A trembling or shaking caused by fear, horror, disgust, or the like. – Mother gave a *shudder* when Sally showed her the large black snake.
–*v. shudders, shuddered, shuddering.* Tremble with fear, horror, or disgust.–The ghost story Jack told made us all *shudder.*

shuf•fle (SHUF-əl) *v. shuffles, shuffled, shuffling.* 1. Walk, barely lifting the feet.–The gardener was so tired that he just *shuffled* along.
2. Mix up (cards).–Bob likes to *shuffle* the cards when we play card games.

shun (SHUN) *v. shuns, shunned, shunning.* Keep away from or avoid. – Father *shuns* driving during times when there is heavy traffic.

shut (SHUT) *v. shuts, shut, shutting.* 1. Close. –Please *shut* the door when you leave.
2. Keep out.–The window pane *shuts* out the rain.–Do not *shut* the new boy out of your games.
3. Imprison or close in.–Father *shut* the dog in the garage for the night.
4. Close up.–We have *shut* up our seashore cottage for the winter.
5. Turn (off).–Father forgot to *shut* off the water while he fixed the faucet, and the kitchen got flooded.
–*adj.* Closed.–The store seems to be *shut* for there is no light inside.–Baby's eyes are *shut;* she must be asleep.

shut•ter (SHUT-er) *n. shutters.* A cover for a window, usually on the outside. *Shutters* generally are made of many slats fastened across a frame, and swing on hinges. – We live in a brown house with green *shutters.*

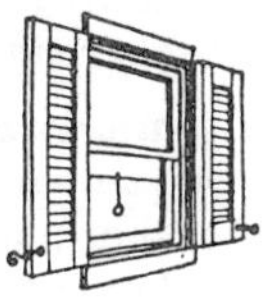

shut•tle (SHUT-l) *n. shuttles.* 1. A sliding thread holder that is used in weaving cloth. The *shuttle* holds the spool of thread that is thrown from side to side between the lengthwise threads.

2. On a sewing machine, the part into which the bobbin or spool that holds the lower thread is put. The *shuttle* goes back and forth when you sew.

3. A train which travels regularly back and forth between two places.

–*v. shuttles, shuttled, shuttling.* Go back and forth regularly.–There is a subway train in New York City which *shuttles* between Grand Central Station and Times Square.

shy (SHY) *v. shies, shied, shying.* 1. Jump to one side; jump away from.–The horse *shied* when it heard the shrill whistle of the express train.

2. Avoid; shrink (away).–Mary is apt to *shy* away from difficult tasks.

–*adj. shyer* or *shier, shyest* or *shiest.* 1. Bashful; uneasy in front of people, especially strangers.–George is very *shy.* He hides in his room whenever company comes.

2. Easily frightened. – Birds are very *shy.* They fly away if you come too near them.

shy•ness (SHY-nəss) *n.* Bashfulness.–The boy's *shyness* was caused by the fact that he had been brought up in the country and was not used to playing with other children.

sick (SIK) *adj. sicker, sickest.* 1. Not well; ill. –Grandmother is *sick* today. She has a bad cold. – When people have measles, or any other disease, they are *sick.*

2. Sick in the stomach.–Sally often gets *sick* from riding in the car.

3. Tired; bored.–Jack is *sick* of working on his model boat.

4. Miserable.–The girl is *sick* with longing to see her family.–Mother was *sick* with worry the night Jack was late coming home.

sick•le (SIK-əl) *n. sickles.* A farm tool with a sharp, curved blade set into a short handle; it is used for cutting grass.–The farmer cut the grass around the barn with a *sickle.*

sick•ness (SIK-nəss) *n. sicknesses.* Illness; bad health.–The man's *sickness* was serious.

side (SYD) *n. sides.* 1. Edge; outline.–Father put rails around the *sides* of the porch so that Baby could not fall off.

2. Not the front, back, top, or bottom, but one of the other two surfaces.–There are portholes in the *sides* of a ship.–The broken window is on the other *side* of the house.

3. A particular face or surface of anything.– Print your name and age and the date on the other *side* of your picture.

4. A section or part.–Father has to drive to the other *side* of town to get to work.

5. An opinion, position, or part in a game, argument, or fight.–Which *side* are you on in the discussion? Whom do you agree with?– Our *side* won the spelling bee.

–*v. sides, sided, siding.* Take the part of; stand up for.–Bob *sides* with Jack in a quarrel with the other boys; he is on Jack's side.

side show (SYD shoh) *side shows.* A small show, usually one of many accompanying a larger show.–There are many *side shows* at the circus.

side•walk (SYD-wawk) *n. sidewalks.* A path made of cement, stone, brick, or other material, at the side of a street or road, for the people on foot to walk on. – It is safer to roller skate on the *sidewalk* than out in the street.

side•wise (SYD-wyz) *adj.* and *adv.* Toward the side, not toward the front or back.–Look *sidewise* before crossing the street.

si•es•ta (see-ESS-tə) *n. siestas.* A short nap or rest taken at midday or in the afternoon. People take *siestas* in Spain, Mexico, and other countries with hot climates.

sieve (SIV) *n. sieves.* A strainer; a kitchen tool that has a fine, screenlike bottom in it so that juice or very small pieces of anything will go through it, but not the larger pieces.–Mother rinses vegetables by putting them in a *sieve* and running water over them.– She sifts flour through a *sieve* to get all the lumps out of it.

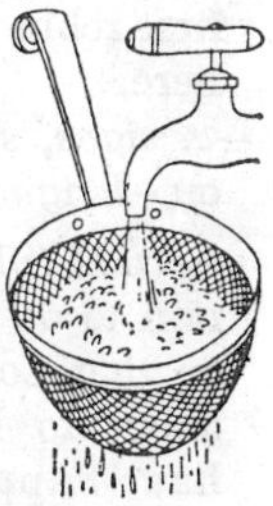

sift (SIFT) *v. sifts, sifted, sifting.* Strain, or put through a screened frame like a sieve, to separate smaller pieces from larger ones.– The workmen *sifted* the gravel.–Mother *sifts* the flour before baking.

sigh (SY) *n. sighs.* A sound made by breathing out a deep, long breath to show that one is tired, sad, or glad, or that something has happened or is over with.
–*v. sighs, sighed, sighing.* Make a sound in this way.–We heard Mary *sigh* as the lecture droned on.

sight (SYT) *n. sights.* 1. Power or ability to see.–People and animals have *sight.* They can see.–Father wears glasses to aid his *sight* when he reads.
2. Something to see.–The flower gardens are a beautiful *sight.*
3. Something seen.–The girl was very happy at the *sight* of her new doll.
4. Aim.–The man took *sight* at the target and then pulled the trigger on his gun.
5. A little piece of metal on the upper side of a gun barrel which helps in aiming at the target.

6. A glimpse; a short look at. – Mother caught *sight* of Bob hiding in the barn.
7. The distance that one can see.–The airplane is now out of *sight.*
–*v. sights, sighted, sighting.* See.–We *sighted* the tall buildings far ahead.

sign (SYN) *n. signs.* 1. A mark or movement used to stand for or mean something.–A red cross on a white background is the *sign* of the Red Cross.–The *sign* for adding is +; – is the *sign* for subtracting.–A nod of the head is a *sign* that one says "yes."
2. A board with lettering on it to advertise goods, name the owner of a shop or office, or tell anything else to people who see it.–Road *signs* say "Slow," "10 Miles to Detroit," etc.

3. A thing that tells that something exists, is about to happen, or has happened. – The first robin is a *sign* that spring will soon be here.
–*v. signs, signed, signing.* Write one's name on.–I *signed* the letter.

sig·nal (SIG-nəl) *n. signals.* A sign or indication to do something, or that something is about to happen, or has happened. – A green traffic light is the "go" *signal.* – The janitor gave the fire-drill *signal.* He rang the bell five times.

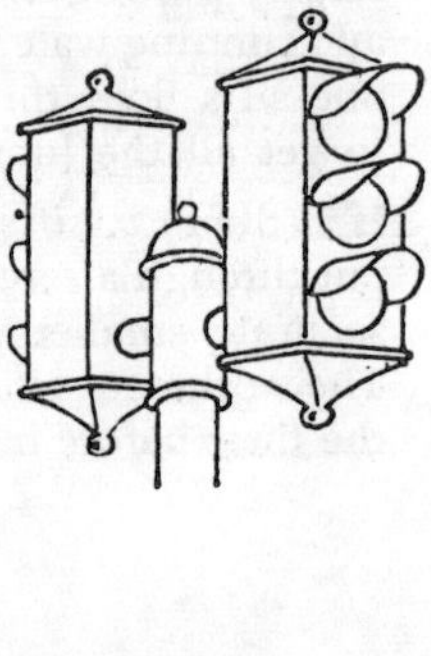

–*v. signals, signaled* or *signalled, signaling* or *signalling.* Tell by means of a signal.–The catcher *signaled* the pitcher to pitch a curve.

sig·na·ture (SIG-nə-cher) *n. signatures.* 1. One's own name, written by oneself. – The teacher put her *signature* on Bob's excuse to go home when he felt ill.

2. A sign written at the beginning of music to tell the time and the key in which the music is written.–The children looked at the *signature* before starting to sing the music.

sig·nif·i·cance (sig-NIF-ə-kənss) *n.* 1. A meaning. – The children did not know the *significance* of the bell's ringing at eleven o'clock.–Do you know the *significance* of the American eagle?
2. Importance.–Father got a letter of great *significance* to his business.

sig·nif·i·cant (sig-NIF-ə-kənt) *adj.; significantly, adv.* 1. Important.–The principal made a *significant* statement today. He said there would be no school tomorrow.
2. Carrying meaning; having meaning. – Father and Mother exchange many *significant* looks around Christmas time.

sig·ni·fy (SIG-nə-fy) *v. signifies, signified, signifying.* 1. Mean.–A red traffic light *signifies* danger.–This sign * next to a word usually *signifies* a note at the bottom of the page.
2. Make known; express.–If you are pleased with the music, *signify* it by clapping.

sign·post (SYN-pohst) *n. signposts.* A post with a sign or message fastened to it. – The sign on the *signpost* read, "No Hunting Allowed."

si·lence (SY-lənss) *n. silences.* A stillness, quietness, or absence of noise or sound.–The *silence* of the country is restful after the noise of the city.
–*v. silences, silenced, silencing.* Make quiet or make still.–Mother *silenced* Baby's crying by feeding her.

si·lent (SY-lənt) *adj.; silently, adv.* 1. Quiet; still; without sound.–The children were *silent* while their teacher read to them.–In *silent* reading we do not say the words out loud. We read to ourselves.
2. Not pronounced. – The "e" in the word "make" is *silent.* It is not pronounced.

sil•hou•ette (sil-ə-WET) *n. silhouettes.* 1. A picture showing only the outline of a form with the rest of the form filled in in black. A *silhouette* is usually painted on or fastened to a light surface so that it will show up easily.
2. Anything that the light strikes in such a way that all you can see is the dark form.—At dusk the tall buildings of the city form a *silhouette* against the sky.

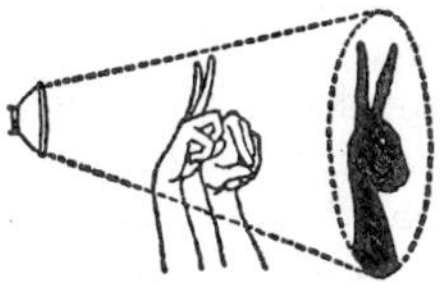

3. Outline.—Mary didn't like the *silhouette* of the skirt she tried on. It was straight and she likes her skirts to balloon out at the sides.

silk (SILK) *n. silks; silken, adj.* A kind of fine, shiny thread made by silkworms. These threads are woven into cloth which is also called *silk.*
—*adj.* Made of silk thread or cloth.—Grandmother wore *silk* stockings.

silk•worm (SILK-werm) *n. silkworms.* A caterpillar that makes a cocoon of silken threads from which silk is made. — *Silkworms* eat mulberry leaves.

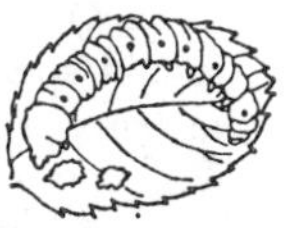

sill (SIL) *n. sills.* A ledge or shelf across the bottom of the frame of a window, door, or building.—Mary set the plants on the window *sill,* where they would get the sun.—Today Mother scrubbed the door *sill.*—When the men tore down the house, they found that the *sills* were rotten.

sil•ly (SIL-ee) *adj. sillier, silliest.* Foolish; giddy. — The children were playing a *silly* game. It didn't make much sense but it was a lot of fun.

si•lo (SY-loh) *n. silos.* A tall, round, towerlike building made of wood, stone, cement, or brick. Sometimes a *silo* is a large hole in the ground.—The farmer puts green food or grain in a *silo* to keep it for his cows. Air cannot get to the grain in a *silo* and so the grain does not spoil.

silt (SILT) *n.* Bits of sand, earth, rock, etc., carried or deposited in water.—The sediment at the bottom of the river contains mud, clay, *silt,* and pebbles.

sil•ver (SIL-ver) *n.* 1. A kind of soft, whitish, valuable metal. — Some knives, forks, and spoons are made of *silver.*—*Silver* shines when it is polished.
—*adj.* 1. Made of silver.—I have a *silver* dollar.
2. Pale gray, bright and shiny.—Grandfather has *silver* hair.

sil•ver•ware (SIL-ver-wair) *n.* Knives, forks, spoons, and other tableware made out of silver.—Mary put the *silverware* on the table for Mother.

sim•i•lar (SIM-ə-ler) *adj.; similarly, adv.* Very much alike; about the same.—Mary did not buy the dress because it was too *similar* to the one she had.

sim•ple (SIM-pəl) *adj. simpler, simplest.* 1. Easy to understand.—This dictionary is very *simple.*
2. Plain; not fancy; not trimmed much. — Mary's new dress is quite *simple.*
3. Weak-minded; stupid. — The clown pretended to be *simple.*

sim•ple•ton (SIM-pəl-tn) *n. simpletons.* A very stupid or weak-minded person.—Simple Simon in the nursery rhyme is a *simpleton.*

sim•plic•i•ty (sim-PLISS-ə-tee) *n.* Plainness; quality of being simple, or of not being complicated.—The *simplicity* of the arithmetic problems made Jack smile. He thought they were too easy.

sim•ply (SIM-plee) *adv.* 1. Plainly. — The woman was dressed *simply.*
2. Just.—It is easy to find our house; you *simply* turn left at the next corner.

sin (SIN) *n. sins.* A wrong-doing; a bad act or deed.—It is a *sin* to kill, steal, or do any other evil thing.
—*v. sins, sinned, sinning.* To do something evil.

since (SINSS) *adv.* 1. From that time until now.—It started raining Sunday and it has rained ever *since.*
2. At some time between that time and now. —Yesterday Father said he could not go, but *since* then he has changed his mind.
3. Before now; ago. — The postman has passed our house long *since.*
—*conj.* Because; seeing that.—*Since* it is your birthday, you may stay up an hour later.
—*prep.* Ever after.—Bob has felt much better *since* last month when he got over his cold.

sin•cere (sin-SIR) *adj.; sincerely, adv.* Honest; not deceitful. – Grandmother is a very *sincere* person. She doesn't try to fool you.

sin•ew (SIN-yoo) *n. sinews; sinewy, adj.* A cord which fastens muscles to bones.–Bob strained the *sinews* in his ankle when he slipped.

sin•ful (SIN-fuhl) *adj.; sinfully, adv.; sinfulness, n.* Evil; wicked.–The man is *sinful.* He does evil, wicked deeds.

sing (SING) *v. sings, sang, singing.* 1. Make music with the voice.–The teacher plays the piano when the children *sing.*–Sometimes they hum and sometimes they *sing* the words.
2. Make a humming or whistling sound.–When the teakettle makes a humming sound, we say that it *sings.*–Birds *sing,* too.

singe (SINJ) *v. singes, singed, singeing.* Burn slightly.–When Mother got her fur coat too near the fire, she *singed* the fur.

sing•er (SING-er) *n. singers.* A person who makes music with his voice.

sin•gle (SING-gəl) *n. singles.* A hit in baseball which allows the batter to get to first base.–Bob's *single* drove in the winning run.
–*v. singles, singled, singling.* 1. Pick.–The policeman *singled* out the boy who had saved the child from being struck by the car.
2. Hit a single in baseball.–Bob *singled* and the boy on third ran to home plate.
–*adj.; singly, adv.* 1. One.–A *single* cookie was left on the plate.
2. Made for one only; having one.–We have a *single*-car garage. It holds only one car.
3. Not married.–My Uncle Alex is married, but my Uncle Paul is still *single.*

sin•gu•lar (SING-gyə-ler) *adj.; singularly, adv.* 1. Only one.–The word "boy" is *singular;* it means only one boy. If we mean more than one boy, we say "boys."
2. Strange; queer. – It is very *singular* that the cat was able to get into the house when all the doors were closed.

sink (SINGK) *n. sinks.* A basin with a pipe to drain off whatever is poured in. – Mary poured the water out of the glass into the kitchen *sink.*

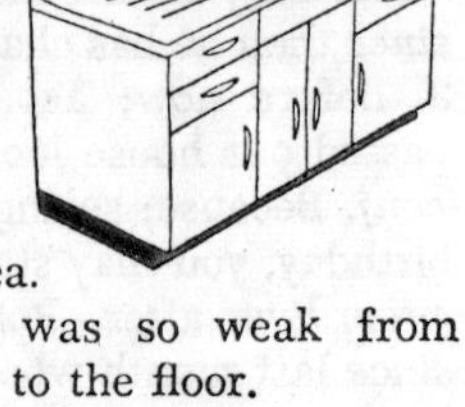

–*v. sinks, sank, sinking.* 1. Go down. – Boats sometimes *sink* to the bottom of the sea.
2. Fall slowly. – Tom was so weak from laughing that he *sank* to the floor.

sink•er (SINGK-er) *n. sinkers.* A small piece of lead put on the end of a fishing line to pull the hook deep into the water.

sin•ner (SIN-er) *n. sinners.* A person who does bad or wrong things.

si•nus (SY-nəss) *n. sinuses.* One of the air spaces in the front of the skull. The *sinuses* are lined with mucous membrane and connect with the passages of the nose. When the mucous membrane of the nose becomes inflamed, the *sinuses* are often affected the same way.

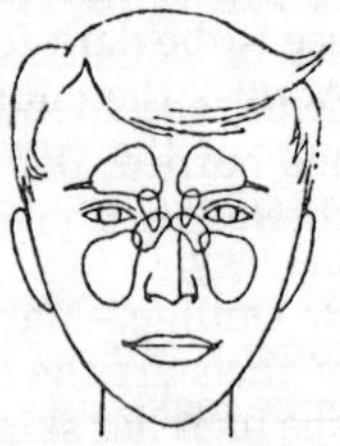

sip (SIP) *n. sips.* A small drink; a swallow.–Take a *sip* of this lemonade.
–*v. sips, sipped, sipping.* Drink slowly in small amounts.–Do not drink ice water too fast. *Sip* it.

sir (SER) *n. sirs.* A title of honor or respect used in speaking to older men or officers of the army or navy.–Bob said to the policeman, "Will you help me, *sir?*"–Mary started her business letter with the words "Dear *Sir.*"

si•ren (SY-rən) *n. sirens.* A kind of whistle which makes a loud noise by whirling around. –After the accident, we heard the sound of the *siren* on the ambulance.–The fire engine had a very loud *siren.*

sir•up or **syr•up** (SIR- *or* SER-əp) *n. sirups* or *syrups.* A liquid made of sugar or other sweet substance.–We eat *syrup* on pancakes and waffles.

sis•ter (SISS-ter) *n. sisters.* 1. A girl or woman born of the same parents as another person. –Mary is Bob's *sister.* Mary and Bob have the same father and mother.
2. A nun.–The *sister* was good to the child.

sis•ter-in-law (SISS-ter-in-law) *n. sisters-in-law.* The sister of one's wife or husband, or the wife of one's brother.–Your mother's sister is your father's *sister-in-law.* – Your father's sister is your mother's *sister-in-law.* –The wife of your mother's brother is your mother's *sister-in-law.* – The wife of your father's brother is your father's *sister-in-law.*

sit (SIT) *v. sits, sat, sitting.* 1. Rest on the backs of the thighs or upper part of the legs. –Bob *sits* in a big chair.
2. Remain; stand; perch.–Chickens *sit* on a roost at night.

site (SYT) *n. sites.* A location; place to put a building or other structure.–A new post office will be built on this *site.*

sit•u•at•ed (SI-choo-ay-təd) *adj.* Located or placed.–An old house is *situated* on top of the hill.

sit•u•a•tion (si-choo-AY-shən) *n. situations.* Set of conditions.–When Mother returned home, she found a bad *situation:* the meat had burned, Baby was sick, and the dog had chewed up a pillow.

six (SIKS) *n. sixes* and *adj.* The number [6] coming after 5 and before 7. – Three and three make *six.*

six•pence (SIKS-pənss) *n. sixpences.* A piece of money used in England and some other countries. It is worth about seven cents of United States money.

six•teen (siks-TEEN) *n. sixteens* and *adj.* The number [16] after 15 and before 17.–Ten and six make *sixteen.*

six•teenth (siks-TEENTH) *n. sixteenths.* One of 16 equal parts.–If you divide anything into sixteen parts all the same size, each part is one *sixteenth.* It may be written 1/16.
–*adj.* Coming as number 16 in a series.–My name was *sixteenth* on the list.

sixth (SIKSTH) *n. sixths.* One of 6 equal parts.–If you divide anything into six parts all the same size, each part is one *sixth.* It may be written 1/6.
–*adj.* Coming as number 6 in a series.–Sue's name is *sixth* on the list.

six•ti•eth (SIKS-tee-ith) *n. sixtieths.* One of 60 equal parts.–If you divide anything into sixty parts all the same size, each part is one *sixtieth.* It may be written 1/60.
–*adj.* Coming as number 60 in a series.–Mike's name was *sixtieth* on the list.

six•ty (SIKS-tee) *n. sixties* and *adj.* The number [60] coming after 59 and before 61. –Thirty and thirty make *sixty.*

size (SYZ) *n. sizes.* The bigness or smallness of a thing; the amount of room or space a thing takes up.–The *size* of an elephant is large compared with the *size* of a dog.–I wear *size* 7 shoes and Mary wears *size* 6 shoes.

siz•zle (SIZ-əl) *v. sizzles, sizzled, sizzling.* Make sputtering and hissing sounds, as frying fat does.–The steaks are *sizzling* on the platter.

skate (SKAYT) *n. skates.* 1. A short runner attached to a shoe for gliding over ice.

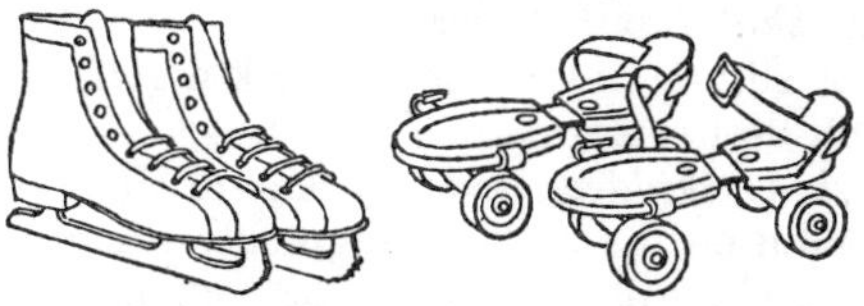

2. A platform with four wheels attached to the shoe for rolling over any smooth surface.
–*v. skates, skated, skating.* Glide on skates or roller skates.–Bob likes to *skate* on the pond in the winter.

skat•er (SKAY-ter) *n. skaters.* A person who skates.–Bob is a good *skater.*

skein (SKAYN) *n. skeins.* An amount of yarn put up in long loops. –Mary helped wind a *skein* of wool into a ball.

skel•e•ton (SKEL-ə-tn) *n. skeletons.* 1. A bony framework. – This picture shows the *skeleton* of a person's body.
2. A framework of any kind.–The *skeleton* of a house is of wood.

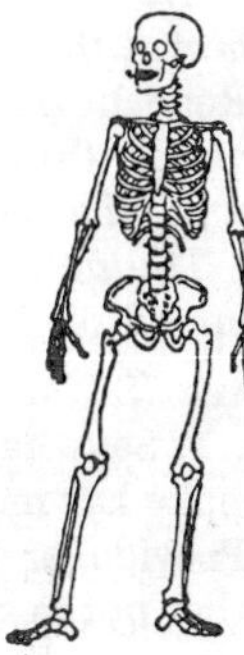

skel•e•ton key (SKEL-ə-tn kee) *skeleton keys.* A key which opens many different locks.

sketch (SKECH) *n. sketches.* 1. A rough drawing.–Bob showed the *sketch* of the plane to Father.
2. A short play or story.–The children gave some little *sketches* about school life as part of their show.
–*v. sketches, sketched, sketching.* Draw a rough picture or outline of.–Jack *sketched* the house.

ski (SKEE) *n. skis.* One of two long wooden runners that are fastened to the shoes for gliding over snow.

–*v. skis, skied, skiing.* Glide on skis.–It is fun to *ski* in winter.

skid (SKID) *n. skids.* 1. A runway to slide something on.–The logs were sent down a long *skid* into the river.
2. A slip; a slide.–The car took a *skid* as it went up the icy road.
–*v. skids, skidded, skidding.* Slip or slide.–Do not put on the brakes too quickly when you are driving on icy streets, or your car may *skid.*

skill (SKIL) *n. skills.* Ability to do a certain thing well as a result of practice.–Bob shows much *skill* in baseball.

skil•let (SKIL-it) *n. skillets.* A heavy, shallow, metal pan with a long handle. A *skillet* is used for frying foods.

skill•ful or **skil•ful** (SKIL-fuhl) *adj.; skillfully, adv.* Expert; having much ability.–A *skillful* workman is one who knows much about his work and does it very well.

skim (SKIM) *v. skims, skimmed, skimming.* 1. Take off from the top. – Mary helped Grandmother *skim* the cream from the milk.
2. Move lightly over. – The speedboat *skimmed* the water.
3. Read hurriedly and not thoroughly.–Bob *skimmed* through the story just to get an idea of what it was about.
–*adj.* The milk that is left after the cream is skimmed off is *skim* milk.

skimp (SKIMP) *v. skimps, skimped, skimping.* 1. Save carefully.–Mother has to *skimp* to make her money last all week.
2. Provide or use too little of. – Bob told Mother not to *skimp* the frosting on the cake.

skimp•y (SKIMP-ee) *adj. skimpier, skimpiest.* Not enough; too little.–Sally gave Ann a *skimpy* portion of green beans. She did not know how much Ann could eat.

skin (SKIN) *n. skins.* The outer covering of the body of a person, animal, vegetable, or fruit. – If you cut through the *skin* on your hand, it will bleed.–Bob cut off the *skin,* or peel, of the orange.

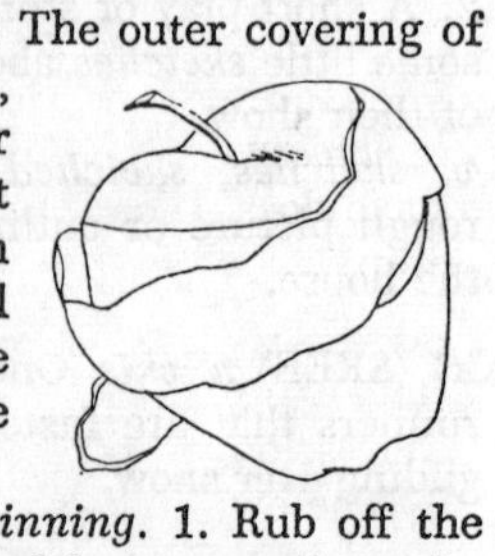

–*v. skins, skinned, skinning.* 1. Rub off the skin of.–Mary *skinned* her arm when she ran into the stone wall.
2. Remove the skin from. – The butcher *skinned* the rabbit so that it could be cooked.

skin•ny (SKIN-ee) *adj. skinnier, skinniest.* Thin; lean; not fat. – The hungry cat is *skinny.*

skip (SKIP) *v. skips, skipped, skipping.* 1. Jump or move with little hopping steps.–Children like to *skip* over a rope.–The girls *skipped* to the music.
2. Pass over.–Bob was so anxious to finish the book that he *skipped* some pages. He didn't read them.–Tom was in such a hurry to finish his speech that he *skipped* some of the points he had planned to make.

skip•per (SKIP-er) *n. skippers.* A commander of a boat or ship.–Bob stood in the pilot house with the *skipper.*

skirt (SKERT) *n. skirts.* The part of a dress that hangs from the waist down.–Mary wears a sweater and *skirt.*

–*v. skirts, skirted, skirting.* Pass along the outer edge of.–We *skirted* the city to avoid the heavy traffic.

skull (SKUL) *n. skulls.* The bones of the head that form a case for the brain and support the face.–The man's *skull* was fractured in the accident.

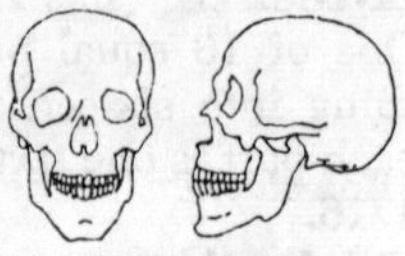

skunk (SKUNGK) *n. skunks.* A small animal that has black fur with white stripes down the back, and a bushy tail. *Skunks* protect themselves by giving off a very unpleasant odor when they are frightened or hurt.

sky (SKY) *n. skies.* The air high above us.–On clear days, the *sky* looks blue.–Birds fly high in the *sky.*–The *sky* is often called heaven, or the heavens.

sky•light (SKY-lyt) *n. skylights.* A window set in a roof or ceiling.–Artists' studios usually have *skylights* to let in more daylight.

sky•rock•et (SKY-rahk-it) *n. skyrockets.* A firework on a stick that shoots high into the sky and then explodes.–On the Fourth of July, we shot off many *skyrockets.*

sky·scrap·er (SKY-skray-per) *n. skyscrapers.* A very tall building.—We saw the *skyscrapers* as we came nearer to the city.

slack (SLAK) *n.* Looseness, or loose part. — When the dog ran he took up the *slack* in the rope.
—*adj. slacker, slackest.* 1. Loose. — The rope walker said the rope was too *slack* to walk on. He asked to have it pulled tighter.
2. Quiet; not active.—Spring is a *slack* season for people who sell ice skates. Not many people buy ice skates in the spring.
3. Careless.—I was *slack* about getting my arithmetic paper in on time. Miss Jones asked me to try and be more prompt the next time.

slack·en (SLAK-ən) *v. slackens, slackened, slackening.* 1. Slow down.—Much work must still be done, so do not *slacken* now.—When one is tired, his energy *slackens.*
2. Become loose.—When it rains, the clothesline *slackens.* When it is dry, it tightens.

slacks (SLAKS) *n. pl.* Trousers; long pants. —When Ruth goes on a hike, she wears *slacks.*

slag (SLAG) *n.* The waste matter left over after metals have been separated from their ores.

slain (SLAYN) *v.* One form of the verb *slay.* —The bear was *slain* by the hunter.

slam (SLAM) *n. slams.* A noise made by shutting something with a bang.—We knew Jack had come home because we heard the *slam* of the front door.
—*v. slams, slammed, slamming.* Shut with a bang or with much force.—Do not *slam* the window. You may break the glass if you do.

slang (SLANG) *n.* Made-up words and expressions that are used mostly in talk.—The sleepy man said, "It's time to hit the hay." He meant it was time to go to bed. — "Step on it!" is *slang* for "Hurry!"

slant (SLANT) *n.* A leaning to one side. — Mother writes without any *slant* to her letters. She writes straight up and down.
—*v. slants, slanted, slanting.* Slope. — Most roofs *slant.*—The flagpole stands straight up, but the roof *slants* downward from the top.

slap (SLAP) *n. slaps.* A blow with the open hand.—Mother gave the dog a gentle *slap.*
—*v. slaps, slapped, slapping.* Hit with the open hand. — When the dog got onto the chair, Mother *slapped* him gently to teach him not to do it.

slash (SLASH) *n. slashes.* A long cut or slit. —The Boy Scouts' tent had a *slash* in one side, and the rain came in.
—*v. slashes, slashed, slashing.* To cut.—Someone *slashed* the tent accidentally with a jackknife.

slat (SLAT) *n. slats.* A thin, narrow bar of wood or metal. — Grandfather nailed some *slats* across the chicken coop to keep the chickens in.—Bedsprings are held up by *slats.*

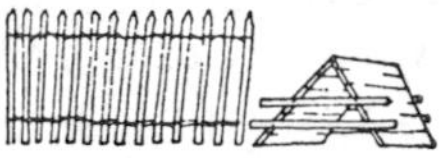

slate (SLAYT) *n. slates.* 1. A smooth blue-gray rock that splits into thin layers.—Our blackboard is made of *slate.*
2. A framed square of slate. — When Father went to school, the children used *slates* to write on.
—*adj.* Bluish-gray. — Mother has a *slate*-colored suit.

slaugh·ter (SLAW-ter) *n. slaughters.* Killing or butchering.—The farmer led the lamb to the *slaughter.*
—*v. slaughters, slaughtered, slaughtering.* Kill; butcher. — The farmer *slaughtered* a lamb today.

slave (SLAYV) *n. slaves.* A person who is owned by another person and can be sold by that person. A *slave* works without pay. There are no *slaves* in this country any more.
—*v. slaves, slaved, slaving.* Work as hard as a slave does.—The mother *slaves* for her children.

slav·er·y (SLAY-və-ree) *n.* 1. Condition of a slave. — The captives of the ancient army were sold into *slavery.*
2. The owning of slaves.—*Slavery* was abolished in this country during the Civil War.

slaw (SLAW) *n. slaws.* A salad made by chopping cabbage into long, fine shreds and then adding vinegar dressing.

slay (SLAY) *v. slays, slew, slaying.* Kill with force.—The stained-glass window shows St. George *slaying* the dragon.

slay·er (SLAY-er) *n. slayers.* A person who kills another.–The police are tracking down the *slayer.*

sled (SLED) *n. sleds.* A low platform on runners that slides easily over snow.–Children like to coast on a *sled.*

–*v. sleds, sledded, sledding.* Ride on a sled.–We went *sledding* after the snowfall.

sledge (SLEJ) *n. sledges.* A large, heavy hammer. – The men drove the posts into the ground with a *sledge.*

sleek (SLEEK) *adj.; sleekly, adv.; sleekness, n.* Smooth and glossy.–The kitten's fur is *sleek.*

sleep (SLEEP) *n.* Slumber or rest. – Father had only four hours' *sleep* last night because he got to bed so late.

–*v. sleeps, slept, sleeping.* Slumber; rest the mind and body; fall naturally into an unawareness of the things around one.–When we *sleep* at night we close our eyes.

sleep·er (SLEE-per) *n. sleepers.* 1. A person sleeping.–Mother was never a late *sleeper.* 2. A railroad car that has berths, or beds, for sleeping.–Father made the long railroad trip in a *sleeper.*

sleep·less (SLEEP-ləss) *adj.; sleeplessly, adv.; sleeplessness, n.* Restless; wakeful; without sleep.–It was so hot that Mother had a *sleepless* night.

sleep·y (SLEE-pee) *adj. sleepier, sleepiest.* Drowsy; ready to go to sleep.–When Baby is *sleepy,* Mother puts her to bed.

sleet (SLEET) *n.; sleety, adj.* Rain that freezes into tiny pieces of ice as it falls. – *Sleet* covered the streets and made them very slippery.–*Sleet* rattled on the windowpanes.

sleeve (SLEEV) *n. sleeves.* The part of a coat, dress, or other garment that covers the arm.

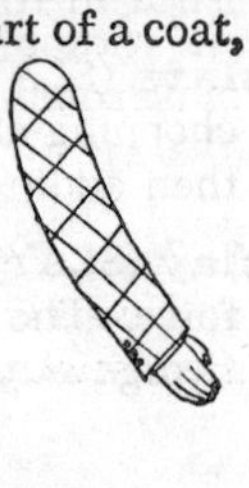

sleeve·less (SLEEV-ləss) *adj.* Without sleeves; ending at the shoulder of the garment. – Men's vests are *sleeveless.*

sleigh (SLAY) *n. sleighs.* A large sled. *Sleighs* are pulled by horses.

slen·der (SLEN-der) *adj.; slenderness, n.* Thin; slim.–Mother is *slender,* but Father is stout.

slept (SLEPT) *v.* One form of the verb *sleep.*–Baby *slept* soundly all night.

slice (SLYSS) *n. slices.* A thin, flat piece. – Mother cut the watermelon into *slices.*

–*v. slices, sliced, slicing.* Cut into thin, flat pieces.–Mary *sliced* the bread for Mother.

slick·er (SLIK-er) *n. slickers.* A raincoat; a waterproof coat.–On rainy days Jack keeps dry by wearing his *slicker.*

slide (SLYD) *n. slides.* 1. Anything on which something can move smoothly and easily.–The picture shows a *slide* for the children to go down.

2. A thin piece of glass on which there is a picture, which may be thrown on a screen by a projector.–Our teacher showed us some *slides* of animals at the zoo.

3. A small sheet of glass to put something on to look at through a microscope.

–*v. slides, slid, sliding.* Move smoothly and easily.–Children like to *slide* down a hill on their sleds.

slight (SLYT) *v. slights, slighted, slighting.* 1. Neglect, or give too little attention to. – Do not *slight* your work, or you may not pass. 2. Neglect, or treat rudely.–Bob *slighted* Sy by not asking him to play.

–*adj. slighter, slightest.* 1. Slim; slender. – Grandmother is *slight.* She's short and thin. 2. Little; small; not great.–The man at the store said there would be a *slight* charge for delivering the table.

slim (SLIM) *adj. slimmer, slimmest.* 1. Thin; slight; slender. – Mary has a *slim* waist. Her waist is not very big around.

2. Small; slight.–We have a *slim* chance of winning the game if Bob does not play.

sling (SLING) *n. slings.* 1. A device for throwing stones or other small objects. It is made of two cords joined by a piece of leather or cloth which holds the stone while the cords are whirled around in the air.–A *sling*shot has a forked stick through which the stone is shot by the force of rubber bands.

2. A piece of cloth looped about the neck.–When Jack broke his arm, he supported it with a *sling*.

3. A chain or heavy rope used to lift heavy things.–Boats are unloaded with *slings*.

–*v. slings, slung, slinging.* Hang. –When Jack goes on a hike, he *slings* his knapsack over his shoulder.

slip (SLIP) *n. slips.* 1. A mistake. – Do not make a *slip* of the tongue and tell Mother about her present.

2. A woman's undergarment.–Mother wears a *slip* under her dress.

3. A cutting; little branches cut from other plants.–These plants grew from *slips*.

–*v. slips, slipped, slipping.* 1. Slide; move quickly and smoothly.–These shoes *slip* on easily.

2. Slide accidentally and fall. – The dish *slipped* through my fingers and fell.

3. To cause to move quickly and easily.–Bob *slipped* the candy into his pocket.

4. Pass quickly.–The day at the farm *slipped* by before we knew it.

5. To move around quietly.–He *slipped* in and out without being seen.

slip·knot (SLIP-naht) *n. slipknots.* A knot made so that if you pull the cord, the knot will slide along the cord.

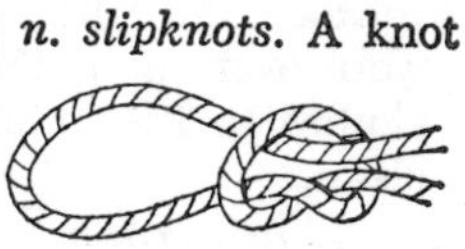

slip·per (SLIP-er) *n. slippers.* A light shoe that slips onto the foot easily.–Mother has silver evening *slippers*.

slip·per·y (SLIP-ə-ree) *adj. slipperier, slipperiest.* Easy to slide or slip on; too smooth to get a firm hold on.–A waxed floor and an icy street are *slippery*.–Fish are *slippery*.

slit (SLIT) *n. slits.* A straight cut, tear, or opening. – A ray of light streamed through the *slit* in the barn door.

–*v. slits, slit, slitting.* Cut a long line in.–The doctor *slit* the soldier's coat so that he could dress his wounds.

sliv·er (SLIV-er) *n. slivers.* A long, thin piece of wood or metal that has been cut off or broken off a larger piece; a splinter. – Father got a *sliver* of wood in his thumb while picking up a log.

slo·gan (SLOH-gən) *n. slogans.* A word, a group of words, or a saying used as a motto.–"We work to win" is the *slogan* of our class.

sloop (SLOOP) *n. sloops.* A sailboat with one mast and at least one mainsail and jib.

slope (SLOHP) *n. slopes.* Slanting land.–The children climbed the *slope* to the top of the hill.

–*v. slopes, sloped, sloping.* Slant. – The hill *slopes* downward to the river.–Since the roof *slopes*, water rolls off it when it rains.

sloth (SLOHTH *or* SLAWTH) *n. sloths.* A hairy animal that lives in South America. It eats leaves and fruits, lives in trees, and hangs upside down.

slouch (SLOWCH) *v. slouches, slouched, slouching.* Move, walk, or sit in a lazy, drooping way.–Do not *slouch* at your desk or you will spoil your posture.

–*slouch, n. slouches.*

slow (SLOH) *v. slows, slowed, slowing.* Go slower; go with less speed. – Always *slow* down when you come to a corner while on your bicycle.

–*adj. slower, slowest; slowly, adv.* 1. Not fast or quick.–Bob is rather *slow* in doing his work. He takes a lot of time.

2. Behind time.–Bob was late because his watch was 15 minutes *slow*. His watch said 8:15 when it was really 8:30.

3. Dull; not bright.–A *slow* person does not learn quickly or easily.

slug (SLUG) *n. slugs.* 1. A slow-moving animal something like a snail, but without a shell. – Mary found some *slugs* in the garden.

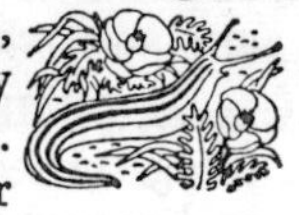

2. A metal bullet.–The hunter had a pocket full of *slugs* for his gun.

–*v. slugs, slugged, slugging.* Hit hard. – The man was *slugged* by the robber and left lying unconscious.

slum (SLUM) *n. slums.* A very dirty and crowded part of a city, where poor people live.

slum•ber (SLUM-ber) *n. slumbers.* Sleep. –Father didn't want us to disturb his *slumber.*
–*v. slumbers, slumbered, slumbering.* Sleep.–Betty *slumbers* ten hours a night.

slump (SLUMP) *n. slumps.* A falling off. –There was a *slump* in trade last month.
–*v. slumps, slumped, slumping.* Fall or sink down suddenly.–The boy *slumped* over when the ball hit him.

slush (SLUSH) *n.; slushy, adj.* Partly melted snow.–We wore rubbers because of the *slush.*

sly (SLY) *adj. slier* or *slyer, sliest* or *slyest; slyly, adv.* Able to do things secretly, or without letting others see or know.–The kitten was *sly* about trying to catch the goldfish. She waited until we had left the room and then she tried to put her paw in the goldfish bowl.

small (SMAWL) *adj. smaller, smallest.* 1. Little.–A *small* child went up to the policeman and asked him the way to the store.
2. Mean and petty.–It was *small* of the man to report the boy who accidentally broke his window.

small•pox (SMAWL-pahks) *n.* A catching disease that causes fever and a breaking out on the body.–Do not go near a person with *smallpox* or you may get it.–People are vaccinated to prevent *smallpox.*

smart (SMAHRT) *v. smarts, smarted, smarting.* Sting or pain sharply.–When the nurse put the medicine on the cut, it started to *smart.*
–*adj. smarter, smartest; smartly, adv.* 1. Stylish and in good taste.–Mother got a *smart* new spring suit.
2. Quick and clever.–Jack is a *smart* fellow.

smash (SMASH) *v. smashes, smashed, smashing.* 1. Break into many pieces.–When Mary dropped the plate, it *smashed.*
2. Break with force.–The runner *smashed* through the other team's line in the football game. He pushed everyone out of his way and rushed through.
3. Crash or fall heavily and noisily. – The airplane *smashed* into the house.

smear (SMIR) *n. smears.* A spot left by something rubbed on.–Mother had a big *smear* on her new apron.
–*v. smears, smeared, smearing.* Spread or rub over.–Mary *smeared* her hands and face with cold cream.

smell (SMEL) *n. smells.* An odor.–The *smell* of tobacco smoke came from the room.
–*v. smells, smelled, smelling.* 1. Get odors of things through the nose.–We *smell* bacon when it is cooking.
2. Give off an odor.–Roses *smell* sweet.

smelt (SMELT) *v. smelts, smelted, smelting.* Melt ore to separate the metal from the slag; remove impurities from metal by melting; refine. – Huge furnaces are used to *smelt* steel.

smile (SMYL) *n. smiles.* A look of amusement or of happiness. – The new puppy brought a *smile* to the boy's face.
–*v. smiles, smiled, smiling.* Look amused or happy by turning the mouth up at the corners.

smith (SMITH) *n. smiths.* A person who makes things out of metal. – A gold*smith* shapes things out of gold. – A black*smith* shapes horseshoes, wagon tires, and other things out of iron.

smith•y (SMITH-ee) *n. smithies.* The workshop in which a person makes things from iron or other metals.–A blacksmith shop is a *smithy.*

smock (SMAHK) *n. smocks.* A loose gown worn over one's other clothes to keep them clean.

smog (SMAHG) *n.* A mixture of smoke and fog.–*Smog* blanketed the city.

smoke (SMOHK) *n. smokes.* The cloud of tiny particles or vapor that rises from anything burning.–*Smoke* poured out of the big chimney.
–*v. smokes, smoked, smoking.* 1. Breathe in and out the smoke from burning tobacco.–Father *smokes* a pipe.
2. Give off smoke.–The stove *smokes.*
3. Cure (meat) or prepare by exposing to

smoke.—Grandfather *smokes* meat. He hangs it in a small room over a small fire that fills the room with smoke.—Meat that has been *smoked* keeps for a long time.

smoke•stack (SMOHK-stak) *n. smokestacks.* A tall chimney to let out smoke from a furnace.—Smoke poured out of the school *smokestack* when the janitor started the fire in the furnace.

smok•y (SMOH-kee) *adj. smokier, smokiest.* 1. Full of smoke. —Places where there are factories are often *smoky.*
2. Covered or darkened by smoke that has settled.—The windows are *smoky.*

smol•der or **smoul•der** (SMOHL-der) *v. smolders* or *smoulders, smoldered* or *smouldered, smoldering* or *smouldering.* Give off smoke but no flame. — The campfire *smoldered* long after we went to bed.

smooth (SMOOTH) *v. smooths, smoothed, smoothing.* 1. Remove bumps, wrinkles, etc. — Mary *smoothed* the wrinkles out of the tablecloth.—The board was rough, so Father planed and sandpapered it to *smooth* it.
2. Make peaceful and calm.—Bob and Mary quarreled this morning, but they have *smoothed* over their troubles now.
—*adj. smoother, smoothest; smoothly, adv.* 1. Level; even; without bumps or roughness.—A pane of glass is *smooth.*—The lake was not *smooth* because the wind made ripples in it.
2. Free from lumps. — Mother stirred the gravy to make it *smooth.*
3. Evenly moving; in a level course. — We had a *smooth* ride in the boat. It was not jerky and bumpy.

smoth•er (SMUTH-er) *v. smothers, smothered, smothering.* 1. Die from lack of air.—Jim cut air holes in the box before he put the chick in. Otherwise the chick would *smother.*
2. Kill or extinguish by cutting off air from. —Father *smothered* the fire by covering it with dirt.

smudge (SMUJ) *n. smudges.* 1. A dirty mark or spot.—When Mary rubbed the soot on her cheek, it made a *smudge.*
2. A fire that smokes but doesn't blaze.—The campers built a *smudge* to drive away the mosquitoes.
—*v. smudges, smudged, smudging.* Smear; make a dirty mark on.—Baby's face was *smudged* with jelly.

smug (SMUG) *adj.* Too sure of oneself or too pleased with one's own position, brightness, or goodness; self-satisfied.—The girl's *smug* attitude is disliked by most of her classmates. They don't think she's quite so great as she thinks she is.

smug•gle (SMUG-əl) *v. smuggles, smuggled, smuggling.* 1. Take anything in or out of a country secretly when it is against the law to do so.
2. Take in or out secretly.—The boy tried to *smuggle* his dog into school.

smug•gler (SMUG-ler) *n. smugglers.* A person who takes things into or out of a country when it is against the law to do so. — The Coast Guard arrested the *smugglers.*

snag (SNAG) *n. snags.* 1. A branch or stump of a tree under the water.—While rowing the boat, the boys struck a *snag.*
2. Unexpected trouble.—Mother couldn't finish Mary's dress on time, because she struck a *snag.* She ran out of material.
—*v. snags, snagged, snagging.* Catch on something rough or sharp.—Mother *snagged* her stocking. It caught on something rough.

snail (SNAYL) *n. snails.* A slow-moving animal that lives in water and on land. *Snails* have a coiled shell into which they crawl for protection.

snake (SNAYK) *n. snakes.* A long crawling animal without legs. Some *snakes* live on the ground, some in the water. They eat insects, small animals, and the like. Some *snakes* have poisonous bites.

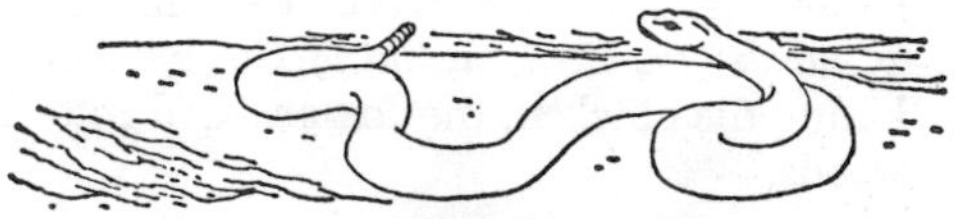

snap (SNAP) *n. snaps.* 1. A quick, sharp noise.—The stick broke with a *snap.*
2. A fastener which clicks when squeezed together.—Some of Mary's dresses have buttons on them and some have *snaps.*
3. A crisp, thin cookie.—Mother makes ginger*snaps.*
—*v. snaps, snapped, snapping.* 1. Make a sudden biting motion; snatch with the teeth.—The dog will not *snap* at you if you do not tease him.—The hungry dog *snapped* up the bone and ran away.
2. Make a sharp cracking noise.—The ice on the branches of the trees made them *snap.*
3. Break suddenly.—The ice made the telephone wire *snap.*

snap·drag·on (SNAP-drag-ən) *n. snapdragons.* A garden flower with blossoms shaped like dragon heads growing along the sides of the stem.

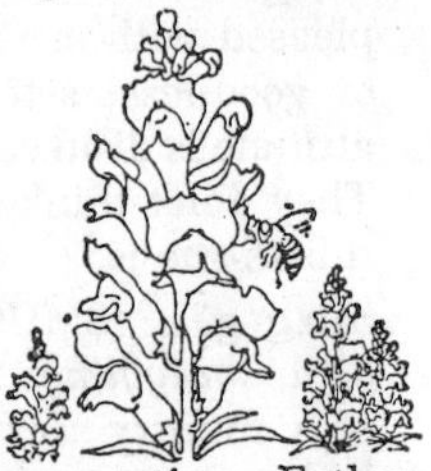

snap·shot (SNAP-shaht) *n. snapshots.* A photograph taken quickly without much preparation.–Father took a *snapshot* of Baby.

snare (SNAIR) *n. snares.* A trap or noose designed to catch birds and small animals.–The trapper caught the rabbit with a *snare.*
–*v. snares, snared, snaring.* Catch with a trap or noose.–The trapper *snares* animals to sell their pelts.

snarl (SNAHRL) *n. snarls.* 1. A growl or curling of the lip.–The lion looked up with a *snarl.*
2. A tangle.–Father could not comb the *snarls* out of Sally's hair.
–*v. snarls, snarled, snarling.* 1. Growl or curl the lip up fiercely.–The little dog *snarled* at the big dog.
2. Tangle.–The kitten *snarled* up Grandmother's yarn by rolling in it.

snatch (SNACH) *n. snatches.* A bit or small part.–Father just read *snatches* of the book.
–*v. snatches, snatched, snatching.* Grab or catch hold of.–A thief tried to *snatch* Mother's purse in the store.–The drowning boy *snatched* at the rope thrown to him.

sneak (SNEEK) *n. sneaks.* A sly, mean person.–The *sneak* who had stolen the money let another man be accused of stealing it.
–*v. sneaks, sneaked, sneaking.* Go slyly.–After killing the chicken, the fox *sneaked* into the woods.

sneer (SNIR) *n. sneers.* A mocking or scornful look or remark.–Bob tries to pay no attention to Bill's *sneers.*
–*v. sneers, sneered, sneering.* Show by the look on one's face that one looks down on a person.–Bill *sneers* at Bob for trying so hard in school.

sneeze (SNEEZ) *v. sneezes, sneezed, sneezing.* Force air out through the nose so hard that it causes a sharp, sudden noise.–A tickling in the nose often causes one to *sneeze.*

sniff (SNIF) *n. sniffs.* Breath; smell.–Take a *sniff* of this perfume.
–*v. sniffs, sniffed, sniffing.* Take little short breaths through the nose.–When a dog smells a rabbit, he *sniffs.*

snip (SNIP) *n. snips.* Quick cut.–With one *snip* Sally cut off the extra string.
–*v. snips, snipped, snipping.* Quickly cut off.–The barber *snipped* Baby's hair.

snipe (SNYP) *n. snipes.* A long-billed bird that lives in marshes.
–*v. snipes, sniped, sniping.* To shoot from a place where one cannot be seen.

snip·er (SNYP-er) *n. snipers.* A soldier who shoots from a place where he cannot be seen by the enemy soldiers.

snoop (SNOOP) *v. snoops, snooped, snooping.* Try to find out about other people's business; pry into things.–Jack likes to *snoop* around in the refrigerator.

snore (SNOR) *v. snores, snored, snoring.* Breathe with a harsh, rough noise while sleeping.–Father *snores* when he naps.

snort (SNORT) *n. snorts.* A sudden noise made by forcing air through the nose.–Jack made a *snort* when Mary said she was going to be the greatest actress in the world.
–*v. snorts, snorted, snorting.* Force air through the nose so that it makes a sudden noise.–Horses *snort.*

snout (SNOWT) *n. snouts.* A long nose that sticks out.–A pig's *snout* is his nose. Other animals have *snouts,* too.

snow (SNOH) *n. snows.* Small, white, star-shaped flakes of frozen water that fall from the sky in winter.–When *snow* melts, it turns into water.
–*v. snows, snowed, snowing.* Drop down snow. –Do you think it will *snow* for Christmas?

snow·ball (SNOH-bawl) *n. snowballs.* 1. A ball made of snow pressed together.–Sally likes to throw *snowballs* at Father.
2. A white flower that grows on a bush.

snow·bound (SNOH-bownd) *adj.* Surrounded by the snow so that one cannot get out. – Grandfather could not go to the city because he was *snowbound.*

snow·drift (SNOH-drift) *n. snowdrifts.* A bank or large pile of snow.–The wind blew the snow into *snowdrifts.*

snow·flake (SNOH-flayk) *n. snowflakes.* One of the small, lacy pieces in which snow falls to the earth.–Mother showed Sally how to catch *snowflakes* on a piece of black velvet.

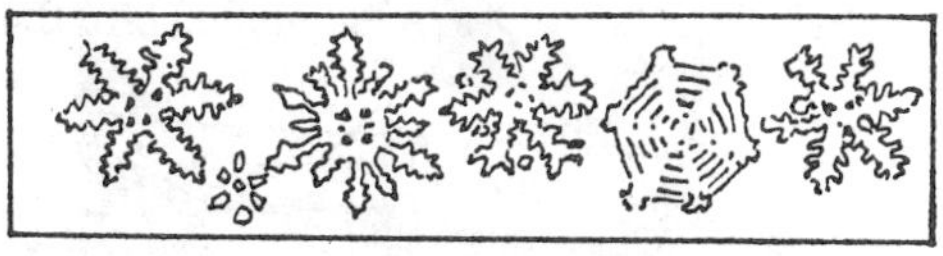

snow·man (SNOH-man) *n. snowmen.* A figure of a man made of snow.–The children put Father's pipe in the *snowman's* mouth.

snow·plow (SNOH-plow) *n. snowplows.* A machine used to push the snow from streets, roads, railroads, and other places.

snow·shoe (SNOH-shoo) *n. snowshoes.* A frame that looks something like a tennis racket. *Snowshoes* are tied to the feet and worn when traveling by foot over deep snow to keep one from sinking into the snow.

snow·storm (SNOH-storm) *n. snowstorms.* A storm during which much snow falls; a blizzard.–We were caught in a heavy *snowstorm.*

snub (SNUB) *n. snubs.* A slight.–Mary usually tries to ignore Jack's *snubs.* When he doesn't say hello to her, she just doesn't pay any attention.
–*v. snubs, snubbed, snubbing.* Slight; treat coldly.–The boy felt *snubbed* because he wasn't invited to the party.
–*adj.* Short and turned up, as a *snub* nose.

snug (SNUG) *adj. snugger, snuggest.* 1. Close-fitting.–Bob has grown so much that his coat is too *snug.*
2. Cozy, warm, and comfortable.–The library is *snug* when there is a fire in the fireplace.

snug·gle (SNUG-əl) *v. snuggles, snuggled, snuggling.* Lie close; cuddle.–The kitten *snuggled* up close to Sally.

so (SOH) *adv.* 1. As.–Bob's story was not *so* good as Mary's.
2. To such a degree or amount.–Do not eat *so* much.–It is *so* beautiful out, that I should like to take a walk.
3. Very.–It is *so* hot today!
4. Likewise.–Jack was talking, and *so* was Bob. Bob was talking, too.
5. In order.–We eat *so* that we will grow.–Father works *so* as to earn money.
6. Referring to something said before.–If Father says *so,* it is true.
–*conj.* Therefore.–I was sick, *so* I could not go.
–*pron.* More or less.–Mary was an hour or *so* late.

soak (SOHK) *v. soaks, soaked, soaking.* 1. Wet through and through.–When Bob waded into the water, he *soaked* his shoes and socks. –Mother *soaked* the soiled clothes in soapy water.
2. Suck; absorb.–A blotter *soaks* up ink.

soap (SOHP) *n. soaps.* A material which makes suds in water. It is used to wash dishes, clothes, and other things, and to bathe with.–*Soap* is made in cake form, in liquid form, and in flakes and powders.
–*v. soaps, soaped, soaping.* Rub soap on.–Mother *soaps* the collars of Father's shirts to get them clean.

soar (SOR) *v. soars, soared, soaring.* Fly upward; fly high.–Some eagles *soar* above mountains.

sob (SAHB) *v. sobs, sobbed, sobbing.* Cry with short, jerky, loud breaths.–We heard the little child *sobbing* pitifully when he lost his tricycle.

so·ber (SOH-ber) *adj.; soberly, adv.* 1. Quiet; earnest.–Bob is a very *sober* boy. He takes things seriously.
2. Not drunk; not having had too much alcohol to drink.–The driver was *sober* when the accident happened.
–*v. sobers, sobered, sobering.* Stop laughing; become quiet.–The children *sobered* down after their mother scolded them.

soc·cer (SAHK-er) *n.* A game played with a round football that is kicked or hit with any part of the body except the hands or arms.

so•cial (SOH-shəl) *n. socials.* A friendly party.–We had an ice-cream *social* at our school.
–*adj.; socially, adv.* 1. Fond of the company of others.–Mary is a very *social* person. She likes to talk and have fun with others.
2. Having to do with people.–*Social* study is the study of people and how they live together. Geography and history are *social* studies.

so•cial•ism (SOH-shəl-iz-əm) *n.* A system of social organization based on the theory that goods and property should be owned and controlled by the community as a whole, not by private individuals. Various means proposed for reaching this goal have usually been based on different historical and local conditions.

so•ci•e•ty (sə-SY-ə-tee) *n. societies.* 1. Company.–Bob enjoys Jack's *society.* He likes being with Jack.
2. All people, living and working together; the way human beings live together.–Scientists do work of great value to *society.*
3. A club or group of people who work together for some purpose.–We have formed a *society* to help others.
4. The rich, fashionable group of people in a community.

sock (SAHK) *n. socks.* Short-legged stocking. –Mother wears long stockings. The children wear *socks.*

sock•et (SAHK-it) *n. sockets.* A hollow part into which something fits.–Father made a *socket* to hold the flagpole. – The light did not work because the bulb was not screwed tightly into the *socket.*

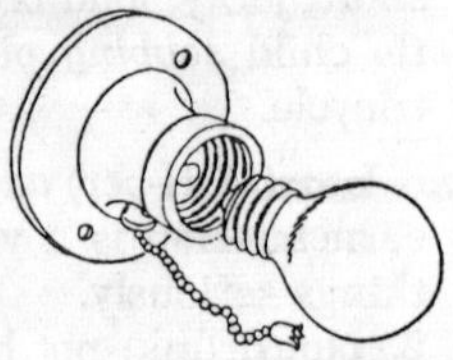

sod (SAHD) *n. sods.* Grassy topsoil that is held together by the roots of the grass.–We put new *sod* on our yard.
–*v. sods, sodded, sodding.* Put sod on.–We *sodded* the yard to make a nice lawn.

so•da (SOH-də) *n. sodas.* 1. A white powder used in cooking.–Baking *soda* is usually used in making cakes that have sour milk in them.
2. (Also called "soda water.") Flavored water that fizzes because it has been charged with carbon dioxide.–Father brought home a case of *soda* for the party.
3. A drink made with ice cream, syrup, and soda water.–Jack likes chocolate *sodas.*

so•fa (SOH-fə) *n. sofas.* An upholstered couch that usually has a back and arms.

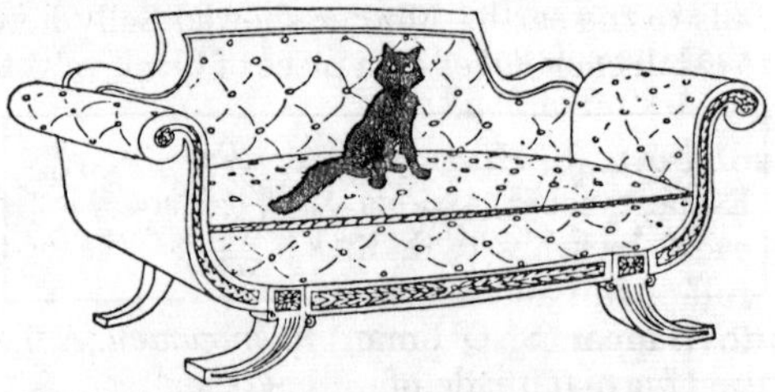

soft (SAWFT) *adj. softer, softest; softly, adv.*
1. Not hard.–The pillow is *soft.*
2. Quiet, gentle, and mild.–A *soft* breeze blew through the trees.
3. The letter "c" in the word "cat" is hard. It has a throaty sound. The "c" in "cent" is *soft.* It is pronounced like an "s."–The letter "g" in "game" is hard. The "g" in "giraffe" is *soft.* It is pronounced like a "j."

soft•ball (SAWFT-bawl) *n.* 1. A ball game similar to baseball, but played with a softer and larger ball.–The boys chose sides for a game of *softball.*
2. The ball used in such a game.

soft wa•ter (SAWFT WAW-ter *or* WAHT-er). Water that is more or less free from the minerals that make it hard to form soapsuds. It doesn't take much soap to make suds in *soft water.*–*Soft water* feels smooth to the hands.

sog•gy (SAHG-ee) *adj. soggier, soggiest.* Soaked; wet through.–The bottom crust of the blackberry pie is *soggy.*

soil (SOIL) *n. soils.* Ground; earth; dirt.–The *soil* in our garden is black and rich.
–*v. soils, soiled, soiling.* Make or become dirty. –Baby *soiled* her clean dress making mud-pies.–Her dress was *soiled.*

so•lar (SOH-ler) *adj.* 1. Measured by the sun. –A sundial is a *solar* clock.
2. Having to do with the sun.–The *solar* system is made up of the sun and all the planets and heavenly bodies that revolve around it.

sold (SOHLD) *v.* One form of the verb *sell.*– Father bought a new house, but now he has *sold* it.

sol•der (SAHD-er) *v. solders, soldered, soldering.* Join metal parts by melting a special metal or alloy and applying it as a glue. The melted metal hardens around the parts and locks them together.

sol•dier (SOHL-jer) *n. soldiers.* A man serving in an army. *Soldiers* fight the enemy in time of war.

sole (SOHL) *n. soles.* 1. Bottom of a shoe.—The *soles* of Bob's shoes were worn out.
2. Bottom of the foot.—Father walked so far that the *soles* of his feet were sore.
3. A kind of fish that is good to eat.

sol•emn (SAHL-əm) *adj.; solemnly, adv.* 1. Earnest; sober; serious.—Bob has *solemn* blue eyes; Jack has twinkling blue eyes that are full of fun and mischief.
2. Happening or done in a serious and formal way.—The inauguration of a president is a *solemn* event.

sol•id (SAHL-id) *adj.; solidly, adv.; solidness, n.* 1. The same all the way through.—A stove pipe or drain pipe is hollow. A baseball bat is *solid.*
2. The same all over.—Mary's new dress is a *solid* blue.
3. Firm and strong.—The parts of a table must be glued together to make it *solid.*—The house has a *solid* foundation.
4. Firm and hard.—Water is liquid. When it freezes, it becomes *solid.*

sol•i•tar•y (SAHL-ə-tair-ee) *adj.* 1. Alone; living or being apart from others.—A hermit leads a *solitary* life.
2. Lonely; not visited.—He lives on a *solitary* isle.

sol•i•tude (SAHL-ə-tood *or* -tyood) *n.* State of being alone; peace and quiet.—Jerry often goes into the garden to find *solitude.* He goes there to be alone in a quiet place.

so•lo (SOH-loh) *n. solos.* A piece of music to be played or sung by one person at a time. —*adj.* Without companions. — The airplane pilot made a *solo* flight. He flew all alone.

so•lo•ist (SOH-loh-ist) *n. soloists.* A person who sings or plays a piece of music alone.

sol•u•ble (SAHL-yə-bəl) *adj.* 1. Able to be dissolved.—Sugar, salt, and many other food products are *soluble* in water.
2. Capable of being solved, as a problem, or a mystery.—The riddle is *soluble.*

so•lu•tion (sə-LOO-shən) *n. solutions.* 1. Finding the answer to something, as a puzzle or mystery.—The *solution* of the crime was difficult.
2. The answer or explanation.—There seems to be no *solution* to the problem.
3. The act or process of dissolving something, as sugar in water.—*Solution* of the powder was made easy by the use of boiling water.
4. The liquid in which a substance has been dissolved.—The *solution* is too thick.

solve (SAHLV) *v. solves, solved, solving.* Find the answer to.—Mary tried to *solve* the arithmetic problem.—The police tried to *solve* the mystery.

som•bre•ro (sahm-BRAIR-oh) *n. sombreros.* A high-crowned hat with a broad brim worn by men in Mexico; some other parts of America, and Spain.

some (SUM) *adj.* 1. A number of.—*Some* sailors came to town.
2. Any.—Tell *some* policeman about your accident.
3. Any amount of.—Put *some* sugar on Baby's oatmeal.
4. Any number of.—*Some* apples are red.

some•bod•y (SUM-bahd-ee) *pron.* 1. Some person, not named or not known.—The mother bear said, "*Somebody* has been eating my porridge."
2. A person of importance.—Father always says to Bob, "Be *somebody,* son."

some•how (SUM-how) *adv.* By some means; in one way or another.—Father will get to work *somehow* while the car is being repaired.

som•er•sault (SUM-er-sawlt) *n. somersaults.* A heels-over-head turn.—Some children can turn a *somersault* backwards.

son (SUN) *n. sons.* A boy or man as related to his father and mother. A boy is his father's *son.* Your father is your grandfather's *son.*

song (SAWNG) *n. songs.* A short piece of music with words to be sung.—"America" is the name of a *song* we sing at school.—Some poems are set to music. Then they are *songs.*

son-in-law (SUN-in-law) *n. sons-in-law.* The husband of a person's daughter.—Sister's husband is the *son-in-law* of Father and Mother.

soon (SOON) *adv. sooner, soonest.* 1. Before long; at a time not far away.—Dinner will be ready *soon.*
2. When; at the time.—As *soon* as the bell rings, the children are quiet.
3. Rather.—I would *sooner* sleep than eat.

soot (SUHT) *n.* A black dust formed when something burns.—*Soot* from the furnace fire collects on the window sill.

soothe (SOOTH) *v. soothes, soothed, soothing.* 1. Relieve; remove pain from.—This medicine will *soothe* the burn.
2. Calm; comfort; quiet.—Mother tried to *soothe* the lost child.

soph·o·more (SAHF-ə-mor) *n. sophomores.* A student in the second year of high school or college.

so·pran·o (sə-PRA-noh *or* sə-PRAH-noh) *n. sopranos.* 1. A woman or girl who has a high singing voice; one who can sing high notes.
2. The highest kind of voice.–Mother sings *soprano,* but Father sings bass.
–*adj.* The highest part in a piece of music written for more than one voice or instrument.–The violin often plays the *soprano* part.

sor·cer·er (SOR-ser-er) *n. sorcerers.* A person who is supposed to have magical powers obtained from evil spirits.–*Sorcerers* often are found in fairy tales.

sor·cer·ess (SOR-ser-əss) *n. sorceresses.* A female sorcerer; a witch.

sore (SOR) *n. sores.* A painful spot where the skin is broken or bruised.–The *sore* on my hand hurts.
–*adj. sorer, sorest.* Painful.–The cut on Bob's finger is *sore.*

sor·ghum (SOR-gəm) *n.* Any of several types of cereal grasses grown in the tropics of the Eastern Hemisphere. One kind of *sorghum* is used as a cereal. Other kinds are used to make syrups and fodder.

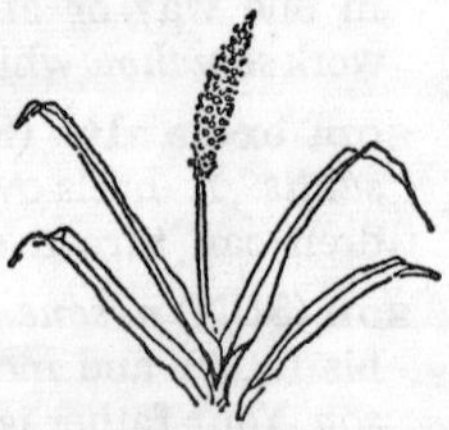

so·ror·i·ty (sə-ROR-ə-tee *or* sə-RAHR-ə-tee) *n. sororities.* A club or society for women, especially at a college or university.

sor·row (SAHR- *or* SOR-oh) *n. sorrows.* 1. Grief; sadness; unhappiness.–Much *sorrow* was caused by the accident.
2. Trouble; something which makes one feel sad.–The old king had many *sorrows.*

sor·ry (SAHR- *or* SOR-ee) *adj. sorrier, sorriest.* 1. Filled with sadness or sorrow.–I am *sorry* that you are sick.
2. Politely regretful.–I am *sorry* I was standing in your way.

sort (SORT) *n. sorts.* Kind or type.–What *sort* of ice cream would you like for dessert?
–*v. sorts, sorted, sorting.* Separate things and put like things together in groups.–Bob helped the teacher *sort* the children's papers.

soul (SOHL) *n. souls.* 1. A person.–Not a *soul* heard the bell.
2. Deep feeling; strong spirit.–Mary puts her heart and *soul* into her piano playing.
3. The part of a person concerned with his thinking and feeling.–Many people believe that the *soul* is not part of the body and that the *soul* can never die.

sound (SOWND) *n. sounds.* A noise.–The room was so quiet you could not hear a *sound.*
–*v. sounds, sounded, sounding.* 1. Make a noise.–The squeaking door *sounds* like the squeak of a mouse.
2. Cause to make a noise.–*Sound* the fire alarm!
3. Seem; appear.–The news *sounds* bad.
–*adj.* Stable; healthy.–The boy is *sound* in body and mind.

sound·proof (SOWND-proof) *adj.* Capable of keeping sound in or out.–The studio is *soundproof.* Sounds cannot pass through the walls, ceiling, or floor.

sound wave (SOWND wayv) *sound waves.* A vibration or disturbance in the air caused by any sound. *Sound waves* carry sounds to our ears.

soup (SOOP) *n. soups.* A liquid food made by boiling meat or vegetables in water or milk, with seasonings.–I like creamed tomato *soup.*

sour (SOWR) *v. sours, soured, souring.* Become acid; spoil.–Do not leave the milk out of the icebox, or it may *sour.*
–*adj.* 1. Not sweet.–Sugar is sweet. Lemons are *sour.*
2. Spoiled; gone bad.–The soup has turned *sour.* It has mold on the top.

source (SORSS) *n. sources.* The place from which anything comes; the starting place.–Farms are the *source* of most of our food.–The *source* of the river is a spring high up in the mountains.

south (SOWTH) *n.* 1. One of the four main directions. *South* is opposite north. The sun rises in the east. Turn your face to the east. Your left hand is to the north, and your right hand to the *south.*

2. (Usually spelled with a capital "S.") The southern part of a country.–Father's family lived in the *South.*
–*adj.* and *adv.* Toward the south.–We live *south* of Main Street.–The birds fly *south* in the summer.–That window is on the *south* side of the house.

South Car·o·li·na (SOWTH kar-ə-LY-nə) *n.* A state on the east coast of the United States noted principally for the cotton and tobacco raised there, for its large amount of shipping, and for the manufacturing of thread and cotton goods.

South Da·ko·ta (SOWTH də-KOH-tə) *n.* A farming and grazing state in north central United States. The largest gold mine in the United States is found in the Black Hills of *South Dakota.*

south·east (sowth-EEST) *n., adj.,* and *adv.* The direction halfway between south and east.

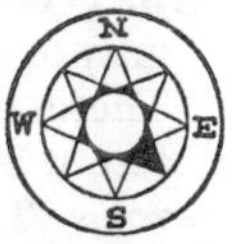

south·ern (SUTH-ern) *adj.* Of the south; toward the south.–We live in the *southern* part of town.–Father's family was *Southern.* They lived in the South.

south·west (sowth-WEST) *n., adj.,* and *adv.* 1. The direction halfway between south and west.
2. (Spelled with a capital "S.") The southwestern portion of the United States, usually considered as centering on Arizona and New Mexico.

sou·ve·nir (soo-və-NIR *or* SOO-və-nir) *n. souvenirs.* A keepsake; something to bring back memories.–Uncle Ned brought Mary a *souvenir* of New York. It was a scarf with pictures of buildings on it.

sov·er·eign (SAHV-rin) *n. sovereigns.* 1. The highest ruler of a country, such as a king, queen, or emperor.
2. A former British coin, worth one pound.
–*adj:* 1. Independent (of a country).–The United States is a *sovereign* nation. It runs its own affairs without help from other nations.
2. Supreme.–The keeping of peace in the world is of *sovereign* importance.

sow (SOW) *n. sows.* A fully grown female pig.–Grandfather's *sow* has a litter of little pigs.

sow (SOH) *v. sows, sowed, sowing.* Plant by scattering seeds; scatter.–The farmer *sows* the grain in the spring.

soy·bean (SOI-been) *n. soybeans.* A kind of bean used for food, and for making flour, oil, and many other things.

space (SPAYSS) *n. spaces.* 1. Room; place.–There is *space* in the icebox for one more dish.
2. A blank; an empty place; a distance.–I wrote one word on the typewriter, then skipped a *space* and wrote another.–The teacher asked us to leave a *space* at the bottom of the page.–Telephone poles have short *spaces* between them.
3. Sky; nothingness.–Airplanes fly in *space.* –The horse and rider plunged off the cliff into *space.*
4. Time.–During the earthquake houses collapsed within the *space* of a minute.
–*v. spaces, spaced, spacing.* To place with certain distances between.–Jack *spaced* the paragraphs in his composition to make it look neat.

space·ship (SPAYSS-ship) *n. spaceships.* A vehicle designed to travel through space to other planets and to the moon.

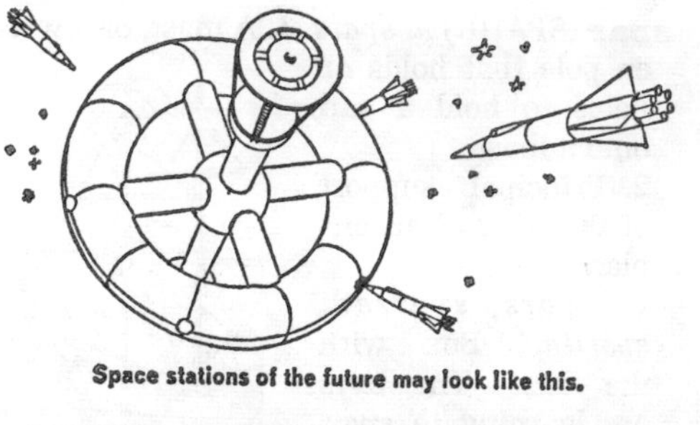

Space stations of the future may look like this.

space sta·tion (SPAYSS STAY-shən) *space stations.* A proposed base to be "stationed" or placed in orbit around the earth. *Space stations* would serve as stopping points or service stations for spaceships traveling through space.

spa·cious (SPAY-shəss) *adj.* Large; roomy.–We have a *spacious* living room.

spade (SPAYD) *n. spades.* A gardening tool with a shorter handle and a flatter blade than a shovel. – We use a *spade* to dig up earth.
–*v. spades, spaded, spading.* Dig up.–Father *spaded* the earth to look for angleworms.

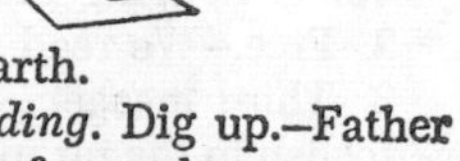

span (SPAN) *n. spans.* 1. The distance from the tip of the little finger to the tip of the thumb on a grown person's hand when the hand is stretched out. It is about nine inches.
2. The distance or space from one support or foundation to the next on a bridge or an arch.

bridge span

span of horses

3. A pair of horses or mules driven together. –Grandfather has a *span* of sorrel horses.
4. A period of time.–Father and Mother lived in the city for the *span* of three years.–The fortuneteller told the man that his *span* on earth was far from over.
–*v. spans, spanned, spanning.* 1. Extend or stretch across.–The bridge *spans* the river.
2. Measure by one's stretched-out hand.

span•iel (SPAN-yəl) *n. spaniels.* A medium-sized dog with long, wavy hair; long ears that hang down, and short legs.

spar (SPAHR) *n. spars.* 1. A mast, or a wooden pole that holds or helps to hold a sail onto a mast.
2. Principal support of the wing of an airplane.
–*v. spars, sparred, sparring.* Box with the fists. – The boys are learning to *spar.*

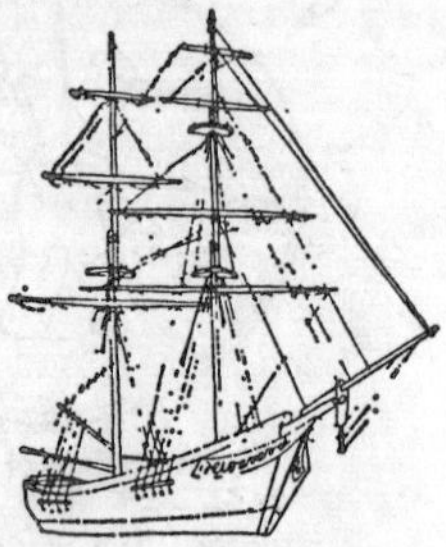

spare (SPAIR) *n. spares.* An extra.–I bought two flashlight batteries and one *spare.*
–*v. spares, spared, sparing.* 1. Lend; give up; get along without.–Since Mother was sewing, she could not *spare* her thimble.–I can *spare* a glass or two of jelly; I have plenty.
2. Have mercy on; not punish or hurt.–The hunter *spared* the deer. He did not shoot the deer, even though he could have.
–*adj.* 1. Extra.–We have a *spare* tire for our car. We keep it to use only when one of the others is being repaired.
2. Free.–We read stories in our *spare* time.
3. Thin; meager. – His *spare* figure looked foolish in the fat man's clothing.

spark (SPAHRK) *n. sparks.* 1. A little piece or bit of fire. – The Boy Scouts watched the *sparks* from the campfire to see that they did not start another fire.
2. A little flash of fire.–When Mother pulled the plug out of the wall socket, we saw *sparks.*

spar•kle (SPAHR-kəl) *v. sparkles, sparkled, sparkling.* 1. Glitter, flash, or throw off little glints of light. – Mother's diamond ring *sparkles.*
2. Twinkle or dance.–Sally's eyes *sparkle* when she is planning something new.
–*sparkle, n. sparkles.*

spark plug (SPAHRK plug) *spark plugs.* A plug used in the cylinders of automobiles to make electrical sparks which will explode the gasoline. These explosions, which take place one right after the other, make the motor run.

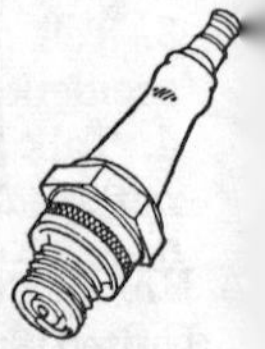

spar•row (SPAR-oh) *n. sparrows.* A small gray or brownish bird. There are many different kinds of *sparrows.* The song *sparrow* has a very pleasant song.

sparse (SPAHRSS) *adj.; sparsely, adv.* Thinly spread or scattered.–*Sparse* patches of grass dot the field.

spasm (SPAZ-əm) *n. spasms.* 1. A sudden, unusual, and involuntary drawing together of a muscle or muscles.–John said he spilled the milk because a *spasm* in his arm made his hand shake.
2. Any short, sudden burst of energy, feeling, or activity.–I had to leave the church because of a *spasm* of coughing.

spat (SPAT) *n. spats.* 1. An outer covering for the ankle and instep, made of cloth and worn over the shoe.
2. A little quarrel. – The children had a *spat* over the ball game.

spat•ter (SPAT-er) *n. spatters.* 1. A spot.–Mary got a *spatter* of grease on her dress.
2. A noise made by the fall of little drops.–We heard the *spatter* of rain on the roof.
–*v. spatters, spattered, spattering.* 1. To splash or sprinkle with water, grease, mud, or other wet substance.–The rain *spattered* the car with mud.
2. Fall on in drops.–Grease from the frying pan *spattered* the stove.

spawn (SPAWN) *v. spawns, spawned, spawning.* 1. Give birth to, usually in great numbers; produce. – Countless numbers of fish are *spawned* each year in the waters of the world.
2. Produce or deposit eggs, especially into water.–The fish seem to be *spawning* earlier than usual this year.

speak (SPEEK) *v. speaks, spoke, speaking.* 1. Talk.–Bob was so surprised that he couldn't *speak.*–The teacher told us always to *speak* clearly.
2. Give a talk or speech.–The President will *speak* on the radio tonight.
3. Tell about.–The policeman *spoke* of the accident.
4. Talk to one another.–Mary and Jack are not *speaking.*
5. Say.–She *spoke* falsehoods.

spear (SPIR) *n. spears.* 1. A weapon with a sharp tip and a long, straight handle. – Guards stood outside the king's palace holding their *spears.*

2. A piece.–Mother gave each of us six *spears* of asparagus.
–*v. spears, speared, spearing.* Put a spear through, or pierce.–It is against the law to *spear* certain kinds of fish.–Father *speared* a piece of potato with his fork.

spe•cial (SPESH-əl) *adj.* 1. Particular. – Making model airplanes is Jack's *special* hobby.–This is a *special* soap. It is good for Baby's skin.
2. Unusual; extra nice.–Father thinks that strawberry shortcake is a very *special* dessert. –Mother wears her blue lace dress for *special* occasions.

spe•cial•ist (SPESH-əl-ist) *n. specialists.* A person who makes a study or a business of some particular subject or line of work. – When Baby had an earache, Mother took her to an ear *specialist.* She took Baby to a doctor who had studied all about, and treated things wrong with, the ear.

spe•cial•ty (SPESH-əl-tee) *n. specialties.* Something one does unusually well.–Making model airplanes is Jack's *specialty.*–Coconut cream pie is Mother's *specialty.*

spe•cies (SPEE-sheez) *n. sing.* and *pl.* A group of plants or animals that are very much alike.–Tiger lilies are one *species* of the lily family.

spe•cif•ic (spə-SIF-ik) *adj.; specifically, adv.* Particular; exact.–If you have no *specific* reason for staying at home, why not come with us?–When Mother told the doctor Baby didn't seem well, he asked her to be more *specific.* He asked Mother to tell him exactly what seemed to be the trouble.

spec•i•men (SPESS-ə-mən) *n. specimens.* A sample.–Our teacher asked each of us for a *specimen* of our drawing to hang up for visitors' week.–Bob collects moths. He took one of his *specimens* to school.

speck (SPEK) *n. specks; specked, adj.* 1. A small spot.–Father cleaned his glasses because they were covered with *specks.*
2. A small bit.–Sally took out a black *speck* that had fallen into her milk.

spec•ta•cle (SPEK-tə-kəl) *n. spectacles.* 1. Sight; show.–The Air Force put on a great *spectacle* over the parade grounds. Planes flew in formation over the area all day.
2. (In the plural) Eyeglasses.–Grandmother wears *spectacles* to help her see better.

spec•ta•tor (SPEK-tay-ter) *n. spectators.* Someone who watches or looks on.–Jack told Mother he did not take part in the rescue, but was just a *spectator.*

spec•tro•scope (SPEK-trə-skohp) *n. spectroscopes.* An instrument used to produce and examine a spectrum. The earliest known *spectroscope* was an ordinary prism. It was used by Sir Isaac Newton in the seventeenth century to examine rays of sunlight.

spec•trum (SPEK-trəm) *n. spectrums* or *spectra.* The series of colors ranging from red through orange, yellow, green, blue, and indigo to violet. White light is really composed of all these colors. You can break a beam of

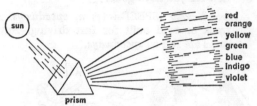

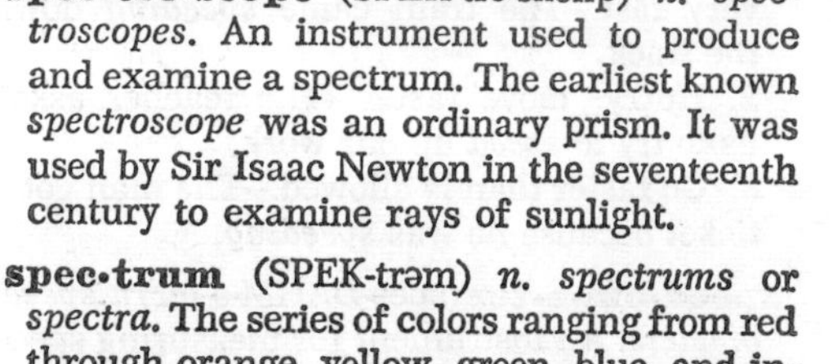

white light into a *spectrum* by passing it through a spectroscope. A rainbow is the result of rain acting as a spectroscope on the sunlight that passes through it.

spec•u•late (SPEK-yə-layt) *v. speculates, speculated, speculating.* 1. Form opinions on the basis of insufficient knowledge.–When she says Mary is leaving tomorrow, she is just *speculating.* Mary hasn't made up her mind to go.
2. Try to make money by taking great business risks.–People with little money should not *speculate.* They may lose everything.
3. Meditate; reflect. – Pioneers in science *speculated* deeply about the universe before undertaking the experiments which led to great discoveries.
–*speculation, n. speculations.*

sped (SPED) *v.* One form of the verb *speed.*–The dog *sped* home when he heard Jack whistle.

speech (SPEECH) *n. speeches.* 1. The ability to speak.–People have *speech.* They are able to speak or talk. Animals do not have *speech.*
2. A talk; what one says to a group of people who have come to listen.–The mayor made a *speech* at the dinner.
3. Way of talking.–John's *speech* shows that he comes from England.

speed (SPEED) *n. speeds.* 1. Swiftness; quickness. – Mary got dressed with all possible *speed.*
2. Rate of motion or movement.–The *speed* limit is thirty-five miles an hour. That is as fast as one may drive.–The *speed* of this train is ninety miles an hour.
–*v. speeds, speeded* or *sped, speeding.* 1. Move very fast.–The train came *speeding* down the track.
2. Hurry; move faster.–The teacher asked us to try to *speed* up our work.
3. Go faster than is allowed.–The man got a ticket because he was *speeding.*

speed•om•e•ter (spee-DAHM-ə-ter) *n. speedometers.* An instrument for measuring speed and distance. You look at the *speedometer* on your car to see how fast you are going and how far you have gone.

speed•way (SPEED-way) *n. speedways.* A track or road built for fast driving.–Auto races are run on *speedways.*

spell (SPEL) *n. spells.* 1. A period; a length of time.–We went to the lake during the hot *spell.*
2. A charm; an enchantment. – The fairy cast a *spell* over the princess.
–*v. spells, spelled, spelling.* 1. Speak or write the letters of words in the right order.–C A T *spells* cat.
2. Mean.–Black clouds *spell* rain.
3. Take the place of (someone) for a short time.–If you are tired, I'll *spell* you at mowing the lawn.

spell•bound (SPEL-bownd) *adj.* Enchanted; fascinated.–The audience was *spellbound* by the magician's tricks.

spell•er (SPEL-er) *n. spellers.* 1. A person who spells.–Mary is a good *speller.*
2. A spelling book; a book with words in it to help you learn to spell.

spell•ing bee (SPEL-ing bee) *spelling bees.* A spelling contest; a contest to see who can spell the best.

spend (SPEND) *v. spends, spent, spending.* 1. Pay out.–Do not *spend* your money just because you have it.–Mother *spent* five dollars for a new hat.
2. Pass (time). – Bob *spends* his holidays making model airplanes.
3. Use up.–All his energy was *spent* after the football game. He just wanted to go home and rest.

sphere (SFIR) *n. spheres.* A ball or globe.–Every part of the outside of a *sphere* is the same distance from the center.–The earth is a *sphere.*

sphinx (SFINGKS) *n. sphinxes.* 1. An ancient Egyptian figure with the head of a man, a ram, or a hawk and the body of a lion. The most famous statue of this kind is near the pyramids of Giza, Egypt, and is known as the Great Sphinx. It is nearly two hundred feet long.
2. A figure in ancient Greek mythology with a woman's head, a lion's body, a serpent's tail, and wings.

SPHINX

spice (SPYSS) *n. spices.* A sharp-tasting seasoning made from the dried leaves, seeds, or bark of certain plants.–Cloves, allspice, cinnamon, and nutmeg are *spices.*–Mother puts many *spices* in her gingerbread.
–*v. spices, spiced, spicing.* 1. Put spice in. – Mother *spices* her apple pie with cinnamon.
2. Make lively.–The lecturer *spiced* his talk with amusing stories.

spi•der (SPY-der) *n. spiders.* 1. A small animal with eight long legs. *Spiders* are not insects, for they have eight legs and no wings; insects have six legs, and usually have wings. *Spiders* spin webs to catch bugs and insects for food.

2. A skillet; a frying pan.

spike (SPYK) *n. spikes.* 1. A long, strong, thick nail.–The men put *spikes* in the railroad ties to hold the tracks in place.
2. A sharp, pointed piece of metal.–Baseball players, runners, and other athletes wear shoes with *spikes* sticking out of the soles.
3. A pointed cluster on a plant.–This is a *spike* of grain. The picture next to it is a *spike* of flowers.

–*v. spikes, spiked, spiking.* Cut or pierce with spikes.–Bob was *spiked* in the leg by an opposing player.

spill (SPIL) *n. spills.* A fall.–We had a big *spill* when our sled hit the bump.
–*v. spills, spilled, spilling.* 1. Let a liquid run out over the edge of its container, or let loose material like sand or sugar fall or scatter about.–Baby often *spills* her milk.
2. Let fall.–The sled ran over a bump and *spilled* the children into the snow.

spin (SPIN) *n. spins.* 1. A whirling.–The falling airplane went into a *spin.*
2. A ride.–Will you go with us for a *spin* in the sports car?
–*v. spins, spun, spinning.* 1. Whirl or make whirl.–Bob likes to *spin* his top. – The top *spins.*
2. Draw out and twist wool, silk, or cotton into threads.–Long ago women *spun* their own thread and yarn on spinning wheels.
3. Make of threadlike strands.–Spiders *spin* webs to catch insects for food.
4. Feel dizzy.–My head is *spinning.* It feels as though it were going around and around.
5. Tell.–The old man loved to *spin* yarns about his youth.

spin•dle (SPIN-dl) *n. spindles.* 1. A long rod that goes round and round. It is used to wind thread when spinning.

2. A long, heavy pin for papers.–The teacher puts papers on a *spindle.*

spine (SPYN) *n. spines.* 1. The backbone. A person's *spine* is made up of many bones fitted together.

2. A thorn, pricker, or sharp point.–A porcupine's quills are *spines.*

spin•ning wheel (SPIN-ing hweel) *spinning wheels.* A machine to spin and wind thread or yarn. It has a large wheel that is turned by hand or by a foot pedal.

spin•ster (SPIN-ster) *n. spinsters.* An aging unmarried woman.

spi•ra•cle (SPY-rə-kəl *or* SPIR-ə-kəl) *n. spiracles.* An opening used for breathing by insects; a similar opening in the heads of sharks and rays.

spi•ral (SPY-rəl) *n. spirals* and *adj.* Something shaped like a coil.–A corkscrew or a coiled bedspring is a *spiral.*

spire (SPYR) *n. spires.* The pointed part of a steeple. – We saw the church *spire* from a distance.

spir•it (SPIR-it) *n. spirits.* 1. Soul or mind; the unseen part of a person concerned with thinking and feeling.
2. A ghost, elf, fairy, or other imaginary being.
3. Way of feeling; nature. – When Father went to work he was in good *spirits.* He was happy.
4. Liveliness; strength. – He defended his point of view with *spirit.*
5. Influence; feeling. – The class showed a *spirit* of cooperation in making plans for the trip.
6. (Usually plural) Liquid containing a large quantity of alcohol.

spir•it•ed (SPIR-it-id) *adj.* Lively; vigorous. –Grandfather has a *spirited* horse. It is full of energy and courage.

spit (SPIT) *n. spits.* 1. The saliva or liquid that forms in one's mouth.
2. A bar, sometimes one which turns, on which meat can be roasted.
–*v. spits, spat* or *spit, spitting.* 1. Throw out saliva or anything from the mouth.–*Spitting* may spread disease.–Baby *spits* out food she doesn't like.
2. Hiss.–Pussy *spat* at the strange dog.
3. Throw forth.–The hot pan is *spitting* fat. Be careful!

spite (SPYT) *n.* An unfriendly feeling.–The man let his dog run in the garden out of *spite* for the person who owned the garden.
–*v. spites, spited, spiting.* Show unfriendly feelings or a dislike for someone.–The boy didn't want the book but he took it to *spite* the other boys.
–*In spite of* means notwithstanding, nevertheless.–John came home *in spite of* the rain.

splash (SPLASH) *n. splashes.* 1. A throwing or scattering of liquid; the noise made by it.–When Bob dived into the water, we heard a big *splash.*
2. A spot made by spattered liquid.–When Father paints, he gets *splashes* of paint on his shirt.
–*v. splashes, splashed, splashing* Throw; dash; scatter (liquid) about.–A passing car *splashed* muddy water on Mary's clothes.

splat•ter (SPLAT-er) *v. splatters, splattered, splattering.* Splash; scatter (liquid). – Do not *splatter* ink on your paper.

splen•did (SPLEN-did) *adj.; splendidly, adv.* Brilliant; excellent; glorious.–The teacher told Dan that she was proud of him because he had done a *splendid* job on the test.

splen•dor (SPLEN-der) *n. splendors.* 1. Brilliance; radiance.–The moon rose in *splendor* over the sea.
2. Magnificence; glory.–The *splendor* of the king's court is beyond compare.

splice (SPLYSS) *n. splices.* Place where two pieces of rope or string are joined by twisting the ends together to make one long piece.
–*v. splices, spliced, splicing.* Join together in this way.–The sailor *spliced* two pieces of rope together.

splint (SPLINT) *n. splints.* A thin strip of wood or other material.–The chair seat is made of *splints.*–The doctor put a *splint* on the boy's broken finger.

splin•ter (SPLIN-ter) *n. splinters.* A sliver of material such as wood or metal.–The nurse took a *splinter* from the child's foot.
–*v. splinters, splintered, splintering.* Break, sliver, or split into long, thin pieces.–The box fell from the truck and *splintered.*

split (SPLIT) *n. splits.* 1. A crack; a long break.–There is a big *split* in the tree where it was hit by lightning.
2. A division.–There was a *split* among the members of the club over the amount of dues that should be charged.
–*v. splits, split, splitting.* 1. Break or pull apart, especially along the grain.–Bob *split* the stick from end to end to make sticks for his kite.
2. Divide.–The boys *split* the candy bar.

spoil (SPOIL) *v. spoils, spoiled, spoiling.* 1. Ruin; damage; destroy. – The hailstorm *spoiled* the lettuce.
2. Become unfit to eat.–Some foods will *spoil* if not kept cold. They may become sour or moldy, or may decay.

spoils (SPOILZ) *n. pl.* Things taken by force or won.–Great works of ancient Greek art were carried away as *spoils* by the soldiers of the Roman Empire.

spoke (SPOHK) *n. spokes.* One of the bars leading from the axle of a wheel to the rim.
–*v.* One form of the verb *speak.* – Mary *spoke* to the teacher about the lesson. – At dinner, the mayor *spoke* on the subject of beautifying the town.

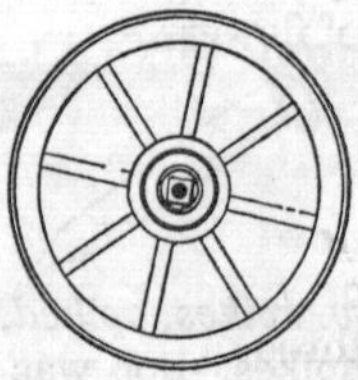

spo•ken (SPOH-kən) *v.* One form of the verb *speak.*–I have *spoken* to her on the telephone, but not face to face.

spokes•man (SPOHKS-mən) *n. spokesmen.* A person chosen to speak for a group.–At the meeting, the students elected Bob as their *spokesman* to present their idea to the principal.

sponge (SPUNJ) *n. sponges.* 1. A kind of animal that lives in the sea.
2. The cleaned and dried skeleton of such an animal.–A *sponge* soaks up much water.
–We use a *sponge* to wash things.
3. A man-made imitation of a natural sponge.

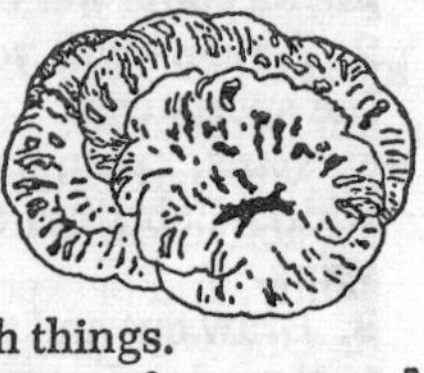

–*v. sponges, sponged, sponging.* 1. Rub with a sponge.–Mother *sponged* Father's suit with a damp sponge.
2. Let someone else pay one's way or do one's work.–It is better to work for yourself than to *sponge* on someone else.

spon•sor (SPAHN-ser) *v. sponsors, sponsored, sponsoring.* 1. Take responsibility for a person or thing.–John is *sponsoring* his friend for membership in the club.
2. Act as a godparent; take vows or answer for an infant at baptism.–Father *sponsored* Mary's child at the christening.
3. Pay the costs for a radio or television program. Business firms *sponsor* programs in return for the privilege of advertising their products.
–*sponsor, n. sponsors.*

spon•ta•ne•ous (spahn-TAY-nee-əss) *adj.; spontaneously, adv.* Arising or happening naturally, as if from some inner force; without external cause.–The audience broke into *spontaneous* applause when the President entered the auditorium.
–*Spontaneous combustion* takes place when something sets itself on fire by internal chemical action.–Piles of paper or rags, especially oily rags, sometimes burst into flames by *spontaneous combustion.*

spook (SPOOK) *n. spooks.* A ghost (said in fun).–On Halloween the children dress up in sheets, and pretend they are *spooks.*

spool (SPOOL) *n. spools.* A short, round piece of wood or metal with a hole through it from end to end. Thread, cord, and wire are often wound on *spools.*

spoon (SPOON) *n. spoons.* A small tool with a bowl and handle for lifting liquids or soft foods.–Baby eats with a *spoon.*

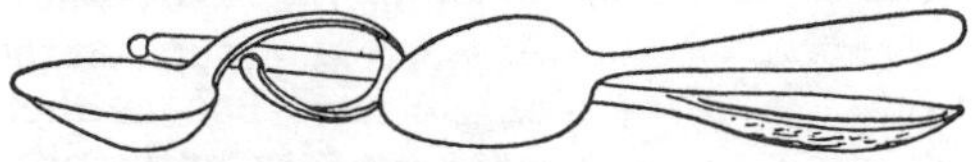

spore (SPOR) *n. spores.* A cell from which new plants grow. Ferns and other flowerless plants have *spores.*

sport (SPORT) *n. sports.* 1. Fun, play, or amusement.–It is good *sport* to go fishing.
2. Any particular kind of game, particularly an active game.–Hockey, baseball, football, skiing, and basketball are *sports.*
3. One who takes troubles well, or is a good loser.–Bob was a good *sport* about missing the game.

sports•man•ship (SPORTSS-mən-ship) *n.* Fair play; ability to follow rules or to accept conditions cheerfully.–To lose gracefully is a sign of good *sportsmanship.*

spot (SPAHT) *n. spots.* 1. A mark, stain, blot, or speck.–It is hard to get ink *spots* out of clothes.
2. One of a pattern of dots or round markings.–A giraffe has *spots.*
3. A place.–We have found a pretty *spot* to put up our tent.
–*v. spots, spotted, spotting.* 1. Stain; get a spot on.–Mother put a bib on Baby so that Baby would not *spot* her clean dress.
2. Locate. – John *spotted* his father in the crowd at the station.

spot•light (SPAHT-lyt) *n. spotlights.* 1. A circle of strong light thrown on something.–The singer stood in the *spotlight* so that everyone could see her easily.

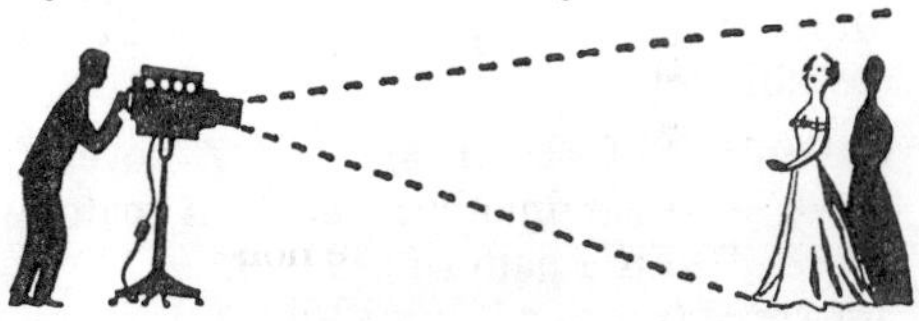

2. The lamp that makes a spotlight.
3. Center of public attention.–The attendance of many world leaders put the United Nations in the *spotlight.*

spot•ted (SPAHT-id) *adj.* 1. Stained; marked with spots.–Baby's bib is *spotted.* She spilled food on it.
2. Covered with spots or marks not of the same color as the rest.–Sally's turtle has a *spotted* shell. Its shell is yellow with black spots.

spout (SPOWT) *n. spouts.* 1. A tube or pipe through which water or other liquids may run or be poured. –Teapots and coffeepots have *spouts.*–Tea pours through the *spout.*

2. Jet or stream.–We could see the whale's *spout* across the water.
–*v. spouts, spouted, spouting.* Pour; gush. –Water *spouts* from the fountain.

sprain (SPRAYN) *v. sprains, sprained, spraining.* Injure by twisting or overstretching the muscles or ligaments.–Bob *sprained* his ankle while playing ball.
–*sprain, n. sprains.*

sprang (SPRANG) *v.* One form of the verb *spring.*–The cat *sprang* at the mouse.

sprawl (SPRAWL) *v. sprawls, sprawled, sprawling.* Lie with the arms and legs stretched out.—The tired boys *sprawled* on the grass.

spray (SPRAY) *n. sprays.* 1. A branch of a plant with its flowers and leaves.—Mary put a *spray* of apple blossoms in the vase.

spray of flowers

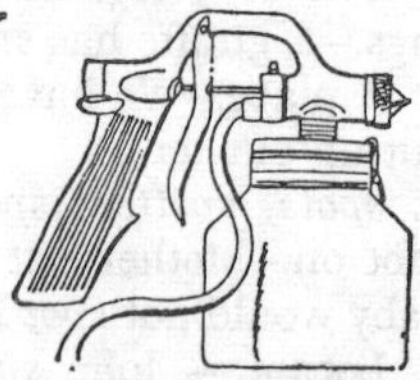

spray gun

2. A kind of gun that pumps out liquid in a misty stream.
3. Fine drops of water.—The wind blew the *spray* from the sprinkler into our faces.
—*v. sprays, sprayed, spraying.* Sprinkle.—The farmer *sprays* his potato plants with a liquid to kill bugs.

spread (SPRED) *n. spreads.* A cover for a bed. — Grandmother made a patchwork *spread* with a pattern of stars.
—*v. spreads, spread, spreading.* 1. Lay smoothly.—Mother *spread* jam on the toast.—Mary *spread* her dress on the ironing board in order to press it.
2. Get further apart.—The captain told the boys on the ball team to *spread* out so that someone would catch the ball.
3. Stretch out; unfold.—The bird *spread* its wings and flew away.
4. Scatter; distribute; reach over a wide area. —News of the accident soon *spread* far and wide.—Scarlet fever *spreads* fast.

spring (SPRING) *n. springs.* 1. Ability to stretch and then go back to the usual size.—A rubber band has *spring.*
2. A coil or strip of metal that gives under pressure and then jumps back to its original shape.—These are *springs* for a chair or bed. Push them down and then let go, and they will jump back to their usual size.

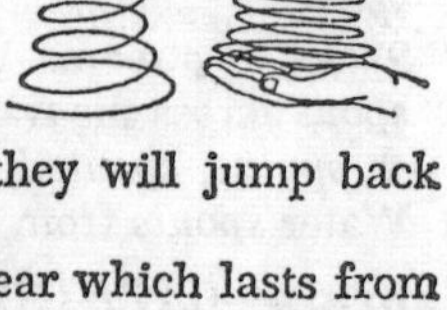

3. The season of the year which lasts from March 21 to June 21.—The four seasons of the year are *spring,* summer, autumn, and winter.—The farmer plants his seeds in the *spring.*
4. A bubbling stream of water coming out of the ground.—The Boy Scouts found a *spring* in the woods.
5. A leap.—With one *spring,* Jack was out of bed.
6. Energy; vigor.—The tired girl's step has lost its *spring.*
—*v. springs, sprang* or *sprung, springing.* 1. Jump; leap.—Have you ever seen a cat *spring* at a mouse or a bird?
2. Come up quickly; shoot up.—Mushrooms *spring* up overnight.

spring·board (SPRING-bord) *n. springboards.* A diving board; a springy board from which a swimmer dives or jumps.

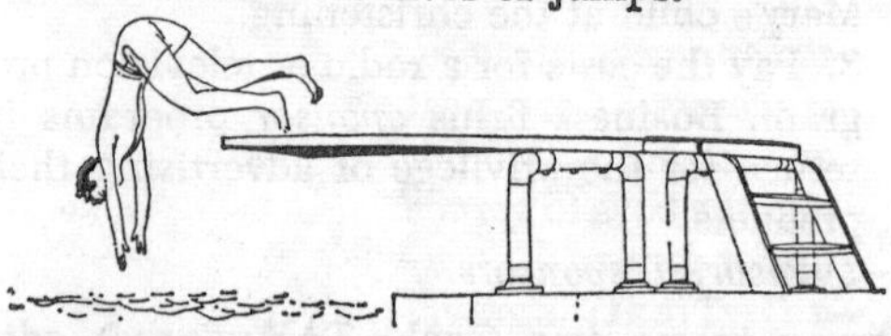

spring·time (SPRING-tym) *n.* The spring of the year.

spring·y (SPRING-ee) *adj. springier, springiest.* Able to be pressed down or together and then go back to its usual shape and size when the pressure is gone.—The mattress on Mother's bed is soft and *springy.*

sprin·kle (SPRING-kəl) *n. sprinkles.* 1. A light rainfall.—We had a *sprinkle* this morning, but the sun is shining now.
2. A very small amount.—Mother put just a *sprinkle* of pepper in the soup.
—*v. sprinkles, sprinkled, sprinkling.* 1. Scatter drops or small bits.—Mother *sprinkled* the clothes with warm water.
2. Spray; put liquid on by sprinkling.—Father *sprinkled* the garden.
3. Rain a little.—It started to *sprinkle,* so we went into the house.

sprin·kler (SPRINGK-ler) *n. sprinklers.* 1. A device fastened to a hose, for spraying. — Father uses a *sprinkler* to water the lawn.

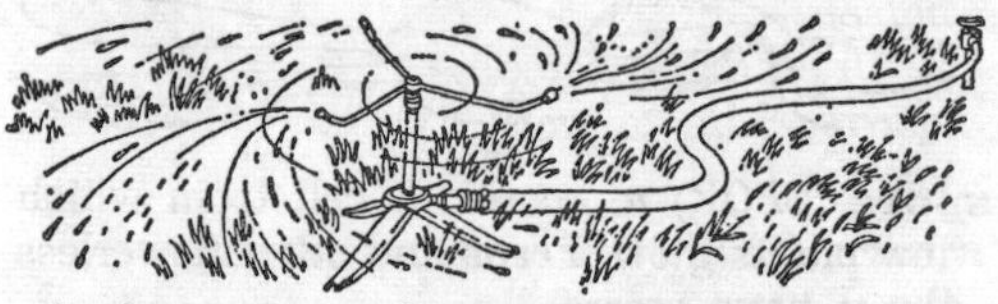

2. A water truck or cart with tanks from which water is sprayed on the pavement.— Men sprinkle the city streets with *sprinklers* to keep down the dust.

sprint (SPRINT) *n. sprints.* A fast, short race.—The boys had quite a *sprint* across the playground.
—*v. sprints, sprinted, sprinting.* Run fast. — Jack *sprinted* up the path.

sprite (SPRYT) *n. sprites.* Fairy or elf.–The water *sprites* are supposed to have long, pale green hair.

sprout (SPROWT) *n. sprouts.* A tiny new stalk from a seed or another plant.–Mother started this plant from a *sprout.*
–*v. sprouts, sprouted, sprouting.* Start to grow. – Beans *sprout* very soon after they are planted.

spruce (SPROOSS) *n. spruces.* An evergreen tree. A *spruce* has cones.
–*v. spruces, spruced, sprucing.* Get neat and clean. – Mother told the boys to *spruce* up for dinner.
–*adj.* Neat; smart; trim. – Father looks very *spruce* in his new suit.

sprung (SPRUNG) *v.* One form of the verb *spring.*–Jack looked behind the bush from which the little rabbit had *sprung.*

spry (SPRY) *adj. sprier, spriest; spryly, adv.* Quick; lively; full of life. – Grandfather is *spry* for his age.

spur (SPER) *n. spurs.* 1. A pointed device fastened to a horseman's heels with which to jab the horse and make it go faster.

2. Anything that forces, urges, or drives one to do a thing.–The man's hunger was a *spur* that drove him to work.
3. Any point that sticks out like a horseman's spur.–The rooster dug his *spurs* into Grandfather's hand.
–*v. spurs, spurred, spurring.* 1. Prick a horse's sides with spurs.–The cowboy *spurred* his horse.
2. Urge; drive; force. – The man's hunger *spurred* him to work hard in order to get enough food.

spurn (SPERN) *v. spurns, spurned, spurning.* Refuse scornfully.–Father *spurned* the dishonest man's offer.

spurt (SPERT) *n. spurts.* 1. A gush.–A *spurt* of flame from the stable reached the hayloft above.
2. A short burst (of energy, activity, effort, etc.).–Ann had a *spurt* of interest in stamp collecting, but she soon tired of the hobby and gave it up.
–*v. spurts, spurted, spurting.* 1. Squirt or gush. –Water *spurted* out of the hole in the hose.
2. Make a sudden, increased effort. – The black horse *spurted* ahead and won the championship race.

sput•nik (SPUHT- *or* SPUT-nik) *n. sputniks.* One of the first man-made satellites launched from Russia. *Sputnik* I was launched October 4, 1957; *Sputnik* II was launched November 3, 1957; and *Sputnik* III was launched May 15, 1958.

sput•ter (SPUT-er) *v. sputters, sputtered, sputtering.* 1. Make a spitting, hissing sound. –Hot dogs *sputter* when roasting.
2. Talk fast and in a way that cannot be understood.–Jack was so excited that he *sputtered,* and we could not understand what he was trying to tell us.
–*sputter, n. sputters.*

spy (SPY) *n. spies.* A person who secretly watches to find out something.–In time of war, a *spy* tries to get information about the enemy. He tries to find out the enemy's plans and positions.
–*v. spies, spied, spying.* 1. See; find with the eyes.–When Mary found the thimble, she cried, "I *spy* it."
2. Watch secretly; act as a spy.–The policeman *spied* on the robbers.

squad (SKWAHD) *n. squads.* A small group of as many people as are required for some activity.–A *squad* of workers cleaned up the city park. – A football *squad* includes the team of eleven players and a number of substitutes.

squad•ron (SKWAHD-rən) *n. squadrons.* A fighting unit of airplanes, warships, or cavalry.–A *squadron* of airplanes flew over the city.

squall (SKWAWL) *n. squalls.* 1. A sudden, strong, whirling rush of wind, usually with rain.
2. A loud squawk or cry.–The duck let out a *squall* when the dog chased it across the barnyard.
–*v. squalls, squalled, squalling.* Cry out loudly.–The cats on the back fence *squalled* at the sight of the dog.

squan•der (SKWAHN-der) *v. squanders, squandered, squandering.* Waste; spend unwisely.–The man did not *squander* his money. He saved it.

square (SKWAIR) *n. squares.* 1. A flat shape with four sides of the same length and four corners all alike. – A checkerboard is divided into *squares.*

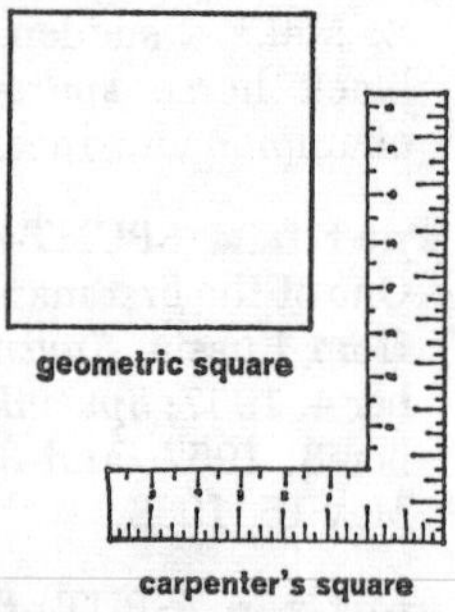

2. A carpenter's tool for measuring corners to make sure that they are perfectly square, that they are like the corners of the figure in the picture.
3. A city block; place or space in a city with streets on all four sides.
–*v. squares, squared, squaring.* 1. Make the four sides even, and the four corners alike.–The carpenter *squared* the board.
2. Settle; make right.–Bob *squared* his debt with Father.
3. Correspond. – His story doesn't *square* with the facts.
–*adj.* 1. Having four equal sides and four corners alike.–The table top is *square.*
2. Honest and fair.–Grandfather says that it pays to be *square* with everyone.

squash (SKWAHSH) *n. squashes.* A vegetable that grows on a vine as a pumpkin does. *Squashes* are yellow or green.

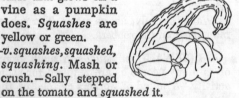

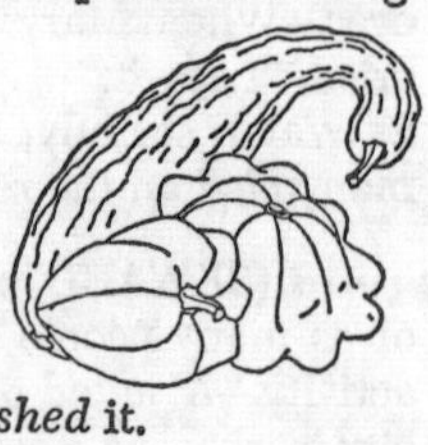

–*v. squashes, squashed, squashing.* Mash or crush. – Sally stepped on the tomato and *squashed* it.

squat (SKWAHT) *v. squats, squatted, squatting.* Sit on one's heels. – Grandfather *squatted* down to weed the garden.
–*adj. squatter, squattest.* Short and thick. – One pitcher is tall and slender; the other is *squat.*

squaw (SKWAW) *n. squaws.* A name for an American Indian woman or wife.

squeak (SKWEEK) *n. squeaks.* A short, shrill noise. – The *squeak* of the barn door kept Grandmother awake.
–*v. squeaks, squeaked, squeaking.* Make a sharp, shrill sound.–A door with hinges that need oiling often *squeaks.*

squeal (SKWEEL) *n. squeals.* A sharp, shrill cry.–We heard the *squeal* of the little pig.
–*v. squeals, squealed, squealing.* Make a sharp, shrill cry.

squeeze (SKWEEZ) *v. squeezes, squeezed, squeezing.* 1. Press hard.–You make orange juice by *squeezing* oranges.
2. Get (through or into a crowded or tight place). – She *squeezed* through the narrow opening.–I've *squeezed* all I can into the suitcase.

squeez•er (SKWEEZ-er) *n. squeezers.* A device for pressing the juice out of oranges, lemons, and the like.–Mother uses a *squeezer* to make lemonade.

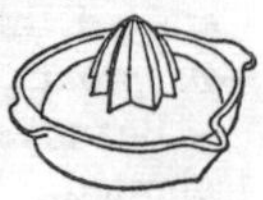

squint (SKWINT) *v. squints, squinted, squinting.* Look with eyes partly shut.–The sun was so bright that I had to *squint* to see at all.

squirm (SKWERM) *v. squirms, squirmed, squirming.* Wriggle, twist, and turn this way and that.–Do not *squirm* at the dinner table.

squir•rel (SKWER-əl) *n. squirrels.* A small red, black, or gray animal with a long bushy tail. *Squirrels* can run fast and climb trees. *Squirrels* put away nuts to eat in winter.

squirt (SKWERT) *v. squirts, squirted, squirting.* Cause liquid to shoot out in a jet; spurt. –Harry accidentally *squirted* ink from his fountain pen onto his desk.

stab (STAB) *n. stabs.* 1. A jab or thrust.–The robber made a *stab* at the policeman with his knife.
2. A wound made by something pointed.–The child had a small *stab* in his hand from the point of the pen.
–*v. stabs, stabbed, stabbing.* Pierce with a pointed weapon.–The man *stabbed* a potato with a knife.

sta•ble (STAY-bəl) *n. stables.* A barn or building in which horses or cattle are kept.–The farmer has three *stables* for his animals.
–*adj.* Firm; steady.–Let me get you a more *stable* chair. Yours looks as though it might collapse.

stack (STAK) *n. stacks.* 1. A large pile.–Little Boy Blue was under the hay*stack* fast asleep. – Mary carried a big *stack* of plates out to the dining room.

2. A chimney (usually of a factory or other large building, or of an engine).–Smoke from the furnace goes out through the smoke*stack.*
–*v. stacks, stacked, stacking.* Arrange in a pile.–Mother *stacked* the dinner dishes in the sink.

sta•di•um (STAY-dee-əm) *n. stadiums.* An outdoor field with many rows of seats built around it.–Football and baseball games are often played in *stadiums.*

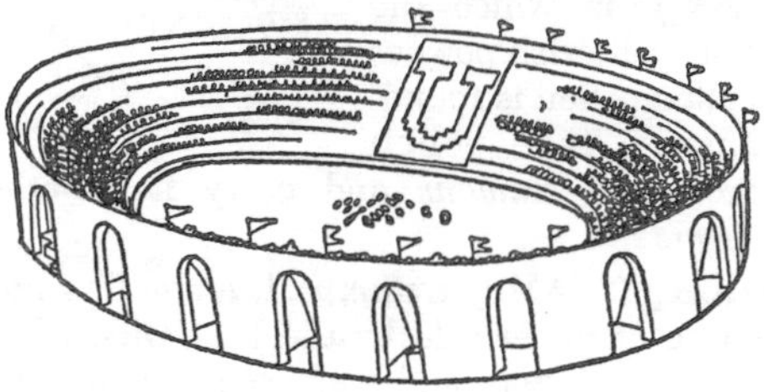

staff (STAF) *n. staffs* or *staves.* 1. A pole, stick, or rod.–Little Bo-Peep carried a *staff* to guide the sheep.–The Boy Scouts raised the flag on the flag*staff*.–Tommy made a walking *staff* for Grandfather.
2. (*pl. staffs*) The four spaces and five lines on which notes are put in written music.

3. (*pl. staffs*) A group, especially of workers. –A hospital has a *staff* of doctors.–A school has a *staff* of teachers.
–*v. staffs, staffed, staffing.* Provide workers for.–It is sometimes difficult to *staff* hospitals in Africa because of the lack of doctors and nurses there.

stag (STAG) *n. stag* or *stags.* A male deer that is fully grown. *Stags* have horns.

stage (STAYJ) *n. stages.* 1. A raised platform or floor for public performances.–The children went onto the *stage* to sing "The Farmer in the Dell."
2. The theater; acting.–Mary wants to go on the *stage.* She wants to be an actress more than anything.
3. Degree or period.–A frog goes through a tadpole *stage* of development.–We climbed the mountain by easy *stages.* We would go up a little way, stop to rest, and then go on.
–*v. stages, staged, staging.* Arrange; bring about; put on (a stage).–The boys *staged* a boxing match. They made all the arrangements for having it in public.

stage•coach (STAYJ-kohch) *n. stagecoaches.* A coach or carriage used in olden times to carry passengers and mail.

stag•ger (STAG-er) *v. staggers, staggered, staggering.* 1. Walk unsteadily, or sway back and forth or from side to side.–The sick man *staggered* down the sidewalk.
2. Arrange alternately.–The principal *staggered* our lunch hours. He arranged them one after another so that everyone in the school would not be eating at the same time.

stag•nant (STAG-nənt) *adj.* Not flowing; foul from standing still.–Mosquitoes breed in *stagnant* water.

stain (STAYN) *n. stains.* 1. A soiled spot.–Do not spill blackberry juice on your dress or it will make a *stain.*
2. A coloring or finish.–Father used a maple *stain* for the table.
–*v. stains, stained, staining.* 1. Make a spot.–The juice will *stain* your dress.
2. Color, or put a finish on.–Father *stained* the unpainted table.

stair (STAIR) *n. stairs.* A step.–We go down a flight of *stairs* to get to the basement.

stair•way (STAIR-way) *n. stairways.* A set of steps.–The *stairway* leading to the second floor has a rail at the side.

stake (STAYK) *n. stakes.* 1. A pointed stick or rod pounded into the ground.–The goat was tied to a *stake.*
2. An issue; a thing to be won or lost.–The soldier's life was at *stake.*
3. An interest.–Every citizen has a *stake* in the future of the town.
–*v. stakes, staked, staking.* 1. Mark off with stakes.–Bob *staked* out his garden. He drove sticks into the ground around it to show where his garden ended.
2. Risk.–I would *stake* my life on the prince's loyalty to the king. That is how much I believe in the prince's loyalty.

sta·lac·tite (stə-LAK-tyt) *n. stalactites.* An icicle-shaped formation hanging from the ceiling of a cave. *Stalactites* are formed over very long periods of time by dripping water that contains lime. The water evaporates, but the lime is added to the growing *stalactite.*

sta·lag·mite (stə-LAG-myt) *n. stalagmites.* A formation of lime that looks like an upside-down icicle rising from the floor of a cave. *Stalagmites* are formed over long periods of time by the build-up of lime from water that has dripped to the floor of the cave.

stale (STAYL) *adj. staler, stalest.* 1. Not new or fresh.—This cake is *stale.* It is old and dry.
2. Not keen or vigorous.—Bob played baseball badly because he was *stale* from overtraining and from playing in too many games.

stalk (STAWK) *n. stalks.* The main stem of a plant. — Mary broke the *stalk* of the lily.—Bob ate a *stalk* of celery.

—*v. stalks, stalked, stalking.* 1. Try to get near an animal or person without letting that animal or person know it.—The hunter *stalked* the deer in the woods.
2. Walk slowly and proudly. — The cat *stalked* through the door.

stall (STAWL) *n. stalls.* 1. A space in a barn or stable for one horse or one cow.—The horse stands in his *stall* and eats hay from a rack.

2. A booth, or small enclosed counter.—The girls had a *stall* from which to sell candy at the fair.
3. A seat for a member of a church choir.—The minister faced the choir *stalls.*
—*v. stalls, stalled, stalling.* 1. Stop when you don't want it to.—Our motor *stalled* and we couldn't get it started.
2. Delay on purpose.—Mother told Jack to stop *stalling* and to get ready.

stal·lion (STAL-yən) *n. stallions.* A male or he horse.

sta·men (STAY-mən) *n. stamens.* The part in the middle of a flower on which the fine, yellowish powder called pollen is found. Insects take pollen from the *stamens* and carry it to other flowers.

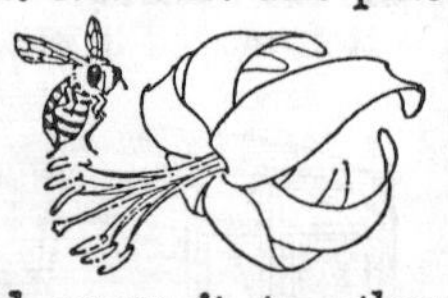

stamp (STAMP) *n. stamps.* 1. A small printed piece of paper sold by the Post Office. It is glued to letters and packages to show that one has paid for sending them.—Before mailing letters or packages, you must put *stamps* on them.

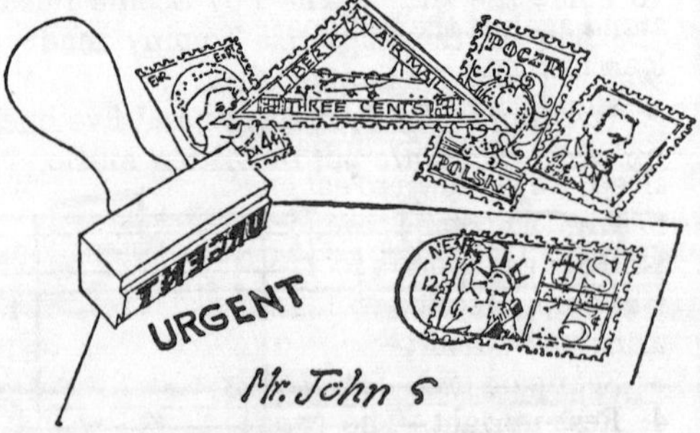

2. A block (usually rubber) with a name, picture, or some other design on it. You can press the *stamp* on an ink pad and then print the design on paper.
3. A mark, signature, or the like pressed upon anything.—The teacher puts a *stamp* on our report cards.
—*v. stamps, stamped, stamping.* 1. Mark with a stamp.—She *stamps* her name on the cards.
2. Put a stamp on.—Remember to *stamp* the letter before mailing it.
3. Beat the ground with the foot; pound or crush with the foot. — The hungry pony *stamped* noisily. — Some little children believe that if you *stamp* on an ant, it will rain.
—*Stamp out* means get rid of.—The mayor did much to *stamp out* crime in the city.

stam·pede (stam-PEED) *v. stampedes, stampeded, stampeding.* 1. Cause to run, scatter, or flee in a sudden rush.—The fire in the barn *stampeded* the cattle.
2. Flee in panic; run headlong in a body.—The crowd *stampeded* out of the smoke-filled theater.

stand (STAND) *n. stands.* 1. A position.—The member of the Safety Patrol took his *stand* at the corner to help the little children cross the street.—What *stand* do you take on this subject? What do you think about it?

2. An outdoor counter where things are sold. –We bought a pound of big red cherries at the fruit *stand.*

bedside stand

fruit stand

3. A small table; a base that something stands on.–Mother put the lamp on the bedside *stand.*
4. A stop to face a military foe.–Custer's last *stand* against the Indians is famous in American history.
–*v. stands, stood, standing.* **1.** Rest on one's feet with the body upright.–We lie down to sleep; we sit down to eat our meals; we *stand* to sing "The Star-Spangled Banner."
2. Rise; get to one's feet.–Our teacher has us *stand* up, face the windows, and stretch our arms every hour.
3. Set up on end.–*Stand* the broom there.
4. Rest upright.–The candlestick *stands* on the sideboard.
5. Bear or endure. – Mother cannot *stand* hearing Baby cry.
6. Hold good; remain. – Mother's promise still *stands.*
7. Take or have a position.–Where do you *stand* in your class? How do you compare with the others?

stand•ard (STAN-derd) *n. standards.* **1.** A banner or flag.–The boy who carries our flag is our *standard*-bearer. He carries the *standard.*

2. Any post, pole, or the like that stands up straight to support or hold up something.–A flagpole is a *standard.*
3. Something by which things can be judged, measured, or compared; something set up as a rule or model.–Bob's mark on the arithmetic test was not up to his usual high *standard.* He does better most of the time.
–*adj.* **1.** Conforming to the usual rule.–The *standard* size for typewriter paper is eight and a half by eleven inches.
2. Of a value generally recognized. – They studied the *standard* authors.
–*Standard time* is the time that has been chosen by law for use by all people in a part of a country or in a whole country.–Detroit has Eastern *Standard time.* The city of Chicago has Central *Standard time.*

stan•za (STAN-zə) *n. stanzas.* A group of lines of a poem, especially of a poem set to music. In a song, the tune is sung once for each *stanza.*–We learned one *stanza* of "The Star-Spangled Banner."

sta•ple (STAY-pəl) *n. staples.* **1.** Most important products raised.–Coffee and rubber are the *staples* of parts of South America.
2. A U-shaped piece of metal with the ends pointed.–The farmer fastened the wire fence to the posts with *staples.*

3. A piece of wire that bends over at each end to fasten papers together.–The teacher fastened the pages together with *staples.*
–*v. staples, stapled, stapling.* Fasten with staples.–She *stapled* the booklet. She put the papers together with staples.
–*adj.* Most important; chief.–Among the *staple* articles in a grocery are coffee and tea.

star (STAHR) *n. stars.* **1.** A five- or six-pointed figure.–The teacher puts *stars* on our spelling papers if the words are spelled right.
2. A *star* is a large sphere of glowing gas in space. Our sun is a *star.* Other *stars* are so far away that they are seen only as points of light in the night sky.
3. A leading actor or performer. – Mickey Mouse was the *star* of the movie we saw.
4. A person who can do something exceptionally well.–Babe Ruth was a baseball *star.*
–*v. stars, starred, starring.* **1.** Be the chief performer.–Mickey Mouse *starred* in the moving picture.
2. Put a star on. – The teacher *starred* the good spelling papers.

starch (STAHRCH) *n. starches.* **1.** A white substance found in certain plants that has no taste or odor.–Potatoes, macaroni, rice, and many other foods contain *starch.*
2. A white powder made of this, used to stiffen clothes. – Mother puts *starch* in Father's collars.
–*v. starches, starched, starching.* Stiffen with starch.–Starch is mixed with water and used to *starch* shirts and other clothes before they are ironed.

stare (STAIR) *n. stares.* A steady look with wide-open eyes.
–*v. stares, stared, staring.* Look straight and steadily with eyes wide open.–The hungry girl *stared* at the food on the table.

star•fish (STAHR-fish) *n. starfish* or *starfishes.* A star-shaped animal that lives in the sea.

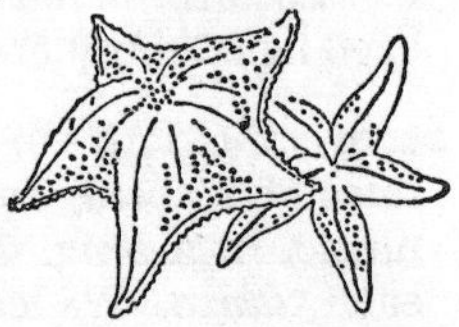

star•light (STAHR-lyt) *n.* Light coming from the stars.–The *starlight* helped us find our way through the woods.

star•ling (STAHR-ling) *n. starlings.* A brownish-black bird whose feathers look greenish and purplish in the sunlight.

Stars and Stripes (STAHRZ ən STRYPSS). A name for the flag of the United States.

start (STAHRT) *n. starts.* 1. A sudden, startled movement.–A loud crash of thunder made me awake with a *start.*

2. A setting out; beginning. – The whistle blew and Bob was off to a good *start* in the race.

3. A lead.–She had a five minutes' *start,* but I caught up to her.

4. A place of beginning.–In studying world trade, we'll look at our village stores for a *start.*

–*v. starts, started, starting.* 1. Begin; set out. – I *start* to school at eight o'clock. – I *start* working on time. – Bob turned on the radio and the music *started.*

2. Set in motion.–Father *started* the car.

start•er (STAHR-ter) *n. starters.* 1. A person who tells others when to start or begin doing something.–The person who blows a whistle for a race or a game to begin is a *starter.*–A man at the bus station who tells the driver when to start is a *starter.*

2. A mechanical device to set something in motion. – Father worked the *starter* in the car to start the motor.

star•tle (STAHR-tl) *v. startles, startled, startling.* Shock; surprise; frighten for a moment.–The ringing of the doorbell *startled* Mother.

star•va•tion (stahr-VAY-shən) *n.* Being without food.–The farmer's pigs died of *starvation.* He had no food and could not feed them.

starve (STAHRV) *v. starves, starved, starving.* Be without food; die of hunger.–If you do not eat, you will *starve.*

state (STAYT) *n. states.* 1. A group of people who work and live under one government, or the territory in which these people live and work.–The United States is made up of fifty *states.*–The United Nations is made up of member *states,* or countries.

2. A condition. – Mary was in an excited *state* on the night of the class play.

3. Way in which a person of wealth or position lives; grandeur; magnificence. – The Oriental prince lives and travels in *state.*

–*v. states, stated, stating.* Say something by writing or speaking.–The doctor *stated* that Baby had the measles.

–*adj.* Governmental; formal; official. – Mr. Harris is studying the *state* papers of Abraham Lincoln.

stat•ed (STAY-tid) *adj.* Fixed or definite; set. –Most clubs meet at *stated* times and places. Our club meets on Monday evenings at eight in the school gymnasium.

state•house (STAYT-howss) *n. statehouses.* (Sometimes spelled with a capital "S.") The building in which a state legislature meets and conducts its affairs.

state•ment (STAYT-mənt) *n. statements.* 1. A report; a formal account, written or spoken. – The man who saw the accident made a *statement* to the police.

2. A listing showing how much money you owe or how much is due you.–According to my bank *statement,* I have $14.36 in the bank.

stat•ic (STAT-ik) *n.* An electrical disturbance in the air that causes crackling sounds and otherwise interferes with clear reception of radio signals.–It was difficult to hear the broadcast because of the *static.*

–*adj.* Stationary; at rest; standing still.–The water in a river is never *static;* it is always moving.

–*Static electricity* is electricity whose charges do not move in a current. It is produced when certain materials are rubbed together, such as silk and glass. When you walk across a rug on a cold day and receive a shock from the metal door handle, its cause is a charge of *static electricity* created by the rubbing of your shoes on the rug. The charge jumps from you to the door handle.

sta•tion (STAY-shən) *n. stations.* 1. A regular stopping place for trains or buses. – A railroad *station* is a building in which people wait for trains.

2. An appointed place of duty.–The Safety Patrol boys stood at their *stations* to help the little children cross the streets.

–*v. stations, stationed, stationing.* Locate for duty.–My brother is *stationed* at an army camp nearby.

sta•tion•ar•y (STAY-shə-nair-ee) *adj.* 1. Fixed in one place; not movable.—Our washtubs are *stationary*. So is the furnace.
2. Not changing in size or number.—The size of our class has been *stationary* all year.

sta•tion•er•y (STAY-shə-nair-ee) *n.* Writing materials, such as paper and envelopes.—Mother keeps her *stationery* in the desk.

sta•tis•tics (stə-TISS-tiks) *n. sing.* and *pl.* 1. (In the *sing.*) The collecting and analyzing of numerical data with the goal of reaching some numerical estimate. One would use *statistics* to estimate anything from how much spinach will be eaten in a certain town in a given year to how many trucks will cross a certain bridge in a given day.
2. (In the *pl.*) Numerical facts or data which have been collected and analyzed.—*Statistics* show that everyone in our town who works is earning twice as much this year as he did five years ago.

stat•ue (STACH-oo) *n. statues.* A carved or molded figure of a person or animal. *Statues* are made of stone, clay, metal, wood, etc. —We saw the *statue* of Abraham Lincoln in Washington.

stat•ure (STACH-er) *n. statures.* Natural height.—Dwarfs are persons of very short *stature*.—Giants are persons of very tall *stature*.

sta•tus (STAY-təss *or* STAT-əss) *n. statuses.* 1. Social or professional position.—He enjoys a high *status* in medical circles. He is highly regarded as a doctor by other doctors. —Mr. Smith's present *status* is that of vice-president of the firm.
2. State or condition; situation.—What is the present *status* of the ball game? Who is winning and what is the score?

stat•ute (STACH-oot) *n. statutes.* A law.—*Statutes* against stealing are part of the law of every land.

stay (STAY) *n. stays.* 1. A time of staying in a place.—We had an enjoyable *stay* at the farm.
2. A support.—*Stays* of rope or wire support the mast.
—*v. stays, stayed, staying.* Remain; live; reside; be (in one place).—You go and I will *stay* here.—Bob has gone to Grandmother's to *stay* for the summer.

stead•y (STED-ee) *adj.; steadily, adv.* 1. Regular; always the same; not jerky.—Grandmother's writing is *steady*.—Father drives the car at a *steady* speed.
2. Firm; not shaky or wavering.—The man's step is *steady*. He doesn't totter or shake when he walks.—The big tree is *steady*.

steak (STAYK) *n. steaks.* A slice of meat (or fish), usually beef, to be fried or broiled.—We got a two-pound *steak* at the butcher's.

steal (STEEL) *v. steals, stole, stealing.* 1. Take something that belongs to another person without his permission.—The Bible tells one not to *steal*.—The dog *stole* the cat's food.
2. Move quietly and secretly.—Bob *stole* into the kitchen to taste the stew.

steam (STEEM) *n.* Water turned into gas or vapor by heat. When water boils, it throws out moisture into the air. This moisture is *steam*. You cannot see *steam*. When *steam* is turning back to water, it forms a white cloud of tiny drops, also called *steam*.—Some homes are heated by *steam*.—Some engines are run by the power of *steam*.
—*v. steams, steamed, steaming.* 1. Treat or cook with steam.—Mother *steams* bread to freshen it. She puts hard bread into a pan with holes in it, sets it over a kettle of boiling water, and covers it up. Foods can be cooked in this way, too.
2. Give off steam.—The water in the teakettle is *steaming*.
3. Go by steam.—The ship *steamed* out of the harbor.

steam•boat (STEEM-boht) *n. steamboats.* A boat which is driven by steam power.

steam en•gine (STEEM en-jən) *steam engines.* An engine driven by steam power. —Many railroad engines are *steam engines*.

steam•er (STEEM-er) *n. steamers.* 1. A ship, boat, or engine that is moved by steam.
2. A kind of pan with holes in it for steaming food.—Mother cooked the pudding in a *steamer*.

steam•ship (STEEM-ship) *n. steamships.* A ship which is driven by steam power.

steed (STEED) *n. steeds.* A horse, especially one of high spirit.—The knight rode a gallant *steed*.

steel (STEEL) *n.* and *adj.* Iron that has been heated and mixed with carbon and other substances to make it harder and stronger. *Steel* is used to make many things that get hard use and must be very strong.—The bodies of most cars are made of *steel.*
—*v. steels, steeled, steeling.* Make strong or tough; make able to resist.—John *steeled* himself against possible disappointment.

steep (STEEP) *v. steeps, steeped, steeping.* Soak.—Tea is better if *steeped* in boiling water.
—*adj. steeper, steepest; steeply, adv.* Slanting sharply.—The boys climbed the *steep* hill.

stee•ple (STEE-pəl) *n. steeples.* The pointed tower on a church roof.

steer (STIR) *n. steers.* The young male of beef cattle.—*Steers* are killed to provide meat.
—*v. steers, steered, steering.* Direct; guide; cause to go in the direction desired.—Bob *steered* his bicycle through the crowded street.—We turn the steering wheel on an automobile to *steer* the car and make it go where we want it to.

stem (STEM) *n. stems.* 1. The main stalk of a plant.—Flowers and leaves are joined to the main *stem* by smaller *stems.*

2. The tube of a smoking pipe through which smoke is drawn into the mouth.
3. A slender support like the stem of a plant.—The glass has a *stem* at the bottom.
—*v. stems, stemmed, stemming.* 1. Remove the stems of.—Jane *stemmed* and pitted the cherries for the pie.
2. Grow out of, as from a stem.—The riots *stemmed* from unemployment.
3. Make headway against.—The ship *stemmed* the tide.
4. Stop; decrease.—The flow of blood was *stemmed* by applying a tourniquet.

sten•cil (STEN-səl) *n. stencils.* 1. A sheet of paper or metal with designs or letters cut through it. When you lay out a *stencil* on paper and brush ink across the *stencil,* the cutout designs or letters will show on the paper.

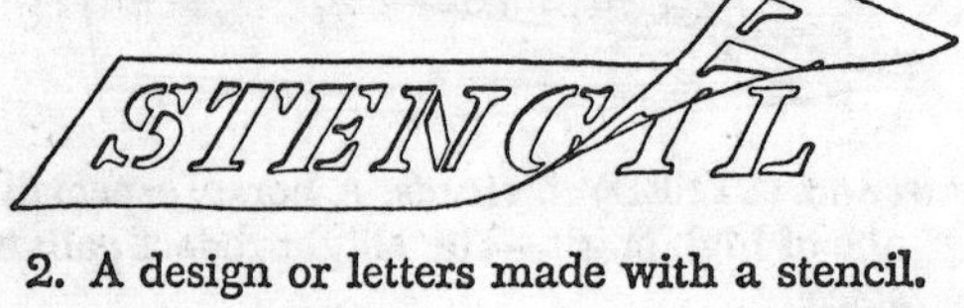

2. A design or letters made with a stencil.

ste•nog•ra•pher (stə-NAHG-rə-fer) *n. stenographers.* A person who can write down spoken words as fast as they are said by a special way of writing called shorthand.

step (STEP) *n. steps.* 1. The placing of one foot forward.—Jack took six *steps* to get to the blackboard.—The distance which one can put one foot forward is also a *step.*
2. A regular movement of the feet in dancing.—Mary taught Jack the new dance *step.*
3. A foot*step* is the sound of feet when walking or running.
4. One footboard of a stairway or ladder.—The first *step* of our hall stairs is covered with a rubber mat.
5. An act; a thing to do; one of a series of such actions.—The first *step* in building a house is to dig the basement.
—*v. steps, stepped, stepping.* Move by placing one foot in a new forward position while the other foot remains where it was, as in walking.—Father *stepped* up one stair.

step•fa•ther (STEP-fah-ther) *n. stepfathers.* The husband of one's mother, but not one's real father.—After Bill's father died, his mother married another man. This man is Bill's *stepfather.*

step•lad•der (STEP-lad-er) *n. stepladders.* A ladder with two parts hinged together so it will stand up by itself. A *stepladder* has flat steps instead of rungs to stand on.

step•moth•er (STEP-muth-er) *n. stepmothers.* The wife of one's father, but not one's real mother.—After Cinderella's own mother died, her father married another woman. This woman was Cinderella's *stepmother.*

steppe (STEP) *n. steppes.* A vast treeless plain, especially one of those in parts of the Soviet Union.

ster•e•o•phon•ic (stair-ee-ə-FAHN-ik) *adj.* Made by a special process for reproducing sounds with great realism.—Father bought an album of *stereophonic* records.

ster•e•o•scope (STAIR-ee-ə-skohp) *n. stereoscopes.* A viewing instrument by means of which two slightly different pictures of the same subject may be seen as one. Pictures seen through a *stereoscope* have a three-dimensional quality, or a feeling of depth.—My grandmother has a *stereoscope.*

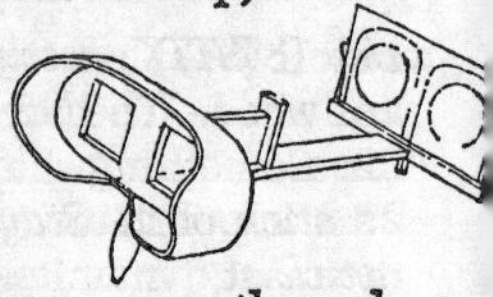

ster·ile (STAIR-əl) *adj.* 1. Free of living germs.–The doctor placed a *sterile* bandage on the wound.
2. Not able to produce crops; not fertile; barren.–It is now possible to irrigate *sterile* desert areas and make them fertile.

ster·i·lize (STAIR-ə-lyz) *v. sterilizes, sterilized, sterilizing.* Make sterile or free from living germs.–The nurse *sterilizes* the doctor's instruments in boiling water.

stern (STERN) *n. sterns.* The back part of a boat.
–*adj. sterner, sternest; sternly, adv.* 1. Strict.–Our teacher plays with us during recess, but during class she is very *stern.* She will not allow any laughing or whispering during our lessons.
2. Harsh; angry.–Jack called his dog away from the smaller dog in a *stern* voice.

steth·o·scope (STETH-ə-skohp) *n. stethoscopes.* An instrument used by doctors for listening to sounds in the body, such as the heartbeat.–The doctor listened to the patient's breathing with his *stethoscope.*

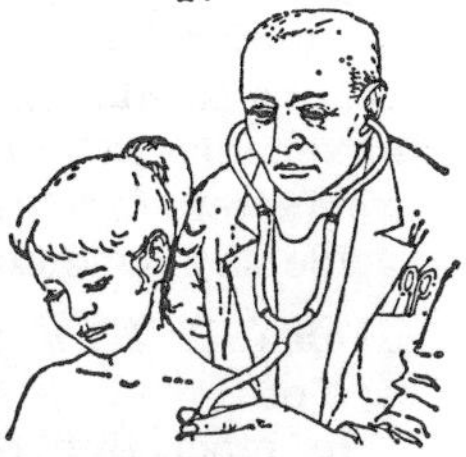

stew (STOO *or* STYOO) *n. stews.* A dish of vegetables and meat boiled together slowly.–Lamb *stew* is Father's favorite dish.
–*v. stews, stewed, stewing.* Cook by boiling slowly.–The cook *stewed* the prunes.

stew·ard (STOO- *or* STYOO-erd) *n. stewards.* 1. An officer on a ship in charge of food and sleeping quarters for passengers and crew.
2. A man on a ship who takes care of rooms, waits on table, and performs other duties, under the direction of a chief *steward.*
3. A man in charge of the dining car on a train.

stew·ard·ess (STOO- *or* STYOO-er-dəss) *n. stewardesses.* 1. A woman steward.
2. A woman on an airplane who looks after the comfort of the passengers and feeds them.

stick (STIK) *n. sticks.* 1. A long, slender piece of wood.–The boys cut *sticks* to make a kite.
2. Something shaped like a stick of wood, as a *stick* of candy, a *stick* of chewing gum, a *stick* of dynamite.–A cane is a walking *stick.*
–*v. sticks, stuck, sticking.* 1. Fasten together with glue or paste.–*Stick* these two pieces of paper together.
2. Hold fast.–The dish *stuck* to the table.
3. Prick; pierce.–Be careful or you will *stick* your finger with the pin.
4. Put or thrust.–The cat *stuck* its nose into the milk.
5. Be unable to continue; fail to work.–The old car *stuck* halfway up the hill.
–*Stick to* sometimes means to keep at.–*Stick to* your work until it is done.

stiff (STIF) *adj. stiffer, stiffest; stiffly, adv.* 1. Not easily bent or moved.–Cardboard is *stiff;* paper is easy to fold.–The boy's sore arm is *stiff* now, but it will soon loosen up as he uses it.
2. Thick; solid; firm.–Gelatin becomes *stiff* when it cools.
3. Hard; harsh.–The troops engaged in a *stiff* battle.–A *stiff* breeze came up.
4. Formal and unbending in manner.–He made a *stiff* bow, without a word of greeting.

stiff·en (STIF-ən) *v. stiffens, stiffened, stiffening.* Make or become stiff or firm.–Mother uses starch to *stiffen* the collars and cuffs on Father's shirts.–The pudding *stiffens* when it cools.–The army's resistance *stiffened* in the face of the attack.

stile (STYL) *n. stiles.* 1. A step or steps used in going over a fence or a wall.–The old woman's pig would not go over the *stile.*
2. A gate that allows only one person to pass through at a time.

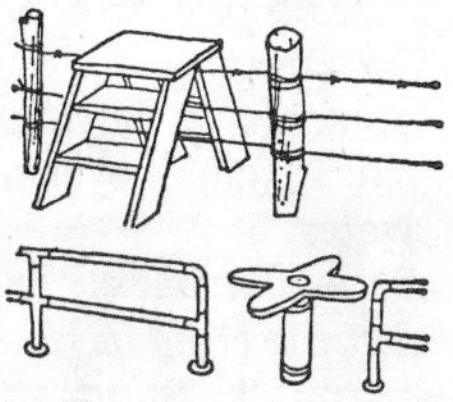

still (STIL) *n. stills.* A device used in purifying water and in making whiskey and other liquors.–You can make fresh water out of salt water with a *still.*
–*v. stills, stilled, stilling.* Quiet; make still.–Mother *stilled* the baby's crying with a lullaby.
–*adj., adv.,* and *conj.* 1. Not moving.–Stand *still.* Do not move.
2. Quiet; silent.–Be *still.* Do not make a sound.
3. Nevertheless; and yet.–Ruth says her tables again and again; *still,* she doesn't seem to know them.
4. Even.–Bob can write well when he writes fast; he can write *still* better when he writes slowly.
5. Yet.–At noon the fire was *still* burning. It had not gone out.

still·ness (STIL-nəss) *n.* Quietness; calm.–The *stillness* of the night is restful.–This lake is known for its *stillness.* The water is never ruffled.

stilt (STILT) *n. stilts.* One of a pair of long poles which has a step or a footrest attached so that the user is elevated above the ground.—Tom learned to walk on *stilts.*

stim·u·lant (STIM-yə-lənt) *n. stimulants.* Something which stimulates, excites, or rouses, usually for a short time.—A cold shower sometimes acts as a *stimulant.*—Various medicines and beverages, including tea and coffee, are *stimulants.*

stim·u·late (STIM-yə-layt) *v. stimulates, stimulated, stimulating.* Rouse to action; stir up; excite.—He was *stimulated* and encouraged by the good news.—The teacher is trying to *stimulate* a classroom discussion.
—*stimulation, n.*

sting (STING) *n. stings.* 1. Bite (of an insect).—Bees and other insects give painful *stings.*
2. The injury made by the bite of an insect.
3. The part of a bee, insect, or animal used for stinging.
4. A sharp, burning pain.—The *sting* of the salt in Jack's eyes made him come out of the water.
5. A sharpness; an intention to hurt.—Tom felt the *sting* of his friend's words of ridicule.
—*v. stings, stung, stinging.* 1. Bite (by an insect).—The mosquito *stung* me.
2. Cause a sharp, burning pain.—Salt *stings* if it gets into a cut on your finger.
3. Hurt by sharpness of word or manner.—Tom was *stung* by his friend's ridicule.

stingray (STING-ray) *n. stingrays.* A flat fish having a long whiplike tail with one or more spines. *Stingrays* live mostly near the bottoms of warm seas. Their tails are used as weapons and are quite dangerous.

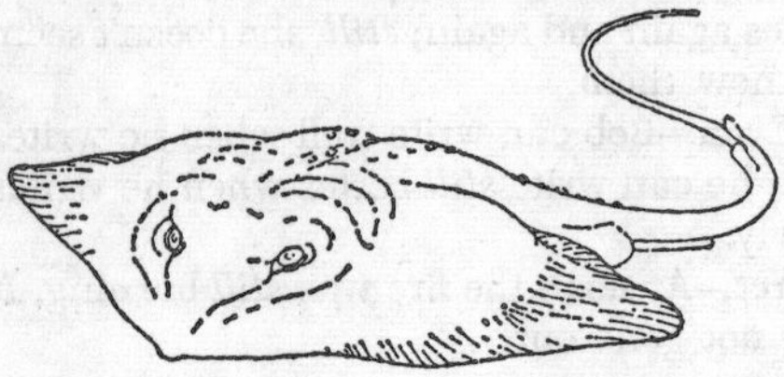

stin·gy (STIN-jee) *adj. stingier, stingiest.* Not generous; unwilling to spend or give away money or other things.—The *stingy* man spends money on nobody, not even himself.

stink (STINGK) *n. stinks.* A bad smell; foul odor.—A leak in the gas pipe caused a *stink* in the house.
—*v. stinks, stank* or *stunk, stinking.* Give off a bad odor.—Garbage, if allowed to stand a long time, *stinks.*

stir (STER) *n. stirs.* 1. Excitement.—The accident in the factory caused a *stir.*
2. Movement.—We could hear a *stir* in the kitchen.
3. A mixing.—She gave the batter a *stir.*
—*v. stirs, stirred, stirring.* 1. Move or mix, as with a spoon.—Mother *stirs* the candy when it is cooking to keep it from burning.
2. Move a little.—The wind made the leaves *stir.*
3. Arouse; excite.—The man *stirs* up trouble wherever he goes.

stir·rup (STER- *or* STIR-əp) *n. stirrups.* One of a pair of footrests or supports for the feet of a person riding horseback. *Stirrups* are fastened to the saddle and hang down on each side.

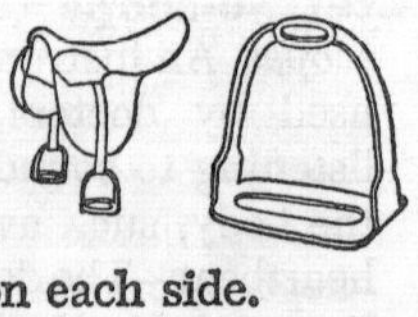

stitch (STICH) *n. stitches.* 1. A single passage of thread through the cloth in sewing.
2. In crocheting or knitting, *stitches* are made by twisting the thread around the needles in certain ways.
3. A sharp, sudden pain.—Grandmother got a *stitch* in her side when she bent over to pick up her glove.
—*v. stitches, stitched, stitching.* Sew; make stitches.—Mother *stitched* the hem in Mary's dress.

stock (STAHK) *n. sing.* and *pl.* Cows, horses, sheep, and other domestic animals.—The farmer keeps his *stock* in the barn.

stock (STAHK) *n. stocks.* 1. Share of investment in a business.—Father buys *stocks,* or lends his money to a business. If the business makes a profit, Father receives a dividend, or share in the profit.
2. Family.—She comes of Irish *stock.*
3. (In the plural) Wooden frame in which wrongdoers in olden times were forced to sit or stand in public for long periods. Many had holes for the hands and feet.
4. A supply, especially of things to sell.—After the Christmas rush, the stores had only a small *stock* left.
—*v. stocks, stocked, stocking.* Have or get a supply of (usually in a store).—Mr. Jones doesn't *stock* hats.

stock•ade (stah-KAYD) *n. stockades.* 1. A defensive enclosure made of high stakes stuck upright in the ground. The early pioneers of America built *stockades* around their dwellings to protect them from Indian attacks.

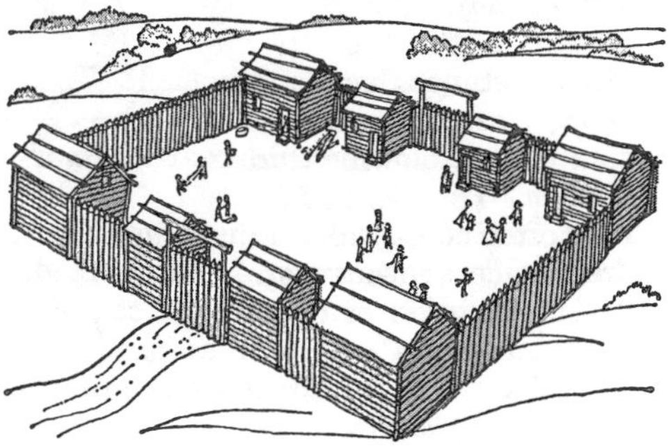

2. Any such high, fenced enclosure.–The cowboy showed us a cattle *stockade.*

stock•ing (STAHK-ing) *n. stockings.* One of a pair of coverings for the feet and lower legs. –Mary wears wool *stockings* in the winter.

stock•yard (STAHK-yahrd) *n. stockyards.* A yard or enclosure where cattle and sheep are kept before they are sent on to markets or slaughterhouses.

stoke (STOHK) *v. stokes, stoked, stoking.* Tend; put fuel in (a furnace, boiler, etc.).–Father *stokes* the coal furnace. He stirs up the fire and puts coal on when it is needed.

stok•er (STOH-ker) *n. stokers.* A person or a machine that takes care of a furnace by putting coal into it. A *stoker* in a factory or on a ship takes care of the fires which heat the boilers.

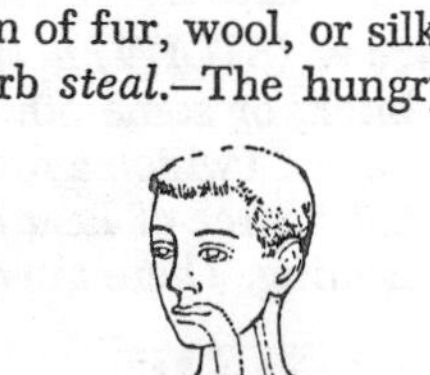

stole (STOHL) *n. stoles.* A woman's scarf or shoulder covering, often of fur, wool, or silk. –*v.* One form of the verb *steal.*–The hungry man *stole* food.

sto•len (STOH-lən) *v.* and *adj.* One form of the verb *steal.* – The jewelry was *stolen.*

stom•ach (STUM-ək) *n. stomachs.* The pouch inside the body into which food goes when swallowed. The *stomach* helps to digest the food.

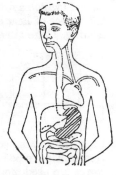

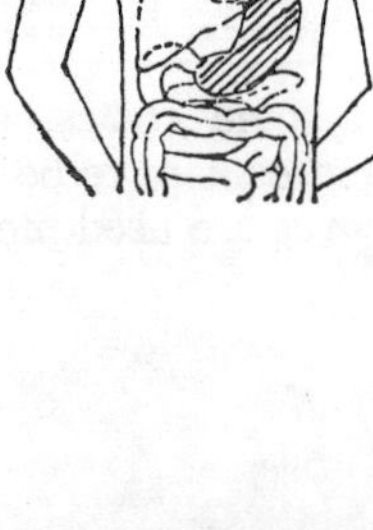

stone (STOHN) *n. stones* and *adj.* 1. A piece of rock.–The house was built of large *stones.*
2. Rock; a hard mineral material found in the earth.–The house was built of *stone.*
3. A gem.–Rubies, opals, and diamonds are precious *stones* used in jewelry.
4. A large seed in a fruit such as the peach or plum.–Mother took the *stones* out of the peaches before preserving them.
–*v. stones, stoned, stoning.* 1. Throw stones at. –In olden times criminals were sometimes *stoned* to death.
2. Take the seeds out of.–Mary helped Mother *stone* the cherries before preserving them.

stood (STUHD) *v.* One form of the verb *stand.*–The boy *stood* by his chair.

stool (STOOL) *n. stools.* 1. A seat without a back.–Mother sits on a kitchen *stool* to mix the cake.
2. A low footrest with legs.

stoop (STOOP) *n. stoops.* 1. A small entrance porch.–In the summer, Mother sometimes sits on the *stoop.*
2. A slumping posture.–That girl does not stand straight; she has a *stoop.*
–*v. stoops, stooped, stooping.* 1. Let the shoulders and head lean forward.–That girl *stoops.*
2. Bend down.–Can you *stoop* and touch the floor with your fingers without bending your knees?
3. Do something unworthy of oneself.–Do not *stoop* to stealing.

stop (STAHP) *n. stops.* 1. A halt; a standstill. –Bring the car to a *stop* at a red light.
2. A stopping place.–The bus *stop* is at the next corner.
3. A device for controlling the tone or quality of tone of a musical instrument.–You can see the *stops* at the side of an organ keyboard.
–*v. stops, stopped, stopping.* 1. Halt; come to a standstill.–*Stop,* look, and listen before you cross the street.
2. Cease; quit.–The bell *stopped* ringing.
3. Close or stuff up.–The boy *stopped* the leak in the dike by putting his thumb into the hole.
4. Block; prevent from moving.–A big, fat man with packages *stopped* the turnstile.
5. Cause to cease or come to an end.–Mother *stopped* the baby's crying by giving her a cracker.–Father *stopped* the water from running by turning off the faucet.
6. Prevent.–Father caught Baby just in time to *stop* her from falling.
7. Drop in (at); visit.–I *stopped* at the bank to cash a check on my way home.

stop•light (STAHP-lyt) *n. stoplights.* 1. A traffic signal light.–The busy intersection has a *stoplight* to control the flow of traffic.

2. A red signal light on the rear end of an automobile.–When a driver steps on his brake, the *stoplight* automatically flashes a warning that the car is slowing or stopping.

stop•per (STAHP-er) *n. stoppers.* A piece of cork, rubber, or glass used to close a bottle or other container.–Mary put the *stopper* in the vinegar bottle.–The perfume bottle has a fancy glass *stopper.*

stop watch (STAHP wahch) *stop watches.* A watch whose hands can be stopped or started at will, usually by pressing a button. *Stop watches* are used especially to time races or other sporting events.

stor•age (STOR-ij) *n.* 1. Being stored; keeping things stored; a place where things may be kept for safekeeping.–We have some furniture in *storage.*–At home our place for *storage* is the attic.

2. The amount paid for storing a thing.–She had to pay twenty-five dollars *storage* on her fur coat.

stor•age bat•ter•y (STOR-ij bat-ə-ree) *storage batteries.* A battery that stores electrical energy. *Storage batteries* can be very easily recharged when they have run down.

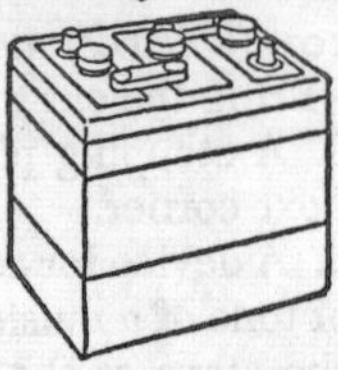

store (STOR) *n. stores.* 1. A shop, or place where things are sold.–Bob went to the fruit *store* to buy a dozen oranges.

2. A supply.–We have quite a *store* of preserved fruit on the cellar shelves.

–v. stores, stored, storing. Put or keep in a special place for later use.–We *store* potatoes, onions, and canned goods in the cellar.

stork (STORK) *n. storks.* A wading bird with long legs, a long neck, and a long bill.

storm (STORM) *n. storms; stormy, adj.* 1. Any strong natural disturbance in the air. Sometimes there is rain, snow, sleet, or hail, and a strong wind blowing during a *storm.*–Thunder and lightning often come with a rain*storm.*–The children made snowmen after the snow*storm.*

2. An explosion or outburst of any kind,–Mary burst into a *storm* of tears.

3. Violent military attack.–The army took the town by *storm.*

–v. storms, stormed, storming. 1. Rush into by force and numbers.–The winners of the ball game *stormed* the schoolroom.

2. Rush angrily.–Jack *stormed* into the room and asked who had taken his bicycle.

sto•ry (STOR-ee) *n. stories.* 1. A report of things that have happened, or of imaginary happenings made up by someone.–Sally likes the *story* of Chicken Little.

2. A falsehood; a lie.–If you do something wrong, do not tell a *story* about it; tell the truth.

3. A floor, or a level, of a building.–We live in a house with two *stories.* It has two floors, on two different levels. The kitchen, dining room, and living room are on the first *story.* The bedrooms are on the second *story.*

stout (STOWT) *adj. stouter, stoutest; stoutly, adv.* 1. Heavily built; fat; thick.–Jack Sprat was thin and his wife was *stout.*–The tramp carried a *stout* stick to defend himself against dogs.

2. Sturdy; strong.–The boy set out to seek his fortune with a *stout* heart.

stove (STOHV) *n. stoves.* A box built of iron, brick, or some other material that does not burn, in which a fire can be made, or an electric source of heat turned on, for cooking or heating. There are electric and gas *stoves.*

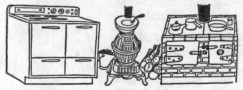

In some *stoves,* coal or wood is burned. Houses used to be heated by *stoves,* but now *stoves* are used mostly for cooking.

strad•dle (STRAD-l) *v. straddles, straddled, straddling.* To spread the legs far apart; to sit on something with one leg on either side. –Bob *straddled* the horse to ride it.–The boy is *straddling* a stool.

straight (STRAYT) *adj. straighter, straightest* and *adv.* 1. Not crooked; without turns, curves, or bends.–The road goes *straight* for five miles, and then it turns.
2. Right; in order.–Our teacher asked us if we had all our lessons *straight*.–Mother told Mary to put the sofa cushions *straight*.
3. Direct; directly.–Go *straight* to school. Go now and go the shortest way.
4. Honest.–That man is *straight*. You can trust him.
5. Serious.–John kept a *straight* face in the classroom, though he wanted to laugh at the antics of the dog outside.

straight•en (STRAY-tn) *v. straightens, straightened, straightening.* 1. Make straight. –The carpenter *straightened* the crooked nail before he hammered it.
2. Tidy; make neat.–The teacher told us to *straighten* up our desks.

strain (STRAYN) *n. strains.* 1. Injury caused by pulling a muscle or ligament.–Father's injury was only a *strain*.
2. Pressure; weight; tension.–The *strain* on the telephone wires caused by the falling tree made them break.–Mother was under a great *strain* when Father and Baby were sick.
3. (Often in plural) Music; melody.–He recognized the *strains* of "The Star-Spangled Banner."
4. Streak; trace.–There was a *strain* of uneasiness in his voice.
–*v. strains, strained, straining.* 1. Stretch; pull too tight.–The clothesline was *strained* by the wet clothes hanging on it.
2. Sprain; injure by pulling a muscle or ligament.–Father lifted a heavy rock in the garden and *strained* his back.
3. Press through a sieve or strainer to remove little pieces.–Mother *strained* the orange juice to get out the seeds and pulp.
4. Try as hard as possible.–Jack *strained* to lift the table.

strain•er (STRAY-ner) *n. strainers.* A kitchen tool with a fine screen or wire net used for straining things; a pan with small holes at the bottom; a sieve.–Tomatoes, fruits, and soups are often pressed through a *strainer* to take out seeds and pulp.

strait (STRAYT) *n. straits.* 1. A narrow, natural channel of water that joins two larger bodies of water.–The *Strait* of Gibraltar connects the Atlantic Ocean and the Mediterranean Sea.

2. (Usually in plural) Difficulty; distress.–The man was in desperate financial *straits* before he found a job.

strand (STRAND) *n. strands.* 1. One of the many fine threads twisted together to make heavier threads, ropes, yarns, and so forth.
2. A string.–Mother wore a *strand* of pearls with her black dress.–Grandmother brushed a *strand* of hair off Mary's forehead.
–*v. strands, stranded, stranding.* 1. Place in a helpless position.–The lost boy was *stranded* in the strange city without money.
2. Force aground.–A ship was *stranded* on the big rocks.

strange (STRAYNJ) *adj. stranger, strangest; strangely, adv.* 1. Not known, seen, or heard of before; new and not familiar.–The man's face was *strange* to Bob.–This part of the city is *strange* to me.
2. Queer; not natural; odd. – Mother felt *strange* after eating the fish. – Mary looks *strange* in a baby bonnet; she's a big girl now.
3. Shy.–The new boy felt *strange* among so many boys he didn't know.

stran•ger (STRAYN-jer) *n. strangers.* 1. A person whom one has never known, seen, or heard of before.–Mother opened the door and found a *stranger* standing on the porch.–This boy is a *stranger* in our school.
2. A person in a place unfamiliar to him.–I am a *stranger* in Boston. Can you tell me how to reach Boston Common?

stran•gle (STRANG-gəl) *v. strangles, strangled, strangling.* 1. Kill or die by choking.–The hero in the story *strangled* the villain. He killed him by holding him tightly by the neck so that he could no longer breathe.–Do not fasten your puppy's collar too tight, or he may *strangle*.
2. Choke; cut off the breath.–Grandfather's cough seems to *strangle* him. It makes him gasp for breath painfully.

strap (STRAP) *n. straps.* A narrow strip of leather or other material that can be bent easily.–Father put a *strap* around the suitcase.–*Straps* of metal are used on boxes to make them stronger.

–*v. straps, strapped, strapping.* 1. Fasten with a strap.–Bob *strapped* the basket onto his bicycle.

2. Whip with a strap.–Long ago students were often *strapped* as punishment.

stra•te•gic (strə-TEE-jik) *adj.; strategically, adv.* 1. Based on careful planning, management, or direction.–The army made a *strategic* withdrawal from the city.–Mary took up a *strategic* position in the school hall, where she could catch Joan and give her a message at lunchtime. She had thought out where Joan would be and how she, Mary, could best reach her.

2. Important or useful, especially in the planning and direction of military projects.–Bridges usually are *strategic* military targets.

strat•o•sphere (STRAT-ə-sfir *or* STRAY-tə-sfir) *n.* The part of the atmosphere that extends from a point about ten miles above earth to a point about sixty miles above earth. Below the *stratosphere* is the troposphere and above it is the ionosphere. Temperature varies very little within the *stratosphere.*

straw (STRAW) *n. straws* and *adj.* 1. A dry stem of wheat, rye, oats, or other grain after the grain has been threshed or taken off.–*Straw* is used as bedding for cattle, to make hats and paper, to pack china, bricks, or other breakable things, and for other purposes.

2. A thin tube of paper.–Bob sips his ice-cream soda through a *straw.*

straw•ber•ry (STRAW-bair-ee) *n. strawberries.* A red berry that grows on creeping vines, close to the ground.

stray (STRAY) *v. strays, strayed, straying.* Wander.–Little Red Riding Hood *strayed* away from the path to pick flowers.

–*adj.* 1. Lost.–Jack found a *stray* puppy.

2. Scattered; loose. – A few *stray* curls showed beneath her hat.

streak (STREEK) *n. streaks.* A line or stripe. –Joe got a *streak* of paint on his face.

–*v. streaks, streaked, streaking.* Mark with long lines or stripes.–The sunset *streaked* the sky with crimson.

stream (STREEM) *n. streams.* 1. A flow of water or other liquid, or gas.–A *stream* of water came from the faucet.

2. A river or brook.–We went to the *stream* to fish.

3. A steady line of people or things. – A *stream* of people poured out of the theater.

–*v. streams, streamed, streaming.* 1. Run or flow.–Light *streamed* from the open door.

2. Wave or blow.–The children marched in the parade with flags and banners *streaming.*

3. Move steadily in large numbers.–Large crowds of people *streamed* out of the theater after the play.

stream•er (STREE-mer) *n. streamers.* A long narrow flag, ribbon, or anything that will wave.–The children carried *streamers* in the parade.

stream•line (STREEM-lyn) *v. streamlines, streamlined, streamlining.* To shape so that surrounding air, water, or gas will pass to the sides without being blocked off, and so not check the speed of movement.–Airplanes must be *streamlined* so that they can fly swiftly.

street (STREET) *n. streets.* An open way in a town or city on which people travel.–Automobiles, bicycles, and people walking filled the narrow *streets.*

street•car (STREET-kahr) *n. streetcars.* A large, public car which runs on tracks in the street.–*Streetcars* are run by electricity.

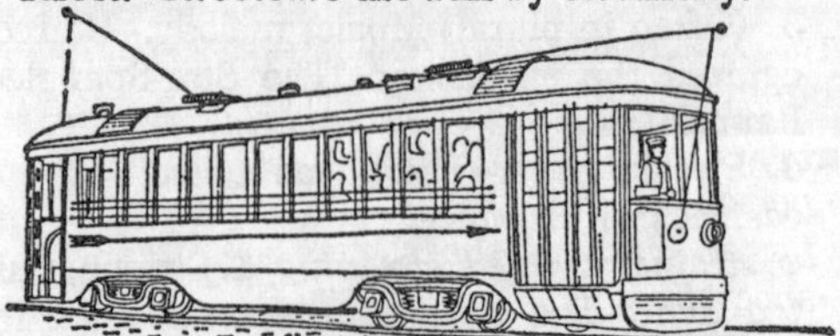

strength (STRENGKTH *or* STRENGTH) *n. strengths.* The quality of being strong.–The workman had great *strength.* He could lift big rocks.–Grandmother didn't have much *strength* after her sickness.–The *strength* of his argument lay in the fact that his idea would save money.

strength•en (STRENGK- *or* STRENG-thən) *v. strengthens, strengthened, strengthening.* Make or grow strong; give strength to.–The men *strengthened* the bridge by putting more timbers under it.

stren•u•ous (STREN-yoo-əss) *adj.; strenuously, adv.* 1. Very energetic; extremely active.–The senator is a *strenuous* fighter for human rights.

2. Marked by great effort.—The candidates are waging a *strenuous* campaign for election to office.

stress (STRESS) *n. stresses.* 1. Emphasis.—In our school much *stress* was put on spelling. In our class much attention was given to learning to spell.
2. A strain; a force.—The rafters in the building are under constant *stress.*
3. An accent.—He put *stress* on the words "as we, and we alone, may decide."
—*v. stresses, stressed, stressing.* Accent or emphasize.—In some music we *stress* the first note of each measure.—In saying the word "kitten," we *stress* the first syllable. — Our school *stresses* spelling.

stretch (STRECH) *n. stretches.* 1. A reaching out; extension.—He cannot be considered tall by any *stretch* of the imagination.
2. A continuous area; a section.—This is a beautiful *stretch* of road.
—*v. stretches, stretched, stretching.* 1. Extend; reach out.—The children *stretched* their arms high over their heads. — The cat always *stretches* when she wakes up.
2. Spread apart.—Bob had to *stretch* his fingers to play the piano.
3. Reach.—Baby *stretched* out her hand for the glass of milk.
4. Make or get larger under strain.—Mary *stretched* the rubber band to get it around her book.
5. Extend or reach. — Our garden *stretches* from the house to the back fence.

stretch·er (STRECH-er) *n. stretchers.* 1. A person or thing that stretches or makes larger.—Father's shoes were stretched on a shoe *stretcher.*
2. A carrier for injured or sick people, made of two poles with heavy cloth fastened between them. A *stretcher* is carried by two men, one at each end.—The injured boy was carried to the ambulance on a *stretcher* and rushed to a hospital.

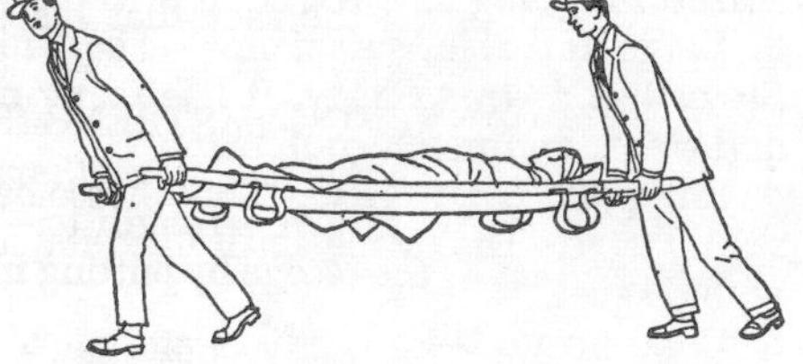

strew (STROO) *v. strews, strewed, strewing.* Scatter.—Do not *strew* your toys all over the house. — When Mary dropped the bag, it *strewed* beans all over the floor.

strict (STRIKT) *adj. stricter, strictest; strictly, adv.* 1. Demanding obedience to rules. — The principal is very *strict.* He makes all the children obey the rules carefully.
2. Exact; just right.—Bob made the measurements for the model airplane with *strict* accuracy.
3. Absolute; total; extremely careful. — The monks observed *strict* silence at their work.

stride (STRYD) *n. strides.* A long step.—Bob measured the field with a hundred *strides.*
—*v. strides, strode, striding.* Walk with long steps.—The teacher *strode* to the back of the room to open the window.

strife (STRYF) *n.* Fighting; struggle; conflict.—The nation was torn by *strife.*

strike (STRYK) *n. strikes.* 1. The sound of a bell or gong.—We heard the *strike* of the clock.
2. A stopping of work by workmen as a group to get more money or better working conditions.—There is a *strike* at the factory now.
3. In baseball, a miss or failure to hit a good pitch when batting.—Bob was called out on *strikes.*
4. In bowling, the knocking down of all the pins with the first ball.—Father bowled last night and had five *strikes* in a row.
—*v. strikes, struck, striking.* 1. Hit; come or bring into sharp contact with.—The boy tried to *strike* me.—The car skidded and *struck* a pole.
2. Light (a match). — Be careful when you *strike* matches.
3. Sound by hitting a bell or gong.—Mary heard the clock *strike* two.
4. Come suddenly to (one's mind).—An idea of how to make a model plane *struck* Bob today.
5. Quit work as a group to get higher pay or better working conditions.—The men at the factory have *struck;* they quit work yesterday and said they would not go back till they were promised more money.
6. Find; come upon.—The miners *struck* gold while digging.—Bob and Mary have *struck* a plan for saving money.
—*Strike out* sometimes means to mark out. —Mary spelled the word wrong and corrected it by *striking out* the wrong letter.
—*Strike out* may mean to start. — The Boy Scouts *struck out* through the woods.
—*Strike out* in baseball means for the batter to fail to hit, or fail to swing at, three good pitches.—Bob *struck out.* The pitcher *struck* him *out.*

string (STRING) *n. strings.* 1. A cord; a light rope; a heavy thread or anything else used for tying or binding.–Bob's kite *string* broke, and his kite blew away.

2. Ornaments on a string.–Mary has a *string* of beads.

3. A fine, strong cord or wire used to make the tones on violins, pianos, and some other musical instruments.

4. A row.–A *string* of stockings was hung near the decorated Christmas tree.

5. Any long, thin piece that looks like a cord. –Mother cooked the candy until the syrup formed *strings* when it dripped from a spoon.

6. A tough threadlike part of a plant.–Beans in the shell, or pod, have *strings* along the sides of the shell.

–*v. strings, strung, stringing.* 1. Remove strings from. – Mother *strings* beans before she cooks them.

2. Put on a string.–Children like to *string* beads to wear when they play "dress up."

3. Put strings on.–The violinist could not play until he had *strung* his violin.

–*String out* means to stretch out like a piece of string.–The parade was *strung out* from the river to the park.

–To *string up* something means to hang up by a string or rope.–The butcher *strung up* a leg of beef.

string bean (STRING been) *string beans.* A pod of beans. Along each side of the pod, or shell, is a stringy part that is pulled off before cooking.

stringed in·stru·ment (STRINGD IN-strə-mənt) *stringed instruments.* A musical instrument in which tones are produced by plucking or bowing strings. The violin, cello, guitar, and harp belong to the family of *stringed instruments.*

strip (STRIP) *n. strips.* A long, narrow piece. –Mary cut off a *strip* of paper to write her spelling words on.

–*v. strips, stripped, stripping.* 1. Undress.– Mother *stripped* Baby to give her a bath.– The doctor asked the boys to *strip* before he examined them.

2. Peel off, or cut off, in strips.–The hunter *stripped* the skin from the rabbit he had shot that afternoon.

3. Make bare or empty.–The hungry children *stripped* the cupboard of all the food that had been in it.

stripe (STRYP) *n. stripes.* A broad line; a long, narrow band or strip.–The American flag has red and white *stripes.*

–*v. stripes, striped, striping.* Cover or mark with stripes. – The boys *striped* the pole with paint so it could be used for a Maypole on May Day.

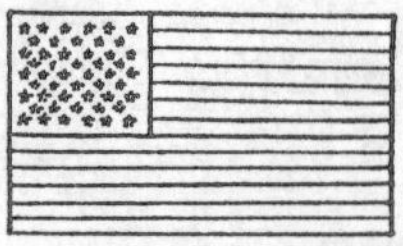

strive (STRYV) *v. strives, strove, striving.* 1. Make a great effort; try or work very hard.– The man is *striving* to complete his task.

2. Battle; struggle; fight.–The firemen *strove* in vain against the flames.

stroke (STROHK) *n. strokes.* 1. A blow. – Bob chopped the piece of wood in two with one *stroke* of the ax.

2. A kind of sudden illness which often makes a person helpless.–The old man had a *stroke* last night.

3. A complete movement made over and over in a certain activity, such as skating, swimming, or rowing.–Tom rowed with long, even *strokes.*

4. A single movement, as the *stroke* of a pen, brush, pencil, etc.; the visible result of such a movement that makes a mark.–The artist's brush *strokes* in that painting are graceful and delicate.

5. A sound caused by striking.–Santa Claus came at the *stroke* of twelve by the clock.

6. A gentle caress.–Tom gave Pussy's head an affectionate *stroke.*

–*v. strokes, stroked, stroking.* Rub gently and caressingly.–Mother *stroked* Baby's head.

stroll (STROHL) *n. strolls.* A slow walk for pleasure.–The girls have gone for a *stroll.* –*v. strolls, strolled, strolling.* Walk slowly for pleasure.–They *strolled* about for an hour.

strong (STRAWNG) *adj. stronger, strongest; strongly, adv.* 1. Not weak; having strength or force.–Prize fighters are *strong.*

2. Forceful.–A *strong* wind is blowing the ships about.–The need of money is a *strong* reason for going to work.

3. Large and able; sufficient. – The United States has a *strong* navy. It has many men and ships, and much equipment.

4. Sharp; keen; powerful.–This cheese has a *strong* taste.–The *strong* smell filled the man with disgust.

5. Concentrated.–Father likes *strong* coffee, but Mother likes it with more water in it.

6. Tough; not easily broken.–The kite string is *strong.*–The old chair is *strong,* however it may look. It will hold your weight.

strop (STRAHP) *n. strops.* A leather strap on which straight razors are sharpened.
–*v. strops, stropped, stropping.* Sharpen on a strop. – The barber *strops* his razor before he uses it.

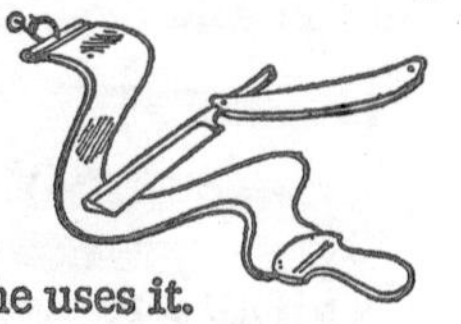

struck (STRUK) *v.* One form of the verb *strike.*–The clock *struck* four.

struc•ture (STRUK-cher) *n. structures.* 1. Anything built, as a factory or bridge. – We saw many large *structures* as we came nearer the city.
2. The way in which anything is formed or shaped.–The *structure* of Mary's face is like that of Mother's.

strug•gle (STRUG-əl) *n. struggles.* A strong effort or fight.–The men put up a great *struggle* to keep the fire from spreading. It was hard work.
–*v. struggles, struggled, struggling.* Work very hard; fight against difficulties.–The poor man had to *struggle* to feed his children.–The lion *struggled* to get out of his cage.

strung (STRUNG) *v.* One form of the verb *string.*–We *strung* popcorn for the Christmas tree.

strut (STRUT) *n. struts.* 1. A brace or support.–One of the plane's wheel *struts* was damaged in the emergency landing.
2. A haughty walk; a proud gait.–The rooster must think he is king of the barnyard, judging by his *strut.*
–*v. struts, strutted, strutting.*–Walk with exaggerated pride.–The peacock *strutted* in the garden, his tail spread wide.

stub (STUB) *n. stubs.* 1. Short, dull piece left after the main part is gone.–Mary has used the pencil down to a *stub.*–Father threw the *stub* of his cigar away.
2. A pen with a blunt point.–Mary likes a sharp pen, but Bob likes a *stub.*
3. A short part of a bill or ticket that is torn off and given to the buyer as a receipt. – Tickets such as theater tickets and train tickets have *stubs.* Checks have *stubs* that are left in the checkbook as a record.
–*v. stubs, stubbed, stubbing.* Bump (one's toe). –Don't *stub* your toe against the low step.

stub•born (STUB-ern) *adj.; stubbornly, adv.* Refusing to give in to others or to change one's mind; obstinate.–Father told Jack he was solving the problem in the wrong way, but Jack was *stubborn.* Jack insisted that he could do it his own way.

stuck (STUK) *v.* One form of the verb *stick.* –Bob *stuck* the stamp on the envelope.

stu•dent (STOO- *or* STYOO-dənt) *n. students.* A person who studies; a pupil.–There are five hundred *students* in our school. – People who study law are *students* of law. – Our minister is a *student* of the Bible.

stu•di•o (STOO- *or* STYOO-dee-oh) *n. studios.* 1. A room where a painter, musician, or other artist works.

2. A place where radio and television programs are broadcast.
3. A place where movies are made.

stud•y (STUD-ee) *n. studies.* 1. A room used for reading, learning, or writing.–The writer went into his *study* to work on his new book.
2. A subject that one tries to learn.–Geography, English, and history are some of Bob's *studies.*
3. A written work produced as the result of research.–The botanist did a *study* on the uses of palm trees.
–*v. studies, studied, studying.* 1. To try to learn or understand by reading, thinking, or practicing.–Ann is *studying* French.
2. Try to figure out; think about.–Bob *studied* the puzzle. He tried to think out a way to solve it.
3. Look at carefully. – Sally picked up the snail and *studied* it closely.

stuff (STUF) *n. stuffs.* 1. The material that things are made of.–Cotton is the best *stuff* for children's clothes. – The teacher thinks Bob has the *stuff* in him to be an engineer.
2. Material or objects of any kind.–If there were less *stuff* in this room, it would look prettier.
–*v. stuffs, stuffed, stuffing.* Fill.–She *stuffed* the doll with cotton.

stuff•ing (STUF-ing) *n. stuffings.* 1. A material used for filling a thing.–Cotton and sawdust are *stuffings* used for dolls.
2. A dressing usually made of bread crumbs mixed with seasonings and put into chicken, turkey, or other meat or food.

stum•ble (STUM-bəl) *v. stumbles, stumbled, stumbling.* 1. Trip by catching the foot.—Mary *stumbled* on the garden hose.
2. Walk unsteadily; walk shakily.—Baby is learning to walk and often *stumbles.*
3. Make a mistake.—Mary *stumbled* in spelling the long word.

stump (STUMP) *n. stumps.* 1. The short part left in the ground after a tree or plant has been cut down. —The squirrel sat on a tree *stump* and ate a nut.—Ed looked at the age rings on the *stump.*

2. The part of anything that is left when the main part is gone.

stump•y (STUMP-ee) *adj. stumpier, stumpiest.* Short and thick like a stump.—A *stumpy* little man came waddling down the street.—Jack's dog likes to thump his *stumpy* tail on the floor.

stun (STUN) *v. stuns, stunned, stunning.* 1. Make senseless or unconscious.—A blow on the head *stunned* the boy. For a time he knew nothing.
2. Shock; surprise.—We were *stunned* by the news of the accident.

stung (STUNG) *v.* One form of the verb *sting.*—A bee *stung* Grandmother.

stunt (STUNT) *n. stunts.* An unusual trick; something that is hard to do.—Acrobats and clowns amuse people by doing *stunts.*
—*v. stunts, stunted, stunting.* Check or stop (growth).—Too little exercise and too little fresh air may *stunt* one's growth.

stu•pid (STOO- *or* STYOO-pid) *adj. stupider, stupidest; stupidly, adv.* Dull; not bright or smart.—Because the child is too shy to talk much, he sometimes seems *stupid.* — The things the thoughtless man said were *stupid.*

stur•dy (STER-dee) *adj. sturdier, sturdiest; sturdily, adv.* 1. Strong; well-made; able to endure things.—This is not a very *sturdy* chair to sit on; it may not hold you.—Mary is not so *sturdy* as Sally; Mary gets sick more easily.
2. Firm.—Jack has a *sturdy* belief that his dog will come back; he really believes it, although the dog has been gone nearly a year.

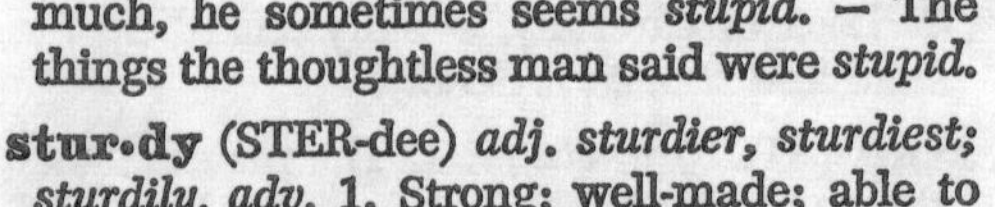

stur•geon (STER-jən) *n. sturgeon* or *sturgeons.* A kind of fish that is good to eat.

sty (STY) *n. sties.* 1. A pen built for pigs. —Mother said the house was as dirty as a *sty.*

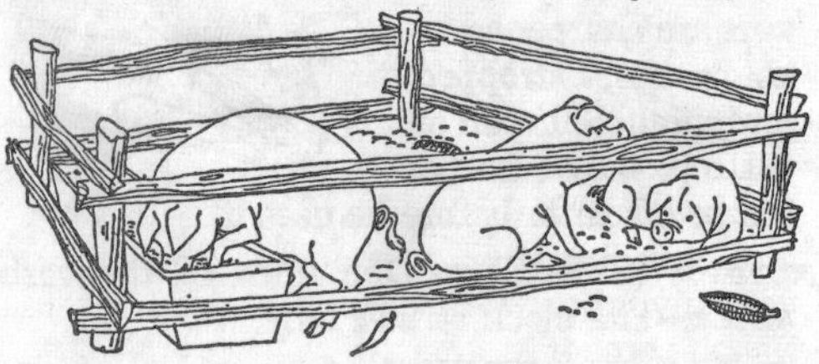

2. A red, swollen sore on the edge of the eyelid.

style (STYL) *n. styles.* 1. Fashion.—High-button shoes are not in *style.*
2. A way of doing something. — There are many different *styles* of handwriting among the students at school.

styl•ish (STYL-ish) *adj.; stylishly, adv.* Fashionable. — *Stylish* clothes are the kind that well-dressed people are wearing.—The clothes worn a hundred years ago are not *stylish* now.

sub•due (səb-DOO *or* -DYOO) *v. subdues, subdued, subduing.* Overpower; conquer. —The sheriff and his deputies *subdued* the band of rustlers.

sub•ject (SUB-jikt) *n. subjects.* 1. The person or thing about which one is talking, writing, thinking, or studying.—The *subject* that Mary and Bob were talking about was the party for Tuesday.—The *subject* of Linda's story was "Life as a Movie Star."—My favorite *subject* is arithmetic.
2. A citizen of a kingdom.—Mr. Jones is a British *subject,* a *subject* of the British Queen.

THE TURTLE (built during the American Revolution)

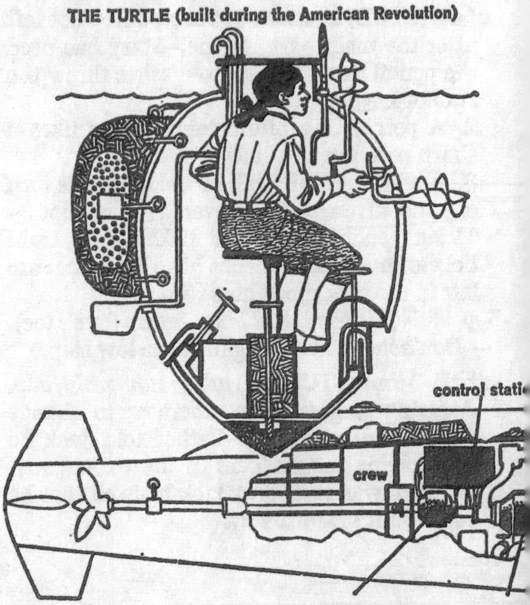

–(səb-JEKT) *v. subjects, subjected, subjecting.* Force to endure or submit.–The explorers were *subjected* to great hardships. – The king's armies *subjected* all the small surrounding countries to his rule.

–(SUB-jikt) *adj.* 1. Apt to have.–Father is *subject* to colds. He catches cold easily.

2. Depending upon or resting on.–I accept your invitation, *subject* to Mother's consent. I shall come if Mother will let me.

sub·ma·rine (SUB-mə-reen) *n. submarines.* A boat that can run under water.

–(sub-mə-REEN) *adj.* Being or used under water in the sea or ocean; having to do with the depths of the sea or ocean.–Scientists study *submarine* life. They study plants and animals that live in the sea.

sub·merge (səb-MERJ) *v. submerges, submerged, submerging.* 1. Cover with water. – The flood *submerged* roads and cars.

2. Sink; dive beneath the surface of the water.–The submarine captain gave the command to *submerge.*

sub·mit (səb-MIT) *v. submits, submitted, submitting.* 1. Give in or surrender.–The boy *submitted* to having his tooth pulled.

2. Hand in or offer.–Mary *submitted* a report to her teacher.

sub·or·di·nate (sə-BOR-də-nit) *adj.* 1. Of a lower rank, position, or order; of less importance.–Tom rose from a *subordinate* job in the firm to the position of office manager.

2. Under the command or authority of a superior.–A private in the army is *subordinate* to his officers.

sub·scribe (səb-SKRYB) *v. subscribes, subscribed, subscribing.* 1. Agree to take and pay for.–Mother has *subscribed* to the daily paper and a monthly magazine.

2. Make a written promise to give a certain amount.–We *subscribed* five dollars to the Red Cross.

3. Agree (to); approve.–I *subscribe* to the proposal that the town build a swimming pool.

sub·scrib·er (səb-SKRYB-er) *n. subscribers.* A person who promises to take and pay for something, as a magazine or newspaper.–Jack now has fifty *subscribers* on his newspaper route.

sub·scrip·tion (səb-SKRIP-shən) *n. subscriptions.* 1. Agreement to take something and pay for it.–Mother has renewed her *subscription* to the paper for another year.

2. An amount promised.–Our *subscription* to the Red Cross was five dollars.

sub·side (səb-SYD) *v. subsides, subsided, subsiding.* Become less.–The wind *subsided* in the evening.

sub·stance (SUB-stənss) *n. substances.* 1. What a thing is made of; a material. – The Indians smeared their faces with a reddish *substance.*

2. The main part. – The *substance* of the committee's report deals with education.

3. The actual meaning; the essential idea or ideas.–The *substance* of his philosophy is "Do unto others as you would have others do unto you."

4. Property; wealth.–Mr. Jones is a man of *substance.*

SUBMARINE

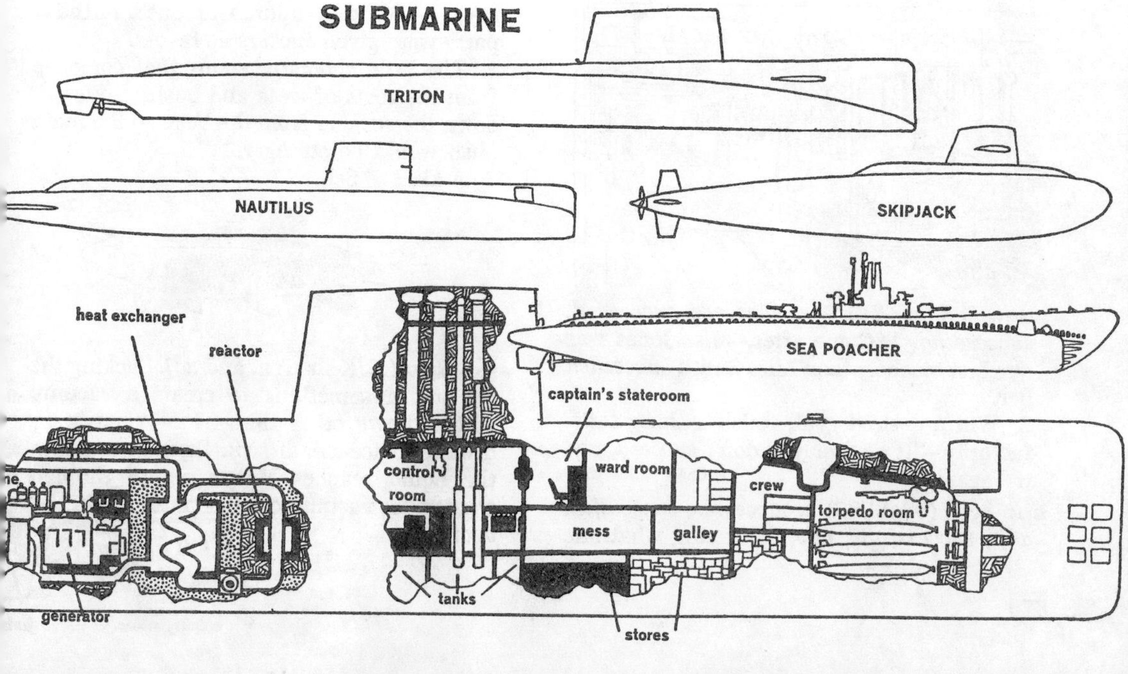

sub·stan·tial (səb-STAN-shəl) *adj.; substantially, adv.* 1. Strong and solid; firm.—It was a small but *substantial* house.
2. Large; considerable. — Harry received a *substantial* increase in salary.
3. Real; not imaginary.—The figure Ann saw proved to be *substantial* after all, and not a ghost as she had thought.
4. Of wealth or means.—Mr. Jones is a *substantial* businessman.

sub·sti·tute (SUB-stə-toot *or* -tyoot) *n. substitutes.* A person or thing serving in place of another.—The doctor could not come, so he sent a *substitute.* He sent another doctor.—Father didn't have a saw, so he used a knife as a *substitute.*—Bill is a *substitute* on the school football team. He sometimes plays in place of one of the regular players.
—*v. substitutes, substituted, substituting.* Provide in place of.—They didn't have chocolate ice cream, so they *substituted* vanilla.
—*substitution, n. substitutions.*

sub·tract (səb-TRAKT) *v. subtracts, subtracted, subtracting.* Take away.—One *subtracted* from four leaves three.

sub·trac·tion (səb-TRAK-shən) *n.* Taking one thing from another.—"One from four leaves three" is an example of *subtraction.*

sub·urb (SUB-erb) *n. suburbs.* A section or small community on the edge of a city. — We could not get a house in the city, so we live in a *suburb.*

sub·way (SUB-way) *n. subways.* An electric railroad that runs under the ground. — We went into the city by *subway.*

suc·ceed (sək-SEED) *v. succeeds, succeeded, succeeding.* 1. Come after.—Miss Jones was our first teacher; then Miss Smith *succeeded* her.
2. Win a desired goal; finish a thing satisfactorily.—"If at first you don't *succeed,* try, try again."

suc·cess (sək-SESS) *n. successes; successful, adj.; successfully, adv.* 1. Getting what one wants; doing what one wants to do satisfactorily.—William had *success* in making his kite.
2. Fame; fortune.—The man won *success* by working very hard.
3. A person or thing that succeeds or turns out well.—The singer was a great *success.* She was famous because she sang well.—The fire drill was a *success.* All the children left the building quickly and calmly.

suc·ces·sion (sək-SESH-ən) *n. successions; successive, adj.; successively, adv.* 1. The happening or coming of one thing right after another.—In the circus parade, the elephants walked in *succession.* They followed one another without anything between them.
2. Right to follow or inherit. — After the king's death, the *succession* to the throne was in doubt. It was not certain who had the right to be the next king.

such (SUCH) *adj.* 1. So bad; so good; so big; so much.—Baby is *such* a comedian!—The boy is *such* an eater!
2. Of a certain kind.—Bob had *such* vegetables as corn, peas, and cabbage in his garden. —Mary reads *such* stories as "The Three Bears" and "Cinderella" to Sally.
—*pron.* 1. This or that which has already been spoken of.—Mother said no, and *such* was her decision.
2. Such a thing or person.—What we thought Bob had meant as a criticism was not intended as *such.*

suck·er (SUK-er) *n. suckers.* 1. A lollipop or hard piece of candy, usually fastened to a stick. — All the children at Sue's birthday party were given *suckers* as favors.
2. The little shoots or stems that come up from the roots of trees and bushes.—We cut down the *suckers* from the bush so the main bush would be stronger.
3. A kind of fish.

suc·tion (SUK-shən) *n.* and *adj.* Sucking the air out of something to create a vacuum which draws other things in.—When Mary drinks an ice-cream soda through a straw, the liquid reaches Mary's mouth through *suction.*—A vacuum cleaner picks up dirt by *suction.*

sud•den (SUD-n) *adj.; suddenly, adv.* 1. Unexpected.–A *sudden* clap of thunder made us jump.
2. Quick; rapid.–Father made a *sudden* trip to the country.
–*All of a sudden* means suddenly or unexpectedly.–*All of a sudden* the door opened.

suds (SUDZ) *n. pl.* Water with enough soap in it to make bubbles.–Mother washed the clothes in *suds.*

sue (SOO *or* SYOO) *v. sues, sued, suing.* Take action against someone through the courts.–The man would not pay for the damage he had done, so Father had to *sue* him. Father started action against him in court to get him to do the right thing.

su•et (SOO- *or* SYOO-it) *n.* Hard fat taken from the meat of cattle and sheep. *Suet* is used for cooking and for making candles.

suf•fer (SUF-er) *v. suffers, suffered, suffering.* 1. Feel great pain.–Grandmother *suffered* when she broke her arm.
2. Endure; undergo.–The poor man has *suffered* many hardships during the cold winter.
3. Be harmed or hurt.–The farmers' crops have *suffered* because we have had no rain.

suf•fi•cient (sə-FISH-ənt) *adj.; sufficiently, adv.* Enough; as much as is needed. – We have *sufficient* coal for the winter. We have plenty of coal for the winter.

suf•fo•cate (SUF-ə-kayt) *v. suffocates, suffocated, suffocating.* 1. Kill or die by stopping the breath.–The killer *suffocated* his victim.
2. Choke or smother. – The firemen wore masks so that the heavy smoke would not *suffocate* them.

sug•ar (SHUHG-er) *n. sugars.* A sweet substance made from sugar beets or sugar cane. –We put *sugar* in coffee, on fruit, and on breakfast food to make them sweet.
–*v. sugars, sugared, sugaring.* 1. Make sweet by adding sugar.–Father *sugared* the cereal for Baby. He sprinkled sugar on it.
2. Turn to sugar.–The jelly has *sugared* from being boiled too long.

sug•ar beet (SHUHG-er beet) *sugar beets.* A large, white kind of beet used in making sugar.

sug•ar cane (SHUHG-er kayn). A plant with tall, hollow stalks that are used in making sugar. It usually grows in a warm climate.

sug•ar ma•ple (SHUHG-er may-pəl) *sugar maples.* A maple tree that gives a sweet sap. When this sap is boiled for a long time, it becomes a sugar called maple sugar.

sug•gest (səg-JEST) *v. suggests, suggested, suggesting.* 1. Bring up or mention as a possible and desirable thing to do. – The teacher *suggested* that we read the story before going home.–Bob *suggested* that we work first and then play.
2. Bring something to someone's mind or attention.–If I say "cloud" to you, what does it *suggest?* It *suggests* rain.

sug•ges•tion (səg-JESS-chən) *n. suggestions.* 1. A thought or idea that someone has and suggests or offers to someone else.–Mary gave us a *suggestion* as to how we might save paper.
2. A bringing to mind; a hint.–There is a *suggestion* of unhappiness in her manner and her speech.

su•i•cide (SOO- *or* SYOO-ə-syd) *n. suicides.* 1. Killing of oneself.–The man's death was not an accident; it was *suicide.* He killed himself purposely.
2. A person who kills himself. – The man was a *suicide.*

suit (SOOT *or* SYOOT) *n. suits.* 1. A set of clothing worn together, as a jacket, vest, and trousers.–Father's new *suit* is brown.
2. In a pack of playing cards, all those cards that have spots of the same shape.–Hearts, clubs, spades, and diamonds are the four *suits.*
–*v. suits, suited, suiting.* 1. Satisfy or please. –A picnic on the last day of school *suited* the children very well. They liked it.
2. Go well with; match.–A yellow dress *suits* a person with brown hair and brown eyes.

suit•a•ble (SOO- *or* SYOO-tə-bəl) *adj.; suitably, adv.* Proper; fit.–Men's straw hats are not *suitable* for winter weather.–Overalls are *suitable* for farm work.

suit•case (SOOT- *or* SYOOT-kayss) *n. suitcases.* A flat traveling bag. – Mother packed our clothes in a *suitcase* when we went to Grandmother's.

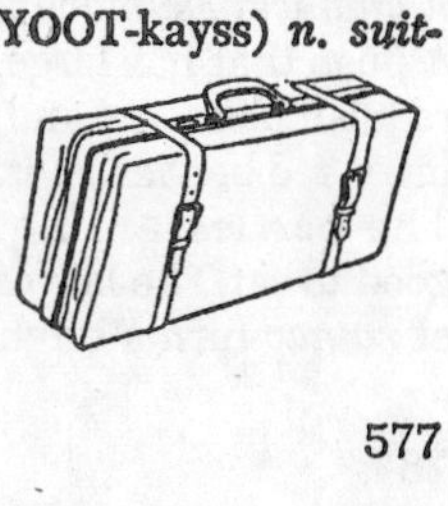

suite (SWEET) *n. suites.* 1. A group or a set. –A special *suite* of hotel rooms is being reserved for the President.–Mother bought a *suite* of furniture for the bedroom.
2. A staff of followers or attendants.–The prince and his *suite* will arrive at the hotel tomorrow.

suit•or (SOO- *or* SYOO-ter) *n. suitors.* A man who wants to marry a certain woman.–The woman's *suitor* called on her every night last week.

sul•fur or **sul•phur** (SUL-fer) *n.* A yellowish substance that burns easily and gives off a strong odor that makes it hard for one to breathe.–The heads of some matches have *sulfur* in them.

sulk (SULK) *v. sulks, sulked, sulking.* Show bad humor by keeping quietly and gloomily to oneself.–The girl *sulks* when she does not get her own way.

sulk•y (SUL-kee) *n. sulkies.* A small, two-wheeled carriage often used for racing.
–adj. sulkier, sulkiest; sulkily, adv. Cross; bad-tempered.–Mother said that no one likes a *sulky* person.

sul•len (SUL-ən) *adj.; sullenly, adv.* 1. Quietly angry.–Baby is *sullen* when she can't have her own way.
2. Dull; gloomy. – The *sullen* skies made everyone feel unhappy at the picnic.

sul•tan (SUL-tn) *n. sultans.* A ruler in certain countries of the East.

sul•try (SUL-tree) *adj. sultrier, sultriest.* Hot and damp.–A *sultry* day is one that is hot and moist, with very little breeze.

sum (SUM) *n. sums.* 1. The number made by adding numbers.–The *sum* of four and two is six.
2. (In the plural) Arithmetic problems.–Bob sometimes has trouble doing his *sums.*
3. An amount of money.–Mary has a small *sum* of money to spend each week.
–v. sums, summed, summing. Sum up means to tell in a few words.–The teacher asked us to *sum up* what we had learned during the day.

su•mac or **su•mach** (SHOO- *or* SOO-mak) *n. sumacs* or *sumachs.* A bush that has large, reddish blossoms and, later, red berries on it. The berries are not good to eat. The leaves of *sumac* turn a bright red in the fall.

sum•ma•rize (SUM-ə-ryz) *v. summarizes, summarized, summarizing.* Briefly give the main points of a speech, discussion, piece of writing, or series of events.–A speaker often *summarizes* at the end of his talk to remind his listeners of the points he has made.
–summary, n. summaries.

sum•mer (SUM-er) *n. summers.* One of the four seasons.–The seasons of the year are spring, *summer,* autumn, and winter.–In our part of the world, *summer* is the hottest season.

sum•mit (SUM-it) *n. summits.* The top; the highest point.–It is a hard climb to the *summit* of the hill.
–A *summit meeting* refers to a meeting of the heads of state of leading nations, usually the United States, Britain, France, and the Soviet Union. The purpose of such a meeting is to discuss world problems in the hope of finding solutions acceptable to all.

sum•mon (SUM-ən) *v. summons; summoned, summoning.* Call or send for.–The teacher *summoned* the boy to her desk.

sun (SUN) *n. suns.* 1. The brightest body we see in the sky; the star which gives the earth light and heat.–The earth goes around the *sun* once in a year.–We see the stars shining at night. We see the *sun* shining during the day.
2. Heat and light of the sun.–The *sun* makes the plants grow.–The living room faces the east, so it gets the morning *sun.*
–v. suns, sunned, sunning. Expose to the light of the sun. – Father sat on the sand and *sunned* himself.

sun•beam (SUN-beem) *n. sunbeams.* A ray of sunlight.–A *sunbeam* danced on the wall.

sun•bon•net (SUN-bahn-it) *n. sunbonnets.* A bonnet with a broad brim.
–A *sunbonnet* is usually worn to keep the hot sun off the face and the neck.

sun•burn (SUN-bern) *n. sunburns.* A burn made by the sun's rays.–Mary put a cream on her *sunburn.*
–v. sunburns, sunburned, sunburning. Have the skin reddened or blistered by the sun's rays.–People with light skins are apt to *sunburn* easily.

Sun•day (SUN-dee) *n. Sundays.* The first day of the week. *Sunday* is the Christian Sabbath, or day of rest.

sun•di•al (SUN-dy-əl) *n. sundials.* An instrument for telling time by the sun's shadow. The sun makes a shadow that points towards numbers on the dial. The numbers on which the shadows fall tell what time it is.

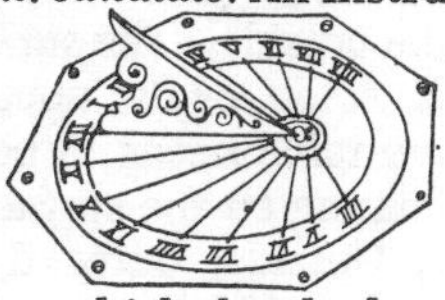

sun•down (SUN-down) *n.* The time when the sun goes down out of sight; sunset.—Mother told us to be home by *sundown.*

sun•fish (SUN-fish) *n. sunfish* or *sunfishes.* A small, somewhat brightly colored fish that is good to eat.

sun•flow•er (SUN-flow-er) *n. sunflowers.* A tall plant that has large, yellow flowers with large, brown centers which are full of seeds.

sung (SUNG) *v.* One form of the verb *sing.* – We sing the song "America" in school. We have *sung* it every day this week.

sunk (SUNGK) *v.* One form of the verb *sink.* – The boat that had *sunk* was lifted up and taken away.

sun•light (SUN-lyt) *n.* Light of the sun.—We sat in the *sunlight* to get warm.

sun•ny (SUN-ee) *adj. sunnier, sunniest.* 1. Filled with sunshine.—This is a *sunny* day.
2. Bright; pleasant.—Sally has a *sunny* smile.

sun•rise (SUN-ryz) *n. sunrises.* 1. The time of day when the sun comes up.—Grandfather gets up at *sunrise.*
2. Dawn; light in the sky when the sun comes up.—We watched the *sunrise* from the mountaintop.

sun•set (SUN-set) *n. sunsets.* 1. The going down of the sun.—Take down the flag just before *sunset.*
2. The changing light and color in the sky when the sun goes down.—We watched the *sunset* over the lake.

sun•shine (SUN-shyn) *n.* Light from the sun.—The *sunshine* came into the window.

su•per•in•tend•ent (soo- *or* syoo-prin-TEN-dənt) *n. superintendents.* A person who oversees or directs workers.—A *superintendent* of schools directs and guides teachers, and sees that school business is taken care of. —The *superintendent* of an apartment house sees that the house is kept clean, heated, and in good condition.

su•pe•ri•or (sə- *or* soo-PIR-ee-er) *n. superiors.* 1. A person higher in position than another. —The principal is our teacher's *superior.*
2. A person better than another or others in some respect.—John is Bob's *superior* at tennis. John plays tennis better than Bob does.
—*adj.* 1. Higher in position. – A major is *superior* to a captain. – A superintendent of schools is *superior* to a teacher.
2. Better.—Our team has *superior* players on it.—Bill thinks he is *superior.* He acts as though he were better than the other boys.

su•per•mar•ket (SOO- *or* SYOO-per-mahr-kit) *n. supermarkets.* A large shopping center or food store, usually operated on a self-service basis.—Mother goes to the *supermarket* once a week to shop for our food.

su•per•son•ic (soo- *or* syoo-per-SAHN-ik) *adj.* Capable of traveling at a speed faster than that of sound, or faster than about 738 miles an hour.—The Air Force has many *supersonic* aircraft.

su•per•sti•tion (soo- *or* syoo-per-STISH-ən) *n. superstitions.* 1. A false belief or fear.—It is an old *superstition* that it is bad luck for a black cat to cross a path ahead of you.—Educated people today know that *superstitions* are not true.
2. The habit of believing in mysterious powers or forces which do not really exist.—*Superstition* makes people think it is unlucky to walk under a ladder.—Science tries to fight *superstition.*

su•per•sti•tious (soo- *or* syoo-per-STISH-əss) *adj.; superstitiously, adv.* Believing in and fearful of unknown powers.—*Superstitious* people think it is bad luck for thirteen people to sit at a table.

sup•per (SUP-er) *n. suppers.* The last meal of the day. – Some people have dinner at noon. In the evening they have *supper,* a lighter meal.

sup•ply (sə-PLY) *n. supplies.* An amount or quantity on hand.—The stores have a *supply* of shoes for the winter season.—Father has our *supply* of coal in the coal bin.
—*v. supplies, supplied, supplying.* 1. Give; produce; provide.—The farmers *supply* food for the people of the city.—City people *supply* clothing, machines, and other things to the farmer.
2. Add or furnish.—Mary got all the words in the puzzle but one. Bob *supplied* that one.
3. Fill.—The store tries to stock enough coats to *supply* the demand.

sup•port (sə-PORT) *n. supports.* 1. Anything that holds something up.—A clothesline pole or prop is a *support* because it holds up the clothesline.
2. Help in getting food, clothing, and the things necessary for living; getting a living.—Children depend on their parents for *support.*
—v. supports, supported, supporting. 1. Hold up; keep (a thing) from falling.—A clothesline pole *supports* a clothesline.—Posts *support* the roof of the porch.
2. Furnish a home, food, and clothing for, or everything necessary for living. — The father *supports* his children.
3. Help; encourage.—The sick man was *supported* by the good wishes of his neighbors. —Mother said she would *support* Jack's plan to go camping.
4. Be in favor of; uphold.—Father *supports* Mr. Jones for mayor.

sup•pose (sə-POHZ) *v. supposes, supposed, supposing.* 1. Believe; guess.—I *suppose* Jack will come to the party.
2. Imagine. — Just *suppose* you were on a desert island. What would you do?
3. Expect or presume.—The children are *supposed* to be in bed. It is their usual time for sleeping, but I do not know if they have actually gone to bed yet.

su•preme (sə- *or* soo-PREEM) *adj.; supremely, adv.* 1. Greatest.—This news is of *supreme* importance to us.
2. Highest in position or power. — In the United States the *Supreme* Court is the highest court.

sure (SHUHR) *adj. surer, surest.* 1. Certain; positive.—Mary is *sure* that she heard Mother call.
2. Dependable. — This is a *sure* recipe for chocolate cake. It will not fail.
3. Confident. — Jack is *sure* of making the team. He is certain he will.
4. Firm; safe. — The mountain climbers crossed the ridge with *sure* steps.

sure•ly (SHUHR-lee) *adv.* Certainly.—*Surely* that was Father we saw; I am sure it was.

surf (SERF) *n. surfs.* Waves of the sea hitting or washing against the shore.—We stood on the rocks and watched the *surf.*

sur•face (SER-fəss) *n. surfaces.* 1. A side; the outside.—The *surface* of a brick is rough.
2. A top, or flat upper part.—The *surface* of the table needs to be painted.—A stick was floating on the *surface* of the water.
3. Outside; outward appearance. — On the *surface,* Mary thought the problem looked easy. But when she began to work on it she realized that it was quite difficult.

surge (SERJ) *n. surges.* A sudden great wave or rush.—A *surge* of water carried the tiny boat to shore.
—v. surges, surged, surging. Roll up and fall. —During the storm, the waves *surged* over the rocks on the coast.

sur•geon (SER-jən) *n. surgeons.* A doctor who operates on people.—A *surgeon* operated on Mary. He took out her tonsils.

sur•plus (SER-pluss) *n. surpluses* and *adj.* Extra amount.—We had a *surplus* of money this week. We had some left over.

sur•prise (ser-PRYZ) *n. surprises.* 1. Something not expected.—Father had a *surprise* in his pocket for Sally.
2. A feeling caused by something that was not expected.—A look of *surprise* came over Bob's face when he saw his new bicycle.
—v. surprises, surprised, surprising. 1. Come upon suddenly and unexpectedly.—The policeman *surprised* the robbers in their hideout.
2. Amaze; take unaware.—Mother was *surprised* to see us.
—adj. Not expected.—We are planning a *surprise* party for our teacher. She doesn't know about it or expect it.

sur•ren•der (sə-REN-der) *n. surrenders.* A giving up.—The *surrender* of the enemy came when their supplies ran out.
—v. surrenders, surrendered, surrendering. Give up.—The enemy held the town for a long time, but at last they had to *surrender* it.—The robbers *surrendered* to the police.

sur•rey (SER-ee) *n. surreys.* A four-wheeled carriage with two seats. *Surreys* are drawn by horses.

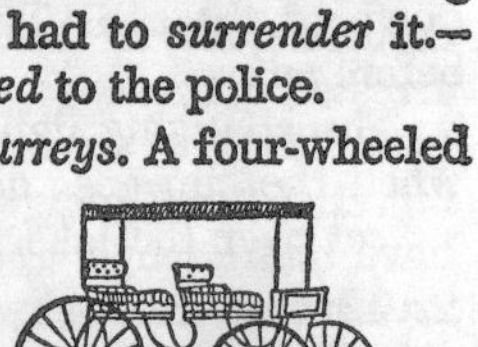

sur•round (sə-ROWND) *v. surrounds, surrounded, surrounding.* 1. Enclose. —A fence *surrounds* the garden. It goes all the way around the garden to keep the chickens from getting in.
2. Close in on all sides.—When the sheriff's men *surrounded* him, Robin Hood blew his horn for his Merry Men to come to his aid.

sur•round•ings (sə-ROWN-dingz) *n. pl.* Things or conditions all about one. – The children have always lived in pleasant *surroundings.* They have had a pretty home in the country, with pleasant neighbors.

sur•vey (SER-vay) *n. surveys.* A study; examination; comparison.–The teachers made a *survey* of the parents' opinion of the progress of their children. They tried to find out what the parents thought.

–(ser-VAY) *v. surveys, surveyed, surveying.* 1. Look over; examine.–The teacher *surveyed* the room to see that everything was neat and orderly.

2. Measure carefully to get the size, shape, and position of an area and to determine where the boundaries are. – The men are *surveying* the lot next to our house.

sur•vey•or (ser-VAY-er) *n. surveyors.* A person who uses surveying instruments to measure land for size, shape, and position.

sur•vive (ser-VYV) *v. survives, survived, surviving.* 1. Remain alive after; live through.–All the families *survived* the flood.

2. Live longer than. – Mrs. Jones *survived* Mr. Jones. When Mr. Jones died, Mrs. Jones was still alive.

3. Last through.–The old flag has *survived* three wars. We still have it.

–*survival, n. survivals.*

sur•vi•vor (ser-VY-ver) *n. survivors.* A person who is still alive.–The ship sank, and two sailors were the only *survivors.* All the others were drowned.

sus•pect (SUSS-pekt) *n. suspects.* A person thought guilty of something.–The policeman arrested one *suspect* for the murder.

–(sə-SPEKT) *v. suspects, suspected, suspecting.* 1. Guess; imagine.–I *suspect* that you have had enough to eat.

2. Think or believe to be guilty without being able to prove it.–The boy *suspected* his pet crow of taking the clip, but he couldn't be sure because he hadn't seen him do it.

3. Doubt.–Father *suspected* the stranger's honesty.

sus•pend (sə-SPEND) *v. suspends, suspended, suspending.* 1. Hang. – The swing was *suspended* from a broad branch of the tree.

2. Stop; put off.–Work on the road was *suspended* because of the rain.

3. Temporarily not allow to attend or to perform one's work.–Bill was *suspended* from school for smoking between classes.

sus•pend•ers (sə-SPEN-derz) *n. pl.* Straps worn over the shoulders and buttoned or clamped onto the trousers to keep them up.– Father wears *suspenders,* but Bob wears a belt.

sus•pen•sion bridge (sə-SPEN-shən brij) *suspension bridges.* A bridge hung from cables.

sus•pi•cious (sə-SPISH-əss) *adj.; suspiciously, adv.* 1. Thinking someone has done wrong, or that something is wrong, without real proof.–The policeman is *suspicious* of the man standing in front of the bank.

2. Causing one to doubt or suspect. – The man's sneaky habits are *suspicious.* They make people think he is not to be trusted.

–*suspicion, n. suspicions.*

swal•low (SWAHL-oh) *n. swallows.* 1. A small bird that flies swiftly and smoothly. –Some *swallows* build their nests in barns.

2. As much as one can drink in one gulp.–The thirsty boy asked for a *swallow* of water.

–*v. swallows, swallowed, swallowing.* 1. Take into the stomach through the throat. – Do you want some water to help you to *swallow* the pill?

2. Believe too easily. – The boy *swallows* everything anyone tells him.

swam (SWAM) *v.* One form of the verb *swim.* –Ducks swim in the pond. One duck *swam* all the way across the pond.

swamp (SWAHMP) *n. swamps; swampy, adj.* Soft, wet, marshy land.–We gathered cattails in the *swamp.*

–*v. swamps, swamped, swamping.* 1. Fill with water and sink.–A big wave *swamped* the little boat.

2. Overwhelm. – Mother said she was *swamped* with work. She had too much to do.

swan (SWAHN) *n. swans.* A large water bird with short legs and a long neck.–The graceful *swans* swim in the pond at the park.

swap (SWAHP) *v. swaps, swapped, swapping.* Trade; exchange.–The girls *swap* books with the other girls after they have read them.–Bob *swapped* a ball for a bat.
–*swap, n. swaps.*

swarm (SWORM) *n. swarms.* A large group; a crowd.–A *swarm* of bees is a group that leaves the beehive and flies away together to form a new colony somewhere else.–*Swarms* of people rushed to the fire.
–*v. swarms, swarmed, swarming.* 1. Gather into a big group.–Bees are *swarming* in the flower garden.
2. Be crowded or full.–The barn is *swarming* with flies.

swarth·y (SWOR-thee) *adj. swarthier, swarthiest.* Dark in color.–People who are outdoors much of the time in the hot sun are apt to have a *swarthy* skin.

swat (SWAHT) *n. swats.* Hard blow or hit.–The boy gave the mosquito a *swat*.
–*v. swats, swatted, swatting.* Hit; knock.–The ballplayer *swatted* the ball out of the park.

sway (SWAY) *v. sways, swayed, swaying.* 1. Move or swing slowly back and forth or from side to side.–The trees *swayed* in the wind.
2. Influence; cause to change one's mind.–Nothing could *sway* the boy from his resolve to become a sailor.

swear (SWAIR) *v. swears, swore, swearing.*
1. Make a statement asking God or some sacred being to witness the truth of what you say.–The witness in court *swore* to tell the truth.
2. Vow or promise.–When Bob joined the Boy Scouts, he had to *swear* to obey certain rules.
3. Curse; use sacred names without reverence.

sweat (SWET) *n.* 1. Perspiration; moisture which comes through the skin.–*Sweat* ran from the man's forehead.
2. Moisture; droplets of water.–*Sweat* formed on the cold glasses of water.
–*v. sweats, sweated, sweating.* 1. Perspire; give off moisture through the skin.–We *sweat* when we run or exercise and become warm.
2. Collect moisture.–Cold water pipes *sweat* when it is very warm. Drops of water form on the pipes.

sweat·er (SWET-er) *n. sweaters.* A knitted wool garment worn on the upper body.–Mother is knitting a *sweater* for Bob.–The teacher asked the children to take off their *sweaters* in school so that they would not get too warm.

sweep (SWEEP) *n. sweeps.* A cleaning with a broom.–Mother said that a daily *sweep* was all that the floor needed.
–*v. sweeps, swept, sweeping.* 1. Brush with a broom.–Mary likes to *sweep* the porch.
2. Push or carry along or away.–The rushing water *swept* away everything in its path.
3. Pass over lightly.–The teacher *sweeps* her hand over her desk each morning to see if there is dust on it.
4. Pass over or through rapidly.–Fire *swept* the forest. It passed quickly through.

sweet (SWEET) *adj. sweeter, sweetest; sweetly, adv.* 1. Of the pleasant taste of sugar.–Sugar is *sweet*. Vinegar is sour.
2. Pleasing.–Roses have a *sweet* smell.
3. Fresh.–Baby likes *sweet* milk, milk that isn't sour or spoiled.
4. Not salted.–*Sweet* butter has no salt.
5. Soft and pleasing.–Mary has a *sweet* voice.–The sounds of the violin were *sweet*.
6. Lovable; good and pleasant.–Baby is *sweet*.

sweet·en (SWEE-tn) *v. sweetens, sweetened, sweetening.* Make sweet by adding sugar or syrup.–*Sweeten* the cherries while they are still cooking.

sweet·heart (SWEET-hahrt) *n. sweethearts.* 1. A loved one.–Baby is Mother's *sweetheart*.
2. A beau.–Aunt Ruth had a *sweetheart*.

sweet po·ta·to (SWEET pə-tay-toh) *sweet potatoes.* A kind of large yellow root that is somewhat sweet. *Sweet potatoes* are good to eat when baked, candied, or boiled.

sweet Wil·liam (sweet WIL-yəm) *sweet Williams.* A kind of flower of many colors that grows in flat clusters. *Sweet William* belongs to the family of pinks.

swell (SWEL) *n. swells.* A long wave or waves out at sea.–The ship tossed in the *swell*.
–*v. swells, swelled, swelling.* Become larger in size, amount, force, or sound.–The mosquito bite made Mary's hand *swell*.–A balloon *swells* when air is blown into it.–The river *swells* when the snow melts.–Music *swells* when it becomes louder and louder.

swell·ing (SWEL-ing) *n. swellings.* A swollen place; a place that is puffed up. – The *swelling* on Father's finger has gone away.

swel·ter (SWEL-ter) *v. swelters, sweltered, sweltering.* Suffer from the heat.–People in the city often *swelter* in the summer.

swept (SWEPT) *v.* One form of the verb *sweep.*–Mary *swept* the front porch.

swift (SWIFT) *adj. swifter, swiftest; swiftly, adv.* 1. Very fast.–The race horse is *swift.*
2. Prompt; quick.–Mother had a *swift* reply to her letter.

swift·ness (SWIFT-nəss) *n.* Speed. – The messenger delivered the letter with great *swiftness.*

swim (SWIM) *n. swims.* A period of swimming.–The boys went for a *swim* in the lake.
–*v. swims, swam, swimming.* 1. Move through the water by moving the arms and legs, or

fins and tail.–A fish *swims* by moving its fins and tail.–A duck *swims* with its feet.
2. Cross by swimming.–The boys could not *swim* the wide river.
3. Glide smoothly.–The balloon went *swimming* through the air.
4. Float about.–Rings of butter *swim* on the soup. They float. They stay on the top.
5. Be covered. – Mary's favorite dessert is berries that are *swimming* in cream.
6. Be dizzy.–My head is *swimming* from excitement.

swim·mer (SWIM-er) *n. swimmers.* An animal or person who swims.

swin·dle (SWIN-dl) *v. swindles, swindled, swindling.* Cheat or get something dishonestly.–The crooked salesman tried to *swindle* Father by selling him a car that was no good.
–*swindle, n. swindles.*

swin·dler (SWIN-dler) *n. swindlers.* A person who gets things by dishonesty or cheating.–Father had the *swindler* arrested for trying to sell him a car that was no good.

swine (SWYN) *n. sing.* and *pl.* A hog or pig.

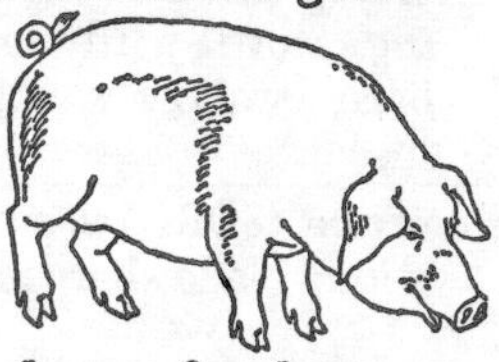

swine·herd (SWYN-herd) *n. swineherds.* A person who cares for swine as a shepherd cares for sheep.

swing (SWING) *n. swings.* A seat hung so that it can move back and forth. – Father hung the *swing* from a branch of the largest tree in our backyard.

–*v. swing, swung, swinging.* 1. Move back and forth in a swing.–Children like to *swing.*
2. Move or cause to move in a circle or part of a circle.–A golfer *swings* the golf club to hit the ball.–Can you stand on one foot and *swing* the other?

swish (SWISH) *n. swishes.* A whispering sound; a rustle. – We heard the *swish* of Mother's taffeta skirt as she entered the room.
–*v. swishes, swished, swishing.* Move with a whistling or rushing noise.–The lion tamer's whip *swished* through the air.

switch (SWICH) *n. switches.* 1. A whip, or a small branch of a tree used for whipping.
2. On a railroad, a mechanical device that shifts part of a track so that a train can move from one track to another.

3. A device for turning off and on.–Electric lights are turned on by a *switch.*
–*v. switches, switched, switching.* 1. Whip.–The cruel man *switched* the dog.
2. Swing back and forth or up and down like a whip.–A cow *switches* her tail to drive the flies off.
3. Change over; transfer. – The engine *switched* from one track to another. – Bob *switched* coats with Jack. Bob wore Jack's coat and Jack wore Bob's.
4. Turn (on or off) with a switch.–*Switch* the light on so you can see to read.

swol•len (SWOH-lən) *v.* One form of the verb *swell.*–John's finger had *swollen* as a result of the infection.

swoop (SWOOP) *v. swoops, swooped, swooping.* Move swiftly and smoothly down.–The barn swallow *swooped* down to catch an insect.

sword (SORD) *n. swords.* A weapon that has a long blade sharpened on one or both edges.

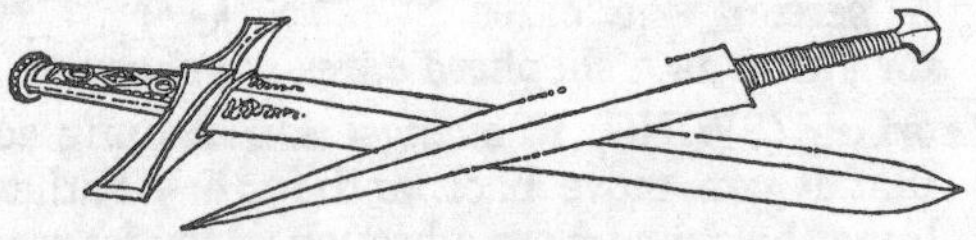

swore (SWOR) *v.* One form of the verb *swear.* –Billy *swore* that he would uphold the rules of the club.

sworn (SWORN) *v.* One form of the verb *swear.*–Billy has *sworn* to uphold the rules of the club.

swung (SWUNG) *v.* One form of the verb *swing.*–The monkey *swung* by his tail from a branch.

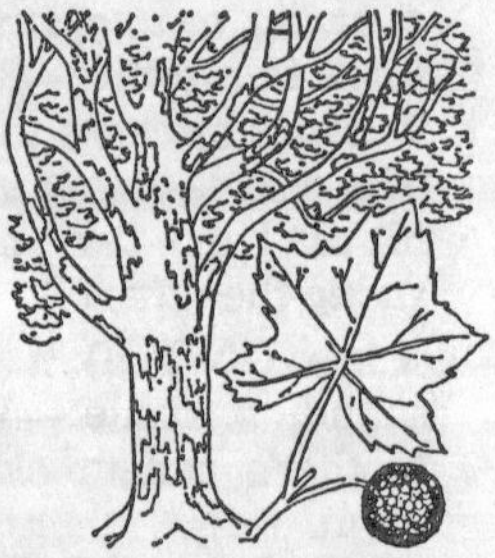

syc•a•more (SIK-ə-mor) *n. sycamores.* A kind of tree with scaly bark.

syl•la•ble (SIL-ə-bəl) *n. syllables.* 1. A part of a word that is pronounced separately. We say the word "sympathetic" in four parts: (sym-pa-thet-ic). Each part is a *syllable.* We say the word "man" in only one part: (MAN). "Man" has only one *syllable.*
2. In writing, a part of a word that can be separated at the end of a line. Each *syllable* contains at least one vowel. In this dictionary these *syllables* are marked by dots in each entry word, as: crit•i•cism. Words that appear without dots, like "man," cannot be separated at the end of a line.

sym•bol (SIM-bəl) *n. symbols.* 1. A thing that stands for something else.–A white flag is a *symbol* of surrender.–The American flag is the *symbol* of the United States.
2. A mark which has a definite meaning.–In arithmetic we use + as a *symbol* for addition and – as a *symbol* for subtraction.

sym•bol•ize (SIM-bəl-yz) *v. symbolizes, symbolized, symbolizing.* 1. Be a symbol of; stand for.–An olive branch *symbolizes* peace to most people.
2. Represent by a symbol.

sym•pa•thet•ic (sim-pə-THET-ik) *adj.; sympathetically, adv.* Sharing the feelings of others, and feeling kindly toward them.–Mother is *sympathetic* toward the sick woman. She seems to know how the woman feels, and feels sorry for her.

sym•pa•thize (SIM-pə-thyz) *v. sympathizes, sympathized, sympathizing.* Feel sympathy for; share the feelings of.–When Bob is sick, he wants you to *sympathize* with him. He wants you to show that you understand how he feels.

sym•pa•thy (SIM-pə-thee) *n. sympathies.* 1. A kind feeling that one person has for another. A person shows *sympathy* for another person when he feels that person's sorrows and troubles.
2. Agreement.–Father is in *sympathy* with our plans for vacation.
3. A state of understanding and sharing ideas and feelings about things.–If music makes both Bob and Mary feel happy at the same time, they are in *sympathy* with each other.

sym•pho•ny (SIM-fə-nee) *n. symphonies.* A long piece of music, usually in four parts, written for an orchestra.

symp•tom (SIMP-təm) *n. symptoms.* A sign; an indication.–The doctor did not find any *symptoms* of measles when he examined the baby; he found no red spots.

syn•o•nym (SIN-ə-nim) *n. synonyms.* One of two or more words that mean the same or nearly the same thing.–"Small" and "little" are *synonyms.*–"Big" and "large" are also *synonyms.*

syr•up or **sir•up** (SIR- *or* SER-əp) *n. syrups* or *sirups.* A thick, sticky, sweet liquid containing much sugar and sometimes fruits and other flavoring.–Mary wanted chocolate *syrup* on her ice cream and Bob asked for pineapple *syrup.*–Bob and Mary always eat lots of maple *syrup* with their pancakes.

sys•tem (SISS-təm) *n. systems.* 1. An orderly plan or method.–Mother has a *system* for doing her housework.
2. A whole body.–The doctor said that Bob's *system* was unusually strong.
3. A network.–Uncle Joe is an announcer for a radio and television broadcasting *system.*
4. An arrangement; an order.–The United States and Britain have democratic *systems* of government.

Tt

T, t (TEE) *n. T's, t's.* The twentieth letter of the alphabet.

ta•ble (TAY-bəl) *n. tables.* 1. A piece of furniture with a flat top resting on legs.–We set lamps on *tables* in the living room.

2. A list of things, or information given in a very short form.–We looked in the *table* of contents in the front of the book to find out what stories were in the book.–In arithmetic we learn the multiplication *table:*

$2 \times 1 = 2$
$2 \times 2 = 4$
$2 \times 3 = 6$

ta•ble•cloth (TAY-bəl-klawth) *n. tablecloths.* A cloth spread on a dining table before the dishes and foods are put on.–Mary put the *tablecloth* and napkins on the table.

ta•ble•spoon (TAY-bəl-spoon) *n. tablespoons.* A large spoon.–Mother serves the vegetables with a *tablespoon.*

tab•let (TAB-lət) *n. tablets.* 1. A pad.–A writing *tablet* has many sheets of paper fastened together at the top.
2. A sheet or thin piece of metal, stone, or wood with something written on it.–The school children put up a *tablet* in the main hall in honor of the first principal of the school.
3. A small, flat pill.–The *tablets* which the doctor gave Father were easy to swallow.

tab•u•late (TAB-yə-layt) *v. tabulates, tabulated, tabulating.* Make a table or arrangement of numbers, words, or facts.–The results of the election were *tabulated* to show at a glance the names of all the candidates and the number of votes each received.
–*tabulation, n. tabulations.*

tack (TAK) *n. tacks.* A short nail with a large flat or rounded head.–The children used thumb*tacks* to fasten their drawings to the wall.

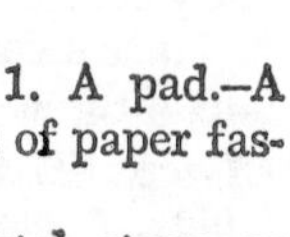

–*v. tacks, tacked, tacking.* 1. To fasten with tacks.–The drawings were *tacked* onto the wall.
2. Sew loosely and temporarily.–Mother *tacked* the hem of Mary's dress. She put in loose stitches until she could sew it permanently.

tack•le (TAK-əl) *n. tackles.* 1. Things used for doing a job.–Fishing *tackle* is the equipment used by a fisherman for fishing.
2. Ropes specially arranged for lifting heavy loads.
3. One of the players on a football team.–John is right *tackle* on the school team.
–*v. tackles, tackled, tackling.* 1. Grab; get hold of.–One football player *tackled* the other.
2. Try to do; undertake.–Father will *tackle* the work that has to be done as soon as he gets home.

tact (TAKT) *n.; tactful, adj.; tactfully, adv.* A person who has *tact* knows how to do and say things without annoying people or hurting their feelings.

tad•pole (TAD-pohl) *n. tadpoles.* The young of a frog or toad. *Tadpoles* have tails which disappear before they become full-grown frogs or toads.

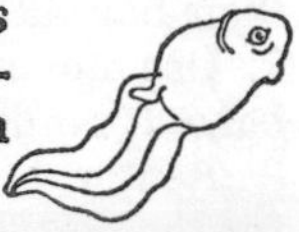

taf•fe•ta (TAF-ə-tə) *n. taffetas.* A stiff silk cloth.–Grandmother has a dress of brown *taffeta* that makes a rustling or whispering sound when she walks.

taf•fy (TAF-ee) *n.* A candy. *Taffy* is made of sugar or molasses, water, and vinegar.

tag (TAG) *n. tags.* 1. A small piece of cardboard fastened to anything to give a name, directions for use, price, etc.–The clerk told us we could find the price of the skates by looking at the *tag.*–The children tied Christmas *tags* to their gifts to tell who was to get each gift and whom it was from.

2. A game in which one player, who is "it," chases the others until he touches one.
–*v. tags, tagged, tagging.* 1. Fasten a tag to.–After the gifts were *tagged,* they were put under the Christmas tree.
2. Follow close behind.–Jack's dog always *tags* after him.
3. To touch in the game of tag.–Mary *tagged* Ruth, and then Ruth was "it."

tail (TAYL) *n. tails.* 1. A part which grows on the back or rear end of many animals.–Cows switch their *tails* to keep the flies away.
2. The last or back part of anything, as the *tail* of an automobile, the *tail* of an airplane, the *tail* of a person's coat or shirt.

tai•lor (TAY-ler) *n. tailors.* A man who makes or alters clothes.–Mother took her suit to the *tailor* to have it shortened.

take (TAYK) *v. takes, took, taking.* 1. Hold; clasp; grasp.–The children *take* each other's hands when playing "The Farmer in the Dell."
2. Accept.–Grandfather said that he would not *take* the money that Bob offered to pay for the pony.
3. Choose; select; pick for yourself.–*Take* the book you want.–*Take* any seat you wish.
4. Carry; bring.–We *take* our lunch to school.
5. Receive; get; win.–Mary will surely *take* the prize for the best story.–The girls won the first game, but the boys *took* the second.
6. Capture.–The police *took* the robbers at their hideout.
7. Use up; need.–Bread *takes* an hour to bake. It needs to be baked an hour.
8. Rent or buy.–The boys will *take* the boat for the day.
9. Accompany; escort.–I will *take* you to school. I will go with you.–Father *takes* Mother out to dinner on Thursdays.
10. Go on.–Father *took* the train to town.
–*Take off* means to remove.–Mother *took* the dishes *off* the table.

talc (TALK) *n.* A soft, soaplike mineral. *Talc* is used in making talcum powder, soap, and lubricating products.

tal•cum (TAL-kəm) *n. talcums.* A kind of smooth white powder used on the face or body to soothe the skin.

tale (TAYL) *n. tales.* 1. A story.–Grandfather told an exciting *tale* about the bear he fought.
2. A bad report about someone, told to get him into trouble.–Mary likes to carry *tales* to Mother about Jack.

tal•ent (TAL-ənt) *n. talents.* A natural ability to do a thing easily.–Mary has a *talent* for music.

tal•ent•ed (TAL-ən-təd) *adj.* Having a special natural ability.–Mary is *talented* in music. She learns music easily and quickly.

talk (TAWK) *n. talks.* 1. A discussion.–Let's have a *talk* about your problems.
2. A speech; a lecture.–The policeman gave a *talk* on safety.
3. A rumor.–There is *talk* of school closing early this year.
–*v. talks, talked, talking.* Speak; put ideas or thoughts into spoken words.–We *talk* to our friends about things we're interested in.

talk•a•tive (TAWK-ə-tiv) *adj.* Likely to talk much; fond of talking.–Some children are *talkative.* They talk a great deal.

tall (TAWL) *adj. taller, tallest.* 1. Long or high from head to foot.–One boy is short; the other is *tall.*–A person who stands seven feet high is very *tall.*
2. High.–The Empire State Building is *tall.*

tal•low (TAL-oh) *n.* The fat of cows, sheep, and some other animals. *Tallow* is used in making soap and candles.

tal•ly (TAL-ee) *n. tallies.* 1. A piece of paper or a card on which a score in a game, or a count of anything, is kept.
2. A score or count.–During the game, Mary kept the *tally.*
3. A mark used in keeping count or score.–Each mark that Mary made was a *tally.*
–*v. tallies, tallied, tallying.* 1. Match or agree.–Bob's answer *tallies* with Mary's; Bob and Mary both think the answer is 369.
2. Make a count; keep score.–Bob and Mary *tallied* the votes for class president.

tal•on (TAL-ən) *n. talons.* A claw, especially of a bird that kills other birds or animals for food.–Hawks have long, sharp *talons.*

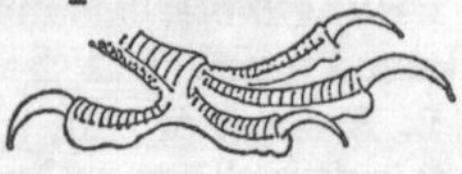

tam•a•rack (TAM-ə-rak) *n. tamaracks.* A tree of the larch family.

tam•bou•rine (tam-bə-REEN) *n. tambourines.* A very small drum with only one head and with flat pieces of metal fastened loosely to the rim. It is played by tapping it with the fingers while shaking it to make the metal pieces jingle.

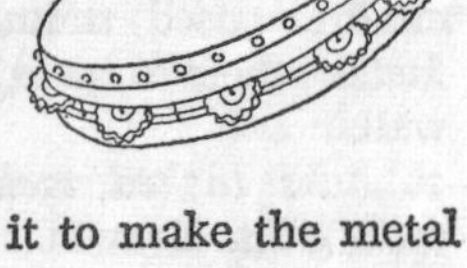

tame (TAYM) *v. tames, tamed, taming.* Make gentle and obedient; accustom to people.—Some animals, such as horses, that were once wild have been *tamed* so people can use them.
—*adj. tamer, tamest; tamely, adv.* 1. Not wild; accustomed to people.—The squirrels in the park are *tame.* They aren't afraid of people.
2. Not exciting; dull.—Mary said the book was so *tame* that she did not finish it.

tam-o'-shan·ter (tam-ə-SHAN-ter) *n. tam-o'-shanters.* A flat, round cap with the top larger than the head band. Some *tam-o'-shanters* are crocheted from yarn and others are made from wool or felt.

tam·per (TAM-per) *v. tampers, tampered, tampering.* Meddle with something; try to fix or repair something without knowing how.—Father never *tampers* with the clock. He has it repaired by someone who is an expert on clocks.

tan (TAN) *n. tans.* A light-brown color.
—*v. tans, tanned, tanning.* 1. Turn to a brownish color from exposure to the sun.—The children played outdoors so much that their faces *tanned.*
2. Make (hides) into leather.—The hides and skins of certain animals are *tanned.*

tan·a·ger (TAN-ə-jer) *n. tanagers.* A kind of sparrow-like bird. The male *tanager* has beautiful, bright-colored feathers.

tan·ge·rine (tan-jə-REEN) *n. tangerines.* A kind of small, sweet orange which peels easily.

tan·gle (TANG-gəl) *n. tangles.* A twisted knot.—Ellen got a *tangle* in her sewing thread and had to break it.
—*v. tangles, tangled, tangling.* Knot and twist together.—Bob has *tangled* the string of his kite so badly that he will have a hard time straightening it.

tank (TANGK) *n. tanks.* 1. A large container for liquid.—We have a hot-water *tank* in the basement.
2. A heavily armored war machine mounted with guns. A *tank* can travel over very rough ground.

tank·er (TANGK-er) *n. tankers.* A cargo vessel fitted with tanks for carrying such things as oil and gasoline.

tan·nic ac·id (TAN-ik ASS-id). A chemical that is used in medicines, inks, tanning, and dyeing. *Tannic acid* is obtained from certain plants, often from oak bark.

tan·ta·lize (TAN-tə-lyz) *v. tantalizes, tantalized, tantalizing.* Tease, as by making promises that are not kept, or by showing something desirable and then keeping it out of reach.—Mother *tantalized* Father with the pie she had baked. She pretended to offer him a piece, but then she told him he could not have any until after dinner.

tan·trum (TAN-trəm) *n. tantrums.* A fit or sudden outburst of bad temper.—The baby had a *tantrum* when she wasn't allowed to have any more cookies. She screamed and cried.

tap (TAP) *n. taps.* 1. A light knock.—We heard a *tap* on the door.
2. A faucet; a valve for controlling the flow of a liquid.—We turned on the *tap* to get a drink of water.

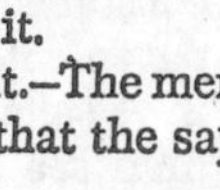

3. A cap that screws on.—The workmen put a *tap* over the end of the pipe to keep the water from coming out.
—*v. taps, tapped, tapping.* 1. Strike or hit lightly.—*Tap* on the box to open it.
2. Make a hole to let the liquid out.—The men *tapped* the sugar maple trees so that the sap would flow out.

tape (TAYP) *n. tapes.* 1. A long, narrow strip of cloth, paper, steel, etc.
2. A narrow strip of paper or cloth with glue on one side.—The teacher mends books with *tape.*—The nurse put *tape* over the cut.
—*v. tapes, taped, taping.* Put a tape on; bind with tape.—The doctor *taped* the boy's foot so that he could walk.

tape·line (TAYP-lyn) *n. tapelines.* A strip of steel or cloth marked off into inches for measuring. It is also called a tape measure.

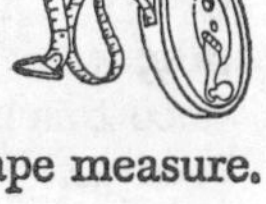

ta•per (TAY-per) *n. tapers.* A long, thin candle.
–*v. tapers, tapered, tapering.* Become smaller toward one end.–The end of a sharpened pencil *tapers* toward the point.

tape re•cord•er (tayp ri-KOR-der) *tape recorders.* An instrument used to record music, voices, or other sounds on a special kind of tape. A *tape recorder* can play back what it has recorded.

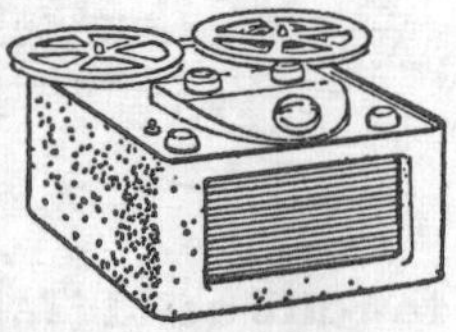

tap•es•try (TAP-iss-tree) *n. tapestries.* A piece of cloth with figures or pictures woven into it. *Tapestries* are hung on the walls just as painted or printed pictures are.

tap•i•o•ca (tap-ee-OH-kə) *n.* A kind of starchy food made from the roots of a tropical plant. *Tapioca* is used to make tasty puddings.

ta•pir (TAY-per) *n. tapirs.* A large hoglike animal found in Central America, South America, and Malaya. The *tapir* has a flexible snout, lives in forests, and eats only plants.

taps (TAPSS) *n.* A traditional tune played on a drum, a bugle, or a trumpet telling soldiers or sailors to put out the lights and go to bed. *Taps* is also sounded when a soldier or a sailor is buried.

tar (TAHR) *n. tars.* 1. A thick, sticky, black substance made from coal.–*Tar* is used in pavements, and to waterproof roofs.
2. A sailor.–The old *tar* likes to tell the children sea stories.
–*v. tars, tarred, tarring.* Put tar on.–The men *tarred* the road.

ta•ran•tu•la (tə-RAN-chə-lə) *n. tarantulas.* A large, hairy spider.

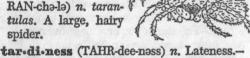

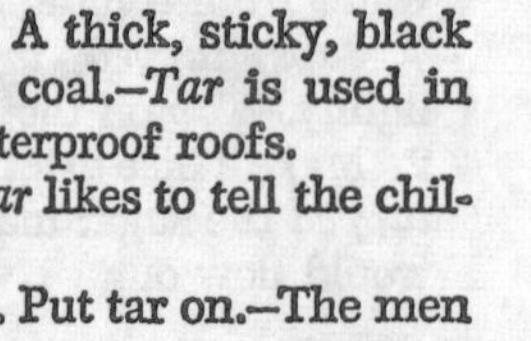

tar•di•ness (TAHR-dee-nəss) *n.* Lateness.–The boy's *tardiness* spoiled the record of the class for promptness.

tar•dy (TAHR-dee) *adj. tardier, tardiest; tardily, adv.* Late.–Mary has not been *tardy* once this school year. She has always been on time.

tar•get (TAHR-gət) *n. targets.* Anything used to shoot or aim at.–The boys put a tin can on the post for a *target;* they tried to hit the can with the stones they were throwing.

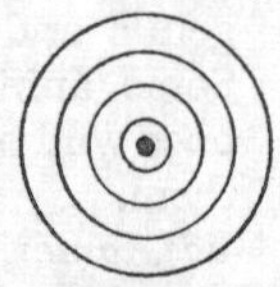

tar•iff (TAR-if) *n. tariffs.* 1. A system of taxes or duties fixed by the government on imported goods.
2. A tax or duty.–What is the *tariff* on bicycles?

tar•nish (TAHR-nish) *v. tarnishes, tarnished, tarnishing.* 1. Lose brightness; turn dark on the surface.–Silver *tarnishes* when left out in the air.
2. Cause to turn dark.–Gas will *tarnish* silver. It will make it lose its brightness.

tar•pau•lin (tahr-PAW-lin) *n. tarpaulins.* A large sheet of waterproof canvas.–When it rains, the grounds keeper at the ball park puts *tarpaulins* over the baseball diamond.

tar•ry (TAR-ee) *v. tarries, tarried, tarrying.* Be slow; waste time; wait.–Do not *tarry* on the way. Come right home.

tart (TAHRT) *n. tarts.* A small baked crust of pastry filled with fruit, jelly, or jam.–Grandmother makes *tarts* from pie crust that is left over from making pies.
–*adj. tarter, tartest.* Sour; biting or sharp to the taste.–Grapes that are not ripe are *tart.*

tar•tar (TAHR-ter) *n.* A substance that gathers and hardens on the teeth. *Tartar* consists of tiny particles of food, saliva, and lime. It is usually removed by the dentist when he cleans your teeth.

task (TASK) *n. tasks.* A piece of work.–If a *task* is once begun, never leave it till it's done.
–Bob's weekly *task* is cutting the grass.

tas•sel (TASS-əl) *n. tassels.* 1. An ornament made of a number of cords fastened together at one end and loose at the other. A *tassel* hangs down.–Mary's hat has a *tassel* on the side.
2. The silky threads on an ear of corn.

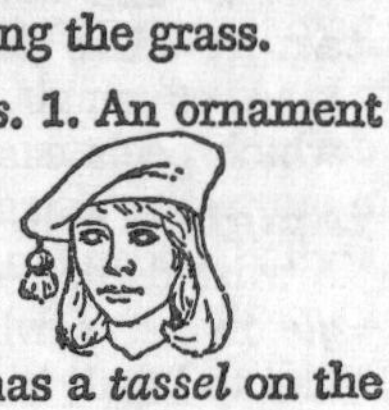

taste (TAYST) *n. tastes.* 1. The sensation or feeling one gets when food or drink is in the mouth.–The *taste* of sugar is sweet; the *taste* of vinegar is sour.
2. Judgment and understanding of beauty, or of what is good or proper.–Mary has good *taste* in clothes. She always picks clothes that are attractive and appropriate.

—*v. tastes, tasted, tasting.* 1. Test the flavor of food or drink by putting a little into the mouth.—Mary *tasted* the soup and said it was too salty.
2. Have a particular flavor.—This medicine *tastes* bitter.—Sea water *tastes* salty.

tat·tered (TAT-erd) *adj.* Ragged and torn.—The scarecrow's clothes were *tattered.*

tat·too (ta-TOO) *v. tattoos, tattooed, tattooing.* Mark the skin with colors which will not come off.—The sailor had a picture of a clown *tattooed* on his arm.
—*tattoo, n. tattoos.*

taught (TAWT) *v.* One form of the verb *teach.*—Mother *taught* Mary how to sew.

taut (TAWT) *adj. tauter, tautest; tautly, adv.; tautness, n.* Tightly stretched.—The clothesline was so *taut* that it broke in two.

tav·ern (TAV-ern) *n. taverns.* 1. A place where beer, wine, and other alcoholic drinks are served.
2. An inn; a hotel.—An old *tavern* stood on the side of the hill.

tax (TAKS) *n. taxes.* Money that must be paid by a person or company to help with the cost of government. Firemen and policemen are paid from *taxes* collected by a city. The Army, Navy, and Air Force are paid for by *taxes* collected by the Federal government in Washington.
—*v. taxes, taxed, taxing.* Require a tax from.—A person is *taxed* according to the amount of money he earns.

tax·i (TAK-see) or **tax·i·cab** (TAK-see-kab) *n. taxis* or *taxicabs.* An automobile, driven by a regular driver, that can be hired to carry passengers. Most *taxis* have a meter to show how long the trip is and how much one must pay.

tax·i·der·mist (TAK-sə-der-mist) *n. taxidermists.* A person who prepares, stuffs, and mounts the skins of animals. The animals stuffed and mounted by a good *taxidermist* look almost alive.

tea (TEE) *n. teas.* 1. A shrub grown mainly in China, Japan, and India; the dried leaves of this plant.

2. A drink made by pouring boiling water over the dried leaves of this plant.—Mother drinks *tea.*
3. A late afternoon party where tea and other refreshments are served.—Mother is going to a *tea* at our neighbor's home.

teach (TEECH) *v. teaches, taught, teaching.* 1. Instruct; show how; help one to learn.—Miss Jones will *teach* you how to sew.—Father *teaches* the boys to play baseball.—Our teacher *teaches* us reading, arithmetic, and spelling.
2. Give lessons in.—Mr. Smith *teaches* art.

teach·er (TEECH-er) *n. teachers.* A person who instructs others, or helps others to learn something.—Mary takes singing lessons from a music *teacher.*

teach·ing (TEECH-ing) *n. teachings.* 1. Instruction; the work of teachers.—Our teacher finds *teaching* very pleasant work.
2. A thing taught or preached.—The *teachings* in the Bible are good rules to live by.
—*v.* One form of the verb *teach.*—Father is *teaching* Bob to skate.

team (TEEM) *n. teams.* 1. A number of people who work, play, or act together.—One *team* plays against another *team.*
2. Two or more horses or other animals harnessed to one carriage or machine.
—*v. teams, teamed, teaming.* Join or work together for something.—Two dancers *teamed* up in one act of the show.

team·ster (TEEM-ster) *n. teamsters.* A person who drives a team of horses or a truck.—The *teamsters* loaded up their trucks and drove off.

team·work (TEEM-werk) *n.* Work or effort performed by a team, or by a group of persons as a whole.—The coach believes that good *teamwork* is the key to victory. He believes that everyone must work together in order to win.

tea·pot (TEE-paht) *n. teapots.* A container something like a kettle, made of metal or china, for making and pouring out tea.—Grandmother has a pretty china *teapot.*

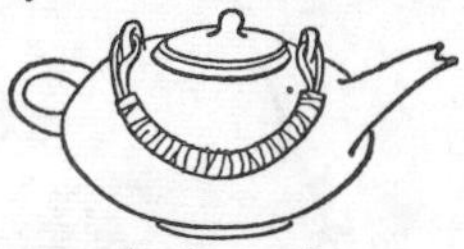

tear (TAIR) *n. tears.* A rough, jagged cut.—Father hit his arm against the saw and made a long *tear* in his sleeve.
—*v. tears, tore, tearing.* 1. Pull apart; rip.—Father *tore* his sleeve on the saw.
2. Pull hard; pull hard on.—The angry artist *tore* down the pictures.—The wind *tore* the leaves from the tree.
3. Run wildly; rush.—Bob *tore* across the field to get his kite.

tear (TIR) *n. tears.* A drop of salt water that comes out of one's eyes.—Big *tears* fell on the baby's cheeks when she cried.

tear gas (TIR gass). A gas that irritates the eyes so that tears begin to flow. *Tear gas* causes temporary blindness. It is used in war, and sometimes it is used by the police as an aid in capturing criminals and breaking up riots.

tease (TEEZ) *v. teases, teased, teasing.* 1. Lightly make fun of.—Mary *teases* Father about getting fat.
2. Beg.—Baby *teases* Mother for lollipops.

tea·spoon (TEE-spoon) *n. teaspoons.* A small spoon.—We use a *teaspoon* to eat ice cream, pudding, and other soft foods.

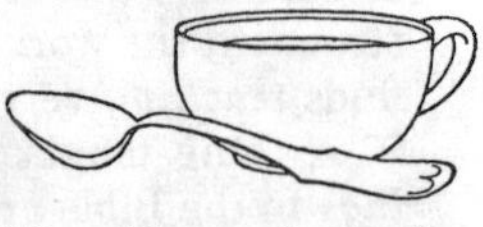

tech·ni·cal (TEK-nə-kl) *adj.; technically, adv.* Having to do with the special methods and skills of a particular science, art, or field. —Jim has always been interested in engineering, but he has not yet had any *technical* training in the field.

te·di·ous (TEE-dee-əss) *adj.; tediously, adv.* Dull, tiresome, and boring.—The long speech was *tedious.*

teeth (TEETH) *n. pl.* More than one *tooth.* The sharp, white, bony points that grow in two rows in the mouths of people and many animals; the points of a rake or a comb.—We chew our food with our *teeth.*—A rake has *teeth* to comb the grass.

tel·e·cast (TEL-ə-kast) *v. telecasts, telecast* or *telecasted, telecasting.* Broadcast by television.—The program is being *telecast* across the entire nation.

tel·e·gram (TEL-ə-gram) *n. telegrams.* Written message sent over wires by electricity.—Father's *telegram* read, "Home Saturday night in time for supper. Love. Father."

WESTERN UNION

tel·e·graph (TEL-ə-graf) *n. telegraphs · telegraphic, adj.; telegraphically, adv.* A device or way by which written messages are sent over wires by electricity.—Father sent Mother a message by *telegraph* when he was away. —*v. telegraphs, telegraphed, telegraphing.* Send a written message over wires by electricity.—Father *telegraphed* Mother.

tel·e·phone (TEL-ə-fohn) *n. telephones.* A device which carries sound, such as that of voices or music, over wires by electricity.—Sally talked to Father on the *telephone.*

—*v. telephones, telephoned, telephoning.* Talk to someone or call someone on the telephone. —Mother *telephoned* Father to ask him when he would be home.

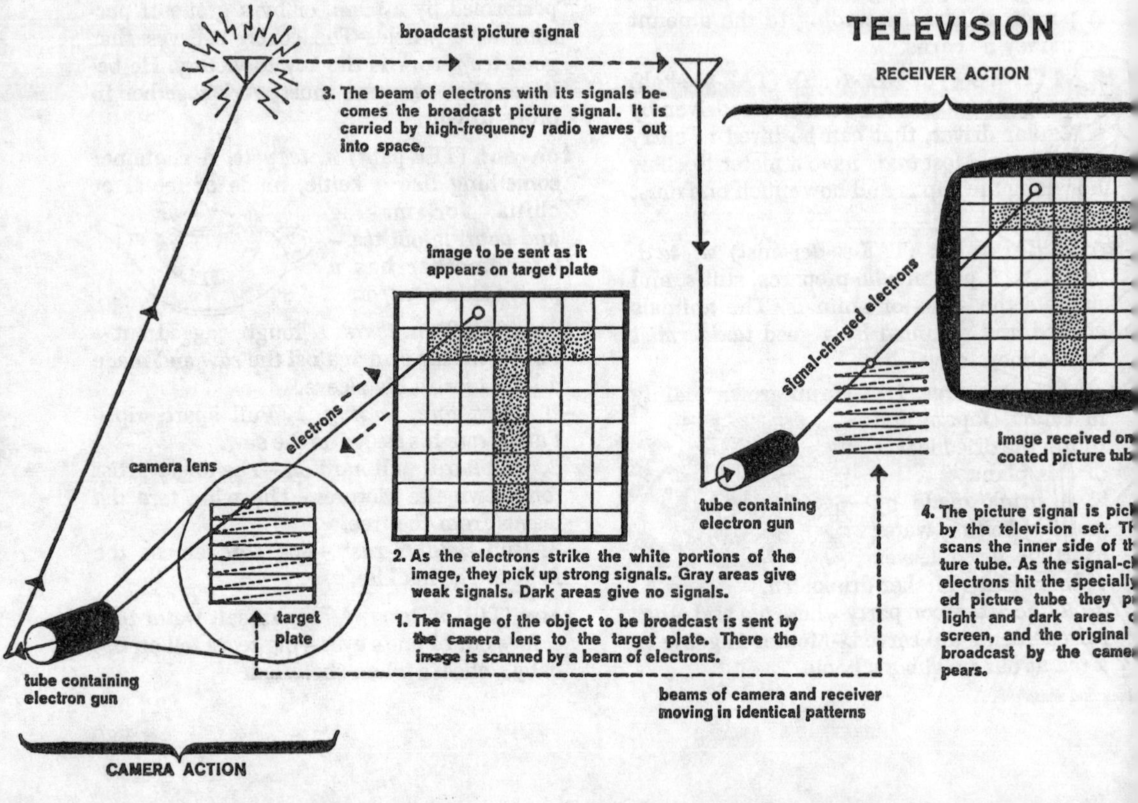
TELEVISION
RECEIVER ACTION
broadcast picture signal
3. The beam of electrons with its signals becomes the broadcast picture signal. It is carried by high-frequency radio waves out into space.
image to be sent as it appears on target plate
electrons
camera lens
target plate
tube containing electron gun
2. As the electrons strike the white portions of the image, they pick up strong signals. Gray areas give weak signals. Dark areas give no signals.
1. The image of the object to be broadcast is sent by the camera lens to the target plate. There the image is scanned by a beam of electrons.
signal-charged electrons
tube containing electron gun
beams of camera and receiver moving in identical patterns
CAMERA ACTION

tel•e•scope (TEL-ə-skohp) *n. telescopes.* An instrument which, when looked through, makes faraway objects look larger, clearer, and closer to you. *Telescopes* are used to study the stars. – We looked through a *telescope* at the moon and saw the mountains on it.

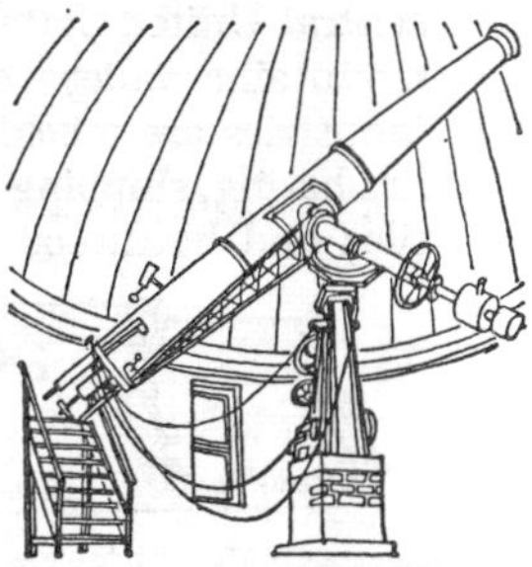

Tel•e•type (TEL-ə-typ) *n. Teletypes.* A telegraphic instrument that works like a typewriter. As the operator types on the instrument's keyboard, the *Teletype* sends out the message letter by letter. The message is received and automatically printed by another *Teletype.*

tel•e•vise (TEL-ə-vyz) *v. televises, televised, televising.* Transmit or receive by television. –The championship fight was *televised* from coast to coast.

tel•e•vi•sion (TEL-ə-vizh-ən) *n.* A method of sending pictures of people or objects in motion by radio waves. The moving pictures appear on a screen which is part of the receiving set.–Father sat at his new *television* set, watching and listening to the baseball game being played in Chicago.

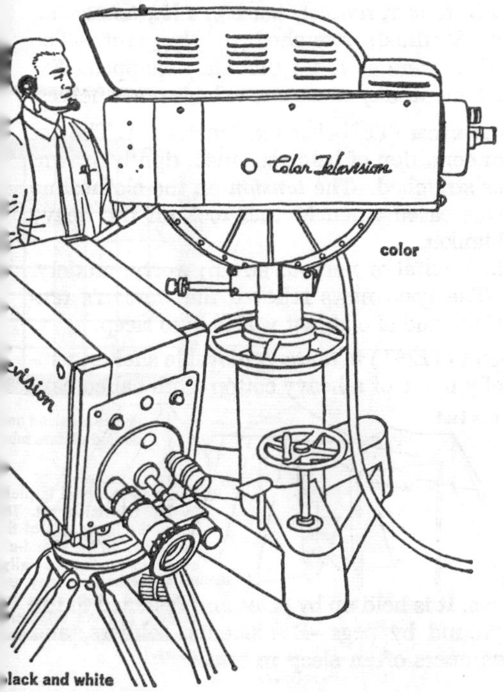

TELEVISION CAMERAS

tell (TEL) *v. tells, told, telling.* 1. Say or speak about something.–I will *tell* you about my trip.–I will *tell* you a story.
2. Show.–The speedometer on the car *tells* how fast you are going.
3. Order; command.–Father *told* the man to leave.
4. Let know; inform.–*Tell* me how far it is to school.

tell•er (TEL-er) *n. tellers.* 1. Someone who tells.–Grandfather is known as a fine *teller* of stories.
2. A bank employee who receives deposits and counts and gives out money.–Frank is working as a *teller* in the bank downtown this summer.

tem•per (TEM-per) *n. tempers.* 1. One's behavior or way of acting.–Mother has an even *temper.* She is calm and is not easily disturbed or made angry.
2. An angry mood.–Jack flies into *tempers* quickly, and he always feels very sorry afterward.

tem•per•ate (TEM-per-ət) *adj.* Mild; not extreme or excessive.–We live in a *temperate* climate, where the weather is not usually very hot or very cold.–Father is a man of *temperate* eating habits; he likes to eat, but doesn't eat too much.

tem•per•a•ture (TEM-per-ə-cher) *n. temperatures.* Heat as measured in degrees; hotness or coolness. *Temperature* is measured by a thermometer.–Mother set the oven control for a *temperature* of 400 degrees (400°).–Water boils when its *temperature* is about 212° Fahrenheit.–When the *temperature* is 0° Fahrenheit, it is very cold.

tem•pest (TEM-pəst) *n. tempests.* A very bad, windy storm.–A *tempest* kept the ships from sailing.

tem•ple (TEM-pəl) *n. temples.* A sacred building used for religious worship.

tem•po (TEM-poh) *n. tempos.* 1. In music, the rate of speed at which a composition is to be played or sung.–The *tempo* increased during the last movement of the symphony.
2. In general, any rate of work or activity; rhythm.–The boy who was behind in his studies tried to work at a faster *tempo* in order to catch up with the others.

tem•po•rar•y (TEM-pə-rair-ee) *adj.; temporarily, adv.* Not permanent; lasting for a little while only.–Jack will take a *temporary* job during his summer vacation.

tempt (TEMPT) *v. tempts, tempted, tempting.* 1. Lead someone to want to do wrong or evil.–The dollar which the man left out on his desk *tempted* the hungry boy to steal.
2. Make one want something; attract.–The cold pool *tempted* the thirsty hiker. It made him long for water.

temp•ta•tion (temp-TAY-shən) *n. temptations.* A thing that leads one to want to do something though he tries not to do it.–An open box of chocolates on the table is a *temptation* to eat.

ten (TEN) *n. tens* and *adj.* The number [10] coming after 9 and before 11.–Five and five make *ten.*

ten•ant (TEN-ənt) *n. tenants.* Someone who pays rent for the use of land or any kind of building.–Grandfather has *tenants* on his farm.–We are *tenants.* We pay rent for our apartment.

tend (TEND) *v. tends, tended, tending.* 1. Look after.–Mary *tends* the baby when Mother is away.–Bob *tends* the front lawn in the summer.
2. Be usually.–Bill *tends* to be lazy; he is usually lazy.

ten•der (TEN-der) *adj. tenderer, tenderest; tenderly, adv.; tenderness, n.* 1. Soft; easily cut or broken.–Some meat is tough, but this piece is *tender.*
2. Not strong; delicate; easily harmed.–Baby has *tender* skin.
3. Kind; easily moved; sympathetic.–Grandmother has a *tender* heart. She shares other people's sorrows and troubles.
4. Sore.–Baby has a *tender* spot on her head where she bumped it.

ten•der•foot (TEN-der-fuht) *n. tenderfoots* or *tenderfeet.* 1. A person without experience; a beginner; a novice.–Newcomers among the pioneers of the United States were called *tenderfeet* by the oldtimers.
2. A beginning rank among Boy Scouts.

ten•don (TEN-dən) *n. tendons.* A strong cord that fastens a muscle to a bone. – The football player pulled one of the *tendons* in his leg and had to leave the game.

ten•dril (TEN-dril) *n. tendrils.* The thin leafless stem by which climbing plants attach themselves to objects for support.–The grape *tendrils* are coiled around the trellis.

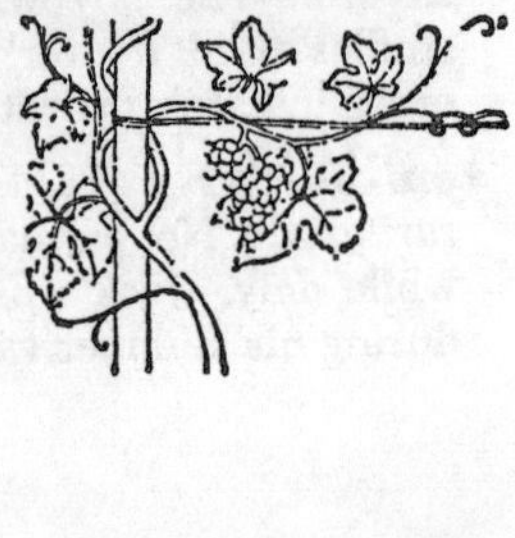

Ten•nes•see (ten-ə-SEE) *n.* A state in south central United States noted for its beautiful mountains, valleys, and plains. Its important industries are mixed farming, cattle raising, lumbering, shipping, and manufacturing textiles and hardwood products.

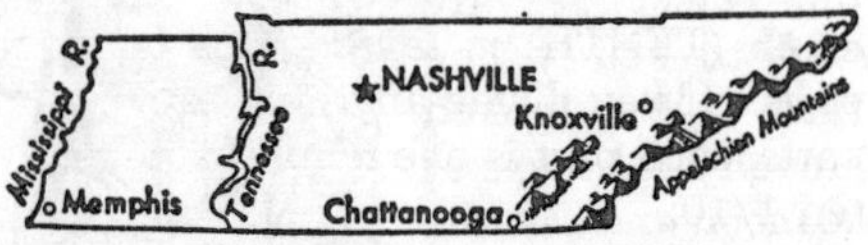

ten•nis (TEN-iss) *n.* A game played by hitting a ball back and forth over a net with a kind of paddle called a racket.

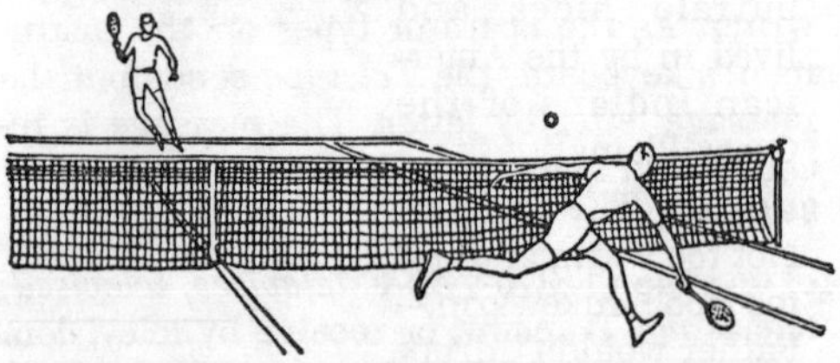

ten•or (TEN-er) *n. tenors* and *adj.* The highest singing voice that a grown man can have; a man with such a voice.–Father sings *tenor.* He is a *tenor.*

tense (TENSS) *n. tenses.* Any of various verb forms used to show the time of an action or happening.–The past *tense* of "come" is "came." John came to see me yesterday. "Came" shows that John's visit happened in the past.
–*adj. tenser, tensest; tensely, adv.; tenseness, n.* Strained; stretched tightly; taut. – The wires were so *tense* that they snapped.–Excitement may cause one to have *tense* nerves.

ten•sion (TEN-shən) *n. tensions.* 1. The act or condition of being strained, tightly drawn, or stretched.–The *tension* on the clothesline was eased when Mother took off the heavy blanket.
2. Mental or nervous strain; worry; anxiety. –The good news relieved the woman's *tension,* and she at last was able to sleep.

tent (TENT) *n. tents.* A movable shelter, usually made of a heavy cotton cloth called canvas. It is held up by poles and fastened to the ground by pegs.–Boy Scouts, soldiers, and campers often sleep in *tents.*

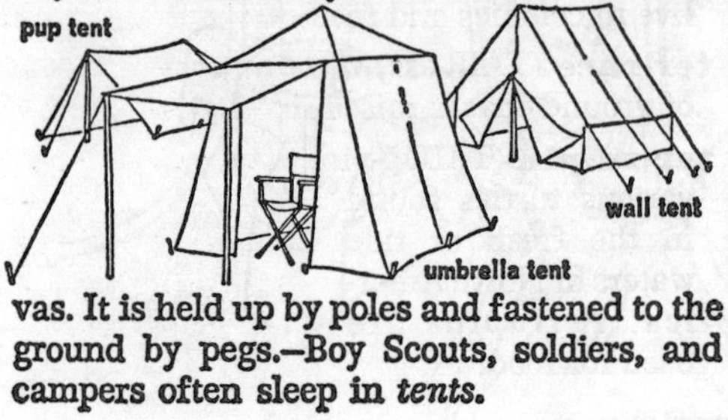

ten•ta•cle (TEN-tə-kəl) *n. tentacles.* 1. A long, flexible projection, usually on the head or near the mouth of an animal; a feeler. *Tentacles* are used for holding, feeling, or moving.–An octopus has eight *tentacles.*
2. Any sensitive hairlike projection on a plant.

tenth (TENTH) *n. tenths.* One of 10 equal parts.–If you divide anything into ten equal parts, each part is one *tenth.* It may be written 1/10.
–*adj.* Coming as number 10 in a series.

te•pee (TEE-pee) *n. tepees.* A pointed tent made of poles and buffalo hides and lived in by the American Indians of the Great Plains.

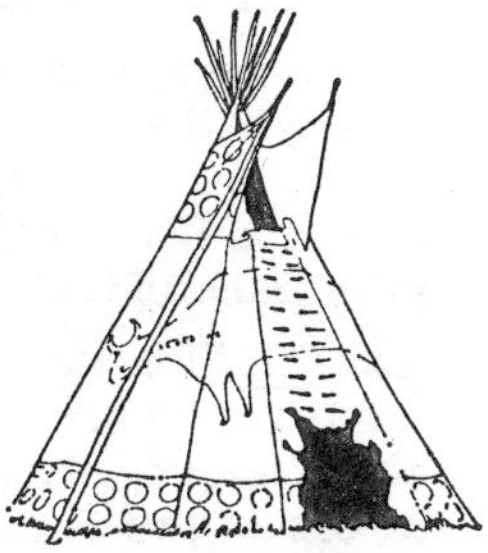

tep•id (TEP-id) *adj.* Not too warm and not too cool; lukewarm.–Father wouldn't drink the *tepid* water. He wanted cold water.

term (TERM) *n. terms.* 1. A set length of time.–In our school the first *term* is from the eighth of September until the last of January.
2. A word or expression.–We must know the meaning of certain *terms* in order to understand arithmetic. Plus, minus, add, and subtract are *terms* used in arithmetic.
3. A condition; a thing agreed to.–Bill did not live up to the *terms* of the bargain.

ter•mi•nal (TER-mə-nəl) *n. terminals* and *adj.* 1. The end; the part which forms an end. –A bus *terminal* is a station at the end of a bus line.
2. An electrical connecting device at the end of a cable or wire.–The television antenna is connected to a *terminal* in back of the set.

ter•mi•nate (TER-mə-nayt) *v. terminates, terminated, terminating.* Put an end to; end or come to an end. – The chairman *terminated* the discussion.

ter•mite (TER-myt) *n. termites.* A light-colored, soft-bodied, destructive insect. *Termites* live in colonies and feed on wood and paper.

ter•race (TAIR-əss) *n. terraces.* A flat piece of ground that is raised like a broad step.

ter•ra•pin (TAIR-ə-pin) *n. terrapins.* Any of various turtles found in the fresh or tide waters of North America. *Terrapins* are used for food.

ter•rar•i•um (tə-RAIR-ee-əm) *n. terrariums.* A gardenlike enclosure, usually glass-walled, in which small land animals are kept. A *terrarium* is for land animals what an aquarium is for fish.

ter•ri•ble (TAIR-ə-bəl) *adj.; terribly, adv.* Causing great fear or awe.–The car crash was a *terrible* accident.

ter•ri•er (TAIR-ee-er) *n. terriers.* A small, short-haired dog. *Terriers* were once used for hunting small animals that live in the ground.

ter•rif•ic (tə-RIF-ik) *adj.; terrifically, adv.* Terrible; awful; dreadful. – A *terrific* fire broke out in the factory.

ter•ri•fy (TAIR-ə-fy) *v. terrifies, terrified, terrifying.* Frighten very much.–The loud barking of the dog *terrified* the baby so much that she shrieked.

ter•ri•to•ry (TAIR-ə-tor-ee) *n. territories.* 1. A large stretch of land; a part of a country. –Some *territory* in North America is covered with forests.
2. A part of the United States which did not belong to any state, but was governed by men chosen by the President.–Alaska and Hawaii used to be United States *territories.* Now they are states.

ter•ror (TAIR-er) *n. terrors.* 1. Great fear.–*Terror* came over the crowd when the lion got loose.
2. A thing that causes great fear.–The escaped lion was a *terror.*

test (TEST) *n. tests.* A trial or examination which shows how much a person knows about a thing.–Our teacher gave us a spelling *test.*
–*v. tests, tested, testing.* Examine by trial.–The teacher *tested* our spelling ability by giving us a test.

tes•ta•ment (TESS-tə-mənt) *n. testaments.* 1. A legal document telling what a person wishes done with his property after he dies; a will.–The lawyer is planning to read the dead man's *testament* to a gathering of his relatives.
2. (Spelled with a capital "T.") One of the two portions of the Bible, either the New *Testament* or the Old *Testament.*

tes•ti•fy (TESS-tə-fy) *v. testifies, testified, testifying.* Make a solemn statement; tell what one knows to be true.–Bob *testified* that he saw the man pay the money.

tes·ti·mo·ny (TESS-tə-moh-nee) *n. testimonies.* 1. A sworn statement made by a witness in court.–The *testimony* of the first witness stated that the accused man had been in Boston on the day of the crime.
2. Proof; evidence.–What *testimony* do you have to support your statement?

test tube (TEST toob *or* tyoob) *test tubes.* A thin tube of glass closed at one end, usually used for containing liquids. – The scientist used a *test tube* to hold the chemical he was about to use in the experiment.

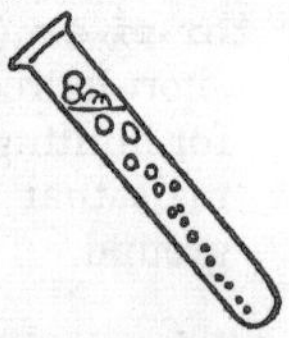

tet·a·nus (TET-n-əss) *n.* A dangerous and often fatal disease, usually caused by infection of wounds. *Tetanus* is marked by pain, stiffness of various muscles, and violent spasms.–Tom has been inoculated to protect him from *tetanus.*

teth·er (TETH-er) *v. tethers, tethered, tethering.* Attach an animal with a rope, chain, or rein so that it can move or graze only within limits.–The cowboy *tethered* his horse to a tree.

Tex·as (TEK-səss) *n.* The second largest state in the United States and the greatest farming state, located in the south central part of the United States. It produces cotton, grain, rice, petroleum, and much meat. *Texas* claims the largest cattle ranch in the world.

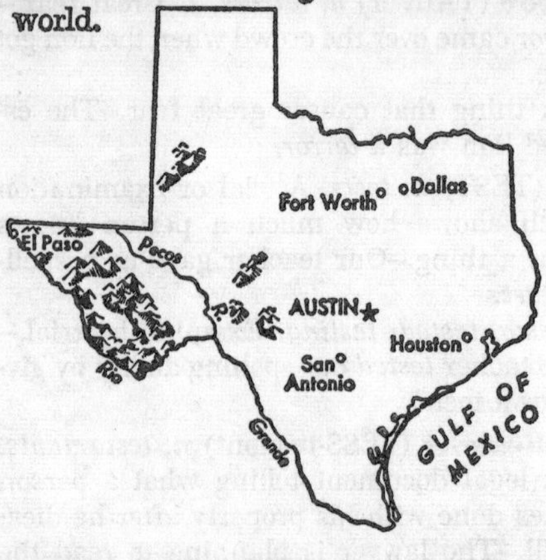

text·book (TEKST-buhk) *n. textbooks.* A schoolbook; a book that one studies from in school.–Our school is using a new *textbook* for geography.

tex·tile (TEKS-til *or* -tyl) *n. textiles.* A woven cloth.–Some *textiles* are woven from wool.
–*adj.* Having to do with weaving.–The big *textile* plant weaves many kinds of textiles.

tex·ture (TEKS-cher) *n. textures.* 1. Structure; arrangement of the parts of a substance. *Texture* may be soft or hard, rough or smooth, coarse or fine.
2. The way a fabric is woven; the arrangement of threads in a woven fabric.–Silk has a fine, tight *texture.*

than (THAN *or* thən) *conj.* The word *than* is used in comparing things.–Baby is smaller *than* Mary.–I would rather sleep *than* eat.

thank (THANGK) *v. thanks, thanked, thanking.* Tell that one is grateful; show gratitude. –Bob *thanked* his grandmother for the gift by saying "*Thank* you."

Thanks·giv·ing (thangks-GIV-ing) *n.* A holiday in the United States on the last Thursday in November. It is a day set aside to give thanks to God for the many things we have to be thankful for.

that (THAT *or* thət) *adj.* 1. A person or thing pointed out or noted before.–*That* boy I spoke about yesterday has returned home.
2. One of two or more persons or things. – Although the shelf was filled with many books, I took only *that* book off the shelf.
3. Opposite of this, usually referring to some thing or person not seen.–*That* tree was a maple; this one is an oak.
–*adv.* To a certain extent or degree; so.–No child should eat *that* much.–I don't want to walk *that* far. It's too far, and I'm too tired.
–*conj. That* is used to connect two parts of a sentence and show how they are related.– Bobby said *that* he would come. – Mother knew *that* Father would be late. She knew because Father had told her.–The baby ate so much *that* she got sick.
–*pron. those.* Who, whom, or which.–He is the boy *that* sells papers.–The boy *that* you saw was Jack.

thatch (THACH) *n. thatches.* Grass or straw used as roofing.
–*v. thatches, thatched, thatching.* Cover (a roof) with straw in overlapping layers. – The farmer *thatched* the roof of the hut.

that's (THATSS). That is.–*That's* the best book I ever read.

thaw (THAW) *n. thaws.* A time when snow and frost melt.–We had an early *thaw* in February.
–*v. thaws, thawed, thawing.* Melt; become soft.–If the ice *thaws,* we cannot go skating.

the (THEE *or* thi *or* thə) *adj.* or *art. The* is used in speaking of some particular person or thing.–*The* dog with Bob is black.–I read *the* book you gave me.

the·a·ter or **the·a·tre** (THEE-ə-ter) *n. theaters* or *theatres.* 1. A building where something is presented for people to see or hear.–Tom saw a play in the new *theater.*
2. Drama.–Mother enjoys the *theater.* She goes to plays as often as she can.

3. A place of action; a place where great things happen.–Europe and the Pacific areas were *theaters* of war in World War II.

thee (THEE) *pron. Thee* is an old way of saying you, meaning one person only. It is used in the Bible, in prayer, and in some poetry.–"Blessings on *thee,* little man, barefoot boy with cheeks of tan."

theft (THEFT) *n. thefts.* Stealing; robbery.–The newsboy reported the *theft* of his money to the police.

their (THAIR *or* thər) *adj.* Belonging to them.–Bob and Jack could see *their* house from the top of the hill.

theirs (THAIRZ) *pron.* Something belonging to them.–This bicycle is yours and that one is *theirs.*

them (THEM *or* thəm) *pron.* The things or animals or people already mentioned or spoken of.–The boys took the dog with *them.* "*Them*" refers to the boys.–Grandmother had three spotted kittens, but she gave *them* away.

them·selves (thəm-SELVZ) *pron.* The children *themselves* prepared the dinner. Nobody helped them.–The boys *themselves* admitted they had done wrong. Even the boys admitted it. – Mother told the children to dress *themselves.* Each child was to dress himself.

then (THEN) *adv.* 1. At that time.–If you want me to come to your house at three o'clock, I will be there *then.*
2. Soon or immediately afterward.–We arrived home, and *then* it started to rain.
3. Next.–First came the band and *then* the horses.
4. Therefore; because of that.–If you play this morning, *then* you must study this afternoon.

the·o·ry (THEE-ə-ree *or* THIR-ee) *n. theories.* 1. The principles, ideas, or methods of an art or science.–Mary has been studying music *theory.* As soon as she has a piano, she will be able to apply and practice what she has learned.
2. A carefully thought-out explanation based on facts or observations.–After the police had studied all the clues, they offered their *theory* of how the crime had been committed.
3. A possible explanation; an opinion or idea.–Everyone seemed to have a different *theory* on how to raise money for the party.

there (THAIR) *adv.* 1. In that place.–Put the basket *there.*
2. At that place.–Stop *there* for lunch.
3. To that place.–The circus is in town. We were just going *there* when it started to rain.
4. Used to point out or call attention to.–*There* is Father now!–*There* is the trouble.
5. *There* are ten more days until Christmas.–Is *there* room for one more in your car?

there·af·ter (thair-AF-ter) *adv.* After that; afterward.–The child burned his hand playing with matches, and *thereafter* he was always careful of matches.

there·fore (THAIR-for) *adv.* For that reason; because of that.–Mary had a bad cold, and *therefore* could not go to school.

there's (THAIRZ). There is.–*There's* a circus in town this month.

ther·mom·e·ter (ther-MAHM-ə-ter) *n. thermometers.* An instrument for measuring one's temperature, or for telling how cold or hot it is. – Mother took the baby's temperature with a *thermometer* when he was sick. – We have a *thermometer* in the kitchen to tell us how warm or how cold the room is.

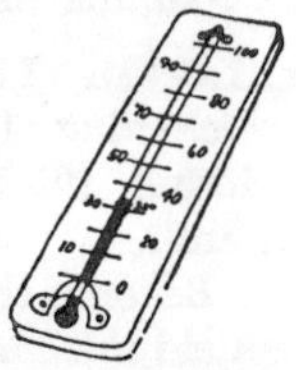

Ther·mos bot·tle (THER-məss baht-l) *Thermos bottles.* Trademark name of a bottle so made that it will keep cold things cold and and hot things hot for hours. – Father carries a *Thermos bottle* of hot soup with his lunch. – The boys took a *Thermos bottle* of cold milk on their hike.

ther•mo•stat (THER-mə-stat) *n. thermostats.* An instrument that makes a heating or air-conditioning unit work just enough to keep a building from getting too warm or too cold.–If you set your *thermostat* for 70°, the temperature in your house will stay near 70°.

these (THEEZ) *adj.* and *pron.* Plural of *this,* used when we point out or speak of more than one person or thing that is nearer to us than some others are.–*These* yellow daisies are from my garden.–*These* are the children who live next door.

they (THAY) *pron. pl.* Used in speaking about persons or things or animals already named. –The boys work hard so that *they* will get good marks.

they'll (THAY-əl). They will.–The girls said they would come early; so *they'll* be here soon.

they're (THAY-er *or* THAIR). They are.–The boys are usually early, but today *they're* late.

they've (THAYV). They have.–We expect the children, but *they've* been delayed.

thick (THIK) *adj. thicker, thickest; thickly, adv.* 1. Not thin; not slender; plump.–One book is thin, the other is *thick.* The *thick* one is wider from cover to cover.
2. Close together; crowded together. – The plants in the garden are too *thick* to have room to grow.–The weeds are *thick* in the garden.
3. Partly solid; not completely liquid.–Water is thin. Gravy is *thick.*
4. Foggy; heavy; clouded.–The air was *thick* with smoke. You could hardly see through it.
5. Husky, deep, or hoarse.–When Father had a cold, his voice was *thick.*

thick•en (THIK-ən) *v. thickens, thickened, thickening.* 1. Make thick or more solid. – Mother *thickens* the pudding with cornstarch.
2. Become thicker. – The ice on the windshield *thickened* as we drove.

thick•et (THIK-it) *n. thickets.* A thick growth of underbrush and bushes.–We had to cut our way through the *thicket* with our jackknives.

thick•ness (THIK-nəss) *n. thicknesses.* 1. Distance from top side to bottom side.–What is the *thickness* of this board? I have measured its length and width, but how thick is it?
2. A layer.–The nurse put six *thicknesses* of bandage on the boy's sore arm.

thief (THEEF) *n. thieves.* A robber; a person who steals.–The policeman caught the *thief* as he left the store with the stolen rings and watches.

thieves (THEEVZ) *n. pl.* More than one *thief;* robbers. – The *thieves* were soon caught.

thigh (THY) *n. thighs.* The part of one's leg between the knee and the hip.

thim•ble (THIM-bəl) *n. thimbles.* A cap usually worn on the middle finger when sewing, to push the needle through the cloth, and to protect the finger. *Thimbles* are made of metal or other hard materials.

thin (THIN) *v. thins, thinned, thinning.* Make smaller, less fat, less thick, or less dense; reduce in size or abundance.–Father *thinned* the carrots in the garden. He pulled out some to give the others more room to grow. – Mother *thinned* the gravy with hot water.
–*adj. thinner, thinnest; thinly, adv.* 1. Slender; not thick.–One book is thick, the other is *thin.* The *thin* book has less distance from cover to cover.–Mother likes bread cut in *thin* slices.
2. Lean; having little flesh or fat.–Mother is *thin,* but Father is stout.
3. Scattered; far apart.–The grass is still *thin* in April. The blades are not close together.
4. (Of a liquid) Easily poured.–We use *thin* cream for coffee, and heavy cream for whipping.
5. Not strong or deep.–The little old lady has a *thin* voice.

thine (THYN) *pron.* An old way of saying *yours.*–The sword was *thine,* not mine.

thing (THING) *n. things.* Any object, idea, deed, or matter. – Furniture, clothes, and other objects are *things.*–There are marbles, pencils, paper, crayons, and many other *things* on the teacher's desk.–He talked of every*thing* except the *thing* on his mind.–Interrupting a person is not a polite *thing* to do.

think (THINGK) *v. thinks, thought, thinking.* 1. Use one's mind.–To work a problem, to learn to spell, or to study anything, one must *think.*
2. Believe.–I *think* it pays to be honest.
3. Get an idea.–Can you *think* of anything to do now that it is raining?

third (THERD) *n. thirds.* One of 3 equal parts of anything. – If an apple is cut into three equal parts, each part is one *third* of the apple. It may be written 1/3.
–*adj.* Coming as number 3 in a series.–Mary was first, Bob was second, and Bill was *third.*

thirst (THERST) *n. thirsts.* 1. A dry feeling in the throat and mouth caused by the need of liquid.–The explorers lost in the desert nearly died of *thirst.*
2. A great desire.–A scholar has a *thirst* for learning about things.

thirst•y (THERSS-tee) *adj. thirstier, thirstiest; thirstily, adv.* Feeling thirst; needing water.–Baby is *thirsty.* She wants a drink.

thir•teen (ther-TEEN) *n. thirteens* and *adj.* The number [13] coming after 12 and before 14.–Ten and three make *thirteen.*

thir•teenth (ther-TEENTH) *n. thirteenths.* One of 13 equal parts.–If a thing is divided into 13 parts all the same size, each part is called one *thirteenth.* It may be written 1/13.
–*adj.* Coming as number 13 in a series.–Jack was the *thirteenth* person in line.

thir•ty (THER-tee) *n. thirties* and *adj.* The number [30] coming after 29 and before 31. –Three times ten equals *thirty.*

this (THISS) *adj.* and *pron. these.* The one at hand or the one just mentioned. The word *this* is used to speak of or to point out a person or thing that is present, very near, or has just been spoken of.–*This* boy is Bob's cousin; that boy over there is *this* boy's friend. – *This* is my book.

this•tle (THISS-əl) *n. thistles.* A prickly plant that has purple flowers.

thong (THAWNG) *n. thongs.* A strip of leather used for fastening, and as the tail end of a whip.–*Thongs* are often used for lacing shoes.

tho•rax (THOR-aks) *n. thoraxes* or *thoraces.* 1. In higher animals (including human beings), the section of the body between the neck and abdomen; the chest; the cavity within the chest, or enclosed by the ribs.
2. In insects, the section of the body between the head and abdomen.

thorn (THORN) *n. thorns.* A prickle; a sharp point on a rosebush or some other plant.

thor•ough (THER-oh) *adj.; thoroughly, adv.; thoroughness, n.* 1. Doing all that should be done.–The girl is very *thorough* with her work. She does it all very carefully.
2. Done completely.–That girl did a *thorough* job.

thor•ough•bred (THER-ə-bred) *adj.* Bred from the finest animals of its kind.–Tom's dog is a *thoroughbred* collie.

thor•ough•fare (THER-ə-fair) *n. thoroughfares.* 1. A public highway or main road. – Turnpikes, freeways, and throughways are *thoroughfares.*

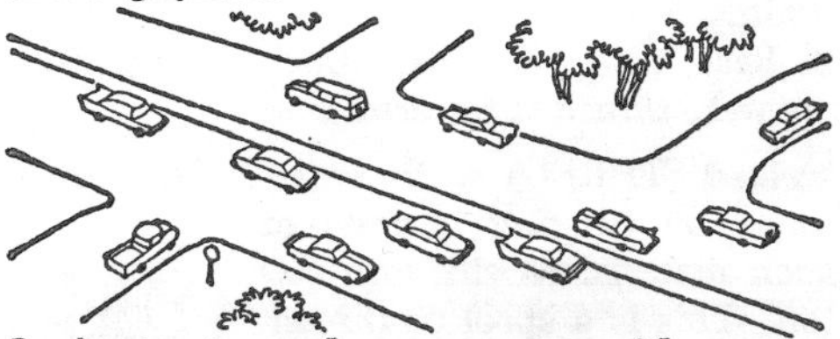

2. A street, road, or passage with an entrance and an exit; a way through.

those (THOHZ) *adj.* and *pron.* Plural of *that,* used in speaking of or pointing out more than one person or thing farther away than some others.–*Those* apples are the best. These are not so good. *Those* apples over there are better than the apples right here.

though (THOH) *adv.* However. – You may have spoken to me; I didn't hear you, *though.*
–*conj.* 1. Even if.–We will come to the party *though* we will be late.
2. In spite of the fact that.–Bob was on time, *though* he got up late.
–*As though* means as if. – Mother spoke *as though* she expected us to go.

thought (THAWT) *n. thoughts.* 1. An idea; anything one thinks about. – He kept his *thoughts* secret.–The man has some good *thoughts* about building airplanes.
2. Thinking; working of the mind.–Father said he would give the problem some *thought.*
–*v.* One form of the verb *think.*–We *thought* of you on your birthday.

thought•ful (THAWT-fuhl) *adj.; thoughtfully, adv.; thoughtfulness, n.* 1. Busy thinking; in the habit of thinking. – George is *thoughtful* about beginning college next month. He has been thinking about it.
2. Careful of the welfare or feelings of others.–Mother said it was *thoughtful* of Mary to send the birthday card to Grandmother.

thought·less (THAWT-ləss) *adj.; thoughtlessly, adv.; thoughtlessness, n.* 1. Careless.–A *thoughtless* person is always making mistakes.
2. Not careful of the welfare or feelings of others.–The *thoughtless* boy played the radio when his father was trying to sleep.

thou·sand (THOW-zənd) *n. thousanas.* The number represented by 1 followed by three zeros. Ten one hundreds make a *thousand.*
100 is one hundred.
1,000 is one thousand.

thrash (THRASH) *v. thrashes, thrashed, thrashing.* 1. Separate grain from its stalk by beating; thresh.–The farmer *thrashes* his grain.
2. Beat; whip.–In olden times some prisoners were *thrashed* for crimes.

thread (THRED) *n. threads.* A fine string made by twisting strands of such material as silk and cotton.–This is a spool of *thread.* –We use *thread* for sewing.

–*v. threads, threaded, threading.* Put thread through (a needle).–Mother *threads* her needle before she starts to sew.

threat (THRET) *n. threats.* A promise to do harm.–Peter was not frightened by the *threat* of force.–The *threat* of rain made us go into the house.

threat·en (THRET-n) *v. threatens, threatened, threatening.* 1. Promise to do harm to. –The pirates *threatened* to attack the ship.
2. Give notice of; warn of.–The wind *threatens* a storm. It warns that a storm may come.

three (THREE) *n. threes* and *adj.* The number [3] coming after 2 and before 4.–Two and one make *three.*

thresh (THRESH) *v. threshes, threshed, threshing.* Separate grain from its stalk by beating; thrash.–The farmer *threshes* his grain. He separates the grain from the straw with a machine.–In olden times, grain was *threshed* by beating it with a jointed stick called a flail.

thresh·old (THRESH-hohld) *n. thresholds.* 1. The piece of wood or stone at the bottom of a doorway.–Baby sat on the *threshold* and watched for Father.
2. Beginning.–The scientist knew that he was at the *threshold* of a discovery.

threw (THROO) *v.* One form of the verb *throw.*–Bob *threw* the ball to Jack after Bill had thrown it to him.

thrice (THRYSS) *adv.* Three times.–The old woman told the prince to knock *thrice* on the door.

thrift (THRIFT) *n.* Avoiding waste; habit of saving.–*Thrift* is a good habit to form.

thrill (THRIL) *n. thrills.* A shivery or excited feeling.–The sight of the flag gave Jack a *thrill.*
–*v. thrills, thrilled, thrilling.* Cause to feel excited.–The music *thrilled* the boy. It gave him a tingling, excited feeling.

thrive (THRYV) *v. thrives, thrived* or *throve, thriving.* 1. Grow strong and be healthy.–The plants will not *thrive* unless you water them.
2. Be successful; grow or improve; get along well.–Father's new business is *thriving.*

throat (THROHT) *n. throats.* 1. Front part of the neck. – Mother puts cream on her *throat* to keep it from wrinkling.–Ed has a bandage on his *throat.*

2. The passage inside the neck.–When one swallows food, it passes through the *throat.*

throb (THRAHB) *v. throbs, throbbed, throbbing.* Beat fast or hard; pound.–The boy's heart *throbbed* after he ran the race.

throne (THROHN) *n. thrones.* 1. A chair, usually on a dais, used by a king, queen, or other ruler.
2. The office or rank of a king.–The boy prince came to the *throne* during the war. He became king.

throng (THRAWNG) *n. throngs.* A crowd.–A *throng* gathered for the game.
–*v. throngs, thronged, thronging.* Crowd. – People *thronged* the ball park.

throt·tle (THRAHT-l) *n. throttles.* A valve, lever, pedal, or other means of controlling the flow of fuel to an engine.–The racer opened the *throttle,* thereby increasing the speed of the motorboat.

through (THROO) *adj.* 1. Express; nonstop. –We took the *through* train to the city.
2. Finished.–Mother will be *through* soon.
–*adv.* 1. The whole distance. – We went *through* to California. We went across the entire United States, from New York to California.
2. From beginning to end; from start to finish.–Have you read that book *through,* or have you only read parts of it?

–prep. 1. In one side and out the other.–The train went *through* the tunnel.–Grandmother put the thread *through* the eye of the needle.–Jim looked *through* the microscope.
2. Among; in the midst of; between.–The birds fluttered *through* the trees.–We walked *through* the tall sunflowers.
3. Along; from one end to the other; in.–We walked *through* the halls to go from one class to another.
4. During; throughout.–The baby cried all *through* the night.–We worked *through* the day. We worked all day.
5. Because of.–Tom became sick *through* overeating.
6. By means of.–I didn't tell you directly; I told you *through* him. I told him to tell you.

throw (THROH) *n. throws.* The act of hurling.–Bob's fine *throw* to first base won the game.
–v. throws, threw, throwing. Hurl; fling; cast; pitch.–The pitcher *throws* the ball to the catcher.–*Throw* your waste paper into the basket.–The car stopped suddenly and we were *thrown* from our seats.

thrush (THRUSH) *n. thrushes.* One of a group of songbirds known for their sweet singing. A robin is one kind of *thrush.*

thrust (THRUST) *n. thrusts.* 1. Hard push.–David threw open the door with a quick *thrust.*
2. Stab.–One *thrust* of the knife killed the wildcat.
–v. thrusts, thrust, thrusting. 1. Push hard; shove.–The boy *thrust* his way through the crowd.–The workman *thrust* his shovel deep into the sand.
2. Stab; pierce.–The hunter *thrust* his knife into the wildcat.

thud (THUD) *n. thuds.* Dull, bumping sound. –We heard the *thud* as the book fell to the floor.
–v. thuds, thudded, thudding. Make a dull, bumping sound. – The book *thudded* onto the floor.

thumb (THUM) *n. thumbs.* 1. The short, thick finger set apart from the other fingers.
2. A place for the thumb.–Mittens have *thumbs* but not separate fingers.

–v. thumbs, thumbed, thumbing. Turn (pages of) with the thumb.–Mary *thumbed* through the book looking for pictures.

thun·der (THUN-der) *n. thunders.* 1. The loud rumbling or cracking sound that often follows a flash of lightning.–The dog hides under the bed when he hears *thunder.*
2. A noise like thunder.–We heard the *thunder* of the enemy's guns.
–v. thunders, thundered, thundering. 1. Make the noise of thunder.–It *thundered* during the storm.
2. Speak very loudly. – "Where have you been?" Father *thundered.*

thun·der·storm (THUN-der-storm) *n. thunderstorms.* A storm with thunder and lightning.–We ran to get home before the *thunderstorm.*

Thurs·day (THERZ-dee) *n. Thursdays.* The day after Wednesday. *Thursday* is the fifth day of the week.

thus (THUSS) *adv.* 1. In this way.–If you do the work *thus,* you will get through sooner.
2. Therefore.–He started early; *thus* he was on time.
3. So; this.–You may go *thus* far, and no farther.

thy (THY) *pron.* Your (used of one person only). *Thy* is used in the Bible, in praying, and in old poems. – Thou shalt love *thy* neighbor as *thy*self.

thy·roid (THY-roid) *n. thyroids* and *adj.* A gland in the neck. The *thyroid* is divided into two round parts, one on each side of the windpipe. The *thyroid* secretes a substance which has a great affect on the body's growth, and on one's physical and mental activity.

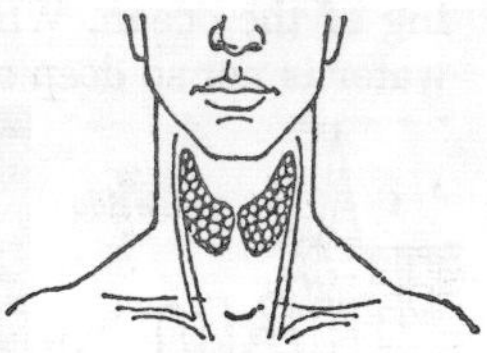

thy·self (thy-SELF) *pron.* An old form of the word *yourself.*

tick (TIK) *n. ticks.* 1. A small insect or spider that sucks the blood of animals and people.
2. A light beat; a sharp, quick click.–We heard the *tick* of the watch.

–v. ticks, ticked, ticking. 1. Make light, quick sounds over and over, like *tick*-tock, *tick*-tock, *tick*-tock.–The clock *ticks.*
2. Make marks to record something; check; count.–The teacher asked us to *tick* off the important points of the things we had copied off the blackboard.–The stop watch *ticked* off the seconds left in the last minute of the game.

tick•et (TIK-it) *n. tickets.* 1. A printed card or paper which shows that one has paid to ride on a train, go into a moving picture, see a football game, etc.
2. A tag.—The clerk put a price *ticket* on each of the different pieces of jewelry.

tick•le (TIK-əl) *n. tickles.* An uneasy, tingling feeling.—Father had a *tickle* in his throat which made him cough.
—*v. tickles, tickled, tickling.* 1. Touch lightly, causing a tingling feeling. — Bob *tickled* Baby's neck with a feather.
2. Amuse; delight.—The clown's performance *tickles* the children. — The kitten's antics *tickled* the whole family.

tick•lish (TIK-lish) *adj.; ticklishness, n.* 1. Sensitive to being tickled. — Sally's feet are *ticklish.*
2. Difficult to do and handle right; requiring tact or great care.—It will be a *ticklish* job to get the teacher's consent to have a party during school hours.—Pasting the small pictures in the scrapbook is *ticklish* work.

tid•al wave (TYD-l wayv) *tidal waves.* A tremendous ocean wave. *Tidal waves* are usually caused by earthquakes or very strong winds. *Tidal waves* can cause great damage when they sweep over the land.

tide (TYD) *n. tides.* 1. The rising and the falling of the ocean. When the *tide* is low, the water is not so deep at the shore line. When

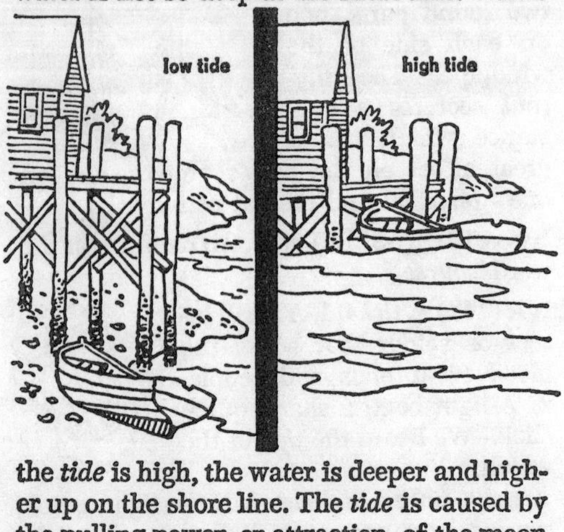

the *tide* is high, the water is deeper and higher up on the shore line. The *tide* is caused by the pulling power, or attraction, of the moon and the sun.
2. A current, or movement of water.—The rowboat was carried out to sea by the *tide.*
—*Tide over* means to help out, carry over, or piece out. — Grandmother loaned us two quarts of milk to *tide* us *over* until the milkman came.

ti•dy (TYD-ee) *v. tidies, tidied, tidying.* Make neat; put in order.—Mary helps Mother *tidy* up the house on Saturday morning.
—*adj. tidier, tidiest.* Neat and in order.—Bob has a *tidy* desk.

tie (TY) *n. ties.* 1. A necktie; a strip of cloth extending around the neck under the collar and knotted in front.—Father likes to wear a red *tie.*
2. An equal score. — The ball game ended in a *tie;* the score was one to one.
3. A large piece of wood to which the rails of a railway are fastened.
—*v. ties, tied, tying.* 1. Fasten; bind; make a knot or bow of.—Baby is too little to *tie* her own shoelaces.—The children *tied* up their Christmas gifts with red ribbon.—The organ-grinder *tied* the monkey to the hand organ.
2. Make the score of one team equal to that of the other.—Jack's home run *tied* the score in the seventh inning.

tier (TIR) *n. tiers.* One of several rows placed one above the other; a layer.—We sat in the top *tier* of seats at the play. — The wedding cake had three *tiers.*

ti•ger (TY-ger) *n. tigers.* A large wild animal of the cat family with yellow fur striped with black. *Tigers* eat the flesh of other animals. At the zoo, the *tigers* are kept in strong cages.

tight (TYT) *adj. tighter, tightest; tightly, adv.; tightness, n.* 1. Close-fitting; too close-fitting; snug. — Baby's feet have grown so much that her shoes are too *tight.*—Screw the nozzle on *tight* if you don't want the hose to leak.
2. Stretched taut.—The clothesline is *tight.*
3. Firm; hard; difficult to undo.—Baby pulled her shoestring into a *tight* knot.
4. A thing that is air*tight* will not let air in. Anything water*tight* will not let water in.
—*adv.* Firmly; closely.—The apples were packed *tight* in the box.

tight•en (TYT-n) *v. tightens, tightened, tightening.* Make firmer, tighter, or more close-fitting. — The workmen *tightened* the rope. They pulled it hard and tied it securely so that it did not sag.—Mother *tightened* the top on the jar.

tight•rope (TYT-rohp) *n. tightropes.* A tightly stretched rope on which one or more acrobats perform. – The circus acrobat rode a bicycle across the *tightrope.*

tights (TYTSS) *n. pl.* A close-fitting garment for the legs and hips, usually worn by acrobats, dancers, and other performers. *Tights* fit smoothly over the skin.

ti•gress (TY-grəss) *n. tigresses.* A female tiger.–The *tigress* defended her three cubs fiercely.

tile (TYL) *n. tiles.* 1. Baked clay or stone in thin pieces, used for roofs, floors, walls in bathrooms, and many other things.
2. A large, earthen pipe for drains and drainage ditches.

till (TIL) *n. tills.* A drawer in which money and other valuables are kept.–The grocer put the money in the *till.*

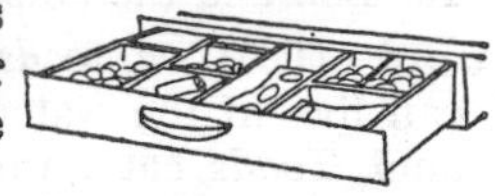

–*v. tills, tilled, tilling.* Plow; turn (earth) to prepare for planting.–The farmer *tilled* the ground before he planted his crops.
–*conj.* Until; up to the time when.–Wait *till* Father gets home.
–*prep.* Until; up to the time of.–Must we wait *till* evening?

tilt (TILT) *v. tilts, tilted, tilting.* 1. Slant; tip; lean to one side.–The telephone pole is not straight up and down. It *tilts.*
2. Tip; set at an angle.–Do not *tilt* your chair back or you may fall.

tim•ber (TIM-ber) *n. timbers.* 1. Wood used for building.–Most houses are made of *timber.*
2. A strong, thick piece of wood.–Large *timbers* were used in building the bridge.
3. Woods or forest where trees grow.–The *timber* burned down.

time (TYM) *n. times.* 1. A measured period that something lasts; duration. – Minutes, hours, days, weeks, months, and years are all measures of *time.* They answer the question "How long?"
2. A part of a measured period.–Morning is a *time* of day.–Spring is a *time* of the year.
3. A definite point or moment (of or in time). –Noon is the *time* for lunch.
4. In music, time means the regular beat.– A waltz is in three-quarter *time.* It has three beats in each measure.
5. An occasion; a repeated happening.–We heard the whistle three *times.*
–*v. times, timed, timing.* Measure the duration or length of.–The teacher *timed* our test. She watched the clock and told us when to start and when to stop.
–*Times* means multiplied by.–Six *times* two is twelve.

time•piece (TYM-peess) *n. timepieces.* A clock or watch.–We tell time by a *timepiece.*

time•ta•ble (TYM-tay-bəl) *n. timetables.* A list showing when trains, planes, buses, etc., arrive and depart.

tim•id (TIM-id) *adj.; timidly, adv.; timidity, n.* Shy; bashful; afraid of people and things. –Baby is *timid* around strangers.

tin (TIN) *n. tins.* A light, soft metal used in making such things as pans, kettles, cans.

tin•der (TIN-der) *n.* Anything, such as paper or soft, dry wood, that catches fire easily.

tine (TYN) *n. tines.* One of the slender, pointed fingerlike pieces on a fork.

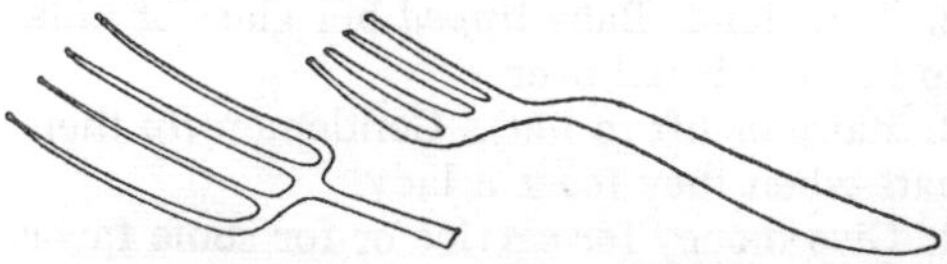

tinge (TINJ) *n. tinges.* A slight color or quality (of).–Mary's hat has a *tinge* of red in it. The hat is mainly blue, but there is some red in it, also.
–*v. tinges, tinged, tingeing* or *tinging.* Add a touch or trace of color to; color slightly; tint. –Mary drew a picture of a sailboat and *tinged* the water with blue.

tin•gle (TING-gəl) *n. tingles.* A stinging or prickly feeling caused by such emotions as excitement or fear.–Bill felt *tingles* running up and down his spine when he entered the haunted house.
–*v. tingles, tingled, tingling.* Have a prickly feeling.–The sound of the fire truck makes Tom *tingle* with excitement.

tin•kle (TINGK-əl) *n. tinkles.* A soft ringing sound.—We heard the *tinkle* of the cowbell.
—*v. tinkles, tinkled, tinkling.* Make or cause something to make ringing sounds.—The boy *tinkled* his knife and fork by hitting them together. The fork *tinkled* when struck.

tin•sel (TIN-səl) *n.* 1. Long strings of glistening threads made of bright metal. — The children trimmed the Christmas tree with *tinsel.*

2. A sparkling cloth with shiny metal threads woven into it.

tint (TINT) *n. tints.* A light or pale color.—Pink, light blue, and pale green are *tints.*—When the sun sets, the clouds have many reddish *tints.*
—*v. tints, tinted, tinting.* Color lightly; put light colors on.—Mary likes to *tint* her pictures with chalks.

ti•ny (TY-nee) *adj. tinier, tiniest.* Very small, as a *tiny* shell or a *tiny* flower.—Baby's hand looks *tiny* next to Mother's.

tip (TIP) *n. tips.* 1. An end.—The seal balanced the ball on the *tip* of his nose.
2. A small piece put on the end of something, as the cap on the end of a cane or umbrella.
3. Money given for service or for some favor done.—Father gave a *tip* to the boy who brought him the message.
—*v. tips, tipped, tipping.* 1. Put a tip on.—Uncle *tipped* his cane with a rubber cap.
2. Tilt; slant.—Baby *tipped* her glass of milk so far that it fell over.
3. Raise or lift (a hat).—Gentlemen *tip* their hats when they meet a lady.
4. Give money for service or for some favor done.—Father *tipped* the boy who brought the message.

tip•toe (TIP-toh) *n. tiptoes.* The end of the toe; the ends of the toes.—Mary walked on her *tiptoes* because the baby was asleep.
—*v. tiptoes, tiptoed, tiptoeing.* Walk on the toes, softly and with caution.—Mary *tiptoed* across the room.

tire (TYR) *n. tires.* 1. An outer rim of rubber that fits onto the rim of a wheel. — Father bought new tires for the car.
2. Any rim on which a wheel rolls. — The wheels of some wagons have iron bands for *tires.*
—*v. tires, tired, tiring.* Become tired or weary.—Do not work too fast or you will soon *tire.*

tis•sue (TISH-oo) *n. tissues* and *adj.* 1. A section of living matter with a particular structure and use, such as bone *tissue,* muscle *tissue,* and brain *tissue.* Your body is made of *tissues.*
2. Tissue paper.

tis•sue pa•per (TISH-oo pay-per) *tissue papers.* Very thin, soft paper.—The children wrapped their gifts in *tissue paper.*

ti•tle (TY-tl) *n. titles.* 1. The name of a book, story, song, picture, etc.—The title of the book is "Man and Power."
2. A special name used before a person's name to show his position or occupation, as "Dr." Smith, "Mrs." Jones, "King" George, "Lord" Byron, "Sir" Galahad.
3. Legal ownership, or papers showing such ownership.—Father paid for the car and has the *title* to it.
—*v. titles, titled, titling.* Name; give a title to.—The author *titled* his new book "Man and Power."

to (TOO *or* tuh *or* tə) *prep.* 1. Give it *to* me. It is mine.
2. I want *to* go. Children like *to* play.
3. Bob walked *to* the woods.
4. Our class won the game four *to* three.
5. Baby can count *to* five.
6. Send the letter *to* Grandmother.
7. The girls danced *to* lively music.
8. Mother rocked the baby *to* sleep.
9. He plays *to* win.
10. Bob tied the horse *to* the post.

toad (TOHD) *n. toads.* A froglike animal. It can live in the water, but usually lives on land. *Toads* eat worms, insects, and slugs.

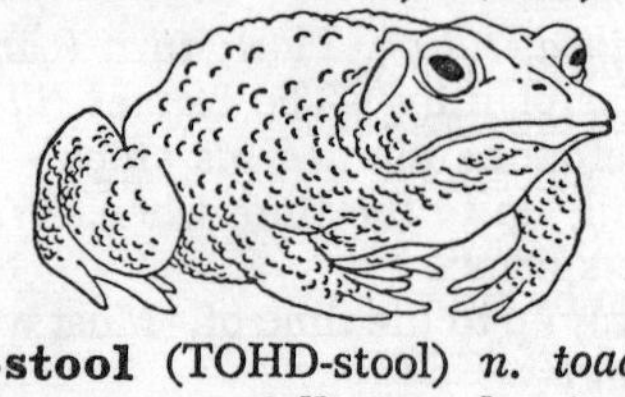

toad•stool (TOHD-stool) *n. toadstools.* A mushroom, especially one that is poisonous.

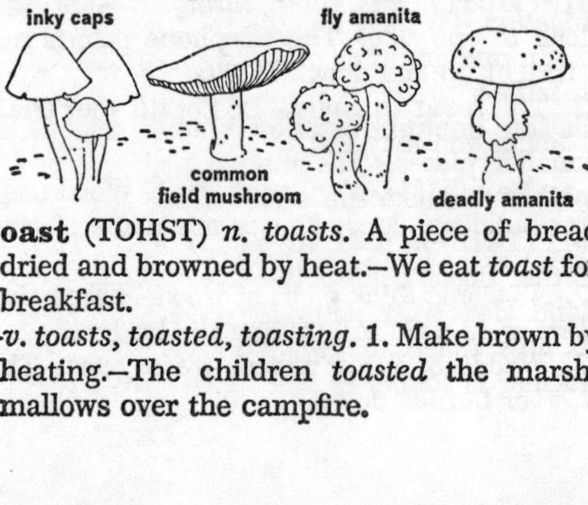

toast (TOHST) *n. toasts.* A piece of bread dried and browned by heat.—We eat *toast* for breakfast.
—*v. toasts, toasted, toasting.* 1. Make brown by heating.—The children *toasted* the marshmallows over the campfire.

2. Make warm. – Grandmother sat by the stove and *toasted* her feet.
3. Drink in honor of something or someone. –Everyone *toasted* Bill. Everyone drank in his honor.

toast•er (TOHSS-ter) *n. toasters.* A device for toasting bread, for browning it by heat.

to•bac•co (tə-BAK-oh) *n. tobaccos* or *tobaccoes.* A plant with large leaves which are dried for smoking or chewing. Cigarettes and cigars are made from the leaves of the *tobacco* plant.

to•bog•gan (tə-BAHG-ən) *n. toboggans.* A flat sled that has no runners.–The children like to slide downhill on a *toboggan.*

–*v. toboggans, tobogganed, tobogganing.* – Slide on a toboggan.–We will *toboggan* down the long hill after school.

to•day (tə-DAY) *n. todays.* This day.–*Today* is Monday.–*Today* Mother does the laundry.
–*adv.* 1. On this day.–It is hot *today.*
2. Nowadays; at the present time.–Many women work in factories *today.* Years ago only men worked in factories.

toe (TOH) *n. toes.* 1. One of the parts at the end of the foot. We have five *toes* on each foot.

2. The end of the shoe, stocking, or boot that covers the toes.–Mary had a hole in the *toe* of her stocking.

to•ga (TOH-gə) *n. togas.* A loose outer garment worn by citizens of ancient Rome.

to•geth•er (tə-GETH-er) *adv.* 1. With one another; in a group.–The children play well *together.*–We sat *together* on the bus.
2. In one group or pile.–We put our money *together.*
3. Into one unit or one large piece made of smaller pieces.–The men put the parts *together* to make the automobile.

toil (TOIL) *n. toils.* Any hard work.–Grandfather doesn't mind the *toil* of plowing the land. He is a farmer and is used to hard work.
–*v. toils, toiled, toiling.* Work very hard.–The farmer is *toiling* in the fields.

toi•let (TOI-lit) *n. toilets.* 1. A bathroom or water closet.
2. A bathroom fixture for disposing of bodily waste matter.
–*Make one's toilet* means to bathe, dress, comb one's hair, etc.

to•ken (TOH-kən) *n. tokens.* 1. A sign.–A white flag is a *token* of surrender.
2. A keepsake; a souvenir. – When Ruth moved away, she gave Ann a ring as a *token.*
3. A piece of metal, shaped like a coin, bought and used instead of a ticket.–You can buy streetcar *tokens* in some cities.

told (TOHLD) *v.* One form of the verb *tell.*– Mother *told* us a story yesterday.

tol•er•ance (TAHL-er-ənss) *n.; tolerant, adj.* The act or practice of being fair towards those whose beliefs, religion, and customs are different from one's own.

tol•er•ate (TAHL-ə-rayt) *v. tolerates, tolerated, tolerating.* 1. Permit or allow. – The police will not *tolerate* violation of the law.
2. Endure; put up with.–It is difficult to *tolerate* people with bad manners.

toll (TOHL) *n. tolls.* 1. Ringing.–Each *toll* of the bell told us that an hour had passed.
2. Money paid for the right to use something. –Father had to pay a *toll* to cross the bridge.
–*v. tolls, tolled, tolling.* Ring or sound, slowly and evenly.–The church bells *tolled* at the end of the wedding ceremony.–The clock is *tolling* the hour.

tom•a•hawk (TAHM-ə-hawk) *n. tomahawks.* A hatchet or a lightweight ax that was used by some Indians in North America. –The Indian hurled his *tomahawk* at his enemy.

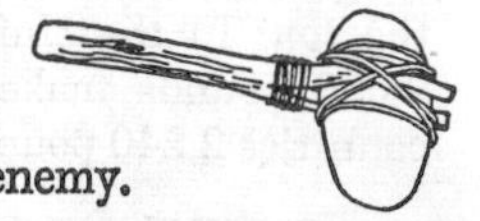

to•ma•to (tə-MAY-toh) *n. tomatoes.* A red or yellow fruit that grows on a low plant or vine. *Tomatoes* have many seeds in them. The juice of *tomatoes* is good to drink.

tomb (TOOM) *n. tombs.* A grave; a place where the bodies of the dead are kept.– *Tombs* are often built of marble or other hard stone.

to•mor•row (tə-MAHR-oh *or* tə-MOR-oh) *n. tomorrows.* The day following today.–Today is Monday. *Tomorrow* will be Tuesday.
–*adv.* On or for the day following today.– Grandmother will arrive *tomorrow.*

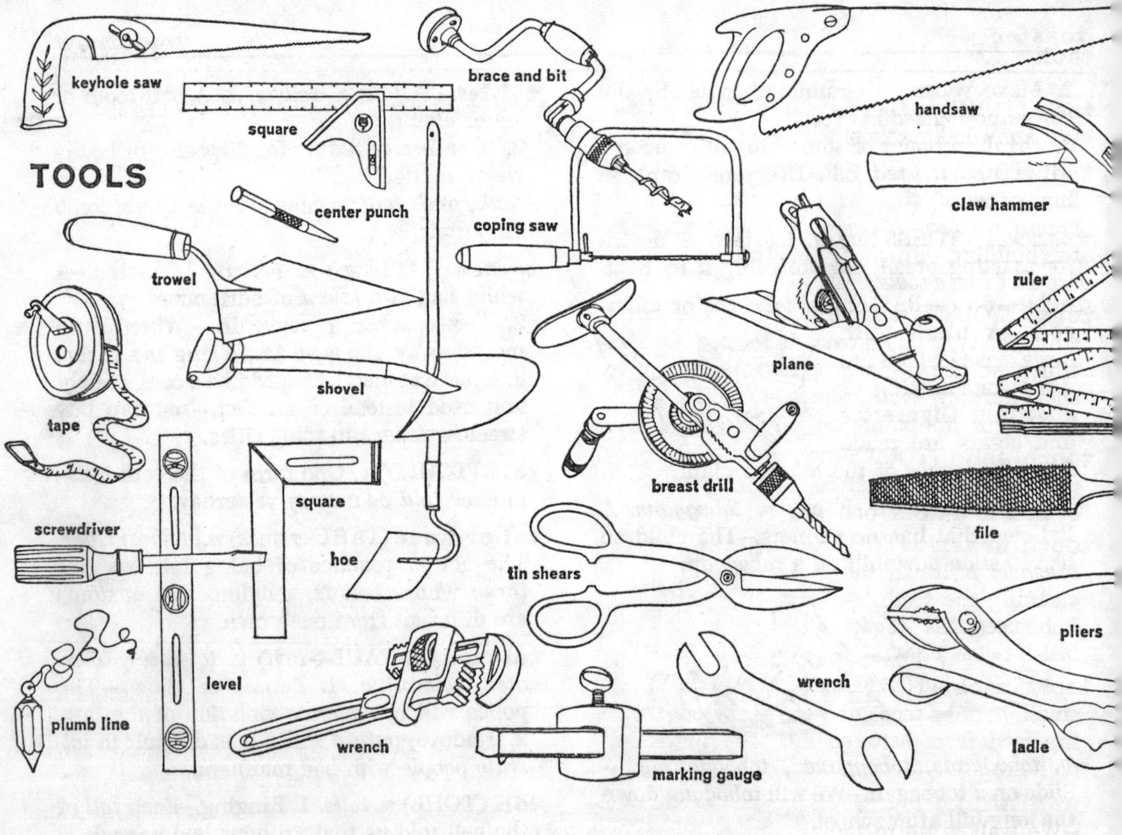

tom-tom (TAHM-tahm) *n. tom-toms.* A kind of drum originally used by primitive peoples. It is beaten with the hands or with sticks.

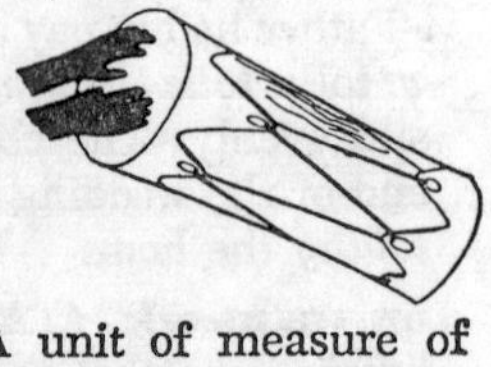

ton (TUN) *n. tons.* A unit of measure of weight. We measure hay, steel, coal, etc., by the *ton.* In the United States and Canada 2,000 pounds make 1 *ton.* In some other countries 2,240 pounds make 1 *ton.*

tone (TOHN) *n. tones.* 1. A sound; a note.–The shrill *tone* of the whistle frightened us.–The sweet *tones* of the organ echoed in the empty church.
2. Manner of speaking; quality of voice; accent.–Mother's soft *tones* soothe Baby.–Jack spoke in an angry *tone.*
3. A shade.–The picture has many *tones* of blue in it.

tongs (TAWNGZ *or* TAHNGZ) *n. pl.* Scissorslike tools used for lifting and holding, as ice *tongs,* sugar *tongs,* wood *tongs.*–Mother used sugar *tongs* to pick up the sugar cubes and drop them into her cup.

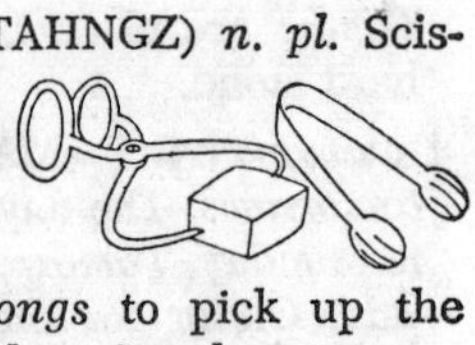

tongue (TUNG) *n. tongues.* 1. The flexible and movable organ in the mouth with which one tastes. We also use our *tongues* in speaking.
2. A language.–The Frenchman spoke in his native *tongue.* He spoke French.
3. A thing shaped or used like a tongue.–The *tongue* of a shoe is the leather piece under the laces of the shoe. – The *tongue* of a wagon is the long pole at the front.

ton•ic (TAHN-ik) *n. tonics.* A medicine or treatment to make one strong and give one an appetite.–The doctor gave Grandmother a *tonic.*–Sunshine and fresh air are *tonics.*

to•night (tə-NYT) *adv.* 1. The night following this day.–We are going to a show *tonight.*
2. This night; the night we are in.–The children seem happy *tonight.*

ton•sil (TAHN-səl) *n. tonsils.* One of two small organs on the sides of the throat at the back of the mouth.

too (TOO) *adv.* 1. Also.–We have a dog, and a kitten, *too.*–I should like to go *too.*
2. More than enough; more than is good. –Tommy ate *too* much candy.
3. Very.–The boy was only *too* glad to come to the party.

took (TUHK) *v.* One form of the verb *take.*–I *took* my doll to school with me yesterday.

tool (TOOL) *n. tools.* Anything used for some kind of work, such as a hammer, a saw, a broom, a ruler.–A carpenter's *tools* are used for building.–Brushes, palettes, and paints are an artist's *tools.*

tooth (TOOTH) *n. teeth.* 1. One of the sharp, white, bony, pointed parts in the mouth with which we chew.–Baby opened her mouth to show her new *tooth.* She now has six *teeth.*
2. One of the points on a rake or a comb.

tooth•ache (TOOTH-ayk) *n. toothaches.* A pain in a tooth.–When food gets into a cavity or hole in a tooth, one may get a *toothache.*

tooth•brush (TOOTH-brush) *n. toothbrushes.* A brush for cleaning the teeth. – Bob uses his *toothbrush* twice a day.

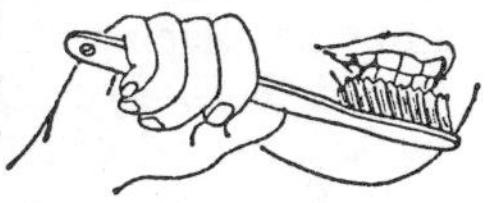

tooth•pick (TOOTH-pik) *n. toothpicks.* A small, pointed piece of wood used for removing food from between the teeth.–It is not polite to use a *toothpick* at the table.

top (TAHP) *n. tops.* 1. Highest point or part. –We walked up to the *top* of the hill.–The weather vane on *top* of Grandfather's barn pointed east.
2. The upper edge or side.–The snow came up to the *tops* of our shoes.–Mother wiped off the table *top.*
3. The head.–Bob is usually at the *top* of his class.

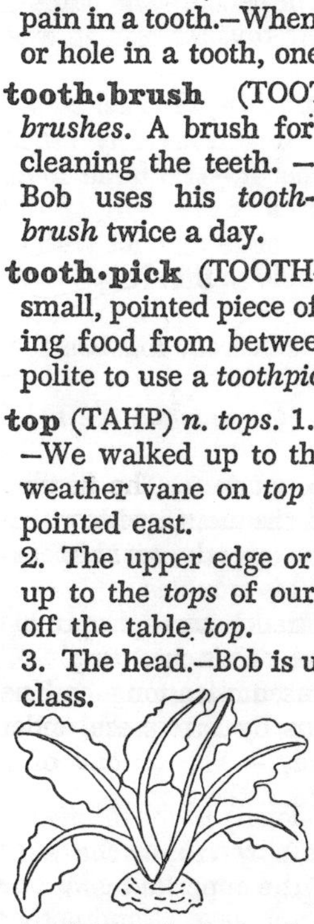

4. A leafy part that grows above the ground on vegetables such as carrots and beets. – Beet *tops* are good to eat.
5. A round toy made with a pointed tip on which it can be spun. –Tommy likes to spin his *top.*

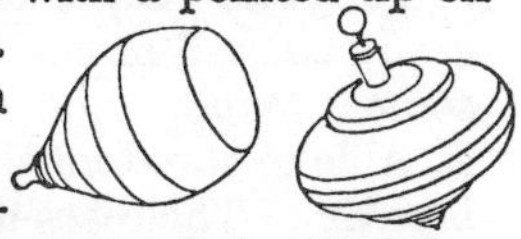

–*v. tops, topped, topping.* Cover. – Mother *topped* the birthday cake with marshmallow frosting.

top•ic (TAHP-ik) *n. topics.* A subject one is talking about, thinking about, or writing about.–The *topic* we were discussing was the ball game. Mary doesn't like baseball and she tried to change the *topic* of conversation.

top•ple (TAHP-əl) *v. topples, toppled, toppling.* Fall forward; tumble.–The tower of blocks *toppled* over because it was too heavy at the top.

top•sy-tur•vy (TAHP-see-TER-vee) *adj.* and *adv.* Upset; upside down.–The playroom was *topsy-turvy* after the party. Nothing was in order.

torch (TORCH) *n. torches.* 1. A light made of something that burns easily and can be carried in the hand, like a stick of wood. – The man carried a *torch.*
2. A flashlight.

tore (TOR) *v.* One form of the verb *tear.*–Yesterday Mother *tore* up two old sheets for dust cloths.

tor•ment (TOR-ment) *n. torments.* Suffering; torture.–The boy's feeling of guilt filled him with *torment.*
–(tor-MENT) *v. torments, tormented, tormenting.* 1. Tease; annoy.–The dog *torments* the cat. He chases her, steals her food, and barks at her.
2. Give pain to.–The sore throat *tormented* the boy all night.

torn (TORN) *v.* One form of the verb *tear.*–The high wind had *torn* the leaves from the trees.

tor•na•do (tor-NAY-doh) *n. tornadoes.* A strong, whirling windstorm that often destroys trees and buildings.

tor•pe•do (tor-PEE-doh) *n. torpedoes.* 1. A large metal shell filled with material that explodes when it hits something. It has a propeller and machinery to drive it forward under water. *Torpedoes* are used to blow up ships.

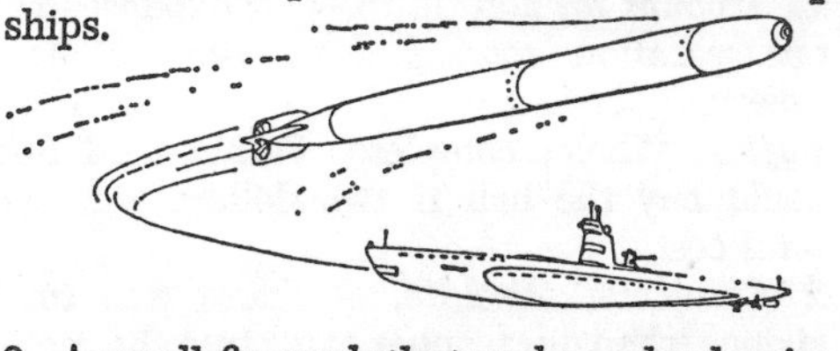

2. A small firework that makes a loud noise when hit against something hard. – On the Fourth of July we had fun with *torpedoes.*
–*v. torpedoes, torpedoed, torpedoing.* Destroy or blow up with torpedoes. – The airplane *torpedoed* the enemy cruiser.

tor•rent (TOR- *or* TAHR-ənt) *n. torrents.* A rushing stream of water. – The boat was caught in the *torrent* and carried down the river.–It was raining in *torrents.*

tor•rid (TOR- *or* TAHR-id) *adj.* Very hot. – The jungles of Africa are in the *Torrid* Zone.

tor•til•la (tor-TEE-yah) *n. tortillas.* A thin, flat cake of corn meal. *Tortillas* are baked on a hot iron plate or stone.

tor·toise (TOR-təss) *n. tortoises.* A turtle, especially one that lives on land or in fresh water.

tor·ture (TOR-cher) *n. tortures.* 1. Great pain. – The victims of the fire suffered much *torture* from their severe burns.
2. The inflicting of great pain.–Flogging is a form of *torture.*
–*v. tortures, tortured, torturing.* Cause (a person or animal) to suffer greatly.–The enemy *tortured* the thirsty prisoners by not giving them water.

toss (TAWSS) *v. tosses, tossed, tossing.* 1. Throw lightly with an upward movement.–Jack *tossed* the ball to Bob.
2. Cause to move up and down, and to and fro.–The wind *tossed* the kites in the sky.
3. Roll back and forth.–The heat made Baby *toss* in her crib.
4. Throw back proudly. – Mary *tossed* her head as she went past Jack.

tot (TAHT) *n. tots.* A wee, tiny child.–Baby is still just a *tot.*

to·tal (TOHT-l) *n. totals.* Entire amount. –Jim's savings reached a *total* of twenty dollars.–If you add 4 + 5 + 2, the *total* is 11.
–*v. totals, totaled, totaling.* 1. Add. – *Total* 4 + 5 + 2, and you get 11.
2. Amount to; add up to.–Our expenses for our vacation *totaled* seventy-five dollars apiece.
–*adj.* 1. Whole; complete.–Father said Bob could buy the ball if two dollars was the *total* cost.
2. Complete; absolute. – There was *total* silence when our teacher came into the room. No one said a word.

to·tem pole (TOH-təm pohl) *totem poles.* A pole erected by primitive people, with animals or other figures carved or painted on it. The token or symbol of the family or tribe was always included.

tot·ter (TAHT-er) *v. totters, tottered, tottering.* 1. Walk with trembling steps.–An old man with a cane *tottered* down the street.
2. Shake as if about to fall.–A sick person often *totters* when he tries to walk.

tou·can (TOO-kan *or* -kahn) *n. toucans.* A brilliantly colored bird of tropical America. The *toucan* has a huge colorful beak. The beak is light and thin in spite of its size. The *toucan* is a fruit-eating bird.

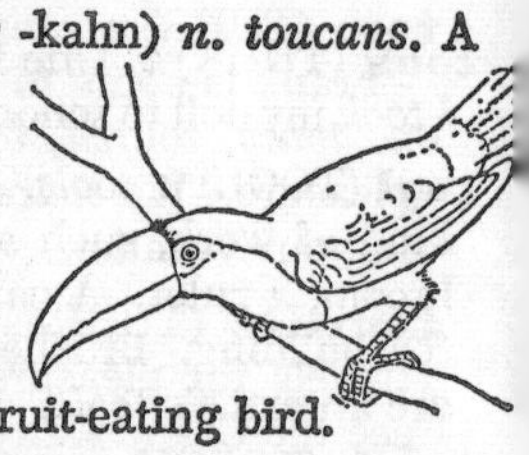

touch (TUCH) *n. touches.* 1. One of the senses of the body.–*Touch* makes us able to learn about things by feeling them.
2. A slight or mild trace.–Bob put a *touch* of salt on his egg.
3. A stroke of a brush or pencil.–The painter gave the picture a few *touches* and it was done.
–*v. touches, touched, touching.* 1. Feel something by placing the fingers or any other part of the body against it.–The blind man *touched* the raised letters of the sign.
2. Be or come together or in contact with.–Put the books on the table so that they *touch* each other.
3. Reach. – Mother's housecoat *touches* the floor.
4. Strike lightly.–Bob just *touched* the ball. He hit it lightly.
5. Lay hands on.–Do not *touch* the kitten.
6. Cause a feeling of kindness, sadness, or pity.–My parents were greatly *touched* by the stranger's story of his troubles.
–*Touch up* means to make small improvements in.–The picture needs *touching up.*
–*In touch* means in communication.–Father keeps *in touch* with us by letters and telephone when he is away.

touch·down (TUCH-down) *n. touchdowns.* Score made in football by taking the ball across the goal line of the opposite team.

tough (TUF) *adj. tougher, toughest.* 1. Not easily chewed or cut.–Some meat is tender; some is *tough.*
2. Able to stand much use or strain without breaking.–The ropes used to tie a ship to the dock must be *tough.*
3. Not pleasant; difficult.–This has been a *tough* winter for the poor family whose home burned down.
4. Sturdy and lasting. – Some plants are *tough;* others die with the first frost.
5. Stubborn and hard to manage.–The prisoner got *tough* when taken from his cell. It took two guards to handle him.
6. Rough and lawless.–The family moved from a *tough* part of the town to a better part.

tour (TUHR) *n. tours.* A journey for pleasure. –Frank is going to take a *tour* of Europe.
–*v. tours, toured, touring.* Travel about for pleasure.–We *toured* the United States during our vacation.

tour•ist (TUHR-ist) *n. tourists.* One who travels for pleasure.–Many *tourists* stop to see the Grand Canyon.

tour•na•ment (TUHR- *or* TER-nə-mənt) *n. tournaments.* 1. A contest or series of contests in which many players take part. –Stephen became the tennis champion by winning the tennis *tournament.*
2. A contest of skill and daring between knights on horseback. – The queen gave a prize to Sir Harold, the champion of the *tournament.*

tour•ni•quet (TUHR- *or* TER-nə-ket) *n. tourniquets.* Something that stops the flow of blood from a cut by pinching the bleeding blood vessel closed. A *tourniquet* can be made by twisting a handkerchief.

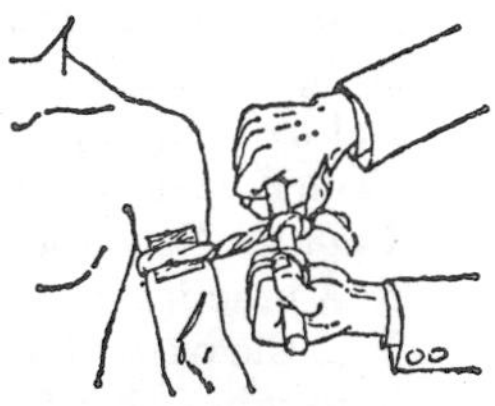

tow (TOH) *n. tows.* 1. Something being drawn along by a connecting rope, chain, or cable. –The bus being pulled is the *tow.*

2. A rope or chain used to pull something.
–*v. tows, towed, towing.* Pull or draw along by a connecting rope, chain, or cable.–The bus had a broken axle and had to be *towed* by a repair truck.
–*In tow* usually means being pulled.–While the bus was *in tow,* the tow rope broke.

to•ward or **to•wards** (TORD *or* TORDZ) *prep.* 1. In the direction of.–The dog ran *toward* the garage.
2. Near; close to.–It is getting *toward* the time to quit work.
3. For the purpose of; to help buy.–Mary gave some money *toward* the sick boy's flowers.–Bob has saved five dollars *toward* a new bicycle.
4. To.–The boy's behavior *toward* his classmates was not polite.

tow•el (TOW-əl) *n. towels.* A piece of cloth or paper used for wiping or drying.

tow•er (TOW-ėr) *n. towers.* A tall, slender part of a building, or a tall, slim building that stands alone. –The church bell is in the *tower.*
–*v. towers, towered, towering.* Be much taller or higher. – The tall boy *towers* above the rest of the class.–The chimney *towers* above the rest of the building.

town (TOWN) *n. towns.* 1. A place where many people live near each other, smaller than a city but larger than a village.
2. The people living in a town.–The whole *town* went to see the circus.

tox•ic (TAHK-sik) *adj.; toxin, n.* Having to do with poison; poisonous.–Many weed- and insect-killing agents are *toxic.* They will poison anyone who drinks them.

toy (TOI) *n. toys.* A thing for children to play with. – There were many *toys* under the Christmas tree.
–*v. toys, toyed, toying.* Play (with); amuse oneself (with).–Baby *toys* with her toes.

trace (TRAYSS) *n. traces.* 1. A sign; a mark; an indication.–He saw *traces* of deer in the woods.
2. A small bit.–The dog licked the plate so clean that not a *trace* of food was left.
–*v. traces, traced, tracing.* 1. Draw an outline of; sketch.–The man *traced* a plan of the playground.
2. Copy by drawing over the lines of.–Mary *traced* the picture by placing tissue paper over it and marking the lines of the picture on the tissue.
3. Follow.–The hunter *traced* the rabbit by its tracks in the snow.

tra•che•a (TRAY-kee-ə *or* trə-KEE-ə) *n. tracheae.* The windpipe. Air passes to and from the lungs through the *trachea.*

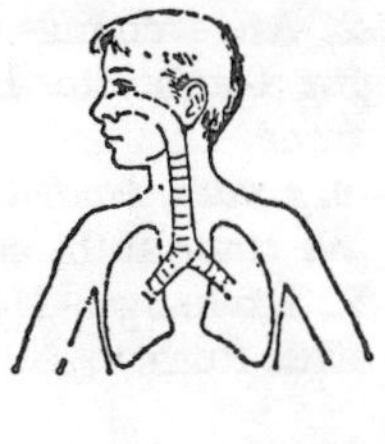

track (TRAK) *n. tracks.* 1. A mark left by the passing of something, as bicycle *tracks*, wagon *tracks*, rabbit *tracks.*–Judy left a *track* in the snow as she walked across the field to Grandmother's house.

2. A road or path.–The hunters followed the narrow *track* to their cabin.

3. A roadway or path, usually circular, built for racing. – The racers roared around the *track.*

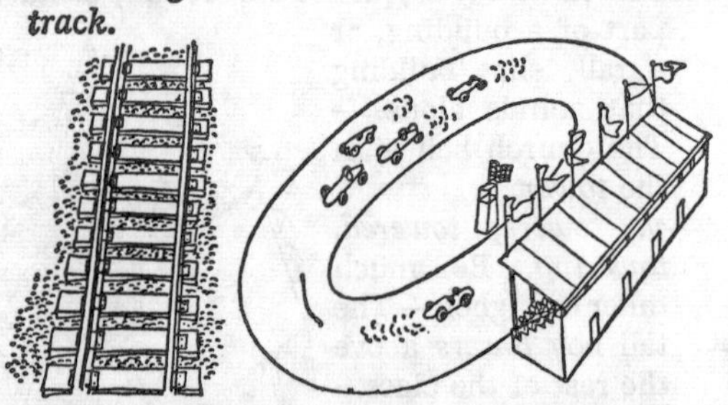

4. A line of steel rails.–Trains run on *tracks.*

–*v. tracks, tracked, tracking.* Trace; follow from clues.–The dog *tracked* the rabbit to the old log.–The policeman *tracked* the robber to his hideout.

tract (TRAKT) *n. tracts.* 1. A region; an area. –The farmer is plowing a large *tract* of land.

2. An area of the body containing related organs or parts.–The nose, windpipe, and lungs are parts of the respiratory, or breathing, *tract.*

3. A pamphlet or little book.–*Tracts* usually are written about religious topics.

trac•tor (TRAK-ter) *n. tractors.* A heavy machine with a motor, used for pulling a plow or some other machine.–Many farmers use *tractors* instead of horses.

trade (TRAYD) *n. trades.* 1. The work one does to make a living.–Father's *trade* is toolmaking.

2. An exchange.–Bob exchanged his knife for Tom's kite. Bob thought it was a good *trade.*

–*v. trades, traded, trading.* 1. Do business.–We *trade* at the corner store.

2. Exchange.–Mary *traded* geography books with Ruth.

trade•mark (TRAYD-mahrk) *n. trademarks.* A name, mark, or picture put on goods by a manufacturer so that one can tell his goods from those made by someone else.

trad•er (TRAY-der) *n. traders.* A person who buys, sells, or exchanges goods.–That man is a horse *trader.* He buys and sells horses.

trade wind (TRAYD wind) *trade winds.* A steady wind blowing over the oceans toward the equator. North of the equator the *trade winds* blow from the Northeast to the Southwest. South of the equator they blow from the Southeast to the Northwest.

tra•di•tion (trə-DISH-ən) *n. traditions; traditional, adj.; traditionally, adv.* 1. Something that has been done for a long time, over and over again, without any written reason. –The Easter Parade on Fifth Avenue is a *tradition* in New York City.

2. A practice, custom, or belief handed down from the past.–John went to the same college from which his father and grandfather had graduated. It was a family *tradition* for all the boys to do so.

traf•fic (TRAF-ik) *n.* Movement of people or of cars, trucks, or other vehicles.–*Traffic* is very heavy on Sundays. Many cars are on the roads.

–*adj.* Having to do with the movement of people or vehicles.–There are many *traffic* accidents on holidays.

trag•e•dy (TRAJ-ə-dee) *n. tragedies.* 1. A play that has a sad ending.

2. A sad happening.–The death of the fireman in the burning house was a *tragedy.*

trail (TRAYL) *n. trails.* A path worn through the woods.–An old Indian *trail* led to the brook.

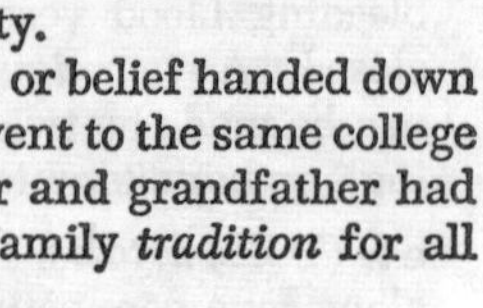

–*v. trails, trailed, trailing.* 1. Drag something along behind.–The runaway horse ran home *trailing* the broken rope.

2. Follow.–The dog *trailed* Jack across the field and into the woods.

3. Track; trace; follow the tracks of. – We *trailed* the rabbit to the hollow log.

4. Fall behind, come after, or follow the others.–Our favorite horse *trailed* in the race.

trail·er (TRAY-ler) *n. trailers.* 1. A vehicle used for living quarters that is drawn by an automobile.—We lived in a *trailer* during our vacation.

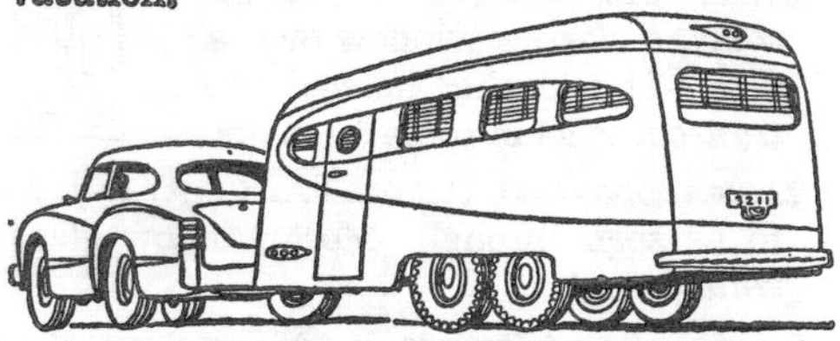

2. Any wheeled vehicle, such as the body of a truck, designed to be pulled by another vehicle with a motor.
3. A plant that crawls along the ground. — Arbutus, a spring flower, is a *trailer.*

train (TRAYN) *n. trains.* 1. A string of railway cars that are joined together and pulled by an engine or locomotive.

2. A part of a skirt that drags on the floor behind the wearer.—The bride's dress had a long *train.*
—*v. trains, trained, training.* 1. Bring up; teach.—The children's good manners showed that they were well *trained* at home.
2. Practice; prepare. — Our runners *trained* for the track meet. They made themselves fit and ready by exercising, by eating properly, and by getting enough rest.
3. Coax or fix in a certain way, till it becomes natural.—Grandmother *trained* the morning-glories over the fence.
4. Aim; point.—The sailors *trained* the ship's guns on the pirate vessel.

train·ing (TRAYN-ing) *n.* Study and practice.—It takes *training* to learn to be a carpenter or a mechanic.—The prize fighter went to bed at nine o'clock while he was in *training.*

trait (TRAYT) *n. traits.* A special feature, quality, or characteristic. — John's honesty, quick wit, and good manners are his outstanding *traits.*

trai·tor (TRAY-ter) *n. traitors.* A person who is not true to his country; one who helps the enemies of his country.

tramp (TRAMP) *n. tramps.* 1. A homeless man who goes from place to place.—A *tramp* came to the farm for food and water.
2. A steamship that goes from one port to another, picking up what freight it can.
3. A walk; a hike.—Bob and Father went for a long *tramp.*
—*v. tramps, tramped, tramping.* 1. Walk; march.—The children *tramped* through the halls.—Policemen *tramp* miles each day.
2. Walk (on) heavily. — The cows *tramped* on the new plants in the garden.

tram·ple (TRAM-pəl) *v. tramples, trampled, trampling.* Step on and crush.—The cows got into the cornfield and *trampled* the corn.

tran·quil (TRANG-kwəl) *adj.; tranquility, n.* Free from disturbance; quiet; peaceful; calm.—Nuns and monks lead *tranquil* lives.—The water on the lake is *tranquil.* There is not a ripple on it.

trans·act (tranz-AKT) *v. transacts, transacted, transacting.* Carry on; attend to; conduct; manage.—The company has been *transacting* business since 1905.—Although he is not feeling well, he can still *transact* his affairs.

trans·at·lan·tic (tranz-ət-LAN-tik) *adj.* Crossing the Atlantic Ocean.—The huge ship is a *transatlantic* liner. It is a ship that travels across the Atlantic Ocean.

trans·con·ti·nen·tal (transs-kahn-tə-NEN-tl) *adj.* Crossing or extending across a continent.—The radio broadcast was heard over a *transcontinental* network. It could be heard from New York to California.

trans·fer (TRANSS-fer) *n. transfers.* A ticket used to ride on another bus or car without paying the whole fare again.—The conductor gave us a *transfer* to another bus.
—(transs-FER) *v. transfers, transferred, transferring.* 1. Move; put in a different place.—Mr. Jones was *transferred* to a different department.
2. Change from one car or bus to another.—We *transfer* at the corner of Main Street and First Avenue.
3. Copy; trace; reproduce. — Mary used tracing paper to *transfer* the picture in the book to her notebook.

trans·form (transs-FORM) *v. transforms, transformed, transforming.* Change from one thing to another.—Cream is *transformed* into butter by churning. — The fairy godmother *transformed* the pumpkin into a splendid coach.

trans•fu•sion (transs-FYOO-zhən) *n. transfusions.* The transfer of blood from one person to another person.

tran•sis•tor (tran-ZISS-ter) *n. transistors.* A tiny device which takes the place of a vacuum tube. *Transistors* are used in scientific and electrical instruments and in pocket-size radios.

trans•late (transs-LAYT) *v. translates, translated, translating.* Change into a different language.–Father *translated* the French letter into English.
–*translation, n. translations.*

trans•lu•cent (transs-LOO-sənt) *adj.* Allowing light to pass through, but not letting objects be seen clearly. Frosted-glass windows and some stained-glass windows are *translucent.*

trans•mit (transs-MIT) *v. transmits, transmitted, transmitting.* 1. Send along; pass on; transfer; forward.–Please *transmit* the information as soon as you receive it.
2. Send out signals by such means as radio, television, and telegraph.–The radio station *transmits* only to a local area.

trans•mit•ter (transs-MIT-er) *n. transmitters.* An instrument by which messages are sent by telephone, telegraph, radio.

tran•som (TRAN-səm) *n. transoms.* A narrow window over a door.–The teacher opened the *transom* to let in some fresh air.

trans•par•ent (transs-PAIR-ənt) *adj.* Able to be seen through.–Most window glass is *transparent.*

trans•plant (transs-PLANT) *v. transplants, transplanted, transplanting.* Move; plant again somewhere else.–We planted tomato seeds in a box in the house. When the plants were large enough, we *transplanted* them into the garden.

trans•port (TRANSS-port) *n. transports.* 1. A ship, a train, a bus, or a truck that carries soldiers and sailors from one place to another.
2. An airplane that carries people and things from one place to another.
–(transs-PORT) *v. transports, transported, transporting.* Carry or take from place to place.

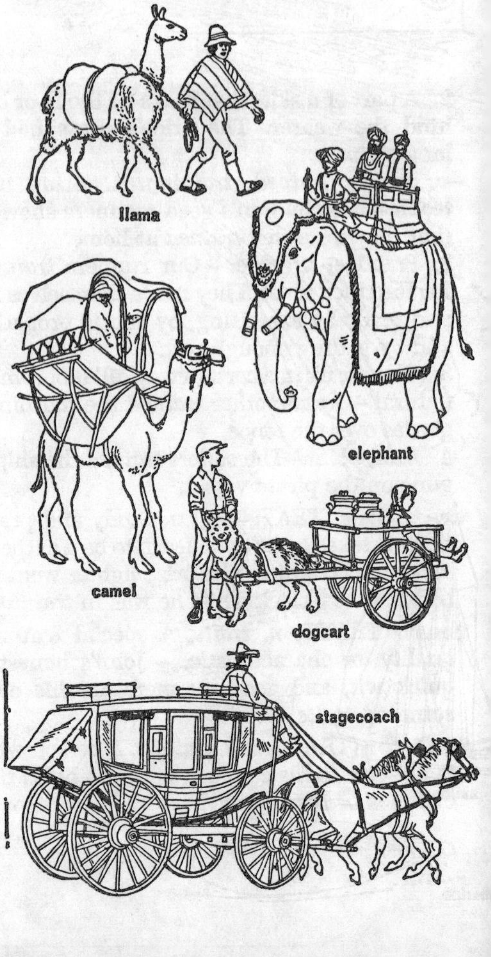

trans·por·ta·tion (transs-per-TAY-shən) *n.* The carrying of goods or passengers from one place to another.–*Transportation* is important to business.

trap (TRAP) *n. traps.* 1. A device to catch animals.–Father caught a rat in a *trap.*

2. A U-shaped pipe in a drainpipe that allows water to pass out but keeps sewer gas from coming back through it.–The plumber repaired the *trap* in the drainpipe.
–*v. traps, trapped, trapping.* Catch in a trap.–The hunter *trapped* the fox.

trap door (TRAP dor) *trap doors.* A door in a floor or ceiling or on a roof. – The man found a *trap door* in the floor.

tra·peze (tra-PEEZ) *n. trapezes.* A swing high above the ground.–The acrobats performed on a *trapeze.*

trap·per (TRAP-er) *n. trappers.* A person who traps wild animals to sell their furs.

trash (TRASH) *n.; trashy, adj.* Rubbish; broken and used-up things.–The barrel in the alley is filled with *trash.*

trav·el (TRAV-əl) *v. travels, traveled* or *travelled, traveling* or *travelling.* Go from place to place. – Mary wants to *travel* around the world when she grows up.

trav·el·er (TRAV-əl-er) *n. travelers.* A person who is going from one place to another.

tray (TRAY) *n. trays.* A large, flat piece of metal, wood, or other material, often with a shallow rim around the edge. Food, dishes, glasses, and so on, are often carried on a *tray.*–Mary served Mother her breakfast in bed on a *tray.*

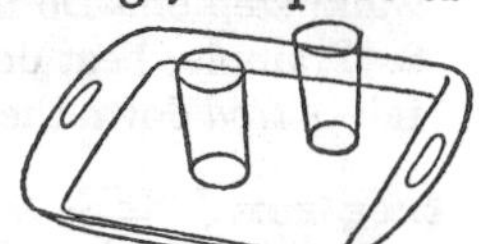

treach·er·ous (TRECH-er-əss) *adj.; treacherously, adv.* 1. Not trustworthy; not reliable; deceiving; not loyal.
2. Having a false appearance of dependability or strength.–The floors of the old building are *treacherous.* The boards look solid but they are rotten in many places and will not hold a person safely.

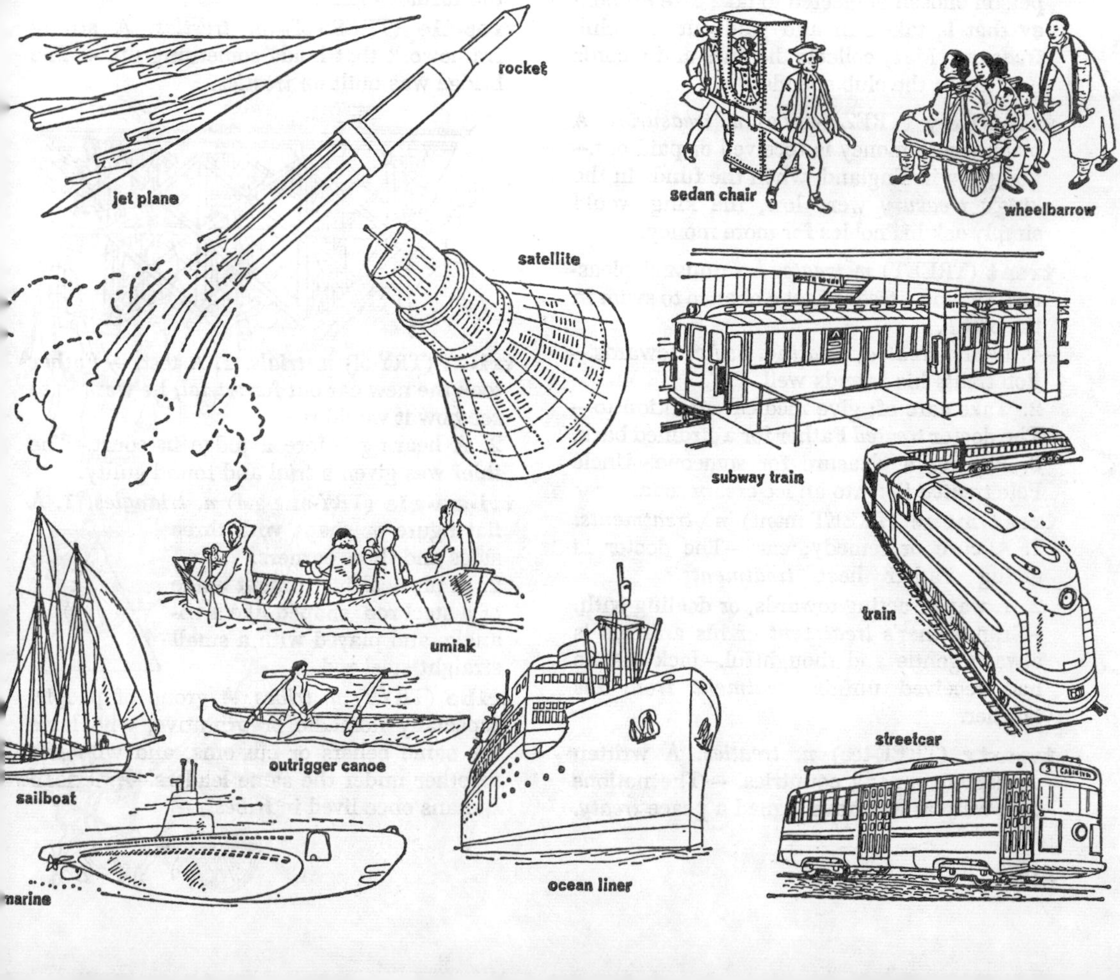

tread (TRED) *n. treads.* 1. Walking; steps.—We heard the heavy *tread* of marching feet.

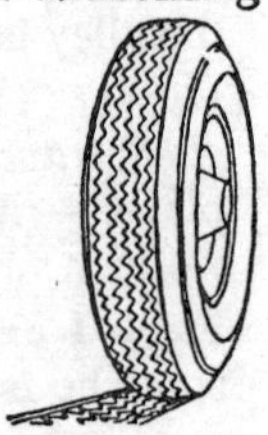

2. The part of a rubber tire that touches the ground.
3. The part of a stair step that one puts his foot on. If the *treads* are narrow, it makes the stairs steep.
—*v. treads, trod, treading.* 1. Step; walk; step on.—Do not *tread* on my toes.
2. Trample; beat down.—The hordes of buffaloes *trod* down the grass with their feet.

trea•son (TREE-zən) *n.* Being untrue to one's country; secretly helping the enemies of one's country. — The man was found guilty of *treason.* He had sold supplies to the enemy.

treas•ure (TREZH-er) *n. treasures.* Money, jewels, or any things of value that have been collected or saved up.—The boys were digging in the cave for *treasure.*
—*v. treasures, treasured, treasuring.* Value dearly.—Mother *treasures* the old picture of Grandmother and Grandfather.

treas•ur•er (TREZH-er-er) *n. treasurers.* A person chosen or elected to take care of money that is taken in and paid out.—As club *treasurer,* Mary collects the dues and records how much the club spends.

treas•ur•y (TREZH-ər-ee) *n. treasuries.* A place where money is received or paid out.—Long ago in England, when the funds in the king's *treasury* were low, the king would simply ask his nobles for more money.

treat (TREET) *n. treats.* An unusual pleasure.—It was a *treat* to get a chance to swim in the ocean.
—*v. treats, treated, treating.* 1. Act towards.—Bob *treats* his friends well.
2. Take care of; give medical attention to.—The doctor *treated* Father for a strained back.
3. Pay for a pleasure for someone.—Uncle Pete *treated* Betty to an ice-cream soda.

treat•ment (TREET-mənt) *n. treatments.* 1. A cure or remedy; care.—The doctor is giving Father heat *treatments.*
2. A way of acting towards, or dealing with.—Grandfather's *treatment* of his animals is always gentle and thoughtful.—Jack felt he had received unfair *treatment* from his teacher.

trea•ty (TREE-tee) *n. treaties.* A written agreement among countries. — The nations that were at war have signed a peace *treaty.*

tree (TREE) *n. trees.* A very large, woody, leafy plant with a stem called a trunk. Some *trees* have fruit or nuts on them. Wood for building houses and furniture comes from the trunks and branches of *trees.* See p. 328.

trem•ble (TREM-bəl) *n. trembles.* Shaking.—We could feel the *tremble* of the house after the explosion.
—*v. trembles, trembled, trembling.* 1. To shake slightly from a strong feeling such as fright, cold, or nervousness. — Jack *trembled* with eagerness as he unwrapped his present.
2. Shake slightly.—The wind made the leaves *tremble.*

tre•men•dous (tri-MEN-dəss) *adj.; tremendously, adv.* Very great.—The fire caused a *tremendous* loss for the owners of the house.

trench (TRENCH) *n. trenches.* 1. A ditch.—The farmer dug a *trench* at the side of the barn to drain the water off.
2. A ditch with a bank of dirt in front for protection.—The soldiers shot from *trenches.*

tres•pass (TRESS-pəss) *v. trespasses, trespassed, trespassing.* Go onto the property or land of someone else without their permission to do so.—Hunters sometimes *trespass* on the farmer's land.

tres•tle (TRESS-əl) *n. trestles.* A strong framework that holds something up. — The bridge was built on *trestles.*

tri•al (TRY-əl) *n. trials.* 1. A test. — Father took the new car out for a *trial;* he wanted to see how it would run.
2. A hearing before a judge in court.—The thief was given a *trial* and found guilty.

tri•an•gle (TRY-ang-gəl) *n. triangles.* 1. A flat figure or shape with three sides and three corners.
2. A musical instrument made of a steel rod shaped like a triangle and played with a small straight steel rod.

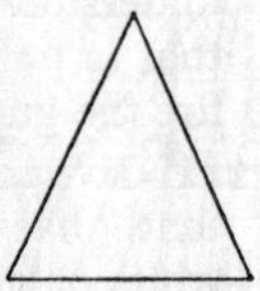

tribe (TRYB) *n. tribes.* A group of people, especially nomadic or primitive, who have the same beliefs or customs, and who live together under the same leaders.—American Indians once lived in *tribes.*

trib·u·tar·y (TRIB-yə-tair-ee) *n. tributaries.* 1. A stream flowing into a body of water larger than itself.–The Ohio and Arkansas Rivers are *tributaries* of the Mississippi River.
2. A person, state, or nation that pays tribute.–The defeated nation became a *tributary* of its conqueror.

trib·ute (TRIB-yoot) *n. tributes.* Thanks; respect; praise. – On Memorial Day we pay *tribute* to the soldiers who gave their lives for their country.

trick (TRIK) *n. tricks; tricky, adj.* 1. A clever act or stunt which amuses people.–The magician's best *trick* was pulling rabbits out of a hat that seemed to be empty.
2. A joke; a prank.–Bill played a *trick* on Mother by filling the salt shaker with sugar.
–*v. tricks, tricked, tricking.* Cheat; deceive. – The man tried to *trick* Uncle Henry into buying an inferior watch.

trick·le (TRIK-əl) *n. trickles.* A thin stream. –A *trickle* of water leaked from the pipe.
–*v. trickles, trickled, trickling.* Run in a fine stream; fall in drops.–It was so hot that perspiration *trickled* down the man's forehead. –Water *trickled* from the leak in the pipe.

tri·cy·cle (TRY-sik-əl) *n. tricycles.* A small, three-wheeled vehicle that is run by pedals and steered by handle bars.

tried (TRYD) *v.* One form of the verb *try.* –I try each day to do a kind deed. Yesterday I *tried* hard.
–*adj.* Proved; sure.–Joe is Jack's *tried* and true friend.

tri·fle (TRYF-əl) *n. trifles.* 1. A little thing that is not important.–Don't fret over *trifles.*
2. A very small amount of money. – We bought this knife for a *trifle;* it cost only ten cents.

trig·ger (TRIG-er) *n. triggers.* The small, movable piece on the underside of a gun that is pulled back to fire the gun.

tril·li·um (TRIL-ee-əm) *n. trilliums.* A plant that has a large, white or pinkish flower with three petals and three green leaves. The flower which grows on the plant is also called a *trillium.*

trim (TRIM) *n.* Good condition.–Our baseball team is in *trim* for the game. All the players are in good shape.
–*v. trims, trimmed, trimming.* 1. Make neat and orderly by cutting some away. – Bob *trims* the rose bushes.–Mother *trims* her fingernails.
2. Decorate; add decoration to. – Mother *trimmed* the birthday cake with pink flowers.
–*adj.* Neat and orderly.–The room is *trim.* Everything is in place.

trin·ket (TRING-kit) *n. trinkets.* A small or cheap toy or piece of jewelry.–The children bought some *trinkets* at the fair.

tri·o (TREE-oh) *n. trios.* 1. A group of three persons or things.–A *trio* of girls sang the song.

2. Music written for three people to sing or play.–The *trio* was played by a violin, a cello, and a piano.

trip (TRIP) *n. trips.* A journey.–We are going for a *trip* in the automobile soon.
–*v. trips, tripped, tripping.* 1. Step lightly and quickly.–The children *tripped* along after the Pied Piper.
2. Catch one's foot; stumble.–Grandfather *tripped* on the edge of the rug and fell.
3. Cause to stumble.–The boy put his foot out and *tripped* the fleeing bandit.

tri·ple (TRIP-əl) *n. triples.* In baseball, a three-base hit.–The batter got a *triple.*
–*v. triples, tripled, tripling.* Make three times as great.–Jack *tripled* his income from his paper route. Last year he made five dollars a week; this year he makes fifteen dollars a week.
–*adj.* 1. Three times as great.–Jack's income this year is *triple* what it was last year.
2. Of three parts. – Some forks are *triple*-pronged. They have three prongs.

tri·plet (TRIP-lət) *n. triplets.* 1. A group of three things that are alike or related; a trio.
2. One of three children born at one birth to the same mother.

tri·pod (TRY-pahd) *n. tripods.* Anything having three feet or legs, like a stool, or a stand. –The photographer mounted his camera on a *tripod.* He set it on a three-legged stand.

tri•umph (TRY-əmf) *n. triumphs.* A victory; a success.—Our ball team celebrated its *triumph* by marching through the streets and singing.
—*v. triumphs, triumphed, triumphing.* Be victorious; win. — We have always *triumphed* over our opponents.

trod•den (TRAHD-n) *v.* One form of the verb *tread.*—The path had been *trodden* by the cows until it was packed hard.

troll (TROHL) *n. trolls.* An ugly fairy dwarf that lives in caves. — A *troll* waited on the bridge for the goat.

trol•ley (TRAHL-ee) *n. trolleys.* 1. An electric bus or streetcar.—We went to town on the *trolley.*
2. The wheel that runs along an electric wire and carries electricity to the streetcar.—The *trolley* came off the wire and the car stopped.

trom•bone (TRAHM-bohn *or* trahm-BOHN) *n. trombones.* A musical instrument made of a bent brass tube, with a section which slides in and out to make different tones.

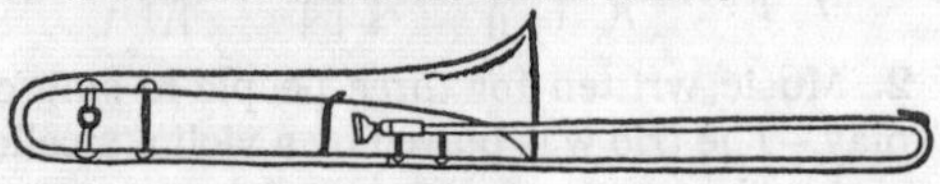

troop (TROOP) *n. troops.* 1. A group of soldiers, or other united group. — A Boy Scout *troop* is camping at the lake.
2. Soldiers. — The general said there were ten thousand *troops* in his army. There were ten thousand men.
—*v. troops, trooped, trooping.* March together. — The children following the Pied Piper *trooped* into the opening in the hillside.

tro•phy (TROH-fee) *n. trophies.* Something given as a sign of victory; something won.—The winner of the race won a silver cup as a *trophy.*

trop•ic (TRAHP-ik) *n. tropics.* 1. A line of latitude lying about 32½ degrees either north or south of the equator. The northern line is called the *Tropic* of Cancer. The southern line is called the *Tropic* of Capricorn. The area that lies between the *tropics* is called the Torrid Zone.
2. (In the plural and usually spelled with a capital "T.") The land that lies in the Torrid Zone.—The weather in the *Tropics* is usually very hot.

trop•o•sphere (TRAHP-əss-feer) *n.* The lowest layer of the atmosphere; the part in which we live. Temperature varies with altitude in the *troposphere;* the higher the altitude, the lower the temperature. Almost all clouds are formed in the *troposphere.*

trot (TRAHT) *n. trots.* A gait of a horse in which a front foot and the opposite hind foot move together.
—*v. trots, trotted, trotting.* 1. Move at a trot.—The cowboy's horse *trotted* slowly along.
2. Run slowly.—The dog *trots* along after its master.

trou•ble (TRUB-əl) *n. troubles.* 1. A worry; a concern; a disturbance.—The girl's mischievous pranks at school make *trouble* for her family.
2. A nuisance; additional work. — We will stay for lunch, if it isn't too much *trouble* for you.
3. A difficulty; something that causes worry, unhappiness, unpleasantness, and so on; misfortune. — That family has had many *troubles.*
—*v. troubles, troubled, troubling.* Worry. — Baby's sickness *troubles* Mother.

trou•ble•some (TRUB-əl-səm) *adj.* Causing trouble, difficulty, disturbance, and so on.

trough (TRAWF *or* TRAHF) *n. troughs.* 1. A narrow box or holder for animal food. — Horses, cattle, pigs, and other animals eat and drink from *troughs.*

2. A gutter or drain.—*Troughs* carry water from the roofs of buildings into drainpipes.

trou•sers (TROW-zerz) *n. pl.* The part of a man's or boy's clothing which covers the body from the waist down.

trous•seau (TROO-soh *or* troo-SOH) *n. trousseaux* or *trousseaus.* A set of clothes and other things, such as bed linen and table linen, that a bride has when she marries.—My sister is going to get married next month, so she is shopping for her *trousseau.*

trout (TROWT) *n. trouts.* 1. A kind of fish that is found in fresh water and used for food.

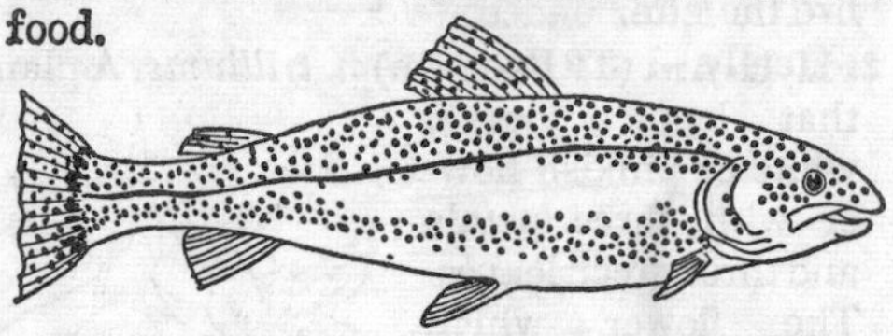

2. A salt-water fish that is something like the salmon.

trow•el (TROW-əl) *n. trowels.* 1. A hand tool with a broad, flat blade used to smooth plaster and cement. –A bricklayer uses a *trowel* for putting mortar between bricks.

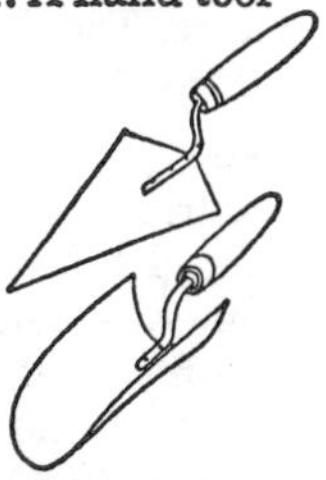

2. A small digging tool.–Mother uses a garden *trowel* for digging up plants.

tru•ant (TROO-ənt) *n. truants* and *adj.* 1. A girl or boy who stays out of school without the consent of his parents. A *truant* officer calls at the home of a *truant* to talk with his parents about his absence.
2. Absent without permission.–Bob was *truant* from school once when he went fishing.

truce (TROOSS) *n. truces.* A pause or short stop in fighting.–The two armies called for a *truce.* During the *truce* the leaders talked about peace.

truck (TRUK) *n. trucks.* 1. A big, powerful vehicle for carrying loads.
2. A group of wheels that holds up one end of a railroad car and let it turn easily.
3. A small platform on wheels that is pushed by hand.–Cases of food are moved about the grocery store on a hand *truck.*
4. Worthless rubbish.–Bob's room was littered with *truck.*
5. Vegetables.–Grandfather sells his garden *truck* to the market in town.
–*v. trucks, trucked, trucking.* Transport or carry on a truck.–The goods were *trucked* to us by the manufacturer.
–*adj.* Vegetable. – Grandfather has a *truck* garden.

true (TROO) *adj.* 1. Correct; real.–This is *true:* the sun shines here in the daytime. This is false: the sun shines here at night.–Mary likes imaginary stories, but Bob likes *true* stories.
2. Sincere; faithful.–Sally is a *true* friend to Mary and Jane.
3. Rightful; actual; real.–The teacher asked us who the *true* owner of the ball was.

tru•ly (TROO-lee) *adv.* 1. Sincerely; faithfully.–The letter ended, "Very *truly* yours."
2. Really.–I am *truly* coming to see you.

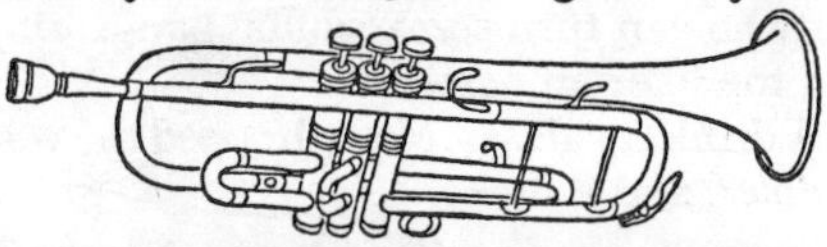

trum•pet (TRUM-pət) *n. trumpets.* A musical instrument sounded by blowing. – The *trumpet* is a wind instrument.

trunk (TRUNGK) *n. trunks.* 1. The main stem of a tree.–The owl lived in the hollow *trunk* of an old oak.
2. The body of a person or animal, not including the legs, arms, or head.
3. The snout of an elephant.–The elephant can pour water over his head with his *trunk.*

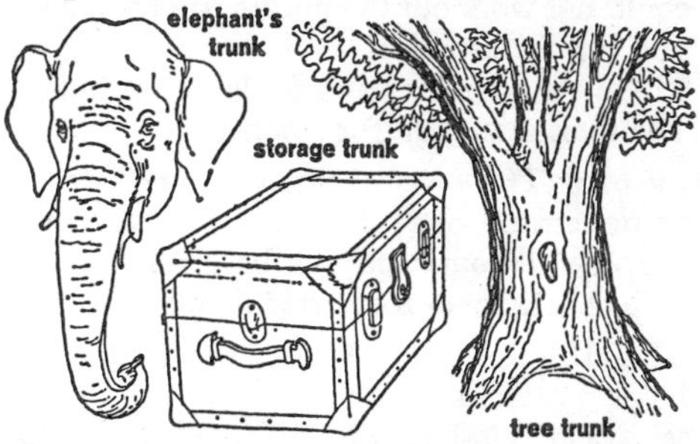

4. A large covered chest for storing or moving clothing or other belongings. – When traveling, we send our clothes in a *trunk.*

trunks (TRUNGKS) *n. pl.* Short, tight pants. –Men wear *trunks* when they swim.

trust (TRUST) *n. trusts.* 1. A duty; something one promises to do.–Bob lived up to his *trust* to take care of the garden.
2. Faith.–The children have complete *trust* in what their teacher tells them.
–*v. trusts, trusted, trusting.* 1. Have faith in; believe in; depend upon. – Children *trust* their parents.–The teacher knew she could *trust* Jack to bring back the book.–We did not have enough money with us to pay for the groceries, but the storekeeper *trusted* us.
2. Hope; expect.–I *trust* you will be coming home soon.

trust•wor•thy (TRUST-wer-thee) *adj.; trustworthily, adv.; trustworthiness, n.* Dependable; true to one's word or duty.–The teacher found the boy to be *trustworthy.*

trust•y (TRUSS-tee) *n. trusties.* In a prison, one who has earned special privileges by his good behavior.
–*adj. trustier, trustiest.* Dependable; not failing.–Robin Hood bent his *trusty* bow and shot his arrow right into the bull's-eye.

truth (TROOTH) *n. truths.* What is true or real; exactly what happened.–Mother taught us to tell the *truth.*–It would not be telling the *truth* to say that the children are perfect.

truth•ful (TROOTH-fuhl) *adj.; truthfully, adv.; truthfulness, n.* Honest; telling what really is so.–It pays to be *truthful.*–In the story, George Washington was *truthful* about what happened to the cherry tree.

try (TRY) *n. tries.* A test or trial.–Mother is giving the new soap a *try* today.
–*v. tries, tried, trying.* 1. Use or test; give a trial to.–If you cannot work out the problem this way, *try* another way.–*Try* one of these candies.
2. Attempt; make an effort. – At first Bob could not work out the puzzle. He *tried* again and finally solved it.
3. Give a court hearing to, before a judge.– The man was *tried* for stealing.

try·out (TRY-owt) *n. tryouts.* A test or trial to determine one's fitness for a particular purpose. *Tryouts* may be held for membership on a team or for parts in a play.

tub (TUB) *n. tubs.* 1. A large, open vessel that holds water in which to wash clothes or bathe. – Bob takes showers, but Jack bathes in the *tub*.

2. A low, wooden, barrel-like vessel. – The grocer had a *tub* half full of butter.

tu·ba (TOO- *or* TYOO-bə) *n. tubas.* A large, low-toned horn.

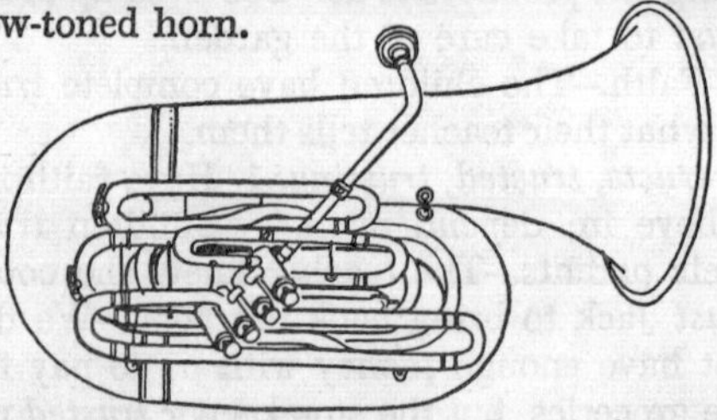

tube (TOOB *or* TYOOB) *n. tubes.* 1. A pipe; a long, hollow piece of rubber, metal, glass, etc.
2. Any hollow stem.–We drink sodas and lemonade through paper *tubes* called straws.
3. A part of a radio that looks something like an electric light bulb.

4. A round container of thin metal with a top that screws on.–Medicines, shaving creams, and toothpastes often come in *tubes*.
5. A tunnel for trains. – Many people travel under the Hudson River through *tubes*.

tu·ber·cu·lo·sis (too- *or* tyoo-ber-kyə-LOH-səss) *n.* A disease, usually of the lungs. When a person has *tuberculosis*, he is often sent to a hospital for treatment and rest.

tuck (TUK) *n. tucks.* A stitched fold. – The sleeves of Father's shirt were too long, so Mother put a *tuck* in them.
–*v. tucks, tucked, tucking.* Place, fit, or squeeze in neatly.–Mother *tucked* Baby's curls into the bonnet.–Mary *tucked* the blankets in.

Tues·day (TOOZ- *or* TYOOZ-dee) *n. Tuesdays.* The day after Monday. *Tuesday* is the third day of the week.

tuft (TUFT) *n. tufts.* 1. A group of threads, hair, feathers, or anything of the kind, fastened together at one end and loose at the other. – The bluejay has a *tuft* of feathers on his head.
2. A bunch of yarn. – The bedspread was white with blue *tufts*.

tug (TUG) *n. tugs.* 1. A small boat that can pull or tow other boats, even those much larger than the *tug* is.

2. A hard pull. – Bob gave just one *tug* and the box opened.
–*v. tugs, tugged, tugging.* Pull hard.–The boys *tugged* at the wagon to get it out of the pool of mud at the bottom of the hill.

tu·i·tion (too- *or* tyoo-ISH-ən) *n.* 1. Instruction or teaching.–Fine *tuition* is available at a great many schools, colleges, and universities.
2. The fee or money paid for instruction.– *Tuition* is payable in advance in many schools.

tu·lip (TOO- *or* TYOO-lip) *n. tulips.* A bright-colored, cup-shaped flower that grows from a bulb. The bulbs are put into the ground in the fall. The flowers blossom in the spring.–Many *tulips* grow in Holland.

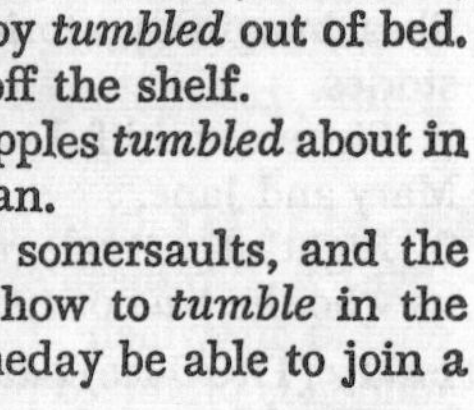

tum·ble (TUM-bəl) *v. tumbles, tumbled, tumbling.* 1. Fall.–Baby *tumbled* out of bed. –The books *tumbled* off the shelf.
2. Roll or toss.–The apples *tumbled* about in the basket when Bob ran.
3. Turn handsprings, somersaults, and the like.–Bob is learning how to *tumble* in the hope that he may someday be able to join a circus as an acrobat.

tum·bler (TUM-bler) *n. tumblers.* 1. A person who can turn somersaults, handsprings, and the like; an acrobat.
2. A drinking glass.–Mary dropped the water *tumbler*, and it broke.

tu·na (TOO-nə) *n. tuna* or *tunas.* A large fish that is good to eat. The meat of *tuna* is canned and sold in stores.

tune (TOON *or* TYOON) *n. tunes.* 1. A melody.—I know the *tune* of "America."
2. A piece of music; a song.—Play a *tune* for us.
—*v. tunes, tuned, tuning.* Bring to the proper pitch or tone.—Mary *tuned* her violin.—Mother had the piano *tuned.*

tung·sten (TUNG-stən) *n.* A rare heavy metal. *Tungsten* has the highest melting point of all metals. It is used for filaments in electric lamps and for hardening other metals against easy melting.

tun·nel (TUN-əl) *n. tunnels.* A passageway made underground.—Trains and automobiles go through a *tunnel* to get through a mountain or under a river.

—*v. tunnels, tunneled, tunneling.* Dig an underground passage.—The mole *tunneled* under the vegetable garden and made the row of radishes sink.

tur·ban (TER-bən) *n. turbans.* 1. A cap with a scarf wound around it.—The man is wearing a *turban.*

2. A scarf wound around the head.—The woman is wearing a *turban.*
3. A kind of small, close-fitting hat without a brim, resembling a wound scarf.

tur·bine (TER-bin *or* -byn) *n. turbines.* An engine in which the motion is produced by the push of water, gas, or steam against a series of curved blades set into a shaft or wheel. As the water, gas, or steam pushes each successive blade, the shaft or wheel rotates.—*Turbines* are often used to provide the power to run ships.

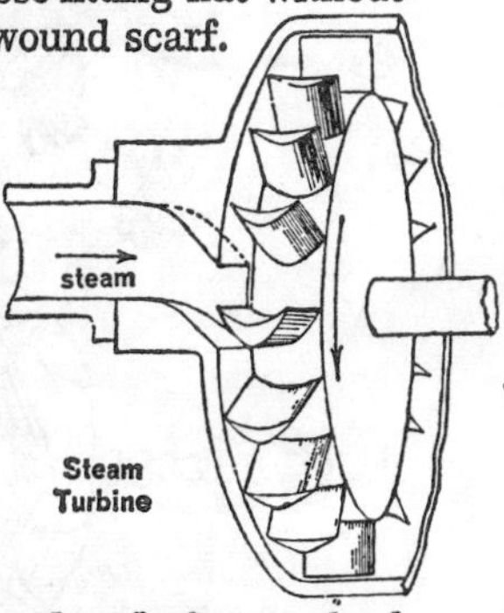

Steam Turbine

turf (TERF) *n.* Sod; grass with its tangled roots.—Men playing golf often dig up *turf* with their clubs.

tur·key (TER-kee) *n. turkeys.* 1. A kind of large bird with wrinkled, red skin on its head and neck. Some *turkeys* are wild.
2. The meat of a turkey.—We eat *turkey* on Thanksgiving.

tur·moil (TER-moil) *n.* Confusion, as of movements, sounds, ideas, etc.; a disturbance.—The barking dog put the barnyard in a *turmoil.*

turn (TERN) *n. turns:* 1. A chance; an opportunity; a time.—We took *turns* batting.—The children formed a line, and each waited his *turn* to get a drink.
2. A deed; an act.—If you will help me now, sometime I will do you a good *turn.*
3. A sudden change.—Bill's behavior takes a *turn* for the better just before Christmas.
4. A complete circular movement.—If you give the clock stem too many *turns* when winding it, it will break.—Father unlocks his safe with two *turns* to the right, and three to the left.
—*v. turns, turned, turning.* 1. Change direction; go a different way.—We were driving west. Then we *turned* a corner and drove south.—Bob *turned* when I called to him.
2. Move in a circle.—The hands of the clock *turn.*—A top *turns.*
3. Change; become.—Ice *turns* to liquid when it gets warm.
4. Transform; change.—The witch *turned* the little girl into a toad in the fairy story.—Caterpillars *turn* into butterflies.
5. Upset.—The sight of a mouse *turns* Mother's stomach.

tur·nip (TER-nəp) *n. turnips.* A kind of plant with a root that is often eaten; the root of this plant.—*Turnips* are sometimes cooked as table vegetables, and sometimes they are eaten raw.

turn·stile (TERN-styl) *n. turnstiles.* A turning gate with crossed bars at the top. Some *turnstiles* register the number of persons passing through. –When going from the depot to the train, we passed through a *turnstile.*–We put our fare in a slot in a subway *turnstile* before we pass through.

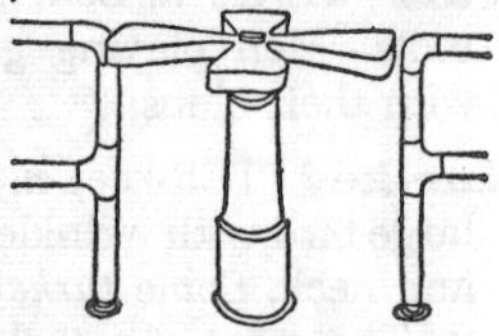

tur·pen·tine (TER-pən-tyn) *n.* An oily substance that comes from trees that have cones. –Father thinned the paint with *turpentine.* –*Turpentine* is sometimes used in medicine.

tur·quoise (TER-koiz *or* -kwoiz) *n. turquoises* and *adj.* 1. A greenish-blue stone.–Hannah's pretty new ring is set with a *turquoise.*
2. Greenish-blue.–Mother has a *turquoise* silk dress.

tur·tle (TER-tl) *n. turtles.* An animal with a hard shell over its back. *Turtles* live both in the water and on the land.

tusk (TUSK) *n. tusks.* A long, pointed tooth. – Elephants have a *tusk* on each side of the head. – Walruses and some other animals also have *tusks.*

tu·tor (TOO- *or* TYOO-ter) *n. tutors.* A teacher who gives private lessons.–The sick boy could not go to school, so he had a *tutor* instruct him at home.
–*v. tutors, tutored, tutoring.* Teach privately. –Father *tutored* the boy in arithmetic.

tux·e·do (tuk-SEE-doh) *n. tuxedos.* A suit worn by men on semi-formal occasions. The coat of a formal suit is long and has tails. The coat of a *tuxedo* is suit length and has no tails.

tweed (TWEED) *n.* A kind of wool cloth with rough threads woven into it.–Father's suit is made of *tweed.*

tweez·ers (TWEE-zerz) *n. pl.* A small implement for pulling, grasping, or picking up objects; a small pinchers.–*Tweezers* are used by jewelers, watchmakers, printers, and doctors.

twelfth (TWELFTH) *n. twelfths.* One of 12 equal parts. If you divide anything into twelve parts all the same size, each part is one *twelfth.* It may be written 1/12.
–*adj.* Coming as number 12 in a series. – Carrie's name was *twelfth* on the list.

TURTLES

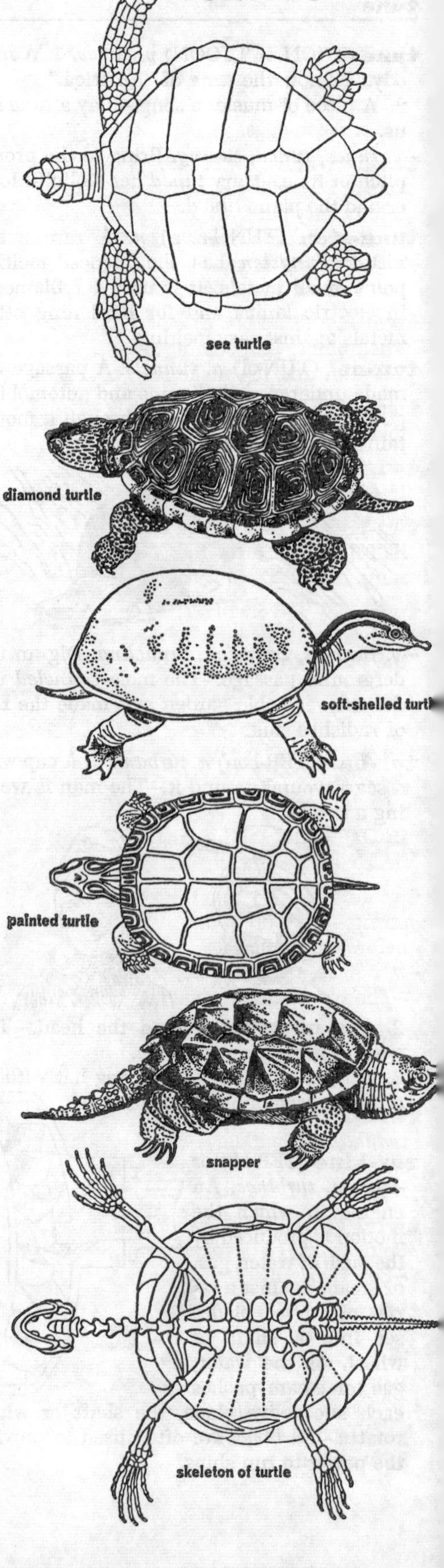

twelve (TWELV) *n. twelves* and *adj.* The number [12] coming after 11 and before 13. –Ten and two make *twelve.*–*Twelve* eggs are a dozen eggs.

twen·ti·eth (TWEN-tee-ith) *n. twentieths.* One of 20 equal parts. If you divide anything into twenty parts all the same size, each part is one *twentieth.* It may be written 1/20.
–*adj.* Coming as number 20 in a series.–Albert's name was *twentieth* on the list.

twen·ty (TWEN-tee) *n. twenties* and *adj.* The number [20] coming after 19 and before 21.–Ten and ten make *twenty.*

twice (TWYSS) *adv.* Two times.–The teacher told us *twice* how to spell the word.

twig (TWIG) *n. twigs.* A tiny branch of a tree.–The sparrow sat on a *twig* of the tree.

twi·light (TWY-lyt) *n. twilights.* Dusk; the half-light just after the sun sets in the evening, or just before it rises in the morning.

twin (TWIN) *n. twins.* 1. One of two children or animals born to the same mother at the same birth. *Twins* often look alike.

2. One of two things that are just alike or nearly alike.–The airplane has *twin* engines.

twine (TWYN) *n. twines.* Heavy cord or string.–We put *twine* around the package before we mailed it.
–*v. twines, twined, twining.* Twist and wind. –The ivy *twines* around the fence.

twinge (TWINJ) *n. twinges.* A sharp, sudden pain.–Jack felt a *twinge* in his leg when he fell down.

twin·kle (TWING-kəl) *v. twinkles, twinkled, twinkling.* Sparkle. – Baby's eyes *twinkle* when she sees something good to eat.–The reflection of the stars *twinkled* in the lake.

twirl (TWERL) *v. twirls, twirled, twirling.* Spin; whirl; go or make go round and round. –Bob *twirls* his key chain when he thinks.

twist (TWIST) *n. twists.* A special thread made by twisting two strands of thread together.–Mother mended the buttonholes in Bob's old coat with *twist.*
–*v. twists, twisted, twisting.* 1. Wind.–The girl stood *twisting* her handkerchief around in her hands.
2. Move restlessly.–The children *twist* and turn in their seats when they are too tired to sit still.
3. Bend around; bend out of shape.–The rim of Bob's bicycle was *twisted* where it had hit the curb.

two (TOO) *n. twos* and *adj.* The number [2] coming after 1 and before 3.–One and one make *two.*

ty·ing (TY-ing) *v.* One form of the verb *tie.* –Baby can't tie her shoe strings, so Mary is *tying* them for her.

type (TYP) *n. types.* 1. A kind; sort.–Children like books of different *types.* Fairy stories are the *type* that Mary likes.
2. Metal blocks with letters on them, used in printing.–Books and papers are printed with *type.*
–*v. types, typed, typing.* Write on a typewriter. –Mother can *type.*

type·write (TYP-ryt) *v. typewrites, typewrote, typewriting.* Write with a typewriter. –Mother *typewrites* all of Father's letters for him.

type·writ·er (TYP-ryt-er) *n. typewriters.* A machine which prints letters and figures by an arrangement of keys which are struck by hand.

ty·phoid fe·ver (TY-foid FEE-ver). An illness caused by a germ usually found in impure water.

ty·phoon (ty-FOON) *n. typhoons.* A very strong or severe whirling windstorm. – The ship was blown ashore by the *typhoon.*

typ·i·cal (TIP-ə-kəl) *adj.; typically, adv.* Showing the regular traits or qualities of a particular type, as: a *typical* teacher, a *typical* day, a *typical* party.–A *typical* student is one who is just about the same in ability and behavior as most other students.

typ·ist (TYP-ist) *n. typists.* A person whose work is writing on a typewriter.–There are many *typists* in the office where Father works.

ty·rant (TY-rənt) *n. tyrants.* 1. A cruel king; an unjust ruler.–The people overthrew the *tyrant* and formed a new government.
2. Any unjust or cruel person with power.– Harry's boss is a *tyrant.* He makes Harry work very hard and pays him very little money.

U u

U, u (YOO) *n. U's, u's.* The twenty-first letter of the alphabet.

ud·der (UD-er) *n. udders.* The large, baggy-looking milk gland from which cows give milk. Some other female animals, such as goats, have *udders,* too.

ug·ly (UG-lee) *adj. uglier, ugliest; ugliness, n.* 1. Not at all pretty; not pleasing to see.—The monster's face was *ugly.*
2. Unpleasant; cross; bad-tempered.—Sometimes Baby is *ugly* when she first wakes up from her nap.
3. Very severe and causing ruin.—A very *ugly* accident happened at the corner of Main and Broadway this morning.

u·ku·le·le (yoo-kə-LAY-lee) *n. ukuleles.* A small musical instrument with four strings, played by picking the strings.

ul·cer (UL-ser) *n. ulcers.* An open sore discharging pus.—A person with stomach *ulcers* must eat very simple foods.

ul·ti·mate (UL-tə-mət) *adj.; ultimately, adv.* 1. Final; last.—Everyone knows that Tom is going to the city, but no one knows where he is going after that. He is keeping his *ultimate* destination a secret.
2. Basic; not capable of further examination or division; elementary.—The *ultimate* necessity of kindness is recognized by all good men.

ul·ti·ma·tum (ul-tə-MAY-təm) *n. ultimatums* or *ultimata.* A last or final proposition; a set of final terms or conditions.—Mother gave Sally her *ultimatum:* finish her homework, or not watch television.

ul·tra·vi·o·let (ul-trə-VY-ə-lit) *adj.* Having to do with the invisible light lying beyond violet in the spectrum.—*Ultraviolet* rays are used in the treatment of various skin diseases, rickets, tuberculosis, and other disorders.

um·brel·la (um-BREL-ə) *n. umbrellas.* A collapsible frame with a cloth covering that is used to keep off the rain or sun.

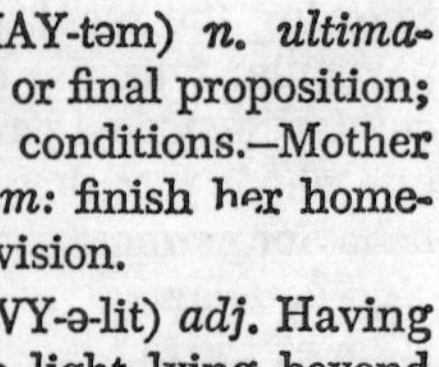

um·pire (UM-pyr) *n. umpires.* A person who decides who is right and who is wrong in games like baseball.

—*v. umpires, umpired, umpiring.* Make decisions as an umpire.—The principal of our school *umpired* our ball game.

un·a·ble (un-AY-bəl) *adj.* Not able; not strong or capable enough.—Mary has been sick and is still *unable* to go to school.

un·ac·count·a·ble (un-ə-KOWN-tə-bəl) *adj.* Not accountable; not responsible; not to be explained; mysterious; without reason. —The man apologized for his dog's *unaccountable* behavior. He said his dog had never growled at anyone before and he didn't know why it was growling now.—An *unaccountable* light was seen in the sky. There didn't seem to be any reason for its sudden appearance.

u·nan·i·mous (yoo-NAN-ə-məss) *adj.; unanimously, adv.* In complete agreement; of a single mind or opinion. — The members were *unanimous* in their choice of a new club location.—The judges handed down a *unanimous* decision. They all agreed that Mary should win the essay contest.

un·a·ware (un-ə-WAIR) *adj.* Not aware; without knowledge. — We were *unaware* of your sickness. We didn't know that you were sick.

un·bal·anced (un-BAL-ənst) *adj.* 1. Not in balance.—The scales are *unbalanced.* They showed my weight as 65 pounds, and I really weigh 72 pounds.
2. Insane; mentally ill.—The poor woman is *unbalanced.*

un·bear·a·ble (un-BAIR-ə-bəl) *adj.* Not bearable; not to be endured or tolerated.—The heat was *unbearable.* It was so great that I couldn't stay in the room.

un•be•liev•a•ble (un-bə-LEEV-ə-bəl) *adj.; unbelievably, adv.* Not to be believed.—The strange tale of witches, monsters, and giants is *unbelievable.* Witches, monsters, and giants don't exist.

un•buck•le (un-BUK-əl) *v. unbuckles, unbuckled, unbuckling.* Undo a buckle; loosen a buckle.—*Unbuckle* your belt.

un•but•ton (un-BUT-n) *v. unbuttons, unbuttoned, unbuttoning.* Loosen or undo the buttons of; remove buttons from their buttonholes.

un•cer•tain (un-SER-tən) *adj.* Not certain; not sure.—I am *uncertain* about my answer. I am not sure it is right.

un•changed (un-CHAYNJD) *adj.* Not changed; remaining the same.—The time for the party is *unchanged.*

un•civ•i•lized (un-SIV-ə-lyzd) *adj.* Not civilized; savage; barbarian.—There still are *uncivilized* people living in parts of the world. Their tools are crude; they have no written language; they have many superstitions.

un•cle (UNG-kəl) *n. uncles.* The brother of one's mother or father, or the husband of one's aunt.—My mother's brother is my *uncle.* —Aunt Sally is my mother's sister; she is married to *Uncle* Joe.

un•clean (un-KLEEN) *adj.* 1. Filthy; dirty. —My shirt was *unclean,* so Mother washed it.
2. Impure; evil.—Boy Scouts are taught to avoid *unclean* thoughts.

un•com•fort•a•ble (un-KUM-fer-tə-bəl) *adj.* Not comfortable; causing or feeling discomfort.—This chair is *uncomfortable.* Bob is *uncomfortable* when he sits in it.

un•com•mon (un-KAHM-ən) *adj.; uncommonly, adv.* Not common; remarkable; unusual; rare.—An eclipse of the sun is *uncommon.* It doesn't happen very often.

un•con•cerned (un-kən-SERND) *adj.; unconcernedly, adv.* Not concerned; not worried; free from care or interest.—Tom was *unconcerned* about the test. He had studied hard and knew he would do well.

un•con•di•tion•al (un-kən-DISH-ən-əl) *adj.; unconditionally, adv.* Without conditions or reservations; absolute.—The general demanded *unconditional* surrender of the enemy.

un•con•scious (un-KAHN-shəss) *adj.* Not conscious; not aware of things about one.—The man was *unconscious* after the accident.

un•con•sti•tu•tion•al (un-kahn-stə-TOO-shən-əl *or* un-kahn-stə-TYOO-shən-əl) *adj.; unconstitutionally, adv.* Not constitutional; not in agreement with, or contrary to, the constitution.—The Supreme Court declared the law *unconstitutional.*

un•cov•er (un-KUV-er) *v. uncovers, uncovered, uncovering.* 1. Take the cover off.—*Uncover* the butter dish, please.
2. Make known; find out.—A big secret was *uncovered.*
3. Take off one's hat. — The boys *uncover* when the flag goes by.

un•der (UN-der) *prep.* The opposite of on or over; beneath; below.—Put your hands on your desk and your feet *under* it.—Miners go *under* the surface of the earth to work.

un•der•brush (UN-der-brush) *n.* Shrubs, small trees, and bushes that grow under larger trees.—The rabbit ran into the *underbrush.*

un•der•clothes (UN-der-klohthz) *n.pl.* Clothes worn next to the body, under other clothes.

un•der•foot (un-der-FUHT) *adj.* and *adv.* Under one's feet; on the ground.—It is often wet and slushy *underfoot* in the winter, especially during a thaw.—Be careful not to fall. It is slippery *underfoot.*

un•der•go (un-der-GOH) *v. undergoes, underwent, undergoing.* 1. Suffer; bear; endure. —The actor *underwent* many hardships before he finally won success and became a television star.
2. Experience; go or pass through.—The big city is constantly *undergoing* changes. Old buildings are being torn down, and new ones are being built.—Aunt Jane entered the hospital to *undergo* an operation.

un•der•ground (un-der-GROWND) *adj.* and *adv.* Under the ground or under the surface of the earth.—Henry's uncle was a coal miner who worked *underground.*

un•der•line (un-der-LYN *or* UN-der-lyn) *v. underlines, underlined, underlining.* Put a line under.—*Underline* the title of the book that you enjoyed most and then *underline* the author's name.

un•der•neath (un-der-NEETH) *prep.* Under; below; beneath.—We found a small snail *underneath* the log.

un·der·pass (UN-der-pass) *n. underpasses.* A place where a road or railroad track goes under another road or railroad track. — We drove through the *underpass* at the same time that a train was going over it.

un·der·rate (un-der-RAYT) *v. underrates, underrated, underrating.* Rate too low; set too low a value on; underestimate.—Never *underrate* the strength of your opponent.

un·der·shirt (UN-der-shert) *n. undershirts.* A shirt worn next to the skin, under one's outer clothing.

un·der·stand (un-der-STAND) *v. understands, understood, understanding.* 1. Get the meaning of. — Mary *understands* the directions for making the box.
2. Know the meaning of. — Father *understands* French.
3. Have heard; have learned that.—I *understand* that you have a new car.

un·der·stand·ing (un-der-STAND-ing) *n. understandings.* 1. An agreement.—Bob and his father have an *understanding* about the work to be done.
2. The ability to know what things mean.—How Mother can do so many things at once is beyond my *understanding.*

un·der·take (un-der-TAYK) *v. undertakes, undertook, undertaking.* Try to do; agree to do.—Mother has so much work to do that she can not *undertake* any more.—Bob *undertook* to find the missing books.

un·der·tak·er (UN-der-tayk-er) *n. undertakers.* A person whose business is getting dead persons ready to be buried and taking charge of funerals.

un·der·tow (UN-der-toh) *n.* 1. An underwater current moving towards the sea.—You shouldn't swim in the ocean when there is a strong *undertow.* It can sweep you out to sea.
2. Any strong current below the surface of an ocean, river, or lake that moves in a different direction from water at the surface.

un·der·wear (UN-der-wair) *n.* Underclothing; clothing worn under one's outer clothes. —Woolen *underwear* helps keep one warm.

un·de·sir·a·ble (un-di-ZYR-ə-bəl) *adj.; undesirably, adv.* Not desirable; objectionable; not to one's liking.—A dirty city is an *undesirable* place to live in.

un·de·ter·mined (un-di-TER-mənd) *adj.* Not settled or decided upon; not fixed.—An *undetermined* number of guests will be invited to the party. The exact number will have to be decided upon later.—The boundary between Mr. Jones' farm and ours is *undetermined.* We don't know the exact point where our farm ends and his begins.

un·do (un-DOO) *v. undoes, undid, undoing.* Loosen; unfasten. — Baby pulled her shoestring into a knot, and Mary tried to *undo* it.

un·done (un-DUN) *adj.* Not accomplished; not finished.—The work was still *undone* at six o'clock.
—*v.* One form of the verb *undo.*—Jack found that Baby had *undone* the knot.

un·dress (un-DRESS) *v. undresses, undressed, undressing.* Take off the clothes. — Mother has to *undress* Baby and bathe her. —*Undress* quickly and go to bed, for it is late.

un·earth (un-ERTH) *v. unearths, unearthed, unearthing.* 1. Dig up from beneath the earth. —The explorers *unearthed* a buried temple.
2. Bring to light; discover; uncover. — The guards have *unearthed* a plot to kill the king.

un·eas·y (un-EE-zee) *adj.; uneasily, adv.* Restless; nervous.—The dog is *uneasy* when his master is away.

un·em·ployed (un-em-PLOID) *adj.* Out of work; without a job.—When times are hard, many people are *unemployed.*

un·e·qual (un-EE-kwəl) *adj.; unequally, adv.* 1. Not equal; not of the same number, size, or value.—A diamond and a piece of glass are *unequal* in value. A diamond has much more value than a piece of glass.
2. Unfair; poorly matched; one-sided.—The tennis match was *unequal* because one of the players had a sore back and couldn't play well.

un·e·ven (un-EE-vən) *adj.; unevenly, adv.; unevenness, n.* 1. Not straight and flat; not level.—The table rocks because the floor is *uneven.*
2. Not the same size.—The pickets in the fence are *uneven.*
3. Odd (of numbers).—The houses are numbered so that the even numbers are on one side of the street and the *uneven* numbers (numbers ending in 1, 3, 5, 7, 9) are on the other side.

un•ex•pect•ed (un-iks-PEK-təd) *adj.; unexpectedly, adv.; unexpectedness, n.* Not looked for; not waited for.–I received an *unexpected* gift from Uncle Jim.

un•fair (un-FAIR) *adj.; unfairly, adv.; unfairness, n.* Not just.–Jack felt it was *unfair* of the teacher to expect him to know the answer to the question when none of the others knew it.

un•faith•ful (un-FAYTH-fuhl) *adj.; unfaithfully, adv.; unfaithfulness, n.* Not true; not loyal.–Do not be *unfaithful* to your old friends. Do not desert them.

un•fa•mil•iar (un-fə-MIL-yer) *adj.* Not known; not seen before.–The man's face is *unfamiliar* to me.

un•fas•ten (un-FASS-ən) *v. unfastens, unfastened, unfastening.* Undo; loosen (as to untie, unlock, unbutton).–Can you *unfasten* this suitcase for me?

un•fa•vor•a•ble (un-FAY-ver-ə-bəl) *adj.; unfavorably, adv.* Not favorable; not to one's advantage; bad.–Bill received an *unfavorable* report card. His conduct and marks were unsatisfactory.–The weather seemed *unfavorable* for a picnic. It looked as if it were going to rain.

un•fin•ished (un-FIN-isht) *adj.* 1. Not all done; not completed.–The model plane is *unfinished;* it hasn't been painted yet.
2. Without paint, varnish, or other finish.–We bought *unfinished* furniture and painted it ourselves.

un•fit (un-FIT) *adj.* Not good; not suitable.–The meat is spoiled and is *unfit* to eat.–Your white dress is *unfit* for traveling on the dusty train.

un•fold (un-FOHLD) *v. unfolds, unfolded, unfolding.* 1. Open the folds of; spread out; open up.–*Unfold* your handkerchief quickly when you feel you may be going to sneeze.
2. Open.–A bud *unfolds* as it becomes a flower.

un•fore•seen (un-for-SEEN) *adj.* Not expected; not looked for. – We shall come if nothing *unforeseen* happens.

un•for•tu•nate (un-FOR-chə-nit) *adj.; unfortunately, adv.* Unlucky; unsuccessful. – The lady is a very *unfortunate* person. She lost her new watch.

un•found•ed (un-FOWND-əd) *adj.* Without foundation; without reason; without basis; groundless.–The rumors are completely *unfounded.* There is no truth in them at all.

un•friend•ly (un-FREND-lee) *adj.* Not liking other people; not wanting to get to know others. – The boy is so shy that he seems *unfriendly.*

un•furl (un-FERL) *v. unfurls, unfurled, unfurling.* Unfold; unroll; spread.–The soldiers stood at attention as the flag was *unfurled.*–The sailors are *unfurling* the sails.

un•grate•ful (un-GRAYT-fuhl) *adj.; ungratefully, adv.; ungratefulness, n.* Not thankful. – The boy is *ungrateful* for the many things you have done for him.

un•hap•py (un-HAP-ee) *adj. unhappier, unhappiest; unhappily, adv.; unhappiness, n.* 1. Without cheer; sad.–Cinderella was *unhappy* because she couldn't go to the ball.
2. Unlucky; unfortunate. – By an *unhappy* chance, Jack had a bad fall the first day he rode his new bicycle.

u•ni•corn (YOO-nə-korn) *n. unicorns.* An imaginary animal that has a single horn in the center of its forehead. The *unicorn* is usually represented as having the head and body of a horse, the tail of a lion, and, at times, the beard of a goat.

u•ni•form (YOO-nə-form) *n. uniforms.* Clothes that are made to show the wearer's occupation or rank, and are exactly like those of other people of the same occupation or rank. – Soldiers, sailors, nurses, policemen, and firemen wear *uniforms.* See page 321.
–*adj; uniformly, adv.* 1. Alike in size, shape, speed or the like.–The telephone poles along the highway are all of *uniform* size.
2. Consistent; even; steady; regular. – The driver drives his car at a *uniform* speed.

u•ni•fy (YOO-nə-fy) *v. unifies, unified, unifying.* Unite; become or make into one; bring together.–After the Civil War, the nation was *unified* once again.

un•in•hab•it•ed (un-in-HAB-ə-təd) *adj.* Not inhabited; not lived in; having no inhabitants.–The old house is *uninhabited.* No one lives in it.

un•ion (YOON-yən) *n. unions.* 1. A joining together of things into one, or the things that have been joined together. – The United States is a *union* of states.
2. A group of workers who are joined together to bring about better working conditions and better wages.

u•nique (yoo-NEEK) *adj.; uniquely, adv.* Standing alone; being without comparison; unmatched; without equal; rare.–This is a *unique* fossil. It is the only one of its kind.

u•nit (YOO-nit) *n. units.* One person or thing, or a group of persons or things considered as one.–We are working on the first *unit* of a number of lessons grouped together to make a course of study.

u•nite (yoo-NYT) *v. unites, united, uniting.* Join together as one.–The children *united* in reciting the poem.

U•nit•ed Na•tions (yoo-NY-təd NAY-shənz). An organization of nations formed in San Francisco in 1945. The *United Nations* has

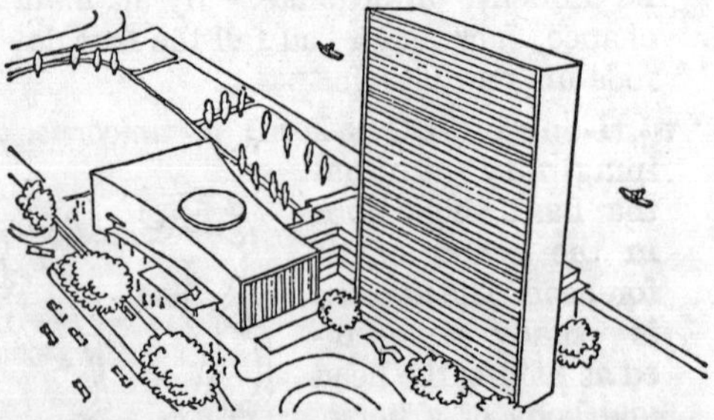

its headquarters in New York City. The members of the *United Nations* have pledged themselves to work for international peace and social progress.

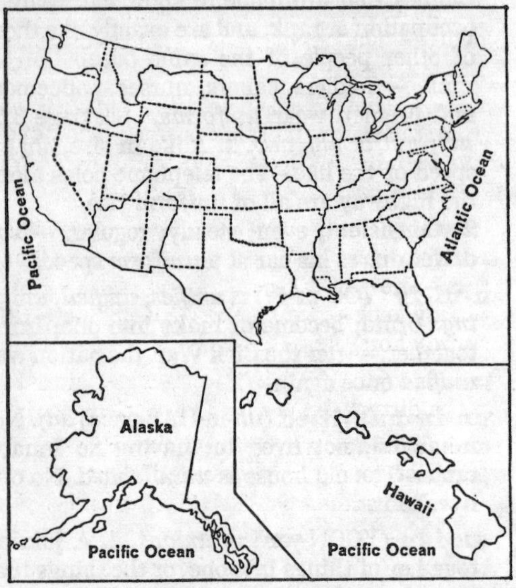

U•nit•ed States (yoo-NY-təd STAYTSS). One of the largest countries in the Western Hemisphere, and the one with the most inhabitants; 193,957,707 people live in the *United States.* It consists of fifty states and the District of Columbia.

u•ni•ty (YOO-nə-tee) *n. unities.* 1. The state of being a single undivided unit; oneness; wholeness.–The United States is proud of its *unity.* Although there are fifty separate states, the country acts as one.
2. Harmony; accord. – The children are playing together in *unity.* They are playing quietly, peacefully, and happily, without argument or disagreement.

u•ni•ver•sal (yoo-nə-VER-səl) *adj.; universally, adv.* 1. Having to do with the universe; present or existing everywhere; to be found anywhere.–Arithmetic is a *universal* school subject. Every school teaches it.
2. Concerning everyone; used or done by all; general.–Eating and sleeping are *universal* needs. Everyone has to eat and sleep.

u•ni•verse (YOO-nə-verss) *n.* 1. The earth, sun, stars, and all other objects in space, considered together.
2. Everything that exists.

u•ni•ver•si•ty (yoo-nə-VER-sə-tee) *n. universities.* A large school made up of several colleges.–Students learn engineering, dentistry, medicine, teaching, law, and many other things at a *university.*

un•just (un-JUST) *adj.; unjustly, adv.* Not fair.–The man is *unjust* with his helpers. He does not pay them enough and he does not treat them well.

un•kind (un-KYND) *adj.; unkindly, adv.; unkindness, n.* Not gentle or considerate; cruel.–The *unkind* boy abused his little dog.

un•known (un-NOHN) *n. unknowns.* A person or thing that is not known; that which is not known.–Bill didn't want to go into the dark room because he was afraid of the *unknown.* But as soon as he turned on the lights, he saw that there was nothing to be afraid of.
–*adj.* Not familiar; not known; strange.–That girl is *unknown* in the neighborhood. She is a stranger.

un•lace (un-LAYSS) *v. unlaces, unlaced, unlacing.* Take out the strings; loosen the laces of.–Baby likes to *unlace* Mother's shoes.

un•less (un-LESS) *conj.* and *prep.* If not.–I can't go *unless* you wait for me.

un•like (un-LYK) *adj.* and *prep.* Not like; different from.–This fruit is *unlike* any I have ever eaten.

un•lim•it•ed (un-LIM-it-əd) *adj.* Not limited; without bounds; not restricted.–Ancient kings and rulers often had *unlimited* power over their subjects.

un•load (un-LOHD) *v. unloads, unloaded, unloading.* Remove the load from. – The farmer *unloaded* his truck.

un•lock (un-LAHK) *v. unlocks, unlocked, unlocking.* Unfasten the lock of.–The key would not *unlock* the door.

un•luck•y (un-LUK-ee) *adj. unluckier, unluckiest.* Unfortunate; having or bringing bad luck.–This is an *unlucky* day for the boy who lost his watch. He was *unlucky.*

un•nat•u•ral (un-NACH-ə-rəl) *adj.; unnaturally, adv.* 1. Not natural; contrary to the normal order of things; not normal; strange. –If a man were to grow wings and fly, it would be most *unnatural.*
2. Very cruel; evil; wicked. – The man trapped under the fallen tree was suffering *unnatural* pain.

un•nec•es•sar•y (un-NESS-ə-sair-ee) *adj.; unnecessarily, adv.* Not needed; useless. – The teacher told her pupils that their noise was *unnecessary.*

un•of•fi•cial (un-ə-FISH-əl) *adj.; unofficially, adv.* Not official; without authority.–The runner set an *unofficial* record in the 100-yard dash. There was no judge present to score his fast time.–The teacher gave the student some *unofficial* advice, not as a teacher, but as a friend.

un•pack (un-PAK) *v. unpacks, unpacked, unpacking.* Take out packed contents.–Mary helped Mother *unpack* the suitcase.–We *unpacked* our lunch and had a picnic.

un•pleas•ant (un-PLEZ-ənt) *adj.* Disagreeable; not pleasant or nice.–When the sun shines, it is a pleasant day. When it rains and is dark, the weather is *unpleasant.*

un•pop•u•lar (un-PAHP-yə-ler) *adj.* Not liked or sought after.–A boy who does not tell the truth is *unpopular.*

un•pre•pared (un-pri-PAIRD) *adj.* Not ready.–The teacher gave us a spelling test, and we were *unprepared* for it.

un•re•al (un-REE-əl) *adj.* Not true; not like actual things. – This is an *unreal* story. Things do not actually happen the way they do in this story.

un•rea•son•a•ble (un-REE-zən-ə-bəl) *adj.* 1. Foolish; not sensible.–The girl was *unreasonable* about spending her money. She paid an *unreasonable* price for the dress.
2. Not fair.–The man is *unreasonable* to his workers; he makes them work too hard and gets angry at them too easily.

un•re•lat•ed (un-ri-LAY-təd) *adj.* 1. Not related; untold.–The man left before he could tell his story. The story, therefore, remained *unrelated.*
2. Without connection; having no relationship.–The two events are completely *unrelated.* They have nothing to do with each other.
3. Not a relative or relation.–Mary is *unrelated* to me. She is not my sister; she is my friend.

un•rest (un-REST) *n.* 1. Lack of rest, peace, or quiet; uneasiness.–His mind is in a state of *unrest.* He is troubled by many problems.
2. Popular disturbance; lack of satisfaction among the people, with the possibility of rebellion.–The heavy taxes caused great *unrest* in the kingdom.

un•roll (un-ROHL) *v. unrolls, unrolled, unrolling.* Roll out or spread out something that has been rolled.–Someone *unrolled* the paper towels.–*Unroll* the ribbon from the spool.

un•rul•y (un-ROO-lee) *adj.* Not easy to rule; hard to control; causing disturbance; lawless.–The police broke up and scattered the *unruly* mob.–The cowboy finally made the *unruly* horse stop kicking.

un•safe (un-SAYF) *adj.* Dangerous; not safe. –The dirty water is *unsafe* for drinking.

un•sat•is•fac•to•ry (un-sat-əss-FAK-tə-ree) *adj.* Not good enough; not sufficient; not up to certain standards.–The teacher said Jack's work was *unsatisfactory.*

un•seen (un-SEEN) *adj.* Not seen; not visible to anyone.–The small child stood *unseen* behind the chair.

un•self•ish (un-SEL-fish) *adj.* Thoughtful; considerate of others; generous.–Selfish people think only of themselves. *Unselfish* people are kind and helpful to others.

un·set·tled (un-SET-əld) *adj.* 1. Upset; not in order.—Father is papering the walls, so our house is *unsettled.*
2. Not inhabited.—The family moved to an *unsettled* part of the country.
3. Uncertain; likely to change.—The weather is *unsettled.*

un·skilled (un-SKILD) *adj.* Without special ability; not trained.—The man wanted the job but he was *unskilled* in that kind of work.

un·stead·y (un-STED-ee) *adj.; unsteadily, adv.; unsteadiness, n.* Shaky; not firm or strong.—The sick man's knees were still a little *unsteady.*

un·think·a·ble (un-THINGK-ə-bəl) *adj.* Not to be thought of or imagined; not even to be dreamt of.—His sudden good fortune was almost *unthinkable.* He had never dreamed of possessing so much money.

un·ti·dy (un-TY-dee) *adj.* Not tidy; not orderly; not neat; sloppy.—Susan is very careful about things. Her room is rarely *untidy.*

un·tie (un-TY) *v. unties, untied, untying.* Unfasten; undo; loosen the knot of.—It is easier to *untie* one's shoestrings than it is to tie them.

un·til (un-TIL) *conj.* 1. Up to (a certain time). —Wait here *until* school is out.
2. Up to (a certain point).—We ate *until* we could eat no more.
—*prep.* 1. Till; to.—We had to wait from noon *until* after four o'clock for the doctor to come.
2. Before.—Bill won't get here *until* noon.

un·u·su·al (un-YOO-zhuh-əl) *adj.; unusually, adv.* Different from most; not ordinary; rare or outstanding.—Mary has *unusual* musical talent.

un·wel·come (un-WEL-kəm) *adj.* Not wanted.—The visitor felt *unwelcome* among so many strangers.

un·will·ing (un-WIL-ing) *adj.; unwillingly, adv.; unwillingness, n.* Not willing; not wanting or consenting.—The workman was *unwilling* to work after six o'clock at night.

un·wise (un-WYZ) *adj.; unwisely, adv.* Foolish.—It is *unwise* to eat too much.

un·wor·thy (un-WER-thee) *adj.; unworthily, adv.; unworthiness, n.* 1. Not deserving. —The bad boy is *unworthy* of your kindness.
2. Bad; not deserving praise.—Some of the early settlers had *unworthy* aims. They wanted to take land belonging to the Indians.
3. Not as good as one would expect; not fitting.—The mayor has done nothing *unworthy* of his position.

un·wrap (un-RAP) *v. unwraps, unwrapped, unwrapping.* Remove the wrappings from; undo or open (as a package). — Mark *unwrapped* his birthday present. He untied the ribbon, tore off the paper, and opened the box.

up (UP) *adv.* 1. To a higher place.—Bob tried to get his kite farther *up* in the sky.
2. Upright; straight; on one's feet. — We stood *up* to salute the flag.
3. To pieces.—Dynamite was used to blow *up* the rocks on the hill.
4. Over; at an end.—Our playtime is *up.*
5. Out of bed; awake.—The farmer gets *up* early each morning.
6. Tightly.—Close *up* your purse.
7. Out of the ground.—The children pulled the weeds *up.*
8. Above the ground. — The spring flowers will soon be *up.*
9. Higher than the horizon.—The sun is *up* in the daytime.
10. Completely; to the end or final point; until finished.—Eat your food *up!*—The house burned *up.*
11. Into sight or view.—My lost watch has finally turned *up.*
—*prep.* 1. To a higher place.—I went *up* to bed.
2. To or near the top of.—"Jack and Jill went *up* the hill to fetch a pail of water."
3. Along. — Our house is just *up* the road from school.
4. Toward the beginning of. — Albany is farther *up* the Hudson River than New York.
—*Bring up* means to improve, educate, or bring to an advanced state or condition.—Mother wants to *bring* us *up* in a small town.
—*Keep up* means to maintain or keep the same rate of speed or progress as another.—Bill tried to *keep up* with Jim in the race, but he couldn't. He was too slow.
—*Ups and downs* means to have a rise and fall in luck or fortune.—Our school's baseball team has many *ups and downs.* Sometimes it wins, and sometimes it loses.

up·hold (up-HOHLD) *v. upholds, upheld, upholding.* Agree to; back up with agreement. —The teacher *upheld* Jack's statement. She agreed that he was right.

up·hol·ster (up-HOHL-ster) *v. upholsters, upholstered, upholstering.* Make cushions and other padded parts of furniture, and cover them with heavy cloth.—The couch in the living room was *upholstered* in deep blue velvet.
—*upholstery, n.*

up•keep (UP-keep) *n.* 1. The act or process of maintaining in good working order, condition, or state of repair.—The *upkeep* of the farm is not difficult. Very few things need fixing.
2. The cost of keeping things in good working condition; general operating expenses. —Our house is large and comfortable, but the *upkeep* is high. It costs a lot to maintain it.

up•on (ə-PAHN *or* -PAWN) *prep.* On; on the top of.—Put the cup *upon* the table.

up•per (UP-er) *adj.* Higher; top.—The *upper* part of anything is the higher part. – The *upper* shelves of a cupboard are the ones near the top.

up•right (UP-ryt) *adj.* 1. Straight up and down; standing.—Two of the telephone poles were blown down in the storm, but the others were *upright*.—Baby can sit *upright* in her crib.

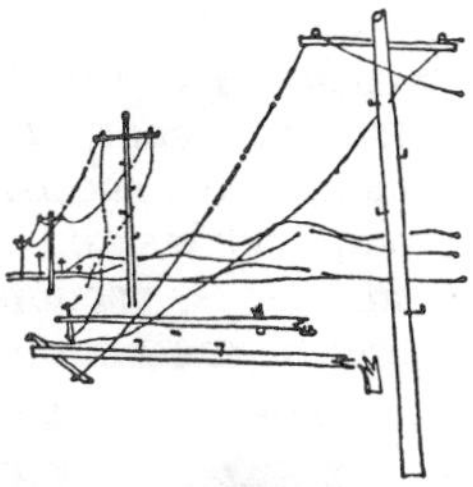

2. Honest.—The mayor is an *upright* man.

up•ris•ing (UP-ry-zing *or* up-RY-zing) *n. uprisings.* A rising up or revolt; a rebellion. – Troops were called to put down the *uprising.*

up•roar (UP-ror) *n. uproars.* A loud shouting; a noise or disturbance.—When the boy got a home run, an *uproar* rose from the crowd.

up•set (up-SET) *v. upsets, upset, upsetting.* Turn over; tip over.—The cat *upset* the can of fish so she could eat them.
—*adj.* Disturbed; worried.—Father was *upset* when Bob got home late from school.

up•side down (UP-syd DOWN). 1. With the upper part or the top side down.—Turn the clean glasses *upside down* on the shelves.

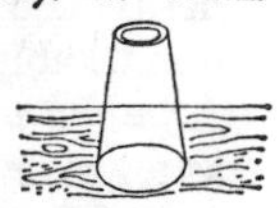

2. Topsy-turvy.—The boys, in searching for the lost key, turned the room *upside down.* They upset everything.

up•stairs (up-STAIRZ) *adv.* 1. On a floor above the first floor.—We cook and eat downstairs. We sleep *upstairs.*
2. Up the stairs; up a flight of stairs.—We go *upstairs* to our bedroom.

up•stream (up-STREEM) *adv.* In the direction from which the water in a stream or river is coming or flowing.—It is hard to row a boat *upstream.*

up-to-date (UP-tə-DAYT) *adj.* In the latest style or fashion.—Mary's suit is *up-to-date.*

up•ward or **up•wards** (UP-werd *or* -werdz) *adv.* To a higher place; away from the ground. – The elevator shot *upward.* – The smoke floated *upward.*

u•ra•ni•um (yuh-RAY-nee-əm) *n.* A hard, heavy, radioactive, metallic element. *Uranium* is found in pitchblende, a black lustrous mineral, and in several other minerals. In certain forms, it is used in making atomic bombs.

U•ra•nus (YUHR-ə-nəss) *n.* 1. In ancient Greek mythology, the imaginary person representing Heaven. *Uranus* was supposed to be the ruler of the world. He is shown in works of art as a bearded old man holding a robe above his head.
2. The seventh planet from the sun. It is the third largest planet and has five moons. *Uranus* takes eighty-four Earth years to complete its journey around the sun.

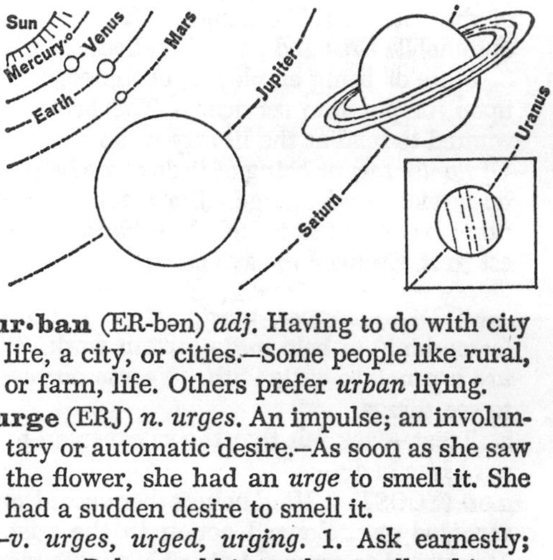

ur•ban (ER-bən) *adj.* Having to do with city life, a city, or cities.—Some people like rural, or farm, life. Others prefer *urban* living.

urge (ERJ) *n. urges.* An impulse; an involuntary or automatic desire.—As soon as she saw the flower, she had an *urge* to smell it. She had a sudden desire to smell it.
—*v. urges, urged, urging.* 1. Ask earnestly; coax.—Bob *urged* his mother to allow him to play football for the school team.
2. Drive; force.—The angry driver *urged* his horse to go faster by using a whip.

ur•gent (ER-jənt) *adj.; urgently, adv.; urgency, n.* Requiring immediate attention; pressing.—This is an *urgent* matter. It must be dealt with at once.

u•rine (YUHR-in) *n.* A watery fluid given off by the kidneys and stored in the bladder of the body. Later it is released from the body.

urn (ERN) *n. urns.* A kind of vessel, usually set on a base.—We have an *urn* for flowers.

us (USS) *pron.* The others and me.—This is our dog. Grandfather gave him to *us.*—Give *us* some books to read.

us·a·ble (YOO-zə-bəl) *adj.* In a condition to be used; fit for use.–Although the handle is broken, the coffee pot is still *usable.*

us·age (YOO-sij) *n.* 1. The way something has been used, said, or done over a long period; usual manner or custom; habit. – A dictionary is a record of language *usage.* It shows how words are used.
2. Handling; treatment.–The packages received rough *usage* before their delivery.

use (YOOSS) *n. uses.* 1. Getting help or work from.–Bob thanked Mary for the *use* of her pen.
2. A need.–We have no *use* for broken baseball bats.
3. A point; a value.–There is no *use* coaxing Father to let you go.
4. A way in which a thing is used or employed.–The teacher asked us to name some of the *uses* of rubber, and Jack mentioned automobile tires and heels for shoes.
5. State of being employed, occupied, acted upon, or put into service. – The book Jim wanted to read at the library was in *use.*
–*Of no use* means being of little or no help; of no service or advantage.–Jim's stamp collection was *of no use* to Bob. Bob had no interest in it. He liked to save coins.

use (YOOZ) *v. uses, used, using.* 1. Cause (something) to help to do certain work.–We *use* a pencil to write with.–We *use* our eyes to see things.
2. Treat.–Jack felt that the salesperson had *used* him badly.

used (YOOST) *v. Used* helps other verbs show repeated or prolonged action in the past.– Mary *used* to wear a hair ribbon. She wore a hair ribbon for many years but she does not any more.
–*adj.* Accustomed.–Grandfather is *used* to getting up early.

use·ful (YOOSS-fuhl) *adj.; usefully, adv.; usefulness, n.* 1. Helpful; of value or service. –The child makes himself *useful* around the house.
2. Of some use or help.–A watch is a *useful* gift, one that can be used by its owner.

ush·er (USH-er) *n. ushers.* A person who shows one to one's seat in a church, in a theater, at a ball game, etc.
–*v. ushers, ushered, ushering.* To lead or bring one to a place. – Mary *ushered* the guests into the living room.

u·su·al (YOO-zhuh-əl) *adj.; usually, adv.* Ordinary; accustomed; same.–We go to school this year at the *usual* time.–We met at the *usual* place.

U·tah (YOO-taw *or* -tah) *n.* A mountainous state in western United States, with rich fruit- and vegetable-growing valleys. Over half the land is usable only for pasturage. Many minerals, especially copper and silver, come from *Utah.* Great Salt Lake, which has water five times as salty as ocean water, is in *Utah.*

u·ten·sil (yoo-TEN-səl) *n. utensils.* A tool, an instrument, or anything that is used in doing some special kind of work.–Pots and pans, skillets and strainers are kitchen *utensils.* Mops, vacuum cleaners, brushes, and brooms are household *utensils.*

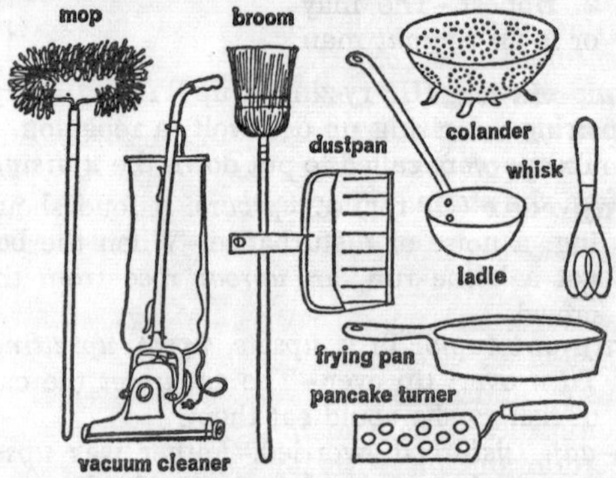

u·til·i·ty (yoo-TIL-ə-tee) *n. utilities.* Usefulness.–The *utility* of a safety pin is quite remarkable.
–A *public utility* is a business company, such as a gas or electric company, which performs a useful public service.
–A *utility room* is a room in which such things as mops and ironing boards are kept or stored.

ut·most (UT-mohst) *adj.* 1. Most distant; farthest.–Pluto is the *utmost* known planet in our solar system.
2. Of the highest sort, degree, quality; extreme; greatest.–The President accepted his adviser's resignation with the *utmost* regret.

ut·ter (UT-er) *v. utters, uttered, uttering.* Speak; say.–No one *uttered* a word.
–*adj.; utterly, adv.* Complete.–The bombed city is in *utter* ruin.

V v

V, v (VEE) *n. V's, v's.* The twenty-second letter of the alphabet.

va•can•cy (VAY-kən-see) *n. vacancies.* 1. An empty space; an empty office, house, or apartment.–The sign on the apartment building said that there were no *vacancies.*
2. An open job; a position waiting to be filled.–When Bob quit his job to go to school, he left a *vacancy* to be filled by someone else.

va•cant (VAY-kənt) *adj.* Empty; not occupied.–The lot next door is *vacant.* There is nothing built on it.

va•ca•tion (vay-KAY-shən) *n. vacations.* A period of time away from school, work, or one's usual occupation to do as one chooses, to have fun or to rest.–Our summer *vacation* lasts three months.

vac•ci•nate (VAK-sə-nayt) *v. vaccinates, vaccinated, vaccinating.* Inoculate a person with a vaccine to make him safe from smallpox or some other particular disease for a number of years.–Mary was *vaccinated* before she started going to school.

vac•cine (VAK-sin *or* vak-SEEN) *n. vaccines.* A specially-made fluid containing disease germs, usually dead ones. When *vaccine* is injected into a person, the body produces antibodies to fight the germs. These antibodies remain in the bloodstream for a certain amount of time and protect the person against the disease should he come in contact with it.

vac•u•um (VAK-yuh-əm) *n. vacuums.* A space that is completely empty, even of air, such as the space inside a radio tube.

va•grant (VAY-grənt) *n. vagrants.* A tramp; a penniless wanderer.–A *vagrant* knocked at our door and asked Mother for some food.
–*adj.; vagrantly, adv.* Having no set course or direction; moving about aimlessly; wandering. – The *vagrant* suggestions that Tim made showed that he did not have any well-thought-out plan for the picnic. He just had a few general ideas.

vague (VAYG) *adj.; vaguely, adv.* Not clear; indefinite; hazy.–The *vague* outline of a ship could be seen in the fog.–Father's vacation plans are still *vague.*

vain (VAYN) *adj.* 1. Proud.–The girl is *vain.* She thinks she is beautiful and likes to look at herself in the mirror.
2. Worthless; useless.–Jack made a *vain* attempt to catch the ball, but it was far over his head.
–*In vain* means without success.–Jack's efforts to catch the ball were *in vain.* He couldn't reach it.

vale (VAYL) *n. vales.* A valley; low land between hills or mountains.

val•en•tine (VAL-ən-tyn) *n. valentines.* A card or other token of love or friendship sent on St. Valentine's Day, February 14.

val•et (VAL-it *or* val-AY) *n. valets.* A man servant who takes care of his master's clothes, aids him in dressing, and so on.–The prince's *valet* helped him prepare for the ball.

val•iant (VAL-yənt) *adj.* Brave.–The *valiant* fireman went into the burning building to save the child.

val•id (VAL-id) *adj.; validity, n.* 1. Backed by facts, knowledge, authority.–Bill's opinion is not *valid.* He does not know the facts. He is only guessing.
2. Legal.–The contract was not *valid* until Father signed it.
3. Based on a good reason. – Bill told his teacher that he was absent from school because he had been sick. The teacher said that it was a *valid* excuse.

va•lise (və-LEESS) *n. valises.* A traveling bag; a suitcase.–Grandmother packed her *valise* to come to the city.

val•ley (VAL-ee) *n. valleys.* Low land between two hills or mountains. – We went down the hill into the *valley.*

val•or (VAL-er) *n.* Great courage.–The sailor received a medal for *valor* for saving his shipmates from drowning. – The fire chief said that Tom's *valor* in rescuing the baby deserved great praise.

val•u•a•ble (VAL-yə-bəl) *n. valuables.* Things of special worth.–The woman keeps her *valuables* locked in a safe.
–*adj.* 1. Worth much money.–A mink coat is *valuable.*
2. Of great worth or necessity.–These papers are *valuable* to the owner although they are worthless to the man who found them.

val•u•a•tion (val-yoo-AY-shən) *n. valuations.* The amount of money a thing is declared to be worth.–The farmer's *valuation* of his farm was eight thousand dollars.

val•ue (VAL-yoo) *n. values.* 1. Worth in money; price.–The *value* of the house is ten thousand dollars; but the owner must sell it quickly, so he will take eight thousand.
2. Worth.–Bob's friendship is of great *value* to Jack.
–*v. values, valued, valuing.* Appreciate; attach worth or value to.–Jack *values* Bob's friendship.

valve (VALV) *n. valves.* A device which controls the pressure or flow of air, gas, water, or other fluid. Some *valves* are operated by pressure within and some are operated by hand.–Water faucets are *valves.*

van (VAN) *n. vans.* 1. A covered truck usually used for carrying furniture.–It took a large *van* to move all the furniture the family had.

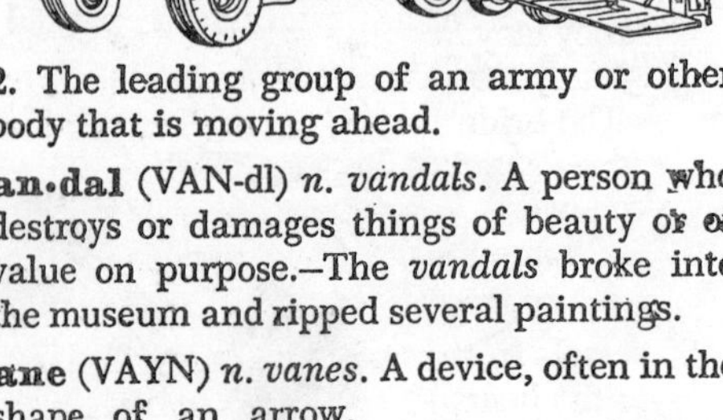

2. The leading group of an army or other body that is moving ahead.

van•dal (VAN-dl) *n. vandals.* A person who destroys or damages things of beauty or of value on purpose.–The *vandals* broke into the museum and ripped several paintings.

vane (VAYN) *n. vanes.* A device, often in the shape of an arrow, which shows the direction the wind is blowing.

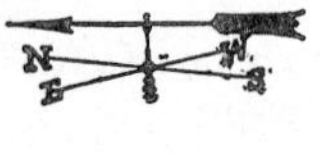

va•nil•la (və-NIL-ə) *n.* and *adj.* A flavoring extract made from the beans of the *vanilla* plant, which grows in warm places. – Mother flavored the candy with *vanilla.*

van•ish (VAN-ish) *v. vanishes, vanished, vanishing.* 1. Suddenly disappear.–The dog ran past us and *vanished* into the woods.
2. Disappear completely.–Mary learned to swim and her fear of the water *vanished.*

va•por (VAY-per) *n. vapors.* Moisture that can be seen.–Fog, mist, and steam are *vapors.*

var•ied (VAIR-eed) *adj.* Of different kinds.–Bob's collection of shells is *varied.* He has many kinds of shells.
–*v.* One form of the verb *vary.* – The sick child's condition hasn't *varied* during the night. His condition has not changed.

va•ri•e•ty (və-RY-ə-tee) *n. varieties.* 1. A wide selection of many different kinds.
2. A kind; a type.–The store has a new *variety* of cabbage for sale.

var•i•ous (VAIR-ee-əss) *adj.* 1. Several; different.–People from *various* countries took part in the program.
2. Varied; of different kinds. – There were *various* styles of dresses in the window.

var•si•ty (VAHR-sə-tee) *n. varsities.* An athletic team representing a university, college, school, etc., in any sport. The *varsity* is usually the first-string squad.

var•y (VAIR-ee) *v. varies, varied, varying.* 1. Change; make or become different.–The direction of the wind *varies* often.–The boy *varies* his handwriting so we won't know whose it is.
2. Be different. – The houses on this street *vary* in size, style, and color.

vase (VAYSS) *n. vases.* A vessel to put flowers in or to set on a table or mantel just for its beauty.

vast (VAST) *adj.; vastly, adv.; vastness, n.* Very large or great, especially covering much space.–A *vast* forest covers the mountains.

vat (VAT) *n. vats.* A tub, a barrel, or other large container for holding liquids.–The grocer keeps a *vat* of vinegar and a *vat* of pickles down in the cellar of his store.

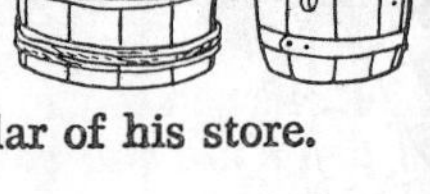

Vat·i·can (VAT-ə-kən) *n.* 1. The palace of the Pope, head of the Roman Catholic Church. The *Vatican* includes a library, several museums, art galleries, and chapels, as well as St. Peter's Basilica and the living quarters of the Pope and his assistants. The *Vatican* is in Vatican City, a section of Rome.
2. The papal power; the authority of the Pope.—The *Vatican* has declared that all men should work toward peace and brotherhood.

vaude·ville (VOHD-vil *or* VAW-də-vil) *n.* A theatrical entertainment or variety show. *Vaudeville* usually features acts or performances that include comedy, songs, dances, and acrobatics.

vault (VAWLT) *n. vaults.* 1. A small room, usually of stone, for keeping the dead.
2. A strong room where things are safe and protected.

veal (VEEL) *n.* Calf meat.—*Veal* is often used for stew.

veg·e·ta·ble (VEJ-tə-bəl) *n. vegetables.* A plant that has parts which are used for food. —Spinach is a leafy *vegetable.* We eat the leaves.—Beans and peas are *vegetables.* We eat their pods or their seeds.—Carrots and beets are *vegetables.* We eat their roots.

veg·e·tar·i·an (vej-ə-TAIR-ee-ən) *n. vegetarians.* Someone who eats only vegetables or vegetable products; someone who does not eat meat. *Vegetarians* believe that human beings should not eat meat.

veg·e·ta·tion (vej-ə-TAY-shən) *n.* Plants, trees, and other growing things.—Where the soil is poor, there is little *vegetation.*

ve·hi·cle (VEE-ə-kəl) *n. vehicles.* A car, truck, bus, wagon, sleigh, or other means used for carrying persons and goods from place to place. *Vehicles* run on wheels or runners.

veil (VAYL) *n. veils.* A piece of very thin or fancy lacy material that you can see through. —Many hats have *veils* on them for trimming. —The bride's *veil* was very long and trailing. —*v. veils, veiled, veiling.* Cover or hide; put a veil over.—In some countries it is the custom for women to *veil* their faces in public.

vein (VAYN) *n. veins.* 1. One of the blood vessels in the body that carry the blood back to the heart.—Look at the under part of your wrist and you can see some of your *veins.*
2. Any line, crack, ridge, or long thin marking, as the *veins* in marble and in leaves, or a *vein* of mineral deposit in a rock.

ve·loc·i·ty (və-LAHSS-ə-tee) *n. velocities.* Speed, or how fast a thing travels.—The weather report says that the *velocity* of the wind today is twelve miles per hour.

vel·vet (VEL-vət) *n. velvets; velvety, adj.* A very soft cloth of silk, rayon, or cotton, with a thick, short nap.—*Velvet* dresses are beautiful.—Baby's skin is as soft as *velvet.*

ven·dor (VEN-der) *n. vendors.* A peddler; a man who sells things from a cart, wagon, or truck.—We bought a bag of peanuts from a peanut *vendor.*

ve·neer (və-NIR) *n. veneers.* 1. A thin layer of good wood laid over a cheaper wood.—This table has a walnut *veneer.*
2. Surface polish.—The boy had only a *veneer* of good manners. The boy behaved well at times, but if he forgot himself he was apt to be rude.

ven·er·ate (VEN-ə-rayt) *v. venerates, venerated, venerating.* Regard with reverence, admiration, or respect; hold in awe; worship.—The students *venerate* their old professor.—Many ancient peoples *venerated* idols.

venge·ance (VEN-jənss) *n.; vengeful, adj.* Punishment in return for injury; revenge.—The natives sought *vengeance* for the killing of their chief.
—*With a vengeance* means with unusual force, violence, or energy.—The hurricane winds were blowing *with a vengeance.*

ven·i·son (VEN-ə-zən) *n.* Deer meat. *Venison* tastes much like beefsteak, but it tastes stronger.—Robin Hood and his Merry Men ate *venison.*

ven·om (VEN-əm) *n.; venomous, adj.* 1. The poison of an animal such as a snake, scorpion, or spider.—Venomous animals inject their *venom* into their enemies by biting or stinging.
2. Spite; envy; general unfriendliness or ill will.—The jealous woman showed her *venom* by her cruel remarks.

vent (VENT) *n. vents.* An opening for letting something out.—Open the chimney *vent* or the room will fill up with smoke.
—*v. vents, vented, venting.* Give free expression to; discharge; let out.—The enraged man *vented* his anger by slamming the door.

ven·ti·late (VEN-tə-layt) *v. ventilates, ventilated, ventilating.* To change the air in an enclosed place by forcing the old, stale air out and letting fresh air in.—At home we *ventilate* the house by opening windows.—At school the rooms are *ventilated* by air pipes.

ven·tri·cle (VEN-trə-kəl) *n. ventricles.* Either of the two lower chambers of the heart. The right *ventricle* pumps used blood to the lungs to pick up a fresh supply of oxygen. The left *ventricle* pumps fresh blood to the arteries that supply the rest of the body.

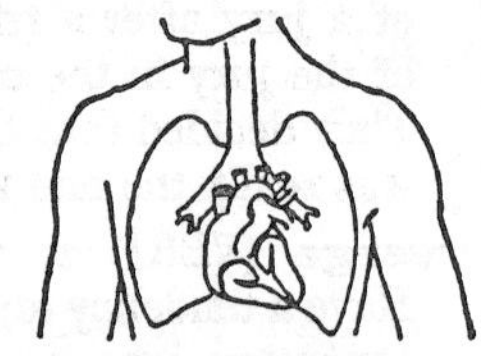

ven·tril·o·quist (ven-TRIL-ə-kwist) *n. ventriloquists.* A person who can speak so that his voice seems to be coming from some other person, animal, or thing.—The *ventriloquist* entertained the audience by carrying on a mock conversation with his wooden dummy.

ven·ture (VEN-cher) *n. ventures.* Something one sets out to do in which there is a danger of injury or loss.—Father's new business *venture* has been a success.
—*v. ventures, ventured, venturing.* 1. Dare; take a chance.—Jack *ventured* to say what he thought about the plan.—Mary did not *venture* a second request for spending money after Father said no.
2. Risk; put in danger.—The fireman *ventured* his life to save Joe from the burning house.

Ve·nus (VEE-nəss) *n.* 1. The ancient Roman goddess of spring, gardens, beauty, and love.
2. The second planet from the sun. *Venus* is the most brilliant of all the planets. At times it can be seen with the naked eye in the middle of the day.

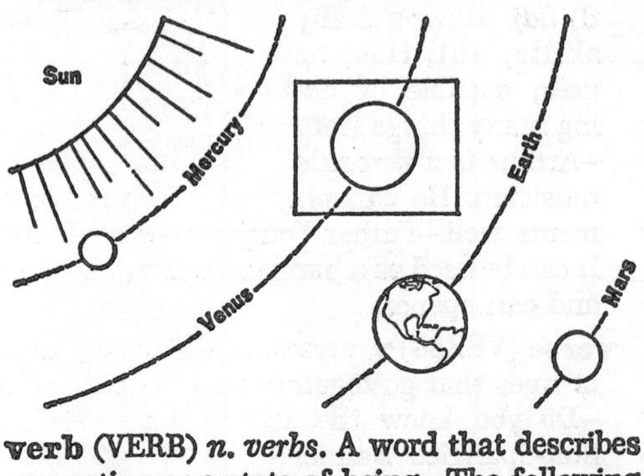

verb (VERB) *n. verbs.* A word that describes an action or a state of being.—The following words are *verbs:* sing, hear, do, ate, is, was.

ver·bal (VER-bəl) *adj.* 1. Dealing with words; in words.—The teacher asked for a *verbal* illustration. She did not want any pictures.
2. Expressed by word of mouth; spoken; oral.—He received *verbal* instructions. He was told what to do.

ver•dict (VER-dikt) *n. verdicts.* The decision of a jury after a trial in court.—The *verdict* of the jury in the murder case was "guilty." They decided that the man who was on trial was really the one who had done the killing.

verge (VERJ) *v. verges, verged, verging.* Have a tendency to; be on the border of.—The confusion was so great that the meeting *verged* on riot.
—*On the verge of* means on the edge of, or at the point after which something else will happen. — Mary was *on the verge of* tears after she found that her new dress was dirty.

ver•i•fy (VAIR-ə-fy) *v. verifies, verified, verifying.* Prove to be true; check the accuracy of.—Bill told his teacher that Tom had started the fight. Tom said Bill had started it. Tom's account was *verified* by two witnesses. Bill had lied.—Please *verify* the spelling of this word. Check to see whether it is spelled correctly.

ver•min (VER-mən) *n. sing.* and *pl.* Insect pests or other small animals that annoy, disgust, or bother people.—Flies, bugs, lice, mice, and rats are all *vermin.*

Ver•mont (ver-MAHNT) *n.* A dairying and vacation state in northeastern United States, particularly known for producing more maple sugar and maple syrup than any other state.

ver•sa•tile (VER-sə-tl) *adj.* Having many skills, abilities, or uses; capable of doing many things well.—Arthur is a *versatile* musician. He can play six different instruments well.—Father bought a *versatile* tool. It can be used as a hammer, screwdriver, file, and can opener.

verse (VERSS) *n. verses.* 1. A stanza; a group of lines that go together in a poem or song.—Do you know the second *verse* of "The Star-Spangled Banner"?
2. Poetry. — Robert Louis Stevenson wrote *verse* for children.

ver•sion (VER-zhən) *n. versions.* 1. A translation, especially of the Bible. — There are several *versions* of the Bible.
2. One side of a story, as related by two or more persons.—Tom's *version* of the argument is different from Bob's.

ver•sus (VER-səss) *prep.* Against (used especially in law and sports). — One of the world's great boxing matches was Joe Louis *versus* Max Schmeling.

ver•te•bra (VER-tə-brə) *n. vertebrae* or *vertebras.* One of the small bones that make up the spine, or backbone.

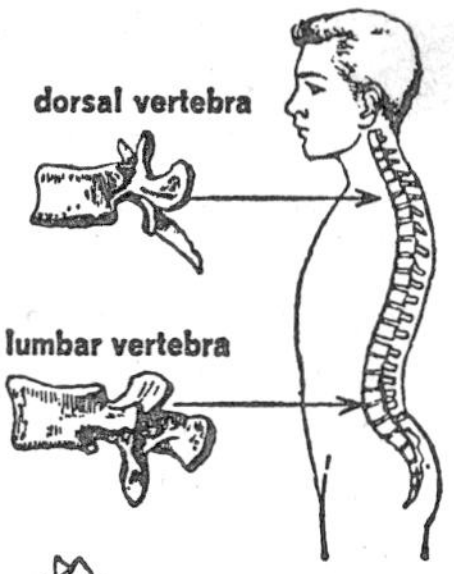

ver•te•brate (VER-tə-brayt *or* -brit) *n. vertebrates.* An animal having a spinal column, or backbone.—Human beings are *vertebrates;* fish, birds, and reptiles are *vertebrates.*

ver•ti•cal (VER-tə-kəl) *adj.; vertically, adv.* Standing straight up and down; not leaning. —The flagpole stands in a *vertical* position.

ver•y (VAIR-ee) *adj.* and *adv.* 1. Extremely; exceedingly.—Mother is *very* kind to us.
2. Same. — The *very* day school started, I came down with the measles.
3. Mere.—The *very* idea of winter makes me shiver.

ves•pers (VESS-perz) *n. pl.* (Sometimes spelled with a capital "V.") Late afternoon or evening prayers; the religious service attending such prayers.—The church bell tolled for *Vespers.*

ves•sel (VESS-əl) *n. vessels.* 1. A pot, bowl, cup, dishpan, or anything that is hollow and will hold liquids or other substances.

2. A ship or boat; any craft that carries people on the water.
3. One of the tubes that carry the blood through one's body.

vest (VEST) *n. vests.* A short, sleeveless garment.—Men sometimes wear *vests* under their suit jackets.

ves•ti•bule (VESS-tə-byool) *n. vestibules.* A hall or passage between the outer door and the inside of a house, apartment, or building.—Mother left her umbrella in the *vestibule.*—There is a candy counter in the *vestibule* of the office building.

vest•ment (VEST-mənt) *n. vestments.* A robe or outer garment, especially one worn by a clergyman.—The bishop put on his *vestments* for the special service.

vet·er·an (VET-er-ən) *n. veterans.* 1. A person who has been in service in the army or the navy.
2. A person who has worked at the same kind of work for a long time.—The old actor is a *veteran* of the stage.

vet·er·i·nar·i·an (vet-rə-NAIR-ee-ən) *n. veterinarians; veterinary, adj.* A doctor who treats the diseases of dogs, cats, horses, cows, and other animals.—When Jack's dog was sick, Jack took him to a *veterinarian.*

ve·to (VEE-toh) *v. vetoes, vetoed, vetoing.* 1. When a President of the United States refuses to sign a congressional bill, he *vetoes* it. A bill which has been *vetoed* by the President can only become a law if two-thirds of the members of both Houses of Congress vote for it.
2. Refuse to approve; not give consent to. —When it started to rain, Mother *vetoed* our plans for a picnic.
3. Vote down.—Any of the five permanent member nations of the United Nations Security Council can *veto* a motion by voting against it. Any negative vote from one of these nations kills a motion.

vex (VEKS) *v. vexes, vexed, vexing.* Make angry; annoy.—The boys' jokes *vexed* their football coach.

vi·a (VY-ə) *prep.* By way of; by a route going through.—The letter was sent *via* air mail.—He went to Mexico *via* Texas. He passed through Texas in order to get to Mexico.

vi·a·duct (VY-ə-dukt) *n. viaducts.* A bridge over a road, a part of a city, a low place, etc. A *viaduct* is built to carry trains, trucks, or automobiles. *Viaducts* improve the safety and speed of transportation.

vi·al (VY-əl) *n. vials.* A small bottle or container, usually of glass. Medicines, chemicals, and perfumes are some of the things kept in *vials.*

vi·brate (VY-brayt) *v. vibrates, vibrated, vibrating.* Shake rapidly; swing or move quickly back and forth.—The strings of musical instruments *vibrate* and give off tones.
—*vibration, n. vibrations.*

vice (VYSS) *n. vices.* An evil or bad habit.—Envy and pride are traditionally considered *vices.*

vice-pres·i·dent (vys-PREZ-ə-dənt) *n. vice-presidents.* The official whose rank is second to or just below that of the president.—The *vice-president* substitutes for the president when necessary, taking over his duties and responsibilities.

vi·ce ver·sa (VY-sə VER-sə). Just the reverse.—Jack likes to play tricks on Mary, and *vice versa.* Mary likes to tease Jack, too.

vi·cin·i·ty (vi-SIN-ə-tee) *n. vicinities.* A neighborhood; a section near or around a place.—Mr. Jones lives in the *vicinity* of the school. He lives near the school.

vi·cious (VISH-əss) *adj.; viciously, adv.; viciousness, n.* Savage; mean; spiteful. — The keeper fed the *vicious* tiger through the bars of his cage. The keeper wouldn't go into the cage for fear of being bitten.

vic·tim (VIK-tim) *n. victims.* A person or animal killed or harmed by a happening.—The *victims* of the hotel fire were removed to a hospital.—Jack the Ripper killed his *victims* with a knife.

vic·tor (VIK-ter) *n. victors.* A winner.—We were the *victors* in the football game.—The *victors* in war are the ones who conquer.

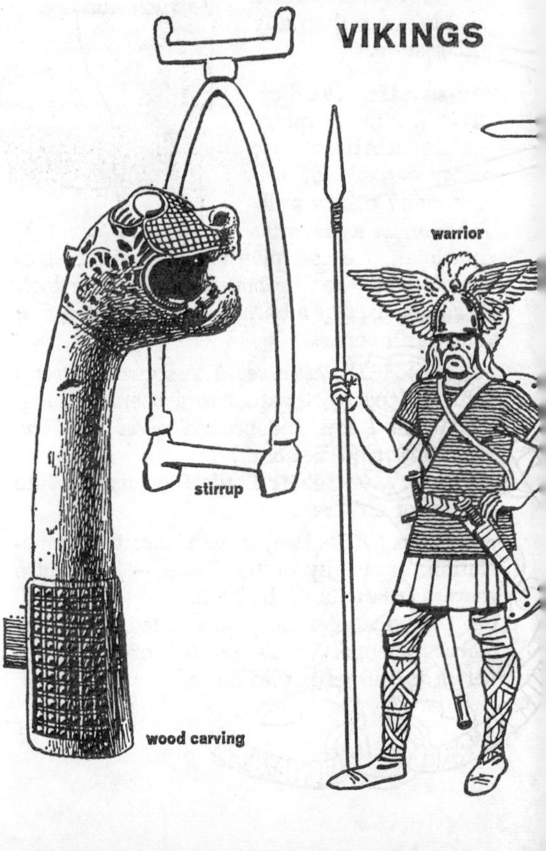

vic•to•ri•ous (vik-TOR-ee-əss) *adj.; victoriously, adv.* Winning; conquering.—Our side was *victorious.* We defeated the other team.

vic•to•ry (VIK-tə-ree) *n. victories.* A success. —Our *victory* in this game made us the champions of the league.

vid•e•o (VID-ee-oh) *adj.* Having to do with television, especially the receiving or sending of an image.—The actors are rehearsing for a *video* performance. They are going to do a television show.

view (VYOO) *n. views.* 1. A scene; that which is seen.—The *view* from the mountaintop was beautiful.
2. A thought; an idea; an opinion.—Father spoke his *views* on the election. — Father asked Mother for her *view* on the color he had chosen to paint the kitchen.
3. Sight.—The airplane soon came into *view.*
—*v. views, viewed, viewing.* 1. Think about; consider.—The doctor *viewed* Mary's illness with alarm. He was worried about it.
2. Look at.—We *viewed* the race from the bridge.

view•point (VYOO-point) *n. viewpoints.* 1. A spot from which a person views something. — He could see the entire valley from his *viewpoint* on top of the mountain.
2. A point of view or attitude; the way a person feels about something.—Your *viewpoint* on certain things may differ from mine, but that does not mean we can't be friends.

vig•il (VIJ-əl) *n. vigils.* 1. The act of staying awake, especially during the hours for sleep; a night watch; a watching at any special time. — The sentry kept a careful *vigil* all through the night.—The doctor's *vigil* was a difficult one. He had to stay awake and give careful attention to his patient all through the night.
2. (Usually plural) An evening church service, especially on the night before a religious festival.—Are you going to take part in the *vigils* on Christmas Eve?

vig•or (VIG-er) *n.* Strength and great energy. —After eating and resting, the man worked with more *vigor.*

vig•or•ous (VIG-er-əss) *adj.; vigorously, adv.* Strong and energetic. — Rest, exercise, and healthful food kept the players *vigorous.*

vi•king (VY-king) *n. vikings.* (Sometimes spelled with a capital "V.") One of the pirates, or sea robbers, who sailed the seas and raided the coasts of Europe during the eighth, ninth, and tenth centuries. The *vikings* came from Scandinavia.

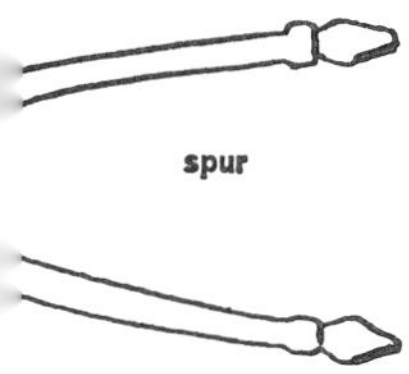
spur

cart

head of bronze pin

inscription on a rune

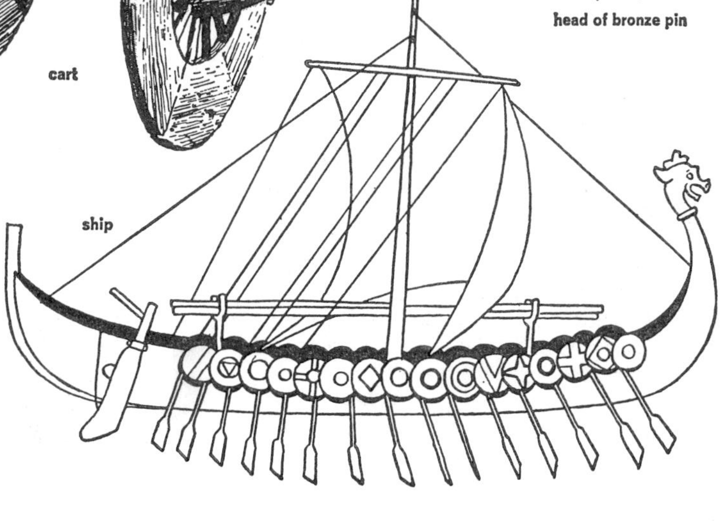
ship

vile (VY-əl) *adj. viler, vilest.* Bad; very bad; wicked.—What a *vile* smell!—He was a *vile* man; nothing seemed to be too evil for him to do or say.

vil•lage (VIL-ij) *n. villages.* 1. A place smaller than a town, where a few people live in dwellings that are close together.
2. The people in a village.—The whole *village* came to put out the fire.

vil•lain (VIL-ən) *n. villains.* A wicked person.—Who took the part of the *villain* in the Western movie you saw?

vine (VYN) *n. vines.* A plant that climbs, or crawls on the ground.—Cucumber *vines* crawl. — Morning-glory *vines* climb.

vin•e•gar (VIN-ə-ger) *n.* A sour liquid used in salads, pickles, etc.—Cider that stands a long time turns into *vinegar.*

vine•yard (VIN-yerd) *n. vineyards.* A place where grapes are grown; a grape plantation. —France is famous all over the world for its fine *vineyards.*

vi•o•la (vee- *or* vy-OH-lə) *n. violas.* A musical instrument that looks like a violin, but is somewhat larger. The *viola* has a deeper, lower tone than the violin.

vi•o•late (VY-ə-layt) *v. violates, violated, violating.* Break (rules or laws).—Children who *violate* the rules of the school may be punished.—Citizens who *violate* the laws of the city may be put into jail.
—*violation, n. violations.*

vi•o•lence (VY-ə-lənss) *n.* Strength; force; roughness.—The storm struck with great *violence;* it hurt many people and did much damage.

vi•o•lent (VY-ə-lənt) *adj.; violently, adv.* Strong; intense; rough. — A *violent* storm lashed the shore and did much damage. — Jack has a *violent* temper.

vi•o•let (VY-ə-lit) *n. violets.* 1. A tiny purple, blue, white, or sometimes yellow flower which blooms in the spring.—We gathered *violets* near the brook.
2. Purplish-blue.

vi•o•lin (vy-ə-LIN) *n. violins.* A musical instrument with strings. The *violin* is played with a bow. It is the highest-pitched stringed instrument.

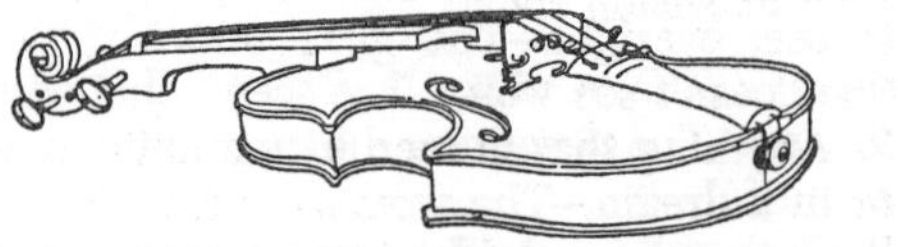

vi•o•lin•ist (vy-ə-LIN-ist) *n. violinists.* A person who plays the violin.

Vir•gin (VER-jin) *n.* Mary, the Mother of Jesus Christ.

vir•gin (VER-jin) *adj.* 1. Pure; spotless.—The hill was covered with *virgin* snow. There were no footprints or marks on it.
2. Not used, touched, or disturbed by man. —The hunter didn't hear or see any sign of another human being in the *virgin* forest.

Vir•gin•ia (ver-JIN-yə) *n.* A forest-covered, mountainous state on the east coast of the United States, important for its farm, dairy,

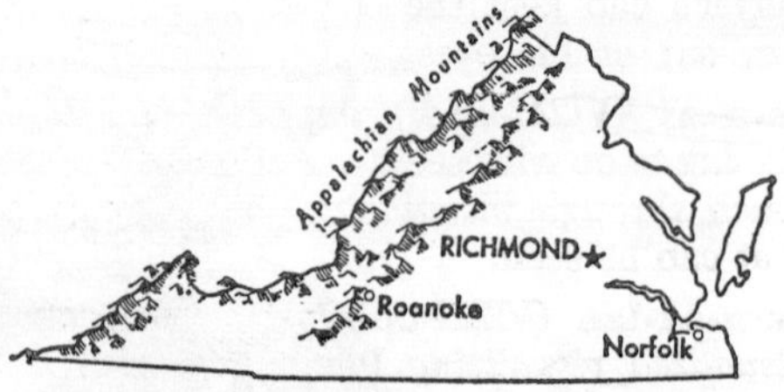

and lumber products, its minerals, and various kinds of building stone. Beautiful natural caverns are found in *Virginia.*

vir•tue (VER-choo) *n. virtues; virtuous, adj.* Goodness; a good quality.—Honesty is a *virtue.* It is a quality one must have to be good.

vi•rus (VY-rəss) *n. viruses.* One of the agents that cause various diseases such as measles, colds, and smallpox. *Viruses* are very tiny and can be seen only with special microscopes.

vise (VYSS) *n. vises.* A clamp used for holding a piece of material while one works on it. It can be opened and closed by means of a screw.—Bob put the wood in the *vise.*

vis·i·bil·i·ty (viz-ə-BIL-ə-tee) *n. visibilities.* 1. Range of vision.—There was so much fog that *visibility* was poor.
2. The clearness with which an object can be seen.—Because of the fog, ground *visibility* was poor. It was hard to see the ground.

vis·i·ble (VIZ-ə-bəl) *adj.* Able to be seen.—The airplane flew so high that it was not *visible* from the ground. It could not be seen from the ground.

vi·sion (VIZH-ən) *n. visions.* 1. The ability to see; eyesight.—The girl's *vision* is poor. She doesn't see well.
2. Anything that is seen in the imagination or in a dream.—The woman had a *vision* of her son, whom she had not seen for years.

vis·it (VIZ-it) *n. visits.* A call; a period of staying as a guest.—We made a short *visit* to our great-grandmother's house.
—*v. visits, visited, visiting.* Go or come to see; be a guest.—Grandma *visited* us. She came to see us and stayed with us awhile. She was our guest.

vis·i·tor (VIZ-it-er) *n. visitors.* A person who comes for a visit; a guest.—Grandmother was a *visitor* at our house.

vi·sor (VY-zer) *n. visors.* The part of a cap that sticks out in front.
—The *visor* on the ball player's cap kept the sun out of his eyes.

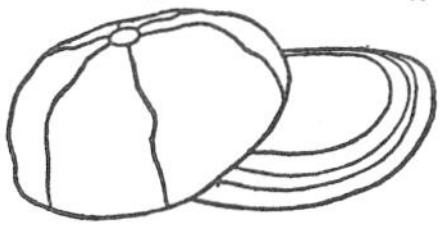

vis·u·al (VIZH-uh-əl) *adj.; visually, adv.* Having to do with seeing or sight.—We learn much through *visual* aids, through things that can be seen.

vis·u·al·ize (VIZH-uh-ə-lyz) *v. visualizes, visualized, visualizing.* Picture in one's mind.
—It is hard to *visualize* something that one has never seen, no matter how well it has been described.

vi·tal (VY-tl) *adj.; vitally, adv.* 1. So important that life depends on it.—Food and rest are *vital* to life.
2. Of great importance.

vi·ta·min (VY-tə-min) *n. vitamins.* Any of certain substances found in foods that are needed to make us well and strong. Different kinds of foods contain different kinds of *vitamins. Vitamins* are named after the letters of the alphabet, as *vitamin* A, B, etc.

vi·va·cious (vy-VAY-shəss) *adj.; vivaciously, adv.* Lively; gay; lighthearted; spirited.—Alice is a *vivacious* girl. She is usually the life of the party.

viv·id (VIV-id) *adj.; vividly, adv.; vividness, n.* 1. Bright; clear.—Mary's dress is a *vivid* blue.
2. Clear; plain.—I have a *vivid* picture in my mind of the hat that I want to buy.

vo·cab·u·lar·y (voh-KAB-yə-lair-ee) *n. vocabularies.* 1. The words that a person knows and uses in writing and speaking.—Our teacher has a large *vocabulary.*—Using a dictionary will help you increase the number of words in your *vocabulary.*
2. A list of words and their meanings, arranged alphabetically, or according to the abc's.

vo·cal (VOH-kəl) *adj.; vocally, adv.* Having to do with the voice; expressed with the voice.
—*Vocal* organs are the parts of the mouth and throat that we use in talking. The tongue, lips, and *vocal* cords are some of the *vocal* organs.

vo·ca·tion (voh-KAY-shən) *n. vocations.* Trade or work; the kind of work one does for a living.—A doctor's *vocation* is curing or healing sick people.—A mechanic's *vocation* is working with machines.—A teacher's *vocation* is teaching.

voice (VOISS) *n. voices.* The sound made by the speech organs (mouth, tongue, throat), as in speaking or singing.—The boy's *voice* was loud and clear. He spoke well.
—*v. voices, voiced, voicing.* Speak; express by saying aloud.—The man *voiced* the reasons he had for voting against the mayor.

void (VOID) *n. voids.* 1. Empty space. — John watched the rocket roar into the *void.* He watched it speed into empty space and disappear from view.
2. A feeling of emptiness due to a loss. — There was a *void* in Tim's life when his dog was lost.
—*v. voids, voided, voiding.* 1. Make something lose its effectiveness. — Our club members voted to *void* the old constitution and pass the new one.
2. Empty; get rid of.—To understand my new idea, you must *void* your mind of all prejudice.
—*adj.* 1. Lacking; empty; being without. — Jim's statement seems to be *void* of meaning. He doesn't seem to have said anything.
—Bill's story was *void* of truth. It didn't have a word of truth in it.
2. Having no legal force. — The Supreme Court declared the law unconstitutional. They declared it *void.*

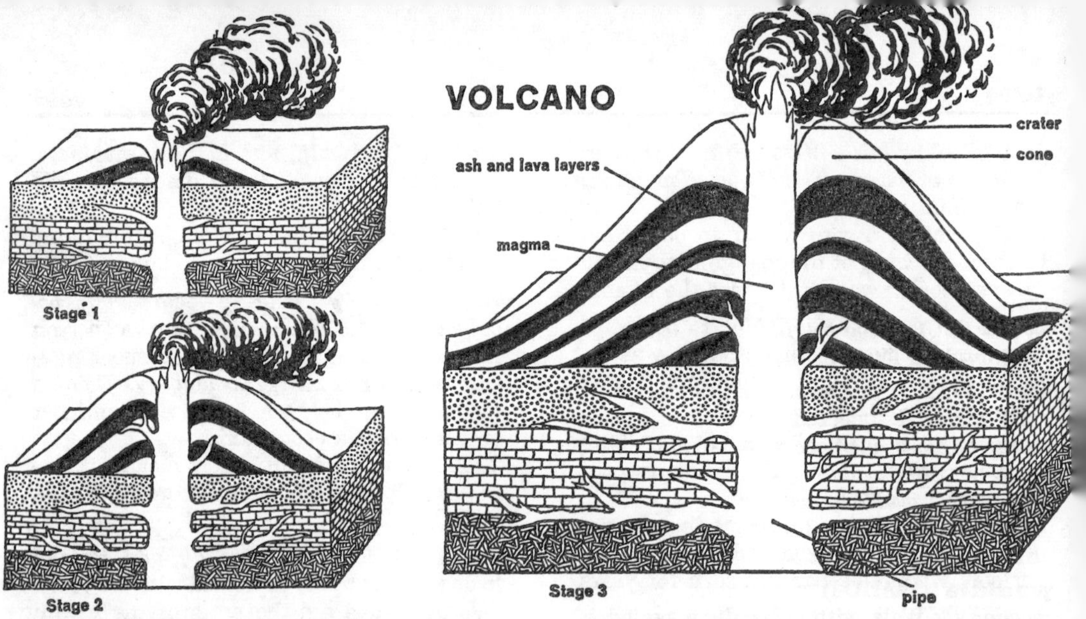

vol·ca·no (vahl-KAY-noh) *n. volcanoes.* A hole in the earth's crust through which lava and gases are thrown out in occasional eruptions. The material thrown out usually builds up into a large cone with a crater in the top.

volt (VOHLT) *n. volts.* A measuring unit that tells you how much force is being used to produce an electric current.

volt·age (VOHL-tij) *n.* Electric power or force, measured in volts.–The radio station has a transmitter of very high *voltage* for broadcasting signals over great distances.

vol·ume (VAHL-yəm) *n. volumes.* 1. A book. –This bookcase holds many *volumes.*
2. One book in a set of books.–Some books are so long that they are printed in several *volumes.*
3. Amount of space occupied; size in cubic inches, feet, etc.–What is the *volume* of this box? How much space does it take up?

vol·un·tar·y (VAHL-ən-tair-ee) *adj.; voluntarily, adv.* Done of one's own choice.–The work Mary did was *voluntary.* No one forced her or asked her to do it. She offered to do it.

vol·un·teer (vahl-ən-TIR) *n. volunteers.* A person who offers to do some task or service. –In small towns the fire department is made up of *volunteers.*
–*v. volunteers, volunteered, volunteering.* Offer to do something; offer one's services without being asked or told to do so.–The man *volunteered* to help put out the fire. – Men *volunteer* to serve as paratroopers.

vote (VOHT) *n. votes.* An expression of one's choice by a method decided on beforehand. Each hand raised or each piece of paper showing what or whom you choose is a *vote.*
–*v. votes, voted, voting.* Express one's choice by a method decided on beforehand, such as raising the hand or writing on a paper called a ballot what you want or whom you choose for an office.–The children who wanted Jack for their captain *voted* for him by raising their hands.

vot·er (VOH-ter) *n. voters.* A person who votes or has the right by law to vote.–Mother and Father are *voters;* their names are registered on a list of people who have the right to vote.

vow (VOW) *n. vows.* A promise.–Mary made a *vow* to study more.
–*v. vows, vowed, vowing.* Make a promise. – Mary *vowed* to Mother and Father that she would study more.

vow·el (VOW-əl) *n. vowels.* The letters a, e, i, o, u, and sometimes y are *vowels.*

voy·age (VOI-ij) *n. voyages.* A trip or journey by sea or over water.–The *voyage* took us across the Atlantic Ocean.
–*v. voyages, voyaged, voyaging.* Travel over water; make a voyage.–We *voyaged* across the Atlantic Ocean.

vul·gar (VUL-ger) *adj.; vulgarly, adv.* Coarse; not nice.–The boy's language is *vulgar.*–*Vulgar* language offends or hurts the feelings of people who have tact and good manners.

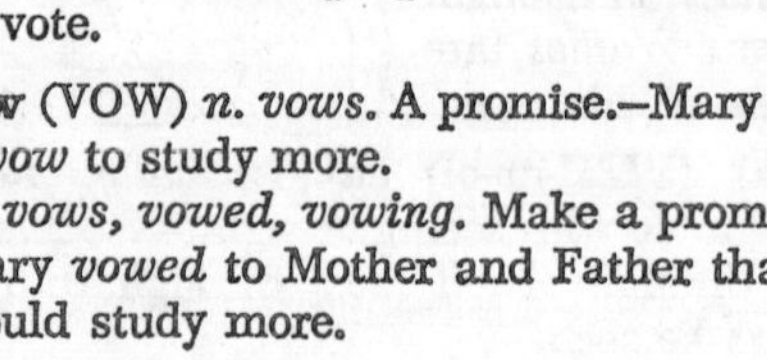

vul·ture (VUL-cher) *n. vultures.* A large bird that feeds on dead animals.

W w

W, w (DUB-əl-yoo *or* -yuh) *n. W's, w's.* The twenty-third letter of the alphabet.

wad (WAHD) *n. wads.* A small amount of any material squeezed together to make a lump or mass, as paper squeezed into a small ball, or paper *wad.*

–*v. wads, wadded, wadding.* Crumple or squeeze into a wad or lump.–The boy *wadded* his paper and put it into the wastebasket.

wad·dle (WAHD-l) *v. waddles, waddled, waddling.* Walk with short steps and swing from side to side.–Ducks *waddle.*

wade (WAYD) *v. wades, waded, wading.* 1. Walk along in water.–Children like to *wade* in the pond.

2. Struggle ahead.–We *waded* through the work in spite of many interruptions.

3. Cross; walk through (a body of water).–The horses *waded* the river.

waf·fle (WAHF-əl) *n. waffles* and *adj.* A cake cooked on a special iron (*waffle* iron) that marks it into small squares. *Waffles* are made of a batter containing eggs, flour, baking powder, and milk.

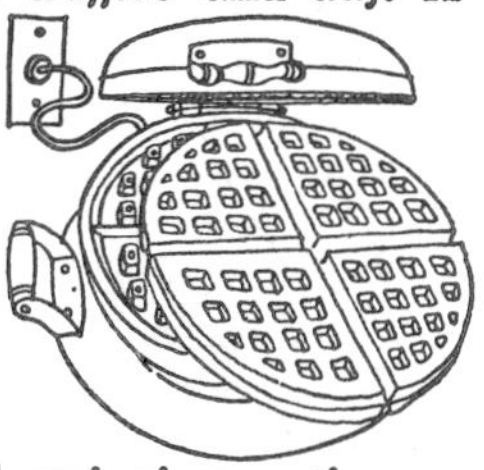

wag (WAG) *n. wags.* A swinging motion. – The dog answered Bob's question with a *wag* of his tail.

–*v. wags, wagged, wagging.* Move or swing from side to side.–The dog *wags* his tail to show that he is happy or friendly.

wage (WAYJ) *n. wages.* Pay; money given for work done, especially if reckoned by the hour.–The boy works for a *wage.* He works for fifty cents an hour.

–*v. wages, waged, waging.* Carry on (war).–The people *waged* war against the rats.

wa·ger (WAY-jer) *n. wagers.* A bet.–Many people make *wagers* on horse races. They bet money that a certain horse will win a race. If the horse they choose wins, they get back more money than they put up. If it does not win, they lose their money.

–*v. wagers, wagered, wagering.* Bet; make a wager.–In some states it is against the law to *wager* on horse races.

wag·on (WAG-ən) *n. wagons.* 1. A horse-drawn vehicle used to carry loads, such as an ice *wagon* or a vegetable *wagon.*

2. A toy vehicle drawn by hand or used for coasting.–Jimmy has a new red *wagon.*

waif (WAYF) *n. waifs.* 1. A lost, homeless person, especially a child.–The woman took the poor, hungry *waif* home and fed him.

2. A stray animal.–The shepherd found the lost sheep and brought the *waif* back.

wail (WAYL) *n. wails.* 1. A loud cry of pain or grief.–The dog gave out a *wail* when he was locked out of the house.

2. A mournful sound.–We heard the *wail* of the wind in the night.

–*v. wails, wailed, wailing.* 1. Cry loudly from pain or grief. – We could hear the woman *wailing* because her child was lost.

2. Make a sad sound.–The cold wind *wailed* in the night.

waist (WAYST) *n. waists.* 1. The middle part of the body, between the hips and the ribs.–A belt is worn around the *waist.*

2. The part of a garment that goes around the waist.–Mother took in the *waist* of her dress.

3. A woman's garment that covers the upper part of the body; a blouse.–A *waist* is worn with a suit or skirt. It covers the body from the hips or the *waist*line to the neck.

wait (WAYT) *n.* The act of staying until something happens; the time spent while being ready for something to happen. – The train was late, so we had a long *wait.*

–*v. waits, waited, waiting.* 1. Stay until some event happens.–You can see Mother if you *wait* for her. She is not here now.

2. Put off; delay.–I'm going to be late. Do not *wait* dinner for me. Do not put off serving dinner until the time that I arrive.

–*Wait on* means to serve.–A kind lady *waited on* us in the store. She sold us some candy.

wait•er (WAY-ter) *n. waiters.* A man who serves food at a table.—The *waiter* at the restaurant served William an extra dish of ice cream for dessert.

wait•ress (WAY-trəss) *n. waitresses.* A woman who serves food at a table.—The *waitress* at the hotel brought me a clean napkin.

waive (WAYV) *v. waives, waived, waiving.* Set aside for the time being; give up freely, as a right to something.—The lawyer *waived* his right to question the witness at that time. He decided to question him later.

wake (WAYK) *v. wakes, waked* or *woke, waking.* 1. Rouse or become roused from sleep; stop sleeping.—I *wake* when the alarm clock rings. The alarm *wakes* me.
2. Stir; begin activity. — The flowers and trees *wake* in early spring. They show signs of life and begin to grow.
3. Become alert; show interest.—The girls *woke* up when the comedy picture was shown.

wake•ful (WAYK-fuhl) *adj.* Sleepless. — Mother had a *wakeful* night. She could not sleep.

wak•en (WAYK-ən) *v. wakens, wakened, wakening.* 1. Wake; rouse out of sleep. — I *waken* when the alarm clock rings. The alarm clock *wakens* me.
2. Stir; begin activity.—The flowers *waken* in the spring.

walk (WAWK) *n. walks.* A trip on foot.—We went for a *walk* in the woods. We didn't ride; we went by foot.
—*v. walks, walked, walking.* 1. Go forward on foot, more slowly than in running.—Do not *walk* on the grass. Do not step on it.
2. Take for a walk.—Bob *walked* the dog around the block. He took him slowly around the block.

walk•ie-talk•ie (WAW-kee-TAW-kee) *n. walkie-talkies.* A radio set capable of sending and receiving messages, yet small enough to be carried about. *Walkie-talkies* were first used by soldiers in World War II.

wall (WAWL) *n. walls.* 1. One of the sides of a room or a building.—Pictures hang on the *walls* of the living room.—*Walls* separate the rooms in a house.
2. A fence built of solid material, such as stone or brick.—Many ancient cities had stone *walls* built around them.

wall•board (WAWL-bord) *n. wallboards.* An artificial board made of cane or wood fiber, or pressed wood shavings or sawdust. *Wallboard* comes in large sheets. It is used instead of wood, plaster, or other materials for such things as walls, closets, and panels.

wal•let (WAHL-ət) *n. wallets.* A leather case, which folds shut like a book, for carrying paper money and personal papers. — Father keeps a picture of his family in his *wallet.*

wal•lop (WAHL-əp) *v. wallops, walloped, walloping.* Hit hard; beat.—The little boy *walloped* the bully. He hit him very hard.

wal•low (WAHL-oh) *v. wallows, wallowed, wallowing.* Roll or wade in.—Pigs *wallow* in mud and water.

wal•nut (WAWL-nut) *n. walnuts* and *adj.* 1. A large nut, good to eat, with a very rough shell.—English *walnuts* are more easily cracked than black *walnuts.*

2. The tree on which walnuts grow.
3. The dark wood or lumber of the walnut tree.—Father's desk and chair are made of *walnut.*

wal•rus (WAWL- *or* WAHL-rəss) *n. walruses.* A large sea animal with tusks. The *walrus* is found in the cold North. Its skin is used for leather.

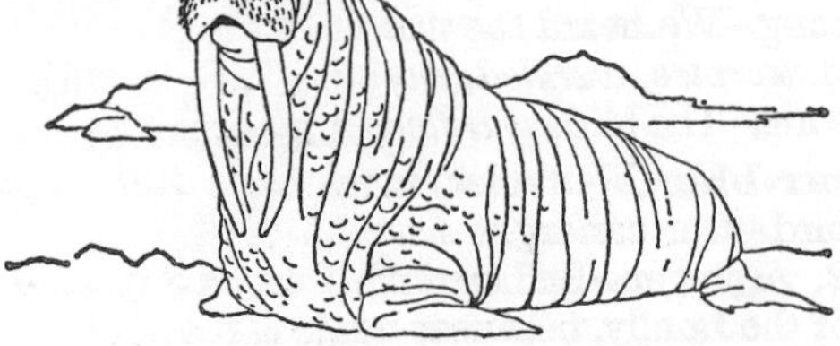

waltz (WAWLTSS) *n. waltzes.* 1. A kind of ballroom dance with a smooth, regular rhythm.—In the old-fashioned *waltzes,* the dancing couples whirled round and round very swiftly.
2. A piece of music written in three-quarter time, or having three beats to a measure.
—*v. waltzes, waltzed, waltzing.* Dance a waltz.
—Mother and Father like to *waltz.*

wam•pum (WAHM- *or* WAWM-pəm) *n.* Beads once used for money and ornament by the Indians of North America. *Wampum* was made of shells of dark purple or white. Dark beads were worth much more than white beads.

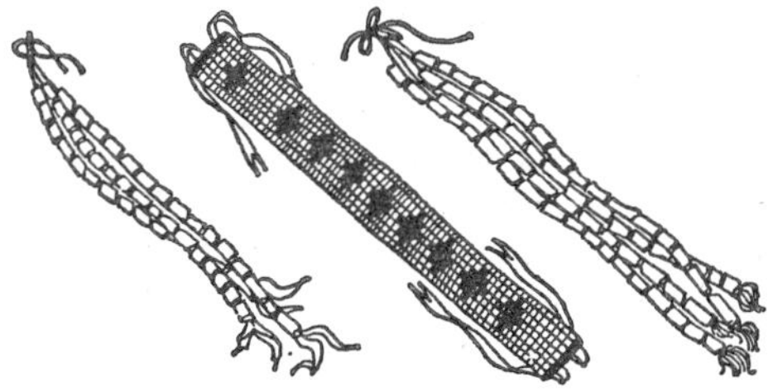

wand (WAHND) *n. wands.* A thin stick to hold in one's hand. – The fairy waved her magic *wand* and the six gray rats became six fine gray horses.

wan•der (WAHN-der) *v. wanders, wandered, wandering.* Roam; ramble; stray.–The children *wandered* through the woods. They went here and there for no special reason.

want (WAHNT) *n. wants.* A need; a thing one has to have.–The child's *wants* are few.
–*v. wants, wanted, wanting.* Desire or wish for.–Susan *wants* a doll with red hair.
–*In want* means to have a need for food, money, clothing, and other necessary things. –That family has always been *in want.* They have always been very poor.

war (WOR) *n. wars.* 1. Fighting over a period of time between two or more countries, or between parts of one country. *War* is carried on with guns, tanks, bomber planes, and other terrible weapons.
2. A planned fight.–Our teacher urged us all to join the *war* on heart disease by giving money.

war•ble (WOR-bəl) *n. warbles.* A trilling song.–We heard the *warble* of the canary.
–*v. warbles, warbled, warbling.*. Sing a trilling song.–The birds *warbled* early each morning.

war•bler (WOR-bler) *n. warblers.* 1. A song-bird.–Our canary is a *warbler.*
2. A singer.–Father calls Mary the *warbler* of the family, because she sings so much.

ward (WORD) *n. wards.* 1. A person left in the care of another person, or of a court.–The orphaned boy is the *ward* of his uncle; his uncle acts as his father.
2. A part of a hospital for certain kinds of patients. – People in a hospital who have catching diseases, such as measles, scarlet fever, or smallpox, are kept in a special *ward* by themselves.
3. A hospital room with beds for many patients.–When Father was in the hospital, he was in a *ward* until there was a private room for him.
4. One of several parts into which a city is divided.–People living in a certain *ward* vote in that *ward.*
–*v. wards, warded, warding.* Prevent; push (off).–He tried to *ward* off the blow with his arm, but he was too slow.–Grandmother is staying in the house today to *ward* off a cold.

ward•en (WOR-dn) *n. wardens.* A chief guard. – A prison *warden* is a person who guards or watches over a prison.–A fire *warden* is a person who sees that fire laws are obeyed.–A *warden* in a college takes care of rules about where the students live, what time they must come in at night, and the like.

ward•robe (WORD-rohb) *n. wardrobes.* 1. A piece of furniture with shelves and hooks for holding clothes.
2. All the clothes one has, or a whole outfit for a particular season or time.–Have you bought your winter *wardrobe* yet?–Mary's *wardrobe* is made up of dresses, sweaters, skirts, shoes, and other articles of clothing.

ware (WAIR) *n. wares.* 1. (In the plural) Goods; things for sale.–Simple Simon asked the Pieman if he might taste his *wares.*
2. Utensils, such as silver*ware*, kitchen*ware*, hard*ware*, copper*ware*, and tin*ware.*

ware•house (WAIR-howss) *n. warehouses.* A building or place for storing goods, machinery, and the like to be sold or used at some later date; a storehouse.–The firm's *warehouse* is located near the railroad yards.

war•fare (WOR-fair) *n.* War; conflict; fighting.–All nations must work together to end all *warfare.*

warm (WORM) *adj. warmer, warmest.* 1. Heated; somewhat hot; not cold.–Winter is cold. Spring is *warm.* Summer is *warmer.*
2. Able to keep or make somewhat hot.–We wear *warm* clothes in cold weather.
3. Hearty; cordial; glad.–Father received a *warm* welcome when he got home. We showed him that we were happy to see him.
4. Close; nearly right. – Tom hid the pen under the table. When Sue started to look under the chair for it, he said she was *warm.*
–*v. warms, warmed, warming.* Heat; make warm.–A fire *warms* a room by heating the air.–*Warm* your hands by holding them near the fire.

warm•blood•ed (WORM-BLUD-əd) *adj.* 1. Having warm blood, as mammals and birds. –Man, dogs, cats, pigeons, and many other animals are *warm-blooded.*
2. Warm in spirit or feeling.–The returning travelers are looking forward to a *warm-blooded* reception from their friends and relatives.

warmth (WORMTH) *n.* Moderate heat.–The *warmth* of the sun felt good on my face.

warn (WORN) *v. warns, warned, warning.* Tell ahead of time about some danger or unpleasant happening. – The boy *warned* the trainmen of a bridge that had been washed away.–Mother *warned* the children not to play with fire.–A dark cloud *warned* us of a storm.

warp (WORP) *n.* The lengthwise threads in cloth. The threads that go from side to side are called the woof.
–*v. warps, warped, warping.* Twist or curve out of shape. – The heat from the radiator *warped* the book that had been left on it.– We could not close the dresser drawer that had been *warped.*

war•rant (WOR- *or* WAHR-ənt) *n. warrants.* 1. A written order that gives one the right to do something.–The policeman had a *warrant* to arrest the man.
2. An excuse; a right; a fair cause.–You have no *warrant* to say such a thing.
–*v. warrants, warranted, warranting.* Justify. –Mary often gets more excited than the cause *warrants.* – The emergency *warranted* a change in the school rules.

war•ri•or (WOR- *or* WAHR-ee-er) *n. warriors.* A man who goes to war and fights.– Soldiers are *warriors.*

war•ship (WOR-ship) *n. warships.* A ship used for fighting in wartime.

was (WAHZ *or* wəz) *v.* One form of the verb *be. Was* is used with other words to help tell of something that has already happened.–I *was* sleepy last night, but I am wide awake today.–Jack *was* hungry before he ate; now he is not.–Rain *was* falling when I left for school, but it isn't now.

wash (WAHSH *or* WAWSH) *n.* A pile of things to be laundered.–Mother had a big *wash* today. There were many clothes to be cleaned.
–*v. washes, washed, washing.* 1. Clean by the use of water or some other fluid.–We *wash* our hands before we eat.–We *washed* our windows and floors today.
2. Carry; sweep. – The hard rain *washed* away the sand on the side of the hill.

wash•board (WAHSH- *or* WAWSH-bord) *n. washboards.* A piece of metal or glass, with ridges on it, in a frame. Clothes being washed are often rubbed on a *washboard* to loosen the dirt.

wash•er (WAHSH- *or* WAWSH-er) *n. washers.* 1. A washing machine.
2. A flat piece of metal, rubber, or other material with a hole in it used at the joints of pipes, hoses, etc., to make them tight and prevent leaking. *Washers* are also used to make nuts and bolts tight. – Father put a *washer* between the hose and the spray to keep the water from spurting out.

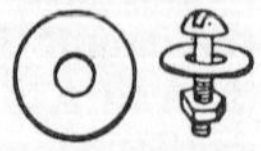

Wash•ing•ton (WAHSH- *or* WAWSH-ing-tən) *n.* 1. The first president of the United States, George *Washington.*

2. *Washington,* D. C.– The capital city of the United States, where the Federal Government is, and where the President lives.
3. A state on the west coast of the United States, the greatest lumbering and apple-growing state in the country. Grand Coulee Dam is in *Washington.*

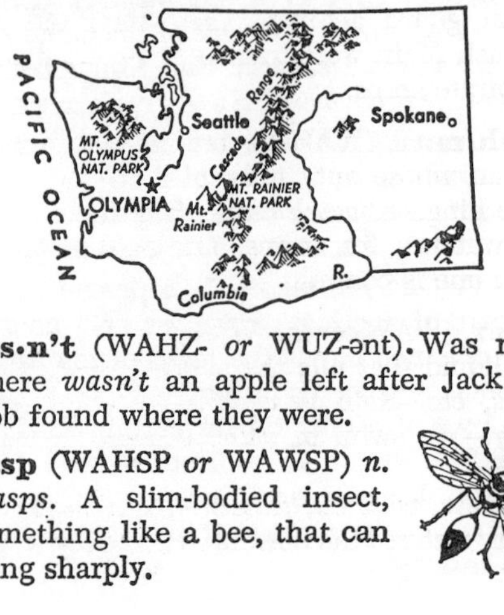

was•n't (WAHZ- *or* WUZ-ənt). Was not.– There *wasn't* an apple left after Jack and Bob found where they were.

wasp (WAHSP *or* WAWSP) *n. wasps.* A slim-bodied insect, something like a bee, that can sting sharply.

waste (WAYST) *n. wastes.* Any material that is left over and cannot be used.–Mother says there is a lot of *waste* on the roast; it has much fat and bone, which cannot be eaten.
–*v. wastes, wasted, wasting.* Not use, or use badly.–Do not *waste* your paper. Use up all of it, and do not take more than you need. Do not throw away anything that can be used again.
–*adj.* Useless; of no value; thrown away after being used.–We throw *waste*paper into the *waste*paper basket.

waste•ful (WAYST-fuhl) *adj.; wastefully, adv.* 1. Causing waste.–The old machines are *wasteful.* The new ones produce twice as much in the same time.
2. Extravagant; spending carelessly. – The rich young man is spoiled and *wasteful.*

watch (WAHCH) *n. watches.* 1. A small clock worn on a strap around the wrist, or in the pocket on a chain. We tell time by a *watch.*
2. A guard.–The Boy Scouts left a *watch* at the camp. He looked after the camp.
3. A turn to stand guard.–From eight o'clock until twelve was Bob's *watch.* He was supposed to stand guard at the camp during those hours.
–*v. watches, watched, watching.* 1. Look at.–We *watched* the circus parade going by.–Susan likes to *watch* Father shave.
2. Mind; care for.–Mary *watched* the baby all day.–Shepherds *watch* their sheep.
3. Look or wait for. – The cat *watched* the house all day for a chance to sneak in through the back door. – The baseball batter was *watching* for a slow pitch so that he could try to hit a home run.
–*Be on the watch for* means to look out for, or be on guard against.–The sailors on the Spanish Main were told to *be on the watch for* pirate ships.

watch•man (WAHCH-mən) *n. watchmen.* A man whose duty it is to watch or guard something.–A *watchman* at a railroad crossing watches for trains, and warns people when one is coming.

wa•ter (WAW-ter *or* WAHT-er) *n. waters.* The liquid that fills the oceans, seas, lakes, rivers, etc.–Rain is *water.*–We drink pure *water.*–We swim in *water.*–Tears are salty *water.*
–*v. waters, watered, watering.* Put water on. –Mary *watered* the flowers so that they would grow.

wa•ter col•or (WAW-ter *or* WAHT-er KUL-er) *water colors.* 1. Paint made for mixing with water.–We paint some pictures with oil paint, or paint mixed with oil, and some pictures with *water colors.*
2. A picture painted in water colors.–Bob likes to paint *water colors* of oldtime sailing ships at sea.

wa•ter•fall (WAW-ter-fawl *or* WAHT-er-fawl) *n. waterfalls.* A stream of water pouring from a high place. – We waded up the brook as far as we could go, and had our lunch by the *waterfall.*

wa•ter lil•y (WAW-ter *or* WAHT-er LIL-ee) *water lilies.* A plant that grows in water. It has white, yellow, or pink blossoms, and large, flat, green leaves that float on the water.

wa•ter•logged (WAW-ter-lawgd *or* WAHT-er-lawgd) *adj.* Containing so much water as to be hard to manage; over-soaked with water.–The canoe was *waterlogged.* The wood had soaked up so much water that it was unable to float.

wa•ter•mel•on (WAW-ter-mel-ən *or* WAHT-er-mel-ən) *n. watermelons.* A large melon with a green rind, and large, flat, black or white seeds. A *watermelon* is a deep pink or red color inside. The juice is sweet.

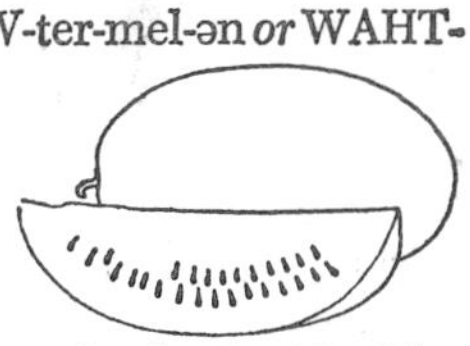

wa•ter•proof (WAW-ter-proof *or* WAHT-er-proof) *v. waterproofs, waterproofed, waterproofing.* Treat something so water will not go through it.–Grandfather put tar on the roof of his barn to *waterproof* it.
–*adj.* Not absorbing water; keeping water out. –Bob's raincoat is *waterproof.*–Galoshes are *waterproof,* too.

wa•ter•shed (WAW-ter-shed *or* WAHT-er-shed) *n. watersheds.* 1. An area from which water is drained, or shed, into lakes, rivers, reservoirs.
2. A chain of hills or mountains separating two or more of these water-shedding areas.

wa•ter va•por (WAW-ter *or* WAHT-er VAY-per). Water spread in the air as a gas; tiny drops of water. *Water vapor* is formed when water is heated to a point just below boiling. At the boiling point, water becomes steam.

wa•ter•way (WAW-ter-way *or* WAHT-er-way) *n. waterways.* A river, canal, lake, etc., on which boats travel.

wa•ter wheel (WAW-ter *or* WAHT-er hweel) *water wheels.* A wheel turned by flowing water to make power to run a machine. – The old mill was run by a *water wheel.*

watt (WAHT) *n. watts.* A unit for measuring electric power.–Light bulbs under sixty *watts* should not be used for reading. They don't transmit enough electrical power to give off sufficient light. They are not bright enough.

wat•tle (WAHT-l) *n. wattles.* 1. The red flesh on the underside of the necks of turkeys, chickens, and some other birds.
2. An easily bent stick or twig. – William stuck some *wattles* together with clay and made a fine hut.

wave (WAYV) *n. waves.* 1. A moving ridge made by the rising and falling of water.–The cork bobbed up and down on the *waves.*

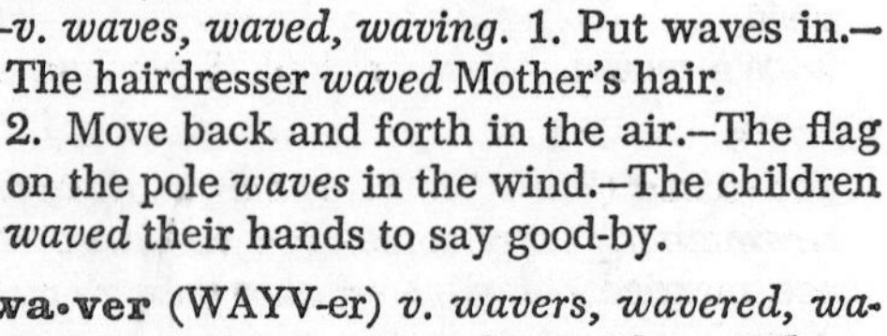

2. A ripple.–The hairdresser set Mother's hair in *waves.*
–*v. waves, waved, waving.* 1. Put waves in.–The hairdresser *waved* Mother's hair.
2. Move back and forth in the air.–The flag on the pole *waves* in the wind.–The children *waved* their hands to say good-by.

wa•ver (WAYV-er) *v. wavers, wavered, wavering.* 1. Sway; move from side to side or back and forth.–The sign hanging over the drug store *wavered* in the strong wind.
2. Shake; tremble; flicker.–When Sue asked Father not to scold her, her voice began to *waver.* Her voice began to tremble. – The flame *wavered.* It flickered.
3. Hesitate; be uncertain or undecided.–Tom *wavered* before making a decision. He wasn't too sure about what he should do.

wax (WAKS) *n.* 1. A yellowish-white substance that is secreted by bees and used in making honeycombs.–*Wax* can be molded when it is warm, and dries solid when it gets cold.–The material that some candles are made of is called *wax.*
2. A polish used on the surface of furniture, floors, automobiles, etc.
–*v. waxes, waxed, waxing.* Put wax on.–Father *waxes* the car to protect the finish.

way (WAY) *n. ways.* 1. A path; a direction.–The cows had trodden a *way* through the pasture.–A large man made his *way* through the crowd.–Show me the *way* to your house.
2. A distance.–It is a long *way* to school.
3. In a certain direction.–The girls went that *way.*
4. A plan; a method; a means.–Bob thought of a *way* to get the rabbit out of the trap.
5. A desire; what one wishes.–Mother didn't want us to go at first, but we got our own *way.* We went in the end.
6. A respect.–Bob's story was the best one in several *ways.* It was exciting, the people in it talked like real people, and it was clearly written.–In some *ways* Mary acts younger than Jack.
7. A manner.–Mother has a sweet *way* about her.–People from other lands have different *ways.*

we (WEE) *pron.* You and I; one or more others and myself.–*We* must hurry or *we* shall be late.–*We* all spelled all the words right in our class today.

weak (WEEK) *adj. weaker, weakest; weakly, adv.* 1. Not strong.–Baby was *weak* after her sickness.–The footbridge is too *weak* to hold many people.
2. Not easy to believe.–The boy's excuse was *weak.* It didn't sound true.
3. Not very good.–We have a *weak* ball team. –Jack is a little *weak* in history.
4. Containing very little of the important part.–*Weak* coffee has much water and little coffee in it.–Adding too much water to soup makes it *weak.*

weak•en (WEE-kən) *v. weakens, weakened, weakening.* Lose strength.–Sickness caused the old man to *weaken.*

weak•ness (WEEK-nəss) *n. weaknesses.* 1. A lack of energy or strength.–After his sickness, the man's *weakness* forced him to rest.
2. A defect.–There is a serious *weakness* in your argument.
3. Something one cannot resist.–Candy is Bob's *weakness;* he cannot help eating it.

wealth (WELTH) *n.* 1. Riches.–Ed is a man of great *wealth.* He has much money and property.
2. Much, or a large amount.–Mary has a *wealth* of dark brown hair.

wean (WEEN) *v. weans, weaned, weaning.* Get a child or young animal used to food other than its mother's milk.–The calves on Mr. Brown's farm have been *weaned.* They no longer drink their mothers' milk. They now eat grass, hay, and grain.

weap•on (WEP-ən) *n. weapons.* Anything used in fighting.–Guns, bows and arrows, swords, and clubs are *weapons.*

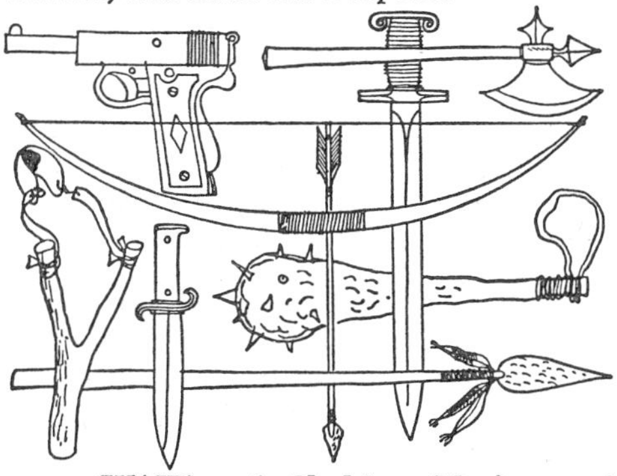

wear (WAIR) *n.* 1. Clothing.–Men's *wear* is sold in the men's department of the store.
2. Service; amount of time something can be used.–This suit will give you good *wear.* It will last a long time.–Father can get a little more *wear* out of his old shoes.
–*v. wears, wore, wearing.* 1. Carry or have on the body, as clothing or an ornament.–People *wear* clothes. They put them on to cover their bodies and to keep themselves warm.–Women *wear* earrings on their ears, rings on their fingers, and bracelets on their arms.
2. Rub or be rubbed away; make or become smaller, thinner, etc., through use. – The eraser on my pencil is *wearing* down. It will soon be all used up.–Mary's shoe *wore* a hole in her stocking.–Running water *wore* away the rocks in the river.

wea•ry (WIR-ee) *adj. wearier, weariest; wearily, adv.; weariness, n.* Tired; worn out. –Father is *weary* after his day's work.

wea•sel (WEE-zəl) *n. weasel* or *weasels.* A quick, small, slender animal that eats birds, mice, and other small animals.

weath•er (WETH-er) *n.* The heat, coldness, wetness, or other condition of the air.–In hot *weather* the air is hot or warm. In rainy *weather* the air is wet. In cold *weather* the air is cold.

weath•er•cock (WETH-er-kahk) *n. weathercocks.* A device, often cut or formed in the shape of a rooster, or a cock, that turns to show the direction in which the wind is blowing.

weave (WEEV) *n. weaves.* A kind or design of weaving. – Mother's skirt has a coarse *weave;* the material is rough.
–*v. weaves, wove, weaving.* Make (cloth or other fabric) by putting threads or strips under and over other threads or strips.–Children *weave* baskets of grass reeds.

weav•er (WEE-ver) *n. weavers.* A person who makes cloth, rugs, mats, etc., by weaving.

web (WEB) *n. webs.* 1. A network.–The picture shows a spider's *web.* Spiders spin *webs* to catch insects in.

2. The skin that joins the toes of certain swimming animals, such as ducks and beavers.

webbed (WEBD) *adj.* Having the toes joined by webs.–Ducks and geese have *webbed* feet. Their toes are joined by skin. *Webbed* feet help them swim.

wed (WED) *v. weds, wedded, wedding.* Marry; become man and wife.–"With this ring I thee *wed,*" said the bridegroom at the wedding.

we'd (WEED). 1. We had.–*We'd* better go now.
2. We would.–*We'd* be cold if we had no coats.

wed•ding (WED-ing) *n. weddings.* A service or ceremony at which a man and a woman are married.–Many *weddings* take place in church.

wedge (WEJ) *n. wedges.* A V-shaped piece of wood or metal used to split wood and to keep objects in position.–We put a *wedge* under the door to keep it open.

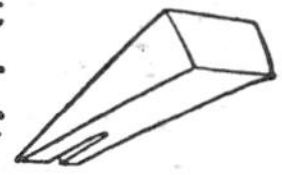

–*v. wedges, wedged, wedging.* Force; push; crowd in.– A stranger *wedged* his way through the crowd.

Wednes·day (WENZ-dee) *n. Wednesdays.* The day after Tuesday. *Wednesday* is the fourth day of the week.

weed (WEED) *n. weeds.* A plant that is useless or that grows where it is not wanted.—*Weeds* crowd out other plants in the garden.
—*v. weeds, weeded, weeding.* Clear of weeds.—Grandfather *weeds* the garden every week. He pulls up the weeds.

week (WEEK) *n. weeks.* 1. The seven days beginning with Sunday.
2. Seven days one right after the other.—Bob has been in the country for a *week.*
3. The five or six working days of the week.—A school *week* has five days in it.

week·day (WEEK-day) *n. weekdays.* Any day of the week but Sunday; or, sometimes, any day of the week but Saturday and Sunday.

week end or **week-end** (WEEK-end) *week ends* or *week-ends.* The holidays at the end of the week, usually Saturday and Sunday.—We go to school during the week and play during the *week end.*

week·ly (WEEK-lee) *n. weeklies.* A magazine or paper printed each week.—We take two *weeklies.*
—*adj.* Occurring every week.—Grandmother pays us a *weekly* visit. She comes to see us every week.
—*adv.* Once a week.—We pay for the newspaper *weekly.*

weep (WEEP) *v. weeps, wept, weeping.* Cry.—When Mary broke the dish, she started to *weep.*

wee·vil (WEE-vəl) *n. weevils.* A kind of small beetle with a hard-shelled back. *Weevils* eat grain, and often get into breakfast foods and flour.

weigh (WAY) *v. weighs, weighed, weighing.* 1. Find out how heavy something is.—Bob *weighed* himself on the scale.—The grocer *weighs* the sugar to be sure that he gives you the right amount.
2. Be of a certain weight or heaviness.—The baby *weighed* six pounds when she was born.
3. Bend or press (down).—The trees were *weighed* down with snow. The heavy snow made them bend over.
—*Weigh one's words* means to carefully consider what one is about to say or write; to carefully choose the words one is going to use in speaking or writing.—*Weigh your words* before you speak. Make sure that you say just what you want to say.

weight (WAYT) *n. weights.* 1. How heavy a thing is; how much a thing weighs on the scales.—Bob weighs eighty pounds. His *weight* is eighty pounds.
2. A piece of heavy material used to hold something down.—Father has a lead paper*weight* on his desk. He puts it on his papers so that wind will not scatter them.

weird (WIRD) *adj. weirder, weirdest; weirdly, adv.; weirdness, n.* Strange; ghostlike; mysterious.—The wind made *weird* sounds as it whistled through the trees.

wel·come (WEL-kəm) *n. welcomes.* A greeting (usually kind or warm).—We gave Father a warm *welcome* when he came home from his long business trip.
—*v. welcomes, welcomed, welcoming.* 1. Greet or receive gladly.—The people of the city *welcomed* the soldiers on their return home.
2. Allow; permit.—I *welcome* you to borrow any one of my books.
—*adj.* 1. Gladly received.—We always feel *welcome* at Grandmother's home.
2. Permitted.—You are *welcome* to stay at my house for the week end.
—People often say, "You are *welcome*" when they have been thanked for something.—When John thanked Mary for her gift, she said, "You are *welcome.*"

weld (WELD) *v. welds, welded, welding.* Join pieces of metal by heating them and pressing them together.—Father will *weld* the ends of the wires together. He will join them by heating them till the metal is soft, and then pressing them together.

well (WEL) *n. wells.* 1. A hole dug or drilled in the ground to reach gas, oil, or water.
2. Anything like a well.—An ink*well* holds ink.
—*adj.* 1. In good health.—Grandfather is *well.* He isn't sick.
2. Right.—It is *well* that you study your spelling words.
—*adv. better, best.* 1. Nicely; in the right or desired way.—Everything went *well* until we came to the obstacle on the road.—Mary sings *well.*
2. Thoroughly. — Chew your food *well* before you swallow it.

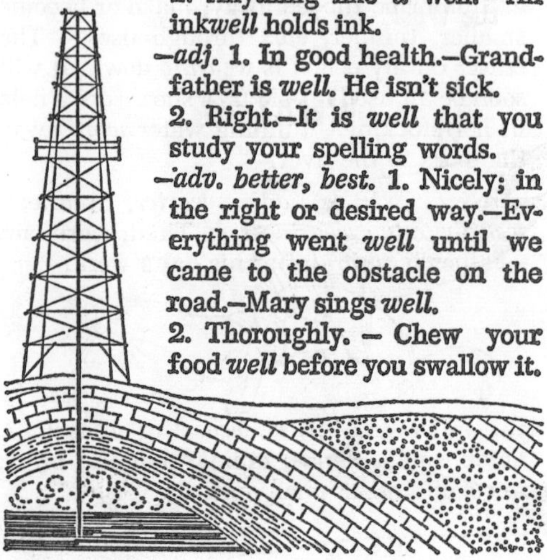

we'll (WEEL). 1. We will.—*We'll* make it to the top.
2. We shall.—*We'll* be late if you don't hurry.

well-known (WEL-NOHN) *adj.* Known by many people.—President Franklin D. Roosevelt was *well-known.* He was known by people everywhere.

welt (WELT) *n. welts.* A long swollen place on the skin caused by a blow.—The cruel man beat the horse until its back was covered with *welts.*

went (WENT) *v.* One form of the verb *go.*—Bob came to school at noon and *went* home at three o'clock.

wept (WEPT) *v.* One form of the verb *weep.* —The children *wept* when their dog was lost.

were (WER) *v.* One form of the verb *be.*—We *were* sorry you didn't come.—You are late today and you *were* late yesterday.—If I *were* hungry, I would eat some food; but I am not hungry, so I shall not.

we're (WIR). We are.—*We're* ready for school now.

weren't (WERNT). Were not.—We *weren't* ready for school when Father left the house.

west (WEST) *n., adj.,* and *adv.*
1. The direction in which the sun sets.—If you stand with your face to the north, *west* is on your left.

2. (Spelled with a capital "W.") The section of the United States lying west of the Mississippi River.—Johnny said that if he could have his wish he would live in the *West* and be a cowboy.
3. (Spelled with a capital "W.") Europe and the Americas are sometimes referred to as the *West.*

west•ern (WESS-tern) *adj.* 1. From, in, of, or to the west.—Bob lives in the *western* part of town.
2. (Spelled with a capital "W.") Having to do with the West.

West Vir•gin•ia (WEST ver-JIN-yə) *n.* A state of forest-covered mountains and rich plateaus in eastern United States, noted for hardwood and tobacco products and the production of soft coal.

west•ward (WEST-werd) *adj.* and *adv.* Toward the west.—The boy turned the corner and went *westward.* He went in a *westward* direction.

wet (WET) *v. wets, wetted, wetting.* Soak, or put a liquid on.—Bob *wets* his hair with water before he combs it.
—*adj. wetter, wettest.* 1. Covered or soaked with water or other liquid.—The grass is *wet* with rain.—The towel is *wet.*
2. Rainy.—We had *wet* weather during our vacation.
3. In liquid form; not hardened; not dry.—The paint is still *wet.*

we've (WEEV). We have.—*We've* six minutes to wait.

whale (HWAYL) *n. whales.* A big sea mammal that looks like a fish. The *whale* is the biggest animal in the world.

WHALES

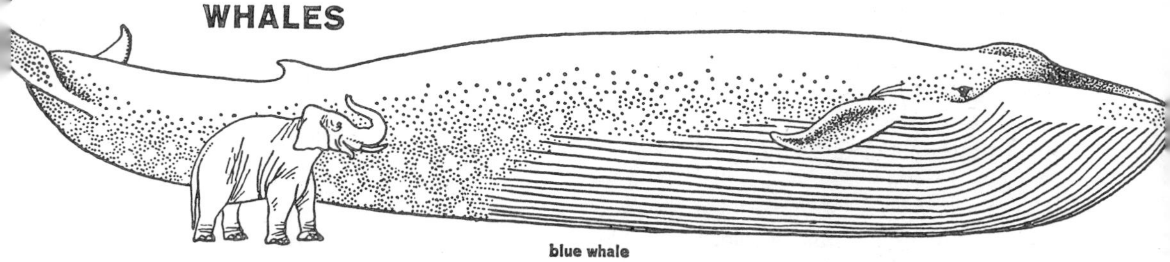

blue whale

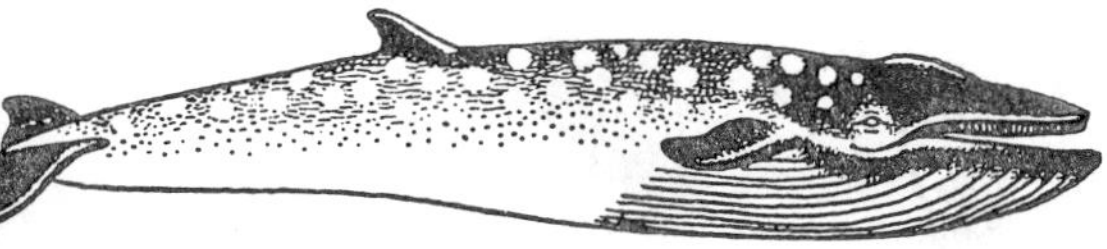

sei whale

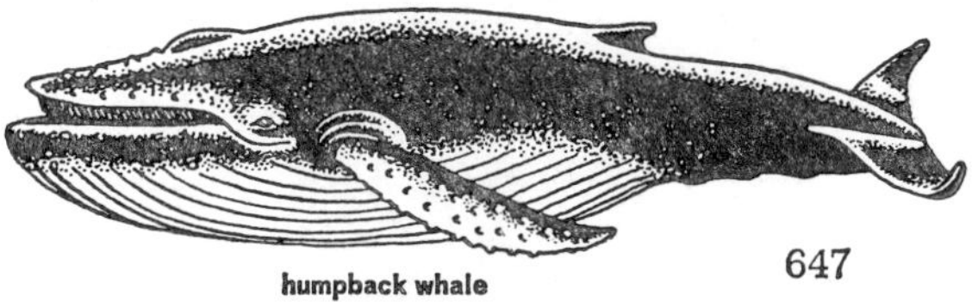

humpback whale

wharf (HWORF) *n. wharves.* A large dock at which boats can load or unload.

what (HWAHT *or* hwut) *adj., adv.,* and *pron.* 1. A word used to ask questions.–*What* is that noise?–*What* is the name of your teacher?–*What* book do you want?–*What* does he mean?
2. Anything that; something that.–Say *what* you want.–The hungry child ate *what* was left over.

what•ev•er (hwaht-EV-er) *adj.* Of any kind. –He may have *whatever* book he wishes.
–*pron.* 1. Anything that.–Eat *whatever* you want to eat.
2. No matter what.–Come tomorrow, *whatever* happens.

what's (HWAHTSS *or* hwutss). What is.–*What's* in the basket?

wheat (HWEET) *n.* An important grain, from which flour, bread, cereals, and other foods are made.–Farmers grow *wheat.*

wheel (HWEEL) *n. wheels.* A round object that turns about its center.–*Wheels* make machines go.–Cars, wagons, and trains run on *wheels.*

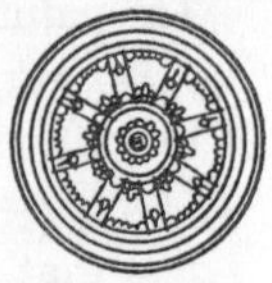

wheel•bar•row (HWEEL-bar-oh) *n. wheelbarrows.* A little vehicle with two legs and one wheel, and pushed by two handles. A *wheelbarrow* is used for carrying small loads.–A man can push a *wheelbarrow* filled with sand, stones, or dirt.

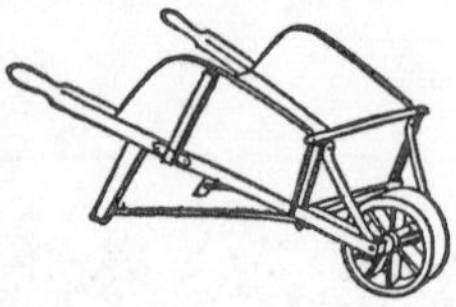

wheeze (HWEEZ) *v. wheezes, wheezed, wheezing.* Breathe heavily with a whistling sound.–When Father has a cold, he *wheezes* and sneezes.

when (HWEN) *adv.* At what time.–*When* do you get up?
–*conj.* 1. At the time that.–We eat *when* we are hungry.
2. After the time that.–Do you want me to throw the ball to you *when* I catch it?
3. Although.–Bob bought two pencils *when* he needed only one.

when•ev•er (hwen-EV-er) *adv.* and *conj.* When; any time that.–Some children eat *whenever* they are hungry.–You may go home *whenever* your work is done.

where (HWAIR) *adv.* 1. In what place.–*Where* did you put your book?
2. At what place.–*Where* did you stop?
3. To what place.–*Where* was the letter sent?
4. From what place.–*Where* did you get that hat?
–*conj.* In or at the place in which.–John is going to sit *where* I usually sit. He is going to sit in my chair.

wher•ev•er (hwair-EV-er) *adv.* Any place that.–*Wherever* you go, I shall go.

whet (HWET) *v. whets, whetted, whetting.* 1. Sharpen by grinding or rubbing, as the edge of a blade or tool.–The hunter was *whetting* his knife with a stone.
2. Stimulate; make keen or eager.–The delicious smell of Mother's cooking always *whets* my appetite. It makes me feel hungrier than I was before I smelled it.

wheth•er (HWETH-er) *conj.* 1. No matter if. –*Whether* it rains or snows, we shall go to the party.–*Whether* you like it or not, I shall do it.
2. If.–Mary didn't know *whether* Bob was home or not.
3. I did not know *whether* to go.

which (HWICH) *adj.* and *pron.* 1. What one. –*Which* girl sits here?–*Which* is the path we should take?
2. That.–We play games *which* we like.

while (HWYL) *n.* A time.–Father will be home in a little *while.*
–*v. whiles, whiled, whiling.* Spend or pass (time).–Bob *whiles* away his time loafing.
–*conj.* 1. During the time that.–*While* we were eating, the doorbell rang.–Tom didn't want to wash the dishes *while* his sister went to the movies.
2. Although.–*While* Mother spoke loudly, I didn't hear her. I was making too much noise.
–*Worth one's while* means that a certain thing that one does is worth doing, that it is worth the time and effort used to do it.–Since Bill was poor in geography, the teacher gave him some extra books to read. She felt that reading them would be *worth his while.*

whim•per (HWIM-per) *n. whimpers.* A sobbing little cry.–We didn't hear a *whimper* from Baby when she fell down.
v. whimpers, whimpered, whimpering. Whine or cry in low, broken sounds.–The dog *whimpers* when he is cold.

whin•ny (HWIN-ee) *n. whinnies.* The cry of a horse.–The pony gave a *whinny* when he saw the apple.
–*v. whinnies, whinnied, whinnying.* Neigh, or give a whinny. – Roosters crow. Dogs bark. Horses *whinny.*

whip (HWIP) *n. whips.* A lash, usually with a handle or grip.–The horseman carries a *whip.*

–*v. whips, whipped, whipping.*
1. Beat; strike.–The cruel man *whipped* the dog for running away.
2. Beat with a beater.–Mary *whipped* the cream to make it thick and fluffy.

whip•poor•will (HWIP-er-wil *or* hwip-er-WIL) *n. whippoorwills.* A bird that flies by night. The *whippoorwill* lives on insects. It seems to say its own name when it calls.

whir or **whirr** (HWER) *n. whirs* or *whirrs.* A buzzing sound.–We heard the *whir* of the engines as we passed the factory.
–*v. whirs, whirred, whirring.* Spin or move fast and make a buzzing sound.–The wheels of Grandmother's sewing machine *whir.*–Sally's top *whirs* when she spins it.

whirl (HWERL) *n. whirls.* A spinning circle. –My head seems to be in a *whirl,* I am so excited.
–*v. whirls, whirled, whirling.* Turn round and round; spin.– A top *whirls.*– The children *whirled* about the room.–The boy *whirled* the rope about his head.

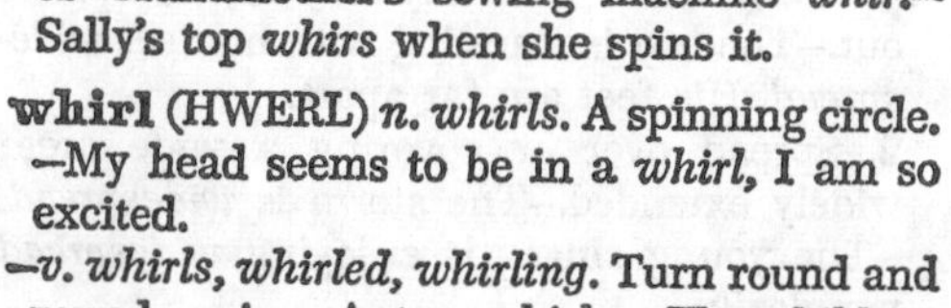

whirl•pool (HWERL-pool) *n. whirlpools.* Water that whirls round and round in a swift circle.–*Whirlpools* often upset boats.

whirl•wind (HWERL-wind) *n. whirlwinds.* Air or wind blowing round and round, fast and fiercely. A *whirlwind* is a violent windstorm.

whisk (HWISK) *n. whisks.* A sweep or brush. –One *whisk* of the hand and Mary's desk was cleaned.
–*v. whisks, whisked, whisking.* 1. Sweep or brush away with a light, easy motion.–Mary *whisked* the scraps of paper from her desk.
2. Dash; dart; quickly move.–When the dog chased the cat, she *whisked* up a tree.

whisk•er (HWISS-ker) *n. whiskers.* 1. A long, stiff hair that sticks out from the sides of the mouth.–Our white kitten has long black *whiskers.*
2. The beard; stiff hair growing on the cheeks, upper lip, and chin of a man.–Father shaves off his *whiskers* in the morning.

whis•key or **whis•ky** (HWISS-kee) *n. whiskies.* A liquor made from wheat or other grains.

whis•per (HWISS-per) *n. whispers.* A soft, hissing sound, under the breath.–Mother has a cold and can speak only in a *whisper.*
–*v. whispers, whispered, whispering.* 1. Speak under the breath with a soft, hissing sound.– When Father is asleep, we *whisper.*
2. Make a low rustling sound.–The wind *whispered* through the leaves on the trees.
3. Tell secretly from one to another.–It was *whispered* about that the teacher wore a wig.

whis•tle (HWISS-əl) *n. whistles.* 1. A little hollow instrument that makes a shrill note when you put it to your lips and blow through it; any device, big or little, for making such a sound. – The policeman blew a *whistle* to tell the children when to cross the street.–The engineer blows the train *whistle.*

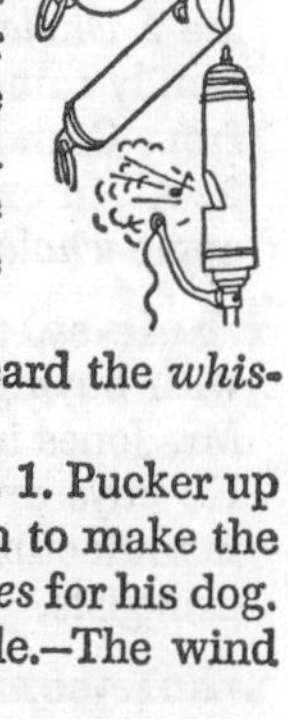

2. A whistlelike sound.–We heard the *whistle* of the whippoorwill.
–*v. whistles, whistled, whistling.* 1. Pucker up the lips and blow through them to make the sound of a whistle.–Jack *whistles* for his dog.
2. Make a sound like a whistle.–The wind *whistles* through the trees.

white (HWYT) *n. whites.* The color of snow. –Mother picked *white* for the color of the house paint.
–*adj.* Of the color white.–Mother's hair is coal-black; Grandmother's hair is *white.*–Wild daisies usually have *white* petals.

whit•en (HWYT-n) *v. whitens, whitened, whitening.* Make white; bleach. – Mother hangs the clothes in the sun to *whiten* them.

white•wash (HWYT-wahsh *or* -wawsh) *v. whitewashes, whitewashed, whitewashing.* Whiten with a liquid substance, usually made of water and lime. – Tom and his friends are *whitewashing* the fence.

whit•tle (HWIT-l) *v. whittles, whittled, whittling.* 1. Cut off chips or pieces of wood with a knife.
2. Carve or cut out in a shape.–Bob *whittled* a doll for Sally.

whiz or **whizz** (HWIZ) *n. whizzes.* A humming sound.–The batter heard the *whiz* of the ball.
–*v. whizzes, whizzed, whizzing.* Fly with a buzzing or humming sound.–Bob threw the ball so hard that it *whizzed* by the boy who was batting.

who (HOO) *pron.* 1. What person; which people. – *Who* would like to go with me? Would you, Mary?–*Who* opened the window?
2. That.–The boy *who* is singing this song is my brother.

whoa (HWOH) *interj.* Stop.–The farmer says "*Whoa!*" to his horses when he wants them to stand still.

who•ev•er (hoo-EV-er) *pron.* Anyone who; any person that.–*Whoever* guesses what I have in my hand may have it.

whole (HOHL) *adj.; wholly, adv.* 1. Complete; entire.–We couldn't play checkers because we did not have a *whole* set of checkers. Some pieces were missing.–The fat man ate a *whole* pie. He ate all of it.–The *whole* family came. Everybody in the family came, from Grandfather to the baby.
2. All in one piece.–Do you want to eat the apple *whole*, or would you like it cut up?

whole•sale (HOHL-sayl) *adj.* Having to do with buying or selling in large quantities.– Mr. Jones is in the *wholesale* drug business. He buys drugs in large quantities from the manufacturers and then sells them to retail druggists.

whole•some (HOHL-səm) *adj.; wholesomely, adv.; wholesomeness, n.* Healthful; good for one's health.–Fruits and vegetables are *wholesome* foods.

whom (HOOM) *pron.* What person; which people.–To *whom* shall I give the book?– *Whom* do you like better, Bob or Jack?

whoop•ing cough (HOO-ping *or* HUHP-ing kawf). A disease, usually of children. *Whooping cough* makes a person cough and whoop. Children catch it by getting near others who are sick with it.

whose (HOOZ) *pron.* 1. Which person's.– *Whose* book is this? To whom does it belong? Is it yours, Mary's, or Jack's?
2. The man *whose* hat blew off is Father.– Mary, *whose* cold was worse, did not go out today.

why (HWY) *adv.* For what reason.–*Why* were you late?–I don't see *why* you don't come with us.

wick (WIK) *n. wicks.* The soft cord in a candle or the loosely woven tape in an oil lamp that draws up the wax or oil to be burned for light.

wick•ed (WIK-id) *adj.; wickedly, adv.; wickedness, n.* Bad or sinful.–The *wicked* king was sorry for his bad deeds when he saw how unhappy he had made the people.

wide (WYD) *adj. wider, widest* and *adv.* 1. Broad.–One path was so narrow that only one person could walk in it. The other was *wide* enough for two people to walk side by side.
2. As far as it will open.–We open the windows *wide* when we go to bed.

wid•en (WYD-n) *v. widens, widened, widening.* Make or become wide.–The workmen will *widen* the narrow street so that more cars can use it.

wide•spread (WYD-SPRED) *adj.* 1. Spread out.–The boy is standing with his feet *widespread.* His feet are far apart.
2. Spread over or covering a wide area; widely extended.–The storm is *widespread.* –The young singer is enjoying *widespread* popularity.

wid•ow (WID-oh) *n. widows.* A woman whose husband is dead, and who has not married again.

wid•ow•er (WID-oh-er) *n. widowers.* A man whose wife is dead, and who has not married again.

width (WIDTH) *n. widths.* Distance across or from side to side; how wide a thing is.– The *width* of my desk is two feet.–The *width* of the river is fifty feet.

wield (WEELD) *v. wields, wielded, wielding.* Hold in the hand and use.–Jack is never happier than when he is *wielding* a paintbrush.

wife (WYF) *n. wives.* A married woman.–Mother is Father's *wife.*

wig (WIG) *n. wigs.* A covering of false hair worn on the head. Some bald-headed people wear *wigs.*–Actors often wear *wigs* to make them look like someone else.

wig•gle (WIG-əl) *v. wiggles, wiggled, wiggling.* Move uneasily back and forth.–Children sometimes *wiggle* in their seats.

wig•wam (WIG-wahm *or* -wawm) *n. wigwams.* A hut made of poles covered with strips of bark. Some Indians of America lived in *wigwams.*

wild (WYLD) *adj. wilder, wildest; wildly, adv.* 1. Not tame. –*Wild* animals are those that are not tamed, those which man cannot control.–Lions and tigers are *wild* animals.

2. Not cultivated; not taken care of by people.–*Wild* flowers are flowers that grow by themselves in the fields and woods, and by the roads.

–*adv.* Without cultivation; without control.–Daisies and violets grow *wild.*–The children ran *wild.*

wild•cat (WYLD-kat) *n. wildcat* or *wildcats.* A fierce wild animal that looks like a large cat. *Wildcats* eat the flesh of other animals.

wil•der•ness (WIL-der-nəss) *n.* A land where no people live.–While riding through the West, Bob and Mary passed through miles of *wilderness.* There was no sign of any people, and the only growing things grew wild.

will (WIL) *n. wills.* 1. Wish or desire; determination.–Tom is intelligent, but he is also lazy. He has no *will* to succeed.

2. A paper written according to law which tells what shall be done with a person's belongings after he is dead.–Grandfather has made a *will* leaving all his possessions to Grandmother.

–*v.* 1. One form of the verb *be.*–Father *will* be home early.–You *will* hear the bells at six o'clock if you listen.–It *will* be getting dark earlier now that winter is coming.

2. Be willing to.–Mary *will* sing if she is asked.

will•ing (WIL-ing) *adj.* Ready; pleased.–Bob is *willing* to do the work.

will•ing•ly (WIL-ing-lee) *adv.; willingness, n.* Gladly.–Mary did the work *willingly.* She didn't mind doing it at all.

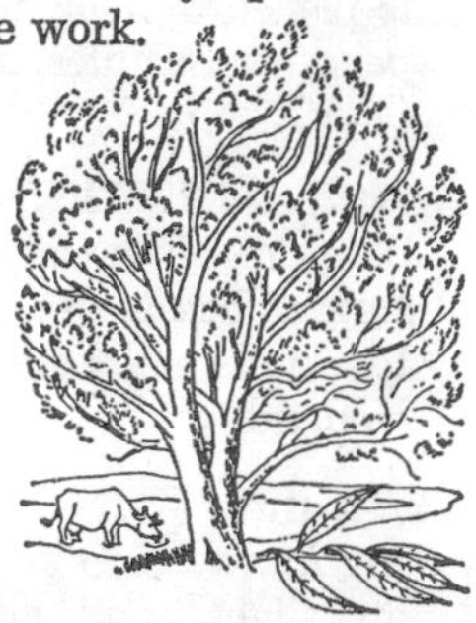

wil•low (WIL-oh) *n. willows.* A kind of tree or bush. – Some *willows* are called weeping *willows.* Their branches bow down as if they were sad.

wilt (WILT) *v. wilts, wilted, wilting.* Wither; droop down; lose strength.–Flowers that are picked and left out of water soon *wilt.*

win (WIN) *v. wins, won, winning.* Succeed; gain a victory; reach a goal.–We *win* ball games by playing better than the other team. –We *win* a spelling contest by spelling better than the other team. – Our team *won* the victory.–Mary *won* the bet from Bob. She was right.

wince (WINSS) *v. winces, winced, wincing.* Shrink or draw back quickly. – The horse *winced* when the driver hit him with the whip.

wind (WIND) *n. winds; windy, adj. windier, windiest.* 1. Air that is moving.–The *wind* blew the apples off the tree.

2. Breath.–The runner was tired and out of *wind* after the race.

–*v. winds, winded, winding.* Make short of breath.–Climbing the stairs *winded* Father.

wind (WYND) *v. winds, wound, winding.* 1. Wrap or twine around; roll up. – The flag *winds* around the flagpole.–Bob *winds* his kite string into a ball.–Mother *winds* thread on the spool.

2. Turn a part of a machine to tighten a spring, so that the machine will go on working by itself.–Grandfather *winds* his watch every night. He turns the stem around and around so that the watch will go on ticking. –The children's phonograph has to be *wound* by hand.

3. Twist; go this way and that way.–A path *winds* through the woods.

wind•break (WIND-brayk) *n. windbreaks.* A shelter or protection from the wind. – A wall, a fence, a tree, a rock, or any other shelter may serve as a *windbreak.*

wind in•stru•ment (WIND IN-strə-mənt) *wind instruments.* A musical instrument that is played by blowing air through it.–Trumpets, horns, flutes, and fifes are *wind instruments.*

wind•mill (WIND-mil) *n. windmills.* A machine run by wind for pumping water.–The farmer has a *windmill* to pump water into his kitchen.–There are many *windmills* in Holland.

win•dow (WIN-doh) *n. windows.* An opening in a wall to let in air, light, and sunshine. – We open our *windows* at night for fresh air.

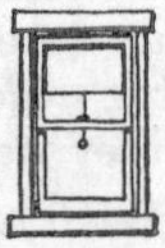

win•dow•pane (WIN-doh-payn) *n. windowpanes.* A piece of glass set in a window to keep out the weather.–The boy tossed a ball through the *windowpane* and broke it.

wind•pipe (WIND-pyp) *n. windpipes.* A tube that carries air from the throat to the lungs.

wind•shield (WIND- *or* WIN-sheeld) *n. windshields.* A heavy, and usually shatterproof, piece of glass in the front of the body of an automobile to keep out rain, snow, dust, and wind.

wine (WYN) *n. wines.* A drink made from the fermented juices of fruits or other plants. *Wine* has some alcohol in it.

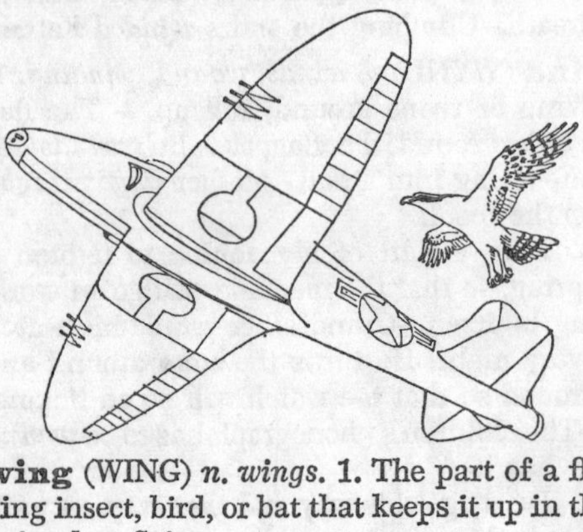

wing (WING) *n. wings.* 1. The part of a flying insect, bird, or bat that keeps it up in the air when flying.
2. Something like a wing in appearance or function, as the *wing* of an airplane.
3. Anything that sticks out from the side of a body or a main part of a thing.–Mother wants to have another *wing* built onto the house because we need more room.
4. A space off the stage at the right or left.–The actors stood in the *wings* until it was time for them to go on stage.
–*v. wings, winged, winging.* Fly. – The bird *winged* its way south.

wing•spread (WING-spred) *n. wingspreads.* The distance between the ends or tips of the wings of a bird, insect, or airplane. *Wingspread* is measured when the wings are stretched out as far as possible.

wink (WINGK) *n. winks.* 1. A quick opening and closing of the eyes; a blink.
2. (In the plural) A brief period of sleep.–Mother was so tired she said she was going to snatch a few *winks* before serving dinner.
–*v. winks, winked, winking.* 1. Open and shut the eyes quickly.–The fly buzzing near the baby's eyes made her *wink.*
2. Open one eye and close it as a signal to someone.–Can you *wink?*
3. Flicker; twinkle.–When Bob opened the door, the candles *winked.*

win•ner (WIN-er) *n. winners.* One that wins or has won.–Our team was the *winner.* It won the game.–Mary's story was the *winner.* It won the prize.

win•ter (WIN-ter) *n. winters.* The cold season of the year.–Spring, summer, autumn, and *winter* are the four seasons.
–*v. winters, wintered, wintering.* Spend the winter.–Our friends *wintered* in the South. They lived there all winter.

win•ter•green (WIN-ter-green) *n. wintergreens.* 1. A small plant with shiny leaves and red berries.
2. A flavoring for candy, ice cream, and cakes made from the oil of the leaves of the plant.

win•try (WIN-tree) *adj.* Having a resemblance to winter; like winter; cold or stormy. –Although the days are warm, the nights are *wintry.*

wipe (WYP) *v. wipes, wiped, wiping.* 1. Make a thing dry or clean by rubbing.–Mary *wiped* the dishes for Mother. – Mother *wiped* the floor with a mop.
2. Rub away. – *Wipe* the jelly from your mouth.

wire (WYR) *n. wires.* 1. A strand or thread of metal.–*Wire* carries electricity for telephones, electric lights, and other things.

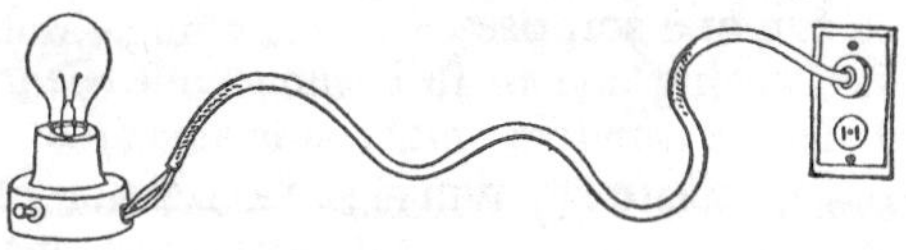

2. A telegraph message; a telegram.–When Father was away, he sent us a *wire* telling us he would be home on Sunday.
–*v. wires, wired, wiring.* 1. Put a wire around.–Father *wired* the box that he sent to Grandmother.
2. Put electric wires in.–We shall *wire* the garage so that we can have a light in it at night.
3. Send a message by telegraph. – Father *wired* us that he would be home on Sunday.

wire·less (WYR-ləss) *n. wirelesses.* A message sent by radio, or without the use of wires.–The ship received a *wireless* from the shore.

Wis·con·sin (wiss-KAHN-sən) *n.* A beautiful, largely agricultural state in north central United States. Dairy farming and general farming, vegetable canning, manufacturing machinery, leather, paper, and furniture are its chief industries.

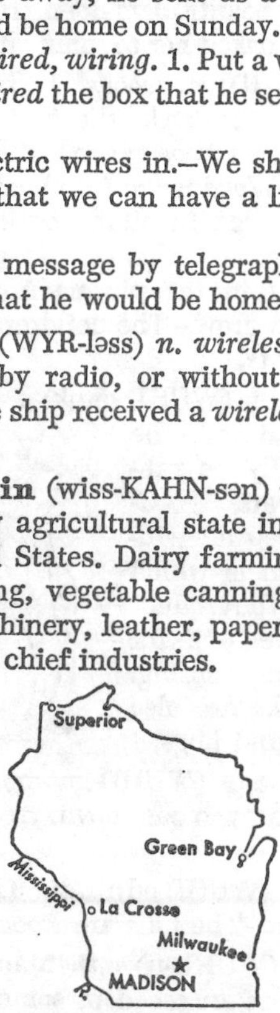

wis·dom (WIZ-dəm) *n.* Good judgment; ability to use one's knowledge to help oneself and others.

wise (WYZ) *adj. wiser, wisest; wisely, adv.* Having wisdom.–Father is *wiser* than Jack because he has lived so much longer. He knows more.

wish (WISH) *n. wishes.* 1. A desire.–John's *wish* is to have a pony of his own.
2. An expressed desire. – Bob made a *wish* when he blew out the candles of his birthday cake. He said he wanted a bicycle.
–*v. wishes, wished, wishing.* 1. Want; desire.–I *wish* I had a dog.–King Midas *wished* that everything he touched would turn to gold.
2. Express hope to (a person) for (something pleasant).–I *wish* you a happy birthday.

wisp (WISP) *n. wisps.* A small strand or bunch of strands.–The bird carried a *wisp* of grass to its nest and wove it in to line the nest.–Bob dropped a *wisp* of hay when he fed the calf.

wit (WIT) *n. wits.* 1. The ability to understand quickly and to express one's thoughts cleverly.
2. (In the plural) Mind; senses.–The Halloween ghost frightened us out of our *wits*.

witch (WICH) *n. witches.* An ugly old woman believed to have magic power.–In fairy tales *witches* ride on brooms.

with (WITH *or* WITH) *prep.* Accompanying; going together. – Mary said to her friend, "Please come *with* me. Let us go together."–We eat butter *with* bread.–Here comes Bob *with* his dog.

with·draw (with- *or* with-DRAW) *v. withdraws, withdrew, withdrawing.* 1. Draw or pull back.–When the cat scratched Mary's foot, Mary *withdrew*.
2. Leave; go away. – The firemen had to *withdraw* from the burning building or be injured.

with·er (WITH-er) *v. withers, withered, withering.* Dry up; become lifeless; fade. – Flowers *wither* unless they have water.

with·hold (with- *or* with-HOHLD) *v. withholds, withheld, withholding.* Hold or keep back; check.–The company *withholds* part of Father's wages each week for taxes.–The police *withheld* the angry mob.

with·in (with- *or* with-IN) *adv.* and *prep.* 1. Inside; inside of.–The boy is hiding *within* the house.
2. Not beyond. – Is the shelf *within* your reach?

with·out (with- *or* with-OWT) *adv.* and *prep.* 1. Not having; not with. – We went *without* lunch. – We can do *without* many things. We can get along even if we do not have many things.
2. On the outside; outside of.–Those within the house called to those *without*.

wit·ness (WIT-nəss) *n. witnesses.* A person who knows and can give proof that something happened.
–*v. witnesses, witnessed, witnessing.* 1. See.–We *witnessed* the fight.
2. Testify to having seen; act as witness.–Father *witnessed* Mr. Jones's signing of the paper. Father wrote his name on the paper to show that he saw Mr. Jones sign the paper.

wit·ty (WIT-ee) *adj. wittier, wittiest.* Having or showing wit; quick, clever, and amusing.–Edward is quite *witty.* He says things that are clever and funny.

wives (WYVZ) *n. pl.* More than one *wife.*–King Solomon had many *wives.* He married many times.

wiz·ard (WIZ-erd) *n. wizards.* A person who is thought to have magic power, or power to do what seems impossible.

wob·ble (WAHB-əl) *v. wobbles, wobbled, wobbling.* Move shakily; tremble.–The sick boy's legs *wobbled* when he walked.

woe (WOH) *n. woes.* Trouble; sorrow.–The knight's heart was heavy with many *woes.*

woke (WOHK) *v.* One form of the verb *wake.* –Baby went to sleep but soon *woke.*

wolf (WUHLF) *n. wolves.* A wild animal that looks something like a police dog.–*Wolves* eat other animals.

wolf·hound (WUHLF-hownd) *n. wolfhounds.* A kind of large dog once used in hunting wolves.

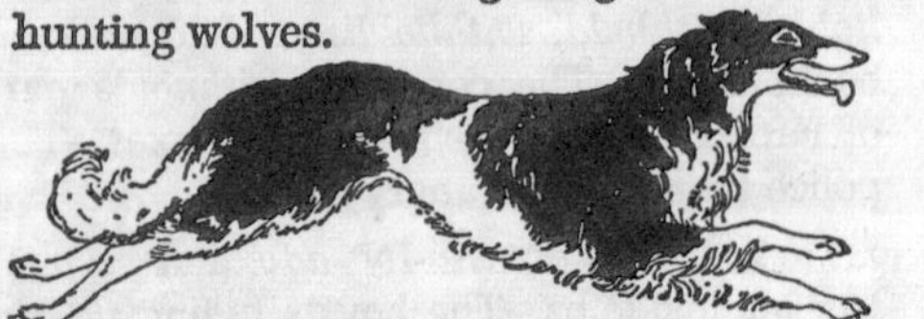

wolves (WUHLVZ) *n. pl.* More than one *wolf.*

wom·an (WUHM-ən) *n. women.* A grown female person.–A girl grows to be a *woman.*–Mother is a *woman.*

wom·en (WIM-ən) *n. pl.* More than one *woman.*–Mother belongs to a club for *women.*

won (WUN) *v.* One form of the verb *win.*–We *won* the ball game. The other team lost.

won·der (WUN-der) *n. wonders.* 1. Surprise. –Bob's eyes opened with *wonder* when he saw his new pony.

2. Awe.–We watched the sunset in *wonder.*

3. Strange, wonderful thing.–Niagara Falls is one of the *wonders* of the world.

–*v. wonders, wondered, wondering.* 1. Want to know.–I *wonder* what my present will be.

2. Be surprised.–I shouldn't *wonder* if it is a new coat.

won·der·ful (WUN-der-fuhl) *adj.; wonderfully, adv.* 1. Full of surprising or delightful things.–Our trip was *wonderful.* It was full of fun and surprises.

2. Causing one to feel wonder. – Niagara Falls is a *wonderful* sight. It is amazing.

won't (WOHNT). Will not.–I *won't* do it.

woo (WOO) *v. woos, wooed, wooing.* Make love to; court.–In the fairy tale the prince *wooed* the beautiful maiden. He made love to her and asked her to marry him.

wood (WUHD) *n. woods.* 1. The part of a tree under the bark; the inside part of a tree.–We burn *wood* to cook with and to keep us warm.–*Wood* is cut into boards and used to build houses, furniture, boxes, and many other things.

2. (Usually in the plural) A place where many trees grow.–The children like to play in the *woods.*

wood·chuck (WUHD-chuk) *n. woodchucks.* An animal of the same family as rabbits and rats. *Woodchucks* sleep all winter in tunnels which they dig in the ground. They come out for food in the spring. *Woodchucks* are also called ground hogs.

wood·cut·ter (WUHD-kut-er) *n. woodcutters.* A man who cuts down trees and chops up wood.

wood·ed (WUHD-əd) *adj.* Covered with many trees.–The hills are *wooded.*

wood·en (WUHD-n) *adj.* Made of wood.–Some houses are *wooden;* some are made of bricks.–The children marched like *wooden* soldiers.

wood·land (WUHD-lənd) *n. woodlands.* Land covered with many trees.–There is a small stretch of *woodland* near our house.

wood·peck·er (WUHD-pek-er) *n. woodpeckers.* A bird that pecks holes in the bark of trees to catch insects that live under the bark. The feathers in a *woodpecker's* tail are stiff to help him in climbing up tree trunks.

woods (WUHDZ) *n. sing.* and *pl.* A forest; a place where many trees grow close together. –The children went to the *woods* to play.

wood wind (WUHD wind) *wood winds.* A wind instrument such as the oboe, clarinet, flute, bassoon, piccolo, and English horn.

woof (WOOF) *n.* The threads that go from side to side across a piece of cloth. The lengthwise threads are called the warp.

wool (WUHL) *n. wools.* The soft, curly hair of sheep.–A sheep's body is covered with *wool.* –*Wool* is made into yarn, cloth, and clothes.

wool•en or **wool•len** (WUHL-ən) *n. woolens* or *woollens.* Clothing made of wool.–The store had a sale of *woolens.*
–*adj.* Made of wool.–*Woolen* clothes are very warm.–*Woolen* blankets keep us warm at night.

wool•ly (WUHL-ee) *adj. woollier, woolliest.* Like the wool on a sheep's back.–Mother has a *woolly* blanket.

word (WERD) *n. words.* 1. A group of letters that stands for one idea. Several *words* that express one thought make a sentence.–The first *word* that Baby spoke was "Mamma."
2. Promise.–I give you my *word* that I will not tell our secret.
3. A message; news.–Father is on a trip, and we have had no *word* from him yet.
4. A short conversation.–Mother had a *word* with Mary's teacher about Mary's work.

wore (WOR) *v.* One form of the verb *wear.*– I wear a clean dress every day. Yesterday I *wore* my best dress.

work (WERK) *n. works.* 1. Anything we do in an effort to make or get something we want.–Bob did some *work* on his model boat.
2. Task.–Father said he had some *work* for Tim. He asked Tim to mow the lawn and to rake the leaves.
3. A trade; a vocation; the thing one does to make a living.–Being a doctor, a mechanic, a clerk, or a teacher is *work.*–Mother's *work* is in the home. She washes, cleans the house, cooks, sews, and takes care of the baby.
–*v. works, worked, working.* Run; operate. – Our car will not *work.* It needs repairs.

work•er (WERK-er) *n. workers.* 1. A person who works.–Bob is a hard *worker* when he is doing something that interests him.
2. A person who works for wages. – The *workers* in the factory asked for higher wages.

work•man (WERK-mən) *n. workmen.* A man who works, especially one who works with his hands.–A gang of *workmen* unloaded the truck.

work•shop (WERK-shahp) *n. workshops.* A shop or room in which work is done.–Santa Claus has many elves in his toy *workshop.*

world (WERLD) *n. worlds.* 1. The earth.– Ships sail round the *world.*

2. All the people living on earth.–The *world* will soon hear the good news.

worm (WERM) *n. worms.* A small, slender animal that wriggles along or through the ground.–Robins eat *worms* that live in the ground and are called earth*worms.*
–*v. worms, wormed, worming.* Wriggle.–The boy *wormed* his way through the crowd so that he could see the parade.

worn (WORN) *v.* One form of the verb *wear.* –I wear this hat every day. I have *worn* it for a year.

worn-out (WORN-OWT) *adj.* Made worthless by wear or use. – Mother threw away Mary's *worn-out* shoes. They had been used until they could be worn no longer.

wor•ry (WER-ee) *n. worries.* An anxious or troubled feeling.–*Worry* over the baby's sickness is very tiring to Mother.
–*v. worries, worried, worrying.* 1. Trouble; bother.–Do not *worry* Baby by teasing her.
2. Feel troubled and anxious.–Mother *worries* when we are late from school.

worse (WERSS) *adj. worst. Worse* means the opposite of better.–Bad, *worse,* worst are the opposites of good, better, best.–Father was sick this morning, and tonight he is *worse.*

wor•ship (WER-ship) *v. worships, worshiped, worshiping.* 1. Show deep or loyal respect for.–We go to church to *worship* God. We pay respect to God.
2. Hold dear.–The man *worships* his little daughter.

worst (WERST) *adj. Worst* means the opposite of best.–Bad, worse, *worst* are the opposites of good, better, best.–Bob is the best boy in school; Bill is the *worst.*–The fire was the *worst* that we had ever seen.

worth (WERTH) *n.* The amount (a sum of money) will buy.–Give me a dime's *worth* of candy.
–*adj.* 1. Equal to in value.–What is your ball *worth?* How much money would it take to buy it?
2. Have a fortune of.–The king is *worth* millions of dollars.
3. Good enough for.–Mary's story is *worth* reading. It is good enough to read out loud.

worth·less (WERTH-ləss) *adj.* Having no value or worth; not usable.–These worn-out clothes are *worthless.*

worth·while (WERTH-HWYL) *adj.* Worth or worthy of time, trouble, interest, or effort. –Reading good books is a *worthwhile* form of relaxation.

wor·thy (WER-thee) *adj. worthier, worthiest.* 1. Deserving.–The soldier's bravery is *worthy* of praise.–The Red Cross is *worthy* of our help.
2. Having worth; admirable.–Abraham Lincoln was a *worthy* gentleman. He was an excellent man whom many people admired.

would (WUHD) *v.* 1. Wished to; wanted to; was willing to.–Bob said that he *would* play ball with our team.
2. *Would* is used to express a condition.–I *would* tell you if I knew. The only reason I don't tell you is that I do not know.
3. Is willing to.–Bob *would* play ball every day if he had time.
4. *Would* is used to show that something went on regularly for some time.–In summer the children *would* go for long walks in the country.
5. *Would* is used to make a request more polite.–*Would* you close the door for me?
6. Wish.–I *would* that I lived in the country.

would·n't (WUHD-nt). Would not. – I *wouldn't* go if I were you.

wound (WOOND) *n. wounds.* An injury, especially from being shot, cut, bruised, or burned.
–*v. wounds, wounded, wounding.* Hurt; injure.–A bullet *wounded* the man in the leg.

wound (WOWND) *v.* One form of the verb *wind.*–Father *wound* the clock last night.

wove (WOHV) *v.* One form of the verb *weave.* –Grandmother *wove* a rug out of strips of colored rags.

wo·ven (WOH-vən) *v.* One form of the verb *weave.*–Cloth is *woven* from threads.

wran·gle (RANG-gəl) *n. wrangles.* A dispute; a quarrel.–The boys got into a *wrangle* over who was to bat first.
–*v. wrangles, wrangled, wrangling.* Quarrel; argue angrily.–Mother told the children not to *wrangle* over their toys.

wrap (RAP) *n. wraps.* An outer garment worn for warmth.–The children took off their wet *wraps* in the hall.
–*v. wraps, wrapped, wrapping.* Cover closely with paper or other material; fasten up.–We *wrap* our presents on Christmas Eve.

wreath (REETH) *n. wreaths.* A ring of leaves or flowers. – Mother hung Christmas *wreaths* in the windows.

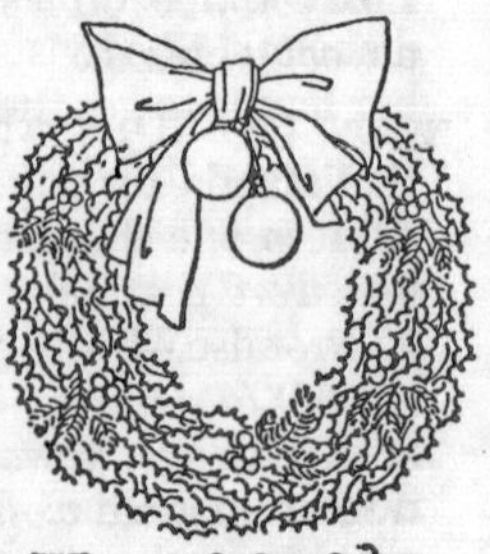

wreathe (REETH) *v. wreathes, wreathed, wreathing.* Encircle; put a ring around.–They *wreathed* their heads with dandelions.

wreck (REK) *n. wrecks.* What is left of anything after it has been damaged badly by a fire, a storm, or some other accident.
–*v. wrecks, wrecked, wrecking.* Destroy or damage badly.–The driver *wrecked* his automobile by running it into a delivery truck.

wreck·age (REK-ij) *n.* What is left after something has been wrecked or badly damaged by fire, storm, or other accident.–We saw the *wreckage* of a boat damaged by a storm.

wreck·er (REK-er) *n. wreckers.* 1. A man who tears down old or damaged houses, machinery, cars, etc. He saves the materials and parts that can be sold and used again.
2. The machine or car a wrecker uses to haul away wreckage.

wren (REN) *n. wrens.* A small songbird. *Wrens* often build nests in birdhouses made for them.

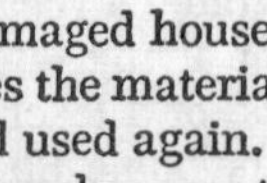

wrench (RENCH) *n. wrenches.* A tool for holding and turning nuts or bolts.–Father tightened the nut on the wheel with a *wrench.*
–*v. wrenches, wrenched, wrenching.* Twist or sprain. – You may *wrench* your back if you carry too heavy a load.

wres·tle (RESS-əl) *v. wrestles, wrestled, wrestling.* Take part in a sport in which each athlete tries to throw the other to the ground. – These boys are *wrestling.*

wres·tler (RESS-ler) *n. wrestlers.* A person who wrestles.

wretch·ed (RECH-id) *adj.; wretchedly, adv.; wretchedness, n.* 1. Very unhappy.–The lonely old man was *wretched* over the loss of his dog.
2. Poor; miserable; uncomfortable. – The poor family was living in a *wretched* house at the edge of town.

wring (RING) *v. wrings, wrung, wringing.* Twist and squeeze. – Mary *wrings* out the dishcloth. She twists and squeezes it between her hands to get the water out.

wring·er (RING-er) *n. wringers.* A machine with rollers that turn in opposite directions, for squeezing the water out of clothes that have been washed.–The *wringer* broke the buttons on Father's shirt.

wrin·kle (RING-kəl) *n. wrinkles.* A little ridge, fold, or line.–The old woman has many *wrinkles* in her face.–Clothes that have not been ironed have *wrinkles* in them.
–*v. wrinkles, wrinkled, wrinkling.* Make folds or ridges in.–Do not *wrinkle* your fresh dress before the party.–Mary *wrinkles* her forehead when she does arithmetic.

wrist (RIST) *n. wrists.* The joint between the hand and the arm.–You wear a watch or a bracelet on your *wrist.*

write (RYT) *v. writes, wrote, writing.* 1. Form letters and words.–Mary likes to *write* on the blackboard with chalk.–*Write* your name at the top of the paper.
2. Think up and set down in words.–Jack *wrote* a story called "The Robber's Revenge."
3. Write a letter.–Father *writes* to Mother every day when he is away.

writ·er (RY-ter) *n. writers.* 1. A person who can write or form letters and words.–Tom is not a good *writer.* He cannot spell very well.
2. An author; a person who makes up stories, poems, or articles, and has them published.–Who is your favorite *writer?*

writ·ing (RY-ting) *n. writings.* Something written.–My favorite author's *writings* fill twenty books.
–*v.* One form of the verb *write.*–Mary is *writing* her name on the blackboard.

writ·ten (RIT-n) *v.* One form of the verb *write.*–My letter to Grandmother is all *written* now. I have finished it.

wrong (RAWNG) *v. wrongs, wronged, wronging.* Do something to someone that is not just.–Sally accused Bob of not returning the book he had borrowed from her. Bob said Sally had *wronged* him; he said he had put the book on her desk that morning.
–*adj.; wrong* and *wrongly, adv.* 1. Not right or good.–It is *wrong* to lie or to steal.
2. Not true or correct. – This answer is *wrong.* It is not the right answer to the question.–That is the *wrong* way to play the game. You are not following the rules.
3. Mistaken; not proper.–It is *wrong* not to thank someone for a present.
4. Not meant to be turned upward or seen.–This wallpaper has a right side and a *wrong* side.–Mary put her sock on *wrong* side out.
5. Not as it should be; out of order.–Something is *wrong* with this watch. It won't work. – Is anything *wrong* with you this morning? Don't you feel well?
6. Not the one wanted or meant. – You brought me the *wrong* book. I wanted a different one.

wrote (ROHT) *v.* One form of the verb *write.* –I write stories in school. Yesterday I *wrote* one about my first piano lesson.

wrought i·ron (rawt Y-ern). A form of iron that can easily be forged, bent, shaped, or welded. *Wrought iron* is used for such things as fences, furniture, and ornaments.

wrung (RUNG) *v.* One form of the verb *wring.* – When I had *wrung* the water out of the washcloth, I hung it up.

Wy·o·ming (wy-OH-ming) *n.* A state that lies within the widest part of the Rocky

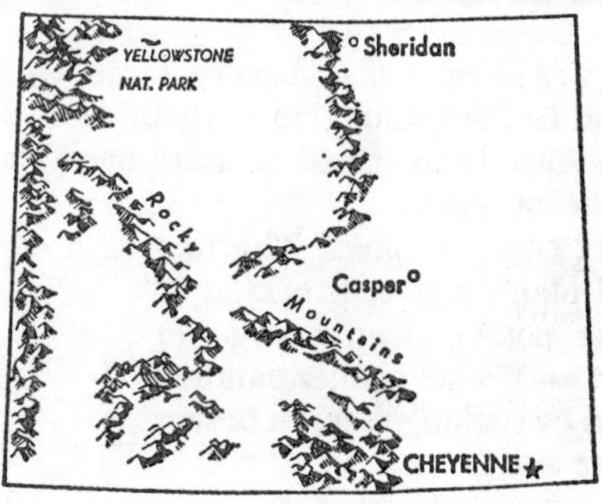

Mountains, in western United States. *Wyoming* is noted for the famous Yellowstone National Park, the oldest national park in the United States.

X x

X, x (EKS) *n. X's, x's.* The twenty-fourth letter of the alphabet.

Xmas (EKS-məss) *n. Xmases.* A short way of writing the word Christmas.–The seal on the package said, "Do not open until *Xmas.*"

X ray (EKS RAY) *X rays; X-ray, adj.* 1. A strong ray, something like light, that can go through certain substances, and even through a person's body. *X rays* are used to see whether bones are broken, or whether the lungs or the roots of teeth are diseased.
2. A picture taken with the help of an X ray. –I saw the X *ray* of Jack's broken arm.
–*v. X-rays, X-rayed, X-raying.* Take an X-ray picture of.–The dentist *X-rayed* Bob's teeth. He examined them by the use of X rays.

xy·lo·phone (ZY-lə-fohn *or* ZIL-ə-fohn) *n xylophones.* A musical instrument which consists of a series of bars of wood or metal. A *xylophone* is played by striking the bars with wooden hammers.

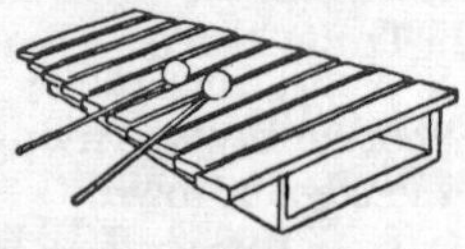

Y y

Y, y (WY) *n. Y's, y's.* The twenty-fifth letter of the alphabet.

yacht (YAHT) *n. yachts.* A boat used for pleasure or for racing.–There was a strong wind blowing the day that we went for a sail on Ed's *yacht.*
–*v. yachts, yachted, yachting.* Sail in a yacht. –Ed and I like to *yacht.*

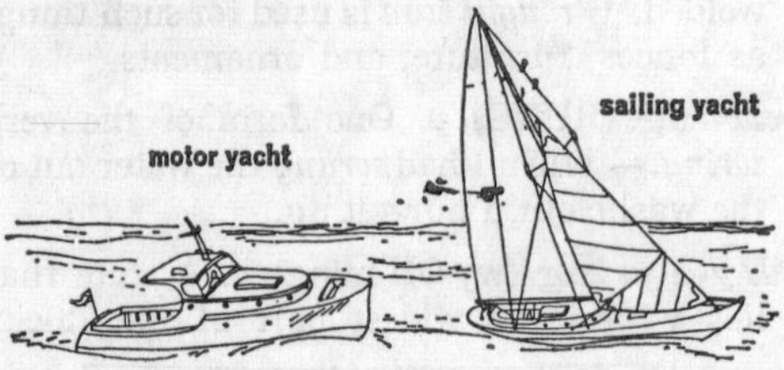

yak (YAK) *n. yaks.* A very large wild ox found in Tibet and other parts of Asia. Some *yaks* have been tamed and are used for domestic purposes.

yam (YAM) *n. yams.* The root of a certain food plant. A *yam* is a kind of sweet potato, deep orange in color. – Mother makes candied *yams* by cooking them in brown sugar and butter.

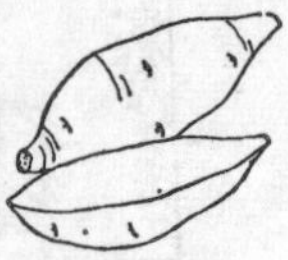

yank (YANGK) *v. yanks, yanked, yanking.* Pull suddenly and sharply; jerk.–The rude boy *yanked* the ball away from his friend and threw it over the fence.

Yan·kee (YANG-kee) *n. Yankees.* 1. A nickname given to people in the northern part of the United States, particularly in the Northeast.
2. A nickname given to the people in the United States by people of foreign countries.

yard (YAHRD) *n. yards.* 1. The space, lawn, or ground around a house.–The children play in the *yard.*
2. An area shut in by a fence or a wall, and used for a special purpose.–The boys built a snow fort in the school*yard.*–We go by the church*yard* on our way home from school.– The cows stood in the barn*yard.*–Trains go to railroad *yards* for repairs.
3. A unit of measure equal to 3 feet or 36 inches. A *yard* is about as long as the distance from a grown person's nose to his fingertips when his arm is held out straight from the shoulder.–Mother bought a piece of ribbon one *yard* long.

yard·stick (YAHRD-stik) *n. yardsticks.* A measuring stick 36 inches long.

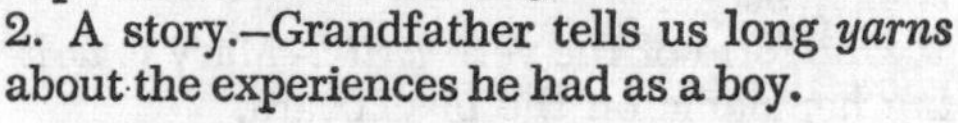

yarn (YAHRN) *n. yarns.* 1. A thread made by drawing out and twisting wool, flax, cotton, or other fiber.–Stockings, sweaters, and caps are often made of *yarn.*
2. A story.–Grandfather tells us long *yarns* about the experiences he had as a boy.

yawn (YAWN) *n. yawns.* Opening the mouth and taking a long breath.–Mary was so tired that she could do nothing to hide her *yawn.*
–*v. yawns, yawned, yawning.* Open the mouth and take a long breath.–When Baby is sleepy, she usually *yawns* and shows her two new teeth.

yea (YAY) *n. yeas* and *adv.* 1. Yes.–When it was time to vote, John voted *yea.* He voted in favor of the resolution. Bill voted against the resolution. He voted nay.
2. Truly; indeed.–*Yea,* that's the way life is.

year (YIR) *n. years.* The time it takes the earth to go around the sun. A *year* has 365 days, 52 weeks, or 12 months in it. Leap *year,* which comes every four *years,* has 366 days in it.

year•ling (YIR-ling) *n. yearlings.* An animal one year old or in its second year of life.–Of all the horses in the stable, the trainer likes the *yearling* most. He likes the one-year-old colt best of all.

year•ly (YIR-lee) *adj.* and *adv.* 1. Once a year.–The Junior Prom is a *yearly* event at our school.
2. Each year.–Bob gets fifty dollars *yearly* for spending money.

yearn (YERN) *v. yearns, yearned, yearning.* Long (for); want very much. – The lonely child *yearns* for letters or post cards from his friends.

yeast (YEEST) *n.* A substance used in making bread. – *Yeast* causes bubbles, which makes bread light. It makes the bread dough rise.

yell (YEL) *n. yells.* A scream; an outcry.–We heard the boy's *yell* from the second-story window of the old house.
–*v. yells, yelled, yelling.* Scream; cry out loudly.–The boys *yelled* when the bear got loose.

yel•low (YEL-oh) *n. yellows.* The color of butter.–Billy thinks we should paint the dining room *yellow.* Lemons and grapefruits are *yellow.*
–*v. yellows, yellowed, yellowing.* Turn yellow. –The old newspaper had *yellowed* with age. It had turned yellow.
–*adj. yellower, yellowest.* Of the color yellow. –The living room is the only *yellow* room in the house.
–*Yellowish* means somewhat yellow.

yel•low fe•ver (YEL-oh FEE-ver). A dangerous infectious disease occurring in warm or tropical climates. *Yellow fever* is carried by a certain type of mosquito and transmitted by its bite.

yel•low jack•et (YEL-oh jak-it) *yellow jackets.* A wasp that has bright yellow stripes on its back. A *yellow jacket's* sting hurts.

yelp (YELP) *n. yelps.* A sharp cry or bark.– The *yelp* of his dog brought Jack running to see what was wrong.
–*v. yelps, yelped, yelping.* Bark sharply.–The dog *yelps* when he is hurt.

yen (YEN) *n. sing.* and *pl.* 1. The unit of money in Japan. One hundred *yen* is about twenty-seven cents in United States money.
2. Desire or longing.–Tom has a *yen* to go to the movies. He has a keen desire to see a motion picture.

yeo•man (YOH-mən) *n. yeomen.* 1. In England, a farmer who owns only a small farm. –The old *yeoman* worked hard, plowing his small field and tending his few crops.
2. An attendant, servant, or guard in the service of a king or a noble. – There are one hundred *yeomen* in the royal army. There are one hundred guards in the royal army.
3. A petty officer in the United States Navy. A *yeoman's* rank is equivalent to that of a sergeant in the United States Army.

yes (YESS) *n. yeses* and *adv.* The opposite of no.–We say *yes* when we agree or are willing.–Will you go with me? *Yes,* I would like to go with you.

yes•ter•day (YESS-ter-dee *or* -day) *n. yesterdays, adj.,* and *adv.* The day right before today; the day just past.–Today is Monday; *yesterday* was Sunday.

yet (YET) *adv.* and *conj.* 1. Up to now; before this time.–The train has not come *yet.* We are waiting for it.
2. Still; even now. – The bells are ringing *yet.* You can still hear them.
3. At some time to come.–I will learn to play the piano *yet.*
4. Still; even.–The wind blew harder *yet* when we turned the corner.
–*As yet* means up to the present time, up till now.–Bill hasn't done it *as yet,* but he will when he gets a chance.

yew (YOO) *n. yews.* 1. An evergreen tree or shrub having fine-grained wood and dark green foliage. *Yews* grow in Europe, Asia, and parts of Africa and North America.

2. The wood of such a tree. – Bows for shooting arrows were generally made of *yew* because the wood is so tough and elastic.

yield (YEELD) *n. yields.* An amount produced.–Four bushels is a large *yield* for a small tree.

–*v. yields, yielded, yielding.* 1. Produce; give forth.–The peach tree *yielded* four baskets of fruit.

2. Give in.–Father *yielded* to Mary's coaxing and let her go to the show.

3. Give up ground; surrender.–The soldiers would not *yield* to the enemy.

yo•ga (YOH-gə) *n.* In the Hindu religion, a union of the human mind with the mind of God. To attain *yoga* a man must control his body and mind to such a degree that he can overcome consciousness of the world around him and release his mind to God.

yoke (YOHK) *n. yokes.* 1. The top part of a dress that is cut separately from the dress. –Sally's yellow dress has a white *yoke* with a bright red ruffle around it.

2. A wooden framework placed over the necks of two animals so that they will work together. – The man fixed the animals' *yoke*.

–*v. yokes, yoked, yoking.* Harness; put a yoke on.–The two oxen were *yoked* together.

yolk (YOHK *or* YOHLK) *n. yolks.* The yellow part of an egg.–Mary likes the *yolk* of the egg best.

yon•der (YAHN-der) *adj.* and *adv.* Over there; at that place. – Look at the sunset *yonder*.

yore (YOR) *adj.* and *adv.* An ancient word meaning olden times, or long ago. The word is used today only in the phrase *"of yore."*– The book contains a dozen tales *of yore*.

you (YOO) *pron. sing.* and *pl.* The person or persons to whom one is speaking or writing. –*You* may go home now.–*You* are bigger than I am.–All of *you* come with me.

you'd (YOOD). A short way of writing you had or you would.–*You'd* see better if you sat nearer to the window.–Before *you'd* walked with us a mile, *you'd* be tired.

you'll (YOOL). You will.–If you do not hurry, *you'll* be late.

young (YUNG) *n.* Babies.–A cat carries her *young* by the backs of their necks.–A dog's *young* are her puppies.

–*adj. younger, youngest.* Not old; not many years old.–Babies are very *young* children.– Boys and girls are *young*.–The peach tree is *young*. It was planted not very long ago.

young•ster (YUNG-ster) *n. youngsters.* A child; a young person.–The *youngsters* at the party played games.

your (YUHR) *adj.* and *pron.* Belonging to the person or persons to whom one is speaking or writing.–*Your* nose, *your* toes, *your* hands are all parts of you. *Your* dress belongs to you.

you're (YUHR). You are.–*You're* taller than I am.–*You're* going to be late.

yours (YUHRZ) *pron.* Something that belongs to the person to whom one is speaking or writing.–This hat is *yours;* that one is mine.–My eyes are blue; *yours* are brown.

your•self (yuhr-SELF) *pron. yourselves.* 1. You alone.–If you want your work done well, do it *yourself*. Don't expect somebody else to do it.

2. Your own self. – Dress *yourself* quickly, for breakfast is ready.

your•selves (yuhr-SELVZ) *pron. pl.* Mother said to us, "You must play by *yourselves* today, for your friends are away."

youth (YOOTH) *n. youth* or *youths.* 1. Older boys and girls.–The high school was built for the *youth* of our town.

2. A young man.–The letter was sent by a *youth* in search of a job.

youth•ful (YOOTH-fuhl) *adj.; youthfully, adv.; youthfulness, n.* Young. – Mother's green dress makes her look *youthful*.–Grandmother is *youthful* in her ideas. She thinks like a young person.

you've (YOOV). You have.–*You've* written to Grandmother, haven't you?

yule (YOOL) *n. yules.* An old-fashioned word for Christmas.

Z z

Z, z (ZEE) *n. Z's, z's.* The twenty-sixth and last letter of the alphabet.

zeal (ZEEL) *n.; zealous, adj.; zealously, adv.* Enthusiasm; warm and active interest; eager desire.—The children worked with great *zeal* to put on the annual school show.

ze•bra (ZEE-brə) *n. zebras.* An animal that looks something like a horse, but has black and white stripes going around its body.

ze•nith (ZEE-nith) *n. zeniths.* 1. That point in the sky directly above any observer or place on earth.
2. The highest point; the peak; the summit. —The actor is at the *zenith* of his career. He is at the top. He has never before been so popular, or earned so much money, or acted so well.

zeph•yr (ZEF-er) *n. zephyrs.* A soft, gentle wind that comes from the west; any gentle wind.

zep•pe•lin (ZEP-ə-lin) *n. zeppelins.* A kind of balloon that can be steered; a dirigible.—People can ride in a *zeppelin.*

ze•ro (ZIR-oh *or* ZEE-roh) *n. zeros* or *zeroes.* 1. The figure [0] which comes before 1. —When the temperature is *zero* [0°], it is very cold.
2. Nothing; none.—Jack has slept all morning. The amount of work he has done amounts to *zero.*
3. A grade meaning that no answer has been correct.—Mary had every answer wrong in the arithmetic test, so her mark was *zero* for that day.

zest (ZEST) *n.; zestful, adj.* Hearty flavor; sharp interest; keen enjoyment.—The hungry boys ate their food with *zest.*

zig•zag (ZIG-zag) *n. zigzags, adj.,* and *adv.* A figure that has short, sharp turns.
—*v. zigzags, zigzagged, zigzagging.* Move back and forth making sharp turns.—The airplane *zigzagged* in the sky.

zinc (ZINGK) *n.* A soft, bluish-white metal.

zin•ni•a (ZIN-ee-ə) *n. zinnias.* A bright-colored late summer flower.—*Zinnias* last for a long time.

zip (ZIP) *v. zips, zipped, zipping.* Fasten with a zipper.—Tom is *zipping* the bag. He is fastening it.

zip•per (ZIP-er) *n. zippers.* A slide fastener. *Zippers* are often used instead of buttons or laces on trousers, skirts, dresses, jackets, etc.

zith•er (ZITH-er) *n. zithers.* A musical instrument having up to forty-five strings stretched over a flat sounding box. — The *zither* is played with the fingers and a small piece of ivory, metal, or other material.

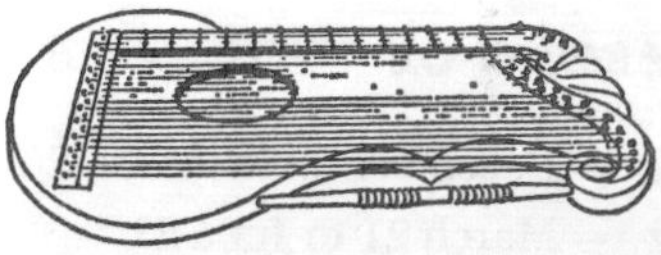

zo•di•ac (ZOH-dee-ak) *n.* In going around the sun, the earth always moves in a certain path. Out in the heavens there is a belt of stars that circles this path. That belt of stars is the *zodiac.* It can be divided into twelve constellations, or picture-groups of stars. Among them are "Taurus, the Bull," "Cancer, the Crab," and "Leo, the Lion."

zone (ZOHN) *n. zones.* 1. An area or place set aside for a special purpose. — The children waited in the safety *zone* for the bus.
2. One of the great divisions of the earth.—It is very hot in the Torrid *Zone.*—We live in the North Temperate *Zone.*—The Frigid *Zones* are very cold.

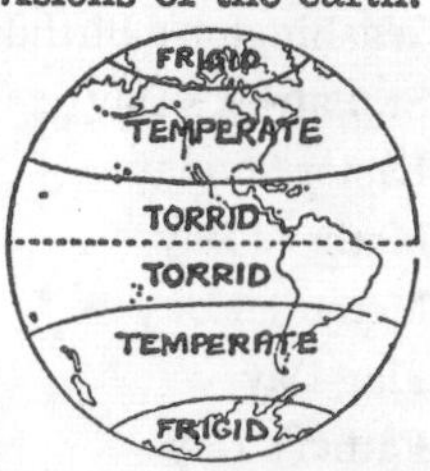

zoo (ZOO) *n. zoos.* A park where wild animals are kept in fenced yards or in cages, so that people can come and look at them. Most large cities have *zoos.* —Father took the children to the *zoo* to see the baby elephant.

zo•ol•o•gy (zoh-AHL-ə-jee) *n. zoologies; zoological, adj.* The science or study of animals and animal life.—Carrie and Hannah are going to college to study *zoology.* They will study everything from one-celled animals to human bodies.

Things You Will Want to Know

DAYS OF THE WEEK

Sunday	(Sun.)
Monday	(Mon.)
Tuesday	(Tues.)
Wednesday	(Wed.)
Thursday	(Thurs.)
Friday	(Fri.)
Saturday	(Sat.)

SEASONS OF THE YEAR

Winter – December 22 to March 20
Spring – March 21 to June 21
Summer– June 22 to September 20
Autumn – September 21 to December 21

MONTHS OF THE YEAR

January	(Jan.)
February	(Feb.)
March	(Mar.)
April	(Apr.)
May	
June	(Jun.)
July	(Jul.)
August	(Aug.)
September	(Sept.)
October	(Oct.)
November	(Nov.)
December	(Dec.)

SPECIAL DAYS

New Year's Day	January 1
Lincoln's Birthday	February 12
Valentine's Day	February 14
Washington's Birthday	February 22
St. Patrick's Day	March 17
Easter Sunday	March or April
Mother's Day	Second Sunday in May
Memorial Day	May 30
Flag Day	June 14
Father's Day	Third Sunday in June
Independence Day	July 4
Labor Day	First Monday in September
Columbus Day	October 12
Halloween	October 31
Election Day	First Tuesday after first Monday in November
Veterans Day (formerly Armistice Day)	November 11
Thanksgiving	Fourth Thursday in November
Christmas	December 25

NAMES OF OCEANS

Antarctic
Arctic
Atlantic
Indian
Pacific

NAMES OF THE CONTINENTS

Africa
Antarctica
Asia
Australia
Europe
North America
South America

MULTIPLICATION TABLE

1	2	3	4	5	6	7	8	9	10	11	12
2	4	6	8	10	12	14	16	18	20	22	24
3	6	9	12	15	18	21	24	27	30	33	36
4	8	12	16	20	24	28	32	36	40	44	48
5	10	15	20	25	30	35	40	45	50	55	60
6	12	18	24	30	36	42	48	54	60	66	72
7	14	21	28	35	42	49	56	63	70	77	84
8	16	24	32	40	48	56	64	72	80	88	96
9	18	27	36	45	54	63	72	81	90	99	108
10	20	30	40	50	60	70	80	90	100	110	120
11	22	33	44	55	66	77	88	99	110	121	132
12	24	36	48	60	72	84	96	108	120	132	144

LONGEST RIVERS IN THE WORLD

name	location	length
Nile	Africa	about 4,100 miles
Amazon	South America	about 3,900 miles
Missouri-Mississippi	U.S.A.	about 3,890 miles
Ob	U.S.S.R.	about 3,200 miles
Yangtze	China	about 3,400 miles

FAMOUS MOUNTAIN PEAKS

name	location	height
Mt. Everest	China-Nepal	29,002 feet
Mt. Aconcagua	Argentina	22,835 feet
Mt. McKinley	Alaska	20,300 feet
Mt. Kilimanjaro	Africa	19,565 feet
Mt. Popocatépetl	Mexico	17,883 feet

LARGEST CITIES IN THE WORLD

name	location	population
Tokyo	Japan	9,683,802
London	U.K.	8,171,902
New York	U.S.A.	7,781,984
Shanghai	China	7,100,000
Moscow	U.S.S.R.	6,354,000
Mexico City	Mexico	4,829,402
Bombay	India	4,152,056
Peiping	China	4,140,000
São Paulo	Brazil	3,850,000
Buenos Aires	Argentina	3,799,000

PLANETS

name	nearness to sun	size
Mercury	1	9
Venus	2	6
Earth	3	5
Mars	4	7
Jupiter	5	1
Saturn	6	2
Uranus	7	3
Neptune	8	4
Pluto	9	8

MEASURES OF LENGTH

12 inches = 1 foot
3 feet = 1 yard
5½ yards = 1 rod
320 rods = 1 mile
5,280 feet = 1 mile

DRY MEASURE

2 pints = 1 quart
8 quarts = 1 peck
32 quarts = 1 bushel
4 pecks = 1 bushel

LIQUID MEASURE

2 pints = 1 quart
4 quarts = 1 gallon

WEIGHT

16 ounces = 1 pound
2,000 pounds = 1 short ton
2,240 pounds = 1 long ton

MEASURES OF TIME

60 seconds = 1 minute
60 minutes = 1 hour
24 hours = 1 day
7 days = 1 week
28, 29, 30, or 31 days = 1 calendar month
12 months or 365 days = 1 year
(Leap year has 366 days)

NUMBERS

12 of anything = 1 dozen
12 dozen = 1 gross

UNITED STATES MONEY

1 cent = 1 penny
5 pennies = 1 nickel
2 nickels or 10 pennies = 1 dime
5 nickels or 25 pennies = 1 quarter
2 quarters or 50 pennies = one half dollar
2 half dollars = 1 dollar
100 pennies = 1 dollar
20 nickels = 1 dollar
10 dimes = 1 dollar
4 quarters = 1 dollar

ABBREVIATIONS

A.D. — in the year of our Lord; after the birth of Christ
Adm. — Admiral
A.M. *or* a.m. — before noon
ans. — answer
ave. — avenue
bbl. — barrel
B.C. — before Christ
bldg. — building
blvd. — boulevard
BSA — Boy Scouts of America
bu. — bushel
c. *or* ca. — about; around
Capt. — Captain
cm. — centimeter
C.O.D. — cash on delivery
Col. — Colonel
ct. — cent
cwt. — hundredweight
doz. *or* dz. — dozen
Dr. — Doctor
e.g. — for example
etc. — et cetera (and so forth)
fl. oz. — fluid ounce
ft. — foot
gal. — gallon
Gen. — General
gm. — gram; grams
govt. — government
gr. wt. — gross weight
GSA — Girl Scouts of America
hf. — half
hr. — hour
ht. — height
i.e. — that is
in. — inch
km. — kilometer
lb. — pound
Lt. — Lieutenant
m. — meter
mi. — mile
min. — minute
mm. — millimeter
mo. — month
Mr. — Mister
Mrs. — Missus
Mt. *or* mt. — mount; mountain
N.B. *or* n.b. — note well
oz. — ounce
Pfc. — Private, First Class
pkg. — package
P.M. *or* p.m. — after noon
P.O. *or* p.o. — post office
P.S. — postscript
pt. — pint
qt. — quart
ques. — question
rd. — rod
ret. *or* retd. — returned
Rev. — Reverend
R.F.D. — Rural Free Delivery
R.R. — railroad
R.S.V.P. — please reply
Ry. — Railway
tn. — ton
U.N. — United Nations
U.S. — United States
yd. — yard
yr. — year

RULES FOR THE USE OF CAPITAL LETTERS

1. The first word in every sentence should begin with a capital letter.	**We go to school.** **Do you like to read?**
2. The first word in every complete line of a poem should begin with a capital letter.	**"How do you like to go up in a swing,** **Up in the air so blue?"**
3. Use a capital letter for "i" when it means oneself.	**You and I went to a show.** **I said that I would come.**
4. The first word and all important words in a title should begin with a capital letter.	**Jack's story is called "The Little Lame Duck on the Pond."**
5. The words north, south, east, and west should begin with a capital letter if they refer to a place.	**Eskimos live in the North.** **John hopes to travel in the West this summer.**

6. Capital letters are used to begin the names of:

(a) persons:	**John Smith**
(b) places:	**Cleveland, Ohio**
(c) months of the year:	**May, June**
(d) days of the week:	**Sunday, Friday**
(e) holidays:	**Thanksgiving, Christmas**
(f) organizations:	**American Red Cross**
(g) political parties:	**Democratic Party, Republican Party**
(h) institutions:	**Washington High School, Columbia University**
(i) buildings:	**Church of Christ, Lincoln Memorial**
(j) deity:	**God, Christ**
(k) titles:	**Mr., Mrs., Dr., Rev.**

7. The first word in the salutation of a letter should begin with a capital letter.	**My dear Ruth,** **Dear Uncle John,**
8. The first word of the complimentary closing of a letter should begin with a capital letter.	**Sincerely yours,** **Very truly yours,**
9. The first word of a direct quotation should begin with a capital letter.	**John asked, "Are you going to a movie tonight?"**

PRESIDENTS OF THE UNITED STATES

name	date of birth	place of birth	years as president
George Washington	Feb. 22, 1732	Westmoreland County, Va.	1789-1797
John Adams	Oct. 30, 1735	Braintree, Mass.	1797-1801
Thomas Jefferson	Apr. 12, 1743	Shadwell, Va.	1801-1809
James Madison	Mar. 16, 1751	Port Conway, Va.	1809-1817
James Monroe	Apr. 28, 1758	Westmoreland County, Va.	1817-1825
John Q. Adams	July 11, 1767	Quincy, Mass.	1825-1829
Andrew Jackson	Mar. 15, 1767	Waxhaw, S. C.	1829-1837
Martin Van Buren	Dec. 5, 1782	Kinderhook, N. Y.	1837-1841
William H. Harrison	Feb. 9, 1773	Berkeley, Va.	1841
John Tyler	Mar. 29, 1790	Greenway, Va.	1841-1845
James K. Polk	Nov. 2, 1795	Little Sugar Creek, N. C.	1845-1849
Zachary Taylor	Nov. 24, 1784	Orange County, Va.	1849-1850
Millard Fillmore	Jan. 7, 1800	Cayuga County, N. Y.	1850-1853
Franklin Pierce	Nov. 23, 1804	Hillsboro, N. H.	1853-1857
James Buchanan	Apr. 23, 1791	Franklin County, Pa.	1857-1861
Abraham Lincoln	Feb. 12, 1809	Hodgenville, Ky.	1861-1865
Andrew Johnson	Dec. 29, 1808	Raleigh, N. C.	1865-1869
Ulysses S. Grant	Apr. 27, 1822	Point Pleasant, Ohio	1869-1877
Rutherford B. Hayes	Oct. 4, 1822	Delaware, Ohio	1877-1881
James A. Garfield	Nov. 19, 1831	Orange, Ohio	1881
Chester A. Arthur	Oct. 5, 1830	Fairfield, Vt.	1881-1885
Grover Cleveland	Mar. 18, 1837	Caldwell, N. J.	1885-1889
Benjamin Harrison	Aug. 20, 1833	North Bend, Ohio	1889-1893
Grover Cleveland	Mar. 18, 1837	Caldwell, N.J.	1893-1897
William McKinley	Jan. 29, 1843	Niles, Ohio	1897-1901
Theodore Roosevelt	Oct. 27, 1858	New York, N. Y.	1901-1909
William H. Taft	Sept. 15, 1857	Cincinnati, Ohio	1909-1913
Woodrow Wilson	Dec. 28, 1856	Staunton, Va.	1913-1921
Warren G. Harding	Nov. 2, 1865	Corsica, Ohio	1921-1923
Calvin Coolidge	July 4, 1872	Plymouth, Vt.	1923-1929
Herbert C. Hoover	Aug. 10, 1874	West Branch, Iowa	1929-1933
Franklin D. Roosevelt	Jan. 30, 1882	Hyde Park, N. Y.	1933-1945
Harry S. Truman	May 8, 1884	Lamar, Mo.	1945-1953
Dwight D. Eisenhower	Oct. 14, 1890	Denison, Texas	1953-1961
John F. Kennedy	May 29, 1917	Brookline, Mass.	1961-1963
Lyndon B. Johnson	Aug. 27, 1908	Stonewall, Texas	1963-1968

Guide to Pronunciation

After each black-type word in this dictionary there is a special spelling of the word which shows you how to say it. The special spelling has parentheses ( ) around it. Here is an example of a black-type word with its special spelling: **cat** (KAT).

On the next page is a guide to the special spellings.

This is how to use the guide. Each line tells about one sound. In the first column you will see the letters that stand for that sound. In the second column are some words in which the sound occurs. If you say those words and listen to the parts in black type, you will hear the sound. In the third column are the special spellings for those words. You can use them to practice sounding out the letters.

Some of the special spellings have both capital letters and small ones.The capital letters are the accented ones. We say them a little louder than we do the others.

In many of the special spellings there is a ə. This is a quiet little sound that is often found in the unaccented, or softly-said, parts of words. ə is just a very weak vowel. The guide will tell you more about ə.

Some of the special spellings give you a choice. They tell you that people very often say a word more than one way. These spellings look like this: (bee- *or* bə-GIN). This means that the first part of the word can be said (bee) or (bə), giving you either (bee-GIN) or (bə-GIN). Sometimes the whole word is spelled out twice, as in (kahn-KREET *or* KAHN-kreet). Then you know that it is either (kahn-KREET) or (KAHN-kreet), as you choose.

Vowel Sounds

a	had, sat	(HAD) (SAT)
ah	far, calm	(FAHR) (KAHM)
air	pear, scare	(PAIR) (SKAIR)
aw	law, cause	(LAW) (KAWZ)
ay	bay, rate	(BAY) (RAYT)
e	met, bet	(MET) (BET)
ee	me, fairy	(MEE) (FAIR-ee)
er	fur, after	(FER) (AF-ter)
i	sit, bid	(SIT) (BID)
oh	go, rowboat	(GOH) (ROH-boht)
oi	oil, boy	(OIL) (BOI)
oo	root, soup	(ROOT) (SOOP)
or	for, border	(FOR) (BOR-der)
ow	how, sound	(HOW) (SOWND)
u	fun, cup	(FUN) (KUP)
uh	could, pull	(KUHD) (PUHL)
y	fly, sight	(FLY) (SYT)
yoo	fuse, view	(FYOOZ) (VYOO)
ə	soda	(SOH-də)
ə	silent	(SY-lənt)
ə	pencil	(PEN-səl)
ə	bacon	(BAY-kən)
ə	circus	(SER-kəss)

Consonant Sounds

ch	church, nature	(CHERCH) (NAY-cher)
g	get, great	(GET) (GRAYT)
j	just, age	(JUST) (AYJ)
ks	mix, six	(MIKS) (SIKS)
ng	king, finger	(KING) (FING-ger)
th	three, thin	(THREE) (THIN)
<u>th</u>	then, further	(<u>TH</u>EN) (FER-<u>th</u>er)
zh	vision	(VIZH-ən)

Say the other consonants just as you always do when you find them in a word.

Every time you see a "y" with a vowel following it, sound it like the "y" in "yoo," just as you do in "yet."